Nancy Dowling

Social Psychology

SOCIAL PSYCHOLOGY

Sociological Perspectives

EDITED BY

Morris Rosenberg & Ralph H. Turner

Prepared by the Section on Social Psychology of the American Sociological Association

Basic Books, Inc., Publishers

NEW YORK

Library of Congress Catalog Card Number: 81–66976
ISBN: 0–465–07904–0 (cloth)
ISBN: 0–465–07905–9 (paper)
Printed in the United States of America
Designed by Vincent Torre
10 9 8 7 6 5 4 3 2 1

Contents

PART IV

Society and Social Behavior

PART V

Society and Personality

Contributors

C. NORMAN ALEXANDER, Jr., is Professor of Sociology at the University of Illinois at Chicago Circle. He has served on the Council of the ASA Section on Social Psychology and on the Editorial Board of *Sociometry.* He has published widely in the area of situated identity theory and research.

KURT W. BACK is James B. Duke Professor of Sociology at Duke University. He has been a Council member of the ASA Section on Social Psychology and a member of the Editorial Board of *Sociometry.* He is co-author of *Social Pressure in Informal Groups* (with L. Festinger and S. Schachter) (1951) and editor of *In Search of Community: Encounter Groups and Social Change* (1978).

CARL W. BACKMAN is Chairman and Professor of Sociology at the University of Nevada at Reno. He has served as Chair of the ASA Section on Social Psychology, as Editor of *Sociometry,* and as Program Director for Sociology and Social Psychology at the National Science Foundation. He is the author or co-author of five books and monographs, including *Social Psychology* (with Paul Secord), and numerous chapters and articles on social psychological research.

DIANE MITSCH BUSH is Assistant Professor of Sociology at the University of Arizona. Her publications include articles on the impact of school structure upon adolescent self-image, on changing attitudes toward sex roles among adolescent girls, and on the routinization of social movement organizations.

SANFORD M. DORNBUSCH is Reed-Hodgson Professor of Human Biology and Professor of Sociology and Education at Stanford. He has been Chairman of the ASA Section on Social Psychology, a member of the Editorial Board of *Sociometry,* and president of the Pacific Sociological Association.

RICHARD EMERSON, Professor of Sociology at the University of Washington, has served on the Editorial Board of *Sociometry.* His work on exchange theory has appeared in the *Annual Review of Sociology* and *Sociological Theories in Progress.*

VIKTOR GECAS is Professor of Sociology at Washington State University. He has written primarily on the topics of socialization and self-concept development.

JACK P. GIBBS is Professor and Chair of the Department of Sociology and Anthropology at Vanderbilt University. He has served as an Associate Editor of *Sociometry* and has been a Council Member-At-Large of the American Sociological Association. He is author of *Crime, Punishment, and Deterrence* (1975) and *Norms, Deviance, and Social Control* (1981), and (with Walter T. Martin) *Status Integration and Suicide* (1964).

CHAD GORDON, Professor of Sociology at Rice University, has been a member of the ASA Section on Social Psychology Council. He is author of *Looking Ahead* (1972), and co-editor (with K. Gergen) of *The Self in Social Interaction* (1968).

STEVEN L. GORDON, Assistant Professor of Sociology at California State University, Los Angeles, has been an NIMH Postdoctoral Fellow in Social Structure and Personality at the University of California, Berkeley.

ALLEN D. GRIMSHAW, Professor of Sociology at Indiana University, is a past member of the Editorial Board of *Sociometry* and of the SSRC Committee on Sociolinguistics. He has also been Editor of *The American Sociologist.* He has published widely on a variety of sociolinguistic topics; a selection of his papers has been published under the title *Language as Social Resource* (1981).

JEROLD HEISS, Professor of Sociology at the University of Connecticut, currently serves as an Associate Editor of *Symbolic Interaction.* His books include *Family Roles and Interaction* (1976) and *The Social Psychology of Interaction* (1981).

RICHARD J. HILL is Acting Provost and Vice President for Academic Affairs at the University of Oregon. He has served as Editorial Consultant, Associate Editor, and Editor of *Sociometry,* and has been Council Member of the ASA Section on Social Psychology, Council Member-At-Large of the ASA, and President of the Pacific Sociological Association.

JAMES S. HOUSE is a member of the Survey Research Center and the Department of Sociology, University of Michigan. Dr. House has served on the Council of the ASA Section on Social Psychology and been a member of the Editorial Board of *Social Psychology Quarterly.* He is the author of *Work, Stress and Social Support* (1981).

HERBERT C. KELMAN is the Richard Clarke Cabot Professor of Social Ethics at Harvard University. He has been Chair of the ASA Section on Social Psychology and has served on the Editorial Board of *Sociometry.* He is recipient of the AAAS Sociopsychological Prize (1956) and of the Kurt Lewin Memorial Award (1972).

BARBARA F. MEEKER, Associate Professor of Sociology at the University of Maryland, College Park, is currently a member of Council, ASA Section on Social Psychology, and serves on the Editorial Board of the

Social Psychology Quarterly. She has published articles on exchange theory and on the relationship of expectation states theory to other theoretical approaches.

GLADYS ENGEL LANG is Professor of Sociology and Political Science at the State University of New York at Stony Brook. She has served on the editorial boards of the *Public Opinion Quarterly,* the *Journal of Communication,* and the *Mass Communications Review Yearbook* and has been a member of the Executive Councils of the American Association of Public Opinion Research and the World Association of Public Opinion Research.

KURT LANG is Professor of Sociology and Political Science at the State University of New York at Stony Brook, a former member of the Editorial Board of *Sociometry,* and winner (with Gladys E. Lang) of the Edward L. Bernays Award of the American Sociological Association for Research on the Effects of Radio/Television on American Life. He is also author or coauthor with G.E. Lang of numerous articles on mass communication, collective behavior, and related subjects.

JOHN LOFLAND, Professor of Sociology at the University of California, Davis, has served as President of the Pacific Sociological Association, Chair of the Section on Collective Behavior and Social Movements of the American Sociological Association, and founding Editor of *Urban Life: A Journal of Ethnographic Research.* His published works include *Analyzing Social Settings* (1971), *Doomsday Cult* (1965), *Doing Social Life* (1976), and *Interaction in Everyday Life* (editor) (1978).

MORRIS ROSENBERG is Professor of Sociology at the University of Maryland, College Park. He has served as Chair and as Council Member of the ASA Section on Social Psychology, as Editorial Board member of *Sociometry,* and as ASA Council Member. In the area of the sociology of the self-concept, his publications include *Society and the Adolescent Self-Image* (1965), *Conceiving the Self* (1979), *Black and White Self-Esteem: The Urban School Child* (with R. G. Simmons) (1972), and *The Social Psychology of the Self-Concept* (co-edited with H. B. Kaplan) (1982).

HOWARD SCHUMAN is a Professor of Sociology and a Program Director, Institute for Social Research, University of Michigan. He is a past Editor of *Sociometry/Social Psychology Quarterly,* and is Chair of the Section on Social Psychology of the American Sociological Association.

MELVIN SEEMAN, Professor of Sociology at the University of California, Los Angeles, has served as Editor of *Sociometry,* and as Advisory Editor for the *American Sociological Review* and the *American Journal of Sociology.* He has been a Member-At-Large of the American Sociological Association Council and a member of the Executive Board of the International Sociological Association Research Committee on Alienation.

ROBERTA G. SIMMONS, Professor of Sociology at the University of Minnesota, has served on the Nominating Committee of the Social Psychology Section of the ASA and has collaborated with Professor Jeylan Mortimer on "Adult socialization," a chapter published in the *Annual Review of Sociology.* She is author of *Black and White Self-Esteem: The Urban School Child* (with M. Rosenberg) (1972) and *The Gift of Life: The Social and Psychological Impact of Organ Transplantation* (with S. Klein and R. Simmons) (1977). She has also edited the first two volumes in the SAI series of research annuals, and she has written many articles on the adolescent self-image.

ELEANOR SINGER is Senior Research Associate at the Center for the Social Sciences at Columbia University and Editor of *The Public Opinion Quarterly.* With Herbert H. Hyman, she edited *Readings in Reference Group Theory and Research* (1968).

NEIL J. SMELSER is a University Professor of Sociology at the University of California. His publications relevant to social psychology include *Theory of Collective Behavior* (1963), *Personality and Social Systems* (with William T. Smelser) (2nd ed., 1970), and *Themes of Love and Work in Adulthood* (1980).

WILLIAM T. SMELSER is Lecturer in the School of Social Welfare at the University of California, Berkeley. In collaboration with Neil J. Smelser, he has edited *Personality and Social Systems* (1970).

DAVID A. SNOW is Assistant Professor of Sociology at the University of Texas, Austin. He has published a number of articles dealing with collective behavior and social movement.

SHELDON STRYKER, Professor of Sociology at Indiana University, has been Chair of the ASA Section on Social Psychology and has twice been elected to the Section's Council. He has served as Editor of *Sociometry,* has been a member of its Editorial Board, and will assume the editorship of the *American Sociological Review.* Recent publications include *Symbolic Interactionism: A Social Structural Version* (1980), "Symbolic Interactionism and Role Theory" (with Anne Statham), in G. Lindzey and E. Aronson, *Handbook of Social Psychology* (forthcoming).

RALPH H. TURNER, Professor of Sociology at the University of California, Los Angeles, has served as Chair of the ASA Section on Social Psychology, as Editor of *Sociometry,* and as President of the American Sociological Association. Currently, he is Vice-President of the International Sociological Association. He has published numerous works in social psychology, including *Collective Behavior* (with L. Killian) (1957, 1972), *Social Context of Ambition* (1964), *Family Interaction* (1970), and *Robert Park on Social Control and Collective Behavior: Selected Papers* (editor) (1967).

MARY GLENN WILEY, Associate Professor of Sociology at the University of Illinois at Chicago Circle, has been a member of the Editorial

Board of *Sociometry.* Her publications lie chiefly in the areas of social psychology and the sociology of education.

CHARLES R. WRIGHT, Professor of Communications and Sociology at the University of Pennsylvania, has served on the Editorial Boards of *Sociometry, American Sociological Review, Public Opinion Quarterly,* and other journals. He was a member of the *ad hoc* committee of sociologists who helped to found the current ASA Section on Social Psychology. *Mass Communications: A Sociological Perspective* (1975) is one of his many published works.

LOUIS A. ZURCHER is Professor of Social Work and Sociology and Acting Dean of the School of Social Work at the University of Texas, Austin. He has served on the editorial boards of seven journals concerned with social psychological topics, and currently is Editor-in-Chief of *The Journal of Applied Behavioral Science.* Many of his articles and three of his books, *Tornado* (1970), *Citizens for Decency* (1976), and *The Mutable Self* (1977), are concerned with collective behavior and social movements.

Preface

Nonsociologists sometimes express puzzlement at the fact that a branch of sociology should be called "social psychology." Yet, whether viewed from the perspective of honored tradition or contemporary theoretical and research activity, social psychology clearly occupies a prominent position in sociology. Historically, it may be noted that (1) the first sociology textbook, published by Small and Vincent in 1894, devoted five chapters to social psychology; (2) as early as 1908, the sociologist E. A. Ross published a book entitled *Social Psychology;* and (3) the universally acknowledged father of sociology, Auguste Comte, is also accorded paternity of the field of social psychology by an eminent authority (Allport 1968). More recently, one can point to the following facts: (1) in terms of self-identification, social psychology currently ranks as one of the foremost areas of specialization among professional sociologists; (2) social psychology is the most common subfield represented in the major sociological journals (Brown and Gilmartin 1969); (3) the American Sociological Association officially sponsors a journal entitled *Social Psychology Quarterly;* and (4) the subject matter is widely taught in sociology departments throughout the country (Segal and Segal 1972).

Sociologists thus share with psychologists an involvement in the field of social psychology. Curiously, however, there is no agreement about what social psychology is. Some authors speak of "two social psychologies" (Stryker 1977) or of "three faces of social psychology" (House 1977). The sense that there is a "psychological social psychology" (PSP) and "sociological social psychology" (SSP) (Boutilier et al. 1980) is increasingly shared. Such language, of course, is figurative. There is only one field of social psychology, whether one defines it, as Allport (1968) does, as an "attempt to understand and explain how the thought, feeling, and behavior of individuals are influenced by the actual, imagined, or implied presence of others," or, as the *Social Psychology Quarterly* (1979) does, "as the study of the primary relations of individuals to one another, or to groups, collectivities, or institutions, and also the study of intra-individual processes insofar as they substantially influence, or are influenced by, social forces." It is concerned, in other words, with how people (and the social forces impinging on them) affect one another's thoughts, feelings, and behavior.

Social psychology is an interdisciplinary field that commands the interest of some of those trained in both parent disciplines. There is nothing in the theory, method, or substance of social psychology that makes it exclusively sociological or psychological; differences are those of interest, emphasis, and approach. Over the years, however, many social psychologists have come to wonder whether there is something distinctive about, or at least characteristic of, the sociological approach to social psychology. In an effort to shed light on this question, in 1976 the Section on Social Psychology of the American Sociological Association decided to sponsor a volume that would set forth the sociological approach—or, perhaps better, the approaches of sociologists—to the field of social psychology. The Section membership was polled and overwhelmingly approved the proposal; Section members made numerous recommendations for chapter topics and contributors; and an editorial board was appointed to assume responsibility for the production of the volume. The editorial board members are Carl W. Backman, Sanford M. Dornbusch, Chad Gordon, Richard J. Hill, Herbert C. Kelman, Barbara F. Meeker, Morris Rosenberg, Howard Schuman, Sheldon Stryker, Ralph H. Turner, and Charles R. Wright. The editorial board elected Morris Rosenberg and Ralph H. Turner to serve as editors.

In preparing this volume, we have scrupulously avoided any attempt to define sociological social psychology or to specify its boundaries, limits, or legitimate areas of investigation. Such efforts at definition would have the effect of encouraging the erection of boundary posts between psychological and sociological social psychology, and nothing could be more alien to our intent. The two fields have generally enjoyed harmonious relations over the years and, we hope, will continue to do so.

Sociological Perspectives

The present work shows how certain sociologists deal with selected social-psychological topics. In some cases, the sociological approach is distinctive and special; in others, it is entirely indistinguishable from the approach adopted by psychologists. It is useful, however, to direct attention to certain of the more distinctive features of sociological theory, method, and substance.

Theory. When a sample of sociologists and psychologists were asked to rank the people who had made the greatest contribution to social psychology, psychologists tended to cite Lewin, Festinger, Schachter, Asch, Campbell, and Allport, whereas sociologists were more likely to cite Mead, Goffman, Freud, Homans, and Bales (Wilson and Schafer 1978). Sociologists, to be sure, are heavily indebted to psychologists for guiding theories; but if any theories may be said to be particularly *characteristic* of SSP, they would be, we believe, symbolic interactionism, social exchange theory, reference group theory, and role theory.

Symbolic interactionism is generally regarded as the most distinctive theoretical contribution to SSP. This does not mean that sociological social psychology rests more heavily on this theoretical base than on others, but rather that sociologists are decidedly more likely than psychologists to utilize it. Although Cooley, Thomas, and Park all made rich contributions to this field, the most seminal work has been that of George Herbert Mead (1934). Human life, Mead contended, is possible by virtue of the human ability to use vocal gestures; these gestures constitute significant symbols and express the same meaning to the person using them as to the person to whom they are addressed. Resting on this fundamental insight, Mead constructed a theory that shed important light on the nature of mind, self, and society. Refinements and elaborations of Mead's insights have been a major thrust of the work of sociological social psychologists in recent years, and interest in this development is at present high. The recently established Society for the Study of Symbolic Interactionism, sponsoring its own publication outlet, is helping to further this development. Unfortunately, some sociologists have elected to equate symbolic interactionism with the totality of SSP theory. The present volume shows that other theoretical orientations also contribute to the understanding of social psychological phenomena.

Since its introduction into sociology in the early sixties (Homans 1961), social exchange theory has also experienced substantial growth, development, and application. Although social exchange is not distinctively sociological (psychologists such as Kelley and Thibaut 1978 have contributed greatly to theory and research in this area), sociologists have been strongly influenced by this theoretical development. For these reasons, chapter 1 by Stryker and chapter 2 by Emerson, in this volume, are devoted to symbolic interactionism and social exchange.

Sociologists have also shared with psychologists a strong interest in reference group theory and role theory. Earlier sociologists had often been puzzled by the frequent discordance between group membership and individual attitudes and behavior. The introduction of reference group theory helped to make sense of hitherto perplexing findings and was thus adopted by sociologists as a central theoretical orientation. Role theory has also been characteristic of the sociological approach. This is understandable, for the role concept is the prime link between social structure, interpersonal interaction, and individual attitudes and behavior. Chapter 3 of this book, by Singer, is thus devoted to reference groups and social evaluation theory and chapter 4, by Heiss, to a consideration of social roles.

None of this is intended to suggest that the sociologist is any less dependent than the psychologist on such fundamental theories as cognitive consistency theory, field theory, psychoanalytic theory, social learning theory, attribution theory, and others. It is simply to say that sociologists are, on the average, more likely to make use of symbolic interactionism, social exchange, reference group theory, and role theory in attempting to account for the social phenomena they observe.

Method. The primary methods of social-psychological research are the laboratory experiment, survey research, field studies, field experiments, and natural experiments. Research findings indicate that, whereas psychologists tend to rely more heavily on laboratory experiments, giving less attention to survey research, precisely the reverse is true of sociologists (Wilson and Schafer 1978). These differences, of course, stem from the substantive interests of the two fields; different problems require different research methods.

It is with reference to method that both psychological and sociological social psychology have experienced the greatest intellectual upheaval in the past decade. Among psychologists this has crystallized into a so-called "crisis in confidence" (Boutilier et al. 1980). All social psychologists recognize, of course, that, except for such deductive systems as logic and mathematics, the strongest model of proof in science is the controlled experiment. In social psychology, however, the experiment has been subjected to three powerful blows.

The first is the growing awareness of "experimenter effects" (Rosenthal 1966) or "demand characteristics" (Orne 1969). The experiment, it is now evident, involves more than a dispassionate test of a scientific hypothesis; it is, in Wuebben et al.'s (1974) terms, a "social occasion." Research subjects are not simply passive objects responding to external stimuli. Instead, they are human beings equipped with cognitive frameworks and motivational systems who are wont to interpret the stimuli in their environments, to react to the characteristics of the investigator, to be alert to the covert communications of the experimenter—in short, to make sense of, and respond to, their environments. The intended experimental stimulus is therefore but one of a number of factors, including social factors, producing the observed response.

A second concern arose from a heightened sensitivity to ethical issues. When Milgram (1963) showed that, upon instruction by an experimenter, a research subject was willing to inflict great pain on another person, he demonstrated the startling degree to which subjects would conform to external authority in the experimental situation. Some social psychologists also raised questions about the ethics of using deception in ways that could be stressful to the research subjects.

Finally, the traditional concern about the limited generalizability of laboratory findings beyond the confines of the laboratory persisted and, in fact, grew. Research frequently showed very different behavior in real-life situations than in laboratory experiments. For one thing, the hierarchical arrangement of the experiment, with an essentially active investigator and passive subject, did not correspond to much of social interaction outside the laboratory. In addition, dispositions measured in the laboratory frequently failed to predict specific behavior in other circumstances (Mischel 1968; but compare Epstein 1979).

Sociologists employing the experimental method necessarily shared the crisis in confidence that assailed their psychologist counterparts. But the chief limitation of the experimental method, from the SSP perspective, was that it was fundamentally poorly adapted to deal with most of the substantive questions of interest to sociologists. Many of these questions required the use of the sample survey. The sociologist's methodological expertise was thus brought to bear on the following critical question: Is it possible to employ the survey method without completely sacrificing the scientific power of the experiment? Compared to the survey, there are two special advantages of the experimental method: (1) it permits the control of extraneous influences, and (2) it provides an unequivocal causal (particularly temporal) ordering of the variables. Controlled laboratory conditions are intended to ensure that the only systematic feature distinguishing the experimental from the control group is exposure to the experimental stimulus; all other differences are random.

Sociologists using the survey method have attempted to approximate, even if they could not match, certain features of the experiment. The first method was to introduce statistical controls in an effort to approximate laboratory controls. Second, the conduct of longitudinal studies enabled them more effectively to establish the time order of certain variables. Third, structural equation modeling enabled investigators to deal with multiple variables within a causal framework. Although causal models could not establish the validity of a causal structure, they could help to clarify and test the investigator's causal reasoning.

The survey method, to be sure, has also not been impervious to attack. Not only is the survey unable to match the conditions of control of the experiment, but it is also fundamentally dependent on verbal behavior which, it has been charged, does not invariably reflect phenomenal reality (Phillips 1971) or predict behavior (Deutscher 1973). These matters have greatly concerned both sociological and psychological social psychologists. Chapter 12, by Hill, sheds light on the relationship between attitudes and behavior.

Other sociological social psychologists also hold that the survey is poorly designed to deal with certain important social psychological phenomena. Many, including the majority of those who call themselves symbolic interactionists, favor instead an ethnographic methodology. The case for this method is developed by Blumer (1969) and many others. According to this view, similar behavior and even identical spoken or written words can have quite different meanings in different situations. Hence one cannot assume, as the survey researcher must do, that short sentences, phrases, and even single words convey standard meanings for all subjects. Even the act of completing a questionnaire or answering survey questions orally creates distinctive social situations, from which generalization to everyday life may be as unwarranted as generalization from laboratory experiments. While there is no way to achieve certainty, the investigator who observes behavior intimately, at length, and repeatedly in its natural setting should come closer to grasping the valid meanings of the acts in question.

Substance thus governs method. Although appreciative of the power of the experiment, SSP has been obliged to step outside the laboratory in order to study social structure and personality, to explore such naturally occurring events as social movements or other types of collective behavior, to study interaction in organizational settings, to conduct sociolinguistic studies of subcultures, to engage in ethnomethodological studies, and so forth. The laboratory experiment has thus played a less central role in SSP than in PSP.

Substance. Given their different disciplinary origins, it is understandable that SSP and PSP should be characterized by certain differences in substantive interests. In general, sociologists are more likely to be concerned with the bearing of the stable persistent features of society on individual behavior, whereas psychologists are more disposed to focus on such intrapsychic processes as cognition and motivation. Thus, the sociologist characteristically begins with a search for order, pattern, and structure in society and attempts to understand how these persistent features of society shape individual personality and behavior. For example, how do social structure, culture, organizations, institutions, norms, values, and so forth impinge upon individual personality and behavior?

Kohn's work (1969, 1977; Kohn and Schooler 1969), discussed in detail in chapter 6 by Gecas, and in chapter 17 by House, is prototypical. The springboard for Kohn's research is the view that the technological and economic imperatives of occupational activity influence the formation of cognitive processes, values, orientations, and so forth in adult life. Kohn is able to demonstrate that people whose occupations involve substantively more complex work develop distinctively different ways of thought. (These differences, furthermore, are not attributable to initial selection into the occupations.) Similarly, when a social psychologist studies the relationship between social class and authoritarianism, between race and self-esteem, or between cultural norms and fatalism, he or she is asking the same order of question, namely, what is the relationship between the patterned features of society and the intrapsychic processes or overt behavior of individuals? Some sociologists are also interested in the effect of personality on social processes (for example, how the authoritarian personality structure may produce an attraction to Nazi political ideology). The connection between social structure and personality is described in chapter 17 by House.

Sociologists are also deeply engaged in exploring the dynamics of social interaction. Perhaps the most distinctive contribution of these studies has been the elucidation of the implicit rules, assumptions, and processes that underpin the everyday interactions of persons. Symbolic interactionism, ethnomethodology, conversation analysis, and the dramaturgical approach are illustrative of work in this area. Two features of this approach are especially worthy of note. The first is that the focus is on dynamic processes rather than on static social or individual structures. The second is the heavy stress on the situation, or, to be more exact, on the individual in the situation. Characteristic of the questions explored by sociologists of this orientation would be the following: What implicit rules do people adopt in presenting themselves to one another? How are social roles played and how are they made (Turner 1962) in human encounters? What are the implicit vocabularies of motive (Mills 1940) employed by people to account to others for their behavior? What linkages or networks of interaction are established in social life? How are role privileges and obligations negotiated in formal organizations (Strauss 1978)? What conversational rules govern communication patterns?

Third, the sociological social psychologist is particularly likely to focus on real-life events—a particular race riot, an assassination, a fad, an election. Certain scientific issues surrounding the studies of real-life events or the ongoing operation of social institutions require special attention.

REAL LIFE EVENTS OR PROCESSES

The focus on natural events or processes has both advantages and disadvantages. On the one hand, it is comparatively free of the problems of experimenter effects and artificiality that afflicts much of experimental research. On the other hand, the conditions of scientific control obviously cannot be imposed on the study of such events; furthermore, such research leaves the social psychologist at the mercy of historical events. In chapter 20, dealing with group movements, sociocultural change, and personality, Smelser and Smelser observe: "As new preoccupations and problems boil up in the larger society, investigators desert old concerns and turn to more timely ones. We note the great fall-off in research on the psychosocial origins of student radicalism, which dominated in the 1960s, and an upsurge of interest in religious cultism in the 1970s." Similarly, the large amount of research on black self-esteem in the recent past, and the increasing recent concern with gender and the self-concept, are consequences of ideological currents in a particular society at a particular time.

Much of sociological social psychology, as the present volume demonstrates, is thus anchored in concrete social processes or events: modernization; desegregation; encounter groups; religious movements. The concern is with what is happening. How does the work experience of people at different stratification levels in the predominantly large-scale organizations in the last quarter of the twentieth century actually influence cognitive processes, values, and behavior? How does school desegregation—for this group at this time in this place—bear upon cognitive processes, self-concepts, and intergroup relations? What features of life on a modern kibbutz or in a tightly knit isolated religious order impinge on human personality in what ways? How have historical changes brought about modifications in self-definitions (Zurcher 1977) or in definitions of the "real self" (Turner 1976)? What are the implicit rules of self-presentation that appear in different societies?

The fact that social psychology is so solidly rooted in culturally and historically bound events has inspired two major critiques of the field. The most radical is that of Gergen (1973), who contends that social psychology's pretensions to scientific status should be abandoned. Holding that efforts to establish transhistorical laws of social behavior are misdirected, he advises us to view "social psychology as history."

Along with sociology's interest in real-life events is its concern with the application of social psychological principles to various organizational and institutional settings. This interest has caused Liska (1977) to contend that sociological social psychology has become "dissipated." Specifically, Liska contends that sociologists characteristically focus on some social phenomenon of interest without taking account of the fact that similar underlying social psychological processes are operating in different circumstances. For example, a sociologist studying prison incarceration will cite literature dealing with prisons, prison structure, prison experience, and so on. But one of the features of incarceration is that it represents a setting for socialization (see chapter 5 by Bush and Simmons and chapter 6 by Gecas), that is, one in which the new recruit must learn a new culture as he adapts to new institutional rules. The features of socialization common to prisons, schools, work places, families, military institutions, and so on, tend to be overlooked. The consequence is that social psychology tends to become dissipated over a series of "social psychology of" subfields.

Must we thus conclude that the social psychologist by focusing on actual events thereby abandons the quest for general principles? We think not. The sociologist studying a real-life event is not simply acting as a journalist or historian. The point of such studies is to *induce* the general underlying principle from the examination of a range of concrete events. It is from the study of specifics that we come to understand the general. By studying soldiers in combat, we develop ideas about relative deprivation (Stouffer et al. 1949a) and of anticipatory socialization (Merton 1968); the study of changing student attitudes sheds light on reference group identification (Newcomb 1943); studies of school desegregation teach us about social comparison processes (Rosenberg and Simmons 1972); the outbreak of the "June Bug" disease among Southern factory workers enhances our understanding of processes of "hysterical contagion" (Kerckhoff and Back 1968).

The abstract principle thus characteristically emerges from the examination of the concrete situation. Such synthetic work, drawing on data from diverse substantive sources, is precisely the focus of this book. As we shall see, the authors of the various chapters have made abundant use of the very diverse materials provided by studies of specific substantive issues to enunciate broader principles. Careful, specific, concrete studies of social events serve as the building blocks for the construction of higher order generalizations. The two chapters on collective behavior (chapter 14 by Lofland and chapter 15 by Zurcher and Snow) are noteworthy illustrations of how the sociologist makes use of concrete social events as the basis for enunciating higher order principles.

In sum, both SSP and PSP make their characteristic contributions to the joint enterprise of understanding the connection between the individual and society. The contributions of psychologists have been carefully synthesized and set forth in a number of works, achieving their definitive expression in the handbooks of Lindzey (1954) and Lindzey and Aronson (1968). No equivalent is currently to be found in SSP. The present work represents an introduction to such an enterprise. It is not our intention in this work to define an area of sociological social psychology that stands in contrast with a psychological social psychology; on the contrary, we flatly reject such an objective. The authors of the following chapters are not self-consciously attempting to bring to bear a sociological perspective on the topics under consideration. They are, instead, sociologists examining social psychological phenomena. In some cases, the sociological approach may be distinctly different from that characteristically adopted by psychologists; in other cases, it is not. To affirm that a given chapter represents a sociological perspective is not to deny that it may equally represent a psychological perspective.

LIMITATIONS OF THE PRESENT WORK

In planning the present volume, a decision was reached to attempt to produce a volume that would be readily accessible to a wide audience. This goal could only be achieved by limiting the work to a single volume of moderate size. Inevitably, then, the work is characterized by certain limitations.

First, not all topics legitimately subsumed by SSP could be represented in this volume. When members of the ASA Section on Social Psychology were polled to elicit suggestions for chapter topics, no fewer than ninety-one different topics were recommended. The present work could accommodate fewer than one-fourth of these. Hence, such developing topics as ethnomethodology, phenomenology, dramaturgical social psychology, social construction of reality, androgyny, social motivation, and social stress and adaptation could not be accommodated as separate chapters. The same was true of such "social psychology of" subfields as the social psychology of large-scale organizations; of work; of the family; of age and aging; of mental illness; of political behavior; and so forth. Although the topics included in this work are important ones, they by no means exhaust the topics of interest and relevance to SSP.

Perhaps the most conspicuous exclusion has been the discussion of methodology. Faced with the option of presenting a limited, and hence inadequate, treatment of social-psychological methodology or none at all, we reluctantly chose the latter course. This decision is regrettable, because few advances have been so consequential for SSP in recent years as its methodology. It is solely space limitations that have prevented us from treating this topic with all the seriousness it deserves.

Second, it has been necessary to keep the chapters relatively short. Authors have been required to limit their discussions to a selection of major points, omitting or radically abbreviating discussions that more extended treatments would have permitted. The strategy has been to retain the main substantive ideas, even if elaborations, exemplifications, and exhaustive literature coverage had to be sacrificed. In many cases, authors have been obliged to pare the references to the bone.

These chapters also do not pretend to the status of definitive treatments of their respective topics. There is no party line, no official position, on these topics. Other sociological social psychologists might certainly have treated these topics differently. This work represents, then, not *the* sociological perspective but *some* sociological perspectives. Some fields, such as symbolic interactionism, are currently in considerable ferment, characterized by different approaches, even schools. Other fields, such as social exchange, are being enriched and deepened through theoretical and empirical advances. Still other areas, such as reference group theory —long-established areas with an impressive research tradition—are in process of re-examination and re-direction. Topics such as the social psychology of the self-concept or sociocultural change and personality are slowly emerging from an amorphous mass of ideas and data and are beginning to achieve rudimentary outline, shape, and form. And some recently emerging fields, such as the social psychology of emotion (see chapter 18 by Gordon), are still in the first exciting bloom of discovery.

SSP, then, is in a dynamic phase of development. The reader will find little here that is fixed in concrete, that is immune to challenge or impervious to modification. SSP is currently mature enough to speak with authority and confidence on the various topics it addresses, but youthful enough to be searching for new directions, attempting to establish frameworks that will comfortably accommodate the abundance of data and ideas that have accumulated in recent decades. SSP might suitably be described as having reached the late adolescent stage of development; as such, it is heir to the various identity crises that so often characterize that developmental stage. This volume, we hope, will assist it in discovering and establishing that identity.

Acknowledgments

In preparing this work, it has been our good fortune to encounter generous cooperation and encouragement at every turn. Our greatest debt is owed to the following colleagues who gave us the benefit of their thoughtful and constructive chapter reviews: Duane F. Alwin, Joseph Berger, Orville G. Brim, Jr., Peter J. Burke, John Clausen, Edward Z. Dager, W. Phillips Davison, Norman K. Denzin, Gordon J. DiRenzo, Glen H. Elder, Jr., Gregory Elliott, David Finkelhor, Arthur W. Frank, David D. Franks, Frank F. Furstenberg, Jr., William A. Gamson, Viktor Gecas, Norman Goodman, F. Roger Higgins, Howard B. Kaplan, Melvin Kohn, Kurt Lang, Otto N. Larsen, Robert Leik, George J. McCall, John McCarthy, Robert F. Meier, Andre Modigliani, Melvin Pollner, James Richardson, Thomas Scheff, Mady W. Segal, James Short, Anselm L. Strauss, Murray Webster, Jr., Eugene Weinstein, L. Edward Wells, Jr., Robin M. Williams, Jr., Milton Yinger, and Don H. Zimmerman.

We are also grateful to Midge Decter and Margaret Steinfels of Basic Books whose support and encouragement helped greatly to bring this work to fruition.

We are also pleased to express our appreciation to Jane Deiter, who coped so efficiently and creatively with the multitudinous secretarial tasks associated with an enterprise of this complexity, and to Michael Wagner, whose assistance proved to be invaluable in the later stages of manuscript preparation.

This work is a project of the Section on Social Psychology of the American Sociological Association. We have been sustained in our efforts by the constant encouragement of the Section members and officers, and we are grateful to them for this support.

PART I

Theoretical Orientations

1 SHELDON STRYKER

Symbolic Interactionism: Themes and Variations

Introduction

Of the theoretical orientations underlying work in social psychology, it is symbolic interactionism that has had its major development among sociologists and that has had major appeal to sociologists. In part, this reflects particulars of the history of the orientation: its early elaboration took place at the University of Chicago during the time that institution played a dominant role in the production of sociologists. In part, however, the appeal of symbolic interactionism to sociologists reflects the fundamental compatibility of this social-psychological perspective with the structural concerns of sociology proper. A theme of this chapter is fit, sometimes neglected and only now being thoroughly exploited, between more general sociological theory and symbolic interactionism as social psychological theory.[1]

This theme is present particularly in a later section of the chapter, where the link being forged between traditional symbolic interactionism and role theory is emphasized and where it is argued that the concept of role serves as the point of articulation—the bridge—between theories that have to do, respectively, with the social structure and with the social person. It is present as well in the section of the chapter that treats a version of current symbolic interactionism that eschews role concepts as too static, non-processual, and insufficiently attuned to the constructed character of social life, and uses the concepts of negotiation and negotiated order to link person and social organization.

As the foregoing suggests, there is considerable internal variation in the content of symbolic interactionism. While there is a core set of theoretical assumptions and concepts which most, if not all, working within this framework accept and use, there are other theoretical ideas relatively peculiar to one or another version. This is equally—perhaps more—true of methodological ideas; the methodological stances of symbolic interactionists range from a thoroughgoing rejection of the ordinary conventions of science as commonly understood to a complete acceptance of these. Such internal variation is another theme of this discussion.

This chapter is concerned more with ongoing and future developments in symbolic interactionism than with history. Some critical sense of the history of this perspective is essential, however, if current emphases are to be understood; and sufficient history must be presented to permit that understanding. What follows this introduction is an abbreviated and selective history of symbolic interactionism that begins with the Scottish moral philosophers and carries the story to the very recent past.[2] To the degree that symbolic interactionist theory in a technical sense exists,[3] it does so in the form of small-scale explanations of relatively limited scope. Although a few such explanations will be briefly treated, the primary concern of this chapter is with symbolic interactionism as a theoretical orientation or as a conceptual framework. That is to say, this chapter is concerned with delineating an approach to the social-psychological world in general, a frame that suggests the terms of and the ways in which explanations of social-psychological events and processes can be formulated. The distinction between theory and theoretical orientation is fundamental; the latter can only be judged on the basis of logical coherence and fruitfulness in suggesting theories that withstand empirical test. Obviously, this assertion implies the belief that specification and test of theories are indispensable to continued adherence to and utilization of a framework or orientation. This chapter is written in the spirit of that belief.

Despite that belief, however, relatively little reference to concrete research will be made. In part, this is because a framework is logically prior to the formation of testable theory and thus to the research that tests theory. In part, it is because a choice had to be made: available space does not permit review and intensive critical evaluation of research; and to simply list researches or present findings uncritically does little justice to the complexities of relating findings of research of varying degrees of sophistication and relevance to theoretical issues. In part, it is because —although there is more good research done from a symbolic interactionist frame than its critics allow—a strong research tradition premised on a symbolic interactionist orientation is still emerging. Thus, the choice made was to concentrate on the framework itself. In the same vein, many of the applications of the symbolic interactionist framework have been in the substantive areas of deviance, of the family, of work (including the professions and occupations), and of collective behavior. Although brief recognition will be given such applications, by and large the focus of the chapter is on the framework abstracted from the substantive areas.

Some years ago, Mullins (1973) essentially wrote off symbolic interactionism as a viable perspective within sociology. His concern was with symbolic interactionism as broader, sociological theory, and he failed to appreciate the degree to which symbolic interactionist ideas have been absorbed into the sociological mainstream. Nevertheless, there have been periods in which symbolic interactionism has waxed, others when it has waned. It waned considerably during the ascendance of a "sociology as hard science" aspiration, doing so in an important degree because many of its most visible adherents were explicitly opposed to the development of rigorous methods espoused by the hard-science advocates. It waned during the period in which functionalism was both intellectually and politically dominant in American sociology.[4] It is now waxing, sparked by the invigorating effects of current efforts to go beyond earlier concern with "proper" interpretations or transliterations of the "masters" and to go beyond sterile debates in which doctrinaire and stultifying positions were taken; by a new concern with theory construction and with test of theory abetted by new and successful attacks on difficult measurement problems; and by new forms of social organization.[5]

The Early Development of Symbolic Interactionism

The fixing of origins of any complex line of thought is arbitrary. Although the label, symbolic interactionism, is a relatively recent invention,[6] the line of thought the term represents can conveniently be traced to the Scottish Moral Philosophers.[7] These eighteenth-century thinkers, as Bryson (1945:1) notes, sought to provide an empirical basis for the study of man and society. While holding diverse views of what was fundamental about the human mind, they—Adam Smith, David Hume, Adam Ferguson, Frances Hutcheson, and others—argued in common that the facts of human association had to be taken into account if a science of man was to be achieved. They turned their attention to communication, sympathy, imitation, habit, and custom in their attempts to develop principles of human behavior. Thus, Adam Smith (1759) writes (discussing the consequences of isolation from others): "Bring him into society, and he is immediately provided with a mirror which he wanted before. It is placed in the countenance and behavior of those he lives with. This is the only looking glass by which we can, in some measure, with the eyes of other people, scrutinize the propriety of our own conduct."[8] David Hume —as well as Smith—saw in "sympathy" the principle through which humans develop their sense of membership in and benefits to be derived from society, and through which they come to be controlled by others. Sympathy, as these Scotsmen conceived it, allows persons to put themselves in the place of others, to see the world as these others do; and sympathy makes possible the communication that initially forms and subsequently reshapes (as we seek the approval of others) who and what we are. As this suggests, society is viewed as a network of interpersonal communication, connecting persons organically. In this manner, the Scottish moral philosophers foreshadowed the symbolic interactionist view of the basic nature of society and of the source of self in society. In addition, they collectively made viewing man as a natural object legitimate, and emphasized the scientific importance of everyday experience. Approaching human behavior from the standpoint of society rather than biology, they appreciated mind as instrumental in human adaptation, emphasized habit relative to instinct, and understood the relation of habit to custom.

The link from the Scottish moral philosophers to contemporary symbolic interactionism proceeds through the American pragmatic philosophers: C. S. Pierce, Josiah Royce, William James, John Dewey, and—of special import—George Herbert Mead. In general terms, pragmatism echoed and elaborated themes already reviewed; it viewed mind as an instrument for adaptation, treated mind and mental activities as natural objects (that is, as open to scientific investigation), saw the organized and internally dynamic character of the human mind, and emphasized the relevance of the natural (including social) world for the emergence of the individual.

More particularly, William James (1890) argues the importance of society as a source of constraints on behavior, doing so through the concept of habit. Particularly relevant to current theoretical extensions of symbolic interactionism, he develops a conception of "self" as both multifaceted and the product of relations with others; and his analyses of the character and sources of self-esteem anticipate current efforts to model the impact on person of society.

John Dewey (1940), by seeing personality organization as primarily a matter of habit and social organization as primarily a matter of custom defined as collective habit, insisted on the intimate relation of person and society. While noting that asserting the priority of society to individual is "nonsensical metaphysics," he observed that nevertheless every person is born into a pre-existing association of human beings, and that habit will consequently reflect a prior social order. Custom and habit are the necessary bases for reflection, for thinking, and thinking occurs in the process of humans adjusting to their environment. Thinking is instrumental; it involves defining objects in one's world in the context of activity and rehearsing possible lines of action in ways instrumental to adaptation. In another influential vein, Dewey rejected a monolithic view of society, instead seeing society as a set of many differential associations.[9]

Putting Mead aside for the moment, the ideas of the philosophers and psychologists reviewed enter sociology largely through Charles Horton Cooley. While Cooley's somewhat more affective orientation has long been neglected by symbolic interactionists relative to Mead's more cognitive emphasis, he still stands as a foremost contributor. Cooley (1902: 84–87) insisted upon the importance of the mental and the subjective in social life, going so far as to define society as a "relation among personal ideas," and "the imaginations which people have of one another (as) the solid facts of society." He called for "sympathetic introspection"—a process by which one uses sympathy to imagine things as others imagine them—as the prime method of discovering these solid facts of society and of other persons as well, since, for Cooley, the individual and society are simply two sides of the same coin: no individual exists apart from society, and there can be no "self" apart from "others." In brief, for Cooley, there is no individuality outside of social order, personality develops from extant social life and the communication among those sharing that life, and others' expectations are central to this development.

A second sociologist, William Isaac Thomas, shares with Cooley preeminence in the early development of symbolic interactionism. Thomas held that accounts of human behavior must incorporate both the subjective and the objective facts of human experience. The objective facts are constituted by situations, circumstances calling for some adjustive response on the part of persons or groups. Intervening between situations and adjustive responses, however, are definitions of the situation, in Thomas's (1937:18) words, "an interpretation, or point of view, and eventually a policy and a behavior pattern." It was Thomas who provided the simple and powerful rationale for the significance of the subjective in social life, and in so doing, provided symbolic interactionism with its prime methodological rule: ". . . if men define situations as real, they are real in their consequences" (Thomas and Thomas 1928:567).

But it is another philosopher, George Herbert Mead, who is the single most important influence shaping symbolic interactionism, in part because he gave more systematic treatment than did anyone preceding him to the ideas being reviewed. Mead's basic social psychological dictum, growing out of evolutionary principles that see mind and symbolic communication among humans as permitting the cooperation essential for survival, is: start with the ongoing social process. From that process, mind, self, and society derive;[10] and the relations among interaction (the ongoing social process), mind, self, and society become the subject matter of his social psychology.

With Dewey, Mead argues that persons initiate activity relating them to their environments, that is, they do not simply respond to "stimuli" existing apart from ongoing activity. Objects become stimuli as they function in the contexts of acts and come to be defined as relevant to completing the act; they acquire meaning in the course of activity. The same principle holds for acts implicating other humans in their completion. Such social acts are the source of personality and of organized social behavior, outgrowths of the social process made possible by communication through language.

Communication involves conversations of gestures, the use by participants in social acts of early stages of one another's acts as indicators or predictors of later stages. From these gestures evolve significant symbols, gestures having the same meaning in the sense of indicating the same future phases of acting to participants. Meaning, for Mead, is thus behaviorally defined: "The meaning of what we are saying is the tendency to respond to it" (1934:67). Significant symbols make possible the anticipation of responses, one's own and others, and adjustment of those responses on the basis of anticipation. We "take the role of the other" through the use of significant symbols and through this process engage in cooperative activity. We come to have minds, to think, through being part of a social process in which significant symbols emerge. These symbols provide the meaning of objects, the meaning to which we are responsible as we incorporate objects into our activities.

The "self" develops through the same social process. Emergent from social interaction, the self—" that which can be an object to itself"—is a social structure existing in the activity of viewing oneself reflexively. Language permits using the standpoint of others to so view oneself.

Once developed, the self becomes critical to the understanding of behavior. Mead envisions two aspects of self: the "me," or the organized attitudes (expectations) of others incorporated into the self; and the "I," or the responses of the person to the organized attitudes of others. For Mead, the "I" represents the creative, spontaneous aspect of human behavior. Important here is the idea that creativity and spontaneity occur within the social process, not outside of it; behavior is the outcome of a dialectic in which the attitudes of others are responded to by the person are responded to by the attitudes of others, ad infinitum. Social control is a necessary condition for the emergence of self-control.

Obviously, for Mead, the development of self is of central importance. In general terms, as noted, the self develops as does any other object. More particularly, it does so through an early "play" stage and a later "game" stage. In play, the child takes the role of particular others. But social life is complex, and for it to proceed one must respond to an intricate pattern of related behaviors by multiple others; thus, Mead's metaphor of the game. To play a game, one takes the role of the "generalized other," the attitudes of the "organized community." One does so, of course, through the symbolic capabilities characterizing humans.

Selves arise out of interaction of persons in organized groups; the prior existence of organized groups is thus implied. But, according to Mead, as society shapes the self, so does the self shape society through the I-me dialectic. Society is through this process continuously being created and recreated; in contemporary language, social interaction is constructed. Social order and social change are aspects of the larger social process.

With Mead's (1934) synthesis, symbolic interactionism entered a period of exegesis, debate with respect to "proper" interpretation, application of the perspective to a variety of issues in sociology and social psychology, the working out of methodological positions, and—to some extent—conceptual development and research designed to examine and test fundamental assumptions. A discussion of the work of two persons, Herbert Blumer and Manford H. Kuhn, will serve both to characterize the period and to bring us closer to the point of contemporary developments.

Self-presented and commonly taken as a straightforward elaboration and specification of Mead, a view devastatingly challenged recently (McPhail and Rexroat 1979),[11] the writings of Herbert Blumer[12] have heavily influenced (particularly, perhaps, in methodological terms) the thought of many sociologists working within the symbolic interactionist frame. Since much of Blumer's writing has the character of a polemic against a sociology he defines in contradistinction to symbolic interactionism, that influence has indeed been consequential both for current issues within sociology and for the character of current attempts to cast symbolic interactionism in more social structural terms.

Mead's analysis of the bases of symbolic interaction, suggests Blumer (1962), presumes that society is composed of individuals who have selves, whose action is constructed through a process of reflexively guiding that unfolding action by indicating the meaning of objects in a social context for prospective action. It also presumes that group action involves the fitting together of individual lines of action through role-taking. Society must be conceived in a manner consistent with these "easily verified" premises, he believes, and he conceives society as consisting of people's actions taking place in and with regard to a situation and constructed by interpreting the situation, identifying and assessing things that must be taken into account, and acting on the basis of the assessment. He insists that even in situations in which there exist common understandings or definitions developed through prior interaction, an interpretive process occurs in which the actions of participants are constructed. He contrasts this view of society with the view held by conventional sociologists, for whom society is a structure or organization. According to Blumer, symbolic interactionism sees social organization as entering action only to the extent that it shapes situations and provides symbols used in interpreting situations. While profound in stable and settled societies, the influence of social organization is less in modern society where crisscrossing lines of action mean situations for which there are no prior standardized actions. From his point of view, seeking to link social behavior to role requirements, expectations, rules, attitudes, and so forth, is inconsistent with recognizing that the human is a defining, interpreting, and indicating creature; Blumer (1969a:1–60) argues that to do so is to have no place for people with selves through which their worlds are handled and action constructed. From his point of view, the articulation of individual lines of action constitutes the social organization of action. Failure to recognize this blinds analysts to the fact that established and repetitive forms of action have to be continuously renewed through interpretation and designation. Analysis in terms of concepts such as culture, social order, norms, values, rules misses the basic point that it is group life that creates and maintains rules, not the other way around.

Blumer's methodological principles are drawn from this vision of the person, organized action, and the environment as fluid, continuously constructed and reconstructed through definitional and interpretative processes; this vision represents "the nature of the empirical world" that Blumer instructs us to respect and to organize our methodological stance to reflect. It is in the name of this vision of the nature of the empirical world that Blumer abjures what he sees as the current, conventional methodology (1969:28–34): adhering to scientific protocol, engaging in replication of research, relying on the test of hypotheses and employing operational procedures. It is also in the name of this vision that he (1954; 1956) instructs sociology to abjure the use of "definitive concepts" and "variables."

Definitive concepts refer to what a class of objects have in common through a clear definition in terms of attributes or fixed bench marks. They contrast with "sensitizing concepts," which, according to Blumer, "merely suggest directions along which to look" rather than "prescriptions of what to see." Blumer suggests that analysis in terms of variables, among other deficiencies, leads one to ignore the processes of interpretation and definition by assuming that an independent variable automatically affects a dependent variable. This assumption fails to recognize that anything that is defined (and everything that is of consequence in social life is, from this point of view) can be redefined, which implies that relationships among "variables" have no intrinsic fixity and that interpretations cannot be given the qualitative constancy required of a variable. It is this same quality of interpretations that rules out the use of definitive concepts.

In place of the experiments, surveys, refined measurement instruments, census data, computer simulation, and "crucial empirical data to test hypotheses" he sees as dominating the methods of conventional sociology, Blumer calls for direct examination of the empirical world of everyday experience. But one must do more than look. Blumer recommends two modes of inquiry to us: exploration and inspection. By definition a flexible procedure not tied to particular techniques, exploration is guided by the maxim to get a clearer picture of what may be going on in an area of social life by any ethical procedure: observation, informal interviewing, listening to conversations, getting life-histories, using letters and diaries, arranging for group discussions, consulting public records, using a resource group of informed persons. In exploration, one constantly tests and revises images, beliefs, and conceptions of the social world being studied. Ultimately, one constructs a comprehensive and intimate account of what takes place in that empirical social world.

Having done so, one then turns to inspection in order to meet the requirements of scientific analysis for clear, discriminating analytic elements and the isolation of relationships among these elements. This involves casting a problem in theoretical form, sharpening connotative referents of concepts, unearthing generic relations and formulating theoretical propositions. Again, the contrast Blumer draws is with his picture of conventional social research, which presumably starts with a theory or model framed in terms of relationships between concepts, uses the theory to select a problem, converts the problem into independent and dependent variables, uses precise techniques to obtain data, discovers relationships between variables, and uses the theory or model to explain these relations. Inspection is the antithesis of such methods; it is flexible, imaginative, creative, unroutinized. It involves looking at empirical instances of given analytic elements in a variety of different ways, viewing them from different angles and from the standpoint of many different questions.

One is indeed to test empirically the basic premises of symbolic interactionism, according to Blumer, but one cannot do so by the "alien criteria of an irrelevant methodology" (that is, by conventional methods). Rather, these premises "can be readily tested and validated merely by observing what goes on in social life under one's nose" (1969:49–50).

Given that the premises of symbolic interactionism are validated, suggests Blumer, certain methodological implications follow: see objects as people see them (since they act on the basis of the meaning the objects have for them) in order to understand their behavior; social interaction must not be compressed into pre-existing forms, rather the forms it takes must be empirically discovered; social action must be analyzed by observing the process of construction, noting how the situation is seen by the actor, what the actor takes into account and how this is interpreted, trying to follow the interpretation that leads to a selection of particular acts. From Blumer's point of view, the study of complex organization or complexly organized social life poses no methodological problem different from those posed when studying individual action.

Many of the tensions, debates, and variations within symbolic interactionism have been described by delineating two "schools," one labeled the "Chicago School" and identified with Blumer and his students, the other labeled the "Iowa School" and identified with Manford H. Kuhn and his students.[13] The contrast between the two has been summarized (Meltzer, Petras, and Reynolds 1975:123, note 4) by saying that the " 'Chicago school' emphasizes process not structure, sympathetic introspection not attitude scales, indeterminacy and emergence not determinacy." As this not entirely apt description does suggest, Kuhn's symbolic interactionism is much more oriented to the development of precisely stated theory and rigorous empirical test of that theory than is Blumer's, and in that sense is considerably closer to the viewpoint of this chapter.

To emphasize his interest in developing generalizations tested by empirical research, Kuhn (1964) chose the label *self-theory* for his version of symbolic interactionism. He regarded his theoretical and conceptual ideas as "orthodox" in their derivation from Cooley, Dewey, and Mead; but he sought to assimilate diverse materials to his perspective. In particular, he assimilated role theory and reference group theory, finding it difficult to distinguish these from symbolic interactionism. He adopted role theory's conception of social structure as consisting of networks of positions and associated roles (expectations). Agreeing that social structure is created, maintained, and changed through symbolic interaction, he also viewed social structure, once created, as constraining interaction. But his identification of role theory and symbolic interactionism is not total; his own emphasis is on role-taking, and on the self as mediating the relation between social structure and behavior. Noting the absence of determinacy in the relation of role expectations and performances, he is more inclined to see determinacy in the relation of self to behavior.

Kuhn treats the self as an object. Observing that for Mead objects are plans of action, or "attitudes," he proposes that the "self" be conceptualized in these terms. The significance of self lies in the need to know subjective definitions of identity in order to predict how people organize and direct their behavior, a requirement growing out of the looseness in secular society of ties between social systems and the individual occupants of statuses in these systems. Attitudes toward self as object are the best indexes of plans of action in general; thus, the most significant object to be defined in a situation is the self.

The core self, a stable set of meaning attached to self as object, takes on central importance in Kuhn's theorizing. It is the core self that provides structure and relative stability to personality and provides continuity and predictability to behavior. However, Kuhn visualizes the self as having a large number of component parts and related aspects, including subjective identification in status terms, attributes and traits, roles, role preferences, role avoidances, role expectations, areas of self-threat and vulnerability, self-enhancing evaluations, patterns of reference selections. Given the complexity of self, Kuhn clearly anticipates no simple relation of self to behavior.

The core self constrains behavior; stability in self results in stability in interaction. Such stability, however, is relative. Kuhn sees opportunity for creativity through the role-taking process, and through the self-control made possible by that process. He also, as noted, sees some slippage between social structure and self-definition, thus opportunity for some volatility in self.

If there is some stability to self, then reliable measurement becomes possible. Kuhn is oriented to conventional science; he seeks general propositions from which specific hypotheses can be drawn and tested, resulting in theory useful in predicting and explaining human behavior and interaction. He sees the route to such theory in sound measurement of the concepts embodied in a tentative theoretical statement in the context of empirical research. To achieve sound measurement, one must start with clear and precise specification of concepts. Kuhn clearly sees no contradiction between the kind of concepts entailed in symbolic interaction theory—concepts that refer to meaning, to the internal and subjective, to symbolic processes—and meeting the requirements for sound measurement; and he sees the contribution he and his students have made to symbolic interactionism in these terms.[14]

While it is convenient to use Blumer and Kuhn as symbols for major themes in the development of symbolic interactionism, bridging the gap from the founding (American) fathers to the relatively recent past and the present, they did not alone fill that interval. It becomes more and more apparent, as symbolic interactionism seeks to develop its incorporation of social-structural concepts, that characterizing the "Chicago School" of symbolic interactionism solely by reference to Blumer's writings is a considerable oversimplification and even distortion.[15] Thus, there is another wing of the school, in part independent of the Blumer wing and in part merging with it, that builds in particular from W. I. Thomas through Robert A. Park and Everett C. Hughes to more recent generations of students. Park's (1955:285–86) insistence on the link, through the concept of role, between self and social structure had major impact. This same insistence is contained in Hughes's (1945) work; and certainly Hughes must be credited with moving Chicago students to participant observation as a principal research form. While the relative neglect in the present context of these figures is justified in part by the fact that Blumer generally has been viewed as *the* spokesman for symbolic interactionism, in part by the strategic requirements of the themes being developed in this chapter, and in part by pragmatic considerations, their continuing influence should not be overlooked.

But there are others who contributed to the ongoing development of symbolic interactionism. Not every (or even many) of these others can be cited, and every person working within the symbolic interactionist frame would construct a somewhat different list of persons and works worthy of being singled out as significant. Nevertheless, and without attempting to locate persons within particular subtraditions, any comprehensive history of the framework would certainly have a place for those in the following account.

Ernest W. Burgess (1926) early adapted the framework deriving from Mead to focus on interactional patterns within marriage and the family, as did Willard Waller (1938).[16] Edwin Sutherland (1939) developed in the differential association theory the implications of this general line of thinking to criminality, and others—for example, Alfred R. Lindesmith

(1947) with respect to opiate addiction; and Edwin M. Lemert (1951)[17] with respect to deviance more generally—extended the application of symbolic interactionist ideas to a variety of forms of deviance.

At a slightly later time, the leads provided by these applications were followed by a "third generation" of students. Thus, Howard S. Becker (1963), Erving Goffman (1963b), and Thomas Scheff (1966) (among others) saw the shaping of the self-concepts or identities of those to whom "society" applied various stigmatizing labels as key to the production of deviance and deviants. In the context of the family, Leonard S. Cottrell (1948), Clifford Kirkpatrick (1955), Ruth Cavan (1953), Reuben Hill (Waller and Hill 1951), Ralph H. Turner (1970), and the present author (1956, 1964) (again, among others) applied and extended the framework in the analysis of husband-wife and parent-child relationships, emphasizing variously the dynamics of role relationships, the significance of role-taking and communicative processes, the importance of symbolic processes. Ralph H. Turner and Lewis M. Killian (1957) and Tamotsu Shibutani (1966) pursued yet another arena of application, collective behavior, basing their treatments to some extent on earlier work by Blumer (1951).

Nor were conceptual and theoretical issues neglected through this period. Perhaps the extremes in theoretical discourse are represented by, on the one hand, John W. Kinch's (1963) effort to formalize the theory of self-concept formation and behavioral impact, and, on the other, Erving Goffman's (1959) subtle portrayal of the processes by which the actor as subject shapes the behavior of others. Influential conceptual distinctions and elaborations are presented in C. Wright Mills's (1940) classic statement on motivation from the perspective of symbolic interaction, Nelson N. Foote's (1951) elaboration of a conception of motivation in terms of identification and identity processes, and Howard S. Becker's (1960) use of the concept of commitment in the interest of a satisfactory interactionist theory of motivation; Walter Coutu's (1951) attempt to clarify the confusion that had grown up around the concepts of role-taking and role-playing; Howard S. Becker and Anselm Strauss's (1956) reintroduction of a significant time dimension in symbolic interactionist thought through the concept of careers; Tamotsu Shibutani's (1955) assimilation of the concept of reference group to symbolic interactionism, and its clarification from the latter point of view; Ralph H. Turner's (1962) reinvigoration of sense of interaction as emergent and constructed through the concept of role-making; Gregory P. Stone's (1962) pregnant development of the conception of situated identity; Eugene A. Weinstein and Paul Deutschberger's (1963) specification of self-presentational processes employing the concept of altercasting; Barney Glaser and Anselm Strauss's (1964) statement on awareness contexts, and Erving Goffman's (1961b) on role distance and role embracement, both seeking to advance our understandings of the impact on behavior of variable commitment to identities.

If there is a highly arbitrary, "personal" quality in the foregoing citations of symbolic interactionist applications and conceptual developments in the period under review, these qualities are necessarily accentuated in citations of research literature.[18] Partly involved is what "counts" as research. If one includes all work that references the empirical world, however anecdotally,[19] the "research literature" growing out of a symbolic interactionist framework is enormous; if systematic and rigorous inquiry is required, the eligibles are relatively few. Further, if systematic and rigorous research that can be interpreted within a symbolic interactionist frame, as differentiated from that which self-consciously and explicitly stems from that frame, is included, the candidates for mention expand greatly. The attempt in the following is only to illustrate various research issues and genres, to make the point that, while the ratio of research to conceptual and theoretical discourse might well have been higher, there has been a continuous stream of research motivated by symbolic interactionism.

One part of that stream seeks to examine the basic premise of Mead's thought, by asking whether the responses of others do indeed shape the self; much of this literature utilizes a survey or an experimental format.[20] The complementary question, whether and how self-concepts do in fact affect further behavior, is studied in a variety of settings and uses a wide variety of research procedures, from informal interviewing to observational to schoolroom questionnaires. So, for example, Alfred R. Lindesmith (1947) uses informal interviewing and an analytic induction procedure to develop his theory of opiate addiction, in which self-concept as addict plays an important role. Donald R. Cressey (1953) uses similar methods and ideas to examine the processes by which persons become embezzlers, as does Howard S. Becker (1953) with respect to marijuana use. Walter Reckless and his associates (1956) focus on the ways in which self concepts as "good" and "bad" boys contribute to the making of delinquents, generating data through questionnaires, as do Michael Schwartz and Sheldon Stryker (1970). Becker (1951) ties the reactions of musicians to their audiences to their conceptions of themselves as musicians, basing his argument on participant observation and informal interviewing. And Schwartz, Fearn, and Stryker (1966) investigate the way in which stable self-conceptions as disturbed contribute to confirming children in emotionally disturbed roles, with data provided by structured instruments.

Since the shaping of the self, and self-concept change, is the heart of the problem of socialization from a symbolic interactionist standpoint, studies already cited are germane to that research topic. So, indeed, are perhaps most researches developing from the frame, particularly if socialization is recognized as a lifelong process. (It is an interesting fact that, until comparatively recently, symbolic interactionists did little with childhood socialization other than cite Cooley's early observations of the evolution of self in his own children and repeat Mead's dicta.) Illustrative researches with direct interest in socialization per se are those of Becker et al. (1961) dealing with medical school students, and Olesen and Whitaker (1968) dealing with nurses, works primarily based on observational and informal interviewing; Brim's (1958) statistical analysis of data relating family structure and the learning of sex roles by children; Norman K. Denzin's (1972, 1975) observational studies of the emergence of self in early childhood; and Thomas and Weigert's (1971) cross-national analysis of adolescent conformity to the expectations of significant others using data from questionnaires administered in classroom settings.

Central to the symbolic interactionist framework, along with the concept of self, is the concept of role-taking. While relatively few researches directly focus on role-taking behavior, some do, among them O'Toole and Dubin's (1968) behavioral demonstration of the reality of the phenomenon in a systematic observational study of mothers feeding their infant children and in an experimental study of body sway; Cottrell's (1971) experimental study of muscular tension in response to observing others' muscular tension; Thomas, Franks, and Calconico's (1972) questionnaire study of the relation between role-taking and power in families; and Stryker's (1956, 1957) work, using structured interviews, on the sources and consequences of accuracy in role-taking.

Finally, this review of research stimulated by a symbolic interactionist framework during the period between the work of the founding fathers and the relatively recent past would be seriously misleading without reference to what have been taken to be characteristic examples of *the* research style associated with symbolic interactionism (Lofland, 1970): qualitative case studies of interaction in diverse social contexts. Examples are Glaser and Strauss's (1964, 1968, 1971) study of the interactions of hospital personnel, family, and dying patients in a hospital setting; Julius Roth's (1963) study of the passage of patients through hospitals, Egon Bittner's (1967) examination of the ways in which police deal with the mentally ill, and—perhaps epitomizing the genre for many[21]—Goffman's (1963b, 1967, 1971) many reports on strategies of interaction.

Current Developments in Symbolic Interactionism

Having traced the history of the symbolic interactionist framework from the Scottish Moral Philosophers to the relatively recent past, it remains to discuss more or less current developments. As a prelude, it will be useful to summarize that framework and to present various criticisms of the framework as it has developed.

As previously remarked, there is no single symbolic interactionism whose tenets command universal acceptance; thus, it ought not surprise that no one summary statement will be acceptable to all. Stone and Farberman (1970:1) delimit the field of social psychology from the standpoint of symbolic interaction in terms of six questions: What is meaning? How does the personal life take on meaning? How does the meaning persist? How is the meaning transformed? How is the meaning lost? How is meaning regained? Manis and Meltzer (1978:5) suggest that the fundamental elements of symbolic interactionism include the meaning component in human conduct, the social sources of humanness, society as process, the voluntaristic component in human conduct, a dialectical conception of mind, the constructive and emergent nature of human conduct, and the necessity of sympathetic introspection. Meltzer, Petras, and Reynolds (1975:54) assert that all varieties of symbolic interactionists take as basic premises that humans act toward things on the basis of the meaning those things have for them, that meanings emerge from social interaction, and that meanings are modified and dealt with through an interpretative process used by persons when responding to things encountered.[22] Jonathan Turner (1978) characterizes the core of symbolic interactionism as consisting in the assertions that humans create, use, and communicate with symbols; they interact through role taking, which involves the reading of symbols used by others; they are unique as a species through having mind and self, which arise out of interaction, and which allow for the interactions that form the basis of society.[23]

The writer (1959) has characterized the common elements uniting symbolic-interactionist thinking in terms of a set of assumptions and a predilection. The assumptions are that human beings must be studied on their own level, and that reductionist efforts to infer principles of human behavior from the study of nonhuman forms are misguided; that the most fruitful approach to the study of human social behavior is through an analysis of society; that the human infant enters life neither social nor antisocial, with the potentialities for human development; and that the human being is an actor as well as a reactor. The predilection is to stay close to the world of everyday behavior, both in the development of the framework and in its application.

George J. McCall (1977) offers the following principles as underlying symbolic interactionism, and the set can be taken as his summarization of the framework:

1. Man is a planning animal, constructing plans out of bits and pieces supplied by culture.
2. Things take on meaning in relation to plans; the meaning of a thing is its implications for plans of action being constructed, so a thing may have different meanings relative to different plans.
3. We plan toward things in terms of their meanings; a plan of action is executed contingent on the meaning for that plan of things encountered.
4. Consequently, every thing encountered must be identified and its meaning discovered.
5. For social plans of action, meaning must be consensual; if meanings are not clear, they are hammered out through the rhetoric of interaction resulting in the creation of social objects.
6. The basic thing to be identified in any situation is the person himself; identities of actors in a situation must be consensually established.
7. Identity, meaning, and social acts are the stuff of drama; as drama involves parts to be played, roles implicit in the parts must be conceived and performed in ways expressive of the role. The construction of social conduct involves roles and characters, props and supporting casts, scenes and audiences.
8. Thus, identification of persons is most often in terms of roles and characters. We identify by placing things in systematically related categories of role systems, status systems, systems of social types, or contrastive sets of social categories.

Another generalized statement of one version of symbolic interactionism has been offered by the writer (1980:53–55). It has the advantage of being less terse and so perhaps more understandable as a summary description of the framework; and it has an advantage in that it incorporates important aspects of recent developments in the framework. Accepting the fundamental reciprocity of society and person, the statement arbitrarily begins with the impact of society on person.

1. Behavior is dependent upon a named or classified world. The names or class terms attached to aspects of the environment, both physical and social, carry

meaning in the form of shared behavioral expectations that grow out of social interaction. From interaction with others, one learns how to classify objects one comes into contact with and in that process also learns how one is expected to behave with reference to those objects.

2. Among the class terms learned in interaction are the symbols that are used to designate 'positions,' which are the relatively stable, morphological components of social structure. It is these positions which carry the shared behavioral expectations that are conventionally labelled 'roles.'
3. Persons who act in the context of organized patterns of behavior, i.e., in the context of social structure, name one another in the sense of recognizing one another as occupants of positions. When they name one another they invoke expectations with regard to each others' behavior.
4. Persons acting in the context of organized behavior apply names to themselves as well. These reflexively applied positional designations, which become part of the 'self,' create internalized expectations with regard to their own behavior.
5. When entering interactive situations, persons define the situation by applying names to it, to the other participants in the interaction, to themselves, and to particular features of the situation, and use the resulting definitions to organize their own behavior in the situation.
6. Social behavior is not, however, given by these definitions, though early definitions may constrain the possibilities for alternative definitions to emerge from interaction. Behavior is the product of a role-making process, initiated by expectations invoked in the process of defining situations but developing through a tentative, sometimes extremely subtle, probing interchange among actors that can reshape the form and content of the interaction.
7. The degree to which roles are 'made' rather than simply 'played,' as well as the constituent elements entering the constructions of roles will depend on the larger social structures in which interactive situations are embedded. Some structures are 'open,' others relatively 'closed' with respect to novelty in roles and in role enactments or performances. All structures impose some limits on the kinds of definitions which may be called into play and thus the possibilities for interaction.
8. To the degree that roles are made rather than only played as given, changes in the character of definitions, the names and the class terms utilized in those definitions, in the possibilities for interaction can occur; and such changes can in turn lead to changes in the larger social structures within which interactions take place.

This version of the symbolic interactionist framework obviously gives greater weight to social structure than do some alternative versions, and does so in a way that permits the elaboration of structural concepts to reflect the complexities of the social world in which humans exist. It also, perhaps not quite so apparently, leaves more room for the routine, habitual, and customary in human behavior than is generally true of contemporary symbolic interactionists despite the importance of such phenomena for their forebears. It opens the door to serious theorizing about the *reciprocity* of self and society, a basic theme of all symbolic interactionism, but one which—because of the way in which it traditionally has been formulated—has not moved much beyond the level of truism to specification of linkages.

In part, recent developments in symbolic interactionism have occurred in reaction to critical appraisals of the framework.[24] Given the internal variations, a portion of these appraisals represent critiques of proponents of one version by proponents of another. Given that internal variation, as well, critiques addressed to one version may or may not be applicable to another,[25] a fact not altogether appreciated by persons evaluating the framework. Too, the worth of critical appraisals must be estimated against the claims made by a theory or theoretical framework: a frame intended to be general is properly subject to criticisms that a frame addressed to a narrow range of issues may not be.

There are basically five kinds of criticisms of symbolic interactionism that recur in the literature, ignoring more or less subtle variations:[26] key concepts are confused, imprecise, and do not lend themselves to sound theory; its concepts are difficult, if not impossible, to operationalize, thus few testable propositions can be formulated, and scientific explanation is rejected in favor of intuitive insight or understanding; emphasizing reflexive thought, symbolic interactionism underplays the import of emotions and the unconscious in social life; the emphases on actors' definitions, on the immediate situation of action, and on the emergent character of organized behavior deny or minimize the facts of social structure and the importance of large-scale features of society, and leave the perspective incapable of dealing adequately with those large-scale features; and the neglect of social structure constitutes an ideological bias.

While no adequate defense of these assertions can be offered here,[27] and however well they may apply to particular statements by symbolic interactionists, there is nothing in the framework that in principle requires conceptual vagueness or imprecision, the rejection of scientific explanation, and so forth; and the fact that testable propositions have been formulated using the framework belies the universal applicability of the first two criticisms. Symbolic interactionism, at least in degree, does neglect the emotions[28] in its emphasis on reflexivity, thinking, and self-consciousness; it also, as noted earlier, neglects habit and custom. Insofar as symbolic interactionism seeks to be a general social psychological framework, such neglect leaves it open to legitimate criticism.

The last two criticisms are closely related, and their validity is a function of two fundamental issues: the extent to which symbolic interactionism is viewed as a general framework for sociological analysis, and the extent to which social structural concepts have been or can be successfully incorporated into symbolic interactionism.[29]

While some make the claim of general sociological utility for the symbolic interactionist framework, others do not.[30] If one does not, the important question becomes whether the framework can incorporate social structural concepts, and whether by doing so it can articulate reasonably to sociological orientations that do attend to such features of broad social organization as status, class, and power.

It is in light of this last question that many recent developments in symbolic interactionism can be viewed. It has been argued (Maines 1977) that symbolic interactionism—that of Blumer as well as of others—has always had more to say about social organization and social structure than its critics contend. However that may be,[31] it is clear that recent work extending the notion of negotiation and that seeking to make use of a modified role theory are attempts to give symbolic interactionism a more adequate sense of social structure, more useful structural concepts, and more reasonable ways of relating interpersonal interaction to large-scale organizational phenomena.[32] The writings of two persons, Anselm

L. Strauss with respect to negotiation and Ralph H. Turner with respect to role theory, will serve to illustrate this development.

Strauss and his co-workers[33] have been largely responsible for the development of a "negotiation" or "negotiated order" framework. This framework, for the most part growing out of his group's studies of interaction in hospital settings and anchored in the application of what has been termed a grounded theory methodology (1967), has been given its most developed statement by Strauss (1978).

Strauss's theoretical problem is rooted in Mead's concern with the question of how change and order in society can simultaneously and continuously exist.[34] He assumes that all social structures continuously break down and are constructed, and that negotiation is key to the construction process in any and all social orders. In brief, all orders are, from this point of view, "negotiated orders."

Negotiation is "one of the possible means of 'getting things accomplished' when parties need to deal with each other to get those things done" (Strauss 1978:2). Somewhat more specifically, the concept is described by central questions one is led to ask when adopting the negotiation framework: Who spoke to whom in what ways and in what sequences, with what responses and results? What negotiation processes occurred? What alternatives and options were considered? Attention is thus focused by the negotiation concept on the nature of some ongoing interaction, the actors involved in that interaction, the tactics and strategies used in the interaction, the "subprocesses" (for example, trading off) used, and consequences. Consequences are new, albeit temporary, organized patterns of interaction; they are new or reconstituted orders that are negotiated orders, and these negotiated orders become context for continuing negotiations.

As this last implies, negotiations occur in contexts, and the concept of context serves the negotiation framework by linking ongoing interaction to social structure. Strauss distinguishes two kinds of context: structural context and negotiation context. The former refers to the general structural parameters within which negotiations occur; the latter to the more specific and immediate properties of situations that bear directly on ongoing negotiations. The former are illustrated by the hospital division of labor, the professional specialty of psychiatry and specializations within the health-care professions that provided the context for the negotiations Strauss and his colleagues observed in psychiatric wings of hospitals. They are also illustrated by features of the American judiciary system and of marketplaces that are context for the covert negotiations of corrupt judges (1978:98–99). The latter, to which Strauss attends more closely, are illustrated by the number, experience, and skills of the negotiators; whether negotiations are open or not; whether negotiations are one-shot or repetitive; the number and complexity of the issues being negotiated; the clarity and separateness of the issues; the relative power and resources of the negotiators, and so forth.[35]

While the negotiation metaphor and the concept of negotiated order do point to aspects of social structure, they do not provide fully for the articulation of symbolic interactionist thinking with more general sociological theory, if only because the negotiation framework (at least to this point) leaves relatively undeveloped the conceptualization of the structural context within which negotiations take place,[36] and because the frame seems more oriented to developing understandings of specific negotiations than explanations couched in theoretical terms.[37] A more likely means by which this articulation can proceed is through role theory; and Ralph H. Turner has, over recent years, been concerned precisely with that articulation.[38]

Turner (n.d.*c*) is working toward the synthesis of symbolic interactionist and role theoretic elements in "something akin to axiomatic theory." His starting point is with criticisms of role theory: the theory offers an overly structured view of human behavior as the enactment of normative scripts; it neglects normal processes of social interaction in its focus on role strain and role conflict; it fails to make adequate use of the concept of role-taking.[39] He seeks to provide role theory with a proper appreciation for the role-taking concept, and so to correct role-theory's overly structured and conformist quality, seeing this core concept as key to the development of theory that can handle both stable, structured forms of social organization and less structured, fluid forms as well.

Human beings act as if others they meet are playing identifiable roles, role-taking to identify these roles. But cultural cues to roles are often vague and contradictory, and so provide only a general outline within which lines of action can be constructed. Under this circumstance, actors make their roles and communicate what roles they are playing in order to permit and to facilitate interaction (Turner n.d. *a;* n.d. *b*).

Actors will behave as though they and others with whom they interact are in particular roles as long as the assumption works by providing a stable and effective framework for interaction. They test the assumption by continuously assessing one another's behavior, checking whether that behavior verifies or validates the occupancy of a position by corresponding to expectations and by demonstrating consistency.

In addition to this emphasis on the concept of role in modified form, Turner retains the symbolic interactionist's emphasis on self. Self-responses emerge from interaction with others, and we present ourselves to others via our self-conceptions. Seeking to infer the roles of others, we seek to inform others through gestures of the role being played, and whether the roles being played are consistent with and invested with self —in brief, we seek to inform others of the degree to which self and role "merge" (Turner 1978).

Unsatisfied with role theory's disparate and unrelated propositions, Turner offers a strategy for theory building: begin with sensitizing concepts, narrow propositions and hypotheses drawn from the research literature, and move to precise definitions and to general, formal theoretical propositions linking empirical regularities and expressing major tendencies of those regularities. Then look for determinants of variation in the regularities, and group-related regularities. Finally, seek common principles to explain why the groupings of regularities should occur. He offers two general explanatory propositions: roles are used to achieve ends efficiently; the playing of roles is a means of achieving personal reward in the form of validation of self, self-esteem, and reinforcement from others.

This strategy is illustrated in his (1978) discussion of role-person merger. Conceptualizing persons as consisting of a hierarchical ordering of all roles in their repertoires, and noting that doing so relates the person meaningfully to social structure, he suggests three criteria of role-person merger: playing a role in situations in which the role does not apply; resisting abandonment of a role despite advantageous alternatives; and acquisition of attitudes and behaviors appropriate to a role. Delineating two types of determinants of mergers, interactive and individual, he then asks: what functions are served for those interacting by viewing one another as persons (that is, as playing roles)? And he concludes that the concept of person is related to the requirements of social control, since effective and lasting social control requires a more stable object than an actor who simply plays a particular role.

This interactive function of role-person merger leads to three interactive principles: in the absence of contradictory cues, people tend to accept others as they appear (the appearance principle); the disposition to see people in terms of their role behavior will vary with the potential effect of the role on interaction (the effect principle); and people will accept the least complicated view of the person that facilitates interaction (the consistency principle). Propositions are then derived from these principles: for example, the more inflexible the allocation of actors to roles, the greater the tendency to conceive the person as revealed by the role; the greater the potential power vested in a role, the greater the tendency to conceive the person as revealed by the role.

A similar analysis of individual functions of role-person merger (to facilitate understanding, predicting, and controlling others by becoming more understandable and predictable to them, to economize effort when playing many roles, to facilitate control and autonomy, to make possible the playing of roles providing gratification, to allow the individual to obtain rewards commensurate with investment) leads again to guiding principles consistent with these functions: people tend to merge their persons into roles by which significant others identify them (the consensual frame of reference principle); selective merger will occur to maximize autonomy and self-evaluation (the autonomy and favorable evaluation principle); and individuals will merge into person those roles in which greatest investment is made or for which return on investment is still to come. Again, propositions are inferred from principles; for example, the more intensely and consistently significant others identify individuals on the basis of a certain role, the more likely will those individuals merge that role and their persons; individuals tend to merge positively evaluated roles with their persons.

Role-person merger speaks to the link between self and social structure. The implications of that link are developed by Turner (1976) in an essay on the "real self": the subjectively held sense that people have of who and what they really are. The link between real selves and social structure should be significant in the functioning of and change in societies, he suggests. To the degree that self has an "institutional" focus, people will see their real selves in feelings, attitudes, and actions that are anchored in institutions, they will recognize their real selves in action when accepting group obligations. To the degree that self has an "impulse" emphasis, people see their real selves in untamed impulse with conformity to institutional norms occurring at the expense of their true selves.

Turner speculates that the past several decades have witnessed a major shift in the locus of self from institution to impulse in American society. If that is true, it has serious implications for the nature of social control and of societal order. Conventional sociological theories of control and order presume actors who locate their real selves in institutions. Turner hypothesizes that the locus of self correlates with a disposition to see either values or norms. Selves tied to institutions lead people to perceive values, and this facilitates control systems of the sort the sociological literature describes. Selves tied to impulse lead people to perceive norms and this does not fit with conventional control systems.

The importance of the foregoing lies, not in whether the substantive theory either stated or implied is correct, but in the ways in which social structure is introduced into social psychological theorizing. Turner uses the concepts of position and normative expectations, albeit cautiously, in order to avoid an overly structured stance. He views larger social structure as both constraint on self and social interaction and as product of self and social interaction. The larger structure organizes relationships, bringing some social circles[40] together and keeping others apart. The articulation of real selves with social structure is a major link in the functioning and change of societies.

A complementary vision of the relation of person and social structure is contained in an essay by Eugene A. Weinstein and Judith M. Tanur (1976). Visualizing the strength of the symbolic interactionism in its sensitivity to the emergent properties of interaction, these authors see this strength as the source of the excesses of one wing of symbolic interactionism. Among the excesses remarked[41] is neglect of the connectedness of the interactive episodes in which social structure finds its concrete expression. Weinstein and Tanur suggest that it is the aggregated outcomes of many prior episodes of interaction in the form of informal understandings, shared meanings, codified rules, and material resources that serve as frameworks for interactions and so link episodes of interaction; it is these aggregated outcomes that give meaning to social structure. Agreeing that the concept of role as it has been used in structural-functional analyses carries too great a theoretical burden, and that the degree to which a social encounter exhibits "role-ness" is variable and problematic, they nevertheless assert that norms and roles are part of the meanings accessible to participants in interaction and usable as resources in that interaction. In brief, the extent, conditions, and means by which social structure is introduced into interaction are to be subject to investigation, but social structure is not to be ignored.

A discussion by the writer (1980) reinforces these themes. Whatever their creative potential, most interactions tend to be with the same or slowly changing casts of others doing the same things on a repetitive basis. Structural concepts like group, organization, community refer to patterns of social life tying particular subsets of persons together and separating others. Structural concepts like class structure, power structure, age structure, and so forth refer to the more abstract social boundaries that operate in similar fashion. The important implication of the generic concept of social structure is that societies are differentiated entities whose differentiation has the consequence that only certain persons interact with one another in certain ways with certain resources in certain settings. Persons do not relate randomly, and the opportunities for and circumstances of social relationships are not randomly distributed.

The person is shaped by interaction, but social structure shapes the interaction. Conversely, when persons creatively alter patterns of interaction, ultimately social structure can change. These obverse assertions define the tasks of a sociologically oriented social psychology and (in part) of sociology, and require the bridging of social person and social structure. It is to meet this latter requirement that aspects of role theory are being drawn into symbolic interactionism.

A root idea of symbolic interactionism from its very beginnings has been the reciprocity of self and society. One way of expressing the criticism of the framework to which the attempt to draw in social structure responds is to say that it failed to respect the complexities of "society" in its conceptualization; and one way to describe sociology's treatment of "society" over recent years is to say that it has incorporated these complexities by imaging society as a multifaceted mosaic of interdependent but highly differentiated parts—groups, institutions, strata—whose relationships run from cooperation through conflict. If society is highly differentiated, and if self reflects society, self, too, must be highly differentiated. It is this insight that underlies another major development of symbolic interactionism, the emergence of identity theory.[42]

Identity theory capitalizes on William James's contention that people have as many selves as there are others who react to them. While Mead shared this sense of the human being with multiple selves, his philosophic premises and hopes led to an emphasis on self as a global, undifferentiated unity. But such an approach to self does not square with the basic symbolic interactionist dictum that self reflects society when the society at issue is complex, as it certainly is. A complex, differentiated society requires a parallel view of self on theoretical grounds.

Empirically, there are issues whose resolution calls for a conception of self as complex and differentiated, yet organized.[43] In particular, there are issues of both behavioral consistency and inconsistency across situations, of explaining the choices that are made when persons are faced with conflicting role expectations, of dealing with the greater or lesser resistance to change exhibited by persons in the face of changing social circumstances.

To meet both theoretical and empirical needs, the concepts of identity,[44] identity salience, and commitment are introduced. Identities are "parts" of the self, internalized positional designations that exist insofar as the person participates in structured role relationships, the consequence of being placed as a social object and appropriating the terms of placement for oneself. Persons may have many identities, limited only by the structured relationships in which they are implicated.

"Identity salience" is one theoretically important way in which discrete identities making up the self can be organized. That is, identities are conceptualized as being organized into a hierarchy of salience defined by the probability of the various identities being invoked in a given situation or over many situations. Directly implied in this definition is the general proposition that an identity's location in a salience hierarchy will raise or lower its threshold of invocation, in interaction with other defining characteristics of situations and (in all probability) other self characteristics as well, for example, self-esteem. Situations that are structurally isolated—through independence of personnel, by virtue of calendar or clock, and so forth—will likely call up only a single identity; conversely, situations that overlap structurally will call up more than one identity, and then the relative salience of those called up becomes a potentially important predictor of behavior.

The underlying symbolic interactionist premise that self reflects society can be made more precise and powerful through this specification of the concept of self. Greater precision and analytic power in specifying society-person linkages is also made possible through the concept of "commitment," defined as the degree to which the individual's relationships to specified sets of other persons depends on his or her being a particular kind of person.[45] By this usage, one is committed to the role of "husband" to the degree that the extensiveness and intensiveness of one's social relationships require that role. So conceived, commitment provides a way of conceptualizing "society's" relevance for interaction, doing so by pointing to social networks—the number of others to whom one relates through the occupancy of a given position, the importance of those others, the multiplexity of linkages, and so on. The general theoretical proposition, one which gives promise of considerably more explanatory potential[46] than its predecessor, is that commitment affects identity salience which, in turn, affects behavioral choices.

This general theoretical proposition leads to a number of testable hypotheses that, collectively, approximate a theory in a technical sense:[47]

- The greater the commitment premised on an identity, the higher that identity will be in the salience hierarchy.
- The greater the commitment premised on an identity, the more positive the evaluation of that identity will be and the higher the identity in the salience hierarchy.
- The more a given network of commitment is premised on a particular identity, as against other identities that may enter that network, the higher that identity will be in the salience hierarchy.
- The more congruent the role expectations of those to whom one is committed by virtue of an identity, the higher that identity will be in the salience hierarchy.
- The larger the number of persons included in a network of commitment premised on a given identity for whom that identity or a counter-identity[48] is high in their own salience hierarchies, the higher that identity will be in the salience hierarchy.
- The higher an identity in the salience hierarchy, the more likely role performances will be consistent with the expectations attached to that identity.
- The higher an identity in the salience hierarchy, the more likely a person will perceive a given situation as an opportunity to perform in terms of that identity.
- The higher an identity in the salience hierarchy, the more likely a person will actively seek out opportunities to perform in terms of that identity.
- The greater the commitment, the higher the identity salience, the greater the impact of role performance on self-esteem will be.

- The greater the commitment, the higher the identity salience, the more likely will role performances reflect institutionalized values and norms.
- The more perceived consequences of projected identity changes are in the direction of reinforcing valued commitments, the less the resistance to change will be, and vice versa.

While its significance is not narrowly limited, Peter J. Burke's work points toward adequate measures of role-identities, thus—among other things—strongly arguing that concepts important to a symbolic interactionist frame are amenable to sophisticated measurement procedures. Schwartz and Stryker (1970) suggest that Osgood's semantic differential technique is a theoretically justified measurement procedure from the point of view of symbolic interactionism; Burke (1980) extends that suggestion by taking seriously the position that measurement processes must be based on theoretical understandings of the phenomena to be measured and by using the semantic differential as the basis of his own procedures (Burke and Tully 1977).[49]

The theoretical properties of the concept of identity, or role/identity in Burke's terms, are that an adequate measure must reflect the ideas that identities are meanings attributed to and by the person to the self as an object in a social situation or social role; that identities are relational; that identities are reflexive; that identities operate indirectly; and that identities are a source of motivation. That one's acts develop meaning through others' reactions and come to call up in the person the responses of others requires a procedure that captures the multiple dimensions of meaning composing the self. Burke conceptualizes the dimensions as a multidimensional semantic space, and develops measurement procedures that use the responses of persons to map that space and to locate persons' role/identities within that space. The relational character of identities implies that identities must be defined (and thus measured) in terms of their relations to counter-identities; Burke's procedures translate this theoretical requirement by measuring identities in terms of commonalities among similarly situated persons and differences from persons in counter-positions.

More programmatic than actualized at this time are Burke's suggestions for meeting the remaining requirements for theoretically adequate measurement procedures. The self is reflexive, implying that although identities influence performances, performances are assessed by the self for their identity implications. The meaning of a performance is compared with the meaning that defines an identity initially. This aspect of self, Burke notes, can be measured by assessing the strength of corrective responses when a performance is off-target and by assessing what it is the person corrects.

The issue of self as process versus self as having temporal stability underlies the conceptualization of identities as operating indirectly. Burke suggests that identities are relatively stable, that we construct self-images as current working copies of identities, and that it is images that have direct influence on performances. Images have the flexibility required by situations and can accommodate role-making as well as role-taking, role construction as well as role enactment. The measurement implication is clear: we must get at both identity and image and find ways to deal with the dynamics of the relations between the two, and among them and performances.

Finally, Burke refines the idea that identities motivate through defining behavior and through the action implications of their meanings. If identities as meanings located in semantic space have action implications, identities close to one another in that space ought to have similar action implications. Further, acts have meanings, and those in the same semantic locations as identities ought to carry implications for those identities. Implied is a measurement procedure that measures both identities and actions in common terms, specifically by locating them in the same semantic space.

Conclusion

It ought to be clear from the preceding pages that symbolic interactionism is alive and at least reasonably well, and that it is pursuing a course in its development that serves to integrate within its general stance a reasonable conceptualization of social structure. In doing so, it is fulfilling both its early promise and the promise of a sociologically oriented social psychology. It is certainly as true today as it was during the height of the Blumer-Kuhn "debate" that there is no symbolic interactionist orthodoxy, no single vision of what the framework "means." In particular, perhaps, the divisions are methodological in the broadest sense of that term. Let us hope, however, that there is more tolerance for alternative styles of work and greater appreciation of the virtues (as well as the limitations) of the various styles. If that is true, it is indeed a hopeful sign, for it implies that less time will be spent in sterile argument addressed to the unwashed both inside symbolic interactionism and outside; that more effort will be expended in the research enterprise on which the framework ultimately rises or falls; that we will exhibit greater willingness to let that research tell us what is and is not useful in the framework; and that there is growing understanding that others—even others writing from the perspectives of alternative frameworks—may have something of value to say. And, if these implications hold, we can look forward to the continued influence and continuing development of the symbolic interactionist framework.

NOTES

1. This theme is also the motif of my more extended treatment (Stryker, 1980) of particular versions of symbolic interactionism, which treatment is used throughout this chapter. See also Handel (1979).

2. For more thorough treatments of the historical development of symbolic interactionism, see Stryker (1980) and Meltzer, Petras, and Reynolds (1975).

3. A theory, in a technical sense, is a set of propositions about some part of the empirical world specifying how this part presumably works, emerging from a set of assumptions or postulates and from a set of concepts used to describe the part of the world the theory purports to explain, and open to checking against empirical observations of that world.

4. I am indebted to Ralph H. Turner (personal communication) for these insights into the relative decline in the influence of symbolic interactionism as a perspective in sociology. Turner sees part of the more recent increased interest in symbolic interactionism as reflecting its role as an alternative to polarization between functionalism and conflict theories.

5. The reference here is to a relatively new Society for the Study of Symbolic Interaction, and its publication *Symbolic Interaction,* as well as to a revived Section on Social Psychology in the American Sociological Association which over the past few years has served to showcase panels on symbolic interactionist themes and topics.

6. Herbert Blumer is responsible for the term, initially using it in a chapter in Emerson P. Schmitt (1937). For some, Blumer's theoretical writings are taken to define symbolic interactionism. For others, the label represents a tradition of thought to which Mead, Cooley, and Thomas are the preeminent early "sociological" contributors, in which Blumer takes his place as an important but not necessarily decisive figure, and which contains a number of contemporary versions methodologically and theoretically distant from Blumer. It is obvious that this chapter is the product of one who holds the latter view.

7. For a detailed argument developing the import of the Scottish Moral Philosophers to American sociology and social psychology, see Bryson (1945).

8. This passage, emphasizing the dependence of conceptions of self on others, anticipates Cooley's discussion of the looking-glass self.

9. See also Dewey (1896, 1920).

10. To use the title of Mead's (1934) influential work, which is actually a compilation of his lecture notes published posthumously.

11. See also the challenge to the common assumption that Blumer's work epitomizes the tradition of Mead implicit in Stryker (1980). Blumer (1980) has written a rejoinder to McPhail and Rexroat, and has in turn been answered (McPhail and Rexroat, 1980).

12. Blumer's views as presented here are taken from essays written relatively late in his career. While these are not always consistent with essays written earlier (or, indeed, internally consistent), their characteristic emphases seem to me to represent accurately the nature of Blumer's influence. Many of his earlier essays reappear in Blumer (1969).

13. Neither label referring to the locales—for much of their careers—of those two symbols of contrasting views fits precisely in the intellectual pedigrees of persons tending to the respective positions the labels are intended to describe. Further, there is a large set of persons whose work is in a symbolic interactionist vein who cannot easily be fitted into either camp. Finally, as will be suggested later, one way of characterizing present developments in symbolic interactionism is to suggest that the divisions implied by the "Chicago" and "Iowa" labels are being bypassed. Too much intellectual energy has been expended in argument that seems to view one or another version of symbolic interactionism more in social movement terms than as a social psychological framework per se.

14. Kuhn and his students were responsible for the development of the Twenty Statements Test, an attempt to achieve a standardized test identifying and measuring self-attitudes. While some equate that specific test and Kuhn's methodology —see Tucker (1966)—and discredit the latter by noting problems of the former, Kuhn's methodological stance does not depend on the success of any particular measurement device.

15. Why the relative neglect of others, some of whom are cited in this chapter, is an interesting question. Perhaps, as with Park, the messages were ones that Blumer tended to deny in his polemical writings; thus, insofar as Blumer is identified with symbolic interactionism, it became "inappropriate" to incorporate

these others. Perhaps it was because Blumer was something of a charismatic figure, at least some of whose students tended to be "disciples."

16. I do not mean to imply, in asserting that Waller adopted Mead's framework, that Mead was the only influence at work on Waller. An identical caveat holds for every other citation in this section.

17. For an intersting and telling response to critics of the "societal reaction" theory of deviance, in which he calls for a much more subtle, structural analysis of society than labeling theorists typically provide, see Lemert (1974).

18. And, indeed, the distinction between this literature, the applications literature, and the conceptual developments literature is itself highly arbitrary.

19. There is a problem here that grows out of style of research and research reporting. Goffman's research may well be systematic and rigorous in the extreme; yet the style of reporting is such that his work looks more like an art form than science. A fair proportion of the symbolic interactionist literature has this characteristic.

20. See, for example, Miyamoto and Dornbusch (1956); Couch (1958); Reeder, Donohue, and Biblarz (1960); Videbeck (1960); Quarantelli and Cooper (1966); Sherwood (1965).

21. Perhaps not entirely fairly. Thus, Glaser and Strauss (1967) draw a strong distinction between the apparently undisciplined approach underlying Goffman's work and their own careful use of what they call the constant comparative method of grounded theory. Glaser and Strauss (1967) has become something of a bible—and the term, *grounded theory,* something of a shibboleth and battle cry—for those whose predilections are toward qualitative research; the book was written in the attempt to undergird qualitative work with the discipline and rigor its detractors have typically denied it.

22. These premises are taken from Blumer's (1969:2–6) characterization of symbolic interactionism.

23. Symbolic interactionists have traditionally asserted the uniqueness of the human species, premising their argument on the presumably unique capacities of humans and the emergence of self. That these presumably unique aspects of humans are indeed unique is severely challenged by recent work with chimpanzees. Apart from undergirding an extreme form of denial of the relevance of work on nonhuman animals for understanding human behavior, however, it is difficult to see what is gained from the assertion of human uniqueness.

24. Space limitations preclude a full review of these critical appraisals. For more complete reviews, together with references to the critical literature, see Stryker (1980) and Meltzer, Petras, and Reynolds (1975).

25. It must be more than apparent by now that criticisms directed at Blumer will not, in general, hold for other versions, and vice versa.

26. These five are reviewed in detail in Meltzer, Petras, and Reynolds (1975).

27. See Stryker (1980: chapter 5) for such a defense.

28. The neglect is relative, not total. See for example the discussion of interactionists' treatment of emotion in Meltzer, Petras, and Reynolds (1975:92), Kirkpatrick's (1963) and Turner's (1970) formulations of an interactionist theory of love, and Shibutani's (1961) discussion of emotion as response to blocked lines of action. See also the suggestion in Stryker (1968) that the self be treated as having conative and cathectic modalities as well as the cognitive modality typically emphasized. There is some indication that more serious work on the emotions is an upcoming item on symbolic interactionism's agenda.

29. This is not true of Huber's (1973) claim of bias in symbolic interactionism based on the argument that an unwillingness to be explicit in its theory leaves symbolic interactionism in the position of tacitly accepting the existing (power) structure of society. Not all symbolic interactionists are unwilling to be explicit in their theorizing.

30. Blumer would fit the first category; the writer, the second.

31. I think Maines overstates the case by ignoring the questions of the depth and adequacy of the treatment of these matters by Blumer and others.

32. Persons seeking to defend symbolic interactionism against the claim that it precludes a concern with macro-social structure cite the work of Hall (1972), Farberman (1975), and Denzin (1977) as counter-instances. These studies do indeed

incorporate both traditional concepts of symbolic interactionism and concepts referring to macro-structure. Whether, however, they resolve theoretically the issues involved in linking the two is moot.

33. See, for example, Bucher and Strauss (1961); Bucher (1962); Strauss, Schatzman, Ehrlich, Bucher, and Sabshin (1963); Glaser (1968); Glaser and Strauss (1965); Glaser and Strauss (1971); Strauss (1971).

34. This is the explicit starting point in Strauss, et al. (1963), which refers to Mead (1936:360–61).

35. While Strauss clearly thinks these aspects of negotiation contexts are reasonably general, the basic principle of the grounded theory approach is to make such matters open and dependent on emergence from the specific situation(s) being researched.

36. My reading of the negotiated order literature leads me to conclude that conventional sociological concepts, such as position, role, role relationship, status, norm, and so forth, are implicitly incorporated into what is said about the social person, interaction, and social structure, but are not explicitly recognized in ways that would be useful in the task of articulating symbolic interactionism and more general sociological theory.

37. I arrive at this judgment in spite of the explicit claims to the contrary to be found in Strauss (1978), through my sense of the basic focus of attention in relevant works.

38. This articulation is also the point of my own efforts, most recently in Stryker (1980). See also Stryker (1964, 1973) and Handel (1979).

39. Turner has another criticism of role theory, that its propositions have little connection with one another, which is less relevant in the present context.

40. Turner uses the term "social circles" to mean what some others mean by "groups," and "social networks," or "role set." His usage stems from Znaniecki (1965) and focuses on those persons involved with the person in the carrying out of her or his role.

41. The other is the injunction against quantitative research as a matter of faith rather than style, and the consequences of that injunction.

42. The outlines of identity theory appear in a paper I presented in 1966 at a meeting of the American Sociological Association which was subsequently published (Stryker, 1968). The same fundamental ideas are elaborated by McCall and Simmons (1966), although with some shifts in terminology and emphasis. The "invention" was entirely independent. I choose to present the theory in my own terms here.

43. The contemporary call for an elaborated conception of self derives only in part from the requirements of the symbolic interactionist framework. For an excellent and compatible vision of the complexities of the self-concept that stems fundamentally from the attempt to deal with empirical puzzles, see Rosenberg (1979).

44. McCall and Simmons (1978) as well as Burke and Tully (1977) use the term *role-identity* in an equivalent way, thus stressing the intimate linkage of self and role.

45. This usage derives from Kornhauser (1962).

46. That potential is now being examined in a research program under way at Indiana University under the writer's direction; preliminary results are highly encouraging.

47. These are taken from Stryker (1980); this statement is based on Stryker (1968).

48. The concept of counter-identity is the analogue of the concept of counter-role as conventionally used by symbolic interactionists. Thus "husband" is a counter-identity to "wife."

49. For an impressive, integrative, theoretical tour de force giving symbolic interactionist ideas central position, based on a research program using semantic differential procedures, see Heise (1977).

Social Exchange Theory

Introduction: The Character and Scope of Social Exchange Theory

If one takes George Homans's essay on social behavior as exchange to be the starting point, then social exchange theory has been part of American social psychology for twenty years.[1] The theory provoked controversy from the start. Morton Deutsch (1964) was critical of the way Homans used operant psychology. Bierstedt (1965) expressed doubt that very much social behavior actually rests upon the calculative rationality some exchange theorists seem to impute to it. The egoistic hedonism of a reward-maximizing, cost-avoiding image of man was found objectionable (Abrahamson 1970). Some exchange "explanations" were criticized (by me and others) as tautological (Emerson 1976). Exchange theory was judged inadequate because it dealt only with dyads (Simpson 1972; Ekeh 1974).

Sociological critics too numerous to mention have been repelled by the psychological reductionism advocated and attempted by Homans. Related to this is a more recent criticism leveled by sociological *collectivists* to the effect that (American) exchange theory is too *individualistic* in its basic conception of man (Ekeh 1974). In the writings of Thibaut and Kelley, Blau, and Homans alike, man (like most other animals) is portrayed as an individual faced with *choices* between alternative lines of action that are differentially rewarding. But the collectivist sees *society* as existing in normative prescriptions that remove choice and decision from action. "Social" action is normatively (collectively) mandated action. Hence, in taking decision-making behavior as its focus, exchange theory systematically fails to engage the social element in human behavior. Peter Ekeh (1974) is the most extreme critic in this respect. For him, exchange behavior *should* express or promote collective solidarity rather than individual benefit. If the theory does not portray it that way, then something is wrong, either with the theory or with the behavior it describes.

All of the critics of exchange theory have had worthwhile points to make. In my opinion, the exchange point of view is gaining broader acceptance in the field partly because it is changing in response to the above criticisms. Some of these changes will become apparent below. Most important among them are (1) increased awareness of the differences between economic and social exchange theory and (2) theoretical extensions beyond the dyad into *n*-person corporate groups and network structures.

THE FOCUS OF EXCHANGE THEORY

Whenever people encounter one another in social interaction, most of the things social psychologists talk and write about are happening *all at once.* Communication is in progress; roles are being formed, enacted, and negotiated; attributions are being made, both to other and to self; and identities are being validated or revised. No theory can possibly encompass it all. No mind can apprehend or comprehend it all at once. Thus, the aim of any theoretical perspective is to separate out a few attributes to be examined in purely analytic isolation. Having traded off claims to comprehensive knowledge, we hope to gain intellectual orderliness within the narrow slice of reality we have chosen to study within a given theoretical approach.

The exchange approach takes as its first focus of attention the *benefits* people obtain from, and contribute to, the process of social interaction. The benefits and losses we refer to have been given more or less technical labels in various disciplines (*reward, utility, valued outcome, positive reinforcement, cost, disutility, opportunity cost, negative reinforcement,* and so forth), yet their core meaning is essentially the same. While each technical term is embedded in its own body of principles and complementary terms, the basic principles involved are fairly similar across several disciplines, notably economics, psychology, anthropology, and sociology.

Three core assumptions in exchange theory. The principles are few in number, providing us with a highly parsimonious yet broadly applicable framework.

1. Beneficial events of all kinds, whether they involve money, goods, smiles, or simply "social attention," are valuable in exactly the same general sense: *people for whom they are beneficial act in a way that tends to produce them.* Such action is often called "rational" behavior.[2] It could also be called "purposeful" behavior or "operant" behavior, depending upon the intellectual tradition one is speaking from.

This is, in part, a definitional matter but it is also an implicit assertion to the effect that people often do, *in fact,* behave rationally (that is, in pursuit of benefits or valued ends). To challenge that assertion is to assert the opposite: that people value nothing. Clearly, this most broad conception of benefit carries with it a very weak and uncontroversial assertion concerning human rationality.

The central concept in exchange theory carries a different name in the various disciplines the theory springs from: *reinforcement* in psychology; *value* in sociology; *utility* in economics and decision theory; *reward, outcome,* or *payoff* in social psychology. I use the simple term *benefit* here, defined broadly enough to cover all of these special terms. The definition given above owes its wording to reinforcement psychology. It handles matters of value or utility in an extremely neutral and theoretically noncommittal way. If a person repeatedly spends money on wine, he is assumed to find benefit in wine—by definition—even though it might be another man's poison. If a person repeatedly invests time and effort in another person's welfare, that person is assumed to benefit from (to place value upon) that other person's welfare. Thus, exchange theory is not and never has been wedded to an egocentric model of human motivation.

Some readers might object to the above definition because it is "circular." Let me repeat that it is a *definition.* It is not an explanation. All definitions are circular when we try to use them as though they were explanations. Whether or not person *A* places value on *B*'s welfare is an empirical question whose answer requires first, a definition of value and second, some observations of behavior guided by that definition. *Why* he should behave in a way that promotes another's welfare is a different question—a question whose answer requires a *theory of values.* Such a theory is discussed below.

The definition of benefit offered above is applicable across the entire range of data on exchange dealt within the various disciplines from which exchange theory derives. A shipload of wheat obtained in return for dollars or human affection obtained in return for reciprocal affection are beneficial in exactly the same generic sense. In building a general theory, the similarities between love and a bushel of wheat can be more important than their obvious differences. (When we discuss the difference between social and economic exchange theory below, the difference is found *in the theories,* not in the kind of benefits they usually study, for example, "material" versus "psychological" benefits. *All* benefits have psychological and material properties.)

2. *Every class of beneficial (valued) events obeys a principle of satiation, value adaptation, or diminishing marginal utility.* The rate of unit value change is, however, a variable. This principle is an empirical assertion subject to test for each class of benefits. It provides, however, a clean conceptual basis for defining different classes of benefits: two events are members of the same class if each satiates the actor for the other. If eating reduces thirst and drinking reduces hunger, an exchange theorist would do well to call food and drink by a single name.

3. The third and final commonality among the various versions of exchange theory in different disciplines is the one that gives this approach its name: *benefits obtained through social process are contingent upon benefits provided "in exchange."* This principle comes to us as a set of empirical generalizations from students in various fields (for example, Gouldner in sociology, Mauss in anthropology, Skinner in experimental psychology). In addition, we have all discovered it for ourselves early in our own social learning. Thus, exchange theory starts with a simple metaphor involving two persons, each of whom provides benefits to the other, *contingent upon* benefits from the other. The capacity to provide some benefit to another is often called a *resource.*

Thus, exchange theory has as its focus the flow of *benefits through social interaction.* Other theoretical frames of reference focus upon various conceptualized features of the *same* empirical situations. For example, symbolic interactionism directs attention to the flow of *information* through symbolic social interaction. The same set of social events usually can be organized in either or both of these (complementary) theoretical frames. Symbolic behavior (in the Meadian rather than the Freudian sense) is operant, benefit-seeking behavior *par excellence.* Seldom is a beneficial event devoid of information, and information, if it is conveyed at all, is usually of value. But information and benefits differ as *concepts* and they are organized into different *theories.* Thus, when Ekeh (1974) insists that gifts exchanged in the Kula ring are symbols and not utilitarian objects, he is describing his own preference for one analytic scheme over another more than he is the ethnographic facts.

Types of social relationships. Much of the descriptive work on exchange, especially in anthropology, has examined some of the forms that principle (3) are known to take. For example, when the benefits enjoyed by exchange partners can be identified as paired events, they are often treated together as a single social entity called a *transaction.* Transactions occur in two distinct forms. A *negotiated* transaction involves *mutually contingent* contributions to the exchange, with both contributions evolving together in some social process. Examples would include two persons making love or the sale/purchase of a piece of real estate as the culmination of a bargaining process. A third example is the simple purchase of an item at a fixed and posted price.

The second type of transaction involves paired but separately performed contributions, only one of which is contingent upon the other. A "free gift," or altruistic act might initiate the process. It is "free" in the sense that it is performed in a noncontingent context (with or without an underlying expectation of return). The other's contribution might or might not occur. If it does occur, and if it is contingent upon (prompted by) the initiating contribution, a *reciprocal transaction* has occurred. If it does not occur, then principle (3) is seen in the fact that the free gift, even though it was truly free, tends not to recur. Long-term exchange relations form (or fail to form) as initiating gifts or altruistic acts prompt (or fail to prompt) reciprocal transactions.

Marshall Sahlins has given us the term *generalized reciprocity* to identify an important form of exchange. Let us develop this concept carefully through a series of steps. Note, first, that the reciprocal transaction, starting with a noncontingent "free gift," can become one of a series of such transactions between two long-term partners. Once such an *exchange relation* has formed between two people, the paired contributions defining a transaction often lose their paired contingency. A helpful act is performed, not in response to any specific benefit received, but rather in honor of the social exchange relation itself, that relation being *a series* of reciprocating benefits extending into the experienced past and the anticipated future. Whether or not accounts are kept, in whatever form, is an empirical question in the given situation. (Institutionalized practices often prescribe forms of accounting and methods of balancing accounts through, for example, the ritual discharge of debts.)

Now let the two-person reciprocating exchange relation described above become a set of three or more such relations among three or more persons, *A, B,* and *C.* Add to that set a special network-wide accounting system in which a benefit received by *B* from *A* can be reciprocated by a helping act *either* to *A* or to *C,* and the system is then an instance of what Sahlins calls generalized reciprocity. By virtue of the above "added" element of network-wide accounting, such an exchange system cannot be reduced to a set of separate dyads. The conditions under which generalized reciprocity will form and survive are worthy of more systematic research.[3]

The last type of exchange relation we must list has been called "incorporation" by Fredrick Barth (1966). It is very similar to what Emerson has called "productive" exchange relations (1976). Barth argues that people engage one another in two qualitatively different modes, a *transactional* mode in which each provides the other with benefit, and a mode called *incorporation* in which both (or all) parties contribute to collective gain. The two modes differ both in social process and in the typical motivation of the participants. Transactions involve reciprocal, but separate, benefits performed by persons motivated to enhance their own gains, as in bargaining over the units in a trading relation. Incorporation, by contrast, is based upon a special form of exchange in which separately obtained benefit is not possible. It takes two to dance the tango. If it is done well by both parties, both parties benefit from a single socially produced event. If either one fails to perform properly, neither one will benefit. Value is produced in the social process from behavioral contributions that have little or no value taken by themselves. Sometimes the benefit is immediately appreciated by all participants (though not necessarily in equal degree), and sometimes the productive process generates a tangible new resource that can be divided through acts of distribution. For example, 400 cavalrymen in the Mughal Army pool their resources in the process of conquering a Hindu fort (the conquest being a *productive* process from the Mughal point of view), and they then *distribute* the booty gained in proportions described by Gamson's theory of coalition formation. Productive exchange (Emerson 1972a, b), coalition formation (Gamson 1961a, b; Caplow 1956, 1959, 1968), and "incorporation" (Barth 1964) are very similar formulations. In Barth's writing, emphasis is placed on the emergence of group gain rather than individual maximization as a motivating strategy.[4]

The descriptive forms of exchange labeled above as negotiated transactions, reciprocal transactions, generalized reciprocity, and incorporated or productive exchange are obviously not a complete list nor are they a logically organized typology. The labels as yet have not even been agreed upon in the field. It is, rather, a first step toward a morphology of exchange relations, giving some sense of the range of phenomena studied within the exchange approach.

THE SCOPE OF SOCIAL EXCHANGE THEORY

Having stated what I believe are the three basic principles at the center of all exchange theories, the scope of the exchange approach could be specified as the range of events across which all three assumptions hold. So defined, the exchange approach would apply to all of micro-economics and much of the subject matter of social anthropology, sociology, political science, and social psychology. That is far too much to deal with in any coherent and in-depth manner. It is, therefore, essential that we take note of some of the major differences between one type of exchange theory and another.

Economic versus social exchange. One of the most troublesome features of social exchange theory in sociology, anthropology, and psychology has been its blurred boundary with micro-economic theory. Economic anthropologists, for example, have argued with one another for decades about the place of Western economic theory. One school, the *formalists,* maintains that neoclassical economic theory applies uniformly across cultures, whereas the *substantivists* maintain that economic institutions in nonwestern socieities are not well described or understood through the use of a Western economic theory.

In other fields as well, efforts have been made to distinguish between economic and social exchange as concretely separate and different forms of exchange behavior. Blau (1964), Ekeh (1974), and Goode (1978) are examples. For systematic discussion of such efforts, see Cook (1979).

It is now apparent, I believe, that no attempt to separate economics from social psychology or sociology of exchange, in terms of the kind of benefits exchanged, can possibly succeed in reducing the confusion. The suggestion that economics studies material or monetary benefits, whereas sociology, psychology, and anthropology study the exchange of more subtle psychological benefits, does an injustice to the power of theoretical concepts in each of those fields. Is a woman obtained through marriage a commodity, or a set of eligible women a market, subject to study through the use of economic theory? Economic anthropologists of the formalist school have every right and very good reason to invoke the theoretical apparatus of economics. Economists will persist in the analysis of what we like to call "social" behavior (see Leibenstein 1976; Williamson 1975), and sociologists will continue to analyze "economic" activity in their own way (see Laumann and Pappi 1976; White et al. 1976).

We must come at the issue from a different direction. Emerson (1976) and Cook and Emerson (1978) have argued that a very sharp distinction exists, not between economic and social exchange *behavior,* but between economic and social theory.

Neoclassical economic theory is based upon the assumption that *transactions are independent events.*[5] That is, if two persons, A and B, conclude a mutually beneficial transaction, the probability of a subsequent A-B transaction is assumed to remain unaffected. As a result, micro-economic theory assumes the absence of long-term relations between exchange partners. Obligations, trust, interpersonal attachment, or commitment to specific exchange partners are all alien topics for neoclassical economic theory. Their existence in empirical economic systems is often viewed as "imperfection" in the system.

No psychologist, sociologist, or anthropologist would advance the assumption of independence among transactions. The entire body of conditioning theory in psychology, regardless of the particular school, predicts that people will form long-term exchange relations composed of a series of *contingent* rather than independent transactions between the same parties. Kelley and Thibaut (1978), taking this noneconomic approach very much for granted, devote their entire scheme to the analysis of recurring transactions between interdependent actors. In anthropology, the same longitudinal orientation is equally clear:

> There is in social anthropology an understandable view that it is the social relation which is primary, which dictates the content and form of the transaction. [Firth 1967:4]

> A material transaction is usually a momentary episode in a continuous social relation. The social relation exerts governance: the flow of goods is constrained by, is part of, a status etiquette. [Sahlins 1965:139]

The mutually dependent, more or less bonded social relation is coming to be the basic conceptual and empirical unit in *social* exchange theory. As a result, it is moving in a direction quite alien to neoclassical economic theory. Cutting through and ignoring long-term relations, economic analysis takes *transactions* as its unit and aggregates them into sets of independent events called *markets.* Cutting through (but *not* ignoring) market processes, social exchange analysis organizes transactions into the interdependent series called an *exchange relation* between specific partners. One of the major tasks the social approach to exchange must address, then, is analysis of systems containing two or more exchange relations—that is, three or more mutually dependent actors. We address that problem below, suggesting that social network analysis can deal with very complex social structures of exchange, with the perfectly competitive market being but one network structure.

Thus, I agree with Goode, who wrote:

> I continue to suppose that the market version of micro-economics is a sub-category of social exchange. Economists do not find it a paradox that at the highest levels of economic interaction (intercorporate exchanges among presidents, international firms, etc.) the micromarket rationality gives way to old-fashioned exchange, in which personal trust, prestige-esteem, favors, favored purchasers or sellers, and so on play a large role. [William Goode 1977, personal correspondence]

Exchange networks are beginning to do for *social* exchange theory what the concept of the competitive market does for *economic* exchange theory. A competitive market is one form of network. I will examine network theory in more detail below.

PLAN OF THIS CHAPTER

Having distinguished between social and economic exchange theory, the rest of this chapter will deal exclusively with social exchange. Economic analysis will be referred to occasionally, but only as a contrasting counterpoint to our central concern.

In part 1, below, we examine the psychological bases of social exchange, turning to dyadic serial interaction in part 2. The remaining three sections deal with theoretical development beyond the dyad. More specifically, in part 3 we discuss productive exchange and *corporate groups* of two or more members. In part 4 we develop some basic principles for the analysis of *exchange networks.* Finally, in part 5 a preliminary discussion of *institutionalized* exchange systems is presented.

Part 1: The Psychology of Social Exchange

It is my contention that sociological exchange theory, far from being *too* psychological, has not incorporated as much psychology as it ought to have. It is a curious fact that despite the psychological reductionism claimed by Homans, his work contains very little individual psychology and a large amount of social interactive substance.

THE OPERANT APPROACH

One reason for this lies in Homans's selection of operant psychology as his source of basic propositions. What sociology wants from any branch of psychology—especially experimental branches—is its *general concepts,* not its operationally defined particulars. But in the case of operant psychology, if one takes away the strictly operational language there is very little "psychology" left. Skinner tried to make his scheme theoretically sparse, if not atheoretical altogether, and he succeeded. As a result, the psychology that entered social exchange theory from Skinner through Homans is reduced to the basic notion that human beings, like almost any other animal form, are self-regulating or cybernetic systems. That is, human beings respond to principles of positive and negative "feedback," or "reinforcement." They tend to act so as to optimize across a set of valued (beneficial) inputs. What do people value? They value whatever it is they optimize. (For a full discussion of this circularity, see Emerson 1976.) For our present purpose it is sufficient to note that such circularity is not a theoretical flaw so long as it is recognized for what it is. It is a definition of a cybernetic system. It is useful because of an existential fact about human behavior: most behavior *is* cybernetically regulated.

But the fact that human beings respond to principles of reinforcement is only a starting point toward a psychology of social exchange. In 1964, Morton Deutsch expressed doubt about the adequacy of operant psychology as a basis for understanding human exchange. Further, he was critical of Homans for having left out the most interesting of Skinner's findings regarding intermittent reinforcement. What seemed desirable, in short, was more rather than less psychology.

TOWARD A THEORY OF VALUE

One of the reasons for the circularity described above is the absence of a theory of *values.* As Homans (and Skinner) suggest, a thing is beneficial, rewarding, or of value if it is reinforcing, that is, if its occurrence strengthens the actions that produce it. The degree of value is the relative strength of one reinforcer compared with others. One can postulate, therefore, a set of valued inputs organized into a value hierarchy.

However, the principle of satiation-deprivation asserts that the unit value of any reward varies inversely with the frequency of (recent) acquisition of that reward. Hence, for Homans, the value hierarchy among rewards is synonymous with a hierarchy of relative deprivation at that moment.

One suspects, however, that there is more to the psychology and sociology of values than momentary deprivation. To advance our knowledge we must take the unit value of reinforcing stimuli as the dependent variable, holding deprivation constant and greater than zero. When a set of independent variables has been specified, we will then have the beginnings of a theory of value suitable for social exchange theory. I suggest three determinants of value over and above deprivation.

Need. Individual actors (either persons or organized groups) can be thought of as functioning "systems." If the system is to function effectively, the system requires or *needs,* in varying degree, a variety of beneficial inputs: food, fluid, oxygen, affection, protection, or whatever, depending upon the kind of system under study. We hypothesize that values develop in some living systems (persons and human groups) as part of the cybernetic system that functions to provide those inputs. The relative need for one input compared to another is the extent to which normal system functioning is objectively contingent upon that input. One variable governing the value attached to an input is the need for that input.

I do not mean to minimize the complexities involved in such system analysis, but I can go no further with the general topic here. My main points are these: (1) Having shied away from the complex notion of need for a variety of reasons, we are left with a poor understanding of values. (2) As a direct result, we often find ourselves talking in a circle: Why does a person perform an act? Because he finds the results rewarding. How do you know it was rewarding? Because he performed the act. Why did he do this rather than that? Because this has greater expected utility than that. How do you know? Because decisions maximize expected utility. An understanding of need and the other determinants of value discussed below is the only avenue of escape from such circularity, other than the atheoretic avenue chosen by Skinner.

While the concept of need is complex, it is not at all mysterious. It is fully amenable to empirical research.

The most notable efforts to avoid the concept of need are found in economics. Almost every textbook author feels called upon to include a section asserting that market *demand* is not to be thought of as consumer *need.* This strategy of avoidance testifies both to the relevance of need in the study of exchange and the complexity introduced, if the concept is included. Avoiding the idea works well in a practical way in economics, but some costs are incurred. Economic theory is left with an oversimplified conception of actors (see Leibenstein 1976); and price theory encounters limits. (Can the street price for heroin be understood without taking addiction into account?) The success that economic theory has achieved, in part because it avoids the notion of need, should not be taken by sociologists and psychologists as reason for adopting the same strategy.

Uncertainty. Assuming that need for a given input is greater than zero, other variables contribute to the value accorded that input. One of those variables appears to be *uncertainty* regarding acquisition of that input.

In previous work I suggested that this hypothesis could be inferred from Skinner's findings regarding intermittent reinforcement. Briefly, Skinner's main line of research dealt with the relative efficacy of different "reinforcement schedules" in producing high rates of behavior. How often will a rat press a lever if every press produces food; if every fifth press produces food; or if effort succeeds *on the average* one out of five times? The latter is an example of a variable ratio schedule involving intermittent and unpredictable reinforcement. It renders the outcome of reward-seeking activity *uncertain.* Under such conditions the rate of activity is high and the behavior is slow to extinguish when reward is no longer forthcoming. Human analogies have been suggested in such high motivation activities as gambling and sports, where winning is possible but problematic.

Taking clues from intermittent reinforcement and elsewhere, I advanced the following definition (Emerson 1972a):

For any class of reinforcers, y, the corresponding class of operant responses has *uncertain* (or "problematic") reinforcement outcomes to the degree $U = 4(p_y q)$; (where p_y is the probability of obtaining y, and $q = 1-p_y$);

followed by the hypothesis that:

The unit value of a class of reinforcers is a direct function of U across the recency-weighted history of exchange.

I suggested the above formal definition of U only as first approximation. So defined, U can assume values from 0.0 to 1.0 and its relation to p_y is nonlinear and symmetrical around $p_y = 0.5$. But the point of maximum uncertainty might better be defined somewhere lower than $p_y = 0.5$ if there is intense *need* for y; or above 0.5 in situations involving a conservative risk-taking policy.

An example will help to make the hypothesis clearer. Let two different persons, B and C, be the sole sources for two different kinds of favors, x and y, valued by A. If A's efforts to obtain x always (or never) succeed, then $p_x = 1$ (or 0), $U = 0$, the value A placed upon x (and upon B) is low, and interaction with B will be infrequent. By contrast, if efforts to obtain y from C sometimes succeed and sometimes fail in an unpredictable way, then $p_y = .5$, $U = 1.0$, the value of y and of C is high and interaction will be frequent with C. The frequency of reward from persons B and C—Homans's "Success" proposition—might well be equal in this example.[6]

Just as need and demand have some affinity, so uncertainty and deprivation are related to, but different from, the economic concept of supply. The economic concepts refer to attributes of market situations whereas the three psychological concepts address a single actor's relation to his environment. Yet, the psychological variables sometimes can be aggregated across members of a population. Most of us *need* medical attention from time to time, and most of us are *uncertain* about gaining effective relief or cure, not because doctors or medicines are in low economic supply, but because they are so often ineffective. Hence, the high status value enjoyed by the medical practitioner; his efforts are valued highly in part *because* they often fail.

Conditioned and generalized reinforcers. A third major source of the value attached to any class of objects or events is the history of their association with other (primary) sources of benefit in a developmental process of conditioning. Thus, in the above example, persons B and C take on value for A. More important for exchange theory, however, is the long-known fact that objects that mediate multiple forms of benefit come to take on affective significance, as though they were of value in their own right. Such objects have been called generalized reinforcers. Money is a common example, as is social approval. So are mothers, lovers, friends, and "significant others."

While the psychological principles involved in such conditioning need not be presented here, their implications for an exchange approach to interpersonal attraction and to exchange relations with social entities such as the church, the party, and to persons who act as their agents (priest and political patron) should be placed at the forefront of exchange theoretical reasoning. We have no need to adopt one or another theory of conditioning, but the psychology of conditioning should be given more prominence in social exchange theory than it has to date.

CONDITIONING VERSUS RATIONAL CHOICE

Another major contribution from individual psychology and economics has been *decision theory* and rational choice viewed as the maximization of subjective expected utility. Anthony Heath (1976) has given us a comprehensive and well-reasoned critique of the place of rational choice in social exchange theory.

Coming to exchange theory through economics, Heath relies heavily upon the cognitive concept of subjective expected utility. The issue of conscious calculation is examined:

> Some writers such as Homans would suggest that it is a *fallacy that a rational decision must be a conscious one,* but I am not sure that I would agree . . . for it raises a curious puzzle: if people do not consciously follow the principle of . . . expected utility maximization, what are the mechanisms which, perhaps magically, manage to produce the "right" results? Of course, if evidence is forthcoming that shows that "conscious and unconscious behavior come out at the same place" (Homans 1961, p. 80), I shall have to accept that such mechanisms do exist. But no one has yet produced that evidence, and I would not care to rely on its appearance. [Heath 1976:78]

What is going on here between Homans and Heath is a contest between a conditioning approach and a decision-theory approach to "rationality."

It is my guess that conscious and unconscious behaviors do *not* "come out at the same place" because they are not alternative ways of dealing with the same situations. Yet, both processes surely lead, most often, to valued outcomes. The "magical mechanisms" by which this happens are at least as well understood in conditioning theory as they are in the theory of rational choice.

Conditioning theory does two things. It addresses the origins of values as discussed above, and it links those values to behavior without going through (in theory) any conscious deliberations. Decision theory takes values as given and assumes some cognitive weighing of *alternative* actions in the process of selecting from among alternatives (decision making). While alternatives play a role in conditioning theory, *the conditioning process removes alternatives* over time. The result is action without "decision"; yet action which *is* beneficial by and large. Such "gut level" behavior might be less efficient in maximizing short-run cognitively labeled goals, yet contain more "wisdom" in its thoughtless pursuit of primordial values. Who can say? On such issues, conditioning theory is no more speculative and no less empirical than decision theory.

The problem before us, however, is not the selection of one or the other approach. Instead, the psychology of social exchange must develop so as to specify the manner in which these two processes—conditioning and decision making—operate together in some situations and are given salience, one over the other, in other situations.

Part 2: The Two-Party Exchange Relation

Because exchange theory has been primarily micro-analytic we will start with individual actors in dyadic exchange. We will then build upward to larger network structures and exchange involving corporate groups.[7]

A. ACTORS, RESOURCES, AND LONGITUDINAL RELATIONS

Throughout this essay I will speak of *actors,* signified by *A, B, C–N,* understanding that actors can be either persons or corporate groups acting through persons as their agents. Actors have possessions or behavioral capabilities. We shall call them *resources* if they are valued by specific other actors. Resources will be signified by *u, v, w–z.* Notice that a resource is not an attribute or a "possession" of an actor in the abstract, *but is rather an attribute of his relation to another or set of other actors* whose values define resources. Therefore, if we write (*Ax*) to mean "actor *A* possesses resource *x,*" the statement is incomplete and potentially misleading. It must contain at a minimum (*Ax;B,*) meaning that "*A* can perform *x* and *x* is valued by *B.*"

To write (*Ax;B*) requires that we know that *B* values *x.* Although there might be several sources of such knowledge (for example, we ask him, we perform an operant experiment to see if *x* is a "reinforcer" for *B,* or we infer his values from the known values of a group he belongs to), *the best evidence involves the behavior which* B *performs for* A *"in exchange" for* x. Thus, the complete expression must be (*Ax;By,*) meaning that *A* and *B* "exchange" *x* and *y.* Recalling the third assumption in the introduction, the behaviors are mutually contingent, *x* upon *y* and *y* upon *x.* Such a contingency can be observed sequentially in the *A–B* social relationship wherein, reflecting what Gouldner called a "norm of reciprocity," *x* at time 1 is tied to *y* at time 2, yielding frequencies over time expressible as an *exchange ratio, x/y.* Or the contingent relation of *x* and *y* can be observed in the bargaining or agreement-forming process which culminates in a single *transaction* at a point in time involving magnitudes which can be expressed as a ratio *x/y.* Research on justice, equity, power, and exploitation all deal with determinants of that ratio.

Thus, we arrive at the *exchange relation Ax;By* as the basic conceptual and empirical unit. The *social* exchange theory discussed below does not consider an observation to be relevant unless it is described as an event within such an exchange relation. The relation is conceived longitudinally, as a series of transactions *between the same actors* over time. This longitudinal feature is important for at least four reasons:

1. The direct behavioral observation of the "value" of *y* to *A* and *x* to *B*—their status as "rewards" or reinforcing stimuli—*requires* longitudinal observation; and
2. The temporal aspects of exchange relations allow the development of "emergent" aspects of the relation, such as trust, commitment, solidarity, "investments," concerns about "justice" and equity, and contractual agreements.
3. The most important single feature of the exchange process is the tendency for actors to become—through exchange—drawn into patterns of more or less lasting mutual dependency.
4. The focus upon serially interdependent transactions provides a clear separation between social and economic exchange theory.

B. INTERDEPENDENCE IN THE DYAD

A significant theoretical format for new research has been presented by Kelley and Thibaut (1978). Their earlier work (Thibaut and Kelley 1959) was the most formal and systematic of the early major writings dealing with social exchange. In this follow-up volume they present a still more formal analysis of two-person interaction. The complexity of their analysis precludes any attempt here to repeat or to summarize it. Instead, I will describe briefly what I see as the major contributions of their work within the larger framework of social exchange theory.

In their first book, Thibaut and Kelley employed a predominantly rational-choice framework in the analysis of dyadic interaction, making extensive use of the outcome matrix as a heuristic device. Their model was a rational-choice model in the sense that (a) it emphasized behavior alternatives (rows and columns in the matrix) requiring some choice; (b) it envisioned alternative social relations for ego to choose between; and

(c) the choices in both instances were assumed to be governed by a tendency to maximize beneficial outcomes. While a fair amount of individual psychology was drawn upon, for example, in their discussion of the evaluational standard called a comparison level, their focus nonetheless was predominantly *social structural.* That is, the two persons were both seen to be acting within an objective or *externally arranged pattern* of interdependence. The outcome matrix described such patterns. The patterns were examined under such concepts as behavior control and fate control. Out of those patterns *dependency,* and therefore *power,* came naturally to be topics of major concern.[8]

In their new work, Kelley and Thibaut are responsive, they say, to colleagues' criticisms of the self-centered rationality that seemed to dominate the first book. They have now enlarged their scheme in major ways which provide for the development, within interdependent social interaction, of what others would call less "rational" social motives: altruism, norms of sharing, value attachment to the welfare of the *group,* and so forth. They have not presented a theory that resolves such issues. Instead, they have formulated a framework for research which can seriously pose and answer questions of this order.

More specifically, their new framework builds upon the old one in two broad ways. First, the objective structural patterns of interdependence represented in outcome matrices are given far more elaborate logical analysis. In this respect the new work is less psychological and more social structural than its predecessor. Their second major elaboration is more important. They give lengthy attention to the fact that persons, placed in an objectively defined initial structure (called the *"given* matrix"), can develop policies, norms, and socialized motives that *transform* the *given* outcome matrix, yielding what they call the *"effective* matrix" within which the people actually conduct their long-term mutually beneficial affair.

C. POWER AND ITS USE IN DYADIC EXCHANGE

Although Kelley and Thibaut introduced the concepts of behavior and fate control, they did not develop in any detail their implication concerning power and the exercise of influence in social interaction. There seem to be two reasons for this. First, their scheme is organized around nonquantitative "behavior sequences" which are either performed or not performed. Hence, degree of influence upon another's actions does not enter as a variable. Second, their attention is focused almost exclusively inside two-party exchange. We will show, in the following discussion, that *power* is a rather vacuous notion in isolated two-person relations. Hence Kelley and Thibaut had little reason to develop the analysis of power processes. I will do so below in the dyad, only as a prelude to analysis of power in systems of three or more actors. A comparison will also be made between economic and social analysis of exchange in isolated dyads.

In the prototypic exchange relation represented as *Ax;By,* person *A* provides some amount of *x* in exchange for some amount or frequency of *y* from *B.* The exchange takes place through a series of transactions between the *same* parties, *A* and *B,* over time. The actual amounts of *x* and *y* are determined through bargaining, whether performed explicitly within the process of a single transaction or implicitly across the series. A major research problem in all exchange theory, whether it be economic or social theory, is to predict or to explain the amounts of *x* and *y* exchanged. As an aid in discussing this problem we present in figure 2.1 a "transaction table" showing some hypothetical quantities which *x* and *y* might take, along with the levels of net benefit to *A* and *B.* (For a more complete discussion of how such a table relates to economic theory on the one hand, and to experimental procedures on the other hand, see Cook and Emerson 1978a.)

In the following analysis we make two assumptions: first, we assume that neither party will repeatedly accept a net loss. Therefore, exchange will not often occur outside the range *c* through *g* in figure 2.1. Second, since we are discussing exchange in an isolated dyad, neither *A* nor *B* has any alternative source of *y* and *x.* Economists have studied such exchange under the label of *bilateral monopoly.*

The outcome of exchange in bilateral monopoly is generally said to be economically "indeterminate." Which of the settlements, *c* through *g,* will occur is said to be governed by the bargaining skill and motivation of the persons or by other possibly random variables which lie *outside the scope of economic theory* (see Coddington 1968).

It is of some theoretical interest, therefore, to show that social exchange theory provides a solution to bargaining outcomes—a kind of "price determination"—in bilateral monopoly. Cook and Emerson (1978a) have shown that power-dependence theory and equity theory both give solutions, and the *same* solution. Equity theory applies to the situation only if:

1. both *A* and *B* know (or think they know) what benefit the other party receives from each possible trade; and
2. both *A* and *B* honor equity as an appropriate distribution rule in the situation at hand.

When one or both of these conditions does *not* hold, then power theory applies; but the predicted outcome is the same either way.

FIGURE 2.1
Schematic Representation of a "Transaction Table."

	Transaction Possibilities										
	a	b	c	d	e	f	g	h	i	j	k
Units of *x* from *A:*	1	2	3	4	5	6	7	8	9	10	11
Net *benefit* to *A:*	7	6	5	4	3	2	1	0	−1	−2	−3
Net *benefit* to *B:*	−1	0	1	2	3	4	5	6	7	8	9
Units of *y* from *B:*	14	13	12	11	10	9	8	7	6	5	4

Note: Since neither actor will accept nonbeneficial trades, g and c are the bargaining limits for *A* and *B* respectively. Neither party knows the other's limit.

Because power will be a major concern throughout the rest of this chapter, it is worthwhile to develop the argument here, quoting at length from Cook and Emerson (1978a):

Let αx and αy be the unit value (i.e., "preference for" or "utility") of the resources x and y to A. Similarly, let βx and βy be the unit value of resources x and y to B. Let X and Y refer to the number of units exchanged. In two-party exchange, equity can be specified quite simply in terms of equal profit:

$$\alpha y\text{Y} - \alpha x\text{X} = \beta x\text{X} - \beta y\text{Y} \qquad (1)$$

If distributive justice or equity is operating, exchange will stablize at outcome: A will give 5 units of x and B will give 10 units of y, with neither party feeling either guilt or anger, as Homans has put it.

But suppose the subjects can't make interpersonal utility comparisons; or suppose they don't care about "equity" as much as they do about their own selfish benefit. We then ask:

Does power theory also offer a solution to the problem of indeterminacy? *Social power* in the dyad can best be conceived as a contest played out along the contract curve—with A pressing for outcomes in [one] direction and B pressing [in the other]. Let us define:

Def. 1. (Power): in any exchange relation *Ax;By,* the *power* of A over B (P_{ab}) is the potential of A to obtain favorable Y minus X outcomes at B's expense.

Def. 2. (Dependence): the *dependence* of A upon B (D_{ab}) is a joint function (1) varying directly with the value of αy minus αx, and (2) varying inversely with the availability of y to A from alternative sources.

These definitions are taken, with minor modifications, from Emerson (1962), where they are linked in the theorem: $P_{ab} = D_{ba}$.

In the power-dependence terms, a bilateral monopoly is the special case in which neither party has any alternative sources. Hence, relative power is based entirely upon the values αy and αx relative to βx and βy. If we assume that:

Both A and B *use* their power,

then it follows that:

X and Y will change over repeated transactions until equilibrium is reached at:

$$\alpha x Y - \alpha x X = \beta x X - \beta y Y \qquad (2)$$

This reasoning follows because the use of power to gain improved outcomes makes the user more dependent and therefore [relatively] less powerful.

Thus, in bilateral monopoly, equity concerns and power processes [lead to the same exchange outcomes]. [p. 723–24]

We derive two major conclusions from the above analysis. First the differences between social and economic exchange theory suggested in the introduction are real and important. Social exchange theory can deal with problems unsolved in economic theory, not because the phenomena under study are different, but because the theories work from different assumptions—notably the presence or absence of dependencies between exchange partners.

Second, we conclude that *social power* as a potentially exploitative relationship is not subject to study at the level of the isolated dyad. If one person is more powerful and uses that power advantage to gain benefits, he becomes more dependent and the advantage is lost. Hence, we have little to learn about power through study of dyadic interaction, for power in any sociologically meaningful sense is a social *structural* phenomenon. We proceed, therefore, to study power as a function of *position* in exchange networks of three or more actors.

Part 3: Beyond the Dyad—Corporate Groups, Agents, and Principals

Simpson (1972) has written that "to apply exchange theory to groups of four or more persons is . . . so thorny a task that no one appears to have accomplished it." It is also an essential task which sociologists working in the exchange area cannot ignore. According to Cook (1979) the problem is not being ignored, and considerable progress is being made.

> The main distinguishing feature of *current* exchange theorizing within Sociology (see Emerson 1972a, b; Cook and Emerson 1978a; Coleman 1972; Ekeh 1974, etc.) is the shift in focus from dyadic exchange relations to more complex exchange systems—exchange networks and corporate groups which, ironically, have been the primary focus of attention within Anthropology from the beginning. [Cook 1979]

The extensions of exchange theory beyond the dyad are forming in two different but complementary ways. One involves *groups* of two or more actors; the other involves *networks* of three or more actors. In this section I will discuss an exchange approach to corporate groups; in the next section, I will examine networks in some detail.

Before examining either groups or networks, the distinction between the two, and their relationship to each other, should be specified. A network is a set of separate but interconnected actors. A corporate group, by contrast, *is* an actor—a *collective* actor composed of two or more persons who, as "members" of the group do not act as "separate" actors. Instead, their group-relevant conduct is prescribed by collective mandates that are more or less consensually valid across the membership of the group. Thus, if a network is portrayed graphically as a set of linked actors forming, for example, a three-actor chain *A-B-C,* or a three-actor loop $\overset{A}{B\text{—}C}$, any letter (or point) in the graph might represent a corporate group or collective actor. The essential features of the corporate group are that (1) it confronts its environment as a single (social) unit, and (2) it is dealt with by actors in the environment as a single unit. The behavioral medium through which corporate actors act is the relationship of *principal* and *agent.* This relationship is itself an exchange relation, (*P*)-*A,* nested inside another exchange relation between the group and an external entity, *E.* Thus, we have [(*P*)-*A*]-*E,* with (*P*) representing the "group" as principal in whose behalf the agent, *A,* deals with *E. E* might be some sector of the natural environment that the group deals with through member *A,* or *E* might be the agent of another group.

Interorganizational exchange (Cook 1977) can be described within the framework

$$[(P_1)\text{-}A_1]-[A_2-(P_2)].$$

Each line is a negotiated exchange relation, and each set of brackets identifies the boundary of a corporate group. In the portion $(P_i)\text{-}A_i$, the negotiation deals with and defines the role responsibilities and rewards of agent A_i in his dealing with A_j. Emerson is nearing completion of an historical case study of imperial rule in Kashmir on an exchange network format of $[(C)\text{-}R]\text{-}Tf\text{-}[W\text{-}(S)]$, where

(S)	=	the central state,
W	=	the "wazir," a disciplined agent of the state,
Tf	=	a "tax farmer," an undisciplined intermediary acting in his own interest in the collection of state revenues from R,
R	=	a raja or regional prince acting as agent for the local petty kingdom, composed of
(C)	=	a set of cultivators from whom all state land revenues derive.

I believe that the analysis of corporate groups requires an explicit boundary with action through agents flowing through the boundary into *specified* external sectors. Such boundaries are represented by brackets in the above notation.

All of the basic features, the collective actor as principal, the agent, the boundaries separating them, and the negotiated exchanges that join them are observable phenomena in natural settings and operationalized phenomena in the laboratory. Cook, Gillmore, and Little (1979) have recently completed an experiment dealing with the conditions under which a network of form 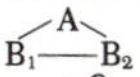 will convert to the structure $[(B_i)\text{-}B_j]\text{-}A$. The process is a special case of coalition formation—which *is* the formation of a corporate group in this case—with one member, B_j, serving as *agent* for the two-person collectivity in subsequent negotiations with A. (The condition that generates this group-formative process is power imbalance in the initial network in A's favor, and the "function" of group formation is power redistribution.)

My main purpose in the preceding paragraphs has been to mix the analysis of corporate groups with discussion of networks that contain groups as actors, thereby giving some sense of the relationship between these complementary forms of social systems. But as abstract forms, groups and networks are vastly different in principle. In some very basic way, the difference can be traced back to the distinction that Fredrick Barth (1966) made between two modes of exchange: "transactions" and "incorporation." I would suggest that networks are based upon the former, while corporate groups require the latter as an exchange basis.

In order to develop this point more precisely, let us separate the related notions of productive exchange (Emerson 1976) from incorporation (Barth 1966). In figure 2.2, matrix I, the resources x and y which enter the exchange *each carry their own value,* 3 and 4 units of value respectively. Therefore, the transaction can be broken down, in principle, into two separately valuable acts. Because they are not equal in value, A and B might negotiate frequencies of behavior to bring about equal benefit. By contrast, resources x^1 and y^1 in matrix II *have no value* taken separately. They "produce" value when properly coordinated through social interaction. For example, when two people play cribbage or engage in a game of tennis, a "productive" exchange results in a valuable *joint* activity that neither actor could produce alone. I would make several observations about such productive exchange relations:

1. The number of *required* participants can readily be increased beyond two without making the analysis any more complex in form. Unlike elementary exchange, productive exchange is not *conceptually* dyadic.
2. All role-systems as we know them in sociology can be portrayed as productive exchange systems. Where role theory focuses upon the structure of normative role-prescriptions, exchange theory focuses upon resource-pooling, benefit-producing, and benefit-distributing processes.
3. Taken as a *given* matrix, the pattern of interdependence involved in productive exchange tends to get "transformed" into what Barth called *incorporation* wherein members identify with the interest of the collectivity (and require that other members do likewise).[9] They attempt to maximize group gain and place a value upon positive group outcomes. Meanwhile, the roots of such group identification reside in the *structure* of organic solidarity implied in the productive interdependence of the underlying "given matrix."
4. Finally, in most productive systems of any complexity, the productive process of resource combination and pooling can be distinguished (analytically or concretely) from the distribution process through which members gain personal rewards (over and above the benefits of identification with a "winning team"). Sahlins (1963) has spoken of a pooling network and a distribution network in economic anthropology. In our notation above, $[(P)-A]-E$, the productive pooling has benefits in A-E transactions, while the distribution of those benefits is handled at the internal level of $(P)-A_1$ transactions.

The distribution of benefits among participants to productive exchange deserves still more discussion. The main issue can be seen in matrix II of figure 2.2. Although the differential value of resources in elementary exchange (matrix I) is theoretically a simple matter, the relative value of contributions to productive exchange is a far more problematic—and interesting—issue. What can the difference between 4 and 3 to A and B be based upon? Their contributions x^1 and y^1 have no value taken in isolation from the process, and each is necessary to the process. (Since 3 and 4 represent net benefit, the costs borne by A and B have been accounted for.)

The issue we are discussing is no less than the reward and status hierarchy of organized groups taken as a dependent variable. One well-known attempt at a theoretical solution is the Davis-Moore notion of

FIGURE 2.2

Matrix Portrayal of "Productive" vs. "Elementary" Exchange Relations.

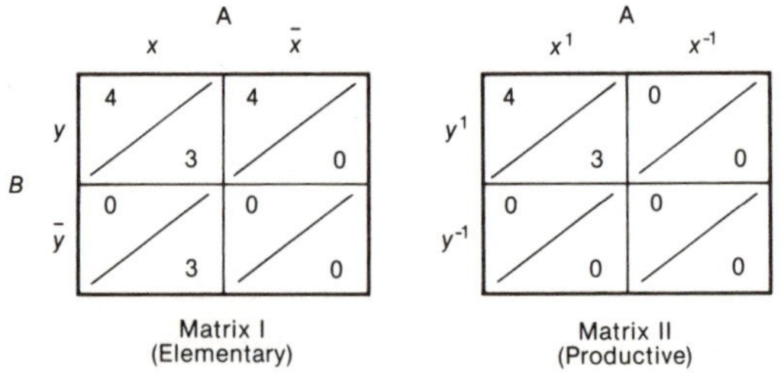

"functional importance." While x^1 and y^1 are both necessary, one might be "more necessary" than the other. This is an empirical possibility and hence an empirical question. One suspects, for example, that a baseball team stands a better chance of winning with an incompetent right fielder than it does with a poor pitcher on the mound.

But the *value* a group assigns to a resource contribution (or the status it grants to a member) is due only in part to its objective importance (see the discussion of *need* above). Another major determinant is the degree of uncertainty, *U,* the group has experienced in obtaining that resource (see the discussion of *U* in part 1, above.) The uncertainty of obtaining a given resource input will be a function of at least two variables:

1. incompetence of role-occupants (as a set) to master the tasks assigned to that role[10]; and
2. the power of role-occupants based upon:
   a. their alternative group affiliations, and
   b. their degree of organization as a class-conscious division of labor.

Thus, we are led back to power.

Part 4: Beyond the Dyad—Power and Position in Network Structures

In an ideal case, a *group* involves *n* persons each of whom holds the social status of a "member" occupying a "role" in a consensually valid normative system of roles. When persons are acting as members of such a group their group-relevant behavior—role performance—is largely prescribed. In sharp contrast, parties performing in a *network* are viewed as relatively autonomous decision-making *actors* occupying *positions* in a structure. Participation in the network is not based upon member status, for unlike corporate groups, networks frequently have no consensually defined boundaries. Indeed, it is often the case that participants in exchange networks have little knowledge of the extent of the network, its members and its boundaries, even though networks *are* empirically bounded social entities, as we shall see.

Space will not allow a review of the rapidly growing literature on social networks;[11] and presentation of a full theory of network structure would be premature. I provide here only a few guiding definitions and comments, as required to provide a framework for the discussion of power and position and institutionalized networks to be introduced in part 5.

NETWORK "CONNECTIONS"

The following quotation from Cook and Emerson (1978a) will establish the basic ideas upon which most of the remaining discussion depends.

It is fairly common in some network research (e.g., sociometric studies of affect structures and communication networks) tacitly to assume that if two relations *A-B* and *A-C* share a member *A* in common then the relations can be joined to form the larger single structure $B - A - C$. This should not be taken as an assumption. For example, if *A* and *C* communicate, whether or not information gets from *B* to *C* through *A* remains to be demonstrated. Similarly, if *A* helps *B* and *B* helps *C*, whether or not *C* is (indirectly) helped by *A* remains to be demonstrated. Instead of making assumptions a priori, systematic study should be conducted concerning a class of empirical phenomena we will call *network connections.* Toward that end we define:

Def. 3. An *exchange network* is a set of two or more connected exchange relations.

Def. 4. Two exchange relations are *connected* to the degree that exchange in one relation is contingent upon exchange (or nonexchange) in the other relation.

(1) The connection is *positive* if exchange in one is contingent upon exchange in the other.

(2) The connection is *negative* if exchange in one is contingent upon nonexchange in the other.

Examples of positively connected networks range from Malinowski's (1922) Kula Ring to vertically integrated markets and channels of distribution (El-Ansary 1972). Family lines can be analyzed similarly with kin-based economic opportunities flowing "down" and filial loyalty and support flowing "up" across generations. Examples of negatively connected networks include competitive economic market structures, dating networks and friendship networks. Most concrete networks involve connections of both types. [p. 424–25]

The contingency defining a connection in Def. 4 can vary in *strength* as well as sign, yielding a continuous variable ranging from 1.0 to – 1.0. As a result

networks have empirically definite "boundaries" at points where the contingency in definition 4 is zero or, relatively speaking, very low. We can then describe complex networks based upon combinations of both positive and negative connections of varying strength. The concept of *network connection* allows us to envision a theory in which events happening at any location in such networks will have mathematically predictable and empirically traceable repercussions to all boundaries of that network. Clearly, such network *connections* must be taken as topics for empirical research in their own right. [Cook and Emerson 1978b]

I can do no more here than hint at the kind of general framework to be used and the sorts of issues to be pursued in such research.

Consider as a bare hint the network and corresponding contingency matrix in figure 2.3. The main feature of this network is that *A*, through

FIGURE 2.3

Network Portrayal of Political Patronage with Associated "Connection Matrix."

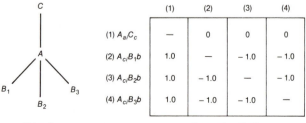

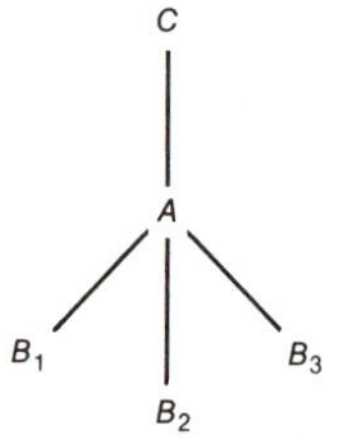

Network

	(1)	(2)	(3)	(4)
(1) $A_{ai}C_c$	—	0	0	0
(2) $A_{ci}B_1b$	1.0	—	– 1.0	– 1.0
(3) $A_{ci}B_2b$	1.0	– 1.0	—	– 1.0
(4) $A_{ci}B_3b$	1.0	– 1.0	– 1.0	—

Connection Matrix

exchange with *C*, obtains something which is valued by, and can be passed on to, any one of several *B*s (for example, having political influence with *C*, *A* can obtain patronage favors for *B*s). In the associated connection matrix the contingencies in row (1) are zero because $A-C$ exchange is (I assume) independent of $A-B_i$ exchange. That is, whatever *A* gets in return for favors is not a basis of his (*A*'s) exchange with *C*. By contrast, in column (1) all contingencies are 1.0 because $A-B_i$ exchange is possible only if there is *A-C* exchange. Thus, the positive connections in this example are *unilateral*. Finally, all three of the A-B_i relations are bilateral negative in their connections to one another because, I assume, any political favor that goes to B_i therefore does *not* go to B_j or B_k. The reader will, of course, think of other illustrations carrying different connecting implications.

What sort of issues are open for research through connected networks of the sort shown in figure 2.3? One of them is the rise of commensal rivalry or competition among *B*s. The most general topic, however, is power and transformations of the network under the impact of power processes. This can be illustrated by applying elementary power-dependence principles (see above) to the connected network shown in figure 2.3. (1) The negative connections among the *B*s enhance *A*'s power advantage over each B_i. Why? Applying the definition of dependence (Def. 2[2], above) it follows that $D_{B_iA} > D_{AB_i}$ and therefore $P_{AB_i} > P_{B_iA}$. (2) The unilateral positive connection linking A-B_i to *A-C* enhances *C*'s power over *A*. Why? Because *A* will depend upon *C* not only for benefits directly from *C* but also for benefits from B_i which *C* indirectly controls. (3) In such a structure *C* has incentive to support and encourage *A* in his use of power over *B*. Why? Because the more *A* gains from *B*, the more dependent *A* becomes upon *C*, giving *C* more power over *A*. (4) But if *A* is excessive in using his power over B_i he might provoke a coalition among *B*s. Why? Because coalition formation will transform the structure of the network, redistributing power to *B*'s advantage (see Emerson 1962; Lawler 1975; Cook, Gilmore, and Little 1979).

"POSITION" IN NETWORK STRUCTURE

Networks are usually more complex than those shown in figure 2.3. It is desirable, therefore, to develop structural concepts that simplify the analysis of network structure by attending to smaller components that are repeated. "Position" is such a concept. In graph theory one can generate from a parent graph, *G*, a *residual* graph RG_i by removing a point (or vertex) v_i. We define a "position" in graph-theoretic terms as follows:

Def. 5. A *position* in a graph is a set of one or more points whose residual graphs are isomorphic.

To illustrate this concept clearly, we introduce the networks in figure 2.4. Positions are labeled by letter and occupants (points) are given numerical subscripts in figure 2.4.[12]

A most valuable feature of the concept of position is that it allows comparisons to be made across networks as well as within networks.

FIGURE 2.4

"Positions" in Network Structure: A network involving (a) four persons in one position; (b) four persons in two positions; and (c) ten persons in three positions.

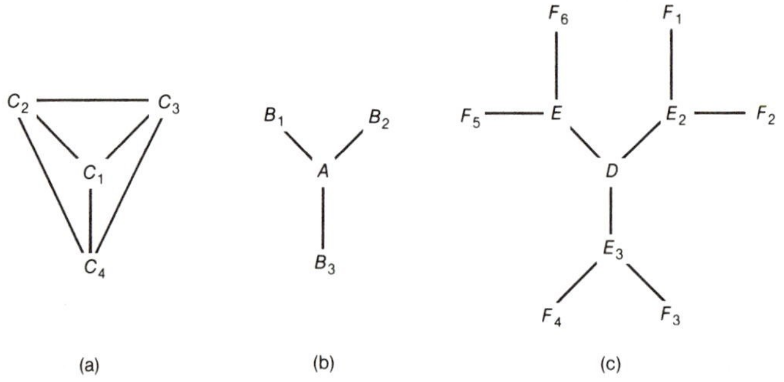

Thus, A and B_1 are describably different in figure 2.4(b) and both are different from *C, D,* and *E* in figure 2.4(a) and (c).

The point of major importance, however, is the fact that every position is defined relative to the *entire structure,* even though the occupants of those positions are ignorant about the structure that surrounds them.[13] This is of immense importance for the study of networks. It is our purpose to show that positions *A, C, D,* and *E,* all of which are "locally" identical, provide the occupant with predictably different amounts of power.

Applying the power-dependence principles given above it can be shown that:

1. Occupants of the same position have equal structurally determined power (for example, the *C*s in figure 2.4(a), whereas occupants of different positions in a given network have unequal power.)
2. Positions *A* and *E* are powerful, and equally so in their respective networks.
3. Positions *B, D,* and *F* are weak, and equally so in their respective networks.

Two experiments provide unequivocal confirmation of these predictions. For details of the theoretical rationale, procedures, and findings, readers are referred to Cook and Emerson (1978a) and Cook, Emerson, Gillmore, and Yamagishi (1979).

POWER AND "CENTRALITY" OF POSITION

It is interesting that the most "central" position in figure 2.4(c), position *D,* is a very weak position, contradicting the common belief that power is a function of centrality. In fact, power-dependence theory applied to such networks gives more refined predictions. With all connections negative in figure 2.4(c), we predict that position *E* will be powerful, and our experiments confirm this. If the connections in that same network were positive, then power-dependence theory would predict that position *D* would be more powerful. Experiments now being designed will test this prediction.

Is there a higher-level principle regarding power in exchange networks which can subsume the above predictions? We believe there is. Position E in a negatively connected network and position D in a positively connected network have one important feature in common: exchange throughout the network *as a whole,* is most dependent upon those two positions. Thus, it appears that Power-Dependence concepts should be raised from the level of *exchange relations,* where it was first developed (Emerson 1962, 1972b), to the more macro-level of networks.

The major step involved will be to define and measure network-wide dependence upon a given postulate therein.

> We suspect that the graph theoretic concept of *vulnerability* (Harary, Norman, and Cartwright 1965) might prove to be useful to us. This general topic deals with the consequences for the entire graph—or for specified subgraphs—of "removing" specific lines and points from the graph. Measuring the consequences of "removal" might reveal the contributions made by—and system dependence upon—the presence of that point. [Cook and Emerson 1978b]

Just as in our definition of *position,* the graph-theoretic concept of residual graph RG_i, the graph that remains when vertex v_i is removed, appears to be useful.

While a formal solution to this problem is premature at this point, the direction for continued formal theory construction can be suggested. First, flow networks (see Busacker and Saatz 1965) are more appropriate than simple graphs because quantitative resource values flow in exchange networks. Residual networks can be employed analogous to the residual graphs mentioned above. We would then develop a definition of *network-wide dependence,* D_{Ni}, in all network structures, involving both positive and negative connections.

Part 5: Institutionalized Exchange Systems

Researchers dealing with exchange network structures, whether in the field or in the laboratory, must face and resolve an issue regarding research strategy. The issue stems from the fact that connected network structures exist in an immense profusion of shapes, forms, and degrees of complexity. It is likely however, that certain structural forms are sociologically more fundamental than others. There are probably some law-like principles which, when understood, will yield the framework for treating certain structure *models* as basic *prototypes.* Theory and research on any immediate issue should always proceed with one eye watching for general structural principles.

For this reason there is merit in focusing research upon fairly stable, long-term, or *institutionalized* exchange systems. In those exchange structures, one would hope, basic sociological principles of exchange will have worked their way to the surface.

In addition to the above strategy concerns, the study of institutionalized forms of exchange promises to inform exchange theory, precisely *because* that theory (in sociology and social psychology) has been subinstitutional in its level of analysis. Homans called it "elementary" social behavior, meaning by that, noninstitutionalized behavior. Finally, some of the most interesting, heated, and as yet unresolved debates in exchange theory involve the analysis of institutionalized systems of exchange. It is fitting that this chapter should end by turning to such topics.

"GENERALIZED EXCHANGE" IN MARRIAGE NETWORKS

In the study of institutionalized exchange, it is not surprising that the social and economic anthropologists have been in advance of sociologists. The seminal work of Karl Polanyi (1957), Marcel Mauss (1954), Malinowski (1922), and Levi-Strauss (1949) has been built upon by a host of others such as Sahlins (1963, 1965).

Concerning the study of structural prototypes, Polanyi and Levi-Strauss stand out from all the rest: Polanyi for the comparative study of reciprocity, redistribution, and market systems of exchange; and Levi-Strauss for the concept of "generalized exchange." Because the latter subject has been the most controversial, I will discuss it rather than Polanyi's work.

Levi-Strauss (1949) studied preferential marriage with mother's brother's daughter (matrilateral cross-cousin marriage) as a cycle of exchange in which women are sent through marriage from group *A* to *B*, from *B* to *C*, from *C* to *D*, and eventually back to *A*. By contrast, preferential marriage with father's sister's daughter (patrilateral) will result in women going from group *A* to *B* in one generation and from *B* to *A* in the next generation. The difference between these two patterns[14] was conceptualized as generalized versus direct exchange. The former is conceived in terms of "univocal reciprocity" wherein the recipient of benefit does *not* give benefit in return (overlooking the various forms of bride-price for the moment), but instead gives benefit to another in a system which eventually completes the circle.[15]

The functional-collectivist position. Based upon the concept of generalized exchange Levi-Strauss advanced a classic functional argument by asserting that (1) generalized exchange, through an open and extensive network of social bonds, promotes society solidarity, and (2) matrilateral is more prevalent than patrilateral cross-cousin marriage *for that reason.*

The "psychological" position. In 1955, Homans and Schneider were not convinced by Levi-Strauss's theory. They developed a far different explanation for what facts are known and assembled some facts of their own. They suggest, in *very brief* summary, that (1) matrilateral marriage is more common because the *person involved* (the potential groom) will develop sentimental preferences for mother's brother's daughter; and (2) what is customary tends to become obligatory.

Needless to say, the Homans-Schneider theory has come under heavy attack as well, notably by R. Needham (1960) and more recently by Ekeh (1974). Space will not permit a full analysis of the pros and cons. The reader is referred to Heath (1976:160–69) for what is by far the most tightly reasoned and balanced analysis of the issues available in the literature.

This discussion is keenly relevant to the topic of this section: institutionalized exchange. For, as Heath observes, one can't get from individual preferences to normative prescriptions in the simple way Homans and Schneider would do it in point (2) above.

> If people do something anyway, there is no need to have a norm prescribing it. The norm is redundant. It is a waste of time prescribing things that people are going to do even if they are not prescribed. [Heath 1976:164]

It follows, then, that if an *institutionalized* practice is to be traced back into the benefit structure of an exchange approach, it must be tied to the benefits of "bystanders" to the behavior, not to benefits enjoyed by the actor on center stage—the potential groom in this case.

The only addition I would make to this argument, based upon the concepts presented in this chapter, is to remind the reader that the actors involved in the marriage process under discussion are corporate groups. The marriage takes place in a structure like the one discussed above:

$$[(P_1)\text{-}G]\text{-}[B\text{-}(P_2)]$$

where G and B are groom and bride, and the principals involved, the norm-forming, norm-enforcing, mate-selecting units are two lineages. The "normative preference" is, I suggest, the expression of a "negotiation" exchange contract committing partners to long-term (that is, reliable) exchange relations. The benefits accrue to P_1 and P_2, not to G. Thus, I am inclined to disagree with Homans and Schneider on both points (1) and (2), above.

But if they are wrong, that does not make Levi-Strauss right. The conclusion Heath comes to seems the only one now possible:

> If Levi-Strauss's assertion is true, there are some interesting implications: generalized exchange does not occur only in the case of matrilateral cross-cousin marriage but also, in a rudimentary form, in the case of blood donations, wedding presents and perhaps with social welfare benefits. Do these institutions generate a greater solidarity than do market exchanges or other (social) forms of direct exchange? It would be nice to think so, but we have no basis for giving an answer at the moment. It is indeed a sad reflection on exchange theorists (myself included) that a hypothesis which has been with us for quarter of a century has not yet received a single decent test. [Heath 1976:166]

KULA EXCHANGE

The Levi-Straussian functional conception of cross-cousin marriage can be discussed a little further, indirectly, through examining Ekeh's attempt to interpret Malinowski's studies of Kula exchange in a similar way, as a form of generalized exchange.

To explain briefly, Malinowski (1922) described the institution of Kula exchange once practiced by the inhabitants of islands in the Western Pacific ocean. One transaction in this vast institutionalized network typically involved a group of people setting out on a trade mission to an established trading partner on another island. Upon arrival, the two head people of these trading groups engaged in the ceremonial act of exchanging a necklace in return for armbands. Those specific items would be held and displayed by the receiving party until they were passed on to some other trading partner in a similar subsequent transaction. Thus, if one were to trace the course of a given necklace, it would travel through a vast network of trade relations, always flowing in the opposite direction to the flow of armbands; and the network would, of necessity, form loops or Kula "rings." By implication, every party eventually would receive a necklace from someone other than the person he gave one to. Ekeh sees in this a pattern similar to the "generalized exchange" of women in the work of Levi-Strauss. At the same time, however, each transaction entails direct exchange (of a necklace for an armband) with a dyad.

I present in figure 2.5 the essential component of the Kula ring, a structural component that is repeated and compounded into a vast network far larger and more complex than the individual participants can realize (so Malinowski asserts).

I want to begin the discussion by allowing what might be disputed, that the network has enough structural points in common with matrilateral cross-cousin marriage to be considered a system of generalized exchange. I would then make a *structural* observation which has not been adequately discussed in the literature on either the Kula or marriage networks. Yet it applies to both. *If for whatever reason a gift* (or good) *received cannot be returned to its sender,* then any network involving that gift or class of objects will of necessity form cycles with a minimum length of three. (Cycles rather than unclosed chains will tend to form for trivial reasons, but also for power-balancing reasons. In the chain *A-B-C, B* has more power than either partner. If the *A-C* partnership forms, giving us the cycle *A-B-C-A,* then power is balanced all around.)

Thus, the Kula *structure* can be explained by two simple facts: (1) enduring trade partnerships form among these islanders; and (2) a necklace cannot be given in return for a necklace from the same partner (nor a bracelet for a bracelet). One need not invoke societal solidarity as its functional contribution if one can give good and sufficient reasons for (1) and (2).

Ekeh (1974) insists that the Kula institution is a strictly noneconomic

FIGURE 2.5
Schematic Representation of the Kula Ring Exchange System.

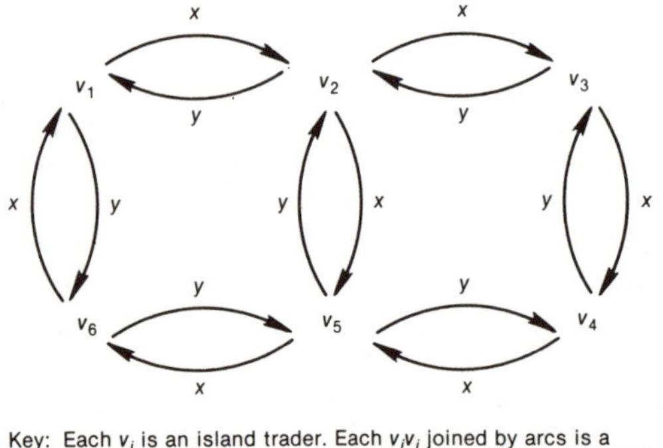

Key: Each v_i is an island trader. Each v_iv_j joined by arcs is a pair of Kula "partners" bound by tradition (that is, committed) to trade armshells (x) for necklaces (y).

ritual-symbolic mechanism either for enhancing collective solidarity or for expressing it. While it entails direct reciprocity between members of a dyad, that is not what the system is all about, as Ekeh sees it. That there might be egocentric motives of status enhancement or other personal gain involved, possibly of an economic sort, is written down by Ekeh as a violation of the "morality" of the Kula and of generalized exchange systems.

I will argue the opposite on all of these points, but *without implying* that the network does *not* enhance solidarity in some sense. The argument will be partly theoretical and partly empirical, drawing upon Malinowski's observations.

The tendency to form partnerships. Turning first to the two premises stated above, the formation of Kula partners is, in Malinowski's words, the result of the "deep tendency to create social ties" through the exchange of gifts (Malinowski, p. 175, quoted by Cook 1979). These are dyadic ties we are talking about. Why do, or did, islanders of the Western Pacific want to form such ties, what exactly were those ties all about as exchange relations?

> The Kula partnership is one of the special bonds which unite two men into one of the standing relations of mutual exchange of gifts and services so characteristic of these natives. Again, the average man will have one or two chiefs in his or in the neighbouring districts with whom he *kulas.* In such a case, he would be bound to assist and serve them in various ways, and to offer them the pick of *vaygu'a* when he gets a fresh supply. On the other hand he would expect them to be specially liberal to him.
>
> The overseas partner is, on the other hand, a host, patron and ally in a land of danger and insecurity. Nowadays, though the feeling of danger still persists, and natives never feel safe and comfortable in a strange district, this danger is rather felt as a magical one, and it is more the fear of foreign society that besets them. In olden days, more tangible dangers were apprehended, and the partner was the main guarantee of safety. He also provides with food, gives presents, and his house, though never used to sleep in, is the place in which to foregather while in the village. Thus the Kula partnership provides every man within its ring with a few friends near at hand, and with some friendly allies in the far-away, dangerous, foreign districts. [Malinowski 1922:91–92]

Why should the islander venture into those dangerous foreign districts at all? The answer will be considered crassly commercial by Ekeh, but it is Malinowski's answer—trade:

> Thus, side by side with the ritual exchange of arm-shells and necklaces, the natives carry on ordinary trade, bartering from one island to another a great number of utilities, often unprocurable in the district to which they are imported, and indispensable there.
>
> The Kula is thus an extremely big and complex institution, both in its geographical extent, and in the manifoldness of its component pursuits. It welds together a considerable number of tribes, and it embraces a vast complex of activities, interconnected, and playing into one another, so as to form one organic whole. [p. 83]

To separate ceremonial exchange out from that organic whole is allowable only in an analytic sense, and sound social analysis must place it *back* inside its proper context. If the exchange of necklaces for armbands is treated as strictly social-symbolic rather than instrumental or economic (Ekeh), then we must know exactly *what* it symbolizes outside of the organic whole that contains it.

Let us turn, then, to network theory. Exchange theory has no problem dealing with the organic wholeness of a many-faceted exchange relation (sometimes called "multiplex" relations in anthropology). Such multiplexity deepens the social bond for reasons stated in part I, above. It intensifies *dependencies* and therefore it raises the level of power associated with participation in the network. Can the system of Kula exchange be subjected to power analysis in a cogent way?

Most of the principles can be seen in figure 2.5. Since each x and y is a specific item traveling through this exchange network, flow v_1v_2 is contingent upon flow v_6v_1, which is contingent upon v_6v_5, and so around the positively connected Kula "ring." However, where rings intersect a negative connection occurs. Thus, v_2v_3 is contingent upon *not* v_2v_5 and vice versa. A further result is that v_1v_2 is contingent upon *either* v_2v_3 or v_2v_5. The implications of such structural features of Kula exchange for power and status in island trade have been overlooked in studies of the Kula system.

Power differentiation in figure 2.5 is unambiguous. The dependence of the network as a whole upon a given point (D_{NI}, above) can be shown to be very high for v_2 and v_5 and quite low for $v_{1,3,4,6}$. If v_2 were removed the "Residual Network", RN_2, would be a chain in which Kula exchange must cease altogether unless or until new partnerships are formed. For example, v_1 and v_3 might form a partnership to close the circle; however, this might not occur if they are on very remote islands. By contrast, if v_1 were to disappear (or refuse to cooperate) only v_6 would be affected, the rest of the network remaining "invulnerable." Power is a function of D_{NI}, which is in turn a function of the number of loops passing through location I. Because every partnership is on a loop, power is a function of the number of partners one has.

Let us turn back to Malinowski now. The number of partners a man has varies with his rank and importance. A commoner in the Trobriands would have a few partners only, whereas a chief would number hundreds of them. In other tribes, where the distinction of rank is not so pronounced, an old man of standing, or a headman of a hamlet or village would also have hundreds of Kula associates, whereas a man of minor importance would have but few. Finally, it is clear from Malinowski's descriptions that participants are free to choose which ornament they will bestow as gift upon which partner; that specific ornaments carry their own relative prestige value, and that a considerable social display follows receipt of the better ornaments upon return from a trade mission.

In conclusion. Whether or not the Kula network binds the larger island society together at an enhanced level of solidarity has not been addressed here. Depending on what one *means* by societal solidarity, it seems quite reasonable that an extended and interconnected network of close partnerships should have some such consequence. But the suggestion that the network formed or survived *for that reason* is a different order of assertion.

Why the Kula system came into being in the form it did, I don't know.

But it was clearly a highly institutionalized exchange system, and the sort of social exchange theory presented here is clearly capable of analyzing such a system.

INSTITUTIONALIZED POWER: THE CASE OF WEBERIAN "TRADITIONAL AUTHORITY"

I will close this chapter by setting forth the research problem in a study which is now in progress, for there is a form of social power that exchange theory has not addressed with any care. Apart from the network analysis presented above, the exchange approach examines power at the *micro*-level of analysis. By contrast, students of power at the *macro*-level have several reasons to doubt the usefulness of the exchange approach. Some of the reasons are worth listing:

1. Exchange theory offers a "soft" interpretation of power. Exchange theory has emphasized *mutually beneficial* exchange rather than coercion. Therefore, power inequalities are seen to result from asymmetric or unilateral exchange (Blau 1964; Baldwin 1978). Stated differently, power inequality stems from unequal dependence (Emerson 1962, 1972). Either way, the exchange approach leads to the important insight that the less powerful party in a relationship is the one who derives the largest benefits from the exchange relation. So why should the less powerful complain? This important principle, sometimes called the "principle of least interest," can be seen to operate even in such extreme cases of power inequality as plantation slavery in the American South and the "debt slavery" of the Jagmani exchange system of South Asia.

But taken by itself, this principle-of-least-interest is only a partial and peculiarly "soft" view of power. It is hardly adequate to handle the "hard realities" of the institutionalized coercion described by Wittfogel, the class domination described by Marx, or the systems of rule analyzed by Max Weber (1978). Therefore, we ask this question: *What, if anything, can the exchange approach provide in the study of institutionalized coercive rule?*

2. Exchange theory has developed largely around voluntary relations involving "rational" decision making. A psychology of choice—whether in the form of expected outcomes calculated prior to action, or in the form of post-action-differential reinforcement—underlies most microexchange theory. Yet power at the macrosociological level involves situations in which persons appear to have little "choice." Members of subordinate classes, relatively speaking, have no differentially rewarding opportunities to choose among. The soldier *must* comply with orders; the subject *must* obey the king; the citizen *must* abide by the regulations of the state. His only "choice" is to comply or to suffer the punishments applied by institutionalized coercive power. Therefore, in view of the emphasis upon voluntary decision making in exchange theory, *what can an exchange approach contribute to the study of nonvoluntary institutionalized systems of power and compliance?*

3. Finally, exchange theory to date is largely micro-theory. Homans, for example, explicitly adopted scope conditions limiting his analysis to "el-

ementary forms" of social behavior. By that he clearly meant subinstitutional behavior. Yet most people recognize that social power also operates at distinctly macroscopic levels, based upon organizational structure and institutional forms. We speak of "positions" of power and of "power structures"; and many of us are skeptical about claims that such structures can be "reduced" successfully to micro-level analysis of individual decisions.

Each of the above three points raises reasonable grounds for doubt about social exchange as an approach to power structures and institutionalized forms of power. As a result, a study now in progress takes as its objective a case analysis of institutionalized coercive rule viewed from an exchange perspective. It was felt that if exchange theory failed to inform the topic, the topic might inform the theory.

Power and authority. Weber began with what now appears to be a fundamental insight: we should distinguish analytically between *Macht* and *Herrschaft;* between *power* in its most general sense, and the particular form involving *domination.* Quoting in part:

A. "Power" *(Macht)* is the probability that one actor . . . will be in a position to carry out his own will despite resistance, regardless of the basis. . . .
B. "Domination" *(Herrschaft)* is the probability that a command . . . will be obeyed by a given group of persons. . . .

For Max Weber "power" is a very general class of social circumstances containing "domination" as a special case. The distinction revolves around the nature of *commands* and the character of social relations in which commands are issued and obeyed. The relation is one of super-subordination between status unequals such as ruler and subject, doctor and nurse, parent and child, military commander and soldier-in-the-ranks. In such relations "commands" are issued with the intention of allowing the recipient no choice. Compliance is socially defined as a duty. Failure to comply is socially defined as a deviant act challenging the validity of the relationship itself. In short, domination is usually found in institutionalized forms of power called *authority,* embedded in or deriving from a "legitimate social order."

Exchange and power. By contrast, nonauthoritative power, or *Macht,* is not confined to such organized relations. It operates as well in the interaction of status equals; between friends, lovers, among equally sovereign states or between autonomous firms; indeed, between *exchange* partners in most any marketplace. For Max Weber, power (as distinct from domination) is founded upon exchange; to yield or comply (as distinct from "obey") is an act of choice taken by a free agent on the basis of personal interest (p. 72–73). Both the weak and the strong party can gain through the yielding act of a weak person. Power, like exchange, can be symmetrical and even equal. Indeed, all of Weber's comments suggest that, had he chosen to analyze *Macht,* he would have found current exchange theory conceptions of power to be quite appropriate.

Exchange and authority. But the relationship between exchange and domination is a very different matter. Domination is fundamentally asymmetrical and therefore cannot be interpreted as an exchange.

Weber gave relatively little attention to the "sociologically amorphous" phenomenon of power, choosing instead to examine the more sociologically relevant topic of domination. His position can be summarized as follows:

1. Domination can take purely coercive forms (see his Bedouin Chief example, p. 53–54), but taken by itself, coercive rule is unstable and costly.

2. Stable and enduring forms of domination are based upon claims of and beliefs in the "legitimacy" of domination (including the *right* to use coercive force). When legitimized, domination is called *authority.*

3. Different bases for legitimacy generate qualitatively different systems of authority.

4. Three "pure types of authority" can be analytically distinguished, deriving their legitimacy from "rational-legal," "charismatic," and "traditional" sources. Concrete empirical systems approximate those types in varying degree.

5. *But none of the forms of domination can be conceptualized properly on the basis of exchange.* For Weber, "power" and "influence" are based upon exchange processes, but "domination" and "authority" are not. Speaking of exchange, Weber asserted:

> No precise concept of domination could be built up upon the basis of such considerations; and this statement holds true for all relationships of exchange, including those of intangibles. [p. 947]

> . . . there are two diametrically contrasting types of domination, viz., domination by virtue of a constellation of interests (in particular: by virtue of a position of monopoly), and domination by virtue of authority. . . . The purest type of the former is monopolistic domination in the market; of the latter, patriarchal, magisterial, or princely power. [p. 943]

In Weber's view, the prince enjoys obedience from his subjects, not as a return for benefits granted, as an exchange approach would suggest, but out of their "absolute duty to obey, regardless of personal motives or interests" (p. 943).

Micro- versus macro-levels. We find a weakness in Weber's argument regarding exchange and domination. His reasons for rejecting an exchange approach are *micro*-social. He uses a language involving the motives *(interests),* actions *(commands),* and attitudes *(duty)* of individual people. At that microlevel no one could disagree with the assertion that *if* a person *obeys* a *command* because of a sense of *duty* (in which case *Herrschaft* is involved by definition), *then* the person is not acting out of personal interest. If exchange is equated with motives of personal gain, then exchange is not the basis for domination.

But if we conceive macroinstitutional forms as mandates which develop over time, transcending the motives and actions of persons at a point in time, then Weber's argument against exchange reduces to an argument about levels. We are left, then, with two questions:

1. Can exchange analysis be raised to the normative, macro-institutional level?
2. If it is so raised, does it inform us about the conditions underlying legitimate domination?

The study now in progress was prompted by these two questions. The research was initiated when we learned that an almost pure case of princely rule had survived in Baltistan (a region of the modern state of Pakistan) from about 1400 until 1972, and that its traces are still available for study. The history of rule in that region promises to provide an ideal-typical case of Weberian traditional authority.

In about A.D. 1400, a military Muslim line from Central Asia conquered the Buddhist agriculturalists of the region. That foreign dynasty maintained unbroken domination for six centuries, without facing any serious peasant revolts; ample time, surely, for truly "traditional" authority to be established. By the time one century had passed, the peasantry had converted to Islam. In the course of time, coercive domination gave way to truly normative compliance wherein it was the *duty* of a peasant household to provide the ruler with up to two-fifths of the agricultural yield and a prescribed amount of labor.

The research issue, then, is very clear: how and why did such norms of compliance emerge? Our study of traditional authority becomes a special case of *norm formation.* Further, from an exchange perspective, norm formation can be treated as a special case of *coalition formation* (see Emerson 1962, 1972). Therefore, the core idea guiding this research on princely rule in Pakistan is a minimal network of three (or more) actors, a prince and two or more subjects, forming the triad.

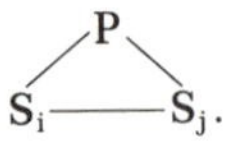

The main research questions, then, become:

1. When P demands from S_i more than S_i is *personally* inclined to give, what does S_j (a "bystander" to that encounter) do? Does S_j
   (a) join with S_i in a "revolutionary coalition";
   (b) support P in his demand, thereby raising the command of P to the level of a collectively legitimized demand—a norm;
   (c) remain a passive bystander? (If he does, then both S_i and S_j separately remain subject to oppressive, coercive rule.)

We know that 1(a) did *not* occur; and we know that such a norm *did* form. Therefore, the next question becomes:

2. Under what exchange network conditions, if any, would the coalition described in 1(b) occur?

Theory provides a tentative answer: when P-S_i and P-S_j are *positively connected* at P (see definition 4(1) above). Such positive connections require that the contribution S_i gives to P provides indirect benefit to S_j.

3. Were peasant subjects positively connected to one another through their prince-ruler?

Historical evidence shows that they *were* so connected through the first five centuries.

After 1948 the network was "disconnected" and, indeed, the normative structure and the authority of the prince have been decaying since that time. Only the memory remains, in the form of oral anecdotes, folk-tales, dances, and songs; and the lingering sentiments of a paternalist system.

Conclusion

Looking back across this Chapter, several very general points seem to have emerged. First, while much has been written about the individual psychological emphasis in social exchange theory, the theory itself has involved very little psychology. Its major concepts are social-relational, and individual actions and motives are viewed within the interactive social relation taken as an irreducible base.

Second, while having obvious points of similarity with economics, the similarity is largely at the gross level of metaphor—both deal with *exchanges,* with mutually beneficial *transactions.* Beyond this, however, economic and social exchange theory are seen to move in very different ways, not so much in their choice of data as in the intellectual framework they build around the data.

The exchange approach has spanned several disciplines. While economic and sociological analyses have pronounced dissimilarities, I find no *important* differences between the work of anthropologists, psychologists, and sociologists in this area. There are differences in method, differences in research setting, and differences in level (micro-macro), but the same intellectual framework seems to be forming in the work of all three disciplines. I expect, for example, to find the Kelley-Thibaut discussion of "transformation" very helpful in a longitudinal case study of traditional rulership.

Finally, it seems clear to me that at both micro- and macro-levels, the approach is moving quite vigorously into interesting research areas.

NOTES

This work was supported by a grant from the National Science Foundation (SOC75-04059). I would like to thank Karen Cook, Bertie Conrad, Mary Gillmore, Toshio Yamagishi, and Morris Rosenberg for helpful comments and editorial advice on this chapter.

1. After Homans (1961), Thibaut and Kelley (1959), and Blau (1964) wrote their first major statements, the exchange approach was given further elaboration in many major writings addressing the theory directly. They include: Gergen 1969; Burgess and Bushell 1969; Emerson 1972a, 1972b; Homans 1974; Ekeh 1974; Chad-

wick-Jones 1976; Emerson 1976; Heath 1976; Kapferer 1976; Befu 1977; Goode 1978; Turner 1978; Kelley and Thibaut 1978; and Cook et al. forthcoming.

2. Whether or not a person acts so as to "maximize" benefits is partly an empirical question of degree and partly a problem of definition which I will not attempt to resolve here.

3. Other writers have coined their own terms for similar exchange systems. Ekeh (1974), for example, writes about "univocal reciprocity," following Levi-Strauss. Ekeh and Sahlins both discuss the diffuse obligations to provide benefit, generated within such exchange systems.

4. In research now under way, Yamagishi (forthcoming) is testing the hypothesis that a distribution of rewards proportional to contributions emerges as a distribution rule under conditions of productive exchange.

5. Economic theory is not a single thing to be so easily characterized. There are many current developments in economics that link directly to social exchange, including Olson (1965); Becker (1974); Williamson (1975); and Leibenstein (1976). Even so, the distinction between economic and social theory advanced here seems to hold true.

6. The general theme involved in this formulation of *value* and *uncertainty* bears a resemblance to notions that have been advanced in widely separated areas. For example, "Effectance motivation subsides when a situation has been explored to the point that it no longer presents new possibilities" (White 1961:315). See also Berlyne (1960), and Atkinson (1957:359–72). As Catton (1966:148) has observed, "Another plausible dimension (of value), that of *probability,* can be traced back to the thinking of Jeremy Bentham. Probability . . . may be regarded as an aspect of the valuer's *relation* to the desideratum. . . . Quite possibly the intensity of striving to attain a goal will be *curvilinearly* related to perceived probability, with less striving for the impossible and less striving for the automatic than for the goal of medium likelihood."

7. This section is based upon Cook and Emerson 1978b.

8. It should be noted that the exchange approach has been especially useful in studying power, influence, control, and related topics. Power emerges as a central theme in virtually all forms of *social* exchange theory. It is notably absent in economic exchange theory for a reason that is well known: the perfectly competitive market is a model of exchange among actors equal in power, and all have zero power. It is a model that assumes that no actor is dependent upon any other actor. It is a model that breaks down when applied to a small number of interdependent actors. It is precisely the latter whom social exchange theory addresses.

9. As Kelley and Thibaut make clear, there is no guarantee that a given matrix will undergo a given transformation. The determining factors are in need of research. Thus, while I hypothesize that productive exchange *tends* to give rise to corporate group formation and associated values and attitudes (Barth's incorporated exchange), we must not equate the two notions.

10. This hypothesis suggests that physicians enjoy high status partly because even the best of physicians knows so little or can do so little about the problems of health. Similarly, even the best pitchers yield home runs. The service both agents provide their principal leaves the principal uncertain about the outcome of the next episode of exchange.

11. Important contemporary contributions by sociologists in this area include Boorman and White 1976; Breiger 1976; White, Boorman, and Breiger 1976; Burt 1977; Coleman 1972, 1973; Laumann and Pappi 1976; Davis and Leinhardt 1972. Much of this work is substantively concerned with power and related topics—elites, cliques, hierarchies, and status levels. In anthropology the concept of network as a concrete social organization form was advanced early (Bott 1957) and has become a standard tool of the trade. See, for example, Boissevain 1969; Boissevain and Mitchell 1973; Wolfe 1978; and Whitten and Wolfe 1971.

12. There is an important similarity between our laboratory-based conception of position and the definition used by Burt (1976, 1977a, b) and White, Boorman, and Breiger (1976) field research.

13. The occupants of network structures usually have limited knowledge about the network they are in, yet they are affected by events in the network beyond their

"field of vision." In our experiments, subjects know only what persons they are themselves engaged in exchange with.

14. The structure of patrilateral marriage is not fully described in this pattern, as Homans and Schneider (1955) observed, but we can overlook this for the sake of the argument.

15. The concept of "generalized exchange" from Levi-Strauss is similar but not identical to Sahlins' "generalized reciprocity" discussed above. The major difference lies in the fixed partnerships involved in Levi-Strauss's case.

3 ELEANOR SINGER

Reference Groups and Social Evaluations

Sociologists and other social scientists have long recognized that attitudes, self-evaluations, and behavior are shaped by the groups to which an individual belongs. The concept *reference group,* which designates the group to which an individual orients himself, regardless of actual membership, calls attention to the fact that such evaluations, attitudes, and behavior may be shaped by groupings other than the person's own. It thus helps to illuminate such central sociological concerns as socialization and conformity, as well as providing clues to processes of individual and social change. As Hyman has put it: "If the groups to which individuals refer themselves . . . are empirically determined, knowledge and prediction of attitude, self-evaluation, and conduct will be enhanced. . . . Such is the hope of reference group theory and research, and the basis of its attractiveness to social scientists" (1968:3–4).

In 1968, Hyman and Singer attempted to organize and make available for systematic development the theoretical and empirical work that had been done on reference groups during the preceding twenty-five years. Some twelve years after the publication of their volume, and almost forty years after Hyman (1942) first coined the term, it must be acknowledged that its explanatory promise has not been fulfilled. There is at present no reference group theory. In part, this may be because the attempt to encompass two disparate concerns—that having to do with socialization and conformity, and that having to do with self- and social evaluation—under the single concept of "reference group" was, at best, premature. This chapter reviews all the research and theorizing that has traditionally been associated with reference groups. But what I shall propose, albeit reluctantly, is renunciation of fully half, perhaps more, of this accretion of work, and restriction of the concept to processes of self- and social evaluation. Only in this way, I believe, can we begin to construct a reference group theory, if by theory we mean what Homans (1961) does —namely, an explanation.

Early History and Conceptual Developments

Although precursors of reference group theory can be found in the writings of Sumner, Cooley, and James, the term, "reference group," was first used by Hyman (1942), who hypothesized that the way individuals evaluate their social status is contingent on their choice of a social framework for comparison. To test this hypothesis, he first ascertained what reference groups and individuals were employed spontaneously, and then determined experimentally the effects of particular reference groups on self-appraisal. At about the same time, Newcomb (1943), seeking to understand processes of attitude change among Bennington college students, explored by interview and repeated testing the ways in which they related themselves to the Bennington community during their four-year college career. These two studies by social psychologists were the first systematic investigations of reference group processes.

In 1949, Stouffer and his associates, in the course of interpreting certain findings in *The American Soldier,* introduced the concept of *relative deprivation,* which is closely related to comparative reference group processes. Attempting to explain paradoxical feelings of satisfaction and deprivation among various groups of soldiers, they postulated that the sense of deprivation or satisfaction was dependent, not on the situation itself, but rather on a comparison the soldiers made between their situation and that of some other group.

The ideas put forward by Hyman, Newcomb, and Stouffer and his colleagues gained prominence among social scientists in 1950, with the publication of Merton and Rossi's "Contributions to the theory of reference group behavior," followed some years later by a more extended treatment (Merton, 1957). By 1968, Hyman and Singer noted that the concept, "reference group," had figured in so many writings that "the more recent history defies brief review. The concept appears in Australia, Israel, and India; in studies of farmers, scientists, drunkards, and newspapermen; it has been applied to problems of mental illness, formal organization, marketing and public relations, mass communication, acculturation, political behavior, consumer behavior, labor relations, and juvenile delinquency, as well as to opinion formation" (1968:7). Although explicit use of the concept appears to have declined since 1968, the processes subsumed under reference group behavior continue to receive attention under other labels. Later in the chapter we will attempt to trace these interrelationships.

With use, the concept was elaborated and refined. Thus, it has been noted that reference functions may be served by *individuals* and by *status categories* (for example, civilians, workers) as well as social groups, and that the individual may orient himself to groups (or categories) to which he or she does or does not belong; that people almost always have *multiple* reference groups, and that these may conflict with or reinforce one another; that relative deprivation may be *egoistic* (experienced on behalf of oneself) or *fraternal* (experienced on behalf of one's group); that reference groups (individuals, and so forth) may serve *negative* as well as *positive* functions (for example, may teach what behavior is to be avoided as well as what is to be emulated). Each of these elaborations has given rise to distinctive research concerns: the relative potency of status categories versus primary groups (and of membership versus nonmembership groups) in inducing conformity; the consequences of multiple group memberships for the individual and for society; the implications for learning, and for changes in status, of negative, as opposed to positive, reference orientations. For a more detailed discussion of these conceptual distinctions and interrelationships, see Merton and Rossi (1950), Merton (1957), and Hyman and Singer (1968).

Basic to all research and theorizing in this area is the distinction drawn by Kelley (1952) between the *comparative* and the *normative* functions of reference groups, according to whether such referents serve as standards of comparison for an appraisal of some sort (self, other, or social arrangement) or as a source of the individual's norms, attitudes, or values.[1] This distinction serves as one dimension along which the discussion in this chapter has been organized.

Because the organization tends to encourage the view that "normative" and "comparative" are distinct types of groups, categories, or individuals, it is worth emphasizing at the outset that these are simply two aspects of what may be the same entity. The very same group may—indeed, often does—serve as the source of the individual's norms, attitudes, and values, and as the standard against which he evaluates the adequacy of his performance, the accuracy of his beliefs, and the justice of his rewards.

To complicate matters further, not only may normative as well as comparative functions be served by the same reference group, but both functions enter into the process of self- or social evaluation, even though this is sometimes regarded as an outcome of comparative reference orientations alone (cf. Pettigrew 1967) and is discussed as such an outcome in this chapter.

Self- (and social) evaluation can come about in two ways. In the first, the individual accepts the evaluations expressed by others and applies them to himself. That is, he accepts these others as normative referents and accepts, as well, their evaluative judgments. As Rosenberg (1979) has pointed out, this concept of "reflected appraisal" has a distinguished theoretical and empirical history, appearing in the writings of Sullivan (1947) and Veblen (1934) and associated especially with the work of George Herbert Mead (1934). No comparisons at all need be involved in this process of self-appraisal.

The second way in which self- (or social) evaluation can come about is through a process of *comparison* with others. An individual's judgment of how well he or she is doing is formed not only directly, on the basis of appraisals by others, but also indirectly, as a result of comparing his or her situation with that of others.

Even in self-evaluations resulting from social comparison, however, normative factors come into play. In the first place, such factors may specify the group with which the comparison must be made. And second, the comparison has consequences for self-evaluation only to the extent that the standard against which an opinion, performance, or situation is compared has normative force—that is, constitutes an *expectation level* that carries with it the implication of "ought" or "should" (Hyman and Singer 1968:24; I. Katz 1967:312).

Thus, although for convenience of presentation this chapter separates the normative functions of reference groups from their comparative functions, it should be remembered that these are analytical distinctions only. In the real world, not only may the same reference object serve both functions, but both functions are implicated in processes of self- and social evaluation.

The second dimension along which this chapter has been organized consists of the dual tasks of reference group theory: namely, (1) to specify the *determinants* of the referents (groups, categories, persons) to which individuals orient themselves, and (2) to elucidate the *consequences* of such orientations for attitudes and conduct. Thus, this chapter reviews and attempts to synthesize research on the determinants and consequences of normative and comparative reference orientations. The aim has not been an exhaustive review of the literature, but instead, one that organizes major theoretical developments and research bearing on them. In the case of social comparison theory and equity theory, work not explicitly related to reference groups has been reconceptualized in reference group terms. Because sociologists have most often concerned themselves with the normative functions of reference orientations, and with consequences rather than determinants, the discussion begins with that cell of the typology.

Consequences of Normative Reference Orientations

Broadly conceived, the consequence of normative reference orientations is conformity. It may be conformity with respect to a belief, an attitude, a value, a behavior; it may be conceptualized as deviance from one set of norms, rather than adherence to another; it may be thought of as conformity to the norms of a group to which the individual aspires to belong rather than to those of one in which he or she currently holds membership. What all of these have in common is a shaping of behavior, feeling, or thought in accordance with that of a referent, and to the extent that such attitudes and behaviors are organized around a particular social status (student, mother, teacher), the consequence of normative reference orientation is socialization or anticipatory socialization.

Although the consequences of normative reference orientations fall in the general area of attitudinal and behavioral conformity, they can also be examined from other perspectives, or used to illuminate more specifically delineated social processes—for example, social mobility, acculturation, attitude change. Many of the classic investigations of reference group behavior have concerned themselves with the consequences of conformity to the perceived prescriptions of some valued group for attitude stability or change. Thus, Newcomb's original investigation (1943) explained attitude change among Bennington students in terms of their orientation to the college as a positive reference group, and his twenty-five-year follow-up study of some of these same students (Newcomb et al. 1967) demonstrates that the stability of their attitudes during this period of time is a consequence of support by significant reference individuals. Hyman, Wright, and Hopkins (1962) used a similar model to account for attitude change and stability among campers at the Encampment for Citizenship. Other studies have shown that experimentally increasing the salience of a reference group can increase a subject's resistance to propaganda directed against the group (Kelley 1955), or increase the frequency of responses conforming to the norms of that group (Charters and Newcomb 1958) or indicating favorability toward the group (Festinger 1947). Still other studies have accounted for the ability to maintain a deviant perspective by its anchorage in a significant reference group or individual (for example, Houseknecht 1977) or have demonstrated that adoption of new reference figures (as through the development of close friendships) is associated with adoption of a new, at times deviant, perspective (for example, Cohen 1977; Kandel 1978; Walsh, Ferrell, and Tolone 1976). More recently, many of the classic experiments on "normative" and "informational" influence (cf. Deutsch and Gerard 1955) have been reinterpreted by Allen and Wilder (1977) in terms of social comparison theory, which, as we shall see, is the main form taken by comparative reference group theory.

While most of the studies cited immediately above have been concerned primarily with attitudes and attitude change, many others have used reference group concepts to account for changes in behavior as well as attitudes, or for changes in behavior alone (for example, Das, Choudhury, and Santra 1973; Rogers 1958; Rogers and Beal 1958). When these changes are designed to bring about conformity with the attitudes and behaviors characteristic of a group or stratum to which the individual aspires to belong, they have, following Merton and Rossi (1950), been referred to as "anticipatory socialization."

In his analysis of changes in attitudes among Bennington students, Newcomb (1943) called attention to identification with the group (that is, taking it as a positive reference group), awareness of its norms, and supporting or conflicting identifications with other groups as mediating the process of attitude change. These three concepts are still useful for summarizing the conditions that facilitate or impede attitudinal and behavioral conformity.

For example, in an elegant field experiment, Siegel and Siegel (1957) demonstrated that attitudinal conformity was greater when a membership group also served as a reference group, and Mannheim (1966) showed that agreement between self-image and the perception of self attributed to other group members was greater when the membership group was also taken as a reference group. Not surprisingly, Fisher and Andrews (1976) demonstrated that a membership group taken as a positive reference group induced more conformity than one taken as a negative reference group.

In the absence of awareness of group norms, however, identification is not enough to produce conformity, and for such awareness to exist, formal or informal communication must take place (for example, Campbell, Gurin, and Miller 1954; Converse and Campbell 1960; Hyman 1960; Kaplan 1955). Even in membership groups, the accuracy with which group norms are perceived is not always high and varies depending on one's position in the group (Chowdhry and Newcomb 1952) as well as on structural properties of the group (Merton 1957).

The third factor identified by Newcomb as mediating conformity was the existence of supporting or conflicting identifications with other groups. Such concepts as cross-pressures, conflicting expectations, and marginality connect normative reference group theory with theories of conflict and integration on both the individual and the societal level. Coser (1956), Simmel (1955), and Ross (1920), among others, have pointed out that the occupancy of several statuses by the individual, and the existence of multiple reference orientations, has potentially different consequences for the person and for society as a whole. For the person, the fact of simultaneous positive orientations to more than one group or social category carries with it the possibility of conflicting expectations, the inability to conform to them all, and therefore the possibility of internal as well as external sanctions for nonconformity. But for society as a whole, the fact that distinct social groupings may be united by overlapping memberships serves to dampen to some extent the potential for conflict among them.

The preceding summary has glossed over serious problems with much of the research bearing on the consequences of normative reference orientations. So far as *measurement* is concerned, investigators have often asserted the influence of a reference group whose psychological presence has been inferred, not measured. Most of the research purporting to show the influence of a reference group on attitudes or behavior has utilized retrospective measurement of both reference groups and the attitudes of those groups, making unambiguous inferences about effects impossible. Too often, analysts arbitrarily attribute causal priority to one of two variables measured simultaneously, failing to consider the possibility that the true causal order may be the reverse of that hypothesized, or that the association between the two may be attributable to still a third variable, antecedent to both. For example, the fact that adolescents who use drugs are more likely to report drug use among their friends does not necessarily mean that such use is a consequence of selecting a particular reference group; the choice of reference group may be contingent on drug-taking behavior, or both may be consequences of particular combinations of residential, social, and other statuses.

Further, the attitudes of referent others are often measured by questioning the individual about them, and the lack of independence in the two measures likewise makes causal inference hazardous. Research by O'Gorman (1975, 1979), O'Gorman and Garry (1976), and Fields and Schuman (1976) has raised serious questions about the usefulness of respondent reports of group norms, and more generally about the relation between perceived norms and "objective norms" (however measured). The notion that one's current friends, for example, should exhibit attitudes more similar to one's own than those of friends one has discarded may be shared by research subjects as well as investigators, and the information given by subjects may be such as to confirm the hypothesis. There are, of course, some notable exceptions to these criticisms, in which researchers have obtained true before-after measures of attitudes and reference group orientations and, in some cases, independent measures of the attitudes of referent others—for example, Newcomb (1943), Hyman, Wright, and Hopkins (1962), Cohen (1977), Kandel (1978).

Aside from questions of measurement, however, serious questions can be raised about the *utility* of invoking the concept, "reference group," for the phenomena discussed in this section. I shall return to this point in the concluding section. For the moment, the reader is invited to consider whether, for example, explaining attitude change in terms of changes in reference groups really explains much of anything at all, or whether it gives the illusion of explanation while simply pushing the crucial explanatory task one step further back.

As already noted, sociologists have been more concerned with the consequences of reference orientations than with their determinants. But in the attempt to move to an explanatory theory, the question of how social referents are selected is crucial. In the next section, we examine the evidence that bears on this question, so far as normative referents are concerned.

Selection and Acceptance of Normative Reference Groups

INTRODUCTION

Some general principles have been identified as influencing the selection and acceptance of groups and individuals that function as normative referents. But before discussing these, it is necessary to make several distinctions that are often blurred.

In the first place, selection does not necessarily involve the same processes as acceptance. To ask how an individual comes to select one group rather than another is to ask about social structures that facilitate or impede awareness and contact, and about norms that may prescribe, proscribe, or remain indifferent to such processes. To ask, on the other hand, how an individual comes to accept as a reference group a group to which he already belongs is to ask how attachments are formed, given awareness and contact.

Second, selection and acceptance of reference groups in the real world may not be governed by the same processes as those investigated in the laboratory, where precision and control are obtained at the price of verisimilitude. In the laboratory, selection is ordinarily reduced to a binary choice: to affiliate with this group or that, that group or none, for a limited time and for a purpose that, from the subject's point of view, may be trivial; and acceptance is similarly measured with respect to groups that are ephemeral rather than enduring, peripheral rather than central to the subject's life. It cannot be assumed that decisions made under these circumstances will necessarily correspond to those made when the consequences carry more weight.

Finally, to ask about processes governing the selection and acceptance of normative reference groups is not identical to asking which set of norms a person will conform to, if two (or more) happen to conflict. Such questions rather involve the relative importance of several different reference groups to the individual, or perhaps simply the relative power of the groups to punish or reward. That is, although "referent power," to use French and Raven's (1962) term, may lead to conformity, conformity may be induced by other than referent power. In the discussion that follows, I shall try to preserve these distinctions.

THE SIMILARITY PRINCIPLE

One important factor demonstrated as influencing the *selection* of new reference individuals (or groups) in the real world is the perceived congruence of their attitudes and values with the person's own (Newcomb 1961). Kandel (1978) concluded that about half the agreement obtaining on a specific attitude within mutually chosen high school friendship pairs at any one time is attributable to similarity on that attitude prior to the formation of the friendship, and about half to subsequent attitude change. This fact, in turn, suggests that attitudinal similarity may be a potent factor in the formation of friendship groups, which subsequently function as powerful reference groups in inducing further attitude change.

Here, as elsewhere, the task of theory building is complicated by reciprocal relations among variables. If similarity leads to liking, so, too, does liking lead to similarity, as both Lazarsfeld and Merton (1954) and Homans (1950, 1961) demonstrated long ago. But, as Lazarsfeld and Merton noted, it is important to distinguish similarity with respect to status ("status homophily") from similarity with respect to values ("value homophily") and related concepts. In general, values and attitudes can be modified more readily than statuses; ascribed statuses such as sex, race, and age cannot be modified at all. Consequently, whereas the proposition that similarity leads to liking may apply to statuses as well as values and attitudes—and similarity of status may, in fact, often be used as a clue to attitudinal similarity—the proposition that liking leads to similarity has more limited applicability, being restricted to those attributes that are, in fact, amenable to change.

Most of the work by experimental social psychologists is only inferentially relevant to reference group selection/acceptance, dealing as it does with the choice of others for limited interaction on a laboratory task, or with expressed liking for others. But, so far as it goes, it, too, supports the similarity principle. For example, see the experimental work on interpersonal attraction summarized in Griffitt (1974).

In short, both laboratory experiments involving the choice of partners for limited kinds of interactions and investigations of friendship choices in the real world have pointed to some sort of similarity as one principle underlying the selection and acceptance of groups that function as normative referents. But the question immediately arises, similarity with respect to what?

To begin with, we might note that social psychologists and sociologists have traditionally adopted different approaches to this question, with social psychologists tending to emphasize similarity with respect to individual values, attitudes, and other personality characteristics, and sociologists, similarity of statuses and roles.[2] But another, perhaps more fruitful formulation, is to ask what part similarity itself plays in the selection process.

From this perspective, it becomes clear that not only the particular dimension of similarity, but similarity itself as a determinant of normative reference group selection, is, in fact, influenced by one of two broad classes of factors. One of these is the *social structure,* which may make one group (individual, category, status, and so forth) more *salient* than another, in terms of its appropriateness or in terms of its power to confer rewards; the other is the *normative structure,* which may define one group (individual, category, status, and so forth) as more appropriate or more rewarding. Existing research on the determinants of reference group selection can conveniently be located within this framework, which at the same time points to some directions for further research.

STRUCTURAL FACTORS

In much experimental research on reference group processes, the *experimenter* structures the situation. Castore and DeNinno's subjects (1977), for example, were required to express a preference for (that is, select) a partner similar in one respect but not in another. In an experimental situation devised by Ofshe (1972), subjects had to conform to one reference figure or another, over a series of trials. In experiments by Kelley (1952), Charters and Newcomb (1958), and Festinger (1947), some group membership (that is, similarity with respect to one status) was deliberately made salient, with the result that subjects were more likely to answer in accordance with that group norm, to resist a counternorm communication, or to vote on the basis of loyalty to the group.

Real life, of course, sometimes mimics these experimental situations. Describing the different friendship patterns in Craftown, a white housing project of some 700 families in New Jersey, and Hilltown, a biracial low-rent project of about 800 families in western Pennsylvania, Merton writes: "The social and cultural context provided by the community went far toward determining both the general extent of selecting status-similars as close friends and the particular statuses for which such selectivity was most marked. Thus, the more cohesive community of Craftown consistently exhibited a lower degree of selection of status-similars as friends; but when such selectivity did occur, it was as likely to be in terms of *acquired* statuses . . . as in terms of *ascribed* statuses. . . . In Hilltown, on the contrary, selectivity was much more marked in terms of ascribed status, since there was less by way of overarching community purposes to focus the attention of residents on locally achieved or acquired statuses" (Lazarsfeld and Merton 1954:22).

The potency of *physical structure* was dramatically demonstrated in a field experiment by Festinger, Schachter, and Back (1950), in which the "functional distance" between apartments turned out to be a powerful determinant of friendship formation among persons who were similar to one another on a variety of social characteristics.

Structural factors also come into play in those situations in which individuals adopt as a point of reference a group whose values are quite dissimilar from their own. The classic instance is that of the "assimilation" of immigrants, or of their children, but other instances have been noted. For example, Inkeles's (1955) study documents that Russian adults "caught between Tsarist and Soviet society" transmitted values to their children different from those they themselves had internalized, and Hyman (1969:7) suggests that the same principle may apply to white parents' deliberate attempts to prepare their children for survival in an integrated South. What seems to be crucial is a perception by the individual of the differential power of similar and dissimilar others to confer rewards. But, as Merton has pointed out, since both the visibility of groups and their ability to confer rewards are socially patterned, the selection of normative reference groups is to some extent patterned by the social structure itself. Thus, a whole body of research bearing on structural factors making for greater or lesser visibility of a group, its norms, and its power to confer rewards—some of which has been alluded to in the preceding section—becomes relevant to the question of how social structure determines the selection of reference groups (for example, Merton 1957:366 ff.).

NORMATIVE FACTORS

One determinant of reference group selection might be termed a normative prescription—the stipulation by a superordinate reference group, or by more general "reference norms" (Eisenstadt 1954), that certain individuals, groups, or categories are to be accepted as authoritative in a given situation. Tomeh (1970), for example, asked some 500 women students in a small, private, liberal arts college in the Middle East who, of eight adults, were most important to them in making decisions in academic, leisure, and financial areas. That fathers were chosen most often for academic matters, and mothers for social matters, does not surprise us, and this absence of surprise, in turn, suggests that each society tends to define appropriate normative referents for its members on the basis, perhaps, of their ability to perform the activity or the legitimacy accorded this performance. The definitions may vary for different statuses within the society, and they may further vary from one subgroup to another.

In a study of spontaneous references to ethnic group membership as a component of the self-concept, McGuire, McGuire, Child, and Fujioka (1978) specifically allude to the role played by social norms. Noting that although, in general, the results supported predictions that persons would selectively attend to those aspects of a complex stimulus that are most distinctive, they point out that there was one exception: blacks were more likely to mention their ethnicity as their proportion in the student population *increased,* rather than decreased. The authors speculate that "what we are seeing is a sociological factor outweighing a psychological one"—namely, a black consciousness-raising movement which develops only if there is a critical mass.

It should be noted that very few of the studies cited above permit clear-cut identification of what actually determines the selection of a normative referent. The determinants are imputed—either by the original analyst, or by me—as a plausible interpretation of the results obtained.

SELECTION AMONG CONFLICTING REFERENCE GROUPS

Until now, we have been considering the problem of selection or acceptance of normative reference groups in the abstract—that is, without taking into account the fact that individuals may have multiple reference groups, and that on occasion their demands may conflict. To ask which of several conflicting expectations the individual will conform to is to raise the problem of reference group selection under these special circumstances.

To review the not inconsiderable literature on role or status conflict resolution is clearly beyond the scope of this chapter. Whether or not all such conflict involves conflicting reference orientations, and under what circumstances it is useful to approach the problem of role conflict from a reference group perspective, is by no means clear. Certainly the problem has often been approached in that way—for example, in the early voting studies by Lazarsfeld and his colleagues (Lazarsfeld, Berelson, and Gaudet 1944; Berelson, Lazarsfeld, and McPhee 1954).

Before leaving this section, we might ask whether anything is gained by seeking the determinants of normative reference orientations *in general.* It is possible that we would do just as well, perhaps better, to stay with the more specific questions posed by many of the studies cited: for example, what determines the selection of friends, the identification with a group, and the resolution of conflicting expectations?

The fact is that much of the research reviewed in this section deals with the selection of concrete entities—friends, coworkers, likable strangers. True, such individuals and groups may subsequently function as norm-givers. But they may equally well serve comparison functions. In that sense, much of the research cited in this section is as relevant to comparative as to normative reference group processes. Such processes are the subject of the next two sections. In the section that follows, I examine the selection of comparison others, returning to the consequences of those comparisons later.

Selection of Comparative Reference Groups

INTRODUCTION

As has already been noted, the comparative function of reference groups is to serve as a standard of comparison for an appraisal of some sort, either of the self or of others. Perhaps because much of the research on the selection of comparison others has been done by social psychologists, it has emphasized primarily motivational determinants. Structural and normative factors have been recognized as playing a role, especially in the work of sociologists, but have been subjected to little systematic investigation.

One motive, postulated by Festinger (1954), is the need to evaluate one's opinions and abilities. In "A theory of social comparison processes," which grew out of a considerable body of experimental work on opinion formation and influence processes in small groups, Festinger accounts for the often observed pressures toward uniformity of opinion in such groups by postulating (1) a universal need to evaluate one's abilities and the correctness of one's opinions; (2) reliance on comparison with other people if more "objective" means are not available; (3) the impossibility of making precise evaluations unless others hold opinions or abilities "close" to one's own. Subsequently, Schachter and his students extended social comparison theory to include the emotions as well as opinions and abilities (for example, Schachter 1959). In social comparison theory as formulated by Festinger, Schachter, and their colleagues and students, the need for realistic self-appraisal leads to a "similarity principle" of comparative reference group selection.

Realistic self-appraisal, however, is only one of several possible motives for comparison. As early as 1942, Hyman, studying the groups and individuals spontaneously used by subjects in making comparative judgments of their standing along a variety of specified dimensions (for example, intellectual, social, economic), found that both similarity and contrast served as principles of selection. Noting that realistic appraisal of one's rank was only one of several motives governing the selection of comparison others, Hyman explicitly commented on two others: status enhancement and status depreciation, both of which involve comparison with others *dissimilar* with respect to some characteristic. Under certain circumstances, individuals may compare themselves with others who are worse off, thus enhancing their self-esteem or satisfaction. Under other circumstances, they may be motivated to make comparisons unfavorable to themselves, selecting as a point of reference others who are better, or better off. Such comparisons, and the resulting dissatisfaction, can act as a lever for change (of jobs, for example) or lead to demands for change (for example, in pay) (See Patchen 1958, 1961).

At the risk of oversimplification, subsequent research on social comparison can be characterized as having followed two diverging paths. Until quite recently, social psychologists have tended to elaborate that branch of social comparison theory emphasizing *cognitive* needs. The research paradigm used most often attempts to arouse uncertainty with respect to some quality of the self, and then requires the subject to make a choice among several comparison others who differ in the degree to which they are similar to the subject along a dimension specified by the experimenter. As a consequence, this version of social comparison theory is applicable only in the special case when (1) the purpose of the comparison is accurate appraisal of one's abilities, opinions, or emotions, and (2) other possible dimensions of comparison have been experimentally held constant. Although the experiments do not deliberately eliminate other variations, they do so for all practical purposes by selecting subjects who *are* similar in significant respects (usually, undergraduates), and by making the experimentally manipulated opinion, ability, or emotion the only salient basis of comparison.

Sociologists, on the other hand, have been much more likely to assume that accurate appraisal is only *one of several possible motives* underlying comparison with others, to investigate what groups or individuals are actually used for comparison in *naturally occurring situations,* and to assume that the selection of comparison others may be largely *determined* by the structure of the situation or the norms operative in it, rather than being entirely, or even primarily, a matter of individual choice. Furthermore, because of their emphasis on statuses and roles, sociologists have explicitly recognized the fact that individuals may resemble others with respect to certain characteristics and qualities, but differ from them with respect to others. Under these circumstances, one wants to know which of several possible bases of comparison is selected as crucial by an individual. In order to evaluate the correctness of his political opinions, for example, will he choose for comparison someone close in opinion but dissimilar in, say, educational and occupational status, or will he rather choose someone close in occupational and educational status but dissimilar in opinion? Even more to the point, in most naturally occurring situations, similarity with respect to one or more statuses may be used as a clue to probable similarity in opinion, attitude, ability, or values.

The different concerns outlined above have given rise to different special theories, all of them based on comparative reference group processes: social comparison theory, equity theory in its various formulations (for example, Homans 1961; Adams 1965; Berger et al. 1972), and relative deprivation theory, which can be construed as a special case of equity theory (for example, Merton and Rossi 1950; Davis 1959; Runciman 1966; Crosby 1976).[3] Of these, only social comparison theory has concerned itself in a systematic way with the *selection* of others for comparison. The other theories have paid much more attention to the *consequences* of different comparisons than to their determinants, and they are discussed in greater detail below. The remainder of this section summarizes what has been learned about the selection of comparison others in both naturally occurring and experimentally structured situations.

SELECTION OF COMPARISON OTHERS IN NATURALLY OCCURRING SITUATIONS

A few studies have addressed the question of what comparative reference groups are used spontaneously by individuals to assess their social situation. Hyman (1942), Stern and Keller (1953), Form and Geschwender (1962), and Runciman (1976), for example, have demonstrated that, with respect to living standards and social status, such spontaneous comparisons tend to be made either with close associates—family or friends—or with people whose class situation approximates that of the respondent's own. Although both Runciman, who investigated reference group processes in Britain, and Stern and Keller, whose study was done in France, suggest that a more mobile society, such as that of the United States, might yield a wider variety of comparative reference groups, the available evidence suggests that there, too, family and close associates constitute the most significant frame of reference for assessing occupational achievement.

Thus, the implication of much research on comparative reference group processes is that spontaneous comparisons tend to be made with persons or groups "close" to the respondent in some way. "Closeness," however, may refer to either similarity or propinquity—that is, geographical nearness. Often, these two factors go together, but what happens when they work in opposite directions? Helen Strauss's analysis (1968) of comparison processes among the blind is particularly interesting because it separates the two. The overwhelming majority of her blind respondents chose to compare themselves with persons who are dissimilar—that is, with the sighted. Surrounded by people who are not blind, they reflect this fact in their choice of a comparative reference group. When their environment and socialization emphasize isolation from the seeing, their reliance on other blind persons increases correspondingly. As noted below, a similar process appears to influence the selection of comparison others among the aged (Rosow 1967, 1970, 1974).

In their study of self-esteem among black and white children in Baltimore, Rosenberg and Simmons (1972) demonstrate the operation of the same principle. Black secondary school students in integrated settings tended to have lower self-esteem than those in segregated settings, presumably because they were more likely to compare themselves and their situation with that of whites in their own school (that is, others who are "close") than with that of blacks in segregated schools (that is, others who are "similar"). The Baltimore findings are supported by a substantial body of other research on the effects of desegregation on the self-concept and the academic self-concept.

These diverse studies suggest that, under some as yet unspecified circumstances, close dissimilars tend to be preferred for comparison to distant similars. The conditions of the studies suggest that this is especially likely to be true when the comparison group constitutes a numerical majority (Davis 1959). Taken together, these studies provide strong evidence for the effects of social structure on the selection of comparison others.

It is tantalizing to juxtapose against these findings the study by McGuire and his colleagues (1978), already cited in the preceding section. The authors postulate that one selectively attends to and encodes those aspects of a complex stimulus that are most distinctive. Specifically, they predict that ethnicity will be more salient to a person who is in the minority; that it will become more salient as the ethnic heterogeneity of a group increases; and that it will become more salient as the proportion of an ethnic subgroup in the larger group decreases. Although their study is concerned with ethnicity, the distinctiveness postulate and its derivatives clearly have broader implications. It means, for example, that women should become more aware of their gender as their proportion in the workplace decreases, and that blind people should be more aware of their handicap among the seeing. Presumably, this process heightens the salience of such statuses, and, as earlier research (Charters and Newcomb 1958; Festinger 1947) has shown, this increased salience in turn makes blacks, women, and the blind (for example) more likely to *act in accordance with the norms associated with such (minority) statuses.* At the same time, however, the tendency to *compare with the majority status appears to be heightened as the proportion of the minority decreases.*[4] In other words, the relative proportions of two complementary statuses (for example, black-white, female-male, blind-sighted, Jew-non-Jew) may have diametrically opposed implications for normative and comparative reference group processes, respectively. Some further implications of this fact are discussed under "Consequences of Comparison," below.

SELECTION OF COMPARISON OTHERS IN EXPERIMENTALLY STRUCTURED SITUATIONS

As stated in the introduction to this section, the early work on social comparison by Festinger, Schachter, and their colleagues and students emphasized a single motive—realistic self-appraisal—under conditions where bases of comparison other than the one manipulated by the experimenter were either eliminated or held constant experimentally. Under these conditions, subjects tend to select for comparison others whose opinions and emotions are similar or whose performance is better.

More recent social psychological research, much of it summarized in Suls and Miller (1977), has begun to broaden this experimental paradigm. Brickman and Bulman (1977), for example, extend the range of motives considered. They acknowledge that at times people may avoid comparison, choose dissimilars, and compare downward, and they propose a model predicting when people will prefer to seek, and when to avoid, comparison. They postulate conflict between adaptive (information-seeking) and hedonic (pleasure-producing) forces, two concepts similar to, but not identical with, distinctions drawn by such previous authors as Thornton and Arrowood (1966) and Hakmiller (1966) between a drive to acquire accurate information and a drive to maintain or improve self-esteem.

Gruder (1977) explicitly considers some of the questions raised by a "two-function" theory of social comparison. Are comparison persons chosen in a way that satisfies both self-evaluation and self-enhancement simultaneously? Is one motive predominant? What situational or personality variables influence the process of choice? He concludes that when self-esteem is threatened, people try to satisfy the motive of self-enhancement rather than that of (accurate) self-evaluation, but most of the questions raised remain to be satisfactorily answered.

Although social psychologists have begun to move beyond the simplified laboratory paradigm in which "everything else" is held constant, they are far from having replaced Festinger's simpler, more limited theory with one that takes new developments into account. At least in part, this is because there is no clear specification of the dimensions along which similarity or dissimilarity is assumed. When Brickman and Bulman (1977), for example, say that people may prefer to compare with dissimilars rather than similars, they certainly do not mean people dissimilar in all respects. They mean people dissimilar in some respects but similar in others. And until the fact of multiple statuses, abilities, attitudes, and values, and the implications of this fact, are clearly conceptualized, there is likely to be no real theoretical progress in this area.

Consequences of Comparison

INTRODUCTION

In examining the consequences of comparison, I have attempted to construct a classificatory scheme general enough to encompass the very diverse kinds of consequences with which different theories have concerned themselves. Three orthogonal dimensions seem capable of generating a property space within which these consequences can be located. The three dimensions are: (1) whether the judgment is cognitive or evaluative;[5] (2) whether the outcome of the comparison is consonant or dissonant, positive or negative; and (3) whether the consequences considered are those for self or for others (cf. table 3.1). In each case, the focal point of the appraisal is assumed to be the self, or some attribute of the self. Thus, for example, "positive" and "negative" evaluations refer to an evaluation of some aspect of the self, and "consequences" refer to the consequences of such evaluations for self and for one's attitude or behavior toward others. "Others" here include those with whom the comparison is made as well as larger social groups, although future work could fruitfully distinguish between various categories of others (cf. Anderson et al. 1969). Here, I shall first give an overview of the several theories—social comparison theory, relative deprivation theory, equity theory, and the status-value version of equity theory—that deal with the consequences of comparison, and then review them in greater detail in relation to the typology shown in table 3.1.[6]

Social comparison theory, as originally formulated, concerned itself primarily with the left-hand portions of table 3.1—that is, with the consequences of consonant and dissonant cognitive comparisons for self and, to a lesser extent, for behavior toward others. The outcomes considered were primarily those that would test hypotheses and derivations from the theory itself: the choice of comparison others among those available; shifts in opinion as a result of comparison; attempts to change the opin-

TABLE 3.1

Consequences of Comparison

Consequences for:	Kind of Judgment			
	Cognitive		Evaluative	
	Consonant	Dissonant	"Positive"	"Negative"
Self	Accuracy Precision Stability Confidence	Uncertainty Unreliability of judgment Change of opinion, estimate Accuracy (if dissonance is reasonable on basis of other characteristics)	Status enhancement Self-satisfaction Guilt (if over-rewarded)	Dissatisfaction with self Striving, achievement Status depreciation Mental, physical illness
Others	Attraction Affiliation	Attempts to induce change Rejection of deviant	"System support"	Anger Dissatisfaction with others Dissatisfaction with social arrangements Crime Prejudice Revolution

ions of others, or, failing that, to reject them as comparison objects. For the first ten to fifteen years after its formulation, social comparison theory might fairly be described as a theory of self-appraisal, where the implications of such appraisal tended to be rather narrowly confined to the cognitive/adaptive realm. As Crosby (1976) has noted, social comparison theory has close kin among such other social-psychological theories as level of aspiration theory, adaptation level theory, and even the various balance theories, but I will not attempt to trace these interrelationships here.

Around 1966, social psychologists began to consider the implications of comparison for self-esteem, or, more generally, to consider the evaluative aspects of comparison. Nevertheless, it remains true that even in this modified form, social comparison theory continues to be concerned more with the implications of comparison for self and for such processes as interpersonal attraction and affiliation than with interactions among groups or with evaluations of social processes. Because comparisons are generally made along a single dimension, which is implicitly assumed to be under the individual's control, issues of equity, justice, or relative deprivation do not ordinarily arise.

Such issues are central to the three other theories considered in this section: equity theory, status-value theory, and relative deprivation theory. Although all three are capable of considering the same range of phenomena, relative deprivation theory has been the most likely to concern itself with (1) consequences of negative evaluations; (2) consequences of comparisons between social groups or categories; (3) consequences for other individuals, groups, or for society as a whole, as well as—or even more often than—consequences for the self. Further, as Crosby (1976) has noted, most of the evidence bearing on relative deprivation theory has come from survey data rather than laboratory research.

In contrast, equity theorists have been more likely to explore justice in the laboratory, and perhaps by virtue of this fact, to consider the implications of injustice for the relations among individuals rather than social groups. To be sure, Berger, Zelditch, and their colleagues are very conscious of the importance of social norms in defining the frame of reference against which the justice or injustice of rewards is appraised. They have, further, deliberately created rudimentary organizational structures in many of their experiments, so that the actions of subjects in those experiments can be ascribed to the social position they occupy, and not to an individual characteristic in an idiosyncratically manipulated situation. Nevertheless, the implications of their work for understanding the consequences of inequity for social groups and for society as a whole remain to be drawn out (cf. K. Cook and Parcel 1977).

In the remainder of this section, I discuss these four theories in relation to the typology shown in table 3.1. Listed in the cells of the table are outcomes that have been found empirically; they represent what is, not an exhaustive compilation of what may be. The discussion begins with a brief recapitulation of theory and research bearing on cognitive judgments, and then moves to a more extended consideration of evaluative judgments, especially negative evaluations.

COGNITIVE JUDGMENTS

So far as it applies to opinions, Festinger's theory of social comparison processes (1954), as well as the research on which it is based and that done soon after its formulation, can be located primarily within the cognitive cells of the typology. As already noted, Festinger hypothesized that in the absence of a more objective means of evaluation, individuals will rely on comparison with others in order to evaluate the correctness of their opinions.

For the self, the outcome of consonant comparisons, Festinger predicted, would be greater precision and stability of judgments, and greater confidence in their accuracy. Attraction and affiliation are the consequences of consonant comparisons for others. If, on the other hand, the outcome of the comparison is dissonant, Festinger predicted that opinions would be held with less certainty and reliability, and that moves would be initiated either to change one's own opinion, to persuade others to change, or to cease comparison with those whose opinion was discrepant.

More recent writers have postulated that, under certain circumstances, dissonant comparisons, too, might result in increased self-knowledge, notably when the dissonance accords with other relevant characteristics of the comparison. For example, in evaluating the "correctness" of one's opinion on government economic policy, it may be as useful to know that someone with different political convictions has a different belief as it is to know that someone with the same convictions has the same belief.

EVALUATIVE JUDGMENTS

Extension of social comparison theory to the abilities, as well as much of the more recent research reviewed in Suls and Miller (1977), explicitly recognizes that many comparisons have an evaluative component, so that judgments of consonance/dissonance are likely to have implications for self-esteem as well. However, while consonance/dissonance can be inferred directly from the comparison itself, the *valence* of the comparison cannot, depending rather on the relationship between the primary dimension of comparison and other relevant dimensions. To take a very simple example, the fact of earning less than someone else does not necessarily have negative implications if the discrepancy is congruent with differences in training or experience (or, perhaps, in needs).

A series of questions about the consequences of comparison arise with respect to evaluative judgments. Under what conditions, for example, will evaluations be positive or negative? Under what conditions will the consequences of comparisons be turned inward, toward the self, and under what conditions will they be turned outward, onto others or onto social arrangements?[7] And what, finally, determines which of the several possible outcomes listed in table 3.1, either for self or for others, will, in fact, occur? In the remainder of this section on evaluative judgments, I will briefly review the theory and research bearing on these questions.

Positive evaluations. Aside from early research on level of aspiration (for example, Lewin et al. 1944), there has been little investigation of the consequences of evaluative comparisons that are positive—that is, those in which one achieves or slightly exceeds one's expected performance. We know that estimates of future performance tend to be more stable when achievement matches expectation than when it exceeds this level or falls short (cf. Festinger 1954). We know also that satisfaction with one's performance or status increases, under certain conditions, when it exceeds some expected level (for example, Hilgard, Sait, and Magaret 1940), or when a lower ranking comparison group is experimentally made salient (for example, Simmons 1969; Dermer et al. 1979). It has also been shown (for example, by Chapman and Volkmann 1939, and by Simmons 1969) that estimated future performance (a cognitive judgment) and self-ranking with respect to certain attributes (an evaluative judgment) can be made to shift upward or downward depending on whether a higher- or lower-ranking comparison group is experimentally made salient.

The fact that certain comparison groups can be made salient, not only in the laboratory but in the social environment, has been used by Rosow (1969, 1970, 1974) to advocate "residential concentration" for the elderly, in order to encourage their use of other older people as both normative and comparative reference groups. Similar reasoning—that is, the greater concentration of like-status others in the environment—has been used by Rosenberg and Pearlin (1978) to explain the lower correlation between self-esteem and social status among children than among adults. It has also been used by E. Singer (1974) to account for the fact that the social psychological consequences of Parkinson's disease weigh much more heavily on younger than on older patients, since the social environment of the latter group includes many more people whose health and activity levels have declined. (Cf. also the discussion of comparison processes among the blind and among black children, under "Selection of Comparative Reference Groups.")

Just as there has been little investigation of the consequences of positive evaluations generally, so there has been no systematic investigation of the circumstances under which such evaluations have consequences for others rather than, or in addition to, oneself. One might speculate, for example, that satisfaction with the outcome of a comparison involving the self would be accompanied by generally positive feelings toward those perceived as responsible for the favorable allocation of tangible or intangible goods. Under conditions of *relative gratification,* in other words, one would expect greater satisfaction with the "system," just as one would expect greater dissatisfaction under conditions of relative deprivation. In a sense, of course, the literature on relative deprivation can be interpreted to make just that point.

The possible exceptions are discrepant comparisons which, though favorable to oneself, imply that the system is inequitable, over-rewarding either the individual or a class of individuals. Unfortunately, we know very little about the circumstances in which individuals *spontaneously* interpret favorable comparisons in equity terms. Most of the research that has been done is based on laboratory situations in which inequity is made salient for the subjects. In these circumstances, the individual may try to restore equity, either by producing more (for example, Adams and Rosenbaum 1962), or by producing work of better quality (for example, Adams and Jacobsen 1964), or even by altering the schedule of payments in the direction of equity (for example, K. Cook 1975). The conditions under which one or another outcome is to be expected, however, remain to be specified, just as do the conditions under which equity considerations will be aroused at all. For example, research by Jasso (1978) shows that under-reward is perceived much more readily than over-reward, and Cook's experiment indicates that when subjects are ignorant of their rank on a task ability, they tend to define their rank on the basis of the reward they receive—that is, no sense of inequity develops. Furthermore, half of those who were over-rewarded with respect to an equal-ability partner revised their estimates of relative ability to reflect the rewards received, thus supporting Homans's (1976) assertion that power underlies equity considerations. Even those subjects who attempted to redress previous inequities did so by rewarding themselves and their partner equally: they did not compensate for past inequity.

In another innovative experiment, Jasso and Rossi (1977) examined what distribution rules are perceived as fair in our society, as far as income is concerned. Using a Baltimore block quota sample and a crossed factorial design in which various characteristics of earners were combined at random into a sample of vignettes, Jasso and Rossi found that sex, marital status, education, occupation, number of children, and amount of earnings all significantly affected judgments of fairness, with the amount of income the most influential factor (the higher the income, the more likely it was to be perceived as excessive). Further, there appeared to be consensus on such judgments among diverse social groups. Finally, the ideal range in income was narrower than the actual one: less discrepancy would apparently have been perceived as more equitable.

Clearly, a great deal of research remains to be done in this area. We know far too little about the conditions that lead to the perception that someone has been inequitably over-rewarded, and far too little about the consequences of such a perception, for self and for several categories of others.

Negative evaluations. By far the greatest attention, in terms of both theory and research, has been devoted to the consequences of comparisons when these result in negative evaluations. In the simplest case, the individual compares himself with a "relevant" other along a single dimension, and finds *himself* wanting. If the dimension is a desirable one, the consequence is dissatisfaction with self which, depending on one's assessment of the chances for bringing about change, may lead to striving for achievement or to emotional or physical symptoms of stress (Crosby 1976). (For a discussion of the conditions under which evaluations will be positive or negative, see pages 84–85, above.)

What is ordinarily not made explicit is that in order for this "simple" process to eventuate, the individual must perceive the dimension along which the comparison is made as lying within his control—as, for example, in the case of certain abilities or other individual characteristics. If, however, the negative outcome is perceived as resulting from an *alloca-*

tion process controlled by others, the consequences are far more complex. In this section, I will discuss three broad strands of theory that all deal with this latter process, noting their similarities and differences and then considering their implications for the question of consequences. The three are relative deprivation theory, equity theory and its antecedents, and the status-value formulation of equity theory.

What all of these have in common is the stipulation that comparisons are made simultaneously along more than one dimension; and that the outcome of the comparison results in some evaluation of the justice, fairness, or equity of the underlying allocation process (Adams 1965). All of these theories, therefore, have implications for the appraisal of the allocating "others," or of social arrangements, though they may have consequences for the self as well.

Relative deprivation theory. Stouffer et al. (1949) and Merton and Rossi (1950) accounted for differences in soldiers' feelings of satisfaction and dissatisfaction during World War II (for example, with army life, with chances for promotion) by reference to assumed comparisons with others. In fact, however, all of these involved a comparison of one's actual to one's expected situation, and, usually, a comparison of these ratios for two (or more) different groups as well. For example, married men who had been drafted were more likely to feel they should have been deferred than single men, presumably because the probability of their being drafted was actually lower and they were aware of this fact. Or again, men in the Military Police evaluated the Army's promotion policies more favorably than men in the Air Corps, presumably because their lower rates of promotion induced lower expectations among them. We do not know whether these expectation levels (that is, subjective probabilities) were derived from observation of one's fellows, or from knowledge of the applicable norms, or from some other source, nor do we know what difference the source of the expectation would make (cf. Merton and Rossi 1950). What is clear is that such expectations, however derived, profoundly affect one's appraisal of the situation.

The term *relative deprivation,* first used to interpret the responses of soldiers surveyed in World War II, has subsequently been used by sociologists, psychologists, political scientists, and economists to account for patterns of satisfaction and dissatisfaction in a wide variety of areas. For example, it has been applied to job satisfaction (Patchen 1958, 1961); attitudes toward social and economic inequalities in twentieth-century England (Runciman 1966); race relations (for example, Pettigrew 1964, 1967; Vanneman and Pettigrew 1972); protest and revolution (Gurr 1968, 1970; Urry 1973; Useem 1975); and mental illness (Parker and Kleiner 1966). For a comprehensive bibliography, see Crosby (1976).

Like the concept of reference group itself, however, definitions of relative deprivation have varied from one study to another. In their attempt to validate the construct as an intervening variable and to differentiate it from other constructs, T.D. Cook et al. (1977) specify four necessary components: not having X; wanting X; social comparison with similar others who have X; and the feasibility of attaining X. They further stipulate that feelings of entitlement, on the one hand, and the absence of personal responsibility for not having X, on the other, will serve to predict when the feelings of dissatisfaction aroused will take the form of anger toward others, rather than being directed toward the self. Their examination of a large number of studies, both in the laboratory and in the field, indicates that for the most part the postulated components, examined one at a time, are related in the predicted direction to expressions of anger.

Cook and his colleagues distinguish between relative deprivation and inequity on the grounds that inequity does not presuppose feasibility, whereas relative deprivation does. In this, and some other details, I believe they are mistaken. The essence of both relative deprivation and the deprivational form of inequity is that a person (group) wants X; does not have it; and feels entitled to it—that is, expects to get it—on the basis of comparison either with similar others or with self at an earlier time, or on the basis of awareness of the norms governing the situation. This expectation has normative force, though it may be based on experience.

The outcome of such feelings of inequity or relative deprivation is a sense of injustice, perhaps accompanied in our society by anger. Only if the person assumes *that the characteristic is within his control*—that is, is *not* the result of some external allocation process—will wanting, not having, and feeling entitled *not* be accompanied by a sense of injustice but may, depending on one's appraisal of the feasibility of bringing about change, lead to either self-deprecation or strivings for achievement.[8]

Equity theory. As formulated by Adams (1965), equity theory explicitly recognizes that what is involved in appraising the justness of a situation is a comparison of two ratios. Adams's formulation derives from Homans's (1961) discussion of "distributive justice," which exists for a dyad when the ratio of A's profits to his investments is the same as the ratio of B's profits to his investments—that is, it involves a comparison of inputs as well as outcomes.

Adams states that inequity exists for Person whenever he perceives that the ratio of his outcomes to inputs and the ratio of Other's outcomes to Other's inputs are unequal. (As we shall see below, however, this formulation will not yet yield an unambiguous definition of justice.) Although he does not consider which person or group will be selected for comparison, nor what outcomes and inputs will be included, Adams does formulate a series of possible "remedies" for the "tension" created by inequity as well as some principles for selection among these remedies (1965:287 ff.). They are limited to a dyadic interaction, and, interestingly enough, exclude the "revolutionary" alternative—that is, changing the rules by which inputs are related to outcomes, or specifying which inputs are to be included in the calculation.

For the most part, equity theorists have concerned themselves with responses to inequity, not with the way in which a situation comes to be defined as just or unjust (Walster, Berscheid, and Walster 1976; Austin 1977). And it might be argued that even the "responses to injustice" which they have concerned themselves with tend to be a limited subclass of situations. As Homans (1976:244) points out, they have generally not concerned themselves with the relations between equity and power, even though it might be argued that power is the more primitive phenomenon: "Justice depends on expectations, and expectations in the long run on actualities. What is, is always becoming what ought to be."

Status-value theory. It has been noted immediately above that equity theory does not permit an unambiguous definition of justice. For example, if Jones is a skilled typist earning $5.00 an hour and Smith is an unskilled clerk earning $5.00 an hour, it is possible that Jones is under-rewarded, that Smith is over-rewarded, or even that both are under- or over-rewarded. By formulating what they refer to as a *status-value* version of equity theory, Berger and his colleagues (Anderson et al. 1969; Berger et al. 1972; Berger et al. 1977) propose to take account of such difficulties. In essence, their theory states that evaluations of justice in a given situation are based on a comparison between characteristics and rewards in a "local" situation and those existing in a "referential structure"—that is, some generalized frame of reference regarded as constituting an appropriate comparison, and yielding normative expectations about the appropriate association of characteristics (for example, sex, age, education) and *goal-objects* (that is, rewards). As a result, an individual comes to believe that "because he possesses a given state of some characteristic he has a *moral* right to a given state of a goal-object. He also acquires beliefs about what states of the goal-object others around him should possess. . . . Justice consists in the realization of these beliefs about what should be. And injustice or inequity exists when moral expectations about how rewards should be distributed are violated. The sociological problem of distributive justice is thus seen to be twofold: first there is the question of how moral expectations about rewards emerge and how these are changed due to changes in the referential structure, and second [there is] the question [of what happens when such expectations are violated]." (Anderson et al. 1969:4).

The virtue of this theory is that, given a referential structure, it is possible to specify the "expected" allocation of rewards to P(erson) and O(ther), and therefore: (1) to distinguish over- from under-reward, and both from justice; (2) to distinguish "collective" from individual injustice—that is, to distinguish those situations where both Person and Other are over- and under-rewarded from those situations where only one of them is; and finally, (3) to distinguish "self" from "other" imbalance, when only one of the two experiences injustice. For example, if an experienced typist should earn $8.00 an hour and a novice half as much, and Jones, who is an experienced typist, earns $8.00 an hour while Smith, who is a beginner, earns $4.00, a situation of distributive justice obtains. If Smith earns less than half as much as Jones, who earns $8.00, Smith is unjustly under-rewarded; if Jones earns $6.00 and Smith $3.00, both are under-rewarded and a situation of collective injustice obtains. For a detailed exposition, see Berger et al. (1972:143 ff.).

Because the theory provides explicit definitions of justice and injustice, over- and under-reward, and collective and individual injustice, it can also talk quite specifically about the expected outcomes of these states (cf. Anderson and his colleagues 1969). Although gains in knowledge are likely to be painfully slow, the approach by Berger and his colleagues has the virtue of systematically identifying and refining theoretical problems.

Like other versions of equity theory, status-value theory has not addressed the question of how referential structures are acquired or changed, or why one rather than another frame of reference is activated in a given comparison. Under what circumstances, for example, will a professor of neurology at a medical school compare his or her salary with that of other professors, and under what circumstances will salary comparisons be made with other neurologists in private practice? Nor has the theory addressed itself to questions first raised by Merton and Rossi thirty years ago: namely, what difference, if any, the source of the referential structure (for example, mass media versus professional associates versus intimate friends) makes to various aspects of the evaluation and its outcomes. Finally, the theory does not address itself to the possibility that different distribution rules exist, and that two conflicting rules—for example, to each according to his ability, or to each according to his need—may be activated simultaneously (K. Cook and Parcel 1977).

Prospects for the Future

Although *reference group* and related concepts have proved enormously fruitful over the past forty years in stimulating sociological and social-psychological research and in explaining sometimes paradoxical findings, it remains true that the potential usefulness of the concept has not been realized. What I would like to suggest at this point is retrenchment and consolidation.

In 1950, Merton and Rossi noted that "reference group theory aims to systematize the determinants and consequences of those processes of evaluation and self-appraisal in which the individual takes the values or standards of other individuals and groups as a comparative frame of reference" (1957:234). Yet only a few pages later, seduced like others by the siren song of the concept, they had turned from the analysis of appraisals and evaluations to the elucidation of conformity and social mobility, suggesting that reference group theory might bear as well "on more general and seemingly disparate patterns of behavior, such as group defection, renegadism, social climbing, and the like." Since then, sociologists have concerned themselves more with normative than with comparative reference group processes, as any search of the published literature and of the dissertations done in the intervening years will show. But no comparison of the early with the more recent work can help noting the contrast between the excitement and sense of discovery prevailing then and the routine and repetitive quality of research done in the last ten, or even twenty, years. Although it is tempting to relate reference group phenomena to many of the major theoretical concerns of sociologists—conformity and deviance, integration and conflict, socialization and social mobility, communication and interpersonal influence—it is not clear, at least from the work to date, that this approach will bear fruit.

Furthermore, it is not clear that the concept is essential to elucidating these processes; certainly it has not done so yet. To say that one conforms to the norms of this group rather than that because one uses it as a positive reference group is to explain nothing, or at any rate nothing that could not equally well be explained without resort to the term. "Reference group," in such a situation, stands for a combination of other characteristics—visibility, salience, reward, to name only a few. Use of the term "reference group" serves to obscure rather than illuminate these characteristics; it begs the question of why conformity occurs.

Matters stand quite otherwise in the case of self- or social evaluation, using "evaluation" to include cognitive processes as well. Such evaluations are very often contingent on comparison; and the selection of a comparison point contributes to, though in itself it does not determine, the outcome of the evaluation.

By proposing to restrict reference group theory to comparison processes, I do not mean to exclude the role of norms from such processes. On the contrary, normative prescriptions undoubtedly play an important role in directing the choice of a comparison point. Furthermore, a norm itself may serve as the standard against which behavior, one's own or that of others, is compared and evaluated. Finally, a comparison has consequences for self- or social evaluation only to the extent that the standard against which performance is evaluated constitutes an expectation level that the individual feels should be met.

I have attempted to demonstrate above, at some length, the convergence of several theories dealing with the consequences of comparison. Since Pettigrew's 1967 essay, very little attention has been paid to the possible relationship of these special theories to a more general theory of social evaluation, and yet the prospects for codification and consolidation and for a synthesis of explanatory propositions seem excellent here. Such a unified theory would draw on social comparison theory and some aspects of relative deprivation theory for propositions about the consequences of comparisons involving characteristics under the individual's own control, and would draw on relative deprivation theory, equity theory, and the status-value version of equity theory for propositions about the consequences of comparisons involving rewards and punishments allocated by others. Inter alia, such a synthesis would bring into sharp relief a previously ignored set of consequences that might be labeled *relative gratification,* constituting the positively valued counterpart of those outcomes considered under the theory of relative deprivation. In such a unified theory, both relative gratification and relative deprivation would emerge as special cases of equity theory. As I have already pointed out, however, the latter needs the specification provided by Berger and his colleagues in order to make explicit the full range of possible outcomes.

Although there has been substantial progress in delineating the *consequences* of social comparison, theory and research on the *selection* of comparison others are in a much more primitive state. Thus, not only would it seem useful to restrict reference group theory to comparison processes, but it may also be wise, at least for the time being, to concentrate attention on the selection of comparison others.

Social psychologists have made some progress in specifying the criteria governing the selection of others for comparison under specialized circumstances, some of which have been described in detail above. It should already be possible to codify their findings in such a way as to make clear what principles of selection apply in a limited class of situations to comparisons undertaken for a limited set of purposes. While this is no small undertaking, it is simply the first task in the development of a theory of referent selection. The next task is to develop a more comprehensive framework within which what is known can be located.

A large step toward development of such a framework might be taken, it seems to me, by considering three factors that influence the selection process: (1) the *object* of the comparison—either an attribute within the control of the actor, or a characteristic that is construed as a reward or punishment for such an attribute; (2) the *motive* for the comparison—accurate appraisal, self-validation, or impetus for change; (3) the structural and normative *constraints* on choice—for example, the number of "similar" others present in the immediate environment.

For those evaluations involving some attribute within the control of the individual, the characteristics of others chosen for comparison might be conceptualized, as a first approximation, in terms of similarity-dissimilarity. As noted earlier, however, it will be necessary to consider similarity with respect to several dimensions, not just one: similarity with respect to the dimension being compared; and similarity with respect to other relevant dimensions.

For those evaluations involving considerations of fairness—that is, evaluations of characteristics seen as allocated by others—the principles governing the choice of a referential structure are more complex. At the same time, far less theory and far less research exist to account for such selection processes. Nevertheless, as suggested above, it seems likely that here, too, the motive for the comparison—whether to provide accurate appraisal, justify an existing state of affairs, or provide an incentive for change—would serve to direct attention to some referents rather than others, within the normative and structural constraints making some comparisons both more salient and more legitimate than others.

"So now," to paraphrase Philip Roth's eminent Dr. Spielvogel, after some forty years and several hundred publications, "vee may perhaps to begin."

NOTES

For the organization of this chapter and the discussion of early research and theory, I have drawn heavily on Hyman and Singer (1968). I would like to express my deep appreciation to W. Phillips Davison, Herbert H. Hyman, Pat Robinson, Morris Rosenberg, Howard Schuman, and Charles R. Wright for their many thoughtful comments on earlier drafts.

1. Shibutani (1955) distinguished three denotations of the term "reference group": (1) that group that serves as the point of reference in making comparisons or contrasts; (2) the group in which the actor aspires to gain or maintain acceptance; (3) that group whose perspective is assumed by the actor. He proposed

limiting the concept to the third usage, which is akin to Kelley's normative function, but with even broader imperatives for defining the situation.

2. Sometimes the relative importance of the two has been tested against each other, as in the case of race and beliefs (Rokeach, Smith, and Evans 1960; Triandis 1961; Hendrick, Bixenstine, and Hawkins 1971). Findings have varied from laboratory to laboratory, apparently because the level of prejudice mediates the importance placed on race (Byrne 1971).

3. Davis (1959) points out that relative deprivation theory and social comparison theory are both "special cases of some more general uncodified theory, which can specify the circumstances" where each of the others applies (1959:282). As noted earlier, Pettigrew (1967) proposed "social evaluation theory" as the more general theoretical formulation.

4. Or, as Davis (1959) puts it, as the proportion of the majority increases. The feelings accompanying this comparison, however, cannot be inferred from the direction of the comparison alone (Hyman 1942; see also the discussion of equity theory, pp. 83, 86).

5. Rosenberg (1979), summarizing the relevance of comparison processes for the self-concept, makes a similar distinction.

6. The review is illustrative rather than exhaustive. For recent comprehensive reviews of research on social comparison processes, see Suls and Miller (1977); on relative deprivation theory, Crosby (1976) and T.D. Cook, Crosby, and Hennigan (1977); on equity theory, Berkowitz and Walster (1976), Walster, Berscheid, and Walster (1976), and Austin (1977); and on status-value theory, K. Cook and Parcel (1977) and Berger et al. (1977).

7. One might speculate that the answer depends in part on the perceived opportunity to bring about the desired change, as well as on the extent to which personal responsibility for consequences is assumed (cf. Patchen 1961).

8. This view closely resembles Crosby's (1976) model of "egotistical relative deprivation," which postulates that intro/extrapunitiveness is the crucial variable determining whether felt deprivation will lead to actions directed outward, toward the environment, or inward, toward the self. Crosby postulates that the sense of personal control and the presence of opportunities further specify whether the result will be constructive social action or self-improvement, on the one hand, or violence or stress symptoms, on the other.

4

JEROLD HEISS

Social Roles

To immerse oneself in the literature on social roles is to get the feeling that one has been transported with Alice behind the looking glass. Only there would one expect to find common words used in such disparate, confusing, and arbitrary ways. In the real world, terms that have become part of the basic vocabulary of the social scientist should have generally accepted meanings.

A major part of the problem is that different authors use varying labels for the same phenomenon. "What Davis defines as a role, Newcomb calls role behavior and Sarbin role enactment" (Gross et al. 1958:17). In addition, one cannot assume that because two authors are using the same term they are speaking of the same thing. "Sometimes role is used to refer to a *social position,* sometimes to the *behaviour* associated with a position. . . . Alternatively role is used to denote *individual* behaviour or to refer to typical behaviour" (Coulson 1972:108–109).

To this I must add that perhaps most frequently role does not refer to behavior at all. Many authors use it to mean what actor[1] is expected to do; the actions considered appropriate for the occupant of a particular position. And to compound the confusion, the expectations referred to are sometimes those of society, sometimes those of reference groups, and sometimes those of the actor.[2]

I am, of course, not the first to note these problems. Beginning in 1951, a succession of writers have discussed earlier practice and attempted to set things right (Neiman and Hughes 1951; Coutu 1951; Sargent 1951; Gross et al. 1958; Goode 1960a; Dahrendorf 1968; Jackson 1972). Nonetheless, the problem still exists. Therefore, there seems to be little to be gained from another catalog and criticism of the definitions that have been offered in the past. Instead, I will attempt to devise a coherent and useful conceptual scheme from the existing literature. I have no expectation that this scheme will win general acceptance, but if the reader will accept it for the time being, we will at least have a universe of discourse that will carry us through to the end of the chapter.

I believe that role should be, in a literal sense, the central variable in any role theory. All role theories should account for roles and also use roles as key factors in the explanation of other phenomena. From this point of view it is preferable to define roles as expectations rather than as behavior. The ultimate dependent variable in social-psychological theory is social behavior, and if roles refer to actual behavior there would be little for roles to explain. Thus, for me, a role is a set of expectations in the sense that it is what one *should* do.[3]

As noted above, theorists who define roles in this way vary as to whose expectations they have in mind; society's, certain others', or actor's. The preference here is for a definition in terms of actor's own expectations. As noted below, it may not be meaningful to speak of society's expectations, but even if this were not so, the suggested usage seems preferable, for actor's own views have the most direct effect on his or her behavior. Others' expectations affect actor's behavior, in part at least, because they influence actor's views.

All role theories start from the assumption that roles are variable and tied to social characteristics. Using the present terminology, this would mean that the expectations people hold for themselves depend upon which of their characteristics are salient at a particular time. In many schemes the individual's positions in the social system are considered to be the relevant characteristics. There are father roles, teacher roles, vice-president roles, and so forth. Without at all denying that there are such roles, I would add that roles *also* exist for social categories that do not refer to formal positions. Nature lover, hard worker, Jew, New Englander, cynic are not recognized positions in social organization, but to a greater or lesser degree they carry with them behavioral expectations. Thus, I would suggest that roles are associated with *identities,* and an identity is any characteristic that individuals use to define themselves.

It is confusing, however, to speak of a role associated with *an* identity, for in actuality people recognize that what is proper behavior depends upon other's identity as well as on actor's. What would be proper for a vice-president when interacting with a foreman differs from what is expected when the other is the president. Some theorists handle this by speaking of a series of subroles that make up the role of vice-president, but I will adopt Merton's (1957) approach. According to his usage a role is a set of expectations attached to a particular combination of actor-other identities (for example, father-son, father-daughter), and all the roles associated with one of actor's identities is that identity's *role-set.*

A unit larger than the role-set is also useful for some discussions, and I would suggest that *role-repertoire* be used to refer to all the role sets of a particular person. Units smaller than role are also needed. A number of different activities are involved in each role, and for each of these activities there are somewhat different assumptions as to what is proper behavior. For example, it is assumed that the interaction of father and son should be different during recreation from what it is during economic exchange. It is useful, therefore, to recognize the existence of *sub-roles,* distinguished along functional lines, for each role. And finally, I would recommend the term *role norm* to refer to the specific behavioral prescriptions which, when combined, make up a sub-role. The socializer sub-role of the father-son role, then, might contain the role norms: never use physical punishment; do not express impatience, and so forth.

As discussed above, a role appears to be a collection of discrete behaviors that are learned and applied in a piecemeal fashion. This does not, however, capture all that is involved in the phenomenon. I am sympathetic to Turner's view which, if I understand it correctly, sees a role as more than the sum of its parts. A role is a guiding principle, a gestalt, perhaps a "deep-structure." A person who really knows a role knows that a particular behavior is, or is not, appropriate without specific socialization on the point.

It should be noted, however, that not all roles are known to this degree, and even when the gestalt is known it is usually a generalization based upon lower level information. We are not taught gestalts; we are taught specific behaviors or, at best, low level principles. Thus, in my discussion of role learning I will focus on the learning of specific norms, and I will only touch on the process of generalization. This will engender a discussion that is less than complete, but I believe we must deal with the elements before we can hope to capture the full complexity of the subject matter.

Structural and Interactionist Approaches to Roles

Traditionally, role theorists have divided into two camps; the structuralists and the interactionists, and according to many there are basic differences between them. It is my view, however, that this is not the case. Recently, the gap has been reduced to such a degree that Merton (1975:31) is probably right when he contends that "ideas in structural analysis and symbolic interactionism are opposed to one another in the same sense as ham is opposed to eggs: they are perceptibly different but mutually enriching." I would contend that though structuralism and interactionism operate at different levels of analysis, they do not contain contradictory postulates and assumptions. In fact, I believe that they supplement each other (see also Handel 1979; Stokes and Hewitt 1976). This is hardly a view that many will accept as self-evident, and therefore I will proceed to a more detailed consideration of the issue.[4]

THE STRUCTURALIST VIEW

Contemporary structuralism suggests that after an actor defines the situation, he is likely to have a conception of the role he wishes to play and an opinion as to what others should do. The actual process of interaction is, however, more than a simple reading out of scripts brought by the interactants to the encounter. If each actor simply recited "lines," the "play" which would emerge would be chaotic more often than not.

This result would occur if actor and other held differing role definitions, and the role-learning process often produces major differences in definitions. An individual's roles are largely learned from other people, and, therefore, actor and other are likely to agree about role definitions *only* if they have been exposed to similar influences. Many theorists assume, however, that there is no societal consensus on most roles, and thus the roles taught actor may very well differ from those taught other (see Gross et al. 1958; Dahrendorf 1968; Merton 1957; Merton and Barber 1963). If interaction is to lead to desired goals, adjustments will have to be made.

Modern structuralists would suggest, moreover, that even if there were consensus, interaction would require more than a mechanical reading of a script. For one thing, there are likely to be large gaps in the roles brought to the interaction, for these roles do not cover many of the eventualities. As far back as 1949, Davis noted that "often, it is true, the details of action are not very clearly defined, so that there is an air of tentativeness about the contact" (Davis 1949:84).[5]

Other structuralists go far beyond this. Much of the recent work on structural role theory is a discussion of why inter-actor consensus and complete scripts would not be enough. Both Merton (1957, 1976; Merton and Barber 1963) and Goode (1960a) give a central place to the idea that the ways roles are structured ensures that actors would face serious problems of *role strain*[6] if they simply attempted to follow set role patterns that they had previously learned.

In part this is so because *sociological ambivalence* is very common (Merton and Barber 1963), and it produces *role conflict.* That is, actors are likely to find that the various roles in their repertoires contain incompatible elements. Performing the behavior considered appropriate for one role or sub-role may make it difficult or impossible to play another role or sub-role, and, even a single sub-role may contain inconsistent norms. Examples are: conflict between the obligations owed to a boss and those owed to a spouse, incompatibilities between the sponsor and evaluator sub-roles of the professor-graduate student role, and conflict between the norms of equity and altruism in many sub-roles.

Goode (1960a) carries the matter a step further by arguing that even if these incompatibilities did not exist, frequent role adjustments would be necessary in order to avoid another form of role strain; the inability to live up to a role's demands because of lack of time, energy, or resources *(role overload).*

Thus, structuralists hold that innovation, flexibility, and ingenuity are required in any interaction characterized by: a lack of consensus, incomplete instructions, role conflict, or role overload. And, it is an essential assumption of "modern" structuralism that the presence of one or more of these conditions is the rule. These conditions are not merely common —they are thought to be inherent in the nature of social structure. Goode (1960a:485) suggests, for example, "Role strain—difficulty in meeting given role demands—is . . . normal. In general, the *individual's total role obligations are over-demanding.*" Merton says essentially the same for sociological ambivalence. A social role is not simply a set of norms, it is a *combination of norms and counternorms* (Merton and Barber 1963).

Structural theory suggests that people adjust to the realities described above by changing the role definition during the interaction, by acting inconsistently with the role, and so forth. This leads one to ask how actors can have the flexibility needed to do this if they have, as the structuralists also claim, internalized a set of role norms. If role norms are internalized and "a part" of actors how can they deviate from them without suffering guilt, loss of self-respect, and so forth?

Goode (1960a) provides an answer to this question in an article whose major focus is on the opposite side of the coin. In attempting to account for conformity he suggests that internalization does not necessarily mean "to develop an undying devotion to." Internalization certainly implies more than cognitive learning; it has a connotation of commitment to and acceptance of the appropriateness of. But the degree of commitment is clearly variable. "We know that ego may feel much or little emotional commitment to a given norm. . . . Many individuals in our own society do not feel strongly committed to various important norms (Goode 1960a:253). Thus, the fact that they must violate internalized norms does not necessarily cause difficulties for people because their commitment to the norms they are breaking may not be very strong. And, I would add, if the breaking of the norm does cause some stress, the gains to be had may represent more than adequate compensation.

This leaves, however, the problem of "systemic stability." If actor and other have different role conceptions, how are their actions articulated? What has been said suggests that they are *capable* of meshing their actions, but it is rather vague about how they do it.

It might seem that an answer is to be found only by paying close attention to the details of the interaction process, but there is relatively little of this in structural writing. In fact, Merton (1957:112) specifically excludes from consideration the question of "how the occupant of a status manages to cope with the many, and sometimes conflicting, demands made of him." In his view, a structural analysis should have as its main task "identifying *social mechanisms* . . . which serve to articulate the role-set more nearly than would be the case, if these mechanisms did not operate" (Merton 1957:111–12, emphasis added). In other words, their special task is not to explain how people manage to solve their interaction problems. Their contribution is made by showing how societal arrangements reduce these problems to manageable proportions.

Somewhat surprisingly, the analysis given is quite specific, unsystematic, and lacking in detail. In brief summary, Merton's (1957) discussion suggests that general social structures increase the likelihood that the actors will be able to solve sociological ambivalence by: (1) providing rules for ordering priorities; (2) creating differences in power and interest between the interactants; (3) setting up conditions that permit actor to be insulated from observation by others; (4) making actor's dilemma apparent to others, which may lead to a moderation of their demands; (5) creating opportunities for actor to form alliances; (6) providing opportunities for actor to leave difficult situations (see also Merton 1976; Goode 1960).

Despite the emphasis upon the analysis of general social forms, I would suggest that there is in the structuralist's analysis of societal forces an implicit description of interaction. Of course, given their goals, it is not highly developed, but its general outline can be seen just below the surface. To give a specific example, when structuralists speak of how structural arrangements make it possible for actors to conceal their activities, we can be sure their attention is directed to that because of an assumption that concealment is one of the mechanisms used by *individuals* in the process of interaction. Furthermore, structuralists often operate below the societal level of analysis, and when they do, they give additional insights into their conception of the interaction process (Goode 1960a). There is no need to go into detail concerning the nature of this view. The key point is that it is based upon the idea that human beings evaluate various courses of action and choose those that they believe will maximize their gain. This is implicit in Merton's discussions (1957; Merton and Barber 1963), and explicit in the introduction to a reprinted version of Goode's role strain article (Goode 1973).

In sum, it seems clear that there is little validity to the oft-repeated contention that structuralists see interaction as the simple playing out of internalized social norms. It is simply not true, "that social action tends to be treated simplistically and explained as an enactment of culture" (Stokes and Hewitt 1976:839; see also Wilson 1970; Coulson 1972). Such a comment *may* have been valid at one time, but it certainly does not hold for the leading contemporary theorists. They start from the assumption that there is complexity and disorderliness in social life. Their explanations may not be complete, but they are not based on oversimplified assumptions.

THE INTERACTIONIST VIEW

Interactionists also postulate that interaction is guided by definitions of situations, that interaction involves creativity on the part of the actors, that role consensus is a sometime thing, and so forth. In fact, to fully describe the interactionist perspective would lead me into a great deal of repetition. I will, therefore, limit my attention to some of the supposed contradictions between the approaches.

It is often suggested that interactionists have an overly dynamic view of human beings and this is said to be inconsistent with the structuralists' approach. Admittedly, there are statements in the interactionist literature that suggest that they believe human behavior to be in constant flux. In defending his use of the term role-making rather than role-playing Hewitt (1976:55) tells us, for example, that "Roles are . . . made anew each time people assemble and orient their conduct toward one another." And Turner (1962:23) "postulates a tendency to *create* and *modify* conceptions of self- and other- roles as the orienting process in interactive behavior" (emphasis added). The impression one gets is that new roles emerge out of each interaction.

Such a position would be antithetical to structuralism, but it is by no means clear that interactionists deny the existence and influence of roles brought to the interaction. Shibutani's (1961) notion of the conventional role, which is getting renewed attention lately (Hewitt 1979; Lauer and Handel 1977) suggests that some identities have attached to them norms that are fairly generally accepted and often used. The individuals will modify these roles, but the conventional roles are clearly the starting points. Hewitt (1979) also makes this clear in his revised statement on role-making. Actors "have ideas, to be sure, about how the script should be written as they go along, and they derive these ideas (in part) from remembering previous such situations" (Hewitt 1979:61; see also McCall and Simmons 1978). Even in Turner's oft-cited 1962 article, one finds a suggestion that role-making is limited. Admittedly they are viewed as exceptions, but Turner does point out that in the military and bureaucracy rigid role boundaries set severe limitations on role-making. I suspect that even then he would have accepted that some limits are found in most situations. And if there is any doubt, a more recent article makes it quite clear that he postulates carryover from one situation to another. In "The Role and the Person" (Turner 1978) the possibility of such consistency is taken as a given, and the discussion is devoted to a consideration of the factors that lead to *role merger*—the situation in which a particular role becomes so much a part of the person that he or she uses it in a wide variety of situations, including ones in which it might be considered inappropriate.

A second source of supposed incompatibility between the two approaches is said to result from the failure of interactionists to recognize that people are embedded in a social system that affects what occurs in their interactions. The notion is that interactionists deny the importance of the elements considered most significant by structuralists.

In response, I would admit that structural considerations have not been a central focus in interactionist thought, but I would also point out that there are indications that this is changing (see Stryker 1980; Maines 1977; Strauss 1978; Hewitt 1979, to give only a few examples). Furthermore, even in their earlier writings interactionists were not "antistructural." As Handel (1979:864) suggests, "relative theoretical disregard of a topic need not be confused with a denial of its existence or importance." And to say these matters were not central is not to say that they were totally ignored. A fuller discussion will be found in Handel (1979), but here I would note that an interest in structural effects on interaction is revealed in discussions of the effect of market conditions upon used-car sales (Farberman 1975), the effect of societal conflict upon actor's definition of other (Shibutani 1970), the many discussions of the effects of power to be found in the literature, and so forth (see also Stryker, chapter 1, this volume). These efforts show, better than any argument could, that a structural focus is compatible with an interactionist perspective.

I would also point out that if we look beyond the surface of the specific discussion we find that interactionism, like structuralism, is based on the assumption that actors' behavior is purposive, and that the general goal they seek is the maximization of their profits. They try to create a situation whose anticipated rewards will exceed the anticipated costs by as much as possible. The principle is not the maximization of rewards; it is the maximization of *anticipated* profits (Simpson 1972). Actors may set their sights lower than the heights because they believe that the costs associated with the higher reward will be so great as to wipe out additional profits or because they are willing to settle for a lower, but more certain or quicker, payoff. This principle is usually not explicitly stated, but it seems to be implicit in the work of both groups.[7]

I have now shown that the structural and interactionist approaches deal with similar issues and that they do *not* contain contradictory ideas.

In order to support the contention that the approaches are supplementary, I must also show that each contains materials that can be added to the other to produce an analysis wider in scope than either of the components. I have already indicated that interactionists are beginning to integrate structural considerations into their analyses, and therefore all that remains is to suggest what the interactionists have to offer the structuralists.

It will be remembered that I noted earlier that structural theory lacks a systematic analysis of the mechanics of the interaction process, and I would now point out that it is on this topic that the interactionists have made their greatest contribution. The details of that analysis will be presented in the section of the chapter on roles and interaction; for now it should be sufficient to assert that a cogent analysis of structural effects requires a precise conception of the details of the interaction process. How can one delineate effects without knowledge of the nature of the thing being affected? The *general* role theory that I foresee for the future will combine the macroanalyses of the structuralists with the microanalyses of the interactionists.

With these preliminary matters taken care of, we may now turn to a presentation of contemporary role theory. The general assumption is that people come to interaction situations with previously learned role repertoires, that they choose particular roles for the encounter, and that those roles serve as guides for their actions. Therefore, I must explain how roles are learned, how preferences are developed, and how roles are used in interaction.

Role Socialization[8]

In general, I would argue that sociologically oriented social psychologists have not developed a distinctive theory of the mechanisms of role learning. They have, however, made important contributions to this subject. They have introduced new concepts, directed attention to new issues, described important processes, and developed some specific theories.

The problem is that this material lacks a strong base in general theory, and thus it seems ad hoc and unintegrated. I believe, however, that the time is ripe to begin the integration. The psychologist Albert Bandura has provided us with a learning theory, social learning theory, that captures some of the complexity of human learning, and, it can, I believe, provide a unifying structure for sociological efforts. A brief summary of the theory will set the stage for the discussion of sociological concerns.[9]

SOCIAL LEARNING THEORY

From the outset Bandura's (1969, 1971, 1977) social learning theory is more complex than most psychological theories. Instead of treating learning as a unitary phenomenon, it starts from the basic assumption that if one is to understand the "learning" of new responses three questions must be answered: How was the response acquired? Why was it retained rather than forgotten? Why was it performed rather than some alternative which was also known? Since the answers to these questions are different, social learning theory is really three interrelated theories.

The basic ideas of the theory are as follows: though the acquisition of new behaviors can occur through direct experience involving trial and error and the selection of effective responses, human beings get most of their ideas by observing the actions of others who serve as models. We learn largely by visual observation of overt responses by others.[10]

It is asserted, however, that the mere performance of a response by an other in the presence of actor will not necessarily lead actor to acquire that behavior pattern. The person must be attentive to the model if he is to learn the relevant characteristics of the model's actions. *Effective contact* with a pattern of behavior is necessary for its acquisition, and effective contact is attentive observation. This is posited to be sufficient for this aspect of learning. *Reward is not necessary for acquisition.*

Given this view, the major theoretical issues of this part of the theory become: "What influences the nature of actor's contacts?" and "What are the factors that influence the degree of attention given to the model?"

The first question is not treated in any depth. It is simply suggested that among the many relevant factors associational preferences are important. "The people with whom one regularly associates delimits the type of behavior that one will repeatedly observe" (Bandura 1971:6). Beyond noting that we tend to associate with people who are attractive to us and who display functional behavior, nothing much is said about associational preferences, an omission that is probably justifiable given the theory's level of analysis.[11]

The specific determinants of attention are numerous, but the anticipation of reward is a major factor. We tend to be attentive to others: (1) when we expect that *they* will be rewarded (vicarious reinforcement); (2) when they are similar to us; (3) when they give responses that seem to have functional value; (4) when we are in greater need of the reward associated with the model's behavior; (5) when we expect to be rewarded for our attentiveness; and so forth. In addition, intense responses are more likely to be observed, training in attentiveness can increase it, and novel responses are more attention-getting.

Attentive observation is sufficient for the acquisition of a new response, but if these responses are to have any long-range effects on behavior they must be retained over time and attentive observation may not be sufficient for long-term retention. An observed pattern is, however, likely to be retained if it is coded in images. Then when the stimulus cue occurs later, actor finds that he can dredge up a vivid visual image of what the model did in the past.

Verbal coding is even more important, particularly when the behaviors are complicated. Thus, rather than trying to retain a mental picture of the turns required to get to our destination we "tell ourselves" to make a left, then a right, then a left, and we find when we are trying to return we can recall what has to be done.

Rehearsal is another aid to retention. The value of overt practice for the mastering of complex behavioral patterns need hardly be defended to anyone who has attempted to learn a manual skill or memorize material, but overt repetition of the desired responses is not the only way to rehearse. Humans are capable of engaging in covert rehearsal; they can "run through" the behavior in their imaginations, and by this means set it in their memories. This procedure is quite effective and our ability to do this is important, for many significant human actions cannot easily be practiced overtly.

The theory then goes on to consider the factors that affect the extent to which coding and rehearsal will take place. These factors are not very different from those associated with variations in attention, and it is postulated that they are relevant because of their connection to anticipated reinforcement. Included are: the level of actor's self-esteem, the level of other's interest, the degree of attraction between actor and other, the novelty of the behavior, and the extent to which actor can obtain privacy.

According to the social learning theorist, the actor will develop a large repertoire of behaviors by these means, but only some will actually be used. The question then becomes, which behaviors will be chosen for performance? Part of the answer lies in simple matters of skill. "The amount of observational learning that a person *can* exhibit behaviorally depends on whether or not he has acquired the component skills" (Bandura 1971:8, emphasis added).

However, even when behaviors that are beyond actor's abilities are ruled out, there will still be many to choose from. Bandura's discussion of why particular behaviors are chosen for performance is long and complex, but the essential point is that people will choose those behaviors that are tied to reinforcement. In contrast to certain other theories, however, the tie is not an automatic one. It occurs because human minds make the connection—awareness is an important element in this view of learning (Bandura 1977:19–22). Moreover, the theory is distinctive in that the reinforcement need not come from external sources and be experienced directly by actor. Humans can learn the lessons contained in the reinforcements received by others (vicarious reinforcement), they can provide their own rewards (self-reinforcement), and they can anticipate the future—they can plan their actions in terms of their expectations as to what will follow from their behaviors.

All of this refers to the acquisition and performance by actors of specific behaviors performed by others. Though we cannot go into detail here, it should be noted that Bandura suggests that human capacities extend beyond this. For one thing there is a place for "creative modeling." When there is dissatisfaction with the behaviors presented by models actors can, and often do, "combine aspects of various models into new amalgams that differ from the individual sources" (Bandura 1977:48). Actors are also creative in other ways. They create opportunities for themselves, and to some degree they determine what they will be taught. And, finally, human beings engage in "abstract modeling." They can extract the abstract principles underlying an observed pattern of behavior, and apply those rules to new situations. Essentially, they can develop a conception of a generalized role from the observation of concrete cases.

In the pages that follow I hope to be able to show that social learning theory can serve as a useful base for sociological analysis. Before doing so, it is only fair to point out, however, that the social learning theorists have something to learn from sociologists. Some of the work of sociologists adds important detail to the above. For example, the sociological concept of role-taking suggests that people can put themselves in the place of others through the use of their imaginations and by this means see the situation from other's perspective. Thus "observation" can occur in the absence of overt behavior on the part of other, and the information obtained in this way may be just as useful as that received through observation of overt behavior.

Sociologists can also contribute something to the discussion of the factors affecting attention. Sociologists' discussions of the nature of interaction would suggest that attention will be much greater when actor is a participant rather than a bystander, for interaction requires a degree of attentiveness that is unusual for an uninvolved observer.

Sociologists also deserve credit for recognizing that in the process of role learning actors learn their own roles *and* the roles of others. This point is closely related to the previous one. In interaction one has to predict the behavior of other, and when actors take the role of the other in an attempt to predict other's action they are given opportunities to learn and practice his or her role.

Finally, sociological social psychologists have discussed an opportunity for rehearsal that has not been emphasized by Bandura. Though many social learning experiments involve children engaged in playlike behavior, the theory does not give much specific attention to play and games as contexts in which rehearsal and innovation take place. Symbolic interactionists, in particular, have written on this subject. They argue that, especially for children, play and games provide an opportunity for practicing specific role behaviors and skills such as the ability to take the role of the generalized other (Denzin 1975; Goffman 1967; Mead 1934).

SOCIOLOGICAL ANALYSES

Much of the sociological literature on role learning starts out by describing one or more of the contexts in which socialization occurs. This is then followed by a more or less ad hoc discussion of the relevance of the context for learning. In the analysis presented here the same issues will be addressed, but it is hoped that the ideas just discussed will provide the basis for a more systematic presentation.

Sociologists have typically classified socialization contexts in terms of the age of the socializee, that is, childhood vs. adolescent vs. adult socialization (Mortimer and Simmons 1978; Brim 1966, 1968; Clausen 1968; Elder 1968); on the basis of variation in actor's incumbency of the position, for example, anticipatory vs. in-service socialization (McCall and Simmons 1978; Thornton and Nardi 1975); or as formal vs. informal (Rosow 1974).

These category systems are, of course, related. For example, one of the major differences between adult and early childhood socialization is that there is more anticipatory and informal socialization in the latter. However, in this presentation we will focus on the incumbency classification because it seems most likely to lead to theoretically significant propositions.

I will, however, deviate from convention by using a more complex system than is usual. The simple dichotomy of anticipatory and in-service socialization has not permitted the unambiguous classification of all socialization situations, and this had led to confusion and variation in usage. The major divisions of socialization context as they will be considered here are: (1) anticipatory socialization—*unintentional* preparation for a role that actor does *not* play and will not play in the immediate future;[12] (2) explicit training—*intentional* socialization for a role that actor does *not* play;[13] (3) in-service or tenancy (Riley et al. 1972) socialization—role learning that occurs while actor is playing the role to which he is being socialized.

Anticipatory socialization. As soon as one begins to ask the questions suggested by social learning theory it becomes clear that anticipatory socialization is too gross a category to be useful. The several types of anticipatory socialization situations have different implications for the social learning theory variables. The key seems to lie in whether or not actor and the model are in interaction with each other. In *noninteractive* anticipatory socialization actor observes the model without overtly interacting with him or her. This would include eavesdropping, watching television, and so forth. In the *interactive* form the other who is unintentionally teaching actor a role is actor's role partner.

In table 4.1, the various socialization contexts are rated on a series of dimensions culled from social learning theory, and it seems clear that the traits associated with the noninteractive form of anticipatory socialization are not conducive to adequate role acquisition. In brief, the table shows, to begin with, that though many roles can be observed in this context it is a matter of chance as to whether or not actor will have contact with a role that he will be called on to play in the future. There is little attempt to match person and role-model. Furthermore, when actors have a chance to observe roles that will be useful, the conditions are such that they are not likely to fully avail themselves of the opportunities. As table 4.1 shows, attention, coding, and rehearsal are likely to be quite low in noninteractive anticipatory socialization. Actor is unlikely to perceive that learning the role will lead to reward; other is unlikely to tie reward to actor's learning; there is unlikely to be a close bond between actor and other; there is little need for role-taking, and so forth.

In fact, under these circumstances too close attention may produce negative consequences. It is not polite to be too attentive to other people's business, and as Merton and Rossi (1957) noted, under some circumstances the members of actor's group may define too great an interest in the behavior of out-group members as a form of treason. Opportunities for overt practice are also likely to be limited and negatively sanctioned, if they are used. "Putting on of airs" is often nothing more than the practice of a behavior that has been observed in a situation such as this.

TABLE 4.1

Characteristics of Socialization Contexts

Anticipatory Socialization		Explicit Training		
Non-Interactive	Interactive	Formal	Informal	In-Service Training
I. Factors Affecting Opportunities for Observing Useful Role Behavior				
A. Likelihood that a future self-role will be performed in actor's presence				
Chance	Chance	High	High	Very High
B. Likelihood that a future other's role will be performed in actor's presence				
Chance	High	Moderate	Moderate	Very High
II. Factors Affecting Attention, Coding, and Rehearsal				
A. Characteristics of actor				
1. Likelihood that actor will perceive that the role will prove useful for future self-roles				
Low	Low	High	Moderate	Very High
2. Likelihood that actor will perceive that this is a socialization situation for future self-roles				
Low	Low	Very High	Moderate	High
3. Likelihood that actor will perceive that he will be rewarded by other for the act of learning				
Low	Low	Very High	High	High
4. Likelihood that actor will perceive that the act of learning will provide self-reinforcement				
Low	Low	Very High	Moderate	High
5. Extent to which actor is in need of the reward associated with performing the role or with the act of learning				
Low	Moderate	High	Moderate	High
B. Characteristics of other				
1. Likelihood that other will make reward dependent upon actor's learning				
Low	Moderate	Very High	High	Very High
2. Power of other relative to actor				
Varies	Varies	Very High	Varies	Very High
3. Likelihood that other is going to be rewarded				
Varies	Varies	Varies	Varies	Varies
4. Number of others presenting material				
Varies	Varies	Varies	Varies	Varies
C. Characteristics of the relation between actor and other				
1. Frequency of interaction				
Varies	Varies	Moderate	Varies	Moderate
2. Degree of formality				
Varies	Varies	Moderate to Very High	Varies	Varies

TABLE 4.1 *(continued)*

Anticipatory Socialization		Explicit Training		
Non-Interactive	Interactive	Formal	Informal	In-Service Training
II. Factors Affecting Attention, Coding, and Rehearsal *(continued)*				
C. Characteristics of the relation between actor and other *(continued)*				
3. Degree of Attraction				
Varies	Varies	Varies	Varies	Varies
4. Degree of Similarity				
Varies	Varies	Moderate	Varies	Moderate
D. Characteristics of the material presented				
1. Clarity of cues				
Varies	Varies	Very High	Very High	Varies
2. Degree of inherent interest				
Varies	Varies	Varies	Varies	Varies
3. Amount of reward associated with learning				
Varies	Varies	High	Varies	Very High
E. Situational imperatives				
1. Extent to which role-taking is required				
Low	Very High	Varies	Varies	Varies
2. Value of role-taking for learning useful self-role				
Varies	Varies	High	High	Very High
3. Extent to which actor is insulated from distractions				
Low	Moderate	High	Varies	High
4. Extent of opportunities for overt rehearsal				
Low	Low	Varies	Varies	Very High
III. Factors Affecting Likelihood of Actor Making Abstractions				
A. Extent to which rules are presented as well as specific acts				
Low	Low	High	Varies	Varies
B. Extent to which actor is motivated to attempt abstraction				
Low	High	High	Varies	High
IV. Factors Affecting Utility of Material Presented				
A. Scope of the material presented				
Varies	Moderate	Wide	Varies	Wide
B. Applicability of material presented to concrete cases				
Varies	Moderate	Varies	Varies	Very High
C. Degree of openness of other				
Varies	Varies	Moderate or High	Moderate or High	High
D. Typicality of other				
Varies	Moderate to Very High	Moderate to Very High	Varies	Moderate to High

About the only positive factors in noninteractive anticipatory socialization are that contact with the model may be frequent and that the behaviors may be inherently arresting. These conditions are, however, by no means universal in this context and the latter, in fact, may be counterproductive. The parts of a role that are most dramatic and attention getting may not be the parts that are most important to learn.

Finally, if actor should acquire the information being offered, it is not very likely that he will attempt to extract the general pattern and thus change a series of discrete phenomena into a role. Other is unlikely to be of any help, and actor is unlikely to see any gain in making the effort.

Though the situation in regard to interactive anticipatory socialization is largely the same, two significant differences make all the difference. In the interactive form, attentiveness and role-taking are likely to be viewed as reward producing, for they lead to smooth interaction. The learning of other's role may be a totally unintended by-product. Similarly, actor may rehearse other's role, but not for the purpose of fixing it in mind for later use. The rehearsal occurs during the role-taking. In a sense it is coincidental that when actor takes the role of the other, "Certain responses (belonging to the role of the other) are in fact made, run through, completed . . . [and] this process adds to the repertoire of possible actions of a person those actions [played] by others in their own roles" (Brim 1958:2). Interactive anticipatory socialization is an important source of role-learning.

Explicit training programs. Use of a social learning theory perspective also suggests that explicit training programs, as defined above, are too varied to represent a useful single category. For example, the classes of a professional school and a parent teaching a child to cook would be included. To be sure, contexts as different as these share some important characteristics. They occur before actor is actually expected to play the role, the purpose of the interaction is socialization, the participants are aware of this, and they accept it as proper. But beyond this the differences are major.

There are a number of ways of subdividing the explicit training context, but for our purposes it appears useful to adapt Rosow's (1974) general categories of formal and informal socialization to the explicit training category. He suggests:

> We may define *formal* socialization as a specific training program of a formal organization designed to induct persons into a role or group. The training is purposive, intended to result in a definite social product: a person of particular skills and beliefs. The major objectives and procedures are usually specified, though often in quite general terms. Responsibility for training is clearly designated. . . . In contrast, informal socialization is much less structured on all these counts. [Rosow, 1974:105–106]

As table 4.1 shows, some of the key characteristics *shared* by the two types are: as compared with anticipatory socialization situations there is much more opportunity to observe useful roles in explicit learning contexts because one of other's goals is the presentation of such material and actor often chooses to enter the situation because of the opportunities it offers. In addition, there should be more attention on the part of actor and a greater tendency to code and rehearse, for, again, the learning of the material is one of actor's major goals. He or she can see that there is reward to be gained from attention, and so forth.

The behavior of other also may be different in an explicit training situation. Because the other defines the situation as a learning situation, it is likely that the material to be learned will be presented more explicitly, and, therefore, even if actor's attention is not increased, it is more likely that he or she will learn.

Beyond these general features of explicit training programs there are numerous differences between the formal and informal types. These differences are again described in table 4.1; here all I will do is to highlight and explain a few.

Though it is by no means characteristic of all formal training programs, these programs may develop into "total institutions," and such institutions can so completely dominate the students' existence that there may be little opportunity to encounter any role definition opposed to the one being put forth by the teachers (Goffman 1961; Zurcher 1967).[14] These contexts also permit the instructors to teach all aspects of the formal role—the socializees do not have to integrate information from several sources, and there need be little concern that ancillary sources of information will fail to perform (Rosow 1974). Along similar lines, the models are more easily able to focus their attention on their presentations since that is their major function. The models also are probably in a superordinate position vis-a-vis actor, and they can tie the major rewards in their possession to actor's acquiring the information presented. All of this is less likely to be true of the informal type.

In-service training. The final context, in-service socialization, refers to the instruction that both novices *and* "old-timers" receive while playing a role. In some cases the training is intended and in other instances it is unintentional and a by-product of the interaction.[15]

Intentional instruction on the job tends to have many of the characteristics of explicit training that is anticipatory, and I will not repeat that material here. In fact, there is also not much new that can be said about the nonintentional form of in-service training, for its characteristics tend to be a blend of those of the previously discussed contexts. For example, because socialization is not the major goal of the interaction the instructional content may not be easy to see; as is the case with unintentional anticipatory socialization. On the other hand, because the information is likely to be clearly of value to actor, it may be easy to capture actor's attention, as is the case in explicit training.

In-service socialization does, however, have a few unique features. For example, self-instruction is more likely to occur in this situation than in the others, for it is in the in-service context that such opportunities come naturally. In such situations, actor will probably face problems for which he has to work out his own solutions. It is also the context that provides the best opportunities for full and realistic practice. (There are, to be sure, risks associated with such practice, for actor may have to take full responsibility for his errors.) To give only a few more examples: (1) in the in-service context the rewards associated with learning are likely to be very high; (2) the material presented is likely to be highly pertinent; (3)

opportunities for learning will be numerous; (4) actor's motivation to learn will be high.

I have only touched on the highlights of the characteristics of the various contexts; table 4.1 presents additional information. It does seem clear, however, that social learning theory provides a framework for the integration of a literature which has been characterized as lacking theoretical development, cumulative findings, and a focus on the general (Mortimer and Simmons 1978).

At the same time it must be noted that sociologists have also devoted attention to differences among the contexts in regard to the *content* of the behavior presented for modeling, and this material is particularly in need of integration. It has been, however, largely beyond the purview of social learning theory. If we are to handle questions of content within our framework, the approach has to be different from that usually used in the literature. Much of the sociological writing in the area poses the question: Is the information obtained in this context likely to be accurate? and the answer is phrased in terms of the likelihood that the model will know and reveal the details of the role. This clearly assumes that there is one "right" way to play the role—a view that was rejected previously. I would suggest that the questions be slightly rephrased: What is the likelihood that the role presented by other will represent a full and accurate presentation of his or her views? and What is the likelihood that the model will hold typical views? The alteration is not great, but it is important to make it. If this is done, social learning theory can be of some help.

It is generally agreed (McCall and Simmons 1978; Thornton and Nardi 1975) that there is a good chance, though by no means certainty, that the information gained in both forms of anticipatory socialization may be neither full nor typical. For one thing, if the source of the socialization is one of the media, the model may have had no experience with the role. Even if the model has experience, the presentation is likely to be focused on the dramatic aspects rather than the routine parts, and this will be quite misleading. In other kinds of noninteractive anticipatory socialization a similar problem may exist. In the presence of an outsider the role may be played in a special "public" way.[16]

Even in the interactive form there may be reason to deceive—to protect secrets and self-image, for example. And in the absence of any desire to mislead, this context gives an opportunity to learn only one role in the role-set because actor's identities limit the breadth of his or her interaction possibilities. A boy cannot learn the father-daughter role by means of interactive anticipatory socialization, but he may need to know that role in adulthood.

If the information presented in the interactive anticipatory context is limited in these ways, it is rich in another way. In this context actors are socialized to both parts of a role when they role-take. Through nonreflexive role-taking they learn other's expectations of people like other and through reflexive role-taking they learn other's expectations of people like themselves. When we speak of anticipatory socialization we are focusing upon the former. It is clear, however, that whenever *interactive* anticipatory socialization occurs, in-service training is going on concomitantly. The boy learns the son and father parts of the father-son role. And, of course, it is crucial that he do so if he is to be an effective interactant.

In explicit training situations many of the problems regarding intentionally distorted presentations may seem unlikely to exist. It would seem obvious that if other is consciously attempting to teach actor a role, he would not try to mislead him or her. On reflection, however, it appears that this may not be the case. Other may quite knowingly teach an idealized version of the role—as many parents and teachers do. And if this is not done intentionally, it may occur anyway—because the teacher is out of touch with current practice, because the teacher has no practical experience, or because the need to give a general preparation leads to the presentation of abstract guidelines that are not applicable to real-life situations (Becker 1964).

During in-service training informal norms are likely to be a major focus, and it is probably true that a person's education cannot be complete without such training (Thornton and Nardi 1975). In this context, people learn to apply the general to the specific and learn what is acceptable deviation. However, in-service training, in the sense we are using the term, may have its own problems. It may do well only as long as the actor stays in that particular organization. He is likely to be taught the typical view of the role as it is played there, but he is insulated from alternative views to some extent *if* there is consensus within the group of socializers. This may cause difficulty when he moves into a new situation. In addition, the material presented to actor may be less than complete and "accurate" because others don't define socialization as "their job," or because actor is used where he is most needed rather than where he can learn the most.

DEVELOPING PREFERENCES FOR DEFINITIONS

Important though it may be, the material considered up to this point represents only a beginning for the discussion. It certainly does not explain role playing, for the form that behavior takes depends upon the general role definition that actor starts with *and* events that occur within a particular interaction. Moreover, and this is the relevant point here, it does not even account for actor's role definition in the early stages of the interaction. What has been said so far suggests that actor often knows several versions of a particular role, and thus he must select the one he wishes to use. The question then becomes, what basis will be used for the choice?

Sociologists have not given this issue a complete and systematic treatment, but the ingredients for such treatment are available. They are provided in discussions of related topics such as the development of identities, specific considerations of particular parts of the present issue, and extensions of the insights of social learning theory.

The starting point of the present discussion is the assumption that actors rank the various ways that they know to play a role along a hierarchy of prominence—an idea that owes an obvious debt to the concept of a hierarchy of prominence for identities as developed by Stryker (1968) and McCall and Simmons (1978). The relevant points here are: all versions of a role have "preference ratings" attached to them and thus they can be ranked; this ordering is relatively stable over time though it is subject to alteration under changed conditions; and actor will be inclined to use the definition that is currently highest on the hierarchy *if* its preference rating is above an acceptable minimum. The major problem is, then, to account for the level of preference associated with each definition.

A simple extension of the ideas of social learning theory would suggest that the general preference level for a particular version of a role is a direct function of the anticipated total profit associated with its performance.[17] And the total profit anticipated from a role performance is the anticipated total reward minus the anticipated associated costs.[18] The total reward expected from a role performance is the sum of the reward anticipated from others (role partners *and* third persons) and the expected self-reward. And the external reward anticipated from a role performance equals the likelihood of its being reinforced by others times the anticipated value of the reward, if it is forthcoming, minus the time one must wait before being rewarded. Thus, for the anticipated reward to be relatively high both the likelihood of reward and its value must be high, and it must be quickly forthcoming.

The likelihood that a randomly chosen other will reward actor is a function of the likelihood that other approves of actor's role choice, and actor's estimate of other's likelihood of approving is a function of his estimates as to the distribution of preferences in a pertinent population. The latter is based upon previous experiences.

More specifically, I would suggest that in the absence of any other information, versions of roles that have been "observed" more frequently will be assumed to be more generally acceptable than versions that have been observed less frequently.[19] "If everyone does it that way that must be the way that people think it should be done, and if I do it that way. . . ."

It is, however, unlikely that if actors have observed a role, they know only that it is the form that is used a certain percentage of the time. They are very likely to know how role partners *and* third persons reacted to the performance and that information will also enter into their calculations. Figuratively speaking, a favorable reaction would be doubly influential for it would suggest that both actor and other favor that version. A negative reaction would be counted less because that would signify that only the actor preferred that version.[20]

In what has just been said the focus has been on actor's observation of the consequences that a role performance has for other actors. However, the present actor may himself have used various versions of the role in the past, and the reactions he has experienced will also affect his judgment concerning the likelihood of his being rewarded in the future. In fact, if actor was the target of the reaction, it should be more consequential than if someone else received the reaction, for the reaction received by oneself is a better clue to what will happen to one in the future than is the reaction received by another, and it is also better remembered. Vicarious reinforcement should be less effective than direct reinforcement. From this it is a short step to the idea that reactions received by others like oneself are more important than the experiences of dissimilar others. These ideas follow basic principles of generalization, but they are particularly relevant to roles, for a role is not simply acceptable or unacceptable. Others' attitudes to a role pattern are importantly influenced by their view of its suitability for a particular category of persons, and those categories are often narrowly defined.

Actor can predict the value of the reward that will be forthcoming for a particular version of a role from knowledge of the identity of the others who approved of it. *Significant others* are persons who control rewards and punishments that are important to actor. Other things being equal, a version of a role preferred by significant others is more likely to be high on actor's hierarchy than is a role version favored by nonsignificant others. To perform the second version will gain actor little or nothing. If he does so in the presence of the significant other, he will receive significant *negative* reinforcement. If he does so in the presence of a nonsignificant other, he will gain little of value. Other will approve, but by definition that approval cannot be translated into a reward that actor will value.

The same reasoning would suggest that if the model for a particular version of a role is a significant other, that version is likely to have a higher preference rating than an alternative presented by a model who is less significant. Under most circumstances an actor may assume that imitating the behavior of an other will bring forth approval from that person. However, approval has much more value when it comes from a significant other.[21]

SELF-REINFORCEMENT

Because of their focus on the social sources of human behavior, many sociologists have tended to slight the possibility that people seek other than social rewards. In this tradition it is almost a tenet of faith that behavior is motivated by a desire for social approval. If actor plays a role in a way viewed as deviant by obvious others, the search begins for different reference groups that actor is trying to please. Without at all denying the strength of external reinforcements, it must be recognized that people can reward themselves; they can react to themselves just as they react to others and others react to them. It would follow, then, that in estimating their potential profits actors will take their own reactions into account. If a particular role pattern holds the promise of providing major self-reinforcement, it may come to be preferred over one that has more social acceptability.

The list of needs that do not *require* external reactions for their satisfaction is long and varied. Included would be the need for variety, rest, challenge, accomplishment, physical comfort, and, very important, self-esteem.[22]

COSTS

In judging profits one must also take into account the costs required to obtain the reinforcement. It is quite possible that actor will prefer a particular version of a role that leads to only small rewards over one that is potentially more rewarding, if the costs he expects to incur in obtaining the latter are so great that the general return is less.

More specifically, the easier it is to perform a role the higher its preference rating is going to be. And I would suggest that, in general, the ease of performing a role is related to such factors as the amount of time required, the quantity of resources that must be expended, and the extent to which the cooperation of others is required. In addition, actor's competence will be a highly relevant consideration. And competence would be related to the extent to which actor has used the role before, the extent to which he has observed others use it, the extent to which it is congenial to his general personality traits, its complexity, and so forth. Most of these suggest a tendency toward consistency of behavior. Old forms are likely to be repeated because they are easier to perform.

INNOVATIVE ROLE DEFINITIONS

A major characteristic of human behavior has not been touched upon in the foregoing discussion. The latter accounts for preferences among previously observed behaviors, but it does not explain how human beings develop innovative responses. "Observers may select one or more of the models as the primary source of behavior, but they rarely restrict their imitations to a single source, nor do they adopt all the characteristics of the preferred model. Rather, observers generally exhibit relatively novel responses representing amalgams of elements from different models" (Bandura 1971:11).

Bandura's (1977) explicit treatment of "creative modeling" is brief, but it is possible to piece together a coherent mini-theory from the general ideas presented. In the average case the tendency is to stay fairly close to the behavior of the observed model or models. Bandura notes that innovative behaviors, including amalgams, are not likely to meet with approval when they are first introduced, and a simple economy of effort principle would also favor repetition rather than invention. However, innovation is likely to occur when none of the previously observed role behaviors has a sufficiently high anticipated profit to make it desirable, and when actor perceives that combining elements from several versions will produce greater profit than staying within a single version. Amalgamation may also occur when the observed role patterns are difficult for actor to perform well, when they do not have much self-satisfaction associated with them, when they do not seem likely to lead to desired goals, and so forth.

Amalgamation is not, however, the only form of role innovation. People often use behaviors that they have been taught are appropriate for one identity when they are utilizing a different identity. This kind of innovation has attracted the attention of sociologists as well as social learning theorists. In fact, Brim's (1958, 1960) work, despite its early date, provides a more developed picture than is to be found in the work of psychologists. Brim suggests that it is not at all unusual to transfer behaviors from one role to another. We do not set up locked compartments and forget all our other roles when we are playing a particular one.

Two specific processes are involved (Brim 1958, 1960): (1) *role assimilation* in which an individual adopts a behavior observed in the actions of an other whose identity is not the same as the one for which actor is going to use the role (for example, an older child who acts toward his sibling as he has seen his parents do); and (2) *role extension,* which occurs when actor is inclined to use a behavior he has learned for one of his roles in another of his roles. A child who acts toward his teacher and father as he has learned to act toward his mother is extending his child-mother role to the student-teacher and child-father roles.

Recently Brim's theme has been picked up and expanded in Turner's (1978) consideration of *role-person merger.* This form of role-innovation strongly resembles Brim's role-extension idea. Both imply an affirmative answer to the question, "Can the attitudes and behavior developed as an expression of one role carry over into other situations" (Turner 1978:1)? However, role-person merger is more extreme than role-extension. The latter implies the transfer of a particular aspect of one role to some other role. When role-person merger occurs, a single role becomes so central that actor is inclined to use it in a wide variety of situations. In fact, it is likely to be used "despite available, advantageous, and viable alternative roles" (Turner 1978:3).

Turner's discussion of the determinants of role merger is long and complex and some of it is not relevant here. It may be noted briefly, however, that part of his analysis is simply a restatement of the basic idea of social learning theory. He starts from the idea that actor will prefer to use the same role behaviors when he or she is in a variety of situations, if it is believed that doing so will produce external and self-reinforcements. Then Turner goes well beyond this by elucidating the conditions under which actor would expect role-person merger to lead to such reinforcement. At a very general level Turner suggests that role-person merger is likely to occur when others expect actor to make the transfer. If others assume that the attitudes and behaviors actor uses in one role represent the *essence* of the person, they will expect him or her to use those attitudes and behaviors in many other instances, and actor will develop a preference for this pattern because he or she is rewarded for doing so. In other words, Turner, in contrast to Bandura, suggests that *some* innovative behavior will meet with approval. If people expect actors to behave in a somewhat unusual manner, actors should try to meet those expectations, if they wish reinforcement.

The use of the same behaviors for many roles may result in self-reinforcement. A role merger often saves effort when many roles are to be played, it gives actor an improved basis for predicting how others will react to him or her, it permits him or her to use a set of behaviors that are particularly satisfying more frequently than would otherwise be the case, and so forth. Turner also notes many specific conditions that lead to the general conditions described, but they cannot be considered here.

With this we are brought back to the starting point. Once innovative responses have been developed, their "preference ratings" will be determined by the same processes that influence the ratings of any role pattern. The assumption is that an innovative role is likely to be rather high on the hierarchy at the outset. It is designed to provide high rewards, and if there were any alternatives that were particularly profitable, there would have been no innovation to begin with. After it is performed for the first time, however, its continued favored status will be re-evaluated in the usual terms.

Roles in Interaction

Much of the work of role theorists is focused on interaction that is problematic, that is, interaction that involves problems of definition, malintegration, inconsistency, or lack of needed resources. To understand interaction, however, it is best to start by considering routine interaction. These situations, "can be readily named, the objects to be dealt with in them can be easily anticipated; the roles represented are known in advance and frequently we know who will make these roles; and, in general, a more or less patterned set of activities will occur, often strongly resembling activities that have taken place on previous such occasions" (Hewitt 1979:123–24). We turn now to a description of an *ideal-type* routine interaction.[23]

The first phase of interaction involves defining the situation.[24] "Human conduct takes place within situations that are defined by participants who act toward one another, the situations themselves, and the objects they contain on the basis of their definitions" (Hewitt 1979:119). In very general terms, it is assumed (Stebbins 1967, 1969; McHugh 1968; Perinbanayagam 1974) that when actor enters an interaction situation he takes note of the various social and physical cues that are present and on the basis of his previous experience assigns meaning to them. From his understanding of the meaning of the cues he will develop a general perception of the situation—"I'm in a church." "It's a hold-up." And this label will help in the defining of an identity for self and for other, a definition of actor's and other's goals, and, of course, a role definition for actor *and* other.[25]

Since this is a routine situation, actor will have little difficulty with these tasks. He will have access to the significant cues, they will "make sense" to him, they will suggest a meaningful definition of the whole, he will be able to choose a role that fits, and so forth. But this does not mean that all is going to be obvious at once. It may be that simple, but the chances are that actor is going to have to work at it, and he will probably need help—even in routine situations.

I would suggest that other is a major source of this help. Of course, the physical appearance and manner of other (Stone 1962) are important cues, but it goes beyond these. Other may quite explicitly suggest a definition of the situation, for it is often in his or her interest that actor define the situation "properly." Moreover, whether other is explicit or not, actor will use role-taking to put himself in the place of other and to deduce, among other things, what other's expectations are. Other's definition need not be accepted, but in a routine interaction it probably would be, because it would be consistent with actor's preliminary dispositions. Whether or not it is accepted, it obviously is of help to actor in developing his own view.

When actor has reached this point he probably has a rather good idea as to what he wants to do for his first act, but before he actually does anything, there is likely to be a momentary pause during which actor considers, again by role-taking, what other's reaction is likely to be if he follows through on his plan. If the conclusion is that the reaction will be an acceptable one, actor will go ahead and carry out his first act. And in a routine interaction the probability is that the anticipated reaction of other will be acceptable, for in such situations role definitions are complementary.

All this time other has also been defining the situation, and actor's act is an additional cue that other takes into account. When he understands the situation, other decides what the reaction should be. He then checks, by role-taking, how actor will "take it," and decides whether to go ahead or revise his plans.

The rest of the interaction will follow this pattern, and this is to say it will not fall into the rut of automaticity. Actor will have to remain alert if he is to develop ideas as to what to do next. He cannot depend on cue cards for his lines, for it is in the nature of roles that they provide only very general guidelines. Furthermore, to say that an interaction is routine is not to say that it is unchanging. There may very well be several occasions when the whole set of definitions has to be changed—perhaps because a goal has been reached and a new phase has been entered, perhaps because the interaction has moved from the routine to the problematic. A sore point may come up, for example, and change the entire complexion of the encounter. Actors must remain attentive and active. If they don't, it is probable that the encounter will move from the routine to the problematic.

PROBLEMATIC INTERACTION

Role theorists see the following as the major problems of intervention: (1) an inability to develop a preliminary definition of the situation; (2) an inability to choose a role either because actor does not know a role appropriate to the situation or he knows several and has no basis for choosing; (3) a lack of consensus between actor and other; (4) role strain because of incompatabilities between roles or within roles (role conflict); (5) role strain because of lack of resources, time, or energy (role overload).

Each of these problems is handled somewhat differently as befits the fact that they are quite different from each other. A lack of resources leads, among other things, to attempts to increase them, a lack of consensus leads to negotiations, and so forth. The details will be presented below.[26]

LACK OF ROLE KNOWLEDGE

Given the nature of role, it is not unusual for actors to find themselves in situations in which they are utilizing identities for which their role knowledge is less than complete. A lack of role knowledge is not sufficient to make a situation a problematic one. Two additional conditions are necessary. The lack of information must be so great that actor feels that he cannot perform at even a minimally acceptable level; and the processes that usually make it possible to fill in the gaps must be inoperative.

Actor is likely to lack role knowledge to this extent only when he or she is a complete novice whose anticipatory socialization has been totally inadequate. I would postulate that the latter condition is most likely to occur under conditions of rapid social and personal change, when people find themselves in situations that neither they nor anyone else expected them to be in. Opportunities for anticipatory socialization are most likely to be available and utilized when there is an expectation that actor will, at some point, be able to put the knowledge to use. As we have seen, anticipatory socialization tends to be ineffective even when it comes to important and commonly occurring situations. Nonetheless such a degree of ignorance of role knowledge is improbable when the situation is even vaguely anticipated.

To find oneself so poorly prepared in a situation does not make for the easiest interaction, but as the discussions of in-service socialization and innovation suggest, there are standard remedies. But in this case, by definition, those solutions are not available, and the question becomes: why might this be so?

It will be recalled that the major mechanisms of in-service socialization are the observation of peers, reflexive role-taking of role partners, and following explicit instructions. Obviously, the first mechanism will not be available when there are no other persons playing the same role, or when their activities cannot be observed by actor, and this is not an uncommon situation. However, there is always a role partner, and actor "should" be able to learn his role by deducing what other expects him to do and by following his advice. Other may, however, be unable to help out. If he, too, is an unprepared novice he may not have any better idea of what to do than actor has. In this situation, explicit instruction will not be forthcoming and reflexive role-taking will not be profitable.

In many other instances the role partner has the needed information, but does not make it available to actor. For example, other may choose not to give instructions because he does not define that activity as part of his role or because actor's ignorance acts to his advantage. However, other's cooperation is usually not necessary. If actor cannot figure out his role it must mean also that there is a failure of role-taking. This failure may be caused by the existence of an adversary relationship that leads other to give off misleading cues, and it would also occur when actor and other lack means of effective communication. Under the latter condition actor will not be able to perceive or decipher the cues other gives; he will not be able to engage in effective reflexive role-taking.

Even if all these conditions exist, actor can still solve the problem by engaging in some form of innovation. He will truly be "stuck" only when none of the roles he knows has any relevance to the present situation and when his problem-solving ability is low.

HANDLING PROBLEMATIC ROLE DEFINITIONS

It appears clear from the above that it is uncommon for a situation to be problematic because of problems of role definition. In most cases actor will have sufficient knowledge or ingenuity to keep this aspect routine, and this is all to the good, because if a situation is problematic in the way described above, there is not much chance of a totally adequate solution. A termination of the relationship may appear to be a tempting alternative, but it does not really represent a solution. It is simply an escape that forecloses the possibility of obtaining the rewards that the encounter might bring. However, if actor can withdraw from this relationship to enter a similar one with a more helpful other, there might be a chance to save the day.

Along the same lines a temporary withdrawal might work if it gave actor an opportunity to prepare himself for a return as a competent role player. However, in situations such as this outside opportunities for learning may be minimal or very costly, and a *temporary* withdrawal may not be possible. Failure in the position may foreclose a return, and these situations are, by their very nature, often not voluntary. Thus all of these possibilities may be closed to actor.

If this is the situation there are only two alternatives open. One possibility is to have the situation redefined, which will permit actor to use an identity for which he knows the role. This can be effective at times, for example, if actor gives up his claim to leadership and plays a follower role. But there are limits to this. Situations can be defined in a variety of ways, but those ways are finite. If actor was not able to find elements in other roles that would permit him to function in the situation as originally defined, actor is probably not going to be able to find an identity he can use and that other will accept.

The final possibility is a resort to trial and error. At best this is a costly approach, and here the conditions are far from being optimal. For one thing, actor is unlikely to know what to try. The most reasonable possibilities are behaviors that have worked in other roles, but in this case they may not hold the solution. To add to this, the cost of errors is likely to be high.

Thus, there are ways out of the situation, but at the same time there will be many instances in which none of them is available for a particular actor. In such cases actor will have to "serve his time" and suffer the negative reinforcements that come from inadequate role playing. But even if it comes to that actor is not without resources. He may be able to reduce the cost of those reinforcements by defining the situation as an unimportant one, by failing to perceive them, and so forth (Rosenberg 1979).

ROLE DISSENSUS AND CONSENSUS

As noted earlier, sociologists have long recognized that at the start of an interaction there may be role dissensus—actor's definition of his own role may not be the same as other's definition of actor's role and other's definition of his own role may differ from actor's definition of other's role. I turn now to a brief consideration of the antecedents, consequences, and reactions to this situation. Most of the recent work has focused on the reaction to dissensus, and after a brief consideration of the first two issues we will turn our attention to it.

Antecedents of role dissensus. The material on role socialization contains an implicit answer to the question: under what circumstances are actor and other likely to disagree about role definitions? If we define situations in ways that we have been taught to define them, anything that increases the possibility that actor and other have had dissimilar socialization would increase the likelihood that they will disagree in their role definitions. Dissimilar socialization would increase the probability that actor and other know different versions and have different preference hierarchies.

The implicit assumption in the above is that actor and other have been socialized by third parties, and the issue is how likely is it that these third parties have taught similar lessons. It should be noted, however, that actor may have developed his role definition in previous interaction with the other with whom he is now interacting. If this is so, role dissensus is not too likely to occur. Thus it would follow that the greater the probability that actor and other have previously engaged in similar interaction, the lower the likelihood of dissensus. And dissensus should be *negatively* related to: the frequency of the interaction; the extent to which the interaction provided the conditions conducive to learning; and the degree of similarity between the previous situations and the present one.

In addition, certain kinds of encounters would be more likely to show consensus. Included would be those that take place in specialized locations such as churches and classrooms, those that are guided by formal contracts, those that are institutionalized, and so forth. No new principle is involved here. Dissensus is less likely in these cases because it is in the nature of these encounters that people have probably been taught to define them in a particular way, regardless of who the socializing agent was.

The consequences of role dissensus. Role theory is clear in its implications regarding the consequences of role dissensus. If it is not removed, the interaction is unlikely to proceed smoothly and satisfactorily. If there are important differences in the participants' roles, their behaviors will not mesh and cooperative action will be difficult to achieve. What actor views as the correct response to his behavior will not be the behavior suggested to other by his role definition. In addition, mutual dislike is likely to develop because each will feel that the other is not behaving properly. In fact, just the knowledge that one's interaction partner sees things differently may be sufficient to cause a significant degree of enmity.

It must be emphasized, however, that role dissensus may not lead to serious interaction problems. As Scheff (1967) notes, the amount of coordination needed and desired may be quite low in some interactions. In fact there may well be a lack of awareness of dissensus. And, finally, under some circumstances role definitions can be different without being in conflict. If my definition prescribes much more kindness than my interaction partner's, this is not likely to result in difficulty for him.

It should also be noted that all that is necessary for smooth interaction under most circumstances is a *working consensus.* There does not have to be a basic and profound agreement. It is not necessary that there be "the kind of consensus that arises when each individual present expresses what he really feels and honestly agrees with the expressed feelings of the others present. This kind of harmony is an optimistic ideal and in any case not necessary for the smooth working of society" (Goffman 1959). All that is required is that there be a willingness to accept, for the time being, a set of definitions that does not seriously conflict with that of the other. The situation becomes problematic only when the differences are great enough to cause disruption, and neither is immediately willing to change. Let us now consider how actors handle problematic role dissensus.

Reactions to dissensus. If the dissensus is so costly that the interactants are motivated to go to some lengths to remove it, there are a number of processes that can be utilized. Strauss (1978) lists some fourteen specific options ranging from asking to killing. These specific reactions may be reduced to six general categories: persuasion, education, manipulation, appeal to rules or authority, coercion, and negotiations (or bargaining). In common with most social psychologists I will focus on negotiations.

Though the concept of negotiations is frequenty used, it is difficult to find an explicit definition of it. Several works devoted largely to the subject simply ignore the definitional problem: a rather dubious procedure given the slippery nature of the concept. The definition offered by Chertkoff and Esser (1976) will be the basis for the present discussion, for it serves to distinguish negotiations from similar phenomena, and it gives some insights into how they work.

Negotiations are a form of interaction designed to reduce differences. In order for them to occur the interactants must have divergent interests, and it must be possible for them to communicate about them. In the kind of negotiations of concern here, each participant prefers his own definition and thus has an interest in maintaining it. If either or both has no commitment to their own view there is no need for negotiations.

These two conditions are obviously not sufficient to separate negotiations from other procedures designed to bring about consensus. Chertkoff and Esser (1976) suggest that three additional conditions are required:

1. There must be the possibility of compromise. One of the participants may succeed in getting his original view to prevail, but the "rules" must not require that one of the original definitions be accepted.
2. It must be possible to make provisional offers and counteroffers. This implies three things. First, offers must be permitted to be conditional on some action by other. Secondly, tentative offers must be acceptable. Actor must be able to suggest a willingness to do something without by that suggestion making a commitment to doing it. And, finally, no previously agreed-upon action can be considered totally binding. Of course, once an offer is made, accepted, and confirmed it becomes difficult to retract it. In principle, however, no issue is ever foreclosed.
3. Both participants must be permitted to reject proposals until they feel their

best interests will be served by acceptance. In a negotiating situation, as compared to a coercive one, neither can impose a solution.

This definition fits in very well with the sequential pattern that Rubin and Brown (1975) suggest is typical of negotiations. Actor will offer a definition of a situation and suggest a proposed course of action. Other will evaluate actor's contribution and decide whether the definition is a valid one, whether the proposed action follows from it, and whether the proposed action has advantages to him that are sufficient to lead him to accept actor's view. On the basis of his conclusions about these points, other will frame his reply. It would involve acceptance or rejection, and if the latter is forthcoming, there would probably be a counterproposal. Then actor would have his turn, and a series of such exchanges will occur until negotiations are broken off or a working consensus emerges. Though the words are different, the general pattern of an interaction can be clearly discerned. Negotiations are simply a specific case of the general process of interaction.

Mechanisms of negotiations. The proposals offered in negotiations are usually accompanied by rationales intended to convince other to accept actor's view. In general these rationales are referred to as *accounts* (Scott and Lyman 1968). Much of the sociological work on negotiations has focused on the nature of these rationales, rather than on the proposals themselves, and sociologists have also considered the conditions which are conducive to the acceptance of the accounts. My main discussion will be devoted to these topics.

Accounts are often designed to convince the other that the action is acceptable in terms of conventional standards any appearances to the contrary notwithstanding.[27] Such arguments are often *justifications*—statements in which actor accepts responsibility for an act, but argues that the act is consistent with agreed-upon criteria despite what other might believe (Scott and Lyman 1968). This is often done by attempting to characterize the motives behind an action in acceptable terms. Aggression can be justified by claiming there is no intention to do any harm, for example, or actions that are not acceptable under normal circumstances may be justified by claiming that the conditions are unusual or that actor is special.

Excuses, on the other hand, admit that the action is in fact normally unacceptable, but they ask that it be accepted because actor "couldn't help it." Actor contends, in one way or another, that he or she has diminished responsibility. More specifically, Scott and Lyman (1968) suggest that excuses may involve: (1) *appeals to accident,* which contend that an action was, or will be, caused by events beyond actor's control—heavy traffic, illness, mechanical breakdown, and so forth; (2) *appeals to defeasability,* which suggest either that (a) actor cannot be held responsible because he cannot know what the results of his action will be or that, (b) actor lacks free will—something or someone forced him to do it; (3) *appeals to biological drives,* which are lack of free-will arguments in which the irresistible force is something internal to the actor (frequently the sex drive and psychopathology are the basis for such arguments); (4) *scapegoating,* which combines elements from two of the excuses mentioned above. The claim is that an internal drive forced actor to do as he did, but the stimulus for that drive was an action of the target. "I went crazy when I found that she . . ." (see also Scott and Lyman 1968).

Other's reactions to accounts. If an account is to have much chance of being accepted it must be *credible.* Other must believe that actor is telling the truth, and this belief is unlikely unless the account is internally consistent. In addition, the argument must be consistent with other facts in the role partner's possession. A person who is known to be highly skilled cannot claim a lack of knowledge. And if an account is to be credible, it must be consistent with other's implicit theory of human motivation. An actor cannot successfully claim to have a particular motive if other believes that a particular action is always motivated by something else (cf. Blumstein et al. 1978).

In addition to being believable an account has to be *legitimate* in other's eyes if it is to do its job; it must be relevant to the action, and if it is an excuse, it must be equal to the gravity of the offense. What will be considered legitimate varies among cultures and among individuals. Each culture has scales of equivalencies that are typical for the group, and individuals within the culture will give their own personal twists to the standard scale. And for any particular situation there will be a different scale, depending upon the identity of actor. A child's accounts, for example, are judged differently from those of an adult, and the same is the case for friends as compared to strangers.

The emphasis upon rational consideration should not lead us to ignore the fact that pressure may also be applied. An account is an attempt to convince, but if an argument cannot convince on its merits, actor is likely to utilize any other resources he may have. The application of pressure is common in negotiations (see Heiss 1981).

ROLE STRAIN

It is a fact of social life that the achievement of a working consensus on role definitions does not guarantee that the rest of the encounter will be routine. Even after there is consensus actor may have to contend with *role strain;* a felt difficulty in meeting the norms of the roles that one accepts. There are various forms of role strain but for the present purpose I will consider only the general types: *role conflict* and *role overload.*

Antecedents of role strain. The fact that actor is experiencing role strain is prima facie evidence that the negotiations process has not worked well for him. The point of negotiating is to gain acceptance of a role definition that one can live with and live by. If role strain develops, it is clear that actor has not been successful. Thus, if we are to understand the sources of role strain we must inquire into the reasons why actor might leave negotiations in an untenable position.

We may assume that actor would not intentionally "paint himself into such a corner" and this makes it clear that the possibility of role strain is inversely related to actor's influence over the negotiating process. Thus, actors who are less powerful and less skillful in the use of negotiating techniques are more likely to experience role strain.

In addition, actor may accept a role definition that is beyond him because he is not aware that it will prove to be so. We cannot always accurately predict the outcomes of our agreements. Given this second source of role strain, I would postulate that strain is more likely to occur when actor lacks experience in the role; particularly when anticipatory socialization is ineffective. However, even experienced actors can be led into this situation by the actions of others. Thus, role strain would also be more likely to occur when other has something to gain from actor's role strain, when other controls the course of the negotiations, when actor's experience with the role is greater than others, when actor's role-taking ability is low, and so forth.

The value of combining general structural and "micro-interactionist" analyses can be well illustrated at this point. Though whether or not there will be role strain depends on the outcome of the negotiations between the interaction partners, structural forces that are largely beyond their control may have an important influence on the outcome.

Such forces may, for example, restrict the range of "possible" agreements. If the role that would be relatively strain-free is opposed to a commonly accepted definition, actor will have difficulty in getting his view accepted. Under such circumstances other's opposition may be particularly strong. Also, other will be better able to resist actor's suggestions because he is likely to have the support of third parties and he can quote the society's value system in his defense.

Furthermore, in many instances the agreement between actor and other has to be "ratified" by outsiders and thus agreements which would be to their mutual advantage may be precluded. If third parties were not intruding into the transactions of interaction partners, bribery would be much more common than it is, for example.

These, then, are a few of the general ways in which structural contexts can limit actor's opportunities for negotiating a strain-free role definition. Among the more specific factors that will affect the extent of this influence is the specificity of the norm system within which the interactants are operating. If the societal norms are detailed and permit few deviations, actor's job will be made more difficult. At the extreme, some things are viewed as not negotiable; for example, behavior in dangerous situations. The person who cannot meet the established standards has little or no chance of getting others to accept a pattern that he can meet.

All of the above refer to the extent to which the options open to a negotiating group are limited by the larger social context in which they are placed. This is, however, not the only way in which the larger society intrudes on negotiations to affect actor's chances of working out a strain-free agreement. As noted previously, the greater actor's control over the negotiations, the greater the likelihood that he can avoid role strain; and it is clear that actor's position in the larger context will affect the extent to which he is able to exercise such control (Goode 1960). The most obvious factor is his general social status; the higher his rank the more likely it is that he will be able to manipulate resources in a way that will lead to an advantageous agreement. There are, however, also some advantages to low status. Actor and his activities may have such low value that others do not bother to impose their definitions on him. This would, for example, be seen in police tolerance of many crimes in lower-class communities. And, to give a final example that does not relate to actor's status, I would note that because there are societal mechanisms designed to minimize role strain, the person whose identity set is more typical will have an advantage. That is, "society" will be more likely to have anticipated his problem and made provision for it.

Reduction of role strain. If actor finds that he is experiencing significant role strain he or she will probably try to reduce or eliminate it by attempting to renegotiate the role agreement. And at first glance it would seem that the chances of obtaining a better arrangement are small. Actor was not successful the first time, and other now has an added advantage because the existence of an agreement can be used by other as the basis for a refusal to consider a change.

It is possible, however, that at this point actor's bargaining position may have improved somewhat. If his difficulty was caused by a lack of awareness of the implications of the role bargain, his experience will have opened his eyes and he is unlikely to make the same mistake again. In addition, the fact that actor is suffering difficulty may be the basis for winning a new "contract." A simple plea for mercy may be effective, but actor does not have to depend upon the kindness of other. Other may have a selfish interest in changing the terms because actor's difficulty in doing his part may make it less likely that other will achieve his goals if cooperation is required. Thus, it may be in other's interest to renegotiate.

Actor's chances of a successful renegotiation may also be improved if the changes he wishes to make at this point are relatively minor. Instead of a complete alteration of identity and/or role definition, all actor may need is a modification of previous understandings. *Exemption* is one of the forms that these modifications may take. In this case actor accepts the general appropriateness of the original definitions, but attempts to get other to agree to free him of some of his obligations under specified circumstances. Along with a request for exemption, actor often makes a suggestion regarding *delegation* (Goode 1960a). If there is someone willing and able to take on the duties from which actor is exempted, and the delegation seems appropriate in other's eyes, the chances of a redefinition are quite good.

If actor cannot redefine the situation and is unwilling to terminate the relationship, his goal would then become the reduction of the strain that he is experiencing. There are two general ways to do that: actor can attempt to change other's *and* his own perception as to the extent of the discrepancy between what he is doing and what he "should" be doing, and/or he can blunt the effects of the external and internal negative reinforcements he receives for inadequate performance. All of these will probably go on simultaneously, but of necessity they will be handled here as if they were discrete processes.

In attempting to reduce the perceived discrepancy, actor may focus his efforts on the perception or on the actual discrepancy. If the former is the case, the goal will be to convince other and himself that the discrepancy is not as great as it appears. Whether the target is self or other the basic techniques are the same: actor attempts to hide the facts or influence the definition of them. In the service of these ends he can use lies, self-deceptions, justification, self-justification, excuses, and so forth.

The other way to reduce the perceived distance between expectations and behavior is to actually reduce it. Though actor may believe that he is doing his best to meet his role agreement, when role strain occurs he may find that previously unexplored possibilities exist. If the problem is that actor cannot meet the requirements of a single role, he may find that it is possible to ease the situation by obtaining additional training or by obtaining an assistant who has the needed skills. Such solutions may be particularly attractive because they will not necessarily require the concurrence of the role partner.

When the problem is role overload because of lack of time and energy, one possibility is to abandon one or more of the roles. This possibility undoubtedly has occurred to actor prior to this point, but under conditions of role strain a further consideration of the matter may reveal a way out. He may discover, for example, that a role that was giving no trouble can be abandoned with little cost and the time transferred to the constellation of roles that is causing problems.

Marks' (1977) analysis suggests some possibilities that are not so immediately obvious. He contends that an individual's time and energy are not as finite as they are believed to be. Some activities, such as recreation, may increase energy directly and others, by leading to greater efficiency, increase the available time. He also suggests that an increase in one's commitment to any activity may increase energy. If this is so, actor should increase his commitment to getting the job done and should take on additional, energy-*producing* roles rather than drop roles.

If the problem is one of role conflict the options are quite limited. The only way that actor can avoid negative sanctions is to renegotiate or to drop one or more of the roles that contain incompatible elements. We may assume, however, that if these possibilities existed actor would have made use of them earlier.

Reducing the costs of role strain. We may now assume that actor has considered all the possibilities but the role strain still continues. Even at this point, however, actor will try to keep his costs to a minimum. Large costs may be inevitable, but he can still attempt to reduce their magnitude, and he may also be able to affect the nature of the costs incurred. The costs associated with failure in different roles differ in amount and type, and actor may be able to choose to fail in the role that is associated with the least cost. Or, in a similar fashion, he may choose to fail the role partner who has the least ability to impose costs, whose demands are considered least legitimate (Gross et al. 1968) or who has the least power.

Finally, I will note again that a possible solution is to terminate the relation. If the problems have not been solved at this point, it seems to me, as it would probably to actor, that the cost of performing the role has increased to such a level that termination might very well be the option with the lowest loss.

Conclusion

This is my view of the nature, sources, and manner of operation of roles. It is to be hoped that the reader will view it as coherent, integrated, and plausible. Even if the discussion is viewed in this light, however, a crucial question remains untouched: is it empirically valid? Space considerations have precluded consideration of the voluminous literature that bears upon the many issues that have been raised. In another work (Heiss 1981) an attempt has been made to cover the relevant empirical data in some detail. Here all I can offer is the conclusion I have reached on the basis of that analysis: nothing that has been said in the preceding pages is in conflict with empirical evidence known to me. More than that, many of the ideas offered have empirical support, though many have not been tested and thus at this point remain speculative.

NOTES

1. The person who is the focus of attention will be referred to as *actor,* the person with whom he or she is interacting is *other,* and persons not directly involved in the interaction are *third parties.*

2. Similar difficulties can be found in the works of a single author. Shifts in meaning, which cannot be attributed to the evolution of an idea, occur from one book to the next (cf. Linton 1936, 1945), definitions are often ambiguous, and usage is frequently inconsistent with formal definitions (cf. Parsons 1961:42–43).

3. If roles refer to expectations rather than behavior, we need terms for the behavior that emerges in interaction under the guidance of a role and words to describe the actions of the person who is exhibiting such behavior. I would suggest role behavior and role performance for the former, and playing a role, performing a role, and role-playing for the latter.

4. There is, of course, the problem that there is no single orthodox position, and views change over time. I will attempt to present a composite of the most recent discussions of the leading proponents of each approach.

5. Banton (1965) describes roles as statements of appropriate activities and associated rights and obligations. The actor has to *work out* what specific actions should be taken to carry out the activities, claim the rights, and meet the obligations.

6. The general term *role strain* is used to refer to any felt difficulty in meeting the requirements of a role (Goode 1960a).

7. In fact, it is implicit in much of sociological and psychological theory, nonetheless, that the maximization principle is controversial. Unfortunately, it is not possible to give a full defense of it here. It may help to suggest, however, that unlike the traditional assumption of "economic man" (Simon 1955, 1956) it does *not* assume that actors use complete and accurate information in a skilled way when they are computing the "payoffs" of alternative actions. Our balance sheets are always incomplete, and even if they were not, we would not have the time, motivation, and ability to process them completely. We act in a way that we *think* will produce maximum reward, but we are very likely to be at least somewhat off the mark. Also, we do not attempt to maximize our store of every desired good. The goal is to maximize our *total profits.* For example, we limit our food intake, because beyond a certain level continued eating leads to the costs associated with indigestion, overweight, and so forth.

8. The analysis is incomplete in that, in the interest of simplicity, I focus on the learning of the self-role. Role socialization also involves learning roles for others. The processes are the same, however, and I hope it will be obvious how the two roles are learned simultaneously.

9. This is not to say that sociological phenomena are necessarily reducible to psychological principles. All that is contended is that psychological theory provides a basis for integrating and explaining some of the matters that have concerned sociologists who have written on role socialization.

10. Bandura is not clear as to whether following verbal instructions should be considered modeling behavior. In one publication (1969:25) he seems to exclude it but in another (1971:10) it seems to be included. In my view the two phenomena are basically similar.

11. Theories of interpersonal attraction (Bersheid and Walster 1969; Huston 1973) can do much to fill the gap, but a full treatment would have to consider social structural factors that serve to limit the "range of eligibles."

12. Anticipatory socialization, one might think, would be defined as any activity that provides information on a role for an identity that is not actor's. Clausen (1968:9) suggests, however, that "most common usage confines the term to experiences and activities that are not specifically designed as role preparation." I will adopt this usage even though it is not used as commonly as Clausen's statement might suggest.

13. Included here would be experiences in socializing organizations such as schools and rehabilitation programs. In addition, socialization programs, such as a pledge system in a fraternity, are included even though they occur in organizations whose major purpose is other than socialization (Mortimer and Simmons 1978).

14. Even in such organizations the peer group is an alternative source of socialization. Usually, however, they simply reinforce the instruction of the formal socializers.

15. The various kinds of on-the-job-training found in industry would typify the intentional form of in-service training. What the boss learns from the subordinate is likely to be of the unintentional type.

16. Such an experience does, of course, contain a lesson. It teaches actor what to do in public situations.

17. Bandura tends to speak of reinforcements and rewards but the concept of profit is quite consistent with the general logic of the theory.

18. More exactly we might distinguish between gross reward, which is the reward received, and net reward, which is reward received minus rewards that would have been obtained from alternative behaviors. This distinction seems to be an unnecessary complication here.

19. Observation is used quite broadly. It would include hearing, reading, and so forth, as well as direct observation.

20. Since a single action can be reacted to by multiple others a behavior may have negative valence.

21. There are a variety of ways that an other can become a significant other by gaining influence over actor's fate. Insofar as material rewards are the coin, persons who control many such rewards are likely to be significant, for they can distribute their surplus. But more often the relevant reward is approval, acceptance, honor, or some other psychic reward. Everyone can give these, but they are not always valuable to their recipients. However, if other frequently interacts with actor, if he is viewed as competent, if he is liked, if he occupies a particular position in the social system his approbation is likely to be something that is sought.

22. It must be noted, however, that the personal standards on which self-reinforcement is based are very likely to have social source. People do not decide for themselves that they should feel good if they reach a particular level or act in a particular way. Personal standards are usually previously experienced *social* standards that have been adopted as one's own.

23. To make this distinction is not to suggest, however, that interaction in problematic and routine situations is *basically* different. Certain processes that occur in problematic interaction are not found in routine interaction because they are not needed, but the two types share a common core. The major difference is that in routine situations it is easier to come up with acceptable solutions to the tasks set by the interaction.

24. The assumption is that actor did not initiate or anticipate the occurrence

of the interaction. If he or she had, much of the defining work could have been done prior to the onset of interaction.

25. There is, of course, a strong tendency to utilize the role version that is highest in the hierarchy of roles for the identity being used. This is, however, only a tendency. Conditions may lead actor to start off with a role definition that is not at the top of the hierarchy. The preference hierarchy determines general preferences, not specific usage. In any particular case actor may decide to abandon the role highest on the hierarchy because in this instance its performance will be particularly costly because, perhaps, of the temporary shortage of a needed resource. Or actor may choose a role version that does not have the highest rating because he anticipates that the rewards usually associated with it will not be given in this case. He may have advance information that this other will act differently from persons he has previously observed. Or he may not be interested in the usual reward because he has a temporary surplus of it, and this may lead him to shift to another version in order to get a reward whose desirability is greater than usual. In fact, a large change in any of the major variables that affect general preferences can lead actor to abandon his "favorite" role from the outset of a particular encounter.

26. For a more detailed discussion see Heiss (1981) from which much of this material is adapted.

27. Accounts can be used prospectively or retrospectively. In role negotiations the former is more likely; we try to gain acceptance of what we plan to do. The latter, however, is also found in such situations. We argue over what has happened, and in the process develop the rules for the future.

PART II

Socialization

DIANE MITSCH BUSH AND
ROBERTA G. SIMMONS

5

Socialization Processes Over the Life Course

All the world's a stage,
And all the men and women merely players.
They have their exits and their entrances;
And one man in his time plays many parts,
His acts being seven ages.
At first the infant,
Mewling and puking in the nurse's arms.
. . . Last scene of all,
That ends this strange eventful history,
Is second childishness and mere oblivion,
Sans teeth, sans eyes, sans taste, sans everything.
WILLIAM SHAKESPEARE
As You Like It

How the "mewling, puking infant" becomes the lover, the soldier, the justice, and finally enters "second childishness" and "mere oblivion" occasioned keen interest long before Shakespeare's characterization of individual change over a lifetime. As the social sciences have developed, the study of socialization has assumed major importance in psychology, anthropology, and sociology. Although each discipline has its own distinctive approach to questions concerning individual growth and change from infancy to old age, in all three fields the part played by socialization processes is treated as a cornerstone both for the maintenance of society and for the well-being of the individual. Our tasks here are to trace the historical antecedents of current approaches to socialization over the life course, to synthesize contemporary formulations, and to raise issues that must be resolved if we are to further advance our knowledge of the way in which socialization processes operate throughout the individual's life. Special attention will be devoted to distinctively sociological contributions to current thought in the field and to the questions of the universality and continuity of processes of socialization.

In order to trace the antecedents of current work and to explore recent theories and research in the area, we must first take a brief look at the concept of socialization and distinguish it from the closely allied notions of maturation and development. Then we will examine early theories that laid the groundwork for more recent formulations. Many of the pioneering theories of socialization stress psychobiological processes rather than social ones. However, we can see the roots of a more sociological orientation in these classic approaches to socialization. Current sociological contributions to the study of socialization processes integrate ideas from a variety of traditions.

There are several important aspects of socialization, such as the role of socialization agents and of differing socialization contexts, that we do not cover here because other chapters in this volume discuss them thoroughly. For an extensive exploration of contexts of socialization agents, see chapter 6.

Definitional Distinctions: Maturation, Development, and Socialization

Distinctions between the concepts of maturation, development, and socialization have been stressed in sociological work on socialization. Maturation is seen to entail a more or less automatic unfolding of biological potential in a set predictable sequence (see Clausen 1968). In contrast, development is viewed as a set of sequential changes from simple to more complex structures within the boundaries set by both biological and social structures (Goulet and Baltes 1970; Nesselroade and Reese 1973; Baltes and Schaie 1973). Many developmental theorists stress that the environment influences the individual and that the individual affects the environment as well (Reese and Overton 1970; Goulet and Baltes 1970; Baltes and Schaie 1973). Positions vary widely with regard to the continuity of developmental processes. On the one hand is the view that human development is continuous in addition to being sequential (Gubrium and Buckholdt 1977). The alternative perspective asserts that although development is sequential, it contains discontinuities. Developmental processes between stages may be different according to this view (Nesselroade and Reese 1973). In part, the concern with allowing the concept of development to include discontinuity seems to stem from a relatively recent interest in research on life-span developmental psychology which will be discussed in greater detail below (see Goulet and Baltes 1970; Nesselroade and Reese 1973; Datan and Ginsberg 1975).

Whereas the concept of development stresses an interaction between individual behavior and the environment and views a behavioral repertoire as the outcome of developmental processes, the concept of socialization generally refers to the ways in which individuals learn skills, knowledge, values, motives, and roles appropriate to their position in a group or a society. In keeping with their disciplinary origins, sociological definitions of socialization tend to emphasize the ways in which the individual learns to fit into society, and, to a lesser degree, how this process changes not only the individual but society as well. Many definitions make the point that processes of socialization vary immensely in terms of explicitness, formality, and specificity (Clausen 1968; Elder 1975), often depending on characteristics of the socializee such as age, the relationship between socializee and agent of socialization, and the context of socialization (see chapter 6). Virtually all sociological definitions of socialization emphasize the distinctly social nature of the processes of socialization. For sociologists, processes such as imitation, identification, and role acquisition are viewed as social interactions; the interaction is reciprocal and the socializee is not passive, but takes an active part in the process.

Among sociologists, there seems to be substantial agreement that socialization serves to maintain social groups by promoting the adaptation of the individual to them; in this sense socialization is beneficial to both the individual and society. Sewell (1963) defines socialization as "processes by which individuals selectively acquire skills, knowledge, attitudes, values and motives current in the groups of which they are or will become members." In this definition and in many others (Baumrind 1975; Zigler and Child 1969; Mortimer and Simmons 1978), socialization is a symbiotic process with some positive outcomes for both the social group and the individual. Likewise, those definitions that emphasize acculturation propose that socialization not only enables the socializee to adapt, but that it is the way in which culture and societies reproduce themselves (Inkeles 1968). Levy makes this point clearly:

> An individual is adequately socialized if he has been inculcated with a sufficient portion of the structure of action of his society to permit the effective performance of his roles in the society. There is adequate socialization in a society if there is a sufficient number of adequately socialized individuals for the structural requisites of a society to operate. [Inkeles, 1968:79]

In order to maintain continuity in social organization, then, appropriate roles, behaviors, values, and attitudes must be transmitted. Without socialization, society would not be reproduced with each succeeding generation.

It is not claimed that all consequences of socialization are functional ones, but that socialization does serve certain key functions for the social group and individual. Clearly, there are instances where socialization is dysfunctional. For example, it may benefit the group at the expense of the individual. Many theorists have pointed to socialization as a process of social control (see Neugarten and Datan 1973; Bowles and Gintis 1976), especially in total institutions (Goffman 1961b).

Two issues related to these themes surface repeatedly in discussions of socialization. The first concerns the degree of continuity and consistency of personality throughout life (Brim 1968). Positions here range from the contention that personality is firmly molded in childhood to the assertion that individuals continue to be quite malleable over the life course. Most sociological approaches emphasize the malleability of the self to some degree, and imply in their definitions of socialization the possibility of continuing change. (Brim and Wheeler 1966; Clausen 1973; Elder 1974).

The second issue revolves around the extent to which socialization processes are similar in childhood and adulthood. A number of distinctions between childhood and adult socialization have been made (Sewell 1963; Brim 1968; Clausen 1968; Mortimer and Simmons 1978). It appears that differences between them involve the content and context of socialization more than actual processual differences. However, role-learning (Rosow 1974; Brim 1968; Brim and Wheeler 1966) and self-initiated socialization (Brim 1968; Mortimer and Simmons 1978) may be more characteristic of adult socialization, whereas early socialization may proceed more through imitation and identification. None of these socialization processes, however, is restricted only to a particular period of development.

Historical Antecedents to Current Theory

As we trace the historical antecedents of current theory on socialization through the life course, we will repeatedly encounter several points of contention. The first point is centered on the continuity or discontinuity of processes of socialization. Are the same processes at work through the lifetime? Does significant individual change continue through the lifetime in reaction to socialization experiences, or is socialization essentially complete upon entrance into adulthood? If socialization continues, through what mechanisms does it proceed? Most classic theories of socialization are concerned primarily with childhood socialization and some view the personality as molded early in life. Implicit in the approaches that have had the greatest impact on sociological theories of socialization is some notion either that the self is amenable to change (G. H. Mead 1934) and thus that socialization processes continue through adulthood, or that role transitions are crucial to development (M. Mead 1928; Benedict 1938; Erikson 1950).

After dealing with the issues of continuity in the self and in socialization processes, we must come to grips with the issue of the universality of socialization processes over time and space. To what extent do socialization processes vary for individuals who live in different historical periods or who occupy different positions in the social structure? Each of the early frameworks here has different implications for these issues, thereby setting the stage for current theoretical positions on each.

FREUD'S PSYCHOSEXUAL STAGE THEORY

Freud's psychoanalytic notions of socialization (1961 [originally published in 1930]; 1966 [essays originally published 1917–33]) have so penetrated Western culture in general and the social sciences in particular that it is sometimes difficult to disentangle them from "commonsense" notions of personality and development. Since we are primarily concerned with Freud's contributions to the issues involved in studying processes of socialization over the life course, we will briefly discuss the structural hypothesis and his theory of the stages of psycho-sexual development. The assumption here is that Freud's theories have had a pervasive influence on the study of socialization from psychological, anthropological, and sociological perspectives.

The structural hypothesis. The structural hypothesis, or the structural theory of personality, provides the basis for Freud's psychoanalytic approach to socialization. There are three inborn structures of the mind or personality: the id, the ego, and the superego. In the newborn, only the id is fully present. The ego and superego are differentiated from the id. As the individual matures, the ego and the superego emerge through the cathexis of innate drives[1] onto particular drive representatives. The development of the ego and superego are the basic tasks of socialization. Various objects of drives and drive representatives are genetically located at different periods in the life cycle, since patterns of cathexis vary according to which personality structure (id, ego, superego) is governing behavior.

Identification. Identification is the key process whereby the individual cathects libidinal energy to successive drive representatives, thereby resulting in the differentiation of the ego and superego as personality structures. Identification is "the act or process of becoming like something or someone in one or several aspects of thought or behavior" (Brenner 1974:41); it is dependent upon experience with one's environment, especially with other people. Freud asserted that in any object relation there is a tendency for the individual to become like the object and that the "more primitive" the stage of ego development, the greater the tendency to imitate.[2]

Psycho-sexual stages. The structural hypothesis along with the process of identification are the key elements of Freud's theory of psycho-sexual stages of development. In essence, each stage of development is defined by where and upon whom the the individual's libidinal energy (drive energy) is cathected at a given time. Libidinal energy moves from the mouth to the anus to the genitalia. Each stage, the oral, anal, and phallic, is characterized by a particular kind of interaction with the environment. Identification is the process whereby the individual moves from each stage to the next; movement through the stages is ordered and invariant. Completion of one stage is the requisite for moving to the next. With the completion of the stages, first the ego develops, then the superego emerges. Once the superego is differentiated, the demands of society have been internalized in "morality" and the individual has become a fully functioning adult (Freud 1961).

Impact of Freud's theory. Freud's stage theory has had substantial impact upon the study of socialization, although much recent work has been a reaction to the theory. Most sociological work on socialization has rejected Freud's assumption that the process of development is a dispositional one in which inborn psychobiological structures dictate the unfolding of the self. Yet, until recently, with the emergence of work on adult socialization (Becker 1964; Brim 1968; Rosow 1974; Riley et al. 1972) and life-span developmental psychology (Goulet and Baltes 1970; Baltes and Schaie 1973), most research on socialization has emphasized childhood socialization, as Freud did. Freud stressed the process of identification, and this process is still seen as a key one for socialization even if the bases for identification are not believed to be the bodily centers of the libido. Freud's discussions of the way interaction with the environment might accelerate or retard movement through the psycho-sexual stages are echoed by the pervasive interest of sociologists in the facilitative impact of environment on socialization. Likewise, Freud's view that a fully socialized individual internalizes many of society's demands has become a basic assumption of socialization theory (Freud 1961). Present disagreements between theories of the life-course and life-stage theories (see below) can be seen as originating in or reacting to Freud's assumption that movement from one developmental stage to the next is ordered and largely invariant.

PIAGET'S COGNITIVE-DEVELOPMENTAL STAGE THEORY

Like Freud's, Piaget's theory of development posits a set of cognitive structures and related stages of development, each of which must be completed before the individual can progress to the next stage. Piaget's cognitive-developmental theory of development is, nevertheless, quite different from Freud's account of the process in two important ways.

Social interaction and reordering of cognitive structures. First, Piaget's (1970; Piaget and Inhelder 1969) theory focuses on experience and social interaction as central in the movement from one stage to another. Freud, on the other hand, emphasizes the social environment in a more negative way; it can retard or fixate progression through the stages, but its positive role is far less clear. This is so, in part, because Freud believed that development was basically a process of maturation; innate structures unfold in a biologically determined fashion in the normal individual.

The second feature of Piaget's theory, which is more developed than Freud's, is the continuity and interdependence of each stage of development. Not only are the stages proposed by Piaget continuous in the sense that mastery of each depends on cognitive structures constructed in prior stages, but each stage is actually viewed as an amplification and reordering of results of the previous stage.

Cognitive structures, assimilation, and accommodation. Briefly, Piaget's cognitive-developmental theory is concerned with the progressive construction and reconstruction of cognitive structures[3] as the child develops. One central assumption of the theory is that intellectual functioning, and therefore behavior, is governed by patterns of cognitive structure known as *schemas.* Individuals develop schemas through experience, the schemas then influence subsequent interpretations of the social and physical world. Through what Piaget calls "equilibration" the child assimilates new experiences into her/his existing schema and accommodates cognitive structures to the new experience.

There is a dynamic equilibrium both between the child and the environment and between assimilation and accommodation. Piaget stresses both the active role of the child or the "subject" in these key socialization processes and the way in which maturation delimits the extent to which a child is able to assimilate or accommodate. To be more precise:

> . . . assimilation (means) that . . . reality data are treated or modified in such a way as to become incorporated into the structure of the subject. In other words, every newly established connection is integrated into an existing schema. According to this view the organizing activity of the subject must be considered just as important as the connections inherent in the external stimuli, for the subject becomes aware of these connections only to the degree that he can assimilate them by means of his *(sic)* existing structures . . . that is to say the stimulus is filtered through a structure that consists of the action-schemes (or at a higher level, the operations of thought), which in turn are modified and enriched when the subject's behavioral repertoire is accommodated to the demands of reality. *The filtering or modification of the input is called assimilation; the modification of internal schemes to fit reality is called accommodation.* [Piaget and Inhelder 1969:5–6; italics added]

Thus, the child actively assimilates and organizes new information according to her or his existing cognitive structures. If the new information cannot be integrated, then the child accommodates her or his cognitive structure. The emphasis, then, in much of Piaget's theorizing is on the developing child as social actor.

Cognitive-developmental stages. Assimilation and accommodation thus produce the cognitive reorganization that constitutes the various stages of development posited in Piaget's theory. Movement through these stages (broadly: sensorimotor, concrete operations, formal operations) represents, in part, a shift from being ego-centered to decentered, and from understanding concrete objects or pairs of objects to comprehending complex relationships (forms rather than concrete substance) as totalities. By ages twelve to fourteen, the individual is capable of deducing propositions about objects she/he has never seen and is able to grasp possible transformations of social and physical reality without ever seeing them. This change is viewed as crucial because: (1) it allows for notions of morality; (2) it makes possible the concern with decisions about the future, notably career choice; and (3) it enables the individual to have affective relationships in which she/he not only realizes that others may have different perspectives from her/his own, but she or he is able to coordinate others' perspectives with her or his own as well. The latter ability is central in role-taking and in a number of other social interaction skills as well.

Piaget's stages of cognitive development and those of moral development culminate somewhere in adolescence, although the processes of assimilation and accommodation operate throughout the individual's life. (Piaget's research and the bulk of his theory, however, are concerned with childhood and adolescence.)

> Finally, after the age of eleven or twelve, nascent formal thought restructures the concrete operations by subordinating them to new structures whose development will continue throughout adolescence and all of later life (along with many other transformations as well). [Piaget and Inhelder 1969:152–53]

Impact of Piaget's theory. Piaget's work has been more influential in child psychology than in sociology (Kohlberg 1969, 1973). However, we can see several ways that the implicitly sociological conceptions from his framework have been incorporated into sociological theory. His emphasis on the individual as an active agent in the process of socialization is stressed also in sociological theorizing (Mortimer and Simmons 1978), especially in the symbolic interactionist tradition (Stone and Farberman 1970). The idea that it is only through social interaction and role-taking that individuals construct a self and a world view is a basic assumption common to Piaget and sociological theorists (G. H. Mead 1934; Clausen 1968; Goslin 1969; Becker 1964). Piaget's conception of the importance of social interaction for learning to role-take is similar to the views of the early symbolic interactionists such as G. H. Mead and Cooley.

MEAD'S THEORY OF THE SELF IN SOCIAL INTERACTION

Both Cooley and G. H. Mead were concerned with the emergence of the self through social interaction as the basic process of socialization.[4] According to Cooley (1902), the self was so integral a part of society that to view it as distinct was "absurd." He and G. H. Mead agreed that the self was composed of two components: the "I" and the "me." For G. H. Mead, these two elements of the self were reflexive. The "I" is the individual as active responder, the spontaneous part of the self; the "me" is the person's conception of him- or herself. "The 'me' is a me which was the I at the earlier time" (G. H. Mead 1934:174). Not only is the structure of the reflexive self open to transformation, but each individual may have a number of selves as well (G. H. Mead 1934:140). However, the generalized other provides unity for the self.

How does this differentiated yet whole self come about? Basically, Mead asserts that the reflexive self evolves as the individual takes the role of the other and understands how the various social roles encountered are interrelated to each other. Mead argues that socialization of the individual is, above all, a process of social interaction. Like Piaget, he emphasizes the active part the individual plays in his or her own socialization and the importance of social interaction in individual development. Unlike Piaget, Mead stipulates that the individual will take society's attitudes, in the form of a generalized other, as her or his own. Taking the attitudes and roles, both of other individuals and of the generalized other, is the basic process of socialization.

The self develops in two stages, according to Mead. First, the self is built through the particular attitudes of other people toward the developing individual or toward one another. The second stage marks the construction by the individual of the generalized other, in addition to taking the attitudes of those she/he interacts with.

Although Mead does not really discuss how the self may continue to evolve throughout a lifetime, his theory strongly implies the potential for such development. Inherent in the cognitive structures and processes he posits is the continuing transformation of the self. Since the reflexive self is inherently changeable through social interaction, it appears plausible to suggest that as the individual takes on new roles and encounters new situations, the self will continue to evolve and change. This conception is precisely the one developed by contemporary symbolic interactionists on the basis of Mead's formulation (Becker 1970; Stone and Farberman 1970), although Mead himself was not concerned with adult socialization per se. Thus, both G. H. Mead and Piaget outline cognitive structures and cognitive processes that are developed through social interaction and that could conceivably lead to continuing change in the self over the life course.[5]

M. MEAD AND BENEDICT ON STATUS TRANSITIONS AND DISCONTINUITIES

Up to this point in our discussion, none of the theories covered has dealt explicitly with status transitions or passages. Although both Freud and Piaget attempt to account for the transition from childhood to adolescence, they do not explicitly view this shift as an example of life transitions or status passages generally. M. Mead (1928) and Benedict (1938) point to the importance of life transitions for individuals and status passages, in particular the passages from childhood to adolescence and on to adulthood. Both theorists were concerned with the ways in which the culture of a given society can affect the character and outcomes of life transitions, even though such transitions may be in part maturational processes.

In *Coming of Age in Samoa,* Mead (1928) posed the question of whether the transitions of adolescence were stressful and full of conflict for girls everywhere. Her answer to the question was that difficulties such as those experienced by Western girls in adolescence were not experienced by Samoan adolescents. The explanation for this finding lies in distinct cultural differences between the two societies, especially in the way in which the adolescent transition is dealt with. Mead (1949:541) asserted that "the extent to which in different cultures individuals are put under pressure at points of maximum or minimum ability to stand those pressures is exceedingly important."

Similarly, Benedict (1938) focused on the extent to which cultures provide continuity or discontinuity for role transitions. Like Mead, she maintained that American culture exacerbated the discontinuities and tensions of role transitions during the life cycle. For example, there is a marked discrepancy in our society between the role of childhood and adulthood. Children must be submissive, sexless, and nonresponsible, while adults must be dominant, sexually active, and responsible. She notes the contrast to many American Indian tribes, where submissiveness is discouraged among young boys and where, instead, these young boys are encouraged to develop more adult-like assertiveness. She also notes societies in which sexual play is encouraged among small children. In addition, Benedict (1938:166) offers a number of examples of ways in which "primitive" societies "furnish adequate support to the individual as he progresses from role to role" through the life cycle. One example of such institutional aid for individual life transitions is graduation "publicly and with honor from one age group to another" (Benedict 1938: 165). The idea that cultural arrangements may help or hinder adjustment to life transitions has been quite influential, particularly in the study of adolescent socialization, aging, and life crises.

Both Mead and Benedict stress that the passages of adolescence are not the only crucial life transitions, but that parenthood, old age, and indeed, "the whole life cycle" bear studying. Moreover, Mead (1949:542) notes that approaches that are most useful for explaining one life transition "should apply to the whole life cycle." Her views are an important foundation for current theories on the life course and life cycles.

ERIKSON'S THEORY OF THE SELF IN SOCIAL INTERACTION

Writing somewhat later than any of the above theorists is Erikson (1950). His conception of "the eight ages of man" is one of the most influential frameworks to deal explicitly with the issue of socialization over the life span. Like Freud, Erikson follows the psychoanalytic tradition and views the ego as the central psychic structure. The ego responds to the social world in particular modes during the various stages of development. At each stage, there is a specific "developmental task" that must be accomplished in order for the individual to progress to the subsequent stages. Erikson (1950) allows for "variations in tempo and intensity" in that "an individual or culture may linger excessively" over one or another stage.[6]

Erikson's (1950) stages of development correspond to notable life transitions, but there appears to be a presumption that each stage must be resolved in a particular way or the individual will experience mental health problems. This theme reappears in current work on the life cycle, much of which has emanated directly from Erikson's theory. His major contribution has been to focus interest on stages and tasks of socialization in both childhood and adulthood.

MANNHEIM'S WORK ON GENERATION

Few of the classical theorists have attended to the effects of one's generation in any great detail;[7] Mannheim (1952) is the exception. He views generation location as a source of social change, in part because individuals who are members of different generations undergo different socialization experiences:

> The fact that people are born at the same time . . . does not in itself involve similarity of location; what does create a similar location is that they are in a position to experience the same events and data, and especially that these experiences impinge upon a similarly "stratified consciousness." [Mannheim 1952:304]

Mannheim stresses that people in the same generation location may see the world in very different ways from their counterparts in earlier generations. The unique experiences common to each generation group allow for social change. If processes of socialization actually involve different experiences for each new generation, it is possible that individuals in successive generation cohorts will be socialized in very distinctive ways. This idea of Mannheim's is a major thrust of current work on socialization through the life course (Riley et al. 1972) and in research on socialization experiences particular to certain generations (Elder 1974).

SUMMARY OF HISTORICAL ANTECEDENTS

In summary, these very diverse classic theories of socialization have shaped the themes that continue to pervade the study of socialization. Freud and Piaget saw socialization as a passage through a series of stages, with most stages completed by adolescence. At present there is more emphasis on the continuities of socialization throughout life. Freud emphasized identification as the key socialization process and Piaget saw assimilation-accommodation as the primary socialization process. Both processes may be viewed as distinctly social ones and, as such, have influenced contemporary sociological theorizing on socialization. G. H. Mead's conceptualization of the emergence of the self allows for significant change throughout adulthood and suggests that role learning is a crucial process in continuing socialization. His contributions are the bases for several current approaches to socialization (Becker 1970; Clausen 1968; Gordon 1972). M. Mead and Benedict illustrate the importance of cultural arrangements for facilitating or hindering major life transitions. This theme has been integrated with notions of role learning in recent work on socialization throughout the life course. Likewise, Erikson's views on passage through life stages, especially those after adolescence, have provided the basis for a whole range of perspectives on socialization as progression through a number of life stages culminating in old age and death. Finally, Mannheim has alerted us to the impact of one's generation upon socialization, a theme echoed and expanded in the current work of Riley (Riley et al. 1972) and Elder (1974).

Current Theory and Research

SOCIALIZATION VIEWED AS A CONTINUING PROCESS

Underlying virtually all of the contemporary sociological views on socialization is the assumption that it is a continuing, lifelong process (Becker 1970; Brim 1968; Clausen 1972; Riley et al. 1972). Although most contemporary students of socialization would agree with this statement, the concrete meanings imputed to it may vary immensely across and even within disciplines. Becker (1964) points out that although most social scientists allow that "people exhibit marked changes as they move through youth and adulthood," some would characterize such change as anomalous and others would see it as a logical extension of values, norms, personalities, or selves formed in childhood and adolescence. Becker (1964:40) argues that both approaches to change through adulthood "err by taking for granted that the only way we can arrive at generalized explanations of human behavior is by finding some unchanging components in the self or personality." Such an assumption is based on the prior notion that individuals have some immutable essence, and that any changes observed are only superficial. On the contrary, Becker (1964), Brim (1968), and others contend that both change and stability characterize adult life, just as both are present during childhood. While neither all change nor all stability can be attributed to socialization processes, role acquisition, loss, and transition seem to be key factors in both stability and transformation over the life course.

ROLE ACQUISITION

More or less implicit in all the classical formulations we have explored here is the notion that the acquisition of social roles is a key socialization process. Although Freud never used the concept of role, the culmination of psycho-sexual development certainly appears to be male and female sex roles (Sales 1978). Piaget's concern with decentering, and the consequent ability to understand and act upon perceptions of the other, seems to stem from the presumption that social roles require such capabilities. In Piaget's discussions of the game of marbles, the importance of the ability to role-take is obvious. Likewise, throughout G. H. Mead's analysis of the reflexive self through games, the concepts of role-taking and role learning are prominent. Clearly, Benedict and M. Mead view role transitions as the decisive points in the socialization process. Additionally, it is reasonable to interpret the accomplishment of the developmental tasks posited in Erikson's framework as the resolution of role conflicts and role transitions.

Given the significance accorded processes that appear to be analogous, if not identical, to role acquisition, it is not surprising that contemporary work on socialization, especially adult socialization, has revolved around processes of role acquisition (Brim and Wheeler 1966; Brim 1968; Becker 1964; Rosow 1974), role conflict (Sales 1978; Gross, Mason, and McEachern 1958), and role transitions (Rosow 1974; Gordon 1972; Riley et al. 1972), including role loss (Rosow 1974). As individuals mature, they are expected to take on a number of different, sometimes contradictory statuses and roles. Such expansion of the status-set and role-set (Merton 1957) continues until old age, at which point the number of roles and statuses contracts (Rosow 1974; Riley et al. 1972; Atchley 1975; Gordon 1972).

It is often said that because modern industrial society is so complex, differentiated, and rapidly changing, individuals today need to understand and perform many more roles than individuals in earlier periods or in less complex societies (Brim 1968; Clausen 1973; Sewell 1963). Not only does this mean that individuals simply cannot become prepared in childhood for all the tasks and roles they will encounter as adults, but it also implies that role definitions are in flux and that new roles emerge frequently. Thus, by definition, role acquisition is tied to role conflict and role transitions.

In most situations, but particularly conflicting ones, *internal* as well as *external* stimuli affect the way persons learn presented roles. As Brim (1968) contends, the demands of self may be as important, if not more so, than demands of other persons or the society. Brim's insights are helpful here:

> There may be small but incremental shifts from time to time in what an individual asks of himself, and the resultant day-to-day alterations in his behavior, rewarded by himself, lead to a cumulative change which over the years makes him much different from what he was when younger . . . until one day he finds himself a person quite different from that of a decade earlier, without knowing how the change occurred. [1968:191–92]

One outcome of such self-initiated processes of change is that an individual may redefine a role in a unique way. Thornton and Nardi (1975) maintain that personal reconception of a role is an integral stage in the role-acquisition process. Indeed, they argue that there are several stages in role acquisition: anticipatory socialization, formal socialization, informal socialization, and personal role expectations. After the role incumbent has anticipated and experienced the role, then she or he may begin to redefine it and develop personally tailored role expectations. Thus, role demands that culminate in changes in the self may emanate from within the self, from others encountered in face-to-face situations, or from socially defined norms. While it is likely that demands from these different sources may be related, they are often incongruent.

ROLE TRANSITIONS AND ROLE DISCONTINUITY

Since role change continues throughout the course of the life cycle, the acquisition of new roles and loss of old ones has been a central theoretical concern. There is, in fact, an abundance of theory and research on the concepts of role transitions and role discontinuity (Clausen 1973; Gordon 1972; Lowenthal et al. 1975; Sales 1978; Simmons et al. 1979). Some theorists, echoing Benedict, have argued that the discontinuity involved in major role transition may be psychologically stressful (Lowenthal et al. 1975; Albrecht 1975; Riley 1976; Rosow 1974). Some, again resembling Benedict, have held that this stress is mitigated by the process of anticipatory socialization (for example, see Gordon 1972; Merton 1957; Albrecht 1975). Still others suggest that the level of stress depends on the nature of the role abandoned or acquired. Finally, there are institutionalized rites of passage that smooth the transition to new roles. We will discuss these ideas in turn, as well as issues of being off-time in role transition and issues of role-clarity and role-conflict.

Role discontinuity as stressful. Role conflict implies conflicting demands at one point in time, whereas role discontinuity (Benedict 1938) refers to a contradiction between demands of a new and an old role.

It is this contradiction in role demands that is presumed to be problematic for the individual, both in terms of confronting her or him with a potentially traumatic situation and in terms of rendering the task of learning and adjusting to new roles more difficult. Riley states that:

> The impact of role transitions on individuals depends further on the degree of compatibility or continuity between the role complexes in contiguous (age) strata. Individuals making the transition from one stratum to the next must not only prepare in advance to cross the threshold, but they must also adjust to the new sets of roles at the next higher age level. The new set may either provide direct substitutes for former roles, compatible with the values and attitudes of the previous

complex; or alternatively, it may present entirely different norms that require restructuring of orientations or activate defense mechanisms leading to potentially deviant adjustments. Thus, much depends upon the degree of normative consonance between roles available in adjacent strata. [1976:209]

Thus, according to Riley, ideally role transitions would involve: (1) continuity between roles whose expectations are compatible with each other and (2) adequate prior preparation for the new role before taking it on. Many theorists have argued that such continuity is lacking in Western industrialized countries (Benedict 1938; Rosow 1974; Gordon 1972; Riley et al. 1972; Foner and Kertzer 1978) and even in some age-set societies (Foner and Kertzer 1978). For example, Western adult males are socialized to value autonomy and productivity; yet, with increasing age and retirement, they must suddenly adjust to a more dependent and unproductive role (Mortimer and Simmons 1978). Work and achievement have been central to the self-image of the adult male and to his family role. Yet, when retirement comes, this central work role is suddenly lost, and the husband becomes a part-time housekeeper along with his wife. Many theorists assert that more adequate preparation for a new role will make the transition into it easier and more complete (Neugarten and Hagestad 1976; Albrecht 1975; Levine and Scotch 1970; Gordon 1972).

Anticipatory socialization and role transitions. Much attention has been focused on the way anticipatory socialization (or socialization prior to role assumption) cushions the shock of role transitions and results in successful role acquisition (Becker 1964; Clausen 1968; Gordon 1972; Rosow 1974). However, Mortimer and Simmons (1978) point out that there is little research concerning the actual effects of prior socialization upon adjustment to new roles. One excellent attempt in this direction is Renee Fox's (1957) analysis of the way medical schools unintentionally prepare students for the life of uncertainty physicians must lead.

Thornton and Nardi (1975) observe that in order for anticipatory socialization to facilitate adjustment to the new role, it must be *accurate.* For example, there seem to be some essential inaccuracies in anticipatory socialization for marital roles in the United States[8] (Gordon 1972) resulting in romanticized pictures of such roles that may create problems for those new to the roles. The child usually has intimate knowledge of only one marital model, his parents; if the father is absent, anticipatory socialization may be severely compromised. Likewise, many occupational roles are either invisible or, as in the cases of the physician and lawyer, are portrayed inaccurately in the mass media, thus making anticipatory socialization difficult (Mortimer and Simmons 1978; Becker 1970; Van Maanen 1977).

It seems that visibility of the future role to nonincumbents is important for anticipatory socialization to be effective. Even if the role norms and demands are visible, anticipatory socialization may not proceed unless the role norms are clear. Rosow (1974) maintains that many of the problems encountered by the aged in adjusting to new roles are caused by normative ambiguity. There is little prescribed activity that attends old age; the role is open and unstructured. However, some theorists view such ambiguities as positive in that they allow individuals to define their own roles in a creative way (Thornton and Nardi 1975; Goffman 1961a).

The assumption underlying the anticipatory socialization concept is that if the individual is prepared ahead of time for the new role, in the sense of understanding the norms associated with the role, having the necessary skills to carry out the role, and becoming aware of expectations and rewards attached to the role, that he or she will move into the new role easily and effectively. One situation that seems to be an exception to this notion of role transition is the case in which role transition involves a loss in status. Even if one is prepared for such a role transition, it may still be stressful (Pearlin and Lieberman 1979). Many of the role transitions of old age are examples of such a situation (Rosow 1974; Riley 1976; Neugarten and Hagestad 1976), as work, activities that depend on health and higher income, and family role relationships are lost (in some cases through death of partners). In addition, Rosow (1974) points out that role transitions involving status loss are often involuntary ones, as in the case of retirement, widowhood, and divorce. (The empirical evidence for such assertions, however, is not without controversy; see Mortimer and Simmons 1978:426.)

The nature of the roles changed. If a loss in status compounds the difficulties of role transition, then it is reasonable to assume that a role transition that involves gains may be less stressful and easier (Rosow 1974; Gordon 1972; Atchley 1975; Riley 1976; Pearlin and Lieberman 1979). The thrill associated with one's first "real job" is one example of such a transition. However, some theorists argue that regardless of whether role transitions involve status gains or losses, they are still stressful and problematic (Albrecht 1975; Lowenthal et al. 1975). A case in point is Durkheim's classic argument that upwardly mobile individuals as well as downwardly mobile ones are likely to commit "anomic" suicide.

Both in the case of role loss and of role gain, the individual must not only adjust to new role relationships and expectations, but she/he must "disengage" from old relationships and expectations. It is presumed, although not totally supported by evidence, that both processes are difficult for the individual.

Impact of rites of passage on role transition. Negative effects of discontinuity between sequential roles and changes in status are believed to be minimized by rites of passage (Benedict 1938; Van Gennep 1908; Glaser and Strauss 1971; Rosow 1974). Such rites of passage reflect institutionalized movement from one part of the social structure to another, a loss or gain of privilege, influence, or power, and a changed identity and sense of self as well as changed behavior (Glaser and Strauss, 1971). These rites of passage marking status changes take the form of marriage ceremonies, graduation, and so on. These rituals are believed to make role transitions easier for individuals by signifying to others that the person's status has changed and that new expectations are appropriate, and by symbolizing the status change for the individual her-/himself.[9] However, most of the evidence for this supposition comes from studies of non-Western cultures (Mead 1928; Foner and Kertzer 1978), which imply that transitions are easier in such cultures than in societies like the United States. Foner and Kertzer (1978) analyze the advantages and problems in twenty-one age-set African societies in which transitions from one key age group to another are more obvious than in the United States. Transitions are generally marked by formalized procedures and accompanied by great public ceremony in which individuals make these transitions, not alone, but collectively, as members of a named group. Empirical work on the impact of rites of passage in Western industrial societies is necessary. It would be desirable to have evidence gleaned from systematic study comparing individuals who experience rites of passage to those making transitions without such rituals.

Being "off-time" in making role transitions and multiple role transitions. In addition to role discontinuity and lack of preparation for new roles, it appears that being "off-time" in taking on new roles or disengaging from old ones may make transitions more stressful, and that taking on multiple roles may be more difficult for the individual than a transition to only one new role or role-set. In most societies, there seem to be social norms regarding the correct age for certain major role transitions or status passages (Riley et al. 1972; Foner and Kertzer 1978; Neugarten 1968; Elder 1976; Wilensky 1961)—the right time to start school, get married, have a child, retire, and so forth. If such role transitions occur earlier or later in life than prescribed by the norms, then stresses associated with them will be exacerbated, and socialization to the new role may be faulty or incomplete (Elder 1975, 1976; Atchley 1975; Sales 1978; Wilensky 1961). The additional strains may emanate from the individual's internalization of age norms or from reactions by peers or family or both (Sales 1978). Clausen (1972) suggests that the question of how being "earlier" or "late" affects the individual is still unanswered and bears further examination. Indeed, Neugarten and Hagestad (1976) illustrate ways in which being off-time may be beneficial, and other situations in which being off-time creates problems of adjustment for the individual. Generally, the latter type of experience seems to revolve around disrupting events that force a role transition, such as early widowhood (Albrecht 1975; Lopata 1973).

Being off-time in major role transitions may help the individual around the potentially stressful problem of having to deal with multiple, simultaneous role transitions. Several authors have commented upon difficulties involved in multiple simultaneous role transitions (Sales 1978; Neugarten and Hagestad 1976), such as the coincidence of parenthood and career building or the entrance into junior high coupled with the advent of dating and onset of puberty (Simmons et al. 1979). Neugarten and Hagestad (1976:51) suggest that by delaying one role transition while making another, the individual may "avoid an overload of role demands." (See below for a discussion of the relationship of being "off-time" and the "life-span" developmental psychology approach.)

Lack of role clarity or role consensus. Among the important problems in transitions to new roles is the lack of role clarity or the presence of role ambiguity, such that the socializee does not know how to behave in the new role. If role partners disagree about role expectations, such lack of clarity will make learning the new role problematic. As noted above, it then becomes difficult for the actor to ascertain the expectations of others during anticipatory socialization. For example, in medical schools, some instructors are Ph.D.'s, others are M.D.'s. The Ph.D. instructors value research highly and may be critical of current clinical practice. Because the views of these instructors often clash with those of practitioners, students are presented with two contradictory pictures of the role they are attempting to learn (Becker et al. 1961; Mortimer and Simmons 1978). In addition to this type of "role dissensus" among role partners holding the same status, disagreement between different types of role partners as to what is expected of role incumbents may also add to the problems of role acquisition. Definitions of the role of teacher may vary among teachers, students, principals, and parents, sometimes creating conflicts in role expectations for new role incumbents (Gross et al. 1958).

Role conflict or status-set conflict. Thus, disagreement among role partners, either those occupying the same role or different roles, as to the rights and obligations of the incumbent in one role can make learning that new role difficult. In addition, as Merton has discussed in his classic work (1957), and as we have mentioned above, the problem may not be one of ambiguity but one of clear conflict of expectations. The individual meets conflict because he occupies multiple statuses: for example, the time demands placed on him by his new job may conflict with those placed on him by his spouse. Or within the same role, both students and fellow-professors clearly expect the new professor to be a productive researcher and an excellent teacher. Yet the time spent in one activity may directly detract from the time spent in the other. These classic cases of role and status-set conflict may make it difficult for an individual to adapt to and modify a new role satisfactorily for himself and others.

More of the empirical research on role-conflict has involved the idea of stress (Levine and Scotch 1970; Lowenthal et al. 1975) than the mechanisms by which individuals in the face of pressure modify roles and the planned socialization processes. However, even the question of the impact of role-conflict on stress is not totally clear. The extent to which such conflict may be beneficial in the long run has been raised (Sheehy 1974; Presidential Science Advisory Commission 1973; Douvan and Adelson 1966; Sales 1978). Simmel once declared that membership in multiple groups that make conflicting demands provides increased opportunities to develop a complex, individuated personality (Lowenthal et al. 1975:10). The scant evidence on the effects of conflicting role demands and role conflicts on later socialization processes is unclear on this issue. Much evidence points to detrimental effects on occupational attainment by married, working women because of role conflicts (Birnbaum 1975; Pearlin 1975; Sales 1978; Bernard 1975). Research on occupational socialization gives inconsistent answers to the question of whether role conflict ultimately has a positive or negative result for either the individual or the organization. Van Maanen (1977) and Lowenthal et al. (1975) provide some support for the notion that coping with stress at one point in life facilitates later development. It appears that the long-term effects of conflicting demands, either within a role or among several roles, on individual development and on role modification are not well understood.[10] (For further discussion of the issues of conflicting role demands and of role strain, see chapter 4 in this volume.)

In summary, much of the discussion of role acquisition revolves around stresses and difficulties associated either with coping with multiple roles that make conflicting demands or with making transitions between roles or sets of roles. Many of the role transitions that are of interest are major life transitions: the movement into adolescence, marriage, parenthood, divorce, retirement, or career changes. Several contemporary perspectives concentrate, to varying degrees, on these age-linked role transitions as the basic events and processes of lifelong socialization. It is to these perspectives we now turn.

LIFE-STAGE, LIFE-SPAN, AND LIFE-COURSE PERSPECTIVES

Recently, three general perspectives or approaches to socialization throughout the lifetime have emerged. First, *life-stage* theories are derived from Erikson's (1950) psychoanalytic-stage theory. These frameworks appear to contend that development proceeds through a set pattern of sequential stages that most individuals experience (Gould 1972, Vaillant and McArthur 1972; Levinson et al. 1974; Levinson 1977). A second perspective is found in the evolving field of *life-span* developmental psychology (Baltes and Schaie 1973; Goulet and Baltes 1970), which is concerned with ontogenetic development from birth to death. Within a third paradigm, the *life-course* orientation, a variety of research has begun (Clausen 1972; Riley et al. 1972; Neugarten and Hagestad 1976). Sociological contributions are most evident in the life-course orientation; it integrates elements from G. H. Mead, Erikson, Benedict, and M. Mead and stresses the impact of social norms, role prescriptions, and group processes upon age-related life transitions. The life-stage or life-cycle perspective has gained currency through popularization (Sheehy 1974) and some work in both the life-span and the life-course areas is a reaction to some of the assumptions of the life-stage approach. Since all three paradigms raise crucial issues for the study of socialization, we will attempt to explicate the issues posed by the three frameworks.

Life-stage developmental theories. The frameworks emerging from psychoanalytic theory concentrate upon development from birth to death, but analyze development within the context of sequential stages (Levinson et al. 1974; Gould 1972). Levinson et al. summarize the basis of this approach:

> We are interested in generating . . . hypotheses concerning *relatively universal, genotypic, age-linked, adult developmental periods* within which variations occur. . . . [1974:244; italics in original]

The stages outlined by Levinson et al. (1974) are essentially similar to those outlined by other theorists (cf. Gould 1972; Vaillant and McArthur 1972); each appears to have a corollary in one of Erikson's (1950) stages.[11]

From his study of adult men,[12] Levinson develops several important generalizations regarding transitions. He maintains that:

> A myth supported by most theories of pre-adult development is that at the end of adolescence you get yourself together and, as a normal, mature adult, you enter into a relatively stable, integrated life pattern that can continue more or less indefinitely. This is a rather cruel illusion since it leads people in early adulthood

to believe that they are, or should be, fully adult and settled, and that there are no major crises or developmental changes ahead. [Levinson et al. 1974:250]

Instead of this rather tranquil picture of adult development, Levinson et al. (1974) and Gould (1972) assert that there are several key issues that must be resolved sequentially through adulthood; one is the process of "becoming one's own man" (Levinson et al. 1974), which includes a relationship with a mentor. Another is the "male mid-life crisis," which has been the focus of much relevant theorizing (Vaillant and McArthur 1972; Levinson et al. 1974; Gould 1972; Sheehy 1974; Brim 1976). It is claimed that unless the individual goes through some level of inner turmoil and reassessment at this time, further development will not occur and overall mental health will be affected adversely. Other theorists question the inevitability of major disruptions during this mid-life period (Clausen 1972; Atchley 1975; Mortimer and Simmons 1978). Levinson and Gould base their sweeping conclusions regarding the universality of this particular sequence of stages upon small samples of relatively well-educated upper middle-class men born roughly in the same generation. Yet findings are generalized to "all societies at the present stage of human evolution" (Levinson 1978:322). Clearly, the universality of these particular stages and crises is debatable (Back 1979).

Gordon's theory: a combination of life-stage and life-course perspectives. In an approach somewhat similar to those of the psychoanalytic theorists, in that it uses Erikson's (1950) notion of certain developmental issues to be solved at successive stages, Gordon (1972) proposes a stage developmental model of role and value development across the life cycle. Following Erikson (1950), Gordon maintains that resolution of the issues at any given stage is connected with successful completion of the previous stage. Unlike the psychoanalytic life-stage theorists just discussed, Gordon's theory emphasizes how socially defined roles and social institutions affect value development across the life cycle.[13]

Gordon's model pictures a sequential series of stages in the life cycle based on the integration of value themes with the self as the individual confronts new roles. The socialization process envisioned by Gordon depends upon successful completion of age-linked prior stages in order for the individual to progress to new roles. Most important for the current discussion, Gordon argues that at each stage a "structurally equivalent process ... is the mechanism [that] produces the new socialized learning and resolution" (1972:72). Thus, although the substantive tasks of socialization may differ at each point in the life cycle, the mechanisms through which each stage is resolved are quite similar. For example, the value-theme pair to be tackled in later adolescence is intimacy vs. autonomy, whereas in early maturity it is stability vs. accomplishment; yet, for both stages, interactions with others, experimenting with new roles, and attempting to resolve conflicting role demands are central ways in which progress is made.

Life-span developmental theories of socialization. The life-span approach differs from the life-stage perspective in that it does not view adult stages of change as universal, irreversible, unidirectional, or primarily age-determined. Nor does it view adult life history as being a series of stages with relatively little change within stages and abrupt change between them, but instead depicts greater variation in patterns among individuals and sub-groups (see figure 5.1).

Originally developed[14] as a counterpoint to theories of developmental psychology that posit irreversible, unidirectional, age-determined change, life-span development psychology is devoted to "the description and explication of ontogenetic (age-related) behavioral changes from birth to death" (Baltes and Goulet 1970:12). Prominent among the premises of this theoretical framework is the notion that age per se is not the most salient variable affecting change (Baltes and Goulet 1970; Baltes 1979). Recently many life-span researchers have emphasized the interaction of individual and social characteristics in explanations of behavioral change. Thus, both theoretical and empirical attention is focused on biocultural or social change and cohort effects (Hultsch and Plemons 1979; Baltes 1979; Baltes and Brim 1979; Brim and Kagan 1980). It is at this point in the intellectual growth of the life-span development orientation that it becomes almost indistinguishable from the life-course perspective. Neither purports to be a theory or a set of theories (Baltes 1979), but rather an orientation to exploring behavioral change. Much of the conceptualization of development throughout the life span is at an abstract level dealing either with the very concept of change (as discussed above) or with general models for studying antecedent-consequent relations over time, using a multicausal view (see figure 5.2).

For example, according to Baltes (1979), three sets of antecedent factors interact with each other, cumulating over time, to produce developmental change. First, there are ontogenetic age-graded (or normative age-graded) influences, that is, biological and environmental determinants highly correlated with chronological age. Second, there are evolutionary (normative history-graded) influences that basically refer to cohort effects. Finally, there are nonnormative influences that refer to events that are significant, but do not necessarily occur for everyone, such as serious illness, divorce, and so on (see figure 5.2).

The research which has come out of the life-span perspective reflects this basic model in which the three sets of influences interact.[15] Early research in this tradition (unlike that in the life-course perspective) concentrated on behaviors usually studied by developmental psychologists, such as cognitive development (Flavell 1970), moral development (Kohlberg 1973), intellectual abilities (Baltes and Schaie 1976). As the life-span perspective has gained currency, a wider range of substantive issues has been investigated using this broad orientation. Research has been concerned with such divergent topics as sex-role development (Emmerich 1973; Huston-Stein and Higgins-Trenk 1978), attachment behaviors (Lerner and Ryff 1978), family development (Hill and Mattessich 1979), and the changing meaning of personal possessions throughout the life-span (Furby 1978). To varying degrees, research done within the life-span perspective stresses the complexity of the interactions between biological, psychological, and historical antecedents as well as the interindividual variability in life experiences.

Until recently, accepted wisdom on adult cognitive development stipulated that there is a plateau and then a gradual decline in abilities

FIGURE 5.1

Conceptualizations of Change and Individual Development through the Lifetime According to Life-Stage, Life-Span and Life-Course Perspectives

Change Issues	Amount of Change Possible	Abruptness of Change	Direction of Change	Universality of Change	Origin of Change
Perspectives:					
Life Stage	Change between stages; little change within	Abrupt between stages	Unidirectional	Universal	Largely internal
Life-Span	Change throughout life but amount varies depending upon individual characteristics, life experiences, history	Varies	Reversible	Relative	Internal and external, emphasis on latter
Life Course	Change throughout life but amount varies depending upon individual experiences, age norms, cohort effects, and history	Varies	Reversible	Relative	Internal and external, much emphasis on latter

FIGURE 5.2

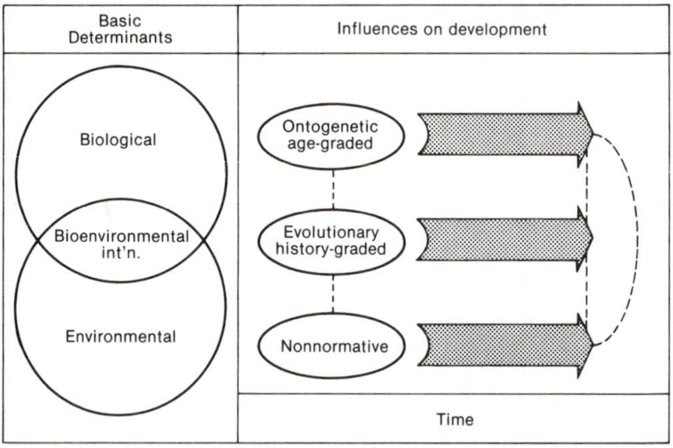

Source: From Figure 2, p. 266 in Baltes, Paul B. "Life-Span Developmental Psychology: Some Converging Observations on History and Theory." Pp. 255–79 in Paul B. Baltes and Orville G. Brim, Jr., eds., *Life-Span Development and Behavior,* vol. 2. New York: Academic Press, 1979.

(Thomae 1979). With the advent of life-span oriented research, this view has been questioned. Nesselroade, Schaie, and Baltes (1972) found that cohort effects accounted for most of the variance in cognitive performance for a sample aged twenty-one to seventy-one years of age. A seven-year follow-up failed to reveal significant changes. Baltes and Schaie (1976) maintain that consistency and change in adulthood is dependent upon a variety of individual, social, and historical variables, in particular, health, education, and socioeconomic status. Schaie (1979) concludes that theories of intelligence throughout adulthood do not take interindividual and cohort variability into account. He states that "it is abundantly clear that reliable decrement until very old age (and by that I mean late 80's) cannot be found for all abilities or for all individuals" (Schaie 1979:104). With regard to cohort differences, Schaie (1979:105) forcefully argues that "variance for ontogenetic change . . . is small relative to that demonstrated for cohort differences."

Another substantive area that has been approached fruitfully from the life-span perspective is attachment behavior. Lerner and Ryff (1978) argue that previously predominant views on attachment focus on early infancy and childhood, assuming that later attachment behavior is primarily dependent on early attachment processes. Such an assumption neglects changes in the nature and causation of attachment. In addition, prior literature has limited the concept of attachment to a dyad rather than a social network and has failed to recognize cultural and historical differences in attachment behavior. According to Lerner and Ryff, infant-caregiver dyads differ considerably from adolescent dating relationships and, in turn, are quite different from marriage relationships both in the nature of the attachment relationships and the process by which they develop. In addition, both infant caregiver and heterosexual attachments are expressed differently in varying cultural and historical milieus. In part, the utility of the life-span approach appears to be the way in which it leads researchers to challenge heretofore accepted assumptions regarding both substance and method.

Similarly, the life-span orientation alerts us to differences in the ways in which individuals experience similar life events. Stressful life events and adaptation to them are a central theme in many investigations of socialization (Holmes and Rahe 1967; Datan and Ginsberg 1975; Lowenthal, Thurnber, and Chiriboga 1975; Lopata 1973; Rossi 1968). As discussed above, role transitions occur because of such life events; much attention in the life-span orientation is devoted to factors or processes that mediate the impact of stressful life events.

Using this approach, Hultsch and Plemons (1979) examine a variety of variables and processes that affect individual response to life events. They look at "individual" and "cultural" events, such as periods of depression, economic prosperity, war, and so forth; the former include marriage, birth of a child, death of a loved one, whereas the latter "are not experienced as a part of the usual life course and (which) affect a larger number of individuals." It is the intersection of these kinds of events that makes the life experience of each cohort unique. For example, Elder's (1974) work on children of the Great Depression reveals that men who experienced this cultural event early in their work careers were more negatively affected in the long run than were those already established. Hultsch and Plemons (1979:21) argue that this finding highlights the importance of concentrating upon timing and sequencing of life events within a historical context.

Thus, we can see that research done within the life-span orientation concentrates upon a variety of factors and processes ranging from the biological to the historical, with an emphasis upon the interaction between ontogenetic, age-graded development and the cultural or historical context.

The life-course perspective on socialization. Similarly, theories now emerging on the life course place emphasis on progression through socially defined, age-linked roles (Neugarten 1968; Riley 1976, 1979; Clausen 1972). Indeed, as figure 5.2 illustrates, there appear to be many similarities between the life-span and life-course approaches. The difference is mainly one of intellectual origin and emphasis. Life-span views originated in the early 1970s within developmental psychology (Goulet and Baltes 1970). At the same time, sociologists (Elder 1976; Clausen 1972; Riley et al. 1972) were voicing similar substantive and methodological concerns. Now the two approaches are quite similar. However, life-span views are still more concerned with age-related development and the degree of stability of personality over time, while life-course views focus more on age-graded norms, generation effects, role transitions, and historical context. Reflecting its origin, life-span developmental psychology places greater emphasis on the individual, whereas the life-course approach concentrates on social structure. However, along certain analytical dimensions, these differences appear miniscule.

Like Gordon's framework and the life-span approach, these life-course perspectives concentrate less on biological bases for transitions than do the psychoanalytic theories. This is so because after the individual reaches adulthood, age per se is viewed as the basis for life-course stages only to the extent that age norms regarding role transitions are clear and widely accepted in a given society (Clausen 1972; Elder 1975). Therefore, the life course is defined by a series of multiple, interlinked roles and transitions (Clausen 1972; Neugarten and Hagestad 1976; Riley, Johnson, and Foner 1972; Elder 1975; Atchley 1975). There is no one particular sequential set of roles outlined by the life-course perspective; rather the life course may be seen as "a crude road map with quite a few alternative routes . . . a successively bigger equation" (Atchley 1975:261–62). However, the character of the completion of a given transition may narrow future alternatives (Atchley 1975; Clausen 1972).

Much attention in this perspective is given to the ways in which social norms and definitions influence the pattern of the life course. Neugarten (1968) and Neugarten and Hagestad (1976) observe that age-related norms provide a social timetable for major role transitions. Although most members of society may shape their life courses by such a social clock, it by no means determines the precise pattern of an individual's life course (Clausen 1973; Atchley 1975). Individual sequencing that is divergent from norms, as well as historical events that upset the age-grading clock, may alter patterns either for individuals or entire age cohorts. An individual may postpone higher education to "find" him- or herself, thus deviating from both the age-grade norms and work ethic norms as well. Historical events, such as wars or depressions, impinge upon the timing of life events, such as marriage, completion of education, and childbearing.

Social definitions of age-appropriate roles and behaviors are one important link between social structure and individuals (Riley, Johnson, and Foner 1972; Riley 1976; Foner and Kertzer 1978). Elder (1975:167) puts it well: "birth, puberty and death are biological facts in the life course, but their meanings in society are social facts or constructions." In addition, the pattern, and even the sequence, of role transitions over the life course are different for those in various positions in the social structure (Clausen 1972; Neugarten and Hagestad 1976; Mortimer and Simmons 1978). For example, possibilities for continued upward mobility within a career are more likely to characterize high socioeconomic status jobs such as those in upper-level management and the professions.

History and social structure may intersect to produce distinctive life-course patterns for members from different birth cohorts (Riley, Johnson, and Foner 1972; Elder 1974, 1975; Riley 1976). Mannheim's (1952) notion that each cohort may have very different socialization experiences and that sub-groups within a cohort may experience historical events differently leads to the hypothesis that the life course may look different for various cohorts and for sub-groups (Elder 1975). Mannheim proposes that intra-cohort differences arise from (1) differential exposure to events; (2) varying interpretations of them; and (3) resultant modes of response. Position in the social structure is related to these three factors. For example, Braungart (1975) uncovers distinctly different attitudes toward the Vietnam War for college and non-college youth of the same cohort.

Elder discovers differences in the impact of the Great Depression upon children from relatively deprived and those from relatively nondeprived families.[16] For boys from deprived families, changes in the family division of labor meant getting a job which resulted in "accelerated movement toward the adult world" (p. 277). Another major change in family relationships involved domination of family relationships by the mother. Both of these changes appear to have made the boys from deprived families more vocationally aware (p. 297) and more likely to view values of job security and family life as important when they became adults.

Another way in which history and social structure interact to affect the life course is through differences in age-graded norms over time. Definitions of childhood and adulthood have changed through history (Ariès 1965). The number of life periods appears to be expanding over time (Neugarten and Hagestad 1976; Riley 1979). For example, adolescence is a relatively new period in the life course (Dragastin and Elder 1975), and as people live to be older and children leave home earlier, there are more distinctive transitions in middle age (Maas and Kuypers 1974; Neugarten and Hagestad 1976).

Changes in timing of life-course events are evident during different historical periods, aside from those attributable to discontinuous social change such as war or depressions. Neugarten and Datan (1973) examine data for 1890 and 1966 that reveal that the median age for life events, excluding leaving school and death of loved ones, has dropped. Neugarten and Datan (1973:66–67) explain that "historically the family cycle has quickened as marriage, parenthood, empty nest and grandparenthood all occur earlier. The trend is toward a more rapid rhythm of events through most of the family cycle."

Finally, as noted above in our discussion of being "off-time" in making role-transitions, dilemmas can be created when life-course transitions for an individual deviate from sequences considered normative for his/her particular sub-group. Elder (1976) discusses the relevant case of unplanned parenthood and Wilensky (1961) analyzes the case of disorderly work careers.

Issues raised by consideration of the life-stage, life-span and life-course perspectives. There are several threads that may tie together the various life-stage, life-span, and life-course approaches to socialization. By examining these threads we may be able to sort out important issues for the study of socialization processes over the lifetime.

The first issue deals with the correspondence of life transitions to biological age. To varying degrees, these perspectives are concerned with sequential role transitions. The extent to which an invariant, time-determined sequence is posited differs considerably with the psychoanalytically oriented theories explicitly matching age periods to particular life stages (Levinson et al. 1974; Levinson 1977; Gould 1972). Within the broad life-course orientation, some theorists argue that although there may be individual variation, life-course transitions are closely linked to age because of age-graded norms in most societies (Neugarten 1968; Riley 1976), whereas others view the connection between age and passage through life-course transitions as more tenuous (Clausen 1972; Atchley 1975).

There is more agreement between the life-stage and life-course perspectives regarding the sequence of major role transitions than on the timing of them. Although the content of stages described by various frameworks may differ, the notion that one transition must be resolved before adjustment to another may proceed appears to be widely accepted (Levinson et al. 1974; Clausen 1972; Gordon 1972; Lowenthal et al. 1975). This is not to say that each period or transition is neatly packaged and disposed of before the individual embarks on further changes, but rather that most issues prominent in a given life period are at least confronted, if not resolved.

Another issue is the question of whether completion of one phase in the sequence of the life course necessitates a "life crisis" (Brim 1976; Clausen 1973; Atchley 1975; Albrecht 1975).[17] As Sheehy (1974) points out, the word *crisis* has a negative meaning in our culture, so some of the confusion about the necessity of a crisis may emanate from the pejorative connotation of the term itself. Sheehy (1974) refers to critical transitions as "passages," whereas Atchley (1975) calls them "turning points." Several authors contend that such transitions need not be characterized by stress and turmoil (Clausen 1972; Atchley 1975; Albrecht 1975; Mortimer and Simmons 1978). For example, there is some evidence that quality of life is perceived as better, not worse, after all children have "left the nest" (Lowenthal and Chiriboga 1972).

A number of factors may make the transitions more or less difficult: that is, variation in the level of anticipatory socialization (Atchley 1975; Mortimer and Simmons 1978; Clausen 1968; Gordon 1972), desirability of the transition (Glaser and Strauss 1971; Pearlin and Lieberman 1979), and multiplicity of changes encountered (M. Mead 1949). Several authors assert that group support for the individual experiencing a life transition may be useful in softening the impact of undesirable or involuntary transitions (Lopata 1973; Atchley 1975). Peers who have already gone through a transition, such as divorce or widowhood, may be helpful. Many life transitions may be positive and/or voluntary, but include distasteful experiences; these may be made less harsh by a set of peers who are going through the transition simultaneously. Professional socialization is an excellent example of such a situation (Van Maanen 1977; Rosow 1974; Becker et al. 1961; Mortimer and Simmons 1978; Bucher and Stelling 1977). For example, medical students overwhelmed by the amount of material to be learned find that the student sub-culture provides guides as to which aspects of study are more important for earning satisfactory grades (Becker et al. 1961; Fox 1957; Van Maanen 1977; Rosow 1974).

Furthermore, Clausen has hypothesized that there might be wide individual variations in the experience of turning points, with some individuals finding them stressful and others experiencing little or no turmoil. Lowenthal et al. (1975) offer support for this generalization and emphasize variations in individual perception of similar events as stressful. Recent research (Pearlin and Lieberman 1979) suggests that the difficulties of life changes in general have been overstated. Rather, Pearlin and Lieberman (1979) find that transitions involving loss are hard to adjust to, but others are not particularly difficult.[18]

As Mortimer and Simmons note:

> The potential problems and strains attending major life cycle changes are well described in the literature and the need for further socialization is clearly im-

plied. Still, there are some studies that question whether all of these role changes are really as problematic and discontinuous as they appear (see Bengtson, 1973; Lowenthal et al., 1975). Adjustment to new parenthood (Deutscher, 1968; Russell, 1974; Fein, 1976), the empty nest (Cain, 1964; Lowenthal and Chiriboga, 1972; Glenn, 1975; Clausen, 1976; Hagestad, 1977) and retirement (Friedmann and Orback, 1974; Maas and Kuypers, 1974; Bengtson et al., 1977) may be relatively positive experiences, at least for certain categories of people. [1978:426]

One other theme that pervades all of the life-stage, life-span, and life-course frameworks is that socialization over the lifetime can be characterized by both continuity and change. Since each transition builds, to some extent, on earlier ones, there is continuity. However, each turning point contains the potential for varying degrees of change. The question, of course, is to determine what factors contribute to each. Maas and Kuypers (1974) find considerable consistency in personality over individual lifetimes (Mortimer and Lorence 1980), whereas Lowenthal et al. (1975) reveal both changes and continuities in value orientations and adaptive responses throughout the life course. They find that men's and women's value orientations change differently across various life stages. The major time of value reorientation for men, according to them, is that of retirement, whereas for women it comes with marriage.

Conclusion

In conclusion, the following prominent themes in the contemporary study of socialization through the life course appear to have originated in the classical antecedents to the topic. First, are there discernible continuities in socialization processes throughout life? Related to this question is the issue of consistency of the self over the lifetime. A second theme that raises a number of questions is that of the universality of life stages. Can we identify socialization experiences and sequences that generalize across time and space? In particular, do members of different birth cohorts, sexes, or social classes encounter similar transitions through their lives? The last theme that underlies virtually all discussion of socialization is the extent to which socialization processes promote change or stability in either individuals or societies. In this concluding section, we discuss briefly each of these themes in turn.

CONTINUITIES IN SOCIALIZATION: CONSISTENCY OF THE SELF

As we have noted, early views of socialization (Freud 1966) argue that the self is established relatively early and that little significant change occurs subsequent to becoming an adult. Following G. H. Mead (1934), more recent approaches view the self as more malleable (Becker 1964; Brim 1968; Clausen 1972). The individual may become "a different person by virtue of changing physique, changing major social roles and changing participation" (Clausen 1972). Research on occupations and values suggests that individuals may shift basic orientations dramatically as they move into different work and family roles (Van Maanen 1977; Mortimer and Lorence 1979). A more pervasive pattern may be that suggested by Brim (1968; see above) and Becker (1964). Small shifts in behaviors, value orientations, and roles may cumulate over years, resulting in dramatic changes over the long run, but continuity over the short term.

CONTINUITY OF SOCIALIZATION PROCESSES

Although the content and context of learning may differ considerably over the life course, it appears that virtually the same processes of socialization are in operation throughout. In the broadest terms, role learning seems to be the basic process of socialization, especially after adolescence. Acquisition of roles is a key socialization process (Gordon 1972; Brim 1968; Rosow 1974) whether we conceive of role learning proceeding through observation of reference groups, modeling (identification theory), the application of previously acquired behaviors and cognitions to new situations (generalization, accommodation), or through situational adjustments (symbolic interaction).

UNIVERSALITY OF SOCIALIZATION PROCESSES AND STAGES

Much research on childhood socialization has involved investigating social class (Kohn 1969; Bronfenbrenner 1958; Rosenberg and Pearlin 1978; Rosenbaum 1975), culture (Inkeles 1968; Inkeles and Smith 1974; Kohn 1969), sex (Maccoby and Jacklin 1974), and historical (Ariès 1965; Elder 1974) differences in content and process. In light of these intensive efforts, it is surprising how little attention is given to the issue of universality of socialization experiences throughout the life course. However, possible differences between birth cohorts, sexes, and social classes have been suggested.

As noted above, much of the literature on life stages (or life cycles) (Gould 1972, 1978; Levinson et al. 1974; Levinson 1977; Maas and Kuypers 1974) relies on data from one birth cohort to make generalizations regarding life-course transitions and socialization processes. Recently, several researchers (notably Elder 1974, 1975; Bengtson 1975; Bengtson and Cutler 1976; Riley et al. 1972; Riley 1976; Neugarten and Hagestad 1976) have pointed out that socialization experiences and life-course transitions may differ considerably among various birth cohorts. In particular, the timing and characteristics of major life transitions, such as completion of schooling, first marriage, birth of first child, or retirement, may vary considerably. Much of the work in this area has revolved around the shifting patterns in women's lives, especially changes in labor force participation and childbearing (Riley et al. 1972; Sales 1978; Elder 1975). That is, the proportion of women who continue to be employed after childbearing or who return to work when children enter school has risen dramatically since the 1950s (Huston-Stein and Higgins-Trenk 1978). Thus, transition to the role of mother has a very different meaning for women from birth cohorts of the 1930s, 1940s, and 1950s than it did for women from earlier cohorts. Instead of exchanging one role (employed person) for another (mother), the individual adds to her role repertoire.

More attention has been given to sex differences in major life transitions than to birth cohort differences (Lowenthal et al. 1975; Maccoby and Jacklin 1974; Sheehy 1974; Riley et al. 1972; Sales 1978; Simmons et al. 1979). It appears that men and women go through life transitions in different orders (Lowenthal et al. 1975; Sheehy 1974; Maas and Kuypers 1974; Sales 1978) and at different ages. Since women traditionally have married men older than themselves, women therefore marry earlier than men, resulting in earlier termination of education.

Class differences in sequence and timing of life transitions are acknowledged in the literature, but not dealt with either theoretically or empirically. Several authors have conjectured that the pattern of life stages may be distinctive for working-class people because they enter the labor market earlier and marry earlier than do middle-class individuals (Atchley 1975; Elder 1975; Levison 1975; Komarovsky 1964; Persell 1977). Beyond stating that there may be class differences in socialization across the life cycle, there is virtually no work on the socialization processes that impinge upon the experience of working-class people throughout their lives. This is especially problematic for the work of the psychoanalytic theorists; the socialization experiences portrayed in their work are based on a decidedly affluent, successful sample of persons (Cain 1979). It is safe to say that the life stages presented in the literature may be representative only of a small group of the population. Therefore, there is a need to study working-class and minority men and women to further our knowledge of socialization processes over the life course.[19]

The assumption that major life transitions must be experienced as crises ignores ways in which history, in the form of generation, and social structure may intersect with socialization processes. Benedict (1938) first commented upon how social institutions or organizations may make life transitions more discontinuous and thus more difficult for the individual. Simmons et al. (1979) present a case in point in their studies of the transition into adolescence. They find that girls who have experienced the coincidence of the onset of puberty, commencement of dating, and entry into a junior high school in seventh grade are at a greater disadvantage in terms of self-image than are girls who are pubertal and date, but have remained in an elementary school for seventh grade. It appears that some features of the junior high type of school organization may make the transition into adolescence for girls more difficult compared to the elementary school context.

Another example of a transition possibly exacerbated by social institutions is the empty nest syndrome (Lowenthal and Chiriboga 1972; Lowenthal et al. 1975). Many women simultaneously enter menopause and lose a central role when grown children leave the home. Although it is not clear to what extent this transition is stressful (Mortimer and Simmons 1978),[20] it is possible that this transition will become less problematic for future generations of women who have a multiplicity of roles remaining after children leave home (Sales 1978; Neugarten and Hagestad 1976), or who view society as allowing for the possibility of new roles and personal growth outside the family (Lowenthal et al. 1975).

SOCIALIZATION, SOCIAL CHANGE, OR STABILITY

An important issue often raised (Riley et al. 1972; Elder 1975; Mortimer and Simmons 1978) revolves around the relationship between processes of socialization and social change. The processes of socialization contain an essential contradiction. Although socialization serves to perpetuate the existing society—its ideology, roles, norms, and values—socialization also contains the seeds for change (Mannheim 1952; Bowles and Gintis 1976; Engels 1972; Elder 1975). At the individual level, a similar contradiction is found. Socialization processes, particularly role acquisition, promote continuity and stability in the self, but at the same time open the possibility for significant individual change (Clausen 1968, 1973; Sales 1978; Thornton and Nardi 1975; Brim 1968).

One of the primary functions of socialization is to reproduce existing forms of social organization (Inkeles 1968; Clausen 1968) and ideology (Bowles and Gintis 1976; Persell 1977; Althusser 1971). Much of childhood socialization is devoted to inculcating societal values, norms, and appropriate social roles so that each successive generation will carry on group goals. Later socialization centers around passage through socially defined patterns and sequences of roles and role sets. Viewing socialization only in this way presupposes a one-way interaction: society molds the individual to fit into existing roles and the individual is seen as a passive receiver rather than an actor.

Obviously such a unidirectional model does not capture the complexity of the process. Yet, until recently, most theories of socialization assumed such a one-way interaction. Not only does it appear that the socializee influences the socializer (Gewirtz 1969), but the individual may redefine social roles and obligations instead of simply accepting them (Thornton and Nardi 1975; Sales 1978; Goffman 1961a). Such a process is credited with bringing about social change over generations (Mannheim 1952; Riley et al. 1972) and redefinition of one role over time (for example, marital roles; see Brim 1968; Hill 1970).

Although there has been considerable research in the areas of role conflict, role ambiguity, and role dissensus, the impact of such factors upon socialization has not been fully explored. One is interested not only in the degree of stress felt in such ambiguous situations, but in the effects on role learning itself and in the extent to which new occupants are able to shape and change such roles.

NOTES

The work of the second author is supported by an NIMH Research Scientist Development Award 1 KO5 MH 41688.

1. "A drive is a genetically determined, psychic constituent which, when oper-

ative, produces a state of psychic tension. This tension impels the individual to activity which is also genetically determined in a general way, but which can be considerably altered by individual experience" (Brenner 1974:17).

2. Individuals may identify with others for a variety of reasons. Freud stressed two basic types of identification: anaclitic identification is based upon dependence, nurturance, and trust; defensive identification or identification with the aggressor is based on fear of a powerful other, classically the fear of the father for the male child (cf. Bandura 1969).

3. "A structure is a system of transformations. Inasmuch as it is a system and not a mere collection of elements and their properties, these transformations involve laws: the structure is preserved or enriched by the interplay of its transformation laws, which never yield results external to the system nor employ elements that are external to it. In short, the notion of structure is comprised of three key ideas: the idea of wholeness, the idea of transformation, and the idea of self-regulation" (Piaget 1970:5).

4. Since there are many sources that serve as summaries of the work of these influential theorists (Stone and Farberman 1970; G. H. Mead 1934; Clausen 1968) and because other chapters in this volume cover them, we will not dwell on them here.

5. It is interesting to note that both theorists use the metaphor of the game—marbles for Piaget and baseball for Mead—to describe the development of the self through social interaction.

6. Briefly, the developmental tasks envisioned by Erikson are: 1. Trust vs. Mistrust; 2. Autonomy vs. Shame and Doubt; 3. Initiative vs. Guilt; 4. Industry vs. Inferiority; 5. Identity vs. Role Confusion; 6. Intimacy vs. Isolation; 7. Generativity vs. Self-Absorption; 8. Integrity vs. Despair. The first five stages correspond to Freud's oral, anal, phallic, latency, and genital periods respectively; the last three are seen as tasks of adulthood. A more detailed description of the stages is given in Erikson (1950:273).

7. Piaget mentions that "equilibration by self-regulation constitutes the formative process of the structures we have described. Child psychology enables us to follow their step-by-step evolution, not in the abstract, but in the lived and living dialectic of subjects who are faced, in each generation, with endlessly recurring problems and who sometimes arrive at solutions that are slightly better than those of previous generations" (Piaget and Inhelder 1969:159).

8. Gordon (1972) argues that in the United States anticipatory socialization is more accurate and visible for parental roles than for marital roles. He observes that everyone has been a child and that many individuals have helped care for younger siblings. Furthermore, he asserts that friends and relatives may be more likely to offer practical advice on parenting than on marital roles. Brim (1968) also comments on the wealth of formal training available to prospective and new parents. See also Rossi (1968).

9. Many authors who discuss rites of passage in the context of role discontinuity concentrate on positive or desirable status passages. However, as Glaser and Strauss (1971) illustrate, some passages may be quite negative for the individual and the rites of passage may then be a form of punitive social control, such as the initial encounters in incarceration.

10. It has been emphasized that the *short-term* effects of such role conflicts are negative for the individual experiencing them, as research in the areas of occupations and sex roles reveals (Van Maanen 1977; Bernard 1975; Gross, Mason, and McEachern 1958).

11. Levinson's stages are: (1) leaving the family (16–20); (2) getting into the adult world (20–24 to 27–29); (3) settling down (29–late 30s–early 40s; (4) becoming one's own man (35–39); (5) mid-life transition (early 40s); (6) restabilization (45–on). These stages are comparable to the last three stages of Erikson's (1950) eight ages of man which are: (1) basic trust vs. mistrust (0–1); (2) autonomy vs. shame and doubt (1–2); (3) initiative vs. guilt (3–5); (4) industry vs. inferiority (6–12); (5) identity vs. role confusion (13–17); (6) intimacy vs. isolation (18–30); (7) generativity vs. stagnation (30–65); (8) integrity vs. despair (65–on).

12. Sales (1978) draws out comparable stages for women using Levinson's and Gould's (1972) outline.

13. In so doing, Gordon integrates concepts and processes from Freud, Piaget, G. H. Mead, and Erikson.

14. There are several good histories of the intellectual evolution of the life-span perspective; one of the most recent is Baltes 1979. Originally the life-span perspective began as a subfield in developmental psychology, but recently theorists have dropped the label *developmental psychology* and replaced it with *life-span development.*

15. For a programmatic statement on the life-span developmental research paradigms, see Baltes and Schaie (1973), Baltes and Goulet (1970), and Baltes (1979).

16. Level of deprivation simply refers to income losses and is not an index of class; it measures a family's loss in income (Elder 1974:276).

17. These ideas are similar to Erikson's (1950) notion that adolescence is a period of necessary "identity crisis."

18. Three interesting findings from Lowenthal et al.'s (1975) longitudinal study could direct further theorizing and research on the issue of the stress involved in life-cycle changes. Lowenthal et al. (1975:174–75) reveal that as people age, events previously viewed as stressful are reevaluated and, in retrospect, are seen as less troublesome. Second, in line with previous work on role conflicts encountered by women, Bernard (1975), Frieze et al. (1977), Lowenthal et al. (1975) report that women enumerate more stressful events at all life stages than do men. Last, the younger respondents reported more positive stresses, whereas older subjects said they experienced more negative stress.

19. There are several pieces that touch upon these issues; see Komarovsky (1964) and Chinoy (1968).

20. Lowenthal and Chiriboga (1972) find that men and women look forward to directing energies previously oriented toward childrearing toward new pursuits when the youngest child is about to leave home. However, in a later work (Lowenthal et al. 1975:235–36), they discover that women approaching "the post parental stage showed signs of desperation—the more so if children gave any indication that they were not choosing to adopt the parental mores and ways of life."

6 VIKTOR GECAS

Contexts of Socialization

Introduction

PERSPECTIVES ON SOCIALIZATION

Within sociology, the concept of socialization has had two fairly distinct meanings. For much of its history, it has been used to denote the individual's adaptation and conformity of one kind or another—conformity to role expectations, to the opinions of others, to the norms and values of society. This conception of socialization has been most closely associated with the structural functionalist perspective, and, in spite of frequent critiques (most notably Wrong's 1961 criticism that it offers an "over-socialized" view of man), it remains prominent in the field (see, for example, Inkeles's view of socialization as social adaptation, 1969:616). This conception tends to view socialization from the point of view of society or the social group to which an individual belongs. Socialization of new members is the means by which a society perpetuates itself.

If the frame of reference is the individual rather than the group, then the concept of socialization takes on a somewhat different meaning. Here the emphasis is on the development of the person, rather than on the transmission of culture. Socialization in this sense refers to the process of development or change that a person undergoes as a result of social influences (Gecas, 1979a:365). Its focus tends to be the development of self-concept, identity and various attitudes, dispositions, and behaviors of the individual. Tallman and Ihinger-Tallman (1977) define socialization as a process of negotiating identities. Similarly, Stryker conceptualizes socialization "largely . . . as a matter of the shaping of self-concepts" (1979:177).

The sociological tradition most closely associated with this view of socialization is symbolic interactionism. Grounded in the social psychological writings of Mead, Cooley, James, and Thomas, this perspective offers a conception of socialization as a continuous process of negotiated interactions out of which selves are created and re-created. The hallmark of this perspective is the emphasis it places on *symbolic* interaction as the natural milieu for human existence; the emergence of mind, self, and social structure out of this interaction process; the active role played by the actor in the construction of self and social situation; the importance of role-taking as a mechanism of self-knowledge and knowledge of others enabling social interaction to take place; and the fluid, somewhat unpredictable, nature of the whole enterprise (see Chapter 1, this volume and Meltzer et al. 1975 for more extensive treatments of this perspective). Symbolic interactionism has had a major influence on sociological thinking about socialization. Along with generating numerous descriptions of socialization processes as they occur in various social settings (for example, subcultures, deviant groups, specific occupations), its influence is conspicuous in some of the contemporary, concept-specific, theoretical offshoots bearing on the analysis of socialization—*self theory, reference-group theory,* and *labeling theory.* Whether these offshoots constitute theory in a formal sense is debatable. But they do refer to important concepts and processes for a sociological orientation to socialization.

In summary, the concept of socialization has two fairly distinct meanings in sociology, stemming from different frames of reference and associated with different intellectual traditions. One point of view stresses the individual's *adaptation* and conformity to societal requirements; the other emphasizes the individual's development into a self-assertive, distinct human being. Both of these perspectives and frames of reference are valid and necessary for an adequate conception of socialization (see Clausen 1968 and DiRenzo 1977b for a review of various conceptions of socialization.) It should also be stressed that these adaptations and identity negotiations typically take place in organized social contexts. The changes that individuals undergo as a result of social influences become sociologically relevant in the context of organized social relationships. In this sense, there is a "membership" component to a sociological conception of socialization. To be socialized is to belong.

This component of socialization is most evident in the concept of identification, one of the key processes in socialization. Two aspects of identification are relevant here: identification *of* and identification *with* (Stone 1962). Both refer to matters of identity. Identification *of* deals with the establishment of identities, that is, the determination of who one is and who the others are in the situation. Identification *with* refers to the emotional and psychological attachment that one has with some person or group. Identification with the socializer or the socializing group makes one more receptive to their influence and motivated to be socialized in accordance with their standards. It is in the interest of socializing agents and agencies to encourage the socializees' identification with their socializers, and in the process, to develop identities appropriate to the group's purposes and goals.

CONTEXTS OF SOCIALIZATION

There is another sociological tradition that has a bearing on the topic of this chapter. The classical tradition in sociology, reflected in the writings of Weber, Marx, and Simmel, has been concerned with the social structural bases of human experience. Focusing on the *contexts* within which socialization takes place, especially the organizational and institutional settings, requires that special attention be given to the *social structural* features of the situations as they affect socialization processes and thereby influence the individuals involved. Social structure is commonly defined as stable patterns of social interaction in a group. But the concept also subsumes other aspects of the group such as its composition (sex and age, for example), and other group features such as size, density, permeability of boundaries, and so forth. Families are different from classrooms, peer groups are different from prisons, and occupational organizations are different from religious conversion settings with regard to the structure of their social relations. One of the tasks of this chapter will be to examine how aspects of the social structure of various socialization settings set the stage for the socialization processes that take place. As Wheeler points out: "Just as individuals may become differently socialized because of differences in past experiences, motivations and capacities, so may they become differently socialized because of differences in the structure of the social settings in which they interact" (1966:53).

The number of contexts of socialization in a complex society is almost limitless. For that matter, *all* socialization is contextual in that it occurs in some social situation. Situations that are occasions for socialization vary in scope and duration, from relatively trivial and fleeting encounters to totally absorbing and enduring experiences. My strategy in this chapter will be first to consider some of the dimensions of social context that can be expected to affect socialization; then to focus on a small sample of socialization contexts selected to reflect variations on some of these dimensions.

SOME DIMENSIONS OF SOCIALIZATION CONTEXTS

Much of the socialization that takes place in our society occurs in the context of social institutions or organizations, such as family, school, prison, and work setting. The explicit goal or mandate of many of these organizations is to change people. Wheeler points out that socialization is increasingly a function of large-scale, bureaucratic organizations (1966:53). One is expected to learn basic cognitive skills in school, to get advanced training in universities, to be treated for mental illness in an asylum, or to be subject to rehabilitation programs in prison.

At the level of general organization goals, Wheeler distinguishes between "developmental socialization systems" and "re-socialization systems." The former refers to organizations, such as family and school, "whose formal purpose is the training, education or, more generally, the further socialization of the individuals passing through" (1966:68). The latter refers to organizations "where the formal purpose is to make up for or correct some deficiency in earlier socialization. These are largely organizations designed to re-socialize the deviant" (1966:68). Wheeler's referents for re-socialization organizations are prisons and mental hospitals. But this category may also apply to religious and political organizations with missionary functions, to military organizations training recruits, and to various rehabilitation groups. One reason this distinction is important is because different processes may be involved when the goal is re-socialization. For example, a process of "unlearning" is frequently described as a necessary step in the re-socialization process. That is, old identities, beliefs, and values may have to be abandoned in the process of creating a new self-concept and world view.

Not all organizations and groups involved in socialization have as their explicit goal the socialization or re-socialization of their members. For some, it is quite an incidental and frequently unintended consequence of group membership. Most occupational organizations are of this nature as are most peer groups or friendship groups. The socialization that takes place within these contexts may be quite consequential for the individuals involved and for the organization or group, as we shall see, but it may also be quite distant from the major purposes of these organizations. Even within organizations whose major purpose is socialization, a great deal of "incidental" learning takes place. As Dreeben (1968:44) observed with regard to the socialization in public schools: what is learned is not always the same as what is taught. This distinction between intentional and unintentional socialization will be important to several of the contexts considered.

Two of the most important elements of the internal structure of socialization contexts are the role system and the power distribution. The role system refers to the configuration of social statuses, along with the behavioral expectations, rights, and responsibilities, operating in a group. It can be quite formal and rigid, as typically found in bureaucratic organizations, or the role system can be loose, amorphous, and emergent, as in peer groups. Roles provide one of the main contents of socialization in that they encompass specific identities (for example, teacher), behaviors (teaching), values (knowledge is good), and beliefs (diligent study leads to knowledge and increased competence). But even more important, roles provide a major link between the social system and the individual. Two characteristics of roles are relevant in this regard: their reciprocity and their embeddedness. Role expectations refer not only to the conduct of the role occupant, but also to various others in their interactions with the role occupant. Merton's (1957) concept of "role-set" captures this reciprocal nature of roles by showing how a particular role is typically located in a whole set or constellation of alter-roles connected to the given role by reciprocal bonds. For example, part of the role-set of "teacher" involves role expectations vis-a-vis students, parents, school administrators, and colleagues. In this way, the role occupant is embedded in a set of interpersonal relationships.

Roles, then, are part of the social environment, embedded in cultural systems and distinguishable to some extent from the individuals who occupy them at any given time. Yet, they are also molded and fashioned by their individual occupants and (to a greater or lesser degree) become sources of personal identity, values, and beliefs. Consequently, roles provide a means for anchoring individuals to social systems. Socialization, especially for adults, is to a large extent the learning of social roles (Brim 1968:186).

The conditions under which individuals become committed to the roles they play, or conversely alienated from these roles, are important considerations for the topic of socialization. Turner (1978) has formulated a number of propositions dealing with the conditions under which person and role are likely to merge: (1) individuals tend to merge with those roles by which significant others identify them; (2) there is a tendency to merge role and person selectively so as to maximize autonomy and positive self-evaluations; and (3) a person is more likely to merge with those roles in which investment has been greatest (1978:13). The first two of Turner's principles are especially relevant to the topic of socialization, as we shall see.

An important element of role systems bearing on socialization is the distribution of power within them. With the possible exception of friendship groups, power tends to be unequally distributed in socialization contexts. The power disparity is especially evident in such institutional role relationships as guard/prisoner, doctor/patient, parent/child, teacher/pupil. Individuals whose formal status in the group involves the socialization of others typically have considerable power over those formally designated as socializees. The latter, however, are not powerless even in the most (formally) asymmetrical of power distributions. Within the context of formal organizations, the power of the socializees is, to a large extent, a function of their numbers relative to the number of staff or agents of socialization. In general, the smaller the socialization ratio (number of agents/number of socializees), the greater the power of the socializees. In such institutional settings as schools, prisons, and mental hospitals where the socialization ratio is quite small and where there are large numbers of people in roughly the same formal status categories, social organization and subcultures among socializees are likely to emerge (Wheeler 1966). Such subcultures frequently develop in directions antithetical to the main socialization goals of the institution.

Along with differences in goals, socialization ratios, and power and role systems, socialization contexts also differ with regard to such other features as intensity and affective climate, degree of self-sufficiency or isolation (total institutions versus more open systems), the nature of the socializee cohort (children versus adults, homogeneous versus heterogeneous), mode of entry for new socializees (voluntary versus involuntary), and physical characteristics (size, density, visibility). These are some of the salient dimensions of socialization contexts which set the stage for the socialization processes and outcomes that result.

In this chapter, a small number of socialization contexts are examined, reflecting variations on most of the dimensions discussed. Five socialization contexts were selected: family, school, peer group, occupational setting, and radical re-socialization settings. Although there are a number of similarities between these contexts on a number of the dimensions, there are also substantial differences. In general, families are more involved in developmental socialization, as are (to a lesser extent) peer groups and public schools, conversion contexts are more involved in re-socialization. Socialization in schools and conversion settings is largely intentional, whereas in peer groups and work settings it is largely unintentional. The role systems tend to be more formal and the power disparity greater in school, family, occupational settings, and re-socialization contexts compared to the power and role systems in peer groups. The socialization ratio tends to be larger and interactions more intense and intimate in family, peer group, and re-socialization contexts, whereas the socialization ratio is smaller in school and, perhaps, work settings (depending on the nature of the job). The scope of socialization is relatively broad in the family, peer, and re-socialization contexts, and narrower in school and occupational settings. Participation in the socialization experience is typically voluntary in work and peer contexts, involuntary in family and school, with both modes of entry represented in re-socialization settings. The socializees are primarily children in family, school, and childhood peer group contexts, and usually adults in occupational and re-socialization contexts. These differences between the various contexts on any one dimension may not be very sharp, but when they are considered in aggregate, it becomes apparent that these contexts represent quite different socialization experiences.

This essay is not meant to be an extensive and thorough review of the socialization literature on each of these contexts. Rather, my aim is to consider some of the key processes and structural characteristics that have a socializing effect on individuals in these contexts. Some of the more specific questions guiding this examination are: What are the important structural features in each context? What aspects of the individual are affected by these structural features? Through what processes or mechanisms of socialization are these effects produced? How are these processes and their outcomes related to the specific functions, goals, or purposes of the organization or group? How are these contexts affected by their larger institutional and historical settings?

Family Context

In the minds of many people, the family is the context most closely associated with the topic of socialization. As an institution, its major function in most societies is the socialization and care of children. The goal of most parents is to develop children into competent, moral, and self-sufficient adults. This is typically undertaken with two objectives or frames of reference in mind: socializing the child for membership in the family group, and socializing the child for membership in the larger society. In the process, of course, parents also become socialized. Relations within the family are intimate, intensive, relatively enduring, particularistic, and diffuse. This is why the socialization that takes place here is usually the most pervasive and consequential for the individual. It is also the first socialization context that most of us experience—the place where we develop our initial sense of self.

SOCIAL ORGANIZATION OF THE FAMILY

The family, in contemporary American society at least, is a relatively simple structure, usually composed of father, mother, and a few children. In fact, the family is becoming increasingly simpler, with the continuing increase of single-parent families through divorce, separation, or premarital pregnancy. This constitutes the major structural variation in families, which has special significance for family socialization. Other structural variations include the number and gender of children and the presence of other adults (usually extended kin).

The major positions in the family are ascribed and tend to be divided along two axes of differentiation: age and sex. There is considerable variation across families regarding the power and authority associated with family positions. But typically, power is unequally distributed within the family, with parents having considerably more power and authority than children (although the power disparity decreases as the children get older), and fathers typically having somewhat more power and authority than mothers—vestiges of a patriarchal system and division of labor in the home that still persist.

Patterns of power and authority in families are also influenced by the size of the family group. As groups increase in size, power becomes increasingly centralized, rules governing duties and responsibilities become more formal and explicit, roles and tasks become more specialized, and there is a greater stress on conformity (Clausen 1966; Bossard and Boll 1956). Elder and Bowerman (1963), in a large sample of high school students, found that the proportion of adolescents reporting their parents to be authoritarian or autocratic increased with family size. The students from large families were also more likely to report that their parents often did not explain the rules that they imposed on the children, were more likely to use physical punishment as opposed to other forms of discipline, and attempted to maintain control over the child longer.[1]

But the large family also offers each child more independence and autonomy from parental supervision than is the case in small families. The greater numbers give a certain amount of protection from parental despotism and emotional absorption by spreading parental attention over more children, thereby diminishing the influence on any one child. Furthermore, to the extent that siblings in a large family can form coalitions and provide a united front against the parents on some issues, their power increases. This is more likely to occur in large families because power is more centralized, and the larger number of children increase the emergence of a "class consciousness."

PROCESSES AND OUTCOMES OF FAMILY SOCIALIZATION

There is a wide range of processes and outcomes of socialization within the family, especially for the child. It is the context in which the child's initial sense of self develops and basic identities, motivations, values, and beliefs are formed. This occurs through most of the major processes and mechanisms of socialization, for example, modeling, reinforcement, role-playing, labeling, and social comparisons, which are enhanced by the general process of identification. The discussion of the various processes and outcomes within this context (as well as the others) is highly selective. Emphasis is placed on those that are most conspicuously affected by the social structural features and dimensions of the family context.

Identification and sex-role identity. A good deal of the socialization that takes place in the family involves learning appropriate role behavior associated with the various family positions. For the child, the most significant of these are sex and age roles. These roles are not only pervasive and diffuse, in that they enter into numerous interaction contexts, but their main significance lies in the consequences that they have for self-conceptions. They are sources of major identities that individuals hold. As such, they are sources of motivation (wanting to act in accordance with role requirements), values (having a positive or negative feeling toward the identity), and, perhaps most important, they engender relatively unshakeable conceptions of reality. They also develop very early in the socialization process, shortly after the acquisition of language. Not long after the appearance of reflective thinking (that is, the ability to view the self as an object—in Mead's sense, to role-take), the child, in categorizing its world and constructing its reality, categorizes itself as *boy* or *girl.* This becomes a statement of fact, not subject to opinion or negotiation—just as the identities of brother, sister, youngest child, and "Benjamin Gecas" become statements of fact that the child forms (Kohlberg 1966). The behavioral consequences of these identities —that is, the role behaviors considered appropriate—take much longer to develop and are much more negotiable. Through processes of reinforcement from parents and others, through identification with various role models, through countless parental admonitions and instructions, the child is socialized into the specific behavioral expectations associated with these roles.

Much of the research on role-learning in the family has dealt with the learning of sex roles (see Maccoby and Jacklin 1974 for a comprehensive review). Some of this literature suggests that the processes involved in sex-role learning might be somewhat different for the two sexes. David Lynn (1969) theorizes that girls learn sex-appropriate behavior through identification with their mothers, whereas boys learn it through identification with a culturally defined masculine role. This difference in processes involved in sex-role learning is a function of the traditional division of labor in the home. As a result, according to Lynn, the process of sex-role learning for girls is rather simple, observing mother and modeling her behavior. But since the father is less visible, the process of sex-role learning is more complicated for boys. Their problem is to determine, on the basis of various sources of information (such as mother's sanctions against "unmasculine" behavior, males portrayed in the mass media, and observations of men in various circumstances), what constitutes appropriate masculine behavior and to use it as a standard for one's own conduct. This involves abstracting from a number of diverse sources of information a general model of masculinity.

The significance of this difference in sex-role learning lies in the consequences that it may have for cognitive functioning. For example, Lynn argues that males tend to be more field-independent than females because of this necessity to abstract from the immediate situation in the learning of their sex role. Females, however, are more field-dependent because of the necessity of being in tune to the immediate situation (mother's behavior) in learning theirs. Lynn's theory seems reasonable. But the extent to which the sex differences in field dependence/independence can be attributed to the socialization process that he proposes is still to be confirmed.

Parents are not the only agents within the family important to the child's sex-role learning. Siblings also have an effect. In a study of sex-role learning in two-child families, Brim (1958) found that children who have a sibling of the opposite sex have more personality traits of the opposite sex than do children from same-sex sibling systems, and that this effect is greater for younger than for older siblings. Furthermore, this process of mutual influence is asymmetrical in the sibling order. Older siblings, because of their greater power and competence, have more influence over younger siblings.

Both Brim and Lynn emphasize identification as a process in the development of sex-role identities. There is no doubt that it is important in the formation of sex-role identities as well as other aspects of self-concept. We develop a sense of who we are by identifying with *and* differentiating from others.

Parenting styles and socialization outcomes. Roles, values, norms, and beliefs are the main cultural contents of socialization that are transmitted from parents to children, more or less intentionally, in congruence with general socialization goals that parents hold. Much of the child's family socialization is of this kind. But much of it is inadvertent, unintentional, and often unconsciously produced by parents. Styles of parental behavior are more likely to be relevant to this aspect of the socialization process.

In the vast literature on child socialization, two dimensions of parental behavior have received considerable attention—the degree and kind of control that parents exert over the child, and the amount of affection and support that they show. Both have been found to have important consequences for the child (for good reviews of this literature, see Rollins and Thomas 1979 and Thomas et al. 1974). The general conclusion from this research literature is that parental support combined with inductive or authoritative (as opposed to authoritarian) control has the most favorable socialization effects on the child, that is, development of high self-esteem, sense of competence, conscience, internalization of adult standards, and high achievement motivation.

A reason for the efficacy of these parental behaviors is that both modeling and identification are affected by them. As Bronfenbrenner points out in assessing the modeling research, the most contagious models for the child are likely to be those who are the major sources of support and control (1970:133). Furthermore, a strong affective relationship between parent and child facilitates the child's identification with the parent (and the parent's with the child). In short, parenting styles that result in a warm, supportive, "reasonably constricting" family environment produce a child who is readily socialized to adult standards. On the other hand, cold, rigid, and coercively-restrictive family environments produce children who are rebellious, resentful, and insecure.

Since the relationship between parent and child is highly reciprocal, parents are also affected in the process. In fact, in the initial confrontation between parent and offspring, the parent is much more influenced by the infant than vice versa. By means of the cry and the smile, infants are very effective at shaping parental behavior (see, for example, Bell 1977; Goldberg 1977; and Rheingold 1969). Socialization into the parental role is largely a matter of on-the-job training, with the child's responses to the parent one of the major processes involved in the role definition of parent.

Family size, configuration, and socialization outcomes. There are several important socialization consequences of family size. A number of studies have found that children from large families have lower scores on intelligence tests than do children from small families, even when the effects of social class are controlled. Also, children from smaller families show higher achievement motivation than do those from larger families (Rosen 1961; Douglas 1964). The most extensive evidence for this relationship is provided by Zajonc (1976). Using records of intellectual performance on various national tests (Scholastic Aptitude Test, National Merit Test) in this country and elsewhere, Zajonc has argued strongly for the negative effect of family size on scholastic aptitude of children. Zajonc's explanation of the association between family size and the child's intelligence is based on the opportunity for interaction with parents available to the child. The basic idea of the "confluence model" proposed by Zajonc is that the intellectual environment of a family depends on the number of family members and their ages. Hence, different family configurations (in terms of number and ages) constitute different intellectual environments. The intellectual environment is conceived as an average of all the family members' mental ages, which changes continually as children grow older, and as additions to or departures from the family occur (1976:227). The research of Zajonc, as well as others (Rosen 1961; Douglas 1964; Olneck and Bills 1979), points to the negative effect of family size on cognitive development through its effect on the quality and quantity of parent/child interaction.

In contrast to the fairly consistent picture of the negative consequences of family size for intellectual development is the chaotic literature on birth order, which has prompted one reviewer to declare that the variable should be abandoned (Schooler 1972). Zajonc (1979), however, has attempted to salvage birth order as a variable by modifying his "confluence model" of the effects of family size and spacing to include *age* of siblings. His data support the proposition that birth-order effects depend on age; firstborns were found to do better than secondborns initially (up until age 4 or 5), then to do worse (until age 12 or 13), and then to do better again (from 13 on). Zajonc concludes that when age of siblings is taken into consideration, birth-order effects on intellectual development become quite patterned and understandable.

This may be an overly optimistic assessment. Zajonc's findings have been criticized because they are based on cross-sectional population data, when longitudinal data on intra-family comparisons are needed to test these ideas (Olneck and Bills 1979; Grotevant et al. 1977). Zajonc's model has also been criticized for the low level of theory upon which it is based. The principal mechanism of influence is equivalent to contagion between family members in proportion to mental level (Olneck and Bills 1979:137). Olneck and Bills's (1979) study is one of the very few studies to consider the effect of birth order by examining *within*-family variations. Their study, based on a sample of 346 pairs of brothers, found no significant effects of birth order on measures of intellectual ability and educational attainment. Family size, however, was significantly related to these variables even when indicators of social class were controlled. An even more damaging critique of the "confluence model" is provided by Galbraith (1979), who questions the mathematics upon which the model is based and the discrepancy between this model and other studies (including Galbraith's own data) of birth-order effects.

In spite of the doubts about the significance of birth order for intellectual development, it would be premature to abandon the variable. Because its significance is questionable regarding intellectual abilities does not mean that birth order is irrelevant to other socialization outcomes. There is enough evidence to suggest that children differently located in the sibling order experience different patterns of interaction with parents and siblings. For example, there are a number of ways in which firstborn children have an advantageous position. Besides the greater amount of parental attention that the firstborn receives (Lewis and Krietzberg 1979), he/she is also more likely to be given responsibility and control over younger siblings and to have higher expectations associated with his/her performance. This combination of high parental support and control, plus high performance expectations, contributes to the greater tendency of firstborns to identify with parents, to internalize parental values, to be more achievement-oriented, to enforce rules, and to be more conscientious (Adams 1972; Clausen 1966; Kammeyer 1967). On the other hand, firstborns are also more likely to be more anxious, conservative, and guilt-ridden.

The distinctive feature about the position of younger children in the birth order is that they are much more subject to child-level interaction than is the firstborn. Since the firstborn is (initially) bigger, stronger, more competent, and able to exert dominance over younger siblings, he/she is likely to serve as a model for them. Thus, we would expect younger siblings to have a greater sensitivity to the moods of older children and to be more peer-oriented once they move outside the family (Clausen 1966;19). This is consistent with Sampson's (1965) observation that the early self-concept of firstborns is based largely on the appraisal of parents, whereas the self-concept of latterborn children is more likely to reflect peer evaluations, provided mainly by siblings.

SOCIALIZATION IN SINGLE-PARENT FAMILIES

The single-parent family is an increasingly frequent phenomenon, having substantial consequences for child socialization. If present trends continue, nearly half of the children born today will spend some time in a one-parent family, usually as a result of separation or divorce (Glick 1978). Research on the consequences of this circumstance for the development of children and parents is sparse. But what there is suggests that the consequences are negative. For example, Hetherington et al. (1976, 1978) found pronounced differences between two samples of middle-class parents (recently divorced and married) in the quality of parent/child interaction. Divorced parents made fewer maturing demands, were less affectionate, and showed marked inconsistency in discipline and control of their children in comparison to married parents. The reciprocity of this relationship and its effects were evident in the similar pattern of negative behavior of the children toward their parents. Hetherington et al. further observed that children living in single-parent homes are more likely to experience problems in cognitive, emotional, and social development than are children in "intact" families.

To the extent that these socialization consequences in single-parent families are true, several explanations could account for them. Along with the practical problems of living, which are frequently aggravated by separation and divorce, especially if the single parent has to work, patterns of parent-child relations become disrupted, especially along the dimensions of control and support. Hetherington et al.'s (1978) observation that control and discipline of children become inconsistent and support and affective interaction become strained suggests that personality and behavior problems in the child would be more likely to occur (recalling the earlier discussion of consequences of parental support and control). Identification with parents and with the family as a unit may also be problematic when the family is no longer an integral whole.

But perhaps most important of all for socialization in single-parent families is the loss of what Bronfenbrenner (1979) calls "second-order effects." Second-order effects refer to the effects that the presence of a third person has on a dyadic relationship. For example, the interaction between mother and child may be different depending upon whether the father is present. Bronfenbrenner (1979:68) observes that second-order effects in family interaction generally seem to be positive. That is, the presence of the other parent tends to have a benign effect on the interaction between parent and child. A mother or father may be less harsh and more "reasonable" in dealing with a son or daughter if the other parent is present. To the extent that this is true, an important source of moderation and temperance in parent/child interaction tends to be lost in single-parent families.

FAMILY SOCIALIZATION IN THE LARGER SOCIAL SETTING

There are a number of factors that affect the family as a context of socialization. Some of these are internal, such as the developmental changes the family system undergoes as a result of life-cycle changes of its members (the chapter by Simmons and Bush in this volume deals with this topic). Others are external and underscore the embeddedness of the family in the larger system of social institutions, cultural processes, and historical developments. This section briefly touches on a few of these external influences.

Social class influences. Various structural features of the family, as well as some of its ideological components, are affected by the family's location in the social class system. It is frequently reported in the literature on social class and family patterns that "lower-class" families and "middle-class" families differ with regard to the conceptualization of family roles, division of labor in the home, power distribution, and socialization values and ideology (Gecas 1979a). For example, middle-class families, compared to lower-class families, are generally found to have a more open and flexible role system, a more egalitarian ideology, a less segregated division of labor, socialization values that emphasize autonomy and individual development over conformity, and less restrictive and less punitive child-rearing patterns. Several scholars have offered explanations for the perceived social-class differences in family socialization patterns. Bronfenbrenner (1958) attributed the increasingly greater flexibility and affective involvement in the child rearing of middle-class families (compared to lower-class families) to the parents' greater exposure and receptivity to mass media and the advice of "experts" regarding patterns of appropriate child rearing. Kohn (1969) located the class difference in parental values in the differential occupational conditions and educational experiences of middle- and lower-class parents (more will be said on Kohn's theory later). Bernstein (1971) argued that the role systems of middle-class and lower-class families differ with regard to degree of openness and flexibility because of differences in the nature of the social networks within which these families are located. These differences in the nature of family roles, in turn, have consequences for types of linguistic codes that parents use in child socialization (see Gecas 1979a for an assessment of these theories). There are also class-associated differences in family patterns because of ethnic, racial, and religious influences. One of the major problems in this area is to disentangle the effects of these various factors.

Historical considerations. The family as a socialization context has been undergoing considerable change over the past few decades, from shifts in child-rearing philosophies to experimentation with alternate family forms. Many of these have had an effect on socialization, but one development that Bronfenbrenner (1970) identifies is especially noteworthy. Bronfenbrenner argues that there has been a progressive decrease in recent decades in the amount of contact between American parents and their children (1970:98). Various social forces (such as urbanization, commuting, working mothers, and the professionalization of child care) have operated to decrease the amount of parent/child interaction, and hence the parent's role as a socializing agent. Bronfenbrenner points to two important consequences of this parental withdrawal. It has produced a vacuum that is increasingly filled by the child's involvement with age peers and with television. Children's peer groups develop independently of (and often in opposition to) adult standards and values (more will be said on this later). They become a frame of reference and a powerful socializing influence for the child. So does television. "The American child spends about as much time watching television as he spends in school, and more than in any other activity except sleep and play" (Bronfenbrenner 1970:102). For Bronfenbrenner, the insidious influence of television is not so much with regard to the behavior that it produces in a child (even though this might be bad enough), but rather the behavior it prevents, that is, the human interaction foregone in the course of being a passive viewer. While the importance of family as a context of child socialization may be decreasing in American society, the importance of school and peer groups has increased. The distinct features of these contexts and their consequences for socialization are considered below.

School Context

The school,[2] like the family, is an institution whose explicit mandate is to socialize people. In each case, this mandate is directed toward children. The school's mission, however, is defined more narrowly than is that of the family. It is primarily concerned with the formal instruction of children and the development of their cognitive skills (but here again, more is learned by the child than that which is explicitly taught). Next to the family, the school is the institution in which the child is most directly involved. And like the family, this involvement is largely involuntary. But in most other respects, family and classroom constitute quite different socialization experiences for the child.

THE SOCIAL ORGANIZATION OF THE CLASSROOM

There are a number of excellent analyses and reviews of the social organization of the classroom (see especially Boocock 1978; Bowles and Gintis 1976; Dreeben 1968; Glidewell et al. 1966; Jackson 1968; Parsons 1964). I have selected from these sources discussions of classroom features and processes that have the most direct bearing on the socialization of children.[3]

Most of this discussion will focus on the classroom since that is where the business of formal education takes place. The typical elementary school classroom (and to a large extent, the high school classroom) is composed of one adult and around twenty-five children of both sexes and approximately the same age, drawn from a relatively small geographical area. The major status distinction is between teacher and pupils—not unlike the major status distinction in the family, although the ratio is quite different. The relationship between teacher and student is more limited in scope (that is, more role-specific) and of shorter duration than is that between parent and child. The procedure of annual promotion from grade to grade provides the child with the experience of establishing and severing relationships with adults at regular periods.

The homogeneous age composition of the class is an especially consequential feature of classroom structure. It provides the child with a standard of comparison for his competencies. It also provides the teacher with a standard for evaluating each student. Formal and public evaluation of performance is one of the hallmarks of the school experience, and, as we shall see, it has substantial consequences for the child's self-esteem. Differentiation among the cohort of pupils is based largely upon differential performance of school tasks. As Parsons pointed out, the school is the first socializing agency in the child's experience that institutionalizes a differentiation of status based on achievement (1964:133).

Another important consequence of a fairly large, age-homogeneous group of socializees in roughly the same formal status and experiencing similar social circumstances is the emergence of a subculture. The content of these subcultures will be considered in some detail in the section on peers as a context of socialization.

PROCESSES AND OUTCOMES OF SOCIALIZATION

Ostensibly, school is primarily concerned with the cognitive development of the child—the acquisition of knowledge, the development of analytical and verbal skills, and other competencies. But in the course of this socialization experience, other things are also learned, such as general norms and beliefs, and other aspects of the child are affected (personality characteristics, self-esteem). The main processes involved are direct instruction, buttressed by a system of costs and rewards (grading, use of praise, and manipulation of self-esteem), social comparison processes, and expectancy effects.

Social reinforcement, expectancy effects, and social comparison processes. The most conspicuous socialization process in the classroom (as, perhaps, in the family) is social reinforcement. Teachers rely on several reinforcers in attempting to shape the student's behavior and development—praise, blame, privileges, and, most important, grades. Grades represent the most concrete evidence of official (teacher's) approval or disapproval of the student's performance.

But grades may also be used to reinforce more than just the development of cognitive competencies. Bowles et al. (1975) suggest that teachers are likely to reward those students who conform to the social order of the school with higher grades and punish violators with lower grades, independent of their respective academic and cognitive accomplishments. In this case, conformity to the social order means that certain personality characteristics are rewarded (for example, dependability, consistency, perseverance, identification with school, punctuality, and tact), while others are punished or disapproved (for example, creativity, aggression, and independence). Bowles et al. (1975) found significant positive relationships between the grade-point average of high school students and the first set of personality characteristics and negative relationships between grade-point average and the second set of characteristics. Similar evidence that grades reflect more than scholastic achievement of students is offered by Holland (1961). In a study of 639 National Merit Scholars, Holland found that differences in scholastic achievement were not related to grades. But two personality variables were significantly and positively related to grades: "citizenship" and "drive to achieve." However, Holland found that neither of these two variables had a significant effect on actual achievement measures, and both were negatively related to measures of creativity and mental flexibility. In short, there is evidence that teachers directly reinforce certain personality characteristics and discourage others through the use of grades and other reinforcers.

Less obvious than social reinforcement, but perhaps no less pervasive, are expectancy effects and social comparison processes. Expectancy effects (Jones 1977), better known as self-fulfilling prophecies, are part of the broader process of defining situations and thereby constructing realities. The concept refers to the capacity of beliefs or expectancies to alter a state of affairs so that it comes to be congruent with the original belief. This notion derives from W. I. Thomas's (1928:527) insight: "If men define situations as real, they are real in their consequences." An extension of this idea to the self-fulfilling prophecy notion is provided by Merton:

> The self-fulfilling prophecy is, in the beginning, a "false" definition of the situation evoking a new behavior which makes the originally false conception come "true." This specious validity to the self-fulfilling prophecy perpetuates a reign of error. For the prophet will cite the actual course of events as proof that he was right from the very beginning. [1957:423]

Merton's statement gives the impression that self-fulfilling prophecies are always negative. In many circumstances they are, as attested by the literature on race relations, deviance, and stereotyping. But often this process can lead to positive outcomes. The research on self-fulfilling prophecies in the classroom demonstrates both effects (Wilkins 1976).

The landmark study on this topic is Rosenthal and Jacobson's influential *Pygmalion in the Classroom* (1968), which tested the proposition that children in the classroom would show greater intellectual growth if their teacher expected it than if he/she did not. The findings were equivocal: teacher's expectations had a significant effect on pupils' IQ gains for first- and second-graders, but not for third-, fourth-, and fifth-graders. The study aroused considerable criticism and controversy. Subsequent replications have produced mixed but generally confirming results (see Jones 1977:104–12 and, for a more critical assessment, Boocock 1978).

The fear that many people have, however, concerning the self-fulfilling prophecy in the classroom is not with regard to the effect of the teacher's *high* expectations, but rather his/her *low* expectations of certain students. Especially in schools where the student body is racially or socioeconomically mixed, parents and policy makers fear that the teacher would have lower expectations for the minority or lower-class student, and that these expectations would be communicated in differential treatment. A careful study by Rist (1970) gives credence to some of these fears. Rist followed a class of black children, in a ghetto school, from kindergarten through second grade. He describes in this report the numerous and subtle ways in which the teacher transmitted her expectations of their competencies or incompetencies to these children in a process that became self-fulfilling.

The other social process of special note in classroom socialization is social comparisons. The process of social comparisons is ubiquitous in the classroom. The age homogeneity and lack of formal status differentiation in the class cohort make it a fertile ground for the operation of social comparison processes as a means of social differentiation. This differentiation occurs largely on the basis of perceived ability and achievement, and each student knows where he stands with respect to his classmates. The class, therefore, serves as a reference group for the student, not necessarily in the normative sense (although it may indeed be a source of norms and values) as much as in the comparative sense (that is, as a standard of evaluation), to use Kelly's (1952) distinction. The family, by contrast, is primarily a normative reference group.

Richer (1976) suggests that reference-group processes (comparison processes) are more likely to operate in the classroom under conditions of greater subgroup differentiation and visibility. This is a classroom condition explored in some detail by Rosenberg (1975) for its effects on students' self-esteem. Rosenberg uses the concept of *contextual dissonance* to refer to the situation of being a member of a minority group in a classroom (or other contexts, for that matter) on the basis of a trait or characteristic that is disvalued by the majority group. In examining the effects of three types of contextual dissonance (social identity context such as race and social class, competence context, and value context), he found that being in the minority subgroup on any of these dimensions had a negative effect on the student's self-esteem. Rosenberg makes a strong case for the negative consequences of minority status *within the immediate interaction context* because social comparison processes operate more forcefully at this face-to-face level rather than when society at large is the frame of reference. This is consistent with the findings of Bachman (1970) and Coleman et al. (1966) showing the negative consequences of school integration for self-esteem of black children, and parallels Kanter's discussion of the negative psychological consequences of minority status on the job.

Classroom organization and the learning of general social norms. Dreeben (1968) argues for the importance of school as a transitional institution between family and job (as do Bowles and Ginitis 1976 from a different perspective). His argument is based upon the observation that conduct in the family and conduct on the job are governed by contrasting normative principles. School provides the bridge between these two institutions by exposing the child to a set of experiences that facilitate learning and internalizing the norms of independence, achievement, universalism, and specificity. The goal of the school, in producing competent citizens, is carried out not only through the formal program of instruction aimed at developing cognitive skills, but also through the less conspicuous development of these four general norms.

Universalism refers to the use of uniform (universal) standards of treatment and evaluation. Its opposite is particularism or special treatment (a norm that operates typically in family relations). In the classroom, the norm of universalism is closely tied to the notion of fairness. *Specificity* refers to the scope of one person's dealings with another. Because the interaction between teacher and pupil is much more role specific, and more temporary, the distinction between the person and the position becomes much clearer in the school than it is in the family. The child comes to see that teachers, unlike mothers, are interchangeable.

Two aspects of classroom structure are particularly germane to the development of the norms of universalism and specificity—size and age homogeneity. Parsons (1964) suggests that because there are so many more children in the classroom than in the family, and because they are concentrated in a much narrower age range, the teacher has less chance than has the parent to treat them in a particularistic manner (1964:136). Along with the sheer logistics imposed by large numbers of socializees, the assignment of similar tasks that all pupils are to perform favors universalistic treatment.

Within the classroom, the norms of universalism and specificity refer primarily to the conduct of the teacher. Independence and achievement are norms that are more relevant to the conduct of pupils, and because they are the basis for evaluating pupils, they have greater psychological consequences for the child. *Independence* refers to doing things on one's own, and connotes such other attributes as accepting responsibility for one's acts and being self-motivated. Cheating and formal testing are two aspects of classroom operations that bear directly on the norm of independence. *Achievement* is perhaps the strongest norm of all. The concept denotes activity and mastery, the striving against some standard of excellence. It is closely tied to the main mission of the school—to teach students and to evaluate the extent of their learning. As a result, the pupil's performance is constantly evaluated in the classroom, and the evaluations are public. The implications of this situation go beyond the mere learning of social norms. They go to the heart of the child's conception of self.

Success, based on one's own efforts, is good for self-esteem and builds confidence in one's abilities. Failure is not, and *public* failure is worse. The school provides numerous opportunities to the child for public failure, as well as for success. It also has fewer resources than does the family for protecting the child's self-respect in the face of failure. But even for those who are more successful on academic criteria, school can be hard on self-esteem. They must constantly work to maintain their status, and few go through this socialization experience without experiencing some failure. In a study comparing levels of self-esteem reported by high-school students with regard to five social contexts (family, classroom, on a date, with friends, and with adults), Gecas (1972) found self-esteem to be lowest in the classroom. Not surprisingly, these students reported feeling least authentic (least "real") in the classroom context. Furthermore, this negative effect of school on self-esteem seems to occur quite early in the child's educational experience. Hales (1980) found second- and third-graders (as well as fourth- and fifth-graders) to have lower self-esteem in the school context than at home or with peers.

Strategies for maintaining self-esteem in the classroom. But students, like other socializees, are not passive recipients of the pressures that they experience. They engage in activities that alter their circumstances, either in fact or by re-defining the situation or both, to make them more favorable to their self-interests and less damaging to their self-esteem. Covington and Beery (1976) propose that two fundamentally different patterns of achievement motivation emerge in schools as a result of these pressures: one is oriented toward success, the other is oriented toward avoiding failure. It is the latter that is considered to be a major obstacle to school achievement. The reason why it is adopted, of course, is to protect one's self-esteem. There are several strategies that students use to avoid failure. The most common are nonparticipation (if you do not participate, you cannot fail); if forced to participate, putting in a minimum of effort; and procrastination, or putting things off until it is too late to do a good job. The objective in these strategies is to disassociate one's performance from one's ability, and certainly to deny that it reflects one's worth. It is a form of role distance, the separation of self from the behavior required of a role occupant. Failure, then, can be attributed to lack of effort or to various external circumstances, and not to one's lack of ability. In a sense, this is viewed as "failure with honor." The irony of these failure-avoiding strategies, as Covington and Beery point out, is that they are self-defeating. In their attempt to avoid *feelings* of failure, these students, by their actions, increase the probability of actual failure. This is one of the serious, unintended, and undesirable consequences of classroom socialization. In the process of socializing students into the norms of independence and mastery (both desirable socialization outcomes from the societal perspective), pressures are generated that lead to patterns of adaptation that are considered undesirable.

CLASSROOM SOCIALIZATION IN THE LARGER SOCIAL SETTING

The socialization that takes place in the classroom is very much affected by the nature of the school system and its place in the larger societal context. Dreeben's (1968) and Parson's (1964) analyses of the development of general social norms allude to the relevance of this larger societal context. Their benign functionalism suggests a happy integration between the school system and the economic system, via the socialization of children for their future participation in the occupational sphere.

A more critical analysis of the relationship between classroom socialization and the economic order is provided by Bowles and Gintis (1976). They also see a functional link between school and the economic system. But in examining the relationship from a Marxian perspective, they deplore the character of both of these institutions as they exist in American society. Bowles and Gintis (1976:12) maintain that the educational system perpetuates the economic order and contributes to the integration of youth into the labor force, mainly through a structural correspondence between its social relations and those of production:

> . . . the relationships of authority and control between administrators and teachers, teachers and students, students and students, and students and their work replicate the hierarchical division of labor which dominates the workplace. . . . Students have a degree of control over their curriculum comparable to that of the worker over the content of his job.

In elaborating on this correspondence, Bowles and Gintis point out that for students as for workers, their degree of autonomy and freedom from supervision increases as they move up the educational or occupational levels.

There is little doubt that the economic system has a powerful influence on the school system and classroom socialization, both because of social structural factors (Bowles and Gintis 1976) and ideological factors (Dreeben 1968). But there are also other important influences from the larger social context that have a bearing on classroom socialization, such as political factors (for example, busing), technological innovations (teaching machines), demographic changes (declining enrollments), and family influences (ethnic diversity). I do not have space to consider these various social factors here. However, the relationship between family and school requires further comment.

Classroom socialization has been treated here as an example of "developmental socialization"—that is, as a progressive continuation of the child's development, building on the foundation established by the family. This is too simple a view. There is enormous variation in the degree to which the transition from family to school is smooth and "developmental" for some children or disjunctive for others. For the majority of children, classroom socialization may indeed be a developmental process. But for children from ethnic-minority families, especially in the poverty segment of society, the school may be a harsh and alien place that devalues much of what they have learned in their family contexts. For these children, the school may be more accurately viewed as a resocialization context.[4]

Childhood Peer Group Context

Within contemporary American society, the emergence of childhood peer groups as socialization contexts is intimately related to the existence of public schools. Along with neighborhoods, the school grounds and adjacent areas are the natural habitat of peer groups. Several features of schools (especially high schools, although this certainly applies to grade schools as well) contribute to the emergence of peer groups among the youth: schools are the locus of a large concentration of children falling within a narrow age range, all are there involuntarily, and all are exposed to similar academic pressures. These are some of the conditions that Wheeler identifies as conducive to social organization and the development of countercultures among the recruits. Cohen (1972) no doubt expressed the sentiment of many schoolteachers when she described the student peer groups as "the netherworld of the classroom."

SOCIAL ORGANIZATION OF ADOLESCENT PEER GROUPS

The most important feature of the peer group is that it is a *voluntary* association. For most children, it is their first. This permits greater freedom of choice regarding associations in the group. The child does have the option to leave the group, a choice much less possible with regard to family or school. As a result, the boundaries of peer groups are more fluid, with individuals drifting in and out.

The peer group is an arena for the exercise of independence from adult control. As such, and to some extent as a reaction against adult control, it is often the context for the development of contra-values and the expression of behavior that is disapproved by adults (such as that described by Coleman 1961, and in much of the literature on juvenile delinquency).

A second important feature of peer groups is that association is between status equals. Consequently, interaction is more likely to be based on egalitarian norms. This is not to say that social differentiation and stratification do not occur in peer groups. On the contrary, informal status hierarchies typically develop based upon achievement in activities considered important by the group. Status within the peer group is more fluid than in more structured contexts and depends much more on negotiation. But the basic relationship within peer groups is not a hierarchical one, but instead is the friendship bond, based on equality, mutual tolerance, and concern. Role-taking is more fully utilized and required in this context because of the greater opportunities for role-making, which requires a greater sensitivity to others in the situation in constructing one's own role (Turner 1962).

A third feature, having special implications for the *content* of socialization, is the observation that adolescent peer groups are typically segregated by sex. Intensive association with same-sex peers and involvement in sex-typed activities strongly reinforces identification and belongingness with other members of the same sex (Parsons 1964). Not only sex-role identity, but much of the sexual socialization occurs in the context of peer rather than parent-child associations (Gagnon and Simon 1973).

PROCESSES AND OUTCOMES OF PEER GROUP SOCIALIZATION

What is fairly distinct about socialization in childhood peer groups is the effect it has on three broad areas of the child's development: (1) the development and validation of the self; (2) the development of competence in the presentation of self through role-taking and impression management skills; and (3) the acquisition of knowledge left residual or avoided by adults in their socialization of children. To be sure, each of these aspects of the child's socialization are also important products and concerns of other contexts (especially family and school). But it is the unique nature of the peer context that makes this context the most effective arena for the development of these three domains.

The key to the importance of the peer group in the socialization of these three domains is the friendship bond. Friendships are based on egalitarian relationships of mutual support and acceptance, where a wider latitude of behavior is allowed than in most other relationships, and where there is no explicit responsibility on the part of friends to change or shape each other's development (in contrast to parent/child relationships). Since a great deal is tolerated in friendships, the individual is freer to explore and express a wide range of behaviors and self-conceptions without fear of condemnation. Fine (1980) argues that friendship relationships are especially appropriate for the mastering of self-presentations and impression-management skills, since inadequate displays will usually be ignored or corrected without severe loss of face. He points out that outside of friendship bonds, preadolescents have a critical eye for each other's behaviors that are managed ineptly. Insults serve the dual purpose of ridiculing outsiders as well as displaying a presentation of self to one's peers. In the development of sex-role identities, for example, boys must learn how to present themselves to male peers as "males," as well as to learn how to interact with females (Fine 1980).

Peer groups are important, not only as contexts for the development of self and interpersonal skills, but also as sources of values, attitudes, and beliefs relevant, especially, to the problems of growing up. They provide the child with a useful stock of knowledge that is typically unavailable from adults. The information acquired by children from such sources as school, family, and mass media is transmitted by adults who generally share a conception of what children should and should not know. There are a number of topics that are of considerable interest to children and adolescents, but about which they typically do not learn from adults, for example, the practice of sex, informal rules of institutions (how to work the system), and how to have excitement and adventure via pranks, mischief, and illegal behavior (Fine 1980). Peer groups fill this void, usually to the dismay of adults.

The peer group is a powerful agent of socialization, not only because it generates strong loyalties and identifications among its members, but also because the socialization ratio is favorable (many-on-one). When the peer group is acting collectively or in concert, the problem for the deviant is that he finds himself at odds with *many* others, whose opinions he values. Indeed, the power of the peer group to exert pressure will become much more apparent when we consider its role in various conversion and identity transformation contexts. The reason why the strength of peer groups as agents of socialization is not as obvious within adolescent peer groups is because they typically lack clear-cut goals beyond the general goal of sociability. When mobilized by an explicit goal, their power to socialize is considerable. When adult institutions are able to channel the power of peer groups toward their own socialization ends, they become much more effective institutions (see, for example, Bronfenbrenner's 1970 description of the utilization of peer groups in Soviet classrooms).

ADOLESCENT PEER GROUPS IN THE LARGER SOCIAL SETTING

Volumes have been written on peer groups and their distinct subcultures among youth in American society. Much of this literature describes the organized alienation of adolescents from adult society—the development of distinct (and frequently opposite) values, norms, language, and tastes from the dominant culture. Coleman's (1961, 1966) significant and extensive studies (as well as Bronfenbrenner 1970) describe the process of age segregation in our society that gives rise to a separate youth culture. Coleman shows that peers constitute an important reference group for the child, both in the normative as well as in the comparative sense. He found that the aspirations of high-school students were mainly determined by the "leading crowd" in school, rather than by their parents or teachers. Success in athletics, rather than in academics, was most important for boys; being popular with peers was most important for girls. Hence, status in the peer group was based upon quite different criteria from that of the classroom. One function that this serves for the pupil is to provide an alternate source of self-esteem and perhaps to repair self-esteem damaged in the classroom (Gecas 1972).

Occupational Context

The previous three contexts of socialization have been relevant mainly to the socialization of children. The next two deal with adults. For most adult men in our society, and increasingly for women, work (in the form of paid employment) is the dominant activity and setting in their lives, outside of the family. It is where much of their time is spent. It is an arena for the development and expression of competence and sense of worth as well as a source of identity. Work provides an interesting contrast to family, school, and peers as a context of socialization.

Typically, the primary goal of work organizations and work settings is not that of socializing those who work in them. The main goal usually involves producing goods or providing services for a certain public. Some of these services may indeed involve socializing various categories of people, for example, students, inmates, patients, and so forth, but typically not the organization's workers themselves. The socialization experienced by workers on the job, therefore, is incidental to the main purpose of the organization and frequently inadvertent.

It should be clear that I am not speaking here of socialization into a profession, such as doctor or teacher. Most of the occupational socialization undergone in preparation or training for a career takes place in specialized schools. These, too, are important contexts of socialization which, if space permitted, would be examined, since they are especially relevant to adult role learning and commitment to occupational identities.[5].

SOCIAL ORGANIZATION OF OCCUPATIONAL SETTINGS

Occupational settings vary considerably with regard to a wide range of features, such as, power and authority relationships, degree of bureaucratization, extent to which co-workers are present and involved in one's job, degree of coordination of work activities, and the nature and complexity of the work involved. Most jobs in contemporary industrialized societies are located in large, bureaucratic organizations, with hierarchical authority and specialized division of labor (Bowles and Gintis 1976). Generally, as jobs increase in status and prestige, they also increase in the degree of autonomy, creativity, and discretion allowed the worker. They also tend to be more satisfying and rewarding. These differences, however, are not strictly linear with regard to the organizational hierarchy. An important categorical distinction, especially within large organizations, is between labor and management, or line and staff positions. This distinction is important, not only because it reflects categorically different patterns of authority and work activity, but also because it reflects differences in worker identification. Workers in management are more likely to identify (and to be identified) with the company or organization; workers in labor are more likely to identify with each other collectively (as in labor unions) and frequently to see their interests in conflict with those of management. These differences in loyalties and identifications between labor and management are an important part of the stratification system of work settings, and they contribute to much of the dynamics of life in work organizations.

PROCESSES AND OUTCOMES OF SOCIALIZATION

A number of scholars have argued that there is a functional relationship between the conditions experienced on the job and the attitudes and values that one holds—that values are adaptations to work requirements. The most persuasive work along these lines is that of Melvin Kohn and his associates (1969, 1973, 1978, 1980). Through a series of impressive studies, Kohn has shown that certain structural features of work (for example, the amount of autonomy, the degree of supervision and routinization, and the amount of substantive complexity experienced on the job) give rise to values of either autonomy or conformity in workers. In general, the greater the freedom experienced on the job and the more complex and challenging the work, the more likely is the worker to place a high value on individual freedom and self-direction. On the other hand, the more constraining, routine, and simple the work, the more likely is the worker to value conformity (that is, obedience, order, and discipline). These work-generated values, Kohn found, become generalized orientations that adults have for themselves and that influence the socialization of their children. Parental values, then, tend to be extensions of the modes of behavior that are functional for parents in their occupational spheres. This transformation of work-generated values into parental practices constitutes an important link between the occupational and the family contexts of socialization. The relationship between occupational conditions and values, along the lines proposed by Kohn, has received rather wide support (see Kohn's review 1977 of these studies published since his original monograph; Gecas 1979a for an assessment of this research literature; and Lee 1977 for a synthesis of cross-cultural research reflecting a similar thesis).

In his more recent writings, Kohn has given more prominence to the substantive complexity of work. He has also expanded his interest in the consequences of this "structural imperative of the job" beyond values per se to a wider range of psychological variables, especially to one called "intellectual flexibility." The argument, again convincingly supported by empirical evidence (Kohn and Schooler 1978), is that substantive complexity of work positively affects the intellectual flexibility of the worker, as well as contributing to the development of values of autonomy. In short, these job conditions that Kohn stresses are instrumental in creating individuals who play a larger part in their own socialization and self-creation.

Important as the occupational conditions identified by Kohn may be in their socializing effects on workers, there are other conditions of work situations that are consequential for the individual. Kanter (1977b) proposes a theory of individual attitudes and behavior in organizations based on three structural features of the work situation: the opportunity structure, the power structure, and the social composition of peer clusters. The adaptation of individuals to their work circumstances, and their degree of commitment to work or alienation from work, is, according to Kanter, largely a function of their location on each of these three structural dimensions. For example, people in work situations that provide little opportunity for upward mobility tend to limit their aspirations, seek satisfaction in activities outside of work, create strong peer associations in which interpersonal relations take precedence over other aspects of work, and develop loyalties to the local unit rather than to the larger organization. The second dimension, being low in organizational power, also has negative psychological and behavioral consequences for the individual. For example, these individuals become pettier, bossier, and more authoritarian; use subordinates for their frame of reference; and rely more on coercive than persuasive techniques of control. The third dimension, the social composition of one's work peers, refers to the proportion of women, men, blacks, ethnic minorities, or some other socially relevant category. Kanter proposes that people who are a minority in the work setting find it harder to be taken seriously; are more isolated and excluded from informal peer networks; and are less effective (1977b:246–49). All three of these clusters represent behavioral consequences of disadvantaged position on the three structural dimensions.

The relationship between social structure and individual behavior is highly reciprocal and dynamic in Kanter's model. It leads to upward cycles of advantage, or downward cycles of disadvantage (1977b:249). Breaking these cycles of development is difficult because: (1) the tendency is for the individual's competence, confidence, and power progressively to increase (or decrease); and (2) the perceptions and expectations that others have of the individual become solidified. Kanter's model, like Kohn's, provides a set of structural conditions that contribute to the development of "self-actualizing" or "self-defeating" people.

Kanter has used her theory of behavior in work organizations to explain the problems of women in male-dominated work organizations. She makes a strong case for the primacy of structural disadvantage in the development of such "typically female" attributes on the job as pettiness, bossiness, low aspirations, loyalty to immediate work groups, and concern with emotional ties with workers. Earlier patterns of sex-role socialization are typically invoked to account for these characteristics of women in organizations. But Kanter (1976) found that they are as descriptive of the behavior of men in structurally disadvantaged positions in the organization as they are of women.

There are a number of similarities as well as some interesting differences between Kanter's theory and Kohn's. Both, in the tradition of Marx, root consciousness in experience, rather than the reverse. For that matter, consciousness (in the sense of beliefs, values, attitudes, self-conceptions) is considered a product of, and an adaptation to, the experience of the work situation, and this consciousness, in turn, has behavioral consequences.

They differ, however, in what each considers the most important features of the work situation and the content of consciousness to which they give rise. The major difference between Kanter's theory and Kohn's is that the former focuses on the larger system of structural (organizational) relations within which a person's job is located. The structure of opportunity, the structure of power, and the social composition of peer clusters as analytical dimensions of the work setting only make sense if the larger organizational context is used as a frame of reference. Kohn's theory, by contrast, focuses essentially on the nature of the work that an individual does (substantive complexity of the job) and the amount of freedom that one has in doing it (degree of self-direction on the job), largely in isolation from the larger organizational context.[6] Another important difference is that Kanter brings a temporal dimension into her analysis. The structure of opportunity brings in the worker's assessment of the future, via prospects for upward mobility, as a factor in present adjustment. Kanter states: "People relate to the present in part in terms of their expectations and prospects for the future . . . to be 'stuck' is a very different work experience than being . . . 'up and coming' " (1977:251). As a result, Kanter focused on *careers;* Kohn on *jobs.*

There are advantages and disadvantages to each approach. Kanter's theory was developed out of an analysis of managerial positions in an organization, and seems to be well suited to this organizational level. It is probably less appropriate to blue-collar workers, and inappropriate to individual entrepreneurs. Kohn's theory, on the other hand, was developed to encompass a wide range of occupational contexts, but at the cost of ignoring the systemic or organizational characteristics within which occupations exist. Taken together, however, they constitute the best current work on socialization in work settings.[7]

WORK IN THE LARGER SOCIAL SETTING

Work settings, like most other socialization contexts, are affected by the larger society within which they exist. The nature of the economic system in a society is one of the most important of these larger contextual considerations. For example, the degree of industrialization, mechanization, and bureaucratization, as well as the predominant form of social relations in the economic system (capitalism, communism, feudalism, slavery), have a pervasive effect on the socialization experience that work provides.

Much of the sociological literature on the psychological consequences of work has dealt with the alienating effects of capitalism (Bowles and Gintis 1976). As developed by Marx, the idea of alienated labor stresses the extent to which the individual has control over his labor and its product. The *ideal* of labor, for Marx, was the active, self-realizing individual in a social process of production where the work is a goal in itself. Labor that is strictly instrumental becomes alienating labor. This is most likely to occur in economic systems where labor is bought or owned (that is, where there is a distinction between owners of the means of production and workers, such as in capitalism, feudalism, and slave economies) and where the work is highly mechanized (as in industrialized societies). These conditions are conducive to the alienation of workers.

There is ample evidence on work in American society to suggest substantial dissatisfaction and alienation of workers from their jobs (Kornhauser 1965; Bowles and Gintis 1976). In a recent Department of Health, Education, and Welfare report (*Work in America* 1973), only 43 percent of white-collar workers and 24 percent of blue-collar workers said that they were satisfied with their jobs.

The socialization consequences of work settings can reflect either processes of relatively passive compliance and adaptation to external exigencies or processes of self-determination and expansion. The Marxian critique of work in capitalist America clearly stresses the predominance of the former process.[8] But in the analyses of Kohn and Kanter, discussed above, it is clear that both aspects of socialization are present. They are not, however, equally distributed across occupations: there is a decided shift from the adaptive/compliant pole to the creative/self-determinative pole of the socialization continuum as one moves from occupations of lower to higher prestige in society.

Radical Re-Socialization Contexts

The focus of this section is on socialization contexts in which the explicit goal is the transformation of the individual. Whereas the previous four contexts could all be viewed as generally reflecting what Wheeler (1966) called "developmental socialization," the contexts considered in this section deal with "re-socialization." The changes which an individual undergoes in these contexts, therefore, represent a more radical discontinuity with the past.

SOCIAL ORGANIZATION OF RE-SOCIALIZATION CONTEXTS

Re-socialization can take place in various institutional settings established for this purpose, such as in prisons, mental hospitals, and compensatory education programs (see Kennedy and Kerber 1973 for an examination of some of these contexts). These institutional contexts, however, are of questionable effectiveness in achieving their re-socialization goals (Wheeler 1969; Kennedy and Kerber 1973). My focus, therefore, will be on re-socialization contexts in which the consequences for the socializees are more radical and dramatic, and, as a result, the socialization processes are more apparent. The specific objectives of these contexts vary from political socialization (or brainwashing) to religious conversions to various types of rehabilitation (such as Alcoholics Anonymous, Synanon, and the Provo Experiment). Participation in some of these contexts is voluntary, and in others involuntary. Most of these contexts can be characterized as involving intense small-group interaction where the socialization ratio is large, and where the interaction environment is totalistic or closed. Under these circumstances, one's sense of reality is most effectively restructured.[9]

PROCESSES AND OUTCOMES IN RE-SOCIALIZATION CONTEXTS

The range of processes and outcomes in re-socialization contexts is about as broad and encompassing as it is in the family. In both settings, the person as a whole is the object of development and change at a fundamental level (that is, basic values, motivations, beliefs, and self-conceptions). In re-socialization contexts, however, the processes of socialization are typically more concentrated, more intense, and directed toward the transformation, rather than the formation, of the person.

Assault on identity: the process of death and rebirth. Within re-socialization contexts, there is an acute focus on matters of identity.[10] The identity in question is usually a pivotal one, involving a core aspect of the socializee's self-concept and sense of reality, such as "American," "professor," "moral person," "Christian." The identities in question tend to be cast in strongly positive or strongly negative terms, and the language in general is heavily charged with value connotations. The new identities toward which the individual is re-socialized are not only different from the old, but typically antithetical to them. A common theme found in the literature on radical re-socialization is that the old self must "die" before the new self can emerge—the old and the new identities cannot coexist.

The agents of socialization in these conversion contexts define the situation as one in which it is their mission to help the socializee "to see the light." They view the socializee as being someone who is in error or in ignorance, and who needs their help in order to be saved. Salvation, however, can be a painful experience, especially if the task involves first dislodging the individual from his old identities. The assault on present and past identities takes place through a combination of physical and psychological coercion, which induces fear and stress in the socializee, and through forced participation in the process of constant self-scrutiny and re-examination of one's past from the perspective of, and with the language provided by, the agents of socialization. The power of the group to influence the attitudes and perceptions of the individual member has been the subject of several classic studies in social psychology (Asch 1940;

Sherif 1936). Its power is that much greater when operating in a closed, totalitarian environment toward a clear goal, such as the ideological conversion of a new recruit.

Lifton's (1961) description of the Chinese Communist program of thought reform or brainwashing is illuminating. Along with the physical coercion, the lack of sleep, and the various forms of psychological stress used to weaken the prisoner's hold on past beliefs and identities, Lifton describes the process of identity casting used in the situation (1961:65–76). From the beginning, it was made clear that the "reactionary spy" who entered the prison must perish, and in his place must arise a "new man" resurrected in the Communist mold. A person's major status identifications, such as doctor, priest, teacher, as well as his name, were undermined and replaced by the identity of "criminal."

Perhaps the most significant assaults upon the prisoner's identity occurred during the process of confession. Confession, which was the major technique employed by the captors to involve the prisoner in the process of his own reform, required thorough and compelling self-examination of every action, attitude, and thought, and always from the "people's perspective." A series of denunciations of friends and associates was required as an essential part of the confession. Making these denunciations not only generated feelings of guilt and shame in the prisoner, but it subverted the structure of his own life. Even when the prisoner was aware that his confession was "wild" and his denunciations invalid, he began to behave as if he were a criminal. The prisoner found himself first announcing, and then experiencing, the refashioned identity that was emerging. This may be considered the "rebirth."

The assault on identities is less dramatic in Empey and Rabow's (1961) description of the Provo Experiment in delinquency rehabilitation, but some of the same elements are present. Like the prisoner of thought reform, the delinquent boy's initial situation was purposely amorphous: "They are left on their own to figure out why authorities are doing what they are doing and what they must do to get out of trouble" (1961:688). The new conscript soon discovered that the only avenue for release was through participation in the delinquent peer group, which was the primary source of pressure for change. The main interactions took place in daily group discussion sessions. In these group sessions, the essential ingredients of identity assault included confession of past transgressions through a minute re-examination of the past, including one's former identities, with the aid of a reform vocabulary and the constant pressure of the peer group. The parallels between this delinquency rehabilitation program and the Chinese thought-reform program have been suggested by several scholars (Gordon 1962 and Empey and Rabow themselves 1962).

Within religious conversion contexts, assault on identity is not as harsh, as concentrated, or as stressful as in these other conversion settings. One reason for this is that the religious contexts are usually voluntary associations—new recruits usually have the option to leave if the situation gets too stressful. But more important, there is less need to use harsh tactics or much effort to alienate the socializee from his past identities. Most of them are already alienated, unhappy with themselves or their lives, lack a strong sense of self and identity, and carry a burden of guilt (Richardson et al. 1972, 1977; Lofland 1965). The main task for the religious group is to channel this discontent into the creation of the new religious self. To be sure, denunciations of past identities and behaviors are still expected, but this is typically done without the coercion reported in forced political conversion contexts. The task of building a "new self" is therefore easier in the religious context. But in both types of re-socialization contexts, it is built largely on the rubble of the old self.[11]

Mechanisms of conversion. There are some striking similarities in the mechanisms used for conversion in the various contexts discussed: total milieu control; group pressure for change; forced participation, either through "discussions" of Marxist doctrine (as in the thought-reform programs of the Chinese) or through group songs and games (as in the Unification Church);[12] and emphasis on self-revelation and the denunciation of one's past.

But there are also some interesting differences in the methods used by the various groups. All of these groups approach conversion initially at the affective rather than the cognitive level. The nature of the affect tends to be either strongly negative or strongly positive. In Lifton's description of the methods of thought reform, the major technique used to make the prisoner receptive to change was fear. Initially, it was simply fear of physical punishment and harassment. But as the effects of confession, self-betrayal, and group attack began to take hold, it became a fear of psychological annihilation (Lifton describes this as hitting rock bottom psychologically). At this point, the group tactics changed in the direction of greater leniency, offering the prisoner a way out of his misery.

By contrast, the method more characteristic of religious conversion groups is to overwhelm the new recruit with positive affect. Lofland describes this initial strategy as used by the followers of the "Divine Principles" as follows:

> The conscious strategy of these encapsulating week-end camps was to drench prospects in approval and love—to "love bomb" them, as the DP's termed it. The cognitive hesitations and emotional reservations of prospects could then be drowned in calls of loving solidarity. [1977:812]

Lofland goes on to observe: "We learn again from looking at the DP's that love can be the most coercive and cruel power of all" (1977:812). Either love or fear can be used to strengthen the group's hold over the individual and make the individual more vulnerable to radical re-socialization.

RE-SOCIALIZATION CONTEXTS IN THE LARGER SOCIETAL SETTING

Since one of the key features of the re-socialization contexts examined in this section is isolation from the larger society, the effect of the larger social setting on socialization in these contexts is minimal compared to the other contexts considered. But even here, the larger social setting has some effect. For example, antagonism or hostility of the larger society to the re-socializing group may have a solidifying effect on group members, strengthening their commitment and identification with the group. On the other hand, where the re-socialization context is supported or even legitimized by the larger society, we would expect a greater reliance on physical coercion of the inmates, especially if they are in the situation involuntarily. In general, however, the more totalistic the re-socialization context, the less it is influenced in its socialization processes and outcomes by the larger society.

Conclusion

Most of the general principles of learning (such as reinforcement, modeling, role-playing, and direct instruction), as well as processes of social influence (such as labeling and expectancy effects, social comparisons and reference-group influences, and group pressure in creating norms and constructing realities), operate to some degree in each of the socialization contexts examined. But it is also apparent, even in this brief review, that these contexts constitute different socialization experiences for individuals. Some of this is undoubtedly due to the association of these contexts with individuals at different life stages: children are more involved with family and school contexts; adults are more involved in occupational and re-socialization contexts.

But the main contention in this essay is that differences in the socialization experiences provided by these contexts are due largely to differences in goals, functions, and social structural features of these contexts. They constitute the parameters within which the two general aspects of socialization (adaptation and self-assertion) take place, and also bear on the effectiveness of the socialization processes. In this regard, the structure of the family, as a small, intimate group of relatively long duration with strongly affective bonds between members, is a relatively effective context for socialization. Processes of modeling, identification, and reinforcement are especially evident in this context, but most of the other processes also apply. Adolescent peer groups are small, voluntary associations between status equals that provide an arena for the exercise of independence from adult authority (especially parents and school). The development of intimate friendship bonds and the ability of the group to exert pressure toward conformity are key features of the socialization experience in this context. School and occupation are not as encompassing or as effective in their socialization outcomes as are family and peers. Yet, individuals spend much of their lives in these settings, and they do leave their mark on the personality. Both school and occupational contexts are more formal, public, and judgmental than are family and peers. Through the individual's adaptation to the particular features of these contexts, they give rise to general norms, values, and behavior patterns. In addition, one of the important things learned in the acquisition of institutional roles is how to maintain self-esteem even under adverse organizational circumstances.

The re-socialization contexts considered here are the most dramatic in their socialization outcomes. They highlight one of the most important features of a socialization context—the socialization ratio. In general, the higher the ratio of agents of socialization to socializees, the more effective is the context of socialization in bringing about changes in individuals. Since one's sense of reality (especially sense of self) is dependent in large part on social confirmation, the concerted efforts of group members to change a person's self-conception can have a powerful effect. In a sense, the radical re-socialization context is a combination of some of the most important socialization features of family and peer group. Like the family, it treats the socializee in holistic terms in the context of intimate, affectively charged relations. Like the peer group, it has the force of numbers in the socialization ratio.[13]

To the extent that the socialization ratio is low, the organization is less effective in achieving its socialization goals. There are two main reasons for this: (1) the agents of socialization have less direct exposure to, and impact on, any one socializee; and (2) the socializee cohort is likely to organize into a context of socialization itself, developing goals and norms that frequently are antithetical to those of the organization. This is evident in such institutional contexts of socialization as schools, prisons, and even within large families.[14]

There are a few other general observations that can be made concerning factors affecting the efficacy of socialization contexts. Mortimer and Simmons observed in their review of the socialization literature (1978: 439) that socialization is most likely to succeed in situations of high affectivity where the socializing agents have considerable power over the socializee. These are conditions most closely approximated by the two most powerful contexts of socialization examined here—family and religious-conversion groups. Within the family, it was found that high parental support combined with high control produced children most effectively socialized to adult standards. Positive affect, however, is not a sine qua non for effective socialization. The political re-socialization contexts suggest that fear combined with total control of the socializee can have similar powerful socialization consequences.

The more the individual can be involved in the socialization process, the more effective is the socialization context. Even if the individual's acts are initially coerced and do not reflect the sentiment or attitude that is desired by the socializers, the appropriate behavior often eventually instills the intended psychological response. This proposition becomes more evident in situations where the socializee becomes responsible for socializing others (a common circumstance for older siblings in the family and for "advanced" socializees in conversion contexts). In the process of socializing others, they become more effectively socialized themselves.

SOME DIRECTIONS AND TRENDS

A number of years ago, Sewell (1963) observed that sociology's contribution to the topic of socialization is its emphasis on the importance of social structure in human development. This has not always been apparent, and some might still disagree with Sewell's assessment. The reason is that much of the sociological work on socialization has been done out of the symbolic interaction tradition which has emphasized social process rather than social structure. One of the promising trends in the area of socialization is a gradual convergence between these two positions—between the classical sociological concern with the social structural bases of human experience and behavior, and the interactionists' concern with social process as the matrix for the creation of meanings. Actually, this is not such a drastic convergence. A number of scholars have argued for the compatability of symbolic interactionism with social structural concerns (Maines 1977; Lewis 1976). Good examples of this convergence can be found in the works of Turner (1976), Rosenberg (1979), and especially Stryker (1980). Focusing on contexts of socialization requires a consideration of both social structure and social process.

But perhaps the most significant trend in the area of socialization (within both sociology and psychology) is an increasing shift from a passive to an active view of the individual. Wrong's (1961) criticism of sociology as having an "over-socialized view of man" is becoming less true. The active, creative self has always been conspicuous in symbolic interaction theory, if not as evident in its research. The problem for the interactionists has been in translating this theoretical stance into research on socialization (Gecas 1979b). The emergence of exchange theory and conflict theory on the socialization scene has given new impetus to the self-as-actor and self-creator themes (Tallman 1976; Mortimer and Simmons 1978).[15] It has led to increased attention to the reciprocal effects between socializers and socializees, between social structure and the individual.

This shift to a more active self in the socialization process is even more evident in psychology. To a large extent, it is associated with the increasing influence of cognitive developmental theories and to the cognitive revolution in psychology in general (see especially Bandura 1977, 1978). As applied to socialization research, there is increasing emphasis on competence, self-efficacy, intrinsic motivation, and the sense of personal causation in determining outcomes. For example, in parent/child interactions, there has been an increased focus on how infants influence parents and how patterns of interaction become stabilized (Zigler and Seitz 1978). There is a clear convergence of sociological and psychological thinking in the direction of a more active self. The direction for future research on socialization is to explicate the reciprocal relationships between the individual and his environment, and, in the process, to show how contexts of socialization shape and are shaped by those passing through them.

NOTES

The writing of this paper was supported in part by Project 0364, Department of Rural Sociology, Agricultural Research Center, Washington State University. Appreciation is extended to Morris Rosenberg, Jeylan Mortimer, Susan Hales, Sheldon Stryker, Darwin Thomas, and Irving Tallman for their helpful comments and criticisms of earlier drafts.

1. We must use caution, however, in interpreting these relationships because differences in family size reflect to some extent differences in the values and goals parents hold, which are related to religion and social class. Yet family size does seem to have an independent effect on family patterns beyond its association with social class and religion (Elder and Bowerman 1963).

2. The reference here is to elementary and high schools, not to colleges and schools for professional or career training.

3. Teachers, of course, are also socialized in the classroom (Dreeben 1973 and Jackson 1968 provide insightful analyses of the teacher's predicament in the classroom), but this focus is more relevant to occupational socialization.

4. In the writings of the "culture of poverty" and "cultural deprivation" advocates, the family is typically seen as the source of the child's inadequacies, which the school must correct and overcome (Valentine 1968).

5. There is a considerable body of research on this type of socialization. See, for example, the work of Becker and his colleagues (1968), and Blau et al. (1979).

6. The closest that Kohn comes to a consideration of the social relationships in the work setting is in his study of "bureaucratic man" (1971). But even here, the major focus is on the content of the job, especially its degree of complexity, rather than on the social organizational properties of the work group.

7. There are, of course, many other important analyses of the effects of work on workers—the literature in this area is quite extensive (see, for example, Shepard 1977 and Blauner 1964 on technology and alienation; Kornhauser 1965 on job stress; and the *Work in America* report 1973 on worker satisfaction).

8. Bowles and Gintis (1976) also point out that the nature of social relations characteristic of capitalist economies is also generally found in communist countries. The worker is just as powerless in the latter countries. The main difference is that control of the means of production and the products of labor is in the hands of the state rather than the private corporation.

9. In this section, I have relied primarily on the following empirical reports of socialization processes in these small, intensive groups: Lifton's (1961) extensive research on "thought reform" of Western civilians and Chinese intellectuals by the Chinese Communists after the Korean War; Empey's (1961, 1971) research on the use of peer groups in delinquent rehabilitation; and Lofland's (1965, 1966, 1977) work on religious conversion.

10. Assault on identity as an initial stage in the re-socialization process is also evident in the context of large, bureaucratic socialization institutions. Goffman's *Asylums* (1961a) is the classic work on this topic. In these settings, it is accomplished less by direct assault than by processes of depersonalization stemming from the regimentation and standardization of life on the ward. Much of Goffman's analysis is an examination of how the institution and the staff strip away the various supports for the patient's self.

11. The voluntaristic, self-determinate conception of religious conversions has been stressed by several scholars (Richardson 1979, 1980; Straus 1976;). Richardson (1979) distinguishes the "old paradigm" of religious conversion from the emerging "new paradigm." The former promulgates a view of the convert as a passive and helpless pawn of forces beyond his control and/or understanding. By contrast, the "new paradigm" offers a view of the religious convert as an active seeker, in search of meaning and purpose, and very much an agent in the process of religious conversion. Translating this distinction into our own terms, the "old paradigm" of religous conversion emphasizes *adaptation* as the socialization or conversion process; the "new paradigm" stresses self-assertion and self-determination. I would also note that aside from intellectual proclivities for one "view of man" or the other, the nature of the context within which conversions take place has a bearing on the predominance of one or the other socialization mode.

12. There is ample evidence in the social-psychological literature that behavior initiated for whatever reasons gives rise to self-attitudes and beliefs (Bem 1972 is most closely identified with this position).

13. Although the socialization in these contexts is more dramatic and occurs

within a shorter period of time than in other contexts, it frequently does not have the same long-term effects. The force of the socialization experience seems to diminish the longer the individual has been away from the closed group context (see Empey 1978:325 for an assessment of the long-term effects of the experiments in group delinquency rehabilitation and Lifton 1961 on those released from the Chinese thought-reform programs).

14. There may even be a "boomerang effect" under these circumstances, in that the socializee may develop in ways *opposite* to those intended by the agents of socialization within these contexts (Rosenberg, personal communication).

15. The concern with the self as cause and as consequence goes back to the very beginnings of sociology as a discipline. Cartwright points out that Comte viewed man as both a creature and a creator of his social world and identified the central problem of social psychology as addressing the question of how the individual can be both the cause and the consequence of society (1979:90).

7 ALLEN D. GRIMSHAW

Talk and Social Control

What is so perilous, then, in the fact that people speak, and that their speech proliferates? Where is the danger in that?

FOUCAULT

Introduction

Language is a truly remarkable phenomenon—arbitrary and yet systematic, obviously learned but apparently on the basis of specific innate capacities, understood by small children, but infinite in its possible variations.

Language is arbitrary in that each one employs only some of the almost infinite range of discrete noises that can be produced by the human vocal system and combines these sounds in different ways to represent meaning. It is arbitrary, too, in that each language has different rules for making these combinations, and the lexicon of each language cuts up the infinite world of possible meanings in different ways. It is systematic in that each language has rules about how its set of noises can be combined, and about how the meaning-bearing combinations of noises can themselves be combined to convey mutually understood meanings. It is systematic, too, in that *all* languages consist not only of minimal units arranged in orderly fashion, with hierarchies of ordered units, but also in that all languages possess certain shared minimal components (for example, nouns, verbs), syntactic and semantic relations among these units (such as subject-object), and functional relations (for example, interrogatives and statements).

Linguistics, the formal study of language, claims as its central foci of investigation the structures of sound and of meaning in human languages and the ties between the two domains. Phonologists study the sound structure of language; syntacticians study its grammatical structure. Both are engaged in a search for the rules[1] that govern the creation of combinations of sounds and of further configurations of sound combinations in communication. With only a few exceptions, linguists historically have studied semantic issues within languages as formal systems and have been interested in issues of, for example, whether transformations (that is, from active to passive voice) preserve meaning, rather than in social dimensions of meaning. Sociologists and anthropologists are, in contrast, interested in language in use in social contexts, and in how speech (and other language in use) simultaneously influences social interaction and has its "meaning" constrained by its interactive context. This paper is concerned with the possibilities for a sociologically informed social semantics; it will be limited primarily to examination of the sociological relevance of speech.

Who people are, whom they engage in spoken discourse, where, when, and what about, all influence the way they talk. The manner of talk, moreover, conditions perceptions of interlocutors, and constrains social relationships and emerging social structures.[2] Causal relations between speech and social structure are complex, and speech can be, simultaneously or serially, (1) an indicator (of, for example, SES attributes of speakers); (2) an independent variable (in determining subsequent behavior of hearer[s]); and/or (3) a dependent variable (in instances where settings constrain code selection, as, for example, in courtrooms, classrooms, or churches).

Some researchers have responded to this complexity by involving themselves primarily in correlational studies of, for example, particularities of speech production associated with categorical membership (class, sex, race, age, and so forth). Others seem to be bogged down in attempts to sort out how much (and which parts) of native speakers' facility in use of their language is innately programmed and how much learned. Some seek the origins of language and keys to its evolution as a human medium. Others continue to wrestle with the nature and limitations of cognitive capacities that are possibly associated with one or another language or code—questions of considerable practical social and political import as manifested in problems of cross-cultural (cross-language) communication and the continuing dispute on deficit theory (see below). Still others (to terminate what could be a much longer list), mostly philosophers but increasingly linguists, psychologists, and social psychologists as well, are deeply involved in questions of meaning and intent.

My own view is that the immediate issues to which a sociological/social psychological sociolinguistics should address itself can and should be more profound and ambitious than the identification of correlations. At the same time, I do not believe that we have the data base or the theoretical resources to attack successfully problems of intention, innateness, or cognitive efficiency (though there are interesting leads on each of these questions). I take it as a given that neither language (speech) nor social structure is causally prior, that they are cooccurring and codetermining (see Hymes 1966 and Grimshaw 1969 or, for a more extended discussion, 1973c) and that our task is to see how speech functions (works) in social interaction. This implies that it works in systematic and *discoverable* ways.[3] I turn now to a discussion of this systematicity, to the notion of rule, and to rule-discovery procedures.

Rules

Linguists share with sociologists the belief that the phenomena they study are orderly. Linguists have long been committed to investigation of universal linguistic functions (to be found in all languages) and of invariance within languages. Linguists use the term *rule* to refer to statements about regularities within languages themselves, for example, about how tenses are formed by inflections or vowels shortened or lengthened in different, and specified, consonantal environments. They believe that language learning consists of discovery, by learners, of the arbitrary but consistent way in which their language is so phonologically and syntactically organized as to meet universal language functions. Some rules of grammar (syntax) and orthography are taught prescriptively, for example, "don't split infinitives" or "i before e, except after c (or before gh, gn, or n!)" but most are discovered by speakers at an unconscious level and are not recoverable without linguistic training (second language training is, of course, much more prescriptive). Grammar is codified, but not (ordinarily) in the prescriptive sense of statutes and regulations governing many other social behaviors. Hearers sometimes respond to rule violations (usually characterized as performance errors rather than as failure to "know" the rules), by treating the rule violator as "careless," or "stupid," or not a native speaker—but *not as in some way morally defective.* (Errors might be fatal if they revealed a speaker's social identity as "enemy." For a putative historical case, see Sibley (1965) on *shibboleth.*) Linguists generally operate as if productive and interpretive rules are isomorphic; this is not the case for other social behaviors (including the interactional accomplishment of conversation, see, for example, Cicourel, 1974a).

That individual languages employ arbitrary "choices" from the infinite inventory of human phonological productive capacity to map meaning onto sound should not obscure the fact that all individual languages share functions which must be performed universally to accomplish the social through talk. Sociologists tend to look at social norms (rules) in terms of the societal functions they meet; we sometimes overlook how individual cultures (societies) have "chosen" modes of fulfillment quite arbitrarily (for example, alimentation, dress, greetings, family structure, and so forth). It may be that some social norms appear to be less arbitrary than linguistic rules simply because the potential range of choices is more limited.

Many contemporary linguists see the grammar of a language as a body of rules for combining sounds into words and words into sentences, "a device," according to Chomsky, "that generates all of the grammatical sequences of [a language] L and none of the ungrammatical ones" (1957: 13). Nouns and verbs and other lexical elements have distinguishing features, and some linguists stipulate a congruence between syntactic well-formedness and meaningfulness (Lyons 1968) such that not all nouns can be combined with all verbs in simple sentences of the form

Noun Phrase + Verb Phrase.[4] Linguists are not concerned with consideration of social acceptability, that is, unacceptability of blasphemous or obscene utterances. More important for us, neither are they concerned with what I will be calling social "appropriateness," that is, whether considerations of social *structure* exclude a syntactically well-formed and interpretable utterance from what Lyons has called use "in normal circumstances" (1968:150). Interactions of the dimensions of syntactic well-formedness, interpretability, meaningfulness, and social evaluation are shown in figure 7.1.

To the extent that "linguistic theory is concerned primarily with an ideal speaker-listener, in a completely homogeneous speech community, who knows its language perfectly" and makes no performance errors (Chomsky 1965:3), it is primarily concerned with the rules that produce sentences such as those in the first row of figure 7.1. The construction of that theory, however, leads linguists to investigate the several varieties of the syntactically anomalous which appear in the several cells of the second row of the figure, that is, the intended violations of grammatically in, for example, metaphor and the performance errors (found in otherwise grammatical sentences) of cell 6 and the ungrammatical (in the prescriptive sense) sentences of socially disvalued dialects or registers of cell 7. Linguists have no particular linguistic interest in cell 2, which contains sentences that are syntactically well-formed and meaningful, but possibly tasteless. Linguistic theory has not considered the special case of cell 3, which contains sentences that are syntactically well-formed and interpretable, but that violate social structural expectations. As will be seen, such examples provide important data for sociologists.

The notions of rule and rule violation are central to any satisfactory understanding of social behaviors, including language; neither linguists nor sociologists have developed widely accepted definitions of the terms themselves or of procedures for study of the behavioral regularities with which they are associated. My truncated treatment here reflects those uncertainties: it is doubtful that they could be resolved even if I had unlimited space. For present purposes, the following discussion is posited on a belief that there are linguistic, sociolinguistic, and social-interactional regularities, that these regularities are in some sense principled or rule-governed, and that the "rules" differ along at least the following dimensions:

1. The extent to which untrained individuals can articulate rules (or principles) underlying behavioral regularities (apparently higher for social behavior than for linguistic production).
2. The degree of socially visible codification (linguistic rules are known primarily to linguists).
3. The occurrence of instrumental-expressive-evaluative distinctions (there are meta-terminologies for these distinctions for language as well as other social behaviors).
4. The occurrence and differential severity of sanctions for violations (generally more severe for social violations).
5. The disciplinary concern with specification of discovery procedures (historically higher in linguistics but shifting as linguists become interested in concommitant variation and sociologists in invariance).

FIGURE 7.1

Some Linguistic and Social Considerations of Syntactic Well-formedness, Interpretability, Meaningfulness, and Social Evaluation[a]

	Interpretable				Uninterpretable and Unmeaningful
	Sensible (meaningful)		Nonsensible (unmeaningful)		
	Approved	Socially Disvalued	Socially Impossible	Biologically Impossible	
Syntactically Well-formed in Standard English	1 David has fathered twins.	2 The ape crapped on the altar.[b]	3 Ford cajoled Nixon into resigning from the presidency.[c]	4 David breast-fed his twins himself.[d]	5 Null
Syntactically Anomalous in Standard English	6 1. My brain is a three-day-old poached egg. (Metaphor) 2. This light creates people to lose gas. (Performance error)	7 Them mens hitted theyselves cruel.[e]	8 Null	9 David breast-fed his twins himself.[d]	10 Purpresture scandium siphonostomatous synergizes.[f]

a. There will be both linguists and sociologists who will disagree with one or more of the illustrations. I am not interested in consensus on labels or on the illustrations themselves as much as in conveying some sense of relevant distinctions among underlying variables.
b. This sentence might, of course, be considered quite "acceptable" if presented in a context that permits it to be interpreted as poetry.
c. This sentence is nonsensible not only because it is historically false but also (and for present purposes, more importantly) because we know that the manipulative strategy "cajole" would not be employed (successfully) to obtain an outcome of such moment by participants with the social characteristics and social relationships these are known to have. See below on *instrumentalities*.
d. Since this sentence violates selectional restrictions (Chomsky 1965; Lyons 1977), some linguists would not consider it to be syntactically well-formed. See note 4 of text. Sentence 1 in cell 6 is also biologically impossible, of course, but meaningful through conversational implicature (Grice 1975).
e. There could be a dialect of English, of course, in which this sentence would be considered syntactically well-formed.
f. Some reader may be able to construct a scenario (context) in which this salad makes sense. See note 1, above.

6. The ease of access to a satisfactory data base (much higher for linguistics: some linguists have employed their own intuitions as a data base; extensive samples of actual speech [or writing] are relatively easy to collect [see Labov 1972a]).

SOCIAL-INTERACTIONAL AND SOCIOLINGUISTIC RULES

Human beings attain social goals through talk. That this gets done (with errors and violations of a magnitude sufficient ordinarily only to reveal the underlying patterns) is itself remarkable. What is even more remarkable is the substantial similarity in how it gets done in what at first appear to be very different cultures and very different modes of talk. Considerations of this nature make cell 3 of figure 7.1 most important to social psychologically oriented sociologists.

The claim that people everywhere accomplish social goals with talk implies two questions: (1) do they everywhere accomplish the same things, namely, is there some set of universal functions; and (2) do they everywhere accomplish them in the same manner, namely, are there sociolinguistic and/or social interactional universals (Grimshaw, 1973a)? I believe that the answer to both is yes; but that there are also both functions and modes of fulfilling functions that are culturally or societally specific. This implies two tasks for social psychologists interested in language in use: (1) specification and differentiation of system-specific and extra-systemic (that is, universal) rules; (2) investigation of the ways in which behavior consonant with these rules gets the socially imperative (or simply desirable) accomplished. Limitations of space will not permit me to address the question of universality in this paper, and the bulk of my illustrative material will be drawn from English usage. The broader question should be kept in mind.

All social interaction involves communication; it is difficult to make a firm distinction between social-interactional and sociolinguistic rules. For preliminary and heuristic purposes I have been using this tentative distinction: (1) social-interactional rules govern the accomplishment of social behavior within social structures with such features as, for example, role, hierarchy, exchange requirements, and so forth; and (2) sociolinguistic rules govern the uses of communicative resources (spoken and written language, kinesic communication, symbolic management, and so forth) within sets of social structural constraints. If this distinction is employed, social-interactional rules are those constraining (1) interactional processes (*forms* in the Simmelian sense), such as the social behaviors associated with the social relations of conflict and accommodation, and more specifically, (2) the *doing* or *accomplishing* of interactional *work* (as these terms have been used by ethnomethodologists), such as the social behaviors associated with requesting, greeting, insulting, remedying rudeness, self-identifying, and the general accomplishment of sustained everyday interaction. The sociolinguistic concern is with the use of language resources in those doings and accomplishings, for example, the ways (and contexts) in which the word "friend" might be used variously to request, greet, insult, and so on (for a further elaboration of this distinction and examples, see Grimshaw 1980a).

The identification and explanation of the social behavior associated with Simmelian forms is an enterprise firmly established in sociology, engaging both scholars using surveys or aggregated statistical data (macro-sociology) and students of, for instance, coalition formation in the small groups laboratory (micro-sociology). Illustrations in this chapter are from the micro level. (For a somewhat dated discussion of some of the "macro" literature, see Grimshaw 1974. For some more recent materials, see Angle 1976; Heath 1977; O'Barr and O'Barr 1976).

In the pages following I will provide examples of speech used as social-psychological (sociological) data. I will focus primarily on the general matter of getting things done with words and then turn very briefly to the question of how we come to be able to do this, that is, the acquisition and modification of linguistic, sociolinguistic, and social-interactional rules. What follows *is* a sampling; readers who do not find attention to topics of particular moment to them can be assured that consideration of language-in-use aspects of those topics probably can be found in the growing literature.

Getting Things Done with Words

As will be seen from the following discussion, much of the literature on the use of language in social control comes from other disciplines. Basil Bernstein is one of a few sociologists who have explicitly addressed issues of language and social control[5] (see Bernstein 1971, 1973, 1975; for extended commentary on this corpus see, inter alia, Grimshaw 1973b, 1976; Hill 1977; Hill and Varenne forthcoming; Poole 1975); he is also one of a very few workers in the field who has offered a theoretical perspective articulating micro and macro questions. The central issue for him is how language is employed as a resource in social control. On the macrolevel he believes that those who control symbols control societies (through their use in "cultural reproduction" [Bourdieu and Passeron 1970] and therefore in continuing class dominance). On the microlevel he believes that families and schools, as principal agents of transmission in cultural reproduction, socialize children into greater or lesser effectiveness in symbol management in "relatively context independent" discourse environments. The greater an individual's "context independence" in speech (through greater facility in Bernstein's now familiar "elaborated" code),[6] the greater her/his ability to disengage from the immediate and the concrete (that is, to attain cognitive detachment), and thus the greater her/his individual autonomy and control over access to life's prizes.

Most of the studies to which I will refer focus, with varying degrees of specificity, on issues related to the use of speech in social control. This issue is at the core of the best-known work of Bernstein and his associates (although other concerns are also addressed, particularly in the writing on "classification" and "frame" in education; see 1975); he is interested in the difference between two principal modes of control, positional and personal (a third mode, the imperative, appears in all contexts and codes), and the linguistic realizations (speech) that accompany each. The positional mode ("Because your mother said so") relies on the authority of the controller, the personal on the "good sense" of the controlled ("Because you could slip and fall and hurt yourself"). Each mode permits variation along the dimension of discretion permitted the controlled, with higher discretion meaning a larger range of alternatives for the controlled and, presumably, some room for negotiation ("Absolutely not" versus "Well, you'll have to walk home if you stay" or "When do you think you'll be 'ready' to leave?"). Controllers use different mixes of control modes and discretion in accomplishing different functions, for example, regulative, instructional, interpersonal, and imaginative (Bernstein's set of four language functions is abstracted from Halliday's [1973a, 1973b, 1975] set), and each child, of course, is exposed to different varieties of control in different functional and socializing contexts.

Bernstein asserts that positional control with low discretion is more likely than other modes of control to invoke shared understandings and to result, therefore, in speech variants with context-dependent meanings. All children (and presumably most adults as well) are doubtless exposed to social control linguistically realized through each of the four possible modes (namely, positional vs. personal *and* high or low discretion). He is simply arguing that the control modes are differently distributed (in terms of actual use) across controllers and those they control, across socializing contexts, and across social class groups. He further argues that some combinations result in greater or lesser effectiveness in certain kinds of speech codes, that variable effectiveness is associated with location in the social structure, and that perpetuation of the social order is a direct consequence. He does not dispute the importance of resource control (power) in the maintenance of class dominance. He argues, however, that raw power and force are unnecessary as long as the dominated have *their* potential power contained through a combination of direct symbolic manipulation and patterns of socialization that reduces *their* capacity to manipulate symbols. To the extent that restricted code permits invocation of shared understandings, moreover, he would acknowledge its very considerable potential for social and political mobilization—to the extent that new symbols could be incorporated as part of the shared base ("Black Power" might be an example).

Bernstein has lacked neither enthusiastic admirers nor sharp critics; many of the latter have actually been more critical of the uses to which the admirers have put Bernstein's work than of the work itself. The criticisms have been methodological, theoretical-substantive, and ideological. Among the methodological criticisms are that his data are unsatisfactory because they are based on reported and/or hypothetical speech rather than actual utterances, and that data have been elicited primarily from mothers (and some children) rather than from all important socializing agents (including, for example, fathers, peers, and teachers—to say nothing of the media). Other critics have complained that neither the conceptualization nor the measurement of elaborated and restricted codes, central to Bernstein's position, are satisfactory. Labov, in a widely reprinted article, has attacked the underlying assumption that some speech codes are less efficient than others. (Labov's [1972b reprinted as chapter 5 in 1972c] attack is actually directed against claims that nonstandard American English is less *logical* than the standard variety, not a claim made by Bernstein. The links are clear, and recognized by Bernstein, who has responded in the paperback edition of his 1971 collection [1973b]. For a comprehensive treatment of this issue see, for example, Edwards 1976, Hill 1977, and Hill and Varenne forthcoming.) More ideologically oriented critics have complained that Bernstein implies that the poor are less intelligent than the rich, and that his perspective denies the possibility of constructive change. Bernstein denies both these charges (see especially 1975).

Bernstein is a controversial figure. He has doubtless made statements of greater generality than his data have warranted. The fact remains, however, that he has raised critically important questions about the relations of class, language, and social control, and that his conceptual apparatus has proved to be extremely fruitful in suggesting new directions of work in a hitherto sociologically neglected area.

STRATEGIES OF VERBAL MANIPULATION

Sociological social psychology has (as does its more psychological cognate) a rich and extensive literature on interpersonal influence; representations of several traditions of work appear elsewhere in this volume. The fact that human social actors spend much of their time with other actors engaged either in attempting to manipulate those others into doing things for them or in themselves being objects of such manipulation is widely recognized. While numerous studies have been made of, for example, persuasion, influence, and compliance, little attention has been paid to the verbal behaviors involved in manipulative acts in social interaction (surprisingly, more attention may have been paid to other channels of communication in such manipulative acts, see section on body communication, p. 224). Given the fundamentally complementary character of social life and its matching of power with weakness, resources with needs, and assertiveness with acquiescence, it is not surprising that much talk is manipulative, with speakers attempting to cause their listeners to alter their behaviors (including speech) or attitudes (for example, experience enhanced or diminished respect for themselves or other actors). Attention to verbal repertoires employed has been modest.

A general formulation for characterizing such manipulative interaction is:

1. SOURCE INSTRUMENTALITY GOAL $\left\{ \begin{matrix} \text{to} \\ \text{into} \end{matrix} \right\}$ RESULT

as in:

2. Jones persuaded Smith to shorten his paper.

where SOURCE is speaker (or manipulator), INSTRUMENTALITY is a mode of talk (typically labeled by a speech-act verb), GOAL is hearer (or target of manipulative move), and RESULT is the outcome desired by SOURCE (that is, an overt behavior by, or a change in attitudinal disposition of, GOAL). It is important to keep in mind that (1) is a *report* of a kind of act, and neither itself such an INSTRUMENTALITY nor a description of the content of such an INSTRUMENTALITY. An instance of an actual INSTRUMENTALITY might be something like:

3. Smith, we simply don't have the space, and as most of our readers won't be interested in speech-act philosophy anyway, couldn't you at least sharply reduce the number of references?

and of content, something like:

4. Jones persuaded Smith to shorten his paper by explaining the space problem and indicating that no one would read the philosophical stuff anyway.

or:

5. Jones persuaded Smith to shorten his paper by saying, "Smith, we simply don't have the space, and as most of our readers won't be interested in speech-act philosophy anyway, couldn't you at least sharply reduce the number of references?"

What content constitutes, e.g. persuasion, is an interesting question; my attention in this paper, however, is directed primarily to constraints on selection of an INSTRUMENTALITY, and to what constraints are considered as reasonable and likely to accurately reflect what actually happened.

Many utterances directed toward manipulating others (in the restricted sense I use here) are neither direct nor obvious. There are, nonetheless, a very large number of INSTRUMENTALITIES for which English has specific labels, as well as a substantial number of recognizable strategies that are not labeled. Since Austin (1962) coined the term *speech act,* philosophers (for example, Searle, especially 1969, 1979, forthcoming; Grice 1975) and more recently linguists (for example, Labov and Fanshel 1977; Cole and Morgan 1975, especially papers by Green, Gordon and Lakoff, Fraser, and Ross) and some psychologists (for example, Bates 1976) and anthropologists (for example, Brown and Levinson 1978) have been doing our work for us. I have no space to treat these contributions in detail; I would like to suggest some developments that are important for consideration of how things get done with talk and then identify critical sociological issues that become more amenable to investigation if these concepts are incorporated into our work.

Most of us employ fairly primitive classification systems in our own ongoing analysis of the talk that permeates our social environment. We make distinctions among, for example, talk for the sake of talking, gossip, serious discussion, and talk as display and are aware of functional difference among utterances, such as questions, statements, and imperatives. While more elaborated classifications of speech acts have been around for some time, it would not be unfair to say that modern speech-act theory began with Austin's (1962) *How To Do Things With Words,* and has received its most useful taxonomic elaboration (for social scientists) in the work of John Searle (for example, 1968, 1969, 1979; see also Sadock 1974). Searle (1979, chap 1) distinguishes utterances with reference to their: (a) propositional content; (b) illocutionary force (what the speaker is "attempting" to get done); and (c) perlocutionary effect (outcomes as manifested, ultimately, in hearers' behaviors). In further distinguishing among different types of illocutionary acts, he invokes twelve dimensions of variation, including, for example, differences in (1) the point (or purpose) of the act; (2) the direction of fit between words and the world (that is, *word-to-world,* such as statements, descriptions, and explanations, and *world-to-word,* such as requests, commands, and promises); (3) expressed psychological states; and (4) force or strength with which the illocutionary point is presented (a critical dimension for sociologists, and one loaded with problems). As will be noted below, other differences noted by Searle are more familiar to sociologists, and have emerged as central in a number of analyses of social control. Further complications are introduced through consideration of, for example, truth conditions on propositional content, speaker-attribute conditions such as "sincerity," and speaker-assigned hearer attributes, such as shared knowledge. As will be noted below, less attention has been paid to hearers than to speakers, and sociologists will need to remedy this neglect if they are to profitably use talk as data (the neglect has not been total, see, for example, Sacks 1972a on "hearers' maxims"). Finally, still another complexity lies in wait for the unwary: the issue of "intention" (which Searle is currently addressing, for example, 1979, forthcoming) or "motive" (on which see Burke 1945). The quotes around "intention," "motive," and "attempting" (above) conceal some major gaps in our understanding of what goes on in talk.

If conversational participants were to rely on the mechanical application of grammatical rules for interpreting the "dictionary" meaning of utterances in discourse, they would be confused, misled, and unable successfully to engage in talk. There are a number of conceptual frames that address the question of how interactants sort out what is meant from what is said. I will note only three here: (1) conversational implicature; (2) comprehensive discourse analysis (as that term has been used by Labov and Fanshel 1977); and (3) the complementary perspectives of "key" (Hymes 1974) and "frame" (Goffman 1974).

Conversational implicature. Grice (1975) observes that much talk is based on a cooperative principle, through which interlocutors who share a concern for maximally effective exchange of information can assume that their partners will make the contributions required in order to achieve a jointly accepted notion of where an exchange is going (he realizes, of course, that there are numerous instances in which purposes of influence or manipulation will militate against operation of the principle—just as the principle itself holds for all rationally cooperative human behavior and not just for talk). In order to cooperate, he argues, interlocutors will ordinarily follow four maxims of: (1) quantity (that is, say as much as and no more than is needed); (2) *quality* (essentially, tell the truth); (3) *relation* (be relevant); (4) *manner* (be clear). Violation of one or another of the maxims can occur because of contradictions (one can't be met without violating another), because of intentional violation of the larger cooperative principle, because of superordinate norms such as enjoining secrecy, or through intentional flouting. It is in this latter instance, where an utterance seems to violate a specific maxim *without intending to violate the larger cooperative principle,* that conversational implicature comes into play. Interlocutors employ conversational implicature to locate the missing in the elliptic, to penetrate the subtleties of understatement, and, in instances of more exotic exploitations of maxim violation, to interpret irony, metaphor, meiosis, and hyperbole. Readers familiar with Cicourel's (1974a) "interpretive procedures" with their properties of "practical reasoning" will recognize their close kinship with Grice's implicature.

Comprehensive discourse analysis. Labov and Fanshel (1977), in their pioneering study of therapeutic conversation, identify the interactional accomplishments of speakers as the end goal of their analyses, that is, "the determination of the *actions* that are being performed by speakers through their utterances" (p. 58). The critical behaviors are, they assert, "not such speech acts as requests and assertions, but rather challenges, defenses, and retreats, which have to do with the status of the participants, their rights and obligations, and their changing relationships in terms of social organization" (pp. 58–59). A critical stage in their analysis (for a fuller explication, see the original or Grimshaw 1979) is *expansion* (synthetic integration of textual materials, prosodic and paralinguistic cues, and analysts' knowledge of ethnographic context) into an elaboration of what is "actually" being *said* (in contrast to what is being *done,* that is, interaction), aiming at no less than a *reproduction of participant's procedures in everyday conversation.*[7] Thus, a spouse's (or parent's or employer's) utterance:

Well, what happened *this* time?

might be expanded (depending on context, and so on) as:

You are late again and this is a topic on which I have previously expressed disgruntlement. You have obligations to meet here and at the very least you should inform me when you are not going to meet them. You have not done so. You frequently claim conflicting obligations. I suppose that you will this time. I am skeptical.

In an actual analysis such expansions are extended, revised, and occasionally rejected as additional materials in a corpus are examined and incorporated.

Concern with what is being *done* is, however, both the central focus of the discourse analysis and its sociological endpoint.[8] In the hypothetical example, this means determining how participants can interpret an utterance in question form not only as a question but also as a complaint, or an accusation, or an attribution (to hearer) of negative qualities, or possibly as an invitation to disputation. In the course of their analysis, Labov and Fanshel locate specific (to the particular events being talked about) and general (extrasituational norms and/or understandings) propositions which appear as recurrent communications (1977:51). They list a number of both local and general propositions and some fifty-six interactional "terms" they have identified in the relatively brief conversational fragment they have analyzed; it is clear that other propositions and other interactional moves are more likely in other varieties of conversation.[9] It *is* interaction that is achieved in conversation, and the kind of analysis done by Labov and Fanshel provides a systematic mapping of the route followed to arrive at the characterization of what it is that participants are *doing.*

Frame analysis. Grice and other students of the logic of conversation and speech acts assume that interlocutors are usually motivated to accomplish maximally effective exchange of information and thus follow the cooperative principle even in the flouting of associated maxims. Labov and Fanshel, although acknowledging that interlocutors sometimes obscure both what they "really" mean and their interactional intent, have studied an interaction in which patient and therapist presumably share a common goal, that is, improvement in the patient's ability to cope. Goffman, in contrast, has devoted much of his attention over the last several decades to what he calls, in the 1974 work from which I have borrowed the title of this section, "vulnerabilities of experience." He has been preoccupied with such social manifestations as "impression management" (1959) and "strategic interaction" (1969) and, most recently, with the benign (and not benign) fabrication, keying, breaking, misrepresentation, and disagreement over the frames (closely akin to definitions of situations) through which interactants order, comprehend, and manage their participation in life's events. He has shown that there are main and subsidiary streams (channels) of events going on simultaneously in every interaction and that each of several channels may have meanings on a variety of levels (laminations; my favorite example is the instance of pretending to pretend, pp. 186–87; see also, Austin 1962, chap. 9), and that, aware of these possibilities, interactants monitor the overt and (intendedly) concealed behaviors of their interlocutors in continuing attempts to discover "what's really going on" (he also notes, however, that we sometimes accept the pretended rather than accept the necessity of confronting implications of sham in the putatively sincere). In directing attention to manifestations of these phenomena in conversational discourse, he concludes in part:

> Talk appears as a rapidly shifting stream of differently framed strips, including short-run fabrications (typically benign) and keying of various sorts. Transformation cues are involved, specifying whether a variation from the typical is to be employed, and if so, what kind. . . . If a participant in a conversation did not constantly apply adjustments for frame, he would find himself listening in on a meaningless jumble of words and, with every word he injected, increasing the babble. [1974:544–46]

Reprise and comment. Talk, in combination with other communicative modes (and its written manifestations), is a critical resource in social control. The meaning of lexically and syntactically identical utterances will differ according to "key" ("the tone, manner, or spirit in which an act is done," Hymes 1974:57), the social context in which the event occurs, and the characteristics of participants. Multiple meanings can be conveyed, intendedly or not, by the same utterance in the same key, the same context, with the same participants.

Cynics may conclude that I am saying that nothing is ever as it appears to be. That is true, of course, but the fact is that while there are clear instances of deliberate fraud and deceit, as well as of unintended communicative ineffectiveness, those who engage in conversation usually expect that their coparticipants *will* discern what is *principally intended* behind the sometimes conflicting appearances and they will provide redundant clues and cues to assure that outcome. There are failures in communication. There are more successes. And as Goffman remarks, the successful, routine, and everyday can come to be understood through examination of exceptions (1974:564).[10]

Instrumentalities

There are many things that can go wrong in communication and Goffman has remarked that "talk is more vulnerable than most activity to keying and fabrication" (1974:502). He has also observed, however, that "the coordination of most social activity, let alone close teamwork, assumes that self-believed, if not correct, statements are possible and even likely . . . " (p. 501). Assuming for the moment that a SOURCE and GOAL share productive and interpretive norms, what questions can we ask about the sociological constraints on that variety of social control exemplified in the formulation:

(1) SOURCE INSTRUMENTALITY GOAL $\left\{ \begin{matrix} \text{to} \\ \text{into} \end{matrix} \right\}$ RESULT.

The following is a non-exhaustive list (I exclude a number of specifically linguistic issues. For a somewhat more fully developed treatment of the "agenda," see Grimshaw 1980d):

1. How does SOURCE select a particular verbal strategy (INSTRUMENTALITY) in seeking desired outcomes (RESULTS) in ongoing interaction, or, put somewhat differently, what independent sociological variables constrain selection of strategies as dependent variables? In still other words, what are *socially appropriate strategies?*
   Comment: I will note some of the findings on this question in the next section. Suffice it to say, at this point, that there are numerous syntactically well-formed sentences, for example, that in cell 3 of figure 7.1, that would fit the above format, but that would sound strange indeed to native speakers. Labov and Fanshel 1977 make a thorough specification of the several conditions on requests. See, especially, pp. 77ff.
2. Under what circumstances do GOALS of different social characteristics and with different relations to SOURCES accede to or resist socially appropriate or inappropriate INSTRUMENTALITIES? What are the behavioral manifestations of resistance? Are there socially appropriate and inappropriate modes?

Comment: GOALS may variously mishear, partially understand, or deliberately misunderstand INSTRUMENTALITY. When INSTRUMENTALITY is acknowledgedly understood, GOALS may accede, refuse, "put off," and so on, doing RESULT, they may or may not mitigate refusals (Labov and Fanshel 1977 list a number of possible resistance modes).

3. What effects does the use (successful or not) of one or another INSTRUMENTALITY have on participants in interaction (SOURCE, GOAL, audience)—and on relationships between or among them?
Comment: Subordinates may resent being ordered; friends may feel embarrassed about asking favors; witnesses may be embarrassed by importuning or outraged by abusive commands. It also happens that people can be "pleased to be asked," and that witnesses can admire the interactional competence of a particularly subtle or tactful SOURCE.

4. Are there kinesic and/or prosodic elements associated with the several verbal INSTRUMENTALITIES that are considered as being socially appropriate or inappropriate? Can the production of some kinesic and/or prosodic behaviors be seen as generating messages contrary to those in the "main" verbal channel? What are they? What are responses to them by participants?
Comment: The military, with its emphasis on "command voice" and "command bearing" has long been aware of the importance of *key* (Hymes 1974, see above); parents tell children to apologize "as if you mean it." It is well known that a wink can deny a denial and the tone of an utterance contradict its dictionary meaning. See, inter alia, Labov and Fanshel 1977:42 ff. on "paralinguistic cues"; Bateson et al. 1956 on the "double bind"; Gumperz forthcoming, on "conversational inference." There are specific literatures on, for example, intonation (for example, Bolinger 1964; Crystal 1969; Halliday 1967) and on the interpretation of kinesic cues (for example, Birdwhistell, 1970; Kendon 1977; Scheflen 1973).

5. What are the distinctive grammatical and other features of jointly produced (that is, by more than one interactant) INSTRUMENTALITIES or responses?
Comment: It not infrequently occurs that SOURCE, because of considerations of deference or concern over the propriety of seeking a RESULT, will use an INSTRUMENTALITY which is so indirect that GOAL will be unable to determine what RESULT is being sought. Third parties may then provide metalinguistic glosses, for example, "What he is trying to say (ask you for) is . . . " and so on. GOALS may themselves help in formulation of an INSTRUMENTALITY. For a consideration of some constraints on requests, see Grimshaw 1973e.

6. What labels (verb names) are assigned to INSTRUMENTALITIES by competent native speakers or how are they otherwise acceptably identified? Do the variables that constrain selection also constrain the acceptability, to other native speakers, of reports of past or ongoing behavior? What is the nature of metalinguistic discussion of strategies by interactants (or audiences)?
Comment: Minor officials don't *order* heads of state to resign, and the latter don't *wheedle* their subordinates into showing them official plans—nor would reporters accept reports that such events had, indeed, occurred. Similarly, students would smile at a peer who reported that he/she would *command* a teacher to cancel classes for the remainder of term. People spend a considerable amount of time planning (even "rehearsing," see Goffman 1974) and discussing INSTRUMENTALITIES past and projected.

7. How are INSTRUMENTALITIES serially employed for the accomplishment (joint or individual) of outcomes superordinate to specific manipulative attempts, that is, how do the latter "fit into" episodes and into the larger speech events (court trials, staff medical sessions, family "conferences," and so forth) of which both INSTRUMENTALITIES and episodes are constituents?
Comment: This is the question of "discourse levels" which led Sinclair and Coulthard (1975; see also Burke 1979) to posit the increasingly comprehensive elements of *act, move, exchange, transaction,* and *lesson.* Similar hierarchies can be elaborated with other speech events (Hymes 1974), such as trial, diagnosis, therapy session, collective bargaining session, dissertation defense, or whatever, at the top level.

8. How are these verbal (and other) manipulative skills acquired? Are there developmental stages in acquisition? Are these skills equivalently acquired by all native speakers of a language?
   Comment: It appears that these complex skills in discourse are acquired in the same developmental manner as language itself is acquired (see, for example, Bates 1976; Corsaro 1979a, b; and articles in Ervin-Tripp and Mitchell-Kernan 1977 and Goody 1978a) and that performance skills are unequally distributed within speech communities (see, for example, Albert 1972 and Grimshaw and Holden 1976).
9. Can the several INSTRUMENTALITIES be mapped into a bounded multidimensional space? Are the dimensions the same as the sociological constraints on strategy selection? How are locations of coordinates to be plotted (that is, how are the sociological variables to be measured)?
   Comment: Some progress is being made on these questions. I will turn briefly to this emerging literature immediately following the discussion, in the next section, of preliminary findings on the sociological constraints on socially appropriate strategies.

THE PRINCIPAL DIMENSIONS

If efficiency of communication were the sole consideration and another person were in a position to facilitate our accomplishment of a desired RESULT, we would simply tell that person what we wanted, or use a simple imperative. Children do simply express wishes, and children do use simple imperatives. They quickly learn, however, that directness is not always efficient, and that consideration (in another sense) for others and sensitivity to their control over resources must be taken into account in selecting an INSTRUMENTALITY.[11] The use of talk in social control requires careful attention to the interacting dimensions of *efficiency* and *politeness,* and both SOURCE and GOAL closely monitor talk for infelicities, improprieties, clues to relevant social characteristics of their interlocutors, and signs of fellow interactants' reactions to ongoing talk. There is now a quite substantial literature, based on a variety of methods and diverse data sets, that indicates that a parsimonious set of sociological variables act to constrain INSTRUMENTALITY selection, not only in the specific case of what I have been calling verbal manipulation, but in all varieties of speech acts (that is, any utterance with propositional content with illocutionary force directed to perlocutionary effect—whether the act itself be representative, commissive, expressive, declarative, *or* directive (per Searle's [1979 chap. 1] taxonomy).

In the immediate case, that is, that of using talk to get others to do (or not do) things that they otherwise would not (or would) do, both selection of INSTRUMENTALITIES and acceptable reports about INSTRUMENTALITIES employed in a past event are constrained by relationships of *power* and *affect* between SOURCE and GOAL (with additional effects introduced by the same relationships with audiences), by the *cost* to GOAL of RESULT, and by RESULT's salience for SOURCE. This is hardly a novel list of variables; their central importance in interaction is based on a tradition as old as the discipline itself and has been treated in detail in the theoretical writings of Heider (1958), Homans (1961), and Blau (1964), and in the empirical work that has tested their several formulations in contemporary attribution and exchange theory (see chapter

2 by Emerson, this volume). What *is* novel is that the variables have been identified in the course of studies of the *accomplishment of social control through talk*—studies, moreover, that attend directly to speech-act characteristics of actual utterances, that is, to the manner in which the several variables are manifested in speech.

Power. Asymmetry appears to be the norm in social relationships and cases of true equality the limiting ones. To the extent that relationships are characterized by superordination-subordination, and to the extent that interactants are aware of asymmetries, different modes of talk, including different selection of terms of address, different access to the floor, and different choice of INSTRUMENTALITIES in manipulative behaviors, will be available to conversational participants. The greater ability of one interactant to get the other to do things he/she would not do without the constraint of unequal power can be either diffuse or specific (Parsons 1951), inherent in roles or positions or an individual attribute (for example, as in charismatic authority), relatively permanent or temporally bounded. Potency (Osgood, Suci, and Tannebaum 1964) is, moreover, a characteristic not only of individuals or roles (Heise 1979) but also of differently named speech acts (Heise 1979), linguistic codes (Bernstein 1971), and of discourse styles or registers (for example, Albert 1972; Frake 1972; Irvine 1974).

An early demonstration of the power dimension in speech, and the one probably best known to readers, is in Brown's publications (see 1965 for a summary) on formal and informal address forms; his findings have been replicated for a number of languages. Other studies have demonstrated that the choice of a language or of dialect, register, or code variants from individual repertoires is similarly affected by power relationships of interlocutors (see especially Blom and Gumperz 1972; Gumperz forthcoming; and Geertz 1960; for more general statements see Grimshaw 1966, 1973d, and 1980a).

Power is a complexly contingent individual attribute, role resource, and situational characteristic. Social relationships of superordination-subordination are unstable to the extent that the subordinate party does not willingly accept the asymmetry. "Stars" in relationships change. There are individual instances in which incumbents of institutionally subordinated roles may, because of dominant personalities or resources external to a particular role relationship, or simply through the passage of time and movement through the life cycle, exercise particularistic power. Power is further constrained by considerations of courtesy, tact, equity, tradition, and so on—as well as by rational apprehension of possible reactions to its abuse—or misperception. All of these qualifications notwithstanding, hierarchy clearly does affect the range of INSTRUMENTALITIES available to interactants. Subordinates do not order or command; superordinates do not ordinarily beg, wheedle, or importune (see Grimshaw 1980b). Nor will manipulative behaviors by the former be labeled as order or command, or by the latter as wheedle, and so on.

The claim has recently been made that there are sets of people who simply do not control ways of speaking that are associated with the exercise of power and authority. Lakoff (1975), in a book widely criticized for its empirical claims, asserts that "women's" speech is more uncertain and trivial, and less clear and forceful, than that of men. Specifically, she claims that women use different adjectives (more "adorables") and more "weak" syntactic forms (for example, "tag" questions, complex request forms, and so on). One study of tag questions (Dubois and Crouch 1975) reports data that flatly contradict Lakoff's claim. Other studies have shown, however, that women *are* more prone to have their speech interrupted than are men (Zimmerman and West 1975), and a number of studies have reported differences in men's and women's speech in both English-speaking (for example, Trudgill 1972 and Brend 1975) and other societies (for example, see Keenan 1974 on Malagasy).

Lakoff remarks in passing that male academics tend, like women, to speak in a manner disvalued by more "masculine" elements in the population. She did not pursue or document her observation; had she done so she would have been constrained to ask some revealing questions, such as: (1) are academics, indeed, more feminine than other males (and on what criteria); (2) if not, are there characteristic features of their lives that constrain them to *act* more like women; (3) if so, are there other groups of men whose lives are similarly constrained so that they also speak more like women than like other men; (4) what are those constraints, and are they shared with women generally, or possibly only with some women; (5) if some women are not so constrained, do they possibly talk more like men? Had it turned out that both men and women varied along a dimension of "femaleness" in their speech, and that that variation was associated with structural conditions of life, Lakoff would have had to consider explaining the variations in speech by structural constraints rather than sex.

Recent work by O'Barr and his associates (for example, Conley et al. 1978; Erickson et al. 1978) has suggested that there are "powerful" and "powerless" varieties of speech—but that both are used by both men and women and that distribution is related primarily, not to sex, but to other SES attributes of speakers. Members of the project collected an extensive corpus of audiotaped courtroom testimony with the purpose of investigating the kinds of talk used by effective attorneys and witnesses. The kinds of speech features that Lakoff had identified as female, that is, those that made speech "more uncertain and trivial, and less clear and forceful," were indeed identified.[12] After listening to many hours of courtroom testimony, however, the investigators discovered that although there were women whose speech manifested many of these features, there were also men who displayed them, and that there were women, as well as men, who manifested few of them. Presence or absence of the features was associated primarily with SES characteristics of education, income, and so on, and not with sex (except, presumably, to the extent that women rank lower on societally valued indices of SES success). Subsequent experiments with several populations of judges demonstrated that those with what they came to call "powerless" speech were judged less favorably on both credibility and measures of attractiveness whatever the sex of the speaker.

In sum: (1) individuals have differential control over modes of speech that have been demonstrated to be differentially effective in gaining one's ends through talk; (2) individuals of different power, whether as individuals or a role resource, have available to them, and use, different INSTRUMENTALITIES.

Affect. The terms *affect, emotion, sentiment,* and *feeling* are often used interchangeably to designate either the character of a relationship between interactants and/or individual attributes, whether perdurable or transient. Feeling-states of an individual, such as happiness or depression and confidence or anxiety, doubtless have an effect on the individual's decisions to enter into interaction and her/his perceptions of the possible which can be accomplished through talk (on emotions, see Gordon, chapter 18, this volume, and Kemper 1979). More important in constraining sociolinguistic selection in speech-act construction, however, are affectual *relationships,* that is, whether interlocutors love or like or dislike or despise one another, and whether they feel admiration or respect or disdain. As is the case with power, truly symmetrical affect is probably rare; cases of gross asymmetry are, however, unstable. Injudicious choice of INSTRUMENTALITY or other infelicitous speech acts can quickly change affect—the relationship between affect and sociolinguistic selection is further complicated by the fact that people are sometimes moody, that there are incompatible goals, unintended differences in understanding, and so on. These transient features of social interaction, along with the more perdurable emotional characteristics that are part of personality, are often incorporated into overall definitions of the affectual relationship. All of these complications notwithstanding, most people, most of the time, have a pretty good idea of how they feel about relevant others—those feelings are usually (correctly) perceived as being reciprocated.

In contrast to the situation described for power, the greater ability of one interactant to get the other to do things he/she would not do where the relationship not one of positive affect tends to be generally diffuse (although there are situations in which we, for example, admire a person's performance in one role and are offended by his/her behavior in another role), and less specific to role relationships (though there are relationships that are culturally defined as positive, for example, certain kin relationships and the informal bonds of friendship). I have already noted that affectual relations can change over time, either quickly (betrayal of trust) or more slowly (gradually emergent ennui in marriage). Although there are doubtless genres of speech acts that reflect positive affectual relations (for example, the intimate exchanges of lovers or baby talk), it is not clear that affect is reflected in selection of linguistic codes.

Brown demonstrates the importance of affectual relations between interlocutors in his pioneering work on address forms. He labels the dimension as one of *solidarity.* His findings on this dimension have also been validated by studies on a number of other languages. Other students, working with other speech acts or with repertoire selection, have also found the affectual relation to be critical in constraining sociolinguistic selection in talk. Brown and Levinson (1978), in their study of politeness universals, refer to *social distance;* Heise (1979), in his study of role relationships and available speech acts, refers to *affect induction;* Katz and Lazarsfeld (1955), in their early study of personal influence, refer to *gregariousness;* in my own work on INSTRUMENTALITIES I have referred to *affect.*

Affect in relationships is, like power, contextually contingent, changeable, and extremely complex. Institutional constraints act to inhibit the expression of favoritism or punitiveness as do considerations of courtesy, tact, equity, tradition, and so on—and as do pragmatic considerations of audience reaction. These qualifications notwithstanding, the affectual character of relationships clearly affects the range of INSTRUMENTALITIES available to interactants. *Ceteris paribus,* individuals sharing positive affectual relationships would rather persuade than order, coax than bully, cajole or sweet-talk than blackmail or con. Systematic investigation of the interaction among SOURCE and GOAL personality characteristics, SOURCE-GOAL affectual relationships (and their histories), and sociolinguistic selection at all levels has barely begun. Such investigation is a critically necessary part of any project on language and social control.

Cost. However much we may chide ourselves or others for engaging in "idle chitchat," truly desultory or aimless talk is a rare phenomenon. Even in instances where someone initiates talk simply to escape from boredom by "passing time" or to reduce tension or embarrassment in a situation of unavoidable copresence and is responded to by his/her addressee only to avoid the appearance of rudeness and rebuff, there is, as Goffman (1967:33) remarks, "no occasion of talk so trivial as not to require each participant to show serious concern with the way in which he handles himself and the others present." The fact is, of course, that most talk is of greater moment, and that most conversational interaction is initiated with some end in mind. The speech act philosophers, moreover, tell us something that is validated repeatedly by our own experience, namely, that speech acts of verbal manipulation will not be initiated unless RESULT is sufficiently valued and cost is seen as being acceptable (see Searle 1969 and, for an extremely sophisticated and comprehensive treatment, Labov and Fanshel 1977). In short, SOURCE will not expend much energy to obtain something she/he doesn't really want, or that she/he doesn't believe GOAL can, or will, provide.

As is the case with relations of power and affect, the considerations of cost which determine whether RESULT will be sought, and *if so how,* are neither obvious nor simple. These considerations minimally include:[13]

1. the strength (intensity, valence) of SOURCE's desire for RESULT:
   a. relative to potential simultaneous "competing" RESULTS;
   b. relative to SOURCE's intensity "range";
2. the possible value of RESULT for GOAL:
   a. as perceived by SOURCE;
   b. as perceived by GOAL;
   c. as perceived by witnesses;
3. the cost of RESULT to SOURCE:
   a. investment, direct, and opportunity cost (Blau 1964). Direct cost includes, for Blau, interactional cost, that is, what Brown and Levinson (see below) refer to as considerations of "face";
   b. relative and absolute;
4. the cost of RESULT to GOAL:
   a. investment, direct, and opportunity cost. Direct cost here includes not only interactional cost but also expenditure of material and other resources;
   b. relative and absolute.

SOURCE's "decision" (it may be conscious, but need not be; it need not be rational, but frequently is) whether to seek RESULT and, if so, how, takes into account, then, a minimum of four factors: (1) desire for RESULT, (2) perceptions of value of RESULT for GOAL, (3) of cost to self, and (4) of cost to GOAL. The aggregate of these values can be labeled *utility.* There are no clear metrics for these values. They vary situationally, they are differently assessed by participants and witnesses, they are a focus of continuing renegotiation by different individuals and groups. In the ongoing interactions in which social control occurs, moreover, perceptions of cost are further influenced by perceptions of relations of power and affect obtaining between SOURCE and GOAL. The interaction facets are complex. None of these complexities, however, invalidates the conclusion that *RESULT itself determines whether an effort directed toward RESULT will be made.*[14]

Interactional costs. A critical concern for a social psychological understanding of social control through talk is the manner in which that talk is converted into *face,* the principal currency of the self. Brown and Levinson (1978) nicely demonstrate that SOURCE's choice of INSTRUMENTALITIES located at varying places on the interacting continua of efficiency and politeness, or of address terms or code or register (Hasan 1973; Blom and Gumperz 1972) is strongly influenced by considerations of face. Following Goffman (1967), they characterize face as "the public self-image that every member wants to claim for himself" (p. 66). They make a distinction between: (1) negative face, a "want" not to be imposed upon; and (2) positive face, the "want" that at least some significant others approve of self. Brown and Levinson argue that some acts are intrinsically threatening; avoidance or mitigation of these face-threatening acts (FTAs) or a willingness to accept their possible consequences in interpersonal stress is at the very core of INSTRUMENTALITY selection. They summarize this neatly in the accompanying figure 7.2. Directness of strategy increases and the likelihood of redressive action decreases with decreasing risks of face loss.

FIGURE 7.2

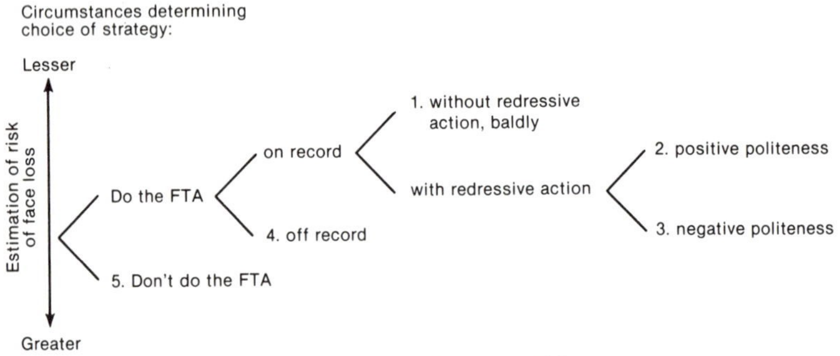

Source: Brown and Levinson 1978:65

SOME SUMMARY PROPOSITIONS

A number of studies have converged on findings that the uses of language in social control (INSTRUMENTALITY selection, selection of address forms, selection from speech repertoires [styles, registers, dialects, languages, and so on]) and the acceptability of reports of those uses are constrained by the relationships of power and affect between SOURCE and GOAL (with additional effects introduced by the same relationships with audiences) and by utility (desirability to SOURCE, value to GOAL, and cost to all parties) of RESULT. Among the findings on which there appears to be agreement are:

1. *Ceteris paribus,* RESULT determines whether manipulation (or other social control through talk) will be attempted. This means that in instances of, for example, equal power and shared positive affect, social control attempts (including manipulation) are most likely when RESULT has high valence for both SOURCE and GOAL and where cost will be low for both. Power is most frequently asymmetrical, and affect not always positive; these variations influence both likelihood and mode of INSTRUMENTALITY (or address form selection, and so forth).
2. Some INSTRUMENTALITIES (or other utterance modes) are not available in instances of mutual positive affect; others in instances of mutual negative affect. The sets are complementary but not mutually exclusive.
3. Hierarchy constrains the range of INSTRUMENTALITIES available (that is, subordinate or equal hierarchical position makes some INSTRUMENTALITIES or other utterance modes unavailable).
4. Within that range, interaction of affect and utility constrain specific selections.

Stated in sometimes quite similar ways, these findings have been validated by several different investigators using data of quite different sorts. The convergence is marked—it is not, on reflection, remarkable. It is unremarkable because it is congruent with both: (1) a host of empirical studies of social behavior that have not considered language and (2) our (naive) individual member's (in the ethnomethodological sense) knowledge about interactional accomplishment in everyday life. As I suggested above, what *does* make it novel is that the convergence has been identified in studies of language phenomena previously neglected by sociologists.

Secondary Social Control: Identity Altering and the Orchestration of Esteem

Most of the research reported thus far has been directed to exploration of the ways in which talk can be used appropriately to get others to do things through the use of named INSTRUMENTALITIES. Much talk, however, has to do with the establishment, maintenance, and altering of self and other identification. Identity-enhancing, maintaining, and denigrating talk can go on within or outside the presence of the person whose qualities are the topic (such talk away from the person discussed is called gossip). Praise, encouragement, reassurance, and the selection of address forms and conversational codes congruent with respect of interlocutor have positive effects; denigration, insult, and impolite repertoire selection have negative effects. Notions of face are heavily implicated in conceptions of self; assigning socially disvalued characteristics to self or others means relinquishing (for self) or denying (to others) the appreciation and approval needed for maintenance of a positive self-image. Labov (1972c, chapter 8) and Mitchell-Kernan and Kernan (1975), among others, have investigated the ways in which insult is accomplished through questioning of identities; Goody (1978a) has shown how inappropriate questioning, with its implications for status violations, can be seen as insulting; examinations of failures in politeness (Brown and Levinson 1978) or in conversational involvement (Goffman 1967, 1971) have shown how these lapses are interpretable as insults. Social psychologists appear to have given no more attention to these dimensions of social control in talk than to more visible instances of manipulative acts involving named INSTRUMENTALITIES.

Toward a Social Semantics

Philosophers have always been interested in meaning, and have contributed to much of the conceptual apparatus used in its discussion (sense, reference, connotation, denotation, intention, intension, and so forth). Problems of meaning are not simple, and for many years linguists seemed willing to let philosophers struggle with them. In recent years, several competing linguistic perspectives on meaning have emerged, and psychologists have also become increasingly interested in semantic uses (see, for general treatments, Steinberg and Jakobovits 1971 and Rosenberg and Travis 1971. Lyons 1968, provides a lucid and accessible introduction to these questions. His more recent two-volume study [1977] is difficult but comprehensive, at least insofar as philosophical, psychological, and linguistic interpretations are concerned). While much recent work has increasingly attended to pragmatics, speech acts, and meanings of language as constrained by social contexts, scholars in the three disciplines have generally focused on meanings of individual words or sentences and used data generated from their own intuitions as native speakers rather than utterances produced by speakers in naturally occurring conversations. Semantic differential studies, for example, ask subjects to make judgments about dimensions of meaning of individual words. This has been the procedure followed by Heise (1979) in his studies of social behaviors (including speech acts) associated with role types.

Some linguists have argued that the meaning of utterances (spoken or written) can only be understood in their social and textual contexts (on social context, see, inter alia, Firth 1968; Lyons 1968; Fillmore 1973. On textual cohesion, see, for example, Halliday and Hasan 1976. On the importance of both for explication of the interactional import of talk, see Labov and Fanshel 1977). Many contemporary linguists, however, see "communication and other social uses of language" as of secondary importance, and an "adequate theory" as needing to show only "how the meaning of a sentence is determined by its grammatical structure and the meaning of its lexical items" (Harman's [1971] characterizations of Chomsky and of Katz and Fodor, respectively). Linguists of the first persuasion, that is, those who insist on the importance of examining language in context, are joining with anthropologists (and a smaller number of sociologists) who have been examining naturally occurring utterances with the goal of discovery and explication of precisely those functions of language that linguists of the second persuasion have seen as "secondary."

There are several sets of researchers who are studying naturally occurring talk, and their efforts have implications both for comprehension of the notion of a social semantics and for understanding of how socially constructed meanings are inextricably implicated in social control through talk. The sets, which are overlapping but distinguishable, include: (1) ethnographers of communication; (2) conversational analysts; (3) cognitive sociologists; (4) ethologists (a gloss for students of nonverbal components of communication); (5) Erving Goffman; and (6) comprehensive discourse analysts.[15]

Ethnography of communication. This label is associated with Hymes (1974) and others (for example, Gumperz and Hymes 1964 and 1972; Bauman and Sherzer 1974) who have investigated a large number of actual speech events (primarily in non-English speech communities) from a perspective that assigns "primacy of speech to code, function to structure, context to message, the appropriate to the arbitrary or simply possible" but with "the interrelations always essential, so that one cannot only generalize the particularities, but also particularize the generalities" (Hymes 1974:9). The unit of analysis has generally been the speech event rather than the speech act (Hymes 1974:52–53);[16] the desired end result of the analysis is understanding of accomplishment of social ends in rule-governed social interaction.

Conversational analysis. This label is associated with Sacks and Schegloff and others (for example, Jefferson 1972, 1974; Sacks 1972a, 1972b, 1974; Sacks, Schegloff, and Jefferson 1974; Schegloff 1972; Schegloff, Jefferson, and Sacks 1977; Schegloff and Sacks 1973; Schenkein 1978; Sudnow 1972) who have investigated conversational exchanges in English (primarily telephone conversations, but also therapy groups) and have: (1) identified and described such features of conversation as, for example, sequencing (including placement of laughter), interruptions, self- (and other) corrections, and so forth, in order to (2) explicate such conversational accomplishments as, for example, gaining and holding the floor, telling acceptable stories, extending invitations, making social categorizations, and so on. In the course of this activity they have developed a rich set of "hearers' (interpretive) maxims,"[17] relevance rules, and a conceptual apparatus sufficiently general to be extended to other types of speech events and to speech events in other speech communities. The unit of analysis is the adjacency-pair (of utterances); the desired end result of the analysis is understanding of how conversations are successfully begun, carried on, and ended (as contrasted to ends extrinsic to an immediate interaction) in rule-governed social interaction.

Cognitive sociology. This label is closely associated with Cicourel (1974a, 1974b, 1974c), who has been investigating "the competence necessary for articulating general rules and the particular social activities that emerge in everyday interaction" through study of "interpretive procedures as invariant properties or principles which allow members to assign meaning or sense to substantive rules called social norms" (1974a:85). These procedures, such as the "et cetera principle" (1974a:87 *et passim*) have been studied by Cicourel and others who have been influenced by his work (although they may not use the designation cognitive sociology; see, for example, Cicourel et al. 1974; Corsaro, 1979a, 1979b; Mehan, 1979) in speech events occurring in school settings, play groups, and medical interviews. The unit of analysis has been the speech event rather than the speech act; the desired end result of the analysis is identification of "sociological cognitive elements of . . . a generative semantics central for an understanding of all human communication" (1974a:74). The concern is not with the semantic elements of lexical items through comprehension of "how participants and *researchers* assign meanings to their own and others' thoughts, objects, and events" (ibid., emphasis added) in syntactic combination but rather with what members of a society (speech community) must be able to do in order to communicate.

Body motion communication analysis. Ethologists and semioticians are interested in the ways in which non-human species communicate; the term kinesics as used by Birdwhistell (1970) to identify human body motion communication behavior has been widely adopted by students who consider the term nonverbal behavior imprecise (see, for example, Kendon 1977; Kendon and Ferber 1973). These researchers emphasize the multi-channel nature of human communication, noting that body behaviors (postural or gestural—voluntary or unconscious) may variously confirm or contradict verbal utterances (see, for example, Condon 1967, 1970; Ekman 1972; Ekman and Friesen 1969a, 1969b; Scheflen 1973; Erickson 1975, 1976; Erickson and Schultz forthcoming; Mehrabian 1972; Speer 1972). This work has been supplemented by Hall's (1966, 1974) work on proxemics with its attention to the availability and processing of communication through other channels (tactile, olfactory, and so forth) and its relation to mutual social location in intimate, personal, social, and public space and by individual studies on specific channels. There is disagreement among researchers as to the relative credibility of verbal and other channels when they are in conflict and there is evidence that the nonverbal can be misread and, as Goffman (1959, 1974) has pointed out, manipulated. The units of analysis have been extremely variable, ranging from uncontexted photographs of individuals, to fairly complete sound-image records of both known and unknown subjects in sustained interactional events; the desired end result of the analyses is understanding of the full range of meanings conveyed (and interpreted) through all communicative channels.

Goffman. Since his first major publication (1959), Goffman has drawn on a diverse literature dealing with elements of socially contexted and constructed meanings and has presented a rich range of actual and fictional accounts of social life in moving toward an increasingly detailed characterization of communication. While Goffman does attend to (primarily scripted or reported) talk, he has devoted his principal efforts to isolating and identifying the ways in which "framing" of events by volitional acts of ratified and casual participants, by attributes of those participants, and by social contexts of the events, constrains participants' and observers' interpretive understanding. He thinks "the first object of social analysis ought . . . to be ordinary, actual behavior"; he seeks to accomplish this analysis through comparative investigation of "realms of being other than the ordinary" which "provide natural experiments in which a property of ordinary activity is displayed or contrasted in a clarified and clarifying way" (1974:564). His units of analysis are his own experience and omnivorous observations and those he vicariously (and voraciously) absorbs; the desired end result of the analysis appears to be nothing less than a descriptively adequate (Chomsky 1965; Grimshaw 1974) characterization of social interaction (at least among the middle class in the United States). An interest in "impression management" and "face work"—in short, social control—is central to his concerns.

Discourse analysis. The ultimate aim of Labov and Fanshel's (1977) "comprehensive discourse analysis" is identification of the *interactional* accomplishment "intended" by interlocutors in ongoing conversational discourse, that is, what gets *done* with what gets said. The penultimate stage of their analysis, that is, specification of what is *meant* by what gets said (their "expansion") is the more traditional aim of a variety of researches in textual or discourse analysis (for a discussion of some past, present, and emerging concerns in discourse analysis, see Hymes 1974, especially p. 97 ff.; for a linguistically informed analysis of dramatic and literary narrative discourse, Klammer 1971; for an application of speech act theory to literary discourse, Pratt 1977; for a treatment focusing more directly on sociological concerns, Corsaro 1981; for an accessible and fascinating discussion of the syntactic devices [for example, reference, conjunction, ellipsis] used to make texts semantically cohesive, Halliday and Hasan 1976). Hymes (1974:99) observes that "much of the coherence of texts depends upon abstract rules independent of specific linguistic form" (that is, understanding of text requires knowledge of interlocutors' or writers' characteristics and ends); he also reminds the reader that "much is to be learnt just from . . . study of syntactic relations." Given the emphasis in this chapter on social elements of communication, it is well to keep in mind that language itself is rule-governed and that lexical items do have dictionary meanings.

More traditional varieties of discourse analysis vary from that of Labov and Fanshel in a second way, namely, in paying more explicit attention to referential (as contrasted to potentially manipulative) functions of writing or talk. Successfully conveying aesthetic reactions or technical information may have the consequence of affecting how hearers perceive the world; such changes in hearers' perceptions may be incidental, unintended, and therefore not a result of manipulation (in the sense I have been using the term). To that extent, the implications for social control are less direct than those discussed earlier.

The units of discourse analysis are texts of any sort; the desired end result of analysis is to determine what is "meant" and "interactionally intended" by the originator of the text. Any comprehensive view of social control through talk must incorporate, at some point, linguistic and literary modes of discourse analysis. This enterprise has yet to be assayed (studies of propaganda notwithstanding).

Reprise. While some students of language continue to study meaning as an intrinsic feature of words, sentences, or more extended texts (spoken, written, or imagined), increasing numbers of investigators have concluded that only a socially informed semantics can comprehensively illuminate *meaningfulness of language in use.* Some of these scholars, those whose work was reviewed in the section on "getting things done with words," are directly attacking questions of the interactional results of talk, that is, what gets *done* with talk. Others, including many of those discussed in this section, are attacking the (prior?) question of what is *meant* by talk. While there is talk that appears to be primarily referential (informative *or* expressive), it seems likely that most, if not all, talk will be found to have implications for social control; the distinction between the two enterprises is, then, a temporary artifact of the underdeveloped nature of our understandings of both talk and social control. This situation will not long obtain.

Acquisition: A Brief Note

The ability to employ talk in social control is, like other speech abilities, learned. Until very recently little has been known about how these skills are acquired—simply because their acquisition (and modification) has been little studied[19] (for some recent exceptions see, inter alia, Gleason and Weintraub 1976; Corsaro 1979a, 1979b; Denzin 1977, several pieces in Ervin-Tripp 1973, and in Ervin-Tripp and Mitchell-Kernan 1977, and Ward 1971).

Linguists do not agree on how language is acquired. Although straight stimulus-response and imitation paradigms have been generally discredited (Chomsky 1959), there is no firm consensus on the extent to which language is genetically programmed (see, however, Lenneberg 1967). Arguments on this issue hinge, in part, on the extent and nature of language universals (more, and more complex, universals supporting more "innateness") and in part on the great complexity of individual languages themselves (that is, it is argued that they are so complex that children could not learn them if they were not genetically fitted to do so). The most widely accepted view appears to be that infants have some sort of innate capacity (sometimes called the LAD or Language Acquisition Device) which permits them to construct "theories" of their language on the basis of the speech data in the world around them. Children's speech capabilities are both well developed and individually differentiated at fairly young ages (five years is frequently seen as a threshold); some investigators have therefore concluded that the LAD begins to "atrophy" at the point at which the fundamentals of language are mastered. Other investigators assert that language learning is a life-long process, and that adaptation and modification of language is continuous (see, for a general statement, Grimshaw and Holden 1976.[20] For two studies that appear to have partially contradictory findings on second language acquisition and dialect modification in adolescence, see Snow and Hoefnagel-Höhle 1978 and Payne n.d., respectively).

Children's rapid acquisition of a wide range of grammatical (phonological, syntactic) skills is well documented. The parallel development of skills children acquire which allow them to use their developing linguistic skills effectively in social interaction, has, until recently, attracted much less research attention. It seems reasonable to assume that the processes *are* parallel; there do seem to be several ways in which the acquisition of social interactional and sociolinguistic rules and skills differs from that of speech itself. I can mention only two of these here.

First, it appears that the bulk of language learning is more compacted than is learning of social interactional or sociolinguistic rules (Cazden 1973). It seems unlikely that this is a consequence of differences in critical ages or periods of learning of the latter rules; there is no reason to expect delayed maturational unfolding of some set of special requisite capacities for these social behaviors as contrasted to speech. A plausible (but untested) hypothesis is that the variation is a consequence of what data are available for a child for the construction of social interactional and sociolinguistic grammars. Speech data for construction of grammars of languages are available for virtually all children. However, exposure to analogous social interactional data (for example, interaction with significant others of widely varying social characteristics in situations with widely varying goals) or sociolinguistic data (for example, interaction with significant others using different dialects and/or registers) varies considerably by location in the social structure in terms of such characteristics as family organization, class status, and area of residence. It thus happens that some persons will learn some social interactional or sociolinguistic skills much later than others (or perhaps never). This variation occurs within as well as across societies. The data availability argument is indirectly strengthened by the existence of the, to many North Americans, precocious interactional sophistication of very young "adults" in poor areas, whose families are unable to afford the luxury of extended dependence of their children. It may be further validated by the fact that some adults simply don't control whole sets of social interactional and sociolinguistic skills, for example, those associated with condolences or (relatively) undisruptive disengagement from intense social relationships.

Second, while I do not want to offend linguists by suggesting that the phenomena they study are not complex, I do believe that social interactional and sociolinguistic rules may be even *more* complex. It is true that several ways of saying the "same thing" are available to speakers, for example, active or passive voice, different verb forms, lexical variants, and so on. These choices, however, are seldom very problematic in ongoing talk—and when they are, the considerations are less likely to be linguistic than sociolinguistic or interactional. Consider the case of getting *others* to do things by talk. The social actor must not only learn a very large repertory of ways of so doing, he/she must also master both rules related to assessments of dimensions of, minimally, power, affect, and utility, and rules related to appropriateness of selection of modes differently located on the politeness-efficiency continua. I suggested above that speaker-member awareness of and ability to recover and articulate rules was higher for social interactional and sociolinguistic than linguistic rules (there may be a continuum) *and* that sanctions are more severe for violations of the former than the latter. If these observations are correct (and only empirical research can make the determination), it is likely that: (1) interactants will be found to be more consciously aware of choices involving appropriateness and possible sanctions for violations; and (2) at least some teaching of these rules will be found to be correspondingly explicit.

These two questions imply a number of related or subsumed issues, for example, (1) explicit instruction versus implicit acquisition (and social bases for differentiation of the two); (2) critical stages for learning; (3) how rule changes (successfully) enter the system; (4) productive versus passive competence; (5) "true" competence versus "routines"; (6) functional specialization in rule acquisition. Answers to these and other questions will be required if there is to be a satisfactory theory of talk and social control.

Coda

Language is a uniquely human social activity; its social use engages us during most of our waking hours. Individuals' production of spoken (and written) language serves simultaneously: (1) to permit their interlocutors to locate them socially; and (2) to facilitate their efforts to influence or control those interlocutors (or readers, as in the current instance). Sociology (and sociological social psychology) generally has neglected language phenomena; this neglect has impeded us in our efforts to understand social control.[21]

Colleagues in other disciplines have been less neglectful, and have made available a number of theoretical and methodological insights and perspectives that can greatly facilitate our exploitation of language in social use as a data resource for study of social control. Their contributions include the linguists' revelations of the autonomous structuring (and logical and aesthetic elegance) of language itself; the philosophers' insights into the formal dimensions of meaning, truth claims, and the structure of speech acts; and the anthropologists' demonstrations of the importance of cultural norms (and their variability) and of cultural context. Our own colleagues have made important contributions to understanding these several aspects of talk in use, particularly with reference to the jointly constructed nature and rule-governed interpretation of that talk and their several roots in shared social knowledge.

The particular concern of sociology is social interaction and the ways in which involvement in that interaction shapes both our ongoing behaviors and our world views (and consequent predispositions for *subsequent* special behaviors). Social control attempts are a critically central feature of many (if not most) interactional events. I have argued in this chapter that we should pay more attention than we have to the talk that constitutes those events *and* to the analytic frames being developed by our colleagues. Such attention, drawing on our own interactional perspectives, will simultaneously enhance our own understanding of social control, contribute to general understanding of language use in social contexts, and facilitate the development of grammars of social interaction.

NOTES

A number of colleagues and several students have identified problems with my argument, my use of terms, and my interpretations of both empirical findings and the literatures of other fields. I thank them all. I am grateful to Aaron Cicourel for extended comments on an earlier draft. I owe a particularly heavy debt to F. Roger Higgins, who has made a valiant effort to protect me from my misreadings of several literatures.

1. The term *rule* has been no less troublesome for linguists than for sociologists. For present purposes it is perhaps best to read the term simply as implying regularities in languages themselves rather than as prescriptions or proscriptions on usage.

2. Carl Couch demurs and writes, "No, the issues are: (1) how do significant symbols emerge from interaction and (2) how are they used (employed) to coordinate social action" (1979 personal communication).

3. There are, of course, instances in which the causal priority of, for example, speech or social structure can be assigned, see, for example, Grimshaw 1973c.

4. Natural language philosophers and linguists find this question of "selectional restrictions" an extremely vexing one; I cannot review their arguments here. See, however, Wiggins's charming discussion (1971:25–34, 50–51), especially his note b., p. 25, in which he anticipates the notion of what I call "social appropriateness."

5. There are numerous sociologists who have studied social control—and a growing number who are studying language in use. Now that the connection has been made, it seems obvious; the fact remains that few past studies of social control attended seriously to language. It seems equally obvious, in retrospect, that any study of language in use would necessarily attend to issues of social control. Some have; it can be hoped that more will. Concern with social control is always latent and sometimes manifest in the work of, for example, Cicourel and his students, Couch and his, and Goffman. It is less evident in the work of the conversational analysts (but see, for example, Atkinson and Drew 1979 or Silverman and Torode 1980). While his focus is on communicative processes generally and not on control, Corsaro's (1980) review of approaches to discourse analysis is richly suggestive for such study.

6. The distinction between "elaborated" and "restricted" is a multidimensional one; the term "code" has a technical meaning in linguistics; Bernstein's own treatment has not always been consistent; and the use of the term "restricted" was ideologically infelicitous. The sorts of differences in typical modes of talk identified by Bernstein *do* exist, a number of reservations notwithstanding (see Hill and Varenne forthcoming, but also Kay 1977); he may have erred in his claims about cross-categorical distribution of modes of talk and in his assessments of

limitations of his "restricted" variety. Whatever the ways of talking are called, however, there are differences in context-boundedness between:

1a: "Aawww riight!"

and

1b: "This cake is truly delicious."

and differences in propositional organization between:

2a: "No, you can't."

and

2b: "It's probably not a good idea because if you stay up you won't get enough sleep and then you won't be alert for your test tomorrow."

Both versions in both sets "get the job done"—it seems likely that in some contexts (particularly educational ones) control over the skills required for producing (and interpreting) sentences of the second type can be valuable (see Grimshaw 1967).

7. Labov and Fanshel are thoroughly circumspect in their discussion of and imputations of intent, noting both its ambiguous status and the fact that their evidence is abstract and indirect (see especially p. 346). Their perspective is, such reservations notwithstanding, quintessentially sociological, as when they observe, "In any over-all view, it is obvious that actions are more important than utterances, since it is actions that have consequences and affect people's lives," and that "The action is what is *intended* in that it expresses how that speaker means to affect the listener, to move him, to cause him to respond" (p. 59).

Questions of intent are sticky ones, and perhaps best left to philosophers. I have tried to demonstrate the sociological relevance of some of their work in Grimshaw 1980c; Searle (1979, forthcoming) addresses some issues of intention in language in social use head on.

8. Cicourel (1980) argues that Labov and Fanshel use their own cultural knowledge and the conceptual apparatus of sociology in interpreting their materials, although they claim that their interpretations emerge, "data driven," from the text itself. His overall view of their enterprise is, nonetheless, favorable (see 1979).

9. Labov thinks, however, that we may end up with fewer rather than more interactional moves. He writes:

> I have always wondered about our very small array of interactional terms at the highest level. Challenge, retreat, support . . . there are only a few. I have always expected that with more thought, a larger battery would emerge, to rival the lower level array of promise, threat, request, refusal, putoff, etc. But that hasn't happened. In fact, I have the nagging suspicion that there are actually too many terms at the highest level, and that we are in fact dealing with a single dimension of human interaction comparable to the psychoanalytic notion of transference and counter transference, and perhaps akin to the simple notion that he who is not for me is against me.
>
> . . . In other words, the moves that unite interaction at the highest level may take place along a single dimension of support or rejection, attack or retreat (1978, personal communication).

Stryker (1979, personal communication) has observed that Labov's conclusion converges with Heider's (1958:200 ff.) conceptualization of unit relation and direction (or sign); Higgins (1979, personal communication) notes a similar convergence with Brown and Levinson's (1978) notions of positive and negative face and Face-Threatening Acts.

10. Although each of the several perspectives just outlined takes characteristics of hearers (or GOALS) into account, it is not unfair to say that interest in recipients of communication has been secondary. It is a truism that communication is a two-way process; it is also a fact that the bulk of attention to the role of talk in social control has treated the communicative target as essentially passive or, if active, as simply compliant, responsive, or resistant. The fact is, of course, that attempts at communication can fail, not only because of unshared knowledge or simply because acoustic signals are inaudible, but also because hearers (GOALS) *intendedly* "don't get the message." Deliberate misunderstanding is an important resource in social control moves. I do not have space to discuss this interesting topic here, see Grimshaw 1980c:31–74.

11. Claudia Mitchell-Kernan has reported (in conversation) an instance in which a child made the following serial requests to her (for threading a needle):

1. "Claudia, would you thread this for me?"
2. "One more time."
3. "Came out again."
4. "This you last time, Claudia."

Bates (1976) and Corsaro (1979a) have reported similar mitigations.

12. For example, "I'm right, aren't I?" (tag); "I'm not sure, but I think she already has her degree" (hedge); "Dr. Smith, I presume?" (superpolite); "I have been unable to ascertain his current location" (hypercharacterized version of "I can't find him").

Not all of the features associated with "powerless" speech are unambiguously so. Intensifiers may be read as "weakening" speech ("Oh, yes, I'm sure")—they can also "strengthen" it ("Certainly!"). Pauses may convey thoughtful consideration as well as uncertainty. Intonation and other prosodic features influence hearers' interpretations, as do contexts (textual and social). That "powerless" features are not always so can be documented by our reactions to such curiosities as:

"God damn it's hot in here! (pause) Isn't it?" where the initial intensifier seems to have a different illocutionary force than do the pause and the tag question.

As to Lakoff's original remark, as mediated through the clarifying notion of O'Barr and his associates, male academics will have to decide for themselves whether their speech is "powerless" or, instead, "thoughtfully cautious."

13. Social psychologists have, of course, prior concerns with the origin of SOURCE's desire (wish, motivation, drive) for RESULT, for example, whether it is: (1) autonomous or induced (in the sense of "false consciousness"); (2) stereotyped (traditional) or emergent from ongoing interaction; (3) self-or collectivity-oriented (in the Parsonian sense).

14. This outline of considerations involved in assessments of cost is not simple—it is simplified. There are RESULTS that are unattainable, or at least not within the power of GOAL to provide or facilitate. More important, manipulative interaction occurs not in ahistorical uncontexted social vacuums but rather in complex, densely contexted situations in which other individuals and possibly organizations potentially have stakes. Either formal or informal organizational norms, for example, may reduce GOAL's ability to provide RESULT—however that ability may be perceived by SOURCE. Cultural norms may constrain SOURCE from attempting to obtain highly desired RESULTS. The latter is true, for instance, in cases of those most affected by secret personnel deliberations.

A somewhat more detailed but still incomplete development of these arguments and some qualifications that could not be included here may be found in my 1980b. See also, particularly, Brown and Levinson 1977.

15. See Corsaro (1981) for a thoughtful and more detailed review and commentary on (2) the conversational analysts, (3) cognitive sociology (particularly in the work of Cicourel), (5) Goffman, and (6) comprehensive discourse analysis. He also covers a further perspective, omitted here because of space considerations, that of "conversational inference" as done by Gumperz (forthcoming) and other relevant literatures. See also, Cicourel 1980.

16. A cocktail party, a church service, a seminar, or a ceremony are speech situations. A conversation, a sermon, an explanation, or an introduction are speech events. A joke, an illustrative story, an interjected question, or a greeting are speech acts. The speech act is the minimal unit; there are instances in which act and event are coterminous.

The difference is an important one—it is that between the analyses of single utterances (or hypothetical sentences) and that of connected discourse in an ethnographic or constraining social context.

17. One such maxim reads essentially: "if utterances or sentences appear in sequence and what happened in a later can be heard (interpreted) as having been caused by what happened in an earlier, hear it that way." Hymes (1974:99) calls this "Sacks's maxim: *post hoc, ergo propter hoc.*" An unenchanted reader of this chapter remarked:

> I find the attribution of these views to Sacks rather amusing, especially the maxim: post hoc, ergo propter hoc. I hadn't realized that Latin was still the language of science in California. I imagine that there's little here that wouldn't have been familiar to an Alexandrian rhetoretician.

Unfortunately, perhaps, the number of sociologists familiar with the Alexandrian rhetoreticians is modest.

18. This may be a matter of emphasis. Many of these researchers are both aware of and concerned with the interactional implications of the phenomena they are studying.

19. There is, in contrast, a vast literature on the acquisition of speech itself. See, illustratively, Bloom 1970; Brown 1973; Halliday 1975; McNeill 1970; Snow and Ferguson 1977; and the rapidly growing literature on "motherese" and speech adjustments made by adults and by older children interacting with younger ones.

20. Higgins (1979, personal communication) comments:

> I do not think that anyone would wish to deny the obvious—that we keep on learning more of our language in some sense as we get older (as well as forgetting much of it, or failing to use it). The problem concerns the kinds of things that we learn more of and the nature of the learning. The generativist would want to say that the discovery of new structures and the unconscious analytic processes which are available to the child for the discovery of new structures are of quite a different order in adults. This is reflected in the rarity of an adult's learning a second language well without explicit instruction and a great deal of conscious effort. Of course some people may manage it; but every (normal) child learns the first language.

PART III

Social Interaction

8 CARL W. BACKMAN

Attraction in Interpersonal Relationships

Introduction

A BRIEF HISTORICAL OVERVIEW

Positive sentiments, liking, loving, and respect, and the development of relationships based on them, have been of interest to philosophers since antiquity. Interest on the part of behavioral scientists in these topics also has a lengthy history. Although it has become fashionable among present-day writers to decry social psychologists' late entry into this area, such a position is based on a somewhat myopic view that equates social psychology with experimental social psychology of the psychological genre. Actually, research and theorizing on attraction and relationships based on attraction can be traced back almost half a century to a number of lines of research by sociologists and psychologists that could easily be classified as social psychological.

These early studies include those in the 1930s and 1940s of factors related to mate selection and marital success and those dealing with the determinants of sociometric or friendship choice. As in other areas of social psychology during this period, the early research focused on individual characteristics, initially those of one person in a dyadic relationship. Only somewhat later did researchers begin to focus on the relationship between partners' characteristics.

The shift to dyadic analysis initiated a number of lines of research revolving around the age-old question of whether similars or opposites attract. Studies of the effects of value and status similarities and of differences in needs or need complementarity dominated the attraction literature during the 1950s and 1960s. Toward the end of this period, the focus began to shift from the characteristics of partners to an examination of processes involved in the development of attraction. Although some process or developmental theories appeared in the sociological literature on the family in the early sixties (Bolton 1961; Reiss 1960), they did not become prominent in the social psychological literature until the early seventies (Murstein 1970; Levinger and Snoek 1972; Altman and Taylor 1973); generally, they were a product of the emphasis on process in exchange theories (Homans 1961; Thibaut and Kelley 1959) that emerged during the preceding decade. As this review suggests, the developmental approach promises to provide the structure for research on attraction during the foreseeable future.

The emphasis on process involved a shift away from an almost exclusive focus on the determinants of the feeling of attraction in the direction of a renewed interest in relationships; their initiation, development, and maintenance or dissolution. Concomitantly, there have been attempts to differentiate between various types of positive sentiments, particularly between liking and loving (Rubin 1970), and with respect to the latter sentiments, between romantic or passionate love and companionate love (Walster and Walster 1978), as well as among various styles of love (Lee 1973; Lasswell and Lasswell 1976).

The increasing focus on the development of relationships has stimulated a renewed interest in power within this context. Recent research suggests that the relative power of potential partners is a factor affecting the likelihood that a relationship will be initiated, and current theories of interdependence and role negotiation are theories concerned with the exercise of power.

The increasing emphasis on process and on a developmental approach to attraction has had a number of consequences, two of which deserve some further comment. The emphasis on process has been accompanied by increasing convergence, both in theory and in method, between the psychological and sociological approaches to the study of relationships. The latter tradition, particularly as represented in symbolic interactionism, has been heavily processual in orientation. Many of the contributions being made by psychologists now have this orientation. Similarly, whereas much of the earlier work on attraction by psychologists had been done on short-term relationships studied in an experimental context, a number of psychologists have turned to studying more extended relationships in the context of everyday life, using essentially survey procedures, but with analytic procedures borrowed from the laboratory that have led to fresh insights into the processes being studied. This move from the laboratory has undoubtedly enhanced the external validity of current research in this area.

Yet there are still limitations on external validity that should be kept in mind. Most of the research to date has been done employing readily available respondents, for the most part college students or others primarily from white middle-class backgrounds, during a particular historical period in which relationships based on attraction, particularly for this population, have been much more central to identity formation than has probably been the case for other times and places. Further, this work has increasingly concentrated on the heterosexual relationships of dating, courting, cohabiting, and marriage to the neglect of other types of relationships. Much of the research and theorizing on attraction has concentrated on the early phases of relationship formation to the neglect of the later stages of maintenance or dissolution, although recently there has been an upsurge of interest in the termination of relationships. While the emphasis in what follows clearly reflects these characteristics of the literature, it is to be hoped that the conclusions drawn will not be too seriously flawed by these limitations.

SOME CURRENT DEVELOPMENTAL THEORIES OF ATTRACTION

As attention has shifted from a focus on attraction to the study of relationships, theories in this area have increasingly incorporated the idea of stages or levels of a relationship. Although these theories differ in the specific stages recognized and in the amount of detail and emphasis devoted to the various stages, they share a common characteristic, the tendency to telescope the total time span of a relationship with the major emphasis placed on conceptualizing the early relationship-forming period to the neglect of later periods of growth or dissolution.

A second characteristic of current stage or developmental theories is that attraction and the growth of a relationship between persons is viewed as a product of the positive and negative reinforcement, rewards and costs, that persons experience as a result of their association. These rewards and costs have four sources. There are those that arise out of the exchange of behaviors between partners. A second source is the reaction of others who respond to the partners' relationship in certain ways. A third source is internal; each person responds to his own behavior in a rewarding or punishing fashion. A fourth source is the affective response of one's partner as well as those affective responses of others that are vicariously experienced. Such an approach is, however, a far cry from traditional models of reinforcement which tended to ignore and, in some instances, deny the role of cognition. Cognitive processes enter in, both as they affect the anticipation of outcomes and in the evaluation of outcomes once experienced. Although various kinds of rewards treated above include some that would not be included in many versions of exchange theory, from which a number of process theories stem, their inclusion is quite consistent with social learning theory and serves to counter the frequent criticism made of exchange theory, that is, that it assumes a selfish hedonistic model of man inadequate for dealing with man's more noble sentiments, such as altruism and caring, typical of relationships based on attraction.

Secord and Backman (1974) have postulated a four-stage process of growth in a relationship, each stage distinguished by the predominant subprocess involved. In the earliest stage, persons engage in various processes of sampling and estimation in which they explore the rewards available in a potential relationship. A second stage, bargaining, involves attempts on the part of both to negotiate the terms of their relationship. A third stage, commitment, is marked by a progressive reduction in the sampling and estimation in alternative relations and increasing dependence on the relationship in question. A final stage is characterized by the process of institutionalization, in which shared expectations emerge, recognizing the rightness and legitimacy of the exclusiveness of the relationship and the patterns of exchange that have developed, these expectations being shared not only by members of the pair but by others in general.

Somewhat in the same vein, Altman and Taylor's (1973) social penetration theory conceptualizes the growth of a relationship in terms of an initial process of exploration involving the forecast of favorable outcomes and their confirmation, along with the accumulation of rewards over time that strengthen the bonds of a relationship.

Murstein's (1976) stimulus-value-role theory similarly conceptualizes the growth of a relationship in terms of three stages: an early stage in which initial attraction is based on the stimulus characteristics of the persons, their physical characteristics, and so forth; a second stage where value consensus is explored and confirmed; and a final stage where the details of their roles within the relationship are worked out to the mutual advantage of the partners.

One of the most extensive of the stage or level theories has been that of Levinger and Snoek (1972), who view the development of a relationship as passing from an initial state of no contact through three stages of increasing pair relatedness. Although all stage theories explicitly or implicitly contain the notion of a filtering process, where what happens in a relationship at one stage determines whether it survives to the next stage, the theory as originally formulated by Levinger and Snoek attempted to delineate those factors and processes that affected the probability of movement from one stage to the next. The developmental theory that provides the organization of this chapter is similar in this respect and has been influenced by this formulation at a number of other points as well.

A FOUR-STAGE THEORY OF THE DEVELOPMENT OF A RELATIONSHIP

In the remainder of this chapter a four-stage developmental sequence will be offered as a way of presenting current research and thinking on relationships based on attraction. As do Levinger and Snoek, we propose to begin with a precontact or preawareness stage in order to allow consideration of a variety of factors that influence homogamy in relationships through their effect on the likelihood that persons with similar characteristics will find themselves in physical proximity. Consideration of a second stage characterized by unilateral awareness will allow for an examination of perceptual processes and self-presentation tactics that influence first impressions, and normative and situational factors that influence the likelihood that unilateral awareness will lead to an encounter and the beginning of an acquaintance, or stage 3. In this stage a number of processes, including exchange and attributional processes, can be related to the growth of the relationship, as they relate to developing interdependence, to role negotiation, and to the defining and evaluation of the relationship. A discussion of stage 4 will allow for consideration of processes related to the maintenance of a relationship or its eventual dissolution.

Stage 1: From No Contact to Unilateral Awareness

THE DETERMINANTS OF PROPINQUITY

Any explanation of the formation and growth of a relationship must start at some point prior to the time when the two individuals meet. Starting at a level of no contact and no awareness, the theory allows for an examination of various factors and processes that affect the likelihood that two persons in a given population will move at least to the stage of unilateral awareness. The crucial variables here are of two kinds. First, there is a variety of institutional structures and processes that determine the physical and temporal location of persons. Social variables, such as social class, that affect residential, occupational, and leisure-time locations, along with the ecological processes of differentiation and segregation that create distinctive location for types of persons and activities, influence the likelihood, frequency, and duration of contact between persons in a given population. Second, there are individual characteristics, such as leisure time interests, abilities, skills, and so forth, that influence the likelihood that persons will encounter each other. These social and individual variables are implicated also in the development of social networks, another source of influence on the likelihood of contact between persons. When a person is linked to a particular network or web of acquaintances, he is more likely to know about and be introduced to others in that network. These variables and processes account in part for the general tendency toward homogamy in relationships because their effect generally is to increase the likelihood, frequency, and duration of contact between persons similar in social and, to some extent, personal characteristics.

THE EFFECTS OF PROPINQUITY

Although perhaps of less interest to social psychologists than variables and processes at a more micro-level, these structural and ecological influences described above are related to attraction through their effects on propinquity, long a focus of interest to attraction researchers. Whether one examines the early research on mate selection that dealt with residential proximity of future spouses (Bossard 1932); the classic study of housing by Festinger, Schachter, and Back (1950) in the 1950s that demonstrated how distance, as well as architectural features that influence traffic patterns within and between buildings, affected acquaintanceship; or studies of attraction among housemates, such as that by Newcomb (1961) in the 1960s; in its effects, the propinquity variable frequently outstripped other social and psychological variables.

Proximity is related in a variety of ways to attraction. In addition to the indirect effect of propinquity on attraction through similarity, physical closeness facilitates a number of processes that contribute to attraction.

To the degree that persons are close, the general process of sampling and estimation is facilitated. When interacting with those nearby, persons are likely to hit upon outcomes sufficiently satisfactory to discourage interaction with those at greater distance (Homans 1961). The interaction with those physically close is much more apt to produce initially favorable outcomes for a number of reasons. First, the physical and psychological costs are likely to be less in such interaction. Whereas the low physical cost is obvious, the low psychological cost requires further comment. In many settings the normative expectations are such as to make interaction between persons spatially contiguous psychologically less costly than with those only slightly more distant.

As Priest and Sawyer (1967) note in their study of dormitory friendships, where persons living on the same floor were separated by distances that were physically quite small, even these small distances were important determinants of friendship:

> In Pierce Tower, a room five doors further away represents more than ten added seconds of travel time; it represents five closer opportunities that must be passed by. When distances are this small, the significance of the closeness, this analysis suggests, is less in the physical distance itself than in its perception. The farther a door is from one's own, the more purposive one's approach must be, and the more such approach tends to require justification. To borrow change for the Coke machine from someone five rooms away may raise the question, "Why didn't he ask someone closer?" [p. 647]

Second, to the degree that proximity encourages frequent observation and interaction, persons are able to predict each other's behavior and avoid the cost of uncertainty and response conflict (Zajonc 1968), reactions which are apt to occur in unfamiliar situations. Third, frequent interaction not only increases the chances of discovering similarities as well as other rewarding characteristics of another person, but allows for the operation of social influence processes that may produce similarity. Finally, a variety of processes emerges in early interaction, that provides a certain momentum favoring a relationship already initiated over later alternatives.

Stage 2: Processes of Sampling and Estimation

At the early stage of unilateral awareness without interaction and in the early stage of interaction, a variety of factors and processes can be subsumed under the general processes of sampling and estimation. At this point, initial attraction and the likelihood that a relationship will be formed will depend upon both individuals' estimates concerning the value of the outcomes to be expected from the relationship, and concerning the probabilities that such outcomes will be realized. These estimates, in turn, will be influenced by a number of tendencies characteristic of person perception and self-presentation, by elements in the situation that influence both, and by a number of interactional processes.

FIRST IMPRESSIONS: PROCESSES OF PERSON PERCEPTION

The findings concerning selective perception and perceptual accentuation suggest that persons will tend, where possible, to notice and distort the characteristics of others in the direction of their current motivational states. For example, it has been demonstrated experimentally (Stephan, Berscheid, and Walster 1971) that males sexually aroused by erotic material will subsequently rate pictures of females as more physically attractive. A second general finding is that the various pieces of information that a person receives about another do not enter equally into determining the total impression of that person. Instead, some kinds of information exert strong effects on how other information is interpreted. Asch (1946) many years ago demonstrated the powerful effects of certain central traits in determining how other traits are interpreted. At about the same time, the sociologist, Hughes (1945), made the same point concerning master statuses. Placement of persons in certain social categories or statuses powerfully constrains the characteristics attributed to them by others.

More recently, the development of attribution theory has provided a number of principles that help explain some of these effects. The general principle of balance, which subsumes the principle of affective-cognitive consistency, appears to explain the tendency for the person to attribute positive traits to those toward whom he has positive sentiments and negative traits to those toward whom he has negative feelings.

A second general principle involving consistency is the tendency to attribute traits of similar value or valence to others. Knowledge that a person falls at the desirable end of the continuum on one trait leads to the attribution of a similar position on other traits.

A third principle is the tendency for persons to infer from the action of a person the existence of underlying dispositions and hence to see other persons' behavior as much more consistent and constant than it actually is. A final principle, that of appropriateness, adds a qualification to the preceding one since it influences the impact of information about others derived from their behavior (Jones, Davis, and Gergen 1961). Behavior appropriate to the situation, and in particular the role requirements in the situation, tends to be disregarded as indicative of the true nature of the person, whereas inappropriate or deviant behavior is used to infer underlying transsituational dispositions.

These various principles are for the most part consistent with the general finding that early information and impressions have greater effects on the perception of others than does later information. Thus, first impressions have considerable impact and, where favorable, provide a certain momentum to the development of a relationship.

FIRST IMPRESSIONS: PROCESSES OF SELF-PRESENTATION AND IDENTITY NEGOTIATION

While attribution theory is consistent with the current emphasis in studies of perception on the active character of the perceiver, by itself it fails to capture the full dynamics of impression formation because it neglects consideration of the active nature of the target, the person being perceived. Not only do persons in interaction attempt to control the kinds of information available to others, but they, as well as others in the situation, may influence the attributions that are finally arrived at. Prus (1975) has argued that attributions, particularly unfavorable ones, frequently are challenged by the target person, and Blau (1964) has suggested that a person initially attracted to another is motivated to impress the other with his or her rewarding qualities. The work of Jones (1964) and his students demonstrated some years ago that if persons are so motivated, they tend to adopt a number of self-presentation strategies or tactics of ingratiation that include, in addition to flattery, conformity in opinion, judgment, and behavior to that of the other and attributing attractive characteristics to themselves directly or indirectly. Two basic processes underlie such tactics: self-presentation (Goffman 1959) and altercasting (Weinstein and Deutschberger 1963), and both of these are involved in the more general processes of identity bargaining (Blumstein 1973) and role bargaining (Goode 1960).

While a discussion of role bargaining will be reserved for later, identity bargaining will be dealt with here. As Blumstein notes, identity bargaining as a process is more sensitive than role bargaining to the momentary fluctuations of social performance in first encounters, where each in the pursuit of his own goals or lines of action attempts to present himself as a certain kind of person and at the same time attempts to cast the other person into an identity that will fit these preferred lines of action. Generally, the identities presented and cast, in first encounters at least, tend to be favorable because positively valued identities are most acceptable and facilitative at this stage. In addition, norms of politeness and consideration that influence the behavior of newly acquainted persons favor this course.

The result of these attributional and interactional processes is often to bring about what Merton (1948) has called the *self-fulfilling prophecy.* While Merton defined the latter as "a false definition of the situation evoking new behavior which makes the originally false conception come true," the emphasis here is not on the trueness or falseness of the identity but on its emergent character. Relationship formation and identity formation, even at this stage, are intrinsic to each other.

While identity negotiations affect the kinds of behavior that each partner displays to another, other factors also affect this aspect of the sampling and estimation process. For the most part, these are situational features that, through their normative definitions, allow, encourage, discourage, or prohibit the display of certain kinds of information, and encourage or discourage inferences from such information. Levinger and Snoek (1972) have noted that persons may be involved daily in a round of segmental interaction without developing a personal relation until something untoward occurs to jolt them out of their role-constrained behavior. In terms of the previously noted principle of appropriateness, when persons are confronted with routine role behavior, they tend not to attribute underlying dispositions to others or to form impressions of what others are really like, nor does routine role behavior allow for or require the kind of interactional leeway that permits the joint creation of a personal relationship composed of two distinct identities. When, however, situational contingencies demand a departure from role routines (a sudden emergency, for instance), this often becomes the occasion for the emergence of a personal relationship as a result of the initiation of interpersonal and intrapersonal processes typical of this early stage of the development of a relationship.

THE COMPROMISE PROCESS

So far, we have mainly examined the effects of various influences on the evaluation of another's characteristics, should a relationship ensue. We have neglected those processes and factors that influence each person's estimate of the likelihood that a relationship can be created and the estimated values attained. Relationship initiation at this stage is always to some degree a compromise made against a background of competing alternatives of varying desirability.

The concept of the compromise process was originally introduced to handle the findings of studies of living groups that friendship choices tended to be made between persons who received roughly the same number of choices from others, and from observations of the rating and dating complex on college campuses, where it appeared that dating partners tended to be ranked similarly on various dimensions of campus prestige (Waller and Hill 1951). As originally formulated by Backman and Secord (1964), the emphasis was placed on the instability of relationships involving persons of different choice status or popularity, the more popular person tending to leave the relationship because of the availability of more attractive alternatives or, when remaining, tending to exploit the person of lower choice status which encouraged the latter to leave.

A similar analysis based on asymmetry in interdependence recently was made by Kelley (1979), and a recent study of the breakup of relationships before marriage (Hill, Rubin, and Peplau 1976) provides support for this interpretation.

While emphasis in the work of the above writers places the compromise process somewhat later in the history of the relationship, the same phenomenon has been studied in the early phase where the focus is on the person's assessment of the likelihood of success or failure in the initiation of a relationship. Here, individuals are thought to take into consideration their own as well as the other person's attractiveness and, depending on their assessments of the likelihood and costs of failure, to decide whether or not to establish a relationship with the other (Huston 1973). Although Stroebe (1977) has noted that the evidence is not entirely consistent, it appears that where the costs of failure in terms of lowered self-esteem are perceived to be real and the relative attractiveness of partners is based on the partners' self-ratings, rather than on ratings made by other persons, people tend to be attracted to those of similar desirability, at least in terms of physical attractiveness, the matching variable on which most recent studies have focused.

NORMATIVE CONSTRAINTS

The immediately preceding discussion has emphasized anticipated consequences, particularly from the persons in the relationship. Actual rewards and punishments and those actual and anticipated ones that stem from the self, as well as from third parties, must also be touched upon, although those actually experienced may be of less importance at the early stage of sampling and estimation than the anticipated ones.

The operation of norms that delineate what has been called the field of eligibles (Winch 1958) in discussions of mate selection influences both self-reinforcement and the reinforcement received from others. As Kerckhoff (1974) has noted, in addition to the role of social factors in determining the likelihood and frequency of contact between persons from various social groups and categories, the subcultures of various groups contain normative expectations concerning the kinds of personal and social characteristics that are considered desirable in a partner in a particular kind of relationship. Thus, similarity in attitudes between mates may be considered desirable by middle-class white Americans where the satisfaction of socioemotional needs is central to the relationship of marriage. Among working-class couples this may not be so essential, because of less emphasis on this function of marriage.

Conformity to the norms of relationship eligibility involves rewards and costs from the self, as well as from others. Early studies of barriers to interfaith marriages clearly illustrate this point. Thus, Hollingshead (1950) reported in the fifties that Jewish women had a very low rate of marriage outside their faith. A well-socialized Jewish girl of that generation may have experienced considerable discomfort over her attraction to a person of another faith—discomfort that arose not only from guilt over violating her own internalized norms concerning endogamy, but from concern over the reactions of friends and family to such a relationship.

The rewarding internal state of enhanced self-esteem and the reward of approval from others are also involved in generating attraction in still another way. To gain and maintain the status of normality, persons are expected by others and themselves to have friends and lovers. As Turner (1970) has noted, regardless of the features of the relationship or characteristics of the persons involved, the fact of having a relationship, such as a marriage, validates one's personal adequacy, heterosexual normality, and personal maturity in the eyes of others, as well as of oneself. Although recent trends toward greater acceptance of the single state for adults in our society may indicate a relaxation of normative pressures in this direction, they still exist.

REWARDS THROUGH FANTASY

Self-supplied rewards are not only involved in conformity processes influencing behavior at this early stage of a relationship, but are implicated in another way as well. Contemporary social learning theory recognizes that persons can, through their control over their own cognitive processes, administer rewards and punishments by imagining certain consequences of their behavior. It is probable that persons contribute to the early growth of a relationship by imagining future rewards and by recounting and, in a sense, replaying in their imagination early pleasurable contacts with their partners. The considerable preoccupation of each partner with the other during the early stage of the courtship relationship probably involves a good bit of this self-rewarding activity.

In the discussion so far, the emphasis has been on process. Before the next stage of the development of a relationship is treated, two variables require a more extended discussion for a number of reasons. Both, although having some influence at later stages, have their strongest effects in the earliest stages of a relationship. Both have been the subject of considerable research on attraction, and this research provides illustrations concerning many of the points that have been or will be made in this portion of this chapter. The first of these variables is similarity and the second is physical attraction.

THE EFFECTS OF SIMILARITY

That similarity is related to attraction has a long history of empirical support. Early sociometric studies (Bonney 1946), as well as the early studies of mate selection (Kirkpatrick 1955), generally found that persons were attracted to others who were similar in social background characteristics and values. More recent studies of friendship (Lauman 1969; Nahemow and Lawton 1975) report the same findings and in addition find similarity between friends in preferences for leisure activities (Werner and Parmelee 1979). A number of longitudinal studies of the growth of attraction in groups (Newcomb 1961; Curry and Emerson 1970) provided further support for the association between similarity and attraction, although not without some qualifications. Finally, an extensive array of experiments (Byrne 1971), in which information concerning the degree of similarity with respect to opinions, personality traits, and social background characteristics of stimulus persons was manipulated, has for the most part supported the similarity-attraction relationship.

Over the years a number of explanations of the relation between similarity and attraction have been suggested. First, agreement with another leads the person to anticipate rewarding interaction, and where it actually facilitates joint pleasurable activities, it also can be expected to lead to attraction. Agreement in activity preferences, attitudes, and values not only ensures that persons will hit upon mutually satisfying activities, but that they will be able to carry them out with a minimum of friction (Werner and Parmelee 1979).

Second, persons are attracted to others who agree with their opinions, but dislike others whose views are divergent. Agreement is rewarding and disagreement punishing, either because liking an agreeing other and disliking one who disagrees provides a balanced cognitive state—one that is psychologically pleasant and comfortable (Heider 1958; Newcomb 1961), or because agreement satisfies a person's affectance needs, the need to feel secure in dealing with the world (Byrne 1971). A third general explanation is that persons tend to anticipate that individuals who are similar to them will like them (Aronson and Worchel 1966).

Several other somewhat artifactual bases of the similarity-attraction relationship should also be mentioned in passing. First, it is generally acknowledged by family sociologists that homogamy or similarity in social background characteristics and accompanying similarity in interests, attitudes, and values in marital partners is in part the result of structural aspects of society that favor higher rates of interaction among persons similar in these respects, leading to increased chances of their forming a relationship regardless of these similarities.

A related element in relationships of this type is the existence of norms of endogamy that encourage persons to select as potential mates in-group members whose social characteristics and attitudes are similar. It is probable that normative pressures of this sort also operate in the selection of friends.

It has also been noted (Murstein 1976) that homogamy in mate selection may also be a product of the compromise process previously described. Similarities on various dimensions of status and correlated value similarities may result from the tendency for persons with similarly valued characteristics and other resources to attempt and succeed in forming relationships.

A final artifactual relationship has been noted by Stalling (1970), Ajzen (1977), and others in connection with the most widely used paradigm to study the similarity-attraction relation—the bogus stranger paradigm (Byrne 1971). In this set of experimental procedures, a participant is given information concerning the opinions of another person in the form of an opinion questionnaire, presumably completed by that person but in reality filled out by the investigator so as to vary the proportion of agreement with items that the participant had previously endorsed. Such a procedure, unfortunately, confounds agreement with the item with the affective value of the item. Thus, it becomes problematic as to how much of attraction in this experimental paradigm is in response to the affective value of the item, either through conditioning or through cognitive processes that influence the likeability assigned to the person, and how much is in response to similarity per se.

Which of these various explanations of the similarity-attraction relationship applies in a given empirical instance will depend on the particular methods employed in demonstrating the relationship, the type of relationship, and the phase of its development. Thus, normative influences on the choice of partners are perhaps stronger in instances of mate selection than in friendship formation. One review of the literature suggests that similarity appears to have stronger effects in the early stages of a relationship than in later stages, and in relationships in socio-emotional groups, rather than in task groups (Secord and Backman 1974). These conclusions should be tempered by the realization that most studies have concentrated on the early phases of relationship formation and have typically dealt with kinds of similarity that may only be remotely related to the kinds of rewards and costs persons experience at later periods in their relationship. In the early phase of a relationship, however, similarity probably enters in principally as a filtering device, as it influences each person's anticipation of future rewards in general, and in particular the reward of being liked. One of the strongest associations in the literature on attraction is the correlation between liking and the perception of being liked in turn. These two variables are also both correlated with the perception of similarity, and although the degree to which each of these three variables is an effect of the other is not entirely clear, the pattern of results from a number of studies suggests that one line of effect is that the perception of similarity induces the anticipation of being liked, which, in turn, increases liking. An early study, Backman and Secord (1959), demonstrated that the experimental induction of the perception of liking on the part of another person does lead the perceiver to be attracted to that person and a later study has provided support for the idea that where persons are insecure concerning their acceptance by others, similarity appears to be a more powerful factor in influencing their choice of associates than when they feel more secure (Walster and Walster 1963). The findings of Kerckhoff and Davis (1962) and Lauman (1969), that the effects of perceived similarity of the type typically investigated, that is, attitudes, seem less important at later points in a relationship when presumably there are other bases for assuming reciprocity of liking, also are consistent with this interpretation.

Not all research has demonstrated a positive relation between similarity and attraction. Under certain circumstances a negative relation occurs. These findings, however, are consistent with the general principle that attraction is influenced by the actual or anticipated consequences of a relationship. Studies that find that persons dislike others who are similar to them in some respects are those where the similar other person is perceived as possessing some undesirable characteristic as well (Peres 1971; Novak and Lerner 1968). In such an instance similarity presumably is threatening. The person might anticipate that rewards from others, particularly their favorable regard, might be reduced if similarity led these persons to conclude that the subject also had this undesirable characteristic.

THE EFFECT OF PHYSICAL ATTTRACTIVENESS

The variable of physical attractiveness has been of increasing interest to social psychologists in recent years. This has come about in part because physical attractiveness has been shown to have effects similar to central traits or master statuses in organizing the perceptions of others (Dion, Berscheid, and Walster 1972), and in part because in investigations of dating, physical attractiveness accounted for a large part of the variance in dating partners' responses to each other, including the desire to continue the relationship (Walster et al. 1966; Stroebe et al. 1971).

A variety of reasons, some with considerable empirical support, have been offered for the fact that physically attractive people are liked. First, attraction may result from the rewards of esthetic satisfaction. Second, persons may receive rewards from others as a result of their forming a relationship with an attractive other, either because this conforms with a cultural norm that the person toward whom one is attracted is supposed to be physically attractive or because one's ability to form a relationship with an attractive other attests to one's own desirability in the eyes of others. Studies have shown that for males at least, information that a male is romantically involved with an attractive female enhances his status (Sigall and Landy 1973; Bar-Tel and Saxe 1976). A third reason already alluded to is the powerful effect of the person's physical attractiveness on the attribution of other traits of similar value.

In the most widely cited study of stereotyping on the basis of physical attractiveness, Dion, Berscheid, and Walster (1972) reported that both males and females attributed personality traits of higher social desirability to pictures of attractive persons than to pictures of those of average attractiveness or those judged relatively unattractive. Respondents also predicted the more attractive would have more favorable life experiences, including higher occupational status, more successful marriages, and in general greater happiness. In addition to the tendency for persons to attribute to others traits having similar values, these findings reflect some of the other principles influencing first impressions. Thus, the physically attractive were seen as sexually warmer and more responsive (Berscheid and Walster 1972), illustrating the effects of selective perception and perceptual accentuation.

Some subsequent research has also suggested that the effects of the cultural stereotype of the physically attractive are often to bring about behavior on the part of the perceiver that, in the manner of a self-fulfilling prophecy, elicits behavior on the part of the perceived person that further enhances the attractiveness of that person. In a rather ingenious experiment, Snyder, Tanke, and Berscheid (1977) demonstrated that males, having been led to believe that the females they were interacting with (over an intercom) were either attractive or unattractive, appeared to elicit from the latter, who were also naive participants, behaviors that another independent group of male subjects rated as consistent with the stereotypes of the physically attractive or unattractive.

The extensive research on the effects of physical attraction as a central trait should not lead the reader to overestimate its importance in organizing the impressions persons form of others. Other studies have shown that physical attractiveness itself may be influenced by other central traits such as personality impressions and perceptions of ability. (Felson and Bohrnstedt 1980). The effects of one characteristic on another also seem to vary depending on characteristics of both the judge and the target person as well as the amount of interaction between the two.

Stage 3: Social Penetration: The Development of Interdependence and Role Negotiation

While the various perceptual and self-presentation processes observed as operative in stage 2 continue into stage 3, they do so at a progressively deeper level and are transformed in the process as the relationship develops. Self-presentation, which originally served as a tactic controlling information given off to others, changes into the process of self-disclosure, a part of the broader process of social penetration (Altman and Taylor 1973). Intermeshed with the process of self-disclosure, in which persons progressively and mutually reveal deeper and more intimate aspects of themselves, are other processes involved in the growth of a structure of outcome interdependence and a shared definition of the relationship.

THE PROCESS OF SELF-DISCLOSURE

If first impressions are sufficiently favorable, persons will be motivated, when they begin to interact, to provide behaviors that will result in favorable outcomes to the other, and to the degree each is successful in this respect, they become progressively motivated to provide rewards that will maintain the relationship. One of the most important rewards that persons exchange as a relationship develops is support for each other's views of themselves as persons, their self-concepts.

The most consistent finding in the empirical literature on attraction is that persons are attracted to others whom they perceive as accepting them as they see themselves and who allow them to behave in a self-validating manner (Newcomb 1961; Curry and Emerson 1970; Secord and Backman 1965). Thus, in the early phases of interaction, each person begins tentatively to reveal himself to the other. The process of self-disclosure involves first, information about the self that each feels relatively confident about and relatively certain that the other will find acceptable. Later, persons reveal more intimate details about which they are less confident, hence in greater need of social validation, and which they are less certain will be regarded favorably.

Revelations at this level play an important part in the process of self-creation. As a relationship develops, each person feels sufficiently secure to try out or tentatively display new elements of identity. Such displays may take the form of revealing hitherto private hopes and fears about the self or, more indirectly, of recounting to the other past or current episodes of behavior where the person behaved in a fashion viewed as confirming some nascent element of self.

Studies of the self-disclosure process (Cozby 1973) generally find that, in the early part of a relationship at least, each person tends to pace the process of disclosure by revealing to the other information at about the same level of intimacy as he is receiving from that person. A number of reasons for this have been suggested, of which two appear to be most plausible. First, as in any other exchange, persons feel obliged to adhere to the norm of reciprocity. To the extent that one person's revelations at progressively more intimate levels are increasingly rewarding in terms of signifying regard and trust to the other partner, the latter feels obligated to return revelations thought to be of equal rewarding value. Second, the process of self-disclosure contributes to another basic interpersonal process, the growth of trust, which in turn further facilitates more intimate disclosure. While there is not complete agreement on a definition of trust, a key element appears to be a sense of certainty that the trusted person will not behave at some point in the future in a way that endangers anticipated favorable outcomes of the trusting person. Each person's revelations of progressively more intimate details concerning himself, and their acceptance and confirmation by the other, give assurance that any resultant vulnerability will not be exploited, either because both partners are equally vulnerable or because each perceives the exchange of progressively more intimate details as a sign of increasingly close interpersonal ties.

The fact that persons perceive the intimacy of disclosure as indicative of attraction allows the self-disclosure process to function as a pacing device in the development of a relationship. By the depth of disclosure to another, a person may indicate his degree of emotional involvement in the relationship.

While our emphasis so far has been on the manner in which self-disclosure allows for maintenance and creation of self-elements, an extremely important reward, self-disclosure provides each partner with information concerning other outcomes as well. Persons learn what kinds of behavior have reward value to each other and which behaviors are costly. This information, in turn, can be used as a guide in arriving at mutually satisfying patterns of exchange that become a part of the structure of interdependence that constitutes the relationship. To this aspect of the social penetration process we now turn.

EXCHANGE, ATTRIBUTION, AND THE DEVELOPMENT OF INTERDEPENDENCE

Once persons actually begin to interact, whether their relationship continues to develop will depend not only on the anticipated outcomes of further interaction, but on the actual outcomes that partners begin to experience as they interact. These outcomes in turn depend on the development of stable patterns of exchange, which can be conceptualized in terms of a structure of interdependence (Kelley and Thibaut 1978; Kelley 1979). This interdependence can be analyzed at three levels. At the first or behavioral level, structure consists of the stable patterns, routines, or combinations of behaviors that make up the day-to-day activities of the pair. The second or normative level of structure consists of the norms and shared understandings that constitute the somewhat unique role structure of the relationship. The third or personal level consists of each partner's personality characteristics, general attitudes, and elements of self relevant to, or embedded in, the relationship.

Elsewhere, Secord and Backman (1974) have outlined a theory of role negotiation that focuses largely on the third of these levels. Their theory combines elements of the role identity model of interaction developed by McCall and Simmons (1966) with contemporary theories of power and negotiation to explain the development of a relationship. More recently, Kelley (1979) has offered a theory that deals with the development of interdependence at all three levels. In this section, elements from both theories will be employed as they relate to the growth of a relationship and those facets of each partner's individuality that are created in that process of growth. We begin with the recent work of Kelley and Thibaut (1978) and Kelley (1979).

INTERDEPENDENCE AND INTERPERSONAL DISPOSITIONS

Basic to Kelley and Thibaut's analysis is the general finding from studies of interdependence that persons do not respond only in terms of their own outcomes, but in terms of the overall pattern of outcomes, which includes those of their partners as well. While this has been demonstrated in studies where participants who were typically unacquainted played games in laboratory experiments (McClintock 1972), Kelley (1979) observes that this also appears to be the case in which persons resolve problems of interdependence in the context of everyday relationships.

Our analysis of the kinds of rewards underlying such relationships suggests that this tendency would be particularly strong in relationships based on attraction. Not only would the manner in which interdependence is resolved influence the exchange of outcomes between partners, but the rewards and punishments, self-imposed or received from others, are affected by norms that prescribe how persons should respond in situations involving interdependence. Vicariously experienced outcomes also influence the ways in which persons respond to interdependency, because as a relationship develops the affective reactions of partners become increasingly salient.

There is also evidence to suggest (McClintock 1972) as Kelley and Thibaut note, that persons differ in the characteristic way in which they react to patterns of interdependence. These individual tendencies Kelley and Thibaut conceptualize as interpersonal dispositions, which they define as a general disposition on the part of persons in situations involving interdependence to resolve the conflict between their own interest and that of their partners in a characteristic manner. Thus, some persons may be basically competitive, tending where possible to maximize their own gains in relation to their partners'. Others may tend toward a cooperative resolution and choose to behave in a fashion calculated to maximize the joint outcomes of the partners, and still others, altruistic, and choose to coordinate their actions with those of their partners so as to maximize the latter's outcomes.

Although persons bring in interpersonal dispositions from other relationships, Kelley suggests that as each relationship develops, interpersonal dispositions emerge that are distinctive to that particular relationship. These arise in part from intraindividual processes of attribution, as each reacts to the manner in which the other chooses to behave in recurring situations of interdependence, and in part from interpersonal processes of identity negotiation.

To illustrate both these points with an example, a basic tenet of attribution theory previously noted is that persons tend to infer from particular acts the existence of underlying causes or dispositions within the individual to behave in certain ways. Thus, when a person chooses to engage in an activity that is not particularly rewarding to him but is rewarding to his partner, the latter is likely to infer that the person is a considerate person who generally tends to respond to the needs of others. On the other hand, persons perceived as acting exclusively in terms of their own outcomes are labeled inconsiderate or selfish. In analyzing the complaints that participants in a study, all of whom were either married or cohabiting, had about their partner's behavior, Kelley (1979) notes that this tendency to attribute underlying dispositions to the partner was particularly marked where the acts of one person had negative consequences for the perceiver.

Kelley suggests that this kind of invidious characterization may be used as a sanction in identity negotiation. By claiming that a partner's acts demonstrate a particularly invidious disposition, the aggrieved person challenges the other to alter his behavior in such a way as to disconfirm the characterization. This latter gambit is a negative variant of the process of altercasting. At this point, however, it is sufficient to note that negotiations at the level of dispositions are not only significant at the personal level, for they result in the creation of facets of identity that have implications for persons' overall view of themselves, but also because the kind of dispositions arrived at influence the resolution of problems of interdependence at the normative and behavioral levels as well.

Conflict and negotiation in a relationship can occur at any level and generally tend to spread from one to the other as persons attempt to work out solutions to their problems of interdependence. In general, the spread is upward. Persons finding themselves at odds at the behavioral level may attempt to resolve this by appeals to norms and role expectations. If they agree that following a particular rule or role prescription is appropriate in the situation, the conflict may be resolved at that level and no further negotiation becomes necessary. If there is still lack of agreement, the conflict may spread to the personal or identity level where each attempts to modify the attitudes and other dispositional characteristics of the other person in a manner that will resolve the problems of interdependence at the lower levels. Thus, the husband who tends toward dominance in relations with others, including his wife, may as a result of processes of identity negotiation begin to change at the dispositional level, allowing him to feel more comfortable in a more equalitarian portrayal of the husband role, which is reflected at the behavioral level by his assuming more of the routine household tasks. Although it is reasonable to expect conflict and negotiation to spread upward from one level of interdependence to the next, both from what is known about attribution processes and the tactics of altercasting and from the fact that solutions at higher levels often provide the basis for solving problems of interdependence at lower levels, this tendency may have deleterious consequences. As partners move from one level to the next, the intensity of conflict is likely to increase because modification at higher levels involves rewards and costs tied to central elements of identity and because the tactics employed at these levels often involve attacks on these elements. As we will note later, just as identity creation is basic to the growth of a relationship, identity destruction generally accompanies its decline.

While Kelley's analysis of interdependence at the behavioral, normative, and identity levels provides for a more fine-grained analysis of interdependence at each of these levels and of the relationship among levels, the theory of role negotiation offered by McCall and Simmons (1966) and Secord and Backman (1974) focuses primarily on negotiation at the level of identity and attempts to relate the results of this negotiation to a number of factors that receive less attention in the approach presented by Kelley. Since power is one of the most important of these factors, some attention must be given to it before describing the process of role negotiation.

DETERMINANTS OF POWER

Although theories concerning the nature and determinants of power in a relationship differ in language and details, most include the central idea that power is a function of the resources, dependencies, and alternatives of the partners. The inclusion of the variable, alternatives, that is, potential sources of rewards in other relationships, suggests that power cannot be explained entirely in terms of the characteristics of members of the pair, but must include factors outside a given relationship. Not only is the presence of alternatives a crucial determinant of each partner's dependency on the resources available from the other partner, but the resources available to each when they attempt to exercise power lie outside as well as within the relationship. In particular, the normative structure, as this influences the partner's responses to their own behavior as well as the responses of others to that behavior, is a significant outside resource.

An understanding of the triadic character of power can be gained if we examine various types of power attempts or strategies that persons employ in their daily activities. Such influence attempts involve changing the actual or perceived consequences of various behaviors in the direction favoring one course of action rather than another. These consequences have three sources: the person's own behavior, the behavior of the other person in the relationship, and that of persons outside the relationship. Various power strategies can be distinguished in terms of these sources. The use of threats or promises as a power tactic are ways of altering one partner's views concerning consequences stemming from the other partner's behavior. Another type of influence attempt is that of one partner altering the other partner's perception of the consequences stemming from the latter's behavior, either because the behavior has certain intrinsic consequences or because it will lead to self-reward or punishment. The admonition to the child that if he eats too much candy he will get sick is an example of the former and the warning that the person won't be able to live with himself in the morning if he does such and such is an example of the latter.

A third type of power attempt is that of one partner altering another partner's perceptions concerning consequences stemming from the behavior of third persons. The admonition that others will not like the partner if he does such and such is a typical example of such a power attempt. The tactic of monopolization also involves third parties. When one person attempts to convince another that he is the only source of a particular reward, he is engaging in this kind of tactic.

Essentially, these strategies involve the same kinds of reinforcement that underlie attraction. They include those that arise out of the exchange of behavior within a relationship, both direct and vicarious, those that stem from the self, and those whose source lies in the reactions of others outside the relationship.

Although the growth of interdependence based on exchange between the two partners in a relationship is undoubtedly the strongest source of power, it is not correct to equate power with such dependency. An important source of power for both parties in a relationship is the normative structure, and persons learn relatively early to use this inexpensive but potent source of power. Invoking norms either directly or indirectly through self-presentation and altercasting brings to bear the influences from others, as well as internal responses of the target person having reinforcing properties. In relationships based on attraction, the development of empathy and the merging of selves makes vicariously experienced reinforcements an increasingly significant basis of power as a relationship develops. Such nonverbal ploys as pouting and putting on a long face are ways of displaying cues that will be vicariously experienced as negative reinforcement by the other member of a pair; to the degree that they engender guilt or threaten the self-esteem of the latter, they involve normative sources of power as well.

The inclusion of sources of reward other than those mediated by the behavior of the other person in a relationship also allows for a consideration of another point, often inadequately dealt with, about power in relationships. Not only does power depend on variables outside as well as within a relationship, but the evolving structure of a relationship in terms of its division of labor, as well as the manner in which outcomes are distributed, is not exclusively determined by the relative power of the parties. As our earlier discussion of Kelley's (1979) work on interpersonal dispositions suggests, persons tend not to maximize the outcomes that their power might allow, but respond by virtue of internalized norms, as well as other determinants of interpersonal dispositions, to the pattern of consequences both to their partners and themselves. Such processes of outcome allocation can be subsumed under the more general canopy of role negotiation, to which we now turn.

A THEORY OF ROLE NEGOTIATION

The theory of role negotiation, as we previously noted, combines elements from the role identity model of McCall and Simmons (1966) with current conceptions of power and influence processes. It identifies a number of constraints operating on processes of role negotiation that influence the final structure of a relationship. These include: (1) the role identities of each partner; (2) situational demands; (3) properties of the role systems that affect the intrusion of other roles; (4) the influence of third parties on the bargaining process; and (5) the power of each of the partners as determined by their respective resources, dependencies, and alternatives.

Role identities are persons' imaginative views of themselves as they like to think of themselves in a particular role relationship. They are somewhat idealized conceptions that incorporate standards that are unlikely to be consistently attained in persons' actual day-to-day role performance. As McCall and Simmons (1966) note, they are most frequently experienced in imagined performances of the role.

But although they are best represented in persons' imagined rehearsals of future acts or in improved-upon replays in the persons' reveries of previous performances, they are not without considerable impact on behavior. Drawing on the work of Lindesmith and Strauss (1956) and Strauss (1959), McCall and Simmons note:

> Role-identities of this sort are not simply idle musings and entertaining daydreams; they exert important influences on daily life. In the first place, they serve as perhaps the primary source of plans of action. The vicarious performances that loom prominently in the substance of any role-identity serve as proving grounds and rehearsal halls for actual performances. The imagined reactions of various others to these vicarious performances constitute important criteria for evaluating any possible plans of *overt* action similar in content to these vicarious performances.
>
> Furthermore, the contents of a person's role-identities provide him with criteria for appraising his own actual performances. Those actions that are not consonant with one's imaginations of self as a person in a particular social position are regarded as embarrassing, threatening, and disconcerting; if possible, they will be discontinued and superseded by actions more in keeping with one's view of self. . . . [1966:69]

These components of the self are not entirely idiosyncratic but reflect in varying degrees the prevailing cultural and subcultural expectations for the role relationship as mediated by the portrayal of particular role models encountered in socialization. They are continuously modified by the results of negotiations in the course of interactions, as our discussion of the development of interpersonal dispositions suggests, and finally are influenced by other features of the person's self-conception, as well as by other features of the personality.

The situational demands and opportunities that influence role negotiations include such occurrences as those that encourage or provide an opportunity for a particular kind of role performance. These may be brief and episodic in character, as when the temporary illness of one partner requires a more solicitous version of the friendship or marital role, or more long-run, as where a wife's employment requires a new division of labor.

The latter example also illustrates another set of influences on the role bargain, namely, the intrusion of other roles. Role systems are rarely so well integrated that persons are not subject at times to conflicting and competing role expectations, stemming in part from the fact that they must simultaneously perform two or more roles. One solution to this dilemma is to enact some compromised version of each. At present, changes in sex roles are having their influence on the enactment of marital roles.

Third parties are also typically involved in the role negotiation process, both directly where they intervene on behalf of one or the other partner or indirectly where they act as sounding boards and sources of advice on how a relationship should be enacted.

Enmeshed in these sets of influences, persons work out their respective roles, the end result reflecting the above constraints, as well as each person's exercise of power and its effectiveness. The latter depends in part on the resources, dependencies, and alternatives of each, as well as each person's interpersonal skills, but only in part. There exists considerable slippage. First, for a number of reasons, persons may not accurately perceive their own resources and their partner's dependencies and alternatives. In fact, many of the tactics of interpersonal bargaining revolve around altering these perceptions. Second, as has been emphasized before, persons are influenced by interpersonal dispositions in the degree to which they exercise the extent of their power. These tendencies are affected by internalized standards and images of self, by agreed-upon rules previously worked out in the relationship, and by empathic concern for their partner's outcomes. Yet, differences in power, predictable from an analysis of resources, dependencies, and alternatives, do help account both for the uniqueness of each relationship and for broad shifts over time in the typical pattern of a relationship in a particular cultural group (Secord and Backman 1974).

At the same time, the role of power differences should not be overemphasized. One recent study (Stafford, Backman, and diBona 1977) of the division of labor in both married and unmarried cohabiting couples found that although the power of both parties influenced to some extent their division of labor, by far the greatest amount of the variance was accounted for by cultural factors affecting their respective role identities. Those holding a more traditional sex-role ideology and those whose parents modeled the more traditional division of labor were most likely to divide household tasks in the traditional fashion. Such situational demands as those arising from the wife's working, although having some impact, had the least effect on the division of labor.

The weight of these various determinants of role negotiation and resultant performance can be expected to vary, depending on the type of relationship. Relationships such as marriage or those involving cohabitation between men and women tend to be much more structured by cultural forms than friendship relationships. Similarly, parent-child relationships are heavily freighted with cultural regulations. In contrast, as Suttles (1970) notes, friendship is preeminently negotiable.

Processes of negotiation, as we have said, involve attempts to change in actuality or in the perception of the negotiating parties the values and the likelihood of consequences resulting from the behavior of each. These consequences arise in the behavior of the originator, the target person, or third parties. Ultimately, negotiations depend upon the pattern of dependencies, alternatives, and resources of both parties in the relationship, including normative resources that each can draw upon, and on each person's interpersonal dispositions.

Negotiations can be understood as occurring as a part of two more general processes, decision making and identity creation. These processes are interrelated in that both what decisions are made and how they are made have implications for each partner's identity; and, as noted previously, one objective of identity negotiation is to fashion interpersonal dispositions that encourage advantageous exchanges.

With respect to identity negotiation, the strategic processes of self-presentation and altercasting are important. Both of these have been commented on before, in terms of how these processes influence early impression formation, and in terms of how altercasting another in terms of an invidious identity can be used as a negative sanction and a tactic designed to elicit desired behavior that disconfirms the negative identity. Positive altercasting, however, is probably more frequent and appears to have a dual function in the development of a relationship. Not only is it an interpersonal tactic that is likely to have stronger effects than negative altercasting on the identity-creating process, but it is a powerful source of rewards, adding to attachment and dependency. If one partner effectively defines the other in terms of desirable attributes, the other's resultant behavior tends to be increasingly rewarding to the former; and to the degree that those favorable definitions are incorporated into the self, they tend to gratify the latter's self-esteem needs.

The creation of identities unique to the relationship and the emergence of habitual routines and ways of making decisions through normatively regulated exchanges constitute the substances and form of a relationship. Habitual routines appear to develop either through a process of mutual reinforcement generally unplanned and unnoticed by the participants or through the emergence of rules that guide interaction. Those rules either arise out of processes of abstraction from recurring events as a part of the learning process (Bandura 1977) or from explicit and conscious bargaining and agreement.

NEED COMPLEMENTARITY IN RELATIONSHIPS

The unique form that each relationship takes explains in part the failure of literally scores of studies to confirm what intuitively appears to be a valid hypothesis, that persons with complementary need structures would be attracted. As initially formulated by Winch (1958), persons high on a particular need, such as dominance, would be attracted to someone low on that need (Type I Complementarity) or persons similarly high or low on two different needs would be attracted to one another, for instance, a person high in the need to take care of others, nurturance, would be attracted to someone high on the need to be taken care of, succorance (Type II Complementarity). While intuitively plausible, the evidence in support of need complementarity has been almost uniformly negative except where the assessment of the personalities of couples has recognized the relationship basis of personality (Secord and Backman 1974).

Standard personality tests, such as the Edwards Personal Preference Scale, the most frequently employed test in such studies, require persons to describe themselves as they are in general rather than as they are in a particular relationship. Such a measurement approach to personality, although consistent with most conceptions of personality that emphasize its transsituational character, fails to capture the facets of personality uniquely tied to a particular relationship.

A variety of interpersonal and intrapersonal processes lead people to underestimate the degree to which the personality of others is in varying degrees different from one relationship to another. They also help explain why outsiders often misjudge the character of a relationship. Not only are many facets of a relationship shrouded in privacy, but an outsider's view is greatly colored by his relationship with each partner. The partners are different persons to some extent when interacting with the outside observer than they are when interacting with each other. Finally, each partner's assessment of a relationship, like its form, is unique, dependent as it is on the distinctive characteristics of the persons involved and the history of the relationship. To the general question of how partners assess their relationship we now turn.

THE ASSESSMENT OF A RELATIONSHIP: THE DETERMINANTS OF EMOTIONAL STATES

The assessment of a relationship can be analyzed as occurring at two levels, the cognitive and the emotional, although variables at each level affect those at the other.

People may experience a variety of feelings and engage in particular behaviors they feel belong with a specific type of relationship. In part, their responses reflect individual differences in personality, including some aspects of identity already discussed, and in part they reflect shared cultural and subcultural definitions of the appropriate feelings and behavior of persons who are linked in a particular relationship, as friends, as lovers, as parents and child, and so forth.

The comparatively intense feelings experienced in the early stage of a love relationship, variously labeled romantic love or passionate love, have been the subject of a number of attempts at explanation and measurement.

As for explanations, two theories have received the most attention from researchers—one based on a reinforcement theory of learning, the other based on a general theory of the determinants of subjective emotional states developed by Schachter (1964), who suggested that in order for a person to experience a particular emotional state, two things must occur. The person must be in a state of physiological arousal, and he or she must label or attribute this state to some cause on the basis of the available situational cues. In a wide-ranging series of investigations, Schachter and his colleagues have been able to manipulate the subjective states of persons, including their feelings of anxiety, anger, euphoria, and hunger, by changing either the person's degree of physiological arousal or the situational cues available.

Berscheid and Walster (1974a) have developed a theory of romantic or passionate love based on this theory of emotions. Observing from anecdotal and literary sources, as well as from the results of experimental studies, that attraction appears to be augmented by both unpleasant as well as pleasant experiences, they have suggested that reinforcement explanations of attraction, although consistent with the latter association, are inconsistent with the former. In contrast to reinforcement theory, their theory posits that, in the manner suggested by Schachter, emotional arousal whatever its source, positive or negative, may under appropriate stimulus conditions be labeled and therefore experienced as attraction or love, and that further, this is particularly likely to happen because of the existence of an ideology in Western culture that suggests how persons in the early phase of a heterosexual relationship are supposed to feel. These ideas about how a person should feel and behave when in love are reflected in popular songs and literature throughout the Western world.

Those who favor an explanation of attraction in terms of learning theory have, however, argued that attraction following aversive or unpleasant stimulation is not inconsistent with learning theory; that attraction results from the reduction of high levels of arousal rather than through labeling. Kenrick and Cialdini (1977) in particular have suggested from research on bonding among infrahuman species that the combination of high levels of arousal and subsequent reduction of that arousal is a particularly potent reinforcement schedule in establishing strong bonds.

Neither reinforcement nor attribution processes and the theories of attraction that rest on them are mutually exclusive, and although those favoring the reinforcement position have argued that their explanation is the more parsimonious, it is difficult to explain why the experience of love occurs as a rule in heterosexual relationships rather than in same-sexed ones without relying on the notion that our culture encourages the labeling of states of arousal and consequently the experiencing of emotion in the former as love. That the development of identity interdependence, along with sexual exploration and other activities typical of courtship, leads to both pleasurable and, at times, uncomfortable states of arousal cannot be denied. In particular, the heightened expectations concerning these matters fostered by romanticism, and the uncertainty of their realization, may explain why the intensity of feeling during this early phase of the initiation and consolidation of a relationship is followed by a more placid phase where uncertainty and unevenness in the rewarding quality of experience are replaced by certainty and routine, and the feelings between partners become more like those identified as companionate love. In fact, the intensity of feeling characteristic of romantic or passionate love does appear to recur, either where the situation is heavily laden with supporting cues and definitions, for example, a couple on a second honeymoon, or during periods of heightened physiological arousal. In particular, arousal associated with the anxiety that accompanies threats or uncertainty regarding the self, such as may occur during life-cycle crises, and the withdrawal of identity support that generally accompanies processes of discord in relationships may prompt the experience of strong emotions reminiscent of the early romantic phase of a relationship.

VARIETIES OF POSITIVE SENTIMENTS

Accompanying the recent theorizing concerning the determinants of the emotional experience of love have been a variety of attempts to measure and distinguish between various kinds of positive sentiments. Initially, Rubin (1970) developed scales that distinguished between liking and loving. The former sentiment appeared to be more akin to respect in that it was prompted by an appreciation of the socially desirable characteristics of another. Segal (1979) has recently made a similar distinction concerning respect.

Loving was conceptualized by Rubin in terms of three components: attachment, the desire to draw close and be with the other; caring, concern for the welfare of the other; and intimacy, the desire for close and confidential communication with the other.

ASSESSMENT OF A RELATIONSHIP: COMMITMENT

Of all the concepts involved in relationship formation mentioned so far, none has received less empirical attention than commitment. It is true that commitment to a particular course of action or belief has been the focus of research on attitudes, particularly within the dissonance tradition, yet this work bears only tangentially on this concept as it is employed in examining the development of relationships. In the latter context it has recently been the target of a number of attempts at conceptual analysis (Rosenblatt 1977; Leik and Leik 1977; Scanzoni 1979), which, unfortunately, reveal considerable disagreement as to its nature. In view of this state of affairs, the definition of commitment employed here is admittedly arbitrary and tentative and the treatment of this topic somewhat speculative.

Commitment can be viewed both as a process and as a state of mind. As the latter, it involves the intention and, some might add, an awareness of a moral obligation (Scanzoni 1979) to remain in a relationship and to continue the same patterns of exchange that have come to characterize it. As a process, it refers to the progressive development of exclusive dependencies between the members of a pair. This involves both coming to terms with or becoming satisfied with the pattern of outcomes associated with the relationship and progressively closing off considerations of patterns of rewards that might be anticipated from alternative relationships. Like self-disclosure, commitment is a reciprocal process, its progressive nature influenced in part by the norm of reciprocity and in part by the growth of trust. Acts of commitment not only increase outcomes and resulting attraction, but are also inherent in the development of power within a relationship. This helps explain why persons tend, at least in the early phase of a relationship, not to reveal a level of commitment in excess of their partner's. To do so might not only depreciate in the eyes of the other the outcomes he is receiving (Blau 1964), but, because commitment involves the giving up of potential alternatives, thus reducing a person's power, until trust is established persons are wary lest such a voluntary reduction in power invite exploitation. That the more committed may be exploited was noted by Waller (1938) some years ago when he formulated the *principle of least interest.* The latter refers to the observation that the person with the least interest in maintaining a relationship; that is, the least committed, generally exercises the greatest power.

The outcomes, the rewards, and cost or punishments involved in the process of commitment are all of the types that have been previously distinguished. They are both actual and anticipated and their source lies within the individual, in the behavior of the other partner, and in the behavior of third parties. Further, both normative and structural variables play a role in the phenomenon of commitment. The exchange of rewards is seldom so perfectly balanced that the norm of reciprocity does not enter into the support of the obligation to continue further exchanges. The costs experienced also may contribute to commitment as they become viewed as investments and are transformed by self-attribution processes into definitions of commitment. These various sources of rewards gained and costs avoided, which underlie the development of commitment, are illustrated in Turner's (1970) discussion of bonding in relationships. He distinguishes, in addition to the kinds of extrinsic rewards or the avoidance of costs that we referred to earlier, that is, those that follow from having a relationship per se irrespective of its character, a number of other consequences. These include outcomes underlying task bonds that are a product of the symbiotic relation between persons represented in the division of labor that grows up between partners carrying on joint activities; those outcomes related to person bonds experienced vicariously as a result of the merging of selves, as well as the support for the self-concept that each provides the other; and outcomes related to crescive bonds. The last named, as the term suggests, involve outcomes that are accumulated products of the unique history of a relationship. Included in this category, Turner suggests, are the investments that each has in a shared future, as well as in the maintenance of a jointly constructed social reality of the past; the unique interdependence coupled with reciprocal incapacity that has resulted from the partner's interlocking roles; the sense of responsibility for each other, as well as for others affected by their relationship, for example, children in a marriage; and finally, the sharing in a depth of communication and a high degree of relaxation in interaction which the security of their relation allows. Moving from the first, the extrinsic bonds, to the last of these bonds, the crescive ones, the rewards and the avoidance of costs associated with them become increasingly dependent on the uniqueness of the relationship—thus, less capable of retrieval in any alternative one, hence, increasingly strong sources of commitment.

Supporting a sense of commitment are both normative and structural barriers to the sampling of outcomes in alternative relations. Thus, in a marriage relationship, norms governing the quantity and quality of interaction with eligible alternatives discourage extensive sampling. These, along with features of everyday joint routines of each partner that develop as a relationship progresses, almost inevitably cut down the time and opportunity for sampling outside the relationship. It is significant that in occupational groups where such routine joint activities are frequently disrupted, or in times of crisis when similar disruption is apt to occur, commitments are weakened and the relationships are more subject to disruption.

Stage 4: Processes Leading to Maintenance or Dissolution of a Relationship

CHANGES IN REWARDS, COSTS, AND COMPARISON LEVELS

Commitment as a state of mind or as a process is rarely complete, nor is it unchanging, but tends to reflect the patterns of reinforcement the person encounters as these are modified by various cognitive processes. Elsewhere, Thibaut and Kelley (1959) and Secord and Backman (1964) have noted that changes over time in the level of attachment or the degree of satisfaction with a relationship can be analyzed in terms of the effects of individual, relational, situational, and cultural factors on three variables: the rewards persons experience, their costs, and their respective comparison levels. While these earlier analyses were largely confined to an analysis of the rewards and costs related to the behavior exchanged by the partners, in the present analysis all forms of reward and costs or punishments are dealt with. The latter include the reinforcing responses of the self and others experienced directly or vicariously, as well as those outcomes simply temporally contiguous with the interaction between partners. With respect to the last named, shifts in mood unrelated to the behavior of the partner or such other rewards contiguous with the relationship, as, for example, the more positive outcomes in general in the lives of the economically more successful, may play a role in determining the overall feelings of satisfaction and attachment in a relationship.

Since the concept of comparison level has not yet been employed in this chapter, a brief introduction is necessary. It has been defined in two complementary ways: as a neutral point on an array or scale of outcomes known to the persons, above which the outcomes are evaluated as satisfactory and below which outcomes are experienced as unsatisfactory; and as a standard by which persons evaluate the rewards and costs in terms of what they feel they deserve. This cognitive standard, which mediates the effects of the amount of positive and negative reinforcement, is influenced by a variety of factors, including the current level of reinforcement, what others, including the partner are receiving, what the levels of outcomes persons believe they might obtain in alternative relations are, as well as various norms and cultural beliefs that influence the choice of others for comparison and persons' reactions to these comparisons. These determinants underscore the contribution of social comparison processes to the growth, maintenance, or dissolution of a relationship.

The tendency of persons to evaluate current outcomes by comparison with the level of those immediately preceding, which is likely not to be too different, may help stabilize levels of satisfaction in the face of shifts in the value of outcomes. The effect of such comparison, as Thibaut and Kelley (1959) note, is for the person's comparison level to rise during periods of increasingly good outcomes and decline during periods of declining outcomes. This may account for a leveling out in noticeable increases in satisfaction during good times and the ability of persons to adapt to declining levels of outcomes during periods of adversity.

Similarly, the tendency for comparisons to be made with others who are similar, particularly with respect to power to obtain resources or avoid costs (Thibaut and Kelley 1959) is a stabilizing influence. Since this tendency narrows the difference between the persons' outcomes and those of comparison others, the result is to add stability to the persons' comparison level.

It was noted earlier that persons tend to form relations with those similar in the social desirability of their characteristics. This tendency facilitates the achievement of equitable exchanges within a relationship, and the degree of equity has been shown to relate to satisfaction in a relationship and, presumably, its stability (Walster and Walster 1978).

While social comparison processes on the whole tend to aid in the maintenance of a relationship, other factors affecting change in the comparison level may be disruptive. At present, changes in ideology concerning sex differences, as well as changes in the opportunity structure for women, have brought pressure for the division of labor and outcomes within the marriage relationship to change toward greater equality. Those changes have resulted in a rise in the comparison levels for many women in the marriage relationship that has contributed to less satisfaction on their part as wives and a greater willingness to leave the relationship. These same changes, particularly as they have made more attractive the alternatives to a current unsatisfactory relationship, have also raised what Thibaut and Kelley (1959) termed the comparison level for alternatives. The latter concept refers to that point on the scale of outcomes known to the person in a relationship where the outcomes expected outside the relationship are no worse than those currently being experienced. Thus, when the outcomes persons are receiving fall below this point, they can be expected to leave the relationship.

Since the degree of satisfaction and resulting attraction to a relationship is determined by the degree to which current outcomes exceed the comparison level, changes in the strength of the relationship and its likely continuation or dissolution will depend not only on variations in each person's comparison level but on changes in the level of outcomes each partner experiences. Those, in turn, are affected by changes influencing the value of rewards and costs that each experiences. Such changes have a number of sources (Secord and Backman 1974). One source is within the individual. As a result of experiences within a given relationship, as well as outside of it, new attitudes, needs, goals, and elements of self may emerge, altering significantly the cost and rewards associated with the enactment of certain behaviors on the part of the person, as well as those associated with the behavior of his partner and those stemming from others as a consequence of the relationship. The housewife and mother who returns to school, develops new interests, and begins to see herself as a budding career person may no longer gain satisfaction from the routines of housewifery and motherhood, and may find appreciation for these roles from her husband, children, and others of less value than support she receives from others for her new emerging identities.

Situational changes are a second source of influences altering the value of rewards and costs of behavior in a relationship. For example, the frugal behavior of a wife may have high reward value for a young struggling executive, but with his later success that behavior becomes embarrassing and costly. The reward and cost associated with the behavior or other characteristics of each of the parties to a relationship may also be modified by their regular association with other rewarding or punishing experiences. Thus, engaging in activity that is of little value for one party may become rewarding because it becomes associated with the rewards provided directly or vicariously by the other person who enjoys the activity. Finally, as a result of exchanges within a relationship, the reward and cost values of various behaviors may be altered. For example, costs may be reduced and rewards enhanced as each becomes increasingly knowledgeable and adept at behaviors that are rewarding to the other party.

INTERPERSONAL PROCESSES AND THE TERMINATION OF A RELATIONSHIP

A number of processes leading to increasing levels of mutually rewarding outcomes have been discussed as we traced the growth of a relationship. Many of these same processes operating in a somewhat reversed fashion appear to account for the successive declines in outcomes that characterize the general process of dissolution of a relationship.

One such process, noted earlier, is the tendency for persons as they begin to anticipate and actually experience increasingly rewarding outcomes as a consequence of a relationship to become motivated to increase the value of outcomes provided to the other, either through reducing the other's cost or by behaving in a more rewarding manner. The reverse often occurs in relationships heading for dissolution. A cycle develops where each in a somewhat tit-for-tat fashion reduces the outcome of the other. This may initially be an aggressive response to frustration whose source lies either within or outside the relationship. It may be in conformity to an eye-for-an-eye and tooth-for-a-tooth version of the norm of reciprocity, or initially it may simply be a power strategy to alter the behavior of the other. Nevertheless, to the degree that such behavior of one partner provokes similar responses in the other, a cycle of punishment and progressive reduction in outcomes occurs.

Often associated with this general process of conflict are a number of other processes whose effects endanger a relationship. The process of identity creation is basic to the growth of a relationship; a prominent process in its dissolution is identity destruction.

Kelley (1979) finds that perceivers are particularly likely to see another's behavior as indicative of some underlying personality trait or disposition when that behavior has negative consequences for them. This perceptual tendency encourages a certain type of attack during conflict in which one partner challenges and denies the validity of the other person's intentions, motives, and various qualities that are central to his identity and imputes negatively valued characteristics instead. In this process, persons have thrust upon them elements of an unwanted identity. Even where such tactics are at a minimum, the avoidance of painful interaction may set in motion the reverse of the process of self-disclosure where each party no longer serves as a confidant of the other because each fears that whatever is revealed may be used against him, or simply because the other can no longer be counted upon to be a supportive audience.

The result is a diminution of trust and a reduction in communication —the reverse of what had occurred during the earlier process of increasingly intimate disclosures. Reduced support for important elements of identity within a relationship may encourage the persons to develop alternative sources of support in other relationships. Where this is successful, the effect is to increase both the person's comparison level and comparison level for alternatives, and to reduce further satisfaction with, and attraction to, the relationship and the likelihood of its continuation.

Other power tactics similarly contribute to the downward spiraling of a relationship. The effectiveness of threats and promises by persons to alter the other person's perceptions of the costs and rewards to be anticipated from the former's behavior rest on their credibility, which, in turn, depends in good part on their being carried out. In the build-up of a relationship, following through on a promise increases the rewards of the other; although the carrying out of a promise may be at some costs to the promiser, those costs are typically balanced out by rewarding behavior from the other. This is generally not the case when threats are employed during the dissolution of a relationship. Not only do they impose costs on the other that are not likely to evoke rewards in return, but they may be made at some considerable cost to the threatener. Often because threats are used as a bluffing tactic, they involve steps that the threatener is not actually prepared to take at the time but, in the face of the noncompliance of the partner, now feels compelled to take so as to insure future credibility. A frequently employed threat is the threat of withdrawal, often employed as part of an attempt to negotiate a definition of the relationship as one in which the threatener is the party of least interest. When such a threat is made, often the person must follow through to support this definition, even though separation may in actuality be quite costly.

In the growth of a relationship, there is a tendency for a person to control his or her involvement so as not to significantly exceed that of the other partner. Where this control is lacking, the relationship is apt to be terminated either because the less involved person leaves the relationship for actual or potential alternatives or perhaps because he or she feels uncomfortable with the demands for reciprocation of the more involved; or the latter leaves the relationship because the former exercises the power of the least interested to exploit the relationship. A study of 103 affairs (Hill, Rubin, and Peplau 1976) that were terminated over a two-year period found, in addition to unequal involvement being a major reason offered by the couples for their breakup, some interesting sex differences on this score. In instances of unequal involvement, men tended more frequently to end the relationship when they were less involved, but rarely did they seek to terminate the relationship when they were the more involved party. Although most women who terminated a relationship reported less involvement than their partners, a sizeable minority, 37 percent, reported greater involvement. Whether this bespeaks the greater rationality of women in relationships of love, as Rubin (1973) has argued, or women's greater dependence on the love relationship for identity support cannot be determined from the data of this study, but both reasons seem plausible and not mutually exclusive.

While the discussion so far has focused principally on costs and rewards inherent in the behavioral exchange between the partners, the anticipated and actual behavior of others as they affect the total pattern of outcomes associated with a relationship must be considered in explaining the decline of a relationship. One of the costs for the more involved party in a relationship is the loss of self-esteem, but, in addition, where differential involvement becomes clear to others, perhaps because of the exploitive behavior of the partner, there is the additional cost of embarrassment.

The destruction of identity support from others that often accompanies public disclosure of a hiterto private rift in a relationship may explain why "going public" appears to accelerate the dissolution of the relationship (Weiss 1975). Disclosure to third persons is often part of a power strategy involving an attempt to bring normative pressures to bear on the partner. Yet, this strategy, like other attempts of persons to employ power to alter their partners' behaviors, although effective in the development of a relationship where involvement is strong and fairly equal, becomes ineffective or even counterproductive in a failing relationship where one party is much less involved than the other. Attempts on the part of the person with greater involvement to employ legitimate power by appeals to norms are ineffective for a number of reasons. First, because guilt, embarrassment, and lowered self-esteem that might result from norm violation can be effectively reduced, given strong motivation to do so, by a variety of accounting devices, justifications, excuses, and other kinds of definitions that serve to blunt the force of moral imperatives in social life (Scott and Lyman 1968; Backman 1976). Second, psychological dependency characteristic of a love relationship, at least, cannot be willed, hence such feelings are unresponsive to threats of reduced outcomes from the self and others. Finally, to the degree that the force of the normative structure is not entirely blunted by appropriate accounts and the other person experiences the costs of guilt, shame, and lowered self-esteem, his outcomes and resultant level of dependency are even further reduced. If the latter occurs, other power strategies that the more involved person may employ to modify the behavior of his less-involved partner further lose their potency. For instance, threats and promises by persons more dependent on a relationship lose their potency either because of a reduction of the value of the outcomes involved in the eyes of their partners or because of their lowered credibility.

Where the attempted exercise of power fails to alter the behavior or feelings of the other or further exacerbates the situation through some of these counterproductive side effects, the more involved person is apt to continue to experience unfavorable outcomes. To the extent that these are sufficiently punishing, attraction and dependency are gradually reduced to the point where the person is willing to leave the relationship, or perhaps becomes the party of least interest. In the latter case, this may prompt behavior that begins a new cycle in the downward spiral leading to dissolution. As the earlier discussion of comparison levels and comparison levels for alternatives suggest, the point of dissolution comes where one or the other party reaches his comparison level for alternatives. Levinger's (1976) concept of barriers, along with our previous discussion of the bonds underlying commitment, suggest some of the factors that determine this point in a relationship.

Barriers to leaving a relationship can be conceptualized in terms of anticipated costs accompanying the termination of a relationship. Levinger, analyzing the barriers to dissolving a marriage, divides these into three categories: the material, symbolic, and affectional. Divorce and its aftermath are financially costly. Not only are there the initial legal costs, but costs of separate maintenance for wife and children, for the male; and the lower earning power of the female often means that both parties face a reduction in their standards of living. The symbolic costs include the reactions of self and others to having broken the marital bond, and vary with the years of investment in the relationship and the attitudes the person and significant others have toward divorce. The affectional costs involve loss of significant relations with others that are based on the marriage, separation from children and other kin by marriage, and often the disruption of friendship networks as well.

That these barriers to marital dissolution are significant in accounting for the lower rate of marital dissolution than for other relations based on attraction can be illustrated by contrasting these barriers to marital dissolution with the much weaker barriers found in the previous study of terminated affairs. These were relationships of relatively shorter duration and consequent investment. They appeared to involve only low levels of personal commitment and were much less buttressed by the expectations of others. In general, those affairs were broken with much greater ease than the typical marriage relation.

A Concluding Note

In this chapter a four-stage developmental sequence has been offered as a way of presenting current research and theory concerning relationships based on attraction. We began with a precontact or preawareness stage in order to allow consideration of a variety of factors that influence homogamy in relationships through their effect on the likelihood that persons will find themselves in close proximity, and the role of proximity in the initiation of relationships. Consideration of a second stage characterized by awareness included an examination of perceptual processes and self-presentation tactics that influence first impressions, and normative and situational factors that influence the likelihood that unilateral awareness will lead to an encounter and the beginning of an acquaintance, or stage 3. In this stage a number of processes, including exchange and attributional processes, were related to the growth of the relationship, through their effects on the development of interdependence, on role negotiation, and on ways partners define and evaluate their relationship. Discussion of stage 4 dealt with processes related to the maintenance of a relationship or its eventual dissolution.

This overview suggests that social psychologists have learned a good deal about this phenomenon. Yet certain gaps and limitations in the body of research and theory should be kept in mind when considering what is currently known and where further research is needed. Most of the research has been done on samples largely homogeneous in age and cultural background during a relatively short historical period. Certainly, much more cross-cultural and historical research will be necessary involving the total life span before the external validity of current knowledge can be assessed. While social psychological preoccupation with the early phase of the heterosexual relationship and to a lesser extent with friendship formation is understandable in our culture, until further attention is directed toward the development of other types of relationships, what is unique to the former or characteristic of relationships per se will remain largely unknown. In addition, a much more fine-grained empirical and conceptual analysis will probably be necessary to delineate further variables and processes underlying the dynamics of relationships. In sum, although this review suggests that a certain amount has been accomplished, there is much more yet to be done.

C. NORMAN ALEXANDER, JR.
AND MARY GLENN WILEY

9

Situated Activity and Identity Formation

Introduction

Social psychology has often seemed less an amalgamation of psychology and sociology than an awkward appendage of each field, pretending to a distinctive domain of common interest, but differing by disciplinary origin "in definition and in execution" (Stryker 1977:145). Thus, members of each branch differ in the topics researched, methods used, journals read, works cited, texts employed, and appraisals of contributions to knowledge in the area (Wilson and Schafer 1978). If this were merely a difference in focus, we should expect to find a heuristic complementarity of emphasis, with psychologists stressing intrapersonal aspects of problems that sociologists approached in terms of role-related interactions. However, where there should be interface there is too frequently irrelevance.

In the area of situated action, where the two social-psychological traditions should merge, the problems and prospects for convergence within the discipline appear (Boutilier et al. 1980). At this analytic level, psychological processes become fully manifest in a distinctly social field and the actions of an individual influence others present. Similarly, the social realities of the environment infuse the activity of the individual who is affected by the presence of others. Thus, at the place where activity becomes a social process, we seek to explore the potential unity of the field.

Despite major differences of theory and method there is general subscription to Allport's definition of social psychology as ". . . an attempt to understand and explain how the thought, feeling, and behavior of individuals are influenced by the actual, imagined, or implied presence of others" (Allport 1968:3). Consideration of this statement leads us to question what it is about the presence of others, in fact or fantasy, that transforms organismic processes into social-psychological phenomena. We believe that an adequate answer to this question involves the fundamental conceptualization of the data with which the discipline deals.

We see the resolution of disciplinary disparities in the adoption of a relational conceptualization of social psychological phenomena. Rather than begin our investigative quests with units of analysis that prejudice the organization of the field into self-contained systems of selves and social structures that ensure boundary disputes, let us begin with the boundary itself. If we start with social acts as units of analysis, we avoid creating conflict between individual responses straining for expression against a repressive social fabric and normative demands requiring sanctioned implementation against resistant psychological forces. We propose that the defining properties of social acts are situated identities. Situated identities are conceived as the attributions that are made from salient perspectives about an actor's presence and performance in the immediate social context. In the following pages, we will explore the bases of this conceptualization, its elaboration into a formally testable model, and studies that embody research on its hypotheses.

Attribution: Behaviorism and Interactionism

Skinnerian behaviorism and Meadian interactionism are, in many essential respects, similar in their view that the transactions between the environment and the organism create the phenomena of ultimate explanatory reference. Mead (1962:77–78) speaks of objects being "constituted" by the actor's purposive relation to them, in the sense that there would be no food if there were no organisms with digestive processes. Similarly, Skinner points out that we have no reason to believe that any particular stimulus configuration would be responded to discriminatively unless the organism were reinforced for doing so (Skinner 1964). The external environment for social-psychological purposes is seen as coming into being and into possession of whatever "qualities" it is assigned by virtue of its inclusion in some functional or pragmatic interaction with a sentient organism. Both theorists take a similar approach to self-knowledge: we come to know ourselves and "qualities" assigned to the internal environment because we learn such responses. Bem's (1972) recent behaviorist theory of self-perception is perfectly compatible with interactionist ideas so long as we recognize that the categories of perception are socially defined.

The emergence of distinctively attributional theories from Heider's work parallels even more directly the issues and the approach we wish to take. Heider (1958) argues eloquently that we respond, not to a world of stimulus configurations, but to a world of organized dispositional qualities: invariant structures and processes. This arises from the continual pressures to attain perceptual economy, maintain stable orientations to the invariant features of variegated experiences, and ensure predictability of events. If we had to attend to the peculiarities of all stimuli manifestations that we encounter, that task alone would overload our capacities and leave us no time to process the inputs and coordinate responses to them. Furthermore, we would be stuck with a meaningless flux of unique and nonrecurrent events that would make anticipation impossible.

To avoid this maladaptive state of affairs, Heider claims that we selectively perceive the world in terms of its dispositional qualities. The phenomena of constancy illustrate the process—we experience an approaching object as possessing the constant dispositional characteristics of shape and size despite variations in distance from it or in angles of view. Two things should be noted. First, the experience is immediately given; it does not require a calculated readjustment of sensory input. Second, the imposition of constancy demands a rather sophisticated implementation of an interpretive system of relational judgments regarding distance, location, movement, and so on. It is this categorization of stimuli into objects with dispositional qualities and knowledge of the lawful relationships among the properties that enables us to progress to prediction. Awareness of what things are is apprehension of how they fit into an orderly sequencing of events: the characteristics of objects are defined by the causal systems connecting them. The advantage for the prediction of events is obvious: active adjustment and manipulative intervention are facilitated.

Heider applied these same principles to the perception of persons who occupy special status as sources or origins of activity. Their activity appears invariant only if we attend to its apparent goal-direction. Activity sources in the inanimate world, such as volcanoes, may explode erratically, but the consequences of an eruption (for example, the lava flow) are grossly predictable and therefore avoidable. However, if a person explodes with anger over something we have done, avoidance of the ensuing harmful consequences is not such a simple predictive matter. An angry person may succeed in harming us in a number of alternative ways, any of which can be adjusted to take account of the avoidance activity we might take. Personal causality possesses what Heider calls equifinality: the means are varied, but the eventual goal is invariant. The dispositional imputations that permit us to predict this goal and take adjustive action to adapt to contingently variable means depend upon our identification of the purposes and intents of the actor. Thus, the dispositional qualities that lend stability, coherence, and predictability to the interpersonal environment involve judgments of aims, wishes, desires, emotions, motives, and other qualities not imputed to the impersonal environment.

From Heider, we glean how the individual attributes dispositional characteristics to others. Like Heider, symbolic interactionists view the person as perceiver of his world. But they regard the stance outlined thus far as a basic framework from which the bulk of analysis proceeds. For this reason, their work aids us in delineating the importance of others' presence for the individual. For example, a key phrase of this perspective, "role-taking" (Mead 1962; Turner 1962), will provide a much clearer understanding of the impact of others' presence (real, imagined, or anticipated) on an individual. Role-taking refers to a central process by which actors take into account the others' responses to them. Heider also recognizes this aspect of the other in his discussion of the other as perceiver. He notes that an actor needs to take into account, not only the dispositional qualities of the other, but the dispositions the other attributes to the actor. For this reason, an actor's perceptions of the other take on a reactive quality. Since Heider does not give this aspect of the process much emphasis, nor does the attribution research based on his work, we depend upon symbolic interactionism to provide a more fully developed view.

The importance of others' dispositional attributions becomes obvious if we think about the total reinforcement we experience in our everyday lives. Much of it flows directly from other persons (acceptance, affection, approval, and so forth) and most of the remainder is mediated by them. During the developmental years this dependency is even more intense. It is during that period that, through the process of role-taking, the self emerges, and the person learns to control and evaluate his or her behaviors. In the same way, the person learns the processes that are effective in self-monitoring and self-evaluation.

From our perspective the paramount thing learned through the process of role-taking is how the self will be responded to by others. As we have seen, others' reactions are a function of the dispositional inferences they make about persons and their actions. Thus, it is evident that in order to anticipate, much less control and manipulate, these responses, the individual must come to view his or her own activity from others' (dispositional) perspectives. Since the ultimate referents of these perspectives are internal qualities, it follows that individuals learn about their internal environment by the same reflexive process. In short, they learn to see themselves in the same dispositional terms and to view their activities and actions as expressing these attributes. The adoption of this perspective transforms mere behavior into conduct.

Behavior, Conduct, and Situated Activity

We will distinguish behavior, conduct, and situated activity, defining the differences between them in terms of their incorporation of social perspectives. This lays the groundwork for the construction of situated-identity theory's conception of social realities as dispositional dimensions relating actors through acts to objects of orientation. We illustrate this with the story, "Brer Rabbit, Brer Fox and the Tar Baby" (Harris 1949).

Once upon a time, Brer Rabbit encounters a tar figure erected by Brer Fox as a trap. Brer Rabbit attempts to carry on a polite conversation with the Tar Baby but gets no response. Brer Rabbit first assumes that this lack of response is due to deafness, but when he shouts the Tar Baby still does not respond. This leads Brer Rabbit to assume that the Tar Baby is "stuck up" and needs to be taught how to "talk to 'specttabble fokes' " (Harris 1949:53). In this attempt, Brer Rabbit punches the Tar Baby and becomes hopelessly stuck. And so Brer Fox catches Brer Rabbit.

Before Brer Rabbit leaves home, his behavior may range from stretching and scratching to fixing breakfast. He may be engaged in mere *behavior,* psychologically oblivious to others' presumed or potential presence. This kind of behavior is irrelevant for social psychology. We are concerned only with events that occur when an actor orients himself to a field in which others are psychologically present. This latter type of event we will call *conduct* to distinguish it from behavior (McCall and Simmons, 1966:39–62). Brer Rabbit's conduct begins when he leaves his home and prances down a path aware that at any moment he may be observed. The imagined presence of others is presumed to activate an orientational set to perceive the environment in psychologically dispositional terms. At the most fundamental level, this orientation of the person toward himself and events does not require perception by others, nor others' actual awareness of, or responsiveness to, the perceiver. In acts we categorize as conduct, it is possible that the entire process is imaginary: it is not necessarily conscious or self-reflexive.

What characterizes the orientation of a person who is engaged in conduct is what Heider calls the arousal of "a general readiness to perceive psychologically . . ." (Heider 1958:57), and what interactionists generally regard as internalized "role-taking." It means primitively that the individual apprehends himself as related to the environment in terms of his own dispositions. Conduct is roughly equivalent to what Goffman (1963) calls an "interactional tonus," a general level of motor activity and disciplined management of personal front that signifies the readiness of a person to be observed by others. As he notes, this is such a general and pervasive orientation that a person is most likely to be totally unaware of it—for example, the diffuse maintenance of ". . . a certain level of alertness as evidence of his availability for potential stimuli, and some orderliness and organization of his personal appearance . . ." (Goffman 1963:30) as evidence of self-control.

Brer Rabbit's conduct becomes *situated activity* when he notices the Tar Baby and identifies it as a potentially sentient other. Now his conduct occurs from an orientation that includes particular others' perspectives, where particular refers not only to specific individuals but to types or categories of persons as well. Conduct becomes situated activity when it is anchored outside the self and constrained by presumed monitoring. Thus, we define situated activity as conduct in the symbolically defined space and time within which an actor presumes that events are being or might be monitored by another. The monitoring does not have to coincide with the action, as when traces are left or accounts are planned, and, as with the Tar Baby, it does not have to be actual monitoring, merely presumed or potential.

The important aspect of situated activity is that it provides the conditions under which identity formation occurs. Brer Rabbit could not have passed the Tar Baby in that sociocultural milieu without facing the choice between greeting and silent disregard. This choice translates to characterization along dimensions of rude-polite, respectful-disrespectful, and so forth. He becomes in a sense inextricably engaged in situated activity by the mere presence of a potential monitor, less pointedly and dramatically so than the Tar Baby who is directly addressed, but unavoidably so nonetheless. Goffman puts it nicely: "Whatever an individual does and however he appears, he knowingly and unknowingly makes information available concerning the attributes that might be imputed to him and hence the categories in which he might be placed . . . the physical milieu itself conveys implications concerning the identity of those who are in it" (Goffman 1961:102). Further, an individual's action "... *inevitably* expresses something about him, something out of which he and others fashion an image of him" (Goffman 1961:97, emphasis added).

Goffman (1959) has stressed that it is necessary for people to establish their respective identities almost before they proceed with interaction, since "who one is" in an encounter defines how he or she is expected to act and how others are obliged to treat him or her. In general, identity claims set the pattern for status, affective, evaluative, and power relationships that will prevail during any activity sequence. With the major dimensions of social responsiveness at stake, it is not surprising that people attend to identity claims.

Dispositional inferences are continuously being made about persons. However, what is *done* is often less important than how it is done. Even when a person acts in perfect accord with normative expectations, he or she still acts with a certain style, timing, vitality, and so on. Furthermore, information is conveyed even in the absence of "events" by a person's dress and demeanor and by the fact that he or she is present (or absent) at a particular time and in a particular place (Stone 1962). Although what causes an event is of interest, an understanding of the dispositional nature of persons, as ongoing sources of causality, is more important for the prediction of a wide range of future events.

Situated Identity Theory

Situated identity theory emerges from the idea that identity formation is the fundamental process of social perception and the cornerstone of interaction. This theory proposes that we define the phenomena of social action in terms of the dispositional attributes that flow from the perspectives of given perceivers of the event field. Situated activity is conceived as an ongoing process of establishing, affirming, modifying, and sometimes destroying situated identities. Situated identities are not properties possessed by or imposed upon persons, nor are they located in some externalized environmental structure. Instead, they define the relationships between the actor and the environment at any given point. The social reality at any moment is the complex of situated identities generated from all of the perspectives that are relevant to the events in a social field.

Although we anticipate that the model eventually will be elaborated to deal with multiple and divergent perspectives, it seems advisable to focus initially on relatively simple situated activity sequences involving similar perspectives. This idea of similar perspectives immediately suggests normative action sequences. Such an interpretation may at first appear to limit severely the range of a social psychologist's investigation. However, this emphasis on normative action sequences is not a serious limitation on initial inquiries, if we accept that most situations are socially defined and that norms are continually emergent and, therefore, relatively pervasive.

Thus, we restrict our investigations to situated activities that meet a consensus criterion—people must agree on the particular attributional dimensions that are relevant to an act, and they must further agree on how to characterize the act along each dimension. When these conditions are met, we can say that the activity is normatively structured.

When an activity sequence has a coherent normative structure, then certain attributional dimensions become relevant to describe participants whereas other dimensions are not salient. For example, performance at a solitary task of personal interest may lead to inferences about an individual's persistence, competence, and carefulness, but it is unlikely to generate any impressions about his or her friendliness, reliability, or cooperativeness. These latter attributions would become relevant if the task were joint and the outcome of mutual importance. However, it is still unlikely that routine performance would generate attributions about honesty, courageousness, and so forth.

The existence of consensual definition also depends on agreement about how an action is to be evaluated along the relevant dimensions. For example, suppose that our solitary task performer makes a series of mistakes. Some people may see the performer as essentially competent, but careless. Others may attribute his or her errors to incompetence, but continue to characterize the performer as careful. The same two dimensions will be relevant for both groups, but they will not agree on how to rate the actor. Since there is lack of consensus on relevant dimensions, we do not have the formation of a normatively structured situated identity.

The issue thus addressed by situated identity theory becomes how potential actions dispositionally characterize an actor for similar others who are taking the role of the actor. Our focus of inquiry is upon the relationship between the dispositional imputations that others make about each of a set of alternatives at a choice-point in the flow of situated activity, and their expectations about the choices that actors make when faced with such a decision. In a particular sense, we are asking for normative definitions of the social action field from the perspective of similar others. Since most attributional dimensions are evaluative, the mere perception of action in these terms is usually an evaluation of it as well. Even if the consequences of actions carry no other sanctions, these evaluations are sufficient justification for calling the emergent expectations *normative.* Once formed, these normative definitions are then compared with expectations about the actor's choices.

Thus, we have alternative choices faced by an actor that are similarly perceived in situated identity terms by similar others. These observers face the problem of deciding which option the actor will choose. It may be that the alternatives are similarly valued, even to the point of being identical. If this is so, and the observer knows nothing about the personality, past, or preferences of the actor, there would be no basis for formulating an expectation of what the actor might do. However, to the extent that alternatives are differentially valued, we suppose that the observer expects the individual to choose the action that is socially desirable. Therefore, in the absence of any other criteria, normative expectations about conduct should be a function of the social desirability of alternatives.

The procedures that operationalize these ideas can best be presented by describing an early study that differs from most subsequent work in that it involves a non-laboratory setting. A naturalistic setting allows us to show that situated identity processes operate under conditions in which the person cannot be viewed as giving a self-conscious presentational performance for public consumption. Given widespread concerns about evaluative apprehension (Rosenberg 1969) in the laboratory and the feeling that it amplifies normal levels of concern about social approval by providing continuous observation, it is important to explore situated identity formation when respondents and their responses are anonymous. Carl Hovland and others (see for example Hovland et al. 1953) conducted extensive research on persuasive communications in natural settings. G. Knight and C. N. Alexander (unpublished data) adopted this approach to study respondents who were members of an audience hearing an impersonal persuasive appeal concerning a private medical problem. The appeal recommended that a preventive action be taken outside the context of the message presentation without the knowledge of the persuasive source.

Situated Identity Formation in Natural Settings

Janis and Feshbach (1953) originally suggested that excessively frightening messages would trigger "defensive avoidance" reactions and reduce compliance with a recommendation to act, despite the increased threat from consequences of noncompliance. Some research continued to support these findings, but an overwhelming number of subsequent studies has shown a positive relationship between the magnitude of fear aroused and the tendency to intend to or actually comply with the recommended preventative action (McGuire 1969; Leventhal 1970). Since none of the previous fear-appeal studies manipulated efficacy of the recommendation in an adequate way, we created our own stimulus materials and varied the efficacy of the recommendation as a cross-cutting, independent variable.

Although there are problematic exceptions, the relationship between fear arousal and attitude or behavioral change has often been positive when recommendations have been highly efficacious—that is, efficiently preventive and relatively easy to follow. Inverse relationships have been found when the recommended actions entail only slightly efficacious behaviors—actions that are difficult, demanding, and uncertain in preventive outcomes. We defined efficacy as the perceived probability of preventing the negative consequences associated with noncompliance and as the costs involved in following the recommended action. Efficacy, so conceptualized, is not only independent of the magnitude of threat, but also independent of the amount of loss if noncompliance is chosen.

One hundred twenty-eight unmarried Stanford undergraduates were recruited to participate voluntarily in an "Experimental Impressions Study." Subjects listened to an authoritative lecture on birth defects, entitled "The Disinherited Children." It dealt with congenitally deficient children whose impairments were traceable to nonhereditary origins: if parents had sought appropriate pre-pregnancy advice, these defects could have been foreseen and averted. A "Uterine Tap" was recommended for mothers-to-be; this examination could detect the imbalance in a woman's endocrine system that was alleged to cause the birth defects.

There were four control versions of the arousing lecture, and four experimental versions. Sixteen subjects responded to each of the eight versions of the persuasive communication. The level of threat (fear-arousal) was varied independently of the recommendation's efficacy. For the first seven minutes, each version presented an identical discussion of nature's physiological preparation of females for motherhood and the importance of proper hormone balance in insuring a healthy, normal conception and birth. During the last seven minutes, the messages departed radically to effect manipulation of the relevant variables. Although much of the information as presented was essentially fictitious, the contents of the tapes were loosely related to medical fact so that they sounded plausible to anyone not specifically knowledgeable on the topic. Factual distortions and exaggerations were freely employed to assure successful manipulations of the independent variables.

In the Low-Fear condition, remarks were confined to a review of the functions of the female endocrine system and a summary of medical research techniques in the area. The High-Fear condition, however, placed considerable emphasis on the unpleasantness of the deformities that arise from pregnancies during periods of hormone imbalance. Apart from miscarriage, the potential consequences included: discolored teeth, massive birth marks, dwarfed limbs, blindness, mongolism, and Siamese twins.

In both versions the recommended Uterine Tap could not cure hormonal imbalance, but it could indicate whether conception should be risked at any given point. In the High-Efficacy condition, the Tap was described as quite painless, easily and quickly done, available at local doctors for a moderate fee, and accurate in detecting significant imbalance 85 percent of the time. By contrast, the Low-Efficacy description noted that it was a new technique, still rather clumsy, and might require repeated samplings. The Low-Efficacy Tap did not involve much pain, was understood to be within most couples' financial means, and was available at a few hospitals in the area. Its accuracy of diagnosis was not conclusively specified, but it was estimated to be around 60 percent.

Our respondents were told that the presentation was excerpted from a longer lecture heard by an audience of young couples attending adult sex-education programs sponsored by church groups, public education series, and the Planned Parenthood Association. The stimulus couples were reported to be either contemplating marriage or recently married but presently childless.

Based upon both the persuasive communication and the description of the attending couples, subjects in each experimental condition estimated the percentage of "audience" women who would comply with the recommendation to secure the Uterine Tap. Half of each experimental group evaluated a stimulus woman who chose to comply, while the other half judged one who decided not to comply. Each stimulus woman was rated on nineteen bipolar adjective scales, the adjective pairs (attribute dimensions) having been selected by the experimenters. Finally, subjects were asked to circle the five dimensions they found most relevant to forming an overall impression of the woman they had evaluated.

To establish the effectiveness of the manipulations, portions of the tapes were played to four control groups who rated the communication's characteristics as they believed the audience would. Two control groups heard the first seven minutes of the tape (neutral information) and either the Low-Fear or High-Fear segment, but without the final portion that described the efficacy of the recommended preventive action. It was evident that the fear segments created the intended impressions: the two messages differed significantly in their disturbingness ($p < .01$), but not in their other measured qualities—convincingness, interestingness, and factual recallability. Another two groups heard the opening information and the reported efficacy of the preventive action, but they did not hear the five-minute fear manipulation. As expected, the efficacy control groups revealed differential impressions of the recommendation's characteristics: the components of accuracy ($p < .01$), availability ($p < .05$), and painlessness ($p < .01$) were all significantly greater under high efficacy, and inexpensiveness was in the same direction—though not significantly so. Control groups perceived the stimulus qualities as intended, and we concluded that our construction of the tapes successfully manipulated the variables of experimental interest.

Observers in the High-Efficacy conditions estimated that 83.1 percent of the women hearing the high-fear message and 63.8 percent hearing the low-fear message would comply. In Low-Efficacy conditions, 53.8 percent compliance was expected for High-Fear, 67.5 percent for Low-Fear. Both differences by Fear were significant at the .01 level by t-test. Thus, increases in fear arousal were directly associated with compliance estimates in High-Efficacy conditions, but inversely associated in low efficacy.

Differences in the mean evaluations of compliant and noncompliant women on the five dimensions selected as most relevant in each of the four conditions parallel the estimated compliance.[1] This rank-order coincidence is what we hypothesized: the more positive the dimension ratings associated with compliance rather than noncompliance, the greater the percentage of persons expected to comply.

Additional situated identity studies in natural settings have stressed the reactions of others as well as the role of events in constructing situated identities. In one early study, Alexander and Epstein (1969) showed the effects of others' reactions on the situated identities of an actor who always made the same choice. They created a role-conflict situation in which a young boy was torn between pitching in a ball game or preparing a term paper due for a class the next day. The boy discussed his dilemma with alter, who was either a fellow student or the teacher. He always decided to pitch, and alter reacted with either approval or disapproval. To the extent that disapproval was anticipated and received, the boy was characterized as more dynamic and motivated to take the action he decided upon. More recently, Rudd (1976) looked at informal persuasion attempts by interacting peers in natural settings and found that the acceptance or rejection of an influence attempt changed the situated identities of both participants.

These themes of the role of events and the reactions of others in shaping the alternative situated identities available to the actor reappear in the laboratory situations, which have been used more frequently than natural settings for situated identity studies. Despite its "fish bowl" atmosphere at times, it is important to test hypotheses about situated identity formation in laboratory settings because they are intentionally created to be free from normative standards that govern behavior. Experimenters typically strive to construct situations that are unfamiliar and novel, precisely to deprive subjects of extra-experimental social standards for conduct and previous expectations about appropriate behavior. Thus, a demonstration that situated identities emerge in these artificially contrived situations would provide powerful evidence for the pervasiveness of these processes. We turn now to those studies.

Situated Identities in Laboratory Settings

Alexander and Knight (1971) simulated an experiment conducted by Carlsmith et al. (1966) to replicate and extend the now classic study by Festinger and Carlsmith (1959) about the effects of counterattitudinal forced compliance on attitude change. The scenario of these experiments involves a subject who first performs dull, boring tasks and is then asked to make favorable statements about them for differential reward. In the extended replication he not only makes these statements to another, allegedly naive subject, but in another set of conditions puts them in an essay for the experimenter only.

Dissonance theory predicts that the subject's subsequent liking for the tasks will vary inversely with the amount of reward he is given for lying about them. This was the relationship found in the original experiment, its replication, a simulation by Bem (1967), and the situated identity study for the face-to-face conditions. However, when the tasks were favorably described in an essay for the experimenter, a direct relation obtained between task liking and payment level in both the experimental and the situated identity studies. The result was not predicted by dissonance theory, which could not specify the crucial difference between the types of presentational conditions.

Alexander and Knight obtained dimensional evaluations of stimulus persons who chose one of the five middle response categories (−2 to +2) on the 11-point task-liking scale. Each response category was assigned a score equal to the mean rating received on the most relevant situated identity dimensions. These scores were correlated with the percentage of people who estimated that each response category would be chosen. The average Pearsonian correlation of these two sets of scores in the four conditions was .9, showing clearly that the desirability of the situated identity associated with a response category related closely to the proportion expecting that category would be chosen. In every condition the situated identity scores predicted the modal response.

Madaras and Bem (1968) were able to explain the risky-shift phenomenon in terms of the dispositional evaluations of those whose choices ranged from risk to conservatism following small group discussions. The tendency for groups to advocate higher levels of risk-taking than did their individual members acting alone was explained in terms of our cultural predisposition to consider and favor risk-accepting positions. Risk-takers were rated as being stronger, faster, harder, and more active, successful, masculine, good, and sociable than those rejecting risks. Changes in the description of the decision-making situation, introducing the possibility of harm to others, produced the opposite effect, shifts toward conservatism in group opinions. The investigators found that these changes shifted the dimensions controlling the decision to moral aspects of the choice, so that risk-takers were characterized as significantly less good and more cruel.

Alexander and Lauderdale (1977) examined one experiment (Zelditch et al. 1980) in a systematic series of studies of the relationship between status characteristics and expectation states (Berger et al. 1972). In this study, two subjects thought they were responding together to a judgmental task. The induction phase of the experiment led them to believe that one had high ability and the other low ability. They were then shown stimulus patterns and asked to judge them, after which they saw how the other person had responded. Each stimulus pattern was shown a second time, and they were given the opportunity of staying with their initial decision or changing it. The independent variable was the ability status of the judge, and the dependent variable the number of times the judge's final and initial choices were the same on twenty critical disagreement trials (alter's responses were controlled by the experimenter for both subjects).

The actual number of changes in the original study and the number of changes estimated in the simulation were virtually the same, and there was a high positive correlation between the situated identity evaluations of stay-patterns and the estimations of their frequency of occurrence. Again, the absolute number of cases per response category and, therefore, the shape of the distribution of responses corresponded closely to the distribution of the situated identity ratings in both conditions.

Alexander and Weil (1969) found the Prisoner's Dilemma game ambiguous enough to permit players to choose diverse goals, from cooperative maximization of both players' gains to cut-throat efforts to maximize the difference between one's own score and that of the other. The study presented an example game in which one player won decisively over the other, and asked subjects to characterize both players in terms of two very differently biased sets of situated identity dimensions. On one list the winner could be seen as clever, enterprising, and intelligent, whereas the loser had to appear naive, gullible, and submissive. On the other list, however, the winner's attributes were greediness, exploitativeness, and selfishness; the loser was seen as considerate, friendly, and generous. When the subjects played the game after seeing the latter list, cooperation rates tripled. The addition of money to the game shifted player goals toward cooperation, but it altered the relevance of the situated identity lists, producing unexpectedly similar cooperation rates in the two list conditions. Nevertheless, the results established that subjects played this experimental game to create the most favorable situated identities and were willing to risk losing the game to obtain positive evaluation.

Focusing on the effects of alter's situated identity, Alexander and Sagatun (1973) interpersonally simulated Gerard and Mathewson's (1966) extended replication of the Aronson and Mills (1959) experiment dealing with the effects of initiation severity on subsequent liking for a group. They hypothesized that the instructional manipulations, interacting with the level of shock employed to manipulate severity, changed the identity of the experimenter to produce differential regard for him.

When the experimenter provided a rationale for the stimulation (either the elaborate discussion-group initiation or a simple justification of the importance of the experiment and the subject's participation in it), it was felt that subjects accepted his concern and the need for electrical shock. When he cursorily presented a set of stimuli to see what effects they would have, as in the noninitiation condition, subjects were likely to experience the events as arbitrary and to become hostile toward the experimenter when he administered painful shocks. In the former justified conditions, an increase in shock level reinforced perceptions that the experimenter was seriously and sincerely concerned to take whatever steps, even painful ones, were necessary to conduct a valuable study.

This is what was found. The justified experimenter who gave stronger shocks received higher ratings as warm, friendly, personal, casual, honest, and interesting. The arbitrary experimenter was rated more negatively on these dimensions when he increased the intensity of the shocks. Evaluations of the experimenter correlated positively with liking for the group discussion across all six conditions of the experiment, and these variables also showed consistent and substantial correlations within each condition. The results parallel the original findings that initiation severity increases attraction to the group, while the unrelated presentation of aversive stimulation decreases the attractiveness of subsequent exposure to the same group discussion.

Rosenthal (1966) summarized the effects of experimenter variations in warmth on subjects' responses with a succinct "like me, like my stimuli" hypothesis, and this fits the above data as well. That hypothesis is actually a situated version of the more generally hypothesized association between similarity and attraction (Newcomb 1961; Byrne 1969). This relationship was explored in a situated identity study by Touhey (1974), who followed the attraction-similarity paradigm in designing a study in which persons exchanged opinions about twelve issues. In three different conditions, subjects found that they agreed with the other person on none, half, or all of the issues. Observers estimated the attraction subjects felt toward the other as a result of varying similarity and replicated the positive association between similarity and liking.

In the fifteen conditions constructed to obtain situated identity ratings, subjects were shown expressing one of five levels of interpersonal attraction toward the other, cross-cutting the three levels of attitudinal similarity. Persons who were more attracted to the other than their similarity warranted were described as submissive, dependent, passive, trusting, and naive. When they were less attracted than expected on the basis of similarity, they were rated as cold, dominant, indifferent, and suspicious. Positive characterizations were reserved for those who showed levels of liking expectationally appropriate to the degree of similarity. Touhey's data thus revealed that specific levels of attraction are expected to correspond to particular degrees of similarity, such that situated identity evaluations predict precisely the association between attraction and similarity.

Problems of Social Desirability

These early studies in situated identity formation have stressed that the context and sequence of events leading up to the dependent variable choice have created response alternatives that differ in social desirability. Although the situations we examined were designed to test various theories, we find that the results from those situations are more parsimoniously and precisely explained by the social desirability differences that characterize the situated identities associated with response options. The interpretation of this state of affairs is exactly analogous to employing judges to determine whether or not the items in a psychological scale are biased by social desirability.

In scale construction, the judges determine potential bias by characterizing item responses in terms of social desirability, just as our observers characterize situational response alternatives. If respondents to the item alternatives on the scale—analogues of respondents to the dependent variable choices in experimental settings—show a preference for those responses that are socially desirable, we do not draw any conclusions about the characteristics the scale was intended to measure (in experiments, about the hypothesized causal relationship the dependent variable responses were supposed to establish). The scale is declared invalid, and the researcher must go back and reconstruct it to eliminate the social desirability bias.

Relationships between an invalid scale and other variables are not thereby discredited; they are simply regarded as improperly tested. Similarly, none of the situated identity studies refute any of the theories that have been tested in the experimental situations we have examined; they merely show that appropriate tests have not been made. In those particular settings, situated identity theory provides an obvious, more comprehensive, and compelling explanation of the results.

The only solution for those who wish to demonstrate the operation of psychological processes in social fields is to construct fields that do not imbue response alternatives with desirability loadings that favor response selections supporting the theory's hypotheses. We feel that the evaluative factor so pervades the realms of social stimuli (Osgood, Suci, and Tannenbaum 1957) and response settings that investigators should feel obliged to demonstrate that their manipulations and measures are not contaminated *before* they extend claims of support for this or that hypothesis (see Alexander and Scriven 1977). Although we believe situated identity formation can better account for a wide range of previous experimental findings, there is no particular benefit for the development of the theory to continue demonstrating this in one experimental setting after another.

We began to search for nonambiguous situations in which the response alternatives did not so frequently produce differentially desirable situated identities. This is not an easy task. Even sociologists are likely to underestimate the extent to which socially defined situations are normatively structured in terms of the differential evaluations accorded alternative actions. However, these circumstances do exist and, as the theory would predict, do not produce expectations that favor the choice of one over another alternative.

Our goal was to test derivations of the theory's postulate that situated identity dimensions provide the bases for expectation formation. To do this, it is necessary to show that the particular dimensions associated with a choice alternative are responsible for the selection or rejection of that action. When the dimensions related to each alternative are bound together by the halo effect of differential desirability, this cannot be done convincingly. Otherwise unrelated dimensions become intercorrelated to the extent that they have evaluative similarities. With social desirability equalized, we can examine the comparability of situations in terms of their particular dimensional components.

There are two sources of information relevant to expectation formation in this kind of response situation: the characteristics of the person or knowledge about that person's previous behavior. Thus, we either described a person in terms of situated identity dimensions variably related to the choice alternatives in the situation or provided information about past behavior involving alternatives of varying similarity to those presently confronted. The crucial question is the adequacy of our definition and measurement of relevance. Elaborating the implications of this focus leads us to propose specific conceptual and operational definitions of situational comparability and of the validity of manipulations and measures. That is the aspect of situated identity theory that we will discuss next.

Situational Comparability

Situated identity theory defines two situations as equivalent if the choice alternatives in each are characterized respectively by the same ratings on the same relevant dimensions. When the dimensions of relevance differ or the ratings on relevant dimensions differ, they cease to be equivalent, but they may be regarded as comparable. It is the function of theory to define the criteria of comparability for the hypothesis being tested.

In a study by Alexander and MacMurray (unpublished data), we defined comparability of experimental conditions in terms of the rank equivalence of the rated importance of trait dimensions and similarity of mean ratings on those dimensions. We constructed seven everyday situations that had clearly defined, situated identities associated with two choice alternatives. The choice-points in the two situations were said to be comparable if (1) roughly the same dimensions were chosen as most relevant in both and (2) ratings on these dimensions were similar. Noncomparability resulted when no alternatives were similar. We found that observations of choices in one situation related to prediction of choices in the other to the extent that comparability existed. Predictions were no better than chance in the noncomparable situations, but were 89 percent accurate with comparable situations. When situated identity descriptions were substituted for previous behavior, similar results were obtained. Predictions ranged from chance levels for subjects provided with descriptions on "noncomparable" dimensions to 85 percent accuracy when the dimensions used in the descriptions were identical to the most relevant dimensions in the situations.

Alexander and Rudd (1980) conceptualized items from the Machiavellian scale as response situations and performed a situated identity variation of "item analysis" with them. They found that items correlating most highly with the rest of the scale evoked dimensions central to the Machiavellian syndrome, and responses to those items were differentiated by ratings along the dimensions. Items that correlated poorly with the rest of the scale did not elicit the relevant dimensional components of Machiavellianism, and responses to them did not show rating differentials. In consequence, observers were able to reproduce total scale scores from knowledge of how respondents had answered discriminant items, but were unable to make accurate predictions based on responses to nondiscriminant items.

This approach to situational comparability enables us to define rather precisely what we mean by that term when it is used to refer to comparisons across experimental conditions or to the creation of "conceptual" replications of conditions. Such precision in definition and the ability to measure situational comparability should reduce the need to rely on intuition and assumption. One area in which it can be most helpful involves the interpretation of the effects of independent variable manipulations. When creating experimental and control conditions, researchers attempt to follow identical procedures and present identical event sequences in both conditions except for whatever is necessary to effect the manipulation of the independent variable. Frequently, the possibility arises that the manipulation actually destroyed the comparability of the conditions.

For example, in the original Festinger and Carlsmith (1959) experiment discussed earlier, subjects were offered either one or twenty dollars to make positive statements about the tasks. Critics charged (Chapanis and Chapanis 1964) that the twenty-dollar payment was so large that it produced incredulity, suspicion, and even resentment (at being bribed to lie) on the part of subjects. In other words, subjects in the high reward condition became different persons (characterized by disbelief, mistrust, hostility, and so forth) from those in the low reward condition. If this did occur, they might be responding to the dependent variable in terms of these characteristics rather than in terms of the intended effects of differential reward. To avoid this possibility, replications and subsequent studies employed less extreme reward differences. More reasonable incentive levels were assumed to diminish the risk of destroying conditional comparability.

Unfortunately, our study showed that even with smaller reward differences, there were still widespread and unintended changes reflected in the relevance of the situated identity variables. Only two of these could be considered acceptable in terms of the aims of the manipulation—increased materialism and justification were associated with increased reward level. Even though this modest manipulation of money seems like a relatively pure and abstract manifestation of the conceptual variable of differential reward, it produced substantial situated identity changes in this particular situation. Significant differences were found in the relevance of the following dimensions: intelligent/simple, sportsmanly/unsportsmanly, sincere/insincere, positive/negative, cooperative/competitive, flexible/rigid, independent/dependent, and self-confident/self-doubting. Such far-reaching effects discredit the validity of the manipulation.

For a particular manipulation to have validity it must selectively differentiate conditions in terms that are theoretically specified. Although information at the point when the dependent variable responses are made is not sufficient to establish the validity of the independent variable manipulation, it does set necessary criteria that cannot be violated if that validity is to exist. The manipulation can be invalidated if it does not alter the relevance and ratings of specified dimensions as theoretically required, or if it alters the relevance of, and ratings on, situated identity dimensions other than those specified.

The same thing can be said for the "conditions under which" hypothesized relationships are expected to obtain. For example, in the forced compliance studies, dissonance is supposed to be created by the subject's misrepresentation of task enjoyment. When the task-liking response to indicate true attitude is finally expressed, one would presume that the response would reflect on the subject's honesty or at least consistency. Yet neither is a relevant dimension. There is no indication from the situated identity data that the veracity of the subject was seen as a salient issue.

This indicates that the events probably did not create the conditions assumed necessary for dissonance arousal.

On the other hand, there are indications that the conditions created by face-to-face and essay differences in presentation of the counter-attitudinal statements were successful. Friendliness, warmth, pleasantness, likability, and maturity are attributes more relevant to describe the subject when statements are made directly to another person. Intelligence, activity, and materialism are more relevant to the construction of an essay for the absent experimenter. The last two dimensions may result from the activity's aim of producing a substantive item for which payment will be received. Thus, despite the complex changes in actions and audience between these two types of conditions, we find the situated identity data straightforward and commonsensical. We have no reason to doubt the validity of the manipulations from the effects they have on the dependent variable responses.

Defining the Situation

It should be evident, however, that we cannot completely define the validity of independent variable manipulations in terms of the effects that appear only at the time dependent variable responses are made. Manipulations may have effects that are not manifest in dependent variable responses. To assess them it is necessary to gather situated identity information at the time they are introduced. The flow of situational events is a continual process that creates and transforms situated identities from moment to moment. In fact, the nature and impact of an event is defined in terms of the changes it effects in the situated identities of participants. Therefore, these consequences must be measured at the time of impact.

The immediate effects of an event do not exhaust its influence, however, as we have stressed with regard to assessing manipulation validity in terms of the situated identities associated with dependent variable responses. Subsequent events in a sequence are structured, in part, by the events that precede them. The implications of an event that falls early in the sequence may not be evident until later response possibilities emerge. Everyday life is no stranger to events that seemed inconsequential at the time of their occurrence, only to be regarded as crucial later. These effects are no less real for being unrecognized at the actual moment the original event took place.

Thus, situated identities are not static: they emerge and are elaborated through the total sequence of events within a situation. Situated identity theory follows Meadian interactionism in conceiving of objects as situationally constituted from the perspectives of the participants in the ongoing activity. Objects exist within the context of the situation by virtue of the action orientations of participants toward them. We conceptualize response categories as prototypical objects that are constituted by action sequences; hence, what they are is determined by attribute dimensions the sequence makes relevant to define them.

The proverbial example of an item serving as either food or missile is frequently used (McCall and Simmons 1966:51–52) to illustrate this with a physical object. The tomato becomes a truly different object depending on actor orientations. If hungry, the person attends to its ripeness, color, taste, cleanliness, and perhaps even its past history of fertilization and pesticide exposure. If angry, he or she is more likely interested in its firmness, weight, and size. The object is defined by different sets of properties under the different conditions. Furthermore, preference ratings along the same dimensions may vary with orientation. If you were going to eat the tomato you would not pick one that was either very hard or rottenly mushy. These qualities, however, make the most desirable missiles, and the choice between them depends on one's relative interest in inflicting injury or insult.

Such examples are helpful in disabusing us of the ordinary notion that objects possess fixed qualities, but they do not convey the full meaning of the conceptualization involved. The social reality we envisage is defined by relationships among actors and objects of orientation, rather than a world composed of organisms and things defined in terms of their qualities. It is by virtue of involvement in ongoing activity sequences that organisms and things become persons and objects defined in fundamentally relational terms. However, the flow of events in the locally realized situation is not the only process that creates and transforms situated identities.

Actors enter settings with portions of their identities already established. This identity information can come from a person's previous actions outside the present situation, or, in the absence of information on action choices, social characteristics (such as age, sex, and race) as well as social categories (such as occupation and group membership) serve as cues to "packages" of identity information. These packages can be seen as culturally established summaries of previous events and actions. They are not necessarily reflective of "true" pasts, but they function in the same manner as information about past events. And, like past events, they modify or transform the situated identities created by event sequences.

Previous research has dealt with the power of situated events to determine the possible identities of persons whose characters emerge within the situation. Actors in these studies have typically been without distinctive personal and social characteristics, relevant pasts and futures, or extra-situational ties to ongoing events outside the immediate focus. We need to investigate processes of situated identity formation with actors who possess character and potential apart from the situated aspects of their activity and with actions and object orientations that occur trans-situationally.

A comprehensive approach to defining the situation requires specification of the principles by which actors organize the relevant perspectives that define their relations to the environment. This organization or configuration of the situated identities generated from all relevant perspectives constitutes the definition of the situation. Thus, propositions need to be developed to explain how situated identity configurations emerge, accommodate new elements, and change over time.

Summary

The individual becomes fully engaged in processes of relevance for social psychology when oriented to a field of events in which others are psychologically present. Conduct becomes situated activity when it is anchored outside the self by the presumed monitoring of a specific other or type of other whose perspective on events is recognized through role-taking. The psychological presence of a particular other sustains a coherent orientation toward the sequence of events that occurs in the symbolic time and space where monitoring possibilities are implied. From such orientation to an event sequence, situated identities emerge.

A situated identity is the set of dispositional imputations that are made from a given perspective about an actor on the basis of the actor's relationship to objects of orientation. The term, *dispositional,* refers to properties of events that relate to the invariant structures and processes of the interaction of actors or objects with their environments. The dispositional characteristics of persons reflect their capacities and inclinations for acting on, and responding to, events. These are the dimensions in terms of which actors are perceived as equipped for, and oriented to, action possibilities.

The definition of the situation for a given actor is the configuration of situated identities that is created by each of the perspectives that are salient for him or her. We view this social reality as a continual flow of sequential choice possibilities, at each point of which the actor confronts an array of actionable alternatives. Each alternative is defined by the situated identity it can actualize. Thus, the actor chooses the personage he or she will become at each choice-point in an activity sequence. Under certain specified conditions, situated identity theory predicts that actors will prefer an alternative to the extent that it is more socially desirable than the others available.

We have reviewed support for this hypothesis from both naturalistic and laboratory settings derived from studies designed to test propositions in diverse areas of social psychology: responses to fear-arousing persuasive appeals, role-conflict situations, interpersonal influence attempts, dissonance, group decision making, conformity, cooperation and competition, experimenter effects, and interpersonal attraction. This research has recently been extended to circumstances in which alternative choices are similar in the social desirability of their situated identity implications. Under these conditions actors are expected to choose alternatives that affirm the identities they have established by previous actions in comparable situations. Specifying precisely how situational comparability can be defined is a major contribution of this effort.

In future development of situated identity theory there will be consideration of circumstances in which there are multiple, possibly conflicting perspectives that define the situated identities associated with a given response alternative. This can come from the simultaneous presence of others with different perspectives. It also arises when the situated identity implications of past or future activity or of social characteristics and category memberships imply the choice of a present alternative that is less than optimally desirable. This development will focus on principles that govern the integration and organization of the total configuration of situated identities that define the situation for the actor at a given time.

Situated identity theory is ultimately concerned with the principles that govern change over time in these configurational structures. The unfolding of events and the elaboration of activity sequences make the situated identities available to actors contingent upon the pasts generated. The nature of current activity is also affected by the careers and characteristics that participants bring with them from other situations. And both the personnel and interactive setting are influenced by the larger patterns of social activities in which they are embedded. These patterns are the roles and institutions within which social interaction occurs.

NOTES

1. Dimensions selected as most relevant vary from condition to condition. Sincerity is relevant in all conditions; flexibility in all but High Fear/Low Efficacy; cautious in all but High Fear/High Efficacy. Rationality is relevant in both High-Efficacy conditions, friendliness in Low Efficacy, and anxious in High Fear. Believing, curious, interested, and active are relevant in one condition each.

Expectation States and Interpersonal Behavior

Introduction

Expectation states theory is primarily the work of Joseph Berger, Bernard P. Cohen, Morris Zelditch, Jr., and their colleagues and students at Stanford University. One of its most important applications, status characteristics theory, merges Berger et al.'s work with work by several other Stanford-affiliated sociologists on stratification systems and formal organizations. This chapter includes a discussion of expectation states theory and of status characteristics theory. I have not been able to include a complete review of all research related to expectation states. Other applications include Asch-type conformity processes (for example, B. Cohen and Lee 1975), relationships between expectations and distributive justice (for example, Berger, Zelditch, Anderson, and Cohen 1972; Cook 1975; McCranie and Kimberley 1973), stability of authority structures (for example, Berger and Zelditch 1962; Zelditch 1972), mathematical work (for example, Fararo 1968, 1973; Foschi and Foschi 1976; Mazur 1975), and essays combining or contrasting expectation states theory with other theories (for example, Archibald 1976; Meeker and Weitzel-O'Neill 1977; Ridgeway 1978). An extensive bibliography of references to these areas of research, as well as to a large body of unpublished research, can be found in Berger and Zelditch (1978).

Power and Prestige Structures

DESCRIPTION OF THE PHENOMENON

To understand the origins of expectation states theory, it is useful to begin with a brief inventory of the generalizations from small group research that describe the phenomenon that expectation states theory seeks to explain.

To begin with, we shall limit attention to initially leaderless groups, that is, to groups in which no formal structure has been imposed from outside, and, we shall also consider only groups in which members are homogeneous in background and status. In such groups, differences in behavior patterns among members emerge out of the process of interaction among members; some members talk more, are more influential, are better liked, whereas others arouse more hostility or are less active and influential.

Research conducted by Bales and his associates (Bales 1950) described the development of group structure, and formed a basis for the later development of expectation states theory. A "Bales group" was typically a group of three to seven previously unacquainted male undergraduate students who were invited into a small groups laboratory for a study in group decision making. They usually met for several one-hour sessions, during each of which they were given a complex human relations problem to discuss, with instructions to try to reach consensus.

From behind a one-way window, observers would record the interaction according to the Bales Interaction Process Analysis. This coding system requires the observer to record for each act (act defined as the smallest meaningful unit of behavior, usually, but not necessarily, a sentence or phrase): who initiated the act, to whom it was addressed, and into which of twelve categories it fell. The twelve categories involve a basic distinction between task (that is, instrumental, goal-directed behavior) and social (that is, expressive, emotional) behavior, as well as a distinction between questions and answers in the task domain and positive and negative reactions in the social domain. These four basic categories—task questions, task answers, positive reactions, negative reactions—are further cross-cut by a three-way dimension to give a total of twelve categories into which any act can (with sufficient training and admitting some unreliability) be classified. Following the hour discussion, each group member was asked to fill out a questionnaire on which he was to rank each other member on dimensions such as who provided the best ideas, who did the most to guide the group, who was the leader, and whom he liked best.

Studies such as Bales's typically find that by the end of an hour's interaction marked inequalities have developed within an apparently homogenous group of strangers. The most talkative group member not only talks much more than less talkative members, but also receives more acts from other group members. The members who are the most talkative tend to be the ones who are chosen most often on the questionnaire as having contributed the best ideas and the most guidance.

We may note some exceptions to this pattern: first, in some groups the distribution of choices on liking did not correspond to the distribution of choices on task contributions (ideas, guidance, leadership); and second, in some groups there appeared to be a "power struggle" with lack of consensus on ranking in the questionnaire items. Since the distribution of choices for best liked is sometimes different from the distribution of choices on the other items, many researchers have concluded that emotional and instrumental structures develop according to different processes (for example, Slater 1955; for a more recent critique, see Lewis 1972). Expectation states theory deals only with the task (instrumental) processes.

Since differentiation has been observed in homogeneous groups of strangers, it is not surprising that almost all other groups on which observations have been made show a pattern of differentiation in amount of interaction, perceived value of individuals' contributions to the group, and influence over others in the group. Some of the correspondence between amount of activity and evaluations by other group members of quality of activity may be explained by suggesting that more active members actually have higher-quality contributions to make, and that the more contributions attempted, the more likely it is that some high-quality contributions will be included. In addition, however, there is evidence that group members actually overestimate the quality of acts by higher status group members and underestimate the quality of acts by lower status or less active group members (for example, Sherif, White, and Harvey 1955; Harvey 1953). There is also evidence that sheer amount of talking is related to influence and to perceived value of contributions, even when controlling for the actual quality of acts (for example, Marak 1964; Riecken 1958).

REFORMULATION

The work of Joseph Berger,[1] which led to the development of expectation states theory, began with the recognition that the variables described above—amount of action initiated, degree of action received, evaluation of quality of contribution, and influence—can be conceived of as aspects of a single phenomenon that requires a single theoretical explanation. Berger labels the phenomenon "power and prestige structure," thus including the idea of leadership or power (amount of influence one individual has over the behavior or beliefs of others); the idea of status (the prestige or respect with which an individual is regarded by others); and domination of interaction by sheer quantity of acts produced. Power and prestige structures are both differentiated and stable; thus an explanation must cover both the development and maintenance of differentiation.

The explanation begins with an examination of the ways in which elements of group structure are related to each other. The structure of a group can be conceptualized as having two sets of components; those that are shared by all members, and those that are scarce or unequally distributed among the group members. In the first set—things that characterize all members of a group—we may include (1) beliefs about the world of fact, the existence and characteristics of physical and social objects, and the nature of cause and effect; and (2) goals or values, that is, statements about what states of the world are desirable and what the ends or goals of behavior are. In any actual group there are varying degrees of consensus on these elements; consensus on beliefs and goals is assumed to be an important intervening variable in the theoretical development that follows.

In a group that meets for the purpose of accomplishing a specific task, the goal is successful completion of the task, while some beliefs about the world of fact are statements about what sorts of actions may or may not bring about the successful completion of the task. Examples of goals in such a situation are: "we have to reach consensus" or "we have to finish in fifteen minutes"; examples of beliefs about means to goals are: "we should elect a secretary" or "we should hear a report from Jean." Goals may also include such things as maintaining group loyalty, winning athletic contests, improving an academic program, and other states of the world internal and external to the group.

An important aspect of the concept of goal is that it implies that there is a state defined by group members as "success" and another defined as "failure"; group members desire to achieve success and to avoid failure and regulate their behavior accordingly. The combination of goals and beliefs about cause and effect produce valued behavior standards; these are standards by which group members assess how likely an act is to lead to success. Beliefs about what actions lead toward or away from success in meeting a goal need not be veridical; they may be contrary to fact or simply refer to matters that are not easily tested. Likewise, goals may range from those for which there is a readily available external standard for judging success to those for which there is no external standard. In the latter case, "success" and "failure" are judged by standards developed within the group, and the task is referred to as *intrasystemic.*

The second set of components that make up the structure of a group are features that are scarce or unequally distributed. In a power and prestige structure there are two types of inequalities. First, there is an unequal distribution of rights, privileges, and opportunities; some group members have more influence, are granted more rights to control the attention of others, to use their time to initiate action for the group and make decisions that are binding on the group, and to resolve disagreements among other group members. Second, there is an unequal distribution of social rewards, the positive feelings and their expression in action variously termed esteem, respect, popularity, or approval.

The two sets of components of group structure—values and beliefs that are shared, and rights and rewards that are unequally distributed—are related. Groups develop shared beliefs about who occupies what place in the structure, and the maintenance of the structure of inequality can become one of the group goals. (Some good examples of these processes can be found in Whyte's 1955 participant observation study of a street-corner group of young men; he describes the group responding unanimously and negatively to attempts by lower status members to behave like higher status members even when such behavior would ostensibly be related to one of the group's goals, such as winning an athletic contest.)

The sets of components of group structure are related in another way, and a statement of this relationship is the fundamental theoretical proposition of expectation states theory:

Other things being equal, an individual's position in a power and prestige structure is a function of his or her performance in relation to valued behavior standards of the group; the more likely other group members think it is that the individual's actions will lead to success in a goal, the higher is the individual's position in the power and prestige structure.

The other things that are equal include the existence of a general consensus on at least some beliefs and goals and on the power and prestige structure; the ability of the group to establish its own (internally generated, not externally imposed) standards for behavior; and some stability in the activities and structure of the group. In this view, the development of differentiated power and prestige structures is a product of the group's shared aspirations to achieve success in a goal and their beliefs about what actions will lead to success. Expectation states theory itself is a set of theoretical statements designed to explain this fundamental principle of human behavior.

RELEVANT PSYCHOLOGICAL THEORIES

There are two complementary psychological theories that are important in expectation states theory: a social exchange model and a cognitive consistency model. The social exchange model (Homans 1961) explains why persons who are seen as more competent might be encouraged to initiate more acts and also might be granted more influence; the rights they are granted enable them to engage in behavior that results in rewards to other group members and the rewards they are given reinforce the behavior that contributes to the group goal. The strict exchange argument does not explain why group members should distort their judgment about the quality of acts to give more "credit" to persons with higher power and prestige positions. Nor does the strict exchange argument tell us how expectations for quality of performance are established in ambiguous task situations. The second psychological theory is the cognitive balance or consistency model (Heider 1958), which could explain why an act performed by the more respected group member should be assigned a higher value than the same act performed by a less respected member. The balance model, however, does not explain how some group members become more respected in the first place. The exchange and balance models together form the basis for Berger's theory of expectation states.

Some common social psychological approaches are not used by expectation states theory. It does not, for example, look at individual personality traits (or, from a more sociological perspective, socialization histories) that make people behave like leaders or make them attractive to others. Although this might help explain why particular individuals occupy high or low positions in a particular power and prestige structure, it does not readily explain why power and prestige structures always develop and have similar properties across a wide range of different arrangements of personalities. Expectation states theory also differs from social psychological approaches that emphasize the emotional states of individuals (for example, the psychoanalytic approach, which might interpret power and prestige phenomena as manifestations of ambivalence toward authority figures). The focus in expectation states theory is on task behavior.

A Formal Theory of Expectation States

Expectation states theory explains the development and maintenance of power and prestige structures as a result of the development and maintenance of differentiated performance expectations for self and other. The theory has three parts: a set of scope assumptions that specify conditions under which the theory is assumed to hold; definitions of concepts; and statements of the assumptions about the process. Although these are expressed in the language of a formal theory, each arises naturally out of considerations described in the less formal discussion above.

SCOPE ASSUMPTIONS[2]

The theory is assumed to hold under the following set of conditions:

1. There is a small group without formal structure which is homogeneous in the background characteristics of its members.
2. The group is task-oriented. This means that the members envision future events or states of the world that their present activities may help bring about or prevent, and they define some possible future events or states of the world as "success" and others as "failure." We need not assume they know exactly what constitutes success, merely that they assume that when the time arrives they will know whether they have succeeded or not and that their present activities are related to the future outcome.
3. The group task is at least partially intrasystemic. This means that the standards for evaluating success or failure are developed within the group rather than being imposed from outside. An ambiguous task (for example, writing a story to accompany a picture) is one case of an intrasystemic task, but even tasks for which there are clear objective standards may be intrasystemic, if the group is able to redefine the meaning of a particular outcome or the importance of the task ("he had a bad day," "we didn't really care about that after all"). The crucial point is that the rules for evaluating a task outcome are developed by the same persons who are part of the power and prestige structure.
4. The group members are collectively oriented. This has two components: one, that the group members are interdependent, that is, they need to take into account other member's acts; and two, that it is legitimate to seek and give advice, to be influenced by or attempt to influence others. The requirement of consensus under which Bales's groups worked provides an example of a collective orientation; if any group member refused to accept a solution, the group failed in its task. The term collective orientation as used here does not precisely mean cooperative orientation (all goals shared so that something that rewards one group member rewards all). People could have a collective orientation in some cases of competition; in fact, there are competitive elements in face-to-face groups, especially the competition for time and attention imposed by the necessity to limit talking to one person at a time.

BASIC CONCEPTS

Some of the basic concepts are terms that have been introduced in the scope assumptions. These include: *actors* (the group members); a *task* (characterized by possible future states of success or failure); *behavior* (acts performed by group members); and *standards for evaluating behavior.* In addition to these, the theory requires four concepts that refer to observable behaviors, two concepts that refer to outcomes of observable behaviors, and two that refer to unobservable mental states.

The four observable behaviors are derived from the Interaction Process Analysis coding categories. They are: (1) action opportunities (any chance to perform granted by one group member to another, including verbal acts such as questions and also nonverbal acts such as questioning looks and momentary silences); (2) performance outputs (any act by one member that is an attempt to contribute to success in the task); (3) positive reactions (especially expressions of agreement or approval); (4) negative reactions (expressions of disagreement or disapproval).

The two concepts that refer to outcomes of behaviors are *disagreement* and *influence.* Disagreement occurs when two members produce conflicting performance outputs or when one tries to get the group to reject a performance output presented by another. A disagreement is distinguished from a simple negative reaction in that it requires a resolution in favor of one person and against another. Negative reactions often lead to disagreements, but not always, for groups sometimes try to avoid having to resolve a conflict and simply ignore or redefine the issue. Influence is defined as the direction of the resolution of a disagreement; the person whose idea is accepted is said to have influenced the one who accepts it. The term influence is not synomymous with control; a person whose performance output is accepted without challenge has obviously exercised control over the group, but since there was no disagreement, influence has not occurred.

Two of the fundamental concepts of the theory refer to unobservable mental states. These are treated in the formal theory as hypothetical constructs. That is, although they are necessary for the development of the assumptions that, taken as a set, produce an explanation of the development and maintenance of power and prestige structures, they are not concepts for which measures or indicators must be developed in order to test the theory. Although some of the empirical work on expectation states uses behavioral indicators of performance expectations, most does not use any attitudinal measurement. (For two exceptions, see Zeller and Warnecke 1973; Webster and Driskell 1978).

The first concept is *performance expectation.* A performance expectation is a prediction about the quality of a performance output of a group member. An individual may hold a performance expectation for his own behavior (a self-expectation) and/or for the behavior of another (other-expectation). The value of an expectation is defined as high (prediction that the performance output will move the group toward success on its goal) or low (prediction that the act will move the group toward failure on its goal).

A *performance expectation state* is defined as a set of performance expectations for two (or more) persons relative to each other. A performance expectation state for person *P* in which *P* thinks he is more likely than the other person (referred to as person *O*) to perform well is called a High-Low expectation state, and is denoted [+ −]. By convention, the expectation state for self is always written first. High-Low thus means high expectation for self, low for other, and Low-High or [− +] means low for self and high for other. A state in which *P* expects both self and other to do well would be High-High or [+ +] and one in which *P* expects both self and other to do poorly would be Low-Low or [− −]. We assume for the sake of simplicity in the initial development of the theory that *P* and *O* have consensus on the expectation state, so that if *P* is [+ −] *O* will be [− +]. A state in which expectations are undefined is also recognized, and denoted [oo]. A performance expectation state exists before a particular performance output occurs, and is a prediction about what the consequences of an act relative to a group goal will be.

The second concept referring to an unobservable mental state deals with the situation immediately after a performance output has occurred. A *unit evaluation* is *P*'s evaluation of the quality of a performance output immediately after it has occurred. Evaluations are called "unit" evaluations because they apply only to a single performance output. The concept does not include global evaluations of persons or their characteristics.

The concept of expectations is basic in sociology, and its use as a fundamental building block of theory marks expectation states theory as distinctively sociological. Although social psychologists in psychology recognize a comparable concept, usually called "expectancy," the concept is more important for sociologists who tend to see social structures as composed of roles and norms which, in turn, are composed of expectations for behavior. Performance expectations are somewhat different from the usual concept of role expectations, however; performance expectations are predictions of quality only, rather than including predictions about form or content of behavior.

ASSUMPTIONS

These concepts furnish the basis for a complete description of the features of social interaction that are relevant to power and prestige structures. To tie them all together, Berger has adapted one of the elements of Bales's theory, the idea of an action cycle or fundamental sequence of behavior. (Fisek 1974; Berger and Conner 1974). The *full fundamental sequence of behavior* is the sequence composed of: action opportunity-performance output-reaction. A positive reaction closes the sequence, but a negative reaction leads to possible disagreement and resolution of disagreement by influence. After the attempted influence introduced by the negative reaction has been either accepted or rejected, the cycle returns to the starting point with an action opportunity. An individual's position in a power and prestige structure is described by the number of action opportunities received, the number of performance outputs produced, the number of performance outputs accepted without disagreement, and the number of influence attempts (that is, initial negative reactions to performance outputs) resolved by rejection of influence attempts from others. Persons at the top of a power and prestige structure score high on these variables while those at the bottom score low.

The two hypothetical constructs of performance expectation states and unit evaluations enter at different points in the fundamental sequence of behavior; performance expectations before, and unit evaluations following, a performance output. The possible forms of the fundamental sequence of behavior may be diagrammed as shown in figure 10.1 (adapted from Berger and Conner 1974 and Fisek 1974).

Berger and Conner (1974) argue that the fundamental action sequence can also begin with a performance output that is not preceded by an action opportunity. It is fairly common for action sequences to begin at the second step in the process shown in figure 10.1. The process as diagrammed in figure 10.1 assumes two actors, Self and Other, (although Other may include several other persons). We are looking at this from the point of view of Self. There are two deterministic assumptions built into the model diagrammed in figure 10.1; the other assumptions are probabilistic. One deterministic assumption is that actors always react positively to performance outputs to which they give a positive unit evaluation, and also always accept influence after giving a negative evaluation to an act by Self.

Assumption 1. A positive unit evaluation is always followed by a positive reaction, and a negative unit evaluation is always followed by a negative reaction. Likewise, in the resolution of disagreement, a negative unit evaluation of one's own act is always followed by acceptance of influence, and a positive unit evaluation of one's own act is always followed by rejection of influence.

Assumption 1 essentially says that it is assumed that the behavior of the group members reflects their evaluations. The importance of the scope

FIGURE 10.1

Diagram of the Full Fundamental Sequence of Behavior

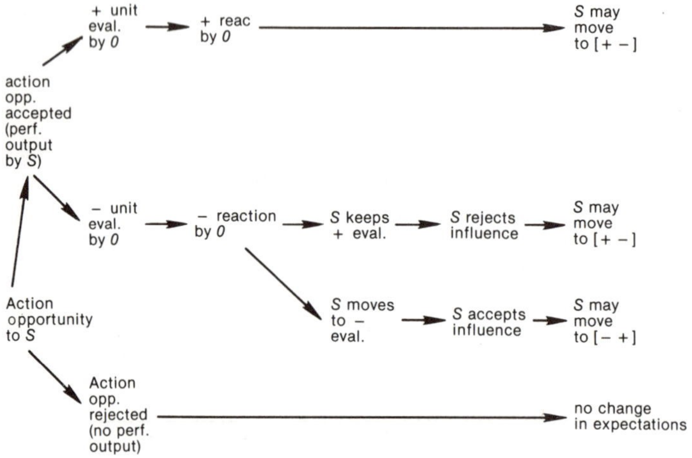

conditions of group task and collective orientation can be seen here, because it is under such conditions that we can assume that people will have no reason to act in a way that is contrary to their evaluations. If they think an act will move the group toward the goal, they accept it; otherwise, not. If it were not legitimate for people to accept influence (perhaps it might be defined as cheating) assumption 1 would have to be modified, and observations of the process would be more complicated. The rest of the assumptions concern the frequency with which each of the possible branches in the tree in figure 10.1 will be taken.

Assumption 2. Effects of expectation states on action opportunities and performance outputs.

(a) If an expectation state is either undefined or undifferentiated (*P* thinks Self and Other are of equal ability, or does not know what their relative abilities are), then Self and Other are:

- —equally likely to receive action opportunities;
- —equally likely to provide performance outputs if given an action opportunity;
- —equally likely to provide performance outputs without being given an action opportunity.

(b) If the expectation state is differentiated, that is, either [+ −] or [− +], then the group member for whom there are higher performance expectations is:

- —more likely to receive an action opportunity;
- —more likely to provide a performance output if given an action opportunity; and
- —more likely to provide a performance output without being given an action opportunity.[3]

These assumptions are based on the exchange model; given that a group is both task and collectively oriented, members should want to provide more action opportunities for the person whose performance outputs are more valuable, and a person with higher expectations for the quality of his own performance should be more likely to try to provide a performance output.

Assumption 3. Effects of performance expectations on unit evaluations. If *P* holds a differentiated expectation state, *P* is more likely to give a positive unit evaluation to a performance output produced by the person for whom *P* has higher performance expectations than to a similar performance output produced by the person for whom *P* has lower expectations.

Assumption 3 is based on a balance model; if a person is expected to do well (positive evaluation of an actor) and that person produces a performance output (positive relationship between actor and act), then it is balanced, tension-free, and stable to give a positive unit evaluation to the act. It is not assumed that expectations always determine unit evaluations; even the most competent person can be expected to make mistakes and to have others catch those mistakes. The assumption is that people feel uncomfortable when this happens, and when possible try to see competent people as producing acts of superior quality and incompetent people as producing acts of inferior quality even when the acts are the same.

Since it has already been assumed (assumption 1) that unit evaluations lead directly to behavior, we can now derive:

Derivation 1. Effect of expectation states on reactions and on influence. If there is a differentiated expectation state, the actor who is expected to do better will

—be more likely to receive a positive reaction for the same performance output; and
—be more likely to reject influence and less likely to accept influence than the person who is expected to do less well.

Finally, we have the last step in the cycle. Since it is imbalanced and hence tension producing and unstable to give a negative unit evaluation to a performance output produced by a person for whom one holds a high performance expectation, and vice versa, we can assume that *P* feels a certain pressure to change some element in his or her set of cognitions at such a point. One possible resolution of the imbalance is to change the performance expectation state to be consistent with the unit evaluation. However (here is the second deterministic assumption of the model), if the unit evaluation is consistent with the performance expectation state, there is no change in expectation state. Thus:

Assumption 4. Effect of unit evaluations on performance expectations. Following a positive unit evaluation of a performance output produced by an actor for whom *P* holds low performance expectations, or for whom *P* has undefined expectations, there is some nonzero probability that *P* will raise his or her performance expectations for that actor. Likewise, following a negative unit evaluation of an act produced by an actor for whom *P* has high performance expectations or for whom *P* has undefined performance expectations, there is some nonzero probability that *P* will lower his or her performance expectations for that actor.

Conversely, following a performance output that receives a unit evaluation consistent with the expectation state for that actor, (that is, a positive unit evaluation for an actor for whom *P* holds high performance expectations or a negative unit evaluation for an actor for whom *P* holds low performance expectations) there is zero probability of a change in performance expectations.

Assumptions 1–3, together with derivation 1, describe the interaction advantages possessed by a person with the high value of a [+ −] or [− +] expectation state. This person is likely to get more action opportunities, to produce more performance outputs with or without being given action opportunities, to receive more positive unit evaluations for a performance output and to win an argument in the event of an initial negative unit evaluation. Once a differentiated performance expectation state is established, this model predicts that it has strong elements of a self-fulfilling prophecy; people act so as to bring about the results they expect.

The last assumption, number 4, completes the model and is probably the most crucial, for it describes how performance expectation states are established and the conditions under which they are either maintained or changed. A positive unit evaluation may nudge an undefined or a low expectation upward and a negative unit evaluation may move a high or undefined expectation state downward. When expectations are undefined, as at the beginning of interaction between strangers, the first person to make a performance output that receives a positive unit evaluation may acquire an interaction advantage over the others.

This model predicts that any factor that causes one actor to receive a positive unit evaluation when another actor does not (including factors that make one actor more likely to receive action opportunities or to produce performance outputs, since there must be a performance output before there can be a unit evaluation) will have the possible effect of creating a differentiated expectation state and hence a power and prestige structure. This can explain why a large variety of personality characteristics, as well as such factors as seating arrangement or etiquette governing interaction, may be found to be associated with "leadership." If one aspect of a power and prestige structure becomes differentiated, all the other aspects will eventually differentiate in a consistent manner. Whatever makes one member talk more than others, talk first, or reject influence more strongly may have the same effect as an initially differentiated performance expectation state.

Empirical Studies of Expectation States

A study reported by Fisek (1974) and Fisek and Ofshe (1970) used the category scheme of action opportunities, performance outputs, positive and negative reactions, and influence to code interaction in a set of small discussion groups. Otherwise, the procedures replicated Bales's methods (groups were three-person groups of male freshmen, previously unacquainted, with no obvious differences in age, class, race, and so forth, who were given forty-five minutes to reach consensus on an open-ended ambiguous problem). The coding system apparently can be used to code interaction, and all groups showed a pattern of differentiation in amount of talking by the end of the forty-five minutes. However, the groups did not show the predicted pattern of gradual development of differentiation over the course of the discussion. About half of the groups showed the predicted pattern (beginning with approximately equal distribution of performance outputs and positive reactions and becoming more differentiated as time went on), but the other half were differentiated from the beginning. Clearly, although the members looked homogeneous to the researchers, in about half of the groups they did not look homogeneous to each other, and group members began the interaction with differentiated expectation states. This study, although showing that the theory does apply to unstructured group interaction, also shows the necessity for controlling for extraneous sources of expectations.

THE STANDARD EXPERIMENTAL SETTING

Most of the empirical studies of expectation states use a variant of a standard experimental setting developed by Joseph Berger. This setting is designed to control for extraneous sources of expectations and also to incorporate theoretically important conditions from both the scope assumptions and the assumptions of the model. Since the major interest is explanation of differentiation in power and prestige, the standard experimental setting focuses on the aspects of the process that produce differentiation. If we consider assumption 4 (effect of unit evaluations on expectation states), we note the importance of disagreements in producing differentiated expectation states. It is when disagreement occurs and must be resolved that actors are forced to make differentiated unit evaluations (either "I'm right and he's wrong" or "he's right and I'm wrong"). Undifferentiated states are unstable under disagreement, which makes disagreement the theoretically appropriate situation to study if one wishes to observe the process of differentiation.

Observing actors who must resolve disagreements has an additional advantage; this is that the rate of acceptance or rejection of influence can be used as an indicator of performance expectation states. The logic here is as follows: given an issue on which there are no objective external standards, and the necessity exists to resolve a disagreement in favor of one actor or another, actors will assign unit evaluations on the basis of performance expectations and, consequently, will accept the act produced by the actor for whom there are higher performance expectations. Thus a high rate of accepting influence should indicate a [$-$ $+$] expectation state ("he's better than I am, so if we disagree, he must be right and I must be wrong; since we are working on a collective task and I want us to succeed, I should accept his choice").

Other requirements for an experimental setting are that the scope assumptions should be met (group must be task-oriented, actors collectively oriented, task intrasystemic); that a differentiated performance expectation state can be created by the experimenter; that it must be possible to assign subjects randomly to high or low conditions of expectation state; and that other sources of expectations can be eliminated.

In the standard experimental procedure, subjects are drawn from a homogeneous population (usually undergraduate students) who have volunteered to participate for pay in a study vaguely described as concerning "group decision making." There are two subjects in a "group" and they are of the same sex, previously unacquainted, and do not have a chance to become acquainted before the study. They are seated on either side of a screen, so they do not see each other during the study. Each has, on a table in front of him or her, a panel equipped with several pairs of buttons and of lights. The experimenter explains that the study involves investigation of a newly discovered ability called Contrast Sensitivity (a variety of other "abilities" have been used; Contrast Sensitivity is the most common). Contrast Sensitivity, the subjects are told, is unrelated to any other known ability but may be quite important to an individual's capacity to perform well on certain kinds of tasks. Some individuals have high levels of this ability, some have low, and others are average.

The experimenter then administers a purportedly reliable test of Contrast Sensitivity. This test consists of a series of (usually) twenty slides, each showing a large rectangle composed of a number of smaller black and white rectangles. Subjects are to estimate whether there are more black or more white small rectangles in the large one, and indicate the estimate by pressing one of two buttons (labeled "black" and "white") on the panel in front of them. Subjects are not told during the test which answer is correct, but at the end of the test, both subjects' scores are reported and posted on a bulletin board; one subject has missed only two ("an unusually high score, indicating a very high Contrast Sensitivity") while the other subject has missed about half the questions ("an unusually low score, indicating very low Contrast Sensitivity"). The administration of the test and report of results is phase I of the study.

In phase II, the subjects are told that they will now be working on a different task, the aim of which is to see how well people can do on a Contrast Sensitivity task when they have additional information. The additional information is the opinion of the other person. The second task is a variant on the first (most usually one in which the slide shows a pair of rectangles composed of black and white smaller rectangles and the subject has to estimate which of the pair has the greater proportion of white rectangles). As in the first test, there are always two choices and the subjects believe one choice must be correct and the other incorrect. On each trial, each subject first makes an "initial choice," and then sees a light informing him or her which alternative the other person has indicated as initial choice. Then both subjects are to make a "final choice." The final choice is the only choice that counts on their score, and they are encouraged to think it is legitimate to change their choices if they want to. Final choices are not exchanged, so neither subject knows whether the other has accepted or rejected influence. There are typically twenty-three to twenty-five trials in phase II, and on twenty to twenty-two of these trials the subjects are informed via the light that the other person has made the opposite choice for initial choice. The disagreements are, of course, arranged by the experimenter and the three to five trials of agreement are inserted to reduce suspicion. (Pretests had indicated that a minimum of three to five agreements are sufficient to produce a situation that seems plausible to the majority of subjects).

Following the end of phase II, subjects are interviewed at some length with special emphasis on discovering any suspicion or misunderstanding of the experimental procedures, and on explaining all the deceptions. A typical rate of suspicion for one of these experiments is about 1/6 to 1/4 of the subjects; the high proportion of disagreement seems to present a severe cognitive challenge that many meet by becoming suspicious. Subjects who are suspicious are normally excluded from analysis, as are any who do not meet the initial conditions of the theory for other reasons, such as confusion about the procedures.

The scope assumptions require a task-oriented situation in which individual performance outputs can lead either toward or away from success. The performance outputs are the final choices, and task orientation is established by telling the subjects they will receive a score (usually a group score) based on the number of correct choices. The task should be ambiguous; this is established by making the actual proportions of black and white small rectangles on each slide very nearly equal so that it is very difficult to tell whether black or white predominates. The slides have been pretested so that the proportion of people choosing black and white is approximately 50 percent. Thus, although the subjects readily believe that there is a single correct answer, there is no external standard by which they can judge whether they are making that correct choice. One of the advantages of the standard Contrast Sensitivity task is that it can easily be made less ambiguous by changing the proportion of black and white rectangles, thereby allowing the experimenter to vary one of the scope conditions. Subjects are motivated to try to achieve success on the task by statements in the instructions that Contrast Sensitivity may turn out to be an important ability, and they are given a collective orientation by working for a group score and/or statements in the instructions that they should feel free to change their choice between initial choice and final choice.

Using an invented ability, described as being unrelated to other known abilities, allows the experimenter to assign subjects randomly to high or low expectation states, since they come in with no preconceived ideas of their own or other persons' abilities at this task. Other sources of expectations are eliminated by making sure subjects do not know each other or talk to each other directly during the study. The format of the experiment keeps constant the number of action opportunities each subject gets and the number of performance outputs each makes since both are required to attempt to answer all questions. The format also ensures constant disagreement, thereby making the only variable in the fundamental sequence of behavior the resolution of disagreements, that is, influence. The basic dependent variable in all these studies, thus, is the proportion of times a subject stays with his or her initial choice (called a Stay response) as opposed to changing to the other person's initial choice (called a Change response). A Stay response indicates rejection of influence, whereas a Change response indicates acceptance of influence.

EFFECTS OF MANIPULATED EXPECTATION STATES

Table 10.1 summarizes the results of two studies using the basic experimental situation with some slight variations. The column labeled "expectation state" is the manipulated expectation state from the subject's point of view; [+ −], for example, means this subject was told he or she got an unusually high score whereas the other person got a low score in phase I. The column labeled "*P(S)*" is the proportion of Stay responses,

TABLE 10.1

Proportion of Stay Responses (Rejection of Influence) by Expectation States, with Two Different Phase II Tasks.

Expectation State	P(S) Meaning Insight Task*	Constrast Sensitivity Task**
[+ −]	.78	.76
[+ +]	.67	.64
[− −]	.65	.66
[− +]	.44	.42

*Adapted from Berger and Conner 1969.
**Adapted from Camilleri et al. 1972.

that is, the percent of trials in phase II on which the subject did not change from initial choice to final choice in the face of disagreement from the other. The first column of results is data reported by Berger and Conner (1969) from an experiment using a fictional ability called Meaning Insight Ability (this requires subjects to decide which of two English words has the same meaning as a supposed phonetic transcription of a word from an obscure foreign language). The second column is from an experiment reported in Camilleri et al. (1972), in which the Contrast Sensitivity task was used. As table 10.1 shows, the results from the two experiments are very similar and in the order predicted by the theory; subjects reject influence most strongly when they believe they have greater ability than the other person and accept influence most often when they believe the other person has more ability, with the undifferentiated states intermediate. The similarity of the results for [+ +] and [− −] provides support for the idea that it is the difference between expectations for self and for other that affects behavior. These results are the basic ones with which results from subsequent experiments can be compared.

Another control condition is reported by Moore (1968, 1969). As one condition of an experiment that will be described in more detail later, Moore had subjects with undefined expectation states work on a Contrast Sensitivity task alone. Instead of receiving information about another person's choice they merely had a five-second period in which they could change a choice if they wanted to. About 75 percent of the trials produced Stay responses under these conditions. In other words, subjects in the [+ −] condition under disagreement change their minds about as often as subjects who do not have to take any other opinion into account. (Compare Moore's results with those shown in table 10.1). Because the task is ambiguous, even persons with a high opinion of their own abilities may be expected to feel uncertain about some of their choices.

Another comparison is reported by Conner (1977). This study tests the hypothesis that expectation states should affect the rate of production of performance outputs if action opportunities are held constant. Verbal latency (speed with which a person responds to a stimulus) has been shown to be related to position in a power and prestige structure. Conner's study built on this foundation by running a standard phase I, in which [+ −] and [− +] expectation states were established, and then informing subjects that in phase II whichever person pushed the button first would determine the group score for that trial. As predicted, more decisions were made by [+ −] than [− +] subjects (55 percent versus 45 percent).

FORMATION OF EXPECTATION STATES

The effects of experimentally established expectation states seem as predicted by the theory. A second set of questions revolves around the problem of how performance expectations are established other than by experimental manipulation. Three types of such situations have been examined experimentally: cases in which there is no information about abilities; cases in which there is only information about abilities that are irrelevant to the task; and cases in which there is conflicting information about abilities.

When subjects with no information about relative abilities are confronted with continual disagreement, they apparently move into a [+ −] state (Conner 1965), but if confronted with two others who disagree continually, some move to [+ −] and others to [− +] (Berger, Conner, and McKeown 1969). Since the performance expectation states are unobservable, a somewhat complicated procedure is required to estimate the proportions of subjects moving into each state, given only the proportion of Stay responses. Berger, Conner, and McKeown (1974) present a Markov process model that incorporates the assumptions of the theory and provides estimates for the probabilities of moving to each differentiated state from an undifferentiated one given the response consistent with that state.

Moving to cases in which more than one ability is involved requires some additional terminology. Any characteristic on which people may form differentiated performance expectations is called a *specific status characteristic;* it is a status characteristic because there are high (high ability) and low (low ability) states; it is specific because it applies to a specific task and group. People who have a high state of ability on a specific status characteristic may or may not have high ability on some other. If I have high Contrast Sensitivity I may or may not be a superior gardener, and if I can grow tomatoes well I may or may not be good at programming a computer. The concept of specific status characteristic will be useful to contrast with the concept of general or diffuse status characteristic, which is introduced later.[4] In the experiments just described, the connection between ability and task success is made for the subjects by the experimenter. If some other characteristic, not explicitly made relevant to success on the task, is seen as relevant by the subject, then the stage is set for balancing processes to initiate a differentiated expectation state. If, on the other hand, a person has a high state of some ability but group members do not associate that ability with task outcomes, then that ability is irrelevant to expectation state processes.

Three related studies have examined the case in which subjects have information about an ability other than the one specifically required for success in the task in phase II. The general procedure is to measure one fictitious ability (for example, Meaning Insight Ability) in phase I and give a different test (usually Contrast Sensitivity) in phase II. In the first study in this series, Berger, Fisek, and Freese (1976) measured Meaning Insight Ability in phase I. Phase II was presented as a separate experiment, in which subjects were to be paid different amounts for their participation. This "separate" study involved Constrast Sensitivity and subjects were told that because time was limited Contrast Sensitivity would not be measured but that the differences in pay would be based on performance on the Meaning Insight test.

Two conditions of relevance of ability in the first test to ability in the second were established: *direct relevance,* in which subjects were told that people with high Meaning Insight Ability usually do well on Constrast Sensitivity; and *indirect relevance,* in which subjects were told nothing about the relationship between the two tests. Under direct relevance, with [+ −] expectation state, *P(S)* = .802 and with [− +] expectation state, *P(S)* = .498. These are very similar to the equivalent expectation states in the standard experiment. Under indirect relevance, *P(S)* in [+ −] = .752 and in [− +] *P(S)* = .602. This shows some differentiation but not so much as under direct relevance.

In a second study, Freese (1976) gave subjects Meaning Insight scores and told them that Meaning Insight was either positively or inversely related to a second fictional ability, which was not tested. Still a third ability, Contrast Sensitivity, also not measured, was required for phase II (presented as a different experiment). Thus, subjects knew that their scores in one experiment could predict performance on some task, but not on the task on which they were working. Direct relevance produced some differentiation: *P(S)* for [+ −] = .73, and for [− +] = .62. However, inverse relevance produced no differentiation (*P*[*S*] = .66 in both [+ −] and [− +]).

In the third experiment in this series, Berger and Fisek (1970) tested two different models of the ways in which people may combine information about status characteristics. A balance model suggests that, faced with inconsistent evaluations about a single object, people will tend to reduce tension by accepting one evaluation and ignoring or redefining the other. In constrast, an averaging model supposes that people simply combine all the information they have. In this study subjects in phase I were given tests of two different fictional abilities, Meaning Insight Ability and Relational Insight Ability (the latter requires matching a phonetic spelling with a picture of an "ancient Japanese ideograph"). Phase II was the standard Contrast Sensitivity task. The two scores in phase I were either *consistent high* (*S* better than *O* at both tasks), *consistent low* (*S* worse than *O* at both) or *inconsistent* (*S* better at one task, worse at the other). For [+ −][+ −], *P(S)* = .821; for [− +][− +], *P(S)* = .533, and for the inconsistent condition, [+ −][− +], *P(S)* = .661. An examination of the variance in the inconsistent condition shows no apparent tendency to the bimodality one would expect if some subjects are ignoring the [+ −] and other subjects the [− +] state; the averaging model is better supported than the balance model.

The conclusions of this set of studies seem to be: (1) people will use information about one specific status characteristic (that is, ability) to predict performance on another characteristic; (2) the more directly relevant the first characteristic is to the second, the more effect information about the first will have on expectations for the second; and (3) people use all information available and average inconsistent information. The information processing model, as a way of describing the process of formation of differentiated expectation states, appears in most recent expectation states research.

SOURCES OF SELF-EVALUATION

A series of experiments (Webster 1969; Sobieszek 1972; Webster, Roberts, and Sobieszek 1972; Sobieszek and Webster 1973; Webster and Sobieszek 1974) has used expectation states theory and the standard experimental setting to investigate another of the perennial concerns of social psychologists, the social context of self-concept. Beginning with the assumptions of Mead and Cooley that individuals develop concepts of themselves through awareness of how others react to them, this line of research asks what some of the attributes are of an "other" that make his or her opinion have an effect on an individual's self-evaluation, and how individuals organize information from more than one other (especially if their opinions conflict).

The particular aspect of the self-concept that is under consideration is the evaluation of one's own ability relative to someone else's at a specific task; it is not a global self-concept. Self-evaluation is measured behaviorally in the standard expectation states experiment, assuming that the subject with a high evaluation of his or her ability will make a high proportion of Stay responses while one with a low self-evaluation will make few Stay responses.

In the standard experimental setting, the other who acts as a source for the subject's self-evaluation is the experimenter, whose opinion is assumed by the subject to be correct in all cases because of the experimenter's access to a list of the correct answers to the problems. Rather than being evaluated by an omniscient experimenter, however, one might be evaluated by persons with varying qualifications to judge the correctness or competence of one's performance. A *source* is defined, for a task situation such as meets the scope assumptions of expectation states theory, as a person not making performance outputs (that is, not contributing to the group task) but who has the right to make evaluations of the performance outputs of the actors who are, and who is believed by *P* (the actor) to be more capable of evaluating performances than *P* is.

The subjects in this series of experiments worked in pairs on the Contrast Sensitivity task, beginning with no prior expectations for relative ability. As a control condition, one set of subjects received no information from any source about their performance outputs; the average number of Stay responses in this condition is .64. (The data reported here and below can be found in Webster and Sobieszek 1974). For the other conditions, the source is described as "a college student like yourselves" and the only other item of information provided about the source is how well he or she did on a test of Contrast Sensitivity; the ability assigned to the source is High or Low. Next, the subjects take a Contrast Sensitivity test which is evaluated, not by the experimenter, but by the source, who reports an estimate of how many slides the two subjects each answered correctly. The source's evaluations are either [− +] (subject did poorly, other did well) or [+ −] (subject did well, other did poorly). The subjects then work on a standard phase II, exchanging initial choices and making final choices, with constant disagreement. In this set of conditions, the proportions of Stay responses are as follows: for a source with High ability, making [+ −] evaluation, $P(S) = .80$; High ability source making a [− +] evaluation, $P(S) = .46$; For a Low ability source the results were: Low ability source making [+ −] evaluation, $P(S) = .65$, and Low ability source making [− +] evaluation, $P(S) = .58$. Apparently subjects' behavior is more affected by the opinions of competent than incompetent evaluators.

When there are two sources, each reporting independently an estimate of how many slides the two subjects answered correctly on the phase I test, the subject seems to accept their evaluations even if they differ in ability (High ability and Low ability source both making [+ −] evaluation produces *P(S)* = .80; both making [− +] evaluation, *P(S)* = .42). When the two sources disagree, there is some tendency for the opinion of the more competent to be weighted more heavily, but both have some effect; that is, when the High ability evaluator makes a [+ −] evaluation *P(S)* = .76 and a [− +] evaluation *P(S)* = .58 under conditions in which a Low ability evaluator makes the opposite evaluation. However, when two High ability sources make opposite evaluations, *P(S)* = .67. In the last case, subjects may be combining the evaluations of the two sources.

Webster, Roberts, and Sobieszek (1972) tested several different models of the ways in which people might be combining information from different sources, and concluded that a simple additive model best describes the process, just as it did with information from one source about two abilities in the research reported in the previous section. Furthermore, there appears to be little evidence from these studies that subjects are attempting to maximize their positive self-evaluations; they do not appear to accept [+ −] evaluations and ignore [− +] evaluations.[5]

UNEQUAL DISTRIBUTION OF RESPONSIBILITY

Another line of research in expectation states presents an apparent paradox. In the standard experimental procedures, the subjects contribute equally to the group score. Several variations on this procedure using an unequal distribution of responsibility have been used. Camilleri and Berger (1967) ran a standard phase I in which [+ +], [+ −], [− +], and [− −] expectation states were induced. In phase II the experimenter told subjects that only one person's choice would count on the group score; this subject was called the *decision maker* and the other subject the *advisor*. In phase II, as usual, subjects exchanged initial choices and experienced continual disagreement. It might seem that having full control over a group score should be associated with a higher power and prestige position and hence with a high rate of rejection of influence. However, just the opposite occurs; subjects with full control have lower rates of Stay responses than those with equal control, and those with equal control have lower rates of Stay responses than subjects with no control, for all four expectation states. (*P*[*S*]) is as follows: for [+ −], full control, .73 and no control, .82; [+ +] full, .60 and none, .71; [− −] full, .52 and none, .73; [− +] full, .24 and none, .43; compare with table 10.1 for equal control results).

This experiment has been replicated several times with variations in subject populations, experimental task, and proportion of control other than equal or all-or-none, and the same phenomenon appears (Balkwell 1969; Camilleri and Conner 1976; Balkwell 1976). Apparently, unequal responsibility, when it occurs naturally in a power and prestige structure, is a result rather than a cause of status differentiation. The researchers listed above (see also Kervin 1974) have explained this using a utility model that posits that subjects get some reward from getting the right answer (regardless of whether it was originally proposed by self or by other), some reward from sticking with own initial choice (whether correct or not), and some reward from deferring to the partner (whether partner is correct or not). According to this model, changing the distribution of responsibility shifts the relative weight of these utilities toward more reward from deferring to partner for the person with higher responsibility for the group score and less reward for the person with lower responsibility.

In future studies, researchers might want to consider the possibility that the effects of shifting responsibility may be related to considerations introduced in the scope assumption of collective orientation. That is, the distribution of responsibility may affect the degree to which it is legitimate to take into account or to ignore the opinions of other group members. One question that remains unanswered is whether an actual change in performance expectations occurs in the unequal responsibility condition. According to the theory, any factor that increases the probability of being influenced will ultimately affect expectations. If this is an example of this process, we should expect that if the phase II of the unequal responsibility conditions were followed by a phase III replicating the standard phase II with equal responsibility, the effects of the unequal responsibility should persist. If the effect is purely a matter of different utilities in the different responsibility conditions, the effect should not persist.

Diffuse Status Characteristics and Expectation States

One of the most important applications of expectation states theory is to a fundamental sociological concern: the effects of large-scale differentiated or stratified structures on individual behavior (Berger, Cohen, Conner, and Zelditch 1966; Berger, Cohen, and Zelditch 1966, 1972; Berger and Fisek 1974; Berger, Fisek, Norman, and Zelditch 1977). The phenomenon to be explained by the theory of diffuse status characteristics is the same in some respects as the phenomenon explained by expectation states theory: the development and maintenance of differentiated power and prestige structures in face-to-face interaction. However, this theory addresses a different type of interaction situation, one in which the members of the group are not initially similar in background.

In groups that are not homogeneous, power and prestige structures develop, but these structures are typically strongly correlated with differences between group members on external characteristics, such as race, sex, occupation, or education. This relationship between external status and position in a small group is referred to as *status generalization* and has been documented in so many different empirical studies that a complete review is impossible. Some examples are: on juries men talk more than women, and persons in professional and managerial occupations talk more than blue collar workers (Strodtbeck, James, and Hawkins

1957; Strodtbeck and Mann 1956). In other mixed-sex problem-solving groups, men contribute more suggestions and have more influence than women (for example, March 1953; Heiss 1962; Leik 1963). In mixed-race groups, whites dominate blacks even when matched in intelligence (Katz and Benjamin 1960; Katz, Goldston, and Benjamin 1958; Katz and Cohen 1962); in psychiatric hospitals, doctors talk more than nurses in staff conferences (Caudill 1958). In air force crews, pilots have more influence on solutions to a puzzle than gunners, even when the pilot's solution is incorrect, the puzzle is unrelated to actual air crew tasks, and the crew is composed of men who do not normally work together (Torrance 1954).

In these and other studies the dependent variables differ, and in each case some particular aspect of the roles involved might be invoked as an explanation (women and men are socialized differently; racial groups experience in-group loyalty and outgroup hostility; managers and professionals have more interest in legal issues than do blue-collar workers; military rank carries certain expectations for etiquette). To status characteristics theory, however, these are all instances of the same phenomenon, that is, the emergence of a differentiated power and prestige structure, and they are explained by proposing that external status differences become translated into differentiated performance expectations.

In general, a *status characteristic* is a dimension on which persons may be ranked or discriminated, and for which it is considered more desirable to have the high state. The *specific status characteristic* that is instrumental to the task is labeled C^* (C for characteristic, and * to indicate it is the particular ability needed to do well on the specific task at hand). Other specific characteristics are labeled $C1$, $C2$, $C3$, and so on. As indicated previously, people may have performance expectations for the C as well as for the C^*, and these expectations may become linked to the performance expectations for C^* especially in the absence of direct information about relative status on C^*.

A *diffuse status characteristic* differs from a specific status characteristic by the possession of two additional features. One is a set of attributes or stereotypes representing specific characteristics that are associated with the diffuse status characteristic. If, for example, sex or gender is a diffuse status characteristic, it means that people expect men and women to have different abilities; men may be expected to be better mechanics, more punctual, more assertive, or stronger than women. The attributes, mechanical ability, punctuality, strength, and so on, are specific characteristics that may or may not be related to any particular task. A diffuse status characteristic may associate higher ability with a lower state of the characteristic for some attributes; for example, women may be expected to be better than men at typing or sewing. However, a diffuse status characteristic is assumed to have a second property called a *general expectation state,* which means that persons with the highly valued state of the characteristic are generally expected to be more competent than people with the less valued state. Thus, if gender is a diffuse status characteristic for an individual, that individual expects that men will, in general, handle most tasks more competently than women.

A diffuse status characteristic is said to be *activated* in a particular task situation if it is a basis of discrimination (that is, of distinguishing among people), and people believe either the general expectation state associated with the characteristic (for example, that men are more competent at most things than women) or if they believe one or more of the specific status characteristics (for example, that men are more punctual or better mechanics than women). If a diffuse status characteristic is not activated, it has no effect on further interaction. Even if it is activated, however, it may not be applied to the particular actors; they may see themselves as exceptions to the general rule. The process of applying a belief in a general rule to specific actors is referred to as the *burden of proof process* by status characteristics theorists. As the name indicates, it is assumed that in the absence of information to the contrary, people will go ahead and apply the general rule to particular people and the burden of proof is on a lower status person to demonstrate that the general rule does not apply to him or her (or on the person with the higher state of the diffuse status characteristic to demonstrate incompetence). Unless halted by such a demonstration, the burden of proof process results in the diffuse status characteristic D becoming *relevant* to C^*; if D is both activated and relevant, then actors assign a high state of C^* to a person with a higher state of D. This final step is called *assignment.*

Once assignment has taken place, a differentiated expectation state exists, and expectation state theory can be used to predict the development of a differentiated power and prestige structure. Although the theory hypothesizes a set of steps, at any one of which the process may be halted, it also hypothesizes that some event must occur to break the chain if the process is to be halted; otherwise, the natural course will be for diffuse status characteristics to determine performance expectations. Note that there are two paths (not mutually exclusive) that the diffuse status characteristic can take to affect performance expectations: either through the general expectation state ("men are usually more competent than women so I'll expect a man to be better at this task") or through one or more of the specific status characteristics associated with the diffuse characteristic ("men are more punctual and better at mechanics and this looks like a task that requires punctuality and mechanical ability").

EMPIRICAL STUDIES OF DIFFUSE STATUS

Sociological social psychologists often experience difficulty in testing causal theories about the effects of social structure on behavior; we cannot randomly assign race, sex, level of education, and so on. Status characteristics theory can be tested experimentally, however, because it hypothesizes that the differences in behavior it predicts are caused by actors' perceptions of difference in status on diffuse status characteristics, translated into differentiated performance expectations. If the theory were concerned with aspects of status inherent in the social role attached to the status (for example, in personality differences due to early socialization or physiological or genetic differences) experimental tests would remain difficult. For example, a person may be better educated than others in one group and less well educated in another, but not college educated in one group and only high-school educated in another.

Status characteristics theory does not suppose that there are no differences in personality created by occupation of different statuses, but instead seeks through experimental design to eliminate these personality factors as causes of the behavior observed.

Moore (1968, 1969) provides an example of the standard format for a study of diffuse status characteristics using the expectation states experimental procedure. Taking a subject population of female junior college students who had volunteered to be in an experiment, Moore randomly assigned them to one of two conditions: either the subject believed her partner was a student at a prestigious university (Low status for self, High for other) or the subject believed her partner was a student at a local high school (High status for self, Low for other). The subjects were, of course, all from the same junior college, and Moore knew that to these students the university was more prestigious than the junior college and the junior college more prestigious than the high school. In this experiment, there was no manipulation of performance expectations; the experiment began with a standard phase II sequence of initial choice, disagreement, and final choice on a Contrast Sensitivity task (Contrast Sensitivity was called, at that time, Spatial Judgment).

When subjects had only the information about their relative statuses, the proportion of Stay responses were: High-Low, .75; and Low-High, .63. When subjects in Low-High were also told explicitly that university students usually do better at the task than junior college students $P(S) = .58$ and when High-Low subjects were told that junior college students usually do better than high school students, $P(S) = .75$ (Moore 1969). Where subjects had only information about relative educational status, some differentiation in power and prestige structure occurred; the external status characteristic had the same general effect as creating a differentiated performance expectation state. However, the effect was stronger when the step of relevance was explicitly taken for the subjects.

The general effect of diffuse status on rate of acceptance of influence in the standard experimental setting has been replicated a number of times with different subject populations (although mostly high school or college students), with minor variations in procedures, and with other diffuse status characteristics such as age (Freese 1974; Freesé and Cohen 1973); race (Webster and Driskell 1978); army rank (Berger, B. Cohen, and Zelditch 1972); prestige of school (see several studies described in Berger, Fisek, Norman, and Zelditch 1977); and sex (Ruch and Newton 1977; Lockheed 1977—these latter two studies used other experimental designs). All these studies show that telling a person that someone else's status on a diffuse characteristic external to the group is higher (or lower) is equivalent to announcing that the other person is better (or worse) at a specific task on which the group is working. Furthermore, this cannot be attributed to any actual differences in skill, because the ability is imaginary and high or low status is randomly assigned.

The situation in which people are differentiated on only one diffuse status characteristic is called the *elementary status situation.* Having established that diffuse status characteristics affect behavior in the elementary status situation, researchers have turned to more complex questions. One question is what conditions strengthen the effect of diffuse status differences on power and prestige behavior. In a study reported by Berger, B. Cohen, and Zelditch (1972), air force staff sergeants worked on a standard Contrast Sensitivity task with a partner who was described as a captain (subject is Low-High) or an airman third class (subject is High-Low).

To test the assumptions of activation, burden of proof, and assignment, three conditions of information were created: subjects with no additional information; subjects who were told that their partner's army general classification score (a general measure of intellectual ability) was very high or very low, consistent with the partner's relative status, but not whether that score was relevant to the Contrast Sensitivity task; and subjects who were told their partner's score on the general test and that score on the test usually predicted Contrast Sensitivity. Differentiation in $P(S)$ appeared between High-Low and Low-High in all three information conditions, but the only effect of information was on the High-Low subjects, who produced a higher $P(S)$ when told both their partner's score and that the score was relevant to the task. This study and the one reported previously by Moore suggest that the effect of diffuse status characteristics on behavior is stronger when the diffuse characteristic is explicitly made relevant to the task.

Under what conditions might the effect of diffuse status characteristics be weakened? A series of studies has addressed this question. These studies build on some of the research reported in the last section on situations in which subjects of equal status on diffuse characteristics have information about their relative abilities on several different specific status characteristics. The argument is that the process of status generalization can be inhibited by providing information about specific status characteristics that contradicts the general expectation state attached to the diffuse status characteristic. Freese and Cohen (1973) told college student subjects that their partner was either much older (thirty-eight years old) or much younger (eleven years old) than themselves; this produced the expected differentiation in $P(S)$. However, when told that the partner, though young, was good at the task (or, though older, was poor at the task) the effects of the diffuse status characteristic were diminished. Even when told that the partner, though young, was better than the subject at a task unrelated to the task the pair was working on, the effect of diffuse status was diminished, and the more other abilities for which this information was provided the less effect diffuse status had. Freese (1974) produced the same result by telling subjects in this experiment that other persons similar in age to the partner had performed either better or worse than the subject. Webster and Driskell (1978) report being able to inhibit status generalization based on race by providing contrary information about specific abilities.

All the studies mentioned above have used differentiated statuses; that is, have informed subjects that they and the partner differ in some socially important way. What is the effect of information that the two partners are the same on some diffuse status characteristic; does this reduce the effect of the differences that they also know about, or is this information ignored? Earlier research had suggested that equating characteristics (for example, subjects are told they are the same age but of different races) does reduce the effect of differentiating characteristics

(Berger, B. Cohen, Zelditch 1972). Some later research, however, suggests that information about equating characteristics is simply ignored, and that the earlier interpretation had not been justified by the data (Webster 1977). The question of equating characteristics is related to the assumption that diffuse status characteristics must be activated in order to have an effect on interaction; part of activation is that the characteristic must be a basis of discrimination between actors. This suggests that race is only a diffuse status characteristic in mixed-race groups, sex in mixed-sex groups, and so forth. It also suggests that trying to mitigate the effects of diffuse status characteristics by pointing out to people how similar they are in other ways will not be very effective.

As with the research on formation of performance expectations and on sources of self-evaluation, an important theoretical question is how people combine information from several possibly conflicting sources to create expectation states. Berger, Fisek, Norman, and Zelditch (1977) have developed a model to describe the information-combining process. The activation, burden of proof, and assignment processes are included in the model, to provide a description of the ways in which information becomes treated as relevant to expectation states. Berger et al. further hypothesize that information that has become relevant to expectation states in a particular task situation is combined to produce expectation states according to three principles: (1) inconsistency—this means that a single item of inconsistent information has greater weight than an item of consistent information (a single factor that contradicts a stereotype will considerably change people's expectations); (2) attenuation—this means that each additional consistent item has less effect; and (3) organized subsets—this means that all negative items (factors that would lead to a low expectation for performance in this task situation) are combined into one subset, and then all positive items (factors that would lead to a high expectation for performance) are combined, and then the two subsets are added together. The result will be an expectation advantage for self over other if there are more positive items for self and/or more negative items for other. If the total for self and other results in a higher expectation for other than self, then there is an expectation advantage for other.

The expectation advantage thus calculated is subsequently used as part of an equation that (when two other parameters are estimated according to methods provided by Berger, Fisek, Norman, and Zelditch 1977) provides an exact estimate of the proportion of Stay responses in an experiment. This model seems to fit data from previous experiments well, although the estimation procedures for some of the parameters are, as the authors admit, in need of further development. Some additional work has been stimulated by this model (Webster and Driskell 1978; Fox and Moore 1979) and more will presumably appear in the future.

INTERVENTION STRATEGIES

A practical consequence of this theory and associated research results is that, although we must expect that in the absence of contradictory information diffuse status differences will be translated into interpersonal power and prestige structures, we may also expect that status generalization can be inhibited by providing the necessary contradictory information. The research, furthermore, suggests that information about specific status characteristics (abilities) can be effective. Two groups of researchers have successfully used expectation states theory in applications to mixed-race elementary and secondary school classrooms. These applications also provide more empirical support for the theory by testing hypotheses derived from it in nonlaboratory settings using different operationalizations of the concepts.

As an example of the work of one of these groups of researchers, E. Cohen and Roper (1972) report that in groups of black and white boys the whites typically dominate a discussion. However, if the blacks are given special training (in this case, being taught how to assemble a radio) and their superiority on this specific status characteristic is made clear to both the black and the white boys (the black boys teach the white boys to assemble a radio), the power and prestige position of the blacks and whites is approximately equal in subsequent interaction. The intervention is only effective, however, if both races are provided with information about the specific status characteristic. Training the blacks without making their superior skill clear to the whites merely produces conflict as the blacks attempt more performance outputs only to have their outputs rejected by the whites. Expectation training thus differs from "assertiveness training," and the theory explains why the difference is necessary. (For reports of other research on expectation training by this group, see E. Cohen 1970, 1972, 1973, 1976; Lockheed-Katz and Hall 1976.)

Another set of research/intervention studies is reported by Entwisle and Webster (1974a) (see also Entwisle and Webster 1972, 1973, 1974b, 1978; Webster and Entwisle 1976). Typically, these studies use the frequency with which a child raises his or her hand in a group discussion, for example, in a group that is supposed to construct a story, as an indicator of frequency of attempted performance outputs. After observing this rate in untreated groups, some children in some groups are given special training in the specific task on which the group is working, or on some other task. The control groups consist of children, none of whom are given special training. Then the rate of raising hands is observed again. Generally, the expectation training does increase the rate of volunteering compared to children who have not had the training, with interesting interactions with race of teacher and rural-urban location of school.

Discussion

For the purposes of this volume, some comment is in order about the distinctively sociological aspects of this body of research as well as the features that make it different from other sociological social psychology. Expectation states theory and its expansion to status characteristic theory are focused on a fundamental sociological problem: the explanation of the origin and maintenance of structured social inequality at the microlevel (power and prestige structures in small groups), at the societal level (social class, race, gender) and in formal organizations (bureaucratic rank). Other features that make the work sociological are the idea that behavior can be explained by expectations, the notion that people organize their behavior in pursuit of collectively defined goals, and the idea that expectations are relative to particular task situations and particular other persons. This last point distinguishes expectation states theory from some of the more psychologically oriented theories that also deal with the relationship between successful or unsuccessful task performance and feelings about the self, or with self-consistency. According to expectation states theory, the effect on behavior is similar for an individual who does poorly on a task on which everyone else does poorly and for an individual who does well on a task on which everyone else does well. Also, the types of intervention strategies suggested by expectation states theory are quite different from those suggested by more psychological theories that suppose that behavior is the result of invariant personality traits or predispositions. For example, if one assumes that gender differences are the result of early socialization, intervention in later life will be supposed to be of little effect, whereas if gender is seen as a diffuse status characteristic, the types of expectation training just described may be supposed to be quite useful in overcoming gender inequality.

Expectation states research differs from much sociological research, however, in its research and theory construction methodologies. One difference is the extensive use of experimental method. Researchers using experimental techniques to study social structure sometimes become defensive (see for example, Zelditch 1969) about the common perception among sociologists that "you can't generalize from laboratory studies; they are too artificial." Since the theory appears to work quite well at predicting the results of intervention in real-life situations, such as integrated classrooms, this criticism does not seem justified in application to this body of research. To look at this issue in another way: since the independent variable is perception of differences in ability or in external status, which may be manipulated by providing information to subjects, it is possible for an experimenter to use random assignment of individuals to conditions. This provides more information about causal processes than do research designs in which the effects of factors associated with the independent variable cannot be eliminated by randomization. Laboratory studies, of course, do not provide descriptive information about social structures; we learn nothing from the status characteristics experiments about what structural or demographic variables are associated with race or sex in the contemporary United States. I suspect that it is descriptive generalization that sociologists are looking for when they complain about inability to generalize from experiments, whereas it is causal generalization that experimental social psychologists mean when they make the same complaint about surveys.

Finally, a distinctive feature of the expectation states and status characteristics research is its emphasis on theory construction techniques. This means, for one thing, using the formal language of definitions, including hypothetical constructs, assumptions, and derivations, moving toward mathematical models where possible. It also means moving from simpler to more complex situations as the theory develops and results of empirical studies either confirm simpler hypotheses or force modifications. The establishment of explicit scope conditions, the initial assumptions about conditions under which the theory applies and may be tested, is part of the strategy. The scope assumptions themselves later become the focus of investigation, as, for example, in the extension from groups with homogeneous background characteristics to those with differences in external status. Another distinctive feature is the application of the theory to social intervention; the theorists and laboratory experimenters who work with expectation states do not consider applied research merely the work of engineers who are making use of scientific results, but rather an integral part of the development and testing of the scientific theory.

The use of formal theory, the development of a standard experimental setting, and the inclusion of applied research are all aspects of a "theoretical research program." (This concept is adapted from the works of the philosopher of science, Lakatos 1968, 1970. Berger, Conner, and Fisek 1974, chapter 1, and Cohen 1980, describe expectation states theory in terms of a theoretical research program, and point out the ways in which the various elements of the program support each other.) One result of this deliberate emphasis on theory and method is that although the concepts and assumptions have been modified as the work has developed, there has been a minimum of the sorts of problems that inhibit development in some areas of research: different researchers defining concepts in different ways, incompatible operationalizations of the same concept, tests of hypotheses that are supposedly derived from a theory but not recognized as such by other researchers, and so forth. The theoretical research program model warrants consideration by sociological social psychologists who are interested in the systematic development of theory and research.

NOTES

1. Most of the material in this section is based on lecture notes from Joseph Berger's graduate courses at Stanford University during the period 1961 to 1965.

2. The explicit use of scope assumptions is part of the "Stanford approach" to theory construction (Cohen 1980 describes this approach and its application to expectation states theory). The aim is to develop the theory under the simplest possible conditions, and then to expand it by relaxing some of the scope assumptions. By stating scope assumptions, the theorist does not mean that the theory does not apply at all under different conditions, but rather that additional assumptions will need to be made to describe the way the process works itself out under different conditions. The scope assumptions also provide an abstract statement of the conditions that will need to be built into a situation designed to test hypotheses derived from the theory, that is, the variables that must be held constant or controlled.

3. More precisely, the probabilities of action opportunities and of performance outputs are distributed as follows:

$$[+\ -] > [+\ +] = [-\ -] = [oo] > [-\ +]$$

4. The distinction between diffuse and specific traces to Parsons, as does much of the conception of interaction here. If I am hiring a research assistant, I would be said to value diffuseness if I will not hire someone I do not like as a whole person, whereas I would be said to value specificity if I will hire anyone who is good at programming a computer.

5. Since the subjects' feelings about themselves were not measured, it is possible that those who accepted the [− +] evaluation were engaging in some other mental process that maintained self-esteem in a more global sense. They were, however, behaving like persons with a low position in a power and prestige structure. It also may be that Contrast Sensitivity is not a central enough component of the self-concept to activate processes that maintain high self-esteem

Small Groups

Individuals, Groups, and Society

Small groups are the intermediate units between the individual and the larger society. This intermediate position defines their importance, but it also makes the study of groups a marginal science, with all that marginality implies. Although we have a clear idea of what individuals are and what societies are, we are less clear about a definition of groups. Several questions occur immediately: Are groups just the creation of people who want to study them? What do we mean by the reality of groups? Is there something peculiar to groups, different from other units? Is the study of groups just a border zone between sociology and psychology?

In the course of this chapter, we shall reach some answers to these questions. Throughout the discussion, the ambivalent position of the study of small groups will be evident. There are two rather different reasons for undertaking this study: one reason is the presence of small conglomerations of people, the existence of small groups, as a feature of the social environment; the other is that small groups are convenient places to study many social phenomena; they are laboratories of social life, literally so in the experimental work of social psychology. Thus, each group represents a reality of social life, in addition to exemplifying more abstract principles of group dynamics.

Vaguely, we know what we mean when we speak of groups, and this commonsense knowledge must suffice for the present. "Small" is defined as small enough for all members to interact simultaneously, to talk to each other or at least be known to each other. Another requirement is a minimum conviction of belonging to the group, a distinction between "us," the members of the group, and "them," the nonmembers. Experimenters have used simple statements, telling people that they belong in one group or another, in order to create considerable differences in cognition and behavior (Breakwell 1978). Similar effects are seen in actual situations, a fact that advertisers use with great effect ("We Tareyton smokers . . .").

While it is sometimes quite obvious what a small group is and who belongs to it, difficulties arise with the borderline conditions. For instance, not all members may be in contact with other members, as in face-to-face groups, although networks exist connecting them. Sometimes, also, a criterion of felt cohesion does not coincide with the actual interaction. These difficulties relate to the questions we have raised as to whether groups are real or artifacts.

The question of the reality of groups was heatedly discussed in the early years of group study. In part, this discussion was weakened by some extreme positions that were taken: on the one side, groups were regarded as super-individuals with their own minds ("group mind"); the other side saw group characteristics simply as components of the cumulative characteristics of group members; for instance, the aim of the group is simply the total of the aims of the individual members, and the group cannot be said to have a goal (Allport 1924; Cattell, Saunders, and Stice 1953; Horowitz and Perlmutter 1953; Warriner 1956). Both these extreme positions are easily discredited. A more reasonable contrast can be formed in terms of systems theory. The group certainly consists of individuals; the question persists whether the group has traits that cannot be traits of individuals. Thus, a group may have structure or norms, which cannot be said of the individuals composing the groups. For analysis, then, we cannot talk of individuals only, but we have to talk of a different level of organization. In fact, some biologists would claim that organisms are groups of quite independent cells (Thomas 1974).

The group concept may be necessary for analysis, but this excuse will not satisfy those who look for the palpable reality. A remarkable attempt to approach the question of the existence of groups was done by Donald Campbell (1958), who introduced the criterion of common fate, which can be taken as basic to the other definitions.

As a first step, let us define two particles, two units, as part of a bigger unit in the following way; if we know what happens to one particle, we can predict better what will happen to the other. This can be just as true in the description of a physical object as of a social unit. For instance, if we have a rigid physical object and we know the location of two of its particles, we know that if we move one, this determines to a great degree the movement and the final location of the other. Even if the relation is more flexible, such as between drops of water in a glass, this limiting condition still exists. We can define members of a social group in a similar way, for instance, by saying that if one member's opinion is changed, this will affect the opinions of the other members of the group, or if one member is excited, this will spread to other members of the group. This, of course, is just as true of different parts of the individual, for instance, of various organ systems, or of larger units of a society, of social classes, or of ethnic groups. But Campbell's definition gives a specific meaning to the reality of groups—the commonality of fate. He then adds other criteria that make them "small" according to our initial definition. These are: similarity, proximity, resistance to intrusion, or amount of internal diffusion and communication. All these features are indices of small groups. They may exist jointly, or, under different conditions, only some of them may be present. The unity of groups is just as "real" as the unity of any other object we may specify.

It is also fruitful to look at the small group as an extension of an individual in space or time. After all, the individual could not exist without the tradition of human culture as it has been developed, or without any other fellow human beings to keep him in the human condition. Many traits that make us human are only developed and take on meaning from association with others, and from their meaning beyond individual lives. Examples of this would be the capacity for language and for nonverbal communication, the agility necessary for tool use, which depends on cooperation, and the capacity of the young to learn the culture of their society. The young, especially, by being born unprotected and needing a social group for a long time, assure human continuity. A child learns that obtaining real satisfaction is possible only through the medium of another person, and thus the circle between perception of a need, such as hunger and its gratification, includes signaling and influencing another person who can supply nourishment. Freud constructed an early model of this interpersonal relationship as a basic part of the individual self (Pribram 1976).

In many other ways, the development of a complete human being is emotionally as well as instrumentally incomplete without direct interaction with others. Moreno's term, *social atom* (Moreno 1953), captures well the meaning which we are trying to express here. However, in distinction from physical atoms, each individual can belong to many different kinds of social atoms. Thus, groups can be studied according to their common features as types of social atoms. One can also classify groups into different types according to their function in the social world, and according to some characteristics, such as their existence in time and space, the relationship between the members and between groups, or by abstract characteristics. We shall follow both approaches to groups, showing the common traits of groups as well as constructing appropriate typologies.

Methods

The peculiarity of groups as agglomerates of individuals has made it necessary to devise specific and frequently novel techniques to combine data on several individuals, their interactions, and the characteristics that emerge as traits only from the combined action of individuals.

The development of methods for studying groups has been helped as well as hindered by the peculiar position of the group in human thought. As every individual, certainly every scientist, is part of a group, objectivity toward groups is hard to maintain. Typically, the motivation for studying groups has been to do something about them, and the methods proposed combine analysis and action. Only when work was further developed could analysis and action be separated. Sociometry, one of the earliest examples of a method designed for the study of groups, was invented by Moreno as an adjunct to psychiatry, using the organization of institutionalized groups as a therapeutic device (1953). Sociometry, as originally used by Moreno, consisted of asking individuals about their associative preferences in taking specific actions, such as playing football, making masks, or rooming with others in a dormitory. In later use, generalized questions—whom do you like—became acceptable. Moreno insisted on concreteness of questions, both in their specificity of content and in their use for organizing groups according to the results of the test. For him, the test was meaningless or even immoral if not used in this fashion. Today, however, the tests are being used abstractly, asking for general preferences as well as dislikes. Moreno (1948), in a polemic, directed attention to this issue. He accused Lippitt and White, who used the sociometric test to equalize groups in a study of leadership style, of destroying the method. The children were asked general questions but given specific tasks. How could one know whether they would like the same partner for making masks as for playing games? Moreno acknowledged grudgingly that the intended study *had* been completed, though according to him, uselessly. He contrasted this experiment with a study by Helen Jennings that carefully classified the children by interviews and observation, at school, at meals, at play, according to a variety of criteria; the results became so complex that apparently the data were never used.

If one views sociometric measures simply as a device to obtain abstract measures of connection between two people and of group structure, the data of sociometry can be treated by algebraic methods. Links can be transformed into variables, most simply as *1, 0,* measures for presence and absence of linking. Sums of linking can be used as a measure of popularity, the whole group structure can be represented in a matrix and manipulated according to the rules of matrix algebra. Matrices can then be divided into types that characterize structures. Network theory and graph theory have become special branches of mathematics with mathematical terms drawn from groups such as cliques or pseudocliques (Leinhardt 1977). Analysis of sociometric data can be combined with other measures for understanding group functions. An example of this would be the contiguity ratio by which one can determine whether people who are linked within a group are more similar in their attitudes, achievement, or cognition than people who are not (Winsborough 1963). Sociometry in this way has developed into a powerful analytic technique that is clearly adapted to the study of groups, as well as other structures.

We should recall, however, Moreno's original ideas as a necessary caution. The varieties of the content of the questions establishing links, and the overriding importance that Moreno gave them, cannot be done justice in research, but total neglect may lose much important information, though it may lead to elegant mathematics.

The conflict over the field of sociometry is just one example of the ambivalence of the fields of small group research; on the one hand, we are interested in groups as social phenomena, which implies naturalistic description, interest in their functioning, and even belief in their values. On the other hand, we look at groups as simplified social relationships, which implies that the groups ought to be described in a way that is generally applicable, eliminating the particular circumstances of the group studied, but using generalized, abstract language. This latter point of view shows itself in the development of network theory (Leinhardt 1977) from Moreno's therapeutic measure. Sociometry has become part of normal science, but has lost—for better or for worse—its messianic flavor. Nobody today would call a treatise on sociometry *Who Shall Survive?* as Moreno did.

Group Experiments

Group experiments are another offspring of social fervor and scientific method. At first, the two aims of the experiment were combined—understanding of group functions and the reconstruction of society through group dynamics were the joint aims. One of the earliest studies, the study of group atmosphere by Lewin, Lippitt, and White (1939) had both aims in mind: an understanding of how authoritarian, democratic, and laissez-faire leadership works (incidentally justifying democratic ideology), and the development of efficient democratic groups. This combination was called action research. In later years, group dynamics' two meanings separated, and some followers emphasized action, some research. The two branches have gone their separate ways, and today we distinguish between experimental social psychology and applied group dynamics. Here we shall discuss only the first aspect, returning to action and ideology at the conclusion of this survey.

The main aim of group experiments is to create groups in isolation and do it according to a theoretically relevant principle. Theory may require the scientist to distinguish different types of groups. Their composition may be different; the action of groups may be distinguished by experimental instruction, for example, members may be told that this is the first of many sessions or that it is a one-shot experience; or an event may be introduced in the course of the experiment, for example, one member —a confederate—may at a certain point act in an obnoxious way. An experiment may impose quite extreme conditions because the experiment is insulated from real consequences. In this sense, participation in an experiment can be looked upon as playing a game. The experiment is an activity that is free, separate, uncertain, governed by rules, unproductive, and make-believe; these are the characteristics that Roger Caillois (1961) has taken to be the definition of games, and such experiments have been called analyses of games (Back et al. 1964; Caillois 1961). The task of the experimenter is, therefore, to have people play a game in which certain generalizable relationships are exhibited. The experimental group does not need to resemble any group functioning in society. The extreme conditions may never be as clear-cut in actual life; what is wanted is the understanding of the effect of particular variables, not a simulation of social conditions. The action is a new creation, invented particularly for the purpose of study. For this reason, however, it represents the general attributes of groups, those aspects that all groups—regardless of their origins—have in common.

The condition of the experiment lies in the willingness of the subject to play the game, to accept the conditions, to follow the rules, and then to act in a way that makes it possible for the experimenter to translate the actions into universally valid statements about groups. The danger of group experimentation lies, paradoxically, not in the failure of the experimenter to define the conditions correctly and secure the cooperation of the subjects (if that fails, the research will simply be a failure and the researcher has to start afresh) but in the excessive success of the technique. Experimenters become overly skilled in conducting the experiments, which then do not lead to generalizations about groups, but only to further experiments on the model of the earlier one. The end result is a perfecting of the rules of a particular game or a skill in creating a special type of group.

As a reaction to this game-playing technique, some methodologists have claimed that the main value of group experimentation is not in the model of the game, but in the play. Subjects do not know the rules, but the aim of the experiment is for the experimenter to perform as stage manager and to show how people can be managed in different interactions, initial attitudes, and actions (Denzin 1970). From this point of view, the experimenter acts as a play director who does not reveal the plot to the actors. He or she only sets the scene in a manner that will ensure that the desired action will occur. This perspective on small groups corresponds best to the isolation of the group as an entity in itself. The immediate staging area, the drama itself, is dominant; the actors must conform to the plot, although there may be variations in the manner in which they perform. We may learn more about the actions of the group from the difficulties and necessary adjustments in staging a scene than from a measurement of outcomes in a routine experimental procedure.

However, social psychologists are not always happy to be told that they write scenarios; they want to show that they represent reality. They do not want to demonstrate which human actions could happen, but establish which actions do happen under what conditions and why. As a consequence of looking for more and more accuracy in explaining actual events, the social psychologist will add more and more variables to the research. These include personality traits as well as the social characteristics under which the experiment occurs. Thus, a host of practical problems is added that makes group experimentation, and even the study of groups, difficult. Explanation seems to become more difficult than designing a new society in which the variables will hold true; again we see the tension between social research and social engineering.

Field Study

Because of the strictures on pure experimental methods, some researchers have tried to look at groups in a naturalistic context without obvious stage management. Such observation could become formalized: for this purpose, one needs techniques to describe groups in action. Formal group observation techniques were developed by Bales (1950), Chapple (1949) for verbal exchanges, and by Birdwhistell (1970) for nonverbal interaction. Early hopes that these techniques would lead to a standardized description of groups have failed, as have so many hopes of cumulative knowledge of groups. But these methods have been used in many contexts and have been adapted for a variety of situations. They are analogous to nonaction techniques, codifying the relations between individuals and in this way measuring changing group structures. Like sociometry, the quality of the interaction is consistent to a varying degree; Chapple's system works only on length of statements, which makes it easy to use for practical application. Bales included more descriptive or expressive statements and questions and answers. Many similar techniques have been adapted from these basic designs.

Like any observation techniques, group processes observation faces methodological and ethical problems. How far can one observe morally vulnerable and reactive human beings without infringing on their rights to privacy and dignity? This consideration leads to special limitations on applying this technique from observation studies to a wide variety of groups. The naturalistic observation of juries, which would be an ideal, real-life, decision-making group, has been prohibited by law. On the other hand, groups might act differently if they knew they were being observed (Wilson 1969). For example, the members might represent themselves as more goal-oriented and rational. Still, in various implementations, group observations have been valuable in introducing reality to the study of groups.

Types of Groups

If we proceed from the general abstract measures to data that give the flavor of the group interaction, we gradually abandon the search for general principles applicable to all groups and work on categories. As the distinction is formulated in the study of living systems, distinctions appear between morphology and physiology on one side and taxonomy and ethology on the other. Up to this point we have considered only the common features in definition and method; it is now appropriate to discuss a taxonomy of groups.

A taxonomy of small groups is to a degree arbitrary. We cannot establish an evolutionary scheme or a definite, immediately perceiveable typology as in biological taxonomy. However, the history of theory in this field has shown some attempts to find a basic type of group and to derive all other groups from this base. We can use the insight of these thinkers to establish a classification of groups and, from this, to gain a more general appreciation of the varieties of group experience. Four different types that show significant contrasts are the family, the work group, the community, and the circle.

FAMILY

The family is one of the oldest and most persistent forms of human association. Among its most intriguing characteristics are its biological necessity, the permanent affiliation of its members, its history through the members' lives, and the strong bonds, positive and negative, that hold members together. Using our definition of groups, the main characteristic of the family is the extension of the individual through time. This characteristic links the individual with his ancestors and descendants, providing a continuity, and transmits the biological as well as social and cultural traits. The family has been a favorite metaphor for group formations and even for larger human associations. Thus, within organizations, we see some groups characterized as families or even as sibling or cousin relationships; and even in more abstract relations we find phrases like "job families," or colonies referred to as "daughters of the mother homeland."

The family is, therefore, an obvious choice for some investigators as a model for group interaction. The theorist who had the greatest influence from this point of view was Freud. In his entire clinical and individual psychological work, Freud stressed the importance of the family. He used the term "family romance" as the basic story that humans let play out over and over: the relationship to the mother and then to the father are the basic conditions of human socialization, as well as of its failures. It is not surprising that in his two books devoted most closely to social psychology, *Totem and Taboo* (1920) and *Mass Psychology and the Analysis of the Ego* (1921), he tried to develop all human associations from the model of the family, and even suggested that they developed historically from it.

In the first of these books, Freud tried to depict a history in which family conditions become the basis of all human social organizations. For this purpose he used the model of the primal horde that had been proposed by Lang (1905) shortly before Freud wrote *Totem and Taboo.* Lang proposed that the original organization of the proto-human primate consisted of one dominant male, his wives, and immature children. This arrangement persisted until the male became too weak to assert his dominance, at which time the sons, or one of the sons, was able to kill the father and assume his status. Freud considered this succession as the original, basic trauma of humanity. The sons got together to kill the father, then felt guilty, jointly ate the father at a totemic feast, and also tried to prevent the recurrence of the same event by establishing a taboo against eating the father or the animal that represents the father of the horde. This combination of guilt, identification, and prohibition, connected with power and succession, became a basic dynamic system of human association, especially the relationship to power.

In the research on groups, the family type represents a situation in which strong emotions, both positive and negative, can be expressed, and where relative positions are fixed over a long time, even when contact is interrupted for a long period. The terms for family relations—father, daughter, sibling—have intuitive meaning in regard to power and affect, which carries over into analogous situations. Therapy situations that are based generally on the family model are well described this way. Other associations can be seen in family terms if emotional or power relations are stressed. Other models may be more appropriate if other factors, such as group goals or group identification, become important.

Here we see the extent and limit of the model. In addition, it is relatively easy to find fault with Freud's model, which is based on questionable sources. One example is his acceptance of the now generally discredited concept of the primal horde. We shall do better, however, if we do not take his speculations too literally. Freud himself, in reply to criticism that his description in *Totem and Taboo* (1920) was on the level of Kipling's *Just So Stories,* replied that it required creativeness to make a good story. The use of such a reconstruction of the past is more a metaphorical device of transposing features that are fundamental to the present situation into a distant past than a literal interpretation of that past. Group leaders have found Freud's writings more useful as guides to the dynamics of current seminars and workshops than as descriptions of the ancient history of humanity (Bennis and Shepard 1956; Slater 1966). What we can find in Freud's work, and in general in those theories that take the family as a model of groups, is the emphasis on dominance relations and their connection with strong affect, particularly the ambivalence leaders and followers feel toward each other. Therefore, when positive and negative feelings are aroused, the succession struggle is the ritualistic way of handling emotions in groups.

WORK GROUPS

A contrast to the family, which persists mainly through time, would be the model of a group that functions through spatial contiguity. The paradigmatic example is the work group, in which individuals achieve an immediate aim through concerted action. A theory of groups based primarily on this situation is that proposed by George Homans in *The Human Group* (1950). In a way similar to that in which Freud uses Lang's primal horde as a model, Homans uses Roethlisberger and Dickson's study of a group of workers wiring transformers in a Western Electric plant (1946). The interaction of this group, especially its two-fold orientation toward getting the work done and toward semi-jocular, semi-aggressive personal relationships, is taken as a model of what happens in small, informal groups. The meaning here is interplay of sentiment, positive and negative, with the required work cooperation.

A main purpose in looking at groups following this model is to analyze the relationship between goal-oriented and emotional behavior, between action and sentiment. This model is hospitable to group observation techniques because it traces relatively short-term behavior in a bounded space. The formal structure of interaction analysis was developed early by Bales and designed with this model in mind. Analysis schemes divide interactions into "instrumental" and "expressive" and are therefore able to handle the problems symbolized by the bank wiring room.

The work-group model stands intermediate between social and individual interpretation of the small group. Theoretically it owes much to Parsons, especially in the distinction between instrumental and expressive variables; this distinction was incorporated into Bales's interaction process analysis scheme. But Homans explicitly acknowledges B.F. Skinner's influence and he tries to build up group actions from individual reinforcement schemes. The model thus lets group action emerge from compromises of individual rewards, but includes group contributions in their own right, especially the instrumental-expressive contrast.

The instrumental-expressive relationship can be visualized as a two-dimensional field, the axes being affective and instrumental rewards (Coleman 1960). Each position in this field has a corresponding force to maximize rewards of both kinds. One finds, as in a physical analogy, that the two conditions of equilibrium may occur. One will be in the weak area of personal sentiment, but this is unstable—if the group moves away from the equilibrium only slightly, it may well move farther away. The other is a point of high positive sentiment, and this is stable. This mathematical analysis corresponds to commonsense knowledge of groups: groups can function with a minimum of affect and interaction, but then they disintegrate easily as there is no particular reason to stay together; or they command strong positive affects with much instrumental interaction. If they can achieve this situation, difficult though it may be, the relation is likely to stay permanent and the work group will achieve a time dimension.

The characteristics of the work-group model follow from Homans's explanation of group memberships and interactions coming from the motivations of individual members. Group membership is seen as a means to an end, and thus the relationship of the group to its environment, including other competing groups, becomes important. Even within the group, cooperation is based on a compromise so that all members are satisfied to a certain degree; one could almost call cooperation the lesser evil because the possibility of conflict is squarely faced, but usually judged to have too high a cost. The relationships within the group will depend on which members have needs and which members have resources. These will determine the relative power positions, which may be equal or stratified. Finally, the group so described is likely to be a special-purpose group.

COMMUNITY

Both family and work theorists look at the group as a means of solving individual problems. Other theorists start from the opposite end, taking groups as primary, and model their theory on examples of groups whose identity is established prior to individual membership. The kind of association that leads to a common identity because of membership can best be called community. The theorist who based his work on this aspect of groups was Kurt Lewin (1951). His theoretical language was visual and geometrical, showing the group as a spatial and temporal field in which individuals can be placed. In introducing the concept of life space, he separated the personally effective part of the environment, alien factors that are in the environment but are subjectively irrelevant. The life space is not only a spatial extension of the person, but involves the psychological past and the psychological future as well. Using this same imagery, Lewin constructed what he called topological psychology, which translated the emotional interpersonal relationships into a geometrical picture, giving geometrical metaphors to the motives and to the means by which motives are realized, to conflict situations, and to overlapping group membership. Positions within a group, such as centrality or peripherality, can thus be given an exact meaning, and many terms of social psychology have derived their meaning from this kind of geometry.

An important consequence of this approach is that the individual is not necessarily the focus of the theory. One can look just as easily at larger conglomerations, such as settlements and households, as the units of discourse. Groups become definite units, subspaces of a larger society, and the individual is no more privileged as an obvious unit than groups or societies would be. Duration of existence, time perspective, are aspects of the group as well as of the individual. In addition to the spatial relationship, Lewin emphasized the dynamic aspect, the temporal dimension. The exact working out of the spatial and dynamic relationship could not, in Lewin's time, be expressed mathematically, but it showed the kind of mathematics that would be needed in social and behavioral analyses. One needs a geometry to express the spatial relations of individuals and groups as well as the dynamics that keep systems stable and provide changes. New development of systems theory and dynamic topology may make it possible to undertake a serious effort in this direction (Poston and Stewart 1978; Woodcock and Davis 1978). The nature of the conditions that bring and hold groups together are basic events, and descriptions of the relations become the basic work of group dynamics. One can then investigate the kinds of conditions that have come into being through those forces and the consequences those forces might have.

The spatial characteristics of the image that Lewin used become valuable in discussing what he called the state of the group at a certain time and place (1943). Minute attention to this situation was very influential in the development of group experiments, which are attempts to form groups and to direct them in a miniature time and place system. The theory is also relevant to those problems that communities face: attitude change, relationships between different kinds of subgroups and the larger groups, training and therapy situations, and loyalty and relationships to outgroup members.

The kind of group that emerges from this model is one that has meaning for the members and that is especially effective in producing or preventing attitude change in its members. The model thus examines the conditions under which members change and begin to exhibit attitudes and beliefs common to the group, or to act in a similar way. The concrete examples of this model are those groups created for the purpose of producing an attitude or a personality change: therapy groups, therapeutic communities, or the small groups assembled for controlled experiments. This is not surprising, for Lewin's interest was in investigating conditions that could produce attitude and habit changes. Two features that we have noted in the previous models, (1) the strong, emotional, cathectic relation among the members and (2) their individual motives, are given less importance in this model; the group by itself and the fact of membership in it are considered to be of overriding importance. This model has been applied especially to industrial, community, and training situations.

The characteristics of Lewin's model derive from factors that hold a group together at any particular moment. There is an attempt to play down conflict within the group, either by rational discourse or by subdividing the group. In this and some related models, purely personal relationships are said to be detrimental to the group (Bion 1959). Rosabeth Kanter (1972), for example, found in her study of nineteenth-century communitarian societies that those communes, such as the Shakers, that eliminated family life lasted longer than those that permitted strong family bonds; family ties took precedence over allegiance to the group and membership splintered away. In his futuristic novel, *Nineteen Eighty-Four,* British author George Orwell (1949) envisions a society in which the individual's bonds to the community are much stronger than his bonds to his family, a manipulation designed to prevent allegiance to any competing group.

The community is best visualized in space. Some communities, however, are not visible as spatial configurations but are nonetheless connected in other ways such as those we discussed in Campbell's "community of fate." In this case, duration of association through many vicissitudes is a persistent sign of community, as in ethnic or religious communities. Lewin recognized the importance of time and duration in groups, but he looked at time as a succession of structural conditions, in contrast to Freud who looked at specific events in the emotional history of the individual. The meaning of the group as an extension in time of the individual will differ accordingly and correspond to the differences in the family and community.

THE CIRCLE

Although family, work, and community may be the most distinctive examples of groups we find around us, they do not exhaust the varieties of existing groups. There is a residual of other groups that have members and whose variety helps to integrate society and assure its continuation. We may call these "circles" or "sociability groups" because one of their main origins seems to be voluntary social interaction among the members. The theorist who developed a general theory of groups from this point of view is Georg Simmel (1955). Simmel tried to look at purely sociable groups—or circles as he called them—in associations and unions of various kinds and find the structure of these groups, the conditions under which they could exist and continue.

In these circles, a variety of feeling tones may exist among members. The basis of the group formation is not necessarily strong attraction among the members, but a factor which brings them into contact, ranging from common beliefs or common interests to a habitual mode of conflict. Simmel could recognize the importance of conflict within and among groups that might eventually lead to regularized procedures and viable conventions. An interpreter of his, Louis Coser, tried to formalize Simmel's theory under the title of *The Functions of Social Conflict* (1956).

Simmel draws attention to the many groups in which people are only partially involved and which can easily be overlooked if you ask people about the important groups in their lives. What he calls "the web of group affiliation" (1955), however, is very important from the social point of view. Each group membership involves a little of the individual's loyalty and time. Collectively, all this makes possible the existence of larger societies, the interaction of large groups of people and the possibility of contact between people in large socieities that might otherwise be broken up into individual families, or groups and communities. Simmel's method, if it can be called such, was adapted to this particular program. It was the insightful observation of what went on around him, using language, social customs, and historical evidence to construct a morphology of groups and of human relationships which could not be captured in a snapshot or series of snapshots or the intentional research methods of the clinician and the experimentalist. The kinds of problems to which Simmel addressed himself were questions of rules of conduct, accommodations to the importance of certain situations that then became natural to the individual and to the society. These groups form the ground in which the other, more emotion-laden groups become the prominent figures.

We have tried to make the pattern of different groups concrete by attaching each type to a well-known group and also attaching it to a theorist who seems to look at this group as the basic idea of group formation. In fact, however, they represent different structural and dynamic constellations that are best exemplified in these theories. One can propose a pattern of these relationships that shows the different group types, the contrasts and similarities, and in this way can show the range of groups and the various problems associated with them.

The groups we have discussed fall into different pairs, according to the intensity of the involvement of membership. The family and the community involve the individual completely and at times demand complete loyalty. The work group and the sociability group in general form only part of a person's involvement, which in the latter case can be almost at will. One looks askance at the workaholic *and* the compulsive socializer for whom this kind of activity threatens to involve the whole person. Within those two pairs, however, the situation, and even more the theory, approaches the group from a different point of view. Theories of the family and of the work group look at the group as created from individual needs and desires. Psychoanalysis and behavior theory, the theories of Freud and Homans, are also basically theories that reduce the group to the individual level. Community and sociability groups deal with the problems of society and try to structure the society into smaller units, taking groups as units per se without having to justify them by descending to the smaller unit of the individual. Thus, we can classify those four types in two ways: by the amount of involvement they require and the point of view or the level of discourse on which they are conceived.

The Affective Dimension

The four models that we have shown as representative examples of actual groups and prototypes of theory can be organized as a classification of two different ways of looking at groups. We can talk of groups that involve the whole person (the family and community) and contrast them with special purpose groups (the work group and the circle). Another division distinguishes groups that give their members an extension in time and those that are based on purely spatial arrangements. On the other hand, a classification by the individual or social origins of the groups presents a different division, separating family and work groups from community and circles. This division turns out to be convenient in two respects: it represents a wide range of groups and ideas through theoretically important factors; it also defines important relationships in other aspects of the group life, such as the affective.

We can divide emotional interactions in two ways by their types, positive and negative, and by the direction of those feelings, namely, whether they are directed toward the ingroup or the outgroup. The family, we have already noticed, is basically a self-sufficient unit, at least in its ideal model. Therefore, all the emotions—and they are strong in this group—are directed inward toward the individuals of the family; this is true of positive as well as negative feelings. In fact, this ambivalence of feelings among members of the family is one of the cornerstones of Freudian theory. The intensity of reciprocal relationships leads to cliques and subgroups with the danger of fission. However, in the intense, emotional relationship within the family, which by its nature endures over a long time, a breakup for this reason is infrequent although violence within the family is a recurring problem. The dynamic problems of the family model are the management of emotions, frequently ambivalent within the group, and the integration of the family into the rest of society, where no obvious link exists. The diverse therapeutic models that analyze the family show the threat of emotional mismanagement. One of them would be Bateson et al.'s theory of the "double bind" in schizophrenia (1956); the intense ambivalence of relationship in which the child is both punished and gratified at the same time for the same reason can lead to disorganization of the person, that is, schizophrenia. R.D. Laing has driven the description of these situations to an extreme, and consequently made the family seem to be an extremely unhealthy environment (1964). To avoid such emotional mismanagement the family system will be organized in a way that the expression of different emotions among members does not lead to completely incompatible situations.

Philip Slater (1963) has dealt with the need of society to integrate the family. He sees three problems with which society must deal: social norms must draw the individual into a social group outside the family; the married couple must be brought to recognize the superior claims of social demands; and, finally, social norms have to integrate the nuclear family into a larger unit. Slater identifies three universal mechanisms which have been used to deal with these problems in every viable society to counteract complete self-absorption and the extreme strength of the ego. First, the process of socialization subordinates the ego to the needs of society. Second, the claims of the couple are subordinated to the social pattern of the institution of marriage which, in its rituals and processes, asserts the claim of society over any intense love and sexual relationship. And, finally, the breaking up of society into small nuclear families is prevented by the incest taboo which forces family members to seek outside relationships and thus links different families to the social order.

In contrast to the other models, the work group needs little positive affect for its functioning. Ideally, the interaction is determined by the requirements of the work itself and the motivation by individuals to enter this group. As we have seen, there are two equilibrium conditions in the work group. There are no necessary positive feelings of members toward each other; on the contrary, it is more likely that there may be competitive, negative feelings among them if not all can reach the goal for which they entered the group, for instance, if the rewards—pay or possibility for promotion—are limited to some of its members. On the other hand, within the larger framework of the organization there have to be positive links joining a specific work group to others so that the organization—the factory, corporation, or agency—may produce. Durkheim (1933) has called the kind of organization that depends on the complete division of labor an *organic* one. He stresses here also the harmonious interrelationship among the organs of society, but not necessarily the relationship of members within the same group.

The community as a type relies principally on positive affect. In fact, the concept of group cohesion, group membership, and identification were all developed within this framework. Community identification can be strong, but it is usually not strong enough to resist negative affect. The ambivalence of the family is absent here, and if ambivalence is found, the situation is usually put in family terms. Conflict will generally break up a community group, and lead to intergroup conflicts. Frequently, communities are kept together as much by positive sentiments within as by negative sentiments from outside.

The distinction between family and community in this way is striking. Whereas the family establishes its relationships through formal roles (parents, children, siblings) and looks for connections with other families, communities find their internal relations through affect and try to maintain their own distinct boundaries and identities. The sociometric method of group-structure analysis is dependent upon affective choice, and sometimes confuses familial and community criteria. Thus, the therapy-group (familial) orientation uses mutual choice as a measure of mental health and adjustment. Community orientation and even community-oriented therapy look at mutual choices as disruptive, that is, as possible sources of cleavages—cliques—within the group. An even spread of choices within the whole community makes mutual choice less likely as a measure of community integration.

Sociometric measures of group integration are usually constructed by comparing the choices individuals make outside of groups to those made inside of groups; in cohesive groups people will choose their friends from within the group. However, if group membership is all-important, then the choices should be made randomly within the group, and no particularly central configuration leading to fission will occur. Thus, a group will be more cohesive if it has fewer mutual choices; a measure adjusted for a deleterious effect of mutual choices has been shown to be more efficient (Festinger, Schachter, and Back 1950). Similarly, Bion (1959) has shown that, in his training group, pairing is an activity that is opposed to the general efficient group process, just as fighting—interpersonal aggression—is. Social critics have seen this point intuitively. Orwell's *Nineteen Eighty-Four* opposes individual love to group solidarity with Big Brother; similarly in Fourier's social units, pairing was distributed over all possible combinations of 1,600 men and women.

The final type of group—the circle—is predicated on the possibility of using groups to regularize conflict. Interpersonal interaction is used to mediate different interests, beliefs, or safe identifications. The conflict may be the basis of creating the groups themselves and adjusting relations to other groups. Here is a situation in which the affective relationships become secondary to some other principles, a belief, an ideal, or an interest. For a short time, the interest may become dominant and involve the whole person, producing strong affect. Thus a union may go on strike, a political club may leave the party, an athletic club might fight for a championship. Under these conditions, interest groups or sociability clubs may become all-involving and arouse positive or negative emotions. However, the persistence of these groups as the fabric of social life depends on low individual involvement. They provide either personal pleasure, as in purely social groups, or promote aims and interests that are only intermittently important to their members. The kind of groups that Simmel, who is mainly interested in structures, describes best are those that are compatible with low emotions or none at all. They are pervasive in the social fabric, and the sum of large numbers of weak links becomes extremely important in everyday life.

In summary, we may say that we have seen a variety of emotional relationships that can characterize groups. In the extreme cases, certain patterns of emotional relations fit more closely to the prototypes of different groups. Groups that contain all their feelings, both positive and negative, within their members fit more closely to the model of the family and are really what Freud was talking about in his theories. Groups that distinguish strongly between an in-group and an out-group, reserving their positive feelings for their own members and negative ones for outsiders, become the prototype of the community and are what Lewin largely expressed in his discussion. Groups that are held together through the necessity of common work, and whose members are negative, or at least indifferent toward each other, but fit easily into a larger organization, are the model of the work group, depending on individual reinforcement, and exemplify those characterized by Homans's discussion of the Western Electric plant groups. Finally, groups that form to promote the common interest and, frequently, to ameliorate conflict, are the kind of groups that Simmel discusses in his social geometry. However, a pure form of group is rarely a part of our actual experience. One might find some groups that resemble the typical family, particularly the work group, but in general it is better to look at these types as possible elements that can be combined in several proportions to construct actual groups. Or, conversely, we might look at several emotional configurations and see how similar they are to different types, or how easily they can be discussed within the framework of different theories.

Types of Group Structure

The classification of groups that we have considered up to now started with different groups found in nature and various scientists' work based on these groups. From this we were led to different types of dynamics within groups. We can also begin to classify groups according to abstract measures, which leads to typologies; we can see whether types derived theoretically lead to the identification of actual groups. This approach is especially valuable in discussing the structural aspects of groups.

In defining a set of possible boundaries, a system of conditions devised by Mary Douglas (1970, 1978) and Basil Bernstein (1971) has been useful in making a classification. This classification is based on individual action as well as on group behavior. The dimension of individuation is called *grid,* the strength of rules that govern group interaction by the position of the individual within the group. In high-grid conditions, the individual person is classified by ascribed features that leave little room for personal choice of behavior; in low-grid conditions, individual initiative is maximized, and expressed through such mechanisms as autonomy, control, and competition. "Group" is defined by the investment of time and energy of the individual members and agreement among the group members as to the boundaries of the group—who is "in" and who is "out." High-group conditions mean complete involvement in one group for all activities and definite rejection of all people outside its well-defined boundaries: low-group is a condition in which "a person finds himself the center of an environment of his own making which has no recognizable boundaries" (Douglas 1978). Both group and grid define possible social environments.

Grid conditions will be relevant to the boundaries around the person, but they are not simply analogous to the relations of the outer boundary to group dimensions. High-grid conditions imply the importance of self-presentation, as interaction is governed completely by the assignment to social position which depends on the social self. Low-grid conditions, however, do not imply an open self. Interaction becomes intensely competitive and private belief is increasingly valued as a resource, as any other possession might be.

We may suspect from the definition of group and grid that we will find these conditions are correlated. Societies and groups that distinguish themselves from the rest of the world also have many inner distinctions, and societies that do not classify individuals by in-groups and out-groups generally have fewer corresponding rules within. Frequently, we find stable permanent groups and societies where either group and grid are low or both are high. However, having boundaries, as well as transcending them, has its cost. There are always some pressures on and by the individual to vary the socially determined boundary system; within each type of society there may be a reaction that changes the type of organization structure. We can look at the high-high and low-low societies as statistical norms passing through inconsistent conditions, and see how changes occur in them both individually and collectively. Societies in which both group and grid are high are what are called tribal or traditional societies. Here everyone has a distinct position and the boundaries are well-kept. The tribe and the rest of the world are rigidly separated. Each status is clearly defined: transitions from one status to another are marked by specific changes and ceremonies; contacts between persons in different statuses are well regulated. There are definite joking, aggressive, or emotional relationships among statuses.

The low-low society corresponds to the modern, rational society. Here the society is open to other cultures and exchanges knowledge and traditions. Within the society, statuses are defined according to the functions a person can perform and do not impose any barriers irrelevant to the performance. Professionalism and the impersonality of modern society are the consequences of this low-group and low-grid condition. For instance, the provider of medical care is a person trained in a certain way, independent of sex, race, or family background. There is no special sacred knowledge or pattern factor peculiar to a particular status which must be preserved.

Like any pure concept, these extreme conditions are seldom completely realized. Impenetrable barriers, as well as complete openness, are not found in human society; persons as well as social units are by their nature open systems (Allport 1960); complete enclosure or complete openness puts too much strain on the individual. Deviations occur and reactions set in. We can find conditions where either grid or group is emphasized, as in transitions between tribal and modern society or as reactions to them. Two additional types can be distinguished. If the grid condition, the interpersonal relations alone, is emphasized, we find societies that are open to an outsider, but extremely careful and strict in the behavior of individual members toward each other. We may find a romantic revolutionary system that wants to create a new world for everybody; in this case, the behavior of the members toward each other becomes of extreme importance and is firmly controlled. Thus the social self—self-presentation—becomes crucially important and well defined. There is corresponding pressure on social rules to make self-presentation identical with the private self, that is, to open the private self to inspection. Authenticity, public self-analysis, and communal living become accepted life styles. At the other extreme are societies that overemphasize group conditions. These societies stress duty toward society, show suspicion of outsiders, use magic to protect their personal boundaries, and distrust having new ideas come in or having their own knowledge go out. These societies accept structure; the role of the individual is underemphasized. These two conditions—grid and group—will characterize deviant phenomena in the tribal as well as in the modern society (Back 1973). Thus, in our society, unease with the extreme situation-defined, low-group, low-grid pattern leads to reaction to all three other kinds of groups: the open avowal of tribal cultures, as in communes; the formation of distinct sects (Hare Krishna or Jonestown); and the culture of sensitivity, the encounter group.

Groups and the Individual

It is not surprising that the actual groups found in nature and taken as a model by theorists are not identical with a scheme that is based on boundaries of different strength and rules of interaction between the group members. These are some correspondences we may find. Families are similar to the high-group, high-grid conditions which would control structurally the intense emotions between their members; the low-group, low-grid conditions are represented approximately in loose interactions of the circle. It would not do to force these correspondences too closely, but the varieties expressed in the two schemas show the strength and weakness of the study of groups, namely, the all-pervasiveness of small groups in the relation of individuals and society as well as the radically different patterns in which we may observe common features.

Group membership has consequences for the person, and these consequences are what make groups in society so important. We can represent this aspect of group membership by the statement that "a group has power over its members." There is something distinctive in this power: it goes beyond the power one individual may have over another; the channel of influence of one person over another cannot account fully for the effect of various group members on each other. There is something in the group as an entity which in itself is a source of power (Cartwright and Zander 1968).

The group itself is the source of power above and beyond the power of the individuals composing it. In this sense, the group has an individuality, a separate meaning for its members. This meaning may be given by a name, "our family," "our community," but also by goals that membership in the group can mediate, say, prestige through being in a select circle, making congenial friends through being members of the community (Back 1951). We speak of this attraction to the group itself as "cohesion." The average strength of the motives enforces group cohesion, is an aspect of any group, and can be used to compare different groups. In fact, it is usually easier to measure this strength than to trace the various bases of cohesion and their different manifestations and consequences. Loyalty to a group may differ over space and time; family and community cohesion may last over a long time and is often reinstated when it is lost. But even weak cohesion, dependent on a short, common experience can be reinstated; alumni of one event, such as one blizzard, will arrange meetings after years.

Group cohesion is a characteristic of all groups, but because groups are so diverse, different measurements of cohesion may be necessary, depending on the institution. In groups such as circles or communities where a network can be established, the density of the network, how closely all members are connected with each other, can be determined; in clubs and organizations, members can be asked about this loyalty to the group, and if group discussions can be observed, the mention of "we" can be noted; other behavioral measures include time spent in the group, preferences for in-groups in giving awards, gain for members for staying in the group, or turnover of membership (Cartwright 1960). Like many fundamental concepts of social life, the individual measures of cohesion may not agree, although they tap the same concept and lead to similar consequences. The measures represent what Bruner (1956) has called "family resemblances"; as pairs they have something in common, but there is no one trait that can be called the unique measure of cohesion.

By being part of cohesive groups, a person accepts a willingness to cooperate as the price of staying a member. Thus, membership in a group leads to openness of influence by the group. A certain uniformity in behavior or attitudes results: this may be expressed quite formally—members of a group wear certain clothes or a certain badge or profess certain beliefs. Circles, especially, are founded on common beliefs. In determination of attitudes, communities are seen to be important; in fact, if we could determine the meaningful communities, our potential and market surveys could be more precise (Festinger 1950).

A series of experiments established some principles of the relation of group cohesion to influences and consequent conformity (Schachter 1951; Back 1951; Festinger and Thibaut 1951). A central principle is that the stronger the cohesion, the stronger the influences toward conformity in general. This rule is not uniform over all potential issues, but only on issues that are important to the existence of the group. A church group may allow differences on supporting baseball teams; a fan club may include people of different religions. In fact, the longer and more intensely a group exists, the more easily can important and unimportant issues be distinguished. A secure, established group can tolerate differences about peripheral issues that a new, insecure group cannot.

Even without formal rules, the group is still able to enforce conformity in informal ways. Conversation within the group will establish an unspoken base of understanding, a frame of reference, that is a source of strength for group members. For many attitudes, values, and beliefs that cannot be checked objectively, group members are dependent on the agreement of those who are members of those intimate groups. In fact, people may join groups to obtain this reinforcement. When this core of belief is established, an effort will be made to have all members of a group accept these standards. Efforts will be made to convince those who disagree, but if these fail, deviates will be excluded from group membership (Schachter 1951; Festinger, Schachter, and Back 1950).

The principle of internal power, particularly the relation of conformity to cohesion, the segmentation of issues according to centrality for the group, the increasing efforts to convince deviates, and the ultimate rejection of deviates are all generally applicable to groups. These hypotheses are derived from work on experimental groups and also some special situations, such as student living projects, which are thought to reflect common principles of all groups (Festinger, Schachter, and Back 1950; Festinger 1950). Widely different groups that exist in society apparently obey these same laws but present special constellations. Thus, the groups that are part of a person's life identity will ensure conformity to basic values during a vulnerable condition of the individual, typically in childhood in the socialization process. The family becomes the strongest group, one that can accept deviations from many standards, secure in the ultimate adherence of the individual. Consequently, if a split occurs, such as the disowning of a child, it is most severe and traumatic. A similar situation occurs in the community; since communities are defined primarily by contrast to other groups and by their strong boundaries, the principal opinions for which conformity is required are those that assert the identity of the group.

In contrast to these all-involving types, work groups and circles are less secure about core values. Work groups, and groups similar to them, have as their core the basic task of the group, and the core values will be centered around this instrumental issue. This kind of effect has been shown in the role of the leader, who, paradoxically, has similar characteristics to the deviate. In order to lead, the leader must be different from the group in certain respects. Hollander (1958) has illuminated this problem with his concept of idiosyncrasy credit. He has shown that by having been helpful to the group in achieving their goal, certain group members obtain the right to violate some of the rules and assume the leadership. Members who violate the same rules without previous achievements are rejected. Thus, some behavior that makes a member without previous achievements a deviate makes another a leader in the group.

The same ambiguity of conformity and leadership is shown in the structurally weakest group, the circle. This group is held together by a common belief or a common aim, but frequently this core has appeared as a result of some previous conflict. This group will also try to enforce conformity to its ostensive aim, but be insecure in its structure and easily susceptible to change. A theoretical model (Schindler 1957–58) developed for therapy groups captures this aspect quite graphically. The group members are classified according to status within the group from alpha, the leader (usually the therapist), to beta, leaders within the group, to gamma, the mass of group members, down to omega. This last, who fills the role of deviate or scapegoat, represents the suppressed values of the group. With slight upsets, such as failure of leadership or an unanticipated event, the values that omega represents can become dominant and omega become the leader.

Consideration of the effect of the group on individuals, including conformity, deviance, and leadership, has shown the barriers to general laws of group formation; the relation of the individual to the group depends not only on the formal condition of group action, but in the nature of the group, on the meaning of the group in the larger society. Better understanding of groups will come from understanding the relation of groups to their role toward individual development and social structure. Putting order into the seemingly endless variety of groups is an important contribution of a sociology of small groups.

Groups as Symbols of Value

A discussion of small groups and their place in society would be incomplete without considering the symbolic importance of groups in society. Sociological theory has described the development of modern society in terms of rationalization, of establishing purposeful relationships between individuals, on the one hand, and amorphous mass society, on the other. The small group becomes the nostalgic symbol of lost support in the frustrations of modern society. The mythology of modern economic society started with Robinson Crusoe, the self-sufficient individual who could build up a viable existence by himself. This ideal of making the individual the economic and social unit dispenses with groups, and, in fact, Robinson is not even able to sustain a dyad (Watt 1951). Social development since Defoe has not quite led us to this extreme, but it has led to a weakening of small group ties and to a stress on the hardy, self-sufficient individual in a normative society. Correspondingly, nostalgia for the never-never land of the lost, pre-industrial society has mounted (Williams 1973; Laslett 1965).

For sociologists, research interest in small groups has been the answer to this supposed trend, showing the enduring importance of groups even in our society, for example, the importance of the family in socialization or work groups in setting output (Katz and Lazarsfeld 1955). But an even more significant reaction has the stresses on the value of the group as such. A group movement has created groups as short-term experiences in special centers. Furthermore, there have developed organizations of groups in many areas of life such as group living, sects, or group meetings. These groups for group's sake have, for better or worse, become a part of the current scene. As a side effect, they give new insights into the group experience.

Groups today are not only social phenomena that are worthy of attention to the social psychologist and sociologist, but endowed as they are with value and symbols become important as major social objects and goals. We must therefore look at groups as social objects, endowed with intrinsic value in today's society. The group as a social object has become an important sociological question.

We have discussed the variety of group settings that limit conclusions concerning conditions that pertain in any group. The general rules of group behavior, which were stated in the 1930s and 1940s, included the synthesis of the group and the individual, the effectiveness of the group in achieving its aims, and the place of the group in transmitting the norms of society (Zander 1979). In addition, positive effects of group membership were noted, especially the comfort of protection by the group, as in the family model, and assertion of identity, as in the community model.

Because of these positive effects and helpful mechanisms inherent in groups, the period witnessed the creation of settings in which groups could be used consciously to effect designated changes in their members or to lead them to accepted goals. In the conduct of these group laboratories a curious phenomenon was observed. Discussions of the events in the group—so-called feedback—and especially reliving of the emotional undertones, turned out to be an intense emotional experience for the participants. Soon the experience was sought for its own sake, not simply as a means to an end.

The combination of new knowledge of existing groups and the striking effects of group membership have turned attention to groups as part of society. Thus, out of the social-psychological discussions of groups by men such as McGregor (1960), Sherif (1936), and Lewin (1948) has come a brand of group dynamics which, in its extremes, looks toward the reorganization of society in terms of groups. This objective has led to group activities, which can be called a group movement, that culminated in the decade 1965–75. During this time a number of centers opened that catered to the desire for group experiences that lasted from a day to several weeks. These recreational centers, the most famous of which was Esalen in Big Sur, California, were supplanted by other centers in which group activities were fused with other aims. These could be managerial efficiency, education for helping professions, and therapy. But the main feature was the symbol of the group itself; if traditional culmination of effectiveness showed minimal results, then the indubitable experience of membership was significant enough for recruitment of new members and a repetition of group process.

The group as a symbol of a particular event in a particular time cannot be the same as the generalized group that we have seen in its various manifestations. Groups in this sense are mainly modeled on the family and community, that is, groups that try to take exclusive possession of the person (Coser 1974); in fact, the theorists most mentioned as precursors are Freud and Lewin. The pragmatic goal orientation of the work group and the eclecticism of the circle are less attracted to the group movement. In fact, one of the aims of their movement is to imbue work and interest groups with the personal and group dynamics of the other models. The techniques developed by the group movement are mechanisms to give group membership an overwhelming influence, be it only for a short time: isolation, physical attraction, emotional self-revelatory scenes (feedback), emotionally and physically exhausting exercises, and a special language of groupness (which has now been parodied to death).

The effort of the group to inject intense relationships into the everyday life of modern society reminds one of the reactions to the low-group, low-grid model that we have discussed previously. This reaction may well be the social setting which, added to the discoveries of group processes, made the group such a powerful symbol for a while. Kenneth Benne, an early philosopher of the group movement, showed in an article, "Men and Moloch" (1964), how four popular novels described the helplessness of the individual against large organizations—*The Castle, A New Life, One Flew Over the Cuckoo's Nest,* and *Catch-22*—with always a hint of more human, smaller group substitutes for the perversion of aims in these "Moloch" organizations. The group movement then became powerful in industrial, educational, therapeutic, and military organizations.

The group movement has shown, at its best, the possibilities of the group as a tool for solving individual problems. Like any tool, it is no quick fix, and has its dangers as well as its benefits in application. The publicized group settings ended in fraud in the case of Synanon, and terror or worse in Jonestown. Colleges that concentrated on group experiences neglected to teach even basic skills (Grant and Riesman 1978), and instances of varieties of these group experiences multiplied. However, the group as a symbol of a certain orientation has remained. The small group has become not only a focus of social-psychological study, but a social fact of our time.

PART IV

Society and Social Behavior

12 RICHARD J. HILL

Attitudes and Behavior

Introduction

A long history of debate surrounds the proposition that attitudes are related to behavior. Our literature contains periodic assessments of that postulate (for example Allport 1935; McGuire 1966; Wicker 1969; Liska 1975; Schuman and Johnson 1976; Ajzen and Fishbein 1977; Eagly and Himmelfarb 1978), and these appraisals have arrived at widely divergent conclusions. In 1935, Allport accorded the concept of attitude a lofty perch in the hierarchy of social-psychological ideas: attitude is ". . . the most distinctive and indispensable concept in contemporary American social psychology" (1935:798).

At the time of the Allport review there were already established giants in the area. Thurstone (1929) had set forth certain basic principles of psychophysical measurement that he extended to the attitudinal domain. The Thurstone and Chave (1929) monograph advanced simplified and easily applied measurement strategies. Bogardus (1925) had begun his inquiry into ethnic and racial attitudes.

This period also provided a forecast of the ensuing disagreement and debate. In 1934, LaPiere published his now classic field research dealing with the receptions given to a Chinese couple by hotel managers and restaurant proprietors. No single piece of research in the area has attracted more attention or created more furor. LaPiere failed to find a relationship between written replies to his inquiries regarding accommodations for Chinese and the treatment received by his Chinese companions when they actually presented themselves and required services. That troublesome finding now has a history of persistent attention. For example, three decades later, Linn (1965) attacked the work on methodological grounds. Deutscher (1969) made the work a crucial element in his critical review of social-psychological validity, and Wicker (1969) gave the work a central place in his assessment of the pertinent literature. In a recent Nebraska Symposium paper, Kelman (1978b) provided a conceptual reanalysis of LaPiere's procedures and results.[1]

If we take the work of Thomas and Znaniecki, Thurstone, Bogardus,

LaPiere, and Likert as the beginning of serious social-psychological concern with the attitude-behavior relationship, we encounter more than findings that are inconsistent. We find conceptual confusion and a lack of methodological consensus. An attitude is "the disposition to behave in particular ways toward specific objects" (Gergen 1974:620). An attitude is "the degree of positive or negative affect associated with some psychological object" (Edwards 1957:2). An attitude is "the predisposition . . . to evaluate some symbol or object" (Katz 1960:168). An attitude is "a delimited totality of behavior with respect to something" (Guttman 1950:51). The list, of course, could be extended, and the obvious confusion would be increased by such an exercise.

That conceptual disagreement has characterized our inquiry was argued convincingly by DeFleur and Westie in 1963. In the seventeen years that have followed that analysis, only questionable progress has been made to clarify the conceptual confusion and reach conceptual consensus. Much of the most recent literature ignores the issue of definition, and the implicit assumption seems to be either that we agree on the matter or that somehow the lack of conceptual consensus is not a serious issue. To even raise the issue may seem to some to be obstructionistic. Nevertheless, it simply is the case that there continue to be unresolved conceptual issues.

If, like Gergen, we conceptualize an attitude as a "disposition to behave in particular ways toward specific objects," then we would not be led to make distinctions between attitudes, beliefs, and behavioral intentions (Fishbein and Ajzen 1975), for beliefs and intentions as well as attitudes are dispositional concepts (see Rosenberg 1979b). If, like Guttman, we actually are convinced that an attitude is a "delimited totality of behavior with respect to something," then the question of the relationship of attitude and behavior toward an object would become tautological. The definitional problem involves not only a lack of agreement as to referent (for example, disposition, affect, behavior, and so forth) but also disagreement regarding the concept's scope. Some have defined the concept so broadly that attitudes include the complete range of dispositional variables (for example, Gergen 1974), whereas others have more narrowly delimited the concept so that it refers only to affective or evaluative orientations (Edwards 1957). The confusion remains despite critical analysis like that forwarded by DeFleur and Westie (1963), and pleas such as Wicker's that ". . . it is essential that researchers specify their conceptions of attitudes" (1969:75).[2]

The substantive debate and the lack of conceptual consensus has been accompanied by methodological disagreement. Measurement practice is illustrative. On the one hand, increasingly sophisticated measurement models have been advanced by Thurstone (1929), Likert (1932), Guttman (1950), Edwards (1957), and Osgood et al. (1957). On the other hand, there remains little or no consensus on which, if any, of these techniques is most appropriate for use when a substantive issue is of central concern. Of course, if the various measurement strategies resulted in identical findings, our concern with this issue would disappear. The problem is that the little evidence available suggests that the correlations we observe are in part a function of the measurement strategy we employ (for example, see Tittle and Hill 1967a; Alwin 1973).

The issues surrounding the selection of some "best" measurement strategy are made increasingly complex by the continued lack of conceptual consensus. Most operational approaches to the measurement of an individual's attitude result in the location of that individual at some point on a continuum. Researchers in the tradition of Hovland and Sherif argue that such measurement strategies are conceptually naive and lead to inaccurate and misleading research results. Obviously, if attitudes necessarily involve varying latitudes of rejection as well as differing latitudes of acceptance, point estimates of attitudinal position are inadequate (see, for example, C. W. Sherif, M. Sherif, and Nebergall 1965).

At various points in the saga, critical scholars have reached conclusions which, if heeded, might have terminated the search for empirical links between attitudes and behaviors. In 1955, Blumer stated without qualification that no empirical connection between attitudes and subsequent acts had been demonstrated. In 1965, Sherif, Sherif, and Nebergall characterized the study of attitudes as being plagued by "theoretical stagnation and confusion" (1965:94). McGuire's 1966 review included the conclusion that, "Attitude research has long indicated that the person's verbal report of his attitude has a rather low correlation with his actual behavior toward the object of the attitude" (1966:156). In 1968, a panel at the Pacific Sociological Association meetings focused on the question, "Is 'attitude' an obsolete concept for sociology?" Panelist DeFleur argued that "while attitude may not be entirely obsolete for sociologists, it may very well become largely irrelevant" (1968:2); panelist Turner stated: "The concept of attitude is now obsolescent, except in a delimited sense that applies to certain kinds of situations" (1968:1). The views of these sociologists were supported by the carefully documented and frequently cited review by the psychologist Wicker. Basing his conclusion on a consideration of the most important contributions to the area, Wicker wrote, "The present review provides little evidence to support the postulated existence of stable, underlying attitudes within the individual which influence both his verbal expressions and his actions" (1969:75).

Given such a negative prognosis, confirmed by both sociologists and psychologists, one might expect rational scholars to turn to other matters. Even a cursory examination of the literature that has accumulated in the decade following these discouraging pronouncements will convince the reviewer that these evaluative assessments were not accurate predictors of the behavior of social psychologists. Work on the problem has increased. Some significant progress has been made in several areas, and some shifts in emphasis have occurred. Eagly and Himmelfarb are convinced that "interest in the attitudes area is increasing once again" (1978:517). Schuman and Johnson conclude:

> Our review has shown that most A-B studies yield positive results. The correlations that do occur are large enough to indicate that important causal forces are involved, whatever one's model of the underlying causal process may be. [1976:199]

Kelman proclaims: "Attitudes are alive and well and gainfully employed in the sphere of action" (1974).

Despite the confusion, pessimism, and negative evidence of the 1960s, some social psychologists refused to give up their commitment to the belief that attitudes and behaviors must be related. Research in the area did increase in the 1970s, new models emerged, new conceptualizations of the problem have appeared. Once again the pronouncement of Thomas and Thomas (1928) is verified. As a minor corollary of the 1928 law, we have clear evidence that if social psychologists define a relationship as real, it will direct their research.

Attempts to Assess the Attitude-Behavior Relationship

Although there have been a variety of attempts to provide general assessments of the evidence pertaining to the relationship between attitudes and behavior, a convenient point at which to begin an assessment of the assessments is the Wicker (1969) review. Wicker examined thirty-three research publications, several of which reported multiple attempts to measure this relationship. His conclusion was:

> Taken as a whole, these studies suggest that it is considerably more likely that attitudes will be unrelated or only slightly related to overt behaviors than that attitudes will be closely related to actions. Product-moment correlation coefficients relating the two kinds of responses are rarely above .30 and often are near zero. Only rarely can as much as ten percent of the variance in overt behavioral measures be accounted for by attitudinal data. [Wicker 1969:65]

The sample of studies analyzed by Wicker was not exhaustive, but it had several characteristics that increase one's confidence in the work. The attitudes and related behaviors were measured on separate occasions, and the behavioral measures were not retrospective self-reports.

Benninghaus (1976) repeated and expanded Wicker's analysis. While there is a slight tendency for more recent studies to report somewhat higher associations, the distributions of relationships reported by Benninghaus are essentially similar to those found by Wicker (see table 12.1).

Ajzen and Fishbein (1977) have conducted a similar analysis. While their classification of the magnitudes of association differ from those used by Benninghaus, the distribution they report is similar to those found in the Wicker and Benninghaus reviews. Of the 142 attitude-behavior relationships analyzed by Ajzen and Fishbein, 32.4 percent were not significant, 40.1 percent were "low or inconsistent," and 27.5 percent were "high."[3]

Interpretations of such results are not without disagreement. Wicker's negative conclusions have been cited above. The shift from the pessimism of the 1960s to the more optimistic view of the 1970s that we have described in the introduction is well illustrated by the more recent interpretations of Schuman and Johnson:

> The correct descriptive summary of the past literature, therefore, is that in most cases investigated, attitudes and behaviors are related to an extent that ranges

TABLE 12.1
*Measures of Association between Attitudes and Behavior**

Association	Wicker's Original Sample		Benninghaus's Additional Studies		Total	
	N	%	N	%	N	%
Inverse	3	7	4	7	7	7
No Relationship	17	38	10	18	27	26
Small Positive Relationship (Association below .30)	11	24	23	40	34	33
Positive Relationship (Association between .31 and .50)	9	20	12	21	21	21
Positive Relationship (Association above .50)	5	11	8	14	13	13
Total	45	100	57	100	102	100

*Adapted from Benninghaus (1976) Tables 4.53 and 4.54, pp. 263–64.

from small to moderate in degree. . . . For now, to keep in perspective the small to moderate correlations generally reported in past A-B investigations, let us note that no more than moderate sized correlations are found for the relationship between father's occupational status and son's occupational status in America (Blau and Duncan 1967), for the association between academic aptitude scores and college grades (Cronbach 1970), and for most other nonartifactual associations of interest to social scientists. [Schuman and Johnson 1976:168]

For Schuman and Johnson, then, a judgment informed by the evidence must conclude that attitudes and behaviors are related under a variety of conditions and over a range of substantive areas. There is something to this relationship that is sufficient to suggest the operation of causal forces.

Such different interpretations suggest that a collection of data like that illustrated by table 12.1 is somewhat more similar to a projective test than it is to a summary of scientific evidence. The summarized evidence seems to suggest that relationships of about 0.30 between measures of attitudes and behaviors are not uncommon, and after all, this is about as good—or as bad—as we frequently observe when we examine relationships between social variables.

It should be noted that the variables being related in the studies included in such summaries have been measured in a variety of ways and over a wide spectrum of contexts. They include measures of attitudes that range from a single item on a survey, to personal letters, to multi-item scales. The variety of behavioral measures include field observations, task performances, archival records, and the self-reports of daily activities. Again, interpretations vary. A skeptical critic might argue that such attempts to synthesize actually have no sound basis for any conclusion because of the great variation in the methodologies and substantive concerns of the studies included. The hopeful optimist might argue that the distribution, given its mode of about 0.30, demonstrates that in most instances some relationship is found regardless of the specific measurement techniques employed or the substantive area involved.[4]

In the remainder of this discussion, I shall make the assumptions of the optimist. It is assumed that attitudes, narrowly defined as *evaluations of objects,* are related to behavior. This assumption serves to focus attention on two immediate questions. First, what accounts for the modest level of the associations that have been reported? Second, what accounts for the variability in these associations?

The Modest Relationship

When modest relations between variables are found repeatedly, social scientists frequently recite a litany of reasons that might explain the results. The measures of the variables are unreliable. The measures are inappropriate or invalid. The independent variable is only one of several determinants of the dependent variable. If time elapses between the measurement of the independent and dependent variable, other variables intervene to mask the relationship or alter the variables under investigation. In one way or another, social psychologists have involved all of the above explanations for their findings regarding the relationship between attitude measures and behavioral criteria.

It is not the intent of this discussion to exhaust the methodological issues involved, but it is appropriate to identify some problems that remain unresolved. Alwin's (1973) analysis demonstrates the possibility of significant attenuation in the observed relationship due to the unreliability of measurement. The model offered by Alwin is of particular interest because it is directed simultaneously at the consequences of measurement unreliability and actual change in attitude over time. The influence of temporal instability in attitude clearly can have important consequences for the observed association of that attitude and behavior (for example, see Schwartz 1978).

The predictive efficiency of various measurement strategies has been examined by several researchers (for example, Kothandapani 1971; Ostrom 1969; Tittle and Hill 1967a). The available evidence does not lead to any firm conclusion about the relative superiority of the techniques examined. If we are concerned about increasing the reliability of our measures, then the psychometric law regarding the length of a test and its reliability ought to be used to justify the construction of multi-item measures of attitude, and the practice of many survey researchers of using single-item measures ought to be questioned. Unfortunately, even this advice cannot be given without qualification. Pressor and Schuman (1976) have raised questions about the use of multiple-item Likert techniques with samples drawn from the general population. Apparently, education is inversely related to susceptibility to acquiescence in the survey situation.

Although most of the concern with measurement has been focused on the reliability and validity of attitude assessment, the measurement of behavioral criteria also is subject to error. The use of self-reports of behavior has been widely criticized by students of deviant behavior. Even in areas where no confession of deviant action is requested, the conformity of self-reports and actual behavior is imperfect. For example, with respect to the relatively innocuous act of voting in a student election, Tittle and Hill (1967b) found that 15.6 percent of those who claimed to have voted actually had not done so. Retrospective self-reports also seem to be affected by intervening events. For example, following the assassination of President John F. Kennedy, 65 percent of an N.O.R.C. national sample claimed to have voted for him in the 1960 election. This is compared to Kennedy's actual plurality of slightly over 50 percent (Sheatsley and Feldman 1965). Similar differences between actual voting behavior and retrospective reports are also suggested in a survey of Dallas residents. When interviewed following the assassination, 57 percent of those sampled claimed Kennedy was their preference in the 1960 election, whereas in the actual election the Kennedy-Johnson ticket received about 38 percent of the Dallas county vote (Bonjean, Hill, and Martin 1965). Thus, in these three instances, differences of at least 15 percent have been found between self-reports of behavior and other indications of actual behavior. Tucker's recent study (1978) of such mundane behavior as buying soft drinks and detergents casts additional doubt on the validity of the self-report of behavior.

Additional problems associated with the measurement of behavior in the survey situation are suggested in a paper by Crane et al. (1979). These researchers attempted to predict television viewing using a single-act criterion measure of behavior. A single-item, general attitudinal measure was more highly related to the behavior at time two than was the same behavior at time one:

> The weak relationship between the behavioral measures at times one and two calls into question the stability of the behavior we are trying to predict. If we consider the two behavioral measures in terms of test-retest reliability, their correlation ($r = .07$) suggests that we have a very fallible criterion. . . . This suggests that our modest capacity to predict behavior from attitude variables is largely attributable to the temporal instability (unreliability) of the criterion behavior. [Crane et al. 1979:11]

Such failure to find impressive correlations between behavioral measures taken on separate occasions is a general problem. For example, in his research in the area of personality, Epstein (1979) argues that most single items of behavior have a high component of measurement error and that normally it is not possible to predict single instances of behavior (see also Bem and Allen 1974).

There are, then, a set of methodological issues and measurement problems that face researchers in this area. Most of the pertinent work that has been done in this area has been conducted within the framework of the theory of tests and measurements. Much of this work, although carefully pursued, suffers from a failure to analyze the basic concepts involved. As an illustration of the type of methodological analysis required, I will examine the 1977 review of Ajzen and Fishbein. In this review, conceptual analysis led to refined measurement recommendations that, in turn, made possible the suggestive reanalysis of previous research findings.

The general model offered by Fishbein and Ajzen will be discussed at a later point in this review. Within this framework, an attitude is a bipolar evaluative judgment about some object. The concept refers to subjective judgments, likes and dislikes, about the range of objects in an individual's world. For the purpose of the present discussion, it is important to note that the object of an attitude can be a behavior. People have attitudes toward dancing as well as toward dancers and dancehalls.

Assume that the researcher is concerned with predicting political action in connection with a political campaign. General attitudes toward the incumbent are obtained, and the interest is in predicting a range of behaviors, such as making a contribution, canvassing a neighborhood, and placing one's name on a newspaper advertisement endorsing the incumbent. The expectation is that the more favorable one's general attitude toward the incumbent, the more likely it is that the person will engage in a supportive action. Assume that the researcher selects canvassing as the behavior to be predicted. The reality may be that some who hold favorable attitudes toward the incumbent will detest canvassing. In such a situation, the general attitude measure would demonstrate little predictive power.

Fishbein and Ajzen have distinguished between attitude toward a target (the incumbent) and attitude toward an action (canvassing). The argument is that a favorable attitude toward a target may be predictive of a set of supportive behaviors taken as a class, without being predictive of a specific behavior that is a member of the class.[5]

Such considerations have led Fishbein and Ajzen to introduce the notions of attitudinal and behavioral entities. Each entity consists of four distinct elements: "the *action*, the *target* at which the action is directed, the *context* in which the action is performed, and the *time* at which it is performed" (Fishbein 1978:384).[6]

A measure of one's general attitude toward the incumbent specifies only the target element. If the behavioral criterion to be predicted is canvassing (action) for the incumbent (target) in a central city area (context) between 10:00 A.M. and noon on Saturday, the first of November (time), a failure to find an association between the general attitude measure and the very specific behavioral criterion would hardly be surprising. What is surprising, at least in retrospect, is that so many of the studies cited in discussions of the attitude-behavior relationship are based on the use of attitudinal entities that are not fully specified in the effort to predict a much more fully specified behavioral criterion.

If attitude toward a target is to be used as a predictor, then the behavioral index should be based on observations of a range of actions. If a single act is to be predicted, then attitudinal entities specifying action, target, context, and time should be employed if the attitude-behavior relationship is to be adequately examined.

This line of argument led Ajzen and Fishbein (1977) to a reanalysis of the literature on the attitude-behavior relationship. Only the target and action elements of the attitudinal and behavioral entities were considered. The expectation was that the observed relationship between attitude and behavior would be high when there was a high degree of correspondence between the attitude measure and the behavioral criterion. High correspondence was considered to be present under two conditions:

> . . . attitudes toward targets will predict multiple-act criteria, provided that the attitudinal and behavioral entities involve the same target elements. Similarly, attitudes toward actions are expected to predict single-act criteria if the target and action elements of the attitudinal entity are identical to those of the behavioral entity. [Fishbein 1978:387]

The analysis was based on an examination of 143 reported relationships between attitudes and behaviors.[7] The results are impressive even though Ajzen and Fishbein recognize that some of their classifications could be challenged. Of the 45 relations characterized by high correspondence, all achieve statistical significance and 78 percent exceed the magnitude of 0.40. If instances of questionable measurement methodology are eliminated from this subset of 45, then 26 relations remain and all are above 0.40. Equally impressive is the finding with respect to relationships characterized by no correspondence: 26 of these 27 relationships failed to reach statistical significance. When the target and action elements defined by the behavioral criterion are the same as those that have been incorporated in the measure of attitude, a relationship between attitude and behavior was found consistently in those studies reviewed by Ajzen and Fishbein.

These findings regarding the importance of element correspondence further our understanding of earlier results regarding the effects of levels of specificity. A widely accepted generalization is that the relationship between attitudes and behaviors is enhanced if the attitude measurements and behavioral criteria are at an equivalent level of specificity. For example, Liska (1974) provided evidence that a multiple-act criterion was predicted better by an equally general measure of attitude than it was by measures of attitudes toward specific behaviors. Supportive findings have been presented by Fishbein and Ajzen (1974) and Weigel and Newman (1976).

The other end of the "specificity principle" also has received support. The study by Heberlein and Black (1976) of gasoline-purchasing behavior is illustrative. Specific attitudinal measures were related to a single-but-repeated-act criterion more highly than was the most general measure of the attitude. Additional support for the principle can be found in a series of studies including Liska (1974), King (1975), and Weigel, Vernon, and Tognacci (1974).

The above findings fit nicely with the correspondence principle offered by Fishbein and Ajzen. If the attitudinal entity and the behavioral entity correspond with respect to target, action, context, and time, then the attitudinal measure and the behavioral criterion will be at the same precise level of specificity.[8]

It is tempting to be uncritical in the face of what is clearly a cumulative growth of findings and an increasingly precise conceptualization of what only a decade ago was seen as a theoretical and empirical quagmire. The literature cited above is not without flaw. For example, some of the samples used provide questionable grounds for external validity; and in some studies, the measures of attitudes and behaviors were obtained on a single questionnaire, which could have resulted in spuriously inflated relationships. Nevertheless, in a variety of substantive areas, in survey research, field observation, and laboratory studies, moderate relations between attitudes and behaviors have been found consistently when attitudinal measures and behavioral criteria correspond on the dimensions of target and action.[9]

Attitude as an Independent Variable

THE FISHBEIN-AJZEN MODEL

Social-psychological researchers have treated attitudinal variables in two rather distinct fashions. Clearly, many early researchers were primarily concerned with the explanation of behavior, and they treated attitudes as independent variables in their efforts to achieve the desired explanations. There is, however, a second concern that has generated an equally prolific literature. If it is assumed that attitudes are important variables, then the explanation of the development, crystallization, and change of such subjective evaluations becomes a legitimate social-psychological concern. Attitudes then become dependent variables demanding explanation. Kelman, for example, stresses the importance of attitudes, "because they have come to serve as *the* dependent variable par excellence for the major categories of social-psychological research" (1974:310).

A variety of theories or models has been offered in the attempt to incorporate attitudes as one of the determinants of behavior. While work continues to be directed by a number of these perspectives, one model emerged in the 1970s as a particular focus of attention. This is the model developed by Fishbein, Ajzen, and their associates. It would be an overstatement to claim that this model has become the dominant one in the area. It is the case that during the last half of the past decade, social psychologists devoted more research attention to this formulation of the problem than to any other.

In somewhat oversimplified form the Fishbein-Ajzen model is represented in figure 12.1. Fishbein's (1978) recent discussion of the concepts involved serves to specify and illustrate the referents of the model.

A *belief* is a probability judgment that links some object or concept to some attribute. The terms "object" and "attribute" are used in a generic sense and both terms may refer to any discriminable aspect of an individual's world. For example, I may believe that *cigarettes* (an object) are *harmful to health* (an attribute) or that *my quitting smoking* (an object) will *reduce my capacity to work* (an attribute). The content of the belief is defined by the object and attribute in question, and the strength of the belief is defined by the person's subjective probability that the object-attribute relationship exists (or is true).

FIGURE 12.1

Fishbein-Ajzen General Model Relating Beliefs, Attitudes, Intentions, and Behaviors with Respect to a Given Object (Fishbein and Ajzen 1975).

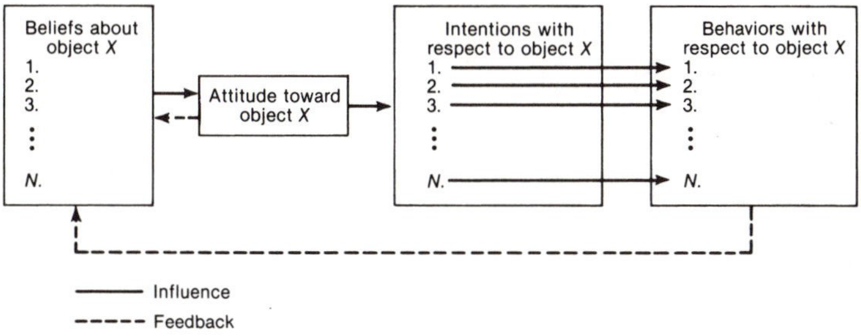

> An *attitude* is a bipolar evaluative judgment of the object. It is essentially a subjective judgment that I like or dislike the object, that it is good or bad, that I'm favorable or unfavorable toward it. Once again, the term "object" is used in a generic sense. Thus I may have attitudes toward people (e.g., smokers), institutions (e.g., the Federal Trade Commission), events (e.g., the release of the Surgeon General's report on smoking), behaviors (e.g., my quitting smoking), outcomes (e.g., gaining status in the eyes of my friends), and so on.
>
> An *intention* is a probability judgment that links the individual to some action. An intention can be viewed as a person's belief about his or her own performance of a given behavior. Intentions can be general (e.g., I will quit smoking) or specific (e.g., I will not smoke any cigarettes at John's party tonight), and they vary in intensity. Like other beliefs, intentions are usually measured by obtaining some index of the individual's subjective probability that he will perform the behavior in question. [Fishbein 1978:378]

Figure 12.1 formulates the problem at a general level. It should be stressed that a set of behaviors constitutes the dependent variable. Thus one's attitude toward an incumbent should be related to such behaviors as making a political contribution, canvassing, endorsing the candidate in a newspaper advertisement, volunteering to do clerical work in connection with the campaign, and voting for the incumbent, when these various behaviors are considered as a totality.

If the concern is with the prediction of a single member of the behavioral set, the model becomes further specified. The crucial attitudinal variable involved now becomes the attitude toward the behavior associated with the object. No longer is general attitude toward the incumbent the appropriate predictor variable. If the dependent behavioral variable is making a political contribution to the incumbent, then the independent variable should be attitude toward making a contribution to that incumbent. The more specific model is illustrated in figure 12.2.

For the case in which a specific behavior is to be predicted, Fishbein and Ajzen also refine the general category of beliefs. The individual has certain beliefs about the probable consequences of the specific act that are the determinants of the attitude toward that act. In addition, the actor attributes specific behavioral expectations to reference groups, individuals, or other social agents. The totality of these expectations as perceived

FIGURE 12.2
Fishbein-Ajzen Model for Predicting Specific Intentions and Behaviors (Fishbein and Ajzen 1975).

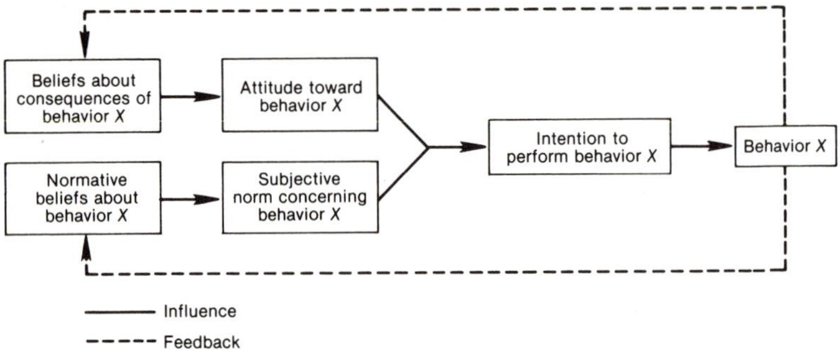

by the individual constitute the "subjective norm" concerning the behavior in question. "Thus a person's behavioral intention is viewed as a function of two factors: his attitude toward the behavior and his subjective norm" (Fishbein and Ajzen 1975:16).

It is important to emphasize that according to this model, norms and attitudes are predictive of behavioral intentions. Thus, the ability of attitudes to predict behavior is dependent upon the strength of the link between behavioral intentions and behavior. The importance of this postulate of the model is underscored in the exchange between Songer-Nocks and Fishbein and Ajzen (Songer-Nocks 1976a, 1976b; Fishbein and Ajzen 1976a, 1976b). Fishbein and Ajzen argued that Songer-Nocks had misrepresented their model by assuming "that the model postulates a strong *empirical* relation between intention and behavior" (Fishbein and Ajzen 1976a:579). In this exchange, the central function of the theory is clarified. "The model's central concern is the predictions of intentions from two major factors: a personal or attitudinal factor and a social or normative factor" (Fishbein and Ajzen 1976a:580).

If it is assumed that there is a strong relationship between attitude and behavioral intention, then what becomes problematic is the relationship between intention and behavior. The experimental work of Fishbein, Ajzen, and their associates does demonstrate that under certain laboratory conditions there is a close relationship between attitudes and behavioral intentions and a similar relationship between behavioral intentions and behavior. Under such conditions, attitudes and behaviors obviously are also closely related. What Songer-Nocks demonstrated was that under modified laboratory conditions, the relationship between attitudes and behaviors was not impressive. According to Fishbein and Ajzen, this does not constitute negative evidence with respect to the model because Songer-Nocks did not examine the strength of the relationship between behavioral intentions and behaviors.

The original social-psychological problem of determining the degree to which attitudes are causal determinants of behaviors has been transformed by Fishbein and Ajzen, but the fundamental issue has not been resolved. To fully examine the adequacy of the Fishbein and Ajzen model, the factors determining the strength of the link between behavioral intentions and behaviors must be specified and the nature of the influence of these factors on the link must be examined. Some work on this problem has been reported.

One variable that can have an effect on the strength of the relation between behavioral intentions and behaviors is the time that has elapsed between the measurements of the intentions and the observations of the behaviors (Ajzen and Fishbein 1973; Fishbein and Jaccard 1973). The importance of the "history" that intervenes between time-one and time-two measures has been discussed by a number of researchers (see, for example, Campbell and Stanley 1963; Alwin 1973). The problems encountered by attitudinal researchers in this regard are similar to those experienced by other social scientists engaged in longitudinal research. Among the problems involved are the stability of the independent variable (intentions) and the operation of unanticipated situational factors that reduce the relationship between the variables of immediate concern.

Fishbein and Ajzen (1976a) suggest two other types of variables that can effect the strength of the link between intentions and behavior. First, the relationship is contingent upon a high degree of correspondence in the levels of specificity at which both behavioral intention and behavior are measured. Second, this relationship depends upon the degree to which the individual's behavior is under volitional control.

The last of these constraints on the model may well limit its applicability to nonlaboratory situations. In most situations of interest to sociologists, contextual constraints do limit the choices available to the actor. If the model is correct, the operation of contextual variables would reduce the relationship between behavioral intentions and behavior, which, in turn, would reduce the association between attitudes and behaviors.

The Fishbein-Ajzen model has been examined in some nonlaboratory settings. The investigation of behavioral intentions with respect to family planning by Jaccard and Davidson (1975; see also Crawford 1974) is of particular interest because it compares the Fishbein-Ajzen model with an alternative developed by Triandis (1971). Measures of attitudes toward various acts and beliefs about the performance of those acts were combined to predict behavioral intentions. The findings are impressive: multiple correlations with behavioral intentions were between 0.730 and 0.842 for the Fishbein-Ajzen model and between 0.727 and 0.832 for the model developed by Triandis. For these and other comparisons, the Fishbein-Ajzen model showed slight but consistent superiority over the Triandis alternative.

There is, then, a cumulative body of research evidence that supports the Fishbein-Ajzen model. There are some conceptual issues that remain to be resolved. For example, there is some evidence that the incorporation of measures of personal normative beliefs (that is, the degrees to which individuals feel that they personally should perform the behavior in question) would improve the predictive power of the model (Schwartz and Tessler 1972; Jaccard and Davidson 1975). There also are unresolved questions about the importance of variables, and interactions among variables, that are now excluded from the model (for example, Songer-Nocks 1976a, 1976b). It seems likely that such issues can be resolved without altering the fundamental structure of the model when the model is applied to situations in which actors are free to select alternatives.

A crucial issue that remains centers on the applicability of the model to situations in which there are constraints on voluntaristic behavior. As Schuman and Johnson (1976:172) point out, some of the laboratory-based evidence generated by Fishbein and Ajzen is not particularly compelling to those who examine a more complex world. The issue is *not* that of the trivial nature of much of experimental social psychology (see Fishbein and Ajzen 1975:518). The issue is one of determining the general utility of the model, even if it is correct under conditions where a high degree of voluntaristic behavior is possible. Few sociologists would accept without serious qualification the postulate of a voluntaristic world. This being the case, the applicability and utility of a theory that incorporates an assumption of voluntarism are subject to question. That question has not yet received sufficient attention.

A consideration of the influence of "social pressures" on the attitude-behavior relationship illustrates the type of issue that remains unresolved. The degree of consistency between attitudes and behavior can be manipulated by the use of confederates who either provide arguments that contradict the individual's attitudinal position or act in ways that contradict that position (for example, see Norman 1975; Frideres, Warner, and Albrecht 1971). In order to incorporate such findings within the Fishbein-Ajzen model, at least one of the following would have to be demonstrated:

1. The situational variables altered the individual's beliefs about the consequences of the behavior which, in turn, resulted in a change in attitude.
2. The situational variables altered the individual's normative beliefs which, in turn, resulted in a change in the subjective norm.
3. The situational variables reduced the association between behavioral intentions and behavior.

Any of the alternatives, alone or in combination, can be incorporated within the logic of the Fishbein-Ajzen model, but the precise dynamics have not been established.

If it is necessary to invoke repeatedly the third alternative to save the model, then the rescue will be seen by many as not worth the effort. The original problem was, and for many still is, to account for behavior, not behavioral intentions. If the link between behavioral intentions and behavior is tenuous, then a model that predicts behavioral intentions may be of limited interest to those still concerned with the prediction of behavior.

MULTIVARIATE APPROACHES

If the goal of attitude-behavior research is to explain the variance in behavior, then the typically moderate associations between these two variables fall short of the mark. When faced with such explanatory failure, social scientists frequently invoke the image of a complex, multivariate world. This image provides an orientation toward much of the research that has been done on the relationship between attitudes and behaviors. Such work continues to lack the guidance of a general theoretical perspective, and what one encounters is a large but unintegrated body of empirical findings. The impact of this work may be suggestive, but the multitude of findings resembles a pile of jackstraws.

Dispositional factors. Various researchers have combined measures of attitudes with measures of personality traits, values, beliefs, or perceived norms in the attempt to explain additional variance in behavioral criteria. Other workers have combined different measures of attitudes or have analyzed the dimensionality, structure, or salience of the attitude under investigation.

The work of Sample and Warland (1973) is illustrative. The influence of such variables as encouragement by friends, knowledge, previous reading, and organizational membership was investigated. The effect of these variables on behavioral intentions and behavior was mediated by the structure of the attitude, "attitudinal certainty." For individuals who were certain about their attitudes, the other personal variables analyzed had little or no ability to improve predictions. For those characterized by low attitudinal certainty, the additional variables did improve predictive ability.

These findings are suggestive and are consistent with those of the Sherifs and their associates regarding attitude change. The probability of attitudinal change is greater when the individual is unfamiliar and not highly involved with the attitudinal object (Sherif, Sherif, and Nebergall 1965:244). Such results suggest that predicting the behavior of the uncertain, uninvolved, and uninformed may require knowledge of more variables than are needed to predict the behavior of those who are certain, involved, and informed (see also Weigel and Amsterdam 1976).

The use of measures of more than one attitude to predict behavior is illustrated by the work of Rokeach and Kliejunas (1972). In their study of the act of "cutting" a college class, Rokeach and Kliejunas were able to improve the prediction of behavior by combining a measure of attitude toward the act with a measure of attitude toward a particular professor (object). Essentially the same finding has been reported by other researchers. For example, Weinstein (1972) improved the ability to predict the signing of a petition by combining attitude toward the act with attitude toward the object. It should be noted that such results are not incompatible with the Fishbein-Ajzen model (Fishbein and Ajzen 1975:347–51).

The attempt to improve behavioral prediction by measuring various components or characteristics of attitudes is illustrated by the work of Norman (1975) and Brown (1974). Norman examined the affective and cognitive components of attitudes and found that behavior could be more accurately predicted for those characterized by high affective-cognitive consistency than for those lacking such consistency. Brown found that adding a measure of the salience of the object increased the relationship between four attitudinal measures and self-reported behavior.

The review of studies that incorporate multiple measures of dispositional variables could be extended to much greater length. The picture is one of many variables being examined and, at least in the published research, of many of these variables having some influence on the observed relationship between attitude and behavior. What remains to be accomplished is a conceptual integration of such work.

Situational variables. Even if attitudes are highly stable, salient, personal characteristics, we should not expect high correlations between attitudes and behaviors under all conditions. Fishbein and Ajzen (for example, 1976a) stress the importance of volitional control which obviously varies across situations. The work of such people as Barker (1968) and Bem and Allen (1974) suggests the fundamental importance of situational variation and the interactions between individuals and situations. Stable individual dispositional characteristics simply should not be expected to predict behavior without regard to situational conditions.

One attempt to incorporate situational constraints into a prediction model of behavior can be found in Wicker's (1971) study of individuals' relations to their churches. In addition to attitude toward the church, Wicker measured the perceived consequences of behavior, the evaluations of behavior, and the judged influences of extraneous events. While an additive combination of all four measures was the best predictor of the behavioral measures, the judged influence of extraneous events was the best single-measure predictor. Fishbein and Ajzen (1975:348–50) have reanalyzed Wicker's findings, arguing that judged influence of extraneous events can best be viewed as the subject's behavioral intention, and that the other three measures are imperfect measures of attitude toward the behavior. They conclude that Wicker's findings are, in fact, perfectly consistent with the Fishbein-Ajzen model. The reanalysis of the findings appears sound, but a less well-known study by Brislin and Olmstead (1973) raises certain questions.

Brislin and Olmstead used variables similar to those employed by Wicker as well as the components of the 1969 version of Fishbein's model (attitude toward the act, personal norms, social norms, and motivation to comply). Judged influence of extraneous events was again the best single predictor of behavior. The combination of the Wicker-type variables predicted the behavioral criteria better ($R = 0.49$) than the combination of the Fishbein components ($R = 0.39$). Brislin and Olmstead found that the best multivariate predictor of behavior was a combination of attitude toward the act, behavioral intention, *and* judged influence of extraneous events. If Fishbein and Ajzen are correct in defining judged influence of extraneous events as a measure of behavioral intention, this last finding is difficult to explain. It may be better to view such measures as the perceived influence of events as a perception of volitional control that conditions the link between behavioral intention and behavior.

Crespi (1971) analyzed three situations in which survey measures of attitudes related highly to behavioral criteria: prediction of election results, movie attendance, and consumer brand preference. While the data are limited, Crespi's conclusions are suggestive:

> . . . attitudes have predictable relationships with behavior to the extent that the actor has *reliable* expectations of the behavioral situation. It would follow that in loosely structured situations, such as occur when crowds gather and in time of rapid social change, pre-existing attitudes are far less determining of behavior than the dynamics of the situation itself. [1971:334]

If this conclusion holds, then, at best, we should expect modest correlations between attitudes and behaviors in novel situational contexts. One does not often pose for intimate, interracial photographs to be published in *Life* magazine, and it is hard to imagine anyone playing Prisoner's Dilemma outside the laboratory. It should be noted that reliable expectations apparently do develop rapidly in simplified situations like that of the Prisoner's Dilemma, and these expectations do influence the attitude-behavior relationship in ways that are congruent with Crespi's hypothesis (for example, Ajzen 1971; Songer-Nocks 1976a).

If the behavior being examined involves a choice under either highly institutionalized or highly routinized conditions, then, according to Crespi (1971), that behavior can be predicted from knowledge of appropriately measured attitudes.[10] Tittle and Hill (1976a) forwarded a similar suggestion, arguing that the most predictable behaviors are those that are patterned and that occur under typical social circumstances. It is perhaps precisely this character of the act of voting that has led to the positive results that have been so encouraging to researchers (for example, see Schuman and Johnson 1976:168–70). Even in this area other situational factors can affect attitudes and the attitude-behavior relationship. As Lazarsfeld, Berelson, and Gaudet (1948) demonstrated in their now classic study, the situational location of the individual can introduce conflicting cross-pressures. Behavioral predictions are most subject to error for persons experiencing such pressures.

The recent study of the California Coastal Commissioners by Wyant (1980) analyzes behavior within an institutionalized, rule-governed situation. Wyant found a strong relationship between the general environmental attitudes of these commissioners and a measure of their accumulated negative votes on applications for permits to develop coastal land ($r = 0.65$). Wyant also incorporated eight situational variables into her prediction equation. When combined with general attitude, the multiple correlation with behavior increased to 0.92.[11] The contextual variables that were most highly weighted were the type of development permit being requested and the region of California being represented by the commissioners.

Situational variables also have been manipulated by a number of investigators in an effort to explore the impact of such variables on attitudinal-behavioral consistency. For example, consistency can be influenced by direct interpersonal pressures (for example, Frideres, Warner, and Albrecht 1971; Norman 1975) and apparently by anticipated behavioral visibility or disclosure (Warner and DeFleur 1969; Green 1972; but see Frideres, Warner, and Albrecht 1971).

Again, the discussion could be extended. The situational context within which data are collected is important (for example, Schuman and Johnson 1976). The apparently crucial significance of reference groups also could be covered in connection with the general importance of situational variables. Again, the findings are multitudinous, and again the image of jackstraws emerges. Making sense of this chaos should be a first order of business if the goal is to predict behavioral variation.

Some convergence of findings suggests generalizations that have at least the status of plausible hypotheses. Songer-Nocks (1976a) found that attitude toward the act predicted laboratory behavior significantly only after the individual had had experience with the experimental games (also see Ajzen 1971). Sample and Warland (1973) found that when an individual is certain about his or her attitudes, knowledge of selected other variables does not improve the correspondence between attitude and behavior. Sherif, Sherif, and Nebergall (1965), in summarizing their various studies, conclude that the individual who is informed and involved is resistent to attitudinal change. Lack of dispositional conflict (Campbell, Gurin, and Miller 1954) or cross-pressures (Lazarsfeld, Berelson, and Gaudet 1948) leads to increased predictability of voter behavior. In situations where the individual has reliable expectations, attitudes and behaviors are related (Crespi 1971).

There are suggestive themes in such a collection of findings. If the individual's attitude is based on knowledge about an object and familiarity with a situation involving choice, and where such knowledge and familiarity do not involve inconsistent dispositional or cognitive elements, the individual's attitude should be characterized by a high degree of certainty, and attitude should be predictive of behavior. Such a generalization has received consistent empirical support.

Attitude as the Dependent Variable

A BRIEF HISTORICAL INTRODUCTION

Almost as soon as the concept of attitude was introduced into the mainstream of social psychology, researchers began to treat attitudes as dependent variables, and a very early focus of this research was on attitude change. Particular attention was directed toward determining the consequences of various types of communication on the attitudes of those receiving messages. The year 1934 may well have been a vintage year, for along with the appearance of the LaPiere classic came Wilke's (1934) finding that the same communication could have different and opposite effects on audience members.

The early literature devoted to the effects of communication on attitudes was characterized by inconsistent results (Murphy, Murphy, and Newcomb 1937). Some studies reported little or no communication effects. A larger number reported attitudinal shifts toward the position communicated. For some, powerful propaganda was seen as having the capability of molding opinion. An interpretive problem was introduced by a significant number of studies reporting that some subjects changed toward the position advocated while other subjects altered their attitudinal positions in the opposite direction.[12]

Research focusing on the effects of persuasive messages on attitudinal position is now a well-established tradition. A number of attempts have been made to integrate the numerous empirically grounded generalizations that have been established. These include the theory of social judgment (Sherif and Hovland 1961), McGuire's (1968, 1969) two-factor model of opinion change, attribution theory (Kelley 1967), and integration theory (Anderson 1971). Kelman (1961) has considered the phenomena from a functional perspective, and Fishbein and Ajzen (1975) have attempted to incorporate many of the findings within their theory of behavior.[13] Although the desired theoretical synthesis remains to be accomplished, considerable conceptual clarification has been achieved, and much has been demonstrated about the importance of such variables as type of appeal, source credibility, and the reciprocal relationship between communicator and the audience. More important for the purposes at hand, the persuasion research literature has demonstrated the utility of attitudes as dependent variables for the examination of theoretical issues and the generation of conceptual propositions.

The importance of attitudes as dependent variables in experimental social psychology was reinforced significantly by the appearance of Festinger's (1957) theory of cognitive dissonance. The theory became an important focus of research during the 1960s and 1970s with the results generating both theoretical and empirical controversy. Some results interpreted as supporting the dissonance formulation could not be replicated, and alternative explanations were developed.[14]

For example, Bem (1965, 1972) forwarded a formulation of the attitude-behavior relationship that, among other things, offered an alternative explanation for the results of dissonance research. Fundamental to Bem's approach is the notion that individuals evaluate their own behavior as do other observers of that behavior, an assumption readily accepted by those sympathetic to the symbolic-interactionist orientation. If individuals act toward some object in a given way, they will infer or attribute to themselves an attitude that is consistent with the behavior. Thus, at least under certain conditions, people become cognizant of their attitudes on the basis of an *ex post facto* analysis of their behavior. The provocative question becomes one of determining the degree to which people are aware, if at all, of their subjective evaluations prior to engaging in some behavior. On balance, I believe that Bem's position is too extreme, and that alternative formulations of the problem have greater potential for achieving an understanding of the behavior-attitude change relationship.[15]

There is no question that attitudinally discrepant or counterattitudinal behavior can change the relevant attitude under certain conditions. There also is no question that after engaging in certain actions we may experience a greater awareness of our relevant attitudes. Once we have behaved in a certain fashion, the behavior is a part of the totality upon which we can reflect. The significance of these change processes is not fully captured within the limits of either dissonance or self-attribution theory. What is needed is a general framework that can incorporate both pro- and counterattitudinal behavior and the conditions that influence awareness within the formulation of the attitude-behavior problem. I have selected the recent work of Kelman (1974, 1978a, 1978b) as being suggestive.

KELMAN'S ATTITUDE-ACTION APPROACH

In order to further illustrate the conceptual and theoretical issues surrounding the construct of attitude, I have elected to examine Kelman's framework in some detail. I have three major reasons for this selection. First, Kelman has emphasized the use of attitude as a dependent variable, labeling it as the "dependent variable par excellence for the major categories of social-psychological research" (1974:310). Second, despite his focus on attitudes as dependent variables, Kelman's formulation is clearly interactive and involves what I believe to be the realistic if troublesome assumptions of social process and rapid, if not instantaneous, feedback. Third, Kelman has done research in a variety of settings: he has done experimental work on the effects of counterattitudinal behavior; he has analyzed attitude change that occurs in therapeutic situations; and he has engaged in fieldwork in natural settings.[16]

Kelman's work also illustrates certain burdens that are associated with the further development of the field. Some of his conceptualization lacks precision, and is, at best, what Blumer (1954) has described as "sensitizing." Nevertheless, I believe that Kelman has suggested the complexity of the interrelationship between dispositions and behaviors, and that his formulation does indicate important avenues that should be taken by theorists and researchers.

Kelman's orientation is derived in part from the reinterpretation of the effects of counterattitudinal behaviors on attitudes. According to Kelman, the process of attitude change is stimulated when the individual is confronted with a discrepancy between attitude and some new item of information:

> Three major types of discrepancy conducive to attitude change can be identified, corresponding to the three types of information about an attitude object . . . a) discrepancy between the attitude and information about reality . . . ; b) discrepancy between the attitude and the attitudes of significant others; and c) discrepancy between the attitude and one's own actions. [Kelman 1974:317]

This typology of discrepancy permits a reasonable classification of attitude change research based upon very broad generalizations about the conditions under which such change should be expected. Kelman (1974) focuses his review on the third type of discrepancy, that between attitude and action.

Kelman identifies three components of actions: the context of the action; the contemplation of the action; and the consequences of the action. Again, consider the situation of action in support of a political candidate. Suppose that there are several candidates whom I find to be equally acceptable. I am approached by a good and valued friend who seeks support for one of these. In the course of my friend's persuasive attempts, I may well examine the issues involved and the relative strengths and weaknesses of the candidates. If the request for support results in such a process of reexamination, attitude change may occur. My prior ambivalence about the several candidates would not lead to the prediction of my support for Candidate X. However, given the context of the action, and the resulting attitude change within that context, there may be no discrepancy between attitudes and behavior at the time the action is taken.

Kelman suggests the conditions under which such attitude change is likely to occur:

A high degree of choice about the induced action is particularly conducive to attitude change. . . . If the person is undecided as to whether to carry out the action, then the higher his degree of choice, the more likely he is . . . to reexamine his attitudes and to marshal forces in support of the action that he finally selects. . . . The fact that he is given the choice may force him to engage in a process of active self-persuasion to find attitudinal support for the action he has already decided to take. [1974:318]

Let us suppose that my friend persuaded me to add my name to an advertisement in support of Candidate X. The process that Kelman identifies as contemplation of the action can lead me to raise questions about the implications of my behavior. If the action was discrepant to my previous attitudinal position, my contemplation of the act is likely to generate justification processes leading to attitude change.

When the advertisement appears, I then have to contend with the consequences of the action. As Bem would predict, I am now likely to attribute to myself an attitude that corresponds to that behavior. Contrary to some of Bem's interpretations, this does not mean that I did not have attitudes prior to the action, nor does it necessarily mean that I was unaware of those attitudes prior to engaging in the behavior. The act of having my name appear in public in support of Candidate X has a range of possible consequences. Other friends who favor Candidates Y and Z may well confront me in the attempt to demonstrate my error of judgment. In preparing for this possible necessity of explaining my action, I may review the grounds for that behavior. I may seek and develop arguments that are supportive, and in the process my attitudes may evidence additional change.

Such a conception of the process of attitude change emphasizes the dynamic nature of the attitude-behavior relationship. In his Nebraska Symposium paper, Kelman describes certain assumptions about the nature of this relationship:

Attitudes are constantly shifting and changing as people interact with the attitude object and with their social environment. . . . Attitudes flow from social interaction and evolve in the course of it. In turn, attitudes feed into social interaction and help to guide the interaction process. . . . Attitudes [are] links between individuals and the various collectivities to which they belong. . . . The formation, expression, and functioning of attitudes simultaneously represent both individual and collective processes. [1978b:2]

Kelman's analysis of the attitude-behavior relation can be distinguished from most other formulations in terms of the attention he devotes to the concept of action. Behaviors differ in the degree to which they have the character of action. For Kelman, action is overt behavior that produces some change for the actor. He also identifies certain characteristics of behavior that are postulated to increase the action-character of that behavior:

. . . the more public, irreversible, active, and committing the behavior is, the greater the change it produces in the environment and the more real-life consequences it has for the actor. . . . It is non-trivial actions . . . characterized by active participation, public commitment, and important real-life consequences—that I have in mind as the usual context for significant attitude change. [1978b:3–4]

One point may appear obvious: some behaviors are of greater consequence than others for a range of individual dispositions, including attitudes. Nevertheless, if the impact of behaviors on attitudes is to be clarified, greater conceptual attention to behavior is required. Kelman suggests some of the behavioral dimensions that deserve further consideration.

In his analysis of the interrelationship between action and attitude, Kelman emphasizes the importance of situational demands, and he identifies two general classes of such demands. At the social-system level, the action situation is constrained by social-structural demands. In addition, within the immediate interactional situation the requirements of the microsystem place further constraints on individual action.

Kelman uses this distinction to suggest a possible reinterpretation of LaPiere's (1934) findings. In responding to LaPiere's letter of inquiry, managers may have been acting primarily as representatives of their organizations and their behavior could have been dictated by the system-level policies of their organizations. When directly confronted by well-dressed and well-spoken potential clients, the situational demands might well have been those norms that govern social interaction in a public place. Perhaps neither the written replies nor the direct responses to the request for accommodations accurately reflected the attitudes of the individuals involved.

It could be argued that Kelman has not introduced considerations that differ from other general formulations of the attitude-behavior relationship. For example, his analysis of the consequences of discrepant information can be interpreted as alterations in the individual's beliefs about the object, the behavior toward the object, or the relevant behavioral norms. Further, the emphasis that Kelman gives to situational demands can be seen as a specification of conditions that affect the relationship between behavioral intentions and behavior. Thus, much of Kelman's discussion could be incorporated into the general model forwarded by Fishbein and Ajzen.

What distinguishes Kelman's work from many other discussions is his emphasis upon the close, dynamic interrelationship between attitudes and actions. Attitudes are constantly forming, developing, and shifting as the course of action proceeds. Kelman considers attitude change within the process of individual socialization, a process that he describes as continuous within the context of action. His emphasis on the dynamic character of attitudes and the close interrelationship between attitudes and behaviors introduces important difficulties. If attitudes are constantly shifting during the course of action, then the determination of the magnitude of the relationship between attitude and behavior becomes problematic. Kelman's formulation suggests that if we are to determine the magnitude of this relationship, our observations should be made simultaneously. Unfortunately, given the available techniques of attitude measurement and behavioral observation, such simultaneous measures would result in relationships that would be suspect. For a variety of reasons, relationships based on simultaneous measures could be spuriously inflated.

An additional problem with Kelman's approach stems from his definition of the concept of attitude. For Kelman, an attitude represents a "range of commitment": "One might think of a person's range of commitment as the range of relationships with or actions toward the object that person finds acceptable" (1978b:23). I have no objection to the view that an attitude is an evaluative range rather than a point on an evaluative dimension. As Kelman notes, such a conceptualization is suggested by previous research, especially that associated with the Yale studies in attitude and communication (Sherif and Hovland 1961).

What is unsatisfactory about Kelman's definition is its lack of substantive specificity. As stated, beliefs, norms, intentions, and evaluations would be involved in determining an individual's range of commitment; as a result, attitude becomes an unnecessarily vague, dispositional concept. Fortunately, Kelman's discussion of the relationship between attitude and action can be applied to attitudes defined more specifically as evaluations of objects.

Despite my disagreement with Kelman on the matter of definition, his approach to the attitude-action problem is insightful. Viewing the connection between attitudes and behavior as a dynamic interactional relationship introduces vexing complexities into the design of appropriate research. Nevertheless, such a conceptualization seems closer to reality than the linear determinism that characterizes many alternative formulations.

Attitudes as Indicators of Social Change

If attitudes change in the course of social action, then we should expect important social events to have an impact on the attitude distributions of those involved in such events. For example, Kelman analyzes the impact of President Anwar Sadat's visit to Jerusalem in November, 1977. He concludes, "There is no question that the immediate changes in attitude produced by this event were large and significant" (1978b:11). This immediate change in public attitude was not maintained as the course of events in the Mideast unfolded, but Kelman argues that Sadat's visit and the events subsequent to it produced a fundamental shift in Israeli attitudes. This shift, in turn, led to the public support of further negotiations between the two nations.

Such an analysis reflects a general concern with social change at a macro- or societal level, and the use of attitudinal data in the effort to monitor or assess such change. The level of concern shifts. The problem now becomes that of determining the interrelationships between aggregated measures of attitude and indices of the behavior of collectivities. Analyses of trends in sex-role and racial attitudes are illustrative of the utility and the limitations of such research.

Thornton and Freedman (1979) have analyzed changes in certain sex-role attitudes for a panel of Detroit women over the period 1962 to 1977. They note that during this period significant changes have occurred in the American family structure and the distribution of occupational roles. They specifically note such changes as the increase in the number of women who combine paid employment with more traditional family roles, the increased divorce rate, the decline in fertility, the increase in the age at marriage, and the increase in female educational attainment.

Longitudinal data are available for four survey items pertaining to the sexual division of labor or authority. These items deal with authority in family decision making, the acceptability of a woman's activity outside the home during the child-raising period, the division of labor in the area of housework, and the acceptability of defining some work as the province of men and other work as women's work. For this panel of women, the data indicate a consistent and impressive shift toward egalitarian sex-role attitudes on all four items.

The panel was subdivided according to the woman's education, age, religion, number of children, work experience, husband's education, and husband's income on the basis of data collected in 1962. While there was some variation in the magnitudes involved, every subgroup examined registered increases in egalitarianism. "The events of the past 15 years have been of such magnitude and importance that they have affected all groups of women irrespective of their experiences and characteristics" (Thornton and Freedman 1979:841). This finding of a general shift in sex-role attitudes receives support from other sources. For example, results from surveys of national samples conducted by Response Analysis (1980) indicate a marked decline between 1971 and 1979 in the respect that women have for the role of housewife and an increase in the desire for the independence that working outside the home affords. For United States society in general, data consistently give support to the conclusion that attitudes toward women's roles have become liberalized during the course of the last two decades (see, for example, Mason, Czajka, and Arber 1976; Ferree 1974).

Here is an instance of consistent change in both significant behaviors and attitudes at the societal level. How is this relationship between attitudinal shift and behavioral change to be interpreted? While Thornton and Freedman found that all subgroups within their panel shifted in the egalitarian direction, the magnitude of the change was associated with certain socioeconomic and experiential variables. For example, women who acquired additional education between 1962 and 1977 and those with more years of work experience shifted toward the egalitarian position to a greater degree than did others. Thornton and Freedman are concerned about the direction of the causality involved.

> . . . conclusions about the direction of causality are more problematic. It is not clear if the attitudinal change caused the experiences during the 15 years or if the experiences caused the attitude change, since we do not know when the sex role attitudes changed, but only the overall differences between 1962 and 1977. [Thornton and Freedman, 1979:839]

If there is a clear direction of causality involved, Thornton and Freedman are correct that the inability to fix temporal order makes the determination problematic. I would argue that the implied desired search is misdirected. If both attitudes and actions are processes, and if these processes are closely interrelated, then it is unrealistic to expect that we will discover clear, temporally ordered, causal sequences that are dramatic in their explanatory power. Further, the failure to find such linear patterns may only indicate that our model of causation is not sufficiently complex to capture the interrelated processes involved.

The analysis of trends in racial attitudes illustrates other strengths and limitations of the use of survey data as a base for the study of longitudinal patterns in attitude and behavioral change. Taylor, Sheatsley, and Greeley (1978) analyzed data from four national surveys conducted in 1963, 1970, 1972, and 1976. They find that since 1963 the attitudes of white Americans have moved toward greater approval of racial integration. The rate of change was greater between 1970 and 1972 than it was in either the earlier or later periods, but the direction of change toward more liberal racial attitudes was consistent. As in the case of attitudes toward sex roles, the vast majority of the research on racial attitudes supports the conclusion that the attitudes of the American public have become increasingly liberal. Further, the available evidence indicates that this liberal shift has been a slow but steady movement at least since 1942 (Hyman and Sheatsley 1964).[17]

Some social psychologists have interpreted this trend in a fashion similar to Thornton's and Freedman's interpretation of the shift in attitudes toward sex roles. Attitudes, institutional action, legal developments, and public behavior have moved in a consistent direction. For example, Schuman concludes:

> I am confident that a careful tracing of events will show that in government, in the armed forces, on television, on college campuses, and in most public spheres of life, racial change in white individual and institutional behavior has occurred at a rapid and visible pace in ways quite consonant with the attitude survey data. [Schuman 1978:374]

The hypothesis of consistency between general attitudinal changes and macro-level social movement is seductive. In the case of racial attitudes, the careful tracing that Schuman calls for leads to some troublesome findings.

In considering the period between 1964 and 1971, Greeley and Sheatsley (1971) have written the following description:

> . . . the U.S. has experienced what is probably the most acute crisis in race relations since the end of the Civil War. City after city suffered racial violence. . . . Martin Luther King . . . was assassinated and another spasm of riots shook the nation. King was replaced on the television screen by a far more militant brand of black leader. . . . Newspapers carried accounts of blacks arming for guerrilla warfare. The Black Panthers appeared on the scene, and in several cities there were gunfights between the police and the Panthers. Columnists, editorial writers and political analysts worried publicly about the "backlash." George Wallace did well in several primaries, and in the presidential election of 1968 he made the most successful third-party showing in many decades. . . . *Concurrently with these dramatic events the attitudes of white Americans toward desegregation continued to change almost as though nothing was happening.* [Greeley and Sheatsley 1971:13; emphasis added]

The consistency hypothesis can be saved in this instance only by the *ex post facto* intellectual equivalent of fancy footwork. Perhaps white Americans, given their increasingly liberal attitudes, interpreted the violent acts of blacks as a justified expression of rage. This interpretation might then have led whites to the conclusions that, to prevent further disruption, a more integrated society was a social necessity. Perhaps this is what occurred, but such a reinterpretation goes beyond the available survey data. Further, such a reinterpretation reinforces the view offered here that the interrelationship between attitudes and behaviors is more complex than that suggested by linear, deterministic models. Finally, the reinterpretation reasserts the powerful capacity of attitudes in the definitional process that determines social reality.

The longitudinal analysis of racial attitudes also provides an exemplary illustration of a basic methodological issue: the long-term utility, validity, and precision of indices. The 1963 N.O.R.C. survey included a seven-item Guttman scale developed by Donald Treiman (Greeley and Sheatsley 1971). By 1978, certain items had lost their utility for multivariate analysis because of the lack of variability in white responses to these items:

> They had to do with the integration of public facilities, an issue that was problematic not so many years ago but then became so settled in the public mind that it was difficult to find whites who would not endorse the principle. If the racial climate continues to improve, other questions in the scale will presumably become less effective and will have to be dropped as new items, reflecting current issues such as busing for school integration, are added to the bottom of the scale. [Taylor, Sheatsley, and Greeley 1978:43]

If *variability* in white attitudes toward integration is to be measured in the future, there seems to be no alternate to the strategy described by Taylor, Sheatsley, and Greeley. High costs are involved: strict, long-term comparability will be lost.

A more subtle problem in index interpretation is also illustrated by the Treiman scale. The item consistently receiving the lowest prointegration response in the surveys of 1963, 1970, 1972, 1976, and 1977 was "Blacks shouldn't push themselves where they're not wanted."[18] White response to this item was less prointegrationist in 1970 than it was in 1963. Greeley and Sheatsley (1971:14–15) suggest that this may have been one indication of backlash and was a response to black militancy.

The same item caused Taylor, Sheatsley, and Greeley interpretive difficulties. The item:

> . . . elicited a more negative response in 1972 than in 1970, and its integrationist percent is about the same now as it was in 1963, whereas the other items show unambiguous trends in the prointegration direction. We believe [this] question may not measure the same dimension of racial attitude as it measured when the scale was first administered, but rather other dimensions or values such as politeness and conventional social behaviors. [Taylor, Sheatsley, and Greeley 1978:43]

Such change in the "meaning" of survey items has been anticipated by measurement theorists. Guttman specifically addressed this issue:

> A universe may form a scale for a population at a given time and may not at a later time. . . . Such a change in time would tend to indicate that a change is one of *kind,* rather than *degree.* A new meaning has been added to the previous single variable. [Guttman 1950:82]

If the troublesome item on the Treiman scale does indicate a change in kind in the domain of racial attitudes, how has this change influenced white response to the other items? Has this index of attitude changed significantly in terms of how respondents define the meaning of what they are being asked? Such questions must be addressed before the longitudinal change in response patterns can be interpreted unambiguously.[19]

A different issue is raised by the response pattern to the Treiman item on neighborhood integration.[20] From 1963 to 1976, whites responded in a fashion that was consistent with an increasingly pro-integrationist position.[21] How is this attitudinal change to be interpreted in face of the fact that, at least until very recently, large central cities have become increasingly black, patterns of segregation have been maintained in the suburbs, and some evidence of "white flight" is available? The work of Farley et al. (1978) suggests that the item upon which this attitudinal analysis is based may be the culprit. Farley and his associates asked standard survey questions of Detroit area residents and the resulting pattern suggested widespread white acceptance of residential integration. Using more sensitive measures reflecting the patterns and the amount of acceptable neighborhood integration, white responses were less suggestive of a pro-integrationist stance. Apparently, the principles of integration can be accepted, and the degree of integration debated:

> Our techniques . . . allowed respondents to go beyond reacting to general values and move toward how they would personally feel in specific situations, what they would actually do, and why. For this mode of inquiry, we obtained a different picture—one closer to the "reality" of high levels of racial residential segregation. [Farley et al. 1978:343]

The trends in general attitudes concerning sex roles and race relations apparently have moved in an egalitarian, liberal direction. Perhaps these shifts are but part of a general societal trend toward greater tolerance, as has been suggested by Davis (1975). In much of the analysis based on survey research, the data apparently warrant such conclusions.

I continue to be cautious and skeptical. I view such conclusions as essentially optimistic hypotheses. Further testing requires more precise, valid, and frequent measurements of both the attitudes of our population and relevant macro-level behavioral indices.

Conclusions

A careful consideration of the research devoted to the interrelationship between attitudes and behaviors leads to greater optimism than that which characterized assessments of the area a decade ago. The debate over the existence or nonexistence of the interrelationship can be put to rest. Under a variety of conditions, attitudes have at least modest utility in predicting behavior, and behavior has at least modest utility in predicting attitude change. On balance, the evidence remains convincing despite differences in the methods employed, the populations studied, and the situations analyzed.

This optimistic view needs to be tempered by certain serious qualifications. Wicker's (1969) plea for conceptual clarification and specification warrants repetition. In the literature devoted to attitudes, too many scholars continue to write about too many different things. If attitude is to serve as something other than a synonym for disposition, we need to sharpen the distinctions that are made between attitude, belief, norm, and value. We need to clarify further the difference between evaluation and expectation. And we must develop methodological strategies that reflect such conceptual distinctions.

I would argue that the concept *attitude* should refer to evaluations of objects and only to such evaluations. Our measurement procedures frequently confound what an individual knows about an object and his or her evaluations of that object. Similarly, some have combined measures of what an individual believes should happen in a situation with evaluations of the expected outcome. Meaningful conceptual distinctions can be made between cognitions, norms, beliefs, and attitudes. Of course, an individual can have attitudes about norms, cognitions, and beliefs. Further, norms, cognitions, and beliefs are interrelated with attitudes. Such interconnections reinforce the demand for clear conceptual distinctions.

Where appropriate conceptual distinctions have been made, promising theoretical models have emerged. The Fishbein-Ajzen model is illustrative. The model has received empirical support in controlled experimental situations. The utility of introducing the notion of behavioral intentions as a variable linking attitudes to behavior has some appeal. Fishbein and Ajzen have been able to provide a common interpretative framework enabling them to integrate a variety of research findings. Despite this progress, much remains to be accomplished before the general validity and utility of the model can be assessed.

We have argued that attitudes and behaviors are interactive processes. The incorporation of feedback loops within the Fishbein-Ajzen model explicitly recognizes the possibility of interaction, but the argument offered is that the effects of behavior on attitude are the indirect consequence of the impact that behavior has on beliefs. Certainly alternative hypotheses can be entertained and deserve investigation.

The link between behavioral intentions and behavior also remains problematic, and much additional work is needed before the utility of the model outside of the laboratory is determined. The importance of contextual or situation variables requires explicit recognition. There are situations in which we should not expect to find a relationship between behavior and attitude or any other dispositional factor. In situations governed by policy and bureaucratic operational rules, knowledge of an individual's attitude may not enhance the ability to predict behavior. In general, to the degree that the behavioral choice available to the individual is constrained by system-level norms, the predictive utility of attitudes will be reduced.

Where choice is available to the individual, other features of the situation should be considered in attempting to understand the interrelationship between behavior and attitude. In routinized choice situations, such as voting, if the individual is familiar with the behavioral requirements of the situation, if his or her behavior is not subject to public scrutiny, and if the social context does not introduce dispositional conflict, then attitudes should be highly predictive of behavior. The ability of attitudinal surveys to predict United States election outcomes within 2 or 3 percent of the actual vote provides support for such expectations.

The incorporation of such considerations into the Fishbein-Ajzen model has not been accomplished. Within the model, knowledge of situational conditions could influence one's beliefs about the consequences of one's behavior. Alternatively, situational considerations could determine normative beliefs about the behavior, and thus affect the subjective norms concerning the behavior. A third possibility exists. On the basis of their exchange with Songer-Nocks (1976a, 1976b), Fishbein and Ajzen (1976a) explicitly recognize that contextual variables can effect the link between behavioral intentions and behaviors.

If the central concern is to understand the interrelationship between attitudes and behaviors, then a model linking attitudes to behavioral intentions is unsatisfactory unless the conditions affecting the relationship between behavioral intentions and behavior can be specified. The available evidence suggests the importance of situational variables as determinants of the magnitudes of such connections. Again, much additional work is required, and to be convincing at least a significant portion of that work must be conducted outside of the laboratory.

Kelman's work suggests other promising avenues. The interactive dynamic character of the interrelationship between attitude and behavior that is emphasized by Kelman has considerable intuitive appeal. Here the immediate problems are of a different order. Kelman's work is suggestive and insightful, but his conceptualization of the problem lacks precision. Further, Kelman's orientation introduces methodological difficulties for which solutions are not readily available. For example, if attitudes are processes that occur in the context of action, obtaining independent measures of the variables may not be possible. Under such circumstances, determining the relationship between attitudes and behaviors introduces vexing problems (for example, see Alwin 1973).

Analysis of the relationship between aggregated measures of attitude and indices of societal change offer another promising direction for continued research. While many social psychologists continue to be primarily concerned with the relationship between individual attitudes and behaviors, the analysis of such relationships at the systems level deserves equal time and attention. The specific conceptual and methodological concerns that impinge upon the two levels of analysis may differ, but eventually the findings concerning the individual should be compatible with those pertaining to collectivities. If the situation proves to be otherwise, it would suggest that the social psychology of individual action is fundamentally different from the social psychology of collective behavior.

There are, then, directions of research focused on the interrelationships between attitudes and behaviors that hold significant promise. Because of the limitations of space, I have elected to focus the discussion on a limited number of problems and approaches. In the process, the contributions of others have been slighted. I believe that the selection does serve to indicate needed directions for both conceptual and empirical work. I agree with Kelman that "Attitudes are alive and well," but much remains to be accomplished before attitudes are well understood or even unambiguously defined.

NOTES

1. The continued focus on LaPiere's field study might make an interesting case study in the history of sociology. LaPiere certainly was not alone in questioning the ability of attitudes to predict behavior. See, for example, Corey (1937), Dunham (1940), and Merton (1940). See also LaPiere (1938, 1969).

2. The conceptual analysis that characterizes the work of Guttman (1950) provides an early illustration of the type of conceptual analysis that is needed. While I disagree with some of Guttman's basic conclusions, the analysis does clarify certain issues. For example, Guttman fails to find utility in the conceptual distinction between attitudes and opinions. I share that conviction and will not treat opinions as something distinct from attitudes, on the one hand, or statements of belief, on the other.

3. The magnitude of relationship dividing the "low or inconsistent" category from the "high" category was 0.40.

4. Schuman and Johnson (1976:183) point out another limitation of such attempts to summarize research findings. Researchers have used a variety of measures of association, and the unqualified comparison of these measures is not justified.

5. Other researchers also have placed considerable emphasis on the distinction between attitude toward the object or target and attitude toward the act or behavior. See, for example, Rokeach (1968), Rokeach and Kliejunas (1972) and Weinstein (1972).

6. The importance of situational or contextual variables is central to the work of other theorists. For example, Smith (1969) discusses the importance of situationally engaged attitudes and beliefs. According to Smith, it is only these situationally engaged dispositions that are perceived by an individual as relevant for behavior at a given time and in a particular social context that are predictive of behavior.

7. The data reported by Fishbein (1978:389) include 143 cases. A similar table presented in Ajzen and Fishbein (1977:913) includes 142 cases. The discussion here is based on the 1978 summary.

8. As Fishbein (1978:389) points out, correspondence is not the equivalent of specificity. Nevertheless, if attitudinal measures and behavioral criteria have a high degree of correspondence, they also have the same level of specificity, be that level high or low.

9. Our conclusion here is somewhat more cautious than that reached by Ajzen and Fishbein (1977:912–13) and by Fishbein (1978:389).

10. Crespi's position on attitude measures corresponds to a number of others and has suggestive similarity to Fishbein and Ajzen's position. Attitudes should be measured as "highly specific combinations of beliefs, preferences, and intentions, each held with varying degrees of intensity" (1971:333).

11. Wyant also used a measure of behavioral intention concerning growth and development along the coast. This measure was a good predictor of behavior ($r = .55$) but not as good as the measure of general attitude.

12. For a review of this early literature, see Sherif and Sherif (1956).

13. For a recent review of persuasion research, see Eagly and Himmelfarb (1978).
14. For a summary of this literature, see Wicklund and Brehm (1976).
15. There have been other significant attempts to locate the effects of counterattitudinal behavior within more general theoretical frameworks. Among the alternatives offered are balance theory (Insko et al. 1975), response contagion theory (Nuttin 1975), and impression management theory (Tedeschi, Schlenker, and Bonoma 1971).
16. I actually have a fourth, and very subjective, reason for electing to review Kelman's work. Kelman has a passionate and tenacious devotion to the concept that is reflected in the title of his suggestive article, "Attitudes are alive and well and gainfully employed in the sphere of action" (1974). If continued progress in this problematic area is to be achieved, such devotion is required.
17. Condran's (1979) recent analysis suggests that data from 1977 may indicate a slight reversal of this trend in certain specific areas.
18. The item originally was worded, "Negroes shouldn't push themselves where they're not wanted." The change in wording from "Negroes" to "Blacks" is itself an interesting indication of attitudinal change and the effect of such change on language usage.
19. For a substantive interpretation of the pattern of responses to this item, see Condran (1979).
20. The item is, "White people have a right to keep blacks out of their neighborhoods if they want to, and blacks should respect that right."
21. A reversal of this trend in 1977 is reported by Condran (1979).

13 MELVIN SEEMAN

Intergroup Relations

Introduction

This chapter concerns the area of minority relations, with two notable restrictions in scope being established at the outset: the emphasis is on American rather than comparative materials; and the perspective is resolutely social psychological. Thus, we are only peripherally concerned with the contrasts in intergroup relations outside the United States; and the focus is on the social psychological features of prejudice, stereotyping, minority identity and self-esteem, marginality, ethnocentrism, and the like. That hardly means that questions of social structure are avoided, since they are heavily implicated in these social psychological phenomena; but it does mean that the emphasis is on attitudes and orientations rather than on structural factors such as ecological patterns, organizational relations, or legal developments.

SOME DEFINITIONAL ISSUES

In one form or another, the idea of "prejudice" has engaged the social psychological researcher for decades. Perhaps as good a sign as any of that continuity of concern lies in the fact that William Graham Sumner's "now indispensable" idea and treatment of ethnocentrism (Leyburn 1968), which dates back to the turn of the century, has only recently been used by Levine and Campbell (1972) to develop a systematic series of propositions about ethnocentric attitudes (for example, that in-group attitudes tend to be seen as universal, intrinsically true, and centrally human). As with many other sociological concepts (the notions of social structure and social norms come readily to mind), we tend to operate with a quick pass at formal definition, assuming that we have a serviceable enough common understanding of what we mean by prejudice.

It is not at all certain that we do, particularly when we begin to examine closely the instruments that are intended to measure prejudice, and when we begin to make distinctions (as the literature recently has begun to do; for example, Sears and Kinder 1971) between "symbolic" and traditional prejudice. The key ideas that are regularly invoked to establish that a prejudice exists are the following: incorrect attribution; resistance to change; categorical (rather than individual) assessment; emotionality; and normative deviation. The simplest version of prejudice is Allport's notion that it involves "thinking ill of others without sufficient warrant" (1954:7); but that was clearly too crisp for his own comfort, since it came too close to saying that prejudice equals simple error or any prejudgment. Hence, he adopted the view that the prejudice that truly concerns us is marked by resistance to the claims of new evidence: "Prejudgments become prejudices only if they are not reversible when exposed to new knowledge" (Allport 1954:9).

A popular view is that prejudice occurs when a distinctively individual assessment is superseded by a categorical judgment (about "Chicanos," "professors," or "women" rather than a given individual and his/her capabilities). But that individualistic view is not terribly helpful since, as Williams (1947) long ago noted, prejudice in that general sense—the attribution of characteristics to a category—is an inevitable part of contemporary life. Hence, the analyst finds it necessary (as did Allport) to distinguish the prejudice that is truly problematic—in effect, to distinguish simple prejudgments from prejudices. The preferred distinctions posit that the categorical usages of importance are those that are basically inaccurate (stereotypes), or so emotionally engaged that they are rigid (irreversible on new evidence), or those that violate established normative standards (regarding equality, fairness, and so forth in social relations).

Thus, Simpson and Yinger (1972:24) choose to include an emotionality component in defining prejudice as "a rigid, emotional attitude toward a human group," whereas Klineberg (1968:439), apparently skeptical of both emotionality and of Allport's reversibility criterion, considers prejudice as an "unsubstantiated prejudgment of an individual or group, favorable or unfavorable in character, tending to action in a consonant direction." Including a tendency to action complicates things, since many would agree that it comes too close to equating prejudice and discrimination, while at the same time there is reluctance to omit the action tendency because that leaves prejudice a "mere attitude" without a direct counterpart in actual behavior. My own inclination is to stand with Klineberg in ignoring the emotionality, reversibility, and normative criteria, and to insist (without reluctance) that the tendency to action is another matter—that discrimination is not necessarily a sign of prejudice. It can be equally well a sign of the priority the actor assigns to values other than ethnic equality—the value of conformity, social mobility, or what have you.

As far as prejudice is concerned, the key point is that social categories are wrongly conceived to have qualities that inhere in the very nature of the category: women as a biological-sexual category are wrongly taken as having given qualities, as are blacks as a racial category, Jews as a genetic and/or cultural-historical category, psychiatrists as an educational training category, and so forth. The error comes in misconceiving and misjudging such groups, and the individual members thereof, as a consequence of misreading the nature of the category involved. Often enough the misreading occurs because the cultural and historical sources of supposed category qualities are not taken into account or are attributed to irrelevant features of the category, that is, to blackness, Jewishness, and so on. What makes all this extremely tricky is that (a) it is difficult to demonstrate what, in fact, the appropriate characterizations are for the social categories we find it necessary to employ; and (b) given the powerful control that majorities exercise, pressures are generated that tend to socialize the members of a given category into the very features we discern: to make Jews "intellectual," blacks "hostile," Chicanos "indolent," and women "dependent." Thus, though demonstrable *relevance* (correctness) of the attributed qualities to the category is critical, there is typically a *seeming* relevance (a misread relevance) that beclouds the issue both for the participant and the analyst.

These considerations have a concrete bearing on the interpretation of research in intergroup relations. Thus, Selznick and Steinberg (1969) wrestle with the problem of anti-Semitic beliefs that "have at least some basis in reality" (p. 19). They compare, for example, an item that reads "Jews don't care what happens to anyone but their own kind" (with which 26 percent of the national sample agreed), with an item that reads "Jews stick together too much" (52 percent agreement). Obviously, these items are different, not least of all in the facts and connotations that surround the notion of clannishness. But Selznick and Steinberg caution: "It would be a mistaken view of prejudice, and its viability, to define only a false ascription as prejudice" since above all, "a prejudiced ascription is a differential ascription" (p. 20). A trait that is applicable to various groups is selectively applied to the minority; and the "social grammar" of antiethnic ideology encourages a connectedness among beliefs so that the belief in clannishness ("by itself no evidence of anti-Semitism or hostility toward Jews"; p. 20) becomes part of an interwoven and more noxious pattern of anti-Semitic beliefs. The existence of this patterned ideology makes it "a short step from accepting a quasi-factual belief in normal times to embracing an anti-Semitic belief system in times of crisis" (p. 20). However, the question remains: the trail in Selznick and Steinberg from an idea not anti-Semitic in itself, to "a quasi-factual belief," to a truly anti-Semitic ideology is not clearly delineated, and it appears to remain the case that the falsity of the attribution to the social category in question is the key to the designation "prejudice."[1]

The concept of discrimination carries many of the same problems. Insofar as the differential treatment of those considered to belong to a given category is part and parcel of daily life, the issue becomes one of establishing the relevance of the treatment to the nature of the category. As with prejudice, the discrimination we are concerned about may be defined as not simply differential treatment (an everyday occurrence) but categorical discrimination—meaning by that, differential access to desired goals on the basis of irrelevant (incorrect) attributions concerning a social category. The simple cases are easy to comprehend (for example, denial of equal educational access to blacks on the grounds of inherent intellectual incompetence); but, as with prejudice, matters soon become delicate and difficult. People can and do discriminate without prejudice (as, for example, in refusing to sell their homes inter-racially strictly for fear of what their neighbors will do); and they may also put the attitudes of others into the service of discrimination by arguing that (let us say) hiring a minority salesperson will hurt their business. The alleged injury to business does not avoid the central fact of discrimination merely by showing the relevance of the social category in that way. The contention that hiring a minority person will offend customers simply means that the irrelevant characterizations of customers about the minority in question are being taken by the actor as the ground for action: in short, in the choice between the value of nondiscrimination and economic success, the actor is choosing the latter. Though some may not be especially happy with these kinds of distinctions (after all, it is said, prejudice without discrimination is an inconsequential attitudinal state; and the idea of discrimination without prejudice may exonerate true prejudice too easily), but it strikes me that both theory and practice command attention to such distinctions. Theoretically, there is no gain in confusing a value choice on the part of the individual with intergroup prejudice; and practically, the United States Supreme Court has made it clear that a definition of discrimination simply in terms of differential outcomes by ethnicity (for example, disproportionate racial balances in the schools) is not adequate: the "soft" standards of aim and intention are an integral part of the definition of discrimination (and there is also the fact that large social outcomes of segregation can obtain despite small differences in motives; see Schelling 1971 and Molotch 1972).

A brief word, finally, about a concept of *minority group* that flows naturally from what has gone before. The idea of a minority group has (contrary to popular connotation) nothing to do with size, but rather refers to behavior. A minority group can most readily be defined as any group against which categorical discrimination (in the sense outlined above) is practiced. Because any observable difference (of speech, dress, appearance, behavior, and so forth) between people can become the basis for such categorical discrimination (that is, differential treatment based upon irrelevant categorical features), it is in some degree an "accident" of history that ethnic, religious, and national categories have constituted the classic minorities, and we are now seeing the emergence of the new minorities: women, gays, children, the handicapped, and the like. What this view makes clear, above all, is (1) that minority status depends upon the existence of any observable difference socially defined as significant for purposes of categorical discrimination; and (2) the shifting circumstances of social interaction may make majority members into minorities (and vice versa) in given situations, depending upon the distribution of power (namely, the power to make discriminatory standards effective in interaction). This quite general behavioral definition need not obscure, however, the differences that surround this great range of minority situations—for example, that women, by the very fact of the unique family-based interdependencies involved, occupy a strategically different place in the stratification system than do the classic minorities.

THEORIES OF PREJUDICE

There are three main lines of theory concerning the social psychology of intergroup relations—personality theory, conflict and Marxian theory, and cultural norm theory—and a brief assessment of their current status as explanations of prejudice and discrimination is undertaken below. That undertaking, however, involves some prior clarity concerning the correlates of prejudice that have been established, especially as far as the major social lines of occupation, income, religion, education, and age are concerned.

A great deal of attention has been given to what might be called the *generality* of prejudice—a matter that has a direct bearing on the theory of prejudice that is favored. Generality, however, refers to a variety of questions that are sometimes confused. In the first instance, it refers to the degree to which an individual's prejudice is generalized in the sense that it includes a wide range of minority groups toward whom hostility or exclusion is expressed: that is, is prejudice relatively group-specific or not? The typical finding is that there is a remarkably high inter-correlation of prejudices yielding a syndrome of (for example) nationalistic, anti-Semitic, anti-Catholic, and anti-black attitudes. As is well known, the ethnocentric syndrome can easily include nonexistent groups (the famously disliked Pireneans, Danireans, and Wallonians; Hartley 1946; Epstein and Komorita 1966); and the correlations among random split-half groupings on a Bogardus-type social distance scale reach into the high .80s and .90s.

No theory of prejudice that depends upon contact experience and its generalization can account for these results demonstrating high cross-group intolerance. Indeed, these consistent findings constitute exactly the kind of evidence that serves as warrant for another notion of generalization and another theory of prejudice; namely, the personality theory that emphasizes the generalized roots of prejudice. The argument is that such a range of cross-group negativisms can hardly be either experiential or rational, hence one must look to deep-lying personality for their source: what binds together these illogical antagonisms is their psycho-logic. As Allport (1954:70–71) put it, "There must be a psychological unity that explains these mental bonds . . . prejudice is basically a trait of personality. . . . The specific object of prejudice is more or less immaterial. What happens is that the whole inner life is affected; the hostility and fear are systematic."

Perhaps. But there are difficulties with the evidence on cross-group generality, and with the generality of roots it is supposed to signify. The instrument contributions to these high correlations are probably massive, given chiefly the fact that the *r*'s derive from social distance instruments and/or prejudice tests that embody highly stereotypic judgments. In effect, they call for the respondent either to be categorical or refuse to respond. Thus, the very language and the response format encourage the kind of ritual responses that the high correlations reflect.

Further, and perhaps more important, the evidence on still another version of the generality of prejudice—generality across situations—argues against a linear, strongly personality-embedded view of prejudice. Old studies (Minard 1952) and newer ones (Campbell 1971) show that it makes a great difference, as far as expressed attitude toward a given minority is concerned, what the issue or situation is that happens to be at stake. Thus, in the fifteen-city study that was undertaken in 1968 under the auspices of the National Advisory Commission on Civil Disorders, the evidence concerning cross-situational variation in attitude toward interracial Negro-white contact is impressive: in a sample of some 3,000 whites, only 10 percent were consistently negative when presented with four different types of contact (working with a black supervisor, neighborhood integration, children's playmates, and personal friendship)—and only 6 percent accepted all four of these interactions. Thus, it is quite clear that the respondents are not very categorical in their response—for example, 86 percent said they would "not mind at all" working with a qualified Negro supervisor; but only 49 percent said they would not mind at all if a Negro family with equivalent income and education moved in next door (Campbell 1971:8).

This selective situationism in ethnic attitudes is not surprising, and it goes hand-in-hand with the specificity of response that has been demonstrated in the literature on attitudes and behavior—again, in both the old evidence (LaPiere 1934; Saenger and Gilbert 1950) and more recent studies (Green 1972; Schuman 1972a). Attitudes are not general enough to predict behavior across even a relatively narrow range of situations, so that the analyst is forced either to narrow the prebehavior measurement drastically to "behavioral intentions" (Fishbein and Ajzen 1975) that are almost directly matched with the behavior that is being predicted ("Do you intend to cut your sociology class on Wednesday?"), or at least to require, not only measurement of one's attitude toward an object, but also an attitude toward the situation in which the object-related behavior takes place (Rokeach 1968a). Hesitancies about the adequacy of conceptions that rely upon stable, predictive personal attributes, such as attitudes, have been common in the sociological literature for a long time (stemming chiefly from the early symbolic interactionists' distrust of preinteractive and cross-situational elements—such as attitudes—as compared with specifically situated and emerging definitions and meanings; for example, Blumer 1953). It is intriguing to find a powerful thrust in this same situational direction emerging among analysts on the psychological side (Rotter 1955; Mischel 1973; Jessor and Jessor 1973). It is not only ethnic attitudes that have been found to be problematic, but a host of other attitudes and personality traits as well; and our theories of prejudice presumably will have to take account of the evidence on distinctiveness rather than generality, and of the centrality of situational analysis.[2]

If that is no surprise to sociologists, the weakness of the variables we regularly count on (and enjoy calling "structural")—especially the class indicators of occupation, income, and education—may be more surprising. The observed relation of prejudice to these standard indicators of social position is not very dependable and quite complex. Not very dependable means that though it is easy enough to find studies in which low status is associated with relative intolerance (for example, Sheatsley 1967), the clarity of this relation dissipates as one examines more carefully the varied ethnic groups and varied social relations under review.

Two relatively recent studies provide examples of this point. In his summation of the Cornell Studies in Intergroup Relations, Williams (1964) notes the general corroboration of the fact that high education is associated with greater tolerance; and indeed, the differences by educational level are sometimes quite impressive. But as Stember (1961) had earlier suggested, when the analysis proceeds to take into account independently the different ethnic objects involved (Jews and Negroes), the tie with the closely related variable of occupation, and the different aspects of prejudice involved (for example, endorsement of stereotypes as contrasted with expressions of preferred social distance in interaction), the results for occupation and education become cloudier—for example, social distance prejudice toward Jews goes with *high* occupation; and those who identify themselves as middle class are somewhat *more* likely than working-class persons to express feelings of social distance toward Jews. The better-educated respondents tend, as one might expect, to reject the (often crudely stated) negative stereotypes, but education is not so linearly related to other types of prejudice items. The conclusion (based not only on the Cornell data, but on a review of the evidence generally): "The pattern of relationships between education and different dimensions of prejudicial attitudes is thus quite complex" (Williams 1964:56).

This surprising inconclusiveness of the evidence on "the social location of prejudice" is again documented in Campbell's study (1971) in fifteen major cities in the United States. The several indicators of ethnic hostility (acceptance of interracial contact, the perception of discrimination, expressed sympathy for black protest, and positive response to legal and economic programs designed to aid the minority) are examined for their association with a series of socioeconomic variables, and what emerges is a series of insignificances: "The differences between Catholics and Protestants in their response to racial questions are very minor" (p. 47); "Church attendance, with whatever exposure to church doctrine this may imply, apparently has no influence on these attitudes" (p. 49); "The racial orientation of white people at different occupation levels differs very little" (with the exception of clerical workers, p. 51); "Whatever income level does tell us about people, it tells us surprisingly little about their racial orientation" (p. 53); "Age in itself explains relatively little of the diversity of attitudes which exists among white adults" (p. 61); and finally, "For that part of the white population whose formal schooling has not gone beyond high school (about three-quarters of these urban white people) years in school has only a modest relationship in racial attitudes . . . the fact that they went to high school or finished high school has surprisingly little effect on the general distribution of their attitudes" (p. 61). The feeble conclusion is that though people obviously differ widely in their racial views, we must turn to "their family backgrounds, their friends, their personal experiences, and other idiosyncratic influences" (p. 61) for an explanation of these differences.[3]

It hardly seems very helpful, however, to count on individual experience or idiosyncratic influences for an explanation of the systematic workings and omnipresence of prejudice. People still express antiminority sentiments with surprising readiness: for example, more than 40 percent say that white people have a right to keep blacks out of their neighborhood, and that blacks should respect that right (Taylor et al. 1978); 56 percent say that "Negroes themselves" (not discrimination) are responsible for their inferior jobs, education, and housing (Campbell 1971); 42 percent agree that "Jews are more willing than others to use shady practices to get what they want" (Selznick and Steinberg 1969).

Perhaps, on second thought, an emphasis on family backgrounds and friends (rather than on the "big" variables such as social class) should not be so disappointing or off the mark. In the first place, our dependence on socioeconomics may have been an over-dependence from the outset. Jessor (1979), for example, shows (contrary to conventional wisdom) that social class indices are of little help in predicting either the "perceived environment" of the respondent or drug-related behavior among adolescents; and he urges that "researchers ought to shift away from class to theoretical variables that operate independently of supposed class differences" (p. 38). In the second place, we have seen recently the re-invigoration of studies highlighting the importance of smaller scale social networks for such varied phenomena as migration (Fischer 1977), work (Granovetter 1973), and community (Laumann 1973); and it may well be that this thrust toward family and informal networks can be more helpful with respect to prejudice and discrimination than we have been given to suppose. Sociologists will find it hard, and probably unwise, to actually abandon social class as a major variable, but they need to reckon with the fact that SES explains prejudice (and other important phenomena) very poorly.

This perspective brings us back to the three main lines of theorizing about prejudice, and in particular to the cultural norm theory, because "family and friends" can basically be seen as a way of focusing on cultural norms as written in early and everyday social interaction. Though the notion of cultural norms is often invoked to explain the generalities discussed above (the widespread attitudes of ethnic rejection, the variety of minorities encompassed, and the stability of stereotypes), it is nevertheless not a very satisfactory explanation when taken at such a global level. Blalock (1967), in fact, points out that, like the notion of "competition" which is so crucial for the Marxian versions of prejudice and discrimination, the notion of culture as a variable that can be used in testing hypotheses is not workable: they are both simply "a general descriptive term referring to a class of phenomena" (p. 74), convenient but not analytical tools.

One might say that the central theme of the cultural norm thesis is the idea of *conformity* (whereas for the conflict theorist the key idea would be *exploitation,* and for the personality theorist, *repression*). But the general emphasis on conformity can be specified and made more workable by focusing upon the more dynamic ideas relating to normative conformity: the ideas of social learning, social acceptance, and differential association, for these are the processes to which normative theorists explicitly or implicitly appeal. And, indeed, the evidence that is typically adduced on these matters—on learning via parental attitudes; on social acceptance via similarities in liking and disliking; on differential contact and subgroup coherences in attitude—becomes rather persuasive regarding the significance of these aspects of the cultural norm approach.

Thus, for example, Epstein and Komorita (1965, 1966) found that the correlations between children's ethnic attitudes and the perceived attitudes of their parents are quite high (in the .6–.7 range), and these findings hold for both Negro and white children. They tie these results to childrearing style in a fairly straightforward social learning fashion, noting that moderate rather than severe discipline is conducive to the modeling of ethnocentric parental attitudes: the consequence of moderate discipline is to incline the child to seek parental approval by internalizing parental attitudes. In a similar way, the effectiveness of differential association as normative reinforcement is suggested by the evidence that indicates that ethnic attitudes are correlated with the person's assessment of the norms that hold among both close friends and larger networks (Fendrich 1967). In both of these illustrations (regarding the relation between children's and parent's attitudes, and between personal prejudice and perceived group norms), the associations can be misleadingly high insofar as they are correlations taken from the same individual—hence, they incorporate a projective element (prejudice the person presumably *wishes* to see in parents and peers). But the evidence indicates that a significant parent-child similarity in politically tinged attitudes is independently verifiable, as is the peer group normative influence (see, for example, Radke-Yarrow et al. 1952; Pettigrew 1958; Sears 1969; and Silvern and Nakamura 1973).

These emphases on social learning, social acceptance reinforcements, and differential association are embodied in a wide variety of materials that are often not explicitly conceived as evidence relating to the social norm thesis. The long-standing data on the effects of equal-status, task-involved and neighborly social contact (Deutsch and Collins 1951; Wilner, Walkley, and Cook 1955), and the newer evidence as well (Williams 1964; Cohen and Roper 1972) go in the same direction, indicating that culturally standardized contacts simply reinforce prejudicial norms, while liking goes with a sense of similarity based on differential association involving interdependent achievement and interpersonal knowledge.

All of this is, of course, within limits and with qualifications—for example, it seems clear, and understandable, that contact has less effect for blacks (Ford 1973; Surace and Seeman 1967). But the normative view, with its emphasis on conformity (including, most recently, conformity to changing legal norms), is substantially buttressed by a long line of studies in social psychology that are not explicitly concerned with interracial attitudes—indeed, with only a small exaggeration one might say that conformity has been *the* theme of contemporary social psychology, from Newcomb's (1943) early study on college socialization, through Asch's (1951) demonstration of the power of conformity in social judgments, to the more recent work on cognitive dissonance, the modeling of "helping" behavior, and even for that matter (though in a somewhat different way) the normative emergence of collective behavior (Turner 1964).

When we turn to the personality-oriented theories in the light of what has gone before, it becomes eminently clear that the several theories of prejudice are not so much in competition with one another as they are answers to rather different questions. As Williams put it, "The prejudice of conformity is not necessarily the active prejudicial hostility of the true bigot" (1964:82). It is one thing to ask about the bigotry that is manifested in strong, situationally unattuned hostility (not the customary pattern, as we have seen), and that which is simply conventional learning. It may well be that the personality theories are best geared to answering the question: why does this person show such unusual consistency in response across situations or circumstances; whereas the normative approach is best geared to answer the question: what accounts for the striking consistency of stereotypes over time and the substantial but situationally discriminating patterns of prejudice and discrimination that exist? In short, it is a question of explaining prejudice that serves a functional deep-lying personality need as compared with prejudice that reflects the everyday and ubiquitous learning of the "right" things to say and do.

If repression is the central theme of the personality approach to prejudice, the mechanisms that support that theme are those of frustration-aggression, projection (of unconscious motives), and rigidity. Since we know that there is a considerable turn these days away from such "trait" language, it is not surprising that a thoroughgoing personality theory of prejudice has lost considerable favor. Its heyday came in the decade following publication of *The Authoritarian Personality* (Adorno et al. 1950) with the myriad of F-scale studies and the sociological (and psychological) critiques thereof. The essence of the matter is that despite the extensive effort and the intellectual stimulation, the work turned out to be unpersuasive (on a variety of methodological and substantive grounds that cannot be reviewed here). One part of the problem was that the F-scale, taken as an index of "deep-lying personality trends," included so many things: pieces of direct prejudice (that is, anti-minority statements), and pieces of various theories of prejudice (including not only projection and frustration-aggression, but also a conventionality factor that overlapped with the social norm theory). It is not so much, therefore, that authoritarianism items (concerning trust, rigidity, obedience, and so forth) do not correlate with prejudice, but rather that the meaning, coherence, consistency, and stability of these correlations were called into question.

These difficulties, however, hardly add up to the view that personality is irrelevant. In several senses that could hardly be so. In the first place, whatever one's theoretical quarrel with the hydraulic images involved, we can hardly dismiss the evidence regarding mechanisms like frustration-aggression, assuming the presence of a cultural specification of minority objects for the displacement of aggression (Berkowitz 1969). The mechanism is certainly complex, certainly does not operate in isolation from situational determinants, and is, at the present juncture, more a matter of plausibility than prediction. It represents the kind of personality mechanism that is at once both real and overclaimed. To argue, for example, that parental anxiety about status produces authoritarian discipline, which in turn produces repression of one's faults and of aggression against authority, and finally the projection of these repressions against minority outsiders, is to construct a chain of plausibilities that remains undocumented.

In the second place, it is clear that attitudes of prejudice are associated with dispositions that are not immediately minority-related—for example, with more generalized personalitylike attitudes of trust, anomie, or status-mindedness (Kaufman 1957). Though some of these demonstrated connections between prejudice and other personalitylike measures may be instrument-born, it seems likely that they also represent a fact of life. They constitute sobering evidence of predispositions relating to prejudice that are quite widespread and potentially virulent. Still, this evidence does not necessarily speak to any depth of personality—for example, the relation between status-mindedness and anti-Semitism is easily understood as an association of compatible learnings, a point that is entirely congruent with Blalock's (1967:62) comment that "status consciousness as a theory of prejudice and discriminatory behavior cannot adequately deal with deepseated feelings and emotions or with extreme forms of aggression . . . it is more appropriate for explaining conventional behavior, conformity, and discrimination based on 'gentlemen's agreements.' "

Thirdly, though the general argument that *any* attitude or behavior is, in some sense, reflective of "personality" is a final possibility, that (not too helpfully) covers the entire field. What is perhaps most instructive here is that the sociological emphasis on the situation as a crucial feature of orientation and action is found now to be an active ingredient in the "personality" domain, with the trait theorists in rather general retreat.

We turn, finally, to the basically economic conflict theories, with an approving nod at the outset to Blalock's (1967:38) comment that "the contrast between economic and status theories, on the one hand, and ideological and personality theories, on the other, has perhaps been overdrawn." Among the reasons for holding that to be the case is that (as already suggested) the several theories (1) address different questions; and (2) where they do not, they imply factors of importance in the supposedly contrasting theory. The central theme in conflict theory is the idea of exploitation, the dynamics of which involves class interest (and manipulation), alienation, and false consciousness. Oliver Cox (1948:393) put it most directly a long while ago: race prejudice ". . . is a social attitude propagated among the public by an exploiting class for the purpose of stigmatizing some group as inferior so that the exploitation of either the group itself or its resources or both may be justified."

What Marxian theory seeks mainly to answer is the (functionalist?) question: why do formations such as group prejudice and discrimination exist in the first place, and why in these places against these groups? As with the theories already discussed, the difficulty lies in firmly establishing the empirical evidence that would allow a choice among putatively rival explanations. It is clear enough historically that the standard minorities have been exploited, that hard economic times or competitive economic situations—as in the case of "middleman minorities" (Bonacich 1973) or in periods of major socioeconomic change (Lipset and Raab 1970)—bring special trouble; and that many have profited (commercially, agriculturally, and so on) at the expense of minorities (as in the Japanese relocation).

But it is not so clear (given the difficulties already alluded to with the idea of competition) that explicit class interests are distinctly engaged, or that elite manipulation is an element in the mix. Many years ago, Paul Kecskemeti (1951) raised a question about the Marxian assumptions in *The Authoritarian Personality,* arguing that the conviction incorporated there concerning calculated management of ethnic hostility by the dominant economic interests was suspicious on at least two counts: (1) neither the evidence nor the logic that such management would, in fact, be beneficial to the elites in the way proposed by the "liberal" ideology was convincing; and (2) the image of a relatively small cabal managing to dupe the masses had an uncomfortable resemblance to right-wing arguments concerning clandestine Jewish control and organized massive deception. It is not assumed that he meant to deny that states and powers (in colonial situations, for example) use political means to encourage or repress racial attitudes to suit their economic gain; the question, instead, concerns the necessity of the idea of elite manipulation for understanding the origin and resurgences of intergroup hostility.

The issues in this debate have not been very well advanced since Kecskemeti's time. The typical stance is to acknowledge the obvious but partial truth of the exploitation theory (noting, for example, the congruent evidence to be found in the relatively high social distance against Jews among their most direct middle-class competitors; Williams 1964:54), but to raise questions about the adequacy of economic competition as an explanation of the range of groups and the range of gains involved—for example, the attitudes towards Quakers and Mormons, or the attitudes of Europeans toward Indians in South Africa (van den Berghe 1962); the widespread upper-class support—both black and white—for tolerance and emancipation (Marx 1967); and the variety of non-economic gains that are served by prejudice and discrimination.

At that point, the more elusive (and one might say, less vulgar) features of the competition theory come into play, via the proposal that direct economic competition is not necessarily the issue. It is, the argument goes, to be expected that a capitalist substructure would produce the kind of generalized alienation (Marx's "alienation of man from man") that is expressed not only in economic terms and not only among the subjugated classes—in a sense, the idea of alienation covers the flanks and the waterfront since generalized alienation softens the necessity for evidence regarding direct competition and exploitation per se. And the idea of false consciousness (not unrelated, for some, to the idea of alienation; Touraine 1973) brings a way of reading what the "natural" intergroup attitudes will be when freed of economic and manipulative constraints (as in the early Reconstruction period, and to a considerable extent in labor union contexts).

The difficulty of obtaining empirical evidence that would allow any real choice among these (at least in some sense) rival explanations is plain.[4] They are not, in fact, mutually exclusive—given, for example, that the social psychology of scapegoating is used to explain the flow of hostility toward middleman minorities under conditions of economic stress; or that social psychological conceptions like the sense of *relative deprivation* are rightly recognized as being embodied in the Marxian view. And if the structuralist imports social-psychological principles, the same is true on the other side—for example, the social psychologist presumably does not expect relative deprivation or normative conformity to operate independent of institutional and organizational structures, the existence and mobilizability of resources, family and social networks, or situational contexts. The end result is not necessarily a straightforward theoretical democracy ("no single theory works; each has some bearing"), but a still remaining task of specifying (1) which of several questions one is seeking to answer (as sketched above in a preliminary way); (2) what key themes or concepts are invoked in the given explanation, and what is their overlap (as suggested above in the commentary about the situation-specific drift of personality theory); and (3) under what conditions the several theoretical alternatives seem to carry a differential explanatory power (for example, the conditions that heighten conformity pressures, or those that make economic and status gains primary considerations).

SOCIAL MOBILITY AND PREJUDICE

Some aspects of this confluence of theories are exhibited in the work centering on social mobility. This work took its impetus from both the explanatory weakness of the standard socioeconomic variables and the failure of (and the sociological hostility to) the personality variables. The cast of its argument was that it is neither personality nor background, but the "structural" fact of having fallen or risen in the class system that is decisive. But if the mobile are more prejudiced, it is the social psychological mechanisms of status frustration or status anxiety that explain such a "structural effect"—the status degradation and frustration of downward mobility leading to prejudice, as does the status concern associated with perilous upward climbing.

The proposition is popular, reasonable, and has some empirical support (for a good summary of early work, see Bettelheim and Janowitz 1964); but it also has been questioned on empirical grounds and with respect to the general assumptions that it embodies (Hodge and Treiman 1966; Seeman 1977). Certainly, the effects of upward and downward mobility seem to be less powerful than has often been supposed, and such findings raise several questions. It may be that intergenerational mobility (which is where much of the effort has been concentrated rather than on career mobility) is too removed to find such effects; or correlatively, that only the extremes of such mobility—which are not well studied—have significant effects. And it may be that mobility effects are limited to particular societies, those that emphasize the importance of status success (as is supposedly the case in the United States).

On the other hand, it may equally be that the postulated connection between social mobility and prejudice represents an altogether too fragile view of people's coping capacities in modern society. I have referred to this matter elsewhere (Seeman 1977) in terms of questioning of the "status assumption" which seems deeply entrenched in American sociological thought. That assumption is characterized by four tendencies, all having implications for ethnicity-related thinking and for the significance attached to social mobility. There is: (1) the still-prominent commitment to the idea of the functional necessity of stratification systems; (2) the readiness to impute status motives to those who are mobile; (3) the dubious assumption concerning a widespread desire for mobility as a first-order priority (see the doubts on this score expressed by Porter 1968); and (4) the quick equation of status and ego.[5]

There is in this domain a kind of "strategy of retreat" that operates to salvage some version of the status assumption when it comes under challenge. One might propose that it is too literal to suggest that people give such priority to where they stand in the *hierarchical* order; but if ladder rank holds no such priority, then at least (it is said) people have a primary concern for *place* in the sense of social acceptance (Blau 1964). And if one questions even the validity of that motive as a general rule, the fall-back position (if social-ladder or social-acceptance concerns cannot be taken for granted), at the very least *self-esteem* is held to constitute a tenable status assumption: that is, people routinely operate so as to maximize their own self-esteem (Rosenberg 1979:188).

Perhaps they do; but this successive weakening of the purview of the status assumption leads as well to a weakening of the argument for prejudice-related social mobility effects. Social class, occupational, or ethnic ranking become a narrow class of many possibilities for establishing self-esteem, and there are many ways in which the individual can weaken their force. All of which may account for the weakness of the demonstrated connection between social mobility and prejudice, though it bears remarking that questioning the data and the assumptions on this point does not amount to saying that mobility and status are irrelevant. The evidence is not wholly negative; and certainly one would expect that people's experience of success or failure in their jobs would have an effect (but not necessarily on their prejudice or discriminatory behavior).

There is another way to look at social mobility and prejudice, in effect to turn the question around and ask not so much what effect mobility has, but what effect prejudice and discrimination have on the mobility of minorities. One answer is obvious, and does not involve a complex social psychology, since all one need do is to compare the occupational and income standing of majority and minority members. But Porter (1974) asked the less obvious question of whether the status attainment *process* is basically the same for blacks as compared with whites—whether white prejudice and discrimination produce different mobility patterns for blacks. Porter invoked Turner's (1960) distinction between "sponsored" and "contest" mobility as a conceptual aid in understanding the observed differences. Black mobility more closely approximates sponsored mobility, the system of prejudice and discrimination apparently generating a different meaning and utility for blacks of ambition and conformity. For blacks, ambition is much more a consequence of conformity—a pattern that Porter interprets as being more consistent with the elite sponsorship version of mobility than with the contest version that he finds more applicable for whites.

In a related search for the social psychological variables that affect achievement and mobility, both Crain and Weisman (1972) and Gurin and Epps (1975) find, as did Coleman (1966) earlier, that the individual's sense of personal mastery over life circumstances is one important ingredient for the achiever. The reasonable presumption (not strongly verified, however; Campbell 1971) is that externality (the sense of low control) is generated by majority prejudice and discrimination and is a significant element in black mobility behavior.

SOCIALIZATION AND MINORITY IDENTITY

There is some irony in the fact that what we know best about socialization has had considerably less policy impact than what has lately come to seem more debatable. What we know best is the fundamental learning of intergroup attitudes via early socialization. I do not propose to review this domain: it is basically unsurprising, and the evidence has been nicely capsuled in a propositional way by Ehrlich (1973:chapter 5). "Unsurprising" simply means that (for example) children develop a sense of the importance and invariance of social categories to which they and others are assigned quite early in the socialization process; they are "helped" in that regard by the existence of emotionally toned edges to neutral designations (such as simple color categories among pre-school children; Renninger and Williams 1966); and they are further helped by the consistency of their parental and neighborly surroundings in these matters—even by the taken-for-granted inattention that is paid to what is being learned via stereotypes, glances, and code names.

A more debatable side of socialization arises in connection with the issue of minority self-esteem. The older literature, which was influential in the school desegregation decision of 1954, documented the damage to self-esteem occasioned by a segregated society. The data (and the legal briefs) of Kenneth Clark (1965) and others emphasized black out-group identifications and the feelings of inferiority engendered in an atmosphere of rejection. The same applied to Jewish self-hatred (Sartre 1948; Lewin 1948). But things do not seem so clear now as the evidence mounts that there are either no differences in minority and majority self-esteem or even more favorable scores among minority members (for example, Rosenberg and Simmons 1972). The puzzle is what to make of this apparent change: are we dealing with errors of fact, differences in method, differential value-guided emphases, or literal changes occasioned by changing historical circumstances?

Again, it does not help simply to be democratic and say that there is a point in all of these explanations; but some of the distinctions that have already been invoked above may apply here. Just as it has been found necessary to distinguish between one's sense of *personal* control and one's judgment about generalized *social* control (or "control ideology"; Gurin and Epps 1975), the distinction between *personal* self-esteem and *racial* self-esteem is an important one (Porter 1961) and one not well made in the earlier studies. To the extent that minority members make such a distinction, the content and context of the measurement of self-esteem can make a very large difference. Similarly, the very idea of a trait called "self-esteem" is called into question by the emerging situationism that has invaded the psychological branch of social psychology (Pettigrew 1978). Greater attention is now called to the social context of measurement and to the specifications in the measurement itself. Thus, it is more complex than the simple argument that times have changed (though indeed they have) as far as minority self-reference is concerned: it is also that times have changed for our theories and measures of self-esteem as well.

We note, for example, that the increased emphasis on reference group and situational perspectives leads to more precise understanding of the comparisons that children make in developing their self-concept; and it seems clear that these are customarily narrower than was earlier supposed. Thus, Baughman and Dahlstrom (1968:460–62), conclude their study of Negro and white children in rural southern Millfield as follows: "the children have a pervasive within-race orientation . . . they look at themselves and their situations not in terms of the full society (not even the limited one that exists in Millfield). . . . When we turn to the self-concept of these children, their interview statements about themselves are markedly positive. This is particularly true for the Negro children, a fact that is at variance with the widely accepted belief that the self-esteem of the Negro is inevitably damaged." The Rosenberg and Simmons (1972) data in Baltimore support the same conclusion: that black self-esteem shows no damage under conditions of steady reference group support.[6]

Though all this may constitute a helpful and constructive revisionism, two points need to be kept in mind: (1) it hardly solves the problem to (as Adam 1978 put it) simply "exonerate" minorities from the stigma of low self-esteem where what is needed is more daily life detail on how minority members actually cope with subordination; and (2) self-esteem (especially as currently measured) is not a privileged value and it may be that the in-group solidarity and narrow reference-group behavior that seem to generate high minority self-esteem constitute too great a price to pay (at a cost in social integration and substantive equality).

CHANGES IN INTERGROUP ATTITUDES

The late 1950s brought the first dramas of school desegregation, followed in the 1960s by urban insurrection and the war in Vietnam, and in the 1970s the steady northern and western (for example, Boston and Los Angeles) court-sponsored extension of desegregation. It would be surprising, in light of all that, if American intergroup attitudes were not significantly altered; and indeed, they have been—as have other attitudes not irrelevant for interethnic relations (for example, attitudes concerning political trust and powerlessness).

Though these attitudes have changed in rather different ways, the changes seem collectively to be reasonable—that is, they appear to be changes that respond to the history of the period. Thus, with respect to attitudes toward racial integration, and antiminority attitudes in general, the evidence is consistent in showing a considerable liberalization over the past two decades. These changes have been most systematically monitored in a series of N.O.R.C. studies (Greeley and Sheatsley 1971; Taylor et al. 1978) which support the following general conclusions: (1) over the past twenty years, opinions have changed so that some of the scale items are becoming obsolete because of the near-unanimity of support (for example, questions concerning approval of the integration of public facilities and integration of the schools); (2) though there has been a great deal of talk about a "white backlash," the data do not confirm its existence: the pace of liberalization has not slowed—indeed, they remark upon a short period of faster change (a "liberal leap") in the early 1970s; (3) these changes are coordinate with liberalization in cognate domains involving attitudes toward political and civil rights (Davis 1975); and (4) the changes are not simply the result of replacements in the population involving younger and better-educated cohorts—there is also a significant general liberal drift across cohorts.

If this sounds a bit too good to be true, it is—when one begins to look more closely at the provisos. For one thing, some of the parallel changes in the political climate on which intergroup relations depend have been far less sanguine. It is often argued that positive change depends upon the firmness and legitimacy of political authority; and here we have witnessed a steady decline in Americans' sense of trust in officialdom, and a steady increase in their sense of powerlessness (House and Mason 1975). The full significance of these changes for intergroup relations remains to be documented; but it seems likely that they are not innocuous given the known sensitivity of minority relations to political and economic circumstances (and the fact that, for both blacks and whites, the sense of powerlessness goes with anti-outgroup sentiment; Seeman et al. 1971).

Another hesitancy regarding the bright picture of change arises from doubt concerning the operative importance of what may be simply conformity to a new climate of expression concerning minority matters. It is not enough to say that even the sensed need to verbalize progressive attitudes is important; that may be, but the brightness dulls when the same attitude measured in another way yields a considerably less positive picture. That is the case, for example, with questions dealing with neighborhood integration. In 1976, the pro-integration response was given by some 60 percent of a national sample (the statement was: "White people have the right to keep blacks out of their neighborhoods if they want to, and blacks should respect that right"). This figure is not inconsistent with that obtained (somewhat earlier) in the fifteen-city study: 49 percent said they would "not mind at all" if a Negro family with about the same income and education moved next door. But there is more recent evidence that these liberal answers concerning hypothetical black neighbors can be quickly subverted when the prospect of real integration is at hand: more than half of the white respondents (57 percent) indicated they would "feel uncomfortable" in a neighborhood that was depicted as one-third black; but more than 80 percent of blacks make such a neighborhood their primary or secondary choice (Farley et al. 1978). The conclusion: given these white and black preferences, which focus on reactions to specific situations rather than general expressions of sentiment, stable neighborhood integration is not likely to occur, despite the improved endorsement of generalized statements regarding integration.

Still another element of doubt is raised by those questions that are both low in acceptance and low in change. The item, "Blacks shouldn't push themselves where they're not wanted," (part of the Treiman scale used in the N.O.R.C. studies) is a case in point. Perhaps, as Taylor et al. (1978) remark, that item is just too ambiguous, and many might affirm the same principle about pushy teachers, preachers, and sociologists. But it is instructive that other samples say as well that "Negroes have been pushing too fast for what they want" (67 percent agree in the fifteen-city study), and it thus begins to appear that this may be an instance of the distinction between traditional and "symbolic" prejudice. Sears and Kinder (1971) use that distinction to make the point that though the traditional prejudices (regarding inferior intelligence, public accommodations, and so forth) show sharp decline, they have been supplanted by a form of racism that is symbolic in the sense that the hostility is not reflective of a direct personal threat to one's life space (housing, schools, personal safety, and so forth) but a threat to accepted values and rules (for example, the minority is not justified in its claims, is too pushy and demanding, does not sufficiently respect the proprieties, and so forth). It is the latter kind of prejudice that is found to be associated, then, with anti-black voting (in the Bradley-Yorty race in Los Angeles), with conventional religiosity, and conservative party identification.[7] The evidence on secular change, taken as a whole, is both impressive and cautionary: it shows the movement in attitudes that social changes should have wrought, and it shows at the same time the subtlety in adaptation that entrenched intergroup relations can exhibit. Though attitudes may not directly predict behavior (see below), the massive residential segregation that persists in the United States, and the continuing resistance to school desegregation, can certainly be taken as powerful evidence of the persistence of *some* kind of troublesome race-related attitudes.

MINORITIES AND COLLECTIVE ACTION

The mix that made the sixties so dramatic was the combination of a Western youth movement along with two uniquely American contributions: the Vietnam anger and minority protest. The latter played a key role, building via a long series of civil rights struggles to what amounted to a kind of urban insurrection. These events occasioned a host of study commissions, research programs, and theoretical evaluations. For our purposes, the most relevant distillates of this almost unsummarizable literature lie in the re-evaluation that occurred concerning the going models of collective behavior (especially questioning the components of irrationality and marginality embedded in the classic versions), and the controversy over the role of social-psychological as against structural factors in collective violence.

These two concerns are linked in the fact that the structurally oriented "resource mobilization" approach stresses the rational organization and allocation of resources in these events, as against such notions as the accumulation of tensions or resentments and their expression in disorderly outbursts. The concept of relative deprivation has served as an excellent vehicle for this debate, being heavily used in the interpretation of American racial violence (for example, Pettigrew 1971; Sears and

McConaghy 1973), made into an essential element in rebellion generally (Gurr 1970), and then challenged both as to its predictive power and its theoretical propriety (McPhail 1971; Tilly 1978). A substantial effort has been mounted (especially when one gets beyond case studies and into a series of events and historical periods) to show that indices of relative deprivation explain very little—so Spilerman (1970) found in his review of episodes of American urban revolt; and so, too, was the case for a much longer period of French upheaval (Snyder and Tilly 1972).

But there is an unnecessary element of fuzziness and fractiousness in the debate, and troubles that both sides apparently wish to ignore. For one thing, the structuralists (and, sometimes, both sides) do not typically derive indices of the *sense* of relative deprivation; they measure structural variables (for example, the movement of economic rates: wages, prices, productivity) that are taken to be indicators of the individual-level variables at issue. But as we should have guessed, the relationship between subjective evaluations of well-being and external objective conditions is itself so filtered through individual circumstances that there is little evidence of a systematic effect of macro-environmental conditions upon overall sense of well-being. In short, it is difficult to get to relative deprivation from economic conditions alone, since structural variables are only weak indicators at best of the personal experience of relative deprivation (Campbell et al. 1976).

More important, perhaps, the argument generally conceals a certain reversibility or commonality in the two positions. Though it seems apt to say that widespread grievance begets rebellion, social psychologists are constantly reminding themselves of a thoroughly correct proviso that goes back to Marx: grass-roots grievance does not typically translate into mass action without social organization and mobilization processes (that is, leadership, political alliances, memberships and cadres, and so forth) and without regard for situational constraints (for example, the visibility and level of official counter-reaction); hence it makes little sense (even to most social psychologists) to pose simply an individualistic accumulation-discharge model of relative deprivation. And on the other side, granting the importance of such factors as political mobilization and the apparatus of state control, one wonders whether the notions of relative deprivation and individual grievance must indeed remain so foreign to resource mobilization. Once the image of an irrational outburst among discontented marginals in society is discounted, there remains, nevertheless, a variety of deprivation and discontent: in a sense, the structuralists simply substitute politically oriented deprivation—call it the struggle for power, if you will—as a motive (rather than economic, ethnic, or other deprivations). In short, there is no reason (as Gamson and Fireman 1979 have recently argued) for social psychologists interested in the micro-social processes of mobilization for collective action to abdicate that ground to the structuralist argument. A contextually sensitive and situationally aware social psychology is surely in order, but that is where, in principle, the emphasis on the sociological side has been for a long while, whatever the difficulties of making that perspective operational in empirical work.

Once these theoretical issues are cleared away (as they certainly have not yet been, here or elsewhere), the main empirical conclusions in the literature on minorities and collective action are probably ones on which all sides will substantially agree. I refer, for example, to the general agreement that the participants in the American racial disorders were not disturbed deviants or rootless marginals; nor were they an economic and educational underclass of the ghetto; nor was it a case of irrational expressive rebellion (a point on which the considerable approval of non-participants bears some witness). It is also plain that demographic factors, such as the sheer concentration of blacks, strategic factors, such as the spread of the initial tactic of violence-oriented demonstrations to other minorities, social control factors relating chiefly to police activity, and the general unavailability of alternative institutionalized avenues of communication in a segregated society played an important role.

Still, it also appears to be true that the riot participants were distinguished at the individual level as well, and here the idea of alienation becomes relevant. The disaffection of what Caplan (1970) has (a bit grandly) called "the new ghetto man" could be discerned, for example, in their relatively high level of political distrust (of both black and white officials), in the strength of their black in-group identification, and in their sense of powerlessness in American society.

In the latter regard, however, there is an object lesson that more or less parallels some of the discussion above concerning self-esteem, in that the too-quick application of a general principle in the absence of essential distinctions can lead one astray. In both cases (self-esteem and powerlessness) there has been an over-readiness to apply the principle that self-definitions are reflections of significant others: we tend to think too readily in majority-oriented terms. But people make finer distinctions as to *which* others are significant, for which definitions, in what circumstances. With regard to powerlessness, the expectation that there should be large differences between blacks and whites, given their objectively different circumstances and the assumed inefficacy that black social subjugation should engender, have not been consistently verified. Though there is some evidence to that effect, the weight of the evidence goes more in the direction of emphasizing that blacks (and presumably other minorities as well) make a clear distinction between what has been called "personal control" and "control ideology" (or, as the Gurins call it, "system blame" for minority disabilities). Thus, the sense of control in one's own life in the daily interactive situations of family or job competence is one thing, and the sense of control as a minority member in American society is another—and the two ought to be discriminable in predicting black activism.

The evidence shows that minority members do discriminate in this way; and, on the whole, it shows as well that an "external" orientation so far as *social* control is concerned (that is, a sense of powerlessness before majority social agencies) is associated with activism, riot participation, and the like (Gurin et al. 1978). With regard to the sense of *personal* control, the relation to minority-related activism remains in question, as does the utility of a further related distinction, that between *expressive* and *instrumental* action. Caplan argues that the black activists of the sixties were *un*alienated in the sense of personal control (though high in *social* powerlessness); but Gurin and Epps (1975:284) contend that things have changed in that regard: "In 1970 the issue of personal powerlessness was simply irrelevant for student activism" (though earlier some relation had been obtained). Their emphasis is on the importance of control ideology and system blame for activism.

Since the distinction between expressive and instrumental action is difficult to operationalize in research, it remains unclear whether that distinction is a viable one in distinguishing how personal and social control operate in different kinds (and periods) of activism. One can readily project a scenario in which those who are characterized by a combination of high personal control (the sense that what the individual does can make a large personal difference) and low social control (the sense that individual decision is systematically hampered by institutional discrimination against minorities) would be the most readily mobilizable element; whereas the sense of personal control might become less relevant as norms concerning the rightness of the movement and participation in it are generated on a wider scale. My own data (based on a longitudinal study of participants in the French events of May 1968) go in that direction: most especially, the early participants were distinguishable by their relatively high sense of personal control. Whatever the necessary situational qualifications that may be required, minority activism is probably tied in predictable ways to such variables as the sense of relative deprivation and to the powerlessness version of alienation.[8]

ALTERNATIVES TO "RACE" RELATIONS

In view of the racial dramatics discussed above, it may seem strange that a significant literature has developed examining the question of whether, in fact, race and ethnicity serve so importantly as the criteria for exclusion and discrimination. That literature offering alternatives to "race" relations is fairly substantial and takes a variety of forms. It is symptomatic of this "revisionism" to note Williams's comment (1975:126) that "... revised accounts of U.S. urban history imply that 'powerlessness' rather than 'race' or 'ethnicity' per se may be the primary condition needing further analysis."

One line of investigation concerning such alternatives developed in the sixties, taking its inspiration from the literature on the relation between interpersonal liking and belief similarity. The argument was that race simply stands as a proxy for differences in values and beliefs that are the actual basis for differential choice. Rokeach (1968b) sought to test the relative strength of race and perceived belief dissimilarity, and concluded that race as a determinant of choice had been overestimated and belief similarity underestimated. It was not an isolated finding—for example, parallel findings led Hendrick and his associates (1971:257) to comment, ". . . at the level of human-to-human interaction, many variables may be more important in determining attraction than racial membership; in fact, race may not be a very important variable at all." And as usual, once postulated, additional research became available to specify for whom and in what circumstances belief similarity appeared to be more significant than race—thus, Triandis and Davis (1965), and others, showed that the belief variable was more operative in choices involving non-intimate interaction; and, not surprisingly, that race was more influential for more highly prejudiced subjects.

This literature on belief as an alternative to race basically flowed from the psychological social psychologists, and, as Fairchild and Gurin (1978) have noted, seems a bit strained both theoretically and practically in a society with the racial and ethnic history of the United States. The evidence, in fact, shows a considerable consensus between blacks and whites with respect to some of the most fundamental values relating to occupational goals, family life, education, and the like (see, for example, TenHouten 1970; Miller and Dreger 1973; Rokeach 1973), and the differences that do obtain (for example, black political distrust) are more like reactions to subordination than they are expressions of basic belief dissimilarity. The result is that in good part the belief dissimilarity thesis reverts to being not so much an alternative to race but a projective and stereotyping phenomenon (concerning presumed minority differences), which in itself needs to be explained.

On the sociological side there have been similar searches for nonracial interpretations, most particularly in the literature on social class and status distinction as alternatives to race. Wilson's (1978) analysis of "the declining significance of race" is an illustration of the continuing sociological interest in "structural" inquiries regarding group cleavage that clearly involve questions of a social-psychological character (that is, attributions, situational definitions, and intergroup hostilities). In Wilson's case the argument is that as a consequence of post-war structural change (in economic and legal systems chiefly) status and class considerations have come to predominate over race per se in defining the nature of black-white relations (influencing intra-group relations as well). It is an argument that is paralleled in a variety of smaller scale investigations. These range from early efforts (for example, Westie 1952) to show that the socioeconomic status of the object of prejudice is a primary consideration in intergroup rejection, to emphasis on status elements in prejudice (Lipset and Raab 1970), to demonstrations that choice is frequently guided more by class standing than by ethnic identification (Epstein and Komorita 1965).

Recently, the issue of race versus class has arisen in connection with the problem of "white flight." Frey (1979:427), for example, argues the reasonability of the view that, whatever the historical reasons may have been, "*current* white flight is largely a response to deteriorating economic and environmental conditions" rather than, as the conventional wisdom has it, to racial motivations. His own data do not allow a discounting of the racial factor, but they do highlight the importance of nonracial (fiscal and ecological) factors. Frey's argument is not inconsistent with the conclusion in another study of some 200 integrated neighborhoods in the United States (Bradburn et al. 1971), in which the importance of feared economic effect rather than racial composition is seen as critical in changing areas, nor with Marshall's (1979) emphasis on the "pull" of the suburbs (rather than the "push" of race-related central city factors).

Finally, these considerations about "alternatives" come back ultimately to the discussion of theories of prejudice and discrimination. Although we are interested in the phenomenal attributions that people may make (their nonracial "reasons" for friendship or neighborhood choice), these are always doubtful, and we regularly seek to go beyond such surface attributions to the underlying causes. That is what analysts seek to do in establishing, let us say, that the hostility to middleman minorities (the Jews in Europe and the United States, the Indians in East Africa) is not primarily an ethnic matter but is rooted in specified economic settings (that is, is found in societies exhibiting a 'status gap' between elite and mass). Complications derive from the fact that the alternatives interact and condition one another—for example, ethnic solidarity is affected by the class situation of minorities. Gordon's (1978) "ethclass" may not represent an elegant solution, but it clearly signals some of this complexity. A further complexity is that the various proposals reviewed above can be construed not so much as *alternatives* to race but as specifications of the *components* of race-related ethnocentrism (that is, rejection based on the assumption that blacks think differently, that ethnicity is inherently tied to socioeconomic incapacity, and so forth).

ATTITUDES AND BEHAVIOR

Our inheritance from LaPiere (1934) is a problem and a debate that will not go away. The literature on the attitude-behavior relationship has been summarized frequently (one might even say insistently, for example, Deutscher 1973; Liska 1975; Wicker 1971), usually asserting the dim prospects of predicting what people will do from what they say. There is no need here for one more such summary, especially in view of a recent survey of this domain by Schuman and Johnson (1976) and the contribution by Richard Hill in the present volume. These are detailed, sophisticated, perceptive, and balanced reviews of the matter—and, in keeping with recent trends, somewhat more upbeat about the utility of attitude measurement.

The upbeat attitude derives less from any technical improvements we have made in the measurement process than it does from a more analytical perspective on both the attitude and the behavior side. On both sides, we owe part of that improved conception of the issue to Donald T. Campbell. On the attitude side, his treatment of the LaPiere finding in terms of "situational thresholds" (Campbell 1963) instead of as a discrepancy between attitude-behavior helped to loosen the hold of a too literal formulation that anticipated that a general attitude toward an object ought to predict to a particular interaction regardless of circumstances. And on the behavior side, his insistence on the need for multiple measures to establish discriminant validity (Campbell and Fiske 1959) carried the message (not often implemented, unfortunately) that it is fruitless to develop a technically precisioned multiple-item attitude measure and expect that its connection with behavior can be appropriately assessed by evidence regarding a single act such as (let us say) petition-signing.

The act of voting is one of those single behaviors that attitude indices can predict quite well, and though it is a rather special kind of action, it can be instructive regarding the basic issues as they relate to intergroup relations. In the first place, to make such predictions we do not ask people about their general attitudes toward politics or politicians; we ask about the specific object (this candidate or party versus another) or about their behavioral intentions regarding the object (for whom do you plan to vote?). The point concerning specificity is made strongly by Fishbein and Ajzen (1975) and it conforms with the proposal that it is (and was) naive to construe attitude measurement as an effort to get at an elusive one-to-one correspondence between generalized attitudes toward ethnic objects and individual behavior toward those objects in concrete social situations. It is no small gain to put that false version of attitude research behind us; but the gain via this narrowing of focus can easily be neutralized by the fact that requiring a tight specificity of attitude to action can make the predictions theoretically uninteresting.

The voting case likewise illustrates the fact that normative circumstances make an important contribution relating to the attitude-behavior tie. Given the institutional stability and consensus surrounding voting, it is hardly necessary (as it is in the case of intergroup behavior) to be concerned over the normative pressures that might tend to dissociate attitude from act. People's perceptions of what the cost and gains may be in a given setting—for example, social network costs or perceived authority constraints—are influential and problematic in intergroup affairs. Schuman and Johnson (1976:187) cite a series of studies, some dealing with civil rights actions and open housing, whose gist is to suggest that attitude has an independent effect on behavior though additional variance can be explained via reference group measures.

Since the attitude-behavior question comes back in good part to the prejudice-discrimination distinction made earlier, the modesty of the attitude-behavior correlations and the necessity for adding the provisos discussed above should be in no way surprising or disturbing. Merton (1949) long ago constructed the fourfold table that included the unprejudiced discriminator and prejudiced non-discriminator, and Campbell (1963) viewed the matter much like a Guttman behavior scale composed of successively higher hurdles, as it were, for consonant behavior to be manifested (see also Linn 1965; and Fendrich 1967). Once the aim of discovering one-to-one correspondence between attitude and behavior is abandoned, the attention to attitudes is directed toward the discovery in all its subtlety of how people think and act (and coordinate the two) in realistic social settings.

It then follows that attention turns away from measurement of ethnic attitudes per se toward an interest in attitudes that connect both with intergroup behavior and with broader conceptions of human interaction. I refer, for example, to the large range of studies bearing on locus of control (or the sense of powerlessness) discussed above in connection with minority activism. These are attitude-behavior studies, but not in the sense commonly proposed. They reflect the broader interests that attitude studies in the intergroup arena have come to embody. A concrete example of this rather different interest in attitude and behavior is found in Bullough's study (1967) showing that, with appropriate controls, a relatively low sense of powerlessness among blacks (1) distinguished those who had, in fact, moved out of the ghetto into integrated neighborhoods; (2) correlated with learning more about one's rights and opportunities in the housing market; and (3) was associated with reported behavior that reflected an "integration" orientation.

The conclusion is that "some such concept as attitude (is) essential for social-psychological analysis" (Kelman 1974), not especially for the specific attitude-behavior connections that can be reliably predicted (though those are of interest) but for the understandings of intergroup dynamics that are generated. Though there is some resistance among sociologists to the attitude concept, it would seem to be generally the case that (1) something like such a concept is imported into what we are wont to call structural analyses; and (2) notions very much like attitudes, though by other names (whether called sentiments, self-concepts, or the like) are integral to the favored social psychological viewpoints in the sociological literature. In short, attitudes are with us, whether they connect directly to behavior or not.

Two further points need to be briefly mentioned. First, quite apart from any predictive or theoretical aim, the study of change in intergroup attitudes has its purpose. The behavioral implications of the drift toward pro-integration attitudes are important; but even in itself such a drift is of considerable interest simply as a reflection of institutional change and the climate of opinion surrounding it. More important, our interest in attitude influences on behavior should not discount or minimize the reverse process wherein behavior change affects attitudes. We have, of course, a massive literature on this behavior-attitude effect in the once-popular studies of cognitive dissonance (now supplanted on the psychological side by "attribution theory"),[9] and a portion of this work has documented directly the short-term changes in minority-related attitudes that behavioral induction can produce (Taylor 1975). Naturally, the longer term in situ change involved in the desegregation of recent years is more impressive for sociologists. Certainly the presumption is that the pro-integration attitudes of the late 1970s are radically different from the 1950s in good part because pro-integration behavior was required by law; and the same principle is at work in the contact studies already reviewed, where respondents who were presumably initially equivalent in race attitudes are shown to differ as a consequence of contact behavior.

It would be pleasant to be able to describe the desegregation process overall in such a favorable light, but the literature on school desegregation does not sustain such a consistently positive portrait. The numerous studies of the desegregation process that have become available since 1954 have been summarized often of late as the court battles and public stir over mandatory busing have taken on a new vigor. The positive outcomes of desegregation behavior are considerably more restricted and in doubt than the social sciences briefs in *Brown* v. *Board of Education* implicitly promised. I refer chiefly to four such outcomes: school attitudes and achievement; self-esteem; sense of control; and intergroup attitudes. The evaluative tone of the summarizers of this literature varies considerably—for example, Stephan (1978) is not impressed with the improvement either in the attitude of whites and blacks toward one another, or in self-esteem (he comments that "the self-esteem of blacks rarely increases in desegregated schools"; p. 217); though Weinberg (1977), in the most inclusive of these assessments, is much more sanguine,[10] whereas St. John (1975) is simply unenthusiastic.

Is it that the social psychological principles we thought were operative simply don't work? That conclusion is hardly warranted despite the disappointments and doubts generated by the desegregation evidence; indeed, the very absence of massive confirmation encourages clearer attention to what those principles really involve.

1. A careful review of pupil achievement, with close attention to the adequacy of the methodologies employed, suggests that desegregation has the expected beneficial effect (Crain and Mahard 1977). But these effects are often quite modest—which is one ground for disappointment, and one ground for the differing opinions as to whether segregation "works" since that is an evaluation that depends on the gap one had hoped to close. Further, whether it works or not depends on school and community contextual variables (another ground for disappointment, if one had hoped that desegregation would simply "work").

2. The conflicting evidence about improvement in self-concept and improvement in intergroup attitudes should not be surprising. The hope for unilinear improvement across a whole range of qualities represents a common but misguided conception of the coherence of "good effects," and we have evidence (not only in intergroup relations) that more often than not such coherence does not obtain. Situations are too complex, and people too discriminating in their responses, for such linearity to obtain with any frequency. Furthermore, there is the problem of short-run versus long-run effects; in the short run, self-esteem may well suffer, whereas over the long haul the expected improvement can occur. The strained community circumstances that have often surrounded desegregation efforts certainly work against producing any overall short-run effect of the kind that has been hoped for. Finally, as Rosenberg and Simmons (1972) effectively argue, the principles that we depend on ought to include some understanding of the reference group processes that obtain in the concrete situation; especially in the short run, these processes can help in understanding when desegregation may have a negative effect on such variables as self-esteem and minority attitudes. We may not appreciate the result when newly integrated minority students compare themselves unfavorably with majority members, but the result does not invalidate social-psychological principles relating to reference group and social comparison processes.

3. With regard to the individual's sense of control, an idea that was highlighted in the Coleman Report (1966), the evidence appears again to be mildly confirmatory—that is, the short-run evidence concerning newly integrated school children is not inconsistent with the longer term evidence that a higher sense of control over the environment goes with integration experience (Crain 1971; Crain and Weisman 1972; Bullough 1967). The evidence quite generally shows that favorable control-related experience improves the person's sense of control (Seeman 1975); but it also shows that the learning regarding control is a differentiated matter. It is not *any* favorable experience that generates improvement; it is

control-relevant experience (for example, successfully managing a job hunt) that improves the sense of control. The same principle should hold with respect to desegregation, in that the experience must not only be generally favorable, but have a perceived control-relevant content to be effective in generating some change in locus of control. It may be (as Crain and Mahard suggest 1977:35) that the development of an improved sense of control ("a greater amount of self confidence from discovering that they can cope") is one of the preconditions for the occurrence of other kinds of minority gains, socially and academically, from the desegregation process.

4. The great bulk of recent studies have not, in fact, studied the process of desegregation. The model most generally applied has been that of the laboratory, with desegregation of the schools in a given community being the supposed experimental manipulation. But a compilation of results from such "experimental" interventions is almost guaranteed to be cloudy and contradictory. As St. John remarks (1975:121), "desegregation is a multi-faceted phenomenon," and it is not only so in the sense that it can be beneficial in some respects and harmful in others, but also in the sense that "it" is always accomplished in a specific school and community context (with specific teachers, facilities, curricula, planning, controversy, political leadership, and so forth). The result is that we are misled from the outset: "desegregation is not a treatment" (Crain and Mahard 1977:31), but we focus our attention on "treatment" effects and gloss over the essential details of the process phenomena.

5. The evidence tends to confirm the idea that an early start on desegregation (that is, in the lower school grades) is more effective in achieving the kinds of attitude change we seek. That idea has been widely proposed from the outset, the social psychological principles involved being rather self-evident, even if the political practicalities frequently are not. But even "early start" optimism must be tempered by an awareness of the deep embeddedness of school desegregation in the larger community—in the housing market, in local and national politics, and in our occupational system. Being misled by the image of a "desegregation experiment" has meant, in part, that we have underplayed how significant it is that education is entangled in these larger economic and political issues.

Ethnicity in American Life

The phrase "consciousness of kind" (Giddings 1896) has an anachronistic ring, but perhaps it was more prophetic than quaint; certainly it is still appealed to, both directly and indirectly, in the analysis of contemporary minority relations. Thus, Hannerz (1969:12) begins his ethnographic study with the question, "What makes the ghetto a community?" his answer being one that stresses "its own consciousness of kind . . . which allows for little confusion" as to who belongs and who is an outsider. The surprise for many analysts has been the tenacity of minority solidarities in American life, especially in view of the power and pervasiveness of mainstream cultural definitions.

The surprise is especially acute in view of the thinness of basic subcultural differences on which ethnic consciousness appears to rest. Consciousness of kind involves a certain sympathetic identification with others in the same category; but the basis of that identification is not necessarily, or even typically, any difference in shared values, but more a matter of in-group associational ties in the context of out-group distance and discrimination. This point is captured in Gordon's (1978) distinction between behavioral and structural assimilation—the former referring to the absorption of the values and behavior patterns of the host society, and the latter to entrance into the social networks and organizational life of the receiving society. Gordon comments: ". . . while behavioral assimilation or acculturation has taken place in America to a considerable degree, structural assimilation, with some important exceptions, has not been extensive" (1978:204).

To be sure, there are ethnic and race-based differences that can be discerned. Hannerz (1969:179) recognized distinctive elements of the "culture of poverty" in such ghetto features as "gregariousness, informal credit among neighbors, a high incidence of alcoholism, the use of violence in settling quarrels, consensual unions," and related items (for example, "a cult of masculinity"), and Liebow (1967) found similar phenomena on Tally's Corner; but the idea of the culture of poverty does not help much in understanding these features, nor do they constitute any essential value ground or differentiation on which racial identity is built. For the Mexican-Americans, a similar kind of relatively thin difference is noted; for example, Grebler et al. (1970) describe the continuing importance of Spanish language and in-group awareness based upon it (see also Lopez 1976), but comment as well: "Mexican-Americans do not appear to possess distinctively traditional values of the kind frequently attributed to them" (1976:438).

The differences in "structural assimilation" that do obtain are important. They certainly play a role in American political life; and as Light (1972) has shown, the internal solidarities and strong associational mechanisms in the American Asian community help to explain their small-business success in comparison with other minorities. Certainly these solidarities play an important role, too, in relation to the current ferment over neighborhood schools, with a not inconsiderable sentiment among minorities themselves against such community-threatening policies as metropolitan or city-wide busing. It takes some stretching to conceive of the "separate sociological structures" (Gordon 1978:205) that a good many minorities retain in the United States as a version of "colonialism" (Blauner 1972), but these structures and the identity convictions that go with them are continuing evidence of the deeply grained pluralism that persists in contemporary American life.

If that persistence has been somewhat surprising, it is also surprising to recognize how perspectives have changed regarding the marginality that such pluralism may engender. Park (1928) emphasized the psychological cost of marginality (while recognizing the potential gains, especially the insight and perspective occasioned by the individual's looser grounding in the majority culture), and for a long time the literature evoked variations on the Park theme. These variations were visible in the concerns about Jewish self-hate (Lewin 1948) and inauthenticity (Sartre 1948; Seeman 1966), and in the extensive literature already cited on the low self-esteem of minorities generally. But the change in emphasis in the self-esteem literature is paralleled in the virtual disappearance of the marginal man thesis: the positive attitude prevails, having been stimulated by the relative success of the civil rights movement and the ethnic awareness that surrounded the long period of activism. The disappearance is probably also due to an increased awareness on our part as analysts of the subtleties of the reference group process among minority members—that is, how positive in-group attitudes can survive in a hostile world. We do not know how much of the change in this marginality literature is a matter of altered "community" (increased black pride, and so forth) or of altered perspectives among sociologists.

In any event, there is no occasion here for a round of applause on either side: the dominations, discriminations, and social distances in American minority life are still firmly entrenched, and we have the difficult task of developing theories and practices that wed democratic process with ethnically separated minority communities that do not wish to disappear. In a certain sense, "the American dilemma" (Myrdal 1944) remains, and is symbolized by the increasing governmental affirmation of ethnicity (for example, the Spanish-English dual-language voting instructions in California). The experience of other countries (Belgium, Ireland, and others) teaches that cherished ethnic identities regularly produce political trouble; and the thrust of ethnicity is, more or less, taking us down the same road, though in the American context joining ethnicity with political community may be considerably more successful.

Summary

My interest, finally, is not so much in a literal summary of the foregoing, but in identifying (briefly, even cryptically) the main themes that emerge for sociologically oriented social psychologists:

1. We often forget how new are the sociological concepts that we now apply with regularity in the domain of intergroup relations. Though we tend to think of them as "classical," such concepts as social norms, reference group, alienation, self-esteem, relative deprivation, and the like, are for the most part missing from the first edition of the *Encyclopedia of the Social Sciences,* which is one way to mark the fact that we have been working seriously with these ideas for a relatively short time. It should be no surprise, therefore, that (for example) the subtleties of reference group phenomena are not well understood, and that reference group mechanisms might explain what appears to be a counter-intuitive finding of high self-esteem among minority members.

2. Sociologists are devoted to demographics—the "structural" variables of social class, education, age, occupation, and so forth, but there is room for doubt in the literature on intergroup relations (and elsewhere) that these "distal" variables, removed as they are from the interpretation and behavior of social factors, are of as much direct importance as is often presumed. For social psychologists, this implies the necessity of discovering the means whereby these factors become specifically and circumstantially relevant to intergroup behavior.

3. We have discerned an important congruence between the sociological and psychological branches of social psychology in their mutual current emphasis on the situated character of behavior. For sociologists, this has been historically the case (one is reminded of Coutu's 1949 largely ignored effort to establish the concept of *tinsit*—tendency-in-situation—as the fundament of social psychology); but the emphasis on situational analysis has come in force to the psychological side as well: "the environment of personality" (Feshbach 1978) is receiving its due, and sociologists ought to be fully aware of this development.

4. A comparable congruence has taken place, not so much in conception (as with the situational emphasis) but in subject matter interests. I refer to the new literature on "attribution theory" (Kelley and Michela 1980) and the generally revived interest among social psychologists on the psychological side in cognitive phenomena bearing on how individuals define the situation in the course of their action. The earlier focus on "cognitive dissonance" had very little affinity with the long-held sociological stress on symbolic interaction, but the current work on the attribution of meanings, causes, connections, and qualities of objects and persons (including the self as actor or observer) is coordinate with the classic sociological concerns inherited from the Chicago school of social psychologists. I have noted above that how "race" is defined in interaction is included in this attributional work.

5. There has been a change in the trait-like notions of "attitude" that dominated the earlier literature. The old interest in attitude scales that might provide something approaching a one-to-one correspondence with behavior (for example, anti-Semitic scales to predict behavior toward Jews) has given way to what one hopes is a more sophisticated interest in understanding the more or less stable orientations and processes that contribute to action under given conditions. Thus, though a relation to behavior is at stake, such constructs as "locus of control" or "self-esteem" are not intended as mirror-images of attitude to behavior in the way that (let us say) religious attitude scales were once employed to predict church attendance. We know what some of the difficulties are in seeking to go from an attitude test to personal behavior (and how to increase the correlation via specificity in many cases), but except for certain instances (for example, voting or consumer behavior) the attitude-behavior analysis is more an interest in developing theoretical constructions of interaction than one of predicting behavior in relation to social categories like Catholics or Chicanos.

6. There has been some emphasis of late on the failure of social-psychological variables—most notably, in the literature on protest and civil disorder, where it is said that resources, mobilization, and political con-

flict (not relative deprivation, alienation, or individual disaffection) are the critical matters. The dismissal of social psychology in this domain is premature and unnecessary, and the arguments not very well put on either side. The social psychologists claimed too much, without making clear the specifications of "structural" circumstances within which the dynamics (let us say) of relative deprivation were presumed to work; and the structuralists have simply been uninterested in the micro-mobilization social psychological processes to which their data by its very nature cannot speak.[11]

7. In a certain sense, the difference just described represents an interest in different questions rather than in competing theories; and the same may be said in good part for the different "theories of prejudice" that are found in the literature. It is not so much a matter of competing testable theses regarding prejudice and discrimination that distinguishes the personality, cultural norm, and group conflict theories, but of different questions that form the focus of their attention: why this group rather than some other is the attacker; why the change in attitude or action here and not there; why the development of this form of segregation in one circumstance and not another?

8. We all know that what we do as social psychologists carries with it a set of assumptions about how interaction works, and we have had occasion recently to become more sharply attuned to what those assumptions are and how they influence our work. Two examples:

(a) The influential studies and testimony on negative black self-esteem have recently come under question, revealing what may have been an unjustified assumption about minority dependence on, and conformity to, the going majority definitions. It would not have been the first or only time that a heavy emphasis on the "conformity assumption" was in evidence in American social psychology (on both the psychological and sociological sides).

(b) Studies in social mobility and prejudice continue to question the "status assumption" that is built into our predictions about the consequences of mobility and migration. That is not to say that mobility (over class lines or organizational lines) has no effect; but it does imply that the effects are more limited and specific than this literature has customarily implied on the basis of status-minded conceptions of self and behavior.

9. For a good while, the literature on intergroup relations (along with a substantial segment of sociological literature generally) tended to ignore the significance of social networks in modern society. Committed to the idea of "mass society" and taken with macro-theories of one sort or another ("postindustrial society" or some variant of systems theory), attention to the social psychological significance of micro-organization in modern society tended to flag, and it is only recently that we have seen a re-invigorated interest in the study of social networks. The implicit interest in this phenomenon that is represented in the traditional studies of the effect of intergroup contact on attitudes has now become a central theme in current research, perhaps precisely because the network idea is one that can join social-psychological interests in the person with structural interests in the situation and its broader social context.

10. Finally, it is no news but still important to remember that our

investigations of intergroup relations are themselves carried out in a historical context. Thus, our changing interpretation of minority self-esteem, our current assessment of the importance of ethnicity or the reality of minority stereotypes, our revised judgments about the character and consequences of slavery, and so on, are themselves products of a societal situation. That is one reason, among others, to insist that a good deal more truly comparative work on social psychology of intergroup relations (and in social psychology generally) is required if we are to avoid a certain provincialism that still remains our fate in this field. Though there are, to be sure, numerous non-American studies, the comparative perspective is not strongly developed in social psychology.[12] Perhaps that is the next story that needs to be told in the area of intergroup relations—though it probably cannot yet be told very convincingly, given the generally constrained focus that has been our history.

NOTES

I wish to acknowledge the valuable bibliographical assistance provided by Marnie Sayles and a helpful critical reading of an earlier draft by Jeffrey Prager (UCLA).

1. For a review of some of the difficulties involved in coming to an acceptable definition of prejudice, see Ehrlich (1973), who prefers a quite general version: "Prejudice can then be defined as an attitude toward any group of people" (1973:8). For a consideration of social psychology's overemphasis on the absence of differences, and of the ways in which real differences between groups can be translated into prejudicial error, see Campbell (1967).

There are difficulties with all of these "solutions" to the definition of prejudice, whether one emphasizes rigidity, emotionality, norm violation, categorical treatment, or (as I do) the criterion of factual relevance. In the latter case, the counterargument is made that (1) unequivocal evidence about imputed category characteristics is rarely available, and (2) the terms typically applied (for example, clannish or loyal; stubborn or principled) are different evaluations of the same facts (favorably or unfavorably interpreted). Though I do not find these arguments persuasive (that is, they do not lead me back to rigidity, emotionality, or categorical treatment as the decisive criterion), the important thing in this discussion is not which definitional choice is made, but that it is made with some clarity concerning the implications of the choice.

2. For a recent analysis that goes in the same direction, emphasizing situational variation and the need to "decompose" the conative, affective, and cognitive features of prejudice, see Jackman (1977).

3. The "striking" (Campbell 1971:68) absence of difference associated with precollege school experience is true also for college experience *except* for the most recent post–World War period, where the recent college-attending generation has encountered a more liberating experience. It is important to remember that some recent evidence is considerably more positive about educational and occupational effects (for example, Taylor et al. 1978).

Since this section has been cast in terms of surprises, it is relevant to note that in a companion to the Campbell study, on attitudes toward militancy and violence on the part of Black respondents (Campbell and Schuman 1968:57), the authors find no evidence that educational attainment is associated with advocacy or moderation regarding racially oriented violence; and they comment: "Since education in turn is fairly closely related to income and occupational status, these results suggest that neither of the latter socio-economic indicators taken alone will explain very much of the data. Advocacy of violence appears to be surprisingly *un*-related to measures of current socio-economic achievement."

4. With respect to false consciousness, for example, it is striking that so little has been done in an empirical way. For two rather different approaches to the matter, see Mann (1970) and Seeman (1966).

5. The clearest enunciation of that equation is found in Lipset and Zetterberg (1956:162). "Since any ranking is an evaluation by the society, it will be reflected in a person's self-evaluation; since any person tries to maximize his self-evaluation, he tries to maximize his rank. The basic idea is that persons like to protect their class positions in order to protect their egos, and improve their class positions in order to enhance their egos."

6. For further evidence regarding widespread positive affirmations of black identity, see Campbell and Schuman (1968), especially chapter 2 on black views of racial issues, and for a comprehensive review of reference group issues as applied to attitudes of the black population in the United States see Hyman (1972).

7. Changes in the attitudes of minorities have not been well monitored over the same period. It is worthwhile to note that for the period 1964–70, with a substantial sample of black men and women from traditionally black colleges, Gurin and Epps (1975) found little change in student aspirations, expectation, self-confidence, or sense of personal efficacy. The review of black attitudes in Campbell et al. (1976:448) is not very conclusive, given the relatively small sample, but the conclusion seems to be that the dramatic events of the recent past "have not enhanced black people's sense of well-being," and that blacks as a whole (especially young blacks) are more negative and distrustful politically.

8. Eisinger (1974) has called attention to the likelihood that participation in protest movements has a very different character for blacks and whites, the attitudes of the black community being more likely to support protest participation and foster expectations of its effectiveness (the latter expectation being an aspect surely of the powerlessness-control question at issue here).

9. This literature is not appropriately reviewed here, but it is relevant to general sociological interests (for example, to the long-standing symbolic interactionist interest in "definition of the situation") and to intergroup matters in particular. For an example of the latter, see Taylor's work (1978) on differences in race-related attitudes based upon differential salience of minority members in group settings.

10. In an introduction to the Weinberg work (1977:iii), Karl Taeuber writes: "Desegregation works. It works for black children and it works for white children. It works for academic achievement and it works for development of racial tolerance."

11. For an instructive review bearing on this thesis, see R. M. Williams's (1976) commentary on "tension" and "structural" explanations of conflict.

12. The new six-volume *Handbook of Cross-Cultural Psychology* should be of considerable help in assessing where this comparative work stands at present and in stimulating further investigation (see, especially, Triandis and Brislin 1978).

Collective Behavior: The Elementary Forms

Introduction

QUESTIONS AND EMPHASIS

As used by sociologists, the term *collective behavior* refers roughly to "emergent and extra-institutional social forms and behavior,"[1] panic-stricken, riotous, and ecstatic crowds being among the more dramatic of its myriad expressions.

In a manner logically identical to other fields of inquiry, students of this subject seek to isolate *forms* and *causes* of collective behavior; *processes* of its operation; the functions it performs or the *consequences* it has for other social forms and for participants; and *strategies* people employ toward and in the context of it, among other concerns.

Each of these and still other foci are valid and indispensable moments in the full round of analysis in all fields of inquiry. But for reasons we may reserve for the scrutiny of the sociologists of knowledge and science, not all are accorded equal attention by investigators at each point in the history of a specialty, and such an imbalance is particularly noticeable in the field of collective behavior. Specifically, in more recent decades, collective behaviorists have displayed a marked preoccupation with questions of causes and some aspects of questions of process to the relative neglect of other questions, especially the question of form (Marx and Wood 1975; Aguirre and Quarantelli 1979; Marx 1979). I believe that this pronounced neglect of forms is having a critically retarding effect on the development of the field of collective behavior, and I attempt in this chapter to begin to redress the imbalance.

One can, of course, challenge the assertion that lack of attention to forms critically retards the study of collective behavior. In its favor, let me point to several matters. First, without articulate taxonomy, there is little guidance for cumulating relevant empirical inquiries. Important studies suffer inattention because no scheme, by its logic, directs attention to them. Among other forms described below, I refer, for example, to lynching and the more abstract pattern it exemplifies, a pattern that goes virtually unconsidered in recent treatments of collective behavior. Indeed, an important mission of this chapter is *genetic rescue* or, more accurately, *generic rescue,* an effort to save the varieties of collective behavior from death by citation neglect in the midst of publication overkill. I try to construct a metaphorical Noah's ark in which to keep the creatures safe in an ocean of informational glut swept by waves of selective attention. Second, without a strong sense of context provided by articulate taxonomy, study of process becomes highly indefinite and prone to loggerheaded and even sterile debate. I fear this has happened, specifically, in debates over the relative merits of the contagion, convergence, emergent norm, and rational calculus views of processes in crowd behavior (Turner 1964; Perry and Pugh 1978; Tierney 1980). I suggest that the next large step in that debate will take the form of specifying the taxonomical (and temporal) location of the operation of each of those four processes. The traditional topics of *milling* and *rumor* are also likely to advance in that manner. Third, I expect that a more complex and variegated rendering of forms will also have a salubrious effect on the study of causes. Undisciplined by taxonomy, causal statements tend either to be extremely general and virtually vacuous or, on the other side, situationally idiosyncratic ("historistic"). Stronger efforts at midrange types and causal treatments so geared are likely to stimulate attention to new kinds of variables. I think, in particular, of Albert Bergesen's (1976 and 1980) excellent work on "official riots" and his attendant innovations in causal thinking (see below). (It is for such contextualizing purposes that I, in what follows, sometimes depart from a strict form-focus, especially as regards study of process.)

For these reasons, then, my treatment is quite selective and somewhat different from most recent efforts. Because it is, I fear that many scholars of collective behavior who have focused on other questions, and who have made outstanding contributions to answering those questions, will be offended by my relative neglect of their achievements. I want to stress that my admitted neglect in this chapter proceeds not from ignorance or cavalier dismissal, but from a belief that expanding initiatives are in order. Expanding initiatives are not necessarily incompatible with existing concerns—at least not in this case—and my larger aim is to enrich the study of collective behavior rather than to displace or ignore what exists. My selectivity arises, instead, from the constraints of space and time and an assessment of priorities within such limits.

THE NATURE OF COLLECTIVE BEHAVIOR

The most basic question of "form" is, of course, that of collective behavior itself as a form relative to other social forms. Employing the "ideal type" or "idealization" (Lopreato and Alston 1970) strategy of theorizing, I think it is helpful to conceive the "pure" case of collective behavior as a limiting instance. Such a case may never (or rarely) be encountered in the empirical world, but the ideal typical model provides a bench mark in terms of which we can gauge the empirical cases we do see. In ideal-type logic, the features of the model are in fact variables—aspects that are more or less present in specific cases. Five such aspects may be pointed to in providing a definition of collective behavior.

Adhering to the spirit of historic ideas and sensitized by a decade of reality constructionist and related thought, a first component is cognitive and concerns how people are defining a situation. As the phenomenologically inclined have urged us to see, ordinary actors go about their ordinary lives within something these analysts call "the attitude of everyday life" (Berger and Luckmann 1966). Within such an attitude, the emerging events of experience are labeled "nothing unusual is happening" (Emerson 1970). For whatever reasons and with whatever consequences, certain actors at times label an emergent situation as to some degree outside "everyday life." They begin to label a situation as "something *un*usual is happening." The attitude of everyday life is to some degree suspended; the frame of ordinary reality, the taken-for-granted world, is made consciously problematic. A situation is to some extent defined as unordinary, extra-ordinary, and perhaps, as unreal. Such a suspension is the begining point of the possibility of collective behavior, but it is not yet collective behavior. The attitude of everyday life is probably suspended most frequently by individuals or by very small groups rather than by collectivities of significant size. Episodes of robbery, mugging, interpersonal violence, grave financial loss, illness, and dying are typical situations of suspending the attitude of everyday life, but their private and individual character make of them scenes of deviance, crime, or mere personal crisis rather than of collective behavior. Second, collective behavior requires suspension of the attitude of everyday life by relatively large numbers of people—by crowds and masses. What is a relatively large number of people? We are speaking of a continuum, of course, and there are, therefore, a set of ambiguous cases between mere personal crises on the one side and full collective behavior on the other. Suspension of the attitude of everyday life is accompanied by increased levels of emotional arousal in participants. This level is highly variable in the same individual over time and from individual to individual at the same time and over time. In their strongest form, states of emotional arousal may approach what we ordinarily label panic, rage, or ecstasy. There are obviously also many states that fall short of these. Completing the ancient trinity of intellectual, emotional, and physical, in collective behavior episodes the emerging definition and affective arousal is accompanied by action defined by participants and observers as outside the ordinary. The degree to which action is extra-ordinary is itself a variable and at the extremes we can conceivably point to such behavior as uncontrolled flight, indiscriminate violence, and complete loss of voluntary control during states of exaltation. Finally, the proportion of a collectivity suspending the attitude of everyday life in varying degrees, and experiencing emotional arousal in varying degrees differs over time. In the ideal-typical case, the proportion and degree of suspension and the proportion and degree of arousal is maximum and sustained.

The idealized profile of collective behavior, then, is unanimous, and maximum suspension of the attitude of everyday life in a collectivity combined with uniform and maximal emotional arousal and universally adopted extraordinary activities. Obviously, this ideal-typical situation rarely, if ever, occurs. It is useful as a domain-marking approach exactly because it is so rare, and, as formulated, turns collective behavior into a variable, something that is measured across participants and is a matter of degree in concrete instances.

In so constitutionally incorporating the idea of diversity within and between collective behavior episodes, one of the major contributions of the emergent norm approach is elevated to a preeminent consideration. As pioneered by Ralph Turner (1964), that approach stresses the lack of unanimity in collective behavior episodes. By stressing that fact at the outset, we are better prepared to develop a more systematic intra- and inter-episode comparative perspective. Although I elect to treat forms, below, in terms of level of dominant emotional arousal, other reasonable directions include scales for measuring the presence of collective behavior that encompass a wider array of relevant indicators (cf. McPhail and Pickens 1975).

PRIMARY VARIATIONS

Attuned simultaneously to the received literature in collective behavior (my "generic rescue" concern) and the emerging logic of the field (just treated), three primary variations may be employed as vehicles for preserving the former while hopefully advancing the latter, albeit with some tension between the two.

Dominant emotion. From among the several basic features of collective behavior just described, I am impressed with the usefulness of employing an episode's dominant emotion as the most basic classifying variation. The notion of *dominant emotion* refers to the publicly expressed feeling perceived by participants and observers as most prominent in an episode of collective behavior. For an emotion to be publicly most dominant—to have become the reigning definition of the emotional situation—is not to say that an especially large portion of that collectivity feels that emotion. Indeed, following the lead of Ralph Turner's formulation of emergent norm theory (1964), the dominant emotion is almost always far from a matter of uniform, unanimous, or even majority inner feeling. In so referring to what is publicly communicated and socially shared, the idea of dominant emotion has much the same logical status as that of the emergent norm. The shift here is simply away from the cognitive (that is, the notion of norm) to the affective.

If we are to focus on dominant emotion, there is then the question of what emotions are to be employed. There are at least two approaches to deciding this. First, we can scrutinize the accumulated literature on collective behavior, asking what emotions appear dominant. Second, we can ask what emotions theorists of emotions per se would offer us. Happily, there is a reasonable accord between these two rather independently developed bodies of theory and research.

Without anyone making a strongly conscious effort, collective behavior studies have moved—haltingly and inarticulately—toward organization around three fundamental emotions: fear, hostility, and joy. This half-century trend is signaled most clearly in Neil Smelser's monumental *Theory of Collective Behavior* (1963), which organizes the field in terms of types of "generalized beliefs" and the quite special topics of the "panic", "hostile outburst," and "craze." Ostensibly about belief, the titles of the forms themselves are also clearly suggestive of dominant emotions. In codifying a vast literature around those three kinds of beliefs, Smelser was being responsive to the long-standing and wide use of something similar to such a trinity in collective behavior studies. Considered the single most important work in collective behavior for many years after its publication in 1963, Smelser's demarcation of the field has persisted, albeit revolving around matters more cognitive than emotive.

Turning to students of emotions per se, we discover several competing schemes of fundamental emotions, but virtually complete agreement that these three are among the most fundamental and even, moreover, transspecific (for example, Izard 1977; Plutchik 1962). Irrespective of these two sources of wisdom, only a modest amount of reflection on social life is required to recognize that these are ubiquitous and central emotions, and emotions that are especially entailed in collective behavior.

But why these three, and why only three? A fully appropriate answer would require an excursus into the sociology of knowledge, because, for better or worse, the historic concerns of the received literature have run largely along these lines. To the degree we take the literature seriously, our actions are constrained.

There are, nonetheless, other basic emotions that can become dominant in collective behavior. Among them are grief, disgust, surprise (Plutchik 1962), and shame (Izard 1977). Although there are some studies relevant to these emotions, they are so few that I will not attempt to treat them, save briefly to mention grief as an uneasy variation on fear (see below). One future task is expansion of the basic divisions of collective behavior in terms of other basic and dominant emotions.

Last, there is the question of the use of dominant emotion as a means of classifying forms of collective behavior. Indeed, some people would observe, the most recent movement in the field is quite explicitly away from concern with emotion because such a stress asserts or implies unusual or peculiar psychic state or mechanisms such as "contagion," "circular reaction," (Blumer 1969a:70–71; Turner 1964), cognitive "short-circuits" and "compressed" ways of acting (Smelser 1963:71). Imputations of "crudeness, excess and eccentricity" arise along with characterizations of collective behavior as ". . . the action of the impatient" (Smelser 1963:72).

I have no quarrel with those who reject such images of collective behavior and fear that they are a consequence of a stress on emotions. My concern, instead, is that stress on the cognitive (and behavioral) commits the opposite error, that of reducing the field to exercises in cognitive theory or, even more extremely, to a species of behaviorism in which the study of collective behavior is merely the study of human coordination (for example, Couch 1970; McPhail 1978). At bottom, though, it is probably impossible to decide rationally which course to take because the longer term consequences of the cognitive, affective, or behavioral stresses are impossible to assess beforehand and the fruitfulness of each changes as each emergently takes account of the others. And in the end, certainly, effort to integrate all three must be made.

Organizational form. Cross-cutting each of the dominant emotions are questions of the organizational form in which collective behavior arises. Historically, the field stressed distinctions among the *crowd,* the *mass,* the *public,* and the *social movement.* Over recent decades the latter two have come increasingly to be treated as separate specialties, especially so in the case of the public and public opinion. (Virtually alone, Turner and Killian's text [1972] continues to treat public opinion.) It is indicative that the present volume provides each its own chapter.

In many recent treatments, even the distinction between the crowd and the mass has been deemphasized in favor of addressing collective behavior per se (for example, Perry and Pugh 1978). Neil Smelser's (1963) grand synthesis appears to have started this trend by defining its main dependent variables—the panic, craze, and hostile outburst—in a way that rendered crowd and mass forms irrelevant.

Nonetheless, the distinction is critical to understanding forms of collective behavior in relation to dominant emotions. A crowd may be thought of as a relatively large number of persons who are in one another's immediate face-to-face presence. A crowd is a special kind of *encounter* as that term has been defined and analyzed by Erving Goffman (1961b) and others (Lofland 1976:chapter 8). A crowd is an "overpopulated" encounter in the sense that it presents an exceedingly complex array of mutual monitoring possibilities and constraints. Informed by the new sensitivities that scholars such as Erving Goffman have provided us about encounters, it is to be hoped that we can again begin to take crowds seriously. Features of the mass are less clear than those of the crowd, and it tends to be defined residually, that is, as whatever is left over after we have looked at crowds. More positively, the term refers to a set of people who attend to a common object, but who are not in one another's immediate physical vicinity.

The two dimensions of dominant emotion and organizational form provide a framework for organizing detailed types of collective behavior. The intersection of these two dimensions is shown in figure 14.1, "Elementary Forms of Collective Behavior," a figure that also provides a synoptic overview of the patterns treated in the sections that follow.

Level/form. Pursuant to conceiving collective behavior as a variable, more specific forms within each of the six master types (so to speak) ought to be arrayed in terms of level of dominant emotional arousal. And pursuing ideal-type logic, the highest level dominant emotions ought to be presented first, moving through successive and lesser degrees or forms of dominant emotions. On the assumption that, overall, crowd situations possess a potential for dominant emotional arousal exceeding those of mass situations, crowd forms need to be treated prior to mass ones.

These principles lead us to envision three pure anchor points to which the paler empirical instances of real world crowds and masses can be contrasted. These may be labeled, in order, *crowd panic, rage,* and *ecstasy,* terms taken to be, by definition, the highest levels of fear, hostility, and joy, respectively. By bearing the pure possibilities in mind, we will have a clearer conception of how far we are straying from the center in our analytic travels. In accordance with this conception, explication within each of the three main domains will proceed, insofar as the materials make this feasible, from the strongest dominant emotions to the weakest, from forms and behavior that are consensually collective behavior to phenomena that probably ought not be discussed in the context of collective behavior.[2]

Having outlined principles from which ideally to proceed, I must now demur and report that the obdurate world of existing materials has not always allowed me to execute these principles. I often need to revert to the prior and more primitive task of simply sorting important forms without judging the level of dominant emotion. This reversion is seen most clearly in the treatment of mass fears and crowd hositilities. When forced to a choice between the dual aims of this chapter (generic rescue and expanding initiative) I have preferred generic rescue. One consequence is that, in order to rescue forms irrespective of dominant emotion, I invoke classificatory principles in an ad hoc fashion. In one instance I even switch from emotion to behavior in ordering forms. In this I subscribe to Erving Goffman's admonition that we treat sociological concepts "with affection," tracing each in its own terms, sensitive to the materials themselves and not merely to logical consistency. As Goffman has put it: "Better, perhaps, different coats to clothe the children well than a single splendid tent in which they all shiver" (Goffman 1961:xiv).

Collective Fears

By means of the term *collective fear* I seek to isolate occasions of collective behavior where the dominant emotion is, in dictionary terminology, the "anticipation or experience of pain or great distress." The term fear is used because it is the most general and least intensity-specific of a family of terms that are relevant: dread, fright, alarm, dismay, consternation, panic, terror, horror, trepidation. Fear seems most accurately to overarch and to capture the spectrum of arousal possibilities.

CROWD FEARS

Crowd fears, as a class, involve by definition a relatively large number of persons in one another's immediate face-to-face presence, each of whom must deal with the fact of mutual presence as a critical contingency entailed in how each can deal with an anticipated or existing pain or significant distress.

Panic. The classic, ideal-typical, and pure level of fearful crowd arousal is, of course, the so-called crowd *panic.* The archetypal illustration is the panic rush from the burning theater and the oft-repeated

FIGURE 14.1

Elementary Forms of Collective Behavior

		Dominant Emotion		
		Fear	Hostility	Joy
Organizational Form	Crowd	Panic Terror Dread Horror Dismay	Political $C \rightarrow I$, e.g., mob attacks $C \rightarrow C$, e.g., political clashes $C \rightarrow E$, e.g., protests $E \rightarrow I$, e.g., bourbon lynchings $E \rightarrow C$, e.g., official riots Leisure $C \rightarrow C$, e.g., intrafan violence $C \rightarrow E$, e.g., resort disorders Emergent $C \rightarrow I$, e.g., proletarian lynchings $C \rightarrow C$, e.g., communal riots $C \rightarrow E$, e.g., ghetto riots Captive $C \rightarrow C$, e.g., inmate clashes $C \rightarrow E$, e.g., pre-planned bids	Ecstatic upheavals Ecstatic conventions Ecstatic congregations Euphoric moods Revivalist crowds Reverent crowds Revelous crowds Excited crowds

Organizational Form	Mass	True dangers Environmental disasters, e.g., earthquakes Social disasters, e.g., revolutionary situations Environmental trends, e.g., eco-hysteria Social trends, e.g., red scares False dangers Environmental disasters, e.g., industrial hysteria Social disasters, e.g., space invasions Environmental trends Social trends, e.g., crime waves	Mass vilification Mass rioting	Crazes El Dorado rushes and booms Promised land migrations Fashions Lifestyles Activity systems Items Fads Objects Ideas Activity People Events

Abbreviations: C = citizens; I = Individual; E = Establishment; → = against.

example is the burning of the Iroquois Theater in 1903 (for example, Turner and Killian 1957: 96–97). A large but older literature addresses the two questions of the nature of the mental state of the panic-stricken person and the conditions under which crowd panic occurs (Smelser 1963:chapter 3).

Although relatively little research has been done on panic in recent years, two directions of work seem particularly important. First, the category of crowd panic is itself probably more heterogeneous than is fruitful. A resurrection of older partitionings, such as that between *escape* and *acquisitive* forms (using Roger Brown's terms 1954:859ff.), might be productive. Further, within escape panic the organizational context of occurrence—the dissolution of a formal organizational effort (as in the collapse of a military attack) versus the flight of unorganized gatherings, such as audiences—seems an important dimension, oft-mentioned but rarely pursued. Second, and more important, the understanding of the psychology of the panic participant may be advanced by a more tenacious pursuit of process explications of the panic situation. The last stab in this direction seems to date from 1938 when LaPiere strove to articulate a three-phase "psychological sequence" in crowd panic, a sequence reported by Roger Brown in his important statement of 1954, but since ignored (LaPiere 1938:445ff; Brown 1954:859). Other than that effort, process analysis of crowd panic remains largely at the level of a distinction between what Smelser terms the "real" versus the "derived" phases (Smelser 1963:154). The real phase is viewed as a response to the initial definition of danger, but the derived phase is importantly a response to the perception that others in the crowd situation are acting in an agitated, if not panicky, manner.

Terror. Attention to crowd panic has meant a relative lack of attention to lesser levels of dominant crowd fears. Such lesser, dominant arousals are, nonetheless, of interest. I think in particular of crowds taken hostage, especially aboard airliners, by terrorist organizations, thereby creating terrorized crowds even if not crowd panic. Such a trapped terrorized crowd often has a rather long existence which is likely to display its own processes, as distinct from crowd terrors where there is no entrapment and where orderly withdrawal from what is feared or orderly convergence on the feared object for the purpose of subsequent withdrawal is possible.

Dread. At a lower level than crowd terror—which connotes a focused and proximate fear—is the pattern of crowd dread, a persistent and chronic apprehension of a more diffuse danger. I have in mind the situation of a crowd trapped by physical mishap rather than by other human beings who are acting in what may seem to be a capriciously violent manner. Small groups trapped by mine cave-ins, by unexpected storms (as with the Donner party), and by mechanical failure are prominent concrete types. Such crowd situations are especially interesting when they are prolonged and thus truly come to require, not just gestures toward a new social order, but the actual construction of one. Such new orders do not often seem to evolve along the lines of the *Lord of the Flies* (Golding 1959), but narrower adaptive innovations, such as cannibalism, drinking urine, and novel codes of morals, do seem to occur. One of the most exhaustive and careful accounts of such a situation has been produced by Rex Lucas in his *Men in Crisis: A Study of a Mine Disaster* (1969).

Horror. Crowds are sometimes witness to fearful and dangerous events that are socially and psychologically disruptive but do not significantly and directly endanger members of the crowd. The explosion of the Hindenburg in 1937, a nearby plane crash, an unusually large crack-up during an automobile race may serve to upset crowds without arousing or endangering them to the extent of the forms previously mentioned. One especially vivid instance occurred at a concert of the Boston Symphony Orchestra on November 22, 1963, when the audience was informed that the president of the United States had been assassinated. As we still lack a careful language for depicting the features and process of such a crowd, it must suffice to say that it begins with a collective and astonished, mournful outcry.

Dismay. On the morning of Monday, November 27, 1978, the mayor of San Francisco, California, and a member of the County Board of Supervisors, an avowed homosexual and advocate of civil rights for homosexuals, were assassinated by a disgruntled public official. That night, thousands of San Franciscans, drawn heavily from nearby homosexual bar and residential districts, marched carrying candles to the front of the City Hall where singer Joan Baez and the Acting Mayor led an emergent memorial ceremony. Wednesday, at noon, a similar ceremony was held in the same place and attended by multiple thousands of a diverse public.

In a more refined treatment of collective behavior, episodes such as this would perhaps better be viewed as having a dominant emotion of grief, sorrow, or mourning. Short of the day there is enough material to establish a fourth division, we can allow such patterns to huddle here as mild forms of fearful crowd arousal. Without debating the intricacies of emotions and their expression, it might even be suggested that fear of a sort is involved in the mourning-grief-sorrow complex in the sense that the sudden loss of revered figures renders standing social arrangements problematic and presages the need to reconstruct understandings in order to take account of the abrupt loss. Leaders, especially, are survivors of intricate processes of selection, compromise, and promises. Sudden removal means that the process must begin anew, especially in the context of a high degree of social fragmentation and conflict.

These types and levels of crowd fears are obviously tentative and crude. They *are* things that exist "out there," however, and must in one or another way figure in more refined depictions of their nature and better and more elaborate schemes of scaled types.

MASS FEARS

The bulk of episodes relevant to the dominant emotion of fear seem not to involve crowds. Crowds may coalesce from time to time within a larger mass configuration, but mass fears occur decidedly more frequently, at least judging from the skewing of the literature.

Consistency and ideals of elegance require that mass fears be treated in terms of the same or similar levels of arousal as those of crowd fears. The materials of mass fears do not, unhappily, yield to such treatment and other partitioning principles must be employed. Explained at appropriate points, there are three of these:

True dangers. The first principle is the truth or falsity of the danger identified as fearful, a distinction that will be explained when I address *false dangers.* The second principle is the space-time visibility of that for which a collective alarm occurs, distinguishing sudden space-and-time-circumscribed dangers (labeled *disasters*) from slow, space-and-time-dispersed *trends.* The third principle is the source of the asserted danger, varying for these purposes in terms of being *environmental* in the strict sense or *social organizational.*

ENVIRONMENTAL AND SOCIAL DISASTERS. The most intensively worked area of mass fears is without doubt that of collective alarm in the situation of environmental disaster, situations where the physical environment has more or less suddenly and momentously gone awry. There are of course important variations within this category relative to the scale, duration, degree of prior warning, and suddenness of danger. One of the more frequently repeated substructions has been that of L. J. Carr, who distinguishes the instantaneous-total, instantaneous-partial, progressive-diffuse, and progressive-focal patterns (Carr 1932). Codifications may in the future take such patterns or some successor to them seriously, as has been attempted by Allan Barton in *Communities in Disaster* (1969:chapter 2) and Russell Dynes in *Organized Behavior in Disaster* (1970:chapter 3). For whatever reason, such schemes do not seem actually to be used in organizing data on environmental disasters; they tend to stand, instead, alone in their separate sections as interesting schemes.

Human beings can sometimes produce collective trauma through assault on their own social organization. Among these, what are called "revolutionary situations" rank at or near the top of any scaled list of mass fear arousals. In these situations, a wide array of routine activities are physically disrupted or merely suspended. The high degree of ambiguity about the nature and fate of the social order renders ordinary and mundane activities temporarily meaningless, as documented by Bowden (1977) for certain years in Ireland and Palestine. Rapid increase in violence that is random from the point of view of the ordinary citizen thus provokes widespread fear (save perhaps among the revolutionarily dedicated who, in contrast, may be experiencing ecstatic joy) (Brinton 1957, especially chapter 7, "Reigns of Terror").

The more diffuse social disarray of revolutionary situations is to be distinguished from sharply focused space-time social events that serve to suspend a sense of "business as usual." In one variety of such sharp jolts, a few days of significant suspension of ordinary life is followed by a quick return to it. The prototypical case might be the sudden loss of a venerated leader. Upon the assassination of American President John Kennedy, for example, a great deal of ordinary life simply ceased, and, indeed, one professional sports team that insisted on playing a scheduled game was widely criticized for an "inappropriate attitude" (Sheatsley and Feldman 1964).

ENVIRONMENTAL AND SOCIAL TRENDS. Environmental and social disasters involve by definition sharply visible and objective changes in natural and/or social arrangements. They can literally be pointed to because they occupy circumscribed space and time. The collective alarm observed is more or less calibrated to the rise of objective danger. As the danger subsides, so does the collective alarm. That pattern needs to be distinguished from situations in which collective alarm is observed in the absence of any sharply visible and highly dangerous event that is responsible for the alarm. Moreover, those alarmed do not assert the existence or portent of any such event. Instead, they claim to discern a trend, a critical cumulation of ominous events that foretell a disastrous future. And less involved observers can assess that there is, in fact, a trend. The alarmed are pointing to something real, something that is, in fact, enlarging or increasing, as they claim. Such observers may not subscribe to the predictions the alarmed make about the future of a trend, and they may not subscribe to the import, interpretation, or meaning the alarmed read into the objective trend in question, but they can agree on the narrow fact of the trend.

Given that dire trends are often quite long-term and sometimes subtle, and that alarm about them is highly variable and sporadic, the key sociological question about given alarms becomes, "Why *now* that alarm?" Why not a decade earlier, or later, or at all, for that matter?

The distinction between *environmental* and *social organizational* dangers is especially pertinent with regard to trend alarms in modern societies. Environmental deterioration in the wake of industrialization and urbanization in America has been well documented and rather widely seen and appreciated for several decades, but the complex, fearful clamor about it that has been called eco-hysteria did not burst forth until late 1969 and early 1970. Mixed with collective hostility and joy, fear of environmental destruction quite importantly possessed Americans. One indicator of its collective behavior character was suspension of the ordinary activities of the educational system, from top to bottom, on "Earth Day" (April 22, 1970) and the closing of many governmental units as well as some businesses. Rallies, marches, and dramatic acts were ubiquitous. Public television provided more than six hours of coverage. But the collective clamor waned almost as fast as it waxed, leaving, however, a new complex of laws and organizations in its wake (Downes 1972). Why 1970 and not 1965 or 1975 or some other year? Why at all?

More common are collective alarms over developing aspects of social arrangements, beliefs, or actions. As a class, these quickly shade off into mere matters of routine public debate and public opinion (important matters nonetheless). The most aroused levels of alarm, though, seem to operate in ways that are almost qualitatively different from those found in the ordinary play of public opinion. Perhaps the historical lenses are distorting, but the approximately eighteen-month episode in American history, commonly called "the Red scare" (1919–20), strikes one as providing an almost ideal-typical case against which we can gauge degrees of fearful arousal found in other social trend alarms. Prior to and during part of that period there seemed, in fact, to be an objective increase in liberal and radical thought and action in American society; that is, the mass fear known as the Red scare was responsive to a real and not imaginary trend. And there seems to have been, in late 1919 and early 1920, a public definition of a national situation requiring extreme and emergency action in order to deal with that trend. Large segments of the society bracketed liberal and radical thought and action together as equally threatening. Grave counter-measures had to be mounted. These included large-scale raids on, and roundups of, alleged radicals, deportations, and refusal to seat properly elected but publicly suspect legislators. Sedition and red flag laws proliferated and mob attacks on radicals occurred, most spectacularly in the Centralia Massacre of November, 1919 (Murray 1955). If we can trust historians' accounts, the level of fearful arousal documented in the Red scare is rather rare. Certainly the so-called McCarthy era seems not to have approached it. Such fears, though, may occur in specific locales and fail to gain society-wide currency.

The analytic problem for collective behavior is where to draw the line between such mass fear and ordinary public opinion. For the sake of analytic purity, I am inclined to draw it at quite high levels. Thus, the Gallup and other polls regularly ask Americans questions such as, "What do you think is the most important problem facing this country today?" The lists of matters commonly elicited are seemingly routine problems. They provide clues to what might become objects of true alarm, but they are not yet alarms.

False dangers. The reality constructionism of much sociology in recent decades has been analytically useful but it also has definite limits. If social analysis is to have any credibility, analysts are in the end forced to make judgments about the degree to which environmental and social dangers are actually "out there" in the empirical world. The disaster and trend fears and their associated alarms just reviewed seem quite real in the sense that we can discover independent evidence of the dangers about which participants are alarmed. The dangers identified by the participants are more or less those that observers are able to identify. In the case of trends, if there is disagreement with participants, it is over the degree of appropriateness of defining the degree of danger rather than over the existence of the trend.

ENVIRONMENTAL AND SOCIAL DISASTERS. This discussion is considerably more than merely theoretical, for, among other reasons, there are a surprisingly large number of episodes that display a pattern of mass (and quasi-crowd) fears of environmental disarray that seem not to be "real," at least not real in the terms asserted by participants. The best-known case is perhaps that studied by Kerckhoff and Back and reported in their book, *The June Bug* (1968). In the summer of 1962, within the space of about a week, sixty-two persons employed in a clothing manufacturing plant "suffered what purported to be insect bites . . ." (Kerckhoff, Back, and Miller 1965:3). The physical symptoms were quite real, but government investigators could discover no physical cause for them. Other such episodes in which there was a seemingly phantom physical cause accompanied by observable symptoms of a physical sort have involved merphose (McLeod 1975), "mystery gas," (Stahl and Lebedun 1974), food poisoning (Pfeiffer 1964), and assorted, vague odors (Cohen et al. 1978). Indeed, the advent of the Federal Government's National Institute for Occupational Safety and Health has caused an upsurge in the reporting and documentation of such cases in the United States (Colligan and Stockton 1978). Investigators are amazingly in accord that the symptoms observed have a psychological rather than a physical origin, and in plant settings refer even to "industrial hysteria" or "assembly-line hysteria." Affected workers are typically those who must perform "under great pressure," have "poor relations with supervisors," little opportunity for expressing grievances and effecting change, and associated problems (Cohen et al. 1978:15). "Having been left with no resource to cope with the situation, an objective physical stressor . . . can serve to provide justification to display somatic symptoms . . ." (Cohen et al. 1978:15).

Scrutinized from a process point of view, false collective perceptions of social disaster differ quite markedly in the focus of their primary or initial phase (Smelser 1963). On the one hand, there are a set of episodes that are similar to environmental false alarms in that the onset events consist of a sequence of people manifesting unusual physical symptoms that have no easily identifiable physical cause and that seem best viewed as episodes of conversion hysteria. The classic case is, of course, the "phantom anesthetist" of Mattoon, Illinois (Johnson 1945), but there are many other such instances of epidemic hysteria (for example, Knight, Friedman, and Sulianti 1965; Schuler and Parenton 1943; Tan 1963; Rankin and Philip 1963). Their common feature is a rapid spread of hysterical symptoms that are attributed to some mystery attacker, "mysterious ailment," the sighting of ghosts, or nothing in particular. The affliction is manifested only by a minority—a quite small minority—of the community involved and reaches a peak, after which few or no new crises are reported. The social response to this "blip" of unusual behavior is one of excited fearfulness and search for remedy. The atmosphere may be "tense and electric" (Tan 1963:72), provoke "unreasoning rush" (Schuler and Parenton 1943:234), and the disorganized activation and scurrying of authorities (Chaplin 1959:111–17). But because the affliction does not spread, the fear seems to subside rather quickly and ordinary social life resumes. (All of this is also the pattern commonly displayed by the environmental false alarms reviewed above.)

On the other hand, the primary phase of such false alarms may be merely cognitive in the sense of being only a report that some fearful event is happening or is about to happen. The most dramatic form is supplied by the media of mass communication, technologies with unique capacities simultaneously to misinform masses of persons. The archetypical episode is Orson Welles's misheard broadcast of the "War of the Worlds" (Cantril 1940). Other documented false media alarms include the "Barseback Panic" (Rosengren et al. 1975) and the "phantom slasher of Taipei" (Jacobs 1965). Analysis of process in such episodes obviously requires accurate descriptions of how many people of given social locations did what, at what point in time, after the alarm. For many years Hadley Cantril's characterization of relatively widespread flight and associated panic behavior in response to the Welles broadcast has been accepted in the literature. Recently, however, studies of a similar incident in Sweden found very little "on-the-ground" citizen response, a finding that has prompted a close rereading of the Cantril reports and a questioning of the characterizations drawn from them (Rosengren et al. 1975). The new reading suggests that a tiny minority of people act in an extraordinary fashion, rumors (false reports) of extraordinary behaviors flourish, and local telephone systems overload temporarily, but that is about the extent of immediate reaction. In the view of the Rosengren group, the key feature is, instead, *exaggerated media processing* of the isolated and short-lived panic behavior. Public officials and a variety of policy-conscious persons are drawn in on the basis of the exaggerations, accepting them as accurate. The secondary phase then consists of fault-finding and blame-laying over the then unquestioned "fact" of the alleged panic. Whatever may turn out to be the case, the efforts of the Rosengren group teach us, at minimum, the need to be extremely cautious about media processing of alarms. The pressures under which media people work promote distorted portrayals, which are then taken by media viewers as accurate.

ENVIRONMENTAL AND SOCIAL TRENDS. The episodes examined above often involve assertion of disaster where there is, in fact, no threat at all. These are *pure* false alarms. In other cases, though, *something* may be happening—as in chain-reaction conversion hysteria—but it is not the threat the participants define it to be, nor is it as threatening as they define it. Both such patterns of false disaster alarms need to be distinguished from cases in which a long-standing feature of a social order, one that has been more or less constant over time, is suddenly fixed on and redefined as a dangerous *trend* that warrants drastic action.

The selectivity of collective social focus and agenda-setting means that only a few trends are at any time defined as meriting such treatment (Cobb and Elder 1972). The interesting obverse of this seemingly banal observation is that at any time there are *also* a multitude of standing conditions that are suppressed from public and collective awareness but about which reasonable numbers of people have significant anxiety. The collection of such conditions form a social ante- or stockroom of matters that, under given conditions, emerge as objects of collective fear. The key point is that the condition itself need not have changed, only the collective assessment of the degree to which it is a threat. The reassessment, however, is quite likely to be accompanied by the assertion that the condition is not merely a stable condition but exhibits features of trend.

The crime wave is one of the best documented and recurrent instances of this process of asserting "false trend dangers." It appears there is, in fact, rarely if ever such a thing as a crime wave (Bell 1961:chapter 8; Sutherland and Cressey 1966:chapter 11). Sporadic collective belief in and alarm over crime waves are a fact, however, and the key sociological question is how a constant comes to be treated as a variable.

An alarm requires an alarmer and in the case of the crime wave the alarmists have been clearly identified as various of the mass media. In his typical let's-not-mince-words fashion, criminologist Donald Cressey has declared "most 'crime waves' are fabrications of the press . . ." (Sutherland and Cressey 1966:259). Following on that idea, Mark Fishman and his associates have made a signal contribution to understanding how media crime waves are precipitated by tracing a "crime wave against the elderly" in the New York City media. Working as part of a team of observers in a New York City television station, Fishman observed the unsurprising fact that media people organize "news" in terms of "themes" and, more interestingly, newspeople rely heavily on viewing one anothers' productions to decide what themes "deserve" or "require" coverage. Further, police try to cooperate with media by organizing and presenting daily reports to them. These reports are constructed to emphasize certain kinds of crimes: crimes in public places, "crimes between strangers and crime specific to age" (Fishman 1978:540). The intersection of these practices produces a steady stream of stories on "crimes against the elderly." They are "normal news." Then a media editor decides to feature that steady-state theme as a problem. Other media see the feature, find, indeed, that there is such a thing and follow suit in order to "meet the competition." Enter, now, public officials who feel they must comment and act. The crime theme has then become a crime wave. The Fishman analysis points up two main questions about such alarms. (1) How is information structured and routed in a way that determines that some rather than other things become objects of alarms? Fishman suggests, for example, that police reporting is structured to conduce alarms only about street crimes. The police "wire" Fishman studied did not, for example, report consumer fraud, environmental pollution, or political bribery. (2) From such a prestructured pool, what, more specifically, are the dynamics of selection and the timing of such selection?

Collective Hostilities

Hostility is the second emotion often dominant in collective behavior episodes, an emotion ordinarily defined as "antagonism, opposition, or resistance in thought or principle." Associated terms are animosity and enmity as well as the concept of anger and its family of terms: wrath, rage, fury, frenzy, ire, and mere displeasure.

The core cases of this broad pattern are well established in the literature under such rubrics as acting crowd, hostile outburst, collective violence, and riot. These and other such concepts are both too narrow and too abstract as dependent variables. They are frequently too narrow in identifying violence and disorder as the sine qua non of collective hostility when there are many varieties that are neither violent nor disorderly. These concepts are frequently too abstract, even within this narrowness, because quite diverse occurrences of violence and disorder are grouped together, occasions that need to be separated for their best understanding. We need, therefore, to broaden and differentiate the view.

In order to establish the range of relevant phenomena, three levels of collective hostility may be described. The first and lowest is *symbolic*, the range of ways people speak and act to communicate their displeasure short of physically interfering with the property and bodies of those toward whom they feel hostility. Disregarding the crowd-mass distinction for the moment, varying levels within symbolic hostility may be arrayed from weakest to strongest in this fashion: written declarations, speeches to crowds, protest marches and rallies, mau-mauing (Wolfe 1971), taunting, crowd baiting. Many of these are, of course, most often quite marginal as collective behavior, *but* they may set the stage for collective behavior and, to inexperienced participants, they might *be* collective behavior. In totalitarian countries the symbolic level of collective hostility is definitely collective behavior.

A second level of collective hostility is directed toward real and personal property and ways in which their uses can be hampered and hamstrung: confiscation of objects (for example, looting); boycott (of objects or persons); strike; occupation or takeover of a place (for example, sitting in, storming); destruction of objects or places (for example, firebombing). The third and highest level is directed to the bodies of other human beings, in the direct forms of capture, assault (for example, clubbing, torturing), and murder.

CROWD HOSTILITIES

Within the area of crowd hostilities, empirical work has focused heavily on the two higher levels, that is, on interferences with property and bodies. While clearly important, that focus is too narrow and probably results from the tendency to relegate "lower level" episodes to the study of social movements because such episodes are often the creatures of social movement strategy. However, we need only to distinguish between encounters and formal organizations as units of analysis to appreciate the relevance of symbolic hostility to the study of collective behavior.

Unlike the other two domains of collective behavior, literature on crowd hostilities yields a number of articulated types. The task, therefore, is less one of discerning and more one of systematizing. Two basic principles can be employed. (1) Episodes of crowd hostility start from significantly different definitions of the situation of assembly. The careers and consequences of episodes vary as a function of the on-the-scene notion of "what the assembly is about" and "what the assembly is." The four main varieties of such "standing definitions of the situation" may be labeled the political, leisure, street, and captive. Each is explained at an appropriate point, below. (2) Cross-cutting these on-the-scene definitions and associated variations in social organization are variations in who is contending. Who is expressing hostility toward whom? In episodes of collective hostility there are three basic parties: a single *individual* (or perhaps a small group of them); a significant segment or category of the *citizenry;* and the *establishment* by which I mean people in positions of political authority and those who associate themselves with such persons. It takes two parties to contend, of course, and the resultant typology provides nine situations of contention, only some of which are collective-behavior relevant (for example, individual to individual contentions involving high levels of hostility are labeled "crime" or "deviance," individuals initiating high levels of hostility against citizens or the establishment are coded "mad dog killer" or some variant thereof). Further, contentions tend to be initiated and dominated by one party. Of course, both parties tend to claim the other party "started it" by reason of long-persisting and nefarious actions or by a recently committed provocative action. Acknowledging such complications, it is still possible to isolate the more initiating and active party in particular episodes.

Political crowds. Crowds assemble under *political* definitions in the sense that "everyone" understands before and at the assembly that the object is to make a statement of some sort about social arrangements. Common instances are demonstrations, rallies, and marches. More broadly, a political crowd is any assembly that is trying "to get particular other people to do particular things," to quote Charles Tilly whose conception of a "collective action" is similar to that of a political crowd except that for Tilly not all collective actions seem to involve crowds (Tilly 1978:143, 1979). Using Tilly's language, political crowds are assembled to make *claims* where, ordinarily, there is an articulate and pressed conflict of interests as defined by the parties in contention.

Not untypically, members of such crowds are relatively well known to each other or at least leaders are known to one another and people participate as members of cliques. The crowds are clique-composites and are led through pre-designed routines by previously evolved leadership.

Of the nine logical types of parties in contention, five have been documented at one or more levels of dominant hostility.

CITIZENS AGAINST INDIVIDUALS (E.G., MOB ATTACKS). Robert C. Meyers's well-known case study of an "anti-communist mob action" (1948) provides a near-prototype of a high level of dominant crowd arousal where citizens are arrayed against an individual or a small set of them. The 1947 event, it will be recalled, involved thousands of emotionally worked-up veterans of World War II assembled vocally and physically to comment on three members of the Communist Party scheduled to speak at a Trenton, New Jersey, auditorium. Such high levels of dominant arousal between parties of this sort seem rather more rare in recent decades although lesser levels in which liberal/radical students harass conservative speakers on college campuses have not been unusual.

CITIZENS AGAINST CITIZENS (E. G., POLITICAL CLASHES). Likewise, high-level dominant arousal involving citizens against citizens in political crowds have seemed in decline in Western societies in recent decades, particularly in the United States. Accounts of the Red scare period, for example, suggest rather frequent and high levels of mob violence between "socialists" and "patriots" in the context of each appearing at the others' political gatherings. One of the most violent was perhaps the famous clash between the Wobblies and an American Legion parade in Centralia, Washington, on Armistice Day, November 11, 1919 (Murray 1955:183–85). The political clash of crowds remains, however, a potent tool, and, indeed, there are suggestions of its resurgence in encounters between conservative whites and liberal/radical blacks.

In a somewhat relaxed conception of political crowds, we might attend to those occasions on which territorial units and groupings come into overt conflict over alleged instances of offensive behavior. For example, in urban slum settings displaying a "segmentary system" (Suttles 1968: 31), there are recurrent rumors or acts of interethnic or neighborhood offensiveness in which "more and more people are involved in the anticipated conflict" (Suttles 1968:198). "Frequently this takes the form of a predicted 'gang fight' " (Suttles 1968:201). Infrequently, there is an actual confrontation of two named street-corner groups. In form, it is not unlike the violent conflicts sometimes occurring between youth of rival towns of a bygone rural world (cf. Tilly 1978:145, 1979).

CITIZENS AGAINST ESTABLISHMENTS (E.G., PROTESTS). The great "growth industry" among political crowds in recent decades seems to have been in episodes of citizens against the establishment, establishment meaning those citizens who are imputed to control important social units, to make decisions in the name of, or almost in the name of, society, or to be direct agents of such persons. The dominant level of arousal of such crowds has been, on the whole, quite low or at the first or symbolic level identified above (Etzioni 1970). This level is itself quite complicated and one important line of advance is identification of its more detailed forms and levels. A key sourcebook for that effort is Gene Sharp's monumental *The Politics of Nonviolent Action* (1973), a tour de force of case study compilation. Unfortunately, Sharp's coverage is constrained by his moral preference for nonviolent protest. Ruthlessly empirical inquiry will articulate the full range of what people actually do. Something of the breadth required is suggested by historians such as George Rudé, whose *The Crowd in History* (1964a) is extremely instructive regarding repertoires of crowd actions in political situations and the complexity of the view of political crowds we will need to develop. As he concludes, the political crowd of early modern Europe was "violent, impulsive, easily stirred by rumor, and quick to panic; but it was not fickle, peculiarly irrational, or generally given to bloody attacks on persons" (Rudé 1964a:257).

ESTABLISHMENTS AGAINST INDIVIDUALS (E.G., BOURBON LYNCHINGS). The notion of the political crowd calls attention to pre-crowd scene organization that has a political definition. There is a deliberate and coordinated movement to a physical site for the purpose of making a claim or a demand. It is a pre-planned expression of hostility aimed at achieving or stopping a change. The level and form of hostile action that ensues is, of course, problematic. The Bourbon lynching is perhaps the most prominent pattern of such a crowd within the more restricted category of the establishment crowd mobilizing against an individual. As developed by Arthur Raper (1933) and treated by Hadley Cantril (1941) it is a "relatively exclusive and well-regulated" affair "often engineered by leading citizens with the knowledge of law-enforcement officers" (Cantril 1941:94). The small crowd is orderly and quiet. Even though it engages in an act of murder, the level of *overt* emotional arousal is reportedly not high.

ESTABLISHMENTS AGAINST CITIZENS (E.G., OFFICIAL RIOTS). The classic images of crowd hostility depict segments of the downtrodden citizenry and assorted underclasses "rising up" against the powers-that-be. Closer attention to parties in contention suggests, however, that the powers-that-be may have been as active in collectively assaulting citizens as being assaulted by them. Collective behavior scholars have simply not turned their attention in this direction albeit the concept of the "program" does appear, in a minor way, in the literature.

One of the more recent and acute efforts to correct this omission has been provided by Albert Bergesen in his re-analysis of the Detroit and Newark ghetto riots of 1967. He is able to document that violence by officials escalated faster than citizen violence and it became "random, indiscriminate and personal in the clear absence of corresponding civilian violence. There seems to have been an increasing lack of organizational or normative control over the actions of officials, which suggests the presence of an 'official riot'" (Bergesen 1976:9). That is, there were "two separate riots."

Bergesen (1976) also provides some fresh causal thinking on crowd hostilities in calling attention to the similarities of the French grain riots to the racial disorders of the American 1960s. Both involved the drawing of new categories of citizens into the national state and the concomitant undermining of the authority of local establishments. He isolates three stages of this process in the American case: (1) federal intervention in local politics, actions that "disequilibrated the local states' order"; (2) the onset of status uncertainty that was associated with the rise of black protest; and (3) the riot of threatened whites.

Leisure crowds. A second genus assembles under a definition of its situation as *leisure.* Its object is to witness a sporting or other entertainment, or simply to lounge, as on beaches. Although contentions over social arrangements, decisions, and rights may emerge during assembly, such conflicts are not the pre-decided objects of the assembly per se, in contrast to the political case just discussed. Here, also, individuals tend to be part of cliques, although somewhat smaller. Leadership is more tenuous, absent, or socially remote (such as mere loudspeaker announcers). In both types, though, members have pre-planned their participation.

Following Goffman (1961b), focused may be distinguished from unfocused leisure crowds, a distinction that in the case materials correlates highly with two common patterns of the parties who are in contention.

CITIZENS AGAINST CITIZENS (E.G., FAN VIOLENCE). Focused crowds assemble to witness some kind of event, most commonly a contest between two sporting teams or persons. In one of its forms of higher dominant arousal, stagers of the event desire and expect the crowd to achieve an overt but orderly level of hostile arousal. Participants apparently also arrive with that expectation and are disappointed if it does not occur. Further, reports on British football, especially, suggest that the organized fan clubs have shared and predictable routines for "whipping" themselves into "frenzied" states of hostile arousal and creating an "electric atmosphere" (Marsh et al. 1978:119). This involves more or less set chants, singing, gestures, and other devices. The mood is sometimes described as one of "fun and excitement" combined with hatred (Smith 1975:310, 316ff.). Such hostile arousal is channeled by roles, rules, and shared meanings that extend to occasions of violence between fan categories and toward officials and players. "Fights . . . do not start up randomly. They occur in circumstances which fans are able to specify and which are seen as legitimizing their actions" (Marsh et al. 1978:107). (Moreover, the hatred combines with fear when violent encounters are in the offing.)

CITIZENS AGAINST ESTABLISHMENTS (E.G., RESORT DISORDERS). Unfocused leisure crowds congregate on a common site without a single and overt object of attention, as on beaches, in parks, and at certain promenades. The pattern in which such crowds become hostilely aroused against an establishment is most familiarly identified with the midsixties phenomenon of hordes of late adolescent youth converging on the beach resort towns of East Coast America. Milling by the thousands, typically on a Saturday night or other major holiday evening such as Labor Day, some provocative event transformed the diffuse search for "action" into focused hostility. Commonly, a police action was the offending event after which an array of violent acts ensued.

In a too-neglected analysis, Thomas Smith has documented the process through which the Labor Day adolescent crowds of Ocean City, Maryland, even evolved into yearly occasions of ritualized crowd expression of hostility. After an initiating disorder on Labor Day, 1959, in succeeding years:

> A crowd would form at Ninth Street; the police would instantly surround and capture it; a few arrests would be made, and the police, in the process of cooling off the crowd, would get "dumped-on" to the delight of on-lookers and retreating participants. The newspapers would feature the story the next day and grind subsequent features out of it for weeks after that. The police would get a slap on the back, and for the following year the teenagers would talk excitedly about what had happened. [Smith 1968:177]

Emergent street crowds. The third major context of crowd hostility evolves in unplanned *street* situations where there is no preplanning of participation. The crowd is "accidental" in the sense that the individual "comes upon" the matters that begin to occupy his or her attention. There is little prior definition of "what the assembly is about." The hostile meaning, if it occurs, is *emergent.* There is little pre-existing internal social networking and pre-established leadership as compared with political and leisure crowds. Leadership, if any, is emergent. The degree of social organization that might be displayed evolves over the course of the situation.

CITIZENS AGAINST INDIVIDUALS (E.G., PROLETARIAN LYNCHINGS). In one ideal typical pattern of emergent citizen crowds against an individual, the offending act or acts of an identifiable and locatable person becomes the object of face-to-face talk among persons who have congregated without pre-plan or design in a public place. In the absence of predesignated leaders, talk and associated physical and emotional milling increase feelings of hostility or outrage. The more vocal of the emergent leaders or keynoters speak in voices loud enough to be heard widely and to suggest hostile courses of action. Under certain micro-ecological conditions facilitating crowd growth and stimulated by focusing events, such emotions are translated into acts of an escalating hostile character. In the most extreme case, the offending individual is taken by force from the custody of authorities and subjected to various acts of violence and to murder. Durwood Prudens's account of the 1930 Leevile, Texas, lynching is no doubt still the most detailed chronicle available on one of the more gruesome trajectories of such events (Pruden 1936; Cantril 1941: chapter 4).

CITIZENS AGAINST CITIZENS (E.G., COMMUNAL RIOTS). In the situation of relatively active street life and pedestrian traffic (which is not yet a crowd, but which provides a recruitment flow for one), a few categorically opposed citizens may fall into hostile and perhaps violent exchange. This provides the focus for a crowd or crowds to form and for additional clashes to start. The scene may be multinucleated in the sense that several small crowds are engaging in intercategorical violence along with "citizens against individuals." The literature has of course focused on interracial instances and prompts the label *race riot.* Conceived more generically, the term *communal riot* (Janowitz 1968) seems more accurate, because the common background and process of these clashes involves competition of citizen categories for the scarce resources of housing, employment, and recreation.

Conspicuous features of such specifically interracial clashes as reported by Grimshaw (1960) and others include concentration of violence "along borders of contested areas" and "at transportation transfer points" (McCall 1970:346), a relatively high degree of physical violence between the races, and relatively little property damage. Fogelson (1971) has characterized the white-initiated part of the violence as "reactionary" in the sense that it is directed to stopping the movement of blacks into previously white-controlled housing, jobs, and public accommodations.

CITIZENS AGAINST THE ESTABLISHMENT (E.G., THE GHETTO RIOT). The type of collective behavior that caused so much concern in the American sixties was the hostility of citizens against the establishment. It has been labeled the "ghetto riot" and while black ghettos were the most obvious instances, at least some of the disorders that took place in university cities can be viewed as emergent street-crowd hostilities of the "youth ghetto" (Lofland 1968). One of the better-known episodes is that documented by Quarantelli and Hundley (1975) with regard to emergent crowds of students and their hostility to jaywalking laws in the illustrious youth ghetto of Columbus, Ohio.

The ideal-typical pattern entails disorder and violence *within* the ghetto rather than along its borders and a relatively small amount of body-directed violence relative to a large amount of property destruction and appropriation. Direct intercategorical clashes are relatively infrequent. The initiating incident is an interchange between an agent of the establishment (almost always the police) rather than between ordinary members of opposed segments of the citizenry (McCall 1970; Quarantelli and Hundley 1975).

Captive crowds. The three crowd contexts just described have in common the fact that they occur in "civil society," by which I mean the participants are involved in a more or less space-and-place segregated round of life, that is, they work, sleep, eat, and recreate in separate places. In contrast, the integrated place-rounds identified by Erving Goffman as "total institutions" involve ". . . a place of residence and work where a large number of like situated individuals, cut off from the wider society, . . . together lead an enclosed, formally administered round of life" (Goffman 1961a:xiii).

Total institutions create peculiarly tight and alienating situations of life and of associated crowd formation and functioning. Physical and/or social and legal barriers do exist and the hot house character of social life within them, produces a uniquely sensitive, systematic, and socially reverberating structure. Once a social order of some sort has evolved and achieved a working consensus, efforts to change parts of it appear to have severe hostility-provoking consequences. Surveying studies of crowd hostilities in total institutions, Norman Denzin has classified such disorders as stemming from *changes* in (1) division of labor, (2) channels of communication, and (3) normative structure (Denzin 1968). One finds, in particular, the anomaly that reform measures in prisons and mental hospitals are productive of disorders because such innovations upset existing social arrangements, providing new advantages for some inmates while depriving others of previously favored situations.

The citizens-against-citizens/citizens-against-establishments distinctions are equally relevant to the context of captive crowds. Indeed, the recent history of American prisons can be written in terms of the decline of the latter and the rise of the former. That is, inmate organization has come increasingly to be based on antagonistic racial categories rather than on solidaristic opposition to prison authorities—the establishment (Irwin 1980). (The rise of one has not, however, meant the disappearance of the other.)

It can now be suggested that these four differences in contexts of crowd hostilities identify a wide variety of ways in which episodes differ with regard to causes of crowd assembly, participants' definitions of the situation and motivations for participation, triggering events for the escalation of hostility, reactions of authorities, subsequent public perception of and response to episodes, among many others. One important line of advance will be the specific comparative analysis of episodes with regard to such contexts and their correlates.

MASS HOSTILITIES

Crowd hostilities, especially the higher levels of arousal, have been extensively researched, but mass hostilities have hardly been speculated about, much less probed empirically. Two kinds of effort must suffice to suggest lines along which this area might fruitfully be developed.

The first direction is illustrated by Orrin Klapp's discussion of the mass villain and the process of vilification in the context of the "urbanized mass," as well as in other contexts (Klapp 1971:chapter 10). He distinguishes four major phases of vilification in terms of the "symbolic tasks" entailed. First, there is a period from the start of social unrest to emergent definition of a "crisis or problem of a kind calling for a villain" (Klapp 1971:86 and Bergesen and Warr 1979 on threat and "boundary crisis"). The second phase is "growth of a demand for a specific villain to fit the moral alarm." Third, action must be organized and carried out, involving debate over the nature of that action. Fourth, there is the "creation of a consummatory dramatic image of the treatment of the villain" (Klapp 1971:87 and Bergesen and Warr 1979 on "ritual persecution"). Klapp's formulation is open-ended and needs adaptation and elaboration with empirical cases, as has begun in the work of Albert J. Bergesen (Bergesen and Warr 1979) and James M. Inverarity (1976).

In a second direction, several types of crowd hostilities, especially those involving violence and disorder, seem to occur in "disorder curves." That is, after the first few, there is a rapid spread in place of occurrence and rise in their number, followed by a precipitous decline and virtual cessation. Such was, for example, the curve of both the American race and youth ghetto disorders of the sixties. Similar "waves" have been documented in the history of American prisons (Irwin 1980) and in the "swastika epidemic" of 1959–60 involving anti-Semitic markings and vandalism (Smelser 1963:257–60). Even though the crowd (or small group) remains the basic "acting unit," there is at minimum a mass-like quality to the manner in which later disorders have the form of earlier ones and follow so close upon them. The mass media are obviously critical in the dissemination of physical images and definitions of the emerging situation. There is some suggestion in the work of Spilerman (1976) and others that, in the case of black ghetto rioting (and perhaps in other curves), local conditions of disadvantage and deprivation become less predictive of disorder the farther along in the series a given disorder occurs. That is, there is perhaps such a contradictory and seemingly impossible thing as a mass riot in the special sense that mass media make it possible for crowd actions to have quite remote inspiration, inspiration not closely geared to specific and particular circumstances at hand (albeit obviously related to them in a general way). Specifically, " . . . incidents [of black ghetto disorder] tended to cluster in time following a few dramatic events such as the massive Newark disorder in July 1967 and the assassination of Martin Luther King in April of 1968" (Spilerman 1976:790). Further, Spilerman asserts "there is considerable evidence that skyjackings, prison riots, bomb threats and aggressive crime of other sorts have been spread by television and other mass media" (Spilerman 1976:790).

Collective Joys

We move from the unpleasant and grim matters of fear and hostility to the positive and even enthralling matter of joy. By joy is meant "the emotion evoked by well-being, success or good fortune or by the prospect of possessing what one desires." It is a "state of happiness or felicity." Associated terms include delight, gaiety, pleasure, jubilation, merriment, and bliss.

The joys of interest are collective in either of two senses: the dominant emotion of a face-to-face assembly (a crowd), or a shared emotion among a dispersed set of persons attending to the same object at more or less the same time and who are aware that other people are attending. These foci exclude a host of private, personal, dyadal, and small-group joys, such as religious, sexual, and kindred ecstatic states, excitements associated with deviant acts, adventures of risk-taking sports such as parachuting, and drug highs, among others. However, to the degree that any one of these becomes a crowd or mass focus, it becomes relevant to collective behavior analysis. The exclusion of any of these is based on empirical rather than analytic grounds.

CROWD JOYS

Joy is a variable, and one prime task is the identification of an ordered and orderly set of dominant levels of arousal. We may point to five dimensions of variation, the several values of which can serve to provide profiles of dominant arousal. First, temporarily leaving aside the number or proportion of the crowd displaying a given behavior, there is variation in the amount of overt motor activity combined with display of emotion socially defined as joyous. A modest level of arousal is suggested by such acts as hand clapping, dancing, singing, foot stomping, and cheering. Higher levels are suggested by unintelligible screaming, body shaking, glazed eyes, tranced demeanor, and fainting with indications of strong emotion and signs of ecstatic states. The greater the frequency of such acts, the higher the state of crowd arousal.

Second, crowds vary in the proportion of members displaying varying levels of these acts. At lower levels, only leaders and performers display them to a silent audience. At the highest levels the audience-performer "polarization" (Brown 1954:843) disappears and the behavior becomes generalized.

Third, the social definition of the nature, meaning, and import of the arousal varies. At higher levels, the psychophysical features of the first dimension are defined as sacred, profound, and of supreme existential or religious consequence. They are viewed as the special and unique communications of a divine realm and the joyous situation at hand is viewed as warrant for suspending ordinary routines of life or even of abandoning one's previous way of life. At more modest levels, such definitions are evoked, but conclusions requiring personal or social upheaval are not drawn. At the lowest levels, the psychophysical manifestations are viewed as merely "fun" or "leisure" or "recreation."

Fourth, occasions of crowd joy differ in the degree to which they are institutionalized in the sense of being pre-designed, planned, and regular in their occurrence. At the highest levels, they are a surprise to all involved, participants, on-lookers, investigators, and others. They are in that sense "pure" collective behavior. At more modest levels—and more marginally collective behavior—"everyone" knows more or less what will happen when the crowd assembles, and the expected more or less does, in fact, happen.

Fifth, crowd joys vary in the duration of a single occasion of arousal and in the degree to which such joys are or are not linked in a *rapid series* of occasions of arousal. The higher levels involve quite long occasions—perhaps eight or more hours—that are spaced back to back over an unbroken series of days. Or, if the series is broken, it may extend over weeks or months.

These five dimensions only *tend* to increase and decrease in a uniform fashion. It is probably most common for occasions to be high on one or two dimensions and relatively low on the others. To be high on all five, though, is to have achieved the ultimate in crowd joy—the pure instance of ecstatic collective behavior. It is also likely that no human crowd has ever achieved (or fallen into or regressed to?) maximal arousal on all five dimensions. Indeed, maximal arousal is probably impossible, entailing as it does an emergent and totally tranced and ecstatic crowd sustaining such states day after day. Even if it somehow did emerge, outsiders would likely intervene. Instead, empirical cases are merely approximations.

Ecstatic upheavals. Among the higher orders of approximation let me first point to a pattern that has no established label but which might be called the *ecstatic upheaval.* Unfortunately the crowd aspect of this pattern is obscured by scholars who view it as an aspect of a social movement, applying such labels as *crisis cult,* and *revitalization movement.* Social movements may or may not rise out of ecstatic upheavals, but at the start they are emergent, joyous crowds. Perhaps the most famous instance is the late 1919 episode starting near the village of Vailala in the then-British territory of Papua (New Guinea) and known as the Vailala Madness (Williams 1923).

Numerous other instances have been reported; Felicitas Goodman's account of a "trance-based upheaval in the Yucatan" (1974) is among the more recent and closely documented. It centered on the congregation of a small Apostolic church, a group whose new minister encouraged glossolalia, the crowd practice of which escalated and encompassed a large portion of the membership. In an episode extending about a month in the summer of 1970, emergent leaders received visions of the imminence of the Second Coming. The congregation accepted this prediction and glossolalic gatherings became frequent and intense. The church was frequently crowded and "the pulsing noise level, the rhythmic pounding of the many glossolalia utterances [boosted] . . . everyone's trance level. This effect appeared to be quite uncontrollable for the individual participant, assuming an autonomous aspect" (Goodman 1974:306). Ordinary routines of life were suspended, a few people went to preach the Second Coming to nearby villages, and several messages mandating throwing out of Bibles, the elimination of all colored objects, and other unusual acts were received and variously acted on. The beginning of the end started when one of the more faithful was accused by the others of being unfaithful. Shocked, she called in a regional church authority who informed the congregation it had been possessed by demons. The status quo ante was quite quickly reinstated.

Ecstatic conventions. Some societies and other social organizations have apparently harnessed ecstatic crowd energy into regularized and multi-day occasions of crowd ecstasy. The dominant level of arousal is quite high, but it is planned and even though defined as serious it is not seen as profound enough to justify overthrowing the existing social order. The existing order is, instead, suspended for a time. The most familiar but oddly ignored depiction of the ecstatic convention appears under the caption social "effervescence" in Durkheim's *Elementary Forms of the Religious Life* (1915:214ff.). Drawing on several reports, he uses terms such as the following to characterize them:

Crying . . . shrieking, rolling in the dust, brandishing . . . arms in a furious manner . . . a sort of electricity . . . extraordinary degree of exaltation . . . violent gestures, cries, veritable howls and deafening noises of every sort. . . . The sexes unite contrarily to the rules governing sexual relations . . . violent super-excitation [and they] finally fall . . . exhausted. . . . [Durkheim 1915:215–16]

Durkheim rightly stresses that such multi-day ecstatic conventions were defined by participants as apart from—as radically different from—ordinary life. People "set themselves outside of and above their ordinary morals." (Durkheim 1915:216). Participants were left with the "conviction that there really exists two heterogeneous and mutually incomparable worlds. . . ." In one "his daily life drags wearily along." But the person gains access to the other by ". . . entering into relations . . . that excite him to the point of frenzy" (Durkheim 1915:218). Durkheim focused on certain simple societies of Australia, but ecstatic conventions are reported elsewhere, including the early phases of the Native American Ghost Dance movement and the American pioneer Camp Meeting (Davenport 1905:38ff.; Pratt 1920; LaPiere 1938:476).

Ecstatic congregations. Several degrees below ecstatic upheavals and conventions there is the relatively routine and repetitive assembly of circles of believers for the purpose of expressing devotion to and emotional involvement in a religious purpose. Such assemblies last less than a day and mostly for a few hours only. Unlike upheavals and conventions, ecstatic congregations may be viewed directly by interested observers almost anywhere in the world. Weston LaBarre's (1962) description of services at Zion Tabernacle may be taken as prototypical. The participants know one another, they have a leader, hold services, and have a specific and performed sense of "what a service is." In outline it involves a "minister" speaking and reading from the Bible, guitar playing, and the gradual escalation of enthusiastic hand clapping and singing. As these build, "shaking reactions" begin to occur and some members begin "jerking their heads and bodies around wildly." Several stand up and "perform a vivacious dance. . . . The minister begins to speak in unknown tongues, as do others." In some services of this particular group, poisonous snakes are brought out and handled. A "mood of general excitement" prevails. People are described as "shaking violently . . . dancing around . . . sobbing, shouting and singing" and there is a laying on of hands in healing (LaBarre 1962:6–9).

It is with some hesitation that I have used the term *ecstacy* to label the three patterns above. The term is perhaps too strong for the reality, but the reality is headed in that direction and the term does suggest the proper order of experience. By ecstacy is meant a state that is "beyond reason and self control" associated with "overwhelming emotion, especially rapturous delight" and "intense emotional excitement." Other aspects include "a state of exaltation" and "a trance state in which intense absorption in divine or cosmic matters is accompanied by loss of sense perception and voluntary control." A portion of the crowds described above appear to approach such states, but a large portion also clearly do not; hence my misgivings.

These three forms of the ecstatic crowd are set apart from the next three in terms of the intensity of their dominant arousal. The three to be considered involve emotional arousal but it is not displayed with as much physical abandon. All six are alike, however, in defining the crowd occasion as having a cosmic and ultimate existential meaning.

Euphoric moods. The euphoric mood is outwardly quite mild or even invisible but inwardly of deep and intense significance. As reported by Benjamin Zablocki with regard to the Bruderhof settlement he studied, new "waves" of the euphoric mood in that community are occasioned by "success in the decision-making process" (Zablocki 1971:188). The Brotherhood's decisions must be unanimous and inwardly accepted by everyone. This requires long and repeated meetings in which there is an air of crisis but also of a slow-building euphoria as the community approaches consensus. When consensus is achieved, ordinarily late of an evening, "there is a feeling of exultation in the air. Perhaps some stirring communal songs are sung" (Zablocki 1971:189). But they do not spend the night in "joyous celebration." Rather, they retire, but the days that follow are permeated with "fresh remembrances of their common euphoria. Each member throws himself into his work with new vigor" (Zablocki 1971:189). According to Zablocki, Bruderhof life is importantly characterized by a "crisis-euphoria" cycle in which crises are expected and "more important [they] expect the joyful end of all crises, even when this is nowhere in sight" (Zablocki 1971:191).

In Zablocki's view, the Bruderhof have adroitly built "the collective behavior experience" into their way of life by muting the intensity of its expression at a given moment and spreading it "out instead as a glow over life" (Zablocki 1971:189). He contrasts this with more common social arrangements into which the collective behavior experience does not fit and "merely erupts" (as in ecstatic upheavals) or is confined to special, institutional occasions such as those I have described above. Such an integration and permeation is not easily achieved, however. It requires a variety of conducive social arrangements, the detailed features of which Zablocki brilliantly presents in chapter four of his report, *The Joyful Community.* It will suffice here to say that these arrangements involve the thoroughgoing subjection of self to the collective and deep immersion in a totalistic religious system.

Revivalist crowds. The revivalist crowd is the most commonly occurring—the garden variety or weed if one prefers—crowd joy with a claim to existential import. It is associated with such famous evangelists as Dwight Moody, Aimee Semple MacPherson, Billy Sunday, and Billy Graham. Careful and sophisticated planning goes into its staging, and the assembled crowds are emotionally aroused in an orderly and constrained manner. There is some audience participation in the form of singing and hand clapping, but there is little or none of the abandon associated with the ecstatic congregation. A strong polarization of performer and audience is maintained. The strongest form of audience participation is the "calling forth" of sinners and/or of the sick to be saved and/or healed.

James Pratt's characterization of the revivalist crowd continues to be one of the best, calling attention as it does to the use of hymns that are joyful but not gay, and tunes that are catchy as in Billy Sunday's favorite "Brighten the Corner" (Pratt 1920:177ff.). The revivalist's address tends classically to play on many emotions—humor, pathos, and sorrow among them—but most centrally on fear and love: fear of damnation and love of the divine (Pratt 1920:178). Unlike the crowd forms already examined, the revivalist, him- or herself, is critical to the crowd process. It is a situation of star performing as much or more than mutual crowd facilitation. McLoughlin has observed of Dwight Moody, "... the rapidity with which he jerked audiences from tears to laughter to solemnity and anxiety was the essence of his pulpit technique" (McLoughlin 1959:240).

Reverent crowds. Least overtly agitated, but aroused nonetheless, is the pattern of crowd joy associated with *reverence,* the quiet, worshipful coming together of people to give homage to what is defined as the cosmic and to make requests of the cosmic. The more purely collective behavior versions of this are emergent in the sense that some new reverable object is declared and people are drawn from diverse points to a new place in order to give homage. What Tumin and Feldman (1955) call "the miracle at Sabana Grande" is the classic episode, a gathering of over 100,000 people at Rinçon, Puerto Rico, May 25, 1953, in order to see the reappearance of a virgin saint. The saint elected not to materialize, exactly, but that day and subsequent days were apparently quite moving crowd events involving much prayer, singing, and chanting.

Reverence as a mode and level of cosmic crowd arousal is transferable to the political realm, a transfer effected most successfully in modern times by the German Nazi party under Adolf Hitler. Despite having an ersatz quality to outsiders, Nazi rallies and festivals were designed to be and were experienced by many as much more than mere political demonstrations. They brought their multitudes, in the words of Hitler, "under the spell of a deep prayer" (Sinclair 1938:583). A "mystic effect" was intended and achieved. The scale of devices for achieving such an effect remain astounding to this day: huge public spaces and gigantic symbols (especially flags and banners); massed choirs and drum corps; adroit use of lighting; hundreds of thousands of people deployed in precise marching and singing movements carrying perhaps 25,000 flags. The rallies at Nuremberg were reportedly stunning, and for a week each fall in the late 1930s "nearly every other event [in Germany] went into obscurity" (Sinclair 1938:528; see also Mosse 1975).

The foregoing six varieties of joyful crowds define their emotional arousal as having an existential, religious, sacred, or cosmic meaning. Variations in such meaning include seeing the joy as caused by the cosmic, as a manifestation of the cosmic, as a direct communication with the cosmic, and as an act of soliciting the help of the cosmic. We now make a transition to a cluster of joyfully aroused crowds in which the joy is not defined in such a grandiose manner. Words such as ecstatic, reverent, and awed are less appropriate than are terms such as amused, delighted, excited, revelous, and merely happy.

Revelous crowds. The highest level of collective arousal among "noncosmic" crowds seems best labeled *revelous,* a term denoting a "wild party or celebration" and connoting abandon. The prototypical revelous scene is one in which thousands of people dance and otherwise cavort in the public streets hour after hour, day after day. Richard Critchfield reports that something of the sort occurs for six days each spring in Salvador, Brazil, a period when "an entire city of a million people goes mad dancing up and down the main street day into night" (Critchfield

1978:53). Critchfield strives to represent that "carnival" using words and phrases such as these:

> Shrill shouts ... rhythm pulsates from the drums ... flashing lights ... sparks fly, ... mists of confetti drift ... thunder rising from the pavement ... eyes flashing, faces filled with laughter ... ear splitting, all obliterating din. [Critchfield 1978:53, 57]

Critchfield characterizes carnival arousal as "fun" in the sense of a "bodily and mental experience that occurs completely independent of your rational self. With an intense physical and emotional realness, you are scarcely aware of your own presence and movement ... it is compulsive and it is marvelous" (Critchfield 1978:57).

Excited crowds. The *excited crowd* is among the most constrained and ordinary of aroused crowds, a pattern of arousal so constrained and orderly that it barely merits mention in the context of collective behavior. The garden variety example of the excited crowd cheers, sings, chants, and otherwise expresses itself in favor of a person, team, or other contestant. The ordinary excited crowd, that is, is responding to a *staged contest* in which there is a "simple but dramatic form of conflict" (LaPiere 1938:477). The conflict is socially related to the spectators in such a way that they become vicarious participants in it, especially when the contestants are symbolic representations of the social identities of the spectators (LaPiere 1938:477). The collective behavior aspect is expressed more clearly when the spectators begin to take the conflict literally, rather than vicariously or symbolically, either in celebratory revelry (above) or in hostile attack, as reported of fan violence in the discussion of collective hostilities.

These depictions of dominant emotions only identify more intense levels and more commonly occurring varieties. Many others might usefully be articulated, including crowds of adoration, ersatz revival (for example, Peven 1968), and comic varieties.

MASS JOYS

Mass joys vary in three ways; a cross-classification of these ways can assist us in achieving a more systematic apprehension of their most familiar forms, the *craze,* the *fashion,* and the *fad.* First, like crowd joys, they vary in the dominant level of emotional arousal. Second, they vary in the degree of seriousness with which they are invested. Third, there is variation in the scope, duration, and regularity of the participants' involvement. Put differently, the degree of obtrusiveness into participants' ordinary lives differ from the craze to the fashion to the fad (cf. LaPiere 1938:chapter 19).

Mass excitements: crazes. A *craze* is an exciting mass involvement that is quite serious in nature and consequence and in which people are more or less encompassingly involved for relatively long periods (cf. Brown 1954:868). The word craze is one of a family of terms none of which comfortably characterizes the empirical instances ordinarily associated with them. The other terms are: *fever* ("heightened or intense emotion . . . transient enthusiasm . . . unstable condition of mind or society"); *madness* ("extreme folly . . . rashness . . . complete involvement"); and *mania* ("excessive or unreasonable enthusiasm"). Craze itself is sometimes defined as a "transient infatuation." Tradition sanctions the use of any of these terms and in the interest of continuity it seems reasonable to continue the usage despite my misgivings that even the mildest of these words—craze—denotes a level of arousal and mindless abandon that is difficult to document in the episodes ordinarily so classified.

Following LaPiere (1938), two patterns of crazes should be distinguished.

THE EL DORADO RUSH AND THE BOOM. The rush to El Dorado centers on the belief that sudden personal wealth is in the offing if one will only physically or socially "go for it" *now* (to use the seventies vernacular) (La Piere 1938:495–96). The physical form involves actually rushing to a specific place in order to take possession of wealth. The California gold rush of the 1850s is perhaps the most famous instance. The most important recent contribution to our understanding of this form is Gary Hamilton's "The Structural Sources of Adventurism" (1978), an analysis in which the social type of the adventurer is developed and interpreted as an adaptive response to societies stressing "particularistic achievement" (Hamilton 1978:1478).

In the social form, certain commodities or investments are defined as sudden sources of wealth and, further, the rush to possess it sets up the well-known "boom dynamic" in which people acquire an object "because they expect others to buy at a higher price; and these others buy at that higher price because they fully expect others to buy from them at a still higher price" (LaPiere 1938:502). A limit is inevitably reached and people shift from buying to selling; they shift, that is, from positive excitement to alarmed escape.

PROMISED LAND MIGRATIONS. LaPiere's brief discussion of what he calls the "mass movement" is one of the few efforts to analyze waves of mass decision making and migration based on the idea that "peace and security" are to be had in a new land. Unlike the fabled departure of the Israelites from Egypt, which had qualities of a social movement, true mass migrations have no central coordination. Individuals and families independently decide to seek a "land of milk and honey," and they do so in large numbers or over a relatively short period of time. In more recent decades, the rural commune migration of the American sixties had the qualities of such a movement.

Mass pleasures: fashions. A fashion is a pleasurable mass involvement that participants and observers define as important but not critical, and in which people are variously engaged depending on the particular fashion. The fact that almost all collective behavior treatments include fashion is an anomaly, for one of its most commonly asserted features is that of being a "prevailing or accepted style" "believed to be superior practice" and to have superior merit in some field (Blumer 1969b:286). This means that "fashion has respectability [and] . . . carries the stamp of approval of an elite . . ." (Blumer 1969b:272). A fashion, moreover, need not be recognized by participants as such. It is often only "from the detached vantage point of later time" that fashions are detected (Blumer

1969b:288). Fashion is associated with moderate levels of dominant emotional arousal, and pleasure mingles with a "careful and discerning" attitude (Blumer 1969b:277). "While people may become excited over a fashion, they respond primarily to its character of propriety and distinction" (Blumer 1969b:277). And even though fashion has serious consequences and is important, such judgments do not reach the critical levels we associate with crazes. Fashion, then, is relatively "institutional" in character as opposed to "collective behavior". However, it must also be acknowledged that its study has no other analytic (or actual) home and it must perforce remain with the collective behaviorists because, although marginal, it has a certain relevance for the reasons stressed by Blumer (1969b) regarding "collective ambiguity" and the merits of "competing models" of practice and belief.

Efforts to specify types or patterns of fashion have mostly pointed to the multi-institutional occurrence of these types, eschewing the idea that fashion has only or largely to do with matters of personal adornment and household decoration. In fact, it is rife in even such sacred areas as physical science, religion, and business as well as in such venal domains as politics, sex, and social science. Taking that point as given, the next step would seem to be the breaking down of the global notion of fashion along more generic lines. I am inclined to do this in terms of the third mode of mass joy variation, scope-duration-regularity. This requires asking several interrelated questions: (1) How broad is the "package of elements" that compose the fashion? (2) How long is the typical involvement in a fashion and the life of the fashion itself? (3) How regular is participation: full time, brief time daily, once a week, occasionally, no special time because of its character? (4) How obtrusive into prefashion life is the new fashion? The concrete fashions of the empirical world, of course, vary infinitely along these lines. Simplification is necessary and three patterns may be suggested: life style, activity system, and item.

LIFE STYLE. Life style fashions entail a relatively rich package or cluster of items in dress, speech, activity, belief, and social relations. The participants define the package as a distinctive and coherent cluster. Participation is constant or, at minimum, many times a week and participation requires, at least, a gradual giving up of one's prefashion life style. If there is any doubt about the respectability of the life style, there is also possible the claim of superiority and avant-gardism. Among the most respectable and snobbish of life style fashions, mention may be made of Marin County Trendy (made famous by Cyra McFadden in *The Serial* 1977), Post-hippie, Bourgeois Bohemians, and Upper-Middle Class Trendies. (For these I am indebted to the keen eye and description of John Irwin 1977:64–71.) Although of marginal and controversial respectability, the Hippie Style, the Surfer Scene (Irwin 1977), the Dandy Life (Smith 1974), the Singles Life and associated "emerging alternative lifestyles" (Butler and McGinley 1977) all illustrate past and present "posing packages."

ACTIVITY SYSTEM. Activity-system fashions are less encompassing. Participation is likely to be regular but segregated in the individual's round of life. Joining involves devoting interspersed hours during a week or on weekends rather than the holistic assumption of an altered daily round, language style, and clothing pattern. Following Irwin's use of the idea of activity system, conspicuous examples are: "tennis, . . . car racing, cooking, skate-boarding, transcendental meditation, nudism, skydiving, stamp collecting . . ." (Irwin 1977:27).

Like life style fashions, these are involvements that participants define as important, but not apocalyptic or critical. Entry and exit from them is relatively private and voluntary, lacking in the kinds of transition trauma we associate with social movement involvements and the main-line institutions of the family, work, and education. While both types of fashion may have a competitive element, sometimes highly competitive, it is not quite the same kind of devastating competition associated with the main line institutions. Fashion may provide, nevertheless, a basis of pride, as in the report that in some parts of America "possession and display of the snowmobile has become a badge of distinction proclaiming that the owner has made it and knows 'where its at' " (Martin and Berry 1974:109). (Such an attitude is of course the essence of fashion.)

ITEMS. Particular and specific cultural items are, of course, the kinds of things that more ordinarily come to mind when using the term fashion. The archetypical item is the human female dress and, concretely and oddly, its length and breadth. A signal feature of item fashions is their relative lack of obstrusiveness into the participant's life. Indeed, the concept of the participant becomes less appropriate than that of the user. Participants have to go out of their way to "get into" something, as was said in the American seventies, whereas users import items to "where they are."

1. Among item fashions, the best known kinds are physical objects, particularly clothing, such as (in recent years) the T-shirt, Levi jeans, and neck chains. Facial hair is also in this class. Beyond these are fashions in items of household decoration, for example, houseplants, design (such as two-car garages), food items and preparation (slow cookers, bottled water), consumer toys (CB radios), and so forth.
2. Ideas, like physical objects, are matters of fashion. More elaborated and enduring ideas—philosophies—may be fashionable as long as a decade or so. Most ideas, however, are not as complicated and robust and have far shorter lives, as in such once-fashionable phenomena captured by such concepts as "radical chic" (Wolfe 1971), environmental salvation (Downes 1972), and nostalgic reminiscence (F. Davis 1979). The narrowest of idea fashions involve mere words and expressions, as in the succession of ways in which American youth has expressed approval: *swell* (circa thirties); *neat* (fifties); *right on* (sixties); *really* (seventies).
3. Discrete forms of activity may be in or out of fashion, interesting instances being regular exercising (Gallup 1977), bicycling (Harmond 1972), genealogical searching, and karate (Gehlan and Doeren 1976). To the degree an activity is elaborated and associated with public settings of action and contact it "graduates" to being an "activity system" as mentioned above and discussed by Irwin (1977:27–28).
4. Specific people (or categories of them à la the adorations of radical chic) may be in or out of fashion. In the dead hero category, for a period in the midseventies, Harry Truman was fashionable, as evidenced in his more or less simultaneous celebration in a song, bumper sticker, book, play, television special, and the placement of his dusted-off portrait in the White House cabinet room. The living are, however, more likely the beneficiaries of fashion, especially in the entertainment, sports, and political realms (Klapp 1964).
5. Finally, for purposes of expanding the conception of fashion, elaborately staged events may be infused with the approving aura of fashion. At a purely mass level, such multi-evening television happenings as the "Roots" of 1977

and the "Holocaust" of 1979 were very much in fashion. Combining mild crowd joy arousals with mass joys, there are the more regularly recurring fashions of the televised Superbowl and "Sun Day."

MASS AMUSEMENTS: FADS. A fad is an amusing mass involvement defined as of little or no consequence and in which involvement is quite brief (cf. Turner and Killian 1972:129; Brown 1954:868). Words often associated with the term include: madcap, hijinks, antics, lark, silly, funny. The notion of a "fancy" is not inappropriately connoted, a "liking formed by caprice rather than by reason," something that is "whimsical [and] irregular." Fad objects have no serious impact on anyone's life (save perhaps to produce a fortune for promoters/manufacturers). Further, fads tend to be shorter lived than crazes or fashions. They tend both to boom quite rapidly and to die out with equal rapidity.

These features bear on the complexity, elaboration, and organization achieved by, or found among, fads. As seen above, crazes and fashions can become quite complicated. Crazes may entail prolonged and arduous travel, novel equipment, or sequences of investment decisions. Fashions are sometimes almost complete life styles or activity systems. Little or none of this is found in fads. From the point of view of the ordinary participant (user?), fads are largely confined to the complexity identified among fashions as the item level.

In spite of these guidelines, the notion of a fad is actually quite slippery and subject to debate when applied in concrete instances. A brief listing of candidate fad items may serve to join the issue of how, more operationally, to identify them. Such candidates may be arrayed in terms of the same categories used to array item fashions.

1. Recent object fads have included blacklight and drug-extolling posters, message bumper stickers, the round, yellow, smiling face, biolators, pop rock, the pet rock, and gnomes. Older clothing fads include beer jackets, rope beads, raccoon hats, and hooded blouses (Horn 1968:179).
2. Recent idea fads include the rumor of the death of Paul McCartney (Suczek 1973) and the practice of astrology and interest in witches. (Marcello Truzzi [1972:22, 26] characterizes interest in the latter two as "highly irreverent, almost playful . . . fun . . . [and] non-serious.")
3. Activity fads include the oft-mentioned miniature golf, yo-yo playing, telephone booth stuffing, and, most spectacularly, streaking (Miller and Evans 1975).
4. Fad people are also spoken of as *fad-heroes,* people who are not quite seriously adored despite the fact that their faces are briefly ubiquitous. An indicator of their unseriousness is their absence from lists of "people most admired" that are generated by public opinion polls. (The people on such lists are fashionable rather than faddish.) Recent fad heroes include the Fonz (actor Henry Winkler), Farrah Fawcett-Majors, and assorted figures grouped under the heading "punk rock."

Concluding Reiterations

I would like to conclude by reiterating the aims of this chapter. First and foremost, I have tried to make at least modest progress in the task of delineating forms of collective behavior, an aspect that seems to me to be egregiously neglected. In pressing that task, I may well have produced, as critics would have it, a "mere catalogue of cryptic accounts" based on an assortment of unrelated principles of classification. But even so, there is a fundamental mission of generic rescue to be performed, and I am satisfied that I have at least begun that work. A decent portion of the relevant array has been minimally displayed.

Second, and less centrally, I have tried to bring emotions back into the study of collective behavior by using their substance and "dominant level of arousal" as principles of classification. It is to be hoped that such an approach is compatible with the more common cognitive and behavioral conceptions popular in the field at present.

I want to urge, finally, that these two tasks ought not be confused with my specific modes of addressing them. As is often and rightly observed, care must be taken not to throw a baby out with its bathwater. Regardless of the usefulness of the present effort to specify elementary forms and to reintroduce an emotive component, those two tasks abide. It is, indeed, from its own ashes that the phoenix arises in youthful freshness.

NOTES

Several scholars have been exceedingly generous of their time in criticizing an earlier version of this chapter. I have profited greatly from their suggestions, but (for better or worse) I have not accepted a great deal of their good advice. I therefore absolve them from guilt by association and I express my deep appreciation to each for having cared to make an effort to save me from the errors of my ways: Richard Gambrell, Lyn H. Lofland, Enrico Quarantelli, Morris Rosenberg, Neil Smelser, Ralph Turner, and several anonymous reviewers. Most of all, I am indebted and grateful to Lyn H. Lofland.

1. Quoted from the by-laws of the Section on Collective Behavior and Social Movements, American Sociological Association, 1980.

2. The similarity of this "ideal-type anchoring" to certain aspects of Neil Smelser's (1963) formulation may be noted. Smelser's effort to portray (and to account for) the panic, hostile outburst and craze also moves in the direction of ideal-type logic. Throughout, he mentions other and lesser "outcomes" without specifying what these might be. The three that he does treat involve high, or fairly high, levels of dominant emotions (and three that are fairly rare in actual occurrence). I have tried to take that logic further by thinking of maximal levels of dominant emotions and the character of "other and lesser" outcomes.

15 LOUIS A. ZURCHER
AND DAVID A. SNOW

Collective Behavior: Social Movements

Introduction

Sociology has been described as "a humanistic discipline because it allows people to understand their social positions and achieve some degree of freedom; a radical discipline because it emphasizes the relativity of truth; and a discipline that combines a critical perspective with a commitment to action" (McNall 1974:361). If this characterization is accurate, then sociological interest in social movements is quite understandable. Nowhere is the reciprocity between the individual and social structure more conceptually and empirically obvious than in the operation of social movements. Nowhere is the notion of the relativity of belief systems and the critical emphasis on praxis more apparent than in social movements.

Social movements are organized collective manifestations of issues for which people have considerable concern. The purpose of the movement is to "do something" about the concern. Movements deliberately attempt to promote or resist change in the group, society, or world order of which they are a part. They do so through a variety of means, not excluding violence, revolution, or withdrawal into utopian communities.[1] Depending upon the degree of correspondence between the goals of a movement and the value orientation of the observer, a movement can be heroic or despicable, on the side of the angels or in league with the devil. Some movements are more dramatic than others; some are more successful than others; and some are more significant than others in terms of the range and depth of their consequences. But seldom are they bland or without controversy. Seldom do they not reflect the ongoing dialectic between the individual and society. Seldom do they not demonstrate the relativity of belief systems and the importance of human agency or social action in the ebb and flow of social life.

These observations will anchor our argument, presented throughout this chapter, that the study of social movements can function as an important bridge for understanding the relation between the individual and society, between structure and process, and between psychology and sociology. Indeed, we will argue that not only does the sociological study of social movements have much to contribute to social psychology, and vice versa, but that exclusively sociological or exclusively psychological analysis yields a truncated understanding of the dynamics of social movements.

In his introduction to *Studies in Social Movements: A Social Psychological Perspective,* McLaughlin (1969:2), a psychologist, explained why he included readings from sociology, anthropology, and history, though the "point of view" of the book "is basically psychological." To take a psychological approach, he advised, "has its hazards, since the psychological mode of analysis tends to over-simplify the variety of motives causing individuals to ally themselves to social movements, and to neglect developmental features such as the evolution of organizational structure and the growth of morale." McLaughlin's caution reflected the earlier concerns expressed by Allport (1968:10–40) in his review of the history of social psychology. Allport observed that around the turn of the century, when social psychology was becoming a recognized subfield, theorists usually emphasized one of five *simple and sovereign explanations* for social behavior: hedonism, egoism, sympathy, imitation, or suggestion. Hedonism was the drive to experience pleasure and avoid pain. Egoism was the pursuit of power and control. Sympathy was the need for affiliation, belonging, empathy, or altruism. Imitation was the proclivity to copy the behavior of others. Suggestion was the tendency to shape one's own behavior according to the intended influence of others. More often than not, an instinct was postulated as the source of the need, motive, tendency, drive, or proclivity, for example, the "instinct for sympathy."

How well has the sociological study of social movements informed social psychology about the hazards of simple and sovereign explanations for social behavior? Have some sociological analyses of social movements depended upon such explanations? If so, how can the deficiencies be remedied without, metaphorically speaking, "throwing out the baby with the bath water?" These questions guide our inquiry. We address them by critically discussing theory and research pertaining to the processes of movement participation and organization, aspects that encompass most of the central issues in the study of social movements. These aspects also constitute the focal areas of social-psychological and sociological analyses, the former being primarily concerned with questions about movement participation, the latter with movement organization and mobilization.

The Processes of Participation in Social Movements

Although not all social movements are equally concerned with expanding their ranks, most set few if any limits on their recruitment designs.

This is not only because movements tend to be "convinced of the rightness of their cause and the inherent attractiveness of their message," but also, and perhaps primarily, because people-power is one of the most important resources movements need in order to advance their interests (Wilson 1973:169). If a movement is to make any headway in its goal-attainment efforts, it must reach out, make contact with, and secure potential participants, and then transform at least some of the new recruits into committed members or devotees. Although those processes tend to merge and overlap in actuality, for analytical purposes they can be distinguished and dealt with separately—the former referring to the recruitment process, and the latter referring to the commitment-building and conversion processes. In this section we first examine the recruitment issue, and then turn to a consideration of commitment and conversion.

RECRUITMENT: WHO JOINS AND WHY?

Among the various issues relating to the study of social movements, few have generated as much discussion and research as the issue of differential recruitment: why do some people rather than others join or participate in already existing social movements? Throughout the large body of literature pertaining to religious cults and movements, revolution, political protest, student activism, or status crusades (Morrison and Hornback 1976), the issue of differential recruitment surfaces repeatedly as one of the dominant focal concerns, both theoretically and empirically. As Marx and Wood (1975:388) noted in their review of theory and research in collective behavior, "one of the most prominent characteristics of collective behavior research in recent years has been the proliferation of quantitative recruitment studies."

Whether conducted by psychologists or sociologists, much of the research and related theorizing (especially earlier investigation) concerning social movement recruitment has sought explanation at a social-psychological-motivational level of analysis. Referred to as "convergence theory" by Turner and Killian (1972) and as the "hearts and minds of the people" approach by Leites and Wolf (1970), the basic underlying assumption is that movement joiners differ importantly from nonjoiners in terms of personality characteristics and/or cognitive orientation. The numerous works operating on this assumption implicitly or explicitly posit a psychofunctional linkage among (1) problematic structural conditions and changes (commonly referred to as structural strains); (2) the social-psychological attributes of potential and actual participants (often conceptualized as predispositions or susceptibilities); and (3) the goals and ideology of movements (frequently construed as appeals). Admittedly, the works of this genre differ significantly in terms of substantive content and theoretical scope, ranging from movement-specific (Almond 1954; Fromm 1941) through middle-range (Davies 1962; Gurr 1970) to more general and inclusive theories (Cantril 1941; Smelser 1963). But inordinate if not exclusive attention generally is given to psychological effects of problematic structural conditions or to the role of attitudinal and personality factors. Those factors are seen as the crucial, albeit intervening, variables in the determination of differential recruitment. Illustrative of this approach is Toch's (1965) psychological examination of the relationship between individual predispositions, susceptibility, and types of movement appeal. For Toch, the appeal and growth of movements centered in their potential to improve the life conditions or ease the psychological strains of a particular constituency or group of individuals. Although Toch did not posit a specific motivational orientation or personality type as conducive to movement susceptibility, other scholars have.

Pursuit of meaning. Cantril (1941:63–65) emphasized the pursuit of meaning as the major motivational force behind movement joining and participation. He contended that those "confronted by a chaotic external environment," uninterpretable because of an inadequate frame of reference, are in a state of suggestibility that renders them susceptible to the simplifying ideology of a movement. In his analysis of the Kingdom of Father Divine, for example, he attributed participation in the movement to three kinds of needs, one of which is the provision of meaning:

> . . . Father gives meaning to the environment in which they (the participants) live. Complexity, confusion, hopelessness, and purposelessness are changed into simple understanding, peace, happiness and a faith in the abstract principles embodied in the person of Father . . . (He thus) provides an escape from a tortuous mental confusion caused by complex, conflicting circumstances. He gives meaning to the individual life and to the world. [Cantril 1941:140–41]

Authoritarianism. Lipset (1963) and Lipset and Raab (1973), drawing on the work of Fromm (1941) and Adorno et al. (1950), have argued that authoritarianism is an important precipitant of participation in extremist movements. Individuals who are dogmatic, highly prejudiced, and insecure are seen as being especially susceptible to the appeals of movements on the radical right and left. This mental set or character type also figures prominently in the work of Hoffer (1951). Arguing that submission to an external cause or authority compensates for feelings of self-inadequacy, Hoffer posits a relationship between movement proneness and the desire to escape from an unwanted self. As he writes with respect to one type of "true believer":

> The permanent misfits can find salvation only in complete separation from the self; and they usually find it by losing themselves in the compact collectivity of a mass movement. By renouncing individual will, judgment, and ambition, and dedicating all their powers to the service of an external cause, they are lifted off the restless treadmill which can never lead them to fullfillment. [1951:50]

Search for identity. More recently, Klapp (1969) has argued that underlying participation in various contemporary movements is a collective search for identity. It is a search symptomatic of mass society's failure to generate and sustain meaningful symbols and anchorages, which are seen as the function of rituals. Turner (1969c, 1976) has similarly suggested that the underlying theme of contemporary social movements is the demand that society guarantee each individual a sense of personal worth and dignity. Symptomatic of this theme is alienation from self and a corresponding search for a more satisfactory locus or base for reconstituting the self. Accordingly, participants in such movements as Hare Krishna, the Children of God, and the National Organization of Women are, hypothetically, individuals whose experiences in the various institutional domains of life have not provided a sense of personal worth or dignity. They are thus seeking a new locus for identity, one that provides a sense of personal worth and a more satisfactory basis for organizing life.

Social isolation or quest for community. Another prominent theme pertaining to movement participation is the social isolation or quest for community proposition. Students of millenarian movements (Aberle 1966; Cohn 1957) and mass society movements (Kornhauser 1959; Lipset 1950, 1963; Nisbet 1954) have argued that vulnerability to movement participation is in part a function of being weakly attached or peripheral to existing social networks. Movement participants are seen as those individuals who lack a series of institutional affiliations and group loyalties. In contrast, those people who are well integrated into kinship groups, cohesive local communities, and various intermediate associations are less susceptible to the appeals of social movements. Readiness to participate thus comes from an absence of those conditions that integrate people into the system and constrain them from involvement. With this emphasis on the presumed cohesive and integrative functions of social movements, phenomena as ideologically diverse as the Reverend Sun Myung Moon movement and the civil rights movement are viewed as surrogate families and primary groups. Participation in such movements hypothetically meets the previously isolated participants' needs for social affiliation, a sense of belongingness, and group identity.

Personal powerlessness. The belief that one's life situation is largely a matter of fate or destiny has also been discussed in relation to movement participation. Two divergent lines of thought have developed. It is hypothesized that subjective powerlessness or little internal control renders the person susceptible to movement appeals and participation (Bell 1964; Bolton 1972; Kornhauser 1959; Lipset 1963). In contrast, it has been hypothesized that a strong sense of personal control or efficacy, coupled with low social control or system blame, is more likely to lead to movement participation, particularly when the movement is political in orientation (Almond and Verba 1965; Gamson 1968). Of these two contrasting propositions, the latter, referred to as the political efficacy-trust hypothesis, has received greater empirical support (Forward and Williams 1970; Paige 1971; Seeman 1975).

Status dissonance or inconsistency. Another factor often regarded as an important determinant of movement susceptibility is the frustration or tension that supposedly results from status dissonance or inconsistency (Geschwender 1967; Rush 1967). As Lenski (1954:211) argued in his seminal discussion of the concept, "the more frequently acute status inconsistencies occur within a population, the greater will be the proportion of that population willing to support programs of social change."

Drawing on Weber's related idea of *status threat,* Lipset (1963), Gusfield (1963), and Zurcher and Kirkpatrick (1976) have argued that challenges to the existence and prestige of the life style to which individuals are committed can render those individuals candidates for participation in "status politics" and/or "status crusades."

Relative deprivation. Probably the most popular explanation for movement participation, extending back to at least the time of Tocqueville (1961), is relative deprivation (Aberle 1966; Davies 1969; Glock 1973; Gurr 1970; Worsley 1957). The basic idea is that a sense of acute deprivation arises when what people want or think they should have exceeds what they actually have. That is, "deprivation occurs in relation to desired points of reference, often 'reference groups,' rather than in relation to how little one has" (Morrison 1971:675). When the gap between expectations or aspirations and actual gratifications or attainments suddenly widens and becomes intolerable, people are thought to be especially prone to movement participation.

Overview of the social psychology of recruitment. Whether the preceding cognitive states or motives are conceptualized in the language of alienation, deprivation, or some other frustration-aggression theory, they suggest what can be regarded as the basic social psychological proposition with respect to movement joining and participation: there exists within the larger population a cohort of individuals who are highly susceptible to movement appeals and participation because they share distinctive social psychological attributes.

Given the tendency for several movements to exist on the market at the same time, the question arises as to how a social-psychological-motivational approach accounts for recruitment to and participation in one movement rather than another. There are two contrasting propositions derivable from the works outlined above. The first posits a linkage between particular types of deprivation or alienation and movement ideology. People are regarded as being differentially susceptible to movement appeals by virtue of different social psychological strains or states. Different kinds of motivations and problem-solving perspectives predispose people to different kinds of movements.

Lofland and Stark (1965), for instance, argue that participation in religious cults and movements is contingent on a preexisting religious problem-solving perspective. Feuer's (1969) questionable linkage of unresolved oedipal conflicts with participation in student movements similarly emphasizes correspondence between particular types of strains and problems and particular types of movement value orientations and programs.

In contrast to the ideology-problem correspondence proposition is the idea of movement interchangeability, articulated most clearly in the work of Hoffer (1951) and Klapp (1969, 1972). They argue that movements draw their members from the same reservoir of potential participants; those susceptible to one movement are therefore susceptible to another, regardless of the nature of the movement's value orientation or ideology. Movements are seen as being interchangeable or functional equivalents of one another. They provide similar opportunities for meaning, community, identity, a sense of personal power, and other gratifications. In both the movement interchangeability and ideology-problem correspondence explanations, movement joining is seen largely as a function of social psychological attributes. The central research task remains that of empirically identifying the personality characteristics or cognitive states that supposedly make people vulnerable to movement appeals and that motivate and sustain participation.

AN EMPIRICAL ASSESSMENT OF THE MOTIVATIONAL APPROACH

Certainly there is explanatory merit to the argument that some people will be more predisposed than others to movement joining for one or more of the reasons suggested above. Not all individuals who come into contact with a particular movement will be equally receptive to the movement's program. However appealing this argument, it has a number of shortcomings that call into question its analytic and predictive power.

Much of the sociological literature examining the hypothetical association between preexisting social-psychological strains and participation in movements suggests a relatively indeterminant relationship (Aberle 1965; Hobsbawm 1965; Useem 1975). Measures of alienation, deprivation, and frustration have been linked to apathy and nonparticipation as well as to participation in such disparate collective phenomena as cargo cults, religious movements, reform movements, ghetto revolts, student movements, and political movements on both the right and left. This is not particularly surprising. Not all individuals who were strongly opposed to America's intervention in Vietnam actively participated in the anti-war movement. Nor do all individuals who find their daily lives and routines periodically devoid of meaning or positive feedback experiment with chanting, encounter groups, and other meditative or self-discovery techniques. Given this indeterminacy between specific social-psychological attributes and movement joining, works that posit a direct linkage between the two thus tend to be tautological: movement joining is taken as evidence for the existence of prestructured cognitive orientations that are assumed to be shared by those who participate.

The hypothetical linkage between movement joining and such cognitive states as frustration, deprivation, or alienation has also been called into question by several sociological studies of participation in collective violence and social movements. Petras and Zeitlin (1967) found that the main determinant of Chilean peasant leftism was proximity to radical mining areas and not differential frustration. Portes's (1971b) examination of data collected in lower-class urban slums of Santiago, Chile, suggested that frustration with personal situation—whether it be induced by relative deprivation, rural-urban migration, or lower socioeconomic status—is a consistently poor indicator of leftist radicalism. The research of Tilly and his associates (Rule and Tilly 1972; Snyder and Tilly 1972; Tilly et al. 1975) on rebellion in Europe also challenges the frustration-deprivation-alienation thesis. In *The Rebellious Century, 1830–1930,* the Tillys (1975) present data that suggest that civil strife in France, Italy, and Germany was not importantly related to economic deprivation, strong governmental repression, or short-term but rapid social change. Instead, the Tillys argue that the collective protest was primarily a function of local, regional, and national struggles for power that were stimulated by urbanization, industrialization, and especially state making. Equally revealing is McPhail's (1971) secondary analysis of 173 tests of relationship between individual deprivation and/or frustration and riot participation. Assessing the magnitude of association between these variables, McPhail (1971:1064) found that the majority of associations were statistically significant and in the direction predicted by the deprivation-frustration thesis, but of a consistently low magnitude. These findings prompted McPhail to call for a careful reexamination of the simple and sovereign cliché "that absolute or relative deprivation and the ensuing frustration, or discontent or despair is the root cause of rebellion."

In light of these and similar observations (Moinat et al. 1972; Lewis and Kraut 1972; Orum 1974; Pinard 1967), it seems reasonable to argue that deprivation or alienation only provides a cognitive state that might be conducive to, but is not sufficient for, movement participation. To paraphrase Zawadski and Lazarsfeld (1935:249) in their study of unemployed Polish workers, frustration and discontent "fertilize the ground" for movement participation, but do not lead to it by themselves. If they did, then, as Trotsky (1959:249) once observed, "the masses would be always in revolt."

THE RECRUITMENT CATALYSTS: NETWORKS AND IDEOLOGY

The bridging function of social networks. The preceding observations indicate that the cognitive states or motives verbalized by the recruit or imputed by the social scientist do not sufficiently account for movement participation. That criticism is reinforced by considering participation in one or more movements to be unlikely without prior contact with a recruitment agent. With few exceptions (Balch and Taylor 1978; Straus 1976), the potential participant, whatever his or her interests, socioeconomic situation, cognitive state or motives, has to be informed about and introduced into a particular movement. Even if there were compelling empirical support for the assumption that attitudinal or personality factors constitute the most critical variables in the determination of differential recruitment, an important sociological question remains: which of the outsiders or potential participants are most likely to come into contact with and be recruited into one or more movements, or into one movement rather than another?

The bridging process whereby potential recruits and a particular movement are brought together has generally been glossed over by those works approaching recruitment from a social-psychological-motivational standpoint. Toch (1965), for example, contends that the transaction between individual susceptibility and movement appeals is central to an understanding of who joins and why, but he does not explain how this transaction occurs. Similarly, the numerous works focusing on alienation and relative deprivation as the key determinants of differential recruitment fail to consider the mechanisms by which dispositions, appeals, and ideology are linked together.

In recent years a growing number of sociological studies have suggested the important role of preexisting social relations and networks in the structuring and channeling of movement recruitment. Jackson et al.'s (1960) examination of the mobilization difficulties encountered by an incipient tax-protest movement in Los Angeles, Petras and Zeitlin's (1967) investigation of the emergence of agrarian radicalism, Marx's (1969) findings regarding the emergence of black militancy, Pinard's (1971) study of the rise of the Social Credit Party of Quebec, Freeman's (1973) discussion of the differential spread of the feminist movement among American women, Leahy's (1976) findings pertaining to the recruitment of leadership to the anti-abortion movement, and Zurcher and Kirkpatrick's (1976) examination of antipornography crusades all suggest that primary and secondary associations can function as important recruitment channels. Critical reviews of research on urban disorders (Feagin and Hahn 1973; McPhail 1971), some studies of the civil rights and student movements (Orum 1972; Von Eschen et al. 1971); and several theoretically oriented works (Oberschall 1973; Wilson and Orum 1976) have also alluded to the function of social networks in the emergence and spread of radical or reformist collective phenomena. One study that set out to examine the social-psychological orientations hypothetically predisposing people to participation in the peace movement even reached the tentative conclusion that:

> . . . recruitment into peace groups is less often the result of self-selection of the group by the recruit than of being recruited through belonging to social networks, some of whose members already belong to the peace group. [Bolton 1972:557]

In addition to the above works pertaining to political protest movements and activities, several studies of religious cults and movements point to the importance of overlapping networks and interpersonal ties for movement recruitment and growth. In their study of Pentecostal groups, Gerlach and Hine (1970) found, for example, that new members' first contact with the movement usually followed preexisting social network lines. In two of the Pentecostal churches studied, sixty-one of the seventy-seven members interviewed were recruited into their respective church by means of face-to-face contact with familiar others who were members. Fourteen of the sixteen individuals who indicated that they were recruited through other means and channels reported they were "drawn into the movement by the direct action of God." Subsequent conversation with several of these individuals revealed that significant relationships with relatives or friends had been involved (Gerlach and Hine 1970:79–80). Harrison's (1974) and Heirich's (1977) research on recruitment and conversion to Catholic Pentecostalism similarly revealed "that members of the movement, when recruiting, turn to previous friends and persons they meet at daily Mass" (Heirich 1977:667). Bibby and Brinkerhoff's (1974) findings regarding the recruitment efforts of evangelistic Protestant churches indicated "that evangelism . . . took place primarily through existent ties with family and friends."

Studies of the spread and growth of the Sokagakkai in Japan also reveal that the majority of adherents were recruited by members who were preexisting friends, acquaintances, or kin (Dator 1969; White 1970). Snow's (1976) participant observation study of the recruitment efforts and spread and growth of the Nichiren Shoshu Buddhist movement in America underscores the importance of social networks in relation to recruitment. All but two of the fifteen most active members of the chanting cell with which Snow was affiliated were drawn into the movement by virtue of being linked to a member through a preexisting, extra-movement interpersonal tie. Examination of the modes of recruiting 330 members who subsequently gave testimony in the movement's newspaper similarly revealed that 82 percent were recruited through social networks.

Since social networks constitute micro-structures, these findings suggest the primacy of social structure in the determination of differential recruitment to and the differential spread and growth of social movements. More explicitly, the findings suggest, as Snow et al. (1980) have argued, that the interconnections between movement network attributes and the interpersonal associations of potential participants are just as, and perhaps even more, important in the recruitment process than social-psychological attributes and hypothesized susceptibilities.

The mobilizing function of ideology. It is axiomatic that not all individuals subjected to a movement's recruitment efforts become deployable agents, devoting time and energy to the movement's cause. What factors other than interpersonal ties with participants function as recruitment catalysts? A partial answer is suggested by the concept of ideology and the extent to which it links the prospective participant's life situation to the goals of the movement. Ideology refers to that component of a movement's "universe of discourse" (Mead 1962:88–90) that supports and justifies movement objectives. It provides both a picture of the world as it is and as it should be. It provides a guide for action by which the desired changes can best be achieved. At the same time it underscores what is wrong, attributes blame and responsibility, and addresses the Leninesque question of "What is to be done?"

The social-psychological-motivational approach tends not to consider the role of ideology in relation to movement recruitment and participation. It focuses on susceptibilities and predispositions, suggesting that the tenets of a movement's ideology are self-evident given a particular personality type, developmental background, or set of frustrations and discontents. Such an assumption is sociologically untenable. Not only does it assume a connection between preaffiliation cognitive states and movement ideology that is too immediate and direct, but it ignores the mobilizing function of ideology.

Sociologically oriented works have generally followed Marx in viewing ideology as the sine qua non precipitant of collective action. Moore (1968), for instance, argued that the creation of a doctrine or "charter myth" is usually one of the first steps along the road to radical political action and revolutionary change. Smelser (1962), using the term "generalized belief" in lieu of ideology, also emphasized the importance of new ideas in mobilizing people for collective action. Rudé's (1964) contention that the philosophy of the French Enlightenment provided a basis for a sense of unity among diverse groups illustrated the importance of an alternative ideology as an energizing force. Rudé (1964:74–75) stated that the French Revolution:

. . . needed more than economic hardship, social discontent, and the frustration of political and social ambition to make a revolution. To give cohesion to the discontents and aspirations of widely varying social classes there had to be some unifying body of ideas, a common vocabulary of hope and protest. . . .

A similar example was offered by Hobsbawm (1965) in his discussion of the practical function of millenarian beliefs for mobilizing rural people. The beliefs facilitated mutual awareness and provided a common cause, a sense of exaltation, and a feeling of invincibility. Such beliefs, he wrote:

. . . helped to organize masses of hitherto unorganized people on a national scale, and almost simultaneously. . . . An atmosphere of high exaltation greatly facilitates the spreading of news. . . . It invests even the smallest organizational advance with an aura of invincibility and future triumph. . . . By these means a movement can almost simultaneously mobilize masses over a wide area. . . . [Hobsbawm 1965:105–106]

The interplay between networks and ideology. While emphasizing the importance of ideology or some alternative belief system in relation to movement recruitment and participation, the above examples also indicate the necessity for someone, usually movement members, to articulate and disseminate the ideology. The importance of the articulation and diffusion of ideology in stimulating movement participation was well illustrated by Morrison and Steeves (1967) in their study of National Farm Organization participants. Their findings indicated that the emergence of NFO consciousness among midwestern farmers was not only linked to dissatisfaction with their socioeconomic situation, but was also importantly related to the presence of "leaders who create the initial recognition of structural blocks and who develop and diffuse structural solutions" (Morrison and Steeves 1967:432). Petras and Zeitlin's analysis of the relationship between organized mining workers in Chile and the development of radical political consciousness among the peasantry was equally illustrative. Although the majority of the peasants were poverty-ridden and oppressed, there were important class differences among them which tended to be reflected in differential political orientations and voting patterns. Taking this differential orientation as problematic, Petras and Zeitlin found that proximity to highly organized and politically radical mining municipalities located in the countryside functioned as the main determinant of peasant radicalism. As they explained:

The miners' organizational skills and political competence, the proximity of the mines to the countryside, the sharing of an exploited position, and conscious political choice enable the miners to politicize and radicalize the Chilean countryside. . . . The miners' leadership and ideology provide the peasants with a form of communication and sharing of experience that is necessary for them to recognize and be able to act upon their common interests. [Petras and Zeitlin 1967:584]

Such findings suggest that the tenets of movement ideology are not immediately self-evident. Nor are they brought to the fore by intense frustration, alienation, or deprivation. Rather, their realization seems contingent on intellectual and emotional exposure along the lines of social networks. The ideology provides the cognitive map articulating the problem, focusing blame, and justifying action. However, social networks channel the diffusion of these ideas for action. Social networks and movement ideology function in an interactive manner to determine the spread of social movements.

COMMITMENT

To demonstrate empirically the critical role of social networks and movement ideology in the recruitment process is not to account for sustained participation. As indicated earlier, if a movement is to remain viable and expand or sustain its membership, not only must it reach out and secure potential adherents, but it must also transform these recruits into committed members or devotees.

Once informed about and brought into contact with a movement, the potential participant has, metaphorically speaking, stepped through the portal of another world. Whether the prospect returns to the world whence he or she came, alternates between the two worlds, or steps further inside and closes the door behind, thereby opting for a new or regenerated Weltanschauung, is problematic for both the analyst and the movement. The line of action taken is not merely a function of social-psychological attributes or motivational predispositions. Such dispositions, along with an interpersonal tie to one or more members, may be instrumental in bringing the recruit and movement together, but they do not alone provide the staying power for continued involvement in the movement. The staying power is largely a function of the extent to which the individual's dispositions, interests, and world view become linked to the goals, ideology, and internal requirements of the movement as an organized collectivity. In other words, whether the new recruit leaves or stays is largely dependent on whether he or she becomes committed to the movement.

Kanter (1972:66–67), in what is the most exhaustive sociological examination of commitment in the field of social movements, suggests that it refers:

> . . . to the willingness of people to do what will help maintain the group because it provides what they need . . . commitment means the attachment of self to the requirements of social relations that are seen as self-expressive. Commitment links self-interest to social requirements.

To be committed in this sense is not only to follow a line of action consistent with the expectations of the movement, but it is to follow a line that rigidly circumscribes or cuts off other possible lines of action. To paraphrase Becker (1960), such commitment would constitute an all-encompassing "side bet." Extraneous interests would be colored and influenced by the basic commitment. Or in Goffman's (1961:106) words, such commitment would indicate the absence of role distance and the existence of role embracement; it would be "to disappear completely into the virtual self available, and to confirm expressively one's acceptance of it."

In this sense, commitment is the underlying essence of Durkheim's (1964) "mechanical solidarity," Toennies' (1957) "gemeinschaft" system of social relations, and Simmel's (1964) "secret society." In each instance, the committed individual's tie to the group is of such intensity that it functions as an all-encompassing side bet. When a person is committed to this extent, "what he wants to do (through internal feelings) is the same as what he has to do (according to external demands), and thus he gives to the group what he needs to nourish his own sense of self" (Kanter 1972:66–67).

Defining commitment in this way usefully provides an "ideal type" of what constitutes total commitment. However, it tends to obscure the fact, as Wilson (1973:303) and Turner and Killian (1972:334) have observed, that commitment is a matter of degree; it can vary not only from one movement to another, but also within the same movement. As such, the above definition might be better conceived of as a bench mark against which the degree of commitment between and within movements might be measured.

The heterogeneity of member commitment. A movement that seeks to control the totality of each member's life for its own ends may be regarded as "greedy" (Coser 1974). In contrast are those movements that call for only periodic participation. Where a movement falls on this continuum is largely a function of its ideology and goals and the way in which it is defined or reacted to by the community in which it exists. Movements that are "reformative" (Aberle 1966) or "normative" (Smelser 1962) in orientation and defined as "respectable," for example, are hypothetically less demanding in that membership can usually be scheduled into a fairly normal life pattern. In such movements, commitment may involve little more than the coordination of "roles inside and outside the movement" (Turner and Killian 1972:334). In contrast, the commitment required by movements defined as "peculiar" and "revolutionary" is usually much more demanding and all-encompassing. Participation "normally requires a choice between the movement and normal life" (Turner and Killian 1972:334)—as in the case of Hare Krishna, the Children of God, the Symbionese Liberation Army, and most communal movements.

The sociological finding that different movements vary considerably in terms of the type and degree of member commitment is rather a truism. But the discovery of intramovement differences in member commitment is somewhat surprising. It runs counter to the stereotypic conception of movements as monolithic entities composed of a similarly committed stable of adherents who are distinguishable only in terms of whether they are leaders or followers. The latter view is an oversimplification and is empirically unfounded. Kanter's (1972) study of the differential viability of nineteenth-century utopian communes clearly illustrates that point.

Drawing on Parsons and Shils's (1962:4–5) theory of action, Kanter suggested three different types of commitment, each of which reflects a mode of object-orientation. The first type, referred to as "instrumental" commitment, reflects a calculative or cognitive orientation to the movement in general and the membership role in particular. Continued participation is purely a utilitarian decision. Those recruits who stay and pursue lines of action consistent with the interests of the larger collectivity are those individuals who find that the rewards or benefits of participation outweigh the costs or liabilities. "Cohesion" or "affective" commitment, Kanter's second type, is a function of the emergence of a positive cathectic orientation to movement members. This kind of commitment binds members together emotionally, thereby giving rise to group cohesion and solidarity. Gratification flows from attachment to and involvement with other movement members. The third type of commitment, referred to as "control" or "moral" commitment, reflects a positive evaluative orientation to the movement and its ideology. Here commitment is "to uphold norms, obey the authority of the group, and support its values" (Kanter, 1972:69). Such commitment functions as the basis for one's decision-making and cognitive orientation. Not only is obedience to movement demands viewed as "a normative necessity," but the demands are viewed as an expression of one's own interests and values.

Kanter's tripartite conceptualization of commitment is particularly instructive for a sociological understanding of movement participation. It suggests, in contrast to the popular assumption of motivational and ideological homogeneity, that individuals may participate in movements not only in different ways and for different reasons, but without having internalized the movement's value orientations. Yet, moral commitment or ideological congruence is not an anomaly. Within most movements there is usually a corps of participants who are devoted to advancing the cause on purely "moral" grounds. Simply put, they think it is right. They see it as the "one way." For such individuals the movement's ideology or value orientation functions as their "primary authority" (Rokeach 1960: 43). For some movement participants, moral commitment to a cause represents an extension of prior socialization; for others it is largely a function of conversion. The process of conversion demands further discussion, given the controversy it has generated among lay persons and social scientists in recent years (Conway and Siegelman 1978; Enroth 1977; Richardson 1978).

CONVERSION

Conversion denotes a process through which a new or formerly peripheral universe of discourse comes to function as a person's primary authority. Before detailing a sociological perspective of the conversion process, we will consider the psychological view.

Psychological views of conversion. Most psychological discussions of movement participation contain implicit or explicit reference to at least one of three approaches to conversion. The first approach views conversion from the standpoint of physiological psychology. Rooted in the work of Pavlov and articulated in Sargant's *Battle for the Mind* (1959), this approach holds that conversion is largely a product of a physiological dysfunction of the brain. The individual is rendered receptive to new ideas and physically incapable of judging or evaluating the wisdom or correctness of those ideas.

The *coercion* model of conversion conceptually blends physiological psychology with strands of psychoanalytic theory (Bauer 1957; Lifton 1963; Schein 1961). Stimulated by studies of the brainwashing (Hunter

1956) of United States POW's during the Korean War, the coercion model holds that the key to understanding conversion resides in such factors as information control, personal manipulation, forced confessions, and ego destruction.

Both the physiological and coercive approaches are of limited generality. They ignore conversions that occur in noncoercive situations and in the absence of physical stress and deprivation. Moreover, to argue that conversion occurs primarily under those conditions is implicitly to define as deviant or pathological the groups and movements to which people frequently convert. More specifically, it suggests that no one of "sound mind and spirit" could find appealing the "nonsensical" world views of many movements. Hence the necessity of milieu control and of overstimulating or inhibiting the nervous system by subjecting conversion prospects to extreme physical stress or sensory deprivation.

The third psychological approach to conversion constitutes a *ballistic missile* model. Strong pressures *within* the person are seen as motivating or compelling conversion (Hoffer 1951; Salzman 1953; Toch 1965). The explanatory concern is not so much with the movements or world views to which people convert as with what moved them to go and why they went where they did. Attention is focused on pre-affiliation tensions, personality characteristics, and unique socialization experiences as key factors in accounting for conversion. Toch's (1965:111–29) view is illustrative. Individuals socialized in childhood to a set of absolute values and beliefs are regarded as particularly vulnerable to subsequent conversion. A new set of absolutes or an alternative world view hypothetically promises attainment of the old absolutes because of the disillusionment experienced in the everyday world. The key to understanding conversion resides within the psyche or background of the individual. Some individuals are therefore more susceptible to conversion than others.

The ballistic missile approach ignores the existence of different types of converts and conversion pathways. It supports a stereotypic view of conversion—the sudden adoption and use of a new universe of discourse. The convert is one who has dramatically turned away from one belief system to another form. Ballistic missile conversion focuses attention on some "extraordinary" event or experience that enables the individual suddenly to "see the light." Analogically, this experience, or "moment of awakening" as the Langs (Lang and Lang 1961:157) refer to it, functions much like an electrical switch that has just been turned on, suddenly rendering aglow and objectifying what had been invisible, hazy, or anathema only moments earlier.

Certainly there are some people who seem to experience sudden and "enlightened" conversion. But psychological explanations often take for granted what is sociologically problematic: the process leading up to and making such an event possible. More explicitly, the emphasis on the manifestation of conversion focuses attention on the end point or culmination of the conversion process rather than on the process itself. Thus a part is mistaken for the whole.

Sociological views of conversion. Sociologically considered, conversion is a function of a gradual social learning process rather than a consequence of some dramatic and extraordinary event that affects fertile psychological dispositions. Indeed, to suggest that conversion is only a function of an extraordinary event is to put the cart before the horse. In order to experience conversion and give testimony to it, a person must first learn something about the new interpretive schema. For example, what kind of experience and events are symbolic of conversion?

In addition to arguing that conversion is contingent on learning what might be termed a basic convert role, sociologists have also identified several conversion pathways. The first involves the adoption of a totally new universe of discourse as one's primary authority. Perhaps best exemplified by Paul's embrace of Christianity, this type of conversion usually involves a radical reconstitution of the objects in one's social world. Old facts and aspects of a person's biography, including one's former identity are not only given new meaning, but they are negatively evaluated (Berger and Luckmann 1967; James 1958; Travisano 1970). For the convert, the old past and the new present bear little, if any, resemblance to each other. Since the metamorphosis is fairly dramatic, we can refer to conversion along this pathway as *transformative.*

Not all conversions involve a complete turning away from one world view and the adoption of another. As suggested earlier, conversion may also involve alignment to and the use of a formerly peripheral universe of discourse in an entirely new way. This form of conversion, referred to as *regeneration,* operates when a person turns back to a belief system that he or she previously had abandoned in skepticism, rebellion, or indifference. Nock (1933:261–66) has suggested that Augustine, whose mother's deep religious convictions influenced his early years, was exemplary of regenerative conversion. The convert typically finds that the old orientation, which might previously only have been given lip service, takes on a new significance.

Another type of conversion pathway, suggested by Gordon (1974:166) in his work on the Jesus movement, involves the adoption of a belief system which combines two prior but contradictory world views. Conversion along this path, referred to as *consolidation,* can either be direct or indirect.

Direct consolidation involves conversion to a variant of the universe of discourse from which the convert began. Gordon (1974:166) offered the example of "a person raised in a Southern Baptist Church, who rejected these beliefs for drugs and perhaps eastern religion, and who then became a Jesus person."

Indirect consolidation is conversion to a third or fourth world view that integrates and extends an intervening world view. Gordon (1974:166–67) illustrated that convert as "a person raised as a Catholic, who rejected his Catholicism for the youth culture, and later became a Jesus person."

The observation that conversion is typically a role-learning process, and that there are several distinct pathways to conversion, undermines the stereotype of conversion as a unidimensional process. It involves more than a radical and sudden transformation of one's belief system. This conclusion is further buttressed by studies of participation in and conversion to "the Moonies" (Bromley and Shupe 1979; Lofland 1977; Lofland and Stark 1965), Hare Krishna (Daner 1976; Judah 1974), Pentecostalism (Gerlach and Hine 1970; Heirich 1977), and Nichiren Shoshu Buddhism (Snow 1976; Snow and Phillips 1980). Conversion to each of these contemporary movements was found to be highly improbable in the absence of affective and intensive interaction with other movement converts and members. Such findings suggest that movements function not merely as vehicles for the expression and amelioration of prestructured dispositions and strains, but they also function as important agitational, problem-defining, need-arousal, and motive-producing agencies. Whereas most psychological analyses typically emphasize the former function, the findings described above suggest the importance and perhaps the primacy of the latter function. Just as successful businesses and corporations help create their own demand, so, it appears, do successful movements.

RECRUITMENT, COMMITMENT, AND CONVERSION: A SUMMARY

How far a movement goes in advancing its interests and attaining its goals depends not only on the nature of those objectives and the degree of resistance encountered but also on the ability of the movement to expand its ranks and transform those who join into committed participants. As suggested throughout this section, the readiness to act on behalf of the collectivity is not an automatic concomitant of affiliation. Nor does commitment, whether it is instrumental, affective, moral, or total, flow solely from pre-affiliation cognitive states and background experience. Rather, it is an emergent and interactional phenomenon that must be developed by the movement itself. In this regard, sociologists have argued that commitment to a course of action consistent with the interests of an organization is largely contingent on whether the organization develops mechanisms that lead people to devote more and more personal resources to it while simultaneously closing off alternative courses of action (Becker 1960; Kornhauser 1962; Selznick 1952). The work of Kanter (1972), Gerlach and Hine (1970), and Wilson (1973) in particular suggest that the strength of commitment to a movement is largely a function of the extent to which the movement develops and institutes various strategies and mechanisms: (1) that provide gratifications and rewards for participation (instrumental commitment); (2) that foster a sense of belongingness and a "we" feeling (affective commitment); (3) that anchor the individual's self-conception and world view in the movement (moral commitment); and (4) that circumscribe other possible objects of commitment and reduce the value of outside activities. In her study of the differential durability of utopian communes, for example, Kanter (1972) found that the more successful ones—those lasting thirty-three years or more—were those with a greater variety of commitment-building strategies and mechanisms. In a recent examination of thirteen communes existing in America between 1965 and 1973, Gardner (1978) found mixed support for Kanter's thesis that the success or failure of communal movements is largely a function of the existence of organizational structures that promote commitment to the group. But since the somewhat different findings seemed to be due in part to different formulas for communal success, Gardner (1978:219) concluded that "all things considered, more conservatively structured communes still seem to have a better chance for long-term survival today."

Several other studies of communes and movements have similarly alluded to the import of mechanisms that foster commitment. Those include: cultural and social insulation (Bittner 1963; Simmons 1964); keeping a distinctive language (Hostetler 1968); specific dress (Isichei 1970; Redekop 1969); geographical isolation (O'Dea 1957); witnessing (Gerlach and Hine 1970; Harrison 1974; Shaffir 1978); confession (Zablocki 1973); and various interpersonal influence tactics and strategies (Lofland 1977, 1978; Snow 1976; Snow and Phillips 1980).

These sociological findings suggest that the key to understanding movement recruitment, commitment, and conversion resides in the interaction between the participant and the movement and in "the structural arrangements and organizational strategies which promote and sustain" participation (Kanter 1968:499). Attention is thus shifted from the individual and his or her pre-affiliation psychology to the organizational arrangements, strategies, and commitment-building mechanisms that influence one's cognitive orientation and behavior or both. This is not to suggest that pre-affiliation attributes are irrelevant for understanding movement participation. Instead, it is to emphasize, as Zygmunt (1972:462) has put it, that:

> Predispositions must be ordered, put into the service of the movement, linked with its values, harnessed to its goals, intermeshed with its own internal requirements as an organized collectivity. Pre-existing motives become relevant mainly as points of departure for a process of learning and relearning, which the movement must direct. Personal motives are not necessarily extinguished in this process, but they come to be linked with new patterns of conduct which are relevant to, and supportive of, the collective enterprise which the movement represents.

That is precisely what occurs in the movement recruitment, commitment, and conversion processes. Some movement organizations carry out those functions well, some do not.

The Processes of Movement Organization and Mobilization

ORGANIZATIONAL TRANSFORMATION AND SOCIAL MOVEMENT ORGANIZATIONS

The sociological study of the organizational characteristics of social movements de-emphasizes psychological explanations for movement emergence. Instead, the analytical focus is upon the structural and political factors that contribute to movement growth, change, and decline. Zald and Ash (1966:327) coined the term "social movement organization" and initially concentrated on the dynamics of movement goal transformation, the shift to organizational maintenance, and oligarchization.

Goal transformation included pragmatic leadership's replacing unattainable goals with diffuse goals, thus providing the movement with a broader range of targets. The shift to organizational maintenance meant a preoccupation with sustaining membership, funds, and other structural requirements for continued existence. Oligarchization described the concentration of power among a few of the movement organization's members.

Influenced by the pioneering work of Weber (1946), Troeltsch (1931), Niebuhr (1929), and Michels (1949) on organizational transformation, Zald and Ash (1966:327) observed that as a social movement organization "takes an economic and social base in society, as the original charismatic leadership is replaced, a bureaucratic structure emerges and a general accommodation of the society occurs." The effects of bureaucratization upon movements are illustrated in several sociological case studies, including, Messinger (1955) on the Townsend movement; Wilson (1959) on the Pentecostal movement; Nelson (1974) and Rudwick and Meier (1970) on the civil rights movement; Gusfield (1957) on the Prohibitionist movement; Curtis and Zurcher (1974) and Wallis (1979) on moral crusades; and Piven and Cloward (1977) on poor people's movements.

The character and degree of movement bureaucratization has been related to such organizational variables as: expressive, instrumental or mixed-goal orientations; exclusive or inclusive member recruiting; solidary or purposive incentives for member participation; homogeneous or heterogeneous memberships; broad or restricted contact with the community; and directing or persuading leadership styles (Curtis and Zurcher 1974). The sociological study of social movement organizations has revealed that, in a context of change and transformation, movement organizations manifest a complex pattern of interactions among structural components. The sophistication of that pattern defies exclusively psychological explanations for movement emergence and evolution.

THE MULTI-ORGANIZATIONAL FIELD, VOLUNTARY ASSOCIATIONS, AND SOCIAL MOVEMENTS

Two other sociological research thrusts shaped the study of social movement organizations. Studies of the multi-organizational field indicated that organizations in a community approximated an ordered, coordinated system (Aldrich and Pfeffer 1976; Curtis and Zurcher 1973; Turk 1970). When present in a community, social movement organizations must become part of that "field," cooperating with, competing with, or attacking other field components. Studies of voluntary action and voluntary associations revealed a network of overlapping organizational memberships in a community (Gordon and Babchuk 1959; Sills 1968; Smith 1975). When a person volunteers for membership in a noncommunal social movement, he or she adds to a set of membership roles. The person must balance the time, energy, and commitment allocated among the roles in the set (Zurcher 1978). Furthermore, he or she must attend to the degree of overlap in or conflict between organizational expectations associated with different memberships. Membership in most social movements does not exist in an organizational or a community vacuum.

THE RESOURCE MOBILIZATION OF SOCIAL MOVEMENTS

Perspectives drawn from studies of organizational transformations, multi-organizational fields and voluntary associations have recently been combined with constructs drawn from economic theory and political sociology to form a *resource mobilization* perspective on social movements. This approach is based on the convergence of the work of a number of students of social movements, particularly Gamson (1968, 1975), McCarthy and Zald (1973, 1977), Oberschall (1973, 1978), and Tilly (1978), but is most clearly articulated by McCarthy and Zald.

Currently described as the "leading edge" of social movement theorizing and research, resource mobilization "examines the variety of resources that must be mobilized, the linkages of social movements to other groups, the dependence of movements upon external support for success, and the tactics used by authorities to control or incorporate movements" (McCarthy and Zald 1977:1213). Resource mobilization "adopts as one of its underlying problems Olson's (1968) challenge; since social movements deliver collective goods, few individuals will 'on their own' bear the costs of working to obtain them. Explaining collective behavior requires detailed attention to the selection of incentives, cost-reducing mechanisms or structures, and career benefits that lead to collective behavior" (McCarthy and Zald 1977:1216).

In their presentation of a "partial theory" of resource mobilization, McCarthy and Zald defined the central concepts as follows:

> A *social movement* is a set of opinions and beliefs in a population which represents preferences for changing some elements of the social structure and/or reward distribution of a society. A *countermovement* is a set of opinions and beliefs in a population opposed to a social movement. [1977:1217–1218]
>
> A *social movement organization* is a complex, or formal organization which identifies its goals with the preferences of a social movement or countermovement and attempts to implement those goals. [1977:1218]
>
> All of the social movement organizations that have as their goal the attainment of the broadest preferences of a social movement constitute a *social movement industry*—the organizational analogue of a social movement. [1977:1219]
>
> In modern America there are a number of social movement organizations which may be thought of as conglomerates in that they span, in their goals, more narrowly defined social movement industries. Common Cause, The American Friends Service Committee, and the Fellowship of Reconciliation are best treated in these terms as each pursues a wide variety of organizational goals which can only with difficulty be contained within even broadly defined social movement industries. The *social movement sector* consists of all social movement industries in a society no matter to which social movement they are attached. [1977:1220]

These definitions clearly differentiate between a population's potential-for-movement behavior and the organizations which mobilize that behavior. The flexibility of these conceptual components is impressive, as is their usefulness for sociological analysis. Social movements, insofar as they are defined as population preferences, may never get off the ground unless the appropriate resources are mobilized by a social movement organization. But the organization exists completely in a setting of social movement industries and sectors, and consequently can be readily restrained, facilitated, or manipulated by political forces outside the organization. In this milieu of "costs and rewards," of give and take, data might be gathered that are pertinent to: how movement beneficiaries are identified and defined; how goals and targets are determined and changed; how members are recruited and made into adherents; how authorities, elites, and entrepreneurs affect a movement; what balance of competition and cooperation between movement organizations is most productive; how the organizations grow, decay and become institutionalized; what kinds of leaders best mobilize what kinds of resources, and when; and what the "zero sum game" for resource mobilization might be (see Zald and McCarthy 1979:1–5, 238–45). The resource mobilization framework might overcome, at least in part, a plague endemic to earlier social movement theory—incapacity to predict the mobilization and outcome of social movements. The understanding of resource mobilization can encourage further research on the factors underlying the *failure* of many social movement organizations. With the exception of such research as that conducted by Gamson (1975), Piven and Cloward (1977), Jackson et al. (1960), and Wallis (1979), studies of movement failure are rare in the literature, despite their importance for theory and application.

RESOURCE MOBILIZATION AND SOCIAL PSYCHOLOGY

The resource mobilization approach shifts the analysis of social movements from the characteristics and dispositions of individual participants to the structure and operation of movement organizations. Viewing movements as operating in a multi-organizational field, it focuses attention on the linkages between a movement organization and other groups or movements within its environment of operation. Rather than concentrating on the initial phases of movements, it focuses attention on their entire life span. Examination of movement outcomes becomes a central element of study. Taken together these focal concerns provide an important corrective to social-psychological-motivational interpretations of social movements. But is the corrective too severe? Have simple and sovereign psychological explanations been replaced by a simple and sovereign sociological explanation?

It might seem so, especially since resource mobilization theorists generally give little attention to the role of ideology, symbolization, and passion in relation to the emergence, operation, and decline of movement organizations. The neglect of ideological and emotional factors is reflected most clearly in the work of McCarthy and Zald (1973, 1977). They tend, for example, to provide a rather unexamined answer to the question of why people devote time and energy to movement organizations. They assume "that the costs and rewards of involvement can account for participation" (McCarthy and Zald 1977:1226). McCarthy and Zald are not the only mobilization theorists to represent a sweeping assumption of motivation for movement participation. Oberschall (1973:162) argues "that the lower the risks and the higher the rewards for an individual and members of a group or social stratum, i.e., the lower the risk/reward ratio, the more likely they are to become participants in a social movement. . . ."

When they attribute movement participation to a rational calculus whereby the costs of participation are weighed against the rewards, McCarthy and Zald (1973, 1977) and Oberschall (1973) ironically invoke the logic of utilitarian economics, the language of behavioral psychology (Skinner 1973), and the formulae of exchange theory (Homans 1958, 1961; Thibaut and Kelly 1959). This suggests that at least some varieties of the resource mobilization approach are rooted in the kinds of "psychologized" domain assumptions they purportedly eschew. It also suggests that resource mobilization is subject to the criticisms leveled against incentive models of behavior. Some of these criticisms warrant further discussion.

RATIONALITY AND TAUTOLOGY

The most obvious shortcoming of incentive models is the tautological character of the rationality assumption. People are supposed to participate in or devote personal resources to movement organizations because it is rewarding to them. Defining participation, rewards, and rationality in terms of each other precludes finding negative cases. The circularity of the argument renders a central component of the resource mobilization approach unfalsifiable. And what is the nature of the rewards? How do they come to have meaning as rewards? How and why do they vary from situation to situation?

Similar difficulties are encountered when the rationality assumption is extended to the organizational level. How is rational collective action to be identified apart from the efficacy of goal-attainment strategies and tactics? Is it possible to assess the rationality of strategies and tactics without assuming that movement goals are well-defined, consensual, and relatively stable? Perhaps the basic problem is that the resource mobilization approach, as reflected in the work of McCarthy and Zald (1973, 1977) and Oberschall (1973), is like other rationalistic incentive models of behavior, basically an optimal theory. It postulates how people and organizations might behave if they had complete information and the ability to process that information in a maximally rational manner. It also assumes some sort of an absolute, consensually validated reward or reward-set. The problem, of course, is that neither individuals nor organizations ever have complete or absolute information regarding the costs and benefits of particular lines of actions. Consequently, the resource mobilization approach is rooted in assumptions that are heuristically rather than descriptively useful.

Even if complete information were available, even if the costs and benefits of a line of action were known a priori, people would not always act in a purely rational or self-interest maximizing fashion. To argue that they would is to assume that all human actions involve calculations, that people always weigh and assess personal costs and rewards in all situations. Such a view of behavior is not only limited; it is repeatedly contradicted. People frequently behave altruistically. Social action in one direction rather than another is frequently prompted by interpersonal loyalties and obligations. And people often act on the basis of principle or moral considerations, as in the case of whites supporting the black movement, "straights" supporting the "gay" movement, and women opposing the draft. Such observations have prompted a number of critiques of the resource mobilization perspective. Fireman and Gamson (1979:21), in particular, have criticized it "for exaggerating the role of self-interest in mobilization while obscuring the role of solidarity and principle." Along similar lines, Jenkins (1977) and Tilly (1978) have argued for the inclusion of "solidary" and "purposive" incentives within the resource mobilization framework. Since it is a sociological truism that social and moral factors are no less important than material incentives in understanding behavior (Parsons and Shils 1962; Etzioni 1975; Kanter 1972), the criticisms put forth by Fireman and Gamson, Tilly and Jenkins seem quite appropriate. However, we do not think the correctives go far enough. Moral incentives, while taken into account, are of secondary importance. The importance of symbols and symbolization is neglected. The function of emotion or passion receives little or no consideration. Both resources and mobilization are conceptualized in a somewhat vague and limited fashion.

SYMBOLS, SYMBOLIZATION, AND MOBILIZATION

Given the centrality of the concept of *resource* to the work of McCarthy and Zald (1973, 1977), Oberschall (1973), Tilly (1978), and Gamson (1975), it is reasonable to expect that the concept would be defined with some clarity. This is not the case. On the one hand, resources are defined so broadly that they "can be anything from material resources . . . to nonmaterial resources" (Oberschall 1973:28). On the other hand, the empirical referent is usually something tangible, such as people, money, and facilities. "Resources," according to Tilly (1978:7), "may be labor power, goods, weapons, votes, and any number of other things, just so long as they are usable in acting on shared interests." In practice, then, the key to determining whether something is a resource seems to reside in its use-value. Such a conceptualization is vulnerable to serious challenge. As with the previously discussed rationality assumption, it smacks of tautology. Can resources be specified independently of their use by movement organizations? If they cannot, how does the resource mobilization perspective avoid the error of self-confirming hypotheses by post hoc identification of resources?

Another problem with conceptualizing resources primarily in terms of their use-value is that the important function of symbolization in relation to mobilization is not fully appreciated. If resources refer to those things that a movement needs to assemble and deploy in order to advance its interests, then some of the most important movement-related resources are those that function primarily in a symbolic manner. That is, their significance or value is based on what they symbolize for movement members, potential supporters, bystanders, and/or targets of influence.

Ideology is probably the best example of a resource that functions in a symbolic fashion and that is importantly related to a movement's mobilization efforts and organizational viability. It is, of course, presumptuous to assume either that mobilization is primarily a function of ideology or that most movement participants carry complex ideologies around in their heads. There is, nonetheless, little question that mobilization is based in part on congeries of ideological phrases and slogans generated and articulated by movement leaders. Such phrases and slogans symbolize the nature and causes of discontent, and provide justification for action. Certainly the repetition of slogans such as "Liberty, equality and fraternity!" "Fight self, fight self-interest," "We shall overcome," "Burn, baby, burn!" and "La raza!" have functioned in this symbolic manner throughout the course of history. Sorel's (1941) advocacy of the general strike was designed to provide exactly that kind of energizing slogan for collective action by the working classes. Though Sorel (1941:137) regarded the general strike as a myth, it was, nonetheless, thought to be a powerful and energizing myth—"a body of images," as he put it, "capable of evoking instinctively all the sentiments which correspond to the different manifestations of the war undertaken by Socialism against modern society." Along similar lines, Fanon's (1965:61–83) advocacy of violence by peasant revolutionaries against the colonial masters can also be viewed as an energizing symbol. For Fanon, the practice of violence functions to bind people together as a whole. "It throws them in one way and in one direction." It is a mobilizing and "cleansing force."

Patterns of rhetoric that are common to most movements can also be construed as symbolic resources. Certainly the rhetoric of justice (Lerner et al. 1975) and equity (Walster et al. 1978) is an important resource that every movement attempts to manipulate to its own advantage in the normative context in which groups contend.

Some strategic patterns of action can be viewed as resources that function in a symbolic manner to secure other symbolic resources. Drawing on data pertaining to the operation of the Nichiren Shoshu Buddhist movement in America, Snow (1979) has suggested that movement accommodation may often be conceptualized as an outward-reaching symbolic gesture or strategy aimed at securing idiosyncracy credit. Idiosyncracy credit (Hollander 1958) symbolizes respectability and legitimacy in the public eye. It is conceptualized as a movement-related resource that has the property of providing some latitude for operation and that can function to expand opportunities for the mobilization of other resources.

The significance and efficacy of terrorism as an insurrectional movement strategy also flow in part from its symbolic functions (Schreiber 1978; Thornton 1964). Although terrorism is frequently employed for direct political purposes, it often functions in a symbolic manner by conveying messages or warnings to opponents, bystanders, or sympathizers. This was clearly recognized by Trotsky (1961:58) when he observed that terrorism "kills individuals and intimidates thousands." Examples of the symbolic value of terrorism abound in the world today. By kidnapping or shooting civilians and public officials, by blowing up buildings and public facilities, and by hijacking modes of public transportation, contemporary terrorists create the impression of ubiquity, urgency, and governmental impotence. Hundreds of thousands of noncombatants may be demoralized; only a handful are killed. In many respects terrorism, whether employed by elites or insurgents, is the ultimate symbolic weapon because it mobilizes and demoralizes at one and the same time, and it does so relatively efficiently.

The importance of symbolization in relation to collective action has also been suggested by studies of looting, rioting, and hostile confrontation between protestors and control agents (Berk and Aldrich 1972; Dynes and Quarantelli 1968; Heirich 1971; Quarantelli and Dynes 1970). Turner and Surace's (1956) examination of the precipitants of the 1943 "Zoot-suit" riots in Los Angeles is particularly illustrative of the connection between symbols and mobilization for collective violence. A content analysis of the *Los Angeles Times* revealed that the symbol *Mexican* tended to be displaced by the symbol *Zoot-suiter* as the period of crowd attacks approached. The symbol Zoot-suiter "evoked only the picture of a breed of persons outside of the normative order, devoid of morals themselves and consequently not entitled to fair play and due process" (Turner and Surace 1956:20). It diminished ambivalence and neutralized norms that might have otherwise inhibited violence against Chicanos. These observations were interpreted as providing support for the basic hypothesis that "hostile crowd behavior requires an unambiguously unfavorable symbol, which serves to divert crowd attention from any of the usual favorable or mitigating connotations surrounding the object being attacked" (Turner and Surace 1956:14).

Although caution should be exercised when generalizing from specific incidents of crowd behavior to the operation of social movements, Turner and Surace's observations suggest the important role of symbols in mobilizing adherents and getting them, metaphorically speaking, from "the balcony to the barricade." Moreover, when such observations are combined with our earlier discussion of the mobilizing functions of ideology, the symbolic character of movement accommodation, and the symbolic consequences of terrorism, there seem to be two inescapable conclusions: not only are some resources purely symbolic, but the symbolic value of many resources is equally, if not more, important than their more tangible use-value. Indeed, it might be argued that the resource most important to a movement's mobilization efforts is a symbol that unifies and empowers, on the one hand, while neutralizing or redefining countervailing orientations on the other.

If the concept of resources should be expanded to include symbols and symbolism, then the concept of mobilization correspondingly needs to be broadened. It should include symbolization, the process through which objects, whether physical, social, or abstract, take on particular meanings. Mobilization is generally conceptualized as involving the accumulation, organization, and deployment of resources for the pursuit of collective goals and interests. Such a conception mistakes a part for the whole. Resources are not only acquired through various outward-reaching strategies and tactics. As we have argued, some are also created or manufactured; some are symbolic productions.

The same can also be said about costs and rewards, interests and incentives, whether material, solidary, or moral. The costs and benefits of participation are not self-evident or fully calculable in advance of actual participation. Rather, they are symbolic productions. Their meaning arises during the course of interaction among movement leaders and members. To argue otherwise is to assume that movement goals, the rewards of participation, and individual interests are initially sufficiently known and sufficiently stable to permit rational assessment of the advantages of participation or of one line of action over another. Such an assumption overlooks the fact, as reported earlier, that the alignment of individual interests and movement goals is often a consequence rather than a precipitant of joining and participation. Additional evidence of this assertion is provided by the existence of consciousness-raising groups and the phenomenon of conversion. The concept of resource mobilization should thus be expanded to include the processes by which meaning and moral incentives are developed and maintained.

The social genesis of meaning is a central problem for symbolic interactionism. The merging of symbolic interactionism with resource mobilization can therefore contribute to a general theory of social movements by helping clarify how individuals assign meanings to the costs and rewards of participation. It could also shed light on how meanings and vocabularies of motive (Mills 1940; Scott and Lyman 1968; Zurcher 1978) are established, modified, and manipulated in social movement settings. Those meanings would be illustrated as emerging from the interaction of principals in the social movement setting—leaders, members, bystanders, targets, opponents, competitors. The processes of interaction could be applied as well, empirically and analytically, to the dynamic networks in social movement industries and sectors. People and their interactions are the linking pins of the networks. Interaction thus conceptually cuts across individuals and organizations, as does meaning as a product of interaction. Such important social movement constructs as rhetoric, ideology, charisma, commitment, and incentive, when put into a framework attending to meaning and resultant action, thereby apply both to individuals and organizations. Symbols, whether verbal or nonverbal, as the currency of meaning are made more fully useful for revealing why people act in a certain way or how they can be influenced to so act.

THE CAST OF CHARACTERS IN SOCIAL MOVEMENTS

Understanding of the operation and the resource mobilization efforts of social movement organizations can also be advanced by closer research attention to movements' casts of characters. The term *cast of characters* is used advisedly. It represents the dramaturgical approach to sociological investigation. The dramaturgical analysis of social behavior, often categorized as a variation of symbolic interactionism (Meltzer, Petras, and Reynolds 1975:67–75), focuses attention on social interaction and the ways in which individuals and "teams" of actors mutually influence each other when physically copresent or engaged in focused interaction (Burke 1965; Goffman 1959, 1967; Messinger et al. 1962). The character and direction of social action, whether at the individual or group level, is seen primarily as a consequence of the adjustments interactants make to the impression they formulate about each other.

Some of the work of resource mobilization theorists suggests, but does not adequately enough exploit, the dramaturgical perspective. Gamson (1975:14–18), for example, discussed social protest as being generated in an interactional setting that involved a challenging group, its constituency and beneficiaries, and the antagonist or target of influence. McCarthy and Zald (1977:1221–22) similarly alluded to constituents, adherents, bystanders, opponents, elites, and potential beneficiaries as the configuration of "characters" that are involved in the operation of movement organization.

What follows is a discussion of research findings that we interpret as bearing upon the dramaturgical cast of characters in social movements. Each of the types of cast members, we argue, can be considered as both resource mobilizers and resources to be mobilized. The discussion will also give us an opportunity to review some of the salient literature on social movement roles, and to comment on its social-psychological relevance.

Leaders and lieutenants. Social-psychological formulations of leaders and leadership have focused on the attributes of the leader position, the personal characteristics of the leader, and leadership as a category of behavior (Katz and Kahn 1966:301). At one extreme has been the "great man-great woman" hypothesis—leaders are born, not made (Bass 1960). At the other extreme has been the situationist perspective—leaders are created by social circumstance. The current social-psychological view of leadership is transactional, cutting across expectations, personal characteristics, and social settings (Hollander and Julian 1970). Fiedler's (1967) "contingency model of leader effectiveness" combines into an analytical matrix such factors as the leader's personal relation with the group, the structure of the group task, and the leader's power over group members.

Weber's (1946) pioneer work clearly has influenced social-psychological explanations of leadership. It would be difficult to find a treatise that did not refer to charismatic, traditional, and legal-rational leadership, or some similar characterizations. Weber's view of leadership was primarily sociological. Authority was legitimated in social settings. The different types of authority were imbedded in contexts of specific organizational forms and of change in those forms. But Weber also noted the contribution that individual personality made to leadership. Charisma was a social phenomenon, but was also the psychological attribute of a person (Friedland 1964:18–26).

Weber's analysis of leadership has profoundly affected sociological discussions of social movements. Charisma seems a natural leadership style for social movements. Weber stated (1946:358–59):

> The term charisma will be applied to a certain quality of an individual personality by virtue of which he is set apart from ordinary men and treated as endowed with

supernatural, superhuman, or at least specifically exceptional powers or qualities. These are such as are not accessible to the ordinary person, but are regarded as of divine origin or as exemplary, and on the basis of them the individual concerned is treated as a leader.

The volatility and crusading goal of many social movements appears to be matched with the volatility and crusading zeal of the charismatic leader. However, as Weber pointed out, and as other scholars (see especially Zald and Ash 1966) have illustrated, charisma almost surely is "routinized" in social movement. It gives way to bureaucracy and bureaucrats. Virtually all of the sociological typologies of social movement leadership reflect the transition from charisma to bureaucracy and, as Weber also suggested, the reemergence of charisma when bureaucracy becomes too rigid and needs changing. Blumer (1951), influenced by Dawson and Gettys (1948), reported the evolution of movement leadership roles from the agitator (during the social unrest stage); to the prophet (during the popular excitement phase); to the statesman (during the formalization stage); to the administrator (during the institutionalization stage). Hopper (1950) and Lang and Lang (1961:241, 517–42) illustrated similar typologies. Brinton (1948:25–26) based his types on what he perceived to be the functions of movement leaders: discovery of ideas; spreading the ideas; creating and holding the loyalty of followers; manipulating situations and events in a manner favorable to the movement. Turner and Killian (1972:391–92) identified leaders who primarily served as symbols and those who primarily served as decision makers. Gusfield (1966:137–56) saw some movement leaders as having an articulation function, some as having a mobilization function. Wilson (1973: 194–225) categorized movement leaders as charismatic, ideological, or pragmatic. Roche and Sachs (1955:248–49) labeled leaders either as "enthusiasts" or "bureaucrats". Killian (1964) observed charismatic, administrative, and intellectual movement leaders.

The diversity of leadership roles in social movements, the manner in which leadership is linked with movement stages, and the changes in leadership style over time illustrate for social-psychological theory the conceptual and empirical flexibility of the term "leadership". There are several different kinds of leader roles, sometimes played by the same actor, more often played by different actors in a dramaturgical setting. Such observations caution against reification of leader types and abstraction of types away from their interactional setting.

Since social movement organizations can be relatively informal and unsettled structures, especially at the onset, the leader roles are both particularly critical and particularly noticeable (Nelson 1971; Zald and Ash 1966; Zurcher and Curtis 1973). Consequently, the social movement setting has been and continues to be fruitful for social psychological studies of leadership. It is particularly important to learn more about how the social movement leader operates in the role of resource mobilizer. The findings could cast some interesting light on the social psychology of entrepreneurship. How does a leader, to use dramatistic language, choreograph the movement? How does the leader orchestrate the "keynoting" important to the emergence of movement norms (Turner 1964; Turner and Killian 1972:89–90)? To what extent is charisma deliberately "put on" by a leader for effect? To what extent is charisma manufactured as an organizational ploy and the property of the structure rather than the person? To what extent, therefore, is it actually "bureaucharisma" (Zurcher 1967:416)?

The study of social movement leadership will continue to be important for the advancement of social-psychological theory as long as it remains at least partly rooted in Weber's original formulations. Both the characteristics of the social setting *and* the characteristics of the individual leader must be considered. The extent to which the characteristics of the individual are shaped by social factors probably will remain a point of constructive debate. The social movement milieu is an excellent stage upon which to observe how social factors influence and are influenced by actors.

With the exception of the work of Lang and Lang (1961), Gerth (1940), and Heberle (1951), little has been written on the role of secondary leaders in social movements or in other organizations. Understanding the division of labor between leaders and lieutenants, the manner in which these roles complement each other, and how their interaction affects leader succession would be interesting social-psychological topics for study, as would be the function of movement cadres or advisory cores.

Rank and file supporters. We shall not discuss here the rank and file participants who devote time and energy to movement organizations. The dynamics underlying the participation of those individuals, referred to by McCarthy and Zald (1977:1221) as the "constituents," were discussed earlier. It is worth repeating, however, that the previously discussed findings and observations suggest that such aspects of participation as conversion and commitment can be best regarded as interactional and emergent phenomena.

Bystanders. The sociological study of social movements has shown that the seemingly passive observers of movement activity can have a significant effect upon the kinds of strategies and tactics sponsored by movement leaders. This is particularly the case with smaller and younger social movement organizations, and with those that have not chosen to isolate themselves as much as possible from society.

Turner (1973) coined the term "bystander public" to describe those individuals who were neither members nor opponents of a movement. They were interested witnesses, or were perceived to be by movement leaders. Basing his observations on a symbolic-interactionist perspective, Turner concluded that leaders attended closely to cues from the bystander public when they formulated courses of action. Three movement mobilization strategies were apparent: bargaining, coercion, and persuasion (Turner 1973:148–49). The choice of those strategies are substantially shaped by what movement leaders thought would "play" to the bystander audience as they judged it.

In addition to illustrating the social psychological pertinence of bystanders in the development of social structures, the sociological data on social movements can be merged with those accrued from psychological studies of bystanders. Darley and Latane (1968), for example, have conducted a series of studies on the effect of bystanders upon helping behavior and response to emergency. Essentially, the psychological findings indicate that the larger the number of bystanders in an emergency situation the more the responsibility for helping action will be diffused and the more likely inaction will result. How empirically and conceptually do those findings fit with the operation of social movements? Are movement participants more inclined toward helping behavior than if they were acting alone? What is the process of "risky shift" in that context (Johnson et al. 1977)? How does the deliberation of equity affect bystander behavior, and the behavior of movement leaders who perceive the reactions of large numbers of bystanders? Sociological and psychological orientations have not yet adequately informed each other in this instance.

Opponents and competitors. We have for the purpose of discussion combined these two types of social movement actors because they fall into the plausible category that Lang and Lang (1961:291–332) referred to as movement social objects.

Opponents are individuals perceived by movement leaders and members to disagree with movement goals and strategies. Opponents take action against the movement to express their disagreement. Sometimes opponents themselves are organized as a social movement which can be called a countermovement.

Agencies or movement organizations that attempt to serve the same goals or beneficiaries can become competitors for limited resources. Opponents and competitors can be generated from within a single movement organization by schism (Firey 1948; Gamson 1975; Wallis 1979).

Sociological findings concerning movement opponents and competitors reveal the manner in which these actors interact, form ad hoc alliances, fracture, evolve, and dissipate. The movement organization is shown to be enmeshed in that evolution, and to influence it. One of the more interesting findings suggests the usefulness of opponents and competitors for maintaining member unity of purpose within the movement organization (Lang and Lang 1961; Shaw 1971).

Further sociological investigation of the interlocking roles of actors who are opponents, competitors, and members of movement organizations can shed light on several issues of interest to social psychological theory. In that research context, data can be found which could help synthesize sociological labeling theory (Schur 1971) with psychological attribution theory (Shaver 1975). Those data could also advance psychological understanding of scapegoating, identification of an "enemy," and processes of dehumanization or depersonalization.

Beneficiaries. Beneficiaries are those members and nonmembers the movement organization appears to serve. Sociological studies of social movements have revealed the manner in which movement leaders select potential beneficiaries—a process similar to movement identification of opponents, competitors, and targets (McCarthy and Zald 1977:1221). Mauss (1975:xvi), using a sociology of knowledge perspective, concluded that "social problems" actually are a kind of social movement. Some human condition is labeled by interest groups as a social problem and action is taken to ameliorate the problem. Beneficiaries are identified as sufferers of the social problem.

To what extent are beneficiaries named by movement leaders primarily for symbolic or strategic rather than for service reasons? How is the choice of movement beneficiaries, and the reasons for the choice, explained by psychological research on altruistic behavior (Macauley and Berkowitz 1970)? How is it explained by what psychologists call the "just-world hypothesis" (Lerner et al. 1975)? There is considerable promise for advancing social-psychological theory through investigations of movement beneficiary choice, as well as by studies of other actors in the movement cast of characters. In turn, such research can further understanding of the intricacies of the mobilization process.

PASSION, ORGANIZATION, AND THE DIALECTIC OF MOVEMENTS

Sociological examination of movement organizations and their mobilization efforts has given limited attention to the reality of emotion in social movements. This is especially true with the resource mobilization perspective. Resource mobilization theorists suggest that people "take to the streets" because of probable payoffs. How strongly they feel about the issues is of little relevance. Movement actors seemingly are bureaucratized. They are organizational functionaries devoid of passion and emotion. Perrow (1979:201) has criticized the work of McCarthy and Zald in this regard, suggesting that theirs is a theory for which "guts, and even praxis" are largely irrelevant. We agree, but do not think the charge pertains only to the work of McCarthy and Zald. Resource mobilization theorists in general neglect the importance of strong passions in relation to the ebb and flow of movement organizations.

Before we discuss the connection between emotion and movement mobilization, we want to emphasize that we are not discounting the importance of organization. To do so would unduly contradict what movement leaders and revolutionaries—from Lenin and Mao to Alinsky and King, from Paul and Wesley to the Reverend Sun Myung Moon—have long known or argued on the basis of first-hand experience: that organization is a sine qua non condition for mounting a serious political challenge or a successful religious propagation drive. The importance of organization has also been suggested in Gamson's (1975) study of factors associated with the success and failure of fifty-three movement organizations that constituted challenging groups in America between 1800 and 1945. Among other things, Gamson found that the more highly organized a challenging group, the more likely it was to realize its goals, that is, to win "new advantages" for its constituency. Organization was defined in terms of two separate indices: bureaucracy and centralization. A movement was considered bureaucratic if it possessed a constitution or charter, kept a formal list of members, and had at least three levels of authority. A group was defined as centralized if power resided in a single leader or central committee. Gamson (1975:95) found that bureaucracy and centralization each contribute to success, but that "the combination is especially potent with respect to gaining new advantages. Three-fourths of the groups that had both gained new advantages while only 15 percent of those which had neither were successful in this respect."

Gamson's findings provide evidence for the necessity of organization if a movement is to realize its goals. But to emphasize the importance of organization too strongly is also theoretically and empirically questionable. Nowhere is this more clearly suggested than in Piven and Cloward's (1977) provocative examination of why poor people's movements sometimes succeed and sometimes fail. Following Michels (1949), Piven and Cloward argue that organization is ultimately antithetical to protest movements. Based on their analysis of civil rights and welfare rights movements and the unemployed and industrial workers' movements, Piven and Cloward (1977:xxi–xxiii, 36–37) contend that:

> Organizers do not create such movements. . . . Efforts to build organization are futile. . . . Whatever the people won was a response to their turbulence and not to their organized numbers. . . . Organizers and leaders who contrive strategies that ignore the social location of the people they seek to mobilize can only fail. . . . Whatever *influence* lower-class groups occasionally exert in American politics *does not result from organization,* but from protest and the disruptive consequences of protest. . . . Organizers and leaders cannot prevent the ebbing of protest, nor the erosion of whatever influence protest yielded the lower class. They can only try to win whatever can be won while it can be won. . . . In these major ways *protest movements are shaped by institutional conditions,* and *not by the purposive efforts of leaders and organizers.* [emphasis added]

If Piven and Cloward are correct, they call into question Gamson's findings in particular and the resource mobilization approach in general. They also challenge conventional sociological wisdom concerning the relationship between movement and organization. What, then, are we to make of Piven and Cloward's conclusions? Can they be reconciled with Gamson's findings, with resource mobilization theory, with what both sociologists and movement leaders have long accepted as an article of faith? If not, how do we choose between one or the other?

We do not choose between them. We think *both* Gamson and Piven and Cloward are largely right. Organization is necessary if a movement is to make any headway in its goal-attainment efforts; yet organization can also lead to acquiescence and frustrate the attainment of goals. The problem is not organization per se, but organizations that fail to develop and maintain a sense of enthusiasm and anticipation. Participants who no longer harbor a sense of expectancy about what tomorrow will bring, participants who no longer feel strongly or passionate about the cause, are participants who can no longer be counted on for action. They are participants who are likely to retreat in the face of adversity. The importance of a sense of anticipation and passion in relation to movement viability has not been lost on movement organizers and revolutionaries. In *The Joyful Community,* Zablocki (1971:149–92) notes that "the secret of the Bruderhof" resides in its ability to develop and maintain a sense of "collective behavior" or enthusiasm and anticipation on behalf of communal members. It can be similarly argued that the secret of Mao's revolutionary genius resided in that ability. Certainly one of the major functions of Mao's Cultural Revolution was to combat the tendency toward bureaucratization, elitism, and complacency by rekindling the fires of passion and expectancy (Mao Tse-tung 1967; Wheelwright and McFarlane 1970). As one observer of the Cultural Revolution noted:

> Mao wished to destroy a party linking a well-defined structure, the principle of working-class leadership and the role of technical expertise. . . . By attaining even partial success he has broken the concentration of power at the top and in the hands of bureaucratically oriented cadres. [Lewis 1970:27]

Given such observations, we think it is reasonable to argue, along with mobilization theorists, that organization is not necessarily antithetical to movement viability and goals. However, we would also argue that organization in the absence of passion leads to stagnation. Indeed, we think the internal dynamics of movements might be best conceptualized in terms of a dialectic between enthusiasm and idealism on the one hand and bureaucratism and pragmatism on the other. Both factors supply a movement with its life-blood. Each by itself is counterproductive. Consequently, movement viability and success is contingent on both organization and passion. The dialectical tension between the two provides movements with dynamism and, curiously, an important kind of stability. This dialectic should constitute a central problem for resource mobilization theory. How do movements resolve the tension between organization and passion? Why are some more successful in this regard than others? What kinds of organizational mechanisms give rise to a sense of passion and expectancy? How are such emotions maintained? What accounts for their demise? How, in short, is passion mobilized, controlled, and utilized?

Summary and Conclusions

In this chapter, we have defined what we mean by social movements and suggested that the study of movements is a fertile endeavor for further understanding the relation between individuals and societies, between social structure and social-psychological processes, and between selected elements of the disciplines of psychology and sociology. We have argued that an exclusively psychological or an exclusively sociological approach to the study of social movements is not sufficient. Either of those exclusive orientations tends to lead to simple and sovereign explanations for the behavior of human beings in social movements.

We divided our discussion into two major sections: the processes of participation in social movements; and the processes of movement organization and mobilization.

Our discussion of the processes of participation in social movements began with an analysis of the recruitment of members. The psychological-motivational explanation for recruitment, that is, the assumption of pre-existing cognitive states as the major motivational basis for participation, was questioned. Specifically, we demonstrated that the following simple and sovereign explanations for participation were not convincingly supported with empirical data: the pursuit of meaning; the inclination toward authoritarianism; the search for identity; the pressures of social isolation and the quest for community; the stress of personal powerlessness; the operation of status dissonance or status inconsistency; and the frustrations of relative deprivation. Those psychological-motivational explanations for movement participation have some merit, but they do not fully enough or consistently enough explain why people choose to be members of social movements. We suggested that other social factors, such as the operation of interpersonal networks and the understanding of ideology, provide bridging functions whereby people are attracted to movements. Individuals almost always have some prior contact with the recruitment agent, himself or herself part of an organizational network, prior to participation. People generally have to be informed about movements as alternative choices of action before they can engage in that action.

We discussed the processes of commitment to a movement, once the members have been recruited. Commitment was shown to be a heterogeneous and not a homogeneous phenomenon. Members dedicated themselves to movement goals and strategies in accordance with their understanding of those goals and strategies. There is no monolithic motivation for member commitment to social movements. Similarly, the conversion of individuals to ardent membership is neither homogeneous nor monolithic. There are several paths to conversion, a diversity of socialization experiences, all of which reveal the importance of considering social processes rather than psychological predispositions toward understanding the fullness of membership.

Participation in social movements, including recruitment, commitment, and conversion, was suggested to be an interactional and emergent process, socially constructed. The social construction is guided in a large part by the nature of the social movement organization and the milieu in which that organization operates.

Our exposition of the processes of movement organization and mobilization began with a discussion of the dynamics of organizational transformation. An assumption of preexisting psychological states among organizational members was not helpful for understanding such transformations. We suggested that structural and political factors better accounted for the operation of social movement organizations, and for their emergence, growth, and decline. Among those structural and political factors, we considered the multiorganizational field and the network of voluntary associations.

Resource mobilization theory is the most important current attempt to explain the operation of social movement organizations. That theory clearly highlights movement activity, and attends to the importance of movement networks and structural processes. However, we argued that resource mobilization theory unduly assumes that movement participants are driven by a simple and sovereign incentive, specifically, the incentive for self-interest. Ironically, resource mobilization theory seems to accept the dictums of stimulus response theory, even though it eschews psychological reductionism. We suggest that resource mobilization, in its present form, is tautological in its conceptions and unrealistic in its positing of an optimal motivational base for human behavior.

We encouraged readers to agree with us that, despite its present shortcomings, resource mobilization promises to contribute importantly to the understanding of participation in and the operation of social movements. Before that promise is realized, however, the theory must go beyond its rationalistic and behavioristic perspectives. Resource mobilization theory ought to incorporate into its conceptions the notions of symbolization, meaning, ideology, conversion, commitment, and, in general, symbolic interaction.

We presented the cast of characters in social movements as an example of the manner in which dramaturgical analysis, a variety of symbolic interaction, might be incorporated into resource mobilization. Among the movement cast of characters we discussed: leaders and lieutenants; rank and file supporters; bystanders; opponents and competitors; and beneficiaries. In our analysis of the cast of characters, we suggested how psychological and sociological theories might be merged productively to understand aspects of social movement performance. Specifically, we referred to: the risky-shift phenomenon; attribution; equity theory; the consideration of leaders in a social context; the just-world hypothesis; and the relation between social movements and social problems.

A consideration of passion or emotion is important, we further suggested, as a component of resource mobilization theory and as a general component of any understanding of social movements. Passion and emotion are not considered to be predispositions for movement participation, but as emergents in the process of movement recruitment and participation. Affect can be considered the catalyst for movement mobilization. Symbolic interactionism provides a particularly useful framework for understanding the emergence of passion and emotion, both in the case of social movements and in the cases of other social phenomena (Schott 1979).

We concluded that the psychological and the sociological approaches to understanding social movements have not well enough informed each other. Until they do, the explanations for the emergence of social movements in the societies will, for the most part, depend upon simple and sovereign explanations, none of which will represent a coherent summary of causes and consequences of movement activity.

NOTES

1. This conceptualization, which blends the definitions suggested by Turner and Killian (1972:246), Wilkinson (1971:27), and Wilson (1973:8), distinguishes social movements from sociohistorical trends (for example, industrialization). Nonetheless, some scholars will undoubtedly find the definition too broad. Roberts and Kloss (1979:57), for instance, include as movements only collective attempts "to influence the labor or property relations of a given society." Similar definitions are suggested by Garner (1977:1–2), Heberle (1951:6), Traugott (1978), and Useem (1975: 6). Since there remains much to learn about the emergence, operation, and conse-

quences of social movements, we see no defensible rationale for limiting the study of social movements to direct political challenges and attempts to alter labor or property arrangements. For further justification of a broad conceptualization, and for a discussion of the distinction between social movements and such collective phenomena as the political party, pressure groups, and voluntary associations, see Wilkinson (1971:26–32). For a more psychological definition of social movements, see Toch (1965) and Milgram and Toch (1969).

The Sociology of Deviance and Social Control

If publications and course enrollments are the criteria, no sociological subject rivals the popularity of deviance. Yet there are only two noteworthy arguments for considering deviance as a central subject for sociology, and both are disputable. First argument: deviance is the antithesis of social order, the very thing that preoccupies sociologists; rejoinder: sociologists seldom depict social order as jeopardized by deviance. Second argument: social change commences as deviance; rejoinder: sociologists rarely study deviance as bearing on social change.

So the popularity of the sociology of deviance cannot be attributed to the *unquestioned* importance of deviance, and references to the field's subject matter as "nuts and sluts" suggest that the field is popular because a prurient market cannot be glutted. Yet interest in the sociology of deviance has been sustained not by a preoccupation with nuts or sluts but, instead by a new perspective and a related major conceptual issue. The new perspective is variously identified as the labeling perspective, labeling theory, or the societal reaction perspective; and the major issue centers on replacement of the traditional normative conception of deviance by a "reactive" conception. The issue's importance beggars exaggeration; it has determined the fate of theories, and the future of the sociology of deviance hinges largely on the resolution.

The present focus on the major conceptual issue entails slighting substantive theories, research findings, and the interrelation between the sociology of deviance and the social psychology of conformity. Given the purpose of this volume, the slighting of the interrelationship is especially unfortunate, not only because of the prospective audience but also because even disciples of Durkheim would grant some possible benefit from a greater integration of the sociology of deviance and the social psychology of conformity. Greater integration is precluded by two largely unrecognized problems: first, social psychologists have only recently commenced showing real awareness of the labeling perspective (for example, Dedrick 1978); and, second, conformity as studied by social psychologists is not simply the obverse of deviance as studied by sociologists.

The present concern with those two problems rather than the literature of social psychology will disappoint some readers; yet there are several recent surveys of the social psychology of conformity, but no confrontation in the literature of the problems in question.

The Normative Conception of Deviance

Prior to the 1960s virtually all sociologists accepted a normative conception of deviance, which reduces to a definition something like this all-too-brief version: deviant behavior is behavior contrary to a norm of some social unit. The definition has two implications: first, deviant behavior is relative, meaning (inter alia) that a *type* of act which is deviant in one social unit (a particular country, company, family, and so forth) may not be deviant in others; and, second, the identification of deviant acts requires reference to norms. The first implication follows from an unquestioned feature of norms, that they vary among social units; hence, no more need be said about it except to emphasize that (critics notwithstanding) the normative conception makes deviance a *relative* phenomenon. But not enough can be said about the second implication, if only because identifying instances of deviance depends ab initio on the definition of a norm.

PROBLEMS WITH THE NOTION OF NORMS

Most definitions of a norm reflect the "superorganic" conception, according to which norms transcend the behavior of particular individuals (the norms are simply somehow "out there"). That conception (Durkheim's legacy) reflects the widespread aversion of sociologists to reductionism, and it generates definitions that promise negligible empirical applicability (that is, little agreement among independent observers in identifying particular norms of particular social units). Consider Blake and Davis's definition of a norm (1964:456): ". . . any standard or rule that states what human beings should or should not think, say, or do under given circumstances." Standard or rule is no more a primitive term than norm, and the definition does not even suggest how instances of norms are to be identified. That suggestion is found only in definitions by sociologists who have no abiding fear of reductionism, George Homans (1961:46) in particular: "A *norm* is a statement made by a number of members of a group, not necessarily by all of them, that the members ought to behave in a certain way in certain circumstances." Homans's definition is the first step toward what may be the only systematic way to identify the norms of a social unit—solicit answers of members to "normative questions," such as: Do you approve or disapprove of smoking marijuana? Unfortunately, that strategy presents a veritable thicket of problems. Homans did not recognize those problems, nor do most sociologists; but they are horrendous nonetheless.

The consensus problem. The assumption of normative consensus is a staple in perennial debates among sociologists (for example, functionalists versus Marxists); and those debates often create the impression that norms and consensus are distinct. Yet if norms are *collective evaluations of conduct,* a norm cannot exist without some degree of consensus. To illustrate, if only 50 percent of Americans voice disapproval of smoking marijuana, it would make no sense to speak of an American marijuana norm. However, it would be unrealistic to require that all members of a social unit make or endorse a statement for it to be a norm in that social unit; hence, the question: What proportion must do so? Any amount less than 1.00 would be arbitrary.

Arbitrariness is only one aspect of the consensus problem; additionally, the distinction between *aggregate* consensus and *structural* consensus must be confronted. Suppose that the normative question about marijuana is posed to a purportedly representative sample of Americans, and 85 percent of that sample voice disapproval. Yet that percentage could vary enormously among families, age groups, social classes, communities, states, and/or race-ethnic divisions; if so, wherein lies the reality of the American marijuana norm? The question's importance is furthered by the assumption that much of human behavior is in some sense normatively determined, but not even Durkheim would argue that the opinions of Vermont Episcopalians determine a Chicano's behavior in Texas. As for the idea that reference groups are the ultimate locus of norms, sociologists will not carry normative relativism that far, nor does that idea solve any problem in formulating procedures for identifying instances of norms.

Normative contingencies. Suppose that someone responds to the marijuana question by voicing approval of that type of behavior. If pressed, the respondent might balk at children smoking pot; but the question does not stipulate "adults," and age is only one of numerous possibly relevant normative contingencies.[1] Everyday experience surely indicates that evaluations of conduct are commonly contingent on the social and personal characteristics of the actor (including attributed intention), the social and personal characteristics of objects of the act (including demeanor), and various situational considerations (for example, time, place).

Most sociological definitions of a norm recognize contingencies (observe the reference to circumstances in both of the preceding illustrative definitions of a norm). However, a normative question cannot stipulate all possibly relevant contingencies, especially since they are unlikely to be the same for all respondents or for all types of conduct.

Differential power. Returning still again to the marijuana question, suppose that one respondent is a wealthy senator and another a skid-row bum. The conventional survey practice (as in public opinion polls) assigns equal weight to the normative opinions of all respondents, but that practice is debatable. Granted that power is a fuzzy notion, in this instance one respondent (the senator) clearly has more of it than the other (the bum). Accordingly, insofar as there is a marijuana norm, the senator would surely have more opportunities to alter it.

Despite doubts about the equality of normative opinions, practical problems alone seemingly preclude an alternative. Even if an empirically applicable definition of power could be formulated, the relative importance of different kinds of power (for example, political, economic) is not likely to be even approximately the same for evaluations of all types of behavior; and there is no prospect of a systematic basis for assigning power weights to each normative opinion.

Other than practical considerations, there is only one rationale for ignoring differential power in soliciting normative opinions (that is, evaluations of conduct). No definition answers empirical questions, such as: why do norms change? Differential power might be part of the answer, but the answer would be a substantive proposition, not a conceptualization. Nonetheless, ignoring differential power in attempting to identify norms appears grossly unrealistic.

What people say and what people do. Although most sociological definitions of a norm are *evaluative* (that is, they focus on collective evaluations of conduct), there are two distinct alternatives. The first, a *statistical* definition, equates a norm with average or typical behavior. Thus, rather than ask individuals if they approve or disapprove of smoking marijuana, the concern would be with the proportion of individuals who do smoke marijuana. Such a definition may have its greatest following among social psychologists, perhaps because of their sensitivity to a particular issue. In applying an evaluative definition of a norm, investigators must solicit normative opinions; and that procedure, as in attitudinal research, ignores the possibility of substantial divergence between what people say and what people do (Deutscher 1973). A statistical definition admits no such divergence, but it makes a normative explanation of behavior circular. Thus, if the rarity of brother-sister marriage makes it contrary to a norm, there would be no point in arguing that such marriage is rare because it is contrary to a norm.[2] Moreover, a statistical definition ignores those subjective states (disgust, indignation, guilt, and so forth) that give a sense of immediate reality to norms as evaluations of conduct; and it ignores this question: Why are some acts concealed?

The problems that haunt an evaluative definition of a norm are not avoided by a statistical definition. Consider this question: With what frequency must instances of a type of act occur before it is a norm? As in contemplating the "consensus problem," any answer would be unrealistic or arbitrary. Then consider the typical American's infrequent attendance of funerals, even though the normative quality of that type of act is suggested by its public character and perceived obligatory nature. Of course, attending funerals is a highly contingent kind of behavior and ostensibly rare for that reason; but it is not clear how contingencies can be recognized by a statistical definition of a norm. Moreover, since instances of types of acts that are contrary to collective evaluations of conduct tend to be concealed, direct counts of those instances are not feasible.

Still another alternative to an evaluative definition is also behavioral in that it focuses attention on actual reactions to acts. Contemplate this brief version of a *reactive* definition: a type of act is a norm of a social unit if, and only if, instances of that type of act are not reacted to punitively. The definition does not rest on the assumption that people "do what they say," nor does it deny that the evaluations of conduct made by some individuals are more influential than the evaluations made by other individuals. Punitive reactions are indicative of what people truly take as important; and assuming that the powerful members of a social unit control sanctions, a reactive definition takes differential power into account indirectly.

A reactive definition appears to confront the problem of normative contingencies, for potential reactors to particular acts presumably take contingencies into account. However, when reactions are *impunitive,* it is not known whether the act itself precluded a punitive reaction or whether it was the context (for example, the social identity of the actor). Similarly, when the reaction is *punitive,* it is not known whether the act itself elicited the reaction or whether it was the context. In brief, normative contingencies are not revealed by the proportion of instances of a type of act that are punished.

Still another reservation stems from (1) recognition that a reactive definition does not *explain* punitive reactions; and (2) the argument that norms in the evaluative sense *determine* punitive reactions. The reservation is disputable because definitions cannot answer empirical questions. Nonetheless, since acts contrary to collective evaluations of conduct tend to be concealed, it is difficult to estimate the proportion of such acts that are punished. One can speak of "acts that would be punished if known to others"; but that terminology introduces conjecture and ignores the relevance of the identity of "others."

Even if all preceding objections were irrelevant, a reactive definition cannot be applied without a criterion as to the necessary frequency of punitive reactions. It would be unrealistic to argue that all instances of a type of act must be punished for that type to be contrary to a norm, or that all reactions must be impunitive for that type to be a norm; but a defensible alternative is wanting.

Normative properties excluded. The evaluative, statistical, and reactive definitions of a norm are all unidimensional. However, contemplate the ultimate argument for the concern with norms—much of human behavior is normatively determined. Yet general observations and everyday experience indicate that in numerous situations individuals orient their behavior (for example, locking car doors) in terms of *expectations* of conduct rather than evaluations of conduct; and, though rare, some definitions of a norm refer to expectations (for example, Secord and Backman 1974:300; Schellenberg 1974:279). Then there is Scheff's contention (1967) that individuals commonly orient their behavior around their perceptions of *others'* evaluations of conduct (see also Schwartz and Fleishman 1978); and such *perceived* collective evaluations are more social than collective *personal* evaluations (even though both are aggregate properties). Since Scheff's argument readily extends to expectations of conduct, one can rightly speak of a distinction between collective personal expectations and perceived collective expectations.

A unidimensional definition of a norm (for example, one that recognizes only evaluations of conduct) is inconsistent with three conventionally recognized types of norms: mores, customs, and laws. Unlike mores, commonly recognized customs (for example, eating breakfast) have no particular affective connotations. They are permissive rather than approved or disapproved behaviors. Yet Americans have expectations as to such behavior, some of them even being surprised on encountering, for example, an adult who does not drink coffee. So customs are norms only insofar as the notion of a norm encompasses both expectations and evaluations of conduct. Then consider what appears to be unquestioned in both the sociology of law and jurisprudence—a law is a type of norm. Although a criminal statute ostensibly expresses an evaluation of conduct, the evaluation may not be shared by even a majority of those subject to that statute. Moreover, if unenforced criminal statutes are not laws, the reactive definition of a norm identifies the relevant normative property.

To summarize, an inclusive definition of a norm would recognize at least five major normative properties: personal evaluations, perceived evaluations, personal expectations, perceived expectations, and reactions to acts. Although each term denotes a property of a given type of act, and each property is collective in one sense or another, it would be extremely difficult to frame an intelligible definition of a norm that recognizes all of those properties; and there is another difficulty in that each property is quantitative. Consequently, as long as sociologists continue to think of a norm as being either present or absent (for example, premarital sexual relations are or are not the norm), the five properties cannot enter into a definition of a norm without the stipulation of some *minimal* amount of each; and any such stipulation is bound to be arbitrary or unrealistic.

A RADICAL SOLUTION

Given the foregoing litany of seemingly insoluble problems, the only solution is to abandon the notion of norms when formulating theories or conducting research and replace it with the notion of *normative properties,* meaning any characteristics of a type of act in a particular social unit having to do with collective evaluations of that type, collective expectations as to that type, and/or reactions to instances of that type. The definition is not precise, but it permits whatever distinctions (for example, personal versus perceived) and specific mensurable variables (for example, perceived evaluative consensus) a theorist may choose to introduce.[3] That is not the case for conventional definitions of a norm, which depict the phenomenon as qualitative and unidimensional.

The proposal is radical, but it would not require that sociologists rewrite their lecture notes. They can continue to teach as if a norm is as real as a fireplug, provided they separate their pedagogy from their theorizing and research.[4] Nonetheless, sociologists who cling to a superorganic conception of norms will dismiss the litany of problems as stemming from the mistaken belief that norms have something to do with the behavior of individuals, but that argument does not even suggest a procedure for identifying norms. Such a procedure would not be required if sociologists used the term to denote a purely theoretical notion (that is, norms do not exist in the real world or they are not subject to observation), but they do not use the term in that manner.

IMPLICATIONS FOR SOCIAL PSYCHOLOGY

The term norm or social norm is used only tangentially (if at all) in numerous reports of studies in the social psychology of conformity (for example, Nosanchuk and Lightstone 1974); and usage of the term tends to be uncritical, the most obvious being the practice of leaving the term undefined. Even when the term is defined (for example, McKirnan 1980:76), the definition typically resembles those formulated by sociologists, and social psychologists appear no more sensitive than sociologists to the problems and issues (see, for example, Moscovici 1976). However, since the term "norm" enters into the traditional conception of deviance (as studied by sociologists), but not into the traditional conception of conformity (as studied by social psychologists), the seeming insensitivity of social psychologists is more understandable. Indeed, there are reasons for doubting whether the term is essential for studies of conformity in the classical mode (Sherif 1936; Asch 1956) of social psychology.

Contemplate the following brief description of a conventional design for research in the social psychology of conformity. Suppose that an experimental group is formed to elicit expressed perceptions of the length of a line from two sets of subjects in each group, the naive (unprompted by the experimenter as to distorting expressed perceptions) and confederates (those so prompted). Such an experiment would throw light on this question: To what extent is an individual's expressed perceptions of a physical object contingent on contrary expressions by others in the same situation? But norms are variables or conditions in such experiments only if one subscribes to the statistical conception of a norm (that is, average or typical behavior, as when all but one experimental subject state that a line of three inches long is four inches). To be sure, naive experimental subjects may well change their expressed perceptions toward the mean or mode of the group, and social psychologists are perhaps justified in interpreting those changes as manifestations of "pressure"; but it surely does not follow that those subjects come to conform to a norm in the evaluative sense (see Allen 1965:136), and that is the sense in which sociologists use the term norm to define deviance. Even the relevance of such perceptual experiments for the sociology of deviance is disputable. Consider the findings that suggest that an increase in the majority beyond three experimental confederates is associated with little or no increase in the conformity of the naive subject (see, for example, Asch 1956; Kiesler 1969). Those findings are undoubtedly important, but they have no obvious bearing on the attempts of sociologists to account for variation in the rate of, say, forcible rape among populations, nor with the distinction between offenders and "conformists."

The foregoing argument is not to be equated with a typical but dubious criticism of experimental studies—that they focus on artificial situations and trivial behavior—let alone an invidious comparison of the sociology of deviance and the social psychology of conformity. Nonetheless, an enormous chasm separates the two fields, and it can be bridged only by social psychologists. As pointed out previously, sociologists have yet to provide a compelling rationale for not defining norms in terms of *perceived* collective evaluations of conduct (that is, some degree of consensus among members of a population in their perceptions of the evaluative beliefs of other members); and that conception of a norm can be transformed into an experimental variable or condition in research on conformity much more readily than can the autonomic conception (that is, some degree of consensus in the members' *personal* evaluations of conduct). A few studies in the social psychology of conformity reflect recognition of the perceptual conceptualization of norms (for example, Schwartz and Fleishman 1978); hence, only two things need be done to realize more integration of the two fields: first, that social psychologists undertake studies of conformity in which perceived evaluations of conduct are expressly an experimental variable or condition; and second, that sociologists actively shift from the traditional concern with consensus in autonomic evaluations of conduct to consensus in perceived evaluations of conduct.

The Contending Conception of Deviance

Despite glaring problems with a normative conception of deviance, a real contender did not emerge until the 1960s.[5] That contender is suggested by the following statements.

> *Becker* (1963:9): The deviant is one to whom that label has successfully been applied; deviant behavior is behavior that people so label.
>
> *Erikson* (1962:308): Deviance is not a property *inherent in* certain forms of behavior; it is a property *conferred upon* these forms by the audiences which directly or indirectly witness them.
>
> *Kitsuse* (1962:253): Forms of behavior *per se* do not differentiate deviants from non-deviants; it is the responses of the conventional and conforming members of the society who identify and interpret behavior as deviant which sociologically transform persons into deviants.

Since the statements are not synthetic (for example, empirical propositions), they must be analytic or conceptual. The suggested conception of deviance is not normative, as no reference is made to "behavior contrary to a norm"; and surely the authors did not write merely to endorse a convention obscurely. True, the statements are not clear-cut definitions, but conceptions suggest definitions; and the statements suggest this: a particular act is deviant if, and only if, it is reacted to distinctively or "so labeled" by members of the social unit in question.

Several defenders of the labeling perspective allege that critics have misinterpreted Becker et al. as advocating a reactive conception of deviance, and some of the statements made by Becker et al. do make their intention disputable.[6] For example, Becker (1963) speaks of secret deviance, which suggests "unreacted to." Ambiguity is also introduced by Becker, Erikson, and/or Kitsuse's reference in stating their arguments to

(1) *creation* of deviance, (2) *audience,* and (3) *behavior.* The creation argument suggests that deviance has nothing to do with behavior; but, alternatively, it may only make the banal point "no norms, no deviance" (Merton 1971:827). Audience may designate either (1) potential reactors to a *particular* act or (2) all members of a social unit who voice normative opinions about *types* of acts. Finally, behavior may denote either a particular act or a *type* of act, and the distinction is crucial. When members of a social unit make evaluative statements (or, put otherwise, express normative opinions) they are reacting to behavior; but norms pertain to *types* of acts, and a particular act is deviant if, and only if, it is an instance of a type contrary to a norm. Yet Becker et al. scarcely speak of types of acts, let alone norms. Accordingly, their arguments seemingly reduce to this: whether a particular act is deviant depends not on its typification (for example, rape, suicide) and reference to a related norm but instead on *actual* reactions to the act. Of course, even a reactive conception suggests that deviant acts are instances of a class, but it is a class defined only by reference to reactions.

OBJECTIONS TO A REACTIVE CONCEPTION OF DEVIANCE

Sociologists have been slow to recognize the reactive conception for what it is—a radical departure from convention. While the reactive conception may become conventional, it, too, is haunted by problems.

What kind of reactions identify acts as deviant? Critics allege that reactivists (advocates of the reactive conception of deviance) have yet to provide an empirically applicable stipulation of the relevant kinds of reactions. That stipulation is not realized by speaking of "distinctive reactions" or "labeled as deviant," and the reactivists are seemingly reluctant to emphasize punitive reactions. Given the reactivists' preoccupation with officials or formal agents of social control, both the content of the reaction and the social identity of reactors may be relevant; if so, whose reactions are relevant? Should the reactivists reply, "formal agents of social control," it would generate issues. For example, if sociologists adopt the reactive conception, how could they identify surveys of self-reported acts as studies of deviance?

Defenders of the labeling perspective (for example, Kitsuse 1975:276) admit that the kinds of reactions that identify acts as deviant remain vaguely specified, but they appear indifferent to the problem. Instead, one defender after another (for example, Schur 1971:14) has made something like this argument: since what is deviant for some members of a social unit may not be for others, a precise definition of deviance would be unrealistic. The argument is consistent with a principle of phenomenology, symbolic interactionism, and ethnomethodology—that the "meaning" of an act is inherently problematical. That principle is introduced not to refute it but instead to suggest that the reactivists' real quarrel is with positivism. If so, the issue may never be resolved; nonetheless, sociologists would profit by recognizing that some things are beyond constructive debate.

The epistemology of reactivists gives rise to a paradox. Kitsuse

(1975:276) argues that regardless of their knowledge of a particular social unit, sociologists are justified in designating a particular act in that unit as deviant only if they consider reactions to that act by the unit's members. The paradox lies in this question: if the meaning of an act is so problematical that a sociologist cannot justifiably classify it as deviant by reference to norms, why is the meaning of a reaction to the act not equally problematical? Surely it would tax credulity to reply that interpretations of reactions can ignore normative considerations.

Is the notion of norms actually avoided? The most compelling argument that can be made for the reactive conception is that it circumvents horrendous problems with the notion of a norm. It does so, however, only if it entails no reference to norms, which is doubtful. Consider Scott's statement (1972:11–12): "there are few natives who actually use the term 'social deviant' as such; most of them, when they confer this property on others, use labels such as 'nut,' 'queer,' 'weirdo,' 'rascal,' 'pervert,' or 'loony.' I employ the generic term 'deviance' to refer to that property that is conferred upon persons whenever labels such as these are used." A complete list of deviant labels is inconceivable; and not even a complete list would answer this question: why do the labels denote deviance? The labels denote *types* of individuals or behavior that numerous members of some English-speaking social units ostensibly disapprove, and that answer reintroduces the normative conception of deviance.

Reactivists cannot argue convincingly that labels alone are decisive. Thus, should a police officer refer to a woman as "a hooker," a label has been applied; but how would we recognize it is a *deviant* label? The problem is compounded because the same label may be indicative of disapproval in one social context but not in others (for example, in certain United States social circles calling someone a "head" is not pejorative). Hence, attempts to punish or reward may be more indicative of deviance than purely verbal labels; but that possibility makes identification of the relevant kind of reaction all the more difficult and debatable, and it is becoming more so. Cullen and Cullen (1978:12) assert that "labeling and not treatment . . . is the kind of reaction that identifies deviant acts and actors," and they further suggest that the harshness of a reaction is irrelevant. Yet how could saying "bad boy" be decisive, but inflicting corporal punishment irrelevant? In any event, far from cleansing deviant labels of normative connotations, Cullen and Cullen (1978:30) actually use the term "norm": "Deviant labels are definitions that announce (correctly or incorrectly) that a behavior or person has violated the norm of a given group." Even if sociologists are to swallow what everyone considers a false "announcement," is the norm's existence irrelevant? Regardless of the answer, it is not clear what constitutes an announcement or who must make it.

Are particular types of acts deviant? The nominalistic character of the reactive conception raises questions about even identifying particular acts as instances of types. Consider Douglas's statement (1967:196): "since there exist great disagreements between interested parties in the categorizations of real-world cases, 'suicides' can generally be said to exist and not exist at the same time. . . ." The implication seems to be that in typifying acts, officials and citizens are not likely to agree in their typifications because the meaning of an act is problematical. In any case, since the participants would use symbols to signify types of acts, how can sociologists know what they mean? So it is that the reactive conception casts doubts on the very idea of identifying acts as instances of types (for example, rape, suicide).

Social psychologists may regard the conceptual issue as moronic. After all, the term deviant is not needed to formulate theories about rape, theft, suicide, and so forth. Yet a synthesis of such special theories would require a delimitation of the class of such behaviors, and no problem would be solved by employing some term other than deviance to denote that class. Nor can reactivists be reconciled to a theory that treats types of acts as objectively real. For that matter, sociologists do not recognize that the reactive conception stems from a general epistemology; thus, just as deviance is any act so labeled, a planet is any object so labeled.

But suppose the reactivists grant that types of acts are real. Can some types in a particular social unit be justifiably designated as deviant by reference to the frequency of some kind of reaction? Assume that the relevant kind is punitive; even so, what proportion of instances of some types of act must be reacted to punitively before that *type* is deviant? As in the case of a reactive definition of a norm, any stipulation of a particular proportion would be arbitrary or unrealistic. So it is not surprising that reactivists refrain from a *reactive definition* of a norm, but without something akin to such a definition they cannot designate *types of acts* as deviant.

What are the prospects for a reactive theory of deviance? Critics of the reactive conception allege that it puts the cart before the horse, meaning that reactions to acts are distinctive (for example, punitive) because the acts are deviant and not vice versa. Imagine a judge saying to a felony defendant at the conclusion of a bench trial: "You have committed a crime because I find you guilty." The point is that the reactive conception does not recognize, let alone explain, obvious relations between acts and reactions. True, that criticism demands what no definition offers—answers to empirical questions; however, definitions can preclude empirical questions, and that consideration generates more doubts about the reactive conception.

Whereas a normative definition admits the possibility of any kind of reaction (including none at all) to a deviant act, a reactive definition does not. Thus, *if by definition* all deviant acts are reacted to punitively, it is illogical to ask: Why do some deviant acts go unpunished? So a reactive definition is not conducive to a theory about variation in the character of reactions to deviance. True, a reactive definition would not preclude this question: Why are some reactions to deviance *more* punitive than others? But reactivists do not emphasize that question, nor show concern with what was once the major question in the sociology of deviance: Why does the rate of deviance vary? A reactive definition of deviance would not preclude an answer; but reactivists apparently harbor doubts about that question, and they have not formulated an alternative. But note the consistency. If deviance is "problematical," then both its definition and questions about it are best left vague.

IN DEFENSE OF THE REACTIVE CONCEPTION

Even granting previous objections, the reactive conception of deviance has several merits. Despite the voluminous literature on the labeling perspective, those merits have not been clearly articulated.

What sociologists actually do. The reactive conception is consistent with the reliance of sociologists on official records in studies of crime, juvenile delinquency, suicide, and mental illness. That reliance is hardly surprising. Sociologists study numerous types of deviance (for example, suicide, robbery) without direct observations of particular instances, and limited research resources alone preclude extensive surveys of self-reported deviance or victimization surveys.

Even normativists use reactive data, but they assume that official rates of deviance are closely correlated with "true" rates. That assumption is debatable because the true rate is unknowable, especially given doubts about self-report and victimization surveys. Yet because of the emphasis in the labeling perspective on the problematical meaning of acts, the contingent character of legal reactions to acts, and the self-serving nature of social control agencies, sociologists are now thoroughly skeptical about the reliability of official rates of deviance. However, they are largely oblivious to the point that a reactive definition of deviance can make official data the only relevant data (for example, the true crime rate *is* what the police report).

Who is a deviant? Extending a normative conception of deviance to a definition of *a deviant* is very difficult. If it is anyone who has acted contrary to a norm of their social unit, then "adult nondeviant" is virtually a null class. Nor is the problem avoided by speaking only of particular *types* of deviants. If theft is deviant behavior, when does a person become a thief and cease being one? Then contemplate the problems in defining a conventionally recognized category of deviants, the mentally ill. Even if psychiatric nosology and diagnostic criteria were empirically applicable, they are not necessarily congruent with relevant social norms, "nonpsychiatric" stereotypes of the mentally ill in particular; and no specific act or condition is by definition (psychiatric or otherwise) common to all individuals who have been "labeled" as mentally ill. Imagine, for example, a definition of a mentally ill individual as "anyone who weeps unpredictably." Clarification of the definition would require an answer to at least this question: How often must an individual weep unpredictably to be classified as mentally ill? Any answer would be as ludicrous as the definition itself.

By contrast, the reactive conception of deviance readily extends to a definition of a mentally ill individual: anyone so labeled. There is a pressing need to clarify "so labeled," including the social identity of relevant labelers; and clarification would be difficult, especially with a view to cross-cultural application. Nonetheless, reactivists face fewer formidable logical problems in defining mentally ill individuals (or any other type of *deviant*) than do normativists.

Avoiding problems with the notion of norms. To silence their critics, reactivists should speak endlessly about problems with the notion of a norm. Only recently have they moved in that direction (see, for example, Kitsuse 1975), and even now they do not stress the possibilities offered by the reactive conception for avoiding problems.

Rather than be crippled by the consensus problem in defining a norm, reactivists could make this argument: if potential reactors do not react to an act distinctively, then they do not truly disapprove of that act. Similarly, far from denying normative contingencies, the argument could be that potential reactors take contingencies into account; and reactions can be interpreted as reflecting differential power.

The advantages of a reactive conception of deviance will remain unexploited until reactivists identify the relevant kinds of reaction and answer this question: What are the criteria for designating *types* of acts and *types* of individuals as deviant? All in all, however, the problems are no more crippling than those that should worry normativists.

Preoccupation with the Issue

The foregoing conceptual issue is conspicuous in the current literature, where sociologists debate it monotonously and busily concoct new definitions of deviance, even attempting to distinguish it from rule breaking. Some recent conceptualizations incorporate a counterfactual conditional notion, something like this: an act is deviant if it has been reacted to punitively or *would have been* reacted to punitively had its commission been known to members of the social unit (for example, Birenbaum and Sagarin 1976:37). Such notions represent a modification of the reactive conception so as to recognize (inter alia) secret deviance. Still other definitions reflect attempts to find middle ground, as follows: an act is deviant if contrary to a norm of a social unit *and* reacted to punitively (see, for example, Schur 1971:24).

Nothing akin to such illustrative definitions will resolve the issue, and more problems are created than avoided. Counterfactual notions invite mere conjecture, especially when the social identity of potential reactors is ignored; and whereas both illustrative definitions identify the relevant kind of reaction as punitive, the reactivists have yet to stipulate the relevant kind. Finally, a compound definition (last illustration) will satisfy few sociologists, because it avoids no objection to either the normative or the reactive conception of deviance.

Virtually all conceptual controversies in the sociology of deviance now reflect the issue in question. As a case in point, sociologists increasingly define deviants so as to include individuals distinguished by physical characteristics (for example, skin color, body dimensions, deformities) and/or origin (for example, ancestral nationality). The rationale is that such individuals are "disvalued" (Birenbaum and Sagarin 1976:37); but contrary to the traditional normative conception, "being deviant" has nothing to do (necessarily) with behavior. Even reactivists may reject the rationale, for it is removed from actual reactions to particular individuals. Nonetheless, in suggesting that acts have nothing to do (necessarily) with deviance, reactivists lend support to the idea that entire categories of individuals may be deviant regardless of their behavior.

Criminologists have been drawn into the debate because the reactive conception applies to crime and juvenile delinquency no less than to extralegal deviance. Stating an illustrative reactive definition of legal deviance briefly: an individual is criminal or delinquent if, and only if, so labeled by a legal official. Should one doubt that such a definition has a following, contemplate Turk's dictum (1969:25): ". . . criminality is not a . . . behavioral phenomenon. . . . Criminality is determined by what the authorities *do,* rather than what they *claim* (or even believe) they are doing in regard to coercing individuals." Other criminologists are busily trying to find middle ground in the debate.[7] Consider Sanders's definition (1976:8): "Juvenile delinquency is the characterization of an act as a violation of delinquency laws." Why not say that juvenile delinquency is an act contrary to a law? Ostensibly because such terminology is normative, whereas "characterization" attributes a reactive quality to delinquency. Yet a question is left unanswered: what constitutes such a characterization and who must do it?

IMPLICATIONS FOR SOCIAL PSYCHOLOGY

Whereas sociologists speak of conformity as though it were simply the obverse of deviance, that logical relation is inconsistent with the *predominant* conception of conformity in social psychology. Consider Aronson's statement (1976:16): "Conformity can be defined as a change in a person's behavior or opinions as a result of real or imagined pressure from a person or group of people." Whatever its merits, that definition is *anormative.* Thus, in obeying a gunman, a store clerk conforms; but few sociologists would regard the clerk's disobedience as deviant. If it be objected that the illustration is irrelevant because a clerk's disobedience in such a situation would not violate a norm, observe that there is no reference, not even an implied reference, to norms in Aronson's statement. Surely it will not do to equate "pressure" with average or typical behavior in a group (even Aronson recognizes that pressure may be applied by one person); and it would do violence to the English language to argue that coercion, authority, punishments, and rewards cannot be "pressure" (see, especially, French et al. 1960; Milgram 1974; Sigelman and Sigelman 1976; Zipf 1960).

Criticism of Aronson is not intended; indeed, insofar as his statement suggests a definition of deviance, that definition would avoid some of the issues that now divide normativists and reactivists. The suggested definition could be worded something like this: deviance is behavior by a person that is contrary to the real or imagined pressure from another person or group of people. True, one may think of norms (as traditionally conceived by sociologists) as "exerting pressure" on behavior; but accepting the suggested definition, no reference need be made to norms (not even in a statistical sense) to identify behavior in *particular situations* as deviant. Yet sociologists are likely to regard the suggested definition as alien to the study of deviance, precisely because it is anormative and seemingly precludes identifying types of acts as deviant. Nonetheless, Aronson's definition is by no means idiosyncratic (see Kiesler 1969:235), and in social psychology, studies of conformity are far more in keeping with that definition than with the obverse of the normative conception of deviance or with the reactive conception (reactivists depict reactions as criteria of deviance, not as "pressures"). Aronson's definition does not stipulate that the person's behavior must change toward the modal behavior of a group; but that requirement would introduce a normative element only if one accepts a statistical conception of a norm, and a reference to "the group standard" in defining conformity (Sakurai 1975:345) is ambiguous.

The Labeling Perspective

If interest in the labeling perspective is now waning, the decline may largely reflect only the usual diminution of novelty. In any case, the issues remain, and the perspective's ultimate impact depends on their resolution.

THREE DISTINCT ARGUMENTS

Most debates over the labeling perspective center on this question: is it really a theory? Those debates are sterile because the question erroneously suggests that the "labeling perspective" is a unitary argument (as any theory must be). To the contrary, sociologists use the term in such a way that it denotes any or all of three distinct and logically independent arguments.

The reactive conception of deviance. Reconsider the notion that an act is deviant if, and only if, so labeled. While most sociologists would recognize that the notion somehow bears on the labeling perspective, some may make this reply. But Lemert (1972), a major figure in the labeling perspective, does not advocate a reactive definition of deviance.

The rejoinder commences with previous quotations of Becker et al., also major figures in the labeling perspective. If those quotations do not suggest a reactive conception of deviance, then the English language should be abandoned. True, they are not explicit reactive definitions, perhaps because Becker et al. were unprepared to bite the bullet. In any event, Kitsuse's position is now (1975:276) more explicit: "The new conception of deviance requires that members of the society perceive, define, and treat acts and persons as deviant *before* the sociologist can claim them as subject matter for study." Had Kitsuse, along with Becker and Erikson, made that statement years ago, a major misunderstanding of the labeling perspective might have been avoided. Be that as it may, Kitsuse's statement is not quoted to refute it, because not even a suggested definition is true or false. Nor is the point that the labeling perspective reduces to the reactive conception of deviance; rather, the conception is a *component* of that perspective.

The theory of secondary deviance. Consider the following summary statement of the theory: if a deviant act is reacted to punitively, the deviant will engage in further deviance as a consequence. That statement grossly oversimplifies; nonetheless, it is an *empirical proposition* and not a definition. So the theory of secondary deviance and the reactive conception of deviance are logically distinct; and even though some advocates of the conception (Kitsuse, in particular) and some advocates of the theory (Lemert, in particular) are major figures in the labeling perspective, they are not making the same argument. So why do sociologists speak of the labeling perspective as though it is unitary? Perhaps because the major figures in the perspective champion the deviant as underdog and/or share a "romantic" view of deviance (Gouldner 1968), but their antipositivism is also relevant. However, whereas the antipositivism of reactivists is reflected in their failure to specify the relevant kinds of reactions, that of Lemert and his followers lies in their avoidance of explicit, falsifiable propositions.

The theory of secondary deviance is far from incoherent; to the contrary, the general assertion is fairly clear: primary deviance is converted into secondary deviance by reactions to the primary deviance. Nor is the theory implausible. To illustrate, it does not tax credulity to suppose that the harsh social degradation of women for the "slightest frailty" adds to the ranks of prostitutes, makes that status irrevocable, and contributes to infanticide (see Lemert 1972:65). Even primary deviance is a fairly clear notion, for in numerous ways Lemert describes it as behavior contrary to a norm and *prior to reactions.*

Nonetheless, the theory defies systematic tests, in large part because of two questions left unanswered by Lemert. First, does the theory apply to all types of primary deviance *and* all kinds of reactions? Second, given a relevant type of primary deviance and a relevant kind of reaction, do all instances of primary deviance become secondary deviance? The theory's plausibility would be diminished by an affirmative answer to either question; but a simple "some" answer would make it unfalsifiable. The general point is that propositions cannot be deduced from the theory; and even if propositions could be deduced, they are not likely to be testable without a clarification of the notion of secondary deviance. Numerous commentators on the theory seemingly equate the notion with *more* deviance; but even that interpretation cannot be construed as "more of what was originally primary," and it is a distortion in any case, though one encouraged by Lemert's assertion (1972:ix) that social control leads to deviance.

The notion is scarcely clarified by Lemert's explicit definitions (1972:48, 63). "Secondary deviation is deviant behavior, or social roles based upon it, which becomes means of defense, attack, or adaptation to the overt and covert problems created by the societal reaction to primary deviation." "Secondary deviation refers to a special class of socially defined responses which people make to problems created by the societal reaction to their deviance." One interpretation is that secondary deviance does not necessarily take the form of "more deviance," and there are even doubts as to whether "more deviance" is necessarily secondary deviance. Hence, there are no prospects for consensus as to the kinds of evidence that would corroborate or falsify the theory.

Societal reaction to deviance. Consider this proposition: in any jurisdictional unit for any given year, the proportion of lower-class individuals arrested is greater than the proportion of other individuals arrested. The proposition does not make arrest a criterion of criminality; so it is distinct from the reactive conception of deviance. Nor does the proposition assert anything about criminality (however defined) *subsequent* to arrest; so it is also distinct from the theory of secondary deviance.

While the proposition has no bearing on either the reactive conception of deviance or the theory of secondary deviance, it does bear on *societal reaction theory.* That theory can be explicated briefly only by a summary statement of what appears to be the central assertion: the character of reactions to a real or alleged deviant act by an individual is primarily contingent on (1) the social identity of the individual; (2) the social identity of the reactors; (3) the operating rules of the reactors' organization; and/or (4) the circumstances before, during, and after the act. The assertion is not a reactive definition of deviance, and tests of it would neither support nor refute the theory of secondary deviance. Some sociologists would identify the assertion as bearing on societal reaction theory or the societal reaction perspective; but most sociologists do not distinguish either term from labeling perspective. Consider Gove's comment (1975:3): "In 1938, Tannenbaum published a statement that was to become a landmark of what is now known as either the societal reaction or the labelling perspective." The comment is entirely consistent with conventional terminology.

Advocates of societal reaction theory evidently do not agree among themselves as to the crucial contingency (for example, social class, race, sex) in reactions to deviance; but it may be premature to demand agreement at this point, and the most relevant contingency may not be the same for all deviance (for example, robbery, homosexuality) or for all reactors (for example, police, psychiatrists). Nonetheless, even if all advocates of the theory should identify one crucial contingency (for example, the "power" or "status resources" of objects of reactions), that agreement would not resolve an issue that stems from the reactive conception of deviance.

Assume overwhelming evidence in support of the foregoing illustrative proposition, that is, in all jurisdictional units the arrest rate is reported as being greater for the lower class. Such reports would only give rise to this question: Why such a difference? One interpretation of the reports would be that the true incidence of crime is greater in the lower class, and that interpretation is a tacit acceptance of the normative conception of criminality, according to which an act is a crime if it is a violation of a criminal law. The interpretation would be rejected not only by advocates of societal reaction theory (the differential arrest rate could be attributed to a postulated predisposition of the police to arrest lower-class individuals), but also by advocates of the reactive conception of crime (who reject the notion of a true incidence of crime, that is, apart from the reactions of legal officials).

So while the illustrative proposition about arrest may appear removed from the debate over contending conceptions of deviance (in this case of crime), when it comes to interpreting evidence that supports the proposition, the issue is just below the surface. That is the case for all similar propositions about deviance, crime or otherwise. Consider the long line of research on differential rates of mental hospitalization by occupation (for example, Rushing and Ortega 1979); and then contemplate another illustrative proposition: in any community for any given year, the rate of involuntary admissions to mental hospitals is greater for the lower class. Given positive tests of that proposition, some sociologists would interpret the findings as supporting the argument that deviance is more a function of social identity than of behavior. However, a normativist or a psychiatrist who subscribes to the disease model of mental illness would advance the counterargument that mental disorders are more severe in the lower class and that severe mental disorders are the most likely to result in an involuntary institutionalization. The general point is that interpretations of tests of societal reaction propositions are bound to be controversial.

CLARIFICATION OF ISSUES

In debating the merits of the labeling perspective sociologists talk past one another because they interpret the perspective in quite different ways. Thus, in his rejoinder to critiques of the labeling perspective, Kitsuse (1975) defended the reactive conception of deviance; but the critiques themselves (Gove 1975) focused on either the theory of secondary deviance or societal reaction theory, without due recognition of the distinction.

Since there is no defensible rationale for limiting the labeling perspective to any one of its three components, the only alternative to more sterile debates is to abandon the term for all but the most casual and general references. Abandoning the term in formulating theories, reporting research, and debating would not resolve the issues, but it would clarify them.

IMPLICATIONS FOR SOCIAL PSYCHOLOGY

The separation of the social psychology of conformity and the sociology of deviance stems primarily from two traditional predominant concerns of the latter, etiological questions about "serious" types of deviance (crime causation in particular) and variation in rates of crime. Neither concern can be investigated through an experimental methodology, the most effective resource of social psychology. However, for reasons indicated subsequently, greater integration of the two fields may be essential for constructive research on the components of the labeling perspective.

The theory of secondary deviance. Contemplate the following proposition: Among individuals convicted of burglary the recidivism rate is greater for those imprisoned than for those placed on probation. Since the theory of secondary deviance is exceedingly vague, the proposition cannot be deduced from the theory by any conventional logic. Yet, the theory seems to suggest the proposition if (1) the theory is construed as implying that severe reactions to primary deviance generate more secondary deviance than do milder reactions; (2) it is assumed that imprisonment is more severe than probation; and (3) recidivism is predominantly secondary deviance. Even so, findings that support the proposition would not corroborate the theory, because legal reactions to crimes tend to be selective, as when offenders who have the worst record (for example, greatest number of previous convictions) are punished more severely. Accordingly, since offenders with the worst record are the most likely to recidivate *regardless* of legal punishments for the previous offense, a direct association between the severity of legal punishment and subsequent recidivism would be characterized by critics as spurious.

The foregoing evidential problem could be lessened by a randomization of legal punishments, but for understandable reasons jurists take a dim view of such a research design in criminal justice studies. Yet a randomization of reactions to deviance, such that some are perceived as more severe than others, could be realized in experimental designs that are familiar to social psychologists; and such experimentation would circumvent still another problem. Even if recidivism is predominantly secondary deviance, there are grave doubts as to the adequacy of official statistics on recidivism (for example, figures on rearrest or reconviction); but social psychologists can devise experimental designs that permit direct counts of deviant acts *after* a reaction to primary deviance. Finally, with a view to improving on the theory of secondary deviance, several central notions in social psychology could be strategic, notably the "self-concept" (see, especially, Wells 1978), the "locus of control" (for example, Cox and Luhrs 1978), and "self-control" (for example, Harvey and Smith 1977:63–82).

Societal reaction theory. Reconsider the proposition introduced in connection with the theory: in any jurisdictional unit for any given year, the proportion of lower-class individuals arrested is greater than the proportion of other individuals arrested. As indicated previously, findings that support the proposition would corroborate the theory only if normativists are willing to assume that there are no substantial class differentials as to the true incidence of criminality. That assumption is unacceptable to numerous criminologists, and similar arguments would surface if the proposition pertained to legal reactions other than arrest and/or to possible contingencies other than social class (for example, race, sex).

Given the problems with surveys of self-reported criminality and victimization surveys, the evidential issue in question cannot be resolved by any methodology familiar to criminologists. However, social psychologists could design experiments in which the imputed or actual social characteristics of confederates and the deviant acts (both number and kind) committed by those confederates in the presence of naive subjects are varied systematically. Naive subjects would be the potential reactors, and the design could extend to a delegation of special "reactive authority" to some of those subjects, with the others treated as "citizen equivalents" (that is, unofficial reactors).

The advantages of such experimentation would not be limited to control over the true incidence of deviant acts. In *observational* research that bears on societal reaction theory, it is commonly impossible to disentangle the various characteristics of alleged deviants so as to identify those characteristics that prompt differential reactions. For example, given evidence that a disproportionate number of blacks are involuntarily admitted to mental hospitals, it would not follow that race is a crucial contingency in reactions. The difference could stem from the association between race and social class, or perhaps something as specific as variation in unemployment rates or marital status by race; and that would be the case even if there were no questions about variation by race in the true prevalence of symptoms of mental illness (indeed, even if there were no questions as to criteria of mental illness). By contrast, in an experimental study the actual or imputed characteristics of confederate deviants could be varied so as to permit an estimate of the "contingency effect" of each characteristic (see, for example, Dedrick 1978). Finally, an experimental design could extend to possibly relevant contingencies other than the characteristics of deviants, such as the circumstances prior to, during, or after a deviant act (see, for example, Dedrick 1978).

Of the three components of the labeling perspective, societal reaction theory stands to gain more from social psychology in the way of concepts and principles; and that gain could well be more important than what the experimental methodology of social psychology has to offer. Specifically, when it comes to speculation as to why reactions to deviance are contingent on the identity of the alleged deviant, the notions of attribution and stereotyping appear immediately relevant; and those notions are central in social psychology. Unfortunately, however, societal reaction theory has not been informed by social psychology, the immediate reason being that sociologists equate it with "labeling theory," which is merely another designation of the labeling perspective. Once it is recognized that societal reaction theory is distinct from other components of the perspective, that recognition may stimulate attempts to state it as a distinct theory, with liberal borrowing from social psychology.

The reactive conception of deviance. Since definitions are analytic statements, it may appear that experimental findings are irrelevant in assessing a reactive definition of deviance. That is not the case, but the relevance of experimental studies cannot be appreciated without examining the genesis of the reactive conception. As pointed out previously, most sociological studies of deviance have made use of official statistics, and those statistics are consistent with the reactive conception. Moreover, even if sociologists had unlimited research resources, they could rarely base their studies of criminality and various extralegal types of deviance on direct observations. Even if they could, in categorizing a directly observed act as a crime sociologists are likely to entertain some assumption as to how members of the population in question and/or legal officials would perceive the act; and that problem is not entirely avoided in using data gathered in surveys of self-reported crimes or victimization surveys.

Granted that a rationale for the reactive conception can be formulated, in suggesting that deviant acts are "created" by reactions, advocates of that conception come close to gross solipsism; and their epistemology runs contrary to their avowed concern with the meaning of events for participants in social life. Consider another version of an earlier illustration, in this instance a police officer arresting an individual after directly observing the individual pointing a gun at a store clerk and demanding money. Given that situation, imagine the police officer saying (or even thinking): "You have committed a crime because I arrested you." Stating the matter more generally, both the citizenry and legal officials think of the quality of acts as determining reactions, and not the reverse.

While the reactivists' argument readily extends to solipsism, there is no defensible basis for rejecting their cardinal principle: whether an act is labeled deviant (or criminal) is problematical. But how problematical is it? That question may well defy an answer; in any case, there is a more important question: What conditions ostensibly determine whether an act will be labeled deviant? For reasons suggested earlier, sociologists can do little in the way of direct observations toward answering that question; and official accounts (for example, police records) rarely extend to acts that are not labeled as deviant, nor do they describe all of the possibly relevant circumstances of acts that have been so labeled. Hence, perhaps only experimental studies of deviance can throw real light on the question, for only that methodology permits investigators to systematically vary possibly relevant conditions. Needless to say, in designing experimental studies to that end all manner of problems would surface, the most immediate one being a question that reactivists have yet to answer: What kind of reaction to acts identify those acts as deviant? It may well be that the conditions of "deviant labeling" depend entirely on the criteria of relevant reactions, but that possibility can best be demonstrated in experimental studies (see Dedrick 1978).

Barriers to relevant experimental studies of deviance. The immediate problem is not the feasibility of experimental studies on the labeling perspective; instead, it is that social psychologists, like many sociologists, appear unaware that the labeling perspective comprises three independent components and, hence, that no experimental finding can bear on all three. To illustrate, in a recent report of an experimental study that purportedly bears on the labeling perspective, Dedrick (1978) introduces the labeling perspective as though it reduces to the reactive conception of deviance, but his experimental findings seemingly bear on societal reaction theory. Similarly, Bord (1976) uses the term "societal reaction theory"; but his experimental findings appear to bear more on the theory of secondary deviance. Even more serious, there are instances where social psychologists have conducted research on conformity or deviance without recognition of the possible implications for any component of the labeling perspective (for example, McKirnan 1980).

Social psychologists should do more than recognize the labeling perspective and its three independent components; they should recognize also that most sociologists conceive of norms as collective evaluations of conduct rather than as the modal behavior of a group. The argument is not that in all studies of the social psychology of conformity the norms are only modal behavior. In some instances it appears that the norms are both evaluative (for example, "procedural rules" imposed by the experimenters) and modal behavior (for example, Wahrman and Pugh 1974). The situation is further complicated by studies of deviance (especially field studies or surveys) in which social psychologists clearly employ the traditional sociological conception of a norm (for example, McKirnan 1980). So there is every reason to argue that the conceptualizations and usages of the terms, norm, conformity, and deviance, by social psychologists are all too uncritical and inconsistent. That situation stems primarily from the practice of tacitly equating "pressure" with "norm." Granted that there are pressures that operate to prevent norm violations and that pressures are commonly applied when norms are violated, the argument is much more intelligible if pressures and norms are both conceptually and operationally distinct. That is not the case when the modal behavior of a group is interpreted as both a norm and pressure; and the conceptual problem is complicated further by recognition of pressures other than the modal behavior of a group (for example, commands, threats of punishment).

Toward a Resolution

Although the labeling perspective has furthered interest in the sociology of deviance, the drift toward conceptual anarchy is not constructive. Sociologists will appreciate that point only when they recognize that their research is being assessed largely in the context of a conceptual issue.

The issue has increased doubts about the reliability of official data on deviance so much that even some normativists advise against their use. As for reactivists, they hardly can endorse surveys of self-reported crimes or victimization surveys; and they tolerate official data only if the reactive quality is made paramount. For example, Douglas (1967:223–27) dismissed positive tests of a theory of suicide by arguing (1) that the independent variable, status integration, is correlated inversely with urbanization, not a variable in the theory; and (2) that urbanization is correlated directly with the official suicide rate because in a highly urbanized population there is less reluctance to label deaths as suicide. Nothing is gained by pointing out that the 1960 *official* United States suicide rate differed little from the 1910 rate, despite enormous increases in urbanization over 1910–60. Nothing is gained because Douglas interprets the official suicide rate as reflecting the predisposition of reactors to label deaths as suicide; hence, he rejects the assumption that the official suicide rate is largely a function of the true suicide rate, which in turn is a function of some "etiological" variable (for example, status integration). Similarly, critics are predisposed to reject works that reflect the reactive conception of deviance, as when Turk is chastised (Gibbs and Erickson 1975:39) for ignoring the actual behavior of men and women in explaining differential arrest rates by sex. All such partisan assessments are harbingers of the degeneration of the sociology of deviance into a debating club.

PROPOSAL OF A STRATEGY

The initial step in circumventing the issue is to take explanation of variation in the *official* rate of each type of deviance (for example, suicide) as the goal of theory; and the second step is to assume that the official rate is a function of two variables: (1) the true rate of the *type of behavior* in question; and (2) dispositions of officials to report instances of such behavior. Hence, theories should treat both the true rate and dispositions as intervening but purely theoretical variables and identify two corresponding sets of mensurable variables: (1) those postulated as antecedent correlates of the true rate; and (2) those postulated as antecedent correlates of the dispositions (for example, possibly the number of police officers per capita).

The *form* of such a theory is suggested by the following graphic representation, where *T* is the true rate of some type of behavior (for example, suicide); *D* is the disposition of officials to report instances of such behavior; *E* is the set of "etiological" variables that are postulated antecedent correlates of *T; S* is the set of sociocultural variables that are postulated antecedent correlates of *D; R* is the *official* rate of the type of behavior in question; → signifies a postulated direct relation, one not subject to observation or measurement; - -> signifies a time-lag statistical association between change in variables; and > or < signifies a multiplicative *or* additive combination of variables.

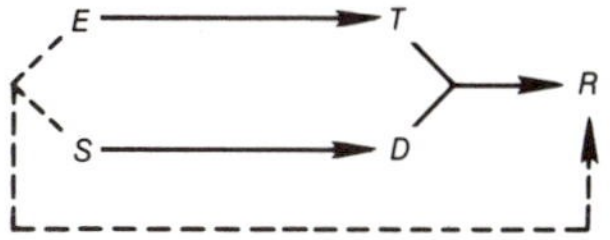

Each theory should pertain to a particular type of behavior (for example, robbery), and the designation of that type must correspond to a label employed by officials in reporting incidence.[8] Such a restriction is hardly a cause for objections, since the pursuit of a *general* theory of deviance has been singularly unproductive. However, if critics reject purely theoretical variables *(T* and *D),* the proposed strategy has no utility.

Neither normativists nor reactivists will adopt the proposed strategy without reservations. Normativists may balk at taking variation in the official rates as the explanandum, viewing that goal as acceptance of the reactive conception of deviance. However, limited resources alone preclude extensive use of unofficial rates, and since official rates are "societal products," they are hardly less real than unofficial rates.

The possible reservations of reactivists are more complex. Should they argue that the strategy equates the true rate of behavior with the true rate of deviance, it would be a misinterpretation. One can speak of the true rate of, say, smoking marijuana without implying that any instance of that *type of behavior* is deviant; and the term "disposition" refers to the inclinations of or opportunities for officials to report instances of behavior rather than the "probability that an instance of a type of behavior will be reported as such by officials." Otherwise, the strategy would suggest that officials report only actual instances of behavior; instead, it admits the possibility that officials report fictional instances. Nonetheless, if reactivists are truly nominalists, they will object to the idea of particular acts being instances of types; but that objection would be relevant only if the strategy called for sociologists to typify particular acts. Instead, the strategy actually treats the true rate of some type of behavior as purely theoretical. Finally, if official data are used in the numerical expression of *E* and *S* (for example, possibly the unemployment rate, number of police per capita), reactivists cannot object that the data reflect a social reality "constructed" only by sociologists.

The most crippling objection would pertain to the very purpose of the strategy, the explanation of variance in official rates of deviance. Given their antipositivistic stance, reactivists may reject "variance explained" as a criterion for assessing theories; if so, the issue dividing normativists and reactivists may never be resolved.

The prescribed strategy would not end the controversy completely, nor should it be so ended, because controversies can be constructive. Even if *E* and *S* jointly explain all variance in *R*, estimating the relative importance of *E* and *S* would be a constructive quest. However, a comparison of the *E*-->*R* and *S*-->*R* statistical associations would not be decisive, because the identification of a variable as *E* or *S* is inherently disputable. To illustrate, suppose that *R* is the official suicide rate and the unemployment rate has been designated as an *E* variable.[9] Even if the measure of statistical association, *M*, between the unemployment rate and the official suicide rate is truly substantial, it would not demonstrate that the unemployment rate is associated with the official suicide rate *(R)* primarily through the true rate *(T)*. Reactivists would argue that officials are more predisposed to label a death as suicide if the deceased was unemployed (Douglas 1967:222); hence, the justification for identifying a variable as *E* or *S* requires evidence beyond M_{er} and M_{sr} (that is, the *E-R* and *S-R* association). That evidence must take the form of unofficial rates *(U)* of the type of behavior in question, with the data gathered in surveys where members of the social unit (excluding officials) are asked questions about their own behavior or that of others. If parties to the debate will assume that the *U* values are closely correlated with *T*, then evidence can be brought to bear on the presumptive identification of variables as *E* and *S*, which is necessary to assess the relative importance of "etiological" and "reactive" phenomena.

Given a *U* value and an *R* value for a social unit, a "dispositional" index *(d)* is the ratio of *R* to *U* (that is, $d = R/U$). That index would be postulated as an epistemic correlate of *D*, meaning that it presumably reflects the inclination of officials to report more (or less) instances of the type of behavior in question than indicated by the unofficial rate. Accordingly, assuming that E is associated with R primarily through T, identifying a variable as E is justified only to the extent that $M_{eu} > M_{ed}$ and $M_{eu} > M_{er}$. Similarly, since any alleged S variable is assumed to be associated with R primarily through D, then its identification is justified only to the extent that $M_{sd} > M_{su}$ and $M_{sd} > M_{sr}$.

If tests of a particular theory stated in the prescribed form indicate that neither identification (E variable or S variable) is justified, then the question of relative importance becomes moot, especially if M_{er}, M_{eu}, M_{sr}, and M_{sd} are negligible. However, if findings justify both identifications, then the relative importance of E and S hinges on the relative magnitudes of M_{er} and M_{sr} and those of M_{ur} and M_{dr}. To the extent that $M_{dr} > M_{ur}$, then the official rates are "reactive phenomena," and to the extent that $M_{ur} > M_{dr}$ the rates are "behavioral phenomena."[10] While esprit de corps may prompt normativists and reactivists to take such comparisons seriously, the more important consideration is the extent to which the multiple association, $M_{r.es}$, exceeds each bivariate association, M_{er} and M_{sr}. If $M_{r.es}$ is substantially greater, then the long-standing controversy will have borne fruit after all; and the protagonists can jointly pursue more constructive work—identifying additional E and S variables with a view to explaining more variance in R.

Major Etiological Theories

The proposed strategy calls for the inclusion of etiological variables in a theory of deviance, and to that end the works of Merton (1957) and Sutherland (Sutherland and Cressey 1974) deserve reconsideration. In contemplating structural determinants of the crime rate, even a Marxist is likely to drift into the orbit of Merton's thinking; and with a view to explaining individual differences as regards criminality, only a genetic determinism would be truly alien to Sutherland's theory.[11] In brief, subsequent carping notwithstanding, the contributions of Merton and Sutherland are enduring, and sociologists with interests in deviance are doomed to rediscover Merton and Sutherland periodically.

ANOMIE AND SOCIAL STRUCTURE

One brief assertion serves to introduce Merton's theory: no American is truly baffled by robbery. Successful perpetrators enjoy a pecuniary benefit, and virtually everyone assumes that motivation. However, Merton's theory is scarcely "psychological," and two additional assertions point to its sociological character. First, possession of material goods is a major *cultural goal* in American society; and, second, robbery would be endemic if there were no stress on and access to institutional means (that is, culturally approved, legitimate) to such possession. Merton would accept both assertions but argue that in the United States means are stressed less than goals. However, he did recognize the *possibility* of a greater stress on means, even though his illustrations of that possibility are not particularly informative, perhaps because of his preoccupation with the United States. In any case, the following postulatory summary of the theory applies to any social unit: The greater the disjunction between institutionalized means and cultural goals, the greater the rate of deviance.

In contemplating the meaning of "disjunction," note that Merton spoke not only of differential stress, but also of access to means; and the two cannot be equated (for example, while unemployment may lessen access to means, it does not reduce stress on means).[12] Access can be subsumed under "disjunction of means and goals"; but Merton did not consistently maintain the distinction between access and stress, and it is a troublesome complexity.

The measurement of disjunction could be guided by this formula: $D = |(Sg)^2 - (Sm)(Am)|$, where D is disjunction, Sg is social stress on some particular goal, Sm is social stress on means to that goal, and Am is the ease of access to those means. The assumption is that the values of each variable range from .00 to 1.00; but far from stipulating how Sg, Sm, and Am are to be measured, Merton did not clearly describe the *logical* connection between D and those three variables (hence, the formula is only suggestive). So systematic tests of the theory are wanting, and numerical expression of Sg, Sm, and Am would be only a first step. Operationalism notwithstanding, measurement procedures do not clarify a theory's logical structure.

If the D value for each cultural goal in a social unit is zero, then the total deviance rate of that unit should approach zero; and if the total D value over *all* cultural goals (that is, ΣD) is the same for two social units, then the *total* deviance rate should be approximately the same for the two units. However, to the extent that $(Sg)^2 > (Sm)(Am)$ for *each* cultural goal in a social unit but $(Sg)^2 < (Sm)(Am)$ for *each* cultural goal in another social unit, the units should differ as to the *predominant* type of deviance but not necessarily as to the total deviance rate. Merton introduced types of deviance in the *second part* of the theory, the last four of his five "modes of adaptation": conformity, innovation, retreatism, ritualism, rebellion. Hence, the theory ostensibly explains variation in the rate of four types of deviance, with each rate being a function of the configurative values of Sg, Sm, and Am. Those rates and not the total deviance rate are central. While the *total* deviance rate is supposedly a function of all D values (that is, overall cultural goals), limited resources alone would preclude computing the total rate.

For reasons just suggested, a test of Merton's theory must be limited to a particular type of deviance. To illustrate, Merton suggested that the rate of innovation (an adaptation mode in which a particular goal is accepted but the means rejected) varies directly with the average overall cultural goals of the disjunction ratio, $Dr = (Sg)^2/(Am)(Sm)$. Unfortunately, however, Merton did not fully clarify the logical connection between the two parts of his theory. The modes of adaptation are not described in structural terms; rather, *individuals* are depicted as accepting or rejecting means and goals, and the implied argument is that they accept only stressed goals and stressed means to which they have access.

Yet, whereas Merton recognized only five modes of adaptation, dichotomized combinations of the three independent variables (for example, low *Sg*, high *Sm*, and low *Am*) yield eight modes; and if the *Sm* – *Am* distinction is ignored, then the dichotomized combinations yield four modes, including conformity.

Even if the connection between the theory's two parts were clear, the modes of adaptation would pose problems. It is doubtful whether agreement can be realized in collating conventionally recognized types of deviance (for example, drug addiction, homosexuality) with Merton's modes, and the difficulty is not just the distinction between instances and classes (for example, only some instances of homicide are murder-for-money). Above all, the distinction between means and goals is troublesome. Thus, if drug addiction is retreatism (as Merton indicates) because it supposedly represents a rejection of both goals and means, what of the argument that happiness or contentment is a goal, and one *perceived* as realizable through drugs? Then what of homosexual behavior: is it a rejection of means, of goals, or both? Now consider what appears to be an indisputable classification—that robbery is innovative deviance. Even so, the robbery rate could not be used to test the proposition that innovative deviance varies *directly* with the disjunction ratio *(Dr)*. There are numerous alternatives to robbery as innovative deviance (for example, burglary, embezzlement), and Merton's theory does not identify the structural determinants of those alternatives. Finally, in focusing tests of the theory on a particular type of deviance (for example, rape, assault, burglary), the relevant cultural goals for that type of deviance would not be readily identifiable, and only in the case of innovation and ritualism is there a clear-cut basis for asserting a relation between the disjunction ratio *(Dr)* and the rate for a type of deviance.

Space limitations preclude even a brief survey of the research inspired by Merton's theory (see Clinard 1964), but that research is a far cry from systematic tests. To illustrate, in a putative study of anomie, Lander reported an inverse relation among subareas of Baltimore between official rates of juvenile delinquency and (inter alia) the percentage of owner-occupied homes (see Clinard 1964:33). That relation may or may not appear consistent with Merton's theory; in any case, it cannot be *deduced* from the theory.

A commentary on Merton's theory should recognize attempts to extend or correct the theory, notably by Cloward and Ohlin, Cohen, and Dubin (see Clinard 1964). No detailed assessment of these works is undertaken here, not only because of space limitations, but also because those works did not solve the logical and measurement problems with Merton's theory.

The demise of the theory. The foregoing dates are telling. Work on Merton's theory effectively ended in the 1960s, but not because of logical defects or negative test findings. Sociologists scarcely demand rigor in theory construction, let alone testable theories. Instead, they accept only theories that are compatible with their preconceptions or "domain assumptions," and with the emergence of the labeling perspective numerous sociologists came to the belief that official crime or delinquency rates are grossly unreliable.

That belief is fatal for theory, because it undermines official data showing a higher arrest or court-appearance rate for the lower class. Merton argued that at least in some social units (the United States in particular) lower-class individuals aspire to cultural goals (money, automobiles, and so forth) that are stressed for all individuals, but lower-class individuals have far less access than others to legitimate means for realizing those goals. Hence, extending the argument, lower-class individuals more frequently resort to illegitimate means for realizing cultural goals, with the result being higher arrest or court-appearance rates for that class. Merton's claim that the class differential supports the theory has been challenged by the argument that lower-class individuals pursue middle-class or upper-class goals less than Merton presumed (see Clinard 1964, especially reference to Hyman). The dispute and its import cannot be assessed properly without using *Sg, Sm,* and *Am* measures in comparisons among social classes, but such research would not satisfy advocates of societal reaction theory. They view arrest rates as reflecting not the "true" incidence of criminality or delinquency but, instead, a predisposition of the police to arrest members of the lower class and race-ethnic minorities for reasons unrelated to the behavior of those members prior to police intervention. The assumption is not incredible, for there is now some evidence (for example, Tittle and Villemez 1977) that the class differential is negligible when the crime-delinquency rates are based on unofficial data (for example, self-reported delicts), though for complex reasons that evidence is disputable (see Hindelang et al. 1979).

DIFFERENTIAL ASSOCIATION

Unlike either part of Merton's theory, the first part of Sutherland's theory focuses primarily on differences among individuals as regards criminality or delinquency. That part appears systematic because Sutherland reduced it to nine premises, but the premises are not logically interrelated such that consequences can be deduced from them, and some of the premises are redundant. Little is lost, therefore, by reducing the nine premises to one: the probability that an individual will commit a given type of criminal or delinquent act is a direct function of the frequency, duration, priority, and intensity of his or her exposure to definitions favorable to that type of act over exposure to unfavorable definitions.

Reduction of the theory to one premise makes it no more testable than Sutherland's full version, but the reduction forces recognition that no prediction about the criminality follows from the theory without observations on "exposures to definitions." In undertaking such observations one would be plunged into a swamp of problems. The immediate problem is realizing empirically applicable criteria of (1) exposure, (2) favorable definition, and (3) unfavorable definition. Whatever those criteria may be, the distinction between favorable and unfavorable definitions must center on the perception of the individuals in question. That problem is complicated by the requirement that definitions (favorable or unfavorable) be assigned values as to frequency, duration, priority, and intensity. Finally, even if all such problems were solved, it is inconceivable that observations could be made on individuals over several years (from birth onward) in such a way that an *F* value (magnitude of favorable definitions) and a *U* value (magnitude of unfavorable definitions) can be assigned to each individual in connection with even one type of delict.

Despite the foregoing commentary, Sutherland's theory is not implausible. To the contrary, unless one entertains the genetic determinism of criminality, the theory borders on a sociological truism. Yet it is another instance where a middle-range sociological theory is no more testable than a grand theory, and that remains the case despite several restatements of Sutherland's theory by friendly critics.

There is no mystery as to why Sutherland's theory once had a large following. It was formulated *after* criminologists abandoned genetic determinism and hedonic rationality but *before* Durkheim's influence made reductionism objectionable in American sociology. Nonetheless, in defending Sutherland's theory, sociologists have employed a disputable terminology. Cressey (Sutherland and Cressey 1974) argues that Sutherland's theory "orders" or "makes sense out of" known facts about crime (for example, higher official rates for urban populations). Since a theory explains facts only when they can be deduced from the theory by explicit logical rules, it is well that Cressey used those terms, because no fact about crime can be deduced from Sutherland's nine premises. To illustrate, suppose one investigator after another reports that the arrest rate for sons of felons is several times the rate for sons of nonfelons. Followers of Sutherland might construe that "fact" as supporting the theory, but how could anyone *deduce* it from his premises? Then what of the possibility of deducing the same difference from a theory that postulates genetic predispositions to criminality? Now suppose there is no difference in the two rates. Would that be negative evidence for the theory? Not at all, for Sutherland's disciples could point out that fathers are only one source of favorable or unfavorable definitions of criminality, and, who knows, perhaps legal punishments of fathers constitute unfavorable definitions for their sons.

Though overly harsh, the foregoing critique is a far cry from the usual unrealistic criticisms of sociological theories, notably the demand that the theory be verified (no theory can), or that causation be demonstrated (it never is), or that an explanation be demonstrably unique (a logical impossibility). The critique is a far cry also from radical operationalization (for example, all variables in a theory must be mensurable). Tests of a theory require only that the variables in the conclusions (theorems) be mensurable, but, again, no conclusions, let alone testable conclusions, can be deduced from Sutherland's premises.

The other part. Sutherland sought an explanation of both individual criminality and variation in the crime rate, but the two parts of his theory are somewhat inconsistent in that he did not assert that the rate is a direct function of the *aggregate* excess of definitions favorable to crime. Instead, he identified the independent variable in the second part of the theory as "differential group organization." The meaning of that term is exceedingly vague, and nothing is gained by the suggestion (Sutherland and Cressey 1974:95–107) that it is somehow different from social disorganization or culture conflict. Sutherland's major interpreter, Cressey (Sutherland and Cressey 1974) furthered clarification by alluding to the independent variable as "normative conflict," but he suggested no measurement procedure.

Neither part of Sutherland's theory is testable, and the second part is not even novel. Specifically, even at the time of Sutherland's formulation, his argument did not go beyond the hoary assertion of a relation between "culture conflict" and crime. Worse still, his argument is a study in uninformative if not circular statements (for example, a high crime rate is a product of a "criminalistic tradition").

Like Merton's theory, work on Sutherland's theory effectively ended in the 1960s, but the termination had little to do with the defects described here. Sutherland clearly accepted a normative definition of delicts; and while the notion of definitions unfavorable to crime suggests a concern with reactions to deviance, Sutherland's theory is far removed from any component of the labeling perspective.

IMPLICATIONS FOR SOCIAL PSYCHOLOGY

Experimental studies by social psychologists have identified numerous possible correlates of conformity, meaning characteristics of situations and/or individuals that ostensibly promote conformity. Sociologists should contemplate recognizing those correlates in formulating theories of deviance; but there are some horrendous problems, and they transcend the *anormative* conception of conformity in most studies by social psychologists.

Consider the following illustrative list of variables, each of which should vary *inversely* with rates of deviance if propositions in social psychology about conformity (Collins 1970) are valid and if their transposition-extrapolation is justified: (1) personal attraction among members, (2) interdependence among members, (3) the public character of the deviant behavior, (4) the difficulty of tasks undertaken by members, and (5) consensus among members. The first variable is alien to macroscopic social units (countries, states, and perhaps even communities) unless restated as "cohesion"; and at the macroscopic level the measure of cohesion must pertain to normative consensus rather than (as in studies by social psychologists) sociometric choices or membership turnover. Even if interdependence can be equated with more conventional terms in social psychology (for example, common fate, shared goals), sociologists view interdependence at the macroscopic level as stemming largely from the division of labor, which appears to vary *directly* with the rate of deviance (assuming any relation at all). While the rate for some types of deviance (for example, smoking marijuana) may be greater than rates for other types because the behavior is not "public," that consideration is largely irrelevant in explaining variation in the rate among social units of the same type (for example, cities). Finally, most commonly recognized types of deviance (for example, assault, mental illness, truancy) are hardly "tasks," and the difficulty of committing or refraining from them probably does not vary appreciably among social units of the same type. So in the illustrative list only consensus appears clearly relevant for both theories of conformity and theories of deviance.

Prospects for greater integration. If the foregoing exaggerates the problems in integrating the sociology of deviance and the social psychology of conformity, the exaggeration stems largely from the failure to recognize that some studies of conformity have more implications for the sociology of deviance than others. While space limitations dictate a concern with the social psychology of conformity in general, such concern is not altogether unrealistic. Integration of the two fields cannot be realized through isolated studies, rather, a general strategy in studies of conformity is required.

The research designs must be such that deviance in the normative sense is the dependent variable, and the comparison groups should differ systematically as to internal normative consensus and perceived or actual social heterogeneity (for example, occupations, race, sex).[13] Such designs might not further social psychologists' understanding of conformity in the sense of the influence of modal behavior; but only complexity would preclude adding experimental controls and variables that are in keeping with classical studies of conformity (for example, Asch 1956; Sherif 1936). In any case, the ultimate purpose of experimental studies of deviance should be tests of sociological theories; and the theories of Merton and Sutherland are prime candidates for two reasons. First, although interest in the two theories has waned substantially, it is difficult to imagine any radically different alternatives. And, second, from the outset both theories have defied systematic tests, in part because the requisite kinds of seemingly relevant data cannot be gathered by conventional sociological methods.

Elaborating on the latter point, the principal variables in both theories (for example, access to means, priority of favorable definitions) are subject to measurement and control (if at all) only in experimental settings. Of course, both theories were formulated to account for actual violations of criminal laws rather than deviance in an experimental setting, and many criminologists will not regard experimental tests as relevant (whatever the outcome). Yet it may be that neither theory can be corroborated or falsified; instead, it may be impossible to go beyond judgments of them as being either consistent or inconsistent with experimental findings. The same is true of virtually all well-known sociological theories, and given the sad state of the field, sociologists should entertain doubts about their traditional indifference to experimental methodology. As for social psychologists, many of them appear inclined to modify traditional experimental designs so as to recognize such things as *social* norms (see, for example, Paicheler 1976); therefore, two purposes would be served in endeavors to assess sociological theories through experimental designs.

In suggesting a division of labor between sociological theorists and social psychologists akin to that between theoretical physics and experimental physics, the implication is not that social psychologists would play the unimaginative or "grubby" role. To the contrary, imagination would be at a premium in designing such experiments, and that is all the more the case since the vast majority of sociological theories cannot be tested (observationally or experimentally) without restating them.

Social Control

The sociological study of *social control* has not been productive, but continued widespread use of the term is indicative of the notion's importance. Paradoxically, however, that very sense of importance makes the conceptualization of social control difficult. The concept's raison d'être is its bearing on a perennial sociological question: How is social order possible? That question preoccupied E. A. Ross (1901), the first to use the term social control extensively, and his conceptualization of social control is little more than a list of "things" (for example, public opinion, law, religion) that supposedly contribute to social order. One must surely wonder how any such list could be complete and why all major institutions (for example, religion) necessarily contribute to social order. Indeed, how can institutions remain viable without social control? Finally, accepting Ross's conceptualization, it becomes illogical to ask if social control contributes to social order.

Only since about 1950 have sociologists realized appreciable consensus in going beyond Ross; prior to that time most definitions (including that of Ross) were intolerably vague and/or impossibly broad. For one, Bernard's definition (1939:11–12) essentially equates control with the influence that any human's behavior has on the behavior of others.[14] Such a definition is very broad in that it admits the possibility of unintentional control and does not distinguish social control from externalistic human control in general (that is, all human control other than self-control). Surely there is some distinction, but it cannot be simply that social control "involves" at least two persons. That distinction would justify identifying all of the following as social control: asking for a pack of cigarettes in a store, a gunman pistol-whipping a bank clerk, inviting a friend over for dinner, performing a lobectomy, hailing a taxi, incarcerating a felon, and rape. Some of those acts are everyday interaction in certain social units, while others are not normative by any definition. But illustrations in the literature clearly suggest that social control is distinct from everyday interaction and normative one way or another, and unless a definition recognizes those qualities, it will be all too broad.

Since 1950 sociologists have come to define social control by reference to the counteraction of deviance. Parsons (1951) promoted that *prophylactic* conception, but an anthropologist, Berndt (1962:11), has supplied the most succinct formulation: "Social control thus covers all the processes and procedures which regulate behavior, in that they exert pressure on persons and groups to conform to the norms."

Such definitions are now so common that a rationale is rarely stated. One ostensible rationale is that the terminology distinguishes social control from externalistic control in general by separating it from everyday interaction and by attributing a normative quality to it. Thus, in light of

Berndt's definition, neither hailing a taxi nor pistol-whipping a bank clerk would be thought of as social control. Moreover, given the conceptual link between conformity to norms and social order, the definition is consistent with a perennial concern in sociology.

The prophylactic conception cannot be interpreted as the *prevention* of deviance, for that term implies *intentional* control, and advocates of the conception (for example, Parsons, 1951:297, 321) do not attribute an intentional quality to social control. While the very idea of "unintended" control borders on a contradiction, it is consistent with a long tradition, one that Lemert (1972:95) rightly characterized as the "assumption of automaticity in the control process." Lemert attributed the assumption to Sumner, but it also stems from Durkheim and Ross. In any case, according to the conception no human behavior (whether a process, practice, or institution) qualifies as social control unless it demonstrably promotes conformity to norms. Thus, wearing wedding rings would be social control (regardless of anyone's perception or intention) given evidence that the custom does promote conformity to some assumed norm (for example, marital fidelity).

The are four major shortcomings of the prophylactic conception. First, even assuming that norms exist, it is extremely difficult to demonstrate that a given practice or institution does or does not promote conformity to those norms. Second, unsuccessful attempts to promote conformity are not social control, because the prophylactic conception makes intention irrelevant; hence, the distinction between successful and unsuccessful attempts at social control is lost. Third, the conception makes it illogical to ask whether social control counteracts deviance.

The fourth shortcoming is the most serious and complicated. All of the seemingly insoluble problems in defining deviance haunt the prophylactic conception, but the advocates write as if deviance is obvious, and rather than confront problems in defining and identifying norms they appear to assume normative consensus or "monolithic" norms. That assumption makes the majority, or a powerful minority, the final arbiters of social control, especially when social control studies focus on law enforcement. Hence, terrorists (a normative minority) are objects but never agents of social control, for they are acting contrary to criminal laws. But contemplate this question: Granted that members of the Ku Klux Klan "counteract" the behavior of blacks, are those actions social control? It will not do to reply that the actions are social control given the Klan's putative norms, for that argument extends to terrorists in general. Indeed, normative consensus is especially dubious in contemplating the Klan, for there are at least six possibly conflicting normative opinions, those of Klan members, blacks, southern whites outside the Klan, southern legal officials (including legislators), federal legal officials, and United States citizens in general. Which opinions constitute *the* norm for judging the Klan's control activities? Advocates of the prophylactic conception simply avoid such questions. True, the problem is not glaring in studies of the counteraction of acts that appear to be disapproved of generally (for example, robbery, rape), but that focus is narrow and makes legislators the final arbiters of social control. So it is not surprising that social control is a "bad name" in certain sociological circles.

Despite shortcomings of the prophylactic conception of social control, there are no real contenders at present. Those who ostensibly reject that conception either leave social control essentially undefined (see Janowitz 1975) or voice doubts as to the feasibility of an alternative (Gibbs 1977). Nonetheless, various problems with theories of social control stem from the prophylactic conception.

THEORIES OF SOCIAL CONTROL

There are only two candidates in the way of major sociological questions about social control. First, why do the features or kinds of social control vary over time and among social units? Second, what is the efficacy of each kind?

Answers to those questions have not been facilitated by the prophylactic conception, and it even raises doubts as to the logical character of the second major question. Since a type of behavior or institution is social control only if it does counteract deviance, then efficacy is attributed to social control *by definition.* Moreover, if the prophylactic conception is accepted, the distinction between a theory of social control and a theory of deviance becomes obscure.

Regard for status. LaPiere's work (1954) represents the first major theory on social control (so-called) after widespread acceptance of the prophylactic conception. His theory is summarized as follows: the amount of conformity to the norms of a social unit is a direct function of the regard for status in that social unit. The summary is a gross oversimplification, but no amount of elaboration would justify identifying LaPiere's work as a theory of social control rather than a theory of deviance. Indeed, unless one denies that deviance is the obverse of conformity, then that work is clearly a theory of deviance. If regard for status is the primary determinant of the conformity rate, then it is the primary determinant of the deviance rate; and if conformists differ from deviants by their regard for status, then the distinguishing characteristic of deviants is given by implication. Stating the argument another way, should social control be conceptualized as a *subclass* of conscious and deliberate attempts to manipulate behavior, LaPiere's work would not be a theory of social control.

The fate of LaPiere's work is another rationale for regarding it as a theory of deviance. It was formulated at a time when Merton's theory and Sutherland's theory still enjoyed a large following. LaPiere's theory was rightly but perhaps dimly perceived by sociologists as a *contending theory of deviance,* and it quickly proved less appealing than its rivals. Had the theory been recognized for what it is, there might have been more attempts to integrate it with the traditional line of work in social psychology and sociology with "status and conformity" (for example, Harvey and Consalvi 1960; Ridgeway 1978). In any case, whatever the reason for its demise, the theory illustrates how a prophylactic conception of social control blurs the distinction between theories of deviance and theories of social control.

Control theories of juvenile delinquency. Concomitant with the waning of interest in anomie and differential association, several theories of juvenile delinquency that emerged in the 1960s purport to identify conditions that inhibit delinquency. Consistent with the prophylactic conception, those theories have come to be designated as *control* theories. The present survey is limited to Hirschi's version (1969), largely because it best illustrates the issue in question (the distinction between a theory of social control and a theory of deviance).

Hirschi's theory does not encompass a conceptualization of control or social control; hence, it appears that either term designates *any condition* that inhibits juvenile delinquency. The theory postulates four inhibitory conditions: (1) commitment to conventional goals, (2) attachment to conventional persons, (3) involvement in conventional activities, and (4) beliefs in conventional norms. To Hirschi's credit, he supplied illustrative procedures for the measurement of corresponding variables. Nonetheless, unless one accepts the prophylactic conception of social control and unless the four conditions do inhibit delinquency, Hirschi's work is not a social control theory. The conditions may render a juvenile more subject to effective control by parents and other "conventional" persons; even so, outside the prophylactic conception, the conditions themselves are not social control.[15] There is no evidence that Hirschi's four conditions are commonly created consciously and deliberately, let alone to prevent juvenile delinquency; rather, the conditions appear largely crescive.

The punitiveness of social control. Despite difficulties in judging punitiveness, it is commonly assumed that legal sanctions are much more punitive in some political units than in others. No less than six theories have been formulated to explain that assumed difference, and space limitations permit only the briefest possible summary of them.[16]

Durkheim attributes punitiveness to a low degree of division of labor and a concomitant high degree of normative consensus. A much more psychological explanation is offered by the *scapegoat theory,* which interprets punitiveness as the sublimation of socially repressed aggressive and sexual urges. The *cultural-consistency theory* is actually a very loose argument that depicts punishment as reflecting general cultural features and conditions of life (for example, when life is harsh, the death penalty is common). From the Marxist perspective (Rusche and Kirchheimer's version in particular) punitive legal sanctions stem from fluctuations in the labor market and the need of the dominant class to maintain exploitative control, with imprisonment flourishing when the labor market is glutted and capital punishment used when social dissent becomes intense. For Ranulf, punitive legal sanctions are concealed expressions of the moral indignation of the middle class, an indignation generated by the assiduous conformity required for members of that class to maintain their social position. Finally, Sorokin views punitive legal sanctions as the manifestation of social ("ethicojuridical") heterogeneity and concomitant antagonistic relations along class, ethnic, racial, or religious lines.

No constructive purpose would be served by describing the merits of and objections to the foregoing theories, because sociological interest in them has effectively ended. The reason was not obvious difficulties in bringing evidence to bear on the theories, or even apparent exceptions to the theories. Instead, consistent with the prophylactic conception, sociologists are prone to think of social control as "that which contributes to social order"; and, rightly or wrongly, they do not see legal sanctions as playing a major role in social order.

Revival of interest in the deterrence doctrine. Commencing about 1968, a small number of sociologists turned to this question: Do legal punishments deter crime? That question had been posed some twenty years before, and the answers after several studies (most concerned with capital punishment) were uniformly negative. Today, in light of recent studies (many by economists), only incorrigible partisans regard the evidence as compelling one way or the other (see surveys in Blumstein et al. 1978; Gibbs 1975). Since space limitations preclude even a summary of the findings, this commentary is restricted to the reasons for inconclusive evidence.

Although seldom recognized, the deterrence doctrine cannot be treated as a unitary theory; rather, it encompasses at least three independent theories: (1) specific deterrence, the postulated impact of punishment on those who have been punished; (2) restrictive general deterrence, the postulated restraining influence of the threat of punishment on those who commit crimes with impunity; and (3) absolute general deterrence, the postulated possibility that the fear of punishment has prevented some individuals from ever committing the type of crime in question. The theories are independent in that evidence falsifying one of them would not falsify the other two (for example, even if there is no specific deterrence whatever, it could still be that some individuals restrict their criminal activities to avoid punishment).

Unfortunately, systematic statements of the theories are wanting, and none of them reduces to a simple proposition, such as: the greater the severity of legal punishments in a jurisdiction, the lower the crime rate of that jurisdiction. To the contrary, in stating a theory of general deterrence (restrictive or absolute) nine properties of legal punishment could be relevant (Gibbs 1975).

Whatever properties of punishment are recognized in a deterrence theory, two problems will haunt tests of it. First, putative evidence of deterrence (for example, an inverse relation among states between the objective certainty of imprisonment and the crime rate) may only reflect one or more of nine nondeterrent mechanisms (Gibbs 1975), such as incapacitation (for example, auto theft is difficult when incarcerated). Second, even if deterrence investigators could control for nondeterrent mechanisms, extralegal conditions that inhibit or generate criminality (for example, perhaps unemployment or the social condemnation of crime) should also be taken into account; but there is no accepted *etiological theory* of criminality that identifies the relevant conditions.

Deterrence could be a strategic subject for social control studies. Granted that social control is not limited to legal punishments, a deterrent penal policy is clearly an attempt at control; hence, deterrence studies have immediate policy implications. Yet the prophylactic conception of social control discourages a concern with deterrence. The reason is not just doubts about the efficacy of punishment, nor the idea that legal punishments are social control only if efficacious. Additionally, the prophylactic conception reflects an assumption—that the crescive features of social life maintain social order. That assumption is a tacit belittlement of conscious and deliberate attempts to control human behavior.

IMPLICATIONS FOR SOCIAL PSYCHOLOGY

All of the preceding leads to this conclusion: greater integration of the social psychology of conformity and sociology can best be realized through the concept social control. That is especially the case if social control is defined at least partially by reference to the manipulation of behavior. However, whereas the manipulation of behavior has an intentional quality, that is not the case for the notion of "pressure" in the social psychology of conformity; but that notion is metaphorical, and to define it in terms of *one effect,* change in the behavior of individuals toward the modal behavior of the group, is both a narrow conception and conducive to tautologies. In any case, all studies in the social psychology of conformity bear directly on this question: What are the various means by which human behavior can be controlled and what is the relative efficacy of each? One can question whether the studies focused on means of social control, but identifying the "social" quality of social control poses unresolved conceptual problems. Granted that a truly defensible alternative to the prophylactic conception of social control has yet to be formulated, no alternative is likely to make the social psychology of conformity irrelevant.

Given the paucity of theories of social control (all the more remarkable since sociologists use the term theory with abandon), propositions about the correlates of conformity (above) are more directly relevant for sociologists with interests in social control than for those with interest in the etiology of deviance. No less important, while the social psychology of conformity is not limited to experimental methods, those methods would make a closer integration of that field and the sociology of social control all the more beneficial. In particular, given the evidential problems that haunt deterrence research, anything approaching conclusive evidence is unlikely without a radical innovation in research designs, and in that connection the negligible participation of social psychologists in deterrence research is unfortunate. Unlike economists, social psychologists would be sensitive to the perceptual character of deterrence, and they have far more skills in experimentation than do sociologists.[17] The latter point is all the more important since the experimental (field or laboratory) simulation of a criminal justice system is a glaring gap in deterrence research.

Conclusion

Since virtually all fields in the social and behavioral sciences are haunted by conceptual problems, the present concern with conceptualization may appear inordinate. However, the conceptual problem examined here is crippling in a general way for two fields. In the sociology of deviance, particular theories and lines of research are now judged largely in terms of one issue—the choice between the normative and the reactive conceptions of deviance—and both contenders are a sea of difficulties. There are scarcely contending conceptions of social control, but that is unfortunate, for the predominant prophylactic conception stands or falls on the resolution of problems in the conceptualization of deviance.

Nothing less than a conceptual innovation will reorient the study of deviance or social control and avoid creeping sterility. Accordingly, sociologists and social psychologists with interest in those subjects should think more and do less. That admonition is radical, but the conceptual problems that haunt the two fields will not cease to be crippling if ignored, nor will a solution be found in conventional research or theorizing.

NOTES

1. This argument is distinct from the notion that a norm "marks off" ranges of tolerable behavior. That "continuum" notion tends to confound three considerations: (1) contingencies, (2) the intensity of evaluations of conduct, and (3) consensus in those evaluations. Hence, far from clarifying, the notion makes it difficult to realize an intelligible and empirically applicable definition of a norm, and the same is true of the term *process,* which appears to have almost magical connotations for some social and behavioral scientists.

2. Yet an individual's perception of behavioral regularities (for example, the modal behavior of an experimental group) may have an impact on his or her behavior, a significant possibility in connection with the interests of social psychologists in conformity (below).

3. The same is true of normative contingencies. Systematic research on normative properties requires answers to normative questions from members of a social unit, but the questions would recognize only contingencies that are relevant *for the research at hand.* Relevance should depend on the theory that guides the research; and the theory should stipulate not only the contingencies to be recognized in the normative questions but also how differential power is to be treated in assessing answers. The strategy departs from the superorganic conception of norms, according to which norms exist independently of theoretical or research interests.

4. A radical alteration of research and theory on deviance would be required. According to the normative conception, a given type of act in a given social unit is either deviant or not, but the proposed strategy would treat virtually any type of act in any social unit as deviant to *some degree.* Moreover, deviance would not be treated as unidimensional; instead, at least five logically independent values would be required to express the deviant character of a type of act, with each value corresponding to one of the five major normative properties (above). Yet the strategy is less radical than it appears. Few sociologists or social psychologists would deny that deviance is somehow a matter of degree, but that recognition is seldom even suggested in conceptualizations of deviance, and it is virtually ignored in research and theory largely because of the inordinate focus in the sociology of deviance on "serious crimes" (for example, murder, robbery, rape). Since the

identification of those types of acts as deviant is scarcely disputable, the focus on them prompts sociologists to overlook problems with the notion of norms and deviance; but the focus is very narrow, and the conceptual problems remain.

5. The normative conception of deviance came to be rejected because of problems with the notion of a norm, even though advocates of the new conception have not made the reasons for their rejection of the older conception explicit. Note, however, that one problem has not been emphasized here—the normative conception makes the identification of instances of deviance difficult because acts contrary to collective evaluations of conduct tend to be concealed. That problem may have encouraged rejection of the normative conception, but it can be avoided only by the incredible denial that deviance has any connection with collective evaluations of conduct.

6. An even more extreme interpretation of the new conception of deviance could be justified. Allusions to *actual* acts as objectively real may be alien to that conception; hence, the illustrative definition should refer to "allegations of acts." However, in recognition that Becker et al. do speak of acts and behavior (not just allegations), the present interpretation is tempered.

7. A failure to find middle ground is conspicuous among "critical" or "conflict" criminologists. Thus, whereas Turk (1969) accepts the reactive conception of deviance, Taylor et al. (1973) reject it. Moreover, the conceptual issue poses a dilemma for this newest school of criminology. It would be paradoxical for those members who profess a Marxist orientation to argue that capitalism is conducive to criminal behavior but at the same time deny that criminality has something to do with behavior. In any case, that school is not treated here because its members diverge on conceptual issues, and that divergence precludes agreement among them when it comes to theories. Insofar as a theory rests on the reactive conception of deviance, it is an implicit denial that behavior has any bearing on deviance, and that denial is likely to make the theory appear implausible. To illustrate, Turk (1969) and Thio (1978) have formulated theories about deviance in which differential power is the principal independent variable, and both theories attribute more power to men and assert that the powerful are *least likely* to be labeled criminals. Yet the official arrest rate of males is several times that of females for various types of crimes (for example, robbery).

8. The problem is that the official label must be a "deviant label"; otherwise, the theory scarcely pertains to deviance. An illustrative list of deviant labels is not an adequate conceptualization, and one alternative is to define deviant labels as "designations of types of behavior which are disapproved by officials who authorize reports of instances of those types." That definition is limited to official data, and it is a partial retreat to the normative conception of deviance, but the *consensus problem* is minimized because no one is likely to deny, for example, that police chiefs both authorize reports of alleged robberies and voice disapproval of robbery.

9. This simple illustration notwithstanding, a theorist may identify several E and S variables, but the variables in each set must be somehow combined. Moreover, the prescribed form does not preclude premises in the theory and *deductions* of the $\rightarrow$ relations in the diagram. Those premises may encompass whatever notions a theorist cares to introduce, and the notions are likely to be more abstract than the present illustrations of E and S variables (the unemployment rate, police officers per capita).

10. The relative importance of the E and S variables cannot be revealed by one comparison (that is, one test of a theory), and it could well be that their relative importance depends on the type of behavior. If so, it will be another instance in the social and behavioral sciences where both camps in a major debate are wrong.

11. Nonetheless, the fact that both theories were formulated over forty years ago should be a source of embarrassment for the sociology of deviance, and perhaps they do not warrant the attention devoted to them here. But the *notions* if not the theories advanced by Merton and Sutherland may well be forever relevant, and with the exception of the labeling perspective and a new school of criminology (note 7, above) there have been few theoretical developments since Merton and Sutherland, nor is there a real prospect for a new leading theory as long as the normativists and the reactivists remain unreconciled.

12. Here, and subsequently, the term *goal* is used in the sense of *culturally approved,* and the term *means* is used in the sense of *institutionalized and legal.*

13. As suggested previously, the conception of norms (or normative properties) that guides experimental studies of conformity should not be statistical; rather, it should be oriented around (1) the notion of perceived collective evaluations of conduct and (2) recognition of the distinction between the two kinds of conformity, normative and modal (for example, Schellenberg 1974:347). Perceived collective expectations of conduct would be an alternative, but most sociologists and social psychologists seem to think of norms more in the *evaluative* sense. In any case, a perceptual conception of norms is more feasible in experimental designs (that is, more readily subject to manipulation) than an autonomic conception (one in which the elementary referent is an individual's *personal* evaluations or expectations of conduct). Briefly illustrating, there is no obvious way in an experimental setting to alter a naive subject's personal evaluations of conduct pertaining to racial or ethnic discrimination, but the description of the confederates in the experiment as, say, "Jews" or "southerners" is likely to have an impact on the naive subject's perceived collective evaluation of conduct as a member of the experimental group.

14. This definition is in keeping with the prevailing conception of conformity held by social psychologists (above). Hence, their studies may be more relevant for sociologists with interests in social control than for sociologists with interests in deviance. Paradoxically, the major line of work in which social psychologists use the term control extensively may be no less relevant for the theory of secondary deviance and societal reaction theory than for the sociology of social control. Those two lines of work are concerned with *perceptions* of the locus of control (see, for example, Cole and Cole 1977) and with self-control (see, for example, Harvey and Smith 1977). Regardless of the line of work, however, social psychologists use the terms control and social control even more uncritically than do sociologists. For the most part they seemingly equate either term with pressure or influence, even in connection with norms and deviance (see, for example, Moscovici 1976), or treat the notions largely in connection with "self-control" (for example, Harvey and Smith 1977:63–82).

15. Hirschi himself occasionally refers to his work as a "bonding theory," a designation more appropriate than "control theory."

16. See Sutherland and Cressey (1974) for a more extensive commentary on each theory.

17. For that matter, the deterrence doctrine is more relevant for social psychologists with interests in conformity than are sociological theories of deviance, especially if they grant that "pressure" is not limited to the modal behavior of groups.

PART V

Society and Personality

17 JAMES S. HOUSE

Social Structure and Personality

Sociology is distinguished as a discipline by its focus on social structure: persisting patterns of behavior and interaction between people or social positions. Thus, a major concern of sociological social psychology must be the relation of social structure to individual psychology and behavior, or what has traditionally been termed the study of social structure and personality. During the formative years of modern sociology and social psychology (1920s to 1960s), social structure and personality was a recognized and recognizable area of specialization; and toward the end of this period Inkeles (1959, 1963; Inkeles and Levinson 1954, 1969) provided several programmatic statements on the nature of and major issues in the study of social structure and personality. For a variety of reasons, however, social structure and personality, as a coherent body of substance and methods within sociology or the interdisciplinary field of social psychology, has more recently become somewhat dissipated.

This state of affairs reflects larger patterns of development in the broad interdisciplinary field of social psychology and its parent disciplines of sociology and psychology. Social psychology has become fractionated into three increasingly distinct and isolated domains or faces, one of which is social structure and personality (cf. House 1977). Psychological social psychology and symbolic interactionism are the other two more widely recognized faces, the former located within the discipline of psychology, the latter within sociology. Although very different in their methodological orientations and in many of their substantive concerns, psychological social psychology and symbolic interactionism both pay scant attention to macro-social structures and processes and how these affect and are affected by individual psychology and behavior. Psychological social psychology has increasingly focused on individual psychological processes (perception, cognition, motivation, learning, and so forth) in relation to social stimuli using laboratory experiments; symbolic interactionism, on face-to-face interaction processes using naturalistic observations.

The relation of macro-social structures (for example, societies, organizations, communities, social classes, racial or ethnic groups, and so forth) or processes (industrialization, urbanization, social mobility) to individual psychological attributes and behavior—the essence of the study of social structure and personality—has increasingly constituted neither a field of its own nor a coherent subfield of social psychology or sociology. The result has been that work on social structure and personality in one area or by one investigator has not contributed much to, or gained much from, related work in other areas or by other investigators. Nor has the study of social structure and personality had much impact on or benefited much from developments in other domains of social psychology.

The study of social structure and personality attained some unity and coherence between the 1920s and 1960s by taking a very "macro" or molar focus with respect to both social structure and personality. Research and theory attempted to relate the characteristics of total societies to holistic conceptions of the personalities of societal members. The comparative study of total societies was characteristic of sociology and anthropology during this early period, as was the comparative study of total personality or character types in psychology and psychiatry. It was natural, probably inevitable, that these two concerns would intersect in the study of society and personality, or what became known as "culture and personality" or "national character."

The evolution of research and theory in culture and personality and in sociology and psychology more generally has, however, moved in the direction of studying *aspects* of societies in relation to *aspects* of individual personality. As its interests have come to center on large and complex societies, sociology has increasingly consisted of a series of rather separate sociologies of work, family, religion, politics, medicine, the arts, leisure, and so forth (cf. Liska 1977). Anthropology appears to this outside observer to exhibit similar, if less marked, trends. Within psychology, holistic study of personality has similarly given way to the separate study of motivation, cognition, learning, psychopathology, and so forth. And students of culture and personality have become concerned with variations in personality *within* societies as well as between societies.

The net result of all these trends was to move the study of social structure and personality away from topics such as the relation between an authoritarian personality structure (manifest in all aspects of a person's life) and authoritarian societal structure (manifest in all aspects of societal life including family politics, and so forth) toward more focused topics such as the impact of achievement motivation on entrepreneurial behavior or the impact of occupational conditions on parental values. Concerns with broad societal patterns and differences in values, attitudes, and behavior have hardly disappeared. Explanation and understanding of such differences is increasingly sought, however, by attending to the component aspects and attributes of both societies and personality.

In light of these developments, this chapter adopts an eclectic and catholic approach to conceptualization of *social structure, personality,* and the relationship between them. This is consistent with the broad and loose usage of these terms in the literature more generally. Social structure commonly refers to any or all aspects of social systems, especially more macro-social phenomena. Similarly, personality is used as a generic label for relatively stable and enduring individual psychological attributes (values, attitudes, motives, needs, beliefs, and so forth). Thus, the relationship between any macro-social phenomena and any individual psychological attribute can be considered an aspect of the study of social structure and personality.

Both social structure and personality, however, also have more specific connotations. As the chapter develops, I follow Inkeles (1959, 1963; Inkeles and Levinson 1969) in distinguishing between social structure and culture as components of a social or sociocultural system. Social structure is defined in this more restricted sense in the opening sentence of the chapter and this conception is elaborated below. The latter part of the chapter focuses on the relation of this more restricted conception of social structure to individual psychological attributes and behavior.

Similarly, personality often connotes something more distinctive than any or all persisting psychological attributes of an individual. Specifically, it suggests that these attributes have a structure or organization and some inherent dynamic properties or tendencies. From the 1920s through the 1950s, psychology and psychiatry were dominated by conceptions of personality as a coherent dynamic system, most notably that of Freud; the same was true of the study of culture and personality or national character. However, both cognitive and behaviorist research and theory have challenged the utility and validity of such a conception of personality, and the study of personality has increasingly evolved into the study of persisting individual differences in a variety of psychological attributes, each of which is generally assumed to be loosely, if at all, linked with most other attributes. Thus, we find little or no emphasis on personality or character "structures" or "types." Rather the concern is with establishing that stable individual traits do exist and have important behavioral consequences. Thus, I feel that using the term personality as a generic label for stable and persisting psychological attributes is quite consistent with current conceptions of personality.[1]

Though conceptions of both social structure and personality have become increasingly loose and multidimensional, I would argue that the study of social structure and personality continues to constitute an important and potentially coherent domain of social psychology in general and of sociological social psychology in particular. What gives the area coherence, however, is not a central substantive focus such as the holistic study of society and personality. Rather, the integrative foci of the study of social structure and personality in the present and future must be a set of general theoretical (or even meta-theoretical) and methodological principles that are applicable to the study of the relationship of any macro-social phenomenon to individual personality and behavior. This chapter attempts to delineate those integrating theoretical and methodological principles and to illustrate their application to a varied, but necessarily select, set of substantive phenomena.

The chapter is divided into five major sections. The first briefly reviews the development of social structure and personality as an area of study from its early sociological origins through the heyday of research on culture and personality or national character. The second traces the recent evolution of research and theory noted above, focusing especially on the work of Alex Inkeles on modernization and modernity, and states three basic analytical principles and related methodological considerations that should guide and integrate current and future work on social structure and personality. The third and fourth sections illustrate the application of these principles, first with respect to a general conceptual distinction between "cultural" and "structural" explanations of relationships between social systems and individual personality or behavior, and second with respect to analyses of the impact of social class on personality. These four sections explore the impact of macro-social phenomena on personality and behavior; the fifth considers when and how personality may affect social structure.

Historical Development: From Comte to National Character

EARLY ORIGINS

The study of social structure and personality is inherently interdisciplinary. Its modern origins trace to the great social analysts of the nineteenth and early twentieth century, whose work has formed the foundation of much of modern social science, most notably sociology. Auguste Comte, Karl Marx, Max Weber, and Emile Durkheim were all centrally concerned with social psychology, especially problems of social structure and personality. This has not been sufficiently appreciated because of tendencies of these writers, often accentuated by later interpreters, to stress the differences between their sociological approach and that of psychologists of their day.

In his classic chapter on the history of social psychology, Allport (1968:7) declared: "If it were possible to designate a single deliberate 'founder' of social psychology as a science, we should have to nominate Comte for this honor." Although Comte is more commonly considered the founder of sociology, Allport (1968:6–10) argues that toward the end of his life Comte was attempting to construct a "true final science" which integrated biology, sociology, and psychology. The focal question Comte posed for this final science is still central to Allport's and my conception of social psychology, and particularly to the study of social structure and personality:

> How can the individual be both a cause and a consequence of society? That is to say: How can his nature depend indisputably upon the prior existence of cultural designs and upon his role in a predetermined social structure while at the same time he is clearly a unique person, both selecting and rejecting influences from

his cultural surrounding, and in turn creating new cultural forms for the guidance of future generations? [Allport 1968:9]

Marx, Weber, and Durkheim also had primary interests in problems of social structure and personality, and their ideas directly influenced more recent work in the area. Two of Marx's earliest and most enduring concepts, alienation and class consciousness, inherently concerned the relationship (both actual and ideal) of societal structure and institutions (for example, industry, government, and the economy) to individual beliefs, motivations, behaviors, and so forth (cf. Fromm 1961; Lukes 1967; Marx 1972a and 1972b). Specifically, Marx saw the structure of the capitalist economic system as not only economically exploitative but also incompatible with the realization of human beings' basic productive natures, at least in the case of workers who did not own or control the means of production. The initial consequence was that workers became alienated from their work, from themselves, and from each other. Marx's early writings focused on these problems of human self-realization and subjective quality of life (cf. Fromm 1961; House 1977).

But Marx hoped and expected that workers would eventually recognize that their deprivation and alienation stemmed from their shared subordinate position in the economic system. That is, they would acquire a class consciousness that would be the foundation of revolutionary collective action to establish a new, nonalienating, social and economic order. Thus, Marx was centrally concerned with (1) the nature and consequences of the "fit" between social structure and the characteristics of individuals, and (2) with how position in the socioeconomic structure shaped values, motives, and beliefs.

Weber, the most explicitly social psychological of the "founders" of sociology, was similarly concerned with the relationship between position in the social structure and individual values, motives, and beliefs (cf. House 1977:169–70). In the *Protestant Ethic and the Spirit of Capitalism,* Weber (1958) turned Marx on his head, arguing that values, motives, and beliefs play an autonomous role in society and can indeed be major causes of dramatic changes in the social structure. Specifically, he posited that the secular ideology spawned by Calvinist theology was a major cause of the rise of capitalism in Western Europe. However, he also recognized that social structures and positions, once established, in turn shape values, attitudes, and beliefs (for example, Weber 1958:72, 181–83).

Durkheim's concern with problems of social structure and personality was less overt but no less real. Inkeles (1959 and, especially, 1963) has masterfully documented the social psychological assertions about social structure and personality that are implicit in what Durkheim (1951) purported to be a purely sociological study, *Suicide.* He also showed how a more explicitly social-psychological approach can clarify Durkheim's theory and data. Lukes (1967) argues that Durkheim's concept of anomie, like Marx's alienation, involves the relationship between "social phenomena" and individual "states of mind," or what are termed here, social structure and personality. Close reading of *Suicide* indicates that Durkheim himself recognized the social-psychological nature of his work, and adopted a militantly sociologistic stance mainly to combat the widespread psychological reductionism of his time (cf. House, 1977:170). Much of Durkheim's work focused on the role of social systems in shaping values and of these values in maintaining social order (cf. Durkheim 1915, 1933).

In sum, the study of social structure and personality was a central concern of the founders of sociology, and their ideas have stimulated further research and theoretical development up to the present. Yet their work, especially Durkheim's, had an anti-psychological component that emphasized the importance and distinctiveness of social phenomena and sociology as a discipline, as opposed to highly individualistic or psychological interpretations of social phenomena that were and continue to be quite prevalent. The subsequent development of sociology in the first half of the twentieth century tended to reinforce this anti-psychological stance. The discipline most concerned with social structural phenomena regarded their relation to individual psychology and behavior as a peripheral activity (cf. House 1977:170–71). This development, along with others, resulted in the study of social structure and personality taking on a peculiarly limited, yet expansive form—what has come to be best known under the rubrics of *culture and personality* and *national character.* In retrospect, this turn of events may have hindered more than it helped the development of the more general study of social structure and personality.

CULTURE AND PERSONALITY AND NATIONAL CHARACTER: THE STUDY OF SOCIETY AND PERSONALITY

Early in this century, anthropologists and later psychoanalysts, psychologists, and psychiatrists became fascinated with the role that individual personality played in understanding the similarities and differences between societies and social systems. Joined subsequently by sociologists and political scientists, they developed the first major cumulative body of theory and research on social structure and personality. The initial impetus in this area came from the anthropologist Franz Boas at Columbia and his students, most notably Margaret Mead and Ruth Benedict. As ethnographers dispersed themselves throughout the world in the early twentieth century, they were struck by the cultural relativity of human behavior and social organization. That is, human customs and practices varied greatly, especially among primitive societies, yet most societies remained quite stable over time. Clearly, there was no universal human nature, nor could genetic or physiological factors explain the variations observed.

Although the validity of some of her ethnographic observations has been questioned (for example, Fortune 1939), Mead's (1935) classic study of *Sex and Temperament in Three Primitive Societies* revealed wide variations in the patterning of behavior and feelings in men versus women among different New Guinea tribes. From these observations Mead derived broad conclusions about the relationship between culture and personality, conclusions that were to be echoed and elaborated by others:

> We are forced to conclude that human nature is almost unbelievably malleable, responding accurately and contrastingly to contrasting cultural conditions. The differences between individuals who are members of different cultures, like the individuals within a culture, are almost entirely to be laid to differences in conditioning, especially during early childhood, and the form of this conditioning is culturally determined. Standardized personality differences between the sexes are of this order, cultural creations to which each generation, male and female, is trained to conform. [Mead 1935:280–81]

Societal patterns, such as sex differences, remained stable over time in the face of constant turnover in societal membership because societies "conditioned" or "molded" (Mead 1939:vii) individual personality to accord with these patterns. Mead felt this molding occurred especially, though not exclusively, during childhood, but failed to specify the influence processes through which it occurred.

Developments in psychology, however, filled this theoretical gap. Despite their differences, the dominant psychological theories of the 1920–50 period, learning theory and psychoanalysis, both emphasized the primacy of child rearing and early experience in the development of personality. Psychoanalysis became central to the study of culture and personality, especially through the collaboration of a psychiatrist, Abram Kardiner (1939, 1945), with anthropologists at Columbia. Kardiner saw the order, coherence, and stability of society stemming from members of society sharing a "basic personality structure" (BPS) which in turn was a product of the "primary" institutions of the society, most notably early child-rearing practices. These primary institutions not only transmitted social and cultural patterns from generation to generation, they were also determinants of these patterns. Social and cultural institutions (for example, religion and ritual) developed and changed as expressions of the needs, tensions, and wishes that characterized the BPS. For Kardiner, the child was the father not only of the man but of many aspects of the society itself. Kardiner's ideas were adopted and elaborated in the later anthropological work on culture and personality by Whiting (Whiting and Child 1953) and Levine (1973).

During and immediately after World War II, anthropologists, psychiatrists, and others, who until then had studied culture and personality largely in primitive societies, were enlisted by their governments in the name of national defense to make similar analyses of modern nations, especially enemy nations, but also allies. The goal was to identify what came to be termed "national character" but was essentially identical to what had been termed basic personality structure or cultural character —the motives, beliefs, and other psychological attributes shared by the members of a given society.

The impact of this work on military or diplomatic policy is unclear, but it did spawn some of the most famous, and in some senses infamous, analyses in the culture and personality literature. Most prominent were studies of America's military adversaries—Japan (for example, Gorer 1943; LaBarre 1945), Germany (for example, Dicks 1950), and later Russia (for example, Gorer and Rickman 1949; Dicks 1952). Although some authors had contact with these societies prior to World War II, these were by necessity analyses of "culture at a distance" (Mead and Metroux 1953) based on knowledge gleaned from historical and current written materials on the society and from interviews with emigrants, prisoners of war, or others who had recently observed or belonged to the society.

Typical of these studies are the quite similar analyses of Japanese national character by Gorer (1943) and LaBarre (1945), both relying heavily on psychoanalytic theory. Though neither had been to Japan, they agreed the Japanese were predominantly anal-compulsive character types, as manifested in their preoccupation with ritual, tidiness, and order, and in their fanaticism and repressed aggression. Guided by psychoanalytic theory, both inferred that the genesis of this character type must lie in severe toilet training experienced by Japanese children as early as four months of age. In a similar analysis of "culture at a distance," Gorer and Rickman (1949) characterized Russian culture as combining discipline and authoritarianism in human relations with occasional periods of almost orgiastic release. This pattern, in turn, derived from shared personality patterns produced by the Russian practice of tightly swaddling infants and then releasing them for brief periods of vigorous kicking and thrashing. Perhaps the most widely disseminated and accepted description of national character among both social scientists and laymen was the "authoritarian personality" of the German people, which helped to explain the rise and rule of the Nazis in Germany during the 1920s to 1940s period (cf. Fromm 1941; Dicks 1950; Adorno et al. 1950).

A simple and seemingly plausible basic theory of society and personality, stated most succinctly by Gorer (1950), underlay these analyses of national character and the earlier work on culture and personality. Figure 17.1 provides a graphic representation of the theory, congruent with both the earlier and the more recent (for example, Levine 1973) approaches to culture and personality or national character, and with the most important sociological work in this area during the post-World War II period, that of Talcott Parsons (1964).[2]

Elements central to all culture and personality analyses discussed above are embodied in the solid boxes *(A–F)* and arrows (1–6) in figure 17.1. The dotted boxes and arrows represent elaborations of the theory made by one or more authors. Box *A* and arrow 1 are not focal concerns, but rather underlying assumptions of all the theories: observed culture and social structure (box *B*) represent the adaptation of a group to its environment—social and nonsocial, present and past (box *A*). The ongoing culture and social structure (or social system), especially those aspects concerned with maintenance of physical survival, determine (arrow 2) the nature of early (largely parental and familial) child-rearing practices (box *C*). These in turn shape (arrow 3) the personality of the child (box *D*) which forms the core (arrow 4) of adult personality (box *E*). Adult personality gives rise (arrow 5) to adult behavior (box 6), the patterning of which constitutes and hence preserves (arrow 6) both the maintenance systems and any emergent expressive institutions such as religion (which Kardiner termed secondary institutions). Varied societies, then, remain stable over time by each socializing its members to "want to act in ways they *have* to act as members of the society" (Fromm 1941:381).

Boxes *A–F* and arrows 1–6 precisely represent the theories of Kardiner

FIGURE 17.1
Theoretical Paradigm of Analyses of Culture and Personality or National Character

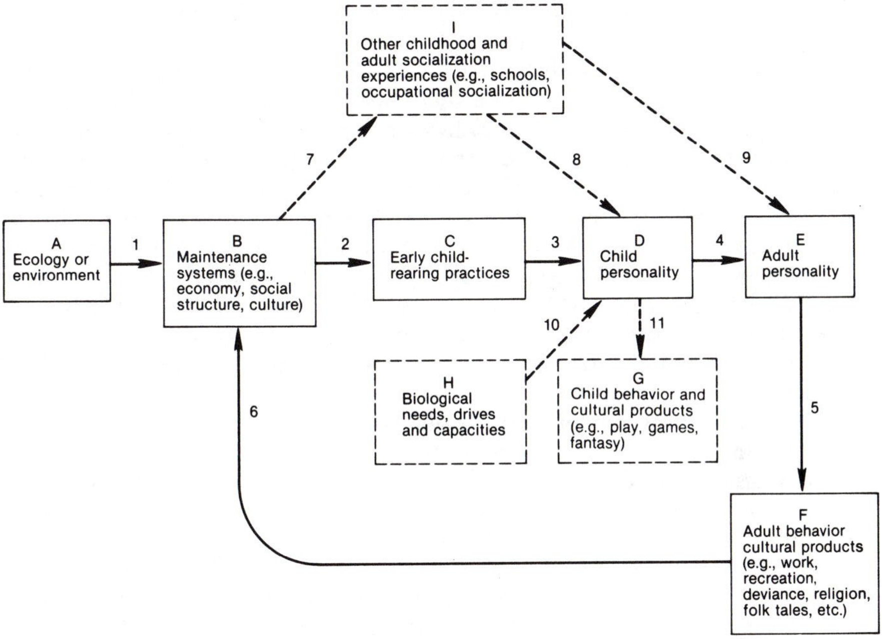

(1945) and Whiting and Child (1953). Levine (1973) uses essentially the same paradigm but explicitly adds biological capacities (box *H*) as something on which child-rearing practices act, so that both jointly affect personality (arrows 10 and 3). He also makes clear what is obviously implicit in the other theories that child personality (box *G*) emerges first, shaping child behavior (arrow 11) and then developing into adult personality. The influence of other childhood and adult experiences (box *H*) on personality (arrows 8 and 9) is allowed for but not emphasized in Mead's work. Since these other influences and child-rearing practices are assumed to arise from the same source (arrows 7 and 2), they largely reinforce each other.

The model of figure 17.1 is a prototype of one major class of theories about the relationships between social systems and the individual discussed below under the rubric of *cultural explanations.* The model is plausible and has desirable properties, most notably a specification of the micro-social interaction and influence processes through which the social system affects the personalities of its individual members (cf. below). The national character studies marked a high-water mark in the development and application of the theory of figure 17.1. They also made manifest, however, the inadequacies of the theory and especially of the empirical evidence purportedly supporting it. A series of articles appeared, beginning in 1950, that were severely critical of both the theories and data on national character or culture and personality (for example, Lindesmith and Strauss 1950; Bendix 1952; Inkeles and Levinson 1954;

Singer 1961; Wrong 1961), that had been produced in what Inkeles and Levinson (1969:441) termed the first period (roughly 1935–55) of work, marked by intensive exploration of single societies by socially oriented psychoanalysts and personality-oriented anthropologists using ethnographic and clinical methods.

The major flaw of these studies was their failure to collect systematic and representative data on the prevalence of either individual personality characteristics or particular child-rearing practices. Instead, personality characteristics and the child-rearing practices that produced them were inferred or deduced from observations of the overt behavior patterns that were also the raw data for inferring the nature of the culture or social structure. Essentially, theories of personality and its formation, such as psychoanalysis, were applied to social and cultural data (Inkeles and Levinson 1969:442). It was assumed, but not empirically demonstrated, that shared behavior patterns were produced by shared personality patterns, which, in turn, were the outcome of shared child-rearing experiences.

These assumptions proved empirically, as well as logically, false. When individual personality characteristics or child-rearing practices were assessed, they were not homogeneous, even in small primitive societies. Nor were the postulated links between child-rearing and personality empirically supported. Lindesmith and Strauss (1950) pointed out, for example, that little evidence supported psychoanalytic propositions about the effects of early child-rearing practices within our own society, much less the validity of applying these same propositions in other cultures. Further, most of the work was not really comparative in that only a single society was considered, and difficult problems of the comparability and translation of concepts and measures across societies were never clearly faced (cf. critical articles noted above for elaboration of these points). Students of culture and personality had largely *assumed* that which they purportedly were to *demonstrate* empirically. Theirs was, in Wrong's (1961) terms, an "oversocialized" conception of people and an "overintegrated" view of society, but one which was influential throughout the social sciences.

Inkeles and Levinson (1969:145) and others (cf. Terhune 1970) saw the application of survey research methods to cross-national samples by Cantril (1965), Lerner (1958), and Almond and Verba (1965) among others as heralding a new period of work on national character that would transcend most of the limitations of the pre-1955 work.[3] These studies did assess psychological attributes of representative samples of persons in different societies, making possible more valid inferences about cross-national differences. Yet, they failed to adequately explain the origins of these differences.

Just as the earlier studies developed a post hoc conception of personality and child-rearing practices that would be congruent with or expressive of their sociocultural data, the later survey studies developed post hoc conceptions of the sociocultural system and its influence on individuals that would be consistent with their psychological survey data. The errors in the latter case are probably not as severe, because conceptions of a sociocultural system can be checked against available social, cultural, and historical data, whereas conceptions of national character cannot be verified in the absence of individual level psychological data on representative samples. Nevertheless, neither approach produces an adequate analysis of the relationship between social structure and personality.

The classic Almond and Verba (1965) study of the "political cultures" of five nations with democratic political systems of varying ages and stability—the United States, Great Britain, Germany, Italy, and Mexico—exemplified the promise and the problems of the survey variety of national character research. The study sought to assess the congruence between each population's political attitudes and each society's political institutions, and to use the degree of congruence to help explain the long-term stability or instability of the various political systems.

A major finding was that the proportion of people who felt they could do something about an unjust law at both the local and national levels was greater in the United States and Britain than in Germany, Italy, or Mexico. In contrast, the proportion who felt they would receive serious consideration if they complained to both the police and a government office was highest in Britain and Germany, somewhat lower in the United States, still lower in Italy, and lowest in Mexico. These differences, and most others in the study, persisted even when educational or other differences across the five national samples were controlled.

Almond and Verba interpret these results as reflecting more general traits of political "competence" produced by the different political histories of the countries that generate different political "cultures." The Germans were particularly notable in having more confidence in the responsiveness of administrative officials than in political or legislative ones. Almond and Verba saw this as due to the early development and stability of bureaucratic efficiency in Germany and the late and unstable patterns of democratic development. In contrast, the revolutionary development of democratic institutions in America was followed by a later and uneven development of a civil-service bureaucracy, explaining why Americans feel more competent with respect to legislative than to administrative institutions. The British have a long and stable history of both democracy and a professional civil service. Hence, they felt relatively competent in regard to either, whereas Italy and Mexico have been disadvantaged in both respects.

This explanation in terms of residues of political history is plausible, but neither as clear nor as convincing as it would be if predictions had been made a priori and the mechanisms by which psychological attributes were acquired more thoroughly studied. For example, how important are socialization factors versus current adult experiences with the political system in generating perceptions of political or administrative responsiveness. If the German police or government bureaucracies are at present more responsive than comparable American bureaucracies, the attitudinal differences are easily explained without recourse to political history (though history may tell us how these institutions got to be the way they are). If, on the other hand, there appear to be no actual German-American differences in police or bureaucratic responsiveness, the sources of attitudinal differences are more plausibly sought in persisting residues of earlier adult experiences and/or childhood socialization. Almond and Verba do not consider such alternatives, and generally are vague about how political institutions and cultures affect individual attitudes. Implicitly, however, they too had adopted a variant of the cultural paradigm embodied in figure 17.1.

FROM NATIONAL CHARACTER TO SOCIAL STRUCTURE AND PERSONALITY

For a variety of reasons, including the political and economic complexities of such research, cross-national survey research on national character became less common throughout the 1960s. Conceptual interest continued in national character as both a cause and consequence of stability and change in cross-national differences in many areas, especially politics (cf. Terhune 1970; DiRenzo 1977a; Inkeles 1978a). Inkeles and Levinson (1969), Terhune (1970), and DiRenzo (1977a:303–307) all speak to the *potential* value of knowledge of the psychological attributes of members of society in understanding the social and political functioning of the society. But these writers present little hard data in support of their propositions, and what data are presented often come from earlier studies of national character or culture and personality. Inkeles (1978a), for example, relies heavily on the Almond and Verba study in his discussion of "continuity and change in the American national character."

Thus, though the study of national character remains conceptually alive, empirically it has diminished greatly in vigor and no longer constitutes the integrative focus of work on social structure and personality it once did. A transition occurred in the study of social structure and personality during the 1960s and 1970s. Research and theory became less holistic in their treatment of both society and personality, more structural and less cultural in their explanatory paradigms, and more concerned with intrasocietal as opposed to intersocietal differences. The origins of this transition traced to a series of analyses, especially by Inkeles and his associates, of differences in psychological attributes of people across societies at varying levels or stages of economic development or modernization.

Toward a New Focus on Social Structure and Personality

FROM CULTURAL TO STRUCTURAL EXPLANATIONS OF "CROSS-CULTURAL" DIFFERENCES: THE WORK OF INKELES

Up to the early 1960s, the theoretical basis of work on culture and personality and national character, whether of the earlier ethnographic or later sample survey varieties (for example, Almond and Verba), was implicitly or explicitly the *cultural* model of figure 17.1. A quite different model, which I term *structural* for reasons elaborated below, was increasingly articulated in the 1960s to explain both intersocietal and intrasocietal differences in personality and behavior. While noting that the idea was hardly original with him, dating back at least to Marx, Inkeles (1960) was the first major recent exponent of this structural approach. In his studies of modernization and modernity he articulated what has come to be known as the "convergence thesis":[4]

> . . . that industrialization leads to common forms of organization in widely differing societies and that these organizations have standard, powerful environments when they produce common values, perceptions, and ways of thinking. Put more generally, institutions with similar *structures* tend to induce common psychic structures or regularities in the personalities of their participants. This is especially true if, as in the case of schools and the work place, the individual spends time in the institutions and they control powerful rewards and punishments. [Suzman 1977:40, emphasis added]

Inkeles (1960:30) viewed the "level of economic and political development" of a nation (that is, levels of industrialization, urbanization, and bureaucratization) and its "distinctive cultural traditions" as "alternative explanations" of the perceptions, attitudes, and values present in its population. He provided initial confirmation of the impact of structural forces, such as industrialization, by showing that persons in similar socioeconomic positions across a wide range of industrialized societies were quite similar, at least relatively speaking, in their values and attitudes.

This analysis was followed by an ambitious survey of about 6,000 industrial and agricultural workers in six developing societies: Israel (focusing on the Oriental or Arabic population), Argentina, Chile, India, Nigeria, and East Pakistan (now Bangladesh). Inkeles and his associates were interested especially in a cluster of psychological attributes that they termed "individual modernity." The central elements of the syndrome were:

> (1) openness to new experience, both with people and with new ways of doing things such as attempting to control births; (2) the assertion of increasing independence from the authority of traditional figures like parents and priests and a shift of allegiance to leaders of government, public affairs, trade unions, cooperatives, and the like; (3) belief in the efficacy of science and medicine, and a general abandonment of passivity and fatalism in the face of life's difficulties; and (4) ambition for oneself and one's children to achieve high occupational and educational goals. Men who manifest these characteristics (5) like people to be on time and show an interest in carefully planning their affairs in advance. It is also part of this syndrome to (6) show strong interest and take an active part in civic and community affairs and local politics; and (7) to strive energetically to keep up with the news, and within this effort to prefer news of national and international import over items dealing with sports, religion, or purely local affairs. [Inkeles 1969:210]

This syndrome of traits was found to cohere within individuals in each society. The problem, then, was to determine the sociocultural influences that produced it. In contrast to the kind of cultural forces emphasized in prior national character research (that is, religion, ethnicity, family socialization, residues of national history), the important determinants of psychological modernity proved to be exposure to aspects of a modern or developed political and economic system: formal education, working in a factory, exposure to mass media, and, to a lesser degree, urban residence and possession of consumer goods (Inkeles 1969, 1978b; Inkeles and Smith 1974). The impact of these factors was remarkably consistent across all six countries, and in Inkeles's view was due less to their deliberately or directly teaching men new ideas and values, and more to their very structure forcing men to respond to and view the world in new ways:

> . . . school and factory produce the same result because both expose individuals to certain common principles of organization, procedures for assigning power and prestige, modes for allocating rewards and punishment, and approaches to the management of time. Individual modernity then becomes a quality learned by the incorporation into the self-system of certain qualities characteristic in certain institutional environments. [Inkeles 1976:122]

Inkeles went on to ask whether different levels of psychological modernity observed in the populations of different societies can largely be explained by differences in exposure to these institutional environments rather than by "national character, religion, or some other cultural factor" (Inkeles 1978b:48). His analysis determined how much of the observed variation and intersocietal differences in psychological modernity could be explained by exposure to the modern institutional environments enumerated above and how much was left to be explained by nationality once these exposures were controlled.

Inkeles found that substantial mean differences in psychological modernity between societies were reduced by 50 percent or more when education, factory experience, mass media exposure, urban residence, possession of consumer goods, and age were controlled. In a regression framework, the impact of nationality on individual modernity was much less than the impact of these six factors, though hardly insignificant statistically or substantively. Inkeles (1978b:61) concluded:

> . . . we were gratified by this outcome because our project, from its very inception, rested on the assumption that an individual's position in social structure, rather than his distinctive culture, would be the *prime* determinant of his psychological modernity. Nevertheless, the finding that this set of individual background factors, such as education and occupation, was much more important than the variable national-cultural milieux, should not be allowed to obscure the fact that the latter are nevertheless quite significant influences in their own right.

Further, Inkeles (1978b:65–67) believes that even these residual national differences reflect a "contextual" effect of living among more modern institutions and people rather than "differences in culture and national character." People in East Pakistan (now Bangladesh) were consistently less modern and those in Israel consistently more modern in their attitudes even after their education, occupational experience, and so forth were equated. But this, Inkeles argues, is a contextual effect of the more modern social structure of Israel (which impinges even on those who, by virtue of education, occupation, and so forth, are not directly exposed to modernizing influences) rather than an effect of different cultural or religious values.

Inkeles's work bridges the earlier holistic approach to society and personality or national character and more recent trends in research on social structure and personality. Although he deals with broad social and individual phenomena—"modernization" and modernity—neither is viewed as the whole of society or personality. Conceptually, both modernization and modernity are broken down into a series of components or facets. In most analyses modernity is treated as a unitary variable, but much attention is paid to the impact of different aspects of modernization (education, factory work, mass media, and so forth). This concern with aspects of society makes analyses *within societies* as important to the study of social structure and personality as analyses between societies. Also, as indicated above, Inkeles emphasized the impact on personality of what may be termed "structural" as opposed to "cultural" aspects of society, though he does not draw the distinction very clearly, either conceptually or empirically. Finally, he sees the necessity for understanding the impact of any macro-social phenomenon on the individual in terms (a) of the proximal social stimuli and interactions it produces in a person's life, and (b) of the psychological processes through which these stimuli and interactions are processed and responded to (cf. Inkeles 1960:1–2, 1963, 1976:118–22). This last interest is, however, only weakly reflected in his actual empirical work.

The remainder of this section will proceed from some of the implicit and explicit ideas in Inkeles's work to formulate three basic principles that should guide and integrate future work on the relationships between macro-social phenomena and the individual, or what is termed social structure and personality in the looser senses of these terms. The succeeding section pursues these principles by: (a) attempting to clarify the important distinctions that Inkeles begins to draw between cultural and structural explanations of the impact of macro-social phenomena on the individual; and (b) intensively exploring the application of these distinctions and principles to the study of one important phenomenon—the relationship of social class to personality.

BASIC ANALYTICAL PRINCIPLES

Understanding of the relationships between macro-social phenomena and individual personality or behavior has been impeded by a general failure to *explicate and test* theories of how and why these relationships occur. Although students of culture and personality and national character constructed one fairly explicit theory of these relationships (that is, figure 17.1), they did not, as noted above, consider alternative theoretical explanations and never conducted adequate empirical tests of their theory. The later survey work of Almond and Verba and others documented attitudinal differences between the populations of different societies. Explanations of what produced these differences, however, were vague, post hoc, and also never explicitly tested. Inkeles's work goes farther in the direction of formulating and testing a theory of how and why differences in modernity are produced, but the empirical tests of this theory are still crude. For example, the effects of education and factory work are interpreted as resulting from the similar *structure* or pattern of activities in those two institutions rather than from the *content* of the values, ideas, and skills that are taught. Yet, no explicit evidence in support of this interpretation is presented. Measures of years of formal education or factory experience tell us nothing directly about the nature of that education or factory experience and what about them modifies people's attitudes.

Survey research is a powerful tool for the study of social structure and personality. But too often the design and analysis of surveys follow a pattern that Blumer (1956) caricatured as "variable" analysis. Specifically, many reports of survey research have consisted almost entirely of bivariate and multivariate analyses of the relationship of a standard set of social-demographic variables—that is, age, sex, race, ethnicity, education, occupation, income (or indices of social class), region, religion, size of place of residence—to individual personality and behavior. Such analyses are a useful and necessary first step. Unfortunately, they are also often the last step in analyses of social survey data. Consequently, we know a great deal about the extent of differences in individual personality or behavior by age, race, sex, and so forth; yet, we know very little about how and why these differences occur. Blumer correctly pointed to this problem in 1956, but he incorrectly suggested that the problem was inherent in quantitative measurement and analysis. In fact, it merely stemmed from a failure to formulate an even minimally adequate conceptual and empirical analysis of how and why a social structure, position, or system could or should affect the individual (and vice versa). Such an analysis involves three key principles.

The components principle. First, we must adequately understand the nature of the social structure, position, or system in question. Such social phenomena almost always have multiple aspects, dimensions, or components, and we must be clear about what they are. Urban versus rural places of residence, for example, differ in multiple aspects of both their "cultures" (for example, shared values and beliefs in many areas) and "structures" (for example, size, density, ethnic or socioeconomic heterogeneity, economic system, political organization, and so forth). We need to be clear which of these aspects or components are most relevant to understanding hypothesized or observed urban-rural differences in particular attitudes or behavior. As the science of social structure, sociology has been surprisingly deficient in this area.

The proximity principle. Second, we must recognize that the effects of social structures, positions, or systems are transmitted to individuals through stimuli that impinge directly on the individual. Therefore, the effects on the individual of large complex structures, systems, or positions, generally must be understood in terms of how they affect the smaller structures and patterns of intimate interpersonal interaction or communication that constitute the *proximate* social experiences and stimuli in a person's life. Differences between age groups, for example, must reflect the differing cultural climates and social experiences to which they are exposed as a function of their different position in the life cycle and/or in the flow of human history (cohort experiences). Any effects of the size, density, or heterogeneity of cities on the person must be produced by the effect that the macro-social or ecological conditions have on the interactions of people with each other and on the stimuli and events they experience in their daily lives. Thus, a major theoretical task in the study of social structure and personality is to trace how macro-social structures and processes affect increasingly smaller social structures (for example, formal organizations) and ultimately those micro-social phenomena that directly impinge on the individual.

The psychological principle. Finally, we must understand individual psychology adequately so that we can specify and test when, how, and to what extent macro-social phenomena and the proximal micro-social phenomena and stimuli they produce (or influence) affect individual personality or behavior. Even if we understand how the characteristics of cities shape the intimate social interactions and stimuli people experience, we will not understand how this does or does not affect their behavior or attitudes unless we understand the psychological processes through which these interactions and stimuli are processed and responded to. Sociologists, based on misreadings of Durkheim (cf. above), have resisted use of psychological theories despite eloquent arguments for their relevance in understanding both individuals and social systems (for example, Inkeles, 1959, 1963; DiRenzo, 1977b). Without such psychological theories, however, we cannot adequately understand the relationship between social structure and personality.

Very simply, the analysis of social structure and personality requires that we understand the nature of social structure (really social systems) and of personality (really individual psychology), and of linkages between them (especially micro-social interaction and small group processes).

METHODOLOGICAL IMPLICATIONS

These conceptual-theoretical principles pose certain methodological issues in measurement and data analysis. We must make advances in the measurement of theoretically relevant aspects of both social structure and personality. We also must develop and use analytic methods for assessing (1) the extent to which the effects of more global or macro-social phenomena are mediated through more specific or micro-social phenomena; and (2) the ways in which the impact of social phenomena on the individual (or vice versa) are conditioned, moderated, or specified by the characteristics of the persons or situations involved (including the problem of "fit" between individuals and social structure). Recent developments in structural equation models (for example, path analyses) have greatly advanced analyses of mediating processes, as in the work Kohn discussed below (cf. Bielby and Hauser 1977, for an overview of these methodological advances). There remains, however, a need for greater attention to ways of conceptualizing and analyzing conditioning or moderating effects. These are statistical interactions and have tended to be neglected in the development of additive structural equation models (cf. Allison 1977 and Southwood 1978 for exceptions to this neglect).

Cultural versus Structural Explanations of Group Differences in Personality and Behavior

CONCEPTUAL DISTINCTIONS

Failure to follow the principles outlined above in both theory and research makes our understanding of the relationship between social structure and personality not only incomplete, but also faulty. We generally cannot, and should not, resist creating post hoc explanations for observed differences in psychological attributes or behavior between social or demographic groups. But such explanations are often formed without adequate consideration of alternative explanations and usually with no empirical evidence for or against the key components of the explanation. I would argue that psychological and sociocultural factors bias such post hoc (and even a priori) explanations in certain directions —particularly in the direction of the kind of cultural model illustrated in figure 17.1. Psychologically, we have a tendency to attribute the causes of behavior to the internal dispositions or personalities of actors (cf. Ross 1977). Similarly, we tend to see group differences in behavior (between nations, races, social classes, and so forth) as rooted in the different beliefs and values shared within each group, which are in turn generally seen to arise from the different ways people in these groups have been socialized from early in life (cf. Schuman 1969).

An alternative explanation of group differences in personality and behavior would emphasize the influence of more contemporaneous situational or structural contingencies and constraints in guiding behavior, and hence influencing personality. I would term this explanatory approach, *structural,* and argue that it has tended to be neglected in work on social structure and personality until recently. Thus, an important, if difficult and imprecise, distinction should be drawn between *culture* and *social structure* as basic aspects of social systems, and between *cultural* and *structural* explanations as basic modes for analyzing the relationship between social systems and individual personality or behavior. Exploration of these two explanatory modes also illustrates the use of the three principles developed in the preceding section.

Though the concepts of social system, culture, and social structure are not easily or clearly separated, and hence are often used loosely and interchangeably (including in this chapter to this point), it is important and worthwhile to distinguish among them for a number of purposes. A social *system,* or what Inkeles and Levinson (1969) term a sociocultural system, is a set of persons and social positions or roles that possess both a culture and a social structure. A *culture* is a set of cognitive and evaluative beliefs—beliefs about what is or what ought to be—that are shared by the members of a social system and transmitted to new members. A *social structure* is a *persisting* and bounded *pattern* of social relationships (or pattern of behavioral interaction) among the units (that is, persons or positions) in a social system. Culture and social structure are closely related—shared values and beliefs shape the definition of social positions and the relations between them (that is, the social structure), whereas the nature of actual social relationships, even if these are primarily responses to physical or biological imperatives, influences our values and beliefs. The correspondence between the two is, however, never perfect. We need to distinguish, therefore, both theoretically and empirically, between what members of a social system collectively believe and what they collectively do. Culture and social structure are generated and maintained by somewhat different forces and they influence individuals in somewhat different ways.

Culture and social structure are both abstractions from observed patterns of human behavior in social systems. However, they differ in their implications and inferences regarding these patterns. A recurring pattern of behavior, such as a religious ritual or the unequal distribution of power or income between workers and managers, is, by definition, an aspect of social structure. To say that such behavioral patterns are also indicative of the existence of culture is to assume that the behaviors are largely a product of, and consistent with, shared values and beliefs. One of the major differences between cultural and structural explanations is in how they account for, or explain, persisting patterns of overt behavior. A cultural explanation, such as the culture and personality model of figure 17.1, sees persisting patterns of social behavior as emanating from shared beliefs and values. A structural explanation, in contrast, need only assert that contemporaneous situational contingencies and constraints exist that motivate the behavior (cf. Bendix 1952). For example, the recurrent flow of people in our society into work organizations between 7:00 and 10:00 A.M. on Mondays could be explained by the combination of inducements for going to work and penalties for not working that are imposed in our society. This pattern of inducements and constraints might emanate from and largely reinforce a widely shared cultural value, but it might equally well emanate from the power that the owners and managers of business have to set work regulations.

A structural approach, however, must account not only for persisting patterns of social behavior, but also for the existence and persistence of shared cultural values and beliefs. A cultural approach, such as that of figure 17.1, explains this largely by the socialization of new members of the social system by older ones. Values and beliefs are transmitted rather directly (though not always consciously or intentionally) from agents of socialization to targets through mechanisms such as learning, identification, or internalization (cf. Kelman 1958). According to Freudian theory, for example, we learn the values of our culture by identifying with parents or others who hold these values and hence take these values as our own. In contrast, a structural approach sees values and beliefs as becoming internalized as a consequence of engaging in a pattern of behavior in response to external contingencies. The psychological literature on dissonance and self-perception (cf. Bem 1972) and symbolic interactionist analyses of the development of self-attitudes provide explanations for such effects. The persistence of values and beliefs can be explained structurally in terms of the persistence of external contingencies that directly shape behavior and indirectly influence values and beliefs.

Where a cultural approach emphasizes the importance of shared values and beliefs in determining socially patterned behavior, a structural approach emphasizes the influence that socially patterned behavior has on shared values and beliefs.

EXAMPLES OF THE DISTINCTION

The distinction being drawn here is hardly novel and has been observed in studies of socialization and of social structure and personality in social systems of varying sizes—from families to formal organizations, to social classes, to societies. Research on socialization within the family indicates that children are sometimes more influenced by the structure of the family (for example, size, birth order, sibling structure, and so forth) than by the values and beliefs that the parents or family share and try to transmit (cf. Gecas, chapter 6 in this volume). In looking at the child's relation to parents and other socializing agents, a structural approach emphasizes the *pattern* of the interpersonal relationship where a cultural approach focuses more on the *content* of the relationship (that is, the ideas and beliefs being communicated). Patterns of discipline (for example, physical punishment versus guilt induction versus reasoning), for example, have been shown to sometimes have greater effects on the child than the values, beliefs, or behavior the discipline is used to promote. Physically punishing children for aggressive behavior tends, paradoxically, to increase their aggressiveness (cf. Becker 1964).

Schools are often viewed as mechanisms for didactically transmitting culturally shared values and beliefs to the next generation. Inkeles (1978a) explains continuities in American national character in terms of this kind of cultural effect of the American public school system. As noted above, however, he interprets the impact of education on individual modernity in developing societies as a structural effect of the way schools are organized and function (Inkeles 1969, 1976, 1978b). Bowles and Gintis (1976) make a similar, but less sanguine, structural analysis of the impact of schools. In their view the American educational system functions, through its structure more than its explicit teachings, to produce a docile labor force for an exploitative, capitalist economic system:

> the educational system operates in this manner not so much through the conscious intentions of teachers and administrators in their day-to-day activities, but through a close correspondence between the social relationships which govern personal interaction in the work-place and the social relationships of the educational system [for example, hierarchical authority and power, use of extrinsic rewards]. [Bowles and Gintis 1976:12]

Research on status attainment demonstrates a quite stable pattern of inheritance of parental educational and occupational status by their offspring (Blau and Duncan 1967). The most common explanation of this phenomenon has been that children of lower socioeconomic status learn different values, skills, and orientations from their families and friends. More Marxian-oriented analysts, however, have noted that this pattern of status inheritance could equally well be explained by structural barriers that impede the educational and occupational achievements of persons from lower SES origins. Kerckhoff (1976) provides a good statement of these opposing viewpoints that closely parallels the cultural vs. structural distinction made here, though he labels them "socialization" versus "allocation": "Rather than differential attainment being seen as due to variations in learned motives and skills, as in a socialization model, an allocation model views attainment as due to the application of structural limitations and selection criteria" (p. 369). Kerckhoff aptly notes that "the two positions are not fully separable" and that evidence is lacking on their relative validity.

Finally, Inkeles's work reviewed above contrasts, if somewhat imperfectly, cultural versus structural explanations for intersocietal differences in modernity, and we will see the distinction recur again below in analyses of the impact of social class on personality. A final detailed example is offered here as a means for spelling out the cultural versus structural distinction and showing that it has important practical and policy implications.

A DETAILED EXAMPLE: CULTURAL VERSUS STRUCTURAL EXPLANATIONS OF POVERTY

A major scientific and policy debate of the 1960s and 1970s, as yet not fully resolved, focused on the importance of cultural versus structural explanations of the persistence of poverty, and the style of life and psychological outlook associated with it, in developed and developing countries. Advances in general economic growth and less dramatic but real, movement toward the equalization of socioeconomic opportunities seemed to be having little effect on the prevalence of poverty, especially in America's urban ghetto areas. One widely accepted explanation of these phenomena was essentially a variant of the cultural model in figure 17.1. An anthropologist, Oscar Lewis (1961, 1968), originated this theory of "the culture of poverty." Lewis argued (1968:7, 10–11) that the social structural conditions to which the poor are exposed ("chronic unemployment and under-employment, . . . low income, lack of property ownership, absence of savings . . . and chronic shortage . . . of food, money, medical care, and other necessities of life") give rise to distinctive patterns of community and family disorganization. These, in turn, produce a distinctive set of beliefs, attitudes, and values (that is, ". . . strong feelings of marginality, of helplessness, of dependence, and of inferiority . . . weak ego structure; confusion of sexual identification; lack of impulse control; strong present-time orientation, with relatively little ability to defer gratification and plan for the future").

To this point Lewis's analysis is largely structural, showing how individual and collective forms of behavior and belief arise in response to social structural conditions (cf. boxes *A* and *B* and arrow 1 of figure 17.1). However, like earlier students of culture and personality, he saw the key to understanding the persistence of the culture of poverty in familial and community patterns of child rearing:

The culture of poverty, however, is not only an adaptation to a set of objective conditions of the larger society. Once it comes into existence, *it tends to perpetuate itself from generation to generation because of its effect on the children.* By the time slum children are age six or seven they have usually absorbed the basic values and attitudes of their subculture and are not psychologically geared to take full advantage of the changing conditions or increased opportunities that may occur in their lifetime. [Lewis 1968:5–6, emphasis added]

The essential elements of Lewis's "(sub)cultural explanation" are embodied in the solid arrows of figure 17.2. Initially (time/generation 1) structural conditions of poverty give rise to subcultural patterns (that is, family and community disorganization), and both of these create in children and adults the patterns of individual personality and behavior characteristic of the poor (for example, "weak ego structure, inability to delay gratification"). For persons who first become poor as adults (for example, as a result of migration, economic depression, drought, and so forth), this personality and behavior pattern is an adaptation to changed structural conditions. However, their children know nothing else and tend to recreate the same subcultural patterns and to pass on these same personality and behavior patterns to their children. And so on for succeeding generations—a shared set of individual beliefs, values, and attitudes ("culture" of poverty) become self-perpetuating and may persist in spite of changes in the larger structural conditions.

Many anthropological and sociological analyses of the persistence of poverty, especially among the black urban poor (for example, Gladwin 1967; Frazier 1940) embodied the culture of poverty thesis, and it entered the arena of policy analysis in the "Moynihan report" (Moynihan 1965). However, empirical evidence for the theory was also widely questioned and criticized by other anthropologists and sociologists (for example, (Goodwin 1972; Hannerz 1969; Liebow 1967) who proposed an alternative structural explanation for the persisting patterns of sociocultural organization and individual personality and behavior observed among the black urban poor. They argued that new generations resemble preceding ones because they confront the same structural conditions and hardships. Early in life poor children generally share the values, beliefs, and attitudes of the larger society, but as they experience the same lack of socioeconomic opportunity as their parents, they adopt the peculiar social and individual modes of response that characterize the "culture" of poverty. This explanation is embodied in the dotted arrows at the upper

FIGURE 17.2

Cultural (→) vs. Structural (-->) Explanations of the Existence and Persistence of Distinctive Patterns of Individual Personality/Behavior across Social Groups or Systems

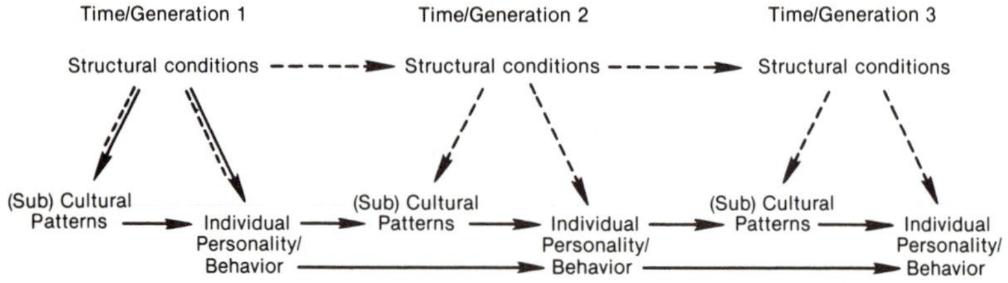

portion of figure 17.2. As long as a set of structural conditions persist, they will recreate the same sociocultural and personality patterns in each new generation. Liebow describes this process for the "street corner" society of the urban black poor:

> . . . the street corner man does not appear as a carrier of an independent cultural tradition. His behavior appears not so much as a way of realizing the distinctive goals and values of his own subculture, or of conforming to its models, but rather as his way of trying to achieve many of the goals and values of the larger society, of failing to do this, and of concealing his failure from others and from himself as best he can. . . . Many similarities between the lower-class Negro father and son (or mother and daughter) do not result from "cultural-transmission" but from the fact that the son goes out and independently experiences the same failures, in the same areas, and for much the same reasons as his father. What appears as a dynamic, self-sustaining cultural process is, in part at least, a relatively simple piece of social machinery which turns out, in rather mechanical fashion, independently produced look-alikes. [Liebow 1967:222–23]

THE COMPLEMENTARITY OF CULTURAL AND STRUCTURAL EXPLANATIONS

At this point we lack the necessary data to evaluate adequately the relative merits of cultural versus structural explanations of the persistence of poverty or of SES more generally, or of the impact of families, schools, organizations, and societies on their members. Most relationships between macro-social phenomena and individual personality or behavior involve both kinds of effects, as Hannerz (1969) cogently argues with respect to the "culture of poverty." Evidence regarding other phenomena noted above is consistent with this view. Caudill (1973:241 cited in Schooler 1976) highlights the importance of both recognizing the differences between cultural versus structural explanations and remembering their complementarity in most situations:

> Middle-class managerial personnel in England and France may have more in common than either group has with working-class machine operators in their own country. At the same time, however, I do not think anyone would say that such Englishmen and Frenchmen are indistinguishable in their approach to work, politics, family life, or sexual activity. They are different in those historically derived and culturally patterned ways of thinking, feeling, and behaving that are passed on, often unknowingly from one generation to the next. . . . I believe that each of these dimensions—position in modern social structure, and continuity of historical culture—exerts a relatively independent influence on human behavior, and that both dimensions need to be considered simultaneously in the investigation of the psychological characteristics of a people.

The cultural versus structural distinction is perhaps most important for sensitizing us to the fact that any macro-social phenomenon has multiple components, some cultural, some structural. These different components imply quite different types of proximal stimuli and interactions through which macro-social phenomena affect the individual. They often also suggest different psychological influence processes. Concern with this distinction in both theory and empirical research should, therefore, promote more adequate scientific analysis of social structure and personality. To the extent that cultural explanations have been, and perhaps always will be, somehow more attractive to us, attention to structural factors is especially needed for both scientific and practical purposes.[5] The next section of this chapter will review selected investigations of the relationship of social class and personality that provide instructive examples of how application of the three general principles (components, proximity, and psychological process) developed above can improve the theoretical quality and empirical validity of structural explanations.

Social Class and Personality: Specification of Components, Linkages, and Psychological Processes

Documenting the importance of *social class* in human life is sociology's most prominent, and perhaps most important, contribution to social science. As Melvin Kohn (1969:3) has noted:

> . . . one aspect of social structure, hierarchical position, is related to almost everything about men's lives—their political party preferences, their sexual behavior, their church membership, even their rates of ill health and death. Moreover, the correlations are not trivial; class is substantially related to all these phenomena.

But Kohn (1969:3) correctly goes on to note:

> These facts are abundant and beyond dispute. What is not at all clear, though, is why class has such widespread ramifications. How do these impressive and massive regularities come about? What specifically is it about "class" that makes it important for so much of human behavior?

Kohn has posed a central problem for students of social structure and personality, and he and his associates have made major contributions to understanding of this problem, especially in specifying components of social class and ways in which these components impinge on individuals, hence influencing their personalities. Their work thus illustrates the promise, as well as some problems, in the application of the first two general principles stated above (that is, the principles of components and proximity). This work is weakest in the area of psychological process, and we thus turn at the end of this section to an analysis by Rosenberg and Pearlin (1978) that illustrates the application of our third principle.

SPECIFYING HOW CLASS IMPINGES ON PEOPLE: THE WORK OF KOHN

Kohn has worked for over two decades with Leonard Pearlin and especially Carmi Schooler to understand the pervasive impact of social class on individual behavior and personality, most notably a syndrome of values and behaviors indicative of *self-direction* versus *conformity.* Because this work grew out of earlier work on social class and schizophrenia, parental values and behavior with regard to their children received particular attention. In several investigations, Kohn (1969) and his colleagues (Pearlin and Kohn 1966; Kohn and Schooler 1969, 1973) found persons in higher social classes (that is, with higher levels of occupation and/or education) consistently more likely than those in lower social classes to value self-direction and concern with internal psychological processes in dealing with children (versus valuing conformity and concern with external appearances). More generally, higher status persons displayed greater intellectual flexibility, were less authoritarian and more open to change, and generally felt more positively about themselves, their jobs, and the world in general.

These results were in many ways not new, being consistent with both earlier and later studies by others (cf. Wright and Wright 1976 and reviews of relevant literature in Kohn 1969, 1977, in press). What has been novel, exciting, and exemplary in Kohn's work is the attempt to show "that the class-values relationship can be interpreted as resulting from class-associated conditions of life, occupational conditions in particular" that people confront in their daily lives (Kohn 1977:xxxiv). That is, Kohn (1977:xlviii) expresses and illustrates the second of my three basic principles: "It is chiefly by shaping the everyday realities people must face that social structure exerts its psychological impact." His work ultimately also provides a good analysis of the concept of *class* and how it must be analyzed into its components to understand its impact on people's daily lives, though there is some confusion, particularly in his early work, on this issue.

The concept and components of class: from confusion to clarity. Kohn's initial work utilized a theoretically and empirically broad conception of social class, but his primary concern has always been with occupation and conditions of work. Kohn's early analyses and publications, like much sociological work of the time, utilized the Hollingshead (1954; Hollingshead and Redlich 1958) index of social class which divides people into five classes based on a weighted combination of occupation and education (with occupation given greater weight). Disaggregation of this index into its components of occupation and education, however, showed that each component had distinctive effects on attitudes and values (Kohn 1969:chapter 8; Wright and Wright 1976). Conditions of work, which were Kohn's focal interest, proved especially important in understanding the impact of occupation on values and attitudes, though they also explained some of the effect of education as well. Thus Kohn's work might better be described as an investigation of the impact of occupation and education, rather than class, on personality.

Kohn's experience illustrates a more general problem with the use of class and other structural concepts in sociology. Much has been written about the effects of class when the data documented only effects of education, occupation, or income. Aggregating such variables into an index of class tends to obscure rather than to clarify the matter. The term class has conceptual and operational meaning only in the context of a theory of class, of which Marx's is the most prominent. Occupation, education, and income are not measures of class in the Marxian sense; control of means of production and/or the labor power of others are (cf. Wright and

Perrone 1977 for appropriate efforts to operationalize Marxian class categories). I would concur with Kohn's (in press) retrospective assessment that occupation, education, and so forth should be considered "dimensions of stratification" and should not be aggregated into indices of class. Further, I would agree with him that the crucial issue is to recognize the complex nature of occupation or education itself and to carefully analyze the aspects or components of each that impinge on and hence affect individual attitudes and behavior.

Components of occupation and the proximate conditions of work. The all too prevalent tendency to utilize indices of occupational prestige or years of education as measures of *occupation* or *education* gives some merit to Blumer's caricature of "variable analysis." Kohn's most important contribution has been to stress that people's occupations define for them a whole set of social conditions and experiences, one of which is the experience of having a given level of prestige. But occupations also give people a position in the organization and economy (for example, owner versus manager versus worker); determine the kinds of things they do for much of each day; expose them to certain pressures, hazards, and uncertainties; provide them with income; and so forth. An index of occupational prestige is a poor or totally inappropriate measure of these other aspects of occupational structure, yet if occupation is scaled in more than a nominal way in research, it is almost always in terms of prestige. Prestige undoubtedly correlates with other occupational conditions and so appears to have a wide range of effects that, in fact, have nothing directly to do with prestige, as Kohn and his colleagues have shown.

They reasoned that values regarding self-direction and related issues would vary by occupational prestige, and to some extent by educational level as well, because occupational prestige and education are associated with people's exposure to occupational conditions which allow self-direction in work. What they hoped to show, and did show, is that (1) these conditions of occupational self-direction could be directly measured; (2) that they would have a strong impact on values regarding self-direction and related issues; and (3) that they would account for, or explain, the association of occupational prestige and education (or the Hollingshead class index) with values. Kohn (1969) developed a series of survey questions regarding three aspects of work that determine opportunities for self-direction: (1) closeness of supervision; (2) the routinization (or repetitiveness) of the work; and (3) the substantive complexity of work. These measures correlate about .80 with independent ratings of some of the same dimensions made for occupations in the *Dictionary of Occupational Titles.*

In his book (Kohn 1969) and a series of later papers (for example, Kohn and Schooler 1973, 1978; Miller et al. 1979), he and his colleagues have shown that among a wide range of occupational conditions, occupational self-direction is the strongest determinant of self-directed values for oneself and one's children and of other related psychological attributes. Further, these studies show that occupational self-direction accounts for almost all of the relation of occupational prestige to these values and for a substantial part (though less than half) of the impact of education on these values. Finally, analyses of complex structural equation models with both cross-sectional and longitudinal data confirm Kohn's a priori arguments (based on limitations of occupational choice, and so forth) that the causal flow is primarily from occupational conditions to values, though the relationship is reciprocal.

Kohn's work is particularly important because it shows that many so-called "class" differences in values and behavior have a structural rather than the cultural interpretation that is often implied in discussions of social class. He has found that the occupation and education of parents or siblings have very weak effects on values once the respondent's occupation and education are controlled, whereas the effects of current occupation are hardly diminished by controls for parental socioeconomic statuses. As Kohn and Schooler (1973:117) aptly conclude:[6]

> ... our findings bear on the issue of whether men similarly located in the structure of society come to share beliefs and values because they experience similar conditions of life or because of some interpersonal process of value-transmission. ... Our findings, emphasizing as they do the structural imperatives of the job and de-emphasizing the importance of interpersonal relatedness, support the argument of the structuralists. A man's job affects his perceptions, values, and thinking processes primarily because it confronts him with demands he must try to meet. These demands, in turn, are to a great extent determined by the job's location in the larger structures of the economy and the society.

Issues of psychological process: how, why, and when do occupational conditions affect people? Kohn's work leaves no doubt that specific structural imperatives of work have profound and pervasive influences on values and behavior. What he has not yet done, as he largely recognizes (Kohn 1977, in press), is to analyze with equal thoroughness the interpersonal and psychological processes through which occupational conditions come to affect values and behavior. He argues (Kohn, in press), much as Inkeles does in explaining the impact of factory experience on modernity, that "the simplest type of learning-generalization process is operating here—a direct translation of the lessons of the job to outside-the-job realities." This, however, only begs the important and interesting questions. We know that the average effects of job conditions are substantial but not overwhelming. This is partly because these values have nonoccupational as well as occupational determinants. It is likely, however, that the impact of occupational conditions of self-direction varies across individuals as a function of both the attributes people bring to their work and of other occupational conditions and interpersonal relations that characterize their life situation. Kohn and his colleagues (for example, Miller et al. 1979) have done only some exploratory analyses of such issues, but he recognizes the need for further work (Kohn, in press).

Several lines of inquiry strike me as especially promising here. First, a substantial body of research and theory in psychological social psychology—especially work on attribution, self-perception, and dissonance—suggests that behaviors in which an individual engages repeatedly are most likely to modify attitudes and values if the person perceives little or no external constraint or justification for his behavior (for example, Bem 1972). It is striking that the same organizational arrangements, which Goffman (1961) termed a "total institution" (involving great deprivation and behavioral control), appear to promote member identification and commitment with some organizations (for example, religious orders, utopian communities, elite military forces) while producing alienation and resistance in others (for example, prisons, conscripted military forces). The major difference in the two cases seems to be that the conditions of the total institution are submitted to voluntarily in one case, involuntarily in the other (cf. Kanter 1968; Sykes 1958). Volunteers are, of course, not only more ready to use their behavior as a basis for forming self-perceptions, they also are more likely to have undergone anticipatory socialization and to be receptive to persuasive communications. Though these effects are not perfectly analagous to those of occupational self-direction, it still seems likely that where individuals perceive their occupational conditions as resulting from their own choice, or at least as their own responsibility, they are more likely to "learn and generalize" from those conditions than if they perceive these conditions as having been imposed against their wishes and efforts.

Greater attention should also be paid to the interpersonal contexts and processes through which individuals experience their occupational conditions. Several aspects of workers' interpersonal relations are captured in Kohn's indices of closeness of supervision and complexity of work with people. However, there is much more that may be relevant. My own work on occupational stress (House 1980) within a factory found the effects of job characteristics on workers' perceptions of occupational rewards and pressures are quite modest (accounting for between 1.5 percent and 15 percent of the variance). This research also indicated that workers with positive, supportive relations with their supervisors and coworkers were generally less affected by job characteristics than workers who perceived their supervisor and coworkers as nonsupportive. Thus, interpersonal relations can modify the degree to which other occupational conditions affect individual personality and behavior. Workers may also have other occupational experiences that modify or compensate for the degree of self-direction in their particular job. Workers in non-self-directed jobs may, for example, participate in union activities or organizational decision making in ways not captured in Kohn's measures (cf. Pateman 1970).

SOCIAL CLASS AND SELF-ESTEEM: A FOCUS ON INTERPERSONAL AND PSYCHOLOGICAL PROCESSES

Rosenberg and Pearlin's (1978:72) study of the impact of social class on self-esteem among children and adults provides an excellent illustration of how principles from psychological social psychology and symbolic interactionism can and should be applied to understand how a social structural or demographic phenomenon "enters the individual's life, is converted into interpersonal experiences, is processed by a particular cognitive structure, and reflects the individual's relationship to his environment." Their work is strongest where Kohn's is weakest, and vice versa. Rosenberg and Pearlin started from the consistent empirical finding of Kohn (1969) and many others that social class, which on theoretical grounds should be positively related to self-esteem, manifests just such a relationship among adults whereas the relationship is weaker among adolescents and nonexistent among younger children.[7] They argue that this pattern occurs because "a social structural variable, such as social class, may signify a radically different set of social experiences and may be endowed with entirely different psychological meanings for individuals of unequal maturity" or who differ on other relevant social psychological factors (Rosenberg and Pearlin 1978:54).[8] Specifically, Rosenberg and Pearlin use four major ideas drawn from psychological social psychology and symbolic interactionism to explain why correlations between SES and self-esteem vary by age. Some of these are tested directly by further analyses of the data, while others are merely shown to be consistent with the observed age differences.

Social comparison processes. Rosenberg and Pearlin argue that SES affects self-esteem because, in line with Festinger's (1954) theory of social comparison processes, we evaluate ourselves in part by comparing our own SES with that of others, specifically other people we know or are aware of. They show that adults are much more likely than children to interact with persons from a wide range of SES levels and to perceive their relative superiority or inferiority. They also show that a substantial part of the total adult relationship between SES and self-esteem is a function of the differences people perceive between their own status and that of others. Since less than 10 percent of children perceive such differences, but this perception increases with age, they infer that invidious social comparison, or the lack thereof of at younger ages, offers a plausible explanation of the age differences in SES-self-esteem correlations.

Reflected appraisal. A major tenet of symbolic interactionism from Cooley and Mead onward is that we see ourselves as others see us. That is, people will see themselves as better or worse as a result of their SES because others communicate such judgments to them in more or less overt ways. Since the proportion of our interactions with status unequals increases with age, at least up to some point in early or middle adulthood, so does our opportunity to receive reflected appraisals regarding our relative superiority or inferiority in this regard. Rosenberg and Pearlin suggest this could also partially explain the increase with age in the correlation between SES and self-esteem, but again do not fully test this hypothesis.

Self-perception theory. Following Bem's self-perception theory, Rosenberg and Pearlin argue that we form our conception of ourselves by observing ourselves as others do. In line with more general theories of attribution, we are likely to attribute to ourselves traits and dispositions that would be consistent with our behavior and its consequences to the extent that we can find no external justification for this behavior and its consequences (cf. Bem 1972). Since the SES of adults is achieved while that of children is ascribed, adults are much more likely to draw inferences about their self-worth from their own SES. Children's self-esteem, in contrast, should be, and is, affected less by SES and more by achievements that are the child's own doing (for example, social, athletic, or academic accomplishments). Rosenberg and Pearlin do not directly test, however, whether the extent to which a person perceives their SES as a personal achievement affects the correlation between SES and self-esteem or explains the age differentials in this correlation.

Psychological centrality. Again, drawing on theorists of symbolic interaction and the self-concept, Rosenberg and Pearlin argue that the impact of particular SES dimensions on self-esteem will vary with the centrality or importance of those dimensions to the individual. Here they provide striking evidence to support this argument. Among adults, the relationship of income to self-esteem is quite strong ($\gamma = .52$) among those who "strongly agree" that "one of the most important things about a person is the amount of money he makes," moderate ($\gamma = .39$ and .37) among those who "agree or disagree somewhat," and weakest ($\gamma = .21$) among those (by far the largest group) who "disagree strongly." Similar though less striking results obtained for occupational prestige and self-esteem among adults. The same analyses could not be done for children. However, Rosenberg and Pearlin do show that young children (for example, eleven or under) tend to deny the existence of social classes, and if they do admit to a subjective class identification, it is unrelated to their parents' SES. Adolescents and adults are increasingly more likely to perceive the existence of social classes and to subjectively identify with a class commensurate with their SES. Rosenberg and Pearlin infer from this that children are much less likely than adults to make other positive or negative judgments about themselves on the basis of their SES.

Social structure and interpersonal or psychological process. The Rosenberg and Pearlin work is notable, and almost unique, in using explicit theories of interpersonal and psychological dynamics to construct and, in some cases, test explanations and predictions regarding the impact of structural phenomena (that is, dimensions of SES) on personality (that is, self-esteem). The logic of their analysis could be extended to any other relationship between SES and individual personality and behavior (for example, self-direction, autonomy, flexibility, class identifications and consciousness, political attitudes), and to the relation between other macro-social phenomena and personality. Appropriate formulation and testing of such propositions will not only improve our understanding of the relation of macro-social phenomena of individual personality and behavior, it will also test the generality of propositions that have largely been developed and tested in laboratory studies of college students or detailed observations of selected individuals.

The Impact of Personality on Social Structure: Actual and Potential

Reflecting the state of the literature, this chapter has focused up to this point on how social systems influence or modify individual personality and behavior. As both Inkeles (1963; Inkeles and Levinson 1969) and

Smelser and Smelser (1970) have noted, research and theory have more often considered the impact of social systems on individuals than the impact of individuals on social systems. This imbalance in the literature is probably a function of both social reality (in which causation actually flows more from social systems to individuals than vice versa) and some deterministic bias on the part of social scientists (Hampden-Turner 1974). Both Inkeles and Smelser and Smelser see two other major problems that a balanced analysis of social structure and personality must address—the impact of individuals on social systems and the effects of *fit,* and especially *misfit,* between personality and social structure. These topics have not been totally neglected in the literature, but they undoubtedly deserve greater attention in the future than they have received in the past.

Both psychology and sociology have increasingly recognized that people are active agents who process inputs from their social environments and respond in ways that are not totally predictable and that may modify the effects of the environment and even the nature of the environment itself. Individuals can alter the nature and effects of social structure in a number of ways. First, individuals select themselves into social structural positions. This self-selection poses difficult interpretive problems for researchers, such as Inkeles and Kohn, who wish to determine the impact of occupational roles on values. Persons high on self-direction or modernity will tend, where possible, to choose occupations compatible with these psychological attributes. Thus, it is not enough to document an association between occupational experience and values. One must, as Inkeles and Kohn attempt to do, design research and analyses to determine the relative impact of roles on personality versus the impact of personality on roles, yet do so without the benefits of experimental manipulation, randomization, and control.

THE NEGOTIATED NATURE OF SOCIAL LIFE

As symbolic interactionists have long emphasized, any social system is a *negotiated* order (cf. Maines 1977). That is, the opportunities, expectations, and demands that social structures pose for individuals are communicated and maintained through a complex interpersonal process in which individuals are active agents. Thus, people not only choose among social positions or roles, they attempt, in varying degrees, to make the social expectations and opportunities confronting them in any given role or position as compatible as possible with their needs, values, and abilities. The effect is often to make the actual or "informal" structure of social life quite different from the apparent or formal structure. Maines (1977) illustrates this process by reference to a series of studies showing that officially bureaucratic organizations often operate in very nonbureaucratic ways. Students of roles and organizations (for example, Blau 1955; Levinson 1959; Turner 1962) have similarly viewed the relation of social roles to personality and behavior as the product of a complex interplay between the characteristics of the person and the structurally given role demands. Aspects of this negotiating process have been studied primarily through qualitative methods, but they can and should be studied quantitatively as well.

A social role is defined by the expectations regarding behavior and even personality of the occupant of a social position held by others who interact with the role occupant. Weber's classic conceptualization of bureaucracy and modern extensions of it are essentially characterizations of the socially shared and communicated prescriptions and proscriptions regarding the behavior of individuals in bureaucratic organizations. To analyze the impact of bureaucracy on personality as Merton (1940) and Kohn (1971) have done is to analyze the effects of occupying a role in a bureaucratic organization.

Role expectations are communicated to individuals by role senders (cf. Katz and Kahn 1978:chapter 7), and the nature of the expectations communicated may vary greatly with different role senders. Even if all, or almost all, role senders for a role communicate the same expectations, such expectations allow varying degrees of latitude of response to the role occupant. Thus, an adequate analysis of the impact of a role on individuals will have to carefully delineate the expectations communicated by role senders and the degree to which these expectations vary across role senders. The larger the number of people occupying a role, the greater the likely variability in the nature of *communicated* expectations. That is, the expectations for a biology teacher in school *X* are likely to be more explicit and consistent across relevant role senders than the expectations for a biology teacher or just a "teacher."

Even where role expectations are strong and explicit, we still find that individual role occupants are able to negotiate definitions of their role that are contrary to, or go well beyond, the expectations held for them by others. Thus, Sykes (1958) shows that even prisoners are able to negotiate the nature of their roles with their captors, and Blau (1955) finds that the social structure of highly bureaucratized government agencies is constantly being modified by informal communication and exchange processes among the members of the organization. Where role expectations and sanctions are less clear and consistent, the opportunity for individuals to influence the nature of their roles becomes even greater. Greenstein (1967) provides a very useful statement of the conditions under which personality is more or less likely to influence political behavior and role performance, and his ideas easily generalize to other social behavior and roles.

Whenever an individual modifies the nature of the expectations or behavior associated with a role, he or she is modifying an aspect of social structure. Such negotiation of social structure is an endemic feature of social life, but its effects on larger patterns of social structure are usually small. However, under certain circumstances, we may observe more profound effects of individuals on social structure. If the role in question is one that has great power, the renegotiation of the nature of that role by a single occupant may have a pervasive impact on the future nature of that role and on many other aspects of social structure. The roles occupied by political elites are of just this sort. Thus, students of personality and politics from the time of Harold Lasswell (1930) have been concerned with how the personalities of political leaders affect their enactment of their roles, and hence the very nature of those roles, and of many other aspects of the political or social system (cf. Greenstein 1967; Terhune 1970; DiRenzo 1977b for reviews of relevant literature). Franklin D. Roosevelt's performance as president, for example, changed the nature of the role of the presidency and of the federal government in American political and economic life. It is difficult to clearly separate how many of these effects should be attributed to Roosevelt's personality and style and how many to the demands and expectations on the president in a time of national crisis. Nevertheless, this has been and will continue to be a fertile area for understanding the impact of personality on social structure.

A large number of individuals occupying the same role may collectively exert a strong effect on social structure, even if none of them individually is especially powerful. Sykes's (1958) analysis of a maximum security prison suggested that the prisoners collectively were able to effect substantial changes in the structure of life in the prison, and that the guards and prison administration collectively acquiesced in these changes. Thus, many of the more annoying formal rules of the prison were not enforced, and prisoners were allowed to exercise substantial authority in conducting their own affairs, as long as they did not challenge the fundamental structure of the prison (for example, try to escape or totally overthrow the prison authority).

The negotiation and renegotiation of the nature of social roles and social structure is a universal phenomenon of social life. Often, however, individuals cannot accommodate themselves to social structures through such a process of peaceful negotiation (or role selection). A state of persistent, consequential, and often increasing incongruence or lack of fit between individual personality and the opportunities and requirements of the social structure comes to exist. Such incongruities have been variously termed *alienation* by Marx, *anomie* by Durkheim, and more recently *social stress* (cf. Lukes 1967; Levine and Scotch 1970). These incongruities produce a state of tension on individuals, the consequences of which may affect both the individual and the social order.

Work on stress and anomie, at least since the time of Durkheim, has tended to emphasize the deleterious individual consequences of such states of incongruity, including decreased physical and mental health (House 1974; Levine and Scotch 1970), deviant behavior, and suicide or homicide (for example, Durkheim 1951; House 1980; Levine and Scotch 1970). These consequences are individual in the sense that they represent individuals' responses to the incongruence between their needs and abilities and the opportunities and demands posed by their social environments. Which responses are chosen by which individuals is determined both by their personalities and the social structures in which they are enmeshed (cf. above references).

The aggregation of a series of such individual responses can constitute a social problem—high rates of crime or of mortality, morbidity and/or disability from mental or physical disorders. The social response to such problems can be to alter the social environment so as to make it more compatible with individual needs and abilities; to alter individuals to make them more compatible with the social order and/or better able to tolerate and cope with incongruence; or to try to better match individuals with environments compatible with their needs. Both Etzioni (1968) and Inkeles (1963; Inkeles and Levinson 1969) have noted that one social consequence of high levels of incongruence between individuals and the social order is the need to expend a greater share of collective resources on processes of socialization and social control.

In contrast to the traditions of research on stress and anomie, research on alienation, reflecting the seminal contributions of Marx, has focused more on the role of incongruence between individuals and social systems in generating collective action for social change, though alienation has also been viewed by Marx and later writers as deleterious to individual well-being (cf. Fromm 1961). Marx and later Marxians saw the alienated state of human existence under capitalism as a major factor in generating a proletarian revolutionary movement. More recent analysts of social and political conflict have also viewed alienation as predisposing people toward participation in collective behavior and social movements directed at changing the status quo (cf. Gamson 1968). Participation in such collective action can be viewed as an alternative to the more individualistic forms of response to incongruence between individuals and their social environment (Solomon et al. 1965) and constitutes a major path through which personality affects social structure.

However, recent analyses of collective behavior and social movements have also emphasized that alienation or other forms of incongruence between the individual and social system are not sufficient or even necessary conditions for the emergence of collective action or individual participation in it (cf. Marx and Wood 1975). Rather, such incongruence merely creates a predispostion toward collective action. Whether that predisposition is converted into behavior depends on a range of other individual and social factors. The same point can be, and has been, made with respect to the relation between stress or anomie and mental or physical health, crime, and so forth. From Durkheim (1951) to more recent analyses of social support (for example, Cassel 1976), supportive social relationships have been known to protect people against the deleterious effects of stress.

Incongruence involves statistical interactions between individuals and social environments. Further, to say that these effects are conditional upon other individual and social factors is to specify a set of second-order interactions. As noted above, too little attention has been paid to statistical interaction in sociological analysis, and recent methodological developments have tended to worsen rather than improve this situation. Recognizing and dealing adequately in both theory and methods with conditional or interactive effects is a major challenge for future research on social structure and personality.

Conclusion

Over the course of this century, the study of social structure and personality has evolved from a fairly exclusive emphasis on the relationship between holistic conceptions of both society and personality, often termed culture and personality or national character research, toward a broad concern with the relation of a wide range of specific macro-social phenomena to a varied array of psychological attributes of individuals. This evolution means that the study of social structure and personality is no longer a field with a singular substantive focus. To some, this may signal a dissipation of this as an area of research and theory.

I would argue, however, that work and workers in the area of social structure and personality are developing, and increasingly should develop, a new integrative focus on theoretical and methodological principles for understanding the impact of macro-social phenomena on the individual. This chapter has suggested three such basic principles: (1) that we delineate the *components* of complex macrosocial phenomena; (2) that we specify the *proximate* social stimuli and interactions through which such phenomena, and components thereof, impinge on individuals; and (3) that we attend to the *psychological processes* through which individuals perceive and respond to these proximate social stimuli. I have tried to illustrate the application of these principles by developing a distinction between two broad models for understanding the relationship between social systems and individuals, cultural versus structural, and by intensively reviewing several areas of research, most notably the impact of modernization and of socioeconomic status on personality. As indicated at the outset, these research areas were selected as illustrations. They do not purport to exhaust the domain of study of concern to students of social structure and personality.

Finally, this chapter has noted that not only does social structure affect personality, but personality may alter social structure. More attention has been focused on the former than the latter type of effect—an imbalance that it is to be hoped will be redressed to some extent in future work. The relation between social structure and personality, properly understood, will undoubtedly prove in most cases to be reciprocal. In all cases, however, such understanding will come from an integration of knowledge of macro-social structure and process, micro-social interaction, and individual psychology. Thus, the study of social structure and personality is the study of social psychology par excellence, and I would hope it will increasingly serve as a meeting ground for those concerned with maintaining a truly broad and interdisciplinary field of social psychology.

NOTES

Alex Inkeles, Gordon DiRenzo, Daniel Katz, Alan Kerckhoff, Melvin Kohn, Morris Rosenberg, and Howard Schuman provided thoughtful and constructive critiques of an earlier draft, and Howard Schuman waded through a revised draft as well. Marie Klatt shepherded the manuscript through several versions. I am grateful for their contributions.

1. Consistent with this view is the definition of personality offered by a major advanced text of the late 1960s (Janis et al. 1969:xxiii–xxiv):

> The major components of personality, according to most psychologists, are those characteristics that most directly affect a person's adjustment to his environment—including his motives, emotions, abilities, and skills in getting along with others. Beyond such a very general definition, however, one encounters disagreement. For as Nevitt Sanford has noted, the leading psychologists in this field do not agree about "what the elements of personality are, how they are organized, what the boundaries of personality are, and how personality interacts with other (psychological) phenomena." [Sanford 1968:587]

A similar argument could be made with respect to conceptions of the self or self-concept among both psychologists and sociologists. The self has largely become a generic label for a variety of persisting attitudes of the person toward him- or herself.

2. Parson's central concern was the old Hobbesian problem of order. In the convergence of the thought of Emile Durkheim, Sigmund Freud, Charles Horton Cooley, and George Herbert Mead upon the concept of *"internalization* (becoming a constitutive part of the structure of personality) of aspects of the normative culture of society in which the individual grows up," Parsons (1964:81) found an explanation for how the behavior of many individuals came to constitute a stable social order.

3. Milgram (1961) creatively used laboratory experiments to assess cross-national differences in personality. Unfortunately his initial efforts were never systematically pursued or developed. This approach gives up the sampling virtues of surveys, but gains the ability to observe actual behavior, even if in a contrived situation. Otherwise, it largely showed the strengths and weaknesses of the survey approach described below.

4. I do not wish to get embroiled in controversies regarding two aspects of Inkeles's and other related work which are not central to my purposes. First is the use of the term *modernization,* which is viewed by many as connoting a superiority of modern over traditional. The structural transformation of society in which Inkeles is interested might preferably be termed development (or industrialization, urbanization, and bureaucratization). The term modernization is used here only because it is the label Inkeles generally uses (though he also refers to development, industrialization, and so forth). Second, many people interpret Inkeles as arguing that "psychological modernity" is a major determinant of modernization. In fact, his argument is quite the opposite—modernization, which is to be explained and understood in social, political, and economic terms, is the major determinant of modernity (cf. Inkeles 1976). There is, of course, some reciprocal causation going on here, as with many relationships of social structure to personality, but the impact of social structure on personality is generally greater than the reverse. Even critics of Inkeles's work in these regards, concur with his basic analysis of the effect of "modern" social institutions on individual attitudes and behavior (cf. Portes 1973).

5. Although I have argued that too often we jump to cultural explanations and fail to test and consider structural ones, there are cases where what seem to be largely structural phenomena turn out to be primarily cultural. This seems to be true for identification with both moderate and radical political parties. Although conventional wisdom and early research in political social psychology (for example, Lazarsfeld et al. 1948) suggested that people's partisan loyalties developed largely out of their social structural position, especially their socioeconomic status, more recent research suggests that early and later political socialization may be equally or more important in shaping party identification with both major parties in the United States (cf. Campbell et al. 1960; Goldberger 1965; Jennings and Niemi 1974) and radical parties in Chile (cf. Portes 1971b). That is, party identification is both a response to one's structural position and a cultural value or belief that is directly transmitted by family, friends, neighbors, and coworkers.

6. It should be emphasized that the most recent work of Kohn and Schooler (1978) shows that the individuals' prior values and beliefs affect the structural degree of self-direction to which they are exposed and vice versa, though the effects of the structure on the person are consistently greater.

7. Rosenberg and Pearlin use the term *social class* rather loosely. They are really referring to dimensions of socioeconomic status (SES), specifically educa-

tion, occupation, and income (cf. above discussions of social class in relation to Kohn's work). For the most part, they are interested in the prestige dimension of these variables rather than the kinds of dimensions on which Kohn has focused. Interestingly Kohn (1969:184–85) finds that occupational self-direction can largely interpret the relation between social class and self-esteem in adults. It still seems more plausible to see prestige as the most important dimension for interpreting relations of SES to self-esteem.

8. It should be emphasized that social class is not really the same thing for children and adults. In the case of children, Rosenberg and Pearlin look at the effects of parental SES on a child's self-esteem, whereas with adults they are looking at the effects of the respondent's own SES on his/her self-esteem. They discuss this difference in various ways (for example, in noting that adult status is achieved whereas children's status is ascribed). Their major arguments, however, hold across age levels within children and across differences on other social-psychological factors within adults. Thus, their findings are not merely an artifact of the difference between effects of own versus others' SES.

The Sociology of Sentiments and Emotion

Introduction

Love, shame, gratitude, contempt, jealousy, and other affective states are experienced frequently and vividly in everyday social life. These states often include a psychic excitement expressed through bodily gestures, and, therefore, may seem to be too private and psychological to bear much relevance for sociology or to be amenable to sociological analysis. The sociological perspective allows us, however, to demonstrate how seemingly individual behavior and experience are shaped by social forces. Although each person's experience of emotion has idiosyncratic features, culture shapes the occasion, meaning, and expression of affective experience. Love, pity, indignation, and other sentiments are socially shared patterns of feeling, gesture, and meaning.

Although sociologists have neglected emotion as a generic dimension of social life, there are important studies of social factors, in particular affective experiences, such as faithfulness and gratitude (Simmel 1950), resentment (Scheler 1961), jealousy (Davis 1936), embarrassment (Goffman 1956), shame (Lynd 1958), love (Goode 1959; Swanson 1965), humor (Coser 1959), and envy (Schoek 1966). Sociologists have shown increased interest recently in developing a comprehensive theory of the social processes common to these diverse emotional experiences (Hochschild 1975a, 1979; Kemper 1978b; Heise 1979; Scheff 1979; Shott 1979). These works proceed from divergent theoretical orientations. The largely incompatible assumptions of the psychodynamic perspective, reinforcement-exchange theory, and symbolic interactionism preclude any synthesis of their insights. Although I will discuss most of these works, space limitations prohibit any treatment that would do justice to the heuristic importance of the original sources, which I recommend strongly.

This chapter begins with a discussion of socially emergent properties of emotion that transcend psychological or physiological explanation. I then distinguish *emotion* as relatively undifferentiated bodily arousal, from *sentiments* as combinations of bodily sensations, gestures, and cultural meanings that we learn in enduring social relationships. Thus, fear is a simple animal emotion, but embarrassment, dread, and hatred are socially distinguished sentiments into which aspects of fear may enter. The greater part of the chapter examines three fundamental social processes that influence all sentiments and are crucial topics for sociological investigation. The first process is differentiation, the establishment and maintenance of qualitative distinctions among sentiments. Differences in feeling, action, and meaning among sorrow, guilt, and love are socially created. Next I examine the socialization of sentiments, the process by which a cultural vocabulary of sentiments becomes an interpretive resource of individuals. Then I consider the management of sentiments, the normative regulation of expression and feeling by individuals and groups.

SOCIALLY EMERGENT DIMENSIONS OF EMOTION

Social life produces emergent dimensions of emotion that resist reduction to properties inherent in the human organism. The social significance of emotion lies in these emergent dimensions, which are explicable only in relation to other social phenomena. I contend that socially emergent dimensions of emotion transcend psychological and physiological levels of analysis in terms of (1) origin, (2) temporal framework, (3) structure, and (4) change.

Origin. Guilt, pity, awe, and other sentiments originate in social relationships, not in the nature of the human organism. Most of the experiences that we usually attribute to human emotional nature are socially constructed. Emotion is merely sensual feeling, Charles Cooley asserted (1962:177), but is refined by communication and sympathetic imagination in primary-group relationships. He continued, "Thus love is a sentiment, while lust is not; resentment is, but not rage; the fear of disgrace or ridicule is, but not animal terror." In contrast to this view, many psychologists locate the origins of emotions in innate response patterns inherent in the human organism. Such models view social factors as merely activating or suppressing the already fixed emotional structures and processes. A psychoanalytic model posits unconscious dynamics among id, ego, and superego in which affect is blocked or discharged by social channels, for example. Such closed-system models make assumptions that may be unnecessary and unjustified for a sociological analysis of emotion, and tend to confine our search for social factors in emotion to whatever stimuli activate or inhibit the fixed organismic system (Allport 1960).

An "open system" approach such as I propose makes the social emergence of sentiments a salient problem for sociological investigation. This approach minimizes assumptions about any fixed, innate emotional structure. We study instead how shame, for example, originates through the organizing influence of social processes upon arousal sensations, bodily gestures, and other emotional elements. If similar sentiments are found in different societies, their origin should be sought in similarities among social relationships, rather than in innate human nature. Gratitude, for example, supplements exchange and reciprocity relationships everywhere, Simmel argued (1950:387), as a powerful means of social cohesion that effects the return of a benefit.

Temporal framework. A second socially emergent dimension of affect is the prolonged time span of love, hatred, resentment, and most other sentiments. In enduring social relationships, previous interactions and anticipations of the relationship's future course influence feeling. These social affects transcend the single situation, while rage, surprise, or terror are confined to the duration of intense arousal and its transient stimulus. In contrast, a feeling like love or hatred reflects the developing properties of the social relationship over time. The significant sociological problem here is how changes in the social relationships are linked with shifts in the associated feelings.

Structure. A third emergent property is that the structural coherence of feeling, gesture, meaning, and occasion for jealousy or indignation is maintained by social, not psychological, forces. The structure or pattern of jealousy, for example, is socially constructed and meaningful, like a social fact in Durkheim's schema. A social fact bears a stable relationship only to other social facts, but its association with psychological factors is usually fortuitous and impermanent (Turner 1969). As a socially recognized pattern of action and meaning, jealousy can be accompanied by diverse psychological dynamics and motives across individuals. One person may be mainly angry at the rival, another person may fear losing his partner, while yet another's jealousy has to be prompted by pressure from concerned friends. The structural coherence of jealousy does not derive from these diverse psychological factors, but from social forces, such as how people respond to expressions of jealousy and how the course and meaning of jealousy are socially defined (see Davis 1936; Clanton and Smith 1977).

Sociologists should study the emergence of a shared pattern of action and meaning out of previously disparate feelings and motives across individuals. Georg Simmel (1950) made an exemplary analysis of the assimilation of psychological diversity into a shared affective pattern. He argued that faithfulness to a relationship gradually supplements the psychic forces that originally brought the relationship about. These initial feelings and motives gradually weaken, but "in spite of all variety of origin, the original psychic states attain, in the form of faithfulness, a certain similarity" (Simmel 1950:381). Even a relationship begun for extrinsic reasons "develops its own faithfulness which, in turn, gives rise to deeper and more adequate feeling states" (Simmel 1950:382).

Change. A fourth socially emergent dimension of emotion is the modifiability of feeling, expression, and meaning in response to social interaction and cultural norms and beliefs. Love, guilt, and compassion are not fixed in innate human nature. Instead, we identify and act upon them in terms of social events, relationships, and values. Psychologists usually conceive of emotion as acting through the person, motivating and directing his behavior and experiences. I suggest that the activation process works mainly in the opposite direction, from consciousness and ongoing action toward feeling and gesture. The social person is sentient, reflecting upon feelings and sometimes changing feelings and how they are interpreted. For example, we may summon up feelings of love, or strive to diminish their intensity. We can also try to mobilize love in another person, directing our gestures to shape their feelings. On a larger, historical scale, love and other sentiments change in how they are expressed, where they are appropriate, and what they mean culturally. These social levels of change in feeling and expression are irreducibly independent from the physiological dynamics of emotion, and are an appropriate and important subject for sociological explanation.

These socially emergent dimensions of origin, temporal framework, structure, and change are not embraced within the concept of emotion as it is used in psychology. In the following section I offer a possible resolution to this conceptual impasse.

SENTIMENTS AND EMOTION

An analytical distinction between emotion and sentiments emphasizes the difference between the psychological and sociological levels of analysis. Consider this representative psychological definition of emotion:

> a complex state of the organism, involving bodily changes of a widespread character . . . and on the mental side, a state of excitement or perturbation, marked by strong feeling, and usually an impulse towards a definite form of behavior. [Drever 1952:80, cited by Strongman 1978:1]

A sociological analysis conflicts with this definition. Grief, love, envy, and hatred are social rather than organic states, and persist beyond the duration of bodily changes. Their mental side is far more complex and differentiated than mere excitement. The behaviors through which grief or love can be expressed are many and varied.

The concept of emotion has a long tradition within philosophy and psychology (see reviews by Gardiner et al. 1937; Hillman 1960; Solomon 1977; Candland 1977). The sociological utility of the concept is diminished not only by its omission of social factors, but also by superfluous connotations that James Averill (1974) called "extraneous psychophysiological symbolism." The concept of "emotion" suggests psychic turmoil and irrationality overwhelming the individual, who reacts to environmental threats or obstacles with reflex-like movements that basically resemble an animal's terror, surprise, or rage.

I recommend "sentiment" as a basic sociological concept for analyzing the socially constructed linkage of bodily sensations and gestures with social relationships and cultural meanings. Sentiment includes bodily and cognitive elements, but is not confined to the psychological level of analysis. The sentiment concept has been used by previous theorists, whose definitions converge on several points. Sentiments organize and integrate the "primary emotions" around objects of action (Shand 1914; McDougall 1920). Sentiments mobilize affect for social objects (Parsons

1949; Davis 1949), and serve as themes for complex and extended actions toward those objects (Asch 1952). Sentiments are "those finer modes of feeling, those intricate branchings or differentiations of the primitive trunk of emotion," wrote Charles Cooley (1964:115). A sentiment is an organized disposition to act toward a personification upon which some type of evaluation is placed (Shibutani 1961:232). A sentiment is a socially defined complex of feeling that indicates a characteristic relationship to a social object and is accompanied by tendencies to behave in the socially appropriate manner (Turner 1970:225).

I define a sentiment as a socially constructed pattern of sensations, expressive gestures, and cultural meanings organized around a relationship to a social object, usually another person. (I will discuss each of these components below). Most of a culture's vocabulary of named affective states are sentiments rather than emotions. Sentiments develop around social attachments, such as parental love, romantic love, friendship, and loyalty. Grief, sorrow, and nostalgia reflect social losses. Compassion and pity are sentiments based on empathy, whereas jealousy and envy reflect notions of possession. Moral sentiments that we feel when judging others include indignation, resentment, and contempt, but also gratitude and pride. Our reactions to how others judge us include shame, guilt, and embarrassment. Patriotism and religious reverence are sentiments for social institutions. Humor, impatience, and enthusiasm are relatively transient sentiments, but are learned socially and are expressed within more enduring relationships to which they contribute meaning. The comprehensive vocabulary of a culture's sentiments will be discussed below.

The socially emergent dimensions of affect and the different qualities of feeling and action that the sentiment concept emphasizes are far more important than whether sociology adopts the specific term *sentiment* to analyze these topics. I will recommend and use the concept, however, in discussing the differentiation, socialization, and management of socially significant feelings, actions, and meanings. An analogous use of such a sensitizing concept was C. Wright Mills's distinction (1940) between motives as socially meaningful explanations of behavior, and motivation as a psychic source of subjective "springs of action" that initiate behavior. (I believe, however, that Mills's analysis, which I discuss below, is somewhat confusing because motive and motivation are so similar linguistically). My definition of sentiment is generally consistent with previous conceptualizations, but some disagreements should be underscored. I reject any linkage of sentiments with instincts, as made by William McDougall (1920) and Vilfredo Pareto (1935). In spite of recent interest in sociobiology, there is little evidence for instinctive determination of behavior in love, hatred, or other sentiments.

I do not rely on George Homans's conceptualization of sentiment variously as internal bodily states (emotions, drives, even thirst or hunger), or as observable behavior expressing feelings, or as a unidimensional continuum of liking-disliking. The first view (Homans 1950:37) is too broad, the second too narrow (Homans 1961:33), and the third omits significant qualitative differences among sentiments, as between liking and loving (see Rubin 1973).

I also reject the reductionist view that sentiments are combinations or derivations of discrete, "basic" emotions (Shand 1914; McDougall 1920), a view also held by some psychologists studying emotion (Plutchik 1962, 1980; Izard 1971, 1977). To argue, as Freud did (1922), that jealousy is a mixture of love, grief, anger, and narcissism may help our intuitive understanding of the sentiment, but does not serve to explain its origin, timing, structure, or change. To speak of "basic" or "fundamental" emotions is a fallacy of misplaced concreteness. As I will argue later in the chapter, psychological evidence suggests that internal sensations, facial expressions, bodily gestures, and emotional experience seem to be relatively independent dimensions. These levels are not sufficiently correlated as to constitute discrete, fundamental emotions with much reductionist explanatory power for analyzing purportedly composite or derived sentiments.

Human capacities for emotional arousal and expression are differentiated socially as sentiments, but much less so innately. Use of the singular form, "emotion," is empirically justified, at least for sociological analyses. Rage, terror, and surprise are sometimes identified as relatively unsocialized emotions that human beings share universally and with animals. I doubt if even these appear in an unsocialized form. For example, even in collective fury or panic, participants' feelings and actions are guided by social interpretations of the situation (Blumer 1946; Turner and Killian 1972:12–25).

Every sentiment is a different socially constructed combination of somatic, expressive, and cultural elements. I will now discuss each of a sentiment's components: relationship to a person, bodily sensations, expressive gestures and signs, and ideological and evaluative beliefs about the sentiment.

RELATIONSHIP TO A PERSON

Every sentiment is organized around a relationship to a social object, usually another person or a group such as a family. We associate a sentiment closely with particular persons or groups. If we try to recall love, pity, or other sentiments, Cooley argued (1964:118), we usually think of people by whom or toward whom these sentiments have been felt. We feel shame, pride, guilt, or embarrassment toward our selves as social objects when we imagine how other people judge our appearance to them (Cooley 1962; Mead 1934). A sentiment may develop around a nonhuman object, such as love for a pet or reverence for a deity, but the object is usually personified with human qualities.

A sentiment establishes a framework of meaning within which specific events, gestures, and sensations can be given a social interpretation. A sentiment is identified through an organization of responses toward a person, not through particular acts viewed separately. For example, a sentiment may be detected by others even when the individual does not acknowledge his feelings. One may deny being in love with a person, but may be imputed the love sentiment by observers who detect a pattern of protection and preoccupation with another person. To use an example from Alexander Shand (1914), we believe that we have detected a man's love for a woman when he demonstrates joy in her presence, sorrow in her prolonged absence, fear when there is danger of losing her, and anger when she is criticized. The characteristic organization of hatred includes being sorry over the enemy's good fortune, feeling anger at his very presence, being happy at his misfortune, and sensing anxiety over his possible successes (Shibutani 1961:347). We interpret, justify, and anticipate acts and feelings in relation to the sentiment's overall pattern.

A sentiment sustains a relationship as an enduring, latent tendency to respond emotionally and overtly toward another person when the opportunity is given. Situational constraints often inhibit direct expression. One factor is our view of what the relationship means to the other person. Sentiments differ in the importance of reciprocal feeling. Reciprocation of hatred will magnify animosity. Failure by the other to reciprocate romantic love may simply heighten the lover's passion as much as reciprocation. The other person may validate a sentiment with an appropriate but different pattern of gesture and feeling, such as showing gratitude for my kindness. The meaning of a sentiment depends on how the other responds to it.

We become highly aware of a sentiment when a controversial discrepancy arises. A single salient act can seem to contradict the whole pattern. Stealing from a loved one, helping an enemy, or cursing a deity are acts that call the sentiment into question. Most acts within a relationship, however, are assimilated into a sentiment and are anticipated and assessed as reflecting its meaning.

BODILY SENSATIONS

Bodily sensations are an intermittent phase of every enduring sentiment. Arousal is more frequent and intense in passionate sentiments, such as romantic love, jealousy, and awe, than in others like kindness, loyalty, and gratitude. These visceral and muscular sensations are essentially autonomic arousal symptoms associated with the flow of adrenaline: heart palpitations, accelerated breathing, flushes, and tremor. However, they may be experienced simply as diffuse, generalized excitement. Arousal does not persist unabated, even in passionate sentiments, but arises intermittently.

Bodily sensations do not define the nature of the sentiment. There are no explicit patterns of arousal that correspond to different sentiments. Instead, we interpret our sensations in terms of the encompassing relationship. A feeling of excitement can be interpreted as indicating the continued vitality of a sentiment, whether love or hatred. We express sentiments more spontaneously when we are aroused. Of course, we feel bodily sensations of various types much of the time, and many of these —dizziness, fatigue, hunger, aches—have nothing to do with social relationships. We are socialized to attend selectively to our own sensations, however, and to sometimes attribute them a social meaning in terms of the course of interaction with another person.

GESTURES AND SIGNS

A sentiment is expressed situationally through a person's conventional gestures, such as kissing, and overt, involuntary bodily signs of arousal, such as trembling. A review of cross-cultural differences in gestures such as hand movements, laughter, crying, and posturing concluded that "there is no natural language of emotional gesture" (LaBarre 1947:55). For facial expressions of emotion, however, there is evidence that anger, disgust, fear, and several other emotions may be expressed and recognized similarly across very diverse cultures (see review by Ekman and Oster 1979). These researchers admit however that in social situations, any natural, innate facial emotion is "masked" beneath culturally conventional expressions.

We interpret a conventional gesture, such as a smile, in terms of situational factors, previous interactions with a person, subtle details in expressive style, and other social criteria. Darwin's (1872) generalization from innate animal expressions to human expressions was criticized by George Herbert Mead (1964:129), who argued that animals do not undertake to express their emotions, but humans do. Human gestures are parts of social communication that become significant symbols when they arouse the same meaning in the observer as in the expressing person. We indicate to ourselves the meaning of our own gestures in terms of the perspective of the other person and shape our gestures according to the meaning we intend them to have. As I will argue below, gestures become meaningful when interpreted as sentiments, which serve as significant categories or symbols held in common by group members.

IDEOLOGICAL AND EVALUATIVE BELIEFS

A fourth component includes ideological and evaluative beliefs about a sentiment, as part of a cultural vocabulary of sentiments. We do not simply feel and express a sentiment, but also interpret, socialize, evaluate, and modify it according to our beliefs and assumptions about it.

Previous theorists have discussed affective vocabularies (Gerth and Mills 1953; Burke 1954; H. Geertz 1959; Levy 1973; Hochschild 1975a), usually guided by C. Wright Mills's work (1940) on motive vocabularies as sets of socially acceptable explanations for our actions. Although Mills emphasized explanations that satisfy other people, a sentiment vocabulary also provides culturally meaningful categories for interpreting one's own sensations and behavior. Sentiments are explanations in self-perception, as well as for other people. A vocabulary of sentiments facilitates and limits the kinds of meanings we can experience for our sensations, gestures, and social relationships.

A vocabulary of sentiments is a selection from the entire potential range of emotional experiences by specialized emphasis. The name for a sentiment is a kind of sensitizing concept. In German *Schadenfreude,* or malicious glee over another's misfortune, is more easily recognized as a common feeling by virtue of the presence of the term. The vocabulary defines our sensations and gestures by naming them, showing us what these mean to other people.

Ideological beliefs about a sentiment are linked with its name in the vocabulary. Like an ideology, these beliefs protect the social reality of a sentiment as a meaningful category, explaining and justifying particular instances of interaction in terms of popular knowledge about the sentiment. For example, how does one recognize envy? Or, what are the rights and obligations of friendship? Is shame natural or learned? Does romance inevitably fade into companionate love? Is it possible to conceal real grief?

I am not contending that people learn precise definitions or complex, formal principles about each sentiment, but they do learn informal theories or folk wisdom. Communication about the sentiment in terms of these popular beliefs preserves each sentiment as an available resource for explaining interaction. More elaborate ideologies surround some sentiments than others. Romantic love has an extensive popular ideology, and religious doctrines explain and justify guilt, reverence, and compassion. In contrast, shame and pity seem to be relatively undefined in our society at present.

The vocabulary also includes evaluative beliefs about each sentiment that influence how we express, label, and identify sentiments. Is pride a mark of self-worth, or one of the seven Christian sins? Depending on the social group, esthetic feeling may be a sign of personal cultivation or aloof snobbery. Our response to a person who reveals or claims a sentiment depends partly on evaluative beliefs about the feeling. "People are encouraged to interpret certain mixed feelings as love," Elaine Walster noted (1971:87), "because our culture insists that certain reactions are acceptable only if one is madly in love." In contrast, envy may be a universally condemned and feared sentiment that few people seriously admit (Schoek 1966; Foster 1972).

The vocabulary within which we communicate about sentiments places boundaries on affective experience, confining it largely to socially significant, shared meanings.

I have argued that each sentiment is a different combination of a social relationship and cultural beliefs with emotional sensations and gestures. Social factors determine which component is most salient at a given time. We become highly aware of bodily sensations when we are physiologically aroused, and I will discuss several types of circumstances that generate arousal. Sensations may also become problematic by their absence, however, when we are apathetic where the socially appropriate reaction would be excitement. Gestures become salient when their meaning is challenged, when we are being socialized into expression, and when we must express deliberately what is not spontaneously felt.

The remainder of the chapter discusses three processes that influence all sentiments. The first is the social differentiation of sentiments. What is the interpretive process by which each sentiment obtains its socially distinctive meaning, differentiating it from other sentiments in our personal experience and social response? Socialization is a second major problem. How do compassion, sorrow, and other sentiments in a cultural vocabulary become capacities and resources of the individual? The third process is the management of expression and feeling according to norms and other social constraints. How do people suppress, magnify, and alter their gestures, feelings, and interpretation of a sentiment?

The Differentiation of Sentiments

The differentiation of sentiments is a social process that combines sensations and gestures together with social relationships and beliefs to form discrete sentiments. We recognize each sentiment, such as shame, as a whole, internally consistent pattern that is different from other affective patterns, such as pity or contempt. We believe that guilt and hatred are different kinds of feelings and relationships. We respond differently in terms of their distinct qualities, although we cannot specify clearly how the boundary between them was established.

This section of the chapter examines the differentiation of sentiments as an emergent property of social interaction. First, I will consider psychological evidence for the biological fixity of certain basic emotions. Then I will discuss the differentiation of sentiments through social interpretation of bodily sensations in terms of a cultural vocabulary of sentiments.

BODILY PATTERNING OF EMOTIONS

Before considering the social differentiation of sentiments, we must examine evidence that basic emotions are patterned independently of cultural learning. Are certain emotions found universally because each is associated with a specific physiological state or an innate gestural pattern? Space limitations prohibit an extensive review of this literature; I recommend reviews by Mandler (1975), Izard (1977), Candland (1977), Strongman (1978), and Plutchik (1980). I will discuss several psychological theories of emotional differentiation, and will suggest where they are relevant to a sociological analysis and where they are incompatible with it.

Charles Darwin argued that facial, gestural, and postural expressions of certain emotions are universal and biologically determined, the product of human evolution (Darwin 1965). These expressive acts formerly had functional utility as internal adjustments needed in emergencies and as signals to one's own species, enemies, and prey. For example, clenching one's jaw in anger is a preparation for, and a warning of, biting. Emotional expressions are basically continuous between human beings and lower animals, but have lost their functional utility for humans and survive as remnants of evolution, Darwin asserted.

Also working within an evolutionary framework, Robert Plutchik (1962, 1970, 1980) saw emotions as retaining functional utility. An emotion, he argued, is a sequence of cognitive appraisal, feeling, impulses to act, and overt behavior that has evolved to cope with the environmental stimulus that triggers the emotion. Destruction of barriers is enhanced by anger, for example, and the avoidance of harmful substances is promoted by disgust. All species have the same basic emotions behaviorally, but the subjective element increases in higher species. Basic emotions combine into mixed emotions. Thus, contempt is a mixture of anger and disgust, according to Plutchik.

Sociologists have proposed that social and psychological levels of affect are functionally integrated, at least for specific sentiments. The organization of emotional elements into different sentiments may be explained partly by the social functions these sentiments fulfill. Kingsley Davis (1936) asserted that sexual jealousy strengthens norms pertaining to property rights, sexual and more generally. Embarrassment also protects social norms, according to Erving Goffman (1956). When norms conflict, a person's embarrassment draws blame onto himself and away from the norms. This temporary sacrifice of identity shows that one is perturbed about his current performance, promises to improve, and recognizes the norms. Sentiments should be analyzed for the adaptive functions they serve for groups and for individuals within a group.

While Darwin had studied the functional differentiation of expressive behaviors, William James (1950) focused on different emotional experiences. He held that an emotion is the outcome and not the cause of bodily reactions: "Bodily changes directly follow the *perception* of the exciting fact, and our feeling of the same changes as they occur *is* the emotion" (Lange and James 1922:13). Each emotion is distinguished in our awareness by its unique physiological correlate, a distinctive pattern of change in the heart, lungs, tear ducts, and other organs. We do not tremble because we are afraid; rather, we are afraid because we tremble. James's theory was criticized on the grounds that visceral reactions are too slow, insensitive, and lack sufficient patterning to stimulate the wide range of emotional qualities we experience (Cannon 1929). Modern psychologists generally agree that although visceral changes contribute to emotional intensity, they are not the source of much differentiation of subjective qualities.

Combining Darwin and James, several psychologists accounted for different emotional qualities in terms of feedback from innate facial patterns (Tomkins 1962; Izard 1971, 1977; Leventhal 1974). The face not only expresses emotion, but also stimulates a corresponding feeling. Unlike the viscera, facial musculature is finely differentiated and can change rapidly. Feedback from facial expressions could therefore stimulate differentiated and immediate emotions. Evidence currently suggests that facial expression can influence emotional intensity, but, as with the viscera, discrete qualities of emotion are not produced (Ekman and Oster 1979).

Facial expressions also have been studied for evidence of an innate, universal set of human emotions, as I mentioned earlier. In a typical study, photographs of posed facial expressions representing selected emotions are shown to subjects in different cultures (Izard 1971, 1977; Ekman, Friesen, and Ellsworth 1972; Ekman and Friesen 1975). Subjects agree substantially in matching each photograph with a label chosen from a short list of emotions. There are distinctive facial expressions for anger, disgust, fear, sadness, happiness, surprise, and possibly other emotions, researchers conclude, and each emotion is expressed the same universally.

Is biological patterning of emotion more "basic" than social differentiation? Crude innate patterning appears developmentally before socialization and remains as a partly autonomous substrate. Social differentiation of primitive rage into resentment and indignation multiplies and refines the possible occasions for antipathy, Cooley wrote (1964:266), but we never lose the simple, animal form of anger. An emotion is not fundamental in the sense that a particular facial expression consistently co-occurs with specific bodily sensations and a distinct affective quality. For example, laboratory studies of facial expressions can only distinguish self-reported pleasant feelings from unpleasant ones (review by Ekman and Oster 1979). Sentiments cannot be explained by reduction to such loosely structured units. If not through biological patterning, how do we know what we feel?

INTERPRETIVE DIFFERENTIATION OF SENTIMENTS

A sentiment is given impulse by bodily arousal, and is given quality and direction by our interpretations of the social situation. As Clifford Geertz wrote (1973:80), human emotional life "is a matter of giving specific, explicit, determinate form to the general, ongoing flow of bodily sensation; of imposing upon the continual shifts in sentience to which we are inherently subject a recognizable, meaningful order, so that we may not only feel but know what we feel and act accordingly." First, I will very briefly review social psychological insights into the cognitive labeling of arousal states. Then I will develop some sociological implications of this perspective, and suggest certain socially emergent properties for future sociological research.

The essence of cognitive labeling theory is that an emotional state is a joint function of physiological arousal and situational cues relevant to the arousal. When we doubt whether the intensity or quality of our emotion is situationally appropriate, we define it by comparing ourselves with how others in a similar situation are reacting (Schachter 1959, 1964). In a well-known experiment, subjects were injected with a chemical that caused physiological arousal, but the nature of this injection was concealed from some of them. Lacking an explanation for their sensations, these subjects tended to feel and behave emotionally according to emotional cues displayed by another person in the situation (Schachter and Singer 1962). Although this study's methods have been challenged incisively (most recently by Leventhal 1974; Kemper 1978b; Marshall and Zimbardo 1979; Maslach 1979), its conclusions are consistent with a large number of subsequent studies to which I refer below (see also review by Harvey and Smith 1977; Liebhart 1979; Kelley and Michela 1980; Pennebaker 1980). These studies testify to the substantial, if not complete, determination of emotional quality by cognitive interpretation.

We interpret our emotional reactions not only by seeing how others react, but also by observing our own behavior (Bem 1972). When internal cues are too weak or ambiguous to identify an emotion, we rely on the same information available to an outside observer: what we did and said in a certain kind of situation. We label an emotional state, not only in terms of its normative appropriateness, but also by making attributions about its likely causes and effects in the situation (Jones and Davis 1965; Kelley 1967; Jones et al. 1972; Harvey et al. 1976, 1978; Kelley and Michela 1980). In order to infer that I am jealous, for example, I must perceive that I feel aroused, attribute this feeling to someone's threat to my love relationship (and not to some internal cause or other external cause), and decide that a twinge of jealousy is normal and appropriate in this situation.

The cognitive labeling model has been applied by psychologists and sociologists to such diverse bodily states as pain (Zborowski 1952), hunger (Schachter 1967, 1971), illness (Mechanic 1972; Kerckhoff and Back 1968), sexual arousal (Storms 1979), insomnia (Storms and Nisbett 1970), and intoxication by alcohol or drugs (MacAndrew and Edgerton 1969; Becker 1953, 1967). In all these studies, the social definition of the situation was a crucial determinant of the meaning people assigned to their bodily sensations.

The labeling model has great heuristic value for sociologists. Even before its refinement by research, Hans Gerth and C. Wright Mills asserted (1953:20): "In order for inner feelings to become emotions these feelings must be linked with socially recognizable gestures, and the person must become aware of them as related to his self. . . . The social definition of the occasion, the meaning it comes to have for certain types of persons, provides the clue to which emotion and which conduct will arise." I will tentatively suggest some problems for future sociological research, based on the socially emergent properties of emotion that I discussed earlier.

How does social interaction structure our perceptions of the causes of bodily feeling? When situational constraints are apparent, people are likely to attribute their sensations and gestures to external causes, not to themselves. The child who is coerced into thanking others will not interpret or internalize gratitude as his own sentiment, but as performed to please his parents. Under different circumstances, a person may perceive considerable freedom of action and feeling, so that her sentiment is her own. The same attribution to self may occur when potent external forces are subtle and not apparent. While going through the motions in "voluntary" school prayer, under subtle peer pressure to conform, a child may attribute his solemn ritual gestures and sensations to his own reverence. By eliminating distractions, rituals make internal cues more salient and attributable to the focal symbolic meaning.

When applied to enduring sentiments, a more complex temporal sequence of arousal and labeling emerges. Arousal and gestures within a relationship are interpreted repeatedly over time. Psychologists have recently proposed a "circular flow" or "feedback loop" model of cognitive labeling, in which each cognition stimulates new arousal, which, in turn, gives rise to new interpretations, and the cycle continues (Candland 1977; Lewis and Rosenblum 1978). The next section of the chapter examines different social contexts and sequences in which arousal occurs.

SOCIAL SOURCES OF AROUSAL

Social conditions generate arousal, which may be interpreted as formation of a sentiment or change in an established sentiment. The following types of social situations make bodily sensations salient in awareness and contribute to sentiment differentiation.

Arousal from interruption or novelty. Arousal often occurs when social events cause an unpleasant interruption in ongoing activity, or a pleasant, novel adjustment in interaction. John Dewey argued (1894) that emotion arises when newer reactions are inconsistent with other impulses that are directed toward goal attainment. I suggest that this arousal is often interpreted by the individual as the presence of a sentiment. Competitive relationships, where each person or group poses an obstacle to others' goal attainment, often generate disjunctive sentiments such as hatred (Shibutani 1961:347). Gordon Allport (1958:340–44) described the transformation of anger aroused when some activity is thwarted into hatred, "composed of habitual bitter feeling and accusatory thought." Repeated frustration by a competitor can cumulate into hatred. George Mandler (1975:226) asserted that "the extreme degrees of disruption and interruption occasioned by the loss of a loved member of one's group are adequate to explain the appearance of grief." Cultural patterns prescribe the meaning, but the arousal's origin is in the interruption of plans that need particular individuals for their completion.

Arousal is often accompanied by a focusing of attention on the existing social relationship. Herbert Blumer (1946) described the elementary, affective processes by which people communicate and define social unrest, which develops over disturbances in their usual form of living or from events that cannot be explained by existing cultural definitions. When conventional norms are ineffective, as in a disaster, sentiments take on greater significance in guiding behavior (Shibutani 1961:384). Ralph Turner noted (1970:332) that when a family's task bonds are ineffective, love rises into mutual awareness, often sustaining the relationship until other bonds can once again stabilize the attachment.

Failure to anticipate a pleasant event is experienced as novelty, because this mild disruption of plans elicits attentiveness, curiosity, and fascination. Gordon Allport (1955:6) believed that all human activities that lead to personal growth and creativity are accompanied by a type of tension or excitement.

Relationship beginnings are characterized by high levels of stimulation. We are highly conscious of the other person and the sentiment that is developing toward him or her (Shibutani 1961:338). Beginnings of romances, for example, pose a choice among alternative love partners. Clear guidelines for choice are lacking, but the decision is regarded as immensely important. Anxious tension accompanies each new romantic involvement, contributing to its passion. Because the ideology surrounding romance describes anxious tension as part of the experience, the sentiment is recognized when these sensations occur. Passionate feelings can be stimulated by sources other than direct attraction, such as guilt, loneliness, and sharply lowered self-esteem. These increase arousal which is attributed to the potential romantic partner in the same setting (Walster 1971; Walster and Berscheid 1971).

Validative arousal. Arousal may be interpreted as undeniable evidence for the continued vitality of a sentiment. We learn that romantic love requires frequent reiteration of its intensity to self and the partner. This testing for latent feeling may also occur in other passionate sentiments such as hatred, jealousy, and religious feeling. Heightened self-monitoring may itself generate or intensify arousal, as an anxious tension accompanying the repeated search for spontaneous feeling, but mainly when one expects to find heightened arousal (Pennebaker 1980).

Love may be validated by shared excitement, quarrels and reconciliations, sex, and other episodes of intense feeling. Parental opposition to their college-age children's love affairs was found to be associated with more intense attachment between the lovers (Driscoll et al. 1972). Emotional turmoil may have contributed to the lovers' passion. Jealousy may be interpreted as evidence of a partner's continued love. A study of women's magazines found that "the woman was told to avoid situations which might make her husband jealous, but to interpret his small expressions of jealousy as evidence of his love" (Clanton and Smith 1977:12).

Arousal is not simply the source of a sentiment, then, but also a criterion by which its continuity can be validated.

Anticipatory arousal. Anticipation of a relationship can stimulate arousal. An individual awaiting a loved one's return may work up feeling for a spontaneously intimate reunion. Imaginative rehearsals stir anxiety, muscular tension, and ready gestures for the forthcoming interaction. Anticipatory arousal is functionally important when immediate, full enactment of a sentiment is required. Parental love cannot be left to gradual, haphazard acquisition. Parents-to-be are primed for the infant's arrival by anticipatory socialization and by the anxiety cued by the mother's pregnancy. The newborn's "amorphous personality" serves as the "perfect screen for the projection of parental emotions," as sentiments long held in abeyance are released "like coiled springs" by the baby's birth (Waller 1938:466).

Anticipation of tragic events, or "worry work," focuses attention on possible dangers and allows planning (Janis 1958). Anticipatory grief precedes the death of a loved one (Lindemann 1944; Glick et al. 1974). This anticipatory sentiment sensitizes survivors to the impending change of relationship, and allows them to "experience part of the emotion appropriate to the disaster before it occurs" (Parkes 1972:74).

Reminiscent arousal. Memories of past interactions and relationships evoke heightened feeling within the extended time frame of sentiments. Reminiscent arousal often develops when members of an enduring group, such as a family, recall shared sentiments from their collective past. Reference to some symbol that designates the whole event triggers an "in-group meaning," including the corresponding sentiment (Turner 1970:24). Through collective worship, Durkheim (1965:-387) contended, faith is created and periodically recreated through rites, as a result of which "men are more confident because they feel themselves stronger, and they really are stronger, because forces which were languishing are now reawakened in the consciousness." Group membership provides the reference points and categories in which memories reside (Halbwachs 1925). Individual memory becomes assimilated to collectively defined and revised memories, which in enduring groups are partial to positive, bonding sentiments.

Empathic arousal. Arousal may be stimulated by observing another person's situation or that person's affective expressions, conventional or innate. Perhaps the important sociological question about gestures is not their origin, but whether natural ones have different social effects than conventional ones. Blumer argued (1946) that rapid transmission and intensification of collective feelings occur when people respond directly to innate gestures instead of interpreting them. This unites people on the most primitive level to overcome problems and occurs in groups where people are sensitized to one another's reactions. Asserting that the basic communicative expressions in rituals are innate signals, Randall Collins held (1975) that people are vulnerable to control by elites who gain power over ritual resources that excite our natural affectivity. Our innate responsiveness to gestures like crying, jeering, and laughter leaves us susceptible to political and emotional manipulation.

An acute responsiveness to others' gestures was a key factor in Durkheim's theory (1965:469) of religious ritual. Emotional arousal is generated by the singing, dancing, chanting, and other ritual actions of people in collective assembly, which awakens religious sentiments upon reaching a certain level of intensity. This social "effervescence" changes the conditions of psychic activity: "vital energies are overexcited, passions are active, sensations stronger." This arousal is socially interpreted. Excitement becomes generalized to religious symbols and meanings, which are imbued with a sacred character as extraordinary as the feelings generated by collective ritual. The person "feels himself transformed and consequently transforms the environment he finds himself in."

Arousal may result from emotional contagion, but soon becomes interpreted according to social meanings. More complex empathic interpretation will be discussed below as a product of socialization. Now I shall discuss the social labels for arousal states.

SENTIMENT VOCABULARIES

Arousal is socially interpreted in terms of sentiment vocabularies, which are sets of meaningful categories that connect sensations, gestures, and social relationships. The total vocabulary of different experiences in our culture is large. Lists compiled by psychologists include hundreds of terms, although some refer to moods ("gloomy") or temperament traits ("excitable") rather than explicitly social feelings (Allport and Odbert 1936; Davitz 1969; Averill 1975). This profusion of terms for sentiments and emotions is certainly greater than the variety of internal sensations we can discern or the number of facial expressions we can identify. However, even a very large vocabulary of sentiments may be smaller than the variety of meaningful distinctions we make among types of social relationships and their associated feelings.

A more important issue than the total number of sentiments is the relative precision of distinctions in different areas of social feeling. Sentiments are finely discriminated for aspects of relationships and personality that are highly valued and strongly regulated. This is seen most easily in cross-cultural studies. Eskimo village life strongly enforces gentleness, mildness, and even-tempered restraint in expressing hostility and affection. Eskimo vocabulary differentiates fine shades of meaning by having many terms for subtle differences in affection and hostility (Briggs 1970). Respect for kin, age, gender, and other status differences is a central theme in Java, where the vocabulary makes fine distinctions among feeling states associated with respectful behavior, such as *sungkan*—a feeling of respectful politeness in which one represses his own impulses so as not to disturb the emotional equanimity of a spiritually superior person (H. Geertz 1959:233).

A vocabulary of sentiments is a linguistic expression of experiences shared by group members, and mirrors their interests and concerns. Each concept imposes meaning on experience as a way of preserving distinctions that are of importance in group life (Sapir 1949; Whorf 1956). Sentiment vocabularies differ among subcultures in a complex society, such as social classes, men and women, and age cohorts. American women distinguish between liking and loving more clearly than men (Rubin 1973:220; Rubin et al. 1981). The socioeconomic implications of mate selection pressure women to be more cautious and interpretive than men in their heterosexual relationships, in order to distinguish male friends from potential husbands. Basil Bernstein's analysis (1972) of language codes suggested that in comparison to the working class, middle-class language contains more words and makes finer, more complex differentiations of experience. This elaborated code permits the middle class to verbalize feelings and react to them more precisely.

Sentiments that are devalued or of little practical importance in a culture are poorly discriminated for lack of an expressive vocabulary. Because moral sanctions in Tahiti operate mainly through teasing, ridicule, and other forms of shame, these feelings "have undergone considerable cultural definition and elaboration . . . in contrast, the feeling of guilt is culturally played down to the point of conceptual invisibility" (Levy 1973:341). Similarly, feelings that we term sadness or longing contradict Tahitian values and are not culturally organized as sentiments. Separation and isolation from others evoke sensations that Tahitians describe in terms of nonspecific, troubled, or subdued bodily states, such as heaviness or weariness. Without meaningful concepts for designating a feeling to self and others, the person's emotional response remains private and socially amorphous. Sensations are severed from their external social cause, minimizing the social significance of the event.

Power and status are the significant relational meanings to which people respond emotionally, according to Theodore Kemper (1978a, 1978b). Cultures and individuals vary in the specific stimuli and language that reflect power and status relations, he argued, but power and status are the basic dimensions to which people are sensitized and that underlie the differentiation of emotions. Space limitations do not allow a full summary of his complex theory, but its essence is that different emotions result from real, imagined, or anticipated outcomes involving excess or deficit in power or status. For example, power deficits produce fear or anxiety; status loss generates anger or depression. Our vocabulary of emotional states is an imperfect reflection of power and status relations. Kemper also discussed and accepted evidence that specific physiological states underlie different emotions to some degree, so that physiological, psychological, and sociological (power-status) levels of differentiation coincide.

A vocabulary includes beliefs about how sentiments are interrelated, and these beliefs guide our labeling of sentiments. One sentiment may be defined as a precondition for another sentiment, so that grief is not regarded as credible or authentic unless the mourner is known to have loved the deceased. Alternatively, the consequent sentiment may be used as a criterion for inferring the precondition. "You must have loved him very much," the mourner is told. One sentiment may be believed to transform into another sentiment consistently. We may believe that men and women cannot be friends without falling in love eventually. Sentiments may be seen as opposites (love and hatred), or as acceptable substitutes from another person (guilt and shame). A belief that humor and awe are incompatible will influence how we respond to humor when we are feeling awe. These beliefs provide ideological support for a sentiment's social reality. Any doubt about one sentiment's reality would have to challenge the whole system of interconnected meanings.

Sentiment vocabularies change historically in content and appropriateness. Aries (1960) detected a shift in culturally approved sentiments toward children. A medieval pattern of harsh egalitarianism changed to a sentiment of tenderness, protection, coddling, and charm over childish antics. Historical forces promoting this change included the higher survival rate of infants, a shift from street life to home life for families, and the emergence of childhood as a distinctive life stage.

Obsolete vocabularies sound trite, hollow, or offensive. They are no longer self-evident, plausible concepts for linking one's feelings and gestures to others' social understanding. Middle-class trends toward women's rights, open marriage, and self-indulgence may be changing the meaning of sexual jealousy (O'Neill and O'Neill 1972; Clanton and Smith 1977; Lasch 1976). Instead of signifying love and commitment, an expression of jealousy may now imply possessiveness or dependency. Jessie Bernard noted (1977:148), "Grief, pain, and humiliation may be experienced at the loss of exclusive love and favors, but if the community does not sanction one's feelings, they can hardly express themselves as jealousy."

Many new shades and varieties of sentiments are developing in modern times, Cooley wrote (1962:178), but with less intense feeling. Refinement of feeling is diffusing from the higher classes to the common people, whose lives are becoming more varied and less crudely determined by primitive conditions. A greater abundance and choice of social contacts diversifies sentiments. Although primitive societies made occasional but severe demands on feeling, with alternations of apathy and explosion, modern emotional life is made up of diverse but mostly mild excitements.

Now I shall discuss several socialization processes through which we learn different sentiments.

Sentiment Socialization

Shame, sorrow, and other sentiments in a cultural vocabulary become abilities and resources of individuals through socialization processes. I define socialization broadly as development of the individual as a social being and participant in society (Clausen 1968:3). How do people learn to interpret sensations and gestures as a sentiment, defined by Cooley (1962:177) as "socialized feeling which has been raised by thought and intercourse out of its merely instinctive state and become properly human?" The topic of affective socialization has been neglected by sociology and psychology. The latter has concentrated on development of behavioral skills and cognitive abilities. The sparse treatment of affective development focuses on innate impulses, such as how the infant's crying and smiling reflexes promote parent-infant attachment, or how sex and aggression drives pose impulse-control problems.

This section begins by examining parallel sequences in sentiment socialization, the emergence of the self-conception, and the development of empathic ability. Sentiment socialization depends on a child's ability to comprehend the meanings of other people's sentiments in relation to self. Then I consider several interactive processes by which we learn sentiments.

Sentiment socialization is part of a larger process that includes development of the social self, the decline of early childhood egocentrism, and the growth of empathic ability. Empathy here means not only the simple emotional contagion discussed earlier, but a self-conscious effort to share and accurately comprehend another person's feelings, thoughts, and their causes (Wispe 1968). My discussion draws from the work of Cooley (1962, 1964), Mead (1934), Jean Piaget (Piaget 1932; Inhelder and Piaget 1958), and Martin Hoffman (1976, 1978, 1979). These separate traditions all analyze the development of social insight in children through interaction with others.

Sentiments are socialized within primary groups, Cooley believed (1964:136), because family and friendship groups promote "entering into and sharing the minds of others." Intimacy, self-disclosure, small size, and enduring interaction facilitate empathy among members. A rudimentary empathy can be observed in newborn infants who will cry upon hearing another baby crying (Hoffman 1976). An emotional contagion of crying often sweeps through maternity wards and nurseries. This primitive arousal is an unself-conscious empathy, a nonsignificant gesture such as animals make (Mead 1934). Infants have not differentiated self from other people; therefore, they respond to crying as though they themselves were in distress. Newborn infants hearing tape-recorded crying were most likely to cry when the recording resembled their own cry (Simner 1971). This primitive empathy is important in the emotional contagion discussed by Durkheim, Blumer, and Collins above, and probably also is a basis for spontaneous feeling within enduring sentiments.

By one year of age, the child is cognitively aware of other people as distinct physical entities, but self remains merged with others affectively. The toddler who encounters a crying child may seek to be comforted by her own mother instead of trying to help (Hoffman 1976:131). If she does help, she egocentrically offers whatever she herself finds most comforting, such as a favorite toy or bringing over her own mother. Her interest in the other child is transitory and inconsistent.

The child gradually learns to regard himself from the standpoint of other people. Meaningless imitation in play of another's role, such as mother or teacher, becomes an ability to view objects from that single other person's standpoint (Mead 1934). The reflexive self, both subject and object, arises through communication. A parallel affective shift is from meaningless imitative empathy to inferring how others feel toward himself. The "looking-glass self" includes "the imagination of our appearance to the other person, the imagination of his judgment of that appearance, and some sort of self-feeling, such as pride or mortification" (Cooley 1964:224). The vestiges of guilt first appear at four or five years of age when children use speech—first aloud, then covertly—to discuss and regulate their own actions (Luria 1961). A child's first fears are over darkness, loud noises, and other material threats, but these are supplanted by "social fears," such as shame and embarrassment (Cooley 1964:266). Self-feeling becomes extended to objects as a sense of appropriation organized around concepts of *mine* and *my*. This sense of possession is basic to the development of jealousy and envy as self-related sentiments.

Viewing herself as someone who arouses definite feelings and thoughts in other people, the child reflects upon her impulses and thoughts. She considers how others would react to them when expressed, and shapes them so as to arouse a desired response from the other. Introspection develops from this selective communication with a view to the other's response, while also reacting to one's own impulses and thoughts from the other's standpoint. Morris Rosenberg's research (1979) found that older children are more likely than younger children to conceptualize the self as a psychological interior of feeling and thought, and also find self-control of impulses to be a greater source of self-deficiency. Children realize gradually that internally experienced affect need not be expressed behaviorally. Older children are more aware than younger children of social norms about appropriate affective expression, and justify those norms in terms of social reasons (for example, politeness) rather than for pragmatic reasons (avoiding punishment) (Saarni 1979).

As self becomes differentiated from other people, the child learns that they have feelings independent of his own. His mother is angry at him, but he does not feel angry toward her. Up to ages nine to twelve, accurate insight into others' feelings depends on how similar the other is to the child, who can simply impute his own probable feeling to the other person (Hoffman 1977). Only gradually does the child consistently recognize sentiments of persons dissimilar to himself, who are in unfamiliar situations.

The child gradually learns to take into account the relations that other people have with one another. Mead (1934) thought this occurs by playing organized games, in which the child has to keep in mind the roles of all other players, including their potential responses toward one another. The parallel affective development is the awareness that the other person has sentiments in life circumstances that transcend the immediate situation and that may differ from the child's own sentiments (Hoffman 1976). Thus, he can understand that his two best friends dislike each other, or that his brother is jealous about a girlfriend.

Heightened capacities for imagination and reasoning allow the adolescent to feel sentiments toward abstract objects, such as patriotism for a nation, reverence for a deity, or compassion for the plight of a class of people (Inhelder and Piaget 1958). He may feel sentiments for persons with whom he has not interacted.

Cognitive development restricts children's abilities to comprehend the adult meanings underlying sentiments. Grief and remorse require cognitive abilities that would enable the child to order past memories and anticipate the future, but such structures are not available until late childhood, David Elkind noted (1979:286). Young children cannot comprehend the irreversible permanence of death, or the special tragedy of accidental deaths, because they lack an understanding of relations of permanence, reversibility, and contingency. Similarly, young children do not take intention into account in the same way that adults do in imputing, admitting, and challenging moral sentiments, such as guilt or indignation.

Sentiment socialization is concentrated in childhood, but continues throughout the life span. Parental love develops upon a foundation of earlier socialization. The new teacher may have to learn how to convey enthusiasm for her subject. The medical student may learn to restrain complete empathy for her patient's sufferings.

SOCIALIZATION PROCESSES

A child learns sentiments by learning to see them as social objects from the standpoints of other persons in the family or friendship groups. One process is a complex type of learning in which one aspect of a sentiment (such as a gesture or feeling) is learned as being consistent with other aspects (such as a situation or the sentiment's name). To be told "you don't sound like you're sorry," or "now that's acting more like a friend" is to be given concrete examples from which the nature and boundaries of "guilt" or "friendship" can be gradually inferred. This indication of consistency and inconsistency among sensations, gestures, situations, and how others react to one's behavior is more explicit and intentional in some families and cultures than in others. Often it is employed with full consciousness of its use, with forceful urging and frequent repetition.

The various components of a sentiment are learned at different rates, but tend to be communicated by the socialization agent in relation to some conception of the whole, larger sentiment. The socializer is attentive for gestures or language that reveal some fundamental comprehension or misunderstanding of the whole sentiment. As Gerth and Mills wrote (1953:55), "We know our own emotions by observations of our gestures and actions, but more importantly, perhaps, by what other people observe and report to us, directly or indirectly by their responses and gestures to the gestures we have made."

Use of its name in conversation reifies a sentiment in the learner's understanding. This name becomes a symbolic designation or focal point around which the consistency of bodily and cultural elements of the sentiment can be cognitively organized. A name makes an otherwise transient impulse or gesture socially significant and memorable. As Hugh Duncan noted (1953:13), "language allows us to convert the brute quality of feelings into conscious emotion. . . . Only as emotions are presented through some symbol system do they become communicable and hence social."

The child experiences a feeling, imputes it to others in relation to some expression and situation, and hears the name along with these elements. As Ralph Turner suggested (1970:179), "When he has been frustrated and his frustration can be attributed to violation of norms by another person, [the child] learns to identify the sensations he is feeling as indignation." Any one element, such as a gesture, comes to imply the remainder of the sentiment. The child thus comes to believe in the sentiment's reality as a social object without endorsing or being able to specify all of its details.

Sensations and gestures that cannot be organized around a name remain diffuse and socially insignificant. Childhood amnesia, our lack of memory about many early experiences, may result from our lack of language in our earliest years (Schachtel 1949). For want of categories, affective and other experiences are soon filtered out of memory.

We learn to feel sentiments in the same "outward to inward" progression as when we learn to empathize with others' feelings. The infant or young child shares another person's crying or other overt expression before she is able to empathize accurately with the other's inner feelings. In learning to feel our own sentiments, facial and gestural expressions and other overt behaviors are mastered before covert feelings and interpretations (Machotka 1964:156). Inchoate, vague sensations and relationship concepts are defined by the reactions of socialization agents, who have access mainly to contemporaneous overt gestures and circumstances of the learner. By being encouraged to correct outward appearances, the child gradually learns which feelings and actions toward a social object are mutually consistent, and what social meaning underlies that consistency.

The rate at which covert elements of a sentiment are learned depends on the emphasis on understanding in socialization. American working-class parents are more likely than middle-class parents to disregard intentions for an action, instead communicating to the child that overt conformity is more important (Kohn 1969). The depth to which sentiments are internalized may vary across subcultures. Emphasis in socialization on outward signs of a sentiment may initially protect learners.

Children and other initiates into a group lack the full inner feeling and understanding of sentiments shared by other members. Gestural and situational elements provide a framework for learning the remainder, and also suffice as substitutes during learning. The child at a funeral who is able to "keep quiet," "stop laughing," and "keep your head down" will be exempted as an affective novice from a deeper feeling and comprehension of grief.

A second socialization process that complements indication of consistency and naming is an interactive socialization of sentiments in association with "personal symbols." The meaning of a sentiment for us is linked with significant persons from whom or for whom we felt the sentiment (Cooley 1962:116). Personal symbols include "facial expression, tone of voice, and other imagery," although Cooley was not more explicit. I infer from his work that personal symbols are interpretive cues that a child uses to recognize and empathize with sentiments of family members and friends. For example, "shame" is learned as meaning the composite of expressions, voice tones, situations, and other symbols that were common among shame experiences in primary groups. These empathic cues are later generalized and modified within other social relationships.

Generalization of a sentiment allows a person to make sense out of a new relationship by analogy to a more familiar one. Compassion, liking, shame, and other sentiments in adulthood are generalized from childhood primary group relations, Cooley argued (1962, 1964). Religious sentiments are generalized from family and clan relationships, according to Durkheim (1965), so that a deity may be imputed moral authority, perpetual dependence by worshippers, and will be visualized as exacting but benevolent, like elders to a child.

The selective combination of personal symbols into a sentiment may cumulate across many relationships. Romantic love, for example, may incorporate a selection of emotional reactions from previous relationships (Kirkpatrick 1955:273). As a composite of previous loves, romantic attraction is felt when a partner is found who reintegrates favorite aspects of family members, friends, and earlier romantic lovers. Romance's intensity is increased by the sudden discovery in one person of these formerly separate, desired qualities associated with previous loves. This discovery evokes the set of earlier love responses simultaneously. Religious feeling may develop similarly through summation of different sensations, memories, and other affective elements into a sentiment, according to Otakar Machotka (1964:166). Religious sentiment builds from a merger of feelings experienced in collective singing, esthetic responses to music and religious adornments, emulation of the service leader's example, the facial and gestural expressions of other worshippers, and other sensations and impressions across many episodes of worship.

In addition to consistency and personal symbols of sentiments, a child learns to apply a sentiment as an interactional technique and resource. The strategic effects of its expression become part of the sentiment's social meaning. For example, shame or guilt are often learned as defensive tactics that deter punishment when they are displayed. Earlier, I discussed the separation of expression from inner feeling as a developmental achievement of the child. Sentiments are learned not only as ideals, but also as practical resources for interaction, depending on how others respond to the child's various attempts at strategic expression. Children's humor is initially a private enjoyment of incongruous symbolic relations among familiar objects (McGhee 1979). If other people are responsive and socially rewarding, children learn to initiate joking and clowning as a social affective resource.

Sentiments are socialized to some degree outside the primary group, through impersonal media such as books, films, and music. A content analysis of "manners books" found that books addressed to the youngest children stressed polite overt behavior and the ideal outcomes of friendships (Cavan 1970). Greetings, honesty, and other overt, ideal means to build friendships were described. Books for adolescents emphasized social techniques and less ideal outcomes. Selfishness and jealousy were portrayed as facts of human nature. The books recommended pretenses, concealment of eagerness, skillful avoidance of undesired friends, and other strategies as effective for friendship and romance.

Impersonal media are especially influential in a complex, literate society such as ours, but are not a new socialization process. The influential love manual, *The Art of Courtly Love,* published in twelfth-century France, socialized readers into the turbulent suffering and ecstasy to be experienced in courtly love (Capellanus 1941). The sentiment was to be expressed through gestures of courtesy and gentility, and only between a married woman and a man of somewhat lower status, readers learned. Stages of love—hesitation, pleading, acceptance, and love service—were described. A list of love's rules was followed by case studies of happy and ill-fated love affairs. Courtly love became the paradigm for modern romantic love (Hunt 1959).

Impersonal media today socialize a diversity of sentiments. Lovelorn advice columns, religious tracts, guides to living, and other media are directed to shape our definition and expression of sentiments. Popular psychology books instruct us how to open up to grief, overcome shyness, read others' body language for erotic attraction, and how to say no without feeling guilty. Most popular songs are about love (Horton 1957). Their lyrics provide love's vocabulary and the symbols through which it can be recognized. Music arouses appropriate moods as one hears how falling in love feels and what course love follows. Motion pictures depict vividly how sentiments begin, develop, and end in a relationship that is compressed into two hours on the screen.

Very little sociological investigation has been directed at the processes by which sentiments are socialized, or at how these processes are related to the child's social development. Now I shall consider the management of affective expression and feeling.

The Management of Sentiments

We evoke, suppress, and transform our sentiments. It is useful to distinguish between management of the outer and inner layers of sentiment. Expression management is the intentional display of gestures that differ from inner feeling. Feeling management modifies the cognitive and somatic experience of a sentiment. Both types of affective control are guided by normative and strategic considerations in social relationships. For example, a wife may believe that she no longer loves her husband as much as she thinks she should. She may increase her expressions of affection toward him so as to conceal her loss of feeling (individual expression management), or may try to regenerate her love feelings by thinking about his virtues and his love for her (individual feeling management). If she tells him that her love is waning, they may decide to just keep up public appearances of affection (collective expression management), or may attempt to revitalize love by seeking new experiences together (collective feeling management). I will discuss expression and feeling management, and will then consider their relationship to the social self, group interaction, and cultural ideologies about sentiments.

EXPRESSION MANAGEMENT

Expression management is guided by conscious strategies to convey a certain impression of ourselves to a social audience (Goffman 1959, 1961:23), and by our more habitual following of display rules, cultural norms for appropriate expressions in a given situation (Ekman and Friesen 1975). Expressive control can be observed even in one-year-old children, who make visible efforts to hold back tears or who smile as a social greeting (Ekman and Oster 1979). Four-year-olds can pose facial expressions upon request and are soon able to explain many norms about situationally appropriate affective expression (Saarni 1979).

Three types of facial display management have been identified (Ekman and Friesen 1975). We often qualify a facial expression by adding a further expression as a comment on the first, such as blending a smile into an angry look. We also modulate a facial expression, showing more or less intensity than we actually feel. We falsify our facial expression in several ways. We may simulate a feeling when we have none. We may show an impassive, neutral face to conceal an inner feeling. Finally, we often mask an expression that we do feel with another expression that we do not feel. This typology may be extended to the analysis of nonfacial gestures, voice tones, postures, and other expressive cues.

FEELING MANAGEMENT

We modify our interpretations of a relationship and may also alter our bodily sensations and reactions to the person. "Affectivity versus affective neutrality" is a choice faced by individuals and groups in forming social acts: what kind of affect and how much of it are appropriate in a given relationship (Parsons 1951). When should impulses be gratified freely, and when should they be subordinated to social interests? Normative and strategic considerations induce us to reflect upon feeling and alter it. In an experimental study, subjects used strategies of cognitive detachment or involvement to self-regulate their affective reactions to filmed stressful situations, and thus altered their bodily reactions, such as heart rate and skin conductance (Lazarus 1974, 1975).

"Feeling rules" are social guidelines that delineate a range of appropriate feeling for a situation or relationship, wrote Arlie Hochschild (1975a, 1979). For example, a brother should love or like his sister, but should feel neither hatred nor romantic passion toward her. We discuss our feelings as if rights and obligations apply to them, and react with approval or disapproval to signs of each others' feelings, Hochschild argued. We try to make our feelings coincide with feeling rules by doing cognitive, bodily, or expressive "work." If we "have no reason to feel ashamed" in front of a person, for example, we may try to change our imagination of how they think of us (cognitive), or try not to wince inside when we see them coming (bodily), or try not to look away or blush as they pass us (expressive).

CONSISTENCY BETWEEN EXPRESSION AND FEELING

Effective social communication does not require feelings to be consistent with expressive gestures. Displaying a gesture in the absence of any corresponding feeling is a form of obeisance to society, showing that one recognizes the appropriate sentiment even if he does not feel it. Mourning is not a natural movement of private feelings, Durkheim asserted (1965:497), but is a duty imposed by the group: "It is a ritual attitude one is forced to adopt out of respect for custom, but which is, in large measure, independent of his affective state." In Javanese society, expression of respect is obligatory, but any consistent feeling is much less important (H. Geertz 1959). Although these examples are from non-Western cultures, Western civilization has been described as the gradual domestication of impulsive expression—an increasing tendency to self-consciously check our behavior and mold it to group standards (Elias 1969). Public expression of affect has been controlled by an intensifying range and rigor of restraints since the Middle Ages. Violations of display rules are met with shame, embarrassment, and disgust in an ever-broadening scope of situations.

Any consistency between expression and feeling should be seen as socially problematic, a product of particular social conditions. Values around child rearing and affective competence in a society are one important condition. The Yanomano Indians of Brazil encourage childish temper and physical attacks against parents as signs of highly valued fierceness (Chagnon 1968). For middle-class American parents, however, childish temper "may signal serious difficulty in children's attempts at self-mastery" (Kohn 1969:106).

Broader ideologies about sentiments and emotions reflect whether social control is aimed mainly at the outer or inner layers of sentiment, at display or at feeling. Colonial Americans believed that feeling can be channeled, but its basic nature cannot be altered (Gadlin 1977:38). Social control was directed at regulating behavior, rather than at shaping inner impulses. A belief that emotion is disclosed involuntarily and inevitably became widespread in the nineteenth century, according to Richard Sennett (1978). If a person were genuinely moved, the feeling would show beyond any power of the person to conceal it. Sennett argued that withdrawal from feeling itself became the only recourse, if one's feelings were not to be read by others in public through gestures, slips in speech, and other cues. Suppression of both feeling and gesture made them consistent. The rising lower classes place greater emphasis on "candor" and "uprightness," noted Gerth and Mills (1953), than do the "sophisticated" upper classes.

These cultural values and beliefs are reflected in expression and feeling management when we indicate their meanings to the social self.

THE SOCIAL SELF IN SENTIMENT MANAGEMENT

We manage our feelings and gestures after indicating to ourselves the probable meaning that they would have for other people. We transform feeling and expression according to their implications for our self-conception, our more stable, continuous, unifying idea of the "real me." A self-conception is a "working compromise" between one's ideals and values and the self-images he infers from how others react to his feelings and behavior (Turner 1968). Some self-images will be accepted as representative of one's self-conception, but other images will be rejected as spurious or unrepresentative of one's real, deeper identity. In situations and relationships that we value in relation to self, we pursue credit for positive images, and seek to avoid responsibility for feelings and acts that generate negative self-images.

We manage expression and feeling by taking our self-conception into account in at least three ways: (1) assuming or avoiding responsibility for a sentiment, (2) detecting social support for the meaning of a sentiment, and (3) committing oneself to a relationship.

Our self-image in a situation reflects the appropriateness of our feeling; we feel proud or guilty about feeling a certain way. Helen Merrill Lynd (1958:42) noted that the incongruity between a trifling event and a deep sense of shame can evoke a "double shame: we are ashamed because of the original episode and shamed because we feel so deeply about something so slight that a sensible person would not pay any attention to it." If we do not modify our feeling into an appropriate quality and intensity, it becomes merged with our moral reaction to it. For example, we may feel a "guilty love" if, as in traditional Japan, love marriages are defined as selfish (DeVos 1960). Even in modern Japan, "individuals who have contracted love marriages are often reported to feel considerable guilt and inner restriction" (Norbeck and DeVos 1972:33). Without feeling management, the original sentiment is "spoiled" by our shame or guilt about it.

Society requires us to undertake many actions for which we do not want to assume full responsibility. These actions may have uncertain outcomes, or conflict with our predispositions not to perform them. Feeling management that intensifies feeling can facilitate these behaviors while shielding the self from responsibility. A "functionally determined emotion" carries one through the situation, Willard Waller wrote (1938), such as "the bitterness which enters into the divorce process and so often disappears just afterwards." The "institutionalized irrationality" of romantic love overcomes self-restraint in courtship and guides lovers into marriage, although rational self-seeking might dictate against this uncertain commitment (Aubert 1965; Greenfield 1965). A socially structured and legitimated passion conquers doubt and gives behavior spontaneity, while exempting the self from full responsibility for its outcome.

How does this intensification of feeling occur? Emotion is the experience of passivity, during which we interpret our behavior as being beyond our control, according to James Averill (1974, 1976, 1980). Deeply internalized desires and aversions erupt as compelling passions. The soldier for whom fury or courage has become second nature rushes into combat in spite of its dangers. Overwhelmed by emotion, we enact socially prescribed behavior although it conflicts with other norms, Averill suggested. For example, by becoming angry we are able to impose socially prescribed punishment even though other norms forbid aggression. The self is not held responsible for violating those norms, however, because it was passive within the experience of emotion. The passive self may be an important interpretation we make within romantic love, jealousy, indignation, and other intense sentiments. For example, a study found that students who believed that life events are generally caused by external forces beyond their control reported falling in love more often than others, and viewed love as a mysterious, emotional experience (Dion and Dion 1973).

The self also enters into feeling and expression management by restraining sentiments that we anticipate would not be validated meaningfully by a particular group. In his study of New York "Bohemians," Waller noted (1930:88) that any display of jealousy was "nothing short of a crime." He wrote, "Bohemia has its code, and if one is hurt in these light affairs, he must expect no sympathy. So if one falls in love, he conceals it from his friends as best he can." Our self-indication of a sentiment's meaning to others may lead us to segregate it from another sentiment that an audience would see as being incompatible. For example, a couple undergoing marital separation often desires to re-unite, at least temporarily, but also seeks to express anger against one another. A common pattern observed by Robert Weiss (1976) was to meet secretly to express affection, concealed from the social circle of kin and friends who had observed the bitter rivalry in the couple and would not understand the contradictory sentiment.

Feeling management may reflect the self as a commitment to a relationship. The "supplementary character of faithfulness," Simmel noted (1950:379), is directed toward the continuance of the relationship, independently of the original forces that brought it about. Communes, families, fraternal organizations, and other groups require love as a voluntary, responsible commitment to enhance the lives and growth of other persons (Swanson 1965). Groups foster love by eliminating sources of seduction, subversion, and competing loyalties. Love is routinized to promote steady, unrewarded care, effort, and self-sacrifice.

People withdraw from commitments by rationing or restricting feeling. Women, more than men, report diminishing their love consciously in faltering relationships (Hochschild 1975b). Women also identify more problems in their heterosexual relationships, and women's scores on a longitudinal measure of love predict relationship outcomes better than do the love scores of their male partners (Rubin et al. 1981). The more vulnerable and emotionally perceptive partner is likely to modulate feeling more consciously in response to relationship trends.

GROUP FUNCTIONS OF SENTIMENT MANAGEMENT

Management of feeling and expression enhances the functioning of groups by allowing continuity of action, building solidarity among members, and indicating status differences. Expressive control allows collective action to continue without the situation becoming redefined as the interrupted action or novelty that emotional arousal implies. For example, expressive control suppresses the potential embarrassment in gynecological examinations (Emerson 1970). Nonemotional voice tones and other nonintimate gestures suppress anxiety, giving the interaction a routine, technical meaning. A similar display rule in public settings shields onlookers from intimate gestures that would disrupt civil comportment. Kissing, fondling, and other gestures between lovers are normally prohibited in public settings (Weitman 1970). Intimate expressions remind onlookers that they are being excluded from a desirable relationship. Violators of this display rule are usually the young, tourists, and others who disregard public sensitivity.

Sentiment management can build group solidarity. The disruptive effects of envy are controlled universally by belief systems that proscribe envy, and by norms that diminish conditions for envy. These norms require that enviable goods be concealed from observation, that people show humility over good fortune, and that enviable objects or events be shared symbolically or materially (Schoek 1966; Foster 1972). Solidarity can also be enhanced by evocation of humor. Laughter and humor among hospital patients were observed by Rose Coser (1959) to be invitations to decrease social distance, emphasizing shared experiences and common definitions of the situation: "The liberating effect of joined laughter consists in the consensus that it brings about in a brief span of time" (Coser 1959:177).

Expression management is a continual affirmation of a group's structure of status and deference. We may claim statuses by displaying affective "coolness" when greater involvement would ordinarily be expected (Lyman and Scott 1970:149). Some male groups admire men who can attract and "conquer" a beautiful woman without becoming involved (Gans 1962:190), or who can engage in homosexual prostitution while displaying affective detachment (Reiss 1961). Business managers are expected to control their emotional reactions, in contrast to ordinary workers who are not believed to be able to do so (Kanter 1977b).

High status includes the power to elicit positive gestures from subordinates and to inhibit their hostile expressions. Smiling and laughter are usually offered upward in status hierarchies, ostensibly indicating pleasant, egalitarian relations and concealing status differences temporarily (Henley 1977:171). These positive gestures are welcomed by superiors only when the latter have invited a decrease in social distance. In traditional Far Eastern cultures, a subordinate was expected to conceal anger or sulking when criticized, and to mask these feelings by showing pleasure at being corrected (Hearn 1894). In contemporary American society, women are more likely than men to smile, even when angered or frustrated (Bugenthal et al. 1971). Women's initial facial expression of anger is masked or covered up instantly (Ekman and Friesen 1975).

Groups manage sentiments through the kinds of information they allow to enter open awareness. Hatred is sustained by emphasizing an enemy's negative qualities, overlooking or explaining away anything favorable, and then directing hatred toward this "contrast conception" (Shibutani 1961:352). Love between parents and their grown children may be strengthened by limited contact that allows earlier conflicts to be forgotten (Waller 1938:473). Generational gaps in attitudes and behavior are accentuated by accurate knowledge about each other, weakening love bonds (Stryker 1957). Selective recall is sometimes a conscious feeling-management technique. College men reported control over jealousy by prohibiting any mention of their girlfriends' previous lovers (Komarovsky 1976:83). The couple jointly censured anyone who indiscreetly disclosed information about the woman's earlier relationships. Sentiments are managed by sensitivity and avoidance within the social framework of memory.

PUBLIC AND PRIVATE CONTEXTS OF SENTIMENT MANAGEMENT

The boundaries of a sentiment vary in their permeability by public observation and involvement in one's feeling. Sentiments expressed in a public or community setting become conventionalized as the individual makes social comparisons about the sentiment's quality and intensity. Private feeling, secret and isolated from social involvement, is less manageable and loses social significance for lack of validation by others. For example, medieval customs required mourners to show sorrow for a fixed period of time (Aries 1974:63). Public ceremonies "tamed" grief, shielding mourners from extreme or prolonged grief. With the privatization of grief, however, the sentiment became idiosyncratic, often "insurmountable" as the mourner languished persistently (Aries 1974; Gorer 1965). In Tahiti, hostile sentiments are expressed publicly in noisy but harmless encounters in which antagonists play to their audience, who intervene if a fight becomes too serious (Levy 1973:281). These exaggerated dramas make hostility appear so intense as to be avoided when possible, and provide support for folk beliefs, such as "Tahitians are terrible when they fight."

Feeling management through public rituals allows the discharge of traumatic emotions, according to Thomas Scheff (1977, 1979). Anger, grief, fear, and embarrassment are unavoidable experiences in social life, but often cannot be discharged or resolved immediately because of social controls. Rituals provide a dramatic frame that restimulates distressful emotion but also gives the person a sense of control or distance from the feeling, so that it may be discharged through catharsis, Scheff argued. Most modern rituals are insufficiently involving in emotion, however, and participants are overdistanced from their distress. An emotional emptiness has developed from a "poverty of identifying rituals," wrote Orrin Klapp (1969:20). Rituals have become formalistic and impersonal because we lack agreement on symbols as collective reference points. We have only shallow feelings for romantic love, religious reverence, and esthetic sentiments, Klapp asserted, because we do not sense that others share the same feeling and meaning.

Summary and Conclusion

The chapter presents a sociological perspective on the organization of emotion into social sentiments, such as love, shame, and jealousy. A sentiment is a socially constructed pattern linking sensations and expressive gestures with cultural meanings, organized around a relationship to another person. The early part of the chapter discusses socially emergent properties that distinguish sentiments from emotion, such as social origin, extended time frame, socially defined content, and social modification. I then consider three major topics for a sociology of sentiments: how they are differentiated, socialized, and managed through social processes. Sentiments are not differentiated through innate bodily patterning, but through interpretation of feeling according to cultural vocabularies of labels and meanings. Sentiment socialization parallels the development of the self-conception and empathic ability. I examine several socialization processes by which we learn sentiments, such as learning to identify consistency among feelings, gestures, and social situations. The third issue I discuss is the management of feeling and expression according to normative and strategic considerations in social interaction. Gestures and feelings are managed in relation to the self-conception, group processes, and cultural beliefs about sentiments.

Every topic in this new field is relatively unexplored and awaits study by the variety of perspectives within sociology. I have also attempted to take into account psychological research, anthropological data, and historical descriptions, particularly where they describe the social actor as sentient, feeling and thinking about those feelings. The social processes that create and shape love, hatred, envy, and other sentiments only enhance the richness and meaning of these experiences.

NOTES

This work was prepared with support from the NIMH Postdoctoral Program in Personality and Social Structure, at the Department of Sociology, University of California, Berkeley. I would like to thank Gordon Clanton, Norman K. Denzin, David Finkelhor, Theodore Kemper, Anne Peplau, Morris Rosenberg, Thomas Scheff, Guy E. Swanson, Joel Telles, and Ralph H. Turner for their critical comments and suggestions on an earlier version of this chapter.

MORRIS ROSENBERG

The Self-Concept: Social Product and Social Force

Introduction

The sociology of the self-concept takes as its subject matter the analysis of the self-concept as a social product and a social force. That the self-concept should be considered a topic of sociological relevance at all may strike us as odd. For in its essence, nothing is more quintessentially psychological; an unequivocally subjective phenomenon, its home is located in the inner world of thought and experience. As such, it may appear to be peculiarly ill-suited as a subject of sociological concern.

The sociological relevance of the self-concept, however, is not obscure. For one thing, social factors play a major role in its formation. It is not present at birth but arises out of social experience and interaction; it both incorporates and is influenced by the individual's location in the social structure; it is formed within institutional systems, such as the family, school, economy, church; it is constructed from the materials of the culture; and it is affected by immediate social and environmental contexts. In other words, the self-concept achieves its particular shape and form in the matrix of a given culture, social structure, and institutional system. Although the individual's view of himself may be internal, what he sees and feels when he thinks of himself is largely the product of social life. But the self-concept, in its turn, exercises an important influence on behavior in various institutional realms. Since the self-concept is acted upon and, in turn, acts upon society, it is relevant to view it as a social product and a social force.

Broadly speaking, two rather different emphases have characterized the sociological approach to the self-concept (Hewitt 1976). One, focusing on the "biographical" self-concept, views the self-concept as a stable, enduring feature of personality or, to be more precise, as "a stable set of meanings attached to self as object" (Stryker chapter 1, this volume). The other, described as the "situated" self-concept, focuses on the self-concept as a shifting, adjustive process of self-presentation in social interaction. This distinction was explicitly recognized in James's landmark work on the subject. In holding to the view of the self-concept as an enduring disposition, James argued that, although the individual's self-esteem may vary from situation to situation, nevertheless "there is a certain average tone of self-feeling which each one of us carries about with him, and which is independent of the objective reasons we may have for satisfaction or discontent" (1950:306). At the same time, James observed, the individual's self also varies from situation to situation. The individual "has as many different social selves as there are distinct *groups* of persons about whose opinion he cares. He generally shows a different side of himself to each of these different groups. Many a youth who is demure enough before his parents and teachers, swears and swaggers like a pirate among his 'tough' young friends. We do not show ourselves to our children as to our club companions, to our customers as to the laborers we employ, to our own masters and employers as to our intimate friends" (James 1950:294).

Although the biographical and situational approaches share a number of fundamental assumptions, there are differences in emphasis. Probably the most extreme exposition of the situated approach is that of Blumer (1969a). However much sociologists may direct attention to stable and persistent features of personality, Blumer insists that the sole social reality is interaction. People's behavior in such interaction "is not the result of environmental pressures, stimuli, motives, attitudes, and ideas," but of how the individual "interprets and handles these things in the action which he is constructing." In the given situation the person must define the self, define the other, guide his own actions by taking the role of the other, and constantly adjust and align these actions with those of the other (as the other person does with regard to him). Actual interaction, then, requires an awareness and control of self, an adjustment to the self of the other, and a dynamic and shifting process that cannot be understood by reference to persistent and stable features of personality.

If one cannot explain social behavior by reference to stable features of personality, no more can one explain it by reference to the stable features of society, according to Blumer. Social system, social structure, culture, social function, and so forth cannot provide an explanation of human behavior. Genuine understanding can only come from comprehending the individual's "interpretation of objects, situations, or the actions of others."

Does this mean that each interaction is unique and idiosyncratic, thereby negating the possibility of generalization? By no means, since it may be possible to discover certain common or general *processes* that recur in diverse situations. A number of social psychologists have elucidated the nature of such processes. Turner (1962), for example, has enriched our understanding of social interaction by describing how (contrary to implicit social structural assumptions) roles are made rather than simply played; the individual does not simply follow a role script, but instead, actively defines and interprets his situation in response to situational dynamics. Goffman (1955, 1959) has presented a rich and vivid description of the implicit rules and strategies humans adopt when interacting with others. According to Goffman, whenever a person enters a situation, he "takes a line," presenting himself as a certain type of person. A convincing performance may require certain props, costumes, and setting; some involve solo performances, others team work; some actions go on front stage, others back stage; verbal, facial, and postural behavior are expressed or repressed; and so on. The essential feature of this approach is its view of social interaction as a matter of "self-presentation" or "impression management." A number of other general social processes have also been shown to characterize interaction: altercasting (Weinstein and Deutschberger 1963), negotiation (Strauss 1978), and the application of various "vocabularies of motive" (Mills 1940), including "disclaimers" (Hewitt and Stokes 1975), "accounts," that is, excuses and justifications (Scott and Lyman 1968), and "techniques of neutralization" (Sykes and Matza 1957).

In contrast to the interactive-situated self-concept approach, the social structural-biographical approach stresses the stable, persistent features of both society and personality. One fairly radical exposition of this position holds that the self-concept is essentially an attitude toward an object —the self—and can be understood within the framework adopted to understand attitudes toward other objects (Rosenberg 1965). Because certain special or distinctive features characterize the self-concept, however, the concept has been broadened to encompass "the totality of the individual's thoughts and feelings with reference to oneself as an object" (Rosenberg 1979). Social psychologists adopting this perspective tend to view the self-concept as a highly complex entity and characteristically study some specific segment of this totality. Some social psychologists are primarily interested in specific self-concept components, for example, traits and statuses; others in the arrangement (structure) of these components, such as their salience or importance in the individual's phenomenal field; still others center attention on certain broader dimensions of the self-concept (for example, self-esteem; self-concept stability; self-confidence; crystallization) which can characterize both the parts and the whole; and so on. The chief aim of this research is to trace various aspects, elements, or dimensions of the self-concept to their social roots.

The social structural-biographical self-concept approach is interested in understanding how patterned features of society operate to shape various aspects of the self-concept and how the self-concept, in turn, influences society. This approach begins with the recognition that societies are organized into systems of interrelated statuses and roles, are characterized by shared norms and values, operate to fulfill important needs and functions, and tend to be arranged in groups or social categories. Societies, in other words, are characterized by social structures, functions, institutions, groups, and cultural elements. The question of interest is: how do these fundamental overarching features of society impinge upon the individual's biographical (dispositional) self-concept, and how does this self-concept influence behavior in important institutional areas?

Both the biographical and the situated identity approaches are complementary ways of exploring the self-concept. Deriving their fundamental insights and drawing their inspiration from the work of Cooley and

Mead, both approaches have yielded important findings concerning the social nature of the self-concept, and each has enriched the other.

Space limitations prevent us from discussing fully the findings yielded by these two approaches. We shall therefore restrict our discussion to four major topics. (1) Interpersonal interaction. The most elementary and ubiquitous feature of social life is face-to-face interaction. How does such interaction influence the formation of the individual's self-concept? (2) Social identity. Among the sociologically most relevant self-concept components are the individual's social identity elements, for example, race, religion, gender, social class. One issue to be considered is the fact that because many of these social identity elements are differentially evaluated in the society, this unequal social prestige might affect the individual's self-esteem. (3) Social context. The question addressed is: how do the qualities or characteristics of *other* people in the environment affect the *individual's* self-concept? (4) Social institutions. How does the individual's involvement in selected institutional areas—economy, polity, educational system, legal system—relate to the individual's self-concept, either as a social product or a social force? This chapter will present some of the systematic empirical research that has addressed each of these questions.

In presenting these data, our approach will be to view the self-concept as encompassing all of the individual's cognitions and emotions relating to the self. So conceived, the self-concept is evidently a great deal broader than self-esteem, with which it is all too often equated. Space limitations bar us from attempting to spell out the diverse aspects, elements, dimensions of this complex entity (for a preliminary effort, see Rosenberg 1979). In the course of this discussion, however, we shall attempt to *illustrate* the diversity of self-concept elements in order to convey a sense of how rich and complex the self-concept actually is.

Social Interaction

A landmark development in the history of the sociology of the self-concept was the publication in 1934 of George Herbert Mead's *Mind, Self and Society.* According to Mead, the fundamental social process—the process that makes society possible and that makes the human being truly human—is communication. In order to communicate, Mead stressed, it is essential to take the role of the other, to put oneself in the other's shoes, to see things, including the self, from the other's perspective. None of us addresses the other in a language that we believe the other does not understand because, in speaking, we adopt the view of the other. But if communication obliges us to see the world from the viewpoint of the other, it inevitably causes us to view the self as well from the viewpoint of the other person. Thus, Mead (1934:68–69) asserted that "we are more or less unconsciously seeing ourselves as others see us."

Although Mead did not intend to imply that the self-concept and actual attitude of the other would be identical, it is a plausible inference to suggest that the attitudes of the other will help shape the self-concept. To say that we come to see ourselves as others see us, however, is essentially a shorthand way of saying that we come to see ourselves as we *think* others see us, for, after all, no one can ever see into the mind of another with unerring accuracy. This point was clearly recognized by the first important sociologist to devote substantial attention to the self-concept, Charles Horton Cooley (1902). No imagery could more vividly represent the idea that we see ourselves through the eyes of others than the couplet "Each to each a looking glass/Reflects the other that doth pass." But, he was quick to add: "A self-idea of this sort seems to have three principal elements: the imagination of our appearance to the other person; the imagination of his judgment of that appearance, and some sort of self-feeling, such as pride or mortification." The self is thus *not* a literal looking-glass image, an exact reflection, but rather an imputed sentiment, the imagination of the evaluation of this reflection within another's mind. We are not only obliged to *interpret* the other's perception of us, but also to interpret his probable response to what he has observed in terms of his own values and attitudes.

The theories of Mead and Cooley are, of course, subtle and elusive, and many of their arguments are not easily subjected to empirical test. The segment of their theory that has been explored most thoroughly has been the principle of reflected appraisals. This principle holds that, as a consequence of seeing ourselves from the perspectives of others, our self-concepts will come to correspond at least partially to other people's views of us. What light has subsequent empirical research shed on the theories of Mead and Cooley?

Before presenting the data, some terminological conventions are needed. Any such interactional analysis involves three components: (1) the self-concept—how the individual *sees himself;* (2) the social (or accorded) self—how other people *actually* see the individual; and (3) the reflected (or perceived) self—how the individual *believes* others see him.

First, the data consistently support the principle of reflected appraisals. For example, Miyamoto and Dornbusch (1956) asked students to rate themselves in terms of four self-concept components: intelligent, physically attractive, self-confident, and likeable. They also asked other members of the individual's group to rate him or her on these characteristics. Since ten groups participated, and each group rated each individual on four traits, forty comparisons were possible. In thirty-five out of forty comparisons, those rating themselves high were more likely than those rating themselves low to be rated higher by the group.

Second, research also shows a strong and consistent association between the reflected self and the self-concept—what we believe others think of us and our self-concepts (Miyamoto and Dornbusch 1956; Reeder et al. 1960; Sherwood 1965). If the individual believes others think well of him, then he tends to think well of himself.

Third, there is a consistent, though imperfect, relationship between the social self (what others actually think of us) and the reflected self (Miyamoto and Dornbusch 1956; Reeder et al. 1960). More often than not, people's views of what others think of them are accurate; but in many cases they also misread the attitude of the other toward themselves (Schrauger and Schoeneman 1979).

Fourth, what we *believe* others think of us (reflected self) is more closely related to our self-concepts than what they *actually* think of us (social self). In the Miyamoto and Dornbusch (1956) study, the prediction that those who rated themselves high were more likely than those who rated themselves low to believe that others rated them high was supported in forty out of forty comparisons. (See also Reeder et al. 1960.)

In general, then, the research unequivocally supports the basic ideas of Mead and Cooley regarding the importance of taking the role of the other in shaping the self-concept. Because this aspect of Mead's theory is general, however, it is imprecise and in need of refinement. For example, although it is true that we tend to see ourselves as others see us, one question is: which others? There are many other people with whom we interact, and since they inevitably view us from different perspectives, we obviously cannot accept *all* their views of us. Second, which self-concept components? Since there are many self-concept components, we may accept a person's judgment of certain of our characteristics, but not of other characteristics. Third: why? Since we internalize other people's attitudes toward us in some circumstances but not in others, the question is: what motivational factors contribute to such differential effects? Research has shed light on each of these questions.

SIGNIFICANT OTHERS

Whether the attitudes of other people toward us affect our self-concepts depends in part on how significant they are to us. The question is: what makes some people highly significant to us, others less so? Two foundations of interpersonal significance will be considered: valuation and credibility.

Valuation. It is reasonable to expect that the opinions of those people who matter most to us—whose opinion we care about greatly—should have a stronger effect on our self-concepts than the views of those to whom we are indifferent. This proposition was examined in a large-scale study of Baltimore school pupils. In this investigation, respondents were asked how much they cared about what certain people in their "role-sets" (Merton 1957) thought of them. The results showed that the relationship between what the child believed his mother thought of him and what he thought of himself was very strong if he cared very much about her opinion of him, but much weaker if he cared little. The same proved to be true with regard to fathers, teachers, classmates, siblings, and friends (Rosenberg 1973).

Credibility. The impact of the other's opinion of us also depends on the degree of faith, trust, or confidence that we repose in that person's judgment. The concept of credibility, although overlapping with that of valuation, is not identical with it. We may be eager to be liked by our classmates, even if we have little respect for their judgment. In the Baltimore study (Rosenberg 1973), the results showed that, with regard to parents, teachers, and best friends, the relationship between the reflected self and the self-concept was stronger if the child had high faith in the other person's knowledge of the self than if he had low faith.

But on what bases do we trust or distrust others' judgments of us? Credibility may rest on at least three different foundations: expertise, imputed motivation, and congruency.

Expertise is an important basis of credibility. For example, Bergin (1962) compared two ways of changing boys' attitudes toward their masculinity. In the high credibility situation, the director of the project told the subjects he would test them by means of an objective measure of their masculinity. In the low credibility situation, the tester was introduced as a high school student whose work represented part of a study in social perception. Not only was the subject more likely to accept the expert's judgment of his masculinity than the high school student's, but he tended to accept the expert's assessment even if it deviated from his own. Similarly, Videbeck (1960) showed that when a bogus "speech expert" evaluated an individual's oral reading ability, the individual readily changed his mind about his skill in this area.

Credibility is also influenced by our attribution of *motives* to others. Whether we will accept the other person's expressed judgment of us depends on whether we consider him or her sincere or false. In Gergen's (1965) study, half of the subjects were told that the interviewer was simply practicing a set of interviewing techniques, whereas the other half were told that the main task of the interviewer was to be as honest as possible. Although both groups of subjects were treated identically, the self-esteem of the first group was less influenced than the group led to believe that the investigator was "sincere, uncalculated and attuned to them as individuals."

Another basis of credibility is the assumed *consensus* of other people's attitudes toward us. Some dissensus, of course, is inevitable, since every other person sees us from a somewhat different perspective. What, then, is the effect of such consensus or dissensus among others on our self-attitudes? In an ingenious experiment by Backman et al. (1963), the investigators attempted to change the subject's views of two self-concept components—one on which consensus was believed to be high, the other on which consensus was believed to be low. If low, the self-concept component proved easy to change, but if high, it was much more difficult to change.

The idea that we see ourselves as others see us is thus a generalization in evident need of refinement. The degree to which it is true depends on how much the judgment of the other is valued and trusted. Certain broader implications of this fact may be suggested. For example, if blacks neither value nor trust the judgments of whites toward their race, but do value and trust the judgments of blacks, then widespread white racial prejudice will not necessarily damage self-esteem among blacks.

SPECIFIC SELF-CONCEPT COMPONENTS

How the attitudes of other people affect our self-concepts also depends on which self-concept component is under consideration. A tennis expert may be highly influential in determining our judgments of our tennis skill, but our parents and friends may be more influential in determining our global self-esteem.

An apt illustration is provided by Denzin's (1966) study of a college population. Using the work of Kuhn (1964) and of Mead (1934) as a springboard, Denzin distinguished between "role-specific significant others," (significant with regard to a specific aspect of the individual's role-set) and "orientational others" (significant in general). To index role-specific significant others, Denzin asked: "Would you please give me a list of those persons or groups of people whose evaluation of you as a *student* on the ——— campus concerns you the *most.*" "Orientational significant others" were assessed by the question: "Would you please give me a list of those persons or groups of people whose evaluation of you as a *person* concerns you the *most.*"

The results showed that, with regard to evaluation of the self as a *student,* respondents tended to mention faculty first, with friends and family members following in that order. But when asked about the views of others toward the self as a *person,* friends were most frequently mentioned, followed by family members, with faculty in third place.

The impact of others also depends on the degree of *crystallization* (Markus 1977) of the self-concept component under consideration. If the component is firmly fixed, others' views may have little impact; but if it is uncrystallized, we may readily accept the other's view of ourselves. This point is most evident when bogus qualities are used. When the professor gives us the results of our performance on a test of "contrast sensitivity" or "perceptual discrimination," informing us that we are deficient or superior in this regard, we readily accept his expert judgment of us. The reason is, of course, that we had no preformulated view of ourselves regarding these qualities. But the same is true of real but uncrystallized self-concept components. Such is the case, for example, when Videbeck (1960) asks his subjects how good they are at "voice control" or "conveying meaning." Experts' judgments are easily accepted with reference to qualities on which we have little or no preformulated opinions. It would be far more difficult to convince us, contrary to an established assumption, that we are a fascist or a moron.

MOTIVES

Finally, whether we accept the other's view of us depends in part on whether or not we are motivated to accept it. Given the self-esteem (Kaplan 1975, 1980) and self-consistency motives (Schwartz and Stryker 1970), it is evident that we would prefer to internalize positive rather than negative, and consistent rather than contradictory, attitudes toward the self. There is evidence to suggest that, in the interests of self-esteem and self-consistency, people engage in (1) selective perception of the attitudes of the other and (2) selective attribution of significance.

Selective perception in the service of self-esteem characteristically involves the belief that others think more highly of us than they actually do. There is, in fact, ample evidence of such a "self-favorability" bias. Virtually every study that has explored the issue finds that people tend to believe that others think more highly of them than these others actually do (for example, Sherwood 1965; Reeder et al. 1960; Wylie 1979). Furthermore, the self-consistency motive contributes to people's tendency to believe that others' attitudes toward them are *congruent* with their own. Backman and Secord (1962) have advanced a theory of "interpersonal congruency" which is said to exist when the individual perceives others as attributing to him a trait that he attributes to himself. This theory was investigated in a study of thirty-one women in a sorority house. Subjects were asked to rank themselves on sixteen paired traits, such as warm-cold, mature-immature, dominant-submissive, and so forth. The subject was asked to indicate the adjectives she thought others would assign to her, those she assigned to herself, and those she assigned to each of the other women. The results showed that the subject *overestimated* the extent to which others saw her as she saw herself, and that this overestimation was strongest for those women whom the subject liked or interacted with most. People thus tend to believe unduly that others—particularly those they know best—see them as they see themselves.

Selective significance is also enlisted in the service of the self-concept motives. Since significance is in the eye of the beholder, it follows that we prefer to attribute significance to those who, we believe, think well (or congruently) of us and to withhold significance from others. Manis (1955) found, for example, that the individual is more likely to be influenced by what he believes his friends think of him than by what he believes his nonfriends think of him. The net result of this interpersonal selectivity is to attribute greater significance to the opinions of those whose attitudes toward the self are more favorable.

In sum, what empirical research has made evident is that the principle of reflected appraisals, though fundamentally correct, is an approximation. Whether we see ourselves as others see us depends on (1) *who* these others are; (2) *which aspect* of the self is under consideration; and (3) whether we are *motivated* to accept or reject their views. The self we see when viewing ourselves through the eyes of others is thus seen through a glass, darkly (Schrauger and Schoeneman 1979).

Social Identity Elements

Social identity elements refer to the groups, statuses, or social categories to which the members of society are socially recognized as belonging. As Stryker (1980) observes, the human being enters a named, classified world, and is immediately sorted into socially relevant categories. Scarcely has the infant entered the world than he or she is immediately classified according to race, sex, religion, nationality, and so forth. In due course, new socially recognized categories, some of his or her own choosing, are added. These are the fundamental bases upon which society, independent of the special and unique features of each individual, orders and arranges its members.

No universally recognized classification of social identity elements is at hand. Without laying claim to exhaustiveness, we suggest that the major social identity elements are (1) social statuses (sex, age, family status, occupation, class); (2) membership groups, such as culture groups (French, Italian, Greek), groups based on common belief systems (Catholic, Baptist, Democrat, Republican), interest groups (unions, professional societies), other organizational affiliations (government employees), and various socially defined categories (married-single, employed-unemployed); (3) social labels, often assigned by some official certifying agency—a judge, doctor, political unit—which places actors into such socially recognized categories as alcoholic, drug addict, mental patient, criminal; (4) derivative statuses, sometimes based on other membership groups, statuses, or labels (ex-convict, widow, war veteran, emeritus professor); (5) social types, based on some socially recognized *syndrome* of interests, attitudes, characteristics, and behavior (intellectual, playboy, Don Juan, eager beaver); and (6) "personal identity," that is, a social classification with a single case (identified by a name, social security number, or similar tagging device).

These social identity elements shape the self-concept in a number of ways. First, to an important extent they define for the individual what he or she is; the individual feels he *is* a male, lawyer, Protestant, father. Furthermore, if the social identity element is ambiguous (for example, is one an adolescent or a young adult? a music student or a musician?) the self-concept is correspondingly ambiguous. Second, these identity elements, because of their associated role standards (Kagan 1964), represent criteria for self-judgment. A boy may condemn himself for lack of courage which a girl may accept without qualm. Conversely, a boy is unembarrassed at his inability to sew, a girl unembarrassed at her ineptitude at catching forward passes. Third, role performances influence social action; this behavior, in turn, comes to constitute an important part of the content of the self-concept. The professor sees himself as a teacher or writer, but the doctor usually does not; the doctor sees himself as a diagnostician or surgeon, but the professor does not. Furthermore, these actions may generalize to broader aspects of the self-concept. Kohn (1969) and Kohn and Schooler (1969), for example, find that men whose work requires them to exercise autonomy, make their own decisions, and assume responsibility are more likely to emerge with higher global self-esteem. Finally, since these social identity elements represent important bases of *social* evaluation, they may influence *self*-evaluation. Since this last point has been of particular interest to social scientists, we have elected to focus on this issue.

SOCIAL ESTEEM AND SELF-ESTEEM

In every society, people are characteristically ordered along a number of dimensions of stratification, for example, occupational, social class, racial, religious, gender, age, and ethnic. Occupations are arranged in a well-recognized hierarchy of prestige (Hodge, Siegel and Rossi 1964); ethnic preferences (including racial) are surprisingly uniform across broad segments of the society and persist over long periods of time

(Bogardus 1959); and so on. Since such stratified positions command unequal social esteem, social scientists have tended to take it for granted that those ranking lower in the various status hierarchies would have lower self-esteem than the more favored members of society. This general assumption would appear to rest primarily on the following three principles of self-esteem formation: (1) reflected appraisals, (2) social comparison, and (3) self-attribution.

The principle of reflected appraisals, suggested by the theories of Mead and Cooley, holds that if others look up to us and treat us with respect, then we will respect ourselves accordingly, but if they derogate or disdain us, then our self-esteem will be low. Rawls (1971:178) minces no words in asserting that "our self-respect normally depends on the respect of others." Hence, insofar as our social class, race, gender, or religion governs the respect with which we are treated by others, the principle of reflected appraisals would suggest a correspondence between social esteem and self-esteem. For example, it is argued that the widespread prejudice against blacks in America ultimately leads to low self-esteem among blacks as they hear "the din of white racists egotistically insisting that Caucasians are innately superior to Negroes" (Pettigrew 1964:9).

The second principle of self-esteem formation is that of social comparison (Festinger 1954). Social comparison is at the heart of social evaluation theory, described by Pettigrew (1967) as follows:

> The basic tenet of social evaluation theory is that human beings learn about themselves by comparing themselves to others. A second tenet is that the process of social evaluation leads to positive, neutral, or negative self-ratings which are relative to the standards set by the individual employed for comparison.

Since it is frequently the case that privilege and disprivilege are cumulative and reinforcing, low position along one stratification dimension may produce a corresponding position along another. A prime example is racial stratification. As a consequence of prejudice and discrimination, black adults in American society are, on the average, less well educated than whites, hold less prestigious occupational positions, and have substantially lower incomes (Willie 1979). In addition, black children are not only victims of the poverty and low occupational prestige of their parents, but they also tend to perform more poorly in school and are more likely to stem from family contexts that are socially stigmatized. Hence, a general consequence of prejudice and discrimination is to bring about *other* conditions of life for minority group members that produce unfavorable comparisons with the privileged majority—comparisons "obviously" damaging to self-esteem.

A third principle of self-esteem formation is self-attribution (Kelley 1967). Bem's (1972) version of this principle, stemming from the radical behaviorist perspective of B. F. Skinner, undertakes to explain behavior without reference to internal psychological processes which, it correctly holds, are inherently unobservable. According to this view, even reports of inner states (such as hunger, anger, excitement, sympathy)—states ordinarily understood to be based on private internal stimuli—may in reality reflect past training in the application of certain descriptive terms to overt behavior and the conditions under which it occurs. Thus, to use Bem's example, the man who, after devouring an enormous meal, concludes that "I guess that I was hungrier than I thought," is drawing conclusions about his level of hunger not by consulting his inner experience but by observing his own behavior or its outcomes. Furthermore, it is not just inner states but any aspect of the self that may be influenced by the individual's observation of his or her own behavior. As Bandura (1978:347) observes: "People derive much of their knowledge [about themselves] from direct experience of the effects produced by their actions." Thus, the minority child who gazes at his poor report card, or the minority adult whose social identity includes a low prestige job, lack of material possessions, or other evidence of failure would be expected to develop low self-esteem.

Because minority group members are victims of prejudice, and hence negative reflected selves (reflected appraisals); because, on the average, they tend to compare unfavorably with the majority in such valued areas as school achievement, educational level, and occupational success (social comparison); and because they may interpret their unfortunate life circumstances and experiences as overt reflections of a lack of essential worth (self-attribution), many writers have simply taken it for granted that people ranking low in the various prestige hierarchies would tend to have lower self-esteem.

The facts, however, speak otherwise. Wylie's (1979) monumental synthesis of this research, involving a review of several thousand studies, offers little support for the conclusion that blacks, Hispanics, women, Jews, or other groups subjected to prejudice and discrimination have appreciably lower self-esteem.

Why have these sound psychological principles failed to yield the expected results? The critical error, we believe, has lain in viewing the situation from the perspective of the broader society rather than from the viewpoints of the minority group members themselves. Investigators have frequently overlooked the advice of Thomas and Thomas (1928) to attempt to understand the individual's "definition of the situation," to gain entry into his phenomenal field or psychological world. To develop this point, we shall consider the finding that, among school populations, black self-esteem is at least as high as white self-esteem (Wylie 1979; Rosenberg and Simmons 1972).

Take the principle of reflected appraisals—that we tend to see ourselves through the eyes of others. But which others? Do children see themselves through the eyes of the broader society or of those with whom they directly interact? The structural arrangements in American society are such that the black child's interaction goes on primarily with others in his role-set, that is, his mother, father, classmates, teachers, and neighborhood peers. Whatever else these particular others may think of the child on other grounds, they are unlikely to derogate the black child on *racial* grounds.[1] Thus, McCarthy and Yancey (1971) correctly observe that blacks are likely to see themselves from the perspective of members of their own group rather than of the dominant majority. Furthermore, these particular others are precisely those likely to be the most significant others. It is thus not the dominant white majority that influences the black child's self-esteem, but primarily other black adults and children with whom he constantly interacts and whose judgment he values and trusts. A study of a school population in Baltimore (Rosenberg and Simmons 1972:142) showed that the relationship between what the child believed his parents, teachers, and friends thought of him and his own self-esteem was very strong for both black and white children and was, in fact, slightly stronger among the black children. The principle of reflected appraisals is thus entirely sound, but has been misapplied by assuming that black children see themselves chiefly through the eyes of the white majority.

The social comparison principle is equally sound and equally misapplied. As noted above, minority children are expected to have lower self-esteem because they compare unfavorably with the white middle-class majority in terms of socioeconomic status, school marks, or intact family. But with whom do the minority children actually compare themselves—the privileged majority or the members of their own group with whom they primarily interact? The evidence strongly suggests that children and adolescents, at least, tend to compare themselves with those in their immediate interpersonal environments. Comparing themselves with others in the same status categories produces the normal distribution of self-esteem. On the other hand, when circumstances *do* stimulate minority children to compare themselves with the majority, their self-esteem does suffer (Rosenberg and Simmons 1972). But only a small proportion of minority children find themselves in such situations.

Third, the self-attribution principle is also sound but misapplied. For example, academic self-concept and, to a lesser extent, global self-esteem tends to be influenced by the child's school marks; in other words, one important basis for assessing one's own worth is to observe one's achievements. But this is precisely why it is so important to recognize that some of the individual's statuses are ascribed, whereas others are achieved. There is evidence to suggest that the chief ascribed statuses—race, ethnicity, gender, religion—show virtually no association with global self-esteem whereas achieved statuses do show such an association (Jacques and Chason 1977). It also explains why social class is unrelated to self-esteem among children, but does show a clear relationship among adults (Rosenberg and Pearlin 1978), namely, that for the child, social class is ascribed, for the adult, achieved.

It is thus apparent that it is not the individual's behavior but his *interpretation* of the behavior that has consequences for self-esteem. The issue, in other words, is one of attribution. Thus, McCarthy and Yancey (1971) observe that one factor protecting the self-esteem of many minority group adults is the "system-blame interpretation." Attribution theorists (Heider 1958; Kelley 1967) have elaborated on the point that, in explaining some behavioral outcome, people may attribute it either to internal properties of the individual or to factors in the external situation. For example, if someone does well on a test, he can attribute this outcome either to the fact that he is smart (an internal characteristic) or to the fact that the test was easy (the external situation). If occupational failure is explained by prejudice and discrimination (external factors), then the lower occupational status of minority group members and women may do no damage to self-esteem.

In sum, any easy and automatic assumption that low prestige in some stratification hierarchy will produce correspondingly low self-esteem is a gross oversimplication. What research has demonstrated is that, although the principles on which this assumption primarily rest—reflected appraisals, social comparison, and self-attribution—are perfectly sound, researchers have tended to overlook the psychological world—the phenomenal field—of the minority group member and, in so doing, have frequently reached erroneous conclusions.

IDENTITY SALIENCE

The bearing of such social identity elements as race, religion, or gender on the self-concept are thus varied and complex. Our understanding of these effects, however, has been appreciably advanced by recognizing that the self-concept is more than a random conglomeration of elements; it is, on the contrary, a *structure* whose elements are arranged in a hierarchy of salience. Some elements are at the center of the individual's concerns, whereas others are more peripheral. For example, Mulford and Salisbury (1964) have shown that the position of mother is more salient to the woman than father is to the man. A number of sociological social psychologists have elaborated on this theme, using such terms as "identity salience" (Stryker 1968), "role salience" and "role prominence" (McCall and Simmons 1978), "role engulfment" (Schur 1971), "role-person merger" (Turner 1978), and "psychological centrality" (Rosenberg 1979). It is relevant to direct attention to several implications of such differential centrality.

First, as Stryker observes, people are more likely to seek to play central than peripheral roles. If "tennis player" ranks high in one person's value hierarchy and low in another's, then the former will be more likely to "perceive a given situation as an opportunity to perform in terms of that identity" (Stryker 1980:84). Thus, a scientist may begrudge every moment spent away from his laboratory, an athlete may champ at the bit in his eagerness to get out on the playing field, and so on.

Second, we are more likely to cultivate the skills or qualities relevant to the role performances of central statuses than of peripheral ones. For example, an athlete may give full attention to ensuring that he is in peak physical condition but show far less concern with whether he is behaving properly as a nephew or brother. The pianist may practice endlessly to improve his musical ability, but make no effort to learn to perform home repairs.

Third, role performance of central statuses may transfer or diffuse to other statuses. This process is aptly described in Turner's (1978) concept of "role-person merger." Turner's social structural formulation views the person as consisting "of all the roles in an individual's repertoire." The question raised is "whether the attitudes and behavior developed as an expression of one role carry over into other situations." For example, "The professional who carries the office bearing and air of authority into family and community dealings has *become* to a considerable degree the professional role played at work" (1978:3). In these circumstances, a particular status moves to the top of one's identity hierarchy; the role standard, or qualities expected of a status incumbent, become of primary concern to the individual, and these qualities generalize to other roles.

Under certain circumstances, in fact, a social identity element may become so important that it overwhelms the others. One expression of this idea is the labeling theorist's concept of "role engulfment" (Schur 1971). This concept suggests that the individual's identification of the self with some labeled category, for example, homosexual, embezzler, or drug addict, may loom so large in his consciousness that all else pales by comparison. His other statuses or characteristics, however admirable, come to count for nothing in his eyes.

Fourth, global self-esteem is more likely to hinge on performance in central than in peripheral roles. This point has been felicitously expressed by William James (1950:310): "I, who for the time have staked my all on being a psychologist, am mortified if others know much more psychology than I. But I am contented to wallow in the grossest ignorance of Greek. My deficiencies there give me no sense of personal humiliation at all. Had I 'pretensions' to be a linguist, it would have been just the reverse."

Finally, our sense of who and what we are tends to hinge more importantly on central than on peripheral identity elements. The woman who loses her identity as wife when her husband dies, or a man who loses his identity as a carpenter or engineer upon forced retirement, may experience feelings of uncertainty about who or what he or she really is. The loss of peripheral identity elements, on the other hand, may have little effect.

For some reason that is not readily evident, sociologists appear to have been more active in developing and elaborating the idea of social identity salience than in examining it empirically. That strongly valued traits have a particularly powerful impact on global self-esteem has been clearly supported by research (Rosenberg 1965:chapter 13). Differential social identity valuation would be expected to show similar effects.

Social Context and Self-Concept

Along with social interaction and social identity elements, social contexts have an important bearing on the self-concept. The special nature of contextual analysis can be highlighted by comparing it with what is doubtlessly the dominant procedure in sociological research, namely, the individual characteristic approach. For example, when we ask about the relationship between race and self-esteem, we are looking at the connection between one characteristic of the individual (a social identity element) with another characteristic of the individual (a global attitude toward the self). When we turn to contextual analysis, on the other hand, the aim is to investigate the bearing of some general property of the *group* on the thoughts, acts, or norms of its constituent members. Instead of asking: what is the impact of the individual's social class on his self-esteem? we might ask: what is the impact of his *neighbor's* social class on his self-esteem? In other words, how does *their* socioeconomic status affect *his* self-concept? The qualities of others structure the individual's experience. For example, it may be a very different experience for a white child to be raised in a black neighborhood than for a black child to be raised in the same neighborhood; for a Catholic child to be raised in a Protestant neighborhood than for a Protestant child to be raised in the same neighborhood; for a middle-class child to be raised in a working-class neighborhood than for a working-class child to be reared in this social context.

By now a substantial body of literature examining contextual effects has accumulated, demonstrating diverse effects. The type of context that appears to be most relevant to the self-concept is the dissonant or consonant context. By consonance or dissonance we refer to the degree to which the individual's characteristics match the characteristics predominant in his environment.

Contexts, of course, may be of varying types. In order to demonstrate the relevance and nature of contextual effects, we shall draw attention to a *range* of contexts ([1] social identity contexts, [2] abilities contexts, and [3] physical characteristics contexts), in relation to a *range* of self-concept effects ([1] global self-esteem, [2] academic self-concept, [3] self-concept stability, [4] self-confidence, and [5] salience of self-concept components).

SOCIAL IDENTITY CONTEXTS

Among sociologists, social identity contexts—racial, religious, and ethnic—have been of particular interest. Although research has usually examined the effects of consonance or dissonance on global self-esteem, some data are also available regarding the bearing of dissonance or consonance on other aspects of the self-concept, namely, self-concept stability, salience of self-concept components, and academic self-concepts. We shall first consider the bearing of the following social identity contexts on global self-esteem: religious, racial, ethnic, and social class.

The bearing of religious dissonance on global self-esteem was investigated in a large-scale survey of adolescents in New York State (Rosenberg 1965). The results showed that Jewish children raised in predominantly Gentile neighborhoods had lower global self-esteem than those raised in predominantly Jewish neighborhoods. Furthermore, Catholics raised in non-Catholic neighborhoods and Protestants raised in non-Protestant neighborhoods also had somewhat lower self-esteem than those reared among their coreligionists. Thus, even people high in religious status manifested some self-esteem decline in dissonant contexts, although the effects were not very strong.

The corpus of research on dissonant *racial* contexts is far more abundant. One point frequently overlooked is that, technically, segregation represents a condition of racial *consonance* whereas desegregation represents a condition of *dissonance.* Research findings in this area have not been entirely consistent, but a number of studies indicate that the global self-esteem consequences of racial dissonance are somewhat negative. St. John's (1975) thorough review of the effects of desegregation found that in nine studies global self-esteem was lower in dissonant contexts, in four studies it was higher, and in seven studies there was no clear difference (p. 51). The weight of evidence suggests that the global self-esteem consequences of racial dissonance tend to be negative, but that the effects are neither powerful nor uniform.

Pitts (1978) provided some evidence that *ethnic* dissonance may bear on global self-esteem. Her study was based on a sample of French Canadian men in Sherbrooke, Quebec, some of whom had been educated in French-speaking and some in English-speaking schools. The data showed that the French who had attended English-speaking schools were more likely than those who had attended French schools to be in occupations of higher prestige but that their global self-esteem was lower. Otherwise expressed, despite the superior achievements resulting from attendance at English-speaking schools, their sense of self-worth appeared to suffer in an ethnically dissonant context.

When we turn to *social class* dissonance, little information is available. One study (Rosenberg 1975) showed that, among white respondents, higher-class children attending lower-class schools had significantly lower self-esteem than higher-class children attending higher-class schools, and lower-class children in higher-class schools had lower self-esteem than lower-class children in lower-class schools. For both upper- and lower-class children, then, dissonant socioeconomic environments appeared hostile to self-esteem. Since this is but a single study, further research is needed.

It should be stressed that, although the weight of evidence indicates that the dissonant social identity context exerts a depressing effect on global self-esteem, this effect is not usually a very powerful one. At the same time we should note that pure and uncontaminated tests of contextual effects rarely appear in nature. Contexts tend to be multidimensional. For a given child, the racial context may be dissonant, but the religious context consonant; the ethnic context may be dissonant, the abilities context, consonant. Hence, the fact that a particular dissonant context may not show a very powerful self-esteem effect does not represent conclusive evidence that the contextual effect is unimportant since, in the case of the specific individual, a dissonance effect may be counterbalanced by a consonance effect.

The reasons for expecting contextual dissonance to have some depressing effect on global self-esteem are not obscure. For one thing, the data clearly show that people in dissonant contexts are more likely to be subjected directly to the ravages of prejudice. A study of New York State adolescents (Rosenberg 1965) showed that those in dissonant religious contexts were much more likely than those in consonant contexts to report that they had been "teased, laughed at, or left out of things" because of their religion. In Baltimore, blacks in desegregated schools were more likely than those in homogeneous contexts to say that they had been subjected to direct racial prejudice (Rosenberg and Simmons 1972). And in Quebec, French-Canadians educated in English-speaking schools were more likely than those in French-speaking schools to report they had experienced ethnic prejudice (Pitts 1978). The reflected appraisals received from those in a dissonant environment may well have damaging global self-esteem consequences.

In addition, the individual socialized in one culture who must judge himself by the standards of another may feel that there is something strange or wrong about himself. Thus, if a French Canadian attending an English-speaking school speaks with a "strange accent" (from the English perspective) or, because of his French background, thinks or acts in ways at odds with others in his English environment, he may, following the self-attribution principle, conclude that there is something wrong with himself. Some inferential evidence suggesting the existence of such a cultural dissonance effect among religious groups has been presented (Rosenberg 1962).

To this point the dependent variable of interest has been *global* self-esteem. But other specific self-concept components may be still more strongly affected by a social identity context. One of these is the *academic self-concept* of the school pupil. Although the data are not abundant, they suggest that racial dissonance may be somewhat more damaging to academic self-concept than to global self-esteem, despite the fact that several studies show that youngsters in desegregated settings perform *better* academically than those in segregated settings. Coleman et al. (1966) found that, although black children in predominantly white schools obtained somewhat higher scores on standardized tests than those in black schools, nevertheless, "for each group as the proportion white in the school increases, the [black] child's [academic] self-concept decreases." St. John's (1975) review of research is consistent with Coleman's findings. In her racial desegregation research, she reported that five studies showed the effects of contextual dissonance on academic self-esteem to be negative and only one study suggested it was positive; in two studies, no clear difference appeared. The chief reason, of course, is that the dissonant racial context provides a damaging comparison reference group for minority children. Studies generally show that black children's school marks tend to compare unfavorably, on the average, with those of whites attending the same schools. It is thus understandable that their *academic* self-concepts should suffer more than their *global* self-esteem under these circumstances.

A third self-concept dimension is *stability.* Although the data suggest that the effect of dissonance on stability is not a powerful one, some evidence indicates that those in dissonant contexts have more unstable, shifting, and uncertain self-concepts. In a study of an urban school system, black children in dissonant racial contexts were conspicuously more likely to have unstable self-concepts than black children in consonant contexts; this proved to be true even when self-esteem was controlled (Rosenberg 1975). The New York State study (Rosenberg 1965) also examined the relationship of religious dissonance and self-concept instability controlling on self-esteem. Although contextual dissonance did not show an association to self-concept stability (independent of self-esteem) among Jewish adolescents, some association between these variables appeared among Protestants, and a definite association appeared among Catholics.

Why contextual dissonance should foster self-concept instability is not certain, but one possibility is that the dissonant context *may fail to provide interpersonal confirmation for the individual's self-hypothesis.* Many self-attitudes require confirmation. Among the various types of evidence confirming or disconfirming a self-hypothesis, probably the most important is interpersonal: others must "legitimate" (McCall and Simmons 1978) the individual's role identity if he is to maintain a stable self-concept.

Thus, with regard to the racial context, the greater self-image instability of black children in dissonant contexts may be attributable to the fact that the white children and teachers in these settings do not provide sufficient confirmation for the black child's self-concept. While he may see himself as physically attractive, mild in disposition, and honest, at least some proportion of the prejudiced white children may not appreciate his good looks and may act as if he is threatening, aggressive, or dishonest. Such behavior could well introduce doubts and uncertainty in the child's mind about who or what he is. But any kind of prejudice—prejudgment—*including the excessively positive,* may have this effect. The "liberal" white teacher who publicly asserts how smart and cute and otherwise wonderful the black child is, whether or not the child actually is like this at all, may generate equal uncertainty and insecurity in the child, thereby fostering an unstable self-concept.

Social identity dissonance has also been shown to have a bearing on the *salience* of social identity elements. For example, at any given point, which of various social identity elements—race, religion, age, gender, occupation, and so forth—is at the forefront of attention? One answer to this question, advanced by McGuire and Padawer-Singer (1976), is that salience is likely to be governed by the "distinctiveness postulate." "The distinctiveness postulate implies that what is salient in a person's spontaneous self-concept is the person's peculiarities, the ways in which one differs from other people in one's customary social environment" (p. 513). For example, a black woman among a group of white women is likely to be conscious of her race; but if she is among black men, she is more likely to be conscious of her gender. McGuire and Padawer-Singer (1976) found that girls in classes in which boys were in the majority, and boys in classes in which girls were in the majority, were more likely spontaneously to mention gender when describing themselves. Ethnic salience also tended to be higher in dissonant contexts (McGuire et al. 1978). Similarly, Herman's (1970) study of American adolescents visiting Israel found that these youngsters were much more likely to be aware of themselves as American when in Israel than when in America. Because of the distinctiveness postulate, social identity components tend to be more salient in dissonant than in consonant contexts.

These data thus suggest that dissonant social identity contexts may have an effect—though not usually a very powerful one—on global self-esteem, academic self-concept, self-concept stability, and salience of identity components. Dissonant contexts may also have some advantageous consequences (Crain and Weissman 1972; Coleman et al. 1966) but these are not generally related directly to the self-concept.

ABILITIES CONTEXTS

The potentially damaging effects of contextual dissonance on self-esteem rests on two rather different foundations. One deals with those ways in which we are different from others; because of prejudice or cultural dissimilarity, such a difference may eventuate in reduced self-esteem. The other effect stems from whether we are better or worse than others; our self-esteem may be damaged if we find ourselves immersed in contexts in which others outstrip us. The latter effect is particularly evident when we consider abilities contexts. How many premier high school students suffer rude blows to their sense of worth when they enter highly select colleges? How many outstanding college football heroes develop feelings of inadequacy upon entering the professional ranks? In other words, it is not only how good the individual is, but how good others around him are that affect his self-attitudes.

In "The American Soldier" studies (Stouffer et al. 1949b), the Research Branch considered the following contexts: inexperienced soldiers in inexperienced outfits, and equally inexperienced replacements in divisions otherwise composed of combat veterans. Among numerous questions put to these soldiers was the individual's confidence in his ability "to take charge of a group of men" in combat. It turned out that the inexperienced soldier in a veteran outfit was less confident that he could take charge of a group of men than was the inexperienced soldier in an inexperienced outfit. Relative to the veterans, the replacements were aware of their inexperience and felt less capable of leadership than did equally inexperienced soldiers in consonant contexts; the competence was the same, but the contexts were different.

The bearing of the abilities context on self-esteem within the classroom is aptly illustrated in a study of the relationship of school marks to self-esteem by Rogers et al. (1978). The authors studied 159 academic underachievers in small special education classes in 17 elementary schools. The data showed that, *within classrooms,* those with higher standardized scores had higher self-esteem, both on the composite self-esteem index and on various subscales. *Across classrooms,* however, objective ratings of pupils showed little consistent relation to their self-esteem. Self-esteem apparently depends on comparison with others within the same classroom, not on comparisons with pupils generally. It is noteworthy that *academic* self-concepts were particularly affected by the contexts.

Parallel results have appeared in studies of handicapped children. Meadow (1969) compared the self-concepts of deaf children with deaf parents with the self-concepts of deaf children with hearing parents; the self-esteem of children with deaf parents (a consonant home context) proved to be higher. Consistent with this result is a study by Craig (1965) showing that the self-esteem of deaf children in residential schools for the deaf was higher than that of deaf children in regular schools for the hearing. It would appear that the damaging self-concept consequences of so stigmatized a disability as deafness appear to be mitigated by immersal in consonant contexts.

PHYSICAL CONTEXTS

One can readily understand why the physical characteristics of those in our environments should affect how we see ourselves. Whether we are tall or short, heavy or light, weak or strong, obviously depends not simply on what we are like but on what others with whom we compare ourselves are like. Research demonstrates that the *salience* of physical characteristics in the self-concept is affected by the context. McGuire and Padawer-Singer (1976) asked 292 sixth-grade pupils in 10 classrooms to "tell us about yourself." One week later the respondents were requested to provide specific information regarding their physical appearance (height, weight, hair color, eye color), and other objective information (sex, birth date, birth place, and household composition). The results showed that pupils either younger or older than average *within their classrooms* were more likely spontaneously to mention their age than those closer to the average; that those born outside the city or outside the country were more likely than natives to identify themselves in terms of place of birth; that redheads and blondes were more likely to mention hair color than the more numerous brunettes or brown-haired subjects; that those with blue or green eyes mentioned eye color more than brown-eyed youngsters; and that those above or below average in weight were more likely to mention their weight. (Unusual height, however, was not more likely to be mentioned.) In other words, self-concept components tend to be salient if they are distinctive—or dissonant—in a given context, independent of whether the quality is ego-enhancing or ego-diminishing.

It is thus evident that different contexts (social identity contexts, abilities contexts, physical contexts) may influence diverse aspects of the individual's self-concept: global self-esteem, academic self-concept, self-concept stability, salience of specific components, and so on. These data offer vivid testimony to the importance of other people in shaping the individual's self-concept. Other people constitute a frame of reference, a backdrop, a perspective from which the self is seen. The self-concept may be as much a product of the quality of the other as the quality of the individual.

Social Institutions and the Self-Concept

To this point we have been primarily concerned with the self-concept as a social product. The fundamental question addressed has been: how do social conditions or experiences—social interaction, social structure, social contexts—shape the individual's self-concept? But the self-concept may also be examined as a social force. The question is: how does the self-concept influence behavior in major institutional areas?

Before addressing this question, it is relevant to say a word about the *personal* consequences of the self-concept. Even if the self-concept had no bearing on society, it would still be important if it influenced people's ability to lead full, rich, satisfying lives. The importance of a healthy self-concept for mental health can scarcely be exaggerated. It is clear that self-esteem is characteristically deeply implicated in the neurotic (though not necessarily the psychotic) process. Whether the research has been essentially clinical or quantitative, the results demonstrate clear and consistent relationships of low self-esteem to psychological depression, anxiety, somatic symptoms, impulse to aggression, vulnerability, negative affective states, and other neurotic symptoms. (For summaries of relevant research, see Wylie 1961, 1979; Bachman 1970; and Kaplan 1976, 1980). The social roots of self-esteem are thus an important topic in the sociology of mental health.

But the sociologist is also properly interested in the influence of personality on society. On theoretical grounds, there is reason to think that the self-concept, at least as a proximal influence is implicated in almost all social behavior. As Shibutani (1961:214–15) expresses it:

> Much of what men do voluntarily depends upon what they conceive themselves to be. . . . Each takes his personal identity so much for granted that he does not realize the extent to which his life is structured by the working conception he forms of himself. The things that a man does voluntarily, and even . . . involuntarily, depend upon the assumption he makes about the kind of person he is and the way in which he fits into the scheme of things in his world.

This section considers how the self-concept is implicated in behavior in four institutional areas—economic, political, educational, and legal—either as cause or effect. Not all aspects of these institutions, of course, are relevant. The economic aspect on which we shall focus is primarily occupational choices and values; the political aspect will focus on political participation and political ideology; the educational aspect will direct attention to school performance; and the legal or normative aspect will focus on deviance. The research presented in this section is intended to be illustrative, not exhaustive. As we shall see, it is not always clear, in the given empirical instance, whether the self-concept is more suitably treated as a social force or as a social product.

OCCUPATIONAL CHOICES AND VALUES

Every society must somehow organize the activities of its members in such a way as to provide for the production and distribution of goods and services. Modern society, which is characterized by a highly refined division of labor, depends on the consistent performance of highly limited and specialized tasks by qualified members. How people get sorted into these various slots is thus monumentally important both for society and the individual. Such sorting depends on the social structure. In caste or estate societies, people are largely assigned to occupations or occupational areas on the basis of birth. In the open-class societies of the contemporary West, on the other hand, individual choice is permitted and encouraged. On what basis, then, do people make the fateful decisions that will occupy so much of their waking lives, constitute so prominent a component of their identities, and contribute so importantly to the functioning of the society?

Among vocational counselors, it is now widely recognized that the self-concept plays a major role in occupational decisions. This idea has been most directly expressed in Donald Super's "self-concept implementation theory of occupational choice." The selection of an occupation, according to Super (1953), depends on a view of the self. The individual making an occupational choice must achieve stereoscopic vision as he attempts to coordinate two images—that of himself and that of the typical or ideal occupational incumbent. Although the answer to the question: what should I become? has important consequences for the occupational system, it always emerges from the ulterior question: what am I like and what do I like to think of myself as? As an obvious example, if girls are socialized to believe that they are incompetent in mathematical ability or assign this talent a low position in their system of self-values, then they will be disposed to avoid occupations such as engineering, physics, and related fields demanding such skills; and, indeed, the facts show them to be strikingly underrepresented in such fields (Gilford and Snyder 1977).

Subsequent research has afforded clear and consistent support for Super's initial insight. People's self-concepts tend to match the stereotypical characteristics associated with their chosen occupations. For example, students planning to enter the field of sales tend to describe themselves as sociable, talkative, aggressive, and having initiative, whereas those selecting accounting are likely to describe themselves as precise, self-controlled, organized, and thorough (Korman 1969). Furthermore, the self-concept is not only consonant with prime occupational choice, but with second occupational choice as well (Leonard et al. 1973). In selecting an occupation, people seek to achieve "self-role" congruence (Sarbin and Allen 1968).

In 1966, Korman proposed a modification of the self-concept implementation theory, holding that it was not universal but was conditional on global self-esteem. Korman provided evidence that, if people had high global self-esteem, then their occupational choices tended to be consonant with their self-concepts, but if their self-esteem was low, the self-concept and the occupational choice were unrelated. In making an occupational choice, people with high self-esteem sought to be true to their pictures of what they were like; people with low self-esteem, on the other hand, tended to make their occupational choices on the basis of other considerations, for example, certain extrinsic rewards of work, such as money, status, or security.

The question of why those with high self-esteem tend to implement their self-concepts whereas those with low self-esteem do not is currently under active debate. Korman has elected to interpret his results within the framework of cognitive consistency theory, but this interpretation has been challenged by Dipboye (1977), who argues persuasively that all the findings can be more meaningfully understood as consequences of the self-esteem motive.

Global self-esteem has also been shown to bear a relationship to occupational aspirations, expectations, and values. A study of high school juniors and seniors showed that youngsters with low self-esteem were more likely to avoid occupations that required the exercise of leadership, to want jobs in which they were free of supervision, and to avoid jobs involving competition (Rosenberg 1965).

Other economic attitudes, orientations, or behavior may also be influenced by the self-concept. Simpson and Simpson (1959) have described how psychiatric attendants reconceptualize the nature of their work for the purpose of enhancing self-respect; Coates and Pelligrin (1957) have studied the self-concepts of executives and supervisors; and Kourvetaris (1971) has shown how historical developments produced changed self-concepts among Greek army officers. Sociological research has also been conducted on the process by which a trainee—say, a medical student (Huntington 1957) or a music student (Kadushin 1969)—comes to see himself or herself as a doctor or a musician. It may be no exaggeration to suggest that the self-concept, in its full rich complexity, pervades virtually every aspect of occupational life.

POLITICAL PARTICIPATION AND ATTITUDES

In the political realm, a number of investigators, seeking to understand how personality factors might bear upon such behavior as political power-seeking among aspiring leaders, have turned their attention to the self-concept as an explanatory variable. Some of the more prominent explanations of the striving for political power can be traced to Alfred Adler's (1956) earlier ideas on compensation for feelings of inferiority. In Adler's view, an individual afflicted with organ inferiority may seek to compensate for his deficiencies in order to overcome his low feelings of self-worth. Demosthenes stuttered as a boy: in order to overcome his handicap, he placed pebbles in his mouth and sought to shout down the waves. Napoleon's drive for power was said to stem from inferiority feelings about his diminutive stature.

Developing the ideas adumbrated by Adler, the pioneering political scientist, Harold Lasswell (1948), in his classic work, *Power and Personality,* advanced the general hypothesis that the power seeker pursues power as a means of compensation against low estimates of the self. But low self-esteem may also be at the root of political apathy, since overwhelmingly low self-esteem might cause the individual to withdraw from the political arena entirely. Similarly, Goldhamer (1950) suggested that political apathy might stem from the fact that the individual is so exhausted by his inner conflicts that he has no interest or energy left for public affairs.

Research findings are consistent in showing that people with low self-esteem are in general more likely to be politically apathetic. One large-scale study of high school juniors and seniors (Rosenberg 1962) showed that youngsters with low self-esteem were less likely to express interest in national or international affairs, to pay attention to political matters in the media, to have much political knowledge, and to be political opinion leaders. Furthermore, even those low self-esteem students who were politically interested were less likely to discuss politics, more likely to feel personally threatened by political discussions, less confident that other people would pay much attention to their political views, and more self-conscious about presenting their political ideas to other people. These low self-esteem youngsters were also more likely to report that they were distracted from public affairs by concern with their personal problems.

Carmines's (1978) study of adolescents extended these findings in a number of ways. Explicitly recognizing that personality would affect political attitudes of youngsters only if they were politically involved, Carmines examined the relationship of self-esteem to political attitudes controlling on political interest. In virtually every case, he found, the relationship of self-esteem to political attitudes was stronger if political involvement was high than if it was low. Furthermore, among those adolescents who were highly interested in political issues, those with high self-esteem were more likely to be knowledgeable about political figures, to have a better understanding of the essentials of democracy, to be less cynical about politics, and to feel more politically efficacious. These findings persisted when grade, sex, socioeconomic status, and intelligence were controlled. Those with low self-esteem, on the other hand, were more likely to support political protest activities.

Qualitative research among adults had added to our understanding of how self-concepts—especially self-esteem—may influence political apathy or participation. One study (Rosenberg 1954–55) showed that some adults were afraid to express political opinions for fear of making fools of themselves. Lacking confidence in their own knowledge and ability, these people retreated from politics. But low political participation also appeared to be fostered by a more fundamental and deep-rooted feeling of inefficacy and insignificance. Some people felt that they did not "matter" (Rosenberg and McCullough 1980), that they made little difference in the broader scheme of things. These people expressed the idea that they were politically unimportant—an ordinary person, an average Joe, a little man. Nothing they could do would make much political difference because the forces that controlled the world, including political forces, were outside their control; political impotence formed the basis of political apathy.

Apathy, of course, is not the only possible outcome of such an attitude. Fromm (1941) has suggested that one reason many Germans were attracted to Hitler was that (like the American subjects described above) they felt ineffectual, impotent, and insignificant in the broader scheme of things. For this reason they attached themselves to a powerful political leader, who not only promised them national glory and, thereby, personal self-esteem, but also preached a doctrine asserting their inherent superiority to all other peoples.

There are many other ways in which the self-concept has been shown to be related to political orientations. Sniderman (1975) showed that people with low self-esteem are more likely to be chauvinistic, ethnocentric, and politically cynical, and to be low on democratic commitment, and Sniderman and Citrin (1971) provide evidence that (among isolationists), those with low self-esteem are more likely to oppose social change, to believe in tradition and social order, to support a position of elitism, and to hold extreme political beliefs. In general, people with low self-esteem tend to hold to political solutions of any political persuasion that makes their confused environments intelligible, orderly, and purposive.

Other studies have also examined self-esteem among elected officials (for example, Barber 1965). But self-esteem is not the only self-concept motive implicated in political behavior; self-consistency also plays a role. The study of adults discussed above (Rosenberg 1954–55) found that some people avoided political activity on grounds of role self-concept incongruence. The individual's view of himself did not match his view of the qualities of a political activist. The political activist was seen as energetic, forceful, and dynamic, whereas the individual saw himself or herself as passive and receptive. This lack of role-person fit was a deterrent to political participation.

In sum, it is plain that the way one thinks about the self influences the way one thinks about the world, including the world of politics. The political institution, like any other, is a realm of action, and whenever people act, their self-concepts are implicated.

ACADEMIC PERFORMANCE

It is understandable that when students of the self-concept turn their attention to the educational institution, they tend to focus primarily on academic performance. School, after all, is the main business of a child's life. Furthermore, there are very few areas of life in which a person is so constantly and explicitly evaluated. Report cards, or school marks, represent a public, "objective," and authoritative assessment of an important aspect of the child's worth. It is thus not surprising to find that there tends to be a positive association between academic performance and self-esteem (though the association is not always strong) (Purkey 1970; Wylie 1979). What is less clear is what this statistical association means. There are at least three questions to be raised in this regard.

The first deals with the aspect of the self-concept under consideration. As we noted earlier, the individual's self-concept includes attitudes toward the self as a whole (global self-esteem) and attitudes toward the specific parts of the self (component self-esteem). The question is: if the self-concept does influence academic performance, is it the individual's overall feeling of worth (his global self-esteem) that is responsible or is it the specific component of academic ability? Research shows that the specific component of self-concept of academic ability tends to be more strongly associated with school achievement (Wylie 1979:406). In other words, it is not one's overall feeling of worth as a human being (which may be based on many things) but one's self-conceived talent in a specific area that is most closely related to performance. For example, the relationship between ability on IQ tests and global self-esteem generally appears to be about $r = .20-.30$. But Brookover, Thomas, and Paterson

(1964) showed that the correlation between school marks and *academic self-concept* was $r = .57$. In general, there is a much higher correlation between school marks and academic self-concept than between marks and global self-esteem.

This observation concerning the part and whole may be generalized beyond school marks. It is Wylie's (1979) judgment—and one in which we concur—that, if specific types of behavior are under consideration, the specific self-concept component will almost invariably be more relevant than the global attitude. Some educators, concerned about the academic performance of minority-group children, have attributed this performance to the lower global self-esteem of the minority-group children and have argued that it is necessary to enhance the minority child's global self-esteem. But if self-concept change is to affect school performance, it will be less through convincing the child that he is generally a person of worth than in persuading him that he has the specific ability to do well on tests. In viewing the self-concept either as a social product or a social force, it is important to keep the distinction between the part and the whole in the forefront of attention.

But even when we find an association between academic performance and self-esteem, the question remains: is self-esteem a *consequence* of academic performance or a *cause* of it? There is theoretical support for both positions. Self-consistency theory, which holds that we tend to behave in accordance with our self-expectations, would view the self-concept as the cause of the behavior. To take Lecky's (1945) example, a child with ample ability may unconsciously make a number of spelling errors because he has developed a view of himself as a poor speller. His poor performance represents an effort to remain true to his self-concept. Self-attribution theory, on the other hand, holds that we draw conclusions about what we are like by observing our behavior or its outcomes. The person who fails in school judges himself, as he would judge anyone else, as academically inept. In this case, the marks are viewed as the cause of the academic self-concept.

Since the self-concept and the behavior may thus affect one another, the question is: which has the greater effect on the other? By means of a cross-lagged panel correlation, Calsyn and Kenny (1977) concluded that academic performance affected academic self-concept more than the other way around; the effect, however, was stronger for girls than for boys. The evidence indicates that the self-concept also affects academic performance, but that this effect is weaker.

Another critical issue involved in interpreting the relationship between academic self-concept and academic achievement is the question of whether the marks are attributable to qualities of the person or components of the self-*concept*. Does someone do well on tests because he *believes* he is academically competent or because he *actually is* academically competent? This issue is widely overlooked. If people who believe they are tall are more likely to be good basketball players, their basketball skill is less attributable to their *views* of themselves as tall than to their actual height. To be able to conclude that the self-concept per se affects behavior, one must equate people in terms of objective characteristics.

This issue was explored in a large-scale study of junior high school pupils by Brookover, Thomas, and Paterson (1964). The question raised by these investigators was whether, *among pupils of equivalent academic talent,* youngsters with positive academic self-concepts did better in school than those with negative self-concepts? For both boys and girls, they found, the zero order correlation between academic self-concept and school marks was .57; controlling on IQ, however, the partial correlation remained .42 and .39 for boys and girls, respectively. *Independent of objective ability,* then, those who viewed themselves as more academically able performed substantially better in school. The self-concept apparently can importantly influence and be influenced by school performance independent of the person's actual abilities. The confidence with which one approaches a task, the amount of effort one devotes to it, and the freedom from disruptive anxiety that interferes with performance may all influence academic achievement. These, in turn, may be strongly influenced by the self-concept.

The self-concept doubtlessly affects and is affected by the educational institution in many other ways as well. Many people have discussed how the teacher's expectations for the child may affect the child's performance. If such effects do, in fact, exist, they are almost certain to be mediated by the child's self-concept. Children have enormous respect for adults (Piaget 1929:378; Rosenberg 1979). If the child believes that the teacher expects him to fail, the child, attributing great wisdom to the teacher, is likely to expect himself to fail. It is thus possible that the teacher's expectations for the child are converted into the child's self-expectations which, following the principle of self-consistency, are converted into academic performance.

DEVIANCE

The self-concept has played an important role in theories of deviance for a quarter of a century (Wells 1978). Its relevance to labeling theory is especially evident. In contrast to earlier social pathologists, who sought the causes of deviant behavior within the individual, the contemporary labeling theorist centers attention on society's reaction to it. The interest of this school is in the effects of society's application of a pejorative tag to the individual (for example, delinquent, convict, drug addict, alcoholic, mental patient), often by some official certifying agency, such as the school, the courts, or hospital officials.

The effects of labeling on the self-concept appear straightforward. First, these labels may become elements of social identity; like most such elements, they are socially evaluated (indeed, denigration is built into the very terms); and because they are associated with norm violation, they are deplored and condemned. Second, as with many other social identity elements, deviants tend to be stereotyped and treated accordingly. These stereotypes are, in effect, "pre-packaged appraisals" (McCall and Simmons 1978) of the individual. Thus, a mental patient labeled "dangerous" may be treated that way by others though his last aggressive act was ten years ago; the labeled delinquent is assumed to be dishonest; the convict, dangerous; the homosexual, effeminate; and so on. The point is that society responds to the individual in terms of the stereotype attached to the label, not in terms of the actual person. Third, the labeled individual may come to develop a corresponding self-concept, and following the self-consistency principle, may behave in terms of it. Hence, by labeling the individual, society fosters the very behavior it deplores. Finally, social labeling may affect the *structure* of the self-concept, when the officially certified label, instead of being one among many social identity elements, becomes central to it. This idea, expressed in the term "role engulfment" (Schur 1971), holds that the deviant identity becomes of overwhelming importance to the individual.

Like academic performance and the self-concept, it is apparent that the association between social deviance and the self-concept is reciprocal; each may affect the other. Meadian theory would lead us to expect deviants to have lower self-esteem for at least two reasons. The first is that, in taking the role of the other, we tend to see ourselves through the eyes of particular others. If they deplore our deviance, our self-esteem would be expected to suffer. But even in the absence of face-to-face interaction, Mead's concept of the "generalized other" would produce much the same result. Internalizing the attitudes of the community as a whole, the deviant views himself from the perspective of the broader society, that is, negatively and stereotypically.

But if deviance affects the self-concept, it is at least equally true that the self-concept may influence deviant behavior. Such an effect would be expected on grounds of the self-consistency motive. Deviant behavior may be a manifestation of the general principle that people behave in accordance with their conceptions of what they are like (Lecky 1945; Epstein 1980). This appears to be the essential principle underlying Reckless et al.'s (1956) influential theory of the self-concept as an "insulator against delinquency." One question that puzzled Reckless was why, in an environment in which delinquency was common, some boys became delinquent whereas others did not. In an attempt to answer this question, Reckless studied a sample of boys in a high delinquency area who, according to their teachers' predictions, were or were not likely eventually to get into difficulty with the law. Reckless et al. (1956) concluded that the critical distinction between the two groups was whether the youngsters conceptualized themselves as delinquents or as "good boys." Subsequent research revealed that these self-concepts were predictive of delinquent behavior. This conclusion was less trivial than it might at first appear. It demonstrated that delinquent behavior could not be explained exclusively in terms of blocked opportunity structure or individual psychopathology. Self-consistency—the striving to be true to one's self-definition as a deviant or a conformist—also played a role.

In addition to self-consistency, the self-esteem motive may also underpin deviant behavior. It has been suggested, for example, that the youngster may engage in delinquent behavior in order to *enhance* his self-esteem (Kaplan 1976, 1980; Rosenberg and Rosenberg 1978). Take a youth who is comparatively unsuccessful as a student, athlete, social leader, and so on. He commands little respect from parents, teachers, and peers, and seeing himself from their perspectives, has low self-esteem. Delinquency may help to enhance his self-respect in several ways. First, it provides him with a peer group—the delinquent gang—who *do* value and respect him; and the greater the deviance, the greater the respect. Second, he may find that he does have the ability (for example, strength, courage, and cunning) to succeed in various forms of delinquent behavior—fighting, pilfering, vandalism—in contrast to his failure as a student or a social leader. Third, in embracing delinquency, the youngster is likely to abandon the members of the straight society as his significant others. Although he may recognize that parents, teachers, and classmates deplore him more strongly than ever before, their views no longer count for him; his self-esteem now rests on the opinion of other deviants. If he wishes to enhance his self-esteem, then, he must behave in a way that commands their respect and approval, that is, behave in a deviant fashion.

The most compelling empirical evidence in support of these ideas is to be found in the work of Howard Kaplan (1980). Kaplan studied 7,618 seventh graders in Houston, Texas, ascertaining both their global self-esteem and their commitment of any of a wide range of deviant acts. Kaplan initially focused on the conformists, that is, those who had *not* committed any deviant acts at the time of the first interview. One year later these subjects were again asked whether they had committed deviant acts. Kaplan found that those with initially low self-esteem were consistently more likely than those with high self-esteem to have committed one or more deviant acts in the subsequent year. These data are consistent with the interpretation that youngsters may turn to delinquency in order to enhance their self-esteem.

Delinquency, of course, is only one type of deviance. Crime, drug addiction, alcoholism, homosexuality, mental illness, and so forth have also been viewed as deviance by various writers. Although the data are very uneven, the evidence is clear (Kaplan 1976, 1980) that the self-concept is implicated in each of these forms of deviance, either as cause or effect.

Future Directions

Society and the self-concept, it is evident, are inextricably intertwined. In this chapter we have attempted to illustrate how interpersonal interaction, social identity, social context, and social institutions all work to shape the individual's self-concept and how the self-concept, in turn, may influence behavior in important institutional areas. Because of space restrictions we have been obliged to slight some of the important insights and findings of the situated self-concept approach. Some of these contributions, fortunately, are well represented in other chapters in this book, most notably in Stryker's chapter on "Symbolic Interactionism" (chapter 1) and Heiss's chapter on "Social Roles" (chapter 4).

Research on the social psychology of the self-concept has now entered a very exciting phase and we may expect advances on a number of fronts in the coming years. Three of these appear particularly worthy of note.

The first is that substantial progress is being made toward understanding the self-concept in its full rich complexity. In the past, sociologists have focused primarily on (1) global self-esteem; (2) the range of specific self-concept components (Kuhn and McPartland 1954; Gordon 1968, 1974); (3) evaluations and typifications of selected social identity elements (for example, race, gender, ethnicity); and (4) self-presentation strategies. Social psychologists are now coming to recognize that the self-concept embraces a good deal more. In recent years substantial progress has been made in the discovery, elaboration, and investigation of a number of new self-concept components or dimensions. These include such concepts as self-consistency (Morse and Gergen 1970), subjective and objective self-awareness (Duval and Wicklund 1972), self-efficacy (Bandura 1977), inner and outer self-esteem (Franks and Marolla 1976), self exteriority-interiority (Rosenberg and Rosenberg forthcoming), schematization (Markus 1977), individuation (Zimbardo 1969), self-monitoring (Snyder 1974), and others. (A number of these concepts are developed in Wegner and Vallacher 1980.) The task still before us is to understand the interplay between social structure or situational circumstances and these diverse aspects of the self-concept.

Although it is difficult to discern a trend, one may hope to see increased attention to the self-concept as a social force. One reason for past neglect, as House notes in chapter 17 of this volume, is that students of social structure and personality have focused overwhelmingly on the impact of society on personality and neglected the impact of personality on society. Yet it is evident that self-concepts may have consequences for the institutional system. For example, if feelings of personal insignificance attract Germans to Hitler, the political institution is shaken to its root; if women's idealized images or desired selves change between the fifties and the eighties, there are inevitable consequences for the family institution. The societal consequences of the self-concept are thus both broad and far-ranging. These consequences are recognized by scholars in a remarkably wide range of fields: vocational counseling, political science, anthropology, education, developmental psychology, criminology, sociology, and many more. That scholars in so many disciplines should find the self-concept relevant to their concerns testifies to the importance of the self-concept as a social force.

Finally, at some point it may prove fruitful to view the self-concept as one of a broader range of self-objectification processes. Mead (1934) was in the forefront of those stressing the importance of self-objectification. The key element of this idea is that the human being is virtually unique in nature in serving as the object of his own observation and action. Not only is the human capable of conceiving of himself, but he is also capable of behavioral interpretation (reflecting on and interpreting one's own behavior), introspection (inspecting one's inner thoughts and feelings), self-regulation (treating the self as an object or instrument of one's purposes), verbal interpretation (responding to one's own verbal expressions), self-reinforcement (punishing or rewarding the self), self-presentation (setting forth a certain self in interaction), and others. Our understanding of these processes may be expected to enlarge and deepen in the years to come.

NOTES

I am grateful to the following persons for their helpful suggestions and criticisms: David Franks, Viktor Gecas, Norman Goodman, Chad Gordon, Howard B. Kaplan, Sheldon Stryker, and L. Edward Wells. The preparation of this chapter was supported in part by Grant MH22747 from the Institute of Mental Health.

1. Teachers constitute the sole possible exception but some evidence suggests that black children are as likely as white children to believe that their teachers think highly of them (Rosenberg and Simmons 1972).

WILLIAM T. SMELSER
AND NEIL J. SMELSER

Group Movements, Sociocultural Change, and Personality

Introduction

In confronting the topic of this chapter, we uncovered a literature that is rich, rooted deeply in the history of social thought, and compelling in its theoretical importance. At the same time we found that literature to be fugitive, noncumulative, subject to vicissitudes of emphasis and ideological loading, and somewhat nightmarish for the methodologically minded.

We hope to illustrate all these contrasting characteristics of the literature here. To mention only the historical dimension at the outset, however, we may note the preoccupation of many of the giants of the sociological and social-psychological traditions with the relations between sociocultural change and personality. Is not one consistent rendition of Marx's theory of alienation (1964) that it altered technological and property relations under modern capitalism and generated deep and destructive effects on the personalities of workers? Was not Durkheim (1951) preoccupied with the isolating and depressing effects of changes in religious life and the disorienting effects of social instability and anomie? Was not Weber (1968) concerned with the depersonalizing and dehumanizing effects of the increase of bureaucracy in modern life? Did not Tocqueville (1945, 1955) argue that the historical victory of the principle of equality—partial in France and nearly complete in America—contributed to envy, resentment, and potential violence on the part of individuals in different social classes in France, and accounted for the characteristics of ambitiousness and restlessness in the American national character? Was not Le Bon (1897) convinced that the decline of traditional religious and political arrangements had permitted the emergence of the base, irrational side of human nature as expressed in the crowd? And did not Freud (1930) hold the march of civilization responsible for the tragic and increasingly deep conflict between impulses and their repression in individuals? The answers to all these queries are, we believe, affirmative, and those answers testify to the historical centrality of the topic of sociocultural change and personality. The explanations invoked by these theorists, moreover, echo loudly into the present and shape the interpretations of many contemporary investigators in the social sciences.

In preparing this chapter we scanned the relevant recent literature in the books and learned journals of sociology, social psychology, psychology, and psychoanalysis. We found that literature to be fragmented and unsystematic. In wrestling with it, we were able to conceive of many different ways of dissecting and classifying our subject for presentation (for example, in terms of different explanatory variables invoked, in terms of different schools of thought, and so forth), all imprecise in varying degrees. In the end we decided to try to order the field in a fairly systematic way, taking "type of sociocultural change" as the main organizing principle.

Following this principle, we shall consider, in order, several types of change that are progressively more comprehensive in scope. First, we shall focus on *individual persons* in the social fabric, including shifts in their rewards and deprivations, their geographical migration within a society, their migration from one cultural setting to another, and their social mobility. Second, we shall consider the dynamics of movements involving *groups,* taking social, political, and religious movements as types. Finally, we shall consider changes in the *social structure* of societies and changes in *culture.*

For each of these types of change we shall pose several questions. What kinds of personality factors contribute to the genesis and development of the change in question? What kinds of impacts on personalities does the change occasion? And can complicated interactive processes, involving both personality and sociocultural factors, be observed? In addressing these questions, we have attempted to proceed consistently on the assumptions that personality and social systems intermesh and interact with one another, that processes at each level are affected in a causal way by processes at the other, and that our understanding and prediction of individual and group behavior, as well as structural arrangements, can be improved by reference to processes at both levels.

Our conception of personality is an inclusive one, necessarily so because of the diversity of definitions and perspectives employed by those investigators dealing with issues of sociocultural change and personality. Lieberman's (1975) definition, for example, deals with adjustment processes, Parker and Kleiner's (1964) with identity of self or group membership, and Etheredge (1978) emphasizes typological issues. Our conception is consistent, moreover, with the position taken by Hall and Lindzey (1978), who argue that "no substantive definition of personality can be applied with any generality," and that any definition of personality flows from the particular *theory* of personality employed by a given investigator (p. 8). Personality theories vary in their relative emphasis on cognition, affect, and perception. A distinguishing feature of personality theory, however (as contrasted with theories of learning, for example) is that it usually involves a general theory of behavior. Smith (1968) has proposed such personality factors as ego defenses and stylistic traits as intervening between the social environment (immediate and distal) and political behavior of the individual. His scheme is applicable beyond political behavior and can serve as a map for understanding social behavior in general. In this chapter we will sometimes invoke personality factors to account for the linkage between social change processes and behavioral outcomes; at other times we will employ them to account for behavior that influences (for example, instigates, enhances, hampers) social change processes.

Social Processes and Personality

We begin by reviewing research on what might be regarded as the simplest kind of social change: shifts in the relationship between a person and the balance of rewards and deprivations in his or her environment. We consider two such shifts—first, changes in fortune arising from abrupt or gradual changes in rewards available or deprivations imposed; and second, changes occasioned by the movement of individuals to new sociocultural settings. We divide the second type into geographical movement within and across societies, and vertical movement or social mobility. These types constitute the sub-headings of this section. The processes are simple in that, considered as such, they do not necessarily involve more general changes in group structure, social structure, or culture.

The notion of social process is not altogether clean analytically for several reasons. First, shifts in rewards and deprivations and movements of persons often occur simultaneously, and it is difficult to discern which, if either, is of primary significance. Second, more general group, structural, and cultural changes often themselves occasion great shifts in resources and people, thus indicating that social process is not a category of change easily separable from other types. And third, cumulative social processes (for example, severe economic loss on the part of important groups in a society) often set in motion reactions that eventuate in more general sociological changes. Despite these ambiguities and qualifications, however, the notion of social processes provides a convenient basis for grouping and interpreting several strands of ongoing research.

In analyzing the individual's relation to rewards and deprivations, economists—and to some extent demographers interested in fertility and migration—posit more or less explicitly certain "utility functions" that specify the kinds of gratifications preferred by individuals, examine the potential "pushes" and "pulls" operating in the environment, and analyze the resultant behavior of individuals as more or less purposive, calculated choices in that environment. By way of contrast, sociologists, anthropologists, and social psychologists tend to focus on shifts in rewards and deprivations that are imposed on individuals—that is, are beyond choice—and on the psychic and human consequences of these shifts. A classic theorem enunciated by Durkheim (1951) illustrates the contrast. Taking precipitous business gains or losses as the starting point of analysis—rather than the phenomena to be explained—he posited that both would prove disruptive and disorienting to affected individuals, and would increase the probability of suicide among them. As we shall see presently, the structure of this kind of argument recurs frequently in research on our topic.

SOCIAL STRESS, SOCIAL GAINS, AND PERSONALITY

Personal stress and death. The ways in which changes in life's fortunes may affect the timing of an individual's death has moved from speculation and folklore to serious empirical investigation in recent years. In a thoughtful review of findings, Rowland (1977) concluded that the death of a significant other and relocation (for example, in a convalescent home) appear to be more important as proximal causes of death for the elderly than retirement as such, though Rowland acknowledged the methodological difficulties in unscrambling and establishing the causal significance of such events. Crisis theory, reinforcement theory, and the concept of "learned helplessness" all appear to be consonant with these differences. With respect to relocation alone, Lieberman (1975), in another review, suggested that certain types of individuals are more vulnerable to death after relocation: those who sense they have little or no choice in relocating, those who experience depression over the move (which is probably directly related to sense of little or no choice), and those who deny the reality of relocation. The last finding revives Janis's (1958) observation that the use of primitive defenses, such as denial, appears to retard recovery from surgery. In another study of the reactions to displacement, Marris (1975) suggested that individual adaptation involves a continuous interplay between the need for stability and the need for change, but that certain types of relocation force an individual beyond the limits of tolerance for the latter.

Economic stress. The personal impact of changes in economic fortunes constitutes a major source of research interest. Robbins (1973) argued that drinking behavior among unacculturated Naskapi Indians (in Canada) is generally a result of loss of economic and social rewards. He refined this argument, however, by distinguishing between those who engage in friendly, social, identity-confirming drinking and those who drink more aggressively. He observed, moreover, that the former are more successful in wage earning than the latter. Speculating further, Robbins suggested that if the Naskapi (and by implication, any other dominated cultural group) were denied access to mechanisms for confirming their own identity, and if the only available reference point for identity was external (in this case, Anglo-Canadian), personal identity would likely be sought in attraction to some sort of millenarian movement. The speculation is interesting in that it suggests that the same objective conditions (for example, economic loss) may contribute to a *variety* of behavior outcomes (drinking, attraction to a utopian movement), and that the main determinant making for selection among them may be some kind of opportunity factor.

Economic deprivation also figures significantly in Elder's (1974) excellent study of the multiple impacts of unemployment in the Great Depression of the 1930s on family structure, family interaction, and personality in 167 families followed longitudinally from 1932 to 1964. He found that the ultimate effect of economic insecurity occasioned by severe unemployment of adults is to generate greater need for stability and security in the lives of their children. He also suggested that economic insecurity leads to familial adaptations that are likely to reinforce traditional attitudes with respect to sex roles, as girls are required to take disproportionate responsibility for helping in the house and boys to generate outside income.

Political stress. Gordon et al. (1976) argued that traumatic sociopolitical situations, such as the draft for the unpopular war in Vietnam, occasion a higher rate of utilization of psychiatry services, and Schubert and Wagner (1975) found that a sample of young adults studied in 1968 manifested more role confusion and more diffuse identity formation than a corresponding sample studied in 1958. They attributed the difference to societal changes of various sorts. Both these studies, however, appear to suffer from a lack of clear definition of sociocultural changes and their effects, as well as the mechanisms by which these may be linked.

Social breakdown. The studies of the effects of bombing and other wartime phenomena in the 1940s and 1950s and the studies of disasters, especially in the 1950s and the early 1960s, firmly established the interest in studying personal reactions to crisis situations. One notable finding of the bombing studies was that severe anxiety reactions (resulting in panic) were not, as had been anticipated, widespread in the face of even heavy continuous bombings (Titmuss 1950). Anxiety reactions tended to be greatest when there was a conspicuous element of ambiguity or uncertainty in the attacks (Denny-Brown 1943; Janis 1958). A similar and also surprising finding of the disaster studies was that debilitating anxiety and outright panic reactions in the face of extreme environmental threats are rare, and that people are likely to engage in various kinds of purposive behavior—particularly efforts to save loved ones—rather than simply fleeing the scene (Killian 1952).

The assassinations of President John F. Kennedy, Robert F. Kennedy, and Martin Luther King generated a burst of research interests into the mass shock and mass bereavement reactions that followed these events (Wolfenstein and Kilman 1966; Greenberg and Parker 1965) and in general, a modest stream of research on reactions to disaster has continued. One of the most recent is Erikson's (1976) vivid and compelling portrayal of a mine disaster in West Virginia and its impact on the community and the individuals affected. Erikson's style of research is phenomenological; he permitted his subjects to tell their own story and ferret out common, communicable reactions, such as initial numbness and extreme guilt for others' suffering—the latter harking back to the importance of extreme guilt reactions of soldiers in battlefield situations (Grinker and Speigel

1945). Erikson also stressed the community's cultural and social history in accounting for individual variations in reactions to objectively identical or similar crisis situations.

Turning to the effects of economic instability, we note Brenner's (1973) historical survey of 127 years of New York State records, in which he found economic instability to be one of the most pervasive and continuous sources of personal stress (as measured by admission rates of mental hospitals). Individuals who consistently lost most in economic and social status during recessions—Brenner focused especially on the lowest socioeconomic class—tended to react with the greatest increase in rates of admission. One apparent anomaly in his findings was that no economic turndown since 1920 (including the depression beginning in 1929) has produced such an increased magnitude of hospitalization; speculating on this, Brenner suggested that individuals in the depression of the 1930s were less likely to experience economic failure as a personal failure, because unemployment was such a widespread and "normal" phenomenon.

Brenner's results run counter in some ways to Goldhamer and Marshall's earlier (1953) research on rates of admission to mental hospitals (for psychoses only) in Massachusetts between 1850 and 1950. They found a general stability of rates of admission, and on the basis of that, argued against the thesis that the increasing complexity of society clearly results in increases in indicators of mental illness. They suggested the possibility, however, of short-term fluctuations reflecting societal changes, and noted some factors other than social and economic change that confound measures of incidence of mental disorders—factors such as mental hospital policies for admission, as well as restrictions on the resources of the hospital, that would limit admissions.

Finally, we cite two studies of the impact of a special type of "breakdown"—the exercise of violence by police and other authorities on participants and observers of protest situations. Adamek and Lewis (1975) stressed the radicalizing effect of such behavior on students' attitudes and behavior, but in a related study, Levenson and Miller (1976) found that, when anticipating more severe actions by authorities, politically conservative students become less politically active, whereas liberal students increase their activism.

Social gains. Recent research on the effects of gains in social rewards has emphasized their positive impact more than their possible psychic costs. This trend was anticipated, perhaps, by the work of Henry and Short (1954) who challenged Durkheim's assertion that extreme prosperity is disorienting, and, in a careful empirical study, attempted to reestablish the more common-sense relationship between boom and low suicide rates on the one hand and bust and high suicide rates on the other. On the basis of further empirical investigations, Pierce (1967) argued for the validity of the original Durkheimian formula, but both his measures and his findings are quite frail. In any event, the main line of research in the past decade has stressed the benign impact of increased education, employment, and income. Citing five sample surveys between 1964 and 1974, Mason, Czajka, and Arber (1976) found consistently that educational attainment and employment of women are positively associated with a more egalitarian sex-role definition. Weston and Ruggiero (1978) found, similarly, that higher levels of education of women correlate positively with attitudes of tolerance toward nonconformists, and that, correspondingly, there was a significant rise in tolerance from 1954 to 1974. A third item along the same lines is that of Hoffman (1977) who cited a number of studies showing that greater education and employment for women, postponed marriage, and reduced numbers of children (see Glick 1977), has led to a change in attitude among women and their offspring that diminishes traditional sex-role differences. Finally, working with a British sample, Marsh (1977) posited that changed economic conditions (especially greater affluence) has qualitatively changed the motivation for political change away from material and civil security and toward greater freedom and participation.

We conclude our discussion of the impact of gains and stress on personality with a substantive question and a methodological observation. While generally accepting the validity of most of the findings we have reported, we would ask whether the general pattern of results is perhaps not too simple-minded in its cumulative emphasis. This general pattern reveals the debilitating features of loss and the beneficial features of gain. We would want to ask, however, about the other side of the coin in each case. Does not, for example, economic deprivation—assuming it falls short of extremes of poverty and hunger—sometimes augment family solidarity and cooperation in a common cause of economic survival and management? And are not the benefits of education, affluence, and emancipation sometimes themselves disruptive of anchors of solidarity and identity? We are suggesting, perhaps, a slight swing of the pendulum back in the direction of Durkheim's stress on the indirect fruits of adversity and the indirect costs of happiness. Surely such a shift would yield a richer and more complex picture of things.

On the methodological side, we may note that the majority of the studies cited are variations on a methodological theme. The theme is that some causal variable is invoked (usually some shift in rewards or deprivations) and some behavioral outcome is posited (in this section we have noted shifts in attitudes toward the self and others, changes in political orientation, drinking behavior, and susceptibility to death). To make sense of the connection, moreover, some intervening personality factor or process is invoked (in the original Durkheimian example, for example, the implicit personality process is the disorientation occasioned by the discrepancy between expectations and rewards). Similarly, Garrity et al. (1977) noted that various personality factors affected not only the experiencing of life changes but also the experiencing of psychophysiological strain associated with them. Social conformists, for example, are less likely to report either life changes or symptoms of strain, whereas individuals classified as "intellectual and sensitive" are more likely to report both. The basic structure of explanation, then, is as follows:

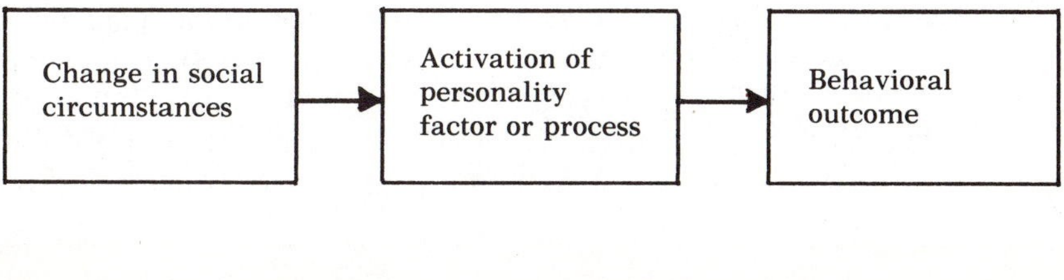

One main variation on this interpretative theme is that the dependent variable is sometimes identified as some kind of simple behavioral outcome (as in the Robbins study of drinking) and sometimes as some kind of personality disposition (as in the Elder study of security needs in children of families suffering from economic hardship). Another variation is found when the investigator systematically investigates the change in the intervening personality factors and processes (as in the Lieberman study of differences in vulnerability to relocation), thus complicating the causal link between social circumstances and behavioral outcome. (Still another variation, to be observed presently, is the treatment of personality factors or processes as having causal primacy in the development of social situations.)

Whatever the combination of theme and variations, this kind of interpretation tends to generate, cumulatively, at least two kinds of methodological vulnerability. The first is that, since on many occasions the intervening personality factors or processes are posited on grounds of plausibility rather than direct measurement, the proportion of unmeasured variation in the research increases accordingly. The second is that, since such a plethora of dispositional and behavioral phenomena are identified on the side of outcomes, the conception of "personality" is forever threatening to lose all analytic shape and become the conceptual dustbin for all that investigators have chosen unsystematically to throw into it through years of research.

MIGRATION

The study of the tribulations of migrants within and across cultures has had a long history among sociologists, who early focused on immigrants coming into the American setting, and among anthropologists, for whom migration has been regarded as one of the principal forms of culture contact. The sources of migration, of course, are rooted in the economic, political, and social forces affecting societies—famines, unemployment, political persecution, and wars. But the main emphases of the traditions mentioned have been on culture shock and confusion, as well as on subsequent adaptation. The tradition continues, and we now examine a modern sample of investigations.

The main assumptions underlying the study of migrants are that the dominant culture into which they migrate exerts pressures to change through culture, institutions, and personal interaction, and that arriving migrants resist this pressure to change. The dominant model, then, is one of marginality and conflict, and the questions that flow from it are: first, what are the personality and behavioral consequences of marginality and conflict; and second, which features of the migrants' traditional culture and personality change rapidly and which slowly, and what accounts for the different rates of change?

A common type of study of migration is to examine some behavioral manifestation on the part of migrants, such as crime, drinking, or symptom of mental disturbance, and to relate it to recency of migration or severity of cultural adjustment. The presumed intervening process—

spelled out with varying degrees of explicitness—rests on an assumption of inner psychological conflict and its expression in disturbed or deviant form. A recent example of this kind of study is the research of Torres-Matrullo (1976), who found that less acculturated and less educated Puerto Rican women immigrants exhibited more stress (as expressed in depression-withdrawal and obsessive-compulsive symptoms) than their more acculturated counterparts. Lasry (1977) found a sample of immigrants from North Africa (into Canada) reporting a disproportionately high number of psychosomatic symptoms, relative to English-speaking North Americans, but not significantly different from French-speaking Canadians or Mexican-Americans. Subsequent findings indicate a decline of such symptoms over time. Christenson (1979), employing a statewide survey of North Carolina, found that value-based forces operate only in a sample seeking a nonmetro to metro move. This sample valued freedom, individualism, and equality more than metro-stayers. On the basis of this finding, Christenson predicted value conflicts arising between these movers and the metro nonmovers (destination sample). Christenson's study is in contrast to the other studies cited in this paragraph, which assess the impact of migration once it has occurred.

What aspects of immigrants' lives are most resistant to change? The evidence is far from definitive, but some studies suggest that deeper personality dispositions and attitudes bred by family experiences are most enduring. Yao (1979), for example, found that among a sample of 133 first-generation Chinese-Americans in metropolitan areas, most had assimilated considerably with respect to *extrinsic* measures such as English proficiency and adaptation to American life style; however, with respect to *intrinsic* traits, such as attitudes toward interpersonal relations, sex education, and women's roles, little deviation from traditional Chinese values was observed. And though Torres-Matrullo (1975) found striking differences in levels of stress according to recency of migration, her subjects showed little change in attitudes toward sex roles. Connor (1974) also found an apparent continuation of dependency needs (presumably intrinsic in their significance) whereas his sample of three generations of immigrants showed considerable difference along a scale of self-rated identity. In another kind of analysis by Pierce et al. (1978), the authors suggested that different generations of immigrants face different kinds of struggles; in their sample of Mexican-American and Japanese-American families in San Francisco, the early generation was preoccupied with the degree to which they should accept or discard their traditional orientations, whereas among later generations the differences involved the degree to which individuals would conform to what the authors called "Anglo Face," or outward behavior manifestations of "American" behavior.

SOCIAL MOBILITY

For a period in the 1950s and 1960s sociologists and social psychologists, influenced mainly by the work of McClelland (1961), focused on the motivational origins of social mobility, particularly the need for achievement (see the summary of literature and issues in Crockett 1966). That kind of interest has fallen off in the 1970s, and more attention has been given to the contribution of race, education, and other sociological factors to individual mobility in societies with relatively open stratification systems. In a recent, interesting variation on the achievement studies, however, De Mesquita (1974) apparently found a linkage between the measured need for achievement of political leaders and a political party's preference for degree of risk taking in elections and coalition formation. Using a varied sample of parties in India, he found that high need-achievement leaders' parties not only took greater risks but also appeared to gain greater electoral success.

Another continuing strand of research concerns the psychic costs of upward and downward mobility. In an excellent study, Parker and Kleiner (1964) found that upward or downward mobility, coupled with high levels of goal striving, were associated with weak or ambivalent ethnic identity as well as mental disorder among urban blacks. Wilensky and Edwards (1959) found that a consistent difference between "skidders" (intergenerationally downwardly mobile men) and others is that the latter appear to be more conservative in their political views. And in a study noted for its ingenious effort to develop a control sample of nonsuicides, Breed (1963) found that the most significant experiential factor in the life of a sample of suicides was downward mobility. In a careful longitudinal analysis of a national sample, Cohn (1978) found that downward mobility (mainly in the form of unemployment) generated dissatisfaction with self, whereas subsequent re-employment restored satisfaction nearly to its original level. These findings parallel Lieberman's earlier (1950) results indicating that upward and downward movement in an industrial organization generated changes in attitudes toward unions and management. However, the consequences of life changes associated with mobility are themselves conditioned by personality variables. One of Cohn's findings is that if an individual does not perceive an external locus of control (presumably to hold responsible for his misfortunes), his experience of loss of satisfaction is relatively greater.

Group Movements and Personality

A conventional—and in many respects sensible—way of looking at social movements is to distinguish between motives for attraction to or joining a movement on the one hand (personality factors as independent variables) and the impact of experience in such a movement, once joined, on its members (personality factors as dependent variables). This distinction appears to have significance for all social movements, but especially for those committed to effecting a radical personal reorientation in the lives of their members, such as Synanon (Yablonsky 1965).

On closer examination, however, we discover this distinction to be ambiguous, difficult to apply, and vulnerable to circular reasoning. For one thing, the notion of "motives" for attraction is too simple, particularly if we regard *both* a movement and its members as having careers. We cannot assume any simple psychology, for example, that either self-esteem, power, or achievement constitutes the sole or main motivation for individuals in groups (Barkow 1975). A movement in a phase of cultic excitement offers something different to potential members than it does in a later state of institutionalization, and those motives that induce an individual to sustain membership in a group movement may be very different from those that led to the initial decision to join (Hiller 1975). Furthermore, it is often tempting to "read backward" from the presumed *effects* of membership (for example, an enhanced sense of belonging) and treat these as original *motives* for joining—an operation that has evident methodological pitfalls (Robbins et al. 1975). Finally, in the absence of measurements taken *before* individuals join movements, investigators run the danger of regarding certain characteristics of members (for example, manifestations of dependency) as constituting *results* of experiences as members, whereas in reality they may have been predispositions that led individuals to self-select themselves into membership. So although we shall divide this section of the chapter into a discussion of the psychosocial origins of group movements and the impact of movements on personality, we acknowledge that the proper unscrambling and understanding of these two processes call for complex interactive models and careful longitudinal empirical studies, both of which are rare in the literature.

PSYCHOSOCIAL ORIGINS OF SOCIAL MOVEMENTS

The literature on social movements reveals an initially confusing array of psychosocial explanations for their rise and persistence; proponents of one explanation, moreover, are frequently critical of the others, but as we hope to indicate, not all the various explanations are incompatible or beyond synthesis. We identify the following types of explanation:

Explanations in terms of predispositional personality variables. One major variant of this kind of explanation is the psychoanalytic. Launched by Freud (1955) and Martin (1920) early in the century, and given impulse in the 1930s by Harold Lasswell's (1930) analysis of the psychopathology of political behavior, that approach has enjoyed a continuing, if waning, existence in the literature. Wangh (1964) developed an account of the Nazi youth movement, and argued for the salience of pre-oedipal defense mechanisms (for example, projection and displacement) during the developmental transition into manhood. In his vigorous effort to explain student protest, Feuer (1969) relied heavily on the notion of the unconscious acting-out of oedipal conflicts.

Other accounts of predispositional variables are not so explicitly psychoanalytic. Block et al. (1969), in their study of the personalities of student activists, emphasized common childhood experiences and dynamics. Edwards (1970) differentiated several personality styles and levels of commitment, as well as socioeconomic backgrounds among participants in the black student movement. Still other studies of predispositions stress cognitive factors. Haan et al. (1968) found wide variations in "moral reasoning" to be a special feature of the personalities of their young subjects who were politically rebellious, and Candee (1974) stressed the affective focus on issues and the low level of complexity of understanding of political processes as characterizing student leftists. The logic common to all these predispositional studies is that the selected characteristic has a high incidence among those who find various kinds of movements attractive, and provides the motive for finding them attractive. Nearly all these studies suffer in one way or another, however, from the difficulty of establishing that the preferred characteristic does not enjoy widespread existence in the larger population of people not attracted to the movement in question.

A final kind of study suggests the importance of attitudinal orientations that predispose individuals to join different kinds of movements. Markle et al. (1978), for example, located a number of general attitudes that are apparently widely shared among participants in the laetrile movement. Among these are a conviction of the central importance of nutrition for physical health, an opposition to or disenchantment with organized medicine, and a right-wing political orientation. Such attitudinal variables, including disapproval of fluoridation, appeared to account more for organization participation than a number of demographic variables. Insofar as these generalized dispositions are important determinants, they suggest that the precise *content* of the protest to which individuals are attracted is less critical than the protest orientation itself, and if this is the case, the same or a similar population of individuals might be found among those attracted sequentially to environmentalist and natural food movements as well as the laetrile movement.

Explanations in terms of generational (Mannheim 1952), cohort (Ryder 1965), and life-course (Clausen 1973) variables. Although overlapping with the personality dispositions just reviewed, these types of variables are specifically tied to the phenomena of age-grading and age-stratification in society.

Needless to say, it is difficult to unscramble the separate effects of generation, cohort, and life cycle. Jennings and Niemi (1975) noted a number of attempts to differentiate among the discontinuous effects of the three. Their own empirical research shows much more extensive change in attitudes among a young cohort over an eight-year period (eighteen to twenty-six) than in the parental generation—and the youths' attitudes also changed in the *direction* of those of their elders—though it is difficult to know whether those changes can be attributed to a diminution of rebelliousness among the young (a generational effect), the passage from adolescence to young adulthood (a life-cycle effect), or to some specific historical situation experienced by the young (a cohort effect).

In his study of young student activists in the 1960s, Flacks (1967) appealed to a specifically generational argument, maintaining that these activists had been socialized in families with liberal, humanitarian values, and rather than rejecting these values, brought them to bear on the diagnosis of social injustices in American society. Lowenberg (1971) referred to the high incidence of psychoanalytically significant experiences (for example, oral deprivation, the absent father) that affected the cohort of German children during and immediately after World War I, and presumably predisposed them to embrace the messages and the leaders of German fascism. And in an interesting but difficult-to-interpret item of research, Phillips (1979) uncovered a tendency for individuals in a similar or same cohort as a publicized suicide victim to have unusually high automobile accident rates subsequent to the suicide; this suggests, at least, a relatively powerful mutual identification among individuals occupying the same cohort. Focusing on life-cycle changes, Fendrich (1976) followed black and white activists of the 1960s during their early adult years in an effort to trace the consequences of past radicalization. Though his research suffered from sampling problems and low response rates, especially from black subjects, there emerged some indication that confrontation politics in youth left a more enduring radicalizing effect on whites than blacks. Fendrich's interpretation was that blacks' political agitation was focused more around the issue of advancing their own race, whereas whites gravitated to a wider range of issues.

In an impressive comparative study of charismatic movements, Cell (1974) first hypothesized and then demonstrated the interaction between psychological determinants that are cohort-specific (for example, the disruption of life experience at a a certain age) and larger social determinants, such as national political crises, in predicting the historical occurrence of such movements. Cell also made an effort to gauge the strength of variables, such as level of nationalism in a society at any given time, rather than rely on cruder, "presence or absence" indices.

Explanations in terms of situational deprivation. The notion that situations of personal distress predispose individuals to seek meaningful solutions in religious or political movements or ideologies found an important place in Weber's (1968) sociology of religion. In a more recent formulation, Glock (1964) attempted to establish a linkage between what he called psychic deprivation or a sense of meaninglessness (as contrasted with material or status deprivation) as motivation for membership in religious cults. But the most influential recent formulation of situational stress has been the notion of relative deprivation, or, more precisely, rising expectations interrupted by some precipitous reversal. Davies's (1962) formulation of the *J*–curve of rising expectations, which is a kind of synthesis of the insights of Marx and Tocqueville, argues that situations of relative deprivation typically precede revolutionary movements. Relative deprivation also occupies a central place in Gurr's (1970) general effort to explain why people rebel. This formulation, too, has been plagued by some methodological problems, particularly the unavailability of direct measures of relative deprivation, and the difficulty in establishing relative deprivation (a subjective condition) on the basis of aggregated objective indicators, such as wage trends or unemployment rates (see Miller et al. 1977). In any event, these formulations of stress and deprivation are analytically distinct from the first set of explanatory factors discussed, in that they stress the current and are invoked without reference to predisposing personality factors.

Explanations in terms of some variant of anomie. As indicated, one of Durkheim's (1951) major types of suicide was anomic, arising from social situations characterized by lack of normative regulation, conflicting expectations, or discrepancies between life situations and normative expectations (the last is perhaps not far from relative deprivation). The anomic factor has survived as an explanation for attraction to political and social movements. Furthermore, it has taken a variety of forms—social marginality, status inconsistency, or, on a more cognitive note, some kind of dissonance or imbalance in an individual's experience. The logic of this explanation is that individuals experiencing some kind of discrepancy in their social environment are inclined to accept beliefs that render their life experience more consistent or harmonious. Those who make use of status-inconsistency as a motive for participation in social movements, however, often see it as interacting with other variables. Thus, Zurcher and Kirkpatrick (1976), who found status-inconsistency an important determinant in predicting who would be attracted to anti-pornography movements, nonetheless insisted that this was only one of several variables to be taken into account. Others, such as Baer et al. (1976), treated status-inconsistency as a general predisposing condition, contributing perhaps either to extreme political activism or extreme political apathy, depending on other conditions. Wilson and Zurcher (1977) identified subtypes of status-inconsistency, and suggested that "over-rewarded inconsistents" are resistant to change-oriented movements (and perhaps attracted to counter-movements), and that "under-rewarded inconsistents" are drawn to change-oriented movements.

For some investigators, the inconsistency is formulated not so much in terms of objective conditions as in terms of individual experiences. Pilarzyk (1978), for example, treated the preconversion individual as trying to interpret a sense of crisis, discontentment, alienation, as well as frequently a disenchanting experience within the youth culture (for example, drug use). More particularly, he interpreted the preconversion syndrome as an unresolved conflict between the contradictory personality needs for autonomy and for belongingness. Heirich (1977), although stressing the importance of situational determinants—rather than psychological stress or prior socialization—in the experience of religious conversion, suggested that conversion typically follows when an individual's rational and nonrational understanding of reality are shattered and a quest for a new understanding arises.

Explanations in terms of some kind of reaction to social constraints or oppression. In the past decade or so there has been a kind of movement among social scientists away from explaining recruitment to social movements in terms of marginality and anomie and toward finding the origins of protest movements in the oppressive social structure or in the unresponsiveness of authorities or other agents of social control. Although not as explicitly "psychological" as some other accounts, this emphasis nonetheless invokes a model of the individual as responding to realistic social situations and opportunities. In a study of black riot participants in the 1960s, Paige (1971) found that sense of political distrust was apparently one of the stronger predictors of propensity to participate, particularly when combined with a sense of efficacy. In his account of the origins of protest among blacks and students in the 1960s, Skolnick (1969) treated their orientations largely as realistic diagnoses of unjust and contradictory social situations in American society. Laqueur (1977), denying that there is such a thing as a "terrorist personality," argued that the motivation for terrorism reflects the quality of the existing social structure; a sense of meaninglessness, for example, may arise as a motive because of disenchantment with elected government. More generally, Laqueur argues that the less clear the political purposes of a society, the greater appeal terrorism has to "imbalanced" persons (a re-introduction of predispositional variables, though in combination with external variables). And in a theoretically sensitive investigation, Lieske (1978), analyzing 334 recent incidents of political disorder, found considerable support for explanations based both on anomic conditions and on the level of unresponsiveness of the political authorities; both in combination appear to make for the highest likelihood of disorder. In addition, Lieske sketched a developmental model of "disorder propensity," which not only incorporated both classes of variables, but treated political unrest and violence as a continuing and changing interaction between the two.

Explanations in terms of social interaction. Although this factor has not occupied as major a role in the study of social movements as some others, we should mention the formulation of Lofland and Stark (1965) and Lofland (1965), which includes personal influence as an important process in bringing individuals into a religious cult. In his study of a small apocalyptic religious cult in San Francisco—which was later to emerge as the Reverend Moon's Unification Church—Lofland found considerable evidence of histories of personal stress and disorganization among the converts to this cult, but also emphasized the importance of past interactions and personal contacts among members as components in initiating and sustaining their membership. Devereux (1961) found processes of interpersonal influence important in determining participation in the Hungarian revolt of 1956.

Explanations in terms of rational calculation. Another perspective recently coming on the scene is the neo-utilitarian model developed by Oberschall (1973). Hostile to explanations that stress depth psychology or personal disorganization, Oberschall regards participation in a protest movement as involving a more or less conscious, rational calculation of anticipated gains and costs. Although perhaps not usually considered as invoking personality factors—indeed, as indicated, antipathetic to them—this model definitely rests on psychological assumptions regarding what an individual perceives as gains (rewards) and costs (deprivations) and how he balances them, as do all explanations based on a variant of economic rationality.

This array of approaches to the psychosocial origins of social movements, discouragingly disparate at first sight, may be capable of systematic synthesis, particularly if we regard the social movement as having some kind of career, during which different kinds of personality factors come into salience at different phases or times. For example, it is likely that general predisposing personality factors, generated in the socialization experiences of a cohort or generation, create a reservoir of candidates for recruitment, though we would not expect all individuals with such predispositions to join, and we would expect a variety of other kinds of attractions to operate as well. Furthermore, it is likely that the timing of a movement might be influenced by some kind of economic, political, or anomic crisis, around which a proportion of that reservoir, along with others, might be mobilized to protest and to correct. Furthermore, it is likely that "cost-benefit" calculations on the part of individual joiners might be of little consequence during the heated and enthusiastic phases of mobilization of a movement, though these kinds of cognitive considerations may become salient when individuals are deciding whether to continue in or leave a movement that has become institutionalized. These observations suggest the advisability of generating combinatorial, interactive, and developmental models of social movements rather than attempting to correlate single types of psychosocial conditions with the incidence of participation in movements or the incidence of movements themselves.

In line with this suggestion, we note a few items of research that rest on a developmental model of social movements and record the changing psychological significance of movements for individuals over time. In interviews with a sample of political party workers, Clarke et al. (1978) differentiated between motives for initiating and motives for sustaining party work. Two-thirds of those interviewed reported differences between these two sets of motives in their own experience; apparently, moreover, expressive or social reasons are more important as reasons for sustaining membership. Social experiences in a movement, however, may generate ambivalence. In an early study of active members of Communist party organizations, Krugman (1952) found the need for belongingness as very important in leading to an initial commitment to the organization; membership itself, however, often thwarted the need for the individual's independent identity and increased the probability of withdrawing. Surely, too, the opportunities for personal gratification—as well as demands on the personality—are different in the revolutionary phase of a successful movement from those that appear when the regime becomes institutionalized (Suedfeld and Rank 1976).

The demands for appropriate personality characteristics may change over time for leaders as well. In a sensitive portrayal of the revolutionary leader, Daly (1972) suggested that in the early phase of a revolutionary movement the leader's capacity to respond quickly to changing situational exigencies is at a premium, whereas as the movement progresses the leader is called upon to deal more with internal doubts and conflicts. Suedfeld and Rank (1976) underscored the need for the leader to engage in and manipulate thinking that has low conceptual complexity during the early phases of revolutionary struggle—thinking, for example, in terms of social reality as dichotomously good or evil. However, the leader must change to a high complexity level during the post-struggle revolutionary phase, presumably to deal with a more complicated, evolving political situation.

IMPACT OF GROUP MOVEMENTS ON PERSONALITY

The other side of the coin of participation in a movement is the effect that experience in a movement has on the participants. On this question we find only a number of scattered studies and speculative essays. Some movements are frankly coercive; Dittmer's (1977) study of the Cultural

Revolution in China focused on "mass criticism" or public degradation ceremonies that were employed to affect moral positions as well as cognitive understandings of a new reality. The degree of coerciveness, however, is variable. Robbins, Anthony, and Curtis (1975) differentiated the brainwashing of POW camps from voluntary religious movements, such as Hare Krishna and Children of God, pointing to the fact that the latter do not normally use physical restraint in their conversion efforts. On the basis of their discussion, Robbins, Anthony, and Curtis posited a mixture of active choice and passive conditions for the members of authoritarian sects. Wieder and Zimmerman (1976) analyzed the process of becoming a "freak" in terms of group-facilitated desocialization. The process involves a disengagement from the conventional culture; doing this, however, as well as dealing with the negative societal labeling of "freaks," generates very high levels of anxiety. On the more positive side, Galanter et al. (1979) recorded an upsurge in the sense of well-being among recent converts to the Moonie organization, with, however, an apparent decline in that sense after a long period of membership. Moreover, those subjects recording a higher distress score before conversion to the movement also reported an increase in neurotic distress during subsequent membership.

In a speculative essay, Roth (1975) expressed a concern for the longer term consequences of what he calls the "new moral mood" of pressing for even greater individual rights and freedoms in contemporary society, arguing that this mood creates a "new unreason" that has been employed to legitimize frankly nihilistic values in various countercultural movements. Gutmann (1973) also expressed apprehension about the generational effects of counterculture membership. He portrayed countercultural converts as psychologically similar to some individuals in the post-empty nest phase of the life cycle, especially with respect to a commitment to diffuse sexuality and a turning away from the instrumental life. He regarded the new morality as militating against the resolution of identity and fostering role diffusion, and creating isolation instead of intimacy; ultimately, moreover, the members of the counterculture are not generative for their own offspring. In short, Gutmann argued, the counterculture morality involves a kind of premature withdrawal or senility, with possibly grave consequences for the future of society.

Social-Structural and Cultural Change and Personality

IMPACT OF PERSONALITY OR BEHAVIOR ON SOCIAL STRUCTURAL AND SOCIAL CHANGE

Despite a lingering appreciation of the importance of the "great man" in historical causation, recent research linking the individual person with processes of social change has been scattered and generally meager. Both the "need achievement" (McClelland 1961 and Hagen

1963) and the psychoanalytically informed "psychohistorical" (for example, Freud and Bullitt 1967 and Erikson 1958, 1969) approaches have enjoyed a certain vitality as ways of linking personal motivation and conflict with processes of economic and political change. Both approaches have faltered, however, in the face of criticisms that they often base sweeping generalizations on minimal data and that they have difficulty in relating the psychoanalytic factors to other causal forces in historical change. Etzioni (1977) has advanced the thesis that social problems (and the possibility of social change) arise when societal forces prevent, rather than advance, the fulfillment of such individual needs as affection, recognition, and self-actualization. He sees such needs as universal and not determined (caused) by social structures, cultural patterns, or socialization processes. Social change arises as a response to personality demands. The response may be inauthentic, moreover, when the social structure merely presents itself as responsive without actually changing.

We single out one recent study because it stands almost alone as a careful attempt to relate the personality of leaders to large-scale political change. In that study, Etheredge (1978) developed a systematic, interpersonal personality typology (based on the variables of dominance and extraversion) of past American political leaders. Further, he tried to show how these personality factors influenced foreign policy decisions of thirty-six leaders from 1898 to 1968. For example, low-dominant extraverts appeared to be consistently more open to social change than low-dominant introverts. Etheredge expressed a certain alarm at a possible implication of his own findings, namely, that personal motives are systematically displaced on to policy issues, and decisions based essentially on personal style are rationalized as being in the nation's collective interest.

Several other studies, more modest in scope, focus on the impact of personality factors on formal and informal organization. Shey (1977) argued that the causes of failure of Danish communes are not to be found in the larger society (which is quite tolerant of the experiments) but their debilitating dropout rate and other indications of failure lie in interpersonal conflicts, bred in part by too strong a commitment to individualistic and impulse-gratifying values. After studying a process of change in a prison setting. Gluckstern and Packard (1977) concluded that different personality styles on the part of agents of change (for example, flexibility, teachability, trust) assume greater salience at different *stages* of organizational change; their observations suggest again the importance of the notion of career in considering both social and individual processes of change. Finally, Kernberg (1979) noted the dysfunctional effects of regressive leadership styles (for example, schizoid, narcissistic) on the organization of a psychiatry department.

AGE, PERSONALITY, AND RECEPTIVITY TO CHANGE

Each research item cited up to this point focuses on some personality factor or personality style of an agent of change. Another kind of influence of personality on change is to focus on the psychological receptivity of persons, considered in the aggregate, to certain types of change. On this score investigators have tended to focus on generational, cohort, and life-cycle differences in attitudes, noting their implications for change. In a very general statement, Brent (1978) suggested that the relative psychological openness of the young and the relative psychological rigidity of the old constitute a functional balance between preservation and change of societal values.

Numerous specific studies, too, suggest a consistent shifting of attitudes in a conservative direction associated with age, but unscrambling the dynamics of this change is a source of persistent difficulty. Hoge and Bender (1974) found large value changes in groups of college males from 1931 to 1952 and from 1956 to 1969. Certain historical events, such as the era of Joseph McCarthy, appeared to generate attitude changes among all groups, but as a general rule changes in personal values were less marked after age forty. In a similar study, Cutler and Kaufman (1975), analyzing two national samples from 1954 to 1972, found a greater tolerance of political nonconformity among all cohorts, with older cohorts more likely than younger ones to adhere to earlier, more conservative attitudes, thus making for a widening gap among cohorts. Similarly, Pederson (1976) found a correlation between age and resistance to change in voting preference in California from 1960 to 1970, noting that with increasing age attitudes become both more rigid and consistent. Following 495 state legislators from 1957 to 1970, Hain (1974) found a certain lag between politicians' age-related failure to advance in politics and their realization of that disadvantage; the general constriction of the perceived opportunity structure for the politicians studied occurred about age fifty; 82 percent of the sample under fifty expressed ambitions, compared to only 27 percent over fifty-five.

Similar findings have emerged with respect to attitudes related to sex roles. Noting the greater propensity for sex-role attitudes to become liberalized in younger cohorts, Waite (1978) suggested that this translates into higher rates of female participation in the work force. In an analysis of national probability samples in 1972 and 1975, Mahoney (1978) also found that the 18–29 age group had the most permissive attitude toward premarital coitus, but the 30–39 group, especially the females, showed the greatest relative shift toward greater permissiveness. Priestnall et al. (1978) found an increasing use of oral contraceptives among unmarried female university students, that usage was greater among political left-wing students than politically right, and that usage was most infrequent among politically uncommitted women. Furthermore, women with a less traditional view of femininity were more likely to use the pill. And in a rare longitudinal study, Willits et al. (1977) traced changes in moral attitudes in a sample over a twenty-four-year span, from 1947 (when subjects were sixteen years old) to 1971 (forty years old). The authors observed a general change in the direction of permissiveness, but not in attitudes toward the behavior of youth. Church attendance appeared to be closely related to degree of resistance to change. The ultimate explanation for these quite consistent findings is not yet available, but in the end it will probably reveal the influence of general cultural drifts (Levine 1973), such as a shift toward impulsiveness and a "disclosing" personal style suggested by Turner (1976), which, however, affects younger age groups disproportionately, on account of the dynamics of generational conflict, position in the life cycle, and the processes of intracohort reinforcement of attitudes.

SOCIOCULTURAL CHANGE AND ITS IMPACT ON PERSONALITY

Modernization and post-industrial society. The lion's share of the literature relevant to our essay falls under this category; and within the category the most persistent preoccupations are with the two topics of modernization and psychological modernity (in which the empirical focus is mainly on the developing countries) and the psychological impact of post-industrial society (in which the empirical focus is expectably on the modern West).

The most influential research on individual modernity is that of Inkeles and his colleagues. As early as 1960 (Inkeles 1960), he stressed the emergence of a distinct psychosocial type in the process of institutional modernization and argued that the individual's occupational status is a more powerful influence on the emergence of modern attitudes and personality characteristics than are his nationality or culture. (By "modern" Inkeles referred to phenomena such as openness to social change, tolerance of social differences, belief in controlling one's destiny, independence from parental generations, and participation in civic affairs.) In a long series of comparative research projects, culminating in a major monograph (Inkeles and Smith 1974), Inkeles has repeatedly hammered home the arguments that a distinctly modern outlook emerges; that the place of work (especially the factory) and the school are the main agents of change in this process; and that—contrary to a tradition that regards factory labor as alienating and detrimental to mental health (Kornhauser 1965)—individuals under modernizing conditions do not experience special stress or special problems of personal adjustment. In connection with the latter point, Suzman (1977), employing Loevinger and Wessler's (1970) ego development scale, found a positive correlation between the individual modernity syndrome and level of ego development (especially for working American women).

Luria (1976) studied the impact of rapid change in the economy in the 1930s and found support, in small villages and collective farms in Russia, for his thesis that there is a shift from concrete to abstract cognitive styles with greater involvement in a more modern economy, Karsh and Cole (1968) found support for the hypothesis that industrial societies are becoming more alike in individual modernity, although they argue that some cultural differences between societies will be preserved. Fliegel (1976), employing a twenty-two-item index measuring eight aspects of modernity and based on interviews with male workers in Ghana, India, Brazil, and the United States, found that most types of workers exposed to greater technological complexity scored higher on the modernity scale. Fliegel also argued that value differences between cultures persist, that Westernization and modernization are not synonymous, and that social-structure convergences among industrial nations are not matched by convergence of cultural values.

Findings by other investigators on the subject of individual modernity point in many different directions, not only because of differences in their assessment and interpretation of data, but because their studies employ a diversity of both independent (modernization) and dependent (attitudinal) variables. To present only a sample, we turn first to two studies making use of Rotter's (1966) Internal-External Scale, designed to locate an individual's conception of and belief about where causal efficacy rests in the world: consistent with Inkeles's emphasis, a high score on Internal would signify a more modern orientation. In one study Nagelschmidt and Jakob (1977) found an increase in women's sense of personal efficacy in a modernizing society. In another study, Reitz and Groff (1974) found workers in two developed countries stressing "internal" efficacy as causes of leadership and success more than did workers from two developing countries. Although generally supportive of Inkeles's position, the authors stressed cultural differences more than he did; for example, workers from Oriental countries (even developed ones like Japan) retain beliefs in "external" efficacy to a greater degree than American workers.

A more diffuse set of consequences was traced by Tallman and Ihinger-Tallman (1979) who concluded, on the basis of a comparison between American and Mexican samples, that poor and developing countries stress materialistic values, whereas industrialized societies place a higher value on interpersonal satisfaction. Furthermore, they argued that with increasing modernization, norms of distributive justice change from an emphasis on solidarity to an emphasis on proportionality or equity. Surely, we would expect cultural differences to influence these kinds of changes as well. And in a more refined study, Guthrie (1977) discovered that among a sample from the Philippines, higher status in society appears to predispose individuals to accept "modern" attitudes more readily.

The measurement of modernity continues to be debated. Inkeles and Smith (1974), as well as Schnaiberg (1970), conclude that modernity is multidimensional, whereas Cohen and Till (1977) and Armer and Schnaiberg (1977) question the convergent and discriminant validity of modernity scales. Gates (1976) has introduced a promising projective method (reliable, replicable) of measuring attitudes toward modernization in Mexican peasant groups undergoing change from traditional agricultural life as new irrigation methods are introduced. Part of her data show a rise in achievement-motivation and self-esteem after some experience with a new irrigation project. She also suggests that her attitudinal measures are more than outcome, and that they can be regarded as indicating a readiness for modernization.

Studies and essays on the impact of sociocultural change in contemporary (or "post-modern") society tend to be less solidly based empirically, and as a consequence, more speculative. They are also informed mainly by some variant of the "anomic" model of social change, treating modern change as overwhelming, disorienting, and productive of a variety of disturbed behaviors. For example, Robertson and Cochrane (1976a, 1976b) proposed to account for increased frequencies of deviant behavior (drugs, attempted suicide) in terms of a conflict between the enhanced expectations on the part of young adults and the scarcity of opportunities for gratification provided by society. Their starting point was the evidence of an apparently rapid increase in recent years in numbers of attempted suicides among males under twenty-five in Edinburgh. They interpreted this phenomenon as manifesting a shift toward a new world view that stresses first, the importance of self-fulfillment, second, the responsibility of society to guarantee this fulfillment, and third, society's inability to do so. In a sample of suicide-attempt youths, the authors found certain evidence of extensive dissatisfaction with society, but no greater than among a group of "controls," or nonattempters with similar characteristics. The suicide-attempt sample did, however, show higher scores on measures of depression.

In another study Johnstone (1975) postulated that rapid social change exacerbates generational conflict; the lag between generations is inevitable because adults do not develop so rapidly as the young, and so their response to social changes is inevitably retarded. Positing that there has been greater social change in French Canada than in English-speaking Canada, he predicted and found greater parent-youth conflict reported by French-speaking youth, especially conflict on issues arising in late adolescence. Dowd's (1979–80) analysis of changes in social and religious values from 1958 and 1971 surveys indicates that older cohorts are less receptive to such changes. He speculates that the older cohorts have a more complex personality system and have been socialized to a certain set of values into which external change is more slowly integrated. Consistent with these findings, Zurcher (1972) posited a high malleability of the self in younger cohorts.

Lauer and Thomas (1976) developed a well-documented case that mental illness increases in incidence as a function of rapidity of social-structural and cultural change. Brenner (1973) identified a specifically American vulnerability to large-scale social changes, namely, the American ethic of individualism and self-sufficiency, which is at variance with the institutional fact that the individual has little control over large-scale societal changes. Caudill (1973) differentiated between social change and cultural change, maintaining that the former has been widespread and rapid in contemporary Japan, whereas cultural change has been much slower; on the basis of this assertion, Caudill outlined a number of problems of personal adjustment for the Japanese.

Changes in family and sex roles. Scholars interested in the fate of the person in modern society have long focused on the family because many personality-affecting forces work through that institution. In an article consistent with a long-standing notion of the disintegration of the family in industrial society, Bronfenbrenner (1974) recorded his alarm over recent changes in the American family, maintaining that family instability (divorce, for example), and a further decline in the family's domestic responsibility (with the spread of ancillary child care, for example) constitute a deterioration of an appropriate social context for nurturing psychological growth in children. Bronfenbrenner attributed what he perceived as an increase in alienated behavior to this trend. In a similar argument, Hsu (in DiRenzo 1977) regarded American society as relying more and more on external controls for behavior and de-emphasizing affective (for example, familial) relationships. Also consistent with Bronfenbrenner, Weigert and Hastings (1977) argued that large-scale social changes (especially the rise in importance of affectless organizations in bestowing individual identity) produce individuals alienated from intimacy and unable to cope with personal loss.

These diagnoses of the fate of the individual in contemporary society, although obviously dealing with most important substantive issues, tend to be short on sensitivity to measurement problems on both the social change and personality levels, short on identifying the precise mechanisms by which the imputed sociocultural changes actually give rise to the presumed personal consequences, and short on comparative and historical analyses. As such, they stand, along with much of the rest of the literature on the impact of society on personality, somewhere in the region between scientific investigation and speculative prophecy.

Recent years have also witnessed a number of efforts to assess the impact of sociocultural changes in modernizing, modern, and post-modern societies on changing attitudes toward and adaptations to sex roles. In an effort to extend Inkeles and Smith's (1974) study to females, Weisner and Abbott (1977) found that in three separate Kenya settings, the combination of women's increased economic *and* domestic obligations (associated with modernizing trends in society) apparently were responsible for generating high levels of psychophysiological stress. Weisner and Abbott also suggested that women over forty appear to experience more stress. And in their study of changes in Japanese women's attitudes toward their roles, Smith and Schooler (1978) described a shift away from defining one's self as related to others or to institutional memberships and toward autonomy and defining one's self in personal, more impulsive ways.

The implication of these changes in sex roles for socialization and the personality of offspring, however, is not altogether clear. Referring to a 1975 follow-up study based on a 1955 sample of Rajput mothers, Minturn et al. (1978) concluded that the later sample is more prosperous economically, and that prosperity has increased their sense of power and status; this, in turn, has given them greater individual control over their children. In any event, whatever consequences such changes might have for children would probably be delayed at least a generation. Numerous investigators (for example, Smith and Schooler 1978) have stressed cultural resistances to changing sex roles—a resistance we noted in our earlier discussion of assimilation of migrants—and Bush et al. (1977), finding little evidence of improvement in females' self-esteem over the past decade, concluded that changes in adolescent perception of sex roles will have to await a new generation of parents and teachers.

Changes in race and education. We note another topical area that has commanded much attention in the literature in the past two decades—the impact of school desegration, specifically on the personality and personal adjustment of pupils. The accumulating research suggests that there is probably no single impact, but instead that the effects of desegregation are mediated through diverse contexts, such as selective closing or building of schools, redistricting, busing; also desegregation may be planned at the local level, or may occur in response to a court order, and this difference, too, would condition any impacts it might have.

Campbell (1977) stressed the multifaceted nature of the desegregation process, involving the family, peer group, and school environment as mediators in influencing racial attitudes and self-esteem for both white and black students. In his research he found that lower socioeconomic status appears to be highly and positively associated with negative racial attitudes, and argued from this finding that a theory based on "deprivation" is a more powerful predictor of resulting racial attitudes than is the fact of social contact between the races. In a two-year follow-up study of desegregated, white elementary school children, Stephan and Rosenfield (1978) found that children of authoritarian and punitive parents developed more negative racial attitudes, while both increases in children's own self-esteem and the amount of interethnic contact appeared to be strongly correlated with positive attitudes toward blacks. And Martinez-Monfort and Dreger (1972) found consistently that negative white attitudes toward blacks appear to be more resistant to modification than negative black attitudes toward whites. It also remains clear, however, that the impact of school desegregation—like that of changing sex roles —is a matter to be discerned not only in the short term, but also in the subsequent adult careers of both blacks and whites who have experienced it and who will rear the next generation.

Desegregation's short-term impact on both racial and personal self-esteem has been the focus of numerous investigations in the past decade, following the 1966 work of Coleman et al. Rosenberg and Simmons (1972) and Rosenberg (1975) found that the personal self-esteem of black children was quite similar to that of white children, and that blacks in desegregated schools had lower self-esteem than blacks in segregated schools. An explanation for these latter findings is found in social evaluation theory, where an immediate social environment that is consonant with the individual's values serves to protect self-esteem (Taylor 1976). St. John's review (1975) supports the findings that the impact of desegregation on the self-concept of minority members tends to be negative or mixed more often than positive. However, St. John also reports that in the longer term desegregation is found to be associated with higher self-esteem.

Wylie (1979), like St. John, criticizes the lack of systematic controls (for example, no control groups) in the designs of most desegregation studies; Wylie also notes the lack of consensual measures of the self and of racial esteem across studies as well as the questionable validity of many of the outcome measures. Wylie's review of the desegregation literature comes to conclusions similar to St. John's, although Wylie is more skeptical of the adequacy of the research designs and outcome measures. Porter and Washington (1979) focus more on studies of change in self and racial esteem. They note the problem of differentiating rise in self-esteem associated with growing older, as in Roberts, Mosely, and Chamberlin (1975) from rise in self-esteem as a result of the black consciousness movement, as in Loomis (1974). Porter and Washington suggest that explanations of changes in racial esteem may differ according to the social class of subjects. For example, relative deprivation theory and socialization into a changing culture may not apply as well as the alienation perspective to individuals at the very bottom of the class structure. Abeles (1976) has attempted to specify the connection between sociological and psychological influences on racial esteem; he finds some evidence that relative deprivation and rising expectations act as mediating variables between improvements in the socioeconomic condition of blacks and black militant behavior. Another such intervening variable is that of blaming the self or the system (one of the dimensions of locus of control). For example, Gurin and Epps (1975) suggest that blame of the system is crucial for high self-esteem of the blacks. Yinger (1977) summarizes such changes as observed by Abeles and Gurin and Epps by noting that depictions of the social character of blacks are moving toward a more creative, adaptive, and active focus than the "injury" approach of such writers as Kardiner and Ovesey (1951).

Adam (1978) notes apparent improvements in blacks' self-esteem over time but contends that current studies of black self-esteem are invalid and gloss over earlier evidence of low black self-esteem. Simmons (1978) responds that earlier studies were based on small, unrepresentative samples, whereas later studies utilize larger, more nearly random samples. In addition, she notes that more recent studies are more global, employ different instruments, and do not focus as exclusively on being black. She argues that the differences between early and later findings are due to actual changes in self-attitudes over time rather than just methodological differences. Pettigrew (1978) agrees that the increase in black self-esteem over the past forty years is more than a reflection of changing political ideological intepretations of research findings.

Acculturative stress. Finally, we note a continuing attention by anthropologists and others to the effects on personality in situations where one society has superimposed itself on another. (These kinds of situations are similar to those discussed under migration and acculturation, but it is important to distinguish the present case from them because of the feature of explicit political domination.) The major themes in this literature continue to be cultural loss, acculturation, and cultural reassertion. In a psychoanalytically oriented study, Hippler (1973) diagnosed the Athabascans' (of interior Alaska) strong external authority system as greatly weakened by Western religious contact, and their social customs as eroded by the loss of the customary potlatch system. According to Hippler's account, the tribe experienced an interim period of apathy and self-destructive, aggressive behavior before attempting to re-establish institutions similar to traditional forms as a way of simultaneously accommodating to and defying the dominant whites. In a finding of similar import, Hackenberg and Gallagher (1972) found those Papago Indians exposed to "most" modernization (higher education, wage labor, Protestant affiliation) manifesting twice the rate of accidental injury as among the traditional Papago. These kinds of studies generally rest on a kind of simple anomic model of social process that posits cultural domination, followed by some kind of disorienting psychosocial impact that is, in turn, followed by a manifestation of some disturbed social behavior.

As we have pointed out on several occasions, this kind of model is fraught with methodological and interpretative problems, and it is heartening to see a few more complicated ways of thinking about reactions to cultural contact and domination appearing in the literature. Morrill (1973), for example, cautioned against interpreting "assertive behavior" in his sample of Thai students in training with American teachers (that is, in culture contact) as "new" behavior acquired from the experience without first determining the differences in the students' assertive behavior *before* cultural contact was established; the obvious alternative explanations made possible by this strategy are that the culture contact had no particular impact on assertiveness and that assertive individuals perhaps self-selected themselves into the training program (in which the cause-effect direction would be precisely opposite to the model of culture contact → impact → behavior). In his study of stress among aborigines, Berry (1978) also took account of variations among those affected. The most traditional aborigines rejecting the dominant society were also more marginal to their own society, more deviant, and experienced more stress. On the basis of this and other research, Berry and Annis (1974) developed an elaborated model of acculturative stress based on the interaction of both cultural and personality variables. The two principles of the model are that the greater the discontinuity between the two cultures, the greater the acculturative stress; and the greater the level of psychological differentiation (complexity) at the personality level, the less the level of acculturative stress. Empirical measures taken on seven American Indian communities tended to verify the first principle, and measures of personality differentiation *within* Indian cultures lent strength to the second principle. These kinds of results led Berry and Annis to reject the notion of a single or universal relationship model between culture contact and acculturative stress. Berry (1978) has subsequently proposed taking base rate measures for a culture prior to a major social change in order to chart the course of subsequent acculturative stress. Also, for communities at different stages of acculturation, different levels of acculturative stress would be predicted for earlier and later periods. One asset of this interactive model is that it makes use of a "career" notion of acculturative processes, rather than a before-after, cause-effect model.

Concluding Remarks

Scanning the recent history of research on group movements, sociocultural change, and personality, we observe a complex mixture of trends—several kinds of discontinuity, but a fundamental continuity as well. The first kind of discontinuity is a tendency for the topics under investigation to shift *over* time, and to shift *with* the times. As new preoccupations and problems boil up in the larger society, investigators desert old concerns and turn to more timely ones. We note the great fall-off in research on the psychosocial origins of student radicalism, which dominated the 1960s, and an upsurge of interest in religious cultism in the 1970s. We note the intensification of research interest in the psychological impact of school desegregation, changing sex roles, and the perceived further disintegration of traditional family forms—all topics of intense debate in contemporary American society. (In line with these observations, we daresay we are now on the eve of the publication of at least a small spate of articles on suicide cults and mass suicide, appearing in the wake of the dramatic Jonestown tragedy in 1978.) Research on change and personality, in short, like many other strands of research in the social and behavioral sciences, mirrors in microcosm the very historical trends and social problems that constitute its subject matter.

The study of social change and personality also shows evidence of discontinuities in paradigmatic emphasis—discontinuities, moreover, that reflect certain general theoretical and ideological developments in the social and behavioral sciences. The fall of the psychoanalytic paradigm from its period of dominance in the 1940s and 1950s is readily observable, particularly in the area known as "psychological anthropology," which has witnessed the dethronement of the psychoanalytically inspired "culture and personality" approach, and the rise of a plethora of phenomenological, cognitive, and other "psychologies" by its side (Spindler 1978). More generally, we perceive that the emphasis on the psychology of inner conflict has given rise to a greater stress on ego-integrative structures and processes, such as identity and personal adaptation. And finally, though this change is perhaps more subtle, we note a tendency for observers to look to determinants that are more nearly external to the individual—determinants such as anomic social situations, repressive social structures, presence or absence of opportunities for individual adaptation—rather than to inner processes. This latter trend, if it is indeed one, may be a reflection of a perceptible increase in emphasis on structural and neo-Marxist emphases among social and behavioral scientists in the late 1960s and into the 1970s.

In regarding these two types of discontinuity and ferment—in topic and in paradigmatic stress—we must report with some sadness that neither kind of change appears to be yielding anything cumulative by way of established theory or valid empirical knowledge. The movements appear to be shifts rather than accretions. The reason for lack of progress, moreover, appears to lie in what we regard as the basic continuity in that area of research relating to sociocultural change and personality. That continuity is the persistence of conceptual and methodological problems involved in the study of the articulation of personality and social systems generally. Among the intractable conceptual problems are a continuing vagueness in the definition of both levels of analysis, continuing difficulties in formulating appropriate kinds of causal relations linking the two levels, and a failure to develop appropriate feedback models of psychosocial processes. Among the intractable methodological problems are difficulties in measuring the important psychosocial variables, the inability to gain control over major sources of variation, and the formidable problems of establishing temporal and, therefore, presumably causal priority of different classes of social and psychological forces. These conceptual and methodological problems are by no means unique to the study of the articulation of personality and social systems, but they are especially severe in this area. We are convinced, moreover, that until quite basic steps are taken to improve the conceptual and methodological fundamentals of this line of research, it will continue to produce flux rather than growth.

GLADYS ENGEL LANG AND KURT LANG

Mass Communications and Public Opinion: Strategies for Research

Introduction

The historical link between the development of the press and the formation of public opinion has been a natural though not the only focus of sociological interest. The continuing development of communication technology has given rise to other sociological concerns, including the role of mass communication as an agent of socialization, the effect of the various media on cognitive processes, their potential for teaching, persuasion, and propaganda, as well as their consequences for leisure time usage, political participation, and other behavior (Weiss 1969; Pool et al., 1973; Wright 1975). We have in no sense attempted to deal here with the total range of sociological issues related to mass media but to focus on the link between the mass media and public opinion. For without the communication facilities that bridge the barriers of geographical and social distance, the mass of people in the Great Society could rarely involve themselves in the central issues of the time. In short, without the mass media, there would be no mass public opinion, only elite opinion.

Early efforts to spell out the relationship between the two were largely speculative and not based on what we would today consider empirical research. Among the founding generation of sociologists, there were those who recognized this lack of data. Thus, in 1910, Max Weber presented to the first Congress of German Sociologists a proposal for extensive research on the role of the press, including an analysis of newspaper content. The project, unfortunately, never got underway, its prime mover having been distracted by a civil suit. Years later, however, after the first World War, Weber's ideas helped shape Harold Lasswell's approach to the study of propaganda. More than most of his contemporaries, Lasswell (1927) was intrigued by the manifold aspects of the relationship between mass communication and public opinion. It is also to Lasswell (1948) that researchers owe the succinct formula under which a large variety of research questions could be conveniently grouped:

Who says *what* in which *channel* to *whom* and with what *effect?* The formula is nothing more than a paradigm for defining the elements in any communication situation, including mass communication. And the terms in the formula also help to define mass communication: the transmission by professional *communicators* of a continuous flow of the same symbolic *content* by means of a complex technological and organizational apparatus *(channel)* to a large, heterogeneous, and physically dispersed *audience.* The definition says nothing about effects, but identifies the elements to be considered in any study of impact. It implies that the communicator or source, the channel or medium, the characteristics of the audience can all greatly influence the reactions to one and the same content, and the content itself can be packaged in different ways. By using the term *transmission,* it sidesteps the question of whether or not there is effective communication in the sense of a meeting of minds. For all that, the question of effect and consequences remains central to the study of mass communication. It is, therefore, all the more surprising that the idea that mass communication has significant effects should have fallen into disrepute and only recently been moved back once more on a track from which it was unfortunately derailed.

Denis McQuail (1977) described half a century of sociological interest in media effects as divisible into three main phases. During the first, which lasted until about 1940, the media were "attributed considerable power to shape opinion and belief, change habits of life, actively mould behavior and impose political systems even against resistance." The second extended to the late 1950s or early 1960s. In this phase, the mass media came to be judged ineffective, impotent, and "unlikely to be major contributors to direct change of individual opinions, attitudes or behaviour." Today, in a third phase, we are told, the case for mass media effects is being revived, with new thinking and a renewed search for evidence. This return thus marks the completion of a media *effects cycle.*

This concept of an effects cycle has a certain aesthetic appeal. Its second phase represents an overinterpretation of findings from research, mainly, but not entirely, the product of projects undertaken by Paul F. Lazarsfeld and his colleagues at Columbia University. These projects discredited once and for all time the view that communication effects could be adequately conceptualized in simple stimulus-effect terms or be directly deduced from the content and the level of exposure to the media. This research helped elaborate a model of the communication process by "documenting the subservience of the mass media to other more fundamental components in any potential situation of [media] influence" (McQuail 1977:73). But its very success led to the undoing of mass communication research. The momentum of the golden era of the postwar years was lost as academics and students, once motivated by their concern over media power and now persuaded that there was none to be found, turned toward other more promising subjects. It was only in the sixties, so it is now said by McQuail and others (Katz 1977), that the earlier minimalist conclusions came under challenge and research once again addressed the problem of media influence.

While McQuail's effort to depict the history of the field in broad strokes has the ring of truth, it is open to question on several counts. Even if, as he contends, we have swung full circle and have now entered a third phase of the effects cycle, we are certainly not far into it. The old controversy continues. Thus, the book in which McQuail heralds the new era in mass communication research (Curran et al. 1977) also includes an article by Tom Burns, a British sociologist, that chides both McQuail and the Langs for concluding that the media influence the public opinion process. Burns (1977:45) notes that social scientists, like specialist writers on mass communication "find it . . . difficult to surrender the belief in the persuasive power of broadcasting despite the accumulation of *almost entirely negative* findings from research over thirty-five years into the extent to which broadcasting actually influences political opinion and voting behavior" [emphasis added]. More recently, Harold Mendelsohn, an American social psychologist, has written about "the futility of searching for direct and one-variable effects," insisting that political communications, like the televised Carter-Ford debates in 1976, influence only those voters who wish to be influenced" (Mendelsohn 1980).

The idea that there are few mass media effects is not easily abandoned. Instead—as typified by both Burns's and Mendelsohn's statements—the myth persists that the search for effects ended some decades ago because none could be found or because, as it is sometimes put, the all-powerful media had proved unexpectedly powerless. Now for a more careful look at the record.

The model that never was. Few, if any, reputable social scientists in the pre-World War II era—that is, during the first phase of the effects cycle—worked with what was later described as the "hypodermic needle model" (Katz and Lazarsfeld 1955). To be sure, there was concern over the fearsome potential of the new means of propaganda—particularly film and radio. This led to some grandiose theorizing. Explanations of Hitler's success invoked the old notions of crowd psychology, as well as newer ones about hypnotism or Pavlovian conditioning (Chakhotin 1939). But this theorizing had little to do with communication research as we know it. On the contrary, the dominant concern of research in the twenties and the thirties was with the techniques of propaganda, with how people could learn to recognize deception for what it was (Lee and Lee 1939). Later, with the Second World War underway, there would be equal concern with how best to inform citizens and soldiers about national needs and programs and to enlist their support for democratic goals.

These researchers understood that for a message to elicit the intended response, at least the following conditions had to be met: the message had to gain the attention of those toward whom it was aimed; it had to be correctly understood; its implications had to be sanctioned by self and/or relevant others: and compliance had to be within their capability. It is understandable that much of the researchers' attention was focused on the kinds of messages that could overcome resistance, but it is also true that, in so framing their research efforts, they neglected other noncontent factors in the communication situation that limit the impact of even the most expertly designed propaganda.

The discovery of effects. In the golden era (Katz 1977) of mass communication research, success seems to have been measured by the number of barriers to direct media influence that could be identified and demonstrated. This indexing of progress had an unexpected consequence: it obscured the fact that, in spite of all the limitations, there were indeed important effects. Even a cursory examination of the literature before 1960 will turn up finding after finding to contradict the then-dominant tendency to downgrade the importance of the mass media.

The detailed examination of how individuals responded to content called attention to "sleeper" effects. The army research unit under Hovland demonstrated experimentally that sometimes the amount of change immediately after exposure was smaller than after several months (Hovland et al. 1949:182 ff.). The increase could be interpreted as reinforcement by cumulative communication activity. Others initiated what later would be labeled the "uses and gratification" approach (Wright 1960, 1974). Here the emphasis was less on persuasion than on a whole range of effects, many not even contemplated by communicators. For example, Warner and Henry (1948) explained how the addiction of some housewives to daytime radio serials (soap operas) enabled them to sustain unrewarding life styles. Their study, as well as those by others, (Riley and Riley 1951) disclosed a relationship between social isolation and the use of mass media fare for personal gratification, more as a substitute for other meaningful contact than as a supplement to social participation. So, too, research found that some readers used the daily newspaper as much (or more) as a source of security in a disturbing world as for information (Berelson 1949). Heavy media use, even if it did not exactly cause passivity, might nevertheless be a convenient substitute for remedial action that required effort or might prove painful or expensive.

These studies not only moved conceptualization beyond the idea of a simple and direct causality, but called attention to other more subtle yet potentially far-reaching consequences of mass communication. It became apparent that some effects were additive. It also became clear that what appeared to be a minor change, occurring only among persons already "disposed" to change, could have serious ramifications when concentrated within a strategic segment of the population, such as the "undecideds" who could swing an election. Of particular interest is a paradoxical finding by Lazarsfeld (1939). Two surveys, one before and one after a speech by Supreme Court appointee Hugo Black about his prior Ku Klux Klan membership, showed that opinion at both times reflected existing social divisions, but the line of division changed. Whereas before the speech the issue was perceived in religious and ethnic terms, Black's radio appeal successfully dramatized its socioeconomic aspects, making the class status of listeners more important than their minority group membership. Here is a case where mass communication changed public opinion by playing into dispositions already present in the audience instead of meeting them head-on. It illustrated what today would be called *agenda setting* and was once known as the power of the media to "structure issues" (Lazarsfeld et al. 1944; Lang and Lang 1959).

Research during this period also helped specify the conditions under which mass communication is more or less effective. One such condition of an essentially sociological rather than psychological character is the strength of other social controls. In one of the seminal studies emerging from the wartime research effort, Shils and Janowitz (1948) were able to show that propaganda leaflets, directed by the Allies at German soldiers in the last months of World War II urging them to desert, had little impact until the bonds of social and organizational cohesion were undermined by casualties to a point where the *Landser* no longer could count on the kind of protection that had sustained him through continuous defeats. His personal fate became less closely related to his immediate group, and loyalty to the soldier's family began to supersede other loyalties. From this point on, both the argument that Germany had lost the war and the promise of safe conduct played into the concern for personal survival. Similarly, the research on the 1940 election reported in *The People's Choice,* usually cited mainly for its discovery of the "opinion leadership" phenomenon, also argued that mass communication had some influence on the votes of persons for whom primary groups did not project homogeneous preferences (Lazarsfeld et al. 1948).

All this accords with the more general view of earlier theorists that mass communication helped liberate people from the narrow perspectives imposed by in-group attitudes. The view received affirmation from research on the Third World. In *The Passing of Traditional Society* (1958), Lerner pointed to the importance of images of American or Soviet standards of living in making Turkish villagers more discontent with their lot in life. This revolution of rising expectations has its counterpart among the poor of America, who measure their own poverty against the affluence shown on television. National coverage also helps sensitize people to standards different from their own. The correlations Tumin (1959) found between the readiness of southerners for desegregation and levels of exposure to mass media, following the landmark Supreme Court decision, were at least suggestive on this point.

The interest in the role the mass media play in situations of tension and potential conflict existed long before the ghetto and youth protest riots in the 1960s. Turner and Surace (1956) showed how the media, in the way they played up the "zoot-suiter," created secondary symbols around which interracial tensions crystallized to the point of open rioting. More moderate effects were documented by Medalia and Larsen (1958). In the psychological atmosphere in which nuclear testing had become an issue, media reports helped trigger a veritable epidemic of calls about mysterious windshield pitting, sufficiently alarming to send the mayor of Seattle appealing to Washington for help. The damage to windshields was no more than normal wear and tear, and calls ceased when the story faded from the newspapers. The case is similar to the more dramatic media-fueled, if not media-created, epidemic of swastika painting in late 1959, that led to political controversy, even at the international level. Again, it was only when newspapers stopped printing stories of scribbled swastikas and of the resurgence of anti-Semitism in postwar Germany that the issue disappeared, though the painting of swastikas, for all one knows, may have continued. This is more than a demonstration effect. The mass media helped legitimate the activity by the attention bestowed on it (Lang and Lang 1961, chapter 14).

What is now remembered as the "no effects" era also produced the most convincing study thus made of the effects of media recognition. This was based on an analysis by Davison (1956) of the blockade the Soviets imposed in 1948–49 on all ground traffic into Berlin, a city that had been divided at the end of World War II among the four occupying powers, each administering its own sector. The full blockade of the land and water routes to the West, which were Berlin's source of supply, was meant to force its surrender to the Russians. The defeat of the Soviet aims came about because of two factors: the success of the Western airlift in supplying the necessities of life to the Berliners, and the willingness of the two million people, crowded into West Berlin, to accept privations and to resist threats and enticements from the Russians who completely surrounded them. The willingness was based on their conviction that they were making history, and the conviction, in turn, was greatly influenced by the media treatment of the crisis. It was largely as a result of exposure to Western-oriented mass media that Berliners came to feel that they were manning the front line with the whole world watching, a feeling that strengthened their resolve. In an altogether different case, the media, by withholding such recognition, helped cause the collapse of a student strike in Washington, D.C., against the implementation of a school desegregation plan. Local papers, at the urging of community leaders, deglamorized the strike, pinpointing the small number of absentees, emphasizing countermeasures taken to limit its spread, publicizing the firm attitude of local officials, and—especially—treating the whole effort as a late summer lark (Mendelsohn 1954).

Little has so far been said about television, still in its infancy as a medium of political communication during the period under discussion. Early research on broadcasting reveals considerable concern over the *actualité* provided by both sound recordings and visual imagery. The content analyses of German radio propaganda by Hans Speier (1941a) and of the German newsreels by Siegfried Kracauer (1947) anticipated many of the issues now raised by the social construction theorists. So did our own study of the televising of MacArthur Day in Chicago (Lang and Lang 1968a). All of these, in one way or another, contrast reality as perceived by a participant with the media image of these same events. In contrasting two perspectives, we tried to show how what was essentially a victory parade for a victorious general was presented as a mass outpouring of sentiment in support of an American supreme commander sacked by President Truman for repeated insubordination. In fact, most people came only for the spectacle and were disappointed even with that. Yet, unlike the Nazi war film, which was a deliberate construction, there was no evidence that newsmen deliberately set out to misrepresent the public mood. They were simply acting in terms of certain preconceptions. In a subsequent study, we were able to show in even greater detail how certain biases intruded unwittingly into the first nationally televised nominating conventions in 1952, giving quite different impressions to persons viewing the same events but on different networks (Lang and Lang 1968a).

Other questions relating to the television personality were raised during the 1952 campaign. While studies that year did not reveal massive vote changes because of mass media exposure, there was evidence that the televised campaign coverage did help shape and change images of political personalities (Pool 1959). This conclusion was underscored, just as the sixties began, by the televised 1960 Kennedy-Nixon debates. Research showed them to have no substantial impact on voting intentions or preferences beyond an acceleration in the movement toward Kennedy after the first debate. But there were some dramatic changes in candidate image that pointed to the possible existence of important sleeper effects, related to the way a political personality builds the kind of credibility that subsequently increases his effectiveness. The long-range effect may have been cumulative rather than direct, based partly on what people heard or read about the debates in the days and weeks following and partly on the enthusiasm the Kennedy performance engendered among campaign workers, who thereafter increased their efforts and made use of the debates as a talking point while canvassing likely voters (Kraus 1962).

Social effects. The evidence available by the end of the 1950s, even when balanced against some of the negative findings, gives no justification for an overall verdict of "media impotence." This evaluation is not just hindsight derived from a reappraisal in the light of more recent findings. The stocktaking of research toward the end of the golden era—by Larsen (1964), Schramm (1949), and the Rileys (1959)—criticized the body of ongoing and past research for certain serious deficiencies. One was the neglect of *social effects,* that is, the society-wide and institutional effects of the media.[1] These had received very little attention in comparison with how *individuals* reacted to media campaigns or were affected by different patterns of media use. The criticism was, in fact, that the research effort had been addressed only to a narrow range of possible effects. Another deficiency was the failure to conceptualize mass communication in interactive terms and as a system. Entranced by the Lasswellian formula, researchers had overemphasized the one-way flow of messages—from a mass media source to a recipient—and the recipient's response to this message as the single relevant stimulus. They had failed to recognize the consequences of feedback from audience to communicator as well as the interactions both between communicators themselves and between members of the audience.

Yet none of these "summings up" concluded that a lack of effect had been demonstrated, only that the focus of research had to be changed, if sociological knowledge was to be advanced. Their remedy was more, not less, research.

Broadly speaking, there were two not incompatible approaches suggested for remedying the inadequacies of past efforts to determine media impact. Those who stressed the need to take feedback into account also stressed the need for a more adequate model of the mass communication process. In an interactive model, members of the audience would be studied as participants in a larger social system embracing the mass communicators as well. If the social relationships of audience members influenced what media content they paid attention to and how they responded, then the communicators, too, as members of groups and organizations, were also subject to influence from one another. The messages transmitted by the media thus had to be studied as responses to a whole host of pressures and demands, including feedback from the audience. This *holistic* or *social context* approach to mass communication was seen as the best way of fitting together the many available pieces of substantive knowledge and of advancing sociological understanding of the precise nature and effects of mass communication. The approach was not so much a sharp departure from past practice as an attempt to fit the Lasswellian model of the process within a model of the larger social system. Though it stressed the need to study the influence of media on social values and beliefs, it did not call for any basic changes in the methods for gauging the potency of the media.

A second approach, focusing mainly on the need to differentiate and expand the kinds of media effects to be empirically studied, emphasized the need to adapt methods to suit research needs, rather than formulating research problems to fit available methods. One basic need, to facilitate the development of suitable research strategies, was to conceptualize impact in terms of units other than the individual member of the audience. The dominant concentration on individual effects, ran the argument, had stemmed in part from the interest of media organizations and advertisers in statistical measures, in part from a commitment of communication researchers to the survey method. Also, much of the pioneer work had been carried out by experimental psychologists whose methods were particularly well suited to isolating and classifying types of effects at the *individual* level. Needed were methodologies suitable for studying responses among segments within the audience (for instance, "taste groups"), responses at the organizational and institutional levels, and at the collective level, as when one speaks of "society" or the "polity." If this approach did advocate a departure from what was then and still is today considered methodological orthodoxy, it did not advocate the abandonment of standards of scientific inquiry and proof.

The general tone of these evaluations was thus constructive and upbeat. The one discordant note was sounded by Bernard Berelson (1959), a Lazarsfeld associate. Speaking at a conference on public opinion, he described the "state" of communication research as "withering away." Though others, in immediate reply (including Lazarsfeld himself, K. Lang, and J. Riley) or later in print (Schramm, Riesman, and Bauer), called the notice premature, Berelson—as others would do—declared the field dead at a time of steady progress in the sociology and social psychology of mass communication.

The mediating factors. There is little doubt that toward the end of the 1950s this advance was about to come to a grinding halt. Most grievously stifled was research on the role of mass media in the public opinion process. One cannot avoid raising the question of why?

Social psychologists long ago learned from W. I. Thomas that to define a situation as real is to make it real in its consequences. And so with mass communication research, and especially that part of it concerned with political effects. The field had not really withered away and died, but had been declared dead. It was not that years of research had demonstrated the impotence of the media, but that interpretation had gradually gained currency. The two works most frequently cited as "proof" both came out of Columbia University's Bureau of Applied Social Research. The first was by Joseph T. Klapper, *The Effects of the Mass Media.* Though not published until 1960, it was an elaboration of an earlier 1949 report (Klapper, 1960). Prepublication drafts had received wide circulation. The many people who still take this book as the definitive statement of the effects of mass communication usually overlook how clearly Klapper specified the limits of his concern: to specific effects on the opinions, values, and behavior of individuals in the audience, and to research using "traditional" social science approaches, mostly surveys and experiments. From this review, he generalized that media influence usually operates in the service of reinforcing existing tendencies and is not to be mistaken as the *sole* agent of change on those relatively few occasions when exposure is followed by conversion. Klapper did not explicitly address himself to the indirect and cumulative effects of the media, except to acknowledge that they might exist, nor did he deal with a whole range of social effects at the aggregate and institutional level. These limitations on his conclusions, acknowledged by Klapper, were largely ignored by others. Larsen's review of the communication literature is one of the few exceptions (Larsen 1964).

Personal Influence by Katz and Lazarsfeld was published in 1955 and may, in its own way, have been an even greater discouragement to further research on the effects of mass communication. It shifted attention from the media to personal influence and opinion leadership. Dealing only with specific effects—how people made decisions or changed their opinions in three areas (marketing, fashion, and movie attendance)—the authors concluded: personal influence as exercised in informal conversation with peers is more potent than influence through exposure to the mass media. The main evidence for this conclusion came from self-reports by respondents about these decisions and changes. Asked what had influenced them, respondents more often named someone they knew than the media as their main source of information or advice. The persons so designated by others, or who nominated themselves, were described as opinion *leaders,* even though they had done nothing more than act as transmitters of news and information, usually of something that had already been in the news or publicized in advertisements.

It is indeed puzzling why these two books should have been invested with so much more authority than was actually warranted. Why, in the one case, was the explicitly narrow scope of the literature review ignored, and why, in the other, were so few readers disturbed by the failure to trace opinion change beyond the specific transaction between opinion leader and follower to the point at which the new information originated? Klapper never concluded that there were no effects to be found. Yet researchers despaired of finding them. For years many political studies scarcely bothered to consider the role of the mass media in the crystallization of votes or, more generally, in the formation of public opinion, despite criticisms of the methodological soundness of the study on which the primacy of personal influence was based (Larsen 1964; Kreutz 1971) and despite the accumulation of contrary evidence (Troldahl 1966–67; Robinson 1976).

Reorientation. Why did the *minimal effects* position gain as much acceptance among media sociologists as it did? Were they justifiably discouraged by what Bogart (1973) has characterized as the "tremendous difficulty of teasing out specific effects from the tissue of surrounding social influences"? Perhaps, but more significant was the almost total constriction of sociological interest to the relatively narrow range of media effects defined by advertisers, public relations specialists, media organizations, the educational, and, sometimes, the medical establishment.

The question is certainly worthy of study as intellectual history. But one thing seems certain: contrary to what has been claimed, the scholar's search for media effects did not end because none were found (Janowitz 1978). Advertisers were, in fact, demonstrating their existence. And, in similar fashion, the revival of interest in effects—the third phase of the cycle—cannot be explained by new discoveries about media power, or even by new methodological approaches to the study of media influence that have altered the researcher's outlook. It is rather a revival of interest in questions some had ceased to ask (Lang and Lang 1968a). Overall, there is considerable continuity. The main strategies for the study of media influence are nothing but variants and elaborations of strategies used during the golden era. The number of strategies is limited.

In the rest of this chapter we shall consider four main strategies that have been followed, and are still being followed, by sociologists in their empirical investigations.[2] Though the emphasis is on effects in the area of politics, it should be understood that public opinion also functions in nonpolitical areas. It represents a form of social control in problematic situations, where consensus cannot be taken for granted but must be actively sought. In this process mass communication play a major part.

Research Strategies: Past and Present

The four strategies for the study of media influence are not in direct conflict and are in certain ways complementary. Each focuses on different elements in the communication situation, but not necessarily to the exclusion of the others. We here identify them as: (1) the study of *audiences;* (2) the search for *correspondences,* mainly relating trends in media content to aggregate changes in society; (3) the concern with *refraction*—how media affect imagery of the world; and (4) the study of *outcomes* in problematic situations where consensus cannot be taken for granted, but must be achieved. Of these four strategies it is the first two that in the past have most often contributed to the "myth of no effects."

STRATEGY I: THE STUDY OF AUDIENCES

In the best-known, most widely utilized, but also most criticized of the strategies, observations are focused on the public as recipients of political communications, that is, on the responses of media audiences. Exposure is the main communication variable; the content of the media is analyzed, if at all, only on the most superficial level. Controlling the exposure variable by manipulating content should not be confused with content analysis.

The objective of the researcher is twofold, depending on whether the communication process is approached from the side of the communicator intent on reaching and influencing members of the audience or from the side of the audience and its needs. From the perspective of the communicator, the objective is to identify the factors that make people receptive or resistant to the intent of the messages produced. From the perspective of the audience, all reactions, whether or not they are intended by the communicator, come under scrutiny. But whatever the side from which the research perspective is defined, the potential recipients remain focal.

The majority of social science propositions about the impact of mass communication have been generated by research designed to meet the operational needs of communicators, not necessarily those of propagandists (Hovland et al. 1953). Atomistic communication events have occupied the center of research interest, the communicators' primary concern being to know more about the audience to whom they direct their messages and the situation in which these are received. They have sought especially information about the perceptual and cognitive processes that govern the responses of the individual in the audience—processes of selection, interpretation, and implementation. Communication is conceptualized as a process in which the individual occupies a terminal point. She/he is the target on whom many competing influences converge.

From a symbolic interactionist perspective, however, recipients of media messages are hardly passive. They can be obstinate, predisposed, or actively seeking to be influenced. It follows that advances in our understanding of how mass communication works have come to be measured, however informally, by the number of factors found to be interposed or mediating between response and content. A response is hardly a simple reaction to some content, nor does effect flow automatically from the fact that a given content is disseminated. One cannot understand the impact of a message on an audience without understanding the phenomenology of the individuals in that audience. The content elicits only responses that are in accord with dispositions, habits, norms, and interests already present or at least not in total contradiction. These function as the *mediators* of responses and can either further or neutralize any change from the content. The research literature has documented how a message can boomerang, eliciting a response directly opposite to that intended by the communicator (Cooper and Jahoda 1947), how the immediate reaction to a message may be nullified as competing social influences come into play, and how the only visible response to a message may be inattention (Hyman and Sheatsley 1947; Star and Hughes 1950), cynicism about the communicator's intention, discounting of its credibility, or rejection of its interpretations or directives (Weiss 1969).

This focus on the audience has yielded two broad propositions: the first is the "minimal effects" theorem, to which we have already referred. This argues that the quantitative predominance of changes produced by the media, including persuasive communications, is in the direction of strengthening existing dispositions. Few changes are disjunctive. Accordingly, communications during a political campaign more often reinforce than convert. Exceptions to this predominant tendency occur when the factors through which responses are mediated and which account for the preponderance of reinforcement effects are themselves in the process of change or when, for whatever reason, they are temporarily neutralized. Pressure toward change builds up during periods of social or political upheaval, especially in severe crises when the whole world as one has known it seems to be crumbling. On the other hand, when individuals are subject to cross-pressures, that is, are pulled in opposite directions by conflicting allegiances or harbor within themselves several contradictory dispositions, their commitment to any particular view is already weakened. This increases the potential for change in response to mass communications.

The above formulation capsulizes the Klapper (1960) conclusions that have had such extraordinary resonance in the world of communication research. It still leaves unresolved a number of questions, questions that were raised at the time and are being considered even more seriously in the present phase of the effects cycle, with researchers once more prepared to take media power seriously.

First, Klapper himself acknowledged that mass media have the capacity to *create* opinions. It is when people have not yet developed firm views that major effects of mass communication are likely to be found and should be sought. Most public opinion research begins only after the issue has already crystallized.

Second, when a new issue emerges, which of several preexisting tendencies will be activated? Which predispositions will be reinforced? Consideration of this problem lies outside the framework of the model with which Klapper worked. Yet the activation or reactivation of one tendency at the expense of another can produce not only short-run but even dramatic opinion change. This is most vividly evidenced at times of impending crisis, as just before American entry into World War II. When American involvement began to appear inevitable, opposition dwindled as people everywhere began to accept that involvement as a fact. Anti-war sentiment, nurtured by the belief that the country had made a mistake in entering World War I, gradually dwindled as coexisting pro-Allied sympathies were activated by media reports of the invasion of Poland, the fall of France, the London blitz.

Third, the implications of what Klapper meant by reinforcement remain somewhat ambiguous. Most of the time, the term seems to imply some degree of continuity and consistency within the individual. At other times, it refers to mass communication as being supportive of the status quo. One need not deny that individual and society are linked together as two open systems to insist on their distinctiveness or to recognize that consistency and continuity on one level are not directly translatable into consistency and continuity on the other. The significance at the societal level of reinforcing a deviant opinion that falls within the range of consensus differs from the reinforcement of an opinion that does not. In the latter case, for example, reinforcement of student opposition to American participation in the Vietnam War intensified conflict to a level that was difficult to accommodate (Mueller 1973). Conversely, the maintenance of the status quo sometimes requires, not reinforcement of prior opinion, but instead, drastic reorientation, as in the adoption of drastic reform programs in the early days of Franklin Roosevelt's New Deal. The more recent reorientation of public opinion toward the People's Republic of China, however, which accompanied a shift in American policy beginning with Nixon's televised visit there in 1971, illustrates the opposite. Both popular fears of Soviet power and inclinations to "follow" the president were activated and translated into a major change of the international status quo.

Focusing on the audience has yielded a second general theorem: effects depend not on what the mass media do to people but, as Katz puts it, on what people do with the mass media. What use do they make of the content or medium? What gratifications do they seek? Where people turn to the media to satisfy some need—to be diverted or to solve some problem—one can expect them to act in a way consistent with previously established patterns. Effect depends on what is sought, and where a need is not met, the message will be ignored. Thus, exposure will have little effect, an expectation altogether compatible with the minimal effects theory. But people also look to the mass media for guidance on matters where they feel an impulse to change (Wright and Cantor 1967) or to learn (Troldahl 1966–67). Where they do, the type of media use works toward change. Media use thus operates merely as another of Klapper's mediating factors.

Blumler and McQuail (1969) incorporated the "uses and gratifications" perspective into a study of communication effects during a political campaign in Britain. Four uses were identified: people sought justification for their political beliefs; tried to keep up-to-date with the latest political developments; looked for guidance on how to vote; or turned to political fanfare for titillation and entertainment. Though this typology of uses did help pinpoint the kind of person whose opinions were most likely to be affected by exposure to campaign communications—the guidance seeker with a strong interest in the campaign—the typology was only an ad hoc construction. The same typology, later used in a survey of Wisconsin voters, retained some of its predictive power, but still lacks the theoretical underpinning through which each use or gratification could be linked to situated motives to explain media habits and preferences.

Like the search for direct conversion effects, the uses and gratifications approach has supported the theorem of minimal effects. Thus, the McLeod-Becker study concludes that "gratifications and avoidances account for considerably more variance [on fourteen political effect variables] than do the exposure variables." But the methodology employed limits the generalizability of such findings: first, it explains only the *differential* impact of a limited range of content over a specifiable time period, and second, the differences found are between individuals and not media situations. Given the methodology employed thus far, the uses and gratifications approach tells us almost nothing about the extent to which the gratifications sought may themselves be media-generated. Here are some examples: puzzling and/or important news events generate surveillance needs and lead to information-seeking activity, as in reports of presidential assassinations, nuclear near-accidents, or mass suicides as in Jonestown. The pressure to keep abreast of the news is especially great among "opinion leaders" who wish to retain this status. Further, when political fare is the only media offering, as when all networks cover a big event like the Senate Watergate hearings, "captive" members of the audience who find the proceedings dramatic or suspenseful learn to regard political spectaculars as potential sources of entertainment (Lang and Lang 1973). The media, by creating political events like debates between presidential candidates, also provide opportunities, otherwise unavailable, for partisans to bring their imagery of the candidates into line with their candidate preferences.

Enthusiasm for the "uses and gratifications" approach drew strength from the disenchantment with the search for direct effects (Swanson 1979). "Gratifications" served not only as a useful intervening variable but as an alternative to the study of "effects." There is some irony in the current affection of some researchers for the uses and gratifications approach. Concerned with curbing the power of big media by democratizing access to and control of technology, they find the conceptualization, though not the methodology, of the approach more compatible with their interests than that of "effects research." The latter, in their view, regards members of the audience as mere passive recipients of messages (on whom the media act) while the gratifications approach looks on them as active participants in the process (doing something with the media).

STRATEGY II. THE SEARCH FOR CORRESPONDENCES

This strategy takes the most direct approach to the complex phenomenon of media effects. It seeks out correspondences (correlations, mutualities) between variations in two aggregate measures: one of a media characteristic, the other of social response. Examples of such two-variable correlations are: between the proportion of editorial endorsements and the proportion of the popular vote received by a candidate (Mott 1944); between the emphasis (amount of space or time) given an issue by the media and its perceived importance among the public (McCombs and Shaw 1972; Frank 1973); between the degree of television penetration (for example, proportion of households with a television set) and electoral participation; and the amount of violence in television drama and amount of violence on the streets. Thus, a belief in such a relationship was the main impetus behind the series of studies on television and violence sponsored by the Office of the United States Surgeon General (Rubinstein et al. 1972). Indeed, in its most familiar form, this strategy has been employed to explore relationships between variations in media content and aggregate trends in public attitudes and opinion (Harris and Lewis 1948; Haight and Brody 1977; Funkhouser 1973).

A third variable is implied. Variations both in the media measure and the social response measure must be observed within some time frame or in communities with contrasting media situations. Thus, differences observed between industrialized and developing parts of the world have been used to draw inferences about the effects of media—for example, newspaper circulation, number of radio sets per 1,000 population, and the capacity of movie houses—on economic growth and entrepreneurial activity (Lerner 1958; Frey 1973) as well as on the emergence of parliamentary forms of democracy and political participation (Fagen 1966). Still, the discovery of patterns, such as correspondences between media development and political participation, only suggest the existence of a relationship that needs to be explained. Not even the presence of a third variable suffices to establish causal influence. So many other social changes accompany media growth that it is difficult, if not impossible, to separate out the specific influence of mass communication from that attributable to rises in literacy, urbanization, the development of political parties or a concerted drive to mobilize the population.

Some studies have used media content as a social (or cultural) indicator rather than as an agent of change (or reinforcer of the status quo). In fact, this may be the more frequent usage. Thus a decline in family size noted in magazine fiction paralleled a real change in the birth rate but hardly explained it (Middleton 1960). Likewise, the profile of television violence—the distribution of perpetrators and victims—reflects the distribution of power in the society. But the attempt to establish a causal link between heavy television viewing and a "belief in a world more dangerous than it actually is seems more questionable, heavy television use being related to a host of other social factors that may help explain the belief (Hirsch 1980).

Long-term trends in media content reflect social change. Leo Lowenthal (1943), in a pioneering study, traced changes in the occupations of persons whose biographies had appeared in popular magazines. Differences between those appearing in the first and fourth decades of this century reflected, according to his analysis, a basic change from a production-oriented to a consumption-oriented society. Between these two periods there was also a change in the tone of war propaganda, from moralizing and emphasis on atrocities to greater sobriety and an emphasis on factual accuracy. According to Kris and Leites (1947), this shift reflected the propagandist's need to counter changes in the society that affected the mobilization capacity of the mass media—the increase in projective distrust and a tendency to withdraw from participation as national leadership failed to satisfy individual demands.

Correspondences between media development and changes in political attitudes have frequently been the focus of study. A 1952 study, explicitly designed to measure the influence of television, then a new medium, compared voter turnout and the two-party distribution of the presidential vote in Iowa counties covered by television with other counties not yet within receiving range of the signal (Simon and Stern 1955). There was no significant difference either in electoral participation or the distribution of votes. This negative finding was less than conclusive evidence of the medium's lack of influence. Candidates, in this first television campaign, continued to rely heavily on more traditional methods with nationally televised speeches only a supplement. Nevertheless, a plurality of citizens questioned in national surveys identified television as the medium "most important for following the campaign."

These negative findings may also reflect a *ceiling effect;* that is, once a rate of political participation reaches a certain level, the possibility of attracting further voters through mass media activity is reduced to a minimum. Nonvoters are either unable to vote because they are ill (even dead) or are simply determined not to participate in the electoral process without coercion (Lang and Lang 1968b). Where there has been room for improvement, as in primaries or in voting for lesser offices, even relatively unobtrusive communications, such as newspaper endorsement of candidates, have proved effective, not to speak of more obtrusive media campaigning made possible by the ability to outspend other candidates (Jacobsen 1975; Mason 1973).

Given the possibility of ceiling effects, the time phase within which correlations between media coverage and political participation are sought makes a difference. Such correspondences are more likely to be discovered when an issue is just surfacing, when a political campaign is just underway, when a country has just won its independence, and so forth.

Correspondences between news coverage of stories and the incidence of related behavior have also been taken as measures of media impact. It is noted, for instance, that hijackings seem to be followed by other, often similar, hijackings (Hamblin et al 1973:122–26). And one sociologist has convincingly demonstrated that the more sensational press accounts of suicides lead to a distinct increase in suicide within the circulation area of the newspapers in which they appear (Phillips 1974). Obviously, here too there is a ceiling effect, for the actual number of hijackings and suicides in relation to the population are rather minuscule. With continuous coverage and/or effective countermeasures, a ceiling would quickly be reached beyond which no further increase could be expected.

The increase in the number of suicides or hijackings represents only one, and not necessarily the most important, measure of public response to news stories about terrorism, strife, crime, corruption, and deviance. The stories do not create these acts, but an increase in the attention paid them by the media can create the *impression* of a crime wave, massive corruption, or widespread lawlessness when, in fact, there has been no change in actual incidence, but only in the number of dramatic stories. In this way, the media signal the existence of a problem. Correlations between the amount of media attention a problem receives and the degree of public concern it arouses have demonstrated that the media do indeed have general effects. By steering attention to certain issues, events, and personalities, the media, collectively, influence not so much what people think, but what they think about. Or, as McCombs and Shaw (1972) have defined the agenda-setting function, people learn from the mass media what the important issues are.

On one level this formulation is self-evident. It is almost impossible for a candidate—beyond the village level—to gain visibility except through the media. The more that is written about the candidate, the more often she/he appears on television, the more important she/he appears to be. Celebrity feeds on itself in this way. The same is true, though not to the same degree, of issues built from events knowable only through the media. It is no surprise that the rising concern over Watergate (as measured by opinion polls) paralleled the increasing attention being paid to the sordid affair by the media. So many people had heard of the Watergate affair a year before Richard Nixon resigned that a ceiling effect had already set in.

On another level the formulation attributes, at one and the same time, too much and too little influence to the media. With regard to issue recognition, it is absolutely essential to distinguish not only between national and local issues, but also among matters that *directly affect nearly everybody,* such as inflation; those where the effects are *selectively experienced,* such as crime, unemployment, ecology, and war; and those where the *effects are quite remote* from almost everyone, such as the plight of the boat people in Vietnam or starvation in East Africa.

Inflation would be recognized as a problem however little attention the media paid it. In this instance, the correlation between media attention and public concern—the fact that the issue is "on the public agenda"—results not from media attention *or* public concern but from a third factor: the recognition of the same problem by the mass *and* the mass media. On the other hand, Watergate, despite coverage by the media during the 1972 election campaign, became an issue, that is, broke through into public consciousness, only when further developments the following year created a real sense of crisis.

The emergence of crime, unemployment, and other more familiar yet selective experiences as issues comes about in different ways. For example, media reports of crime (even television crime shows) can make even those not personally victimized aware that the world may indeed be a dangerous place; publicity given rising unemployment suggests even to job holders that the economy may indeed be shaky. Concern is increased by media reports. But influence may well run in the opposite direction, from growing popular concern, as more and more people are personally affected, to the recognition of the problem by the media. Or, the emergence of an issue can be attributable to events that become "big news"—for example, community conflict activates pre-existent personal concerns (Tichenor et al. 1973).

The necessity to go beyond correlations to a consideration of the reality factor cannot be overemphasized. Lagging recognition of a problem can probably slow the rise of concern, particularly when the number directly affected is small or powerless and inhibits the emergence of an issue. Until the Three Mile Island accident, the potential danger to those living under the shadow of nuclear power plants was seldom publicized by the American media, whereas in Sweden it had been the main issue in an earlier electoral campaign. The report of the Kerner Commission on the riots of the middle sixties criticized the media for underplaying the race problem until it had assumed a truly disturbing magnitude. Still, the opposite can happen. The media can anticipate a problem by speculating about the most dire eventualities. The main effect is on expectations. The stock markets provide daily evidence. Occasionally news reports set in motion a spiraling cycle of fear (as in panic selling or buying) that aggrevates the condition (Kepplinger and Roth 1979); occasionally revelations lead to action that prevents the expectation from coming true (Davison 1956). Once a problem becomes an issue, continuing attention by the media helps keep it alive. The continuing disclosures about Watergate, for example, kept interest from flagging, even when other matters, like the Middle East war, the energy crisis, and inflation competed for attention. Research by Tichenor (1973) and his associates on the effects of media coverage and community conflict are also highly suggestive.

There is good reason to believe that the media do more than just call attention to problems (or teach people what the issues are). By what they emphasize or leave out, they create the political context that transforms a problem or public concern into an issue. In other words, they make the matter politically relevant and provide a reason for taking sides. Concern alone or even knowledge of a problem does not suffice to make an issue. As several studies of the 1972 campaign showed, the one "issue" most decisive for the Nixon electoral landslide did not even appear on the issue inventory of agenda-setting studies (RePass 1976). This was the apparent ineptness and hedging of the Democratic candidate, Senator George McGovern, played up by the media as they searched for "newsworthy" angles, while Nixon and his policies escaped close press scrutiny since he deliberately limited his own public appearances, leaving his surrogates to answer McGovern. Paradoxical as it may seem, the same public that endorsed the dovish position of McGovern on Vietnam had more faith in Nixon to bring about the peace it longed for (Popkin et al. 1976).

It can and has been argued that the media merely transmitted what was there to be shown, that the public would have responded, as it did, to McGovern's personality and issue positions, whatever the press reported. But the candidate has options in utilizing the media, and news organizations exercise judgment in what they select and focus upon. Agenda-setting research needs to pay more attention to these options and focus on those perceptions that influence outcomes. Up to now the efforts to establish direct correspondences between media coverage and issue attention have not probed deeply enough into the complex relationships among content, public perceptions, and response. Such probing requires that researchers make use of content categories sensitive to the way different elements in the content are linked and of politically relevant response measures. Also, researchers must conduct observations at times when candidates are maneuvering for position, the issues are still in flux, and opinions have not yet stabilized near some ceiling, which can only be raised should some crisis occur (Lang and Lang 1959; Jacobsen 1975).

STRATEGY III: THE CONCERN WITH REFRACTION

Here the focus is on the creation of a symbolic environment by the organized media. This focus is fundamental because every group and society lives in a world of meanings, some of which are *mediated.* The objects, events, and personalities these meanings refer to are outside the range of direct experience and known only insofar as knowledge about them is conveyed by others, that is, by communication. The past lives on as history; an oral tradition or written accounts create a collective memory that extends far beyond the life span of any individual member of society. People also pool information concerning events they cannot observe for themselves but that are likely to be of some consequence. They depend on others for advance information of an approaching enemy or a ship nearing the harbor. Such news can arrive in the form of a messenger, through smoke signals, or through drum beats, so that even without mass communication the settings for group activity are always to an extent mediated.

The analytic problem is how the mass media system affects the collectively shared image of the world. The problem is analogous to one that has preoccupied cognitive psychologists. Among them, it has long been axiomatic that discrete sensory impressions attain meaning only when organized under some concept or guiding principle. Themes first developed around the turn of the century in investigations of witness reliability were later elaborated into a variety of "serial reproduction" experiments showing how repeated retelling of a tale tends to transform puzzling and less than clear accounts into rather conventional stories. The process begins with the original observer's own faulty observations and the way these shape his account. Further modifications introduced during transmission are what information theory nowadays calls "noise," present in every system (Mann 1974).

The availability of sophisticated communication technology gives new dimensions to the problem. First, the same symbolic content is transmitted to large numbers. Second, their cognitive horizons are immeasurably extended, making the world more complex and images harder to assimilate to some configuration. Third, the media organizations do not function only as transmitters of messages; their role as producers, even creators, of content is at least of equal importance (Roshco 1975; Gans 1979). They are geared and functionally specialized to observe the increasingly complex world from many different vantage points. The production of news requires that the many observations and reports be brought into focus (Donahue et al. 1972). Inevitably, any focusing involves blowing up some aspects of the reality while leaving others for background. Too close a focus will put some out of range altogether. What the organized news system yields can at best be described as a refracted image; at its worst it results in reports deliberately slanted to fit some self-serving interest (Rosengren et al. 1975; Altheide 1976) or, for better or worse, the public interest as defined by the government (Schlesinger 1978). But whether intentionally distorted or not, the image of the world is always depicted from some perspective, brought into focus through some lens, including the various lenses of the television camera. Hence, we prefer the more neutral term *refraction* to that of *bias* to designate the influence of the communication system on the image disseminated (Lang and Lang 1961:chapter 14).

It is difficult to overstate the extent to which the media-created symbolic environment represents reality. Children too young to discriminate between the make-believe of television drama (fantasy presented as actuality) and the world as it is (fact) often accept the former as an accurate representation of the latter (Greenberg and Reeves 1976). But they are not unique in their inability to separate the two worlds. Observations of audiences (Strategy 1) note how many adults welcome into their homes performers who talk to them via radio and television "as if" they were intimate friends. Audiences cheer them on, advise, admonish, and otherwise respond as they would in face-to-face contact. This pattern of interaction, given its obvious lack of give-and-take between audience and persona, has been aptly characterized long years ago by Horton and Wohl (1956) as "para-social interaction." No less important is it that a good deal of incidental learning results from the viewing of programs with no overt educational (or even factual) content (Bower 1973). For example, a surprisingly large number of people derive their basic ideas of illness and of medical treatment—not from first-aid handbooks or Dr. Spock—but from dramatic serials about hospitals, doctors, and their patients.

Obviously not all or even most of the population considers Johnny Carson or Barbara Walters a close friend, or Marcus Welby an authority on health maintenance, but the media of mass communication are indispensable sources of images about the world of public affairs and about the political discourse, even for the most educated. In fact, the more formal schooling, the greater the cosmopolitan interest which can only be satisfied through involvement in the media. As a result, education does not immunize people against mass-media influence but increases their dependence (Ball-Rokeach and DeFleur 1976).

Finally, nearly everyone will turn to the mass media for information during a crisis or unsettling occurrence. Regardless of the source through which people are first apprised, the mass media provide continuous orientation, as in the aftermath of President Kennedy's assassination, the first moon landing, throughout most of the Watergate controversy, and the resignation of a president. Participation takes place via the media. In the most general terms, the importance of mass communication lies less in what people are told to do (prescriptive and persuasive messages) than in what they convey about the larger world (descriptive communication). The content serves as a common point of reference.

Yet, no matter how strong the commitment of the news media to accuracy and impartiality, the image conveyed never replicates the world "out there" in its full diversity and complexity. The most obvious reason for this refraction is the constraints imposed by limited space and time. Only a small proportion of the information available can ever be accommodated in the print or broadcast newsholes. Some members of media organizations, such as the night editor of a local radio station, function as *gatekeepers,* selecting from the large number of available items the relatively few that seem fit to print or suitable for the next newscasts.

Studies of output provide clues about the characteristics of items that get by these gatekeepers. The first is timeliness. Not only are early news bulletins routinely discarded in favor of later updates, but the closer to the deadline a story breaks, the greater its news value and, hence, its chances of survival (Kristen 1972). The premium on recency can be at the expense of continuity, making the day's news seem a jumble of disconnected stories, a kaleidoscope whose unity consists of a common date line. A second characteristic enhancing survival is the perceived relevance of the news item to the public being addressed. Thus, proximity to the locality within which the audience resides is almost always advantageous (Gans 1979). Policy, stressed by Breed (1955), is a third determinant. Items that fit the editorial position on controversial issues have greater survival power and are more apt to be prominently featured. Of course, policy includes not only political preferences, but an operational code of what is and what is not appropriate news. Selection is further modified by the way editorial responsibility is split into departments. The top items selected by a particular editor have better survival chances than other, possibly more important, items that come under an editor whose daily quota of stories has already been filled (Tuchman 1978; Gans 1979; Rühl 1979). However, all these organizational criteria—deadlines, perceptions of audience relevance, policy, internal politics, and so forth—become less important once a story achieves general visibility through universal attention bestowed on it by the press corps. The big news expresses the tacit consensus of the journalistic fraternity about what is really important in terms of their view of the world (Schlesinger 1978).

Selectivity is only one side of the refraction process through which the media image of the world is constructed. The other is the way newsgathering systems organize to collect the raw material that goes into the image. Refraction is magnified by the way information enters the system through certain more or less definite pathways, on which editors and those sharing their universe of discourse rely. Much remains to be learned about the newsmaking process, but certainly, it cannot be conceptualized simply in terms of accuracy. As Robert E. Park (1940) pointed out, the news falls short of being even a historical record of events. With quick communication, it becomes more and more a social construction with many inputs and feedback on what supposedly is only reported. The process and its product, that is, the image of the present, are influenced by three elements: *professional values* that set the standards for the news gatherers; the *audiences* they address in their reporting; and the routines developed by the *organized news system.* In terms of the Lasswellian formula, we are dealing with the input of communicators, channel, and audience into content.

Studies of the values and ideology of the press corps have accumulated over the years (Tunstall 1971; Gerber and Stosberg 1969; Roshco 1975; Johnstone et al. 1976). All report increasing "professionalism" in the sense of a commitment to factually objective reporting. But "objectivity" means different things: is it to transmit verbatim, without comment or interpretation, statements of the official spokesman or certified expert; to balance two sides of the issue as if equally valid or important; to search out hidden information, as in investigative journalism? The last standard implicitly casts the journalist into the role of adversary, but leaves open the issue of whose cause is advanced by the exposé (Molotch and Lester 1974). The issue of press responsibility—where it begins and ends—is not unique to scandals like Watergate. For instance, Halloran et al. (1970) have criticized the coverage given a major Vietnam demonstration by the British news media, not only for what was emphasized—the public order problems of the huge peace march—but what was underplayed—the anti-government message the demonstrators sought to get across.

The news treatment given events also depends on the communicator's image of the audience. Thus, Pool and Shulman (1959) were able to demonstrate, through an experimental design, that the kind of interlocutor journalism students imagined—the audience response they saw themselves generating by their writing—had a discernible effect on both the type of story produced and on its accuracy. News personnel tend to present ambiguous reality in conformity with expectations they impute to the public (Lang and Lang 1968a). Much yet remains to be learned about the role played by such images. To what extent do reporters shape their stories with an eye on their editors rather than on their public? Are they primarily seeking to please and gain approval or are they determined to attack and expose? How much concern is there about their news sources or for the persons they are writing about? How much effort goes into "scooping" the competition? Into developing a unique angle? And what are the implications for the type of news disseminated? These are serious questions overlooked by the World War II studies that compared unreliable and unverifiable rumor with news stories that had an official seal of approval.

Perhaps the most important influence on news output is the extent to which news operations are conducted within a milieu of uncertainty. It is difficult to predict just where an important story will break. The allocation of limited resources involves complex negotiations between persons with different kinds of editorial responsibility about the importance of a story, its timeliness, whether to dispatch a television camera crew to a scheduled event, and so forth. To anticipate the many contingencies, the collection of information that ultimately becomes news is highly routinized. Most comes from reporters on regular beats and from the steady stream of handouts that flow to media organizations and require no effort on their part (Tuchman 1978; Rühl 1979). Even where news organizations operate autonomously of the government, the way collection of information is organized tends to highlight the activities of individuals and agencies with whom the news organization has already forged communication links. So it is that, in spite of the adversary relationship, news is dominated by an establishment perspective, even where it publicizes problems officials would rather sweep under the rug.

Once a story breaks to become big news, it develops a dynamic all its own. Every editor feels compelled to give it prominence. The events signal a problematic situation that the bulletins from any single source, official or not, can no longer adequately clarify. At such times, one observes the same press corps pooling of information that occurs among populations when information is needed for social orientation in some unusual situation—as in a disaster situation or when rumors of war or peace circulate. Rumor is the improvisation of news when news is hard to come by. Professional specialists with considerable resources, access to establishment networks, and some degree of public accountability, even where improvisation proves necessary, are cautious about unchecked reports, but they can report rumors. None of this prevents spillover from editorial positions into the news columns through selection and rewriting. In fact, there exists rather persuasive evidence that when it comes to public controversies, news organizations tend to emphasize, whether or not by design, those versions of events that favor their own position. The oil spill in the Santa Barbara channel, a local disaster, became a portent of things to come when it was picked up by national media (Molotch and Lester 1975). Given the news emphasis on crisis, such long-term trends—whether ecological, demographic, social, economic—tend to remain unreported until some interesting event serves as a peg on which to hang the larger story.

Media creation of a symbolic environment merits special attention with regard to matters on which there seems to be general consensus. Thus, there are some fascinating case studies of how the press in wartime fostered and lent its prestige to a version of events that, after the war and upon fuller investigation, proved unfounded. But there are other, perhaps more important, questions to be raised. A systematic analysis might attempt to deal with media content as a collective representation, as a map of the mediated environment, with attention on:

1. the activities that appear on the map drawn by the mass media, the distinctions that are made, the way they are labeled, and where boundaries are drawn;
2. the unspoken assumptions that guide the drawing of the various maps and the adequacy of the concepts through which specific elements are linked (Hyman 1974; Speier 1941b);
3. changes over time in this map and in the ease with which it can be modified or assimilate elements not previously incorporated;
4. the degree to which the same maps have currency among different sectors of the population, thereby promoting a single uniform world view or, instead, sharply diverging perspectives.

STRATEGY IV: THE STUDY OF OUTCOMES

The fourth strategy deals with outcomes on the societal level by examining situations in which collective action is oriented toward the media image. It shifts the emphasis away from the degree of opinion change in individuals after having been exposed to certain mass media messages to effects of a cumulative character, such as the result of an election or the course of a controversy. Each can be disproportionately influenced by a minority that tips the balance. Changes that represent only incremental shifts when measured against prior attitudes or which may do no more than reinforce an existing disposition often play an important role. For example, the televised debates that allowed Senator Kennedy to prove himself against Nixon, an opponent with a formidable reputation as a debater, may have shifted few votes, yet provided the indispensable margin of victory. Nor did it matter whether Kennedy's gains were achieved by converting Nixon supporters or by rallying the previously undecided and potential nonvoters to his side (Lang and Lang 1968b). A similarly one-sided mobilization of votes clearly worked in favor of Harry S. Truman. His 1948 upset campaign against Thomas E. Dewey, the clear favorite in preelection polls, successfully played up his Fair Deal policies and brought wavering Democrats back into the fold. Even "nonchange" can be an important media effect (Berelson et al 1954). For example, after his nomination as Democratic presidential candidate in July, 1972, McGovern was no further behind Nixon than was Humphrey at the same stage in the campaign four years earlier. Yet, although Humphrey lost a very close race, the normal Democratic rally to McGovern failed to materialize because McGovern was so consistently outplayed by Nixon in the media campaign.

Electoral campaigns represent only the tip of the iceberg. The study of the media effects on public opinion must include the precampaign period, the primaries and preconvention maneuvering, as well as between-election controversies whenever they are conducted publicly and with an eye toward the public response. The need for a broader and more functional notion of public opinion than an electoral preference is also apparent from questions arising in the aftermath of nearly every election concerning the actual mandate the voters handed the winning coalition. That the presumed mandate is often ignored or nullified suggests that public opinion operates both more subtly and more continuously than during the high media activity scheduled for the campaign period, which has remained the favored site for observing media effects.

Opinions come into play whenever there are options either because of a questioning of conventional wisdom or of the applicability of precedent, and when partisan feelings are mobilized. Such situations can be resolved only by reference to public opinion, conceptualized here as a collective product, a shared image, distinct, on the one hand, from individual opinions that have no force and, on the other, from legal, scientific, and other opinions emanating from persons or bodies with some authority. What we call public opinion can override these "expert" opinions when it endorses activities proscribed by statute or adopts interpretations contradicted by the body of scientific evidence. For this to happen, there need not be unanimity but only a dominant opinion. Public opinion can even be less than majority opinion as long as those who subscribe to it have enough logic, prestige, or force on their side to stifle effective dissent. Conversely, anyone attempting to make or implement public policy must be able to count on a minimum of public support or, at least, public acquiescence (Lang and Lang 1961).

Given the diversity of interests and the diversity of opinions corresponding to such interests, the concepts of coalition and coalition building are as basic to an understanding of the public opinion process as they are to decision making observed in experimental groups, juries, and other deliberative bodies. A decision is gradually reached after various proposals are advanced, often most tentatively and only for the sake of argument or for examination. Alignments on proposals shift until preferences begin to crystallize. Many groups vote only in order to ratify what has already emerged as the viewpoint of the dominant coalition.

Coalitions are as much a part of public life and politics as they are part of these concrete groups. Such coalitions provide the only answer to forming a cabinet when no party holds an absolute parliamentary majority or of assuring the passage of a legislative proposal when party loyalty cannot be counted on to produce the desired result. But this is only part of the story. Every public figure, elected or not, recognizes the value of support from an articulate constituency and, if that is unattainable, the necessity of keeping the murmuring multitude from rocking the boat. Hence, they are compelled to posture for the media in order to build a coalition of followers strong enough to intimidate opponents and to hold it together long enough to translate it into an electoral majority. The media constitute an important political resource to be exploited for one's advantage wherever possible. This view of media influence stands in startling contrast to the minimalist view of media effects based on an examination of shifts in individual opinions.

How mass communication affects this process of coalition building can be set forth categorically:

1. Publicity gives political actors greater *visibility.* Although the actual number attentive to different activities and different personalities varies considerably, publicity significantly enlarges the potential audience, the bystander public (Lippmann 1925).
2. Most of the time, these bystanders do little more than observe and form opinions. Unlike those who make political decisions and formulate policies, their action has no practical relevance. Even when they write letters, sign petitions, join a demonstration, go on strike, or participate in an organized campaign, they are only concerned about *how others should act* or *whether these others have acted correctly.*
3. The distinction between agents and bystanders, between those who act and others who merely react, between insiders who participate in the give-and-take and outsiders who do nothing beyond giving or withholding approval, is absolutely fundamental. To be sure, the roles can change, the line can become fluid. But the bystanders play an important *third-party* role in any political transaction. They can, when mobilized and having aligned themselves, change the power relationship. Even when they do not intervene and refrain from any overt protest, their acquiescence is often essential for the success of any policy.
4. The media of public communication present political actors with a *"looking-glass" image* of how they appear to outsiders. Not that the published reaction is necessarily synonymous with the public reaction. It is nevertheless eagerly scanned as the first clue and possible cause of the more general response. In addition, media recognition, especially if favorable, is an important resource in the political bargaining.
5. The *bystander public* functions as a significant *reference group* for political actors in need of consent or at least acquiescence. Therefore they go to great lengths to control their media appearances so as to align themselves with the largest possible constituency and to avoid stirring up opposition. Many of their activities are deliberately framed with an eye to how these may be reported. The influence of the media on the actions and reactions of those who seek to broaden their base of support through media publicity therefore becomes an important effect to the media on the outcome of a political controversy.

Visibility generates pressure toward conformity. Group experiments have convincingly demonstrated the extent to which at least some individuals yield, against their better judgment, when confronted by unanimous majorities. All experience at least some pressure (Asch 1952: chapter 16). The effects of hierarchical communication are no doubt more subtle, especially since the public and the figure in the limelight are not necessarily subject to the same norms. The deviance of a public figure is often known to other insiders who, even if they disapprove, may be more tolerant than the public as long as the deviance remains unpublicized. Thus, Seymour-Ure (1968) maintains that disclosures in the British press that John Profumo, at the time the minister of defense and a highly respected member of the Conservative establishment, had been involved with prostitutes had far less impact on the public, to whom the information was news, than on the members of Parliament, most of whom already knew about these relationships but considered them insufficient ground for dismissal. Yet Profumo, when called to account because of the press stories, lied about some of these relationships. He denied, in particular, any possible breach of security because of direct or indirect links through his consorts with the Soviet military attaché. But with the full facts out, he became a political liability. The Conservative government did not want to jeopardize the electoral coalition that had given them a parliamentary majority. Official reaction to disclosures about House Majority Leader Wilbur Mills was similar. Although he was revealed to have been stopped by police while drunk and in the company of a woman of questionable character, he was eased out without a major scandal.

Once such peccadilloes are exposed, the public, or some part of it, becomes a relevant reference group. The mere threat of exposure, even before there is any public outcry, may be enough to close the gap between public and private morality (Lazarsfeld and Merton 1948), not only with regard to clear wrongdoing, but also with regard to ordinary political activity. The publicity given to any failure or even to a political trade-off can elicit an adverse public reaction and become a political albatross, something to be avoided (Altheide and Snow 1979). But even if an elite action receives little media attention and/or no articulate opposition has been stirred up, the public nevertheless intrudes as long as political actors are conscious that outside opinion may be mobilized as a reserve force.

Whether subjecting particularistic relationships to general social norms is or is not salutory depends on what opinion public is mobilized. Sometimes negotiators in a protracted industrial dispute see themselves pressured into a settlement by the anticipated third-party reaction to a disruptive strike. At other times, publicity forces each side to play toward a different opinion public, so that bystanders are polarized into antagonistic coalitions rather than forming a dominant third-party pushing toward agreement. In the latter case, reduced flexibility transforms negotiators into mouthpieces for their respective constituencies. Freezing one's position by deliberate leaks is a tactic used to extract concessions, but when both sides play the same game, it is not conducive to effective bargaining.

Political actors, who "go public," rarely go all the way, but try to control the coverage to their own advantage. The relationship between the journalist and his source (Gieber 1960) or that between the president and the press takes on the characteristics of an "exchange," (Grossman and Rourke 1976; Sigal 1973) with each side bargaining over what information to release and what to withhold from the public. The news media also serve an important function as a channel of lateral communication among political actors, where signals may be picked up from both political allies and opponents. The news media become the main battleground for many political controversies. Thus, during Watergate, those somehow involved often used public channels to address one another. Nowhere was this better illustrated than during the events surrounding the so-called Saturday Night Massacre in October, 1973, beginning when Nixon, through his press secretary, ordered Archibald S. Cox, the special Watergate prosecutor, to cease and desist from his quest for tapes of presidential conversations. In reply, Cox called a special press conference, televised on all networks, to put the issue before the nation. In turn, when Nixon ordered the attorney general to fire Cox, Richardson refused and submitted his resignation. His deputy followed his lead, leaving a second replacement to carry out the dismissal. This whole series of events, plus others that followed, were largely enacted over radio and television. Like the general public, official Washington learned by way of the media of Cox's press conference, of the dismissal and resignations, of the FBI's sealing off of the special prosecution force offices, and of Nixon's offer, a few days later, to make some tapes available. Like most of the public, they found the chain of events incredible. The unprecedently heavy flow of phone calls, telegrams, and letters—mainly protesting Nixon's actions—to senators and congressmen, to the prosecution force, and to the White House was a spontaneous reaction to essentially the same experience. Armed with evidence that the public stood behind them, anti-Nixon forces gained unanimous approval from the House, including some very reluctant congressmen, for a resolution that the House Judiciary Committee look into the question of impeachment. A dominant coalition had formed on this one point.

Would the impeachment inquiry have gotten under way so speedily had not both political actors and the mass public been witness to these negotiations through the same media at the same time? Possibly not, but such equalization of access to information does not abolish or even undermine the division of labor between agents and bystanders. The public neither decides nor negotiates. Mass participation in the determination of policy remains limited to saying yes or no once complexities have been reduced to clear alternatives. Usually this means voting for or against a party and the leaders it chooses. Elections are rarely fought over concrete policy issues, with voters' judgments based on careful scrutiny of party platforms and candidates' voting records. This simplification, according to an "investment theory" of voting behavior, results in the "savings" of time and effort for the individual voter who need only decide who can best deal with the problems of the day (Popkin et al. 1976). There is a similar shift toward judging credibility in public controversies other than electoral contests.

Social psychologists have long been aware of the importance of communicator credibility (Hovland et al. 1953), but beyond some general notions about congruence between imagery of public figures and their followers' values and dispositions, we know little about the establishment of credibility. The answer lies less, we suspect, in what people perceive for themselves than in the reputation a public personality is able to develop. This provides the framework through which specific actions are judged. A public figure's reputation is an objective fact, a collective definition that is confirmed by what others, especially those with access to the media, believe. Personalities with whom most people have no other contact need the media to promote a favorable reputation beyond the bounds of their natural constituency.

This poses the broader issue of how much members of the mass public are oriented to opinion beyond the circle of their immediate associates (Fields and Schuman 1976), whether the society at large serves as a meaningful reference group, and what its members are willing to say publicly. The notion of a "spiral of silence" first put forward by Bryce (1891) and recently amplified by Noelle-Neumann (1974, 1977) provides some leads. The spiral develops out of the reluctance on the part of persons to express to strangers opinions presumed to be unpopular and unlikely to receive any support. Such opinions might even provoke strong disapproval. Poll data show that most people have some idea of what the majority view is and that this idea accords broadly with the picture presented in polls (regardless of whether it is actually founded on a reading of polls). Those who believe their own opinion to be in the minority are less likely than others to defend this view in casual encounters with strangers. The spiral works to further weaken a minority viewpoint because their failure to speak out provides the dominant majority with even more visibility. The effect is cumulative. The minority voice is weakened.

Can it be shown that perceptions of public opinion do come mainly from the news media rather than from interpersonal contact? Media depiction of the opinion climate can be far from uniform, and self-selection simply reinforces the perceptions of people moving in different milieus. But sometimes all the media do indeed provide a picture of overwhelming public sentiment in a particular direction, as during the firing of Archibald Cox. Unanimity also characterized news treatment of General MacArthur's homecoming in 1951 after Truman dismissed him. All the country, it appeared, supported and welcomed him back with universal gratitude (Lang and Lang 1968a). During certain periods of what we now know as the McCarthy era, public reaction appeared sufficiently one-sided to intimidate the public expression of contrary views.

It is most unlikely that these appearances of landslide sentiment are derived solely, or even largely, from published polls that provide statistical information on the opinion alignment. However, they do depend on media recognition or neglect of certain activities, with the news media exercising a good deal of discretion in what they choose to report. The media's treatment of a strike can emphasize either the amount of inconvenience it causes or the sense of injustice experienced by the strikers. When a street confrontation ends in a riot, will it be defined as a symptom of long-standing neglect of some underlying condition or as a lawless threat to public order? The readiness with which either image of a riot is embraced by politicians or, for that matter, the news media, depends on its consistency with a preferred strategy; definitions of deviance justify repression, but a definition of protest against conditions gives implicit support to a strategy of remedial intervention (Turner 1969a). Consequently, demonstrators, strikers, and rioters—like other political actors—are understandably concerned over the treatment the media give the activities through which they press their claim. Public opinion, in the broadest sense, includes a wide range of actions designed to influence policy and not just the willingness of private individuals to engage strangers in political arguments on matters of limited interest.

We hypothesize that concern about a general problem will arise when people believe that its existence is generally recognized and remedial action appears sensible and justified (Hubbard et al. 1975; see also Gormley 1975). Two examples are cited in support. One study showed that phone calls protesting noise levels of the Concorde landings and takeoffs at Washington airport rose perceptibly in the two days after major news stories on the subject (Watt and Van den Berg 1978). Most of the calls were spontaneous and apparently triggered by the publicity. A second study, by Kepplinger and Roth (1979) examined coverage by five leading German newspapers of the oil crisis in 1973–74 when the OPEC nations first raised their prices. A sense of panic seized the country and oil supplies dwindled. Yet, it appears that a year before, during the same months, oil imports had risen. Nevertheless, there had been no special news reports and no crisis had ensued. But in 1973–74, newspaper reports suggesting that supplies were endangered raised fears and led to excess buying in anticipation of shortages, creating short-term delivery problems. Government enactment of Sunday driving restrictions further fed these fears. Kepplinger maintains that the oil crisis was media-created and unrelated to the personal experience of the consumers of home-heating oil or of motorists.

Finally, we note that many politically relevant opinions crystallize and mature in group settings, largely on the basis of shared experiences. Media recognition seems to have a catalytic effect on individuals insofar as it encourages them to dispatch telegrams, make phone calls, write letters to relevant authorities, or engage in some other anticipatory activity. Yet, most protest consists of collective, not individual, activity. For organizations, media recognition functions as a morale builder. If a group is facing an uphill battle, its membership will take heart from whatever friendly attention its activities and objectives receive in the media. A sympathetic looking-glass image shows that one's message is getting across, the more so where other news publicizes concurrent protest or the media themselves take up the cause (Gormley 1975). Is there not an analogy with the effect of the one like-minded individual in experimental groups whose presence frees the dissident subject to adhere and express his "true" opinion?

To demonstrate these media effects on a mass scale is difficult, but very few scholars have even attempted it. It requires an imaginative case study, such as the one by Davison (1956) of the Berlin blockade and airlift. The depiction of the heroic stance of West Berliners threatened by the tightening stranglehold took their struggle for survival out of the ordinary. Made conscious by the media that the eyes of the whole world were upon them, viewing them as an outpost of the "free world" against the Soviet effort to expand its hegemony, people were more ready to accept with stoicism the frustrations they faced in their daily lives.

In analyzing the media role in coalition building, the essential strategy is the case study of critical events. Such events are critical because collective definitions are changing. Their study requires innovative combinations and unorthodox use of methodologies in reconstructing the process by which the diverse perspectives of the various political actors, media, and publics coalesce and ultimately affect an outcome.

NOTES

1. For a cataloging of the whole gamut of effects, see Lazarsfeld and Merton (1948).
2. Reviews and updates of the recent literature are to be found in Kraus and Davis (1976), Comstock et al. (1978), and Holz and Wright (1979).

References

Abeles, P. 1976. Relative deprivation, rising expectations, and black militancy. *Journal of Social Issues* 32:119–37.

Aberle, D. 1965. A note on relative deprivation theory as applied to millenarian and other cult movements. In *Reader in Comparative Religion: An Anthropological Approach,* ed. W. A. Lessa and E. Z. Vogt, 2d ed., pp. 537–41. New York: Harper and Row.

———. 1966. *The Peyote Religion Among the Navaho.* Chicago: Aldine.

Abrahamsom, H. A. 1970. Homans on exchange. *American Journal of Sociology* 76:273–75.

Adam, B. D. 1978. Inferiorization and self-esteem. *Social Psychology Quarterly* 41:47–53.

Adamek, R. J. and Lewis, J. M. 1975. Social control, violence and radicalization: behavioral data. *Social Problems* 22:664–74.

Adams, B. 1972. Birth order: a critical review. *Sociometry* 35:411–39.

Adams, J. S. 1965. Inequity in social exchange. In *Advances in Experimental Social Psychology,* ed. L. Berkowitz, vol. 2. New York: Academic Press.

Adams, J. S., and Jacobsen, P. R. 1964. Effects of wage inequities on work quality. *Journal of Abnormal and Social Psychology* 69:19–25.

Adams, J. S., and Rosenbaum, W. B. 1962. The relationship of worker productivity to cognitive dissonance about age inequities. *Journal of Applied Psychology* 43:161–64.

Adler, A. 1956. *The Individual Psychology of Alfred Adler.* Edited by H. L. Ansbacher and R. R. Ansbacher. New York: Basic Books.

Adorno, T.; Frenkel-Brunswik, E.; Levinson, D. J.; and Sanford, R. N. 1950. *The Authoritarian Personality.* New York: Harper.

Aguirre, B., and Quarantelli, E. L. 1980. A critical evaluation of two major critiques of collective behavior as a field of inquiry. Unpublished paper.

Ajzen, I. 1971. Attitudinal vs. normative messages: an investigation of the differential effects of persuasive communications on behavior. *Sociometry* 34:263–80.

Ajzen, I., and Fishbein, M. 1973. Attitudinal and normative variables as predictors of specific behaviors. *Journal of Personality and Social Psychology* 27:41–57.

———. 1977. Attitude-behavior relations: a theoretical analysis and review of empirical research. *Psychological Bulletin* 84:888–918.

Albert, E. 1972. Culture patterning of speech behavior in Burundi. In *Directions of Sociolinguistics: The Ethnography of Communication,* ed. J. J. Gumperz and D. H. Hymes. New York: Holt, Rinehart and Winston.

Albrecht, G. 1975. Adult socialization: ambiguity and adult life crises. In *Life Span Developmental Psychology: Normative Life Crises.* ed. N. Datan and L. Ginsberg, pp. 237–50. New York: Academic Press.

Aldrich, E., and Pfeffer, J. 1976. Environments of organizations. In *Annual Review of Sociology,* ed. A. Inkeles, J. Coleman, and N. Smelser, pp. 79–105. Palo Alto: Annual Reviews, Inc.

Alexander, C. N., and Epstein, J. 1969. Problems of dispositional inference in person perception research. *Sociometry* 32:381–95.

Alexander, C. N., and Knight, G. 1971. Situated identities and social psychological experimentation. *Sociometry* 34:65–82.

Alexander, C. N., and Lauderdale, P. 1977. Situated identities and social influence. *Sociometry* 40:225–33.

Alexander, C. N., and Rudd, J. Forthcoming. Situated identities and response variables. In *Impression Management Theory and Psychological Research,* ed. J. Tedeschi. New York: Academic Press.

Alexander, C. N., and Sagatun, I. 1973. An attributional analysis of experimental norms. *Sociometry* 36:127–42.
Alexander, C. N., and Scriven, G. D. 1977. Role playing: an essential component of experimentation. *Personality and Social Psychology Bulletin* 3:455–66.
Alexander, C. N., and Weil, H. G. 1969. Players, persons, and purposes: situational meaning and the Prisoner's Dilemma Game. *Sociometry* 32:121–44.
Allen, V. L. 1965. Situational factors in conformity. *Advances in Experimental Social Psychology* 2:133–75.
Allen, V. L., and Wilder, D. A. 1977. Social comparison, self-evaluation, and conformity to the group. In *Social Comparison Processes,* ed. J. M. Suls and R. L. Miller, pp. 187–208. New York: Wiley.
Allison, P. D. 1977. Testing for interaction in multiple regression. *American Journal of Sociology* 83:144–53.
Allport, F. 1924. The group fallacy in relation to social science. *American Journal of Sociology:* 688–701.
Allport, G. W. 1935. Attitudes. In *A Handbook of Social Psychology,* ed. C. Murchison, pp. 798–844. Worcester, Massachusetts: Clark University Press.
———. 1954. *The Nature of Prejudice.* Reading, Massachusetts: Addison-Wesley.
———. 1955. *Becoming.* New Haven: Yale University Press.
———. 1958. *The Nature of Prejudice.* Garden City and New York: Doubleday/Anchor.
———. 1960. The open system in personality theory. *Journal of Abnormal and Social Psychology* 61: 301–10.
———. 1968. The historical background of modern social psychology. In *The Handbook of Social Psychology,* vol. 1. ed. G. Lindzey and E. Aronson, pp. 1–80. Reading, Mass.: Addison-Wesley.
Allport, G. W., and Odbert, H. 1936. Trait-names. *Psychological Monograph* 47:1–171.
Almond, G. A. 1954. *The Appeals of Communism.* Princeton, N.J.: Princeton University Press.
Almond, G. A., and Verba, S. 1965. *The Civic Culture.* Boston: Little, Brown.
Altheide, D. L. 1976. *Creating Reality: How TV News Distorts Events.* Beverly Hills, Calif.: Sage.
Altheide, D. L., and Snow, R. P. 1979. *Media Logic.* Beverly Hills, Calif.: Sage.
Althusser, L. 1971. Ideology and ideological state apparatuses. In *Lenin and Philosophy,* ed., L. Althusser, pp. 127–88. New York: Monthly Review Press.
Altman, I., and Taylor, D. A. 1973. *Social Penetration: The Development of Interpersonal Relationships.* New York: Holt, Rinehart and Winston.
Alwin, D. F. 1973. Making inferences from attitude-behavior correlations. *Sociometry* 36:253–78.
Anderson, B.; Berger, J.; Zelditch, M. Jr.; and Cohen, B. P. 1954. Reactions to inequity. *Acta Sociologica* 12:1–12.
Anderson, N. H. 1971. Integration theory and attitude change. *Psychological Review* 78:171–206.
Angle, J. 1976. Mainland control of manufacturing and reward for bilingualism in Puerto Rico. *American Sociological Review* 41:298–307.
Archibald, W. P. 1976. Face-to-face: the alienating effects of class, status, and power divisions. *American Sociological Review* 41:819–37.
Ariès, P. 1960. *Centuries of Childhood: A Social History of Family Life.* New York: Random House.
———. 1965. *Centuries of Childhood.* New York: Vintage.
———. 1974. *Western Attitudes Toward Death.* Baltimore: Johns Hopkins University Press.
Armer, M., and Schnaiberg, A. 1977. Reply to Cohen and Till. *American Sociological Review* 42:378–83.
Aronson, E. 1976. *The Social Animal.* 2d ed. San Francisco: W. H. Freeman.
Aronson, E., and Mills, J. 1959. The effects of severity of initiation and liking for a group. *Journal of Abnormal and Social Psychology* 59:177–81.
Aronson, E., and Worchel, P. 1966. Similarity versus liking as determinants of interpersonal attractiveness. *Psychonomic Science* 5:157–58.
Asch, S. E. 1940. Studies in the principles of judgments and attitudes: II. determina-

tion of judgments of group and ego standards. *Journal of Social Psychology* 12:433–65.
———. 1946. Forming impressions of personality. *Journal of Abnormal and Social Psychology* 41:258–90.
———. 1951. The effects of group pressure upon the modification and distortion of judgment. In *Groups, Leadership and Men.* ed. H. Guetzkow, pp. 177–90. Pittsburgh: Carnegie.
———. 1952. *Social Psychology.* Englewood Cliffs, N.J.: Prentice-Hall.
———. 1956. Studies of independence and conformity: a minority of one against a unanimous majority. *Psychological Monographs* 70: no. 9, whole no. 416.
Atchley, R. 1975. The life course, age grading and age-linked demands for decision making. In *Life Span Developmental Psychology: Normative Life Crises.* ed. N. Datan and L. Ginsberg, pp. 261–78. New York: Academic Press.
Atkinson, J. 1957. Motivational determinants of risk-taking behavior. *Psychological Review* 64:359–72.
Atkinson, J., and Drew, P. 1979. *Order in Court: The Organization of Verbal Behavior in Judicial Settings.* London: Macmillan.
Aubert, V. 1965. *The Hidden Society.* Totowa, N. J.: Bedminster Press.
Austin, J. L. 1962. *How To Do Things With Words.* Cambridge, Mass.: Harvard University Press.
Austin, W. 1977. Equity theory and social comparison processes. In *Social Comparison Processes,* ed. J. M. Suls and R. L. Miller, pp. 279–306. New York: Wiley.
Averill, J. R. 1974. An analysis of psychophysiological symbolism and its influence on theories of emotion. *Journal for the Theory of Social Behavior* 4:147–90.
———. 1975. A semantic atlas of emotional concepts. *Journal Supplement Abstract Service Catalog of Selected Documents in Psychology* 5:330.
———. 1976. Emotion and anxiety. In *Emotion and Anxiety.* ed. M. Zuckerman and C. Spielberger. New York: Wiley.
———. 1980. A constructivist view of emotion. In *Emotion: Theory, Research, and Experience,* ed. R. Plutchik and H. Kellerman, vol. 1. New York: Academic Press.
Bachman, J. G. 1970. *The Impact of Family Background and Intelligence on Tenth-Grade Boys.* vol. 2. *Youth in Transition.* Ann Arbor, Mich.: Institute for Social Research.
Back, K. W. 1951. Influence through social communication. *Journal of Abnormal and Social Psychology* 46:9–23.
———. 1973*a.* The experiential group and society. *Applied Behavioral Sciences* 9:7–20.
———. 1973*b.* *Beyond Words.* New York: Russell Sage.
———. 1979. The waste-land. *Contemporary Sociology* 8:546–47.
———. 1979. Secrecy and the individual in sociological research. In *Regulations of Scientific Inquiry,* ed. K. M. Wulff. Boulder, Col.: Westview Press.
Back, K. W.; Hood, T. C.; and Brehm, M. L. 1964. The subject role in small group experiments. *Social Forces* 43:181–97.
Backman, C. W. 1976. Explorations in psychoethics: the warranting of judgments. In *Life Sentences: Aspects of the Social Role of Languages,* ed. R. Harré. London: Wiley.
Backman, C. W., and Secord, P. F. 1959. The effect of perceived liking on interpersonal attraction. *Human Relations* 12:379–84.
———. 1962. Liking, selective interaction, and misperception in congruent interpersonal relations. *Sociometry* 25:321–35.
———. 1964. The compromise process and the affect structure of groups. *Human Relations* 17:19–22.
Backman, C. W.; Secord, P. F.; and Pierce, J. R. 1963. Resistance to change in the self-concept as a function of consensus among significant others. *Sociometry* 26:102–11.
Baer, L.; Eitzen, D. S.; Duprey, A.; Thompson, N. T.; and Cole, C. 1976. The consequences of objective and subjective status inconsistency. *Sociological Quarterly* 17:389–400.
Balch, R. W., and Taylor, D. 1978. Seekers and saucers: the role of the cultic milieu in joining a UFO cult. In *Conversion Careers,* ed. J. Richardson, pp. 43–64. Beverly Hills, Calif.: Sage.

Baldwin, D. A. 1978. Power and social exchange. *The American Political Science Review* 72:1229–42.

Bales, R. F. 1950. *Interaction Process Analysis: A Method for the Study of Small Groups.* Cambridge, Mass.: Addison-Wesley.

Balkwell, J. W. 1969. A structural theory of self-esteem maintenance. *Sociometry* 32:458–73.

———. 1976. Social decision-making behavior: an empirical test of two models. *Sociometry* 39:19–30.

Ball-Rokeach, S. J., and DeFleur, M. L. 1976. A dependency model of media effects. *Communication Research* 3:3–21.

Baltes, P. 1979. Life-span developmental psychology: some converging observations on history and theory. In *Life-Span Development and Behavior,* ed. P. B. Baltes and O. G. Brim, Jr., vol. 2, pp. 255–79. New York: Academic Press.

Baltes, P. B., and Brim, O. G., Jr. 1979. *Life-Span Development and Behavior,* vol. 2. New York: Academic Press.

Baltes, P. B., and Goulet, L. R. 1970. Status and issues of a life-span developmental psychology. In *Life-Span Developmental Psychology: Research and Theory,* ed. L. R. Goulet and P. B. Baltes, pp. 3–21. New York: Academic Press.

Baltes, P. B., and Schaie, K. W., eds. 1973. *Life-Span Developmental Psychology: Personality and Socialization.* New York: Academic Press.

Baltes, P. B., and Schaie, K. W. 1976. On the plasticity of intelligence in adulthood and old age: where Horn and Donaldson fail. *American Psychologist* 31:720–25.

Baltes, P. B.; Reese, H. W.; and Nesselroade, J. R., eds., 1977. *Life-Span Developmental Psychology: Introduction to Research Methods.* Monterey, Calif.: Brooks-Cole.

Bandura, A. 1969. Social learning theories of identificatory processes. In *Handbook of Socialization Theory and Research,* ed. D. Goslin, pp. 213–62. Chicago: Rand McNally.

———. 1971. *Social Learning Theory.* Morristown, N.J.: General Learning Press.

———. 1977*a*. *Social Learning Theory.* Englewood Cliffs, N. J.: Prentice-Hall.

———. 1977*b*. Self-efficacy: toward a unifying theory of behavioral change. *Psychological Review* 84:191–215.

———. 1978. The self system in reciprocal determinism. *American Psychologist* 33:344–58.

Banton, M. P. 1965. *Roles: An Introduction to the Study of Social Relations.* London: Tavistock.

Barber, J. 1965. *The Lawmakers: Recruitment and Adaptation to Legislative Life.* New Haven: Yale University Press.

Barger, W. K. 1977. Cultural change and psychosocial adjustment. *American Anthropologist* 79:471–95.

Barker, R. 1968. *Ecological Psychology.* Stanford, Calif.: Stanford University Press.

Barkow, J. H. 1975. Prestige and culture: a biosocial interpretation. *Current Anthropology* 16:553–63.

Bar-Tel, D., and Saxe, L. 1976. Perceptions of similarly attractive couples and individuals. *Journal of Personality and Social Psychology* 33:772–81.

Barth, F. 1964. *Models of Social Organization.* London: Royal Anthropological Institute.

Barton, A. 1969. *Communities in Disaster.* Garden City and New York: Doubleday.

Bass, B. 1960. *Leadership, Psychology and Organizational Behavior.* New York: Harper.

Bates, E. 1976. *Language and Context: The Acquisition of Pragmatics.* New York: Academic Press.

Bateson, G.; Jackson, D.; Haley, H.; and Weakland, J. 1956. Toward a theory of schizophrenia. *Behavioral Science* 1:251–64.

Bauer, R. A. 1957. Brainwashing: psychology or demology? *Journal of Social Issues* 13:41–47.

Baughman, E. E., and Dahlstrom, W. G. 1968. *Negro and White Children: A Psychological Study in the Rural South.* New York: Academic Press.

Bauman, R, and Sherzer, J. 1974. *Explorations in the Ethnography of Speaking.* Cambridge: Cambridge University Press.

Baumrind, D. 1975. Early socialization and adolescent competence. In *Adolescence in the Life Cycle,* ed. S. Dragastin and G. H. Elder, Jr., pp. 117–43. Washington, D.C.: Hemisphere Publishing.

Becker, G. 1974. A theory of social interaction. *Journal of Political Economy* 82: 1063–93.

Becker, H. S. 1951. The professional dance musician and his audience. *American Journal of Sociology:* 136–44.

———. 1953. Becoming a marijuana user. *American Journal of Sociology* 59:235–52.

———. 1960. Notes on the concept of commitment. *American Journal of Sociology:* 32–40.

———. 1963. *Outsiders.* New York: Free Press.

———. 1964. Personal change in adult life. *Sociometry* 27:40–53.

———. 1967. History, culture and subjective experience. *Journal of Health and Social Behavior* 8:163–76.

———. 1970. The self and adult socialization. In *Social Work: Method and Substance,* ed. H. S. Becker, pp. 289–303. Chicago: Aldine.

Becker, H. S., and Strauss, A. 1956. Careers, personality and adult socialization. *American Journal of Sociology* 62:253–63.

Becker, H. S.; Geer, B.; Hughes, E. C.; and Strauss, A. 1961. *Boys in White.* Chicago: University of Chicago Press.

Becker, H. S. et al., eds. 1968. *Institutions and the Person.* Chicago: Aldine.

Becker, W. C. 1964. Consequences of different kinds of parental discipline. In *Review of Child Development Research,* ed. M. L. Hoffman and L. W. Hoffman, vol. 1, pp. 169–208. New York: Russell Sage Foundation.

Befu, H. 1977. Social exchange. *Annual Review of Anthropology* 6:255–81.

Bell, D. 1961 *The End of Ideology.* New York: Collier Books.

———. ed. 1964. *The Radical Right.* Garden City and New York: Doubleday/Anchor.

Bell, R. Q. 1977. Socialization findings reexamined. In *Child Effects on Adults,* ed. R. Q. Bell and L. V. Harper. New York: Wiley.

Bem, D. J. 1965. An experimental analysis of self-persuasion. *Journal of Experimental Social Psychology* 1:199–218.

———. 1967. Self-perception: an alternative interpretation of cognitive dissonance phenomena. *Psychological Review* 74:183–200.

———. 1972. Self-perception theory. In *Advances in Experimental Social Psychology,* ed. L. Berkowitz, vol. 6, pp. 1–62. New York: Academic Press.

Bem, D. J., and Allen, A. 1974. On predicting some of the people some of the time: the search for cross-situational consistencies in behavior. *Psychological Review* 81:506–20.

Bendix, R. 1952. Compliant behavior and individual personality. *American Journal of Sociology* 58:292–303.

Benedict, R. 1938. Continuities and discontinuities in cultural conditioning. *Psychiatry* 1:161–67.

Bengtson, V. L. 1975. Generation and family effects in value socialization. *American Sociological Review* 40:358–71.

Bengtson, V. L., and Cutler, N. E. 1976. Generations and intergenerational relations: perspectives on age groups and social change. In *Handbook of Aging in the Social Sciences,* ed. R. Binstock and E. Shanas, pp. 130–50. New York: Van Nostrand.

Benne, K. 1964. Man and Moloch. *Journal of Social Issues* 20:97–115.

Benninghaus, H. 1976. *Ergebnisse und Perspektiven der Einstellungs-Verhaltens-Forschung.* Meisenheim and Glan: Verlag Anton Hain.

Bennis, K., and Shepard, H. 1956. A theory of group development. *Human Relations* 9:415–37.

Berelson, B. 1949. What "missing the newspaper" means. In *Communications Research, 1948–49,* ed. P. Lazarsfeld and F. Stanton. New York: Harper.

———. 1959. The state of communication research. *Public Opinion Quarterly* 23:1–5. Rejoinders by W. Schramm, D. Riesman, R. A. Bauer, ibid. 6–18.

Berelson, B.; Lazarsfeld, P. F.; and McPhee, W. 1954. *Voting.* Chicago: University of Chicago Press.

Berger, J., and Conner, T. L. 1969. Performance expectations and behavior in small groups. *Acta Sociologica* 12:186–98.

———. 1974. Performance expectations and behavior in small groups: a revised formulation. In *Expectation States Theory: A Theoretical Research Program,* ed. J. Berger, T. L. Conner, and M. H. Fisek chap. 4. Cambridge, Mass.: Winthrop.

Berger, J., and Fisek, M. H. 1970. Consistent and inconsistent status characteristics and the determination of power and prestige orders. *Sociometry* 33:287–304.

———. 1974. A generalization of the status characteristics and expectation states theory. In *Expectation States Theory: A Theoretical Research Program,* ed. J. Berger, T. L. Conner, and M. H. Fisek, chap. 6. Cambridge, Mass.: Winthrop.

Berger, J., and Zelditch, M. Jr. 1962. Authority and performance expectations. Mimeograph. Stanford, Calif.: Department of Sociology, Stanford University.

———. 1978. A Bibliography of Expectation States Research, Technical Report no. 67. Stanford, Calif.: Department of Sociology, Stanford University.

Berger, J.; Cohen, B. P.; and Zelditch, M. Jr. 1972. Status characteristics and social interaction. *American Sociological Review* 37:241–55.

———. 1966. Status characteristics and expectation states. In *Sociological Theories in Progress,* ed. J. Berger, M. Zelditch, and B. Anderson. vol. 1. Boston: Houghton Mifflin.

Berger, J.; Conner, T. L.; and Fisek, M. H. 1974. *Expectation States Theory: A Theoretical Research Program.* Cambridge, Mass.: Winthrop.

Berger, J.; Conner, T. L.; and McKeown, W. L. 1969. Evaluations and the formation and maintenance of performance expectations. *Human Relations* 22:481–502.

———. 1974. Evaluations and the formation of maintenance performance expectations. In *Expectations States Theory: A Theoretical Research Program,* ed. J. Berger, T. L. Conner and M. H. Fisek, chap. 2. Cambridge, Mass.: Winthrop.

Berger, J.; Fisek, M. H.; and Freese, L. 1976. Paths of relevance and the determination of power and prestige orders. *Pacific Sociological Review* 19:45–62.

Berger, J.; Cohen, B. P.; Conner, T. L.; and Zelditch, M. Jr. 1966. Status characteristics and expectation states: a process model. In *Sociological Theories in Progress,* ed. J. Berger, M. Zelditch, Jr., and B. Anderson. vol. 1. Boston: Houghton Mifflin.

Berger, J.; Fisek, M. H.; Norman, R. Z.; and Zelditch, M. Jr. 1977. *Status Characteristics and Social Interaction: An Expectation States Approach.* pt. 2. New York: Elsevier.

Berger, J.; Zelditch, M. Jr.; Anderson, B.; and Cohen, B. P. 1972. Structural aspects of distributive justice: a status value formulation. In *Sociological Theories in Progress,* ed. J. Berger, M. Zelditch, Jr., and B. Anderson, vol. 2. pp. 119–46. Boston: Houghton-Mifflin.

Berger, P., and Luckmann, T. 1967. *The Social Construction of Reality.* New York: Doubleday/Anchor.

Bergesen, A. J. 1976. White or black riots. Paper presented at the Annual Meeting of the American Sociological Association.

———. 1980. Police violence during the Watts, Newark, and Detroit race riots of the 1960s. In *Political Deviance,* ed. P. Lauderdale. Minneapolis: University of Minnesota Press.

Bergesen, A., and Warr, M. 1979. A crisis in the moral order: the effects of Watergate upon confidence in social institutions. In *The Religious Dimension,* ed. R. Wuthnow, pp. 277–95. New York: Academic Press.

Bergin, A. E. 1962. The effect of dissonant persuasive communications upon changes in self-referring attitudes. *Journal of Personality* 30:423–38.

Berk, R. A., and Aldrich, H. E. 1972. Patterns of vandalism during civil disorders as an indicator of selection of targets. *American Sociological Review* 37:533–54.

Berkowitz, L. 1969. *Roots of Aggression: A Re-examination of the Frustration-Aggression Hypothesis.* New York: Atherton.

Berkowitz, L., and Walster, E., eds. 1976. *Advances in Experimental Social Psychology.* New York: Academic Press.

Berlyne, D. E. 1960. *Conflict, Arousal and Curiosity.* New York: McGraw-Hill.

Bernard, J. 1975. *Women, Wives and Mothers.* Chicago: Aldine.

———. 1977. Jealousy and marriage. In *Jealousy,* ed. G. Clanton and L. G. Smith. Englewood Cliffs, N. J.: Prentice-Hall.

Bernard, L. L. 1939. *Social Control.* New York: Macmillan.
Berndt, R. M. 1962. *Excess and Restraint.* Chicago: University of Chicago Press.
Bernstein, B. 1971. *Class Codes and Control, vol. 1: Theoretical Studies Toward a Sociology of Language.* London: Routledge and Kegan Paul. (Paperback edition, 1973. Herts, UK: Paladin.)
———. 1972. Social class, language, and socialization. In *Language and Social Context,* ed. P. Giglioli. Baltimore: Penguin.
———. 1973. *Class Codes and Control, vol. 2: Applied Studies Toward a Sociology of Language.* London: Routledge and Kegan Paul.
———. 1975. *Class Codes and Control, vol. 3: Towards a Theory of Educational Transmissions.* London: Routledge and Kegan Paul.
Berry, J. W. 1978. Acculturative stress among James Bay Cree: prelude to a hydroelectric project in Quebec, Canada. In *Consequences of Economic Change in Circumpolar Regions,* ed. L. Muller-Wille, P. J. Pelto, L. Muller-Wille, and R. Darnell, pp. 105–19. Edmonton: University of Alberta.
Berry, J. W., and Annis, R. C. 1974. Acculturative stress: the role of ecology, culture and differentiation. *Journal of Cross-Cultural Psychology* 5:382–406.
Berscheid, E., and Walster, E. H. 1969. *Interpersonal Attraction.* Reading, Mass.: Addison-Wesley.
———. 1972. Beauty and the best. *Psychology Today* 5:42–46.
———. 1974. A little bit about love. In *Foundations of Interpersonal Attraction,* ed. T. L. Huston, pp. 356–81. New York: Academic Press.
Bettelheim, B., and Janowitz, M. 1964. *Social Change and Prejudice.* New York: Free Press.
Bibby, R. W., and Brinkerhoff, M. B. 1974. When proselytizing fails: an organizational analysis. *Sociological Analysis* 35:189–200.
Bielby, W. T., and Hauser, R. M. 1977. Structural equation models. *Annual Review of Sociology* 3:137–62.
Bierstedt, R. 1965. Review of Blau's *Exchange and Power in Social Life. American Sociological Review* 30:789–90.
Bion, W. R. 1959. *Experiences in Groups.* London: Tavistock.
Birdwhistell, R. L. 1970. *Kinesics and Context: Essays on Body Motion Communication.* Philadelphia: University of Pennsylvania Press.
Birenbaum, A., and Sagarin, E. 1976. *Norms and Human Behavior.* New York: Praeger.
Birnbaum, J. A. 1975. Life patterns and self-esteem in gifted family oriented and career committed women. In *Women and Achievement: Social Motivational Analyses,* ed. M. Mednick, S. S. Tangri, and L. W. Hoffman, pp. 127–51. Washington: Hemisphere.
Bittner, E. 1963. Radicalism and the organization of radical movements. *American Sociological Review* 28:928–40.
———. 1967. Police discretion in emergency apprehension of mentally ill persons. *Social Problems* 14:285–90.
Blake, J., and Davis, K. 1964. Norms, values, and sanctions. In *Handbook of Modern Sociology,* ed. R. E. Faris, pp. 456–84. Chicago: Rand McNally.
Blalock, H. M., Jr. 1967. *Toward a Theory of Minority Group Relations.* New York: Wiley.
Blau, P. 1955. *The Dynamics of Bureaucracy.* Chicago: University of Chicago Press.
———. 1964. *Exchange and Power in Social Life.* New York: Wiley.
Blau, P. M., and Duncan, O. D. 1967. *The American Occupational Structure.* New York: Wiley.
Blau, P. M.; Cullen, J. B.; Margulies, R. Z.; and Silver, H. 1979. Dissecting types of professional schools. *Sociology of Education* 52:7–19.
Blauner, R. 1964. *Alienation and Freedom: The Factory Worker and His Industry.* Chicago: University of Chicago Press.
———. 1972. *Racial Oppression in America.* New York: Harper and Row.
Block, J. H.; Haan, N.; and Smith, M. B. 1969. Socialization correlates of student activism. *Journal of Social Issues* 25:143–77.
Blom, J. P., and Gumperz, J. J. 1972. Social meaning in linguistic structure: codeswitching in Norway. In *Directions in Sociolinguistics: The Ethnography of*

Communication, ed. J. J. Gumperz and D. H. Hymes, pp. 407–34. New York: Holt, Rinehart and Winston.
Bloom, L. 1970. *Language Development: Form and Function in Emerging Grammars.* Cambridge, Mass.: The M.I.T. Press.
Blumer, H. 1946. Collective behavior. In *New Outlines of the Principles of Sociology,* ed. A. M. Lee. New York: Barnes and Noble.
———. 1951. Collective behavior. In *The Principles of Sociology,* ed. A. M. Lee, New York: pp. 167–222. Barnes and Noble.
———. 1953. Psychological import of the human group. In *Group Relations at the Crossroads,* ed. M. Sherif and M. O. Wilson, pp. 185–202. New York: Harper.
———. 1954. What is wrong with social theory. *American Sociological Review* 19:3–10.
———. 1955. Attitudes and the social act. *Social Problems* 3:59–65.
———. 1956. Sociological analysis and the "variable". *American Sociological Review* 22:683–90.
———. 1962. Society as symbolic interaction. In *Human Behavior and Social Processes,* ed. A. M. Rose, pp. 179–92. Boston: Houghton Mifflin.
———. 1969*a*. *Symbolic Interactionism: Perspective and Method.* Englewood Cliffs, N. J.: Prentice-Hall.
———. 1969*b*. Collective behavior. In *The Principles of Sociology,* 3d ed., ed. A. M. Lee, pp. 65–121. New York: Barnes and Noble.
———. 1969*c*. Fashion. *Sociological Quarterly* 10:275–91.
———. 1980. Comment: Mead and Blumer: the convergent methodological perspectives of social behaviorism and symbolic interactionism. *American Sociological Review* 45:409–19.
Blumler, J. G., and McQuail, D. 1969. *Television in Politics: Its Uses and Influence.* Chicago: University of Chicago Press.
Blumstein, A. et al., eds. 1978. *Deterrence and Incapacitation.* Washington, D. C.: National Academy of Sciences.
Blumstein, P. W. 1973. Audience, Machiavellianism, and tactics of identity bargaining. *Sociometry* 36:346–65.
Bogardus, E. S. 1925. Measuring social distances. *Journal of Applied Sociology* 9:299–308.
———. 1959. Race reactions by sexes. *Sociology and Social Research* 43:439–41.
Bogart, L. 1973. Warning: the Surgeon General has determined that TV violence is moderately dangerous to your child's mental health. *Public Opinion Quarterly* 36:491–521.
Boissevain, J. 1969. The place of non-groups in the social sciences. *Man* 3:542–56.
Boissevain, J., and Mitchell, J. C., eds. 1973. *Network Analysis: Studies in Human Interaction.* The Hague: Mouton.
Bolinger, D. L. 1964. Intonation as a universal. In *Proceedings of the Ninth International Congress of Linguistics,* pp. 833–48. The Hague: Mouton.
Bolton, C. D. 1961. Mate selection as the development of a relationship. *Marriage and Family Living* 23:234–40.
———. 1972. Alienation and action: a study of peace group members. *American Journal of Sociology* 78:537–61.
Bonacich, E. 1973. A theory of middleman minorities. *American Sociological Review* 38:583–94.
Bonjean, C. M.; Hill, R. J.; and Martin, H. W. 1965. Reactions to the assassination in Dallas. In *The Kennedy Assassination and the American Public.* ed. B. S. Greenberg and E. B. Parker, pp. 178–98. Stanford, Calif.: Stanford University Press.
Bonney, M. E. 1946. A sociometric study of the relationship of some factors to mutual friendship on the elementary, secondary, and college levels. *Sociometry* 9:21–47.
Boocock, S. S. 1978. The social organization of the classroom. *Annual Review of Sociology* 4:1–28.
Boorman, S. A., and White, H. C. 1976. Social structure from multiple networks II. role structures. *American Journal of Sociology* 81:1384–1446.
Bord, R. J. 1976. The impact of imputed deviant identities in structuring evaluation and reactions. *Sociometry* 39:108–16.

Bossard, J. H. 1932. Residential propinquity as a factor in marriage selection. *American Journal of Sociology* 38:219–24.
Bossard, J. H., and Boll, E. S. 1956. *The Large Family System.* Philadelphia: University of Pennsylvania Press.
Bott, E. 1957. *Family and Social Network.* London: Tavistock.
Bourdieu, P., and Passeron, J. C. 1970. *La Reproduction: éléments pour une théorie du systéme-d'enseignement.* Paris: Les Editions de Minuit.
Boutilier, R. G.; Roed, J. C.; and Svendsen, A. C. 1980. Crisis in the two social psychologies: a critical comparison. *Social Psychology Quarterly* 43:5–17.
Bowden, T. 1977. *The Breakdown of Public Security: The Case of Ireland 1916–1921 and Palestine 1936–1939.* Beverly Hills, Calif.: Sage.
Bower, R. T. 1973. *Television and the Public.* New York: Holt, Rinehart and Winston.
Bowles, S., and Gintis, H. 1976. *Schooling in Capitalist America: Educational Reform and the Contradictions of Economic Life.* New York: Basic Books.
Bowles, S.; Gintis, H.; and Meyer, P. 1975. The long shadow of work: education, the family, and the reproduction of the social division of labor. *The Insurgent Sociologist:* 3–22.
Bradburn, N. M. et al. 1971. *Side by Side.* Chicago: Quadrangle.
Braungart, R. 1975. Youth and social movements. In *Adolescence in the Life Cycle,* ed. S. Dragastin and G. Elder, Jr., pp. 255–89. Washington, D. C.: Hemisphere.
Breakwell, G. M. 1978. Some effects of marginal social identity. In *Differentiation Between Social Groups,* ed. H. Tajfel, London: Academic Press.
Breed, W. 1955. Social control in the newsroom. *Social Forces* 33:326–35.
———. 1963. Occupational mobility and suicide among white males. *American Sociological Review* 28:279–88.
Breiger, R. 1976. Career attributes and network structure: a blockmodel study of a biomedical research specialty. *American Sociological Review* 41:117–35.
Brend, R. M. 1975. Male-female intonation patterns in American English. In *Language and Sex: Difference and Dominance,* ed. B. Thorne and N. Henley, pp. 84–87. Rowley, Mass.: Newbury House Publishers, Inc.
Brenner, C. 1973. *An Elementary Textbook of Psychoanalysis.* Revised Edition. New York: Doubleday/Anchor.
Brenner, M. H. 1973. *Mental Illness and the Economy.* Cambridge, Mass.: Harvard University Press.
Brent, S. B. 1978. Individual specialization, collective adaptation and rate of environmental change. *Human Development* 21:21–33.
Brickman, P., and Bulman, R. J. 1977. Pleasure and pain in social comparison. In *Social Comparison Processes,* ed. J. M. Suls and R. L. Miller, pp. 149–86. New York: Wiley.
Briggs, J. L. 1970. *Never in Anger: Portrait of an Eskimo Family.* Cambridge, Mass.: Harvard University Press.
Brim, O. G., Jr. 1958. Family structure and sex role learning by children: a further analysis of Helen Koch's data. *Sociometry* 21:1–16.
———. 1960. Personality as role learning. In *Personality Development in Children,* ed. I. Isroe and H. H. Stevenson, pp. 127–59. Austin: University of Texas Press.
———. 1966. Socialization through the life cycle. In *Socialization After Childhood: Two Essays,* ed. O. G. Brim, Jr. and S. Wheeler, pp. 1–49. New York: Wiley.
———. 1968. Adult socialization. In *Socialization and Society,* ed. J. A. Clausen, pp. 183–226. Boston: Little, Brown and Co.
———. 1976. Theories of male mid-life crisis. *The Counseling Psychologist* 6:2–9.
Brim, O. G., Jr., and Kagan, J. 1980. *Constancy and Change in Human Development.* Cambridge, Mass.: Harvard University Press.
Brinton, C. 1948. The manipulation of economic unrest. *The Tasks of Economic History* 8:21–31.
———. 1957. *The Anatomy of Revolution.* New York: Vintage.
Brislin, R. W., and Olmstead, K. H. 1973. Examination of two models designed to predict behavior from attitude and other verbal measures. *Proceedings of the 81st Annual Convention of the American Psychological Association* 8:259–60.
Bromley, D. A., and Shupe, A. D. 1979. *"Moonies" in America.* Beverly Hills, Calif.: Sage.

Bronfenbrenner, U. 1958. Socialization and social class through time and space. In *Readings in Social Psychology,* ed. Maccoby, Newcomb, and Hartley. New York: Holt, Rinehart and Winston.

———. 1970. *Two Worlds of Childhood: U.S. and U.S.S.R.* New York: Russell Sage Foundation.

———. 1974. The origins of alienation. *Scientific American* 21:53–61.

———. 1979. *The Ecology of Human Development.* Cambridge, Mass.: Harvard University Press.

Brookover, W. B.; Thomas, S.; and Paterson, A. 1964. Self-concept of ability and school achievement. *Sociology of Education* 37:271–78.

Brown, D. W. 1974. Adolescent attitudes and lawful behavior. *Public Opinion Quarterly* 38:98–106.

Brown, J. S., and Gilmartin, B. G. 1969. Sociology today: Lacunae, emphasis, and surfeits. *The American Sociologist* 4:283–91.

Brown, P., and Levinson, S. 1978. Universals in language usage: politeness phenomena. In *Questions and Politeness: Strategies in Social Interaction,* ed. E. N. Goody, pp. 56–289. Cambridge: Cambridge University Press.

Brown, R. 1954. Mass phenomena. In *Handbook of Social Psychology,* ed. G. Lindzey, vol. 2, pp. 833–76. Cambridge, Mass.: Addison-Wesley.

———. 1965. *Social Psychology.* New York: The Free Press.

———. 1973. *A First Language: The Early Stages.* Cambridge, Mass.: Harvard University Press.

Bruner, J. S. 1956. *A Study of Thinking.* New York: Wiley.

Bryce, J. 1891. *The American Commonwealth.* 2d ed. New York: Macmillan.

Bryson, C. 1945. *Man and Society: The Scottish Inquiry of the Eighteenth Century.* Princeton, N. J.: Princeton University Press.

Bucher, R. 1962. Pathology: a study of social movements within a profession. *Social Problems* 10:40–51.

Bucher, R., and Stelling, J. G. 1977. *Becoming Professional.* Beverly Hills, Calif.: Sage.

Bucher, R., and Strauss, A. 1961. Professions in process. *American Journal of Sociology* 66:325–34.

Bugenthal, D. E.; Love, L. R.; and Gianetto, R. M. 1971. Perfidious feminine faces. *Journal of Personality and Social Psychology* 17:314–18.

Bullough, B. 1967. Alienation in the ghetto. *American Journal of Sociology* 72: 469–78.

Burgess, E. W. 1926. The family as a unity of interacting personalities. *The Family* 7:3–9.

Burgess, R. L., and Bushell, D. 1969. *Behavioral Sociology.* New York: Columbia University Press.

Burke, K. 1945. *A Grammar of Motives.* New York: Prentice-Hall.

———. 1954. *Permanence and Change.* Los Altos: Hermes Publications.

———. 1965. *The Psychology of Social Movements.* New York: John Wiley.

Burke, P. J. 1979. Communicative structure, interactive competence and control. Paper presented at the Annual Meetings of North Central Sociological Association.

———. 1980. The self: measurement requirements from an interactionist perspective. *Social Psychology Quarterly* 43:18–29.

Burke, P. J., and Tully, J. 1977. The measurement of role/identity. *Social Forces* 55:881–97.

Burns, T. 1977. The organization of public opinion. In *Mass Communication and Society,* ed. J. Curran et al., pp. 45–49. London: Edward Arnold.

Burt, R. S. 1976. Positions in networks. *Social Forces* 55:93–122.

———. 1977*a*. Positions in multiple network systems. Part One: a general conception of stratification and prestige in a system of actors cast as a social topology. *Social Forces* 57:106–31.

———. 1977*b*. Positions in multiple network systems. Part Two. stratification and prestige among elite decision makers in the community of Altneustadt. *Social Forces* 56:551–75.

Busacker, R., and Saatz, T. 1965. *Finite Graphs and Networks: An Introduction with Applications.* New York: McGraw-Hill.

Bush, D. E.; Simmons, R. G.; Hutchinson, B.; and Blyth, D. A. 1977. Adolescent perception of sex-roles in 1968 and 1975. *Public Opinion Quarterly* 41:459–74.
Butler, E., and McGinley, R., eds. 1977. *The Other Americans: Living in Emerging Alternative Lifestyles.* Buena Park, Calif.: Lifestyles.
Byrne, D. 1969. Attitudes and attraction. In *Advances in Experimental Social Psychology,* ed. L. Berkowitz, vol. 4, pp. 36–89. New York: Academic Press.
———. 1971. *The Attraction Paradigm.* New York: Academic Press.
Caillois, R. 1961. *Man, Play, and Games.* Glencoe, Ill.: Free Press.
Cain, L. D. 1964. Life course and social structure. In *Handbook of Modern Sociology,* ed. R. E. L. Faris, pp. 272–389. Chicago: Rand McNally.
———. 1979. Adding spice to middle age. *Contemporary Sociology* 8:547–50.
Calsyn, R. J., and Kenny, D. A. 1977. Self-concept of ability and perceived evaluation of others: cause or effect of academic achievement? *Journal of Educational Psychology* 69:136–45.
Campbell, A. 1971. *White Attitudes Toward Black People.* Ann Arbor, Mich.: Institute for Social Research.
Campbell, A., and Schuman, H. 1968. *Racial Attitudes in Fifteen American Cities.* Washington, D. C.: U. S. Government Printing Office.
Campbell, A.; Gurin, G.; and Miller, W. E. 1954. *The Voter Decides.* Evanston, Ill.: Row, Peterson.
Campbell, A. et al. 1976. *The Quality of American Life.* New York: Russell Sage Foundation.
Campbell, B. A. 1977. The impact of school desegregation: an investigation of three mediating factors. *Youth and Society* 9:79–111.
Campbell, D. T. 1958. Common fate, similarity, and other indices of the status of aggregates of persons as social entities. *Behavioral Science* 3:14–27.
———. 1963. Social attitudes and other acquired behavioral predispositions. In *Psychology: A Study of a Science,* ed. S. Koch, pp. 94–172. New York: McGraw Hill.
———. 1967. Stereotypes and the perception of group differences. *American Psychologist* 22:817–29.
Campbell, D. T., and Fiske, D. W. 1959. Convergent and discriminant validation by the multi-trait, multi-method matrix. *Psychological Bulletin* 56:81–105.
Campbell, D. T., and Stanley, J. C. 1963. *Experimental and Quasi-Experimental Designs for Research.* Chicago: Rand McNally.
Camilleri, S. F., and Berger, J. 1967. Decision-making and social influence: a model and an experimental test. *Sociometry* 30:367–78.
Camilleri, S. F., and Conner, T. L. 1976. Decision-making and social influence: a revised model and further experimental evidence. *Sociometry* 39:30–38.
Camilleri, S. F.; Berger, J.; and Conner, T. L. 1972. A formal theory of decision-making. In *Sociological Theories in Progress,* ed. J. Berger, M. Zelditch, Jr., and B. Anderson, vol. 2, chap. 2. Boston: Houghton Mifflin.
Candee, D. 1974. Ego developmental aspects of new left ideology. *Journal of Personality and Social Psychology* 30:620–30.
Candland, D. K. et al. 1977. The emotion construct in psychology. In *Emotion,* ed. D. K. Candland. Monterey, Calif.: Brooks-Cole.
Cannon, W. B. 1929. *Bodily Changes in Pain, Hunger, Fear, and Rage.* New York: Norton.
Cantril, H. 1940. *The Invasion from Mars.* Princeton, N. J.: Princeton University Press.
———. 1941. *The Psychology of Social Movements.* New York: Wiley.
———. 1965. *The Pattern of Human Concerns.* New Brunswick, N. J.: Rutgers University Press.
Capellanus, A. 1941 [1184]. *The Art of Courtly Love.* New York: Columbia University Press.
Caplan, N. 1970. The new ghetto man: a review of recent empirical studies. *Journal of Social Issues* 26:59–73.
Caplow, T. 1956. A theory of coalitions in the triad. *American Sociological Review* 21:480–93.
———. 1959. Further development of a theory of coalitions in the triad. *American Journal of Sociology* 64:488–93.

———. 1968. *Two Against One: Coalitions in Triads.* Englewood Cliffs, N. J.: Prentice-Hall.
Carlsmith, J.M.; Collins, B. E.; and Helmreich, R. L. 1966. Studies in forced compliance: I. the effect of pressure for compliance on attitude change produced by face-to-face playing and anonymous essay writing. *Journal of Personality and Social Psychology* 4:1–13.
Carmines, E. G. 1978. Psychological origins of adolescent political attitudes. *American Politics Quarterly* 6:167–86.
Carr, L. J. 1932. Disaster and the sequence-pattern concept of social change. *American Journal of Sociology* 38:207–18.
Cartwright, D. 1979. Contemporary social psychology in historical perspective. *Social Psychology Quarterly* 42:82–93.
Cartwright, D., and Zander, A. 1968. *Group Dynamics.* 4th ed. New York: Harper and Row.
Cassel, J. 1976. The contribution of the social environment to host resistance. *American Journal of Epidemiology* 104:107–23.
Castore, C. H., and DeNinno, J. A. 1977. Investigations in the social comparison of attitudes. In *Social Comparison Processes,* ed. J. M. Suls and R. L. Miller. New York: Wiley.
Cattell, R. B., Saunders, D. R., and Stice, G. F. 1953. The dimensions of syntality in small groups. *Human Relations* 6:331–51.
Catton, W. R. 1966. *From Animistic to Materialistic Sociology.* New York: McGraw-Hill.
Caudill, W. 1958. *The Psychiatric Hospital as a Small Society.* Cambridge, Mass.: Harvard University Press.
———. 1973. The influence of social structure and culture on human behavior in modern Japan. *Journal of Nervous and Mental Disease* 157:240–57.
Cavan, R. S. 1953. *The American Family.* New York: Crowell.
Cavan, S. 1970. The etiquette of youth. In *Social Psychology Through Symbolic Interaction,* ed. G. Stone and H. Farberman. Waltham, Mass.: Ginn-Blaisdell.
Cazden, C. B. 1973. Problems for education: language as curriculum content and learning environment. *Daedalus* 102:135–48.
Cell, C. P. 1974. Charismatic heads of state: the social context. *Behavioral Science Research* 9:255–305.
Chadwick-Jones, J. K. 1976. *Social Exchange Theory: Its Structure and Influence in Social Psychology.* London: Academic Press.
Chagnon, N. 1968. *Yanomano: The Fierce People.* New York: Holt, Rinehart and Winston.
Chakhotin, S. 1939. *La viol des foules par la propagande politique.* Paris: Gallimard.
Chapanis, N. P., and Chapanis, A. 1964. Cognitive dissonance: five years later. *Psychological Bulletin* 61:1–22.
Chaplin, J. P. 1959. *Rumor, Fear, and the Madness of Crowds.* New York: Ballantine.
Chapman, D. W., and Volkmann, J. 1939. A social determinant of the level of aspiration. *Journal of Abnormal and Social Psychology* 34:225–38.
Chapple, E. D. 1949. The interaction chronograph, its evolution and present application. *Personnel* 25:295–307.
Charters, W. W., Jr., and Newcomb, T. M. 1958. Some attitudinal effects of experimentally increased salience of a membership group. In *Readings in Social Psychology,* 3d ed., ed. E. E. Maccoby, T. M. Newcomb, and E. L. Hartley, pp. 276–81. New York: Holt, Rinehart and Winston.
Chertkoff, J. M., and Esser, J. K. 1976. A review of experiments in explicit bargaining. *Journal of Experimental Social Psychology* 12:464–86.
Chinoy, E. 1968. *Automobile Workers and the American Dream.* Boston: Beacon Press.
Chomsky, N. 1957. *Syntactic Structures.* The Hague: Mouton.
———. 1959. A review of B. F. Skinner's "Verbal Behavior." *Language* 35:26–58.
———. 1965. *Aspects of the Theory of Syntax.* Cambridge: The M.I.T. Press.
Chowdhry, K., and Newcomb, T. M. 1952. The relative abilities of leaders and nonleaders to estimate opinions of their own groups. *Journal of Abnormal and Social Psychology* 47:51–57.

Christenson, J. A. 1979. Value orientations of potential migrants and nonmigrants. *Rural Sociology* 44:331–44.

Cicourel, A. V. 1974*a*. *Cognitive Sociology: Language and Meaning in Social Interaction.* New York: Free Press.

———. 1974*b*. *Theory and Method in a Study of Argentine Fertility.* New York: Wiley Interscience.

———. 1974*c*. Interviewing and memory. In *Pragmatic Aspects of Human Communication.* ed. C. Cherry, pp. 51–82. Dordrecht, Holland: D. Reidel Publishing Co.

———. 1980. Three models of discourse analysis: the role of social structure. Mimeograph. San Diego: University of California.

Cicourel, A. V. et al. 1974. *Language Use and School Performance.* New York: Academic Press.

Clanton, G., and Smith, L. G. 1977. *Jealousy.* Englewood Cliffs, N. J.: Prentice-Hall.

Clark, K. B. 1965. *Dark Ghetto: Dilemmas of Social Power.* New York: Harper and Row.

Clarke, H. D.; Price, R. G.; Stewart, M. C.; and Krause, R. 1978. Motivational patterns and differential participation in a Canadian party: the Ontario liberals. *American Journal of Political Science* 22:130–51.

Clausen, J. A. 1966. Family structure, socialization, and personality. In *Review of Child Development Research,* ed. M. L. Hoffman and L. W. Hoffman, vol. 2. pp. 1–53. New York: Russell Sage Foundation.

———. 1968. *Socialization and Society.* Boston: Little, Brown.

———. 1973. The life course of individuals. In *Aging and Society,* ed. M. W. Riley, M. Johnson and S. Foner, vol. 3. pp. 457–514. New York: Russell Sage Foundation.

Clinard, M. B., ed. 1964. *Anomie and Deviant Behavior.* New York: Free Press.

Coates, C. H., and Pellegrin, R. 1957. Executives and supervisors: contrasting self-conceptions and conceptions of each other. *American Sociological Review* 22: 217–20.

Cobb, R. W., and Elder, C. 1972. *Participation in American Politics: The Dynamics of Agenda-Building.* Boston: Allyn and Bacon.

Coddington, A. 1968. *Theories of the Bargaining Process.* Chicago: Aldine.

Cohen, B. P. 1980. *Developing Sociological Knowledge: Theory and Method.* Englewood Cliffs, N. J.: Prentice-Hall.

Cohen, B. P., and Lee, H. 1975. *Conflict, Conformity and Social Status.* New York: Elsevier.

Cohen, B.; Colligan, M.; Wester, W.; and Smith, M. 1978. An investigation of job satisfaction factors in an incident of mass psychogenic illness in the workplace. *Occupational Health Nursing* 26:10–16.

Cohen, E. G. 1970. *A New Approach to Applied Research: Race and Education.* Columbus, Ohio: Charles E. Merrill.

———. 1972. Interracial interaction disability. *Human Relations* 25:9–24.

———. 1972. Sociology and the classroom: setting the conditions for student-teacher interaction. *Review of Educational Research* 42:441–52.

———. 1973. Modification of the effects of social structure. *American Behavioral Scientist* 16:860–78.

———. 1976. Center for interracial co-operation: a field experiment. *Sociology of Education* 48:47–58.

Cohen, E. G., and Roper, S. S. 1972. Modification of interracial interaction disability: an application of status characteristic theory. *American Sociological Review* 37:643–57.

Cohen, J., and Till, A. 1977. Another look at modernity scales: reanalysis of the convergent and discriminant validities of the Armer, Kahl, Smith and Inkeles, and Schnaiberg scales. *American Sociological Review* 42:373–82.

Cohen, J. M. 1977. Sources of peer group homogeneity. *Sociology of Education* 50:227–41.

Cohn, N. 1957. *The Pursuit of the Millennium.* New York: Oxford University Press.

Cohn, R. M. 1978. The effect of employment status change on self-attitudes. *Social Psychology* 41:81–93.

Cole, D. L., and Cole, S. 1977. Counternormative behavior and locus of control. *Journal of Social Psychology* 101:21–28.

Cole, P., and Morgan, J. L., eds. 1975. *Syntax and Semantics* vol. 3: *Speech Acts.* New York: Academic Press.

Coleman, J. S. 1960. The mathematical study of small groups. In *Mathematical Thinking in the Measurement of Behavior,* ed. H. Solomon. Glencoe, Ill.: Free Press.
———. 1961. *The Adolescent Society.* New York: Free Press.
———. 1972. Systems of social exchange. *Journal of Mathematical Sociology* 2: 145–63.
———. 1973. *The Mathematics of Collective Action.* Chicago: Aldine.
Coleman, J. S.; Campbell, E. Q.; Hobson, C. J.; McPartland, J.; Mood, A. M.; Weinfeld, F. D.; and York, R. L. 1966. *Equality of Educational Opportunity.* Washington, D. C.: U. S. Government Printing Office.
Colligan, M., and Stockton, W. 1978. Assembly-line hysteria. *Psychology Today* 12:93ff.
Collins, B. E. 1970. *Social Psychology.* Reading, Mass.: Addison-Wesley.
Collins, R. 1975. *Conflict Sociology: Toward an Explanatory Science.* New York: Academic Press.
Comstock, G., et al. 1978. *Television and Human Behavior.* New York: Columbia University Press.
Condon, W. S. 1967. A segmentation of behavior. *Journal of Psychiatric Research* 5:221–35.
———. 1970. Method of microanalysis of sound films of behavior. *Behavioral Research Methods and Instrumentation* 2:51–54.
Condran, J. G. 1979. Changes in white attitudes toward blacks: 1963–1977. *Public Opinion Quarterly* 43:463–76.
Conley, J. M.; O'Barr, W. M.; and Lind, E. A. 1978. The power of language: presentation style in the courtroom. *Duke Law Journal* 6:1375–99.
Connor, T. L. 1965. Continual disagreement and the assignment of self-other performance expectations. Ph.D. dissertation, Department of Sociology, Stanford University.
———. 1977. Performance expectations and the initiation of problem solving attempts. *Journal of Mathematical Sociology* 5:187–98.
Connor, J. W. 1974. Acculturation and family continuities in three generations of Japanese Americans. *Journal of Marriage and the Family* 36:159–65.
Converse, P., and Campbell, A. Political standards in secondary groups. In *Group Dynamics,* 2d ed., ed. D. Cartwright and A. Zander, pp. 300–18. New York: Harper and Row.
Conway, F., and Siegelman, J. 1978. *Snapping: America's Epidemic of Sudden Personality Change.* New York: J. B. Lippincott.
Cook, K. S. 1975. Expectations, evaluations, and equity. *American Sociological Review* 40:372–88.
———. 1977. Exchange and power in networks in interorganizational relations. *Sociological Quarterly* 18:62–82.
———. 1979. Exchange, power and equity. Didactic Seminar #51, American Sociological Association Meetings, Boston, Massachusetts.
Cook, K. S., and Emerson, R. M. 1978*a.* Power, equity, commitment in exchange networks. *American Sociological Review* 43:721–39.
———. 1978*b.* Experimental studies of exchange networks and corporate groups. Research Proposal. National Science Foundation.
Cook, K. S., and Parcel, T. L. 1977. Equity theory: directions for future research. *Sociological Inquiry* 47:75–88.
Cook, K. S.; Gillmore, M. R.; and Little, J. 1979. Power, dependency and collective action in exchange networks. Technical Report. Institute for Sociological Research: University of Washington.
Cook, K. S.; Emerson, R. M.; Gillmore, M. R.; and Yamagishi, T. 1980. *Centrality and the Exercise of Power in Exchange Networks.* Technical Report. Institute for Sociological Research: University of Washington.
Cook, K. S., and Emerson, R. M. with Gillmore, M. R., and Yamagishi, T. 1980. *The Structure of Social Exchange.* New York: Academic Press.
Cook, T. D.; Crosby, F.; and Hennigan, K. 1977. The construct validity of relative deprivation. In *Social Comparison Processes,* ed. J. M. Suls and R. L. Miller. New York: Wiley.
Cooley, C. H. 1962 [1909]. *Social Organization.* New York: Scribner's.
———. 1964 [1902]. *Human Nature and the Social Order.* New York: Scribner's.

Cooper, E., and Jahoda, M. 1947. The evasion of propaganda: how prejudiced people respond to anti-war propaganda. *Journal of Psychology* 23:15–25.

Corey, S. M. 1937. Professed attitudes and actual behavior. *Journal of Educational Psychology* 28:271–80.

Corsaro, W. 1979*a*. Young children's conception of status and role. *Sociology of Education* 52:46–59.

———. 1979*b*. "We're friends, right?": children's use of access rituals in a nursery school. *Language in Society* 8:315–36.

———. In press. Communicative processes in studies of social organization: sociological approaches to discourse analysis.

Coser, L. 1956. *The Functions of Social Conflict.* New York: Free Press.

———. 1974. *Greedy Institutions.* New York: Free Press.

Coser, R. 1959. Some social functions of laughter. *Human Relations* 12:171–82.

Cottrell, L. S., Jr. 1948. The present status and future orientation of research on the family. *American Sociological Review* 13:370–82.

———. 1971. Covert behavior in interpersonal interaction. *Proceedings of the American Philosophical Society* 115:462–69.

Couch, C. 1958. Self-attitudes and degree of agreement with immediate others. *American Journal of Sociology* 63:491–96.

———. 1970. Dimensions of association in collective behavior episodes. *Sociometry* 33:457–71.

Coulson, M. 1972. Role: a redundant concept in sociology? Some educational considerations. In *Role,* ed. J. A. Jackson, pp. 107–28. Cambridge: Cambridge University Press.

Coutu, W. 1949. *Emergent Human Nature: A Symbolic Field Interpretation.* New York: Knopf.

———. 1951. Role-playing vs. role-taking: an appeal for clarification. *American Sociological Review* 16:180–87.

Covington, M. V., and Beery, R. G. 1976. *Self-Worth and School Learning.* New York: Holt, Rinehart and Winston.

Cox, O. 1948. *Caste, Class and Race.* Garden City and New York: Doubleday.

Cox, W. F., Jr., and Luhrs, J. A. 1978. Relationship between locus of control and alcohol and drug-related behavior in teenagers. *Social Behavior and Personality* 6:191–204.

Cozby, P. C. 1973. Self-disclosure: a literature review. *Psychology Bulletin* 79:73–91.

Craig, H. B. 1965. A sociometric investigation of the self-concept of the deaf child. *American Annals of the Deaf* 110:456–78.

Crain, R. L. 1971. School integration and the academic achievement of Negroes. *Sociology of Education* 44:1–26.

Crain, R. L., and Mahard, R. E. 1977. Desegregation and black achievement. Working paper presented to the National Review Panel on School Desegregation, Amelia Island, Florida, October. Institute of Policy Sciences and Public Affairs: Duke University.

Crain, R. L., and Weisman, C. S. 1972. *Discrimination, Personality and Achievement: A Survey of Northern Blacks.* New York: Seminar Press.

Crane, M.; Manis, M.; Martin, S.; Robins, C.; and Schuman, H. 1979. Attitudes vs. behavior *versus* behavior vs. behavior. Paper presented at the Annual Meetings of the American Sociological Association, Boston, August.

Crawford, T. J. 1974. Theories of attitude change and the "beyond family planning" debate: the case for the persuasion approach in population policy. *Journal of Social Issues* 30:211–33.

Crespi, I. 1971. What kinds of attitude measures are predictive of behavior? *Public Opinion Quarterly* 35:327–34.

Cressey, D. R. 1953. *Other People's Money.* Glencoe, Ill.: Free Press.

Critchfield, R. 1978. Wild at the Carnival. *Human Behavior:* February.

Crockett, H. 1966. Psychological origins of mobility. In *Social Structure and Mobility in Economic Development,* ed. N. J. Smelser and S. M. Lipset, pp. 280–309. Chicago: Aldine.

Cronbach, L. J. 1970. *Essentials of Psychological Testing.* New York: Harper and Row.

Crosby, F. A. 1976. A model of egoistical relative deprivation. *Psychological Review* 83:85–113.

Crystal, D. 1969. *Prosodic Systems and Intonation in English.* Cambridge: Cambridge University Press.
Cullen, F. T., and Cullen, J. B. 1978. *Toward a Paradigm of Labeling Theory.* Lincoln: University of Nebraska Studies. New Series no. 58.
Curran, J., Gurevitch, M., and Woolacott, J., eds. 1977. *Mass Communication and Society.* London: Edward Arnold.
Curry, T. J., and Emerson, R. M. 1970. Balance theory: a theory of interpersonal attraction. *Sociometry* 33:216–38.
Curtis, R. L., Jr., and Zurcher, L. A., Jr. 1973. Stable resources of protest movements: the multi-organizational field. *Social Forces* 52:53–61.
———. 1974. Social movements: an analytical exploration of organizational forms. *Social Problems* 21:356–70.
Cutler, S. J., and Kaufman, R. L. 1975. Cohort changes in political attitudes: tolerance of ideological nonconformity. *Public Opinion Quarterly* 39:69–81.
Dahrendorf, R. 1968. *Homo sociologicus.* In *Essays in the Theory of Society,* ed. R. Dahrendorf, pp. 19–87. Stanford, Calif.: Stanford University Press.
Daly, W. T. 1972. *The Revolutionary: A Review and Synthesis.* Beverly Hills, Calif.: Sage.
Daner, F. J. 1976. *The American Children of Krishna: A Study of the Hare Krishna Movement.* New York: Holt, Rinehart and Winston.
Darley, J. M., and Latane, B. 1968. Bystander intervention in emergencies: diffusion of responsibility. *Journal of Personality and Social Psychology* 8:377–83.
Darwin, C. 1965 [1872]. *The Expression of the Emotions in Man and Animals.* Chicago: University of Chicago Press.
Das, P.; Choudhury, J. B. R.; and Santra, S. K. 1973. Role of reference group in adoption of high-yielding varieties of Paddy. *Society and Culture* 4:85–90.
Datan, N., and Ginsberg, L. H., eds. 1975. *Life Span Developmental Psychology: Normative Life Crises.* New York: Academic Press.
Dator, J. 1969. *Soka Gakkai: Builders of the Third Civilization.* Seattle: University of Washington Press.
Davenport, F. M. 1905. *Primitive Traits in Religious Revivals.* New York: Negro Universities Press.
Davies, J. C. 1962. Toward a theory of revolution. *American Sociological Review* 27:5–19.
———. 1969. The J-curve of rising and declining satisfactions as a cause of some great revolutions and a contained rebellion. In *Violence in America.* ed. H. D. Graham and T. R. Gurr, pp. 690–730. New York: Bantam Books.
Davis, F. 1979. *Yearning for Yesterday: A Sociology of Nostalgia.* New York: Free Press.
Davis, J., and Leinhardt, S. 1972. The structure of positive interpersonal relations in small groups. In *Sociological Theories in Progress,* ed. Berger, Zelditch and Anderson, vol. 2. Boston: Houghton Mifflin.
Davis, J. A. 1959. A formal interpretation of the theory of relative deprivation. *Sociometry* 22:280–96.
———. 1975. Communism, conformity, cohorts, and categories: American tolerance in 1954 and 1972–73. *American Journal of Sociology* 81:491–513.
Davis, K. 1936. Jealousy and sexual property. *Social Forces* 14:395–405.
———. 1949. *Human Society.* New York: Macmillan.
Davison, W. P. 1956. Political significance of recognition via mass media—an illustration from the Berlin blockade. *Public Opinion Quarterly* 20:327–33.
Davitz, J. 1969. *The Language of Emotion.* New York: Academic Press.
Dawson, C. A., and Gettys, W. E. 1948. *An Introduction to Sociology.* New York: Ronald.
Dedrick, D. K. 1978. Deviance and sanctioning within small groups. *Social Psychology* 41:94–104.
DeFleur, M. L. 1968. Is attitude an obsolete concept for sociologists? Paper presented at the Annual Meeting of the Pacific Sociological Association, San Francisco, March.
DeFleur, M. L., and Westie, F. R. 1963. Attitudes as a scientific concept. *Social Forces* 42:20–31.
De Mesquita, B. B. 1974. Need for achievement and competitiveness as determi-

nants of political party success in elections and coalitions. *American Political Science Review* 68:1207–20.
Denny-Brown, D. 1943. Effects of modern warfare on civil population. *Journal of Laboratory and Clinical Medicine* 28:641–45.
Denzin, N. K. 1966. The significant others of a college population. *Sociological Quarterly* 7:298–310.
———. 1968. Collective behavior in total institutions. *Social Problems* 15:353–65.
———. 1970. *The Research Act: A Theoretical Introduction to Sociological Methods.* Chicago: Aldine.
———. 1972. The genesis of self in early childhood. *Sociological Quarterly* 13: 291–314.
———. 1975. Play, games, and interaction: the contexts of childhood socialization. Sociological Quarterly 16:458–78.
———. 1977. *Childhood Socialization: Studies in the Development of Language, Social Behavior and Identity.* San Francisco: Jossey-Bass.
———. 1977. Notes on the criminogenic hypothesis: a case study of the American liquor industry. *American Sociological Review* 42:905–20.
Department of Health, Education and Welfare. 1973. *Work in America.* Cambridge: The M.I.T. Press.
Dermer, M.; Cohen, S. J.; Jacobsen, E.; and Anderson, E. A. 1979. Evaluative judgments of aspects of life as a function of vicarious exposure to Hedonic extremes. *Journal of Personality and Social Psychology* 37:247–60.
Deutsch, M. 1964. Homans in the Skinner box. *Sociological Inquiry* 34:156–65.
Deutsch, M., and Collins, M. E. 1951. *Interracial Housing:* Minneapolis: University of Minnesota.
Deutsch, M., and Gerard, H. B. 1955. A study of normative and informational social influences upon individual judgment. *Journal of Abnormal and Social Psychology* 51:629–36.
Deutscher, I. 1969. Looking backward: case studies on the progress of methodology in sociological research. *The American Sociologist* 4:35–41.
——— (ed.). 1973. *What We Say/What We Do.* Glenview, Ill.: Scott, Foresman.
Devereux, G. 1961. Two types of modal personality models. In *Studying Personality Cross-Culturally,* ed. B. Kaplan. Elmsford, N. Y.: Row, Peterson.
DeVos, G. 1960. The relation of guilt toward parents to achievement and arranged marriage among the Japanese. *Psychiatry* 23:287–301.
Dewey, J. 1894. The theory of emotion. *Psychological Review* 1:553–69.
———. 1896. The reflex arc in psychology. *Psychological Review:* 357–70.
———. 1920. *Reconstruction in Philosophy.* New York: Holt.
Dewey, J. 1940. *Human Nature and Conduct.* New York: Modern Library.
Dicks, H. V. 1950. Personality traits and national socialist ideology. *Human Relations* 3:111–54.
———. 1952. Observations on contemporary Russian behavior. *Human Relations* 5:111–75.
Dion, K. K.; Berscheid, E.; and Walster, E. 1972. What is beautiful is good. *Journal of Personality and Social Psychology* 24:285–90.
Dion, K. L., and Dion, K. K. 1973. Correlates of romantic love. *Journal of Consulting and Clinical Psychology* 41:51–56.
Dipboye, R. L. 1977. A critical review of Korman's self-consistency theory of work motivation and occupational choice. *Organizational Behavior and Human Performance* 18:108–26.
DiRenzo, G. J. 1977*a. We, the People: American Character and Social Change.* Westport, Conn.: Greenwood Press.
———. 1977*b.* Socialization, personality, and social systems. *Annual Review of Sociology* 3:261–95.
Dittmer, L. 1977. Thought reform and cultural revolution: an analysis of the symbolism of Chinese polemics. *American Political Science Review* 71:67–85.
Donahue, G. A. et al. 1972. Gatekeeping: mass media systems and information control. In *Current Perspectives in Mass Communication Research,* ed. F. G. Kline and P. Tichenor, pp. 41–70. Beverly Hills, Calif.: Sage.
Douglas, J. D. 1967. *The Social Meanings of Suicide.* Princeton, N. J.: Princeton University Press.

Douglas, J. W. B. 1964. *The Home and the School: A Study of Ability and Attainment in the Primary School.* London: MacGibbon and Kee.

Douglas, M. 1970. *Natural Symbols.* London: Barrie and Rockliff; Penguin, 1973.

———. *Cultural Bias.* 1978. London: Royal Anthropological Institute.

Douvan, E., and Adelson, J. 1966. *The Adolescent Experience.* New York: Wiley.

Dowd, J. J. 1979–80. Problems of generations: and generational analysis. *International Journal of Aging and Human Development* 10:213–28.

Downes, A. 1972. Up and down with ecology—the "issue-attention cycle." *The Public Interest:* 38–50.

Dragastin, S. E., and Elder, G. H. 1975. *Adolescence in the Life Cycle: Psychological Change and Social Context.* New York: Halsted.

Dreeben, R. 1968. *On What is Learned in School.* Reading, Mass.: Addison-Wesley.

———. 1973. The school as a workplace. In *Second Handbook of Research in Teaching,* ed. R. M. Travers. Chicago: Rand McNally.

Drever, J. 1952. *A Dictionary of Psychology.* New York: Penguin.

Driscoll, R.; Davis, R. E.; and Lipitz, M. E. 1972. Parental interference and romantic love: the Romeo and Juliet effect. *Journal of Personality and Social Psychology* 24:1–10.

Dubois, B. L.; and Crouch, I. 1975. The question of tag questions in women's speech: they don't really use more of them, do they? *Language in Society* 4:289–94.

Duncan, H. 1953. *Language and Literature in Society.* Chicago: University of Chicago Press.

Dunham, H. W. 1940. Topical summaries of current literature: social attitudes. *American Journal of Sociology* 46:344–75.

Durkheim, E. 1933. *The Division of Labor in Society.* Translated by George Simpson. New York: Macmillan.

———. 1915 [1912]. *The Elementary Forms of the Religious Life.* Translated by Joseph Ward Swain. New York: Macmillan.

———. 1951 [1897]. *Suicide.* Translated by John A. Spaulding and George Simpson. New York: Free Press.

———. 1965 [1915]. *The Elementary Forms of the Religious Life.* New York: Free Press.

Duval, S., and Wicklund, R. W. 1972. *A Theory of Objective Self-Awareness.* New York: Academic Press.

Dynes, R. 1970. *Organized Behavior in Disaster.* Lexington, Mass.: Heath.

Dynes, R., and Quarantelli, E. L. 1968. What looting in civil disturbances really means. *Transaction* 5:9–14.

Eagly, A. H., and Himmelfarb, S. 1978. Attitudes and opinions. In *Annual Review of Psychology,* ed. M. M. Rosenzweig and L. W. Porter, vol. 29, pp. 517–44. Palo Alto, Cal.: Annual Reviews.

Edwards, A. D. 1976. *Language in Culture and Class: The Sociology of Language and Education.* London: Heinemann Educational.

Edwards, A. L. 1957. *Techniques of Attitude Scale Construction.* New York: Appleton-Century-Crofts.

Edwards, H. 1970. *Black Students.* New York: Free Press.

Ehrlich, H. J. 1973. *The Social Psychology of Prejudice.* New York: Wiley.

Eisenstadt, S. N. 1954. Studies in reference group behavior. *Human Relations* 7:191–216.

Eisinger, P. K. 1974. Racial differences in protest participation. *American Political Science Review* 68:592–606.

Ekeh, P. 1974. *Social Exchange Theory: The Two Traditions.* Cambridge, Mass.: Harvard University Press.

Ekman, P. 1972. Universals and cultural differences in facial expressions of emotion. In *Nebraska Symposium on Motivation, 1971,* ed. J. K. Cole, pp. 207–83. Lincoln: University of Nebraska Press.

Ekman, P., and Friesen, W. V. 1969*a*. Nonverbal leakage and clues to deception. *Psychiatry* 32:88–106.

———. 1969*b*. The repertoire of nonverbal behavior: categories, origins, usage and coding. *Semiotics* 1:49–98.

———. 1975. *Unmasking the Face.* Englewood Cliffs, N.J.: Prentice-Hall.

Ekman, P., and Oster, H. 1979. Facial expressions of emotion. *Annual Review of Psychology* 30:527–54.

Ekman, P.; Friesen, W. V.; and Ellsworth, P. 1972. *Emotion in the Human Face.* New York: Pergamon.

Elder, G. H., Jr. 1968. Adolescent socialization and development. In *Handbook of Personality Theory and Research,* ed. E. F. Borgatta and W. M. Lambert, pp. 239–64. Chicago: Rand McNally.

———. 1968. *Adolescent Socialization and Personality Development.* Chicago: Rand McNally.

———. 1974. *Children of the Great Depression.* Chicago: University of Chicago Press.

———. 1975. Age differentiation and life course. *Annual Review of Sociology* 1: 165–90.

———. 1976. Forward. In *Unplanned Parenthood: The Social Consequences of Teenage Childbearing.* ed. F. F. Furstenberg, Jr. New York: Free Press.

Elder, G. H., Jr., and Bowerman, C. 1963. Family structure and childrearing patterns: the effect of family size and sex composition. *American Sociological Review* 28:891–905.

Elias, N. 1969. *The Civilizing Process.* New York: Urizen Books.

Elkind, D. 1979. *The Child and Society.* New York: Oxford University Press.

Emerson, J. P. 1970. Nothing unusual is happening. In *Human Nature and Collective Behavior,* ed. T. Shibutani, pp. 208–22. Englewood Cliffs, N. J.: Prentice-Hall.

Emerson, R. M. 1962. Power-dependence relations. *American Sociological Review* 27:31–41.

———. 1972*a*. Exchange theory, part I: a psychological basis for social exchange. In *Sociological Theories in Progress,* ed. J. Berger, M. Zelditch and B. Anderson. vol. 2. Boston: Houghton Mifflin.

———. 1972b. Exchange theory, part II: exchange relations and networks. In *Sociological Theories in Progress.* ed. J. Berger, M. Zelditch and B. Anderson. vol. 2. Boston: Houghton Mifflin.

———. 1976. Social exchange theory. In *Annual Review of Sociology.* ed. A. Inkeles, J. Coleman and N. Smelser, vol. 2, pp. 335–62. Palo Alto, Cal.: Annual Reviews.

Emmerich, W. 1973. Socialization and sex-role development. In *Life-Span Developmental Psychology: Personality and Socialization,* ed. P. B. Baltes and K. W. Schaie, pp. 124–45. New York: Academic Press.

Empey, L. T. 1978. *American Delinquency.* Homewood, Ill.: Dorsey Press.

Empey, L. T., and Lubeck, S. G. 1971. *The Silverlake Experiment.* Chicago: Aldine.

Empey, L. T., and Rabow, J. 1961. The Provo experiment in delinquency rehabilitation. *American Sociological Review* 26:679–95.

———. 1962. Reply to Gordon. *American Sociological Review* 27:256–58.

Engels, F. 1972 [1848]. *The Origin of the Family, Private Property, and the State.* New York: International.

Enroth, R. 1977. *Youth, Brainwashing, and the Extremist Cults.* Grand Rapids, Mich.: Zonderman.

Entwisle, D. R., and Webster, M. A., Jr. 1972. Raising children's performance expectations. *Social Science Research* 1:147–58.

———. 1973. Research note: status factors in expectation raising. *Sociology of Education* 46:116–26.

———. 1974*a*. Raising children's expectations for their own performance: a classroom application. In *Expectation States Theory: A Theoretical Research Program.* ed. J. Berger, T. L. Conner, and M. H. Fisek, chap. 7. Cambridge, Mass.: Winthrop.

———. 1974*b*. Expectations in mixed racial groups. *Sociology of Education* 47: 301–18.

Entwisle, D. R., and Webster, M. A., Jr. 1978. Raising expectations indirectly. *Social Forces* 57:257–64.

Epstein, R., and Komorita, S. S. 1965. Parental discipline, stimulus characteristics of outgroups, and social distance in children. *Journal of Personality and Social Psychology* 2:416–20.

———. 1966. Prejudice among Negro children as related to parental ethnocentrism and punitiveness. *Journal of Personality and Social Psychology* 4:643–47.
Epstein, S. 1979. The stability of behavior: I. on predicting most of the people much of the time. *Journal of Personality and Social Psychology* 37:1097–1126.
———. 1980. The self-concept: a review and the proposal of an integrated theory of personality. In *Personality: Basic Issues and Current Research,* ed. E. Staub. Englewood Cliffs, N. J.: Prentice-Hall.
Erickson, B.; Lind, E. A.; Johnson, B. C.; and O'Ban, W. M. 1978. Speech style and impression formation in a court setting: the effects of "powerful" and "powerless" speech. *Journal of Experimental Social Psychology* 14:207–83.
Erickson, F. 1975. One function of proxemic shifts in face-to-face interaction. In *Organization of Behavior in Face-to-Face Interaction,* ed. A. Kendon, R. Harris and M. R. Key, pp. 175–88. The Hague: Mouton.
———. 1976. Gatekeeping encounters: a social selection process. In *Anthropology and the Public Interest.* ed. P. R. Sanday, pp. 111–45. New York: Academic Press.
Erickson, F., and Schultz, J. J. 1980. *Talking to the Man: Social and Cultural Organization of Communication in School Counseling Interviews.* New York: Academic Press.
Erikson, E. H. 1950. *Childhood and Society.* New York: Norton.
———. 1958. *Young Man Luther.* New York: Norton.
———. 1969. *Gandhi's Truth.* New York: Norton.
Erikson, K. T. 1962. Notes on the sociology of deviance. *Social Problems* 9:307–14.
———. 1976. *Everything in Its Path: Destruction of Community in the Buffalo Creek Flood.* New York: Simon and Schuster.
Ervin-Tripp, S. M. 1973. *Language Acquisition and Communicative Choice: Essays by Susan M. Ervin-Tripp.* Stanford, Calif.: Stanford University Press.
Ervin-Tripp, S. M., and Mitchell-Kernan, C., eds., 1977. *Child Discourse.* New York: Academic Press.
Etheredge, L. S. 1978. Personality effects on American foreign policy, 1898–1968: a test of interpersonal generalization theory. *American Political Science Review* 78:434–51.
Etzioni, A. 1968. Basic human needs, alienation, and inauthenticity. *American Sociological Review* 33:870–85.
———. 1970. *Demonstration Democracy.* New York: Gordon and Breach.
———. 1975. *A Comparative Analysis of Complex Organizations.* New York: Free Press.
———. 1977. Basic characterological needs and changing social systems. In *We, the People: American Character and Social Change,* ed. G. J. DiRenzo, pp. 272–84. Westport, Conn.: Greenwood Press.
Fagen, R. R. 1966. *Politics and Communication.* Boston: Little, Brown.
Fairchild, H. H., and Gurin, P. 1978. Traditions in the social-psychological analysis of race relations. *American Behavioral Scientist* 21:757–78.
Fanon, F. 1965. *The Wretched of the Earth.* New York: Grove Press.
Fararo, T. J. 1968. Theory of status. *General Systems* 13:177–88.
———. 1973. An expectation-states model. In *Introduction of Mathematical Sociology.* New York: Wiley.
Farberman, H. A. 1975. A criminogenic market structure: the automobile industry. *Sociological Quarterly* 16:438–57.
Farley, R.; Schuman, H.; Bianchi, S.; Colasanto, D.; and Hatchett, S. 1978. Chocolate city, vanilla suburbs: will the trend toward racially separate communities continue? *Social Science Research* 7:319–44.
Feagin, J. R., and Hahn, H. 1973. *Ghetto Revolts: The Politics of Violence in American Cities.* New York: Macmillan.
Fendrich, J. M. 1967. Perceived reference group support: racial attitudes and overt behavior. *American Sociological Review* 32:960–70.
———. 1976. Black and white activists ten years later: political socialization and adult left-wing politics. *Youth and Society* 8:81–104.
Ferree, M. M. 1974. A woman for president? changing responses: 1958–72. *Public Opinion Quarterly* 38:390–99.
Feshbach, S. 1978. The environment of personality. *American Psychologist* 33: 447–55.

Festinger, L. 1947. The role of group belongingness in a voting situation. *Human Relations* 1:154–80.
———. 1950. Informal social communication. *Psychological Review* 57:271–82.
———. 1954. A theory of social comparison processes. *Human Relations* 7:117–40.
———. 1957. *A Theory of Cognitive Dissonance.* Stanford, Calif.: Stanford University Press.
Festinger, L., and Carlsmith, J. M. 1959. Cognitive consequences of forced compliance. *Journal of Abnormal and Social Psychology* 58:203–10.
Festinger, L., and Thibaut, J. W. 1951. Interpersonal communication in small groups. *Journal of Abnormal Psychology* 46:92–99.
Festinger, L.; Schachter, S.; and Back, K. W. 1950. *Social Pressures in Informal Groups: A Study of Human Factors in Housing.* New York: Harper.
Feuer, L. 1969. *The Conflict of Generations.* New York: Basic Books.
Fiedler, F. E. 1967. *A Theory of Leadership Effectiveness.* New York: McGraw-Hill.
Fields, J. M., and Schuman, H. 1976. Public beliefs about the beliefs of the public. *Public Opinion Quarterly* 40:427–48.
Fillmore, C. 1973. A grammarian looks to sociolinguists. In *Report of the 23rd Annual Round Table Meeting on Linguistics and Language Studies—Sociolinguistics: Current Trends and Prospects,* ed. R. W. Shuy. Washington, D. C.: Georgetown University Press.
Fine, G. A. 1980. Impression management and preadolescent behavior: friends as socializers. In *The Development of Friendship,* ed. S. Asher and J. Gottman. Cambridge: Cambridge University Press.
Fireman, B., and Gamson, W. A. 1979. Utilitarian logic in the resource mobilization perspective. In *The Dynamics of Social Movements,* ed. M. N. Zald and J. D. McCarthy, pp. 8–44. Cambridge, Mass.: Winthrop.
Firey, W. 1948. Informal organization and the theory of schism. *American Sociological Review* 13:15–24.
Firth, J. R., ed. 1968. *Selected Papers of J. R. Firth, 1952–1959.* Bloomington: Indiana University Press.
Firth, J. R., ed. 1967. *Themes in Economic Anthropology.* London, New York: Tavistock Publications.
Fischer, C. S. 1977. *Networks and Places: Social Relations in the Urban Setting.* New York: Free Press.
Fisek, M. H. 1974. A model for the evolution of status structures in task-oriented groups. In *Expectation States Research,* ed. J. Berger, T. L. Conner and M. H. Fisek, chap. 3. Cambridge, Mass.: Winthrop.
Fisek, M. H., and Ofshe, R. 1970. The process of status evolution. *Sociometry* 33:327–45.
Fishbein, M. 1978. Attitudes and behavioral prediction: an overview. In *Major Social Issues: A Multidisciplinary View,* ed. J. M. Yinger and S. J. Cutler, pp. 377–89. New York: Free Press.
Fishbein, M., and Ajzen, I. 1974. Attitudes toward objects as predictors of single and multiple behavioral criteria. *Psychological Review* 81:59–74.
———. 1975. *Belief, Attitude, Intention, and Behavior: An Introduction to Theory and Research.* Reading, Mass.: Addison-Wesley.
———. 1976*a.* Misconceptions about the Fishbein model: reflections on a study by Songer-Nocks. *Journal of Experimental Social Psychology* 12:579–84.
———. 1976*b.* Misconceptions revisited: a final comment. *Journal of Experimental Social Psychology* 12:591–93.
Fishbein, M., and Jaccard, J. 1973. Theoretical and methodological considerations in the prediction of family planning intentions and behavior. *Representative Research in Social Psychology* 4:37–52.
Fisher, R. J., and Andrews, J. J. 1976. The impact of self-selection and reference group identification in a university living-learning center. *Social Behavior and Personality* 4:209–18.
Fishman, M. 1978. Crime waves as ideology. *Social Problems* 25:531–43.
Flacks, R. E. 1967. The liberated generation: an exploration of the roots of student protest. *Journal of Social Issues* 23:52–75.
Flavell, J. 1970. Cognitive changes in adulthood. In *Life-Span Developmental Psy-*

chology: Research and Theory. ed. L. R. Goulet and P. B. Baltes, pp. 248–57. New York: Academic Press.

Fliegel, F. C. 1976. A comparative analysis of the impact of industrialism on traditional values. *Rural Sociology* 41:431–51.

Fogelson, R. 1971. *Violence as Protest.* Garden City and New York: Doubleday.

Foner, A., and Kertzer, D. 1978. Transitions over the life course. *American Journal of Sociology* 83:1081–1104.

Foote, N. N. 1951. Identification as the basis for a theory of motivation. *American Sociological Review* 16:14–21.

Ford, W. S. 1973. Interracial public housing in a border city. *American Journal of Sociology* 78:1426–47.

Form, W. H., and Geschwender, J. A. 1962. Social reference basis of job satisfaction: the case of manual workers. *American Sociological Review* 27:228–37.

Fortune, W. F. 1939. Arapesh warfare. *American Anthropologist* 41:22–41.

Forward, J. R., and Williams, J. R. 1970. Internal-external control and black militancy. *Journal of Social Issues* 26:75–92.

Foschi, M., and Foschi, R. 1976. Evaluations and expectations: a Bayesian model. *Journal of Mathematical Sociology* 4:279–93.

Foster, G. M. 1972. The anatomy of envy. *Current Anthropology* 13:165–202.

Fox, J., and Moore, J. C., Jr. 1979. Status characteristics and expectation states: fitting and testing a recent model. *Social Psychology Quarterly* 42:126–34.

Fox, R. G. 1957. Training for uncertainty. In *Introductory Studies in the Sociology of Medical Education,* ed. R. K. Merton, P. Kendall and G. C. Reeder, pp. 207–41. Cambridge, Mass.: Harvard University Press.

Frake, C. O. 1972. Struck by speech: the Yakan concept of litigation. In *Directions in Sociolinguistics: The Ethnography of Communication,* ed. J. J. Gumperz and D. H. Hymes, pp. 106–29. New York: Holt, Rinehart and Winston.

Frank, R. S. 1973. *Message Dimensions of Television News.* Lexington, Mass.: Heath.

Franks, D., and Marolla, J. 1976. Efficacious action and social approval as interacting dimensions of self-esteem: a tentative formulation through construct validation. *Sociometry* 39:324–41.

Fraser, B. 1975. Hedged performatives. In *Syntax and Semantics, Volume 3: Speech Acts,* ed. P. Cole and J. L. Morgan. New York: Academic Press.

Frazier, E. F. 1940. *Negro Youth at the Crossways: Their Personality Development in the Middle States.* Washington, D. C.: American Council on Education.

Freeman, J. 1973. The origins of the women's liberation movement. *American Journal of Sociology* 78:792–811.

Freese, L. 1974. Conditions for status equality in informal groups. *Sociometry* 37:174–88.

———. 1976. The generalization of specific performance expectations. *Sociometry* 36:194–200.

Freese, L., and Cohen, B. P. 1973. Eliminating status generalization. *Sociometry* 36:177–93.

French, J. R. P., Jr., et al. 1960. Coercive power and forces affecting conformity. *Journal of Abnormal and Social Psychology* 61:93–101.

French, J. R. P., Jr., and Raven, B. 1962. The bases of social power. In *Group Dynamics.* ed. D. Cartwright and A. Zander, 2d ed., pp. 607–23. Evanston, Ill.: Row, Peterson.

Freud, S. 1920. *Totem and Taboo.* Vienna: Internationaler Psychoanalytischer Verlag.

———. 1921. *Mass Psychology and the Analysis of the Ego.* Vienna: Internationaler Psychoanalytischer Verlag.

———. 1922. Certain neurotic mechanisms in jealousy, paranoia and homosexuality. In *Collected Papers.* vol. 2. New York: Basic Books.

———. 1955. Group psychology and the analysis of the ego. In *The Standard Edition of the Complete Psychological Works of Sigmund Freud,* ed. J. Strachey et al., vol. 18. London: The Hogarth Press.

———. 1961. *Civilization and Its Discontents.* New York: Dorsey.

———. 1966. *Complete Introductory Lectures on Psycho-Analysis.* New York: Norton.

Freud, S., and Bullitt, W. C. 1967. *Thomas Woodrow Wilson: A Psychological Study.* Boston: Houghton Mifflin.
Frey, F. W. 1973. Communication and development. In *Handbook of Communication,* ed. I. De S. Pool and W. Schramm. Chicago: Rand McNally.
Frey, W. H. 1979. Central city white flight: racial and nonracial causes. *American Sociological Review* 44:425–48.
Frideres, J. S.; Warner, L. G.; and Albrecht, S. L. 1971. The impact of social constraints on the relationship between attitudes and behavior. *Social Forces* 50: 102–12.
Fried, M. 1969. Deprivation and migration: dilemmas of causal interpretation. In *Behavior in New Environments: Adaptation of Migrant Populations,* ed. E. B. Brody, pp. 23–71. Beverly Hills, Calif.: Sage.
Friedland, W. H. 1964. For a sociological concept of charisma. *Social Forces* 43: 18–26.
Fromm, E. 1941. *Escape from Freedom.* New York: Rinehart.
———. 1961. *Marx's Concept of Man.* New York: Frederick Ungar.
Funkhouser, G. R. 1973. The issues of the sixties: an exploratory study in the dynamics of public opinion. *Public Opinion Quarterly* 37:62–75.
Furby, L. 1978. Possessions: toward a theory of their meaning and function throughout the life cycle. In *Life-Span Development and Behavior.* ed. P. B. Baltes, vol. 1, pp. 298–336. New York: Academic Press.
Gadlin, H. 1977. Private lives and public order. In *Close Relationships.* ed. G. Levinger and H. L. Raush, Amherst, Mass.: University of Massachusetts Press.
Gagnon, J., and Simon, W. 1973. *Sexual Conduct: The Social Sources of Human Sexuality.* Chicago: Aldine.
Galanter, M.; Rabkin, R.; Rabkin, J.; and Deutsch, A. 1979. The "Moonies": a psychological study of conversion and membership in a contemporary religious sect. *American Journal of Psychiatry* 136:165–70.
Galbraith, R. 1979. Sibling spacing and academic achievement: a within-family analysis. Paper presented to the Society for Research on Child Development Meetings, San Francisco.
Gallup, G. 1977. Exercising doubles in two decades. *Sacramento Union,* October 6.
Gamson, W. 1961*a.* A theory of coalition formation. *American Sociological* Review 25:373–82.
———. 1961*b.* An experimental test of a theory of coalition. *American Sociological Review* 26:565–73.
———. 1968. *Power and Discontent.* Homewood, Ill.: Dorsey Press.
———. 1975. *The Strategy of Social Protest.* Homewood, Ill.: Dorsey.
Gamson, W. A., and Fireman, B. 1979. Micro-mobilization. Paper presented at the 74th Annual Meeting of the American Sociological Association, Boston.
Gans, H. 1962. *The Urban Villagers.* New York: Free Press.
———. 1979. *Deciding What's News.* New York: Pantheon.
Gardiner, H. M.; Metcalf, R. C.; and Beebe-Center, J. G. 1937. *Feeling and Emotion: A History of the Theories.* New York: American Book.
Gardner, H. 1978. *The Children of Prosperity.* New York: St. Martin's Press.
Garner, R. A. 1977. *Social Movements in America.* Chicago: Rand McNally.
Garrity, T. F.; Somes, G. W.; and Marx, M. B. 1977. The relationship of personality, life change, psychophysiological strain and health status in a college population. *Social Science and Medicine* 11:257–63.
Gates, M. 1976. Measuring peasant attitudes to modernization: a projective technique. *Current Anthropology* 17:641–65.
Gecas, V. Parental behavior and contextual variations in adolescent self-esteem. *Sociometry* 35:332–45.
———. 1979a. The influence of social class on socialization. In *Contemporary Theories About the Family,* ed. W. R. Burr et al., vol. I. New York: Free Press.
———. 1979*b.* Beyond the "looking-glass self": toward an efficacy-based model of self-esteem. Paper presented at the Annual Meetings of the American Sociological Association, Boston.
Geertz, C. 1960. *The Religion of Java.* Glencoe, Ill.: Free Press.
———. 1973. *The Interpretation of Cultures.* New York: Basic Books.
Geertz, H. 1959. The vocabulary of emotion. *Psychiatry* 22:225–37.

Gehlen, F., and Doeren, S. 1976. Karate instruction as a type of craze. Paper presented at the Annual Meeting of the American Sociological Association.
Gerard, H., and Mathewson, G. 1966. The effects of severity of initiation on liking for a group: a replication. *Journal of Experimental Social Psychology* 2:278–87.
Gerber, C. P., and Stosberg, M. 1969. *Die Massenmedien und Organisation politischer Interessen.* Dusseldorf: Bertelsmann.
Gergen, K. J. 1965. Interaction goals and personalistic feedback as factors affecting the presentation of self. *Journal of Personality and Social Psychology* 1:413–24.
———. 1969. *The Psychology of Behavior Exchange.* Reading, Mass.: Addison-Wesley.
Gergen, K. 1973. Social psychology as history. *Journal of Personality and Social Psychology* 26:309–20.
Gergen, K. (Chief Academic Advisor). 1974. *Social Psychology: Explorations in Understanding.* Del Mar, Calif.: CRM Books.
Gerlach, P., and Hine, V. H. 1970. *People, Power, Change: Movements of Social Transformation.* Indianapolis: Bobbs-Merrill.
Gerth, H. 1940. The Nazi Party: its leadership and composition. *American Journal of Sociology* 45:517–41.
Gerth, H., and Mills, C. W. 1953. *Character and Social Structure: The Psychology of Social Institutions.* New York: Harcourt Brace and World.
———., eds. 1946. *From Max Weber: Essays in Sociology.* New York: Oxford University Press.
Geschwender, J. A. 1967. Continuities in theories of status consistency and cognitive dissonance. *Social Forces* 46:160–71.
Gewirtz, J. L. 1969. Mechanisms of social learning: some roles of stimulation and behavior in early development. In *Handbook of Socialization Theory and Research,* ed. D. Goslin, pp. 157–212. Chicago: Rand McNally.
Gibbs, J. P. 1975. *Crime, Punishment, and Deterrence.* New York: Elsevier.
———. 1977. Social control, deterrence, and perspectives on social order. *Social Forces* 56:408–23.
Gibbs, J. P., and Erickson, M. L. 1975. Major developments in the sociological study of deviance. *Annual Review of Sociology* 1:21–42.
Giddings, F. H. 1896. *The Principles of Sociology.* New York: Macmillan.
Gieber, W. 1960. Two communicators of the news: a study of roles of sources and reporters. *Social Forces* 39:76–83.
Gilford, D. M., and Snyder, J. 1977. *Women and Minority Ph.D.'s in the 1970s: A Data Book.* Washington, D. C.: National Academy of Sciences.
Gladwin, I. 1967. *Poverty U.S.A.* Boston: Little, Brown.
Glaser, B. G., ed. 1968. *Organizational Careers.* Chicago: Aldine.
Glaser, B. G., and Strauss, A. L. 1964. Awareness contexts and social interaction. *American Sociological Review* 29:669–79.
———. 1965. *Awareness of Dying.* Chicago: Aldine.
———. 1967. *The Discovery of Grounded Theory.* Chicago: Aldine.
———. 1968. *Time for Dying.* Chicago: Aldine.
———. 1971. *Status Passage: A Formal Theory.* Chicago: Aldine.
Gleason, J. B., and Weintraub, S. 1976. The acquisition of routines in child language. *Language in Society* 5:129–36.
Glick, I. O.; Weiss, R. S.; and Parkes, C. M. 1974. *The First Year of Bereavement.* New York: Wiley Interscience.
Glick, P. C. 1977. Updating the life cycle of the family. *Journal of Marriage and the Family* 39:5–13.
———. 1978. Social change in the American family. *Social Welfare Reform, 1977.* New York: Columbia University Press.
Glidewell, J. C. et al. 1966. Socialization and social structure in the classroom. In *Review of Child Development Research,* ed. M. L. Hoffman and L. W. Hoffman, vol. 2. pp. 221–56. New York: Russell Sage Foundation.
Glock, C. Y. 1964. The role of deprivation in the origin and evolution of religious groups. In *Religious and Social Conflict,* ed. R. Lee and M. Martin, pp. 24–36. New York: Oxford University Press.
———. 1973. On the origins and evolution of religious groups. In *Religion in Sociological Perspective,* ed. C. Glock, pp. 207–20. Belmont, Calif.: Wadsworth.

Gluckstern, N. B., and Packard, R. W. 1977. The internal-external change-agent team: bringing change to a "close institution." *Journal of Applied Behavioral Science* 13:41–52.

Goffman, E. 1955. On face-work: an analysis of ritual elements in social interaction. *Psychiatry: Journal for the Study of Interpersonal Processes* 18:213–31.

———. 1956. Embarrassment and social organization. *American Journal of Sociology* 62:264–71.

———. 1959. *The Presentation of Self in Everyday Life.* Garden City and New York: Doubleday/Anchor.

———. 1961*a*. *Asylums: Essays on the Social Situation of Mental Patients and Other Inmates.* Garden City and New York: Doubleday/Anchor.

———. 1961*b*. *Encounters.* Indianapolis: Bobbs-Merrill.

———. 1963*a*. *Stigma: Notes on the Management of Spoiled Identity.* Englewood Cliffs, N. J.: Prentice-Hall.

———. 1963*b*. *Behavior in Public Places.* Glencoe, Ill.: Free Press.

———. 1967. *Interaction Ritual: Essays on Face-to-Face Behavior.* Garden City and New York: Doubleday/Anchor.

———. 1969. *Strategic Interaction.* New York: Ballantine Books.

———. 1971. *Relations in Public: Microstudies of the Public Order.* New York: Basic Books.

———. 1974. *Frame Analysis: An Essay on the Organization of Experience.* New York: Harper and Row.

Goldberg, S. 1977. Social competence in infancy: a model of parent-infant interaction. *Merrill-Palmer Quarterly* 23:163–67.

Goldberger, A. S. 1965. Discerning a causal pattern among data on voting behavior. *American Political Science Review* 60:913–22.

Goldhamer, H. 1950. Public opinion and personality. *American Journal of Sociology* 55:346–54.

Goldhamer, H., and Marshall, A. 1953. *Psychosis and Civilization.* Glencoe, Ill.: Free Press.

Golding, W. 1959. *Lord of the Flies.* New York: Putnam.

Goode, W. J. 1959. The theoretical importance of love. *American Sociological Review* 24:38–47.

———. 1960*a*. A theory of role strain. *American Sociological Review* 25:483–96.

———. 1960*b*. Norm commitment and conformity to role-status obligations. *American Journal of Sociology* 66:246–58.

———. 1973. A theory of role strain. In *Explorations in Social Theory,* ed. W. J. Goode, pp. 97–120. New York: Oxford University Press.

Goodman, F. 1974. Disturbances in the Apostolic Church. In *Trance, Healing and Hallucination,* ed. F. D. Goodman, J. Henry, and E. Pressel. New York: Wiley.

Goodman, P. S. 1974. An examination of referents used in the evaluation of pay. *Organizational Behavior and Human Performance* 12:170–95.

Goodwin, L. 1972. *Do the Poor Want to Work?* Washington, D. C.: Brookings Institution.

Goody, E. N. 1978*a*. Towards a theory of questions. In *Questions and Politeness: Strategies in Social Interaction,* ed. E. N. Goody, pp. 17–43. Cambridge: Cambridge University Press.

———, ed. 1978*b*. *Questions and Politeness: Strategies in Social Interaction.* Cambridge: Cambridge University Press.

Gordon, C. 1968. Self-conceptions: configurations of content. In *The Self in Social Interaction,* ed. C. Gordon and K. J. Gergen, pp. 115–36. New York: Wiley.

———. 1972. Role and value development across the life cycle. In *Role,* ed. J. A. Jackson, pp. 65–105. London: Cambridge Press.

———. 1974. A person-conceptions analytic system for the General Inquirer. Mimeographed.

Gordon, D. F. 1974. The Jesus people: an identity synthesis. *Urban Life and Culture* 3:159–78.

Gordon, D., and Lakoff, G. 1975. Conversational postulates. *Syntax and Semantics Volume 3: Speech Acts,* ed. P. Cole and J. L. Morgan, pp. 83–106. New York: Academic Press.

Gordon, M. M. 1978. *Human Nature, Class and Ethnicity.* New York: Oxford University Press.

Gordon, R. E.; Hamilton, S.; Weber, S.; Gordon, K.; and Plutzky, M. 1976. Psychiatric problems of the 1970's. *International Journal of Social Psychiatry* 22:253–64.

Gordon, W. C., and Babchuk, N. 1959. A typology of voluntary associations. *American Sociological Review* 24:22–29.

Gordon, W. H. 1962. Communist rectification programs and delinquency rehabilitation programs: a parallel? *American Sociological Review* 27:256.

Gorer, G. 1943. Themes in Japanese culture. Translated by *The New York Academy of Sciences* 5:106–24.

———. 1950. The concept of national character. *Science News* 18:105–23.

———. 1965. *Death, Grief, and Mourning.* Garden City and New York: Doubleday-/Anchor.

Gorer, G., and Rickman, J. 1949. *The People of Great Russia.* London: Cresset Press.

Gormley, W. T., Jr. 1975. Newspaper agendas and political elites. *Journalism Quarterly* 52:304–308.

Goslin, D. A. 1969. *Handbook of Socialization Theory and Research.* Chicago: Rand McNally.

Gould, R. M. 1972. The phases of adult life: a study in developmental psychology. *American Journal of Sociology* 129:521–31.

Gouldner, A. W. 1968. The sociologist as partisan. *American Sociologist* 3:103–106.

Goulet, L. R., and Baltes, P. B., eds. 1970. *Life Span Developmental Psychology.* New York: Academic Press.

Gove, W. R., ed. 1975. *The Labelling of Deviance.* New York: Wiley.

Granovetter, M. S. 1973. The strength of weak ties. *American Journal of Sociology* 78:1360–79.

Grant, G., and Riesman, D. 1978. *The Perpetual Dream: Reform and Experiment in the American College.* Chicago: University of Chicago Press.

Grebler, L. et al. 1970. *The Mexican American People.* New York: Free Press.

Greeley, A. M., and Sheatsley, P. B. 1971. Attitudes toward racial integration. *Scientific American* 225:13–19.

Green, G. W. 1975. How to get people to do things with words: the whimperative question. In *Syntax and Semantics Volume 3: Speech Acts,* ed. P. Cole and J. L. Morgan, pp. 107–42. New York: Academic Press.

Green, J. A. 1972. Attitudinal and situational determinants of intended behavior toward blacks. *Journal of Personality and Social Psychology* 22:13–17.

Greenberg, B. S., and Parker, E. B., eds. 1965. *The Kennedy Assassination and the American Public School: Social Communication in Crisis.* Stanford, Calif.: Stanford University Press.

Greenberg, B. S., and Reeves, B. 1976. Children and the perceived reality of television. *Journal of Social Issues* 32:86–97.

Greenfield, S. M. 1965. Love and marriage in modern America. *Sociological Quarterly* 6:361–77.

Greenstein, F. 1967. The impact of personality on politics: an attempt to clear away the underbrush. *American Political Science Review* 61:629–41.

Grice, H. P. 1975. Logic and conversation. In *Syntax and Semantics Volume 3: Speech Acts,* ed. P. Cole and J. L. Morgan, pp. 41–58. New York: Academic Press.

Griffitt, W. 1974. Attitude similarity and attraction. In *Foundations of Interpersonal Attraction,* ed. T. Huston. New York: Academic Press.

Grimshaw, A. 1960. Urban racial violence in the United States. *American Journal of Sociology* 66:109–19.

———. 1966. Directions for research in sociolinguistics: suggestions of a non-linguist sociologist. *Sociological Inquiry* 36:319–32.

———. 1967. Review article of Joyce O. Hertzler, *A Sociology of Language. Harvard Educational Review* 37:302–08.

———. 1969. Sociolinguistics and the sociologist. *The American Sociologist* 4:312–21.

———. 1973*a.* Rules in linguistic, social, and sociolinguistic systems and possibilities for a unified theory. In *23rd Annual Round Table Monograph Series on Language and Linguistics (1972),* ed. R. W. Shay, pp. 289–312. Washington, D. C.: Georgetown University Press.

———. 1973*b.* Language in Society I, review of Basil Bernstein and associates and of William Labov. *Contemporary Sociology* 2:575–85.

———. 1973*c*. Sociolinguistics. In *Handbook of Communication,* ed. W. Schramm et al., pp. 49–92. Chicago: Rand McNally.

———. 1973*d*. Review article of John K. Gumperz, *Language in Social Groups. Language Sciences* 27:29–37.

———. 1974. Data and data use in an analysis of communicative events. In *Explorations in the Ethnography of Speaking,* ed. R. Bauman and J. Sherzer, pp. 419–24. Cambridge: Cambridge University Press.

———. 1976. Polity, class, school and talk: the sociology of Basil Bernstein. A review article of B. Bernstein, *Class, Codes and Control 3: Towards a Theory of Educational Transmissions. Theory and Society* 3:553–72.

———. 1979. What's been done—when all's been said. Review symposium on W. Labov and D. Fanshel, *Therapeutic Discourse: Psychotherapy as Conversation. Contemporary Sociology* 8:70–76.

———. 1980*a*. Social interactional and sociolinguistic rules. *Social Forces* 58:789–810.

———. 1980*b*. Selection and labeling of INSTRUMENTALITIES of verbal manipulation. *Discourse Processes* 3:203–29.

———. 1980*c*. Mishearings, misunderstandings, and other nonsuccesses in talk. *Sociological Inquiry* 50. In press.

———. 1980*d*. INSTRUMENTALITY selection in naturally occurring conversation: a research agenda. In *Conversation, Speech and Discourse,* ed. P. Werth. London: Croom Helm. In press.

Grimshaw, A. D., and Holden, L. 1976. Postchildhood modifications of linguistic and social competence. *Items* 30:33–42.

Grinker, R. J., and Speigel, J. P. 1945. *Men Under Stress.* Philadelphia: Blakiston.

Gross, N.; Mason, W.; and McEachern, A. 1958. *Explorations in Role Analysis: Studies of the School Superintendent Role.* New York: Wiley.

Grossman, M. B., and Rourke, F. E. 1976. Media and the presidency: an exchange analysis. *Political Science Quarterly* 91:455–70.

Grotevant, H. D.; Scarr, S.; and Weinberg, R. A. 1977. Intellectual development in family constellations with adopted and natural children: a test of the Zajonc and Markus model. *Child Development* 48:1699–1703.

Gruder, C. L. 1977. Choice of comparison persons in evaluating oneself. In *Social Comparison Processes,* ed. J. M. Suls and R. L. Miller. New York: Wiley.

Gubrium, J. F., and Buckholdt, D. B. 1977. *Toward Maturity: The Social Processing of Human Development.* San Francisco: Jossey-Bass.

Gumperz, J. J. *Conversational Strategies.* New York: Academic Press., forthcoming.

Gumperz, J. J., and Hymes, D. H. 1964. The ethnography of communication. *American Anthropologist* 66(6). Special publication.

———. 1972. *Directions in Sociolinguistics: The Ethnography of Communication.* New York: Holt, Rinehart and Winston.

Gurin, P., and Epps, E. G. 1975. *Black Consciousness, Identity and Achievement: A Study of Students in Historically Black Colleges.* New York: Wiley.

Gurin, P. et al. 1978. Personal and ideological aspects of internal and external control. *Social Psychology* 41:275–96.

Gurr, T. R. 1968. A causal model of civil strife: a comparative analysis using new indices. *American Political Science Review* 62:1104–24.

———. 1970. *Why Men Rebel.* Princeton, N.J.: Princeton University Press.

Gusfield, J. R. 1957. The problem of generations in an organizational structure. *Social Forces* 35:323–30.

———. 1963. *Symbolic Crusade: Status Politics and the American Temperance Movement.* Urbana, Ill.: University of Illinois Press.

———. 1966. Functional areas of leadership in social movements. *Sociological Quarterly* 7:137–56.

Guthrie, G. M. 1977. A social-psychological analysis of modernization in the Philippines. *Journal of Cross-Cultural Psychology* 8:177–206.

Gutmann, D. 1973. The new mythologies and premature aging in the youth culture. *Social Research* 40:248–68.

Guttman, L. 1950. The problem of attitude and opinion measurement. In *Measurement and Prediction,* ed. S. A. Stouffer et al., pp. 46–59. Princeton, N. J.: Princeton University Press.

Haan, N. M.; Smith, B.; and Block, J. 1968. Moral reasoning of young adults: Political-social behavior, family background, and personality correlates. *Journal of Personality and Social Psychology* 10:183–201.

Hackenberg, R. A., and Gallagher, M. M. 1972. The costs of cultural change: accidental injury and modernization. *Human Organization* 31:211–26.

Hagen, E. E. 1963. How economic growth begins: a theory of social change. *Journal of Social Issues* 19:20–34.

Haight, T. R., and Brody, R. A. 1977. The mass media and presidential popularity: presidential broadcasting and news in the Nixon administration. *Communication Research* 4:41–60.

Hain, P. L. 1974. Age, ambition, and political careers: the middle-age crisis. *Western Political Quarterly* 27:265–74.

Hakmiller, K. L. 1966. Threat as a determinant of downward comparison. *Journal of Experimental Social Psychology,* supplement 1.

Halbwachs, M. 1925. *Les Cadres sociaux de la Memoire.* Paris: Felix Alcan.

Hales, S. 1980. A Developmental Model of Self-Esteem Based on Competence and Moral Behavior: A Longitudinal and Cross-National Analysis. Unpublished doctoral dissertation, University of California, Berkeley.

Hall, C. S., and Lindzey, G. 1978. *Theories of Personality.* 3d edition. New York: Wiley.

Hall, E. T. 1966. *The Hidden Dimension.* Garden City and New York: Doubleday/Anchor.

Hall, P. 1972. A symbolic interactionist analysis of politics. *Sociological Inquiry* 42:35–75.

Halliday, M. A. K. 1967. *Intonation and Grammar in British English.* The Hague: Mouton.

———. 1973*a*. The functional basis of language. In *Class, Codes and Control,* ed. B. Bernstein, vol. 2, pp. 343–66. London: Routledge and Kegan Paul.

———. 1973*b*. *Explorations in the Functions of Language.* London: Edward Arnold.

———. 1975. *Learning How to Mean: Explorations in the Development of Language.* London: Edward Arnold.

Halliday, M. A. K., and Hasan, R. 1976. *Cohesion in English.* London: Longmans Group, Ltd.

Halloran, J. D.; Elliott, P.; and Murdock, G. 1970. *Demonstrations and Communication: A Case Study.* Harmondsworth, England: Penguin.

Hamblin, R. L.; Jacobsen, R. B.; and Miller, J. L. 1973. *A Mathematical Theory of Social Change.* New York: Wiley.

Hamilton, G. 1978. The structural sources of adventurism. *American Journal of Sociology* 83:1466–90.

Hampden-Turner, C. 1974. *Radical Man.* Cambridge, Mass.: Schenkman.

Handel, W. 1979. Normative expectations and the emergence of meaning as solutions to problems: convergence of structural and interactionist views. *American Journal of Sociology* 84:855–81.

Hannerz, U. 1969. *Soulside: Inquiries into Ghetto Culture and Community.* New York: Columbia University Press.

Harary, R.; Norman, R.; and Cartwright, D. 1965. *Structural Models.* New York: Wiley.

Harman, G. H. 1971 [1968]. Three levels of meaning. In *Semantics: An Interdisciplinary Reader in Philosophy, Linguistics and Psychology,* ed. D. D. Steinberg and A. Jakobovits. Cambridge: Cambridge University Press.

Harmond, R. 1972. Progress and flight: an interpretation of the American cycle craze of the 1980s. *Journal of Social History* 5:235–57.

Harris, H., and Lewis, P. M. 1948. The press, public behavior, and public opinion. *Public Opinion Quarterly* 12:220–26.

Harris, J. C. 1949. *The Essential Uncle Remus.* London: Jonathan Cape.

Harrison, M. I. 1974. Sources of recruitment to Catholic Pentecostalism. *Journal for the Scientific Study of Religion* 13:49–64.

Hartley, E. L. 1946. *Problems in Prejudice.* New York: King's Crown Press.

Harvey, J. H.; Ickes, W. J.; and Kidd, R. F., eds. 1976, 1978. *New Directions in Attribution Research,* vols. 1 and 2. Hillsdale, N.J.: Erlbaum.

Harvey, J. H., and Smith, W. P. 1977. *Social Psychology: An Attributional Approach.* St. Louis: C. V. Mosby.

Harvey, O. J. 1953. An experimental approach to the study of status reactions in small groups. *American Sociological Review* 18:357–67.

Harvey, O. J., and Consalvi, C. 1960. Status and conformity to pressure in informal groups. *Journal of Abnormal and Social Psychology* 60:182–87.

Hasan, R. 1973. Code, register, and social dialect. In *Class, Codes and Control,* ed. B. Bernstein. vol. 2. London: Routledge and Kegan Paul.

Hearn, L. 1894. *Glimpses of Unfamiliar Japan.* Boston: Houghton Mifflin.

Heath, A. 1968. Economic theory and sociology: a critique of Blau's exchange and power in social life. *Sociology* 2:273–92.

———. 1976. *Rational Choice and Social Exchange.* Cambridge: Cambridge University Press.

Heath, S. B. 1977. Language and politics in the United States. In *Linguistics and Anthropology,* ed. Saville-Troike, pp. 267–96. Washington, D.C.: Georgetown University School of Languages and Linguistics.

Heberle, R. 1951. *Social Movements: An Introduction to Political Sociology.* New York: Appleton-Century-Crofts.

Heberlein, T. A., and Black, J. S. 1976. Attitudinal specificity and the prediction of behavior in a field setting. *Journal of Personality and Social Psychology* 33: 474–79.

Heider, F. 1958. *The Psychology of Interpersonal Relations.* New York: Wiley.

Heirich, M. 1971. *The Spiral of Conflict: Berkeley, 1964.* New York: Columbia University Press.

———. 1977. Change of heart: a test of some widely held theories about religious conversion. *American Journal of Sociology* 83:653–80.

Heise, D. 1977. Social action as the control of affect. *Behavioral Science* 22:163–77.

———. 1979. *Understanding Events: Affect and the Construction of Social Experience.* Rose Monograph Series. Cambridge: Cambridge University Press.

Heiss, J. 1962. Degree of intimacy and male-female interaction. *Sociometry* 25: 197–208.

———. 1981. *The Social Psychology of Interaction.* Englewood Cliffs, N.J.: Prentice-Hall.

Hendrick, C. et al. 1971. Race versus belief similarity as determinants of attraction. *Journal of Personality and Social Psychology* 17:250–58.

Henley, N. 1977. *Body Politics: Power, Sex, and Nonverbal Communication.* Englewood Cliffs, N.J.: Prentice-Hall.

Henry, A. F., and Short, J. F. 1954. *Suicide and Homicide.* New York: Free Press.

Herman, S. N. 1970. *American Students in Israel.* Ithaca, N.Y.: Cornell University Press.

Hetherington, E. M.; Cox, M.; and Cox, R. 1976. Divorced fathers. *The Family Coordinator* 25:417–28.

———. 1978. The aftermath of divorce. In *Mother-Child, Father-Child Relations,* ed. J. H. Stevens and M. Mathews. Washington, D.C.: National Association for the Education of Young Children.

Hewitt, J. P. 1976. *Self and Society.* Boston: Allyn and Bacon.

———. 1979. *Self and Society.* 2d ed. Boston: Allyn and Bacon.

Hewitt, J. P., and Stokes, R. 1975. Disclaimers. *American Sociological Review* 40: 1–11.

Hilgard, E. R.; Sait, E. M.; and Margaret, G. A. 1940. Level of aspiration as affected by relative standing in an experimental social group. *Journal of Experimental Psychology* 27:411–21.

Hill, C. A. 1977. A review of the language deficit position: some sociolinguistic and psycholinguistic perspectives. *IRCD Bulletin* 12:1–13.

Hill, C. A., and Varenne, H. forthcoming. *Le langage familial et l' éducation scolaire: le modéle sociolinguistique des codes restreints et élabores. Revue Francaise de Pédagogie.* (Mimeo available in English.)

Hill, C. T.; Rubin, A.; and Peplau, A. 1976. Breakups before marriage: the end of 103 affairs. *Journal of Social Issues* 32:147–68.

Hill, R. 1970. *Family Development in Three Generations.* Cambridge, Mass.: Schenkman.

Hill, R., and Mattessich, P. 1979. Family development theory and life-span development. In *Life-Span Development and Behavior,* ed. P. B. Baltes and O. G. Brim, Jr., vol. 2, pp. 161–204. New York: Academic Press.
Hill, R.; Stycos, J. M.; and Back, K. 1959. *The Family and Population Control.* Chapel Hill: University of North Carolina Press.
Hiller, H. H. 1975. A reconceptualization of the dynamics of social movement development. *Pacific Sociological Review* 18:342–60.
Hillman, J. 1960. *Emotion.* London: Routledge and Kegan Paul.
Hindelang, M. J. et al. 1979. Correlates of delinquency: the illusion of discrepancy between self-report and official measures. *American Sociological Review* 44: 995–1014.
Hippler, A. E. 1973. The Athabaascans of interior Alaska: a culture and personality perspective. *American Anthropologist* 75:1529–41.
Hirsch, P. M. 1980. Critique of cultural indicators. *Communication Research* 7. In press.
Hirschi, T. 1969. *Causes of Delinquency.* Berkeley: University of California Press.
Hobsbawm, E. J. 1965. *Primitive Rebels.* New York: W. W. Norton.
Hochschild, A. R. 1975*a*. The sociology of feeling and emotion. In *Another Voice,* ed. M. Milman and R. Kanter, pp. 280–307. Garden City and New York: Doubleday.
———. 1975*b*. Attending to, codifying, and managing feelings. Paper presented at the annual meeting of the American Sociological Association, San Francisco.
———. 1979. Emotion work, feeling rules, and social structure. *American Journal of Sociology* 85:551–75.
Hodge, R. W.; Siegel, P. M.; and Rossi, P. H. 1964. Occupational prestige in the U. S., 1925–1963. *American Journal of Sociology* 70:286–302.
Hodge, R. W., and Treiman, D. R. 1966. Occupational mobility and attitudes toward Negroes. *American Sociological Review* 31:93–102.
Hoffer, E. 1951. *The True Believer.* New York: Harper and Row.
Hoffman, L. W. 1977. Changes in family roles, socialization, and sex differences. *American Psychologist* 32:644–57.
Hoffman, M. L. 1976. Empathy, role taking, guilt, and development of altruistic motives. In *Moral Development and Behavior,* ed. T. Lickona. New York: Holt, Rinehart, and Winston.
———. 1977. Moral development. In *Annual Review of Psychology.* Palo Alto, Calif.: Annual Review Publishers.
———. 1978. Empathy. *Nebraska Symposium on Motivation 26.* Lincoln: University of Nebraska.
———. 1979. Development of moral thought, feeling, and behavior. *American Psychologist* 34:958–66.
Hoge, D. R., and Bender, I. E. 1974. Factors influencing change among college graduates in adult life. *Journal of Personality and Social Psychology* 29:572–85.
Holland, J. L. 1961. Creative and academic performance among talented adolescents. *Journal of Educational Psychology* 52.
Hollander, E. P. 1958. Conformity, status, and idiosyncrasy credit. *Psychological Review* 65:111–17.
Hollander, E. P., and Julian, J. W. 1970. Studies in leader legitimacy, influence, and innovation. In *Advances in Experimental Social Psychology,* ed. L. Berkowitz, vol. 5. New York: Academic Press.
Hollingshead, A. B. 1950. Cultural factors in the selection of marriage mates. *American Sociological Review* 15:610–627.
Hollingshead, A. B.; Ellis, R. A.; and Kirby, E. C. 1954. Social mobility and mental illness. *American Sociological Review* 19:577–85.
Holmes, J. H., and Rahe, R. H. 1967. The social readjustment scale. *Journal of Psychosomatic Research* 11:213–28.
Holz, J. R., and Wright, C. R. 1979. Sociology of mass communications. *Annual Review of Sociology* 5:193–217.
Homans, G. C. 1950. *The Human Group.* New York: Harcourt Brace and World.
———. 1958. Social behavior as exchange. *American Journal of Sociology* 62: 597–606.

———. 1961. *Social Behavior: Its Elementary Forms.* New York: Harcourt Brace and World.

———. 1974. *Social Behavior: Its Elementary Forms.* rev. ed. New York: Harcourt Brace, Jovanovich.

———. 1976. Commentary. In L. Berkowitz and E. Walster, eds., *Advances in Experimental Social Psychology.* New York: Academic Press. pp. 231–44.

Homans, G. C., and Schneider, D. M. 1955. *Marriage, Authority, and Final Causes: A Study of Unilateral Crosscousin Marriage.* Glencoe, Ill.: Free Press.

Hopper, R. D. 1950. The revolutionary process. *Social Forces* 28:270–79.

Horn, M. 1968. *The Second Skin.* Boston: Houghton Mifflin.

Horowitz, M., and Perlmutter, H. 1953. The concept of social groups. *American Journal of Social Psychology* 37:69–95.

Horton, D. 1957. The dialogue of courtship in popular songs. *American Journal of Sociology* 62:569–78.

Horton, D., and Wohl, R. R. 1956. Mass communications and para-social interaction. *Psychiatry* 19:215–29.

Hostetler, J. A. 1968. *Amish Society.* Baltimore: The Johns Hopkins Press.

House, J. S. 1977. The three faces of social psychology. *Sociometry* 40:161–77.

———. 1980. *Occupational Stress and the Physical and Mental Health of Factory Workers.* Report on NIMH Grant No. 1R02MH28902. Research Report Series: Institute for Social Research, University of Michigan, Ann Arbor.

House, J. S., and Mason, W. M. 1975. Political alienation in America. *American Sociological Review* 40:123–47.

Houseknecht, S. K. 1977. Reference group support for voluntary childlessness: evidence for conformity. *Journal of Marriage and the Family* 39:285–92.

Hovland, C. I.; Janis, I. L.; and Kelley, H. H. 1953. *Communication and Persuasion: Psychological Studies of Opinion Change.* New Haven: Yale University Press.

Hovland, C. I. et al. 1949. *Experiments in Mass Communications.* Princeton, N.J.: Princeton University Press.

Howell, R. W. 1965. Linguistic status markers in Korean. The *Kroeber Anthropological Society Papers* 55:91–97.

Hsu, F. L. K. 1977. Individual fulfillment, social stability, and cultural progress. In *We, the People: American Character and Social Change,* ed. G. J. DiRenzo, pp. 95–114. Westport, Conn.: Greenwood Press.

Hubbard, J. C.; DeFleur, M. L.; and DeFleur, L. B. 1975. Mass media influences on public conceptions of social problems. *Social Problems* 23:22–24.

Huber, J. 1973. Symbolic interaction as a pragmatic perspective: the bias of emergent theory. *American Sociological Review* 38:278–84.

Hughes, E. C. 1945. Dilemmas and contradictions of status. *American Journal of Sociology* 50:353–59.

Hultsch, D. F., and Plemons, J. K. 1979. Life events and life-span development. In *Life-Span Development and Behavior,* ed. P. B. Baltes and O. G. Brim, Jr., vol. 2, pp. 1–66. New York: Academic Press.

Hunt, M. 1959. *The Natural History of Love.* New York: Grove Press.

Hunter, E. 1956. *Brainwashing.* New York: Farrar, Straus, and Cudahy.

Huntington, M. J. 1957. The development of a professional self-image. In *The Student Physician,* ed. R. K. Merton, G. G. Reader, and P. Kendall. Cambridge, Mass.: Harvard University Press.

Huston, T. L. 1973. A decision-making model of the initiation of heterosexual pair relationships. Paper presented at the National Council on Family Relations, Toronto, October.

Huston-Stein, A., and Higgins-Trenk, A. 1978. Development of females from childhood through adulthood: career and feminine role orientations. In *Life-Span Development and Behavior,* ed. P. B. Baltes, vol. 1, pp. 257–296. New York: Academic Press.

Hyman, H. H. 1942. The Psychology of Status. *Archives of Psychology,* no. 269.

———. 1960. Reflections on reference groups. *Public Opinion Quarterly* 24:383–96.

———. 1969. Social psychology and race relations. In *Race and the Social Sciences,* ed. I. Katz and P. Gurin, pp. 3–48. New York: Basic Books.

———. 1972. Dimensions of social-psychological change in the Negro population.

In *The Human Meaning of Social Change,* ed. A. Campbell and P. E. Converse, pp. 339–90. New York: Russell Sage.
———. 1974. Mass communication and socialization. In *Mass Communication Research,* ed. W. P. Davison and F.T.C. Yu. New York: Praeger.
Hyman, H. H., and Sheatsley, P. B. 1947. Some reasons why information campaigns fail. *Public Opinion Quarterly* 11:412–23.
———. 1964. Attitudes toward desegregation. *Scientific American* 211:16–23.
Hyman, H. H., and Singer, E., eds. 1968. *Readings in Reference Group Theory and Research.* New York: Free Press.
Hyman, H. H.; Wright, C. R.; and Hopkins, T. K. 1962. *Applications of Methods of Evaluation.* Berkeley: University of California Press.
Hymes, D. H. 1966. Two types of linguistic relativity (with examples from Amerindian ethnography). In *Sociolinguistics: Proceedings of the UCLA Sociolinguistics Conference,* ed. W. Bright. The Hague: Mouton.
———. 1974. *Foundations in Sociolinguistics: An Ethnographic Approach.* Philadelphia: University of Pennsylvania Press.
Inhelder, B., and Piaget, J. 1958. *The Growth of Logical Thinking.* New York: Basic Books.
Inkeles, A. 1955. Social change and social character: the role of parental mediation. *Journal of Social Issues* 11:12–23.
———. 1959. Personality and social structure. In *Sociology Today,* ed. R. K. Merton, L. Broom, and L. S. Cottrell, Jr., pp. 249–76. New York: Basic Books.
———. 1960. Industrial man: the relation of status to experience, perception, and value. *American Journal of Sociology* 66:1–31.
———. 1963. Sociology and psychology. In *Psychology: The Study of a Science,* ed. S. Koch, vol. 6, pp. 317–87. New York: McGraw-Hill.
———. 1968. Society, social structure and child socialization. *Socialization and Society,* ed. J. Clausen, pp. 73–129. Boston: Little, Brown.
———. 1969. Making men modern: on the causes and consequences of individual change in six developing countries. *American Journal of Sociology* 75:208–25.
———. 1969. Social structure and socialization. In *Handbook of Socialization Theory and Research,* ed. D. A. Goslin. Chicago: Rand McNally.
———. 1976. Understanding and misunderstanding individual modernity. In *The Uses of Controversy in Sociology,* ed. L. A. Coser and O. Larsen, pp. 103–20. New York: Free Press.
———. 1978*a*. Continuity and change in the American national character. In *The Third Century: America as a Post-Industrial Society,* ed. S. M. Lipset. Stanford, Calif.: Hoover Institution Press.
———. 1978*b*. National differences in individual modernity. *Comparative Studies in Sociology* 1:47–72.
Inkeles, A., and Levinson, D. 1954. National character: the study of modal personality and social systems. In *Handbook of Social Psychology,* ed. G. Lindzey, pp. 975–1020. Cambridge, Mass.: Addison-Wesley.
———. 1969. National character: the study of modal personality and sociocultural systems. In *The Handbook of Social Psychology,* ed. G. Lindzey and E. Aronson, pp. 418–506. Reading, Mass.: Addison-Wesley.
Inkeles, A., and Smith, D. 1974. *Becoming Modern: Individual Change in Six Developing Countries.* Cambridge, Mass.: Harvard University Press.
Insko, C. A.; Worchel, S.; Folger, R.; and Kutkus, A. 1975. A balance theory interpretation of dissonance. *Psychological Review* 82:169–83.
Inverarity, J. M. 1976. Populism and lynching in Louisiana, 1889–1896: a test of Erikson's theory of the relationship between boundary crises and repressive justice. *American Sociological Review* 41:262–80.
Irvine, J. T. 1974. Strategies of status manipulation in the Wolof greeting. In *Explorations in the Ethnography of Speaking,* ed. R. Bauman and J. Sherzer, pp. 167–91. Cambridge: Cambridge University Press.
Irwin, J. 1977. *Scenes.* Beverley Hills, Calif.: Sage Publications.
———. 1980. *Prisons in Turmoil.* Boston: Little, Brown.
Isichei, E. 1970. *Victorian Quakers.* London: Oxford University Press.
Izard, C. E. 1971. *The Face of Emotion.* New York: Appleton-Century-Crofts.
———. 1977. *Human Emotions.* New York: Plenum.

Jaccard, J., and Davidson, A. R. 1975. A comparison of two models of social behavior: results of a survey sample. *Sociometry* 38:497–517.

Jackman, M. R. 1977. Prejudice, tolerance, and attitudes toward ethnic groups. *Social Science Research* 1:145–69.

Jackson, J. A. 1972. *Role.* London: Cambridge University Press.

Jackson, M.; Peterson, E.; Bull, J.; Monsen, S.; and Richmond, P. 1960. The failure of an incipient social movement. *Pacific Sociological Review* 3:35–40.

Jackson, P. W. 1968. *Life in Classrooms.* New York: Holt, Rinehart, and Winston.

Jacobs, N. 1965. The phantom slasher of Taipei. *Social Problems* 12:318–28.

Jacobsen, G. C. 1975. The impact of broadcast campaigning on electoral outcomes. *Journal of Politics* 37:769–93.

Jacques, J. M., and Chason, K. J. 1977. Self-esteem and low status groups: a changing scene? *Sociological Quarterly* 18:399–412.

James, W. 1950 [1890]. *The Principles of Psychology.* New York: Dover.

———. 1958 [1902]. *The Varieties of Religious Experience.* New York: New American Library.

Janis, I. L. 1958. *Psychological Stress.* London: Chapman and Hall.

Janis, I. L., and Feshbach, S. 1953. Effects of fear arousing communication. *Journal of Abnormal and Social Psychology* 48:78–92.

Janis, I. L., Mahl, G. F., Kagan, J., and Holt, R. R. 1969. *Personality: Dynamics, Development, and Assessment.* New York: Harcourt Brace and World.

Janowitz, M. 1968. *Social Control of Escalated Riots.* Chicago: University of Chicago Press.

———. 1975. Sociological theory and social control. *American Journal of Sociology* 81:82–108.

———. 1978. *The Last Half-Century.* Chicago: University of Chicago Press.

Jasso, G. 1978. On the justice of earnings: a new specification of the justice evaluation function. *American Journal of Sociology* 83:1398–1419.

Jasso, G., and Rossi, P. H. 1977. Distributive justice and earned income. *American Sociological Review* 42:639–51.

Jefferson, G. 1972. Side sequences. In *Studies in Social Interaction,* ed. D. Sudnow, pp. 293–338. New York: Free Press.

———. 1974. Error correction as an interactional resource. *Language in Society* 2:181–99.

Jenkins, J. C. 1977. The dynamics of mobilization: how to repair "resource mobilization" theory. Paper presented at the Annual Meeting of the Society for the Study of Social Problems, Chicago.

Jennings, M., and Niemi, R. G. 1974. *The Political Character of Adolescence.* Princeton, N. J.: Princeton University Press.

———. 1975. Continuity and change in political orientations: a longitudinal study of two generations. *American Political Science Review* 69:1316–35.

Jessor, R. 1979. The perceived environment and the study of adolescent problem behavior. Paper presented at the Symposium on the Situation in Psychological Theory and Research, Stockholm.

Jessor, R., and Jessor, S. 1973. The perceived environment in behavioral science: some conceptual issues and some illustrative data. *American Behavioral Scientist* 16:801–28.

Johnson, D. 1945. The "phantom anesthetist" of Mattoon. *Journal of Abnormal and Social Psychology* 40:175–86.

Johnson, N. R.; Stemler, J. A.; and Hunter, D. 1977. Crowd behavior as risky shift: a laboratory experiment. *Sociometry* 40:183–87.

Johnstone, J. W.; Slawski, E. J.; and Bowman, W. W. 1976. *The News People.* Urbana, Ill.: University of Illinois Press.

Johnstone, J. W. C. 1975. Social change and parent-youth conflict: the problems of generations in English and French Canada. *Youth and Society* 7:3–26.

Jones, E. E. 1964. *Ingratiation: A Social Psychological Analysis.* New York: Appleton-Century-Crofts.

Jones, E. E., and Davis, K. E. 1965. From acts to dispositions. In *Advances in Experimental Social Psychology,* ed. L. Berkowitz, vol. 2. New York: Academic Press.

Jones, E. E.; Davis, K. E.; and Gergen, K. J. 1961. Role-playing variations and their

information value for person perception. *Journal of Abnormal and Social Psychology* 63:302–10.
Jones, E. E.; Kanouse, D. E.; Kelley, H. H., Nisbett; R. E., Valins, S.; and Weiner, B. 1972. *Attribution: Perceiving the Causes of Behavior.* Morristown, N. J.: General Learning Press.
Jones, R. A. 1977. *Self-Fulfilling Prophecies: Social Psychological and Physiological Effects of Expectancies.* New York: Wiley.
Judah, J. 1974. *Hare Krishna and the Counterculture.* New York: Wiley.
Kadushin, C. 1969. The professional self-concept of music students. *American Journal of Sociology* 75:389–404.
Kagan, J. 1964. Acquisition and significance of sex typing and sex role identity. In *Review of Child Development Research,* ed. M. Hoffman and L. Hoffman, 1:-137–65.
Kagan, J. 1977. The child in the family. *Daedalus* (Spring): 33–56.
Kammeyer, K. 1967. Birth order as a research variable. *Social Forces* 46:71–80.
Kandel, D. 1978. Homophily, selection, and socialization in adolescent friendships. *American Journal of Sociology* 84:427–36.
Kanter, R. M. 1968. Commitment and social organization: A study of commitment mechanisms in Utopian communities. *American Sociological Review* 33:499–517.
———. 1972. Commitment and community: communes and utopias. In *Sociological Perspective.* Cambridge, Mass.: Harvard University Press.
———. 1975. Women and the structure of organizations. In *Another Voice,* ed. M. Millman and R. M. Kanter. Garden City and New York: Doubleday/Anchor.
———. 1976. The impact of hierarchical structures on the work behavior of women and men. *Social Problems* 23:413–30.
———. 1977*a. Work and Family in the United States: A Critical Review and Agenda for Research and Policy.* New York: Russell Sage Foundation.
———. 1977*b. Men and Women of the Corporation.* New York: Basic Books, Inc.
Kapferer, B. 1976. Transaction and meaning: direction in the Anthropology of Exchange and Symbolic Behavior. *Commonwealth, Essays in Social Anthropology.* vol. 1. Philadelphia: Institute for the Study of Human Issues.
Kaplan, H. B. 1975. The self-esteem motive and change in self-attitudes. *Journal of Nervous and Mental Disease* 161:265–75.
———. 1976. Self-attitudes and deviant response. *Social Forces* 54:788–801.
———. 1980. *Deviant Behavior in Defense of Self.* New York: Academic Press.
Kaplan, N. 1955. Reference group theory and voting behavior. Columbia University Ph.D. dissertation.
Kardiner, A. 1939. *The Individual and His Society.* New York: Columbia University Press.
———. 1945. *The Psychological Frontiers of Society.* New York: Columbia University Press.
Kardiner, A., and Ovesey, L. 1951. *The Mark of Oppression.* New York: Columbia University Press.
Karsh, B., and Cole, R. E. 1968. Industrialization and the convergence hypothesis: some aspects of contemporary Japan. *Journal of Social Issues.* 24:45–64.
Katz, D. 1960. The functional approach to the study of attitudes. *Public Opinion Quarterly* 24:163–77.
———. 1966. *The Social Psychology of Organizations.* New York: John Wiley.
Katz, D., and Kahn, R. L. 1978. *The Social Psychology of Organizations.* 2d ed. New York: Wiley.
Katz, E. 1977. *Social Research on Broadcasting: Proposals for Further Development.* British Broadcasting Corporation.
Katz, E., and Lazarsfeld, P. F. 1955. *Personal Influence.* Glencoe, Ill.: Free Press.
Katz, I. 1967. Comments on Dr. Pettigrew's paper. *Nebraska Symposium on Motivation* 15:311–15.
Katz, I., and Benjamin, L. 1960. Effects of white authoritarianism in biracial work groups. *Journal of Abnormal and Social Psychology* 61:448–56.
Katz, I., and Cohen, M. 1962. The effects of training Negroes upon cooperative problem solving in bi-racial teams. *Journal of Abnormal and Social Psychology* 64:319–25.

Katz, I.; Goldston, J.; and Benjamin, L. 1958. Behavior and productivity in bi-racial work groups. *Human Relations* 11:123–41.

Kaufman, W. 1957. Status, authoritarianism, and anti-Semitism. *American Journal of Sociology* 62:379–82.

Kay, P. 1977. Language evolution and speech style. In *Sociocultural Dimensions of Language Change,* ed. B. G. Blount and M. Sanches, pp. 21–33. New York: Academic Press.

Kecskemeti, P. 1951. The study of man—prejudice in the catastrophic perspective. *Commentary* 11:286–92.

Keenan, E. O. 1974. Norm-makers, norm-breakers: uses of speech by men and women in a Malagasy community. In *Explorations in the Ethnography of Speaking,* ed. R. Bauman and J. Sherzer, pp. 125–43. Cambridge: Cambridge University Press.

Kelley, H. H. 1952. Two functions of reference groups. In *Readings in Social Psychology,* ed. G. E. Swanson, T. M. Newcomb, and E. L. Hartley, pp. 410–14. rev. ed. New York: Holt, Rinehart and Winston.

———. 1955. Salience of membership and resistance to change of group-anchored attitudes. *Human Relations* 8:275–89.

———. 1967. Attribution theory in social psychology. In *Nebraska Symposium on Motivation,* ed. D. Levine, vol. 15. Lincoln: University of Nebraska Press.

———. 1979. *Personal Relationships: Their Structure and Processes.* Hillsdale, N.J.: Erlbaum.

Kelley, H. H., and Michela, J. L. 1980. Attribution theory and research. *Annual Review of Psychology* 31:457–501.

Kelley, H. H., and Thibaut, J. W. 1978. *Interpersonal Relations: A Theory of Interdependence.* New York: Wiley Interscience.

Kelman, H. C. 1958. Compliance, identification and internalization: three processes of attitude change. *Journal of Conflict Resolution* 2:51–60.

———. 1961. Process of opinion change. *Public Opinion Quarterly* 25:57–78.

———. 1974. Attitudes are alive and well and gainfully employed in the sphere of action. *American Psychologist* 29:310–24.

———. 1978. Attitude and behavior: a social-psychological problem. In *Major Social Issues: A Multidisciplinary View,* ed. J. M. Yinger and S. J. Cutler, pp. 412–20. New York: Free Press.

———. 1980. The role of action in attitude change. In *Nebraska Symposium on Motivation 1979,* ed. M. M. Page. Lincoln: University of Nebraska Press.

Kemper, T. D. 1978*a*. Toward a sociology of emotions. *American Sociologist* 13: 30–41.

———. 1978*b*. *A Social Interactional Theory of Emotions.* New York: Wiley.

Kendon, A. 1977. *Studies in the Behavior of Face-to-Face Interaction.* Lisse, Netherlands: Peter De Ridder Press.

Kendon, A., and Ferber, A. 1973. A description of some human greetings. In *Comparative Behavior and Ecology of Primates,* ed. R. P. Michael and H. H. Crook, pp. 591–668. London: Academic Press.

Kennedy, D. B., and Kerber, A. 1973. *Resocialization: An American Experiment.* New York: Behavioral Publications.

Kenrick, D. T., and Cialdini, R. B. 1977. Romantic attraction: misattribution versus reinforcement explanations. *Journal of Personality and Social Psychology* 35: 381–91.

Kepplinger, H. M., and Roth, H. 1979. Creating a crisis: German mass media and oil supply in 1973–74. *Public Opinion Quarterly* 43:285–96.

Kerckhoff, A. C. 1974. The social context of interpersonal attraction. In *Foundations of Interpersonal Attraction,* ed. T. L. Huston. New York: Academic Press.

———. 1976. The status attainment process: socialization or allocation? *Social Forces* 55:368–81.

Kerckhoff, A. C., and Back, K. W. 1968. *The June Bug: A Study of Hysterical Contagion.* New York: Appleton-Century-Crofts.

Kerckhoff, A. C., and Davis, K. E. 1962. Value consensus and need complementarity in mate selection. *American Sociological Review* 27:295–303.

Kerckhoff, A. C.; Back, K. W.; and Miller, N. 1965. Sociometric patterns in hysterical contagion. *Sociometry* 28:2–15.

Kernberg, O. F. 1979. Regression in organizational leadership. *Psychiatry* 42:24–39.
Kervin, J. B. 1974. Extending expectation states theory: a quantitative model. *Sociometry* 37:349–62.
Kiesler, C. A. 1969. Group pressures and conformity. In *Experimental Social Psychology,* ed. J. Mills, pp. 235–306. London: Macmillan.
Killian, L. 1952. The significance of multiple-group membership in disaster. *American Journal of Sociology* 57:309–14.
———. 1964. Social movements. In *Handbook of Modern Sociology,* ed. R. E. L. Faris, pp. 426–55. Chicago: Rand McNally.
Kinch, J. W. 1963. A formalized theory of the self-concept. *American Journal of Sociology* 68:481–86.
King, G. W. 1975. An analysis of attitudinal and normative variables as predictors of intentions and behavior. *Speech Monographs* 42:237–44.
Kirkpatrick, C. 1955. *The Family as Process and Institution.* New York: Ronald.
———. 1963. *The Family as Process and Institution.* 2d ed. New York: Ronald.
Kitsuse, J. I. 1962. Societal reaction to deviant behavior. *Social Problems* 9:247–56.
———. 1975. The "new conception of deviance" and its critics. In *The Labeling of Deviance,* ed. W. R. Gove, pp. 273–84. New York: Wiley.
Klammer, T. P. 1971. *The Structure of Dialogue Paragraphs in Written English Dramatic and Narrative Discourse.* doctoral dissertation, University of Michigan. Ann Arbor: University of Michigan Microfilms #72–14, 912.
Klapp, O. 1964. *Symbolic Leaders.* Chicago: Aldine.
———. 1969. *Collective Search for Identity.* New York: Holt, Rinehart and Winston.
———. 1971. *Social Types: Process, Structure and Ethos.* San Diego: Aegis Publishing.
Klapper, J. 1960. *The Effects of Mass Communication.* New York: Free Press.
Klineberg, O. 1968. Prejudice: the concept. In *Encyclopedia of the Social Sciences.* ed. D. L. Sills, vol. 12, pp. 439–48. New York: Macmillan and Free Press.
Knight, J.; Friedman, T.; and Sulianti, J. 1965. Epidemic hysteria: a field study. *American Journal of Public Health* 55:858–65.
Kohlberg, L. 1966. A cognitive-developmental analysis of children's sex role concepts and attitudes. In *The Development of Sex Differences,* ed. E. E. Maccoby. Stanford, Calif.: Stanford University Press.
———. 1969. Stage and sequence: the cognitive developmental approach to socialization. In *Handbook of Socialization Theory and Research,* ed. D. Goslin, pp. 347–480. Chicago: Rand McNally.
———. 1973. Continuities in childhood and adult moral development revisited. In *Life-Span Developmental Psychology: Personality and Socialization,* ed. P. B. Baltes and K. W. Schaie, pp. 180–206. New York: Academic Press.
Kohn, M. L. 1969. *Class and Conformity: A Study in Values.* Homewood, Ill.: Dorsey.
———. 1971. Bureaucratic man: a portrait and an interpretation. *American Sociological Review* 36:461–74.
———. 1977. Reassessment, 1977. In *Class and Conformity,* 2d ed. Chicago: University of Chicago Press.
———. 1980. Job complexity and adult personality. In *Themes of Love and Work in Adulthood,* ed. N. Smelser and E. Erikson. Cambridge, Mass.: Harvard University Press.
———. 1980. *Persönlichkeit, Beruf, und Soziale Schichtung: ein Bezugsrahmen.* In *Persönlichkeit, Beruf, und Soziale Schichtung,* ed. K. Luscher. Berlin: Klett-Cotta.
Kohn, M. L., and Schooler, C. 1969. Class, occupation and orientation. *American Sociological Review* 34:659–78.
———. 1973. Occupational experience and psychological functioning: an assessment of reciprocal effects. *American Sociological Review* 38:97–118.
———. 1978. The reciprocal effects of the substantive complexity of work and intellectual flexibility: a longitudinal assessment. *American Journal of Sociology* 84:24–52.
Komarovsky, M. 1964. *Blue Collar Marriage.* New York: Random House.
———. 1976. *Dilemmas of Masculinity: A Study of College Youth.* New York: W. W. Norton.

Korman, A. H. 1966. Self-esteem variable in vocational choice. *Journal of Applied Psychology* 50:479–86.
———. 1969. Self-esteem as a moderator in vocational choice: replications and extensions. *Journal of Applied Psychology* 53:188–92.
Kornhauser, W. 1959. *The Politics of Mass Society.* New York: Free Press.
———. 1962. Social bases of political commitment. In *Human Behavior and Social Processes,* ed. A. M. Rose, pp. 321–39. Boston: Houghton Mifflin.
Kornhauser, W., with the collaboration of O. M. Reid. 1965. *Mental Health of the Industrial Worker: A Detroit Study.* New York: Wiley.
Kothandapani, V. 1971. Validation of feeling, belief and intention to act as three components of attitude and their contribution to prediction of contraceptive behavior. *Journal of Personality and Social Psychology* 19:321–33.
Kourvetaris, G. A. 1971. Professional self-images and political perspectives in the Greek military. *American Sociological Review* 36:1043–57.
Kracauer, S. 1947. Propaganda and the Nazi war film. In *From Caligari to Hitler.* Princeton, N.J.: Princeton University Press. Appendix.
Kraus, S., ed. 1962. *The Great Debates.* Bloomington: Indiana University Press.
Kraus, S., and Davis, D. 1976. *The Effects of Mass Communication on Political Behavior.* University Park, Penn.: Pennsylvania State University Press.
Kreutz, H. 1971. *Einfluss von massenmedien, persoenlicher kontakt and formelle organisation: kritik and weiterführung der these* "two-step flow of communication." In *Sozialisation durch Massenkommunikation,* ed. F. Ronneberger, pp. 172–241. Stuttgart: Ferdinand Enke.
Kris, E., and Leites, N. 1947. Trends in twentieth century propaganda. In *Psychoanalysis and the Social Sciences,* ed. G. Roheim, vol. 1. New York: International University Press.
Kristen, C. 1972. *Nachrichtenangebot und Nachrichtenverwendung.* Dusseldorf: Bertelsmann.
Krugman, H. E. 1952. The appeal of Communism to American middle class intellectuals and trade unionists. *Public Opinion Quarterly* 16:331–55.
Kuhn, M. H. 1964. The reference group reconsidered. *Sociological Quarterly* 5:5–24.
———. 1964. Major trends in symbolic interaction theory in the past twenty-five years. *Sociological Quarterly* 5:61–84.
Kuhn, M. H., and McPartland, T. 1954. An empirical investigation of self-attitudes. *American Sociological Review* 19:68–76.
Labarre, W. 1947. Cultural basis of emotions and gestures. *Journal of Personality* 16:49–68.
———. 1962. *They Shall Take Up Serpents.* Minneapolis: University of Minnesota Press.
Labov, W. 1972*a.* Some principles of linguistic methodology. *Language in Society* 1:97–120.
———. 1972*b.* Academic ignorance and black intelligence. *Atlantic Monthly* 229: 59–67.
———. 1972*c. Language in the Inner City: Studies in the Black English Vernacular.* Philadelphia: University of Pennsylvania Press.
Labov, W., and Fanshel, D. 1977. *Therapeutic Discourse: Psychotherapy as Conversation.* New York: Academic Press.
Laing, R. D. 1964. *Sanity, Madness, and the Family.* New York: Basic Books.
Lakatos, I. 1968. Criticism and the methodology of scientific research programmes. In *Proceedings of the Aristotelian Society* 69:149–86.
———. 1970. Falsification and the methodology of scientific research programmes. In *Criticism and the Growth of Knowledge,* ed. I. Lakatos and A. Musgrave. Cambridge: Cambridge University Press.
Lakoff, R. 1975. *Language and Woman's Place.* New York: Harper and Row.
Lang, G. E., and Lang, K. 1973. Televised hearings: the impact out there. *Columbia Journalism Review* 12:52–57.
Lang, K., and Lang, G. 1959. The mass media and voting. In *American Voting Behavior,* ed. E. Burdick and A. J. Brodbeck, New York: Free Press.
———. 1961. *Collective Dynamics.* New York: Thomas Y. Crowell.
———. 1968*a. Politics and Television.* New York: Quadrangle.
———. 1968*b. Voting and Nonvoting.* Boston: Blaisdell.

Lang, S. 1905. *The Secret of the Totem.* London: Longmans, Green.
Lange, K., and James, W. 1922. *The Emotions.* Baltimore: Williams and Wilkins.
LaPiere, R. T. 1934. Attitudes vs. actions. *Social Forces* 13:230–37.
———. 1938. *Collective Behavior.* New York: McGraw-Hill.
———. 1938. The social significance of measurable attitudes. *American Sociological Review* 3:175–82.
———. 1954. *A Theory of Social Control.* New York: McGraw-Hill.
———. 1969. Comment on Irwin Deutscher's looking backward. *The American Sociologist* 4:41–42.
Laqueur, W. 1977. *Terrorism.* Boston: Little, Brown.
Larsen, O. N. 1964. Social effects of the mass media. In *Handbook of Modern Sociology,* ed. R. E. L. Faris, pp. 349–81. Chicago: Rand McNally.
Lasch, C. 1976. The narcissistic society. *New York Review of Books* 23:5–13.
Laslett, D. P. 1965. *The World We Have Lost.* New York: Scribner.
Lasry, J. C. 1977. Cross-cultural perspectives on mental health and immigrant adaptation. *Social Psychiatry* 12:49–55.
Lasswell, H. D. 1927. *Propaganda Technique in the World War.* New York: Knopf.
———. 1930. *Psychopathology and Politics.* Chicago: University of Chicago Press.
———. 1948. The structure and function of communication in society. In *The Communication of Ideas,* ed. L. Bryson, pp. 37–51. New York: Harper.
———. 1948. *Power and Personality.* New York: Norton.
Lasswell, T. E., and Lasswell, M. E. 1976. I love you but I'm not in love with you. *Journal of Marriage and Family Counseling* (July): 211–24.
Lauer, R. H., and Handel, W. H. 1977. *Social Psychology: The Theory and Application of Symbolic Interactionism.* Boston: Houghton Mifflin.
Lauer, R. H., and Thomas, R. 1976. A comparative analysis of the psychological consequences of change. *Human Relations* 29:239–48.
Laumann, E. O. 1969. Friends of urban men: an assessment of accuracy in reporting their socioeconomic attributes, mutual choice, and attitude agreement. *Sociometry* 32:54–69.
———. 1973. *Bonds of Pluralism: The Form and Substance of Urban Social Networks.* New York: Wiley.
Laumann, E. O., and Pappi, F. U. 1976. *Networks of Collective Action.* New York: Academic Press.
Lawler, E. J. 1975. An experimental study of factors affecting the mobilization of revolutionary coalitions. *Sociometry* 38:163–79.
Lazarsfeld, P. F. 1939. The change of opinion during a political discussion. *Journal of Applied Psychology* 23:131–47.
Lazarsfeld, P. F., Berelson, B., and Gaudet, H. 1948. *The People's Choice.* New York: Columbia University Press.
Lazarsfeld, P. F., and Merton, R. K. 1948. Mass communication, popular taste and organized social action. In *The Communication of Ideas,* ed. L. Bryson, pp. 95–118. New York: Harper.
———. 1954. Friendship as social process: a substantive and methodological analysis. In *Freedom and Control in Modern Society,* ed. M. Berger, T. Abel, and C. H. Page, pp. 18–66. New York: Octagon Books.
Lazarus, R. 1974. Cognitive and coping processes in emotion. In *Cognitive Views of Human Motivation.* ed. B. Weiner. New York: Academic Press.
———. 1975. The self-regulation of emotion. In *Emotions,* ed. L. Levi. New York: Raven Press.
Leahy, P. J. 1976. Mobilization and recruitment of leadership to the anti-abortion movement. Paper presented at the 1976 Annual Meeting of the Southwestern Sociological Association.
Le Bon, G. 1897. *The Crowd.* London: T. Fisher Unwin.
Lecky, P. 1945. *Self-Consistency: A Theory of Personality.* New York: Island Press.
Lee, G. R. 1977. *Family Structure and Interaction.* Philadelphia: J. B. Lippincott.
Lee, J. A. 1973. *The Colours of Love.* Toronto: New Press.
Leibenstein, H. 1976. *Beyond Economic Man.* Cambridge, Mass.: Harvard University Press.
Leik, R. K. 1963. Instrumentality and emotionality in family interaction. *Sociometry* 27:131–45.

Leik, R. K., and Leik, S. A. 1977. Transition to interpersonal commitment. In *Behavioral Theory in Sociology,* ed. R. L. Hamblin and J. H. Kunkel, pp. 299–322. New Brunswick, N.J.: Transaction Books.

Leinhardt, S., ed. 1977. *Social Networks: A Developing Paradigm.* New York: Academic Press.

Leites, N., and Wolf, C., Jr. 1970. *Rebellion and Authority.* Chicago: Markham Publishing Company.

Lemert, E. M. 1951. *Social Pathology.* New York: McGraw-Hill.

———. 1972. *Human Deviance, Social Problems, and Social Control,* 2d ed. Englewood Cliffs, N.J.: Prentice-Hall.

———. 1974. Beyond Mead: the societal reaction to deviance. *Social Problems* 21: 457–68.

Lenneberg, E. H. 1967. *Biological Foundations of Language.* New York: Wiley.

Lenski, G. 1954. Status crystallization: a non-vertical dimension of status. *American Sociological Review* 19:405–13.

Leonard, R. L.; Walsh, W. B.; and Osipow, S. H. 1973. Self-esteem, self-consistency, and second vocational choice. *Journal of Counseling Psychology* 20:91–93.

Lerner, D. 1958. *The Passing of Traditional Society.* Glencoe, Ill.: Free Press.

Lerner, M. J.; Miller, D. T.; and Holmes, J. G. 1975. Deserving versus justice: a contemporary dilemma. In *Advances in Experimental Social Psychology,* ed. L. Berkowitz and E. Walster, vol. 12. New York: Academic Press.

Lerner, R. M., and Ryff, C. D. 1978. Implementation of the life-span view of human development: the sample case of attachment. In *Life-Span Development and Behavior,* ed. P. B. Baltes, vol. 1, pp. 1–44. New York: Academic Press.

Levenson, H., and Miller, J. 1976. Multidimensional locus of control in sociopolitical activists of conservative and liberal ideologies. *Journal of Personality and Social Psychology* 33:199–208.

Leventhal, H. 1970. Findings and theory in the study of fear communications. In *Advances in Experimental Social Psychology,* ed. L. Berkowitz, vol. 5, pp. 119–86. New York: Academic Press.

Leventhal, H. 1974. Emotions. In *Social Psychology,* ed. C. Nemeth, Chicago: Rand McNally.

Levine, R. 1973. *Culture, Behavior, and Personality.* Chicago: Aldine.

Levine, R. A., and Campbell, D. T. 1972. *Ethnocentrism: Theories of Conflict, Ethnic Attitudes and Group Behavior.* New York: Wiley.

Levine, S., and Scotch, N. A. 1970. *Social Stress.* Chicago: Aldine.

Levinger, G. 1976. A social psychological perspective on marital dissolution. *Journal of Social Issues* 32:21–47.

Levinger, G., and Snoek, J. D. 1972. *Attraction in Relationship: A New Look at Interpersonal Attraction.* Morristown, N.J.: General Learning Press.

Levinson, D. J. 1977. Mid-life transition: a period of adult psychosocial development. *Psychiatry* 40:121–30.

———. 1978. *The Seasons of a Man's Life.* New York: Alfred A. Knopf.

Levinson, D. J.; Darro, C. M.; Klein, E. B.; Levinson, M. H.; and McKee, B. 1974. The psychosocial development of men in early adulthood and the mid-life transition. In *Life History Research in Psychotherapy,* ed. D. F. Ricks, A. Thomas, and M. Roth, vol. 3, pp. 243–58. Minneapolis: University of Minnesota Press.

Levison, A. 1975. *The Working Class Majority.* New York: Penguin.

Levi-Strauss, C. 1949. *Les Structures Elementaires de la Parents.* Paris: Presses Universitaires de France.

Levy, R. 1973. *Tahitians: Mind and Experience in the Society Islands.* Chicago: University of Chicago Press.

Lewin, K. 1943. Defining "the field of a given time." *Psychological Review* 50: 292–310.

———. 1948. *Resolving Social Conflicts.* New York: Harper.

———. 1948. Self-hatred among Jews. In *Resolving Social Conflicts,* pp. 186–200. New York: Harper.

———. 1951. *Field Theory in Social Science: Selected Theoretical Papers.* New York: Harper.

Lewin, K.; Dembo, T.; Festinger, L.; and Sears, P. S. 1944. Level of aspiration. In *Personality and Behavior Disorders,* vol. 1, pp. 333–78. New York: Ronald Press.

Lewin, K., Lippitt, R., and White, R. 1939. Patterns of aggressive behavior in experimentally created social climates. *Journal of Social Psychology* 10:271–99.
Lewis, G. H. 1972. Role differentiation. *American Sociological Review* 37:424–34.
Lewis, J. D. 1976. The classic American pragmatists as forerunners to symbolic interactionism. *Sociological Quarterly* 17:347–59.
Lewis, J. W. 1970. *Party Leadership and Revolution in China.* London: Cambridge University Press.
Lewis, M., and Kreitzberg, V. S. 1979. Effects of birth order and spacing in mother-infant interactions. *Developmental Psychology* 15:617–25.
Lewis, M., and Rosenblum, L. 1978. Introduction: issues in affect development. In *The Development of Affect,* ed. M. Lewis and L. Rosenblum. New York: Plenum.
Lewis, O. 1961. *The Children of Sanchez.* New York: Random House.
Lewis, S. H., and Kraut, R. E. 1972. Correlates of student political activism and ideology. *Journal of Social Issues* 28:131–49.
Leyburn, J. G. 1968. Sumner, William Graham. In *Encyclopedia of the Social Sciences,* ed. D. L. Sills, vol. 15, pp. 406–409. New York: Macmillan and Free Press.
Lieberman, M. A. 1975. Adaptive processes in late life. In *Life-Span Developmental Psychology,* ed. N. Datan and L. H. Ginsberg, pp. 135–59. New York: Academic Press.
Lieberman, S. 1950. The effects of changes in roles on the attitudes of the role occupants. *Human Relations* 9:385–403.
Liebhart, E. H. 1979. Information search and attribution. *European Journal of Social Psychology* 9:19–37.
Liebow, E. 1967. *Tally's Corner.* Boston: Little, Brown.
Lieske, J. A. 1978. The conditions of racial violence in American cities: a developmental synthesis. *American Political Science Review* 72:1324–40.
Lifton, R. J. 1963. *Thought Reform and the Psychology of Totalism: A Study of "Brainwashing" in China.* New York: Norton.
Light, I. H. 1972. *Ethnic Enterprise in America: Business and Welfare among Chinese, Japanese and Blacks.* Berkeley: University of California.
Likert, R. 1932. A technique for the measurement of attitudes. *Archives of Psychology* 140:1–55.
Lindemann, E. 1944. Symptomatology and management of acute grief. *American Journal of Psychiatry* 101:141–48.
Lindesmith, A. B. 1947. *Opiate Addiction.* Bloomington, Ind.: Principia Press.
Lindesmith, A. R., and Strauss, A. L. 1950. A critique of culture-personality writings. *American Sociological Review* 15:587–600.
Lindzey, G., ed. 1954. *Handbook of Social Psychology.* Cambridge, Mass.: Addison-Wesley.
Lindzey, G., and Aronson, E., eds. 1968. *Handbook of Social Psychology.* 2d. ed. Reading, Mass.: Addison-Wesley.
Linn, L. S. 1965. Verbal attitudes and overt behavior: a study of racial discrimination. *Social Forces* 43:353–64.
Linton, R. 1936. *The Study of Man.* New York: D. Appleton-Century.
———. 1945. *The Cultural Background of Personality.* New York: Appleton-Century-Crofts.
Lippmann, W. 1925. *The Phantom Public.* New York: Harcourt Brace.
Lipset, S. M. 1950. *Agrarian Socialism.* Berkeley: University of California Press.
———. 1963. *Political Man.* New York: Doubleday.
Lipset, S. M., and Raab, E. 1973. *The Politics of Unreason: Right-Wing Extremism in America, 1790–1970.* New York: Harper and Row.
Lipset, S. M., and Zetterberg, H. 1956. A theory of social mobility. In R. Bendix and S. Lipset, eds., *Class, Status, and Power.* 2d ed. pp. 61–73. New York: Free Press.
Liska, A. E. 1974. Attitude-behavior consistency as a function of generality equivalence between attitude and behavior objects. *Journal of Psychology* 86:217–28.
———., ed. 1975. *The Consistency Controversy.* New York: Wiley.
Liska, A. E. 1977. The dissipation of sociological social psychology. *American Sociologist* 12:2–8.
Lockheed, M. E. 1977. Cognitive style effects on sex status in student work groups. *Journal of Educational Psychology* 69:158–65.
Lockheed-Katz, M. E., and Hall, K. 1976. Conceptualizing sex as a status character-

istic: applications to leadership training strategies. *Journal of Social Issues* 32:111–24.
Loevinger, J., and Wessler, R. 1970. *Measuring Ego Development I: Construction and Use of a Sentence Completion Test.* San Francisco: Jossey-Bass.
Lofland, J. 1965. *Doomsday Cult: A Study of Conversion, Proselytization, and Maintenance of Faith.* Englewood Cliffs, N.J.: Prentice-Hall.
———. 1968. The youth ghetto. *Journal of Higher Education* 39:121–43.
———. 1970. Interactionist imagery and analytic interruptus. In *Human Nature and Collective Behavior: Papers in Honor of Herbert Blumer,* ed. T. Shibutani, pp. 35–45. Englewood Cliffs, N.J.: Prentice-Hall.
———. 1976. *Doing Social Life.* New York: Wiley.
———. 1977. Becoming a world-saver revisited. *American Behavioral Scientist* 20:805–18.
———. 1978. Becoming a world-saver revisited. In *Conversion Careers,* ed. J. Richardson, pp. 10–23. Beverly Hills, Calif.: Sage.
Lofland, J., and Stark, R. 1965. Becoming a world-saver: a theory of conversion to a deviant perspective. *American Sociological Review* 30: 862–75.
Loomis, C. P. 1974. A backward glance at self-identification of blacks and chicanos. *Rural Sociology* 39:96.
Lopata, H. 1973. *Widowhood in an American City.* Cambridge, Mass.: Schenkman.
Lopez, D. E. 1976. The social consequences of Chicano home/school bilingualism. *Social Problems* 24:234–46.
Lopreato, J., and Alston, L. 1970. Ideal types and the idealization strategy. *American Sociological Review* 35:88–96.
Lowenberg, P. 1971. The psychohistorical origins of the Nazi youth cohort. *American Historical Review* 76:1457–1502.
Lowenthal, L. 1943. Biographies in popular magazines. In *Radio Research, 1942–43,* ed. P. F. Lazarsfeld and F. N. Stanton, pp. 507–520. New York: Duell, Sloan and Pearce.
Lowenthal, M. F., and Chiriboga, D. 1972. Transition to the empty nest: crisis, challenge, or relief? *Archives of General Psychiatry* 26:8–14.
Lowenthal, M. F.; Thurnber, M.; and Chiriboga, D. 1975. *Four Stages of Life: A Comparative Study of Women and Men Facing Transitions.* San Francisco: Jossey-Bass.
Lucas, R. 1969. *Men in Crisis.* New York: Basic Books.
Lukes, S. 1967. Alienation and anomie. In *Philosophy, Politics and Society* (3rd series), ed. P. Laslett and W. Runciman, pp. 134–56. Oxford: Basil Blackwell.
Luria, A. R. 1961. *The Role of Speech in the Regulation of Normal and Abnormal Behavior.* New York: Pergamon Press.
———. 1976. *Cognitive Development: Its Cultural and Social Foundations.* Cambridge, Mass.: Harvard University Press.
Lyman, S., and Scott, M. 1970. *A Sociology of the Absurd.* New York: Appleton-Century-Crofts.
Lynd, H. 1958. *On Shame and the Search for Identity.* New York: Harcourt Brace and World.
Lynn, D. B. 1969. *Parental and Sex-Role Identification.* Berkeley, Calif.: McCutchan.
Lyons, J. 1968. *Introduction to Theoretical Linguistics.* Cambridge: Cambridge University Press.
———. 1977. *Semantics.* 2 vols. Cambridge: Cambridge University Press.
Maas, H. S., and Kuypers, J. A. 1974. *From 30 to 70: A 40 Year Longitudinal Study of Changing Life Styles and Personal Development.* San Francisco: Jossey-Bass.
MacAndrew, C., and Edgerton, R. 1969. *Drunken Comportment.* Chicago: Aldine.
Macaulay, J., and Berkowitz, L., eds. 1970. *Altruism and Helping Behavior.* New York: Academic Press.
Maccoby, E. E., and Jacklin, C. N. 1974. *The Psychology of Sex Differences.* Stanford, Calif.: Stanford University Press.
Machotka, O. 1964. *The Unconscious in Social Relations.* New York: Philosophical Library.
Mackie, M. 1980. The impact of sex stereotypes upon adult self-imagery. *Social Psychology Quarterly* 43:121–25.

Madaras, G. R., and Bem, D. J. 1968. Risk and conservatism in group decision-making. *Journal of Experimental Social Psychology* 4:350–65.
Mahoney, E. R. 1978. Age differences in attitude change toward premarital coitus. *Archives of Sexual Behavior* 7:493–501.
Maines, D. R. 1977. Social organization in symbolic interactionism. In *Annual Review of Sociology,* vol. 3 1977, ed. A. Inkeles, J. Coleman and N. Smelser, pp. 235–59. Palo Alto, Calif.: Annual Reviews, Inc.
Malinowski, B. 1922. *Argonauts of the Western Pacific.* New York: E. P. Dutton.
Mandler, G. 1975. *Mind and Emotion.* New York: Wiley.
Manis, J. G., and Meltzer, B. M. 1978. *Symbolic Interaction.* 3d ed. Boston: Allyn and Bacon.
Manis, M. 1955. Social interaction and the self-concept. *Journal of Abnormal and Social Psychology* 51:362–70.
Mann, M. 1974. The social cohesion of liberal democracy. *American Sociological Review* 35:423–39.
Mannheim, B. F. 1966. Reference groups, membership groups, and the self-image. *Sociometry* 29:256–79.
Mannheim, K. 1952. The problem of generations. In *Essays in the Sociology of Knowledge,* ed. K. Mannheim, pp. 276–322. London: Routledge and Kegan Paul.
Mao tse-tung. 1967. *On the Correct Handling of Contradictions Among the People.* Peking: Foreign Language Press.
Marak, G. E. 1964. The evolution of leadership structure. *Sociometry* 27:174–82.
March, J. G. 1953. Husband-wife interaction over political issues. *Public Opinion Quarterly* 17:461–70.
Markle, G. E.; Peterson, J. C.; and Wagenfeld, M. O. 1978. Notes from the cancer underground: participation in the Laetrile movement. *Social Science and Medicine* 12:31–37.
Marks, S. R. 1977. Multiple roles and role strain: some notes on human energy, time and commitment. *American Sociological Review* 42:921–36.
Markus, H. 1977. Self-schemata and processing information about the self. *Journal of Personality and Social Psychology* 35:63–78.
Marris, P. 1975. *Loss and Change.* New York: Doubleday/Anchor.
Marsh, A. 1975. The "silent revolution," value priorities, and the quality of life in Britain. *American Political Science Review* 69:21–30.
Marsh, P.; Rosser, E.; and Harre, R. 1978. *The Rules of Disorder.* London: Routledge and Kegan Paul.
Marshall, G., and Zimbardo, P. 1979. Affective consequences of inadequately explained physiological arousal. *Journal of Personality and Social Psychology* 37:970–88.
Marshall, H. 1979. White movement to the suburbs. *American Sociological Review* 44:975–94.
Martin, E. D. 1920. *The Behavior of Crowds.* New York: Harper and Brothers.
Martin, T., and Berry, K. 1974. Competitive sport in post-industrial society. *Journal of Popular Culture* 8:107–20.
Martinez-Montfort, A., and Dreger, R. M. 1972. Reactions of high school students to school desegregation in a southern metropolitan area. *Psychological Reports* 30:543–50.
Marx, G. T. 1967. *Protest and Prejudice.* New York: Harper and Row.
———. 1979. Conceptual problems in the field of collective behavior. Paper presented at the Annual Meeting of the American Sociological Association.
Marx, G. T., and Wood, J. I. 1975. Strands of theory and research in collective behavior. In *Annual Review of Sociology,* ed. A. Inkeles, J. Coleman and N. Smelser, vol. 1, pp. 363–428. Palo Alto, Calif.: Annual Reviews, Inc.
Marx, K. 1964. Economic and philosophical manuscripts. In *Early Writings.* Translated and edited by T. B. Bottomore, pp. 63–219. New York: McGraw-Hill.
———. 1972a [1844]. Economic and philosophic manuscripts of 1844. In *The Marx-Engels Reader,* ed. R. C. Tucker, pp. 53–103. New York: Norton.
———. 1972b [1848]. The communist manifesto. In *The Marx-Engels Reader,* ed. R. C. Tucker, pp. 335–53. New York: Norton.
Maslach, C. 1979. Negative emotional biasing of unexplained arousal. *Journal of Personality and Social Psychology* 37:953–69.

Mason, K. O.; Czajka, J. L.; and Arber, S. 1976. Change in U. S. women's sex-role attitudes, 1964–74. *American Sociological Review* 41:575–96.

Mason, W. 1973. The impact of endorsements on voting. *Sociological Methods and Research* 1:463–95.

Mauss, A. L. 1975. *Social Problems as Social Movements.* New York: J. B. Lippincott.

Mauss, M. 1954. *The Gift: Forms and Functions of Exchange in Archaic Society.* New York: Free Press.

Mazur, A. 1975. A model of behavior in Berger's standard experiment. *Journal of Mathematical Sociology* 4:83–92.

McCall, G. J. 1977. The self: conceptual requirements from an interactionist perspective. Paper presented at the Annual Meetings of the American Sociological Association, Chicago.

McCall, G. J., and Simmons, J. L. 1966. *Identities and Interactions.* New York: Free Press.

———. 1978. *Identities and Interactions.* rev. ed. New York: Free Press.

McCall, M. 1970. Some ecological aspects of Negro slum riots. In *Protest, Reform and Revolt,* ed. J. Gusfield, pp. 345–62. New York: Wiley.

McCarthy, J. D., and Zald, M. N. 1973. *The Trend of Social Movements in America: Professionalization and Resource Mobilization.* Morristown, N. J.: General Learning Press.

———. 1977. Resource mobilization and social movements: a partial theory. *American Journal of Sociology* 82:1212–39.

McCarthy, J. D., and Yancey, W. L. 1971. Uncle Tom and Mr. Charlie: metaphysical pathos in the study of racism and personal disorganization. *American Journal of Sociology* 76:648–72.

McClelland, D. C. 1961. *The Achieving Society.* Princeton, N. J.: Van Nostrand.

McClintock, C. G. 1972. Game behavior and social motivation in interpersonal settings. In *Experimental Social Psychology,* ed. C. G. McClintock, pp. 271–97. New York: Holt, Rinehart and Winston.

McCombs, M. E., and Shaw, D. L. 1972. The agenda-setting function of mass media. *Public Opinion Quarterly* 36:176–87.

McCranie, E. W., and Kimberley, J. 1973. Rank inconsistency, conflicting expectations and injustice. *Sociometry* 36:152–76.

McDougall, W. 1920. *An Introduction to Social Psychology.* 14th ed. New York: Barnes and Noble.

McFadden, C. 1977. *The Serial.* New York: Knopf.

McGee, P. E. 1979. *Humor: Its Origins and Development.* San Francisco: W. H. Freeman.

McGregory, D. 1960. *The Human Side of Enterprise.* New York: McGraw Hill.

McGuire, W. J. 1966. Attitudes and opinions. *Annual Review of Psychology* 17: 475–514.

———. 1968. Personality and susceptibility to social influence. In *Handbook of Personality Theory and Research,* ed. E. F. Borgatta and W. W. Lambert, pp. 1130–87. Chicago: Rand McNally.

———. 1969. The nature of attitudes and attitude change. In *Handbook of Social Psychology,* ed. G. Lindzey and E. Aronson, vol. 3, pp. 136–314. Reading, Mass.: Addison-Wesley.

McGuire, W. J., and Padawer-Singer, A. 1976. Trait salience in the spontaneous self-concept. *Journal of Personality and Social Psychology* 33:743–54.

McGuire, W. J.; McGuire, C. V.; Child, P.; and Fujioka, T. 1978. Salience of ethnicity in the spontaneous self-concept as a function of one's ethnic distinctiveness in the social environment. *Journal of Personality and Social Psychology* 36:511–20.

McHugh, P. 1968. *Defining the Situation.* Indianapolis: Bobbs-Merrill.

McKirnan, D. J. 1980. The identification of deviance: a conceptualization and initial test of a model of social norms. *European Journal of Social Psychology* 10:75–95.

McLaughlin, B., ed. 1969. *Studies in Social Movements: A Social Psychological Perspective.* New York: Free Press.

McLeod, W. R. 1975. Merphos poisoning or mass panic? *Australian and New Zealand Journal of Psychiatry* 9:225–29.

McLoughlin, W. G. 1959. *Modern Revivalism.* New York: Ronald Press.

———. 1978. *Revivals, Awakenings, and Reform.* Chicago: University of Chicago Press.
McNall, S. 1974. *The Sociological Experience.* Boston: Little, Brown.
McNeill, D. 1970. *The Acquisition of Language: The Study of Developmental Psycholinguistics.* New York: Harper and Row.
McPhail, C. 1971. Civil disorder participation: a critical examination of recent research. *American Sociological Review* 36:1058–73.
———. 1978. Toward a theory of collective behavior. Paper presented at the Symposium on Symbolic Interaction, University of South Carolina.
McPhail, C., and Miller, D. 1973. The assembling process. *American Sociological Review* 38:721–35.
McPhail, C., and Pickens, R. G. 1975. The explananda of collective behavior. Paper presented at the Annual Meeting of the American Sociological Association.
McPhail, C., and Rexroat, C. 1979. Mead vs. Blumer: the divergent methodological perspectives of social behaviorism and symbolic interactionism. *American Sociological Review* 44:449–67.
———. 1980. *Ex cathedra* Blumer or *ex-libris* Mead? *American Sociological Review* 45:420–30.
McQuail, D. 1977. The influence and effects of mass media. In *Mass Communication and Society,* ed. J. Curran et al. London: Edward Arnold.
Mead, G. H. 1934. *Mind, Self, and Society.* Chicago: University of Chicago Press.
———. 1936. *Movements of Thought in the Nineteenth Century.* Edited by Merritt H. Moore. Chicago: University of Chicago Press.
———. 1964. *On Social Psychology: Selected Papers.* Edited by A. Strauss. Chicago: University of Chicago Press.
Mead, M. 1928. *Coming of Age in Samoa.* New York: Morrow.
———. 1935. *Sex and Temperament in Three Primitive Societies.* New York: Morrow.
———. 1939. *From the South Seas.* New York: Morrow.
———. 1949. On the implications of the Gesell-Ilg approach to maturation. In *Personality Characteristics and Cultural Milieu,* ed. D. G. Haring, pp. 534–48. Syracuse: Syracuse University Press.
Mead, M., and Metraux, R. 1953. *The Study of Culture at a Distance.* Chicago: University of Chicago Press.
Meadow, K. P. 1969. Self-image, family climate, and deafness. *Social Forces* 47:1–11.
Mechanic, D. 1972. Social psychologic factors affecting the presentation of bodily complaints. *New England Journal of Medicine* 286:1132–39.
Medalia, N. Z., and Larsen, O. N. 1958. Diffusion and belief in a collective delusion. *American Sociological Review* 33:180–86.
Meeker, B. F., and Weitzel-O'Neill, P. A. 1977. Sex roles and interpersonal behavior in task-oriented groups. *American Sociological Review* 43:91–105.
Mehan, H. 1979. *Learning Lessons: Social Organization in the Classroom.* Cambridge, Mass.: Harvard University Press.
Mehrabian, A. 1972. *Nonverbal Communication.* Chicago: Aldine-Atherton.
Meltzer, M.; Petras, J. W.; and Reynolds, L. T. 1975. *Symbolic Interactionism: Genesis, Varieties and Criticism.* London: Routledge and Kegan Paul.
Mendelsohn, H. 1954. The "student strike" as a social psychological reaction to desegregation. Unpublished paper. Summarized in K. Lang and G. Lang, *Collective Dynamics.* 1961.
———. 1980. Review of Bishop et al., The Presidential Debates. *Public Opinion Quarterly* 44:135–37.
Merton, R. K. 1940. Bureaucratic structure and personality. *Social Forces* 17:560–68.
———. 1940. Fact and factitiousness in ethnic opinionnaires. *American Sociological Review* 5:13–28.
———. 1948. The self-fulfilling prophesy. *Antioch Review* 8:193–210.
———. 1949. Discrimination and the American creed. In *Discrimination and National Welfare,* ed. R. M. MacIver, pp. 99–126. New York: Harper.
———. 1957. *Social Theory and Social Structure.* Glencoe, Ill.: Free Press.
———. 1957. The role-set: problems in sociological theory. *British Journal of Sociology* 8:106–20.
———. 1968. *Social Theory and Social Structure.* enlarged ed. New York: Free Press.

———. 1971. Social problems and sociological theory. In *Contemporary Social Problems,* ed. R. K. Merton and R. Nisbet, 3d ed. pp. 793–845. New York: Harcourt Brace Jovanovich.

———. 1975. Structural analysis in sociology. In *Approaches to the Study of Social Structure,* ed P. M. Blau, pp. 21–52. New York: Free Press.

———. 1976. *Sociological Ambivalence and Other Essays.* New York: Free Press.

Merton, R. K., and Barber, E. 1963. Sociological ambivalence. In *Sociological Theory, Values, and Sociological Change: Essays in Honor of Pitirim A. Sorokin,* ed. E. A. Tiryakian, pp. 91–120. New York: Free Press.

Merton, R. K., and Rossi, A. S. 1950. Contributions to the theory of reference group behavior. In *Continuities in Social Research: Studies in the Scope and Method of "The American Soldier,"* ed. R. K. Merton, and P. F. Lazarsfeld, pp. 40–105. Glencoe, Ill.: Free Press.

Messinger, S. L. 1955. Organizational transformation: a case study of a declining social movement. *American Sociological Review* 20:3–10.

Messinger, S.; Sampson, H.; and Towne, R. 1962. Life as theater: some notes on the dramaturgic approach to social reality. *Sociometry* 25:98–110.

Meyers, R. C. 1948. Anti-Communist mob action: a case study. *Public Opinion Quarterly* 12:57–67.

Michels, R. 1949. *Political Parties.* Glencoe. Ill.: Free Press.

Middleton, R. 1960. Fertility values in American magazine fiction: 1916–1956. *Public Opinion Quarterly* 24:139–43.

Milgram, S. 1961. Nationality and conformity. *Scientific American* 205(6): 45–51.

———. 1963. Behavioral study of obedience. *Journal of Abnormal and Social Psychology* 67:371–78.

———. 1974. *Obedience to Authority: An Experimental View.* New York: Harper and Row.

Milgram, S., and Toch, H. 1969. Collective behavior: crowds and social movements. In *The Handbook of Social Psychology,* ed. G. Lindzey and E. Aronson, vol. 4, pp. 509–610. Reading, Massachusetts: Addison-Wesley.

Miller, J., and Evans, R. 1975. The peaking of streaking. In *Readings in Collective Behavior,* ed. R. Evans, pp. 401–17. Chicago: Rand McNally.

Miller, J.; Schooler, C.; Kohn, M. L.; and Miller, K. A. 1977. Women and work: the psychological effects of occupational conditions. *American Journal of Sociology* 85:66–94.

Miller, K. S., and Dreger, R. M., eds. 1973. *Comparative Studies of Blacks and Whites in the United States.* New York: Seminar.

Mills, C. W. 1940. Situated actions and vocabularies of motives. *American Journal of Sociology* 5:904–13.

Minard, R. B. 1952. Race relationships in the Pocahontas coal field. *Journal of Social Issues* 8:29–44.

Minturn, L., Boyd, D., and Kapoor, S. 1978. Increased maternal power status: changes in socialization in a restudy of Rajput mothers of Khalapur, India. *Journal of Cross-Cultural Psychology* 9:483–97.

Mischel, W. 1968. *Personality and Assessment.* New York: Wiley.

———. 1973. Toward a cognitive social learning reconceptualization of personality. *Psychological Review* 80:252–83.

Mitchell-Kernan, C., and Kernan, K. T. 1975. Children's insults: America and Samoa. In *Sociocultural Dimensions of Language Use,* ed. M. Sanches and B. G. Blount, pp. 307–16. New York: Academic Press.

Miyamoto, S., and Dornbusch, S. M. 1956. A test of the symbolic interactionist hypothesis of self-conception. *American Journal of Sociology* 61:399–403.

Modell, J.; Furstenberg, F. F., Jr.; and Strong, D. 1978. The timing of marriage in the transition to adulthood: continuity and change 1869–1975. *American Journal of Sociology* 84:S120–S150.

Moinat, S.; Raine, W.; Burbeck, S.; and Davison, K. 1972. Black ghetto residents as rioters. *Journal of Social Issues* 28:45–62.

Molotch, H. 1972. *Managed Integration: Dilemmas of Doing Good in the City.* Berkeley: University of California.

Molotch, H., and Lester, M. 1974. News as purposive behavior: on the strategic use of routine events, accidents, and scandals. *American Sociological Review* 39: 101–12.

———. 1975. Accidental news: the great oil spill as local occurrence and national event. *American Journal of Sociology* 81:235–60.
Moore, B., Jr. 1968. Notes on the process of acquiring power. In *Reader in Political Sociology,* ed. F. Lindenfeld, pp. 330–53. New York: Funk and Wagnalls.
Moore, J. C., Jr. 1968. Status and influence in small group interactions. *Sociometry* 31:47–63.
———. 1969. Social status and social influence: process considerations. *Sociometry* 32:145–68.
Moreno, J. C. 1948. Experimental sociometry and the experimental method in science. In *Current Trends in Social Psychology,* ed. W. Dennis. Pittsburgh: University of Pittsburgh Press.
———. 1953. *Who Shall Survive?* 2d ed. Beacon, N. Y.: Beacon House.
Morrill, R. G. 1973. The dynamics of cultural change: the effect of cross-cultural communication on small group behavior in Thailand. *Social Psychiatry* 8: 162–82.
Morrison, D. E. 1971. Some notes toward theory on relative deprivation, social movements, and social change. *American Behavioral Scientist* 14:675–90.
Morrison, D. E., and Hornback, K. E. 1976. *Collective Behavior: A Bibliography.* New York: Garland Publishing, Inc.
Morrison, E. E., and Steeves, A. D. 1967. Deprivation, discontent, and social movement participation: evidence on a contemporary farmers' movement, the NFO. *Rural Sociology* 32:414–34.
Morse, S., and Gergen, K. J. 1970. Social comparison, self-consistency, and the concept of self. *Journal of Personality and Social Psychology* 16:148–56.
Mortimer, J. T., and Simmons, R. G. 1978. Adult socialization. In *Annual Review of Sociology,* ed. R. H. Turner, J. Coleman, and R. C. Fox, vol. 4. pp. 421–54. Palo Alto, Calif.: Annual Reviews.
Mortimer, J. T., and Lorence, J. 1979. Work experience and occupational value socialization: a longitudinal study. *American Journal of Sociology* 84:1361–85.
———. 1980. Self-concept stability and change from late adolescence to early adulthood. In *Research in Community and Mental Health,* ed. R. G. Simmons, vol. 2. Greenwich, Conn.: JAI Press.
Moscovici, S. 1976. *Social Influence and Social Change.* London: Academic Press.
Mosse, G. L. 1975. *The Nationalization of the Masses.* New York: New American Library.
Mott, F. L. 1944. Newspapers in presidential campaigns. *Public Opinion Quarterly* 8:348–67.
Moynihan, D. P. 1965. *The Negro Family: The Case for National Action.* Washington, D. C.: U.S. Department of Labor (Office of Policy Planning and Research).
Mueller, J. E. 1973. *War, Presidents and Public Opinion.* New York: Wiley.
Mulford, H. A., and Salisbury, W. W. 1964. Self-conceptions in a general population. *Sociological Quarterly* 5:35–46.
Mullins, N. C. 1973. *Theories and Theory Groups in Contemporary American Sociology.* New York: Harper and Row.
Murphy, G.; Murphy, L. B.; and Newcomb, T. M. 1937. *Experimental Social Psychology.* New York: Harper.
Murray, R. K. 1955. *Red Scare.* New York: McGraw-Hill.
Murstein, B. I. 1976. *Who Will Marry Whom?* New York: Springer.
Myrdal, G. 1944. *An American Dilemma.* New York: Harper.
Nahemow, T. L., and Lawton, M. P. 1975. Similarity and propinquity in friendship formation. *Journal of Personality and Social Psychology* 32:205–13.
Nagelschmidt, A. M., and Jakob, R. 1977. Dimensionality of Rotters's I-E Scale in a society in the process of modernization. *Journal of Cross-Cultural Psychology* 8:101–112.
Needham, R. 1960. *Structure and Sentiment.* Chicago: University of Chicago Press.
Neiman, J., and Hughes, J. W. 1951. The problem of the concept of role—a re-survey of the literature. *Social Forces* 30:141–49.
Nelson, H. 1971. Leadership and change in an evolutionary movement. *Social Forces* 49:353–71.
———. 1974. Social movement transformation and pre-movement factor effect: a preliminary inquiry. *Sociological Quarterly* 15:127–42.

Nesselroade, J., and Reese, H. W. 1973. *Life-Span Developmental Psychology Methodological Issues.* New York: Academic Press.

Nesselroade, J. R., Schaie, K. W., and Baltes, P. E. 1972. Ontogenetic and generational components of structural and quantitative change in adult behavior. *Journal of Gerontology* 27:222–28.

Neugarten, B. L., ed., 1968. *Middle Age and Aging: A Reader in Social Psychology.* Chicago: University of Chicago Press.

Neugarten, B. L., and Datan, N. 1973. Sociological perspectives on the life cycle. In *Life-Span Developmental Psychology: Personality and Socialization,* ed. P. B. Baltes and K. W. Schaie, pp. 53–71. New York: Academic Press.

Neugarten, B. L. and Hagestad, G. 1976. Age and the life course. In *Handbook of Aging and the Social Sciences.* ed. R. Binstock and E. Shanas, pp. 35–52. New York: Van Nostrand.

Newcomb, T. M. 1943. *Personality and Social Change.* New York: Holt, Rinehart and Winston.

———. 1961. *The Acquaintance Process.* New York: Holt, Rinehart and Winston.

Newcomb, T. M.; Koenig, K. E.; Flacks, R.; and Warwick, D. P. 1967. *Persistence and Change.* New York: Wiley.

Niebuhr, R. 1929. *The Social Sources of Denominationalism.* New York: Holt, Rinehart and Winston.

Nisbet, R. A. 1954. *The Quest for Community.* New York: Oxford University Press.

Nock, A. D. 1933. *Conversion.* London: Oxford University Press.

Nolle-Neumann, E. 1974. The spiral of silence: a theory of public opinion. *Journal of Communication* 24:43–51.

———. 1977. Turbulences in the climate of opinion: methodological applications of the spiral of silence theory. *Public Opinion Quarterly* 41:143–58.

———. 1980. *Die Schweigespirale: Öffentliche Meinung und Unsere Soziale Haut.* München: Piper.

Norbeck, E., and DeVos, G. 1972. Culture and personality: the Japanese. In *Psychological Anthropology,* ed. F. L. Hsu. Cambridge, Mass.: Schenkman.

Norman, R. 1975. Affective-cognitive consistency, attitudes, conformity, and behavior. *Journal of Personality and Social Psychology* 32:83–91.

Nosanchuk, T. A., and Lightstone, J. A. 1974. Canned laughter and public and private conformity. *Journal of Personality and Social Psychology* 29:153–56.

Novak, D. W., and Lerner, M. J. 1968. Rejection as a consequence of perceived similarity. *Journal of Personality and Social Psychology* 9:147–52.

Nuttin, J. M., Jr. 1975. *The Illusion of Attitude Change: Toward a Response Contagion Theory of Persuasion.* London: Academic Press.

O'Barr, W. M., and O'Barr, J. F. 1976. *Language and Politics.* The Hague: Mouton.

Oberschall, A. 1973. *Social Conflict and Social Movements.* Englewood Cliffs, N.J.: Prentice-Hall.

———. 1978. Theories of social conflict. In *Annual Review of Sociology,* ed. R. H. Turner, vol. 4. pp. 291–315. Palo Alto, Calif.: Anual Reviews, Inc.

O'Dea, T. F. 1957. *The Mormons.* Chicago: University of Chicago Press.

Ofshe, R. 1972. Reference conflict and behavior. In *Sociological Theories in Progress,* eds. J. Berger, M. Zelditch, Jr., and B. Anderson, vol. 2. Boston: Houghton, Mifflin.

O'Gorman, H. J. 1975. Pluralistic ignorance and white estimates of white support for racial segregation. *Public Opinion Quarterly* 39:313–30.

———. 1979. White and black perceptions of racial values. *Public Opinion Quarterly* 43:48–59.

O'Gorman, H. J. and Garry, S. L. 1976. Pluralistic ignorance—a replication and extension. *Public Opinion Quarterly* 40:449–58.

Olesen, V. L., and Whitaker, E. W. 1968. *The Silent Dialogue: A Study in the Social Psychology of Professional Socialization.* San Francisco: Jossey-Bass.

Olneck, M. R., and Bills, D. B. 1979. Family configuration and achievement effects of birth order and family size in a sample of brothers. *Social Psychology Quarterly* 42:135–48.

Olson, M. 1965. *The Logic of Collective Action.* Cambridge, Mass.: Harvard University Press.

———. 1968. *The Logic of Collective Action.* New York: Schocken.

O'Neill, N., and O'Neill, G. 1972. *Open Marriage: A New Life Style for Couples.* New York: Avon.

Orne, M. T. 1969. Demand characteristics and the concept of quasi-controls. In *Artifact in Behavioral Research,* ed. R. Rosenthal and R. L. Rosnow, pp. 147–79. New York: Academic Press.

Orum, A. 1972. *Black Students in Protest: A Study of the Origins of the Black Student Movement.* Washington, D.C.: Arnold M. and Caroline Rose Monograph Series, American Sociological Association.

———. 1974. On participation in political protest movements. *Journal of Applied Behavioral Science* 10:181–207.

Osgood, C. E.; Suci, G. J.; and Tannenbaum, P. H. 1957. *The Measurement of Meaning.* Urbana, Ill.: University of Illinois Press.

Ostrom, T. M. 1969. The relationship between the affective, behavioral, and cognitive components of attitudes. *Journal of Experimental Social Psychology* 5: 12–30.

O'Toole, R., and Dubin, R. 1968. Baby feeding and body sway: an experiment in George Herbert Mead's "taking the role of the other." *Journal of Personality and Social Psychology* 10:59–65.

Paicheler, G. 1976. Norms and attitude change I: Polarization and styles of behavior. *European Journal of Social Psychology* 6:405–27.

Paige, J. M. 1971. Political orientation and riot participation. *American Sociological Review* 36:810–20.

Pareto, V. 1935. *The Mind and Society.* New York: Harcourt Brace.

Park, R. E. 1955. *Society.* New York: Free Press.

———. 1928. Human migration and the marginal man. *American Journal of Sociology* 33:881–93.

———. 1940. News as a form of knowledge. *American Journal of Sociology* 45: 669–86.

Parker, S., and Kleiner, R. J. 1966. *Mental Illness in the Urban Negro Community.* New York: Free Press.

Parkes, C. M. 1972. *Bereavement: Studies of Grief in Adult Life.* New York: International Universities Press.

Parsons, T. 1949. *Essays in Sociological Theory.* New York: Free Press.

———. 1951. *The Social System.* Glencoe, Ill.: Free Press.

———. 1961. An outline of the social system. In *Theories of Society.* ed. T. Parsons, E. Shils, K. D. Naegele, and J. R. Pitts, vol. 1. pp. 30–79. New York: Free Press.

———. 1964*a.* The school class as a social system: some of its functions in American society. In T. Parsons, *Social Structure and Personality.* New York: Free Press.

———. 1964*b. Social Structure and Personality.* New York: Free Press.

Parsons, T., and Shils, E. A. 1962. *Toward a General Theory of Action.* New York: Harper and Row.

Patchen, M. 1958. Group standards and job satisfaction. *Human Relations.* 11:-303–14.

———. 1961. A conceptual framework and some empirical data regarding comparisons of social rewards. *Sociometry* 24:136–56.

Pateman, C. 1970. *Participation and Democratic Theory.* Cambridge: Cambridge University Press.

Payne, A. C. n.d. The re-organization of linguistic rules: a preliminary report. *Pennsylvania Working Papers on Linguistic Change and Variation* 1(6).

Pearlin, L. I. 1975. Sex roles and depression. In *Life Span Developmental Psychology—Normative Life Crises,* ed. N. Datan and L. H. Ginsberg, pp. 191–207. New York: Academic Press.

Pearlin, L. I., and Kohn, M. L. 1966. Social class, occupation and parental values. *American Sociological Review* 31:466–79.

Pearlin, L. I., and Lieberman, M. A. 1979. Social sources of emotional distress. In *Research in Community and Mental Health,* ed. R. G. Simmons, vol. 1, pp. 217–48. Greenwich, Conn.: JAI Press.

Pederson, J. T. 1976. Age and change: the case of California, 1960–1970. *Public Opinion Quarterly* 40:153–63.

Pennebaker, J. W. 1980. Self-perception of emotion and internal sensation. In *The*

Self in Social Psychology, ed. D. M. Wegner and R. R. Vallacher. New York: Oxford University Press.
Peres, Y. 1971. Ethnic relations in Israel. *American Journal of Sociology* 76:1021–47.
Perinbanayagam, R. S. 1974. The definition of the situation: an analysis of the ethnomethodological and dramaturgical view. *Sociological Quarterly* 15:521–41.
Perrow, C. 1979. The sixties observed. In *The Dynamics of Social Movements,* ed. M. N. Zald and J. D. McCarthy, pp. 192–211. Cambridge, Mass.: Winthrop Publishers.
Perry, J., and Pugh, M. 1978. *Collective Behavior.* St. Paul, Minn.: West.
Persell, C. H. 1977. *Education and Inequality: The Roots and Results of Stratification in America's Schools.* New York: Free Press.
Petras, J., and Zeitlin, M. 1967. Miners and agrarian radicalism. *American Sociological Review* 32:578–86.
Pettigrew, T. F. 1958. Personality and sociocultural factors in intergroup attitudes: a cross-national comparison. *Journal of Conflict Resolution* 2:29–42.
———. 1964. *A Profile of the Negro American.* Princeton, N.J.: Van Nostrand.
———. 1967. Social evaluation theory: convergences and applications. *Nebraska Symposium on Motivation.*
———. 1971. *Racially Separate or Together?* New York: McGraw Hill.
———. 1978. Placing Adam's argument in a broader perspective: comment on the Adam paper. *Social Psychology Quarterly* 41:58–61.
Peven, D. 1968. The use of religious revival techniques to indoctrinate personnel. *Sociological Quarterly* 9:97–106.
Pfeiffer, P. 1964. Mass hysteria masquerading as food poisoning. *Maine Medical Association Journal* 55:27.
Phillips, D. L. 1971. *Knowledge From What?* Chicago: Rand McNally.
Phillips, D. P. 1974. Influence of suggestion on suicide: substantive and theoretical implications. *American Sociological Review* 39:340–54.
———. 1979. Suicide, motor vehicle fatalities, and the mass media: evidence toward a theory of suggestion. *American Journal of Sociology* 84:1150–74.
Piaget, J. 1929. *The Child's Conception of the World.* London: Routledge and Kegan Paul.
———. 1932. *The Moral Judgment of the Child.* New York: Harcourt Brace and World.
———. 1970. *Structuralism.* New York: Basic Books.
Piaget, J., and Inhelder, B. 1969. *The Psychology of the Child.* New York: Basic Books
Pierce, A. 1967. The economic cycle and the social suicide rate. *American Sociological Review* 32:457–62.
Pierce, R. C.; Clark, M.; and Kaufman, S. 1978. Generation and ethnic identity: a typological analysis. *International Journal of Aging and Human Development* 9:19–29.
Pilarzyk, T. 1978. Conversion and alternation processes in the youth culture: a comparative analysis of religious transformations. *Pacific Sociological Review* 21:379–405.
Pinard, M. 1967. Poverty and political movements. *Social Problems* 15:250–63.
———. 1971. *The Rise of a Third Party: A Study in Crisis Politics.* Englewood Cliffs, N. J.: Prentice-Hall.
Pitts, R. A. 1978. The effects of exclusively French language schooling on self-esteem in Quebec. *Canadian Modern Language Review* 34:372–80.
Piven, F. F., and Cloward, R. A. 1977. *Poor People's Movements.* New York: Vintage Books.
Plutchik, R. 1962. *The Emotions.* New York: Random House.
———. 1970. Emotions, evolution, and adaptive processes. In *Feelings and Emotions.* ed. M. B. Arnold, New York: Academic Press.
———. 1980. *Emotion: A Psychoevolutionary Synthesis.* New York: Harper and Row.
Polanyi, K. 1957. *Trade and Market in the Early Empires.* New York: Free Press.
Pool, I. DeS. 1959. TV: a new dimension in politics. In *American Voting Behavior,* ed. E. Burdick and A. J. Brodbeck, pp. 236–61. New York: Free Press.

Pool, I. DeS.; Schramm, W.; Frey, F. W.; Maccoby, N.; and Parker, E. B., eds., 1973. *Handbook of Communication.* Chicago: Rand McNally.
Pool, I. DeS., and Shulman, I. 1959. Newsmen's fantasies, audiences, and newswriting. *Public Opinion Quarterly* 23:145–58.
Poole, M. E. 1975. Review of Basil Bernstein, Class, Codes, and Control, vols. 1 and 2. *Language in Society* 4:73–84.
Popkin, S. L. et al. 1976. Toward an investment theory of voting. *American Political Science Review* 70:779–805.
Porter, J. N. 1974. Race, socialization and mobility in education and early occupational attainment. *American Sociological Review* 39:303–16.
———. 1968. The future of upward mobility. *American Sociological Review* 33:5–19.
———. 1961. *Black Child, White Child: The Development of Racial Attitudes.* Cambridge, Mass.: Harvard University Press.
Porter, J. R., and Washington, R. E. 1979. Black identity and self-esteem: a review of studies of black self-concept, 1968–1978. In *Annual Review of Sociology,* ed. A. Inkeles, pp. 53–74. Palo Alto, Calif.: Annual Reviews.
Portes, A. 1971*a.* On the logic of post-factum explanations: the hypothesis of lower-class frustration as the cause of leftist radicalism. *Social Forces* 50:26–44.
———. 1971b. Political primitivism, differential socialization, and lower-class leftist radicalism. *American Sociological Review* 36:820–35.
———. 1973. The factorial structure of modernity: empirical replications and a critique. *American Journal of Sociology* 79:15–44.
Poston, T., and Stewart, I. 1978. *Catastrophe Theory and Its Application.* London: Pitman.
Pratt, J. B. 1920. *The Religious Consciousness.* New York: Macmillan.
Pratt, M. L. 1977. *Toward a Speech Act Theory of Literary Discourse.* Bloomington: Indiana University Press.
Presidential Science Advisory Commission, Panel on Youth at President's Advisory Committee. 1973. *Youth: Transition to Adulthood.* Washington, D.C.: U. S. Government Printing Office.
Pressor, S., and Schuman, H. 1976. Question wording as an independent variable in survey analysis: a first report. In the *Proceedings of the 1975 American Statistical Association.* pp. 16–25.
Pribram, K. H. 1976. *Freud's Project Reassessed.* New York: Basic Books.
Priest, R. T., and Sawyer, J. 1967. Proximity and peership: bases of balance in interpersonal attraction. *American Journal of Sociology* 72:633–49.
Priestnall, R.; Pilkington, G.; and Moffat, G. 1978. Personality and the use of oral contraceptives in British university students. *Social Science and Medicine* 12: 403–407.
Pruden, D. 1936. A sociological study of a Texas lynching. *Studies in Sociology* 1:3–9.
Prus, R. C. 1975. Resisting designations: an extension of attribution theory into a negotiated context. *Sociological Inquiry* 45:3–14.
Purkey, W. W. 1970. *Self-Concept and School Achievement.* Englewood Cliffs, N. J.: Prentice-Hall.
Quarantelli, E. L., and Cooper J. 1966. Self-conceptions and others: a further test of Meadian hypotheses. *Sociological Quarterly* 7:281–97.
Quarantelli, E. L., and Dynes, R. 1970. Property norms and looting: their patterns in community crisis. *Phylon* 31:168–82.
Quarantelli, E. L., and Hundley, J. 1975. A test of some propositions about crowd formation and behavior. In *Readings in Collective Behavior,* 2d ed. ed. R. Evans, pp. 538–54. Chicago: Rand McNally.
Radke-Yarrow, M. et al. 1952. The role of parents in the development of children's ethnic attitudes. *Child Development* 23:13–53.
Rankin, A. M., and Philip, P. 1963. An epidemic of laughing in the Bukoba district of Tanganyika. *The Central African Journal of Medicine* 9:167–70.
Raper, A. 1933. *The Tragedy of Lynching.* Chapel Hill: University of North Carolina Press.
Rawls, J. 1971. *A Theory of Justice.* Cambridge, Mass.: Harvard University Press.
Reckless, W. C.; Dinitz, S.; and Murray, E. 1956. Self-concept as an insulator against delinquency. *American Sociological Review* 21:744–48.

Redekop, C. W. 1969. *The Old Colony Mennonites: Dilemmas of Ethnic Minority Life.* Baltimore: The Johns Hopkins University Press.

Reeder, L. G.; Donohue, G.; and Biblarz, A. 1960. Conceptions of self and others. *American Journal of Sociology* 66:153–59.

Reese, H. W., and Overton, W. F. 1970. Models of development and theories of development. In *Life Span Developmental Psychology,* ed. R. L. Goulet and P. B. Baltes, pp. 116–49. New York: Academic Press.

Reiss, A. J. 1961. The social integration of queers and peers. *Social Problems* 9: 102–20.

Reiss, A. L. 1960. Toward a sociology of the heterosexual love relationship. *Marriage and Family Living* 22:139–44.

Reitz, H. J., and Groff, G. K. 1974. Economic development and belief in locus of control among factory workers in four countries. *Journal of Cross-Cultural Psychology* 5:344–55.

Renninger, C. A., and Williams, J. E. 1966. Black-white color connotations and racial awareness in preschool children. *Perceptual and Motor Skills* 22:771–85.

RePass, D. E. 1976. Comment: political methodologies in disarray; some alternative interpretations of the 1972 election. *American Political Science Review* 70:814–31.

Response Analysis Corporation. 1980. Study delineates unfavorable image of housewife. *The Sampler* 16:1.

Rheingold, H. L. 1969. The social and socializing infant. In *Handbook of Socialization Theory and Research,* ed. David A. Goslin. Chicago: Rand McNally.

Richardson, J. T., ed. 1978. *Conversion Careers: In and Out of the New Religions.* Beverly Hills, Calif.: Sage.

———. 1979. A new paradigm for conversion research. Paper presented at the International Society for Political Psychology Annual Meetings, Washington, D.C.

———. 1980. Conversion careers. *Society* 17:47–81.

Richardson, J. T.; Harder, M.; and Simmonds, R. B. 1972. Thought reform and the Jesus movement. *Youth and Society* 4:185–202.

Richardson, J. T., and Stewart, M. 1977. Conversion process models and the Jesus movement. *American Behavioral Scientist* 20:819–38.

Richer, S. 1976. Reference-group theory and ability grouping. *Sociology of Education* 49:65–71.

Ridgeway, C. 1978. Conformity, group-oriented motivation, and status attainment in small groups. *Social Psychology* 41:175–88.

Riecken, C. 1958. The effect of talkativeness on ability to influence group solutions of problems. *Sociometry* 21:309–21.

Riley, J. W., and Riley, M. W. 1959. Mass communication and the social system. In *Sociology Today,* ed. R. K. Merton, L. Broom, and L. S. Cottrell, Jr., pp. 537–78. New York: Basic Books.

Riley, M. W. 1976. Age strata in social systems, In *Handbook of Aging in the Social Sciences,* ed. R. Binstock and E. Shanas, pp. 189–217. New York: Van Nostrand.

———. 1979. Adulthood in the life cycle. *Contemporary Sociology* 8:543–46.

Riley, M. W.; Johnson, M.; and Foner, A. 1972*a. Aging and Society vol. 3: A Sociology of Age Stratification.* New York: Russell Sage Foundation.

Riley, M. W.; Johnson, M.; and Foner, A. 1972*b.* The succession of cohorts. In *Aging and Society: A Sociology of Age Stratification,* ed. M. W. Riley, M. Johnson, and A. Foner, vol. 3, pp. 515–82. New York: Russell Sage Foundation.

Riley, M. W., and Riley, J. W., Jr. 1951. A sociological approach to communications research. *Public Opinion Quarterly* 15:444–60.

Rist, R. C. 1970. Student social class and teacher expectations: the self-fulfilling prophecy in ghetto education. *Harvard Educational Review* 40:411–51.

Robbins, R. H. 1973. Alcohol and the identity struggle: some effects of economic change on interpersonal relations. *American Anthropologist* 75:99–123.

Robbins, T.; Anthony, D.; and Curtis, T. 1975. Youth culture religious movements: evaluating the integrative hypothesis. *Sociological Quarterly* 16:48–64.

Roberts, A.; Mosely, K.; and Chamberlin, M. 1975. Age differences in racial self-identity of young black girls. *Psychological Reports* 37:1263–66.

Roberts, R. E., and Kloss, R. M. 1979. *Social Movements: Between the Balcony and the Barricade.* 2d ed. St. Louis: C. V. Mosby Co.

Robertson, A., and Cochrane, R. 1976*a*. Attempted suicide and cultural change: an empirical investigation. *Human Relations* 29:863–83.
———. 1976*b*. Deviance and cultural change. *International Journal of Social Psychiatry* 22:79–85.
Robinson, J. P. 1976. Interpersonal influence in election campaigns: two-step flow hypotheses. *Public Opinion Quarterly* 46:304–319.
Roche, J., and Sachs, S. 1955. The bureaucrat and the enthusiast: an exploration of the leadership of social movements. *The Western Political Quarterly* 8:248–61.
Roethlisberger, F., and Dickson, W. 1946. *Management and the Worker.* Cambridge, Mass.: Harvard University Press.
Rogers, C. M.; Smith, M. D.; and Coleman, J. M. 1978. Social comparison in the classroom: the relationship between academic achievement and self-concept. *Journal of Educational Psychology* 70:50–57.
Rogers, E. M. 1958. Reference group influences on student drinking behavior. *Quarterly Journal of Studies on Alcohol* 19:244–54.
Rogers, E. M., and Geal, G. M. 1958. *Reference Group Influence in the Adoption of Agricultural Technology.* Iowa Agricultural and Home Economics Experiment Station Project no. 1236.
Rokeach, M., ed. 1960. *The Open and Closed Mind.* New York: Basic Books.
———. 1968*a*. The nature of attitudes. In *Encyclopedia of the Social Sciences.* ed. D. L. Sills, vol. 1. pp. 449–58. New York: Macmillan and Free Press.
———. 1968*b*. *Beliefs, Attitudes, and Values.* San Francisco: Jossey-Bass.
———. 1973. *The Nature of Human Values.* New York: Free Press.
Rokeach, M., and Kliejunas, P. 1972. Behavior as a function of attitude-toward-object and attitude-toward-situation. *Journal of Personality and Social Psychology* 22:194–201.
Rokeach, M.; Smith, P. W.; and Evans, R. I. 1960. Two kinds of prejudice or one? In *The Open and Closed Mind,* ed. M. Rokeach, New York: Basic Books.
Rollins, B. C., and Thomas, D. L. 1979. Parental support, power, and control techniques in the socialization of children. In *Contemporary Theories About the Family,* ed. W. R. Burr et al. vol. 1. New York: Free Press.
Roshco, B. 1975. *Newsmaking.* Chicago: University of Chicago Press.
Rosen, B. C. 1961. Family structure and achievement motivation. *American Sociological Review* 26:574–85.
Rosenbaum, J. E. 1975. The stratification of socialization processes. *American Sociological Review* 40:48–54.
Rosenberg, J. F., and Travis, C., eds. 1971. *Readings in the Philosophy of Language.* Englewood Cliffs, N.J.: Prentice-Hall.
Rosenberg, M. J. 1969. The conditions and consequences of evaluation apprehension. In *Artifact in Behavioral Research,* ed. R. Rosenthal and R. Rosnow, pp. 279–349. New York: Academic Press.
Rosenberg, M. 1954–55. Some determinants of political apathy. *Public Opinion Quarterly* 18:349–66.
———. 1962. The dissonant religious context and emotional disturbance. *American Journal of Sociology* 68:1–10.
———. 1965. *Society and the Adolescent Self-Image.* Princeton, N.J.: Princeton University Press.
———. 1973. Which significant others? *American Behavioral Scientist* 16:829–60.
———. 1975. The dissonant context and the adolescent self-concept. In *Adolescence in the Life Cycle: Psychological Change and Social Context,* ed. S. Dragastin and G. Elder. Washington, D.C.: Hemisphere Publishing Company.
———. 1979. *Conceiving the Self.* New York: Basic Books.
———. 1979. Disposition concepts in behavioral science. In *Qualitative and Quantitative Social Research: Papers in Honor of Paul F. Lazarsfeld,* ed. R. K. Merton, J. Coleman, and P. Rossi. New York: Free Press.
———. 1980. Transient depersonalization. Paper presented at SSRC Committee on Social and Affective Development During Childhood: Conference on the Development of the Self. Mt. Kisco, New York, May.
Rosenberg, M., and McCullough, B. C. 1981. Mattering: inferred significance and mental health. *Research in Community and Mental Health* 2.
Rosenberg, M., and Pearlin, L. I. 1978. Social class and self-esteem among children and adults. *American Journal of Sociology* 84:53–77.

Rosenberg, M., and Rosenberg, F. 1978. The occupational self: a developmental study. Paper presented at Self-Concept Symposium, Boston, Massachusetts, September.

———. Forthcoming. The occupational self: a developmental study. In *Self-Concept Research,* ed. M. Lynch, A. Norem-Hebeisen, and K. Gergen. New York: Ballinger Press.

Rosenberg, M., and Simmons, R. G. 1972. *Black and White Self-Esteem: The Urban School Child.* Washington, D.C.: American Sociological Association.

Rosenblatt, P. C. 1977. Needed research on commitment to marriage. In *Close Relationships,* ed. G. Levinger and H. L. Raush, pp. 73–86. Amherst, Mass.: University of Massachusetts Press.

Rosengren, K. E.; Arvidsson, P.; and Sturesson, D. 1975. The Barseback panic: a radio program as a negative event. *Acta Sociologica* 18:303–21.

Rosenthal, R. 1966. *Experimenter Effects in Behavioral Research.* New York: Appleton-Century-Crofts.

Rosenthal, R., and Jacobson, L. 1968. *Pygmalion in the Classroom.* New York: Holt, Rinehart and Winston.

Rosow, I. 1967. *Social Integration of the Aged.* New York: Free Press.

———. 1970. Old people: their friends and neighbors. *American Behavioral Scientist* 14:59–70.

———. 1974. *Socialization to Old Age.* Berkeley: University of California Press.

Ross, E. A. 1901. *Social Control.* New York: Macmillan.

———. 1908. *Social Psychology.* New York: Macmillan.

———. 1920. *The Principles of Sociology.* New York: The Century Co.

Ross, J. R. 1975. Where to do things with words. In *Syntax and Semantics: Speech Acts,* ed. P. Cole and J. L. Morgan, vol. 3, pp. 233–56. New York: Academic Press.

Ross, L. 1977. The intuitive psychologist and his shortcomings. *Advances in Experimental Social Psychology* 10:173–220.

Rossi, A. 1968. The transition to parenthood. *Journal of Marriage and the Family* 30:26–39.

Roth, G. 1975. Socio-historical model and developmental theory: charismatic community, charisma of reason and counterculture. *American Sociological Review* 40:148–57.

Roth, J. A. 1963. *Timetables.* Indianapolis: Bobbs-Merrill.

Rotter, J. B. 1955. The role of the psychological situation in determining the direction of human behavior. In *Nebraska Symposium on Motivation,* ed. R. Jones, pp. 245–69. Lincoln: University of Nebraska Press.

———. 1966. Generalized expectancies for internal vs. external control of reinforcement. *Psychological Monographs* 80, 1 (whole 609).

Rowland, K. F. 1977. Environmental events predicting death for the elderly. *Psychological Bulletin* 84:349–72.

Rubin, J., and Brown, B. R. 1975. *The Social Psychology of Bargaining and Negotiation.* New York: Academic Press.

Rubin, Z. 1970. Measurement of romantic love. *Journal of Personality and Social Psychology* 16:265–73.

———. 1973. *Liking and Loving: An Invitation to Social Psychology.* New York: Holt, Rinehart and Winston.

Rubin, Z.; Peplau, L. A.; and Hill, C. T. 1981. Loving and leaving: sex differences in romantic attachments. *Sex Roles.* In Press.

Rubinstein, E.; Comstock, G.; and Murray, J., eds. 1972. *Television and Social Behavior.* vol. 4. Washington, D.C.: U. S. Government Printing Office.

Ruch, L. O., and Newton, R. R. 1977. Sex characteristics, task clarity, and authority. *Sex Roles* 3:479–94.

Rudd, J. 1976. Effects of hedonic relevance on the attribution process. Unpublished Master's thesis, University of Iowa.

Rudé, G. 1964a. *The Crowd in History.* New York: Wiley.

———. 1964b. *Revolutionary Europe, 1783–1815.* Cleveland: World.

Rudwick, E., and Meier, A. 1970. Organizational structure and goal succession: a comparative analysis of the NAACP and CORE, 1964–1968. *Social Science Quarterly* 54:9–24.

Rühl, M. 1979. *Die Zeitungsredaktion als organisiertes soziales System.* 2d ed. Freiburg, Switzerland: Universitaetsverlag.

Rule, J., and Tilly, C. 1972. 1830 and the unnatural history of revolution. *Journal of Social Issues* 28:49–76.
Runciman, W. G. 1966. *Relative Deprivation and Social Justice.* Berkeley: University of California Press.
Rush, G. B. 1967. Status consistency and right wing extremism. *American Sociological Review* 32:86–92.
Rushing, W. A., and Ortega, S. T. 1979. Socioeconomic status and mental disorder: new evidence and a sociomedical formulation. *American Journal of Sociology* 84:1175–1200.
Ryder, N. B. 1965. The cohort as a concept in the study of social change. *American Sociological Review* 30:843–61.
Saarni, C. 1979. Children's understanding of display rules for expressive behavior. *Developmental Psychology* 15:424–29.
Sacks, H. 1972*a*. On the analyzability of stories by children. In *Directions in Sociolinguistics: The Ethnography of Communication,* ed. J. J. Gumperz and D. H. Hymes, pp. 325–45. New York: Holt, Rinehart, and Winston.
———. 1972*b*. An initial investigation of the usability of conversational data for doing sociology. In *Studies in Social Interaction,* ed. D. Sudnow, pp. 31–74. New York: Free Press.
———. 1974. An analysis of the course of a joke's telling in conversation. In *Explorations in the Ethnography of Speaking,* ed. R. Bauman and J. Sherzer, pp. 337–53. Cambridge: Cambridge University Press.
Sacks, H.; Schegloff, E. A.; and Jefferson, G. 1974. A simplest systematics for the organization of turn-taking for conversation. *Language* 50:696–735.
Sadock, J. M. 1974. *Toward a Linguistic Theory of Speech Acts.* New York: Academic Press.
Saenger, G. H., and Gilbert, E. 1950. Customer reactions to the integration of Negro personnel. *International Journal of Opinion and Attitude Research* 4:57–76.
Sahlins, M. 1963. On the sociology of primitive exchange. In *The Relevance of Models for Social Research.* ASA Monograph no. 1. London: Tavistock.
———. 1965. Exchange value and the diplomacy of primitive trade. In *Proceedings of the American Ethnological Society.* Seattle: University of Washington Press.
Sakurai, M. M. 1975. Small group cohesiveness and detrimental conformity. *Sociometry* 38:340–57.
Sales, E. 1978. Women's adult development. In *Women and Sex-Roles: A Social Psychological Perspective,* ed. I. H. Frieze, J. E. Parsons, P. B. Johnson, D. N. Ruble, and G. L. Zellman, pp. 157–90. New York: Norton.
Salzman, L. 1953. The psychology of religions and ideological conversion. *Psychiatry* 16:177–87.
Sample, J., and Warland, R. 1973. Attitudes and prediction of behavior. *Social Forces* 51:292–304.
Sampson, E. E. 1965. The study of ordinal position: antecedents and outcomes. In *Progress in Experimental Personality Research,* ed. B. Maher, vol. 2. New York: Academic Press.
Sanders, W. B. 1976. *Juvenile Delinquency.* New York: Praeger.
Sanford, N. 1968. Personality: the field. In *International Encyclopedia of the Social Sciences,* ed. D. L. Sills, vol. 2, pp. 587–606. New York: Free Press.
Sapir, E. 1949. *Selected Writings of Edward Sapir.* Edited by D. G. Mandelbaum. Berkeley: University of California Press.
Sarbin, T. R., and Allen, V. L. 1968. Role theory. In *The Handbook of Social Psychology,* ed. G. Lindzey and E. Aronson, 2d ed. vol. 1. Reading, Mass.: Addison-Wesley.
Sargant, W. 1959. *Battle for the Mind.* New York: Harper
Sargent, S. 1951. Conceptions of role and ego in contemporary psychology. In *Social Psychology at the Crossroads,* ed. J. H. Rohrer and M. Sherif, pp. 355–70. New York: Harper.
Sartre, J. P. 1948. *Anti-Semite and Jew.* New York: Schocken.
Scanzoni, J. 1979. Social exchange and behavioral interdependence. In *Social Exchange in Developing Relationships,* ed. R. L. Burgess and T. L. Huston, pp. 61–98. New York: Academic Press.
Schachtel, E. G. 1949. *Metamorphosis.* New York: Basic Books.

Schachter, S. 1951. Deviation, rejection and communication. *Journal of Abnormal and Social Psychology* 46:190–207.

———. 1959. *The Psychology of Affiliation.* Stanford, Calif.: Stanford University Press.

———. 1964. The interaction of cognitive and physiological determinants of emotional state. In *Advances in Experimental Social Psychology,* ed. L. Berkowitz, vol. 1, pp. 49–81. New York: Academic Press.

———. 1967. Cognitive effects on bodily functioning: studies of obesity and eating. In *Neurophysiology and Emotion,* ed. D. C. Glass. New York: Rockefeller University Press and Russell Sage Foundation.

———. 1971. *Emotion, Obesity, and Crime.* New York: Academic Press.

Schachter, S., and Singer, J. 1962. Cognitive, social, and physiological determinants of emotional state. *Psychological Review* 69:379–99.

Schaie, K. 1979. The primary mental abilities in adulthood. In *Life-Span Development and Behavior,* ed. P. B. Baltes and O. G. Brim, Jr., vol. 2, pp. 68–116. New York: Academic Press.

Scheff, T. J. 1966. *Becoming Mentally Ill.* Chicago: Aldine.

———. 1967. Toward a sociological model of consensus. *American Sociological Review* 32:32–46.

———. 1977. The distancing of emotion in ritual. *Current Anthropology* 18:483–505.

———. 1979. *Catharsis in Healing, Ritual, and Drama.* Berkeley: University of California Press.

Scheflen, A. E. 1973. *Communicational Structure: Analysis of a Psychotherapy Transaction.* Bloomington: Indiana University Press.

Schegloff, E. A. 1968. Sequencing in conversational openings. *American Anthropologist* 70:1075–95.

———. 1972. Notes on a conversational practice formulating place. In *Studies in Social Interaction,* ed. D. Sudnow, pp. 75–119. New York: Free Press.

Schegloff, E. A.; Jefferson, G.; and Sacks, H. 1977. The preference for self-correction in the organization of repair in conversation. *Language* 53:361–82.

Schegloff, E. A., and Sacks, H. 1973. Opening up closings. *Semiotica* 8:289–327.

Schein, E. H. 1961. *Coercive Persuasion.* New York: Norton.

Scheler, M. 1961. *Ressentiment.* New York: Free Press.

Schellenberg, J. A. 1974. *An Introduction to Social Psychology.* 2d ed. New York: Random House.

Schelling, T. 1971. On the ecology of micromotives. *Public Interest* 25:59–98.

Schenkein, J., ed. 1978. *Studies in the Organization of Conversational Interaction.* New York: Academic Press.

Schindler, R. 1957–58. *Grundprinzipien der Psychodynamik in der Gruppe. Psyche* 11:308.

Schlesinger, P. 1978. *Putting "Reality" Together: BBC News.* London: Constable.

Schmitt, E. P., ed. 1937. *Man and Society.* New York: Prentice-Hall.

Schnaiberg, A. 1970. Measuring modernism: theoretical and empirical explorations. *American Journal of Sociology* 76:399–425.

Schoek, H. 1966. *Envy.* New York: Harcourt Brace and World.

Schooler, C. 1972. Birth order effects: not here, not now! *Psychological Bulletin* 78:161–75.

———. 1976. Serfdom's legacy: an ethnic continuum. *American Journal of Sociology* 81:1265–86.

Schott, S. 1979. Emotion and social life: a symbolic interactionist analysis. *American Journal of Sociology* 84:1317–34.

Schramm, W. 1949. The effects of mass communication: a review. *Journalism Quarterly* 26:397–409.

Schrauger, J. S., and Schoeneman, T. J. 1979. Symbolic interactional view of self-concept: through the looking-glass darkly. *Psychological Bulletin* 86:549–73.

Schreiber, J. 1978. *The Ultimate Weapon: Terrorists and World Order.* New York: Morrow.

Schubert, D. S. P., and Wagner, M. E. 1975. A subcultural change of MMPI norms in the 1960s due to adolescent role confusion and glamorization of alienation. *Journal of Abnormal Psychology* 84:406–11.

Schuler, E., and Parenton, V. 1943. A recent epidemic of hysteria in a Louisiana high school. *Journal of Social Psychology* 17:221–35.
Schuman, H. 1969. Free will and determination in public beliefs about race. *Transaction* 7:44–48.
———. 1972*a*. Attitudes vs. actions vs. attitudes vs. attitudes. *Public Opinion Quarterly* 36:347–54.
———. 1972*b*. Free will and determinism in public beliefs about race. In *Majority and Minority: The Dynamics of Racial and Ethnic Relations,* ed. R. Yetman and C. H. Steele, pp. 382–90. Boston: Allyn and Bacon.
———. 1978. Introduction: ambiguities in the attitude-behavior relation. In *Major Social Issues: A Multidisciplinary View,* ed. J. M. Yinger and S. J. Cutler, pp. 373–76. New York: Free Press.
Schuman, H., and Johnson, M. P. 1976. Attitudes and behavior. In *Annual Review of Sociology,* ed. A. Inkeles. pp. 161–207. Palo Alto, Calif.: Annual Reviews.
Schur, E. M. 1971. *Labeling Deviant Behavior: Its Sociological Implications.* New York: Harper and Row.
Schwartz, M.; Fearn; G. F. N.; and Stryker, S. 1966. Note on self-conception and the emotionally disturbed role. *Sociometry* 29:300–305.
Schwartz, M., and Stryker, S. 1970. *Deviance, Selves and Others.* Washington, D.C.: American Sociological Association.
Schwartz, S. H. 1978. Temporal instability as a moderator of the attitude-behavior relationship. *Journal of Personality and Social Psychology* 36:715–24.
Schwartz, S. H., and Fleishman, J. A. 1978. Perceived norms and the mediation of legitimacy effects on helping. *Social Psychology* 41:306–15.
Schwartz, S. H., and Tessler, R. C. 1972. A test of a model for reducing measured attitude-behavior discrepancies. *Journal of Personality and Social Psychology* 24:225–36.
Scott, M. D., and Lyman, S. M. 1968. Accounts. *American Sociological Review* 33:46–62.
Scott, R. A. 1972. A proposed framework for analyzing deviance as a property of social order. In *Theoretical Perspectives on Deviance,* ed. R. A. Scott and J. D. Douglas, pp. 9–35. New York: Basic Books.
Searle, J. R. 1968. Austin on locutionary and illocutionary acts. *Philosophical Review* 78:405–24.
———. 1969. *Speech Arts: An Essay in the Philosophy of Language.* Cambridge: Cambridge University Press.
———. 1979. *Expression and Meaning: Studies in the Theory of Speech Acts.* Cambridge: Cambridge University Press.
———. Forthcoming. *Intentionality and the Use of Language.* Cambridge: Cambridge University Press.
Sears, D. O. 1969. Political behavior. In *The Handbook of Social Psychology,* ed. G. Lindzey and E. Aronson, vol. 5, pp. 315–458. Reading, Mass.: Addison-Wesley.
Sears, D. O., and Kinder, D. R. 1971. Racial tensions and voting in Los Angeles. In *Los Angeles: Viability and Prospects for Metropolitan Leadership,* ed. W. Z. Hirsch, pp. 51–88. New York: Praeger.
Sears, D. O., and McConahay, J. B. 1973. *The Politics of Violence.* Boston: Houghton Mifflin.
Secord, P. F., and Backman, C. W. 1964. *Social Psychology.* New York: McGraw-Hill.
———. 1965. Interpersonal approach to personality. In *Progress in Experimental Personality Research,* ed. B. H. Maher, vol. 2, pp. 91–125. New York: Academic Press.
———. 1974. *Social Psychology.* 2d ed. New York: McGraw-Hill.
Seeman, M. 1966. Status and identity: the problem of inauthenticity. *Pacific Sociological Review* 9:67–73.
———. 1975. Alienation studies. In *Annual Review of Sociology,* ed. A. Inkeles et al., vol. 1, pp. 91–123. Palo Alto, Calif.: Annual Reviews.
———. 1977. Some real and imaginary consequences of social mobility: a French-American comparison. *American Journal of Sociology* 82:757–83.
Seeman, M. et al. 1971. Community and control in a metropolitan setting. In *Race Change and Urban Society,* ed. P. Orleans and R. Ellis, pp. 423–50. Beverley Hills, Calif.: Sage.

Segal, D. R., and Segal, M. W. 1972. How sociological is social psychology? *The American Sociologist* 7:15–16.
Segal, M. W. 1979. Varieties of interpersonal attraction and their interrelationships in natural groups. *Social Psychological Quarterly* 42:253–61.
Selznick, P. 1952. *The Organizational Weapon.* New York: McGraw-Hill.
Selznick, G. J., and Steinberg, J. S. 1969. *The Tenacity of Prejudice.* New York: Harper and Row.
Sennett, R. 1978. *The Fall of Public Man.* New York: Vintage Books.
Severn, B. 1974. *A Carnival of Sports: Spectacles, Stunts, Crazes, and Unusual Sports Events.* New York: McKay.
Sewell, W. H. 1963. Some recent developments in socialization theory and research. *The Annals of the American Academy of Political and Social Science* 349:163–81.
Seymour-Ure, C. 1968. *The Press, Politics, and the Public.* London: Methuen.
Shaffir, W. 1978. Witnessing as identity consolidation: the case of the Lubavitcher Chassidim. In *Identity and Religion,* ed. H. Mol, pp. 39–57. Beverly Hills, Calif.: Sage.
Shand, A. 1914. *The Foundations of Character.* London: Macmillan.
Sharp, G. 1973. *The Politics of Nonviolent Action.* Boston: Porter Sargent.
Shaver, K. G. 1975. *An Introduction to Attribution Processes.* Cambridge, Mass.: Winthrop.
Shaw, M. E. 1971. *Group Dynamics.* New York: McGraw-Hill.
Sheatsley, P. B. 1967. White attitudes toward the Negro. In *The Negro American,* ed. T. Parsons and K. B. Clark, pp. 303–24. Boston: Beacon.
Sheatsley, P., and Feldman, J. 1964. The assassination of President Kennedy. *Public Opinion Quarterly* 28:189–215.
———. 1965. A national survey of public reactions and behavior. In *The Kennedy Assassination and the American Public,* ed. B. S. Greenberg and E. B. Parker, pp. 149–77. Stanford, Calif.: Stanford University Press.
Sheehy, G. 1974. *Passages: Predictable Crises of Adult Life.* New York: E. P. Dutton.
Shephard, J. M. 1977. Technology, alienation, and job satisfaction. *Annual Review of Sociology* 3:1–23.
Sherif, C. W.; Sherif, M.; and Nebergall, R. E. 1965. *Attitude and Attitude Change: The Social Judgment-Involvement Approach.* Philadelphia: W. B. Saunders.
Sherif, M. 1936. *The Psychology of Social Norms.* New York: Harper.
Sherif, M., and Hovland, C. I. 1961. *Social Judgment: Assimilation and Contrast Effects in Communication and Attitude Change.* New Haven: Yale University Press.
Sherif, M., and Sherif, C. W. 1956. *An Outline of Social Psychology.* rev. ed. New York: Harper.
Sherif, M.; White, B. J.; and Harvey, O. J. 1955. Status in experimentally produced groups. *American Journal of Sociology* 66:370–79.
Sherwood, J. J. 1965. Self-identity and referent others. *Sociometry* 28:66–81.
Shey, T. H. 1977. Why communes fail: a comparative analysis of the viability of Danish and American communes. *Journal of Marriage and the Family* 39: 605–13.
Shibutani, T. 1955. Reference groups as perspectives. *American Journal of Sociology* 60:562–69.
———. 1961. *Society and Personality: An Interactionist Approach to Social Psychology.* Englewood Cliffs, N.J.: Prentice-Hall.
———. 1966. *Improvised News: A Sociological Study of Rumor.* Indianapolis: Bobbs-Merrill.
———, ed. 1970. *Human Nature and Collective Behavior.* Englewood Cliffs, N. J.: Prentice-Hall.
Shils, E. A., and Janowitz, M. 1948. Cohesion and disintegration in the Wehrmacht. *Public Opinion Quarterly* 22:280–315.
Shott, S. 1979. Emotion and social life: a symbolic interactionist analysis. *American Journal of Sociology* 84:1317–34.
Sibley, E. 1965. A note on the pronunciation of "shibboleth." *Items* 19 (1):16.
Sieber, S. D. 1974. Toward a theory of role accumulation. *American Sociological Review* 39:467–78.
Siegel, A. E., and Siegel, S. 1957. Reference groups, membership groups, and attitude change. *Journal of Abnormal and Social Psychology* 55:360–64.

Sigal, L. F. 1973. *Reporters and Officials: the Organization and Politics of Newsmaking.* Lexington, Mass.: Heath.

Sigall, H., and Landy, D. 1973. Radiating beauty: effects of having a physically attractive partner on person perception. *Journal of Personality and Social Psychology* 28:218–24.

Sigelman, C. K., and Sigelman, L. 1976. Authority and conformity: violation of a traffic regulation. *Journal of Social Psychology* 100:35–43.

Sills, D. 1968. Voluntary associations: sociological aspects. In *International Encyclopedia of the Social Sciences,* ed. D. Sills, vol. 16. New York: Macmillan and Free Press.

Silverman, D., and Torode, B. 1980. *The Material Word: Some Theories of Language and its Limits.* London: Routledge and Kegan Paul.

Silvern, L. E., and Nakamura, C. Y. 1973. An analysis of the relationship between students' political position and the extent to which they deviate from parents' position. *Journal of Social Issues* 29:111–32.

Simmel, G. 1950. Types of social relationships by degrees of reciprocal knowledge of their participants. In *The Sociology of Georg Simmel,* ed. K. H. Wolff. New York: Free Press.

———. 1955. *Conflict and the Web of Group Affiliations.* New York: Free Press.

———. 1964. *The Sociology of Georg Simmel.* Edited by K. H. Wolff. New York: Free Press.

Simmons, J. L. 1964. On maintaining deviant belief systems: a case study. *Social Problems* 11:250–56.

Simmons, R. G. 1969. The experimentally increased salience of extreme comparative reference groups. *Sociology and Social Research* 53:490–99.

———. 1978. Blacks and high self-esteem: a puzzle. *Social Psychology* 41:54–57.

Simmons, R. G.; Blyth, D. A.; Van Cleave, E. F.; and Bush, D. M. 1979. Entry into early adolescence. *American Sociological Review* 44:948–67.

Simner, M. L. 1971. Newborn's response to the cry of another infant. *Developmental Psychology* 5:136–50.

Simon, H. A. 1955. A behavioral model of rational choice. *Quarterly Journal of Economics* 69:99–118.

———. 1956. Rational choice and the structure of the environment. *Psychological Review* 63:129–38.

Simon, H. E., and Stern, F. 1955. Effect of television upon voting behavior in Iowa in the 1952 presidential election. *American Political Science Review* 49:470–77.

Simpson, G. E., and Yinger, M. J. 1972. *Racial and Cultural Minorities.* 4th ed. New York: Harper and Row.

Simpson, R. L. 1972. *Theories of Social Exchange.* Morristown, N. J.: General Learning Press.

Simpson, R. L., and Simpson, I. H. 1959. The psychiatric attendant: development of an occupational self-image in a low-status occupation. *American Sociological Review* 24:389–92.

Sinclair, J. M., and Coulthard, R. M. 1975. *Towards an Analysis of Discourse: The English Used by Teachers and Pupils.* London: Oxford University Press.

Sinclair, T. 1938. The Nazi Party rally at Nuremberg. *Public Opinion Quarterly* 2:570–83.

Singer, E. 1974. Premature social aging: some psychological consequences of a chronic illness. *Social Science and Medicine* 8:143–51.

Singer, J. E. 1966. Social comparison—progress and issues. *Journal of Experimental Social Psychology* 1:103–10.

Singer, M. 1961. A survey of culture and personality theory and research. In *Studying Personality Cross-culturally,* ed. B. Kaplan, pp. 9–92. New York: Harper and Row.

Skinner, B. F. 1964. Behaviorism at fifty. In *Behaviorism and Phenomenology,* ed. T. W. Wann. Chicago: University of Chicago Press.

———. 1973. *About Behaviorism.* New York: Knopf.

Skolnick, J. 1969. *Politics of Protest.* New York: Simon and Schuster.

Slater, P. E. 1955. Role differentiation in small groups. *American Sociological Review* 20:300–10.

———. 1963. On social regression. *American Sociological Review* 28:339–64.

———. 1966. *Microcosm.* New York: Wiley.

Small, A. and Vincent, G. E. 1894. *An Introduction to the Study of Society.* New York: American Book.
Smelser, N. J. 1963. *Theory of Collective Behavior.* New York: Free Press.
Smelser, N. J., and Smelser, W. T. 1970. *Personality and Social Systems.* 2d ed. New York: Wiley.
Smith, A. 1759. *Theory of Moral Sentiments.* London.
Smith, D. H. 1975. Voluntary action and voluntary groups. In *Annual Review of Sociology,* ed. A. Inkeles, J. Coleman, and N. Smelser, vol. 1, pp. 247–70. Palo Alto, Calif.: Annual Reviews.
Smith, K. C., and Schooler, C. 1978. Women as mothers in Japan: the effects of social structure and culture on values and behavior. *Journal of Marriage and the Family* 40:613–20.
Smith, M. B. 1968. A map for the analysis of personality and politics. *Journal of Social Issues* 24:15–28.
———. 1969. *Social Psychology and Human Values.* Chicago: Aldine.
Smith, M. D. 1975. Sports and collective violence. In *Sport and Social Order,* ed. D. Ball and J. Loy, pp. 281–330. Reading, Mass.: Wesley.
Smith, T. S. 1968. Conventionalization and control: an examination of adolescent crowds. *American Journal of Sociology* 74:172–83.
———. 1974. Aestheticism and social structure. *American Sociological Review* 39: 725–743.
Sniderman, P. 1975. *Personality and Democratic Politics.* Berkeley: University of California Press.
Sniderman, P., and Citrin, J. 1971. Psychological sources of political belief: self-esteem and isolationist attitudes. *American Political Science Review* 65:401–17.
Snow, C. E., and Ferguson, C. A., eds. 1977. *Talking to Children: Language Input and Acquisition.* Cambridge: Cambridge University Press.
Snow, C. E., and Hoefnagel-Hohle, M. 1978. The critical period for language acquisition: evidence from second language learning. *Child Development* 49:1114–28.
Snow, D. A. 1976. *The Nichiren Shoshu Movement in America: A Sociological Examination of Its Value Orientation, Recruitment Efforts and Spread.* Unpublished dissertation. University of California, Los Angeles.
———. 1979. A dramaturgical analysis of movement accommodation: building idiosyncrasy credit as a movement mobilization strategy. *Symbolic Interaction* 2:23–44.
Snow, D. A., and Phillips, C. L. 1980. The Lofland-Stark conversion model: a critical reassessment. *Social Problems* 27:430–47.
Snow, D. A.; Zurcher, L. A.; and Eckland-Olson, S. 1980. Social networks and social movements: a microstructural approach to differential recruitment. *American Sociological Review* 45:787–801.
Snyder, D., and Tilly, C. 1972. Hardship and collective violence in France, 1830 to 1960. *American Sociological Review* 37:520–32.
Snyder, M. 1974. Self-monitoring of expressive behavior. *Journal of Personality and Social Psychology* 30:526–37.
Snyder, M.; Tanke, E.; and Berscheid, E. 1977. Social perception and interpersonal behavior: on the self-fulfilling nature of social stereotypes. *Journal of Personality and Social Psychology* 35:656–66.
Sobieszek, B. I. 1972. Multiple sources and the formation of performance expectations. *Pacific Sociological Review* 15:103–122.
Sobieszek, B. I., and Webster, Jr., M. A. 1973. Conflicting sources of evaluation. *Sociometry* 36:550–60.
Social Psychology Quarterly. 1979. 42:4.
Solomon, F.; Walker, W. L.; O'Connor, G. J.; and Fishman, J. R. 1965. Civil rights activity and reduction in crime among Negroes. *Archives of General Psychology* 12:227–36.
Solomon, R. C. 1977. *The Passions.* Garden City, New York: Doubleday/Anchor.
Songer-Nocks, E. 1976*a.* Situational factors affecting the weighting of predictor components in the Fishbein model. *Journal of Experimental Social Psychology* 12:56–69.
———. 1976*b.* Reply to Fishbein and Ajzen. *Journal of Experimental Social Psychology* 12:585–90.

Sorel, G. 1941. *Reflections on Violence.* New York: Peter Smith.
Southwood, K. 1978. Substantive theory and statistical interaction: five models. *American Journal of Sociology* 83:1154–1203.
Speer, D. C., ed., 1972. *Nonverbal Communication.* Beverly Hills, Calif.: Sage.
Speier, H. 1941*a*. Radio communication of war news in Germany. *Social Research* 8:399–418.
———. 1941*b*. Magic geography. *Social Research* 8:310–30.
Spilerman, S. 1970. The causes of racial disturbances: a comparison of alternative explanations. *American Sociological Review* 35:627–49.
———. 1976. Structural characteristics of cities and the severity of racial disorders. *American Sociological Review* 41:771–93.
Spindler, G. D., ed., 1978. *The Making of Psychological Anthropology.* Berkeley and Los Angeles: University of California Press.
Stafford, R.; Backman, E.; and Dibona, P. 1977. The division of labor among cohabiting and married couples. *Journal of Marriage and the Family* 39:43–57.
Stahl, S., and Lededun, M. 1974. Mystery gas: an analysis of mass hysteria. *Journal of Health and Social Behavior* 15:44–50.
Stalling, R. B. 1970. Personality similarity and evaluative meaning as conditioners of attraction. *Journal of Personality and Social Psychology* 14:77–82.
Stebbins, R. A. 1967. A theory of the definition of the situation. *Canadian Review of Sociology and Anthropology* 4:148–64.
———. 1969. Studying the definition of the situation: theory and field research strategies. *Canadian Review of Sociology and Anthropology* 6:193–211.
Steinberg, D. D., and Jakobovits, L. A., eds., 1971. *Semantics: An Interdisciplinary Reader in Philosophy, Linguistics and Psychology.* Cambridge: Cambridge University Press.
Stember, C. H. 1961. *Education and Attitude Change.* New York: Institute of Human Relations Press.
Stephan, W. G. 1978. School desegregation: an evaluation of predictions made in Brown vs. Board of Education. *Psychological Bulletin* 85:217–38.
Stephan, W.; Berscheid, E.; and Walster, E. 1971. Sexual arousal and heterosexual perception. *Journal of Personality and Social Psychology* 20:93–101.
Stephan, W. G., and Rosenfield, D. 1978. Effects of desegregation on racial attitudes. *Journal of Personality and Social Psychology* 36:795–804.
Stern, E., and Keller, S. 1953. Spontaneous group references in France. *Public Opinion Quarterly* 17:208–17.
St. John, N. H. 1975. *School Desegregation: Outcomes for Children.* New York: Wiley.
Stokes, R., and Hewitt, J. P. 1976. Aligning actions. *American Sociological Review* 41:838–49.
Stone, G. P. 1962. Appearance and the self. In *Human Behavior and Social Processes,* ed. A. M. Rose, pp. 86–118. Boston: Houghton Mifflin.
Stone, G. P., and Farberman, H. A. 1970. *Social Psychology Through Symbolic Interaction.* Waltham, Massachusetts: Ginn.
Storms, M. D. 1979. Sexual orientation and self-perception. In *Perception of Emotion in Self and Others,* ed. P. Pliner, K. R. Blankstein, and I. M. Spiegel. New York: Plenum.
Storms, M., and Nisbett, R., 1970. Insomnia and the attribution process. *Journal of Personality and Social Psychology* 16:319–28.
Stouffer, S. A. et al. 1949*a*. *The American Soldier: Adjustment During Army Life.* vol. 1. Princeton, N.J.: Princeton University Press.
———. 1949*b*. *The American Soldier: Combat and Its Aftermath.* Princeton, N.J.: Princeton University Press.
Straus, R. A. 1976. Changing oneself: seekers and the creative transformation of life experience. In *Doing Social Life,* ed. J. Lofland. New York: Wiley.
Strauss, A. 1959. *Mirrors and Masks.* New York: Free Press.
———. 1971. *The Contexts of Social Mobility.* Chicago: Aldine.
———. 1978. *Negotiations: Varieties, Contexts, Processes, and Social Order.* San Francisco: Jossey-Bass.
Strauss, A.; Schatzman, L.; Ehrlich, D.; Bucher, R.; and Sabshin, M. 1963. The hospital and its negotiated order. In *The Hospital in Modern Society,* ed. E. Friedson, pp. 147–69. New York: Free Press.

Strauss, H. M. 1968. Reference group and social comparison processes among the totally blind. In *Readings in Reference Group Theory and Research,* ed. H. H. Hyman and E. Singer, pp. 222–37. New York: Free Press.

Strodtbeck, F. L.; James, R. M.; and Hawkins, C. 1957. Social status in jury deliberation. *American Sociological Review* 22:713–19.

Strodtbeck, F. L., and Mann, R. 1956. Sex role differentiation in jury deliberations. *Sociometry* 19:3–11.

Stroebe, W. 1977. Self-esteem and interpersonal attraction. In *Theory and Practice in Interpersonal Attraction.* ed. S. Duck, pp. 79–104. New York: Academic Press.

Stroebe, W., Insko, C. A., Thompson, V. D., and Layton, B. D. 1971. Effects of physical attractiveness, attitude similarity, and sex on various aspects of interpersonal attraction. *Journal of Personality and Social Psychology* 18:79–91.

Strongman, K. T. 1978. *The Psychology of Emotion.* 2d ed. New York: Wiley.

Stryker, S. 1956. Relations of married offspring and parents: a test of Mead's theory. *American Journal of Sociology* 62:308–19.

———. 1957. Role-taking accuracy and adjustment. *Sociometry* 20:286–96.

———. 1959. Symbolic interaction as an approach to family research. *Marriage and Family Living* 31:111–19.

———. 1964. The interactional and situational approaches. In *Handbook on Marriage and the Family,* ed. H. Christensen, pp. 124–70. Chicago: Rand McNally.

———. 1968. Identity salience and role performance: the relevance of symbolic interaction theory for family research. *Journal of Marriage and the Family* 30:558–64.

———. 1973. Fundamental principles of social interaction. In *Sociology,* ed. Neil J. Smelser, 2d ed., pp. 495–547. New York: Wiley.

———. 1977. Developments in "two social psychologies": toward an appreciation of mutual relevance. *Sociometry* 40:145–60.

———. 1979. The profession: comments from an interactionist's perspective. *Sociological Focus* 12:175–86.

———. 1980. *Symbolic Interactionism: A Social Structural Version.* Menlo Park, Calif.: Benjamin/Cummings.

Suczek, B. 1973. The curious case of the "death" of Paul McCartney. *Urban Life* 1:61–76.

Sudnow, D., ed. 1972. *Studies in Social Interaction.* New York: Free Press.

Suedfeld, P., and Rank, A. D. 1976. Revolutionary leaders: long-term success as a function of changes in conceptual complexity. *Journal of Personality and Social Psychology* 34:169–78.

Sullivan, H. S. 1947. *Conceptions of Modern Psychiatry: The First William Alanson White Memorial Lectures.* Washington, D.C.: William Alanson White Psychiatric Foundation.

Suls, J. M., and Miller, R. L., eds. 1977. *Social Comparison Processes.* New York: Wiley.

Super, D. E. 1953. A theory of vocational development. *American Psychologist* 8:185–90.

Surace, S. J., and Seeman, M. 1967. Some correlates of civil rights activism. *Social Forces* 46:197–207.

Sutherland, E. H. 1939. *Principles of Criminology.* 3d ed. Philadelphia: J. B. Lippincott.

Sutherland, E. H., and Cressey, D. 1966. *Principles of Criminology.* 7th ed. Philadelphia: J. B. Lippincott.

———. 1974. *Criminology.* 9th ed. Philadelphia: J. B. Lippincott.

Suttles, G. 1968. *The Social Order of the Slum.* Chicago: University of Chicago Press.

———. 1970. Friendship as a social institution. In *Social Relationships,* ed. G. J. McCall et al. Chicago: Aldine.

Suzman, R. M. 1977. The modernization of personality. In *We, the People: American Character and Social Change,* ed. G. J. DiRenzo, pp. 40–77. Westport, Conn.: Greenwood Press.

Swanson, D. L., ed. 1979. The uses and gratifications approach to mass communications research. *Communication Research* 6:3–111 (entire issue).

Swanson, G. E. 1965. The routinization of love: structure and process in primary relations. In *The Quest for Self-Control,* ed. S. Z. Klausner. New York: Free Press.

Sykes, G. 1958. *The Society of Captives.* Princeton, N.J.: Princeton University Press.

Sykes, G., and Matza, D. 1957. Techniques of neutralization. *American Sociological Review* 22:664–70.

Tallman, I. 1976. *Passion, Action and Politics.* San Francisco: Freeman.

Tallman, I., and Ihinger-Tallman, M. 1977. A theory of socialization processes. Paper presented at the annual meetings of the National Council of Family Relations, San Diego.

———. 1979. Values, distributive justice and social change. *American Sociological Review* 44:216–35.

Tan, E. S. 1963. Epidemic hysteria. *The Medical Journal of Malaya* 18:72–76.

Taylor, D. G.; Sheatsley, P. B.; and Greeley, A. M. 1978. Attitudes toward racial integration. *Scientific American* 238:42–49.

Taylor, I. et al. 1973. *The New Criminology.* London: Routledge and Kegan Paul.

Taylor, R. L. 1976. Psychosocial development among black children and youth: a reexamination. *American Journal of Orthopsychiatry* 46:4–19.

Taylor, S. E. 1975. On inferring one's attitudes from one's behavior. *Journal of Personality and Social Psychology* 31:126–31.

———. 1978. Salience, attention and attribution: top of the head phenomena. In *Advances in Experimental Social Psychology,* ed. L. Berkowitz, vol. 2, pp. 249–87. New York: Academic.

Tedeschi, J. T.; Schlenker, B. R.; and Bonoma, T. V. 1971. Cognitive dissonance: Private ratiocination or public spectacle? *American Psychologist* 26:685–95.

TenHouten, W. D. 1970. The black family: myth and reality. *Psychiatry* 33:145–73.

Terhune, K. 1970. From national character to national behavior. *Journal of Conflict Resolution* 14:204–63.

Thibaut, J. W., and Kelley, H. H. 1959. *The Social Psychology of Groups.* New York: Wiley.

Thio, A. 1978. *Deviant Behavior.* Boston: Houghton Mifflin.

Thomae, H. 1979. The concept of development and life-span developmental psychology. In *Life-Span Development and Behavior,* ed. P. B. Baltes and O. G. Brim, Jr., vol. 2, pp. 281–312. New York: Academic Press.

Thomas, D. L.; Franks, D. D.; and Calconico, J. M. 1972. Role-taking and power in social psychology. *American Sociological Review* 37:605–14.

Thomas, D. L.; Gecas, V.; Weigert, A., and Rooney, E. 1974. *Family Socialization and the Adolescent.* Lexington, Mass.: D.C. Heath and Company.

Thomas, D. L., and Weigert, A. J. 1971. Socialization and adolescent conformity to significant others: a cross-national analysis. *American Sociological Review* 36: 835–46.

Thomas, L. 1974. *The Lives of the Cell.* New York: Viking.

Thomas, W. I. 1937. *Primitive Behavior.* New York: McGraw-Hill.

Thomas, W. I., and Thomas, D. S. 1928. *The Child in America.* New York: Knopf.

Thornton, A., and Freedman, D. 1979. Changes in the sex role attitudes of women, 1962–1977: evidence from a panel study. *American Sociological Review* 44:831–42.

Thornton, D. A., and Arrowood, A. J. 1966. Self-evaluation, self-enhancement, and the locus of social comparison. *Journal of Experimental Social Psychology.* supplement 1: 40–48.

Thornton, R., and Nardi, P. M. 1975. The dynamics of role acquisition. *American Journal of Sociology* 80:870–85.

Thornton, T. P. 1964. Terror as a weapon of political agitation. In *Internal War,* ed. H. Eckstein, pp. 71–99. New York: Free Press.

Thurstone, L. L. 1929. Theory of attitude measurement. *Psychological Review* 36: 222–41.

Thurstone, L. L., and Chave, E. J. 1929. *The Measurement of Attitude.* Chicago: University of Chicago Press.

Tichenor, P. J. et al. 1973. Community issues, conflict, and public affairs knowledge. In *New Model for Communication Research,* ed. P. Clarke, pp. 45–80. Beverly Hills, Calif.: Sage.

Tierney, K. 1980. Emergent norm theory as "theory": an analysis and critique of Turner's formulation. In *Collective Behavior: A Source Book,* ed. M. D. Pugh, pp. 42–53. New York: West Publishing.

Tilly, C. 1978. *From Mobilization to Revolution.* Reading, Mass.: Addison-Wesley.

———. 1979. Repertories of contention in America and Britain, 1750–1830. In *The Dynamics of Social Movements,* ed. M. Zald, and J. McCarthy, pp. 126–55. Cambridge, Mass.: Winthrop.

Tilly, C.; Tilly, L.; and Tilly, R. 1975. *The Rebellious Century, 1830–1930.* Cambridge, Mass.: Harvard University Press.

Titmuss, R. M. 1950. *Problems of Social Policy.* London: His Majesty's Stationery Office and Longmans, Green and Company.

Tittle, C. R., and Hill, R. J. 1967*a.* Attitude measurement and the prediction of behavior: an evaluation of conditions and measurement techniques. *Sociometry* 30:199–213.

———. 1967*b.* The accuracy of self-reported data and prediction of political activity. *Public Opinion Quarterly* 31:103–106.

Tittle, C. R., and Villemez, W. J. 1977. Social class and criminality. *Social Forces* 56:474–502.

Toch, H. 1965. *The Social Psychology of Social Movements.* Indianapolis: Bobbs-Merrill.

Tocqueville, A. de. 1945 [1835]. *Democracy in America.* 2 vols. New York: Vintage.

———. 1961. *The Old Regime and the French Revolution.* New York: Harper and Row.

Toennies, F. 1957. *Community and Society.* East Lansing: Michigan State University Press.

Tomeh, A. K. 1970. Reference group supports among middle eastern college students. *Journal of Marriage and the Family* 32:156–66.

Tomkins, S. 1962. *Affect, Imagery, Consciousness,* vol. 1. New York: Springer.

Torrance, E. P. 1954. Some consequences of power differences on decision making in permanent and temporary three-man groups. *Research Studies, State College of Washington* 22:130–40.

Torres-Matrullo, C. 1976. Acculturation and psychopathology among Puerto Rican women in mainland United States. *American Journal of Orthopsychiatry* 46:710–19.

Touhey, J. C. 1974. Situated identities, attitude similarity and interpersonal attraction. *Sociometry* 37:363–74.

Touraine, A. 1973. *Production de la Société.* Paris: Editions de Seuil.

Traugott, M. 1978. Reconceiving social movements. *Social Problems* 26:38–49.

Travisano, R. V. 1970. Alternation and conversion as qualitatively different transformations. In *Social Psychology through Symbolic Interaction,* ed. G. P. Stone and H. A. Farberman, pp. 594–606. Waltham, Mass.: Ginn-Blaisdell.

Triandis, H. C. 1961. A note on Rokeach's theory of prejudice. *Journal of Abnormal and Social Psychology* 62:184–86.

———. 1971. *Attitude and Attitude Change.* New York: Wiley.

Triandis, H. C., and Brislin, R., eds. 1978. *Handbook of Cross Cultural Psychology,* vol. 4. (Social Psychology). Boston: Allyn and Bacon.

Triandis, H. C., and Davis, E. E. 1965. Race and belief as determinants of behavioral intentions. *Journal of Personality and Social Psychology* 2:715–25.

Troeltsch, E. 1931. *The Social Teachings of the Christian Churches,* 2 vols. Trans. Olive Wyon. New York: Macmillan.

Troldahl, V. C. 1966–67. A field test of a modified "two-step flow of communication" model. *Public Opinion Quarterly* 30:609–23.

Trotsky, L. 1959. *The History of the Russian Revolution.* Edited by F. W. Dupee. Garden City and New York: Doubleday.

———. 1961. *Terrorism and Communism: A Reply to Karl Kautsky.* Ann Arbor, Mich.: Ann Arbor Paperbacks.

Trudgill, P. J. 1972. Sex, covert prestige and linguistic change in the urban British English of Norwich. *Language in Society* 1:179–95.

Truzzi, M. 1972. Occult revival as popular culture. *Sociological Quarterly* 13:16–31.

Tuchman, G. 1978. *Making News: A Study in the Construction of Reality.* New York: Free Press.

Tucker, C. W. 1966. Some methodological problems of Kuhn's self theory. *Sociological Quarterly* 7:345–58.

Tucker, L. R. 1978. The environmentally concerned citizen. *Environment and Behavior* 10:389–418.

Tumin, M. M. 1959. Exposure to mass media and readiness for desegregation. *Public Opinion Quarterly* 221:237–51.

Tumin, M., and Feldman, A. 1955. The miracle at Sabana Grande. *Public Opinion Quarterly* 19:124–39.

Tunstall, J. 1971. *Journalists at Work.* London: Constable.

Turk, A. T. 1969. *Criminality and Legal Order.* Chicago: Rand McNally.

Turk, H. 1970. Inter-organizational networks in urban society: initial perspectives and comparative research. *American Sociological Review* 35:1–19.

Turner, J. H. 1978. *The Structure of Sociological Theory.* Homewood, Ill.: Dorsey.

Turner, R. H. 1960. Sponsored and contest mobility and the school system. *American Sociological Review* 25:855–67.

———. 1962. Role-taking: process vs. conformity. In *Human Behavior and Social Processes,* ed. A. M. Rose, pp. 20–40. Boston: Houghton Mifflin.

———. 1964. Collective behavior. In *Handbook of Modern Sociology,* ed. R. E. L. Faris, pp. 382–425. Chicago: Rand McNally.

———. 1968*a.* The self-conception in social interaction. In *The Self in Social Interaction,* ed. C. Gordon, and K. Gergen. New York: Wiley.

———. 1968*b.* Is the concept of attitude obsolete? Paper presented at the annual meetings of the Pacific Sociological Association, San Francisco, March.

———. 1969*a.* The public perception of protest. *American Sociological Review* 34:815–31.

———. 1969*b.* The problems of social dimensions in personality. In *The Sociology of Personality,* ed. S. Spitzer. New York: Van Nostrand.

———. 1969*c.* The theme of contemporary social movements. *British Journal of Sociology* 20:390–405.

———. 1970. *Family Interaction.* New York: Wiley.

———. 1973. Determinants of social movement strategies. In *Human Nature and Collective Behavior: Papers in Honor of Herbert Blumer,* ed. T. Shibutani, pp. 145–64. New Brunswick, N. J.: Transaction Books.

———. 1976. The real self: from institution to impulse. *American Journal of Sociology* 81:989–1016.

———. 1978. The role and the person. *American Journal of Sociology* 84:1–23.

———. n.d.*a.* Role-playing as process. Unpublished paper.

———. n.d.*b.* Role-playing as process. Unpublished paper.

———. n.d.*c.* A strategy for developing an integrated role theory. Unpublished paper.

Turner, R., and Killian, L. 1957. *Collective Behavior.* Englewood Cliffs, N.J.: Prentice-Hall.

———. 1972. Collective Behavior. 2d ed. Englewood Cliffs, N. J.: Prentice-Hall.

Turner, R. H., and Surace, S. J. 1956. Zoot-Suiters and Mexicans: symbols in crowd behavior. *American Journal of Sociology* 62:14–20.

Urry, J. R. 1973. *Reference Groups and the Theory of Revolution.* Boston: Routledge and Kegan Paul.

Useem, M. 1975. *Protest Movements in America.* Indianapolis: Bobbs-Merrill.

Vaillant, G. E., and McArthur, C. 1972. Natural history of male psychologic health: the adult life cycle. *Seminars in Psychiatry* 4:18–50.

Valentine, C. 1968. *Culture and Poverty: Critique and Counter-Proposals.* Chicago: University of Chicago Press.

van den Berghe, P. 1962. Race attitudes in Durban. *Journal of Psychology* 57:55–57.

Van Gennep, A. 1960 [1908]. *The Rites of Passage.* Chicago: University of Chicago Press.

Van Maanen, J. 1977. *Organizational Careers: Some New Perspectives.* New York: Wiley.

Vanneman, R. D., and Pettigrew, T. F. 1972. Race and relative deprivation in the urban United States. *Race* 13:461–86.

Veblen, T. 1934. *The Theory of the Leisure Class.* New York: Modern Library.

Videbeck, R. 1960. Self-conceptions and the reactions of others. *Sociometry* 23:351–59.

Von Eschen, D., Kirk, J., and Pinard, M. 1971. The organizational substructure of disorderly politics. *Social Forces* 49:529–44.

Wahrman, R., and Pugh, M. D. 1974. Sex, nonconformity and influence. *Sociometry* 37:137–47.

Waite, L. J. 1978. Projecting female labor force participation from sex-role attitudes. *Social Science Research* 7:299–317.
Waller, W. 1930. *The Old Love and the New: Divorce and Readjustment.* New York: Liveright.
———. 1938. *The Family: A Dynamic Interpretation.* New York: Cordon Company.
Waller, W., and Hill, R. 1951. *The Family: A Dynamic Interpretation.* New York: Dryden.
Wallis, R. 1979. *Salvation and Protest.* London: Frances Pinter.
Walsh, R. H.; Ferrell, M.Z.; and Tolone, W. L. 1976. Selection of reference group, perceived reference group permissiveness, and personal permissiveness attitudes and behavior: a study of two consecutive panels. *Journal of Marriage and the Family* 38:495–507.
Walster, E. 1971. Passionate love. In *Theories of Attraction and Love,* ed. B. I. Murstein. New York: Springer.
Walster, E.; Aronson, V., Abrahams, D., and Rottman, L. 1966. Importance of physical attractiveness in dating behavior. *Journal of Personality and Social Psychology* 4:508–16.
Walster, E., and Berscheid, E. 1971. Adrenaline makes the heart grow fonder. *Psychology Today* 5:47–55.
Walster, E.; Berscheid, E.; and Walster, G. W., eds. 1976. *Equity Theory and Research.* London: Allyn and Bacon.
Walster, E., and Walster, G. 1963. Effect of expecting to be liked on choice of associates. *Journal of Abnormal and Social Psychology* 67:402–404.
———. 1978. *A New Look at Love.* Reading, Mass.: Addison-Wesley.
Walster, E.; Walster, G. W.; and Berscheid, E. 1978. *Equity: Theory and Research.* Boston: Allyn and Bacon.
Wangh, M. 1964. National socialism and the genocide of the Jews; a psychoanalytic study of an historical event. *International Journal of Psycho-analysis* 45:386–95.
Ward, M. C. 1971. *Them Children: A Study in Language Learning.* New York: Holt, Rinehart and Winston.
Warner, L. G., and DeFleur, M. L. 1969. Attitude as an interactional concept: social constraint and social distance as intervening variables between attitudes and actions. *American Sociological Review* 34:153–69.
Warner, W. L., and Henry, W. E. 1948. The radio day-time serial: a symbolic analysis. *Genetic Psychology Monographs* 37.
Warriner, C. K. 1956. Groups are real: a reaffirmation. *American Sociological Review* 21:549–54.
Watt, I. 1951. "Robinson Crusoe" as a myth. *Essays in Criticism:* 95–119.
Watt, J. H., Jr., and Van den Berg, S. A. 1978. Time series analysis of alternative media effects series. *Communication Yearbook* 2:215–24.
Weber, M. 1946. *From Max Weber: Essays in Sociology.* Edited by H. Gerth and C. W. Mills. New York: Oxford University Press.
———. 1958. *The Protestant Ethic and the Spirit of Capitalism.* Translated by T. Parsons. New York: Scribner's.
———. 1968. *Economy and Society: An Outline of Interpretive Sociology.* Edited by G. Roth and C. Wittich. Berkeley: University of California Press.
Webster, M. A., Jr. 1969. Sources of evaluations and expectations for performances. *Sociometry* 32:243–58.
———. 1977. Equating characteristics and social interaction: two experiments. *Sociometry* 49:41–50.
Webster, M. A., Jr., and Driskell, J. E., Jr. 1978. Status generalization: a review and some new data. *American Sociological Review* 43:220–36.
Webster, M. A., Jr., and Entwisle, D. R. 1976. Expectation effects on performance evaluations. *Social Forces* 55:493–502.
Webster, M. A., Jr.; Roberts, L.; and Sobieszek, B. I. 1972. Accepting "significant others": six models. *American Journal of Sociology* 78:576–98.
Webster, M. A., Jr., and Sobieszek, B. I. 1974*a*. Sources of evaluations and expectation states. In *Expectation States Theory: A Theoretical Research Program.* ed. J. Berger, T. L. Conner, and M. H. Fisek, chap. 5. Cambridge, Mass.: Winthrop.
———. 1974*b*. *Sources of Self-Evaluation: a Formal Theory of Significant Others and Social Influence.* New York: Wiley.

Wegner, D. M., and Vallacher, R. R., eds. 1980. *The Self in Social Psychology.* New York: Oxford University Press.

Weigel, R. H., and Amsterdam, J. T. 1976. The effect of behavior relevant information on attitude-behavior consistency. *Journal of Social Psychology* 98:247–51.

Weigel, R. H., and Newman, L. S. 1976. Increasing attitude-behavior correspondence by broadening the scope of the behavioral measure. *Journal of Personality and Social Psychology* 33:793–802.

Weigel, R. H.; Vernon, D. T. A.; and Tognacci, L. N. 1974. Specificity of the attitude as a determinant of attitude-behavior congruence. *Journal of Personality and Social Psychology* 30:724–28.

Weigert, A. J., and Hastings, R. 1977. Identity loss, family, and social change. *American Journal of Sociology* 82:1171–85.

Weinberg, M. 1977. *Minority Students: A Research Appraisal.* Washington, D.C.: U.S. Department of Health, Education and Welfare (National Institute of Education).

Weinstein, A. G. 1972. Predicting behavior from attitudes. *Public Opinion Quarterly* 36:355–60.

Weinstein, E. A., and Deutschberger, P. 1963. Some dimensions of altercasting. *Sociometry* 26:454–66.

Weinstein, E. A., and Tanur, J. M. 1976. Meanings, purposes, and structural resources in social interaction. *Cornell Journal of Social Relations* 11:105–10.

Weisner, T. S., and Abbott, S. 1977. Women, modernity, and stress: three contrasting contexts for change in East Africa. *Journal of Anthropological Research* 33:421–51.

Weiss, R. S. 1975. *Marital Separation.* New York: Basic Books.

———. 1976. The emotional impact of marital separation. *Journal of Social Issues* 32:135–46.

Weiss, W. 1969. Effects of the mass media of communication. In *The Handbook of Social Psychology,* ed. G. Lindzey and E. Aronson, 2d ed., vol. 5, pp. 77–195. Reading, Mass.: Addison-Wesley.

Weitman, S. 1970. Intimacies: notes toward a theory of social inclusion and exclusion. *Archives Européennes de Sociologie* 11:348–67.

Wells, L. E. 1978. Theories of deviance and the self-concept. *Social Psychology* 41:189–204.

Werner, C., and Parmelee, P. 1979. Similarity of activity preferences among friends: those who play together stay together. *Social Psychology Quarterly* 42:62–66.

Westie, F. R. 1952. Negro-white status differentials and social distance. *American Sociological Review* 17:550–58.

Weston, L. C., and Ruggiero, J. A. 1978. Changes in attitudes of women toward nonconformists. *Pacific Sociological Review* 21:131–40.

Wheeler, S. 1966. The structure of formally organized socialization settings. In *Socialization After Childhood: Two Essays,* ed. O. G. Brim, Jr., and S. Wheeler, pp. 51–116. New York: Wiley.

———. 1969. Socialization in correctional institutions. In *Handbook of Socialization Theory and Research.* ed. D. A. Goslin. Chicago: Rand McNally.

Wheelwright, E. L., and McFarlane, B. 1970. *The Chinese Road to Socialism.* New York: Monthly Review Press.

White, H. C.; Boorman, S. A.; and Breiger, R. L. 1976. Social structure from multiple networks. I. Blockmodels of roles and positions. *American Journal of Sociology* 81:730–80.

White, J. W. 1970. *The Sokagakkai and Mass Society.* Stanford, Calif.: Stanford University Press.

White, R. W. 1959. Motivation reconsidered: the concept of competence. *Psychological Review* 66:297–333.

Whiting, J. W. M., and Child, T. L. 1953. *Child Training and Personality: A Cross-Cultural Study.* New Haven: Yale University Press.

Whitten, N. E., and Wolfe, A. W. 1971. Network analysis. In *The Handbook of Social and Cultural Anthropology.* ed. J. J. Honigman, Chicago: Rand McNally.

Whorf, B. L. 1956. *Language, Thought, and Reality.* Boston: The M.I.T. Press.

Whyte, W. F. 1955. *Street Corner Society.* Chicago: University of Chicago Press.

Wicker, A. W. 1969. Attitudes versus actions: the relationship of verbal and overt behavioral responses to attitude objects. *Journal of Social Issues* 25:41–78.

———. 1971. An examination of the "other variables" explanation of attitude-behavior inconsistency. *Journal of Personality and Social Psychology* 19:18–30.

Wicklund, R. A., and Brehm, J. W. 1976. *Perspectives on Cognitive Dissonance.* Hillsdale, N. J.: Erlbaum.

Wieder, D. L., and Zimmerman, D. H. 1976. Becoming a freak: pathways into the counter-culture. *Youth and Society* 7:311–44.

Wiggins, D. 1971 [1968]. On sentence-sense, work-sense and different word-sense. Towards a philosophical theory of dictionaries, and a reply to Mr. Alston. In *Semantics: An Interdisciplinary Reader in Philosophy, Linguistics and Psychology,* ed. D. D. Steinberg, and L. A. Jakobovits, pp. 14–34; 48–52. Cambridge: Cambridge University Press.

Wilensky, H. 1961. Orderly careers and social participation: the impact of work history on social integration in the middle class. *American Sociological Review* 26:521–39.

Wilensky, H. L., and Edwards, H. 1959. The skidder: ideological adjustments of downward mobile workers. *American Sociological Review* 24:215–231.

Wilke, W. H. 1934. An experimental comparison of the speech, the radio, and the printed page as propaganda devices. *Archives of Psychology* 169.

Wilkins, W. E. 1976. The concept of a self-fulfilling prophecy. *Sociology of Education* 49:175–83.

Wilkinson, P. 1971. *Social Movement.* London: Pall Mall.

Williams, F. E. 1923. *The Vailala Madness and the Destruction of Native Ceremonies in the Gulf Division.* Port Moresby: E. G. Baker.

Williams, R. 1973. *The Country and the City.* London: Chatto and Windus.

Williams, R. M., Jr. 1947. *The Reduction of Intergroup Tensions.* New York: Social Science Research Council.

———. 1964. *Strangers Next Door.* Englewood Cliffs, N. J.: Prentice-Hall.

———. 1975. Race and ethnic relations. In *Annual Review of Sociology.* ed. A. Inkeles et al., vol. 1, pp. 125–64. Palo Alto, Calif.: Annual Reviews

———. 1976. Relative deprivation versus power struggle? "Tension" and "structural" explanations of collective conflict. *Cornell Journal of Social Relations* 2:31–8.

Williamson, O. E. 1975. *Markets and Hierarchies.* New York: Free Press.

Willie, E. V. 1979. *Caste and Class Controversy.* Bayside, N.Y.: General Hall.

Willits, F. K.; Bealer, R. C.; and Crider, D. M. 1977. Changes in individual attitudes toward traditional morality: a 24-year follow-up study. *Journal of Gerontology* 32:681–88.

Wilner, D. M.; Walkley, R. P.; and Cook, S. W. 1955. *Human Relations in Interracial Housing.* Minneapolis: University of Minnesota.

Wilson, B. R. 1959. The Pentecostalist Minister: role conflicts and status contradictions. *American Journal of Sociology* 44:494–504.

Wilson, D. W., and Schafer, R. B. 1978. Is social psychology interdisciplinary? *Personality and Social Psychology Bulletin* 4:548–52.

Wilson, J. 1973. *Introduction to Social Movements.* New York: Basic Books.

Wilson, K., and Orum, A. 1976. Mobilizing people for collective action. *Journal of Political and Military Sociology* 4:187–202.

Wilson, K., and Zurcher, L. A. 1979. Status inconsistency and participation in social movements: an application of Goodman's hierarchical modeling. *Sociological Quarterly* 17:520–33.

Wilson, S. R. 1960. The effect of the laboratory situation on experimental discussion groups. *Sociometry* 32:220–36.

Wilson, T. 1970. Conceptions of interaction and forms of sociological explanation. *American Sociological Review* 35:697–710.

Wilson, W. J. 1978. *The Declining Significance of Race.* Chicago: University of Chicago, Press.

Winch, R. T. 1958. *Mate Selection: A Study of Complementary Needs.* New York: Harper & Row.

Winsborough, H. H. 1963. The similarity of connected observations. *American Sociological Review* 28:977–83.

Wispe, L. 1968. Sympathy and empathy. In *International Encyclopedia of the Social Sciences,* ed. D. Sills. New York: Macmillan.
Wolfe, A. W. 1978. On structural comparisons of networks. *Canadian Review of Sociology and Anthropology* 7:226–44.
Wolfe, T. 1971. *Radical Chic and Mau-Mauing the Flak Catcher.* New York: Bantam.
Wolfenstein, M. 1957. *Disaster: A Psychological Essay.* Glencoe, Ill.: Free Press.
Wolfenstein, M., and Kilman, G., eds. 1966. *Children and the Death of a President: Multi-Disciplinary Studies.* Garden City: Doubleday.
Woodcock, A., and Davis, M. 1978. *Catastrophe Theory.* New York: Dutton.
Worsley, P. M. 1957. *The Trumpet Shall Sound: A Study of Cargo Cults in Melanesia.* London: Macgibbon and Kee. (Reprint 1968. New York: Schocken.)
Wright, C. 1960. Functional analysis and mass communication. *Public Opinion Quarterly* 24:605–20.
———. 1974. Functional analysis and mass communication revisited. In *Uses of Mass Communication: Current Perspectives on Gratification Research,* eds. J. Blumer and E. Katz, pp. 197–212. Beverly Hills, Calif. Sage.
———. 1975. Social structure and mass communication behavior: new directions for audience analysis. In *The Idea of Social Structure,* ed. L. A. Coser. New York: Harcourt Brace Jovanovich.
Wright, C. R., and Cantor, M. 1967. The opinion seeker and avoider: steps beyond the opinion leader concept. *Pacific Sociological Review* 10:33–43.
Wright, E. O., and Perrone, L. 1977. Marxist class and categories and income inequality. *American Sociological Review* 42:32–56.
Wright, J. D., and Wright, S. 1976. Social class and parental values for children: a partial replication and extension of the Kohn thesis. *American Sociological Review* 41:527–37.
Wrong, D. H. 1961. The oversocialized conception of man in modern sociology. *American Sociological Review* 26:183–93.
Wuebben, P. L.; Straits, B. C.; and Schulman, G. I. 1974. *The Experiment as a Social Occasion.* Berkeley: Glendessary Press.
Wyant, S. 1980. Attitudes and behaviors of California coastal commissioners. Unpublished doctoral dissertation, Claremont Graduate School.
Wylie, R. 1961. *The Self-Concept: A Critical Survey of Pertinent Research Literature.* Lincoln: University of Nebraska Press.
———. 1979. *The Self-Concept: Revised Edition.* vol. 2. *Theory and Research on Selected Topics.* Lincoln: University of Nebraska Press.
Yablonsky, L. 1965. *Synanon: The Tunnel Back.* Baltimore: Penguin.
Yamagishi, T. In press. An experimental study of distribution rules, productive structures and the maximization of profit.
Yao, E. L. 1979. The assimilation of contemporary Chinese immigrants. *Journal of Psychology* 101:107–13.
Yinger, J. 1977. Characterological change among Black Americans: a contextual interpretation. In *We, the People: American Character and Social Change,* ed. G. J. DiRenzo. Westport, Conn.: Greenwood Press.
Zablocki, B. 1971. *The Joyful Community.* Baltimore: Penguin.
Zajonc, R. B. 1968. Attitudinal effects of mere exposure. *Journal of Personality and Social Psychology,* Monograph supplement no. 2, pt. 2:1–27.
———. 1976. Family configuration and intelligence. *Science* 192:227–36.
Zajonc, R. B.; Markus, H.; and Markus, G. B. 1979. The birth order puzzle. *Journal of Personality and Social Psychology* 37:1325–41.
Zald, M. N., and Ash, R. 1966. Social movement organizations: growth, decay and change. *Social Forces* 44:327–41.
Zald, M. N., and McCarthy, J. D. 1979. *The Dynamics of Social Movements: Resource Mobilization, Social Control, and Tactics.* Cambridge, Mass.: Winthrop Publishers.
Zander, A. 1979. The psychology of group processes. *Annual Review of Psychology:* 417–52.
Zawadski, B., and Lazarsfeld, P. 1935. The psychological consequences of unemployment. *Journal of Social Psychology* 6:224–51.
Zborowski, M. 1952. Cultural components in responses to pain. *Journal of Social Issues* 4:16–30.

Zelditch, M., Jr. 1969. Can you really study an army in the laboratory? In *Complex Organizations,* ed. A. Etzioni, pp. 528–39. New York: Holt, Rinehart and Winston.

———. 1972. Authority and performance expectations in bureaucratic organizations. In *Experimental Social Psychology,* ed. C. G. McClintock, pp. 484–513. New York: Holt, Rinehart and Winston.

Zelditch, M., Jr.; Lauderdale, P.; and Stublarec, S. 1980. How are inconsistencies between status and ability resolved? *Social Forces* 58:1025–43.

Zeller, R. A., and Warnecke, R. B. 1973. The utility of intervening constructs in experiments. *Sociological Methods and Research* 2:85–110.

Zigler, E., and Child, I. 1969. Socialization. In *Handbook of Social Psychology,* ed. G. Lindzey and E. Aronson, 2d ed., pp. 450–589. Reading, Mass.: Addison-Wesley.

Zigler, E., and Seitz, V. 1978. Changing trends in socialization theory and research. *American Behavioral Scientist* 21:731–56.

Zimbardo, P. G. 1969. The human choice: individuation, reason, and order versus deindividuation, impulse, and chaos. *Nebraska Symposium on Motivation* 17:-237–307.

Zimmerman, D. H., and West, C. 1975. Sex roles, interruptions and silences in conversations. In *Language and Sex: Difference and Dominance,* ed. B. Thorne and N. Henley, pp. 105–29. Rowley, Mass.: Newbury House.

Zipf, S. G. 1960. Resistance and conformity under reward and punishment. *Journal of Abnormal and Social Psychology* 6:102–109.

Znaniecki, F. 1965. *Social Relations and Social Roles.* New York: Irvington Publications.

Zurcher, L. A. 1967. Functional marginality: dynamics of a poverty intervention organization. *Social Science Quarterly* 48:411–21.

———. 1967. The naval recruit training center: a study of role assimilation in a total institution. *Sociological Inquiry* 37:85–96.

———. 1972. The mutable self. *Futurist* 6:181–85.

———. 1977. *The Mutable Self: A Self-Concept for Social Change.* Beverly Hills, Calif.: Sage.

———. 1978. Ephemeral roles, voluntary action and voluntary associations. *Journal of Voluntary Action Research* 7:65–74.

———. 1979. Role selection: the influence of internalized vocabularies of motive. *Symbolic Interaction* 2:45–62.

Zurcher, L. A., and Curtis, R. L. 1973. A comparative analysis of propositions describing social movement organizations. *Sociological Quarterly* 14:175–78.

Zurcher, L. A., and Kirkpatrick, R. G. 1976. *Citizens for Decency: Anti-Pornography Crusade as Status Protest.* Austin and London: University of Texas Press.

Zygmunt, J. 1970. Prophetic failure and Chiliastic identity: the case of the Jehovah's Witnesses. *American Journal of Sociology* 75:926–48.

———. 1972. Movements and motives: some unresolved issues in the psychology of social movements. *Human Relations* 25:449–67.

Name Index

NOTE: Bold face figures indicate inclusive page numbers of chapters.

Subject Index